LEGAL ASPECTS OF
BUSINESS

Texts, Jurisprudence, and Cases

SECOND EDITION

DANIEL ALBUQUERQUE

*Director, Alternative tech Foundation (AtF) of Biodiversity Conservation India Ltd (BCIL),
Bengaluru, India
Visiting professor at the Friedrich Schiller University, Jena, Germany*

OXFORD
UNIVERSITY PRESS

OXFORD
UNIVERSITY PRESS

Oxford University Press is a department of the University of Oxford.
It furthers the University's objective of excellence in research, scholarship,
and education by publishing worldwide. Oxford is a registered trade mark of
Oxford University Press in the UK and in certain other countries.

Published in India by
Oxford University Press
22 Workspace, 2nd Floor, 1/22 Asaf Ali Road, New Delhi 110 002

ISBN-13: 978-0-19-946316-9
ISBN-10: 0-19-946316-6

Typeset in Baskerville
by Ideal Publishing Solutions, Delhi
Printed in India by Nutech Print Services India

For product information and current price, please visit www.india.oup.com

To

Shri Ajit Pershad Jain and Family

Features of

TEXT

It is my desire that there should be uniformity in law and uniformity in sentencing. I even go this far, to grant a three-day stay for those in prison who have been tried and sentenced to death. During this time their relatives can make appeals to have the prisoners' lives spared. If there is none to appeal on their behalf, the prisoners can give gifts in order to make merit for the next world, or observe fasts.

– Ashoka, 273–236 BCE, Pillar Edict Nb4 (S. Dhammika)[3]

Texts from the Acts provide direct acquaintance with the legal language.

Table 1.4 Source of religious laws

Religious groups	Religious laws	Source
Jews	Torah	Bible
Christians	Church Tradition and Canon Law	Bible
Muslims	Sharia and Fiqh	Quran
Hindus	Shruti and Smriti and Social Tradition	Vedas and Sacred Writings, *Manusmriti*

The chapters include interesting and information-rich **Tables** and **Figures** to explain the concepts better.

Jurisprudence

Analytical
- Law as a pure discipline without reference to historical and ethical developments.
- Analysis of the concepts of the state, authority, rights, liabilities, contracts, property, intention, and motive.

Historical
- Study of the legal history, tracing the origins and development of law.
- The historical perspective is important in as much as it helps to understand the application of the law as precedent.

Ethical
- Law based on the ethical value of justice.
- Society established law and its proceedings for those who fail to make the noble ethical standards.
- To protect the rights of every citizen, therefore, justice is the minimum requisite.
- Moral perspective.

Figure 1.1 Interpretation of law

CASE 1.2	PETITIONER: Kohinoor Elastics Pvt. Ltd vs RESPONDENT: Commissioner of Central Excise

DATE OF JUDGEMENT: 4 August 2005*

FACTS: The Central Excise in its notification to the appellant used the terms, 'brand name' and 'trade name', drawn from the Trade and Merchandise Marks Act, 1958.

JUDGEMENT: Use of these terms by the Central Excise for notification is irrelevant.

REASON: The context for notification is Central Excise. It borrowed the terms from another Act that are not relevant to the present instance. The context in which those terms had been used in the Trade Marks Act was not relevant for the purpose of interpreting them in a notification in the Central Excise Act.

The numerous abridged **Cases** impart crisp and vivid legal experience of court proceedings.

Manager's Takeaway highlights the key learning points in context of the topics being discussed that a manager must remember at all times.

MANAGER'S TAKEAWAY
- Be aware of your ever-changing role as buyer and seller.
- Make sure you have the title of the properties in goods, both when you buy and sell.

MANAGER'S TAKEAWAY
- When in doubt, take recourse to the historical perspective of a legal aspect.
- Take the issues of law seriously and not casually.

MANAGER'S TAKEAWAY
- No business is valid without it being at the same time legal.
- Legal framework is a manager's boundary.

the Book

Chapter-end *Exercises* and *Development of Legal Edge* help students to apply and broaden their understanding of legal concepts.

EXERCISES

1. You go to get a no objection certificate (NOC) for your manufacturing plant from the local au-thorities. You give 5 per cent of the value of the land to the authority to expedite procedures and them that the biggest problem in the company that you face is litigation. How will you convince the students the relationship between Business and Law?

DEVELOPMENT OF LEGAL EDGE

- Start a study circle in your college, university, institute, company, or business establishment with some captivating name such as *Legal Cell, Bar at Law, Court Bench, Legal Eagle*, etc.

- In a company or business organisation: Start a legal cell, both to educate and for real help of the employees. This will help them understand their situation in a knowledgeable way. Legal knowledge

In chapter-end detailed *Case Study*, students can experience the complete legal system in action.

CASE STUDY   MINERVA MILLS

No amendment of this Constitution (including the provisions of Part III) made or purporting to have been made under this article [whether before or after the commencement of Sec. 55 of the Constitution (Forty second Amendment) Act, 1976] shall be called in question in any court on any ground.

– Constitution of India, Article 368 (4)

Introduction

The following case, *Minerva Mills Ltd., and Others vs Union of India and Others* dated 9 May 1980, is considered as one of the landmark cases in Indian legal history.[16] The eminent judges of the Supreme Court forming the five-member Bench were Justices Y.V. Chandrachud, A.C. Gupta, N.

power to examine the constitutionality of any Act that is passed by the Parliament.

Courting controversy

The following is a historical development where the Supreme Court had to fight against the Parliament of India

Legal Luminary presents a short profile of a role model who has contributed considerably in the area of the theme of the chapter.

LEGAL LUMINARY

ROHINTON NARIMAN—SPIRITED CORPORATE LAWYER

His nickname, Company Bahadur, says it all. He is a consummate corporate lawyer and for over two decades, he has been a member of the Bar. Rohinton Nariman was made a senior advocate of the Supreme Court at the young age 36, a singular exception in the history of the Supreme Court. According to a Times of India survey, he stands ninth among the top ten lawyers of India.*

The significance of Nariman to you as manager does not lie in his intelligence, success, or pedigree—he is the son of the legendary Padma Vibushan Fali Nariman—but in his attitude to failure. Initially he lost cases. He worked hard. He lost very big cases. He worked harder. He rose to success because he learnt twice from each failure. Moreover,

Glossary provides an exhaustive, ready reference to all the relevant and standard legal terms.

Glossary

A fortiori (*Lt*) With a stronger reason; used in argument to describe a proposition that must be true because it is a subcategory of something that is true
A posse ad esse (*Lt*) From possibility to actuality
A posteriori (*Lt*) From what comes after. Inductive reasoning based on observation, as opposed to deductive,

Abuse To misuse; to wrong or mistreat a person or animal physically, mentally, or sexually, corrupt acts; cruel treatment of another
Accept (Noun—**acceptance**) To receive willingly; to agree voluntarily creating a binding contract; implies the right to refuse

Foreword

According to an old theory of law, jurisprudence is the knowledge of things divine and human, the science of what is right and what is wrong. In simpler terms, it expounds the need for law in society as a regulatory apparatus to dispense justice with equity. The basic assumption for the proper administration of justice is that it does not excuse any citizen of ignorance of law. This eliminates the need to assert the importance of the knowledge of law in so far as a modern day business manager or any other professional is concerned.

In a highly complex and globalized business world, only the rule of law can govern efficiently and effectively. It becomes imperative for every manager to take decisions in the interest of one's corporation in complete compliance of the law. Non-compliance plunges an organization into litigation which is a very costly affair. This in turn reflects on its performance. With costs going up and reputations down, every year we witness how good and renowned companies suddenly find themselves amidst dreadful legal problems that make them bite the dust.

Law has increasingly become a specialist's area. Entrepreneurs, business managers, public administrators, and professionals in all aspects of human endeavour and enterprise find it difficult to decipher the articles and nuances of law. The plethora of legal literature and the abundance of information on the Internet confound the situation. In these circumstances the publisher in his wisdom has decided rightly to bring out *Legal Aspects of Business: Texts, Jurisprudence, and Cases* to help all those who hold responsible positions in the modern organizations.

The title of the book, *Legal Aspects of Business*, clearly defines the scope of the book to laws dealing with business and its affairs. There was a time when managers dealt with some important facets of mercantile law only and to some extent the labour laws. The author has been able to discuss, in a comprehensive manner, not only the classical mercantile law but also the areas of industrial and labour relations, taxation, monetary laws, cyber laws, intellectual property rights, international laws, environmental laws, and human rights. All these aspects are essentially related to modern business.

The author has brought *Jurisprudence* to the forefront. Simply understood, jurisprudence concerns itself with wisdom rather than mere knowledge of the application of law. One is able to achieve such a feat only through the mastery of legal philosophy, a clear understanding of the legal principles, concepts and their application to actual contexts. The sections of the Acts have been highlighted and their brief delineation helps to comprehend the vast implications. The chapter-end exercises ably aid to recapitulate and renew interest in finding solutions to the given problems.

The actual legal *Texts* taken from the legislated Acts acquaint readers to relevant information and legal language simultaneously. Legal language is a specialized field; the entire outcome of a legal dispute depends on it. Although, in principle, legal language is supposed to be plain so that a common man would easily understand, and not flowery and figurative, yet, in essence the concepts are legally exclusive and highly technical. However, this book is highly readable and enjoyable because of the author's innovative style and presentation which has contemporary elegance and flair.

Traditionally, law books have been mere reference books of large, unmanageable volumes containing lengthy cases running into several scores of pages. In this book, one will find abridged *cases*, as is needed to highlight a point. At the same time, one can be satisfied to read the actual text of the judgement. The author has provided a full-fledged case towards the end of each chapter. Its presentation is unique and one is able to experience the courtroom atmosphere while reading the same. It is an unforgettable court drama, chapter after chapter, thirty times. The *Legal Luminary* section at the end of the chapter is like a perfect pudding after a great meal.

Oxford University Press (India) had earlier published *Business Ethics: Principles and Practices* by Dr Daniel Albuquerque. It is fitting that the same author has written on legal aspects of business, because ethics is the conscience of law. While ethics persuades and educates people about the right and the wrong, law applies and enforces its edicts. *Legal Aspects of Business: Texts, Jurisprudence, and Cases* is a right book at the right time for all the responsible stakeholders in the society. Our message to the entrepreneurs, managers, administrators, executives, and to the students or trainees in business management is that this book is a wholesome provision, a comprehensive legal treasure trove. The author has done full justice to the cause of enhancing the comprehension of legal knowledge. With this book, there is help at hand for every manager.

Shri Ajit Pershad Jain

Former Manager, Finance, Indian Airlines
and Founder of a renowned audit firm

Shri Vipin Ajit Jain

Fellow Member of the
Foundation of Chartered
Accountants of India

Preface to the Second Edition

Non in legendo sed in intelligendo leges consistent.
The laws depend not on being read but on being understood.

Dear Friend, while it is a privilege to address you again in the second edition of *Legal Aspects of Business: Texts, Jurisprudence, and Cases*, may I lay the record straight to say that the purpose of this edition is to add four full-fledged chapters of the new Companies Act, 2013. The new law is enacted as an instrument to facilitate business. As the above principle advocates, that it is not merely to be studied as part of the curricula but must be *understood* in a manner that the lawgiver intends. To understand implies to be able to apply it with wisdom and diligence.

This new edition aspires to be a guide to those who study and follow law, especially managers. All good managers deliberate before they act. This book should help such managers to be mentally prepared to take legally sound decisions and implement them.

THE NEW COMPANY LAW

The new Company Law, 2013, is discussed in four exclusive chapters:

Chapter 8: *The Companies Act—Transition from 1956 to 2013* makes a comparative study of both the old and the new acts and discusses the major thrusts and general provisions of the Companies Act, 2013.

Chapter 9: *The Companies Act, 2013—The Context and Constitution of a Company* offers particular discussion on various attributes and characteristics of the new law consisting of the context in which these have been effected, that is, formation, incorporation, commencement, and promotion. There are also several special features such as one-man company and *nidhi* company.

Chapter 10: *The Companies Act, 2013—The Administration and Management of a Company* Administration and management is the job of managers. Prospectus, securities, and share capital are presented at length. Likewise, accounts, audits, and dividends are treated within the given context.

Chapter 11: *The Companies Act, 2013—The Control and Governance of a Company* clearly lays down as to who-is-who within and without a corporation and their relationships. Within the company there are Board of Directors, Directors and Officers of the company, Key Managerial Personnel (KMP), and Independent Directors. Outside the company, there is the Government, the Ministry for Corporate Affairs, the Taxation Authority, and so on.

Further, there are law-enforcing agencies like various courts and tribunals, such as National Company Law Tribunal (NCLT), National Financial Reporting Authority (NFRA), and Serious Fraud Investigation Office (SFIO), where crime and punishment are also studied. Special features like Corporate Social Responsibility get fresh treatment.

All the chapters have examples of on-going cases under the new Act. It will interest you to follow these even outside your workplace and classrooms.

While this edition will discuss the transition from the old Companies Act to the new one, you may access the earlier chapters, exclusively on the Companies Act, 1956, as an online resource to this book, using the following Web-link:

http://oupinheonline.com/book/albuquerque-legal-aspects-business/9780199463169

ONLINE RESOURCES

The following resources are available for the faculty and students using this text:
- PowerPoint slides
- Additional Reading, consisting of exclusive chapters on the Companies Act, 1956
- Manager's Ready Reckoner

GENERAL REVISION

Great care has been taken to revise also the rest of the book where anomalies and incongruities are corrected. You are welcome to share your experience with me at info@seatofwisdom.in.

I wish you a fruitful study and even more successful application through the study of this revised, second edition of *Legal Aspects of Business: Texts, Jurisprudence, and Cases.*

Daniel Albuquerque

Preface to the First Edition

Lex est norma recti.
Law is a rule of right.

INTRODUCTION

Dear Friend, welcome in a special way to this book, *Legal Aspects of Business: Texts, Jurisprudence, and Cases,* where I shall address *you* in second person singular throughout, to share its experience personally. Welcome to the world of business, to its essential core, its centre, called the *contract,* through which all business relationships originate, develop into complex network of deals, transactions, and agreements, cause disputes, disagreements, and cancellation of contracts; where business parties march before an arbitrator appointed by the State in a court of law to seek justice. The following story is an ample demonstration of what awaits you in this book, both as for its objective and the method.

There was a young man who inherited a set of weighing scales from his ancestors made of solid metal and of considerable value. He decided to go to a foreign country in search of better prospects for his career. He needed money for the purpose; he pawned the weighing scales to a moneylender as a security for the borrowed money and it was agreed that he would get his scales back when he returns and reimburses the loan.

The young man became a businessman and prospered. Upon his return, he offered to redeem his wares with the money and interest. However, the moneylender regretted saying that the scales were eaten up by the rats and hence did not exist anymore.

The young businessman reflected for a while, exhibited a friendly and understanding demeanour, and agreed with the moneylender saying that in this world nothing is permanent. In the meantime, the home-returned businessman requested the moneylender to send his son to accompany him to the river for a swim, to which a much relieved moneylender readily agreed.

Upon reaching the river, the businessman hid the young boy in a cave. Seeing him return all alone, the moneylender inquired about his son. The businessman promptly replied saying that a falcon had picked him up and flown away. The moneylender flew into a rage and broke into a fight with the young businessman saying that he is a liar and questioned him as to how such a bird could take away a young boy.

The case was taken to the court and both placed their arguments before the judge. The moneylender explained the impossibility that a bird could take away his son and that the businessman was lying. The businessman countered saying that if rats could eat scales made of solid metal, then a bird could carry away a human being.

After listening to both the parties, the judge passed the order that obliged them to exchange the boy and the scales to their respective holders.

The above is a story from the *Panchatantra* illustrating fair hearing in a dispute and delivering a judgement that is in accordance with reason, thus serving the cause of justice in a business relationship in the society.

ABOUT LAW

In the Indian tradition *dharma* is the rule of life; it is the source of ethical values and justice is one of those values which ensure fairness or *nyaya*. Justice consists of a righteous life that harms none and gives each his or her due. To ensure justice man has created laws which regulate relationships in the society. For instance, Manu has been credited for creating and establishing the code of law; hence, he is honoured as the Lawgiver. Similarly in the Judeo-Christian-Islamic tradition, the Ten Commandments are considered as the foundations of jurisprudence. Ancient Babylonia under Emperor Hammurabi has been regarded as the place where the first code of law originated. Later, the Greek philosophers such as Aristotle and Plato established concepts of justice which are relevant to this day. Upon these is based the Roman law which is a codified law and is the basis of legal systems of all the countries where Civil Code is practised. In the same manner, under the influence of several modern philosophers such as Thomas Aquinas, John Locke, Jeremy Bentham, and others, a common law was framed as *Magna Carta* (Great Charter) in the first parliamentary system developed in Great Britain and was introduced and applied in India and continues to be the current justice delivery system in India.

The genesis of law lies in social contract. In this respect, the Constitution of India is a social contract of the people, by the people and for the people. The object of the law is to apply a standard of behaviour equally to protect the liberty of all those who come under its purview. Contract by its nature assumes the knowledge under which it takes place; hence, it precludes its ignorance.

As it is said above, the object of law is justice and it consists in giving one his or her due. What is this *due*? The due is that which belongs to one as a right. One has an inalienable right to liberty, equality, and fraternity—to live and conduct social and professional relationships. The law is an instrument to protect one's rights.

Law may be explained through the metaphor of a game—cricket. People admit that India is a cricket-crazy nation. One common trait of all these *crazy* people, whether they play the game or not, is their mastery over the knowledge of the game. This knowledge consists of two aspects of the game, the *technique* and the *rules*. Out of these two aspects they are able to draw out everything—from selection of the players, the nature of the pitches, strong and weak points of the opponents, strategies for a win to the rules about bowling, batting, of being given out in various circumstances, exceptions to the rules, rules for various weather conditions affecting the play and even some redundant rules—all that is needed to make a game out of it. A fair game is desired by all. It is figuratively known as a level playing field, in other words, the rules of the game are to be applied equally to all.

Business deals with the economic part of the social contract. A level playing field is what every businessman wants. Just as there is competition in games and sports, so too in business all have a fair opportunity to make money. However, there are rules. There is an umpire who applies the rules by referring to the well-formulated and accepted rules of the game. The rules of the business are formulated by the people's representatives and applied by the government. However, none of them are referees. The system for refereeing is the law. The court of the land and its officers apply the law in the event of any infringement or damage to others.

Our economic life is dominated by work, goods and services, trade and commerce, and finance and money. This is our business; it is what we do for a living. It needs to be governed by law which ensures equity and justice. A corporation or a company is a team and directors and managers in it are players. The law gives them a level field to play.

The State grants legitimacy, through the operation of its law, to its citizens and their activities. Business is one of their essential activities. Business relationship is based on a business contract whose validity is authenticated by law. This is the *fundamental aspect* which a business manager must keep in mind before he agrees or binds himself to a business deal or conducts a business operation. It is a manager's job to make business decisions. The decision is *right* only if it is legally valid.

ABOUT THE BOOK

The objective of this book is to empower managers in legal matters so that they are able to take decisions which are in accordance with the law of the land.

Features of the Book

The book consists of thirty chapters which are divided into six parts; it has an adequate glossary and a helpful appendix. Each chapter of the book has built in a meticulous architecture of legal *Texts* from the Acts which are embedded into *Jurisprudence*, the elucidated principles of law, opening on to the vista of cases which comprehensively capture all the Legal Aspects of Business.

Principle Every chapter begins with a classic legal principle in Latin, its original language, along with its authentic translation. The purpose is to capture the entire subject-matter of the chapter in a single maxim.

Texts The aim of supplying texts from the Acts is to have a direct acquaintance with the legal language.

Jurisprudence The science of acquiring the knowledge of law and applying its principles is the purpose of this work.

Cases The cases are presented in the abridged form of the judgement text as a means to vividly impart the legal experience of court proceedings. The cases, in the initial chapters, have been presented in short summaries and gradually lead to real abridged texts of the court judgements.

Manager's Takeaway Just like lamp posts that you come across at steady intervals, so too, at the end of each section there pop up little text flags which illuminate two main learning points thereof.

Summary At the end of the chapter a short summary is provided to enable recapitulation and internalization of the principles and their application.

Problems and Questions The practical exercises where problems are presented and solutions have been hinted arouse curiosity and exploration into legal texts.

Further Reading Readings and links are suggested to further legal expertise and self-study.

Development of Legal Edge It provides a short guide for practical learning and developing legal skills.

Chapter-end Case The cases within the body of the chapters have the purpose of illustrating a particular concept or a legal principle. The case towards the end of the chapter has a comprehensive purpose where an entire legal problem is treated and one can experience the complete legal system in action.

Legal Luminary The chapter ends with a short profile of a role model who has contributed considerably in the area of the theme dealt in the chapter.

Context and Structure

This textbook is a comprehensive guide to every aspiring and practising manager in the varied and complex world of business. The book is divided into six parts.

Part I Jurisprudence:

Chapter 1 It provides the philosophical context to the entire book and deals with the general principles and application of jurisprudence.

Part II Mercantile Law: Contract, Sale of Goods, Negotiable Instruments, Partnership, Carriage of Goods, Monopolies, Sick Industrial Units, Property, Special Economic Zone, etc.

Chapters 2, 3, and *4* These three chapters deal with the Indian Contract Act, 1872. It is the fundamental law for business and a basis for all the laws which have evolved and developed ever since. These chapters have received an extensive treatment keeping in mind the core legal knowledge that is necessary for a business manager.

Chapter 5 Sale of Goods Act, 1930: Business is identified with sales; hence in this respect this Act is the cornerstone of understanding business deals. Agreements and the various relationships which occur in a business deal have legal significance.

Chapter 6 The Negotiable Instruments Act, 1881 involves exchange of value or money in various forms. From banking to customer relationship in a globalized world, it has both national and international significance.

Chapter 7 The Indian Partnership Act, 1932 was necessitated as Indian entrepreneurship began its modern era in industry. Today, several types of partnerships have grown and have admirably served India's enterprise.

Chapter 8 discusses the transition from The Companies Act, 1956, to The Companies Act, 2013. It includes a comparative analysis of the provisions of the new and the old Acts.

Chapters 9, 10, and *11* discuss the Companies Act, 2013, in detail. These chapters present the rationale of the new Act along with its aim and application. They also elaborate on how this Act affects the context, constitution, and administration of a company and the role of the board of directors, directors, and officers of the company. In addition, they also enumerate the provisions of corporate social responsibility and control and governance by statutory agencies of the government, as per the new Act.

Chapter 12 Fair play implies competition. The Competition Act, 2002 intends exactly to regulate fair business in the market and all the corporations conducting business follow one standard. It sheds light on Competition Commission of India and its Tribunal.

Chapter 13 The Sick Industrial Companies Repeal Act, 2003 and guidelines on insolvency. The law takes cognizance of the financial problems that the companies face in difficult times, such as industrial sickness and disputes. This law clearly lays down guidelines for insolvency.

Chapter 14 Over a period of time several laws have been formed for carriage of goods by land, sea, and air. While today's business largely depends upon supply chain logistics, and the transport of goods in real time facing all sorts of odds on land, at sea, and in the air, the importance of Carriage of Good Laws can never be underestimated.

Chapter 15 Consumer Related Laws such as, Essential Commodities, Black Marketing, Weights and Measures, etc., are dealt here in detail. In some way, all are consumers including both the common people and the companies. Businesses, if they have to succeed, must serve the customers without any violation of their rights.

Chapter 16 Economic Laws of Land and Property are several and all are important to business: from transfer of property to controversial land acquisition problems, from regular stamp duty and registrations to special economic zone—a wide spectrum of laws are discussed in this chapter.

The above 15 chapters (2–16) form a complete whole of mercantile law which should provide for a basic and reliable knowledge to managers.

Part III Financial Jurisprudence: It covers the essential elements of banking, insurance, stock market, and corporate taxation.

Chapter 17 Laws of Securities Contracts Regulation, 1956, the Securities and Exchange Board of India Act, 1992, and the allied laws affecting the capital market are discussed.

Chapter 18 Banking Laws concerning both regulation as well as the Reserve Bank of India Act, 1934 are discussed with an aim to deepen the knowledge of financial regulation in India.

Chapter 19 Laws of Insurance are important because risk management today takes a very high priority both for insurance providers as well as the consumers. Acquaintance with insurance laws and various amendments are dealt in this chapter.

Chapter 20 Laws of Taxation take a very high priority in financial management. Income Tax Act, 1961, Central Board of Revenue Act, 1963, and other important laws such as Central Excise Act, 1944, Customs Act 1962, Transaction Tax, Wealth Tax, and so on, too play their role when a manager's accountability is measured.

Chapter 21 The Laws of Foreign Exchange and Prevention of Money Laundering deal with complex contemporary issues in both national and international trade and commerce. Several laws such as Foreign Exchange Management Act, 1999, Prevention of Money Laundering Act, 2002 have been discussed in this chapter.

Part IV Labour and Industrial Jurisprudence: Industrial relations are governed by the very difficult and human relations, issues of work and wages, working hours and benefits.

Chapter 22 This chapter concerns itself with wage-related laws such as the Payment of Wages Act, 1936 and the Payment of Wages (Amendment) Act, 2005, the Minimum Wages Act, 1948, the Payment of Bonus Act, 1965, the Payment of Gratuity Act, 1972.

Chapter 23 This chapter deals with the workers' social security. The following laws are taken for treatment: The Workmen's Compensation Act, 1923 and The Workmen's Compensation (Amendments) Act, 2000, the Employees' State Insurance Act, 1948, the Employees' Provident Fund and Miscellaneous Provisions Act, 1952 and the Employees' Provident Fund & Miscellaneous (Amendment) Provisions Act, 1996 and the Unorganized Workers' Social Security Act, 2008.

Chapter 24 Two significant laws are considered in this chapter, the study of which is important for every manager interested in industrial relations. These are: The Trade Unions Act, 1926 and the Trade Unions (Amendments) Act, 2001, the Industrial Disputes Act, 1947.

Part V Aspects of New Economy and Jurisprudence: In the area of what is popularly known as the *new economy* three aspects play a major role. These are Information and Communication, Intellectual Property Rights and Issues of Environment and Ecology.

Chapter 25 This chapter mainly deals with two laws—Information Technology Act, 2000, and the Telecom Regulatory Authority of India Act, 1997. The importance of these laws to the concerned industries is enormous, since several of them have been involved in notorious scams.

Chapter 26 Technology is becoming increasingly virtual in nature; goods and services are intangible and easily reproducible. The law comes to the protection of the creators and innovators of new ideas and inventions. The chapter studies the related laws: The Copyright Act, 1957, the Patents Act, 1970, and the Trade Marks Act, 1999.

Chapter 27 This chapter deals with environmental laws and covers the following laws: The Environment Protection Act, 1986 and other Acts Related to Environmental Protection. Industry has been singled out for environmental pollution and destruction.

Managers of industries are made responsible today for any damage to the environment and hence the need to function within the parameters of the law.

Part VI Judicial and Social Jurisprudence: Corporations have social responsibility; corporations do not exist for themselves; they are part and parcel of the society and just as they enjoy their rights to conduct business, they also bear responsibility for their actions. The law applies to them equally.

Chapters 28, 29, and 30 These chapters deal with criminal liability of the corporations, arbitration, and conciliation as dispute resolution and basic human rights. These social issues are of supreme importance to the global society. The businesses have their whole and complete stake in these laws. Knowledge of these, followed by appropriate action, is what is expected of a modern manager.

ACKNOWLEDGEMENTS

The intellectual capital invested in this book consists mainly as follows:

- Literature research from books, periodicals, newspapers, and weeklies
- Electronic resources including the Internet, databases, and television reportage
- Vast background of academic lectures, seminars, discussions, conferences, and peer appraisals

All the resources have been duly acknowledged and documented. The references to electronic media, if not specified, are then to be taken as retrieved within the period of May 2010–May 2012.

Special credits are due to the following agencies and individuals:

- Oxford University Press, New Delhi, the publishers
- Indus Business Academy, Bangalore and Greater Noida
- Shri Ajit Pershad Jain, my guide and philosopher, and Shri Vipin Ajit Jain my friend, for the Foreword
- Dr Wilfred Anthony De Souza, former Chief Minister of Goa
- Shri V.B. Prabhu Verlekar, F.C.A., and Ashish Prabhu Verlekar, F.C.A., Goa
- Prof. Dr Subhash Sharma, Director, Indus Business Academy, Bangalore and Greater Noida
- Prof. Dr K.B. Akhilesh, Department of Management Studies, Indian Institute of Science, Bangalore
- Prof. Dr Nikolaus Knoepffler and Prof. Dr Peter Kunzmann, Friedrich Schiller University, Jena, Germany
- Prof. Dr Willhelm Baumgartner and Prof. Dr Elisabeth Baumgartner, University of Wurzburg, Germany
- Mrs Frieda Meiselbach for assistance and supervision

DISCLAIMER

I would like to state that the law and its adjudication, our courts and justice delivery system are open and freely observed and shared by the public. Further: cases, texts, judgements, places, persons and their names, etc., are from the public domain, such as publications, search engines, websites, print and electronic media and in no way should be interpreted as investigative or referred to as evidence of anything else other than making an academic point solely for learning purposes.

All cases, events, incidences, occurrences, names are not fictional; they are facts examined by the courts, reported in the media belonging to public domain and their utilization is made to illustrate legal concepts in a classroom. In these there is no intention whatsoever to judge, cast aspersions, or formulate an opinion against anyone in any other relation than to study and discuss purely for academic purposes.

The special profiles of legal luminaries, anecdotes, incidences, and stories have laudable intentions of recognizing and honouring their service to the country and to its people and to encourage future leaders to emulate them as role models.

CONCLUSION

Through the operation of its law, the State grants legitimacy to its citizens and their activities. Business is one of their essential activities. Business relationship is based on business contract whose validity is authenticated by law. This is the *fundamental aspect* which a business manager must keep in mind before he agrees or binds himself to a business deal or conducts a business operation. It is a manager's job to make business decisions. The decision is *right* only if it is legally valid. The book awakens you to its principle: *Lex vigilantibus, non dormientibus, subvenit* (Law assists the wakeful, not the sleeping).

You are welcome to share your experience with me at *info@seatofwisdom.in*. Wishing you success in your endeavour to study, appreciate, apply and implement laws related to business enterprise, I remain,

Yours Sincerely,
Daniel Albuquerque

Brief Contents

Detailed Contents

PART I BUSINESS JURISPRUDENCE 1

PART II COMMERCIAL JURISPRUDENCE 45

PART III FINANCIAL JURISPRUDENCE	437

PART IV LABOUR AND INDUSTRIAL JURISPRUDENCE	539

PART

1

BUSINESS JURISPRUDENCE

Business Management and Jurisprudence

Principle: *Ignorantia legis non excusat.*

Ignorance of the law is no excuse.

[You are not excused of your legal liability due to the lack of the knowledge of the law of the land.]

CHAPTER OUTLINE

- Legal Theory and Nature of Jurisprudence
- Definition, Scope, and Classification of Law
- Theories of Law
- Constituents of Law
- Origins of Indian Legal System
- Nature of Indian Legal System
- Administrative Structure of the Indian Legal System

- Relationship between Business and Law
- Principle of Commercial Jurisprudence
- Some Constitutional Aspects
- Manager and the Legal Environment
- Practical Ways to Read and Understand Legal Language
- *Case Study:* Minerva Mills
- *Legal Luminary:* B.R. Ambedkar

1.1 LEGAL THEORY AND NATURE OF JURISPRUDENCE

No person shall be deprived of his life or personal liberty except according to procedure established by law.

– Constitution of India, Article 21

Many a times you must have felt that there is no hope in our country and that it is riddled with crime and corruption. Nonetheless, we suddenly find a reason for hope when we hear and read about the High Courts of the country or the Supreme Court, which step in to correct the Executive or the Government and also not hesitate to show the Legislature or the Parliament its duties. The Constitution of India has empowered the Supreme Court of India under Articles 141, 142, and 144, and the High Courts under Article 226 to safeguard the life, property, liberty, and justice of every citizen. This applies to organizations such as business corporations also—since these too are legal entities (Case 1.1). True justice rests not merely in the letter of the law but also in its spirit.

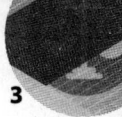

CASE 1.1   PETITIONER: Additional District Magistrate, Jabalpur vs Respondent: S. Shukla etc.

DATE OF JUDGEMENT: 28 April 1976*

FACTS: 1975–77: The Government of India headed by Prime Minister Indira Gandhi declared national emergency, thereby suspending some of the constitutional rights of the citizens. Under Maintenance of Internal Security Act (MISA), 1971, which was amended in 1975, the Government detained political leaders, prominent citizens, and also businessmen arbitrarily. Petitions of habeas corpus, a writ by the court ordering the person to be present in the court to determine that one's freedom is not infringed, pleading invalidation of detention orders, flooded the courts across the country.

JUDGEMENT: High Courts upheld the fundamental rights despite their suspension during the emergency.
Supreme Court overturned the rulings of the High Court.

REASON: Nine High Courts in the country upheld the petitions despite the measures of emergency, suspending the fundamental rights under Articles 14, 19, 21, and 22. But the Supreme Court consisting of a bench of five justices, however, overturned the judgement of the High Courts by 4:1, and held that neither detainees nor anyone on their behalf had the right to move the courts for habeas corpus while under the suspension of fundamental rights.

AFTERMATH: The entire world acclaimed the courage of one judge, Justice H.R. Khanna, for dissenting from the majority judgement by the apex court. The reason for the acclaim being that Justice Khanna showed that under no circumstances, not even emergency, the freedom of the citizens can be compromised. He matched the theory of law to its spirit or wisdom, also known as jurisprudence. After the emergency was over in 1977, the Janata Party Government took measures to correct further such aberrations to the Constitution of India.

*http://openarchive.in/judis/5622.htm (2 February 2010).

Legal theory and jurisprudence are two terms that are used interchangeably in the discipline of law. For the sake of a better understanding, we propose the following perspective.

Legal theory is a systematic study of law. It is the philosophy of law that studies the legal aspects in the context of the society's cultural, political, economic, and other areas. It answers questions about the nature of law, its rationale, or the underlying principle. This science of law is developed not by lawyers but by philosophers and religious and political leaders through their theories and ideologies. Socrates, Plato, and Aristotle were Greek thinkers who established foundations of the legal discipline. Roman thinkers such as Marcus Aurelius, Seneca, and others helped to lay the foundation to modern law. Our own Manu and Kautilya advanced the science of law in India.

Jurisprudentia is the Latin term for jurisprudence—it implies the knowledge of law. As against the theory, it concerns itself with the procedures and application of the law. It

Jurisprudence

Analytical	**Historical**	**Ethical**
• Law as a pure discipline without reference to historical and ethical developments. • Analysis of the concepts of the state, authority, rights, liabilities, contracts, property, intention, and motive.	• Study of the legal history, tracing the origins and development of law. • The historical perspective is important in as much as it helps to understand the application of the law as precedent.	• Law based on the ethical value of justice. • Society established law and its proceedings for those who fail to make the noble ethical standards. • To protect the rights of every citizen, therefore, justice is the minimum requisite. • Moral perspective.

Figure 1.1 Interpretation of law

seeks how to apply the law in individual situations and cases. Jurisprudence is a way of understanding and practising the law in a comprehensive way: it mainly interprets law in three aspects: analytical, historical, and ethical (Figure 1.1)

1.2 DEFINITION, SCOPE, AND CLASSIFICATION OF LAW

'Law' includes any ordinance, order, bye-law, rule, regulation, notification, custom or usage having in the territory of India the force of law...

– Constitution of India, Article 3, Clause (a)

Someone asks you, 'What is the time?' You look at your wrist watch and say, 'Half past ten.' That is the end of the matter. In another instance you are asked, 'What is time?' You feel that you are stuck for an answer. It is clear to you that it is not an inquiry about what time of the day it is; rather, how to understand the concept of time, or more technically, it is about the definition of time. Similarly, when we speak about law in everyday use, we know how to make use of it, but find it difficult if someone asks us to define it. To

MANAGER'S TAKEAWAY

• The law of the land is supreme.
• It applies to all, including every citizen, organisation, association, and corporation formed by citizens.
• The knowledge of law is a must to make legally right decisions and run an organisation.

define, we would have to understand the elements of law through classification, context, and scope (Case 1.2). In short, we define concepts according to their nature in a given context.

At times you may feel that law is all about semantics, that is, how words are used purely to twist and turn facts. There is also the popular belief that lawyers use words cleverly and that they win cases by their sheer command over the language. However, what you need to know is that terms or words have meaning only in their given context. The given context for a particular law is its proper Act (Case 1.2). While this may be perfectly understandable to you as a student, how does one put into context the very first word of this discourse: law? Where or what is its context or scope of action?

CASE 1.2   PETITIONER: Kohinoor Elastics Pvt. Ltd   vs   RESPONDENT: Commissioner of Central Excise

DATE OF JUDGEMENT: 4 August 2005*

FACTS: The Central Excise in its notification to the appellant used the terms, 'brand name' and 'trade name', drawn from the Trade and Merchandise Marks Act, 1958.

JUDGEMENT: Use of these terms by the Central Excise for notification is irrelevant.

REASON: The context for notification is Central Excise. It borrowed the terms from another Act that are not relevant to the present instance. The context in which those terms had been used in the Trade Marks Act was not relevant for the purpose of interpreting them in a notification in the Central Excise Act.

_____

*See: 2005 (188) ELT 3 (SC)http://www.aipma.net/bulletin/dec.htm(5.2.2010); also see: http://www.taxmanagementindia.com/site-map/all/case_laws_court_year.asp?court=&year=2005 (5.2.2010).

Concept of Law[1]

The term 'law' has its root in the Latin term lex, which implies a binding custom or practice of a community. Formally, it refers to a kind of conduct or a prescribed rule that is enforced by a controlling authority. Law, therefore, may be described as that which is imposed by a sovereign authority, where an obligation of obedience on the part of all subjects to that authority is demanded, failing which, an appropriate punishment is awarded. The following are the various terms used to explain the concept of law.

Statute   A law enacted by a legislative body, e.g., Lok Sabha in the Indian Parliament enacts laws for the country.

Rule   Very specific and restricted application of law, e.g., a judgement of the court which is also called a ruling.

Regulation   Prescription by authority to control an organisation, e.g., Securities and Exchange Board of India (SEBI) is a statutory body to regulate securities on the stock exchange.

Precept   It is an advisory, a recommendation; however, it is not mandatory. The government usually issues an advisory to exhort citizens on such matters as foreign travel when danger is perceived, etc.

Canon   Normally in religious context; however, in legal terms, it refers to a principle of law which the courts interpret.

Legal   Something that is according to the law.

Illegal   Something against the law.

Lawful   Something in harmony with the law.

Legitimate   According to the law.

Illegitimate   Contrary to the law.

Licit   Something in accordance with the law.

Illicit   Something not in accordance with the law.

_____
[1]Webster's Dictionary, on law and the related terms (Others, 1983).

Law giver   Those who make or legislate laws are also known as law makers or legislators.

Law abiding   One who is obedient to the law.

Law breaker   One who disobeys the law—an outlaw.

The Law and Its Dilemma

The aforesaid elements of the concept of law teach us that law is that which regulates our conduct in society; it is a rule that is enforced by those who have the authority to do so. Obedience to the law is a must: There is an appropriate punishment awarded to the one who breaks the law. The law is not an end in itself; its object is justice. It does so concretely when it proceeds to protect the liberty and rights of the people. However, the dilemma of law is that while it is bound to protect the liberty and rights of the people, at the same time, in order to uphold its duty, it may have to curb and curtail the liberty and freedom of the others whom it considers as offenders.

Definition of Law

A definition must consist of what the concept both includes and excludes. Thus, the definition of man as a rational animal includes human beings into the category of animals but at the same time differentiates them or gives the exclusive status of being rational as the identity of their species. Clear identification is the objective of the definition of a concept. The essence of understanding law depends upon how clearly one is able to define a concept. Let us define the concept of law itself. Some famous definitions mentioned in Table 1.1. These have been given by well-known legal minds.

Table 1. 1   Famous definitions of the concept of law

Thinkers	Definition*	Remark***
Manu (c. 1500 BCE), the Hindu law-giver	*Dharmashastra*—The sacred law of duty. e.g.: 'Let him, un-tired, follow the conduct of virtuous men, connected with his occupations, which has been fully declared in the revealed texts and in the sacred tradition *(Smriti)* and is the root of the sacred law.' (Verse: 155)**	Religious
Bible (Laws—Ten Commandments and others as interpreted by Jewish Torah and for Christians further consolidated by the New Testament)	The revealed laws of God in the sacred scriptures are to be obeyed as divine commands.	Religious
Sharia (Law as revealed in Koran) and Fiqh (Law as understood in Islamic jurisprudence)	The law as endowed by Allah Himself through His prophet Mohammad.	Religious
Aristotle (384–324 BCE)	The law is natural justice.	Natural

Contd

---

* The following definitions are not the exact quotations of the thinkers unless specified; they are succinct phrases to describe their perspectives; for complete philosophical understanding, see the bibliographical references to the above-mentioned thinkers.

** http://www.bharatadesam.com/spiritual/manu_smriti/.

***Refer Table 1.3.

Table 1.1 *Contd*

Cicero (106–43 BCE)	Highest reason implanted in nature	Idealistic
Thomas Aquinas (1225–74)	Participation in the eternal law discovered by reason	Natural
Emperor Justinian, Rome	The standard of what is just and unjust	Idealistic
John Salmond	The body of principles recognised and applied by the State in the administration of justice.	Idealistic
Immanuel Kant (1724–18)	Its duty is to seek universal justice.	Idealistic
John Austin (1797–1859)	Command of the sovereign	Positivistic
Hans Kelson (1881–1973)	De-psychologised command	Positivistic
H.L.A. Hart	System of social rules and their recognition as such	Positivistic
Daguit	Law is based on social solidarity; it is a social fact and none is above it.	Sociological
Ehrlich	Norms to govern social life	Sociological
Emile Durkheim	An expression and guarantee of society's fundamental values	Sociological
Ronald Dworkin	Law is a matter of facts and moral considerations.	Normative legal positivism
Joseph Raz	Law is an authoritative social institution.	Normative legal positivism

You may now have a fair idea of law from the diverse meanings of the concept of law in different perspectives. These perspectives, of course, have evolved through history and have become more complex and difficult as the life and activity of people becomes multi-faceted and complicated due to fast-paced social, political, and economic progress.

You need to keep in mind that law is a rule to live and conduct business in society. Rule regulates activity. All human activity—eating and drinking, work and play, politics and economics, commerce and trade, art and craft, sports and games, faith and religion—is governed by law.

Scope of Law

There is a law about everything: births, deaths, taxes, marriage, divorce, business, crime, rights and duties, and so on. The scope or the context of law is society. Law is an instrument devised by society to manage its affairs and administer justice. Those who exercise authority in society are to be seen as being none other than managers who manage the affairs of society. Table 1.2 gives a list of the areas that are governed by law.

Table 1.2 The main areas of the law

The Constitution and the fundamental rights	Rights and duties in all forms of social relationship
Persons and kinds of persons and their relationship	Ownership, possessions, titles
Property, kinds of property, inheritance	Commerce, contract, commercial liabilities
Banking and share markets	Carriage, transport
Taxation	Labour, trade unions, and reservation in employment
Civil procedure, criminal procedure	Crime and criminal liabilities
Obligations, procedures, evidence, and probation	Torts and tortious liability
Human rights	Social security, livelihood, insurance
Family, religion, culture	Immigration, refugees, asylum
Public interest litigation	Legal aid
Arbitration	International law

What you must remember is that there is nothing that the law does not cover. If there is no specific law on a particular aspect, it only means that a general law may be applied. When a court of law does apply such a general law, then it becomes a case law. This is the way the law develops and grows.

Classification of Law

It can be seen that we enumerated several types of laws in the scope of law. These may be grouped or classified under definite categories or classes; this would further enable the reader to understand which aspect of our legal life it affects. Strictly speaking, this is not a watertight classification. Just as our life cannot be compartmentalised, the law that governs our life overlaps various aspects of our life simultaneously. However, the following classification (Figure 1.2) will help the reader understand the complex gamut of law.

From the above chart, it becomes clear that law is applicable not only for individuals and group of individuals in a society or a country but also globally. Just as several laws of nation states are reflected internationally, like preservation and protection of indigenous cultures and traditions, similarly, globally accepted laws, such as human rights and environmental laws, are reflected locally—nation states and in even smaller communities. Law is a global phenomenon. For instance, the United Nations Charter: its various international conventions, treaties and pacts, bilateral and multilateral relations between the nations. The law embodies every human being in the world. Hence, today every individual can be rightfully called a citizen of the world. This concept of 'Citizen of the World' was popularised by

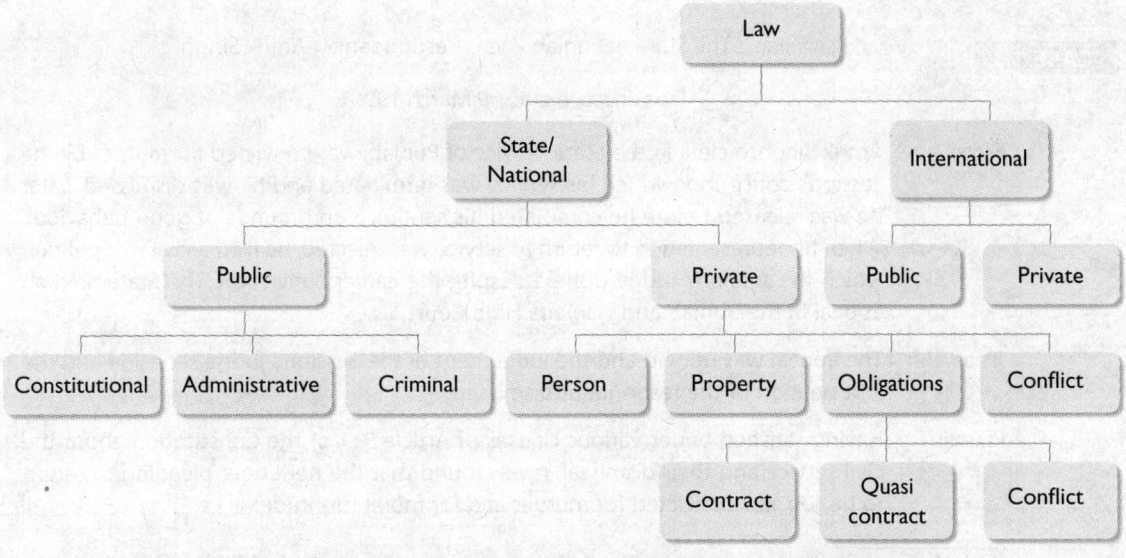

Figure 1.2 Classification of law

Immanuel Kant (1724–1804), the German philosopher, who showed deep insight into law, and held the belief that without it, the society will have no value for its existence. All the categories seen in Figure 1.2 will be discussed in this book as these all relate to business.

1.3 THEORIES OF LAW

TEXT

No person who is a member of a civil service of the Union or an all-India service or a civil service of a State or holds a civil post under the Union or a State shall be dismissed or removed by an authority subordinate to that by which he was appointed.

– Constitution of India, Article 31, 1(1)

One would wonder why he or she should know about the theories of law, because, after all, when one approaches the courts of justice he or she shows his or her faith in it and does not worry about the theory.

In Case 1.3, one experiences how two judges, working under the same law and the Constitution, adjudicate differently because they hold a different view of the law. The session's judge considered the good behaviour of the petitioner and overlooked his criminal liability. He showed an overriding social concern for the petitioner. But the judge of the High Court took into account the criminal liability of the respondent to the appeal and despite several safeguards against the dismissal in the Article 311 of the Constitution, found it reasonable to uphold the appellant's plea and set aside the judgement of the lower court.

MANAGER'S TAKEAWAY

- The law is set in a social milieu and acts as its regulator, just as a manager is responsible for an organisation as a regulator of his area of responsibility.
- All, including the legislators, are the subjects of the law, just as all the rules and regulations of an organisation apply to the managers also.

CASE 1.3

PETITIONER: The State of Punjab vs Respondent: Amrik Singh

DATE OF JUDGEMENT: 9 March 1990*

FACTS: Amrik Singh, a clerk in the State Service of Punjab, was convicted for murder by the session's court upon which his service was terminated and he was dismissed. Later he was released before he completed his sentence on grounds of good behaviour. When his representation to return to service was rejected, he filed a civil writ petition which the session's judge upheld despite the earlier conviction. The State filed an appeal in the Punjab and Haryana High Court.

JUDGEMENT: The appeal was upheld and the judgement of the Session's judge set aside and the writ petition of the respondent dismissed.

REASON: Having satisfied under various clauses of Article 311 of the Constitution about the civil service and their dismissal, it was found that the petitioner pleading to return to his job was convicted for murder and for moral turpitude.

*http://indiankanoon.org/doc/632053/ (2.8.2010).

One has witnessed the different perspectives of judges in Case 1.3. These different perspectives have their source in different schools of thought or theories (Table 1.3).

You may have witnessed in the media that when a judge is appointed—particularly on the Bench of the Supreme Court—there is a deep scrutiny as to what theory of law the judge holds. If you carefully examine any judgement, you will realise that judges have their

Table 1.3 Different theories of law

School of thought	Theory	Thinkers
Historical	Consider law as a part of development of civilisation: customs, culture, religion, language, etc.	Montesquieu, Hugo, Burke, Savigny, Hegel
Religious	The law is revealed by God and interpreted by those in religious authority.	Judaism, Christianity, and Islam
Natural law	Natural law as evidenced in nature and discovered by human reason	Manu, Aristotle, Thomas Aquinas
Analytical	The relevance of the law depends on its analysis under pleasure and pain	Bentham, Austin
Sociological	Law is an important instrument of social progress.	August Comte, Herbert Spencer, Daguit, Durkheim
Realist	View law as pragmatic regulator and reject all dogmatic views	William James, Roscoe Pound, Julius Stone
Positivist	Scientific view of law or also known as pure approach; Does not study applied law	Austin, Kelson, Hart
Communism	The State's authority is supreme; it is a revolutionary legality which will disappear once the classless society is formed.	Marx and Engels, Mao and Communists

individual perspectives which belong to one of the schools of legal thought mentioned earlier. Thus, when you approach the court, it is helpful for you to know the judge's mind.

1.4   CONSTITUENTS OF LAW

TEXT

Order for maintenance of wives, children and parents.
(1) If any person leaving sufficient means neglects or refuses to maintain
(a) His wife, unable to maintain herself... A Magistrate of the first class may, upon proof of such neglect or refusal, order such person to make a monthly allowance for the maintenance of his wife or such child, father, or mother, at such monthly rate[***] as such magistrate thinks fit, and to pay the same to such person as the Magistrate may from time to time direct.[2]

– Code of Criminal Procedure 1973 Sec. 125

MANAGER'S TAKEAWAY

- Lack of sufficient knowledge about the law is like wanting to play a game without knowing the rules.
- It is important to know not only the mind of your lawyer but also that of your would-be judge. Complete preparedness in legal matters would be of great benefit to your company.

A dispute before the court of law may be a simple one but its consequences are usually enormous, because a judgement not only interprets a case in particular but also becomes an instance of reference for every such case in the future. Further, if the said case has some bearing on that person's community, the judgement becomes landmark in character. However, if such a judgement has political and economic implications, it turns out to be complex, complicated, and contentious.

Thus, Case 1.4 shows a very complex phenomenon in society in accordance to which the law is not only applied

CASE 1.4   PETITIONER: Mohd Ahmed Khan   vs   RESPONDENT: Shah Bano Begum and Others*

DATE OF JUDGEMENT: 23 April 1985

FACTS: Shah Bano, a Muslim woman, was divorced by her husband Ahmed Khan in 1978. She was 62 and had five children to support. Since she had no means to support herself and her dependent children, she approached the court to secure maintenance from her husband. The lower courts granted her petition but her husband contested their decision and the case reached the Supreme Court. It pronounced the judgement in 1985, in the seventh year after the divorce.

JUDGEMENT: Upheld the judgement of the lower courts for maintenance by the husband to his divorced wife.

*See for complete judgement, http://www.cscsarchive.org/dataarchive/textfiles/textfile.2008-07-22.2150472804/ file (05 July 2010).

Contd

---

[2]http://www.vakilno1.com/bareacts/CrPc/s 125.htm (12.2.2010), Code of Criminal Procedure 1973 Sec. 125.

Case 1.4 *Contd*

REASON:	The Supreme Court invoked Sec. 125 of the Code of Criminal Procedure, which applies to all, irrespective of caste, creed, and religion.
AFTERMATH:	The application of a pure secular law to a person from a community where personal law applies resulted in a countrywide acrimony and agitation led by both Muslim religious and political leaders. This led the government to enact a specific law called The Muslim Women Protection of Rights on Divorce Act, 1986, which upheld the Muslim Personal Law and nullified any judgement contrary to it.

but also one that develops, taking historical turns and impacting the life of the people of a country. Laws are a result of an intricate and multifarious social, political, cultural, religious, and historical growth.

What constitutes 'X'? It is a scientific question. From the earlier three sections, you must have already gathered a few essential points such as: (a) Society makes laws; (b) there is a system to enforce law; and (c) law develops as does society—historically, culturally, economically, and politically. Thus, whatever constituents or essentials elements there may be for the formation of the body of laws, these must be derived from these basic sources. Figure 1.3 lists down some of the sources from which the law originates.

It provides a distinction, namely, formal and material sources of law. The formal refers to such character of law by which it is validated. A law is null and void if it does not have validity, which comes from authoritative approval. On the other hand, the material source consists of actual objects that you handle in its origin and sustenance.

Common Law and Civil Law

We have read above how the law originates from various sources as well as how it is classified. This, at times, may lead the reader to believe that all laws function the same way; that is, they function as a system. Indeed, they do function as a system; but there is more than one system.

Common law and civil law are secular systems of law (Figure 1.4). In addition to the above, there is a third system, namely, the religious law. Religions are highly codified.

There are several other smaller groups and sects which have their own codes. Generally speaking, secular law has made enough provisions to safeguard the rights of the religious and other communities who are within the jurisdiction of a nation state.

> ⚖ MANAGER'S TAKEAWAY
>
> - Laws tell us how people have been governed, are being governed, and will be governed in the future.
> - No law can be taken lightly, as it impacts the life of not just an individual but the entire society and the world.

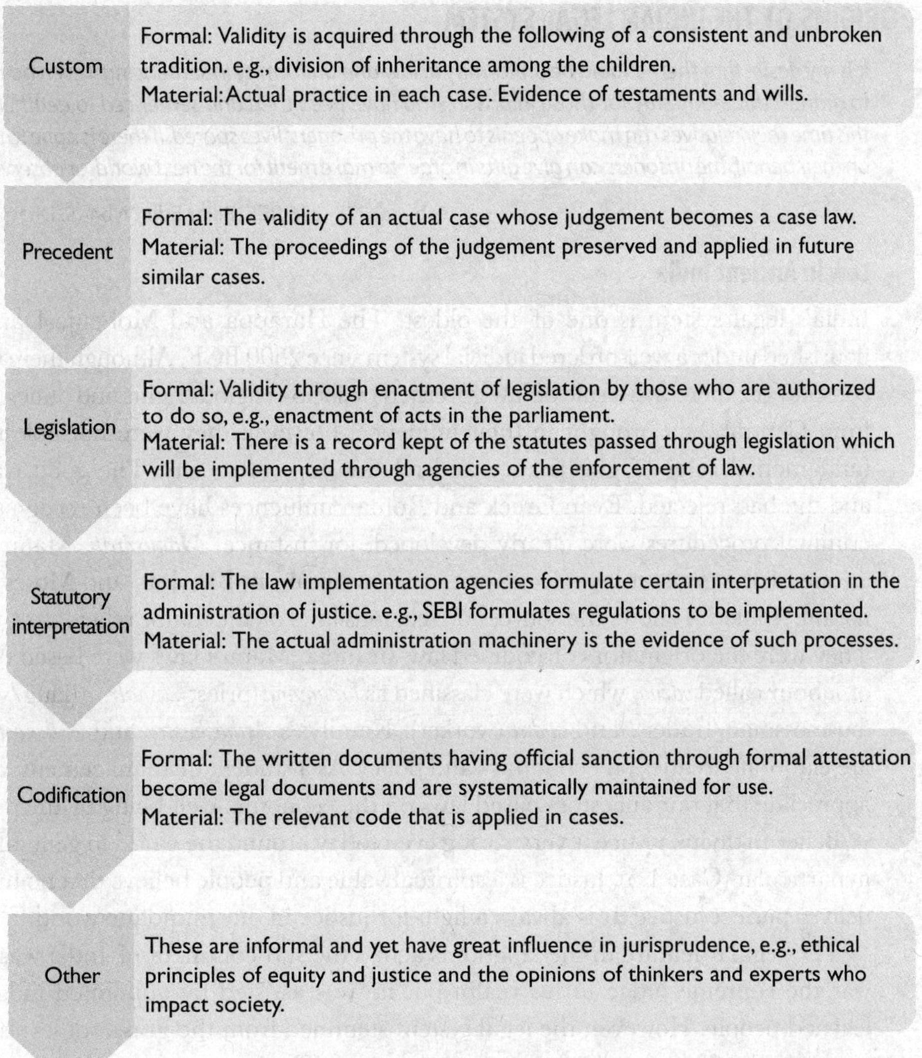

Custom	Formal: Validity is acquired through the following of a consistent and unbroken tradition. e.g., division of inheritance among the children. Material: Actual practice in each case. Evidence of testaments and wills.
Precedent	Formal: The validity of an actual case whose judgement becomes a case law. Material: The proceedings of the judgement preserved and applied in future similar cases.
Legislation	Formal: Validity through enactment of legislation by those who are authorized to do so, e.g., enactment of acts in the parliament. Material: There is a record kept of the statutes passed through legislation which will be implemented through agencies of the enforcement of law.
Statutory interpretation	Formal: The law implementation agencies formulate certain interpretation in the administration of justice. e.g., SEBI formulates regulations to be implemented. Material: The actual administration machinery is the evidence of such processes.
Codification	Formal: The written documents having official sanction through formal attestation become legal documents and are systematically maintained for use. Material: The relevant code that is applied in cases.
Other	These are informal and yet have great influence in jurisprudence, e.g., ethical principles of equity and justice and the opinions of thinkers and experts who impact society.

Figure 1.3 Sources of law

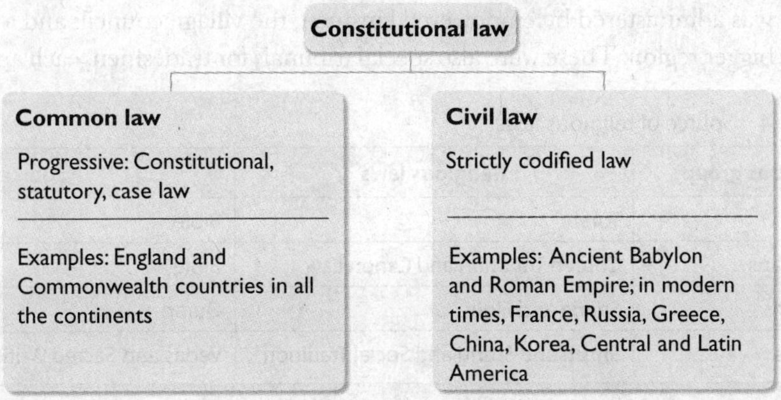

```
                    Constitutional law
          ┌──────────────────┴──────────────────┐
```

Common law	**Civil law**
Progressive: Constitutional, statutory, case law	Strictly codified law
Examples: England and Commonwealth countries in all the continents	Examples: Ancient Babylon and Roman Empire; in modern times, France, Russia, Greece, China, Korea, Central and Latin America

Figure 1.4 Two kinds of constitutional law

1.5 ORIGINS OF THE INDIAN LEGAL SYSTEM

It is my desire that there should be uniformity in law and uniformity in sentencing. I even go this far, to grant a three-day stay for those in prison who have been tried and sentenced to death. During this time their relatives can make appeals to have the prisoners' lives spared. If there is none to appeal on their behalf, the prisoners can give gifts in order to make merit for the next world, or observe fasts.

– Ashoka, 273–236 BCE, Pillar Edict Nb4 (S. Dhammika)[3]

Law in Ancient India

India's legal system is one of the oldest. The Harappa and Mohenjo-Daro civilisations flourished under a well-ordered judicial system since 2500 BCE. Although there was no written constitution, there was a rule of law governed by socio-religious rights and duties. The invasions from Central Asia brought in their influence; however, they were not able to destroy the fundamental rules of governance and relationships in society. The good was assimilated and the bad rejected. Even Greek and Roman influences have been recognised. Civil and criminal procedures were clearly developed, for instance, *Manusmriti*. Manu is considered as one of the greatest law-givers, just as Hammurabi in Babylon, and Moses of the Jewish nation. Table 1.4 shows the sources of religious laws of the major religions of the the world. They were the originators of codified law. In India, Manu's laws were based on the division of labour called *varna*, which were classified as *brahmana* (priest), *kshatriya* (king/warrior), *vaisya* (businessman/trader), and *sudra* (worker). Kautilya's *Arthashastra* and *Nitishastra* (400 BCE) are elaborate treaties on economics and policy. As a student of management, the reader will appreciate that our ancestors based laws on the economic well-being of the people.

Belief in divine justice is very strong even today around the world in general, and in India in particular (Case 1.5). Justice is a spiritual value and people believe that no human law can deliver perfect justice. It is always a fight for justice in our mundane world.

The regular feature in the kingdoms across the sub-continent of India was that the king was the supreme judge in his realm but he was assisted by appointed judges and other learned people. However, the legal system stemmed from the grassroot levels and the king was only the fifth and the final court of appeal. The law was a matter of convention and strict tradition of *varna* ethos. Justice was systematic and not arbitrary. At the lower level, justice was administered by empowered kinsmen, the village council; and a greater council for the bigger region. There were also special tribunals for tradesmen, each according to their

Table 1.4 Source of religious laws

Religious groups	Religious laws	Source
Jews	Torah	Bible
Christians	Church Tradition and Canon Law	Bible
Muslims	Sharia and Fiqh	Quran
Hindus	Shruti and Smriti and Social Tradition	Vedas and Sacred Writings, *Manusmriti*

---

[3]See, http://en.wikipedia.org/wiki/Edicts_of_Ashoka (24.2.2010)

CASE 1.5

Epic Case of Sita's Trial by Ordeal*

FACTS: The Valmiki Ramayana narrates Sita's trial by the test of fire. Her chastity is under suspicion due to her abduction and confinement by Ravana in Lanka.

JUDGEMENT: Test by fire

REASON: Trial by ordeal is the best way to determine innocence.

AFTERMATH: Sita successfully withstands test by fire.

APPEAL: Further aspersions are cast by the people.

JUDGEMENT: Banishment, 14 years of forest exile.

REASON: No immunity from suspicion even to the queen who is pregnant with the heir-apparent and who is already proved innocent.

AFTERMATH: She is rescued by Sage Valmiki and brings up her twin children in his hermitage. Upon the completion of 14 years of banishment, she hands over her sons to the king. Mother Earth opens up and receives Sita in her bosom.

SIGNIFICANCE: Human law may err, but not the divine one.

_____

*For a better appreciation see, http://hindu-texts.suite101 .com/article.cfm/agni_pariksha_of_sita_in_the_ramayana (26.2.2010).

guild of commerce. Arbitration—a mode of compromise and reconciliation—was also in vogue and the panchayat, the five-man council, helped attain justice with equity. The most admirable character of administration of justice lay in its speed; it was quick and effective.

Law in Medieval India

The advent of Islamic rule and the development of its culture had a deep impact and today it occupies a significant part of the contemporary judicial system.[4] Muslim personal law is only one example of such influence. Collections of revenues, infrastructure, management of standing army, agricultural reforms, commerce and trade, etc., were priorities of law during the rule of the Mughal emperors. Although Islamic law was in vogue, except for Aurangzeb, the other kings were tolerant about the Hindu customs and laws. Jahangir, who followed Akbar, established a popular rule of law called the *chain of justice*. A chain with sixty bells was hung outside the palace. Anyone with grievance could tug at it and the emperor himself would appear to dispense justice. Aurangzeb strictly followed *Sharia*, the Muslim law, that clearly distinguishes believers from non-believers *(kafir)*.[5] (See Case 1.6.)

Muslim invasions in India took place as early as the eighth century and Islamic law was thoroughly established. The Mughals in the almost three centuries of their rule institutionalised the *Sharia*. An elaborate system of law was established. The judiciary

_____

[4]For a brief account see, http://www.newworldencyclopedia.org/entry/Mughal_Empire (7.1.2010).
[5]See, http://en.wikipedia.org/wiki/Aurangzeb#Establishment_of_Islamic_law (7.1.2010).

CASE 1.6 — APPEAL OF THE MUSICIANS OF DELHI TO AURANGZEB, THE MUGHAL EMPEROR

FACTS: Upon the orders of Emperor Aurangzeb, there was a raid on the musicians of the Kingdom and all the musical instruments were destroyed. Musicians who were employed for occasions of marriages, festivals, and celebrations by both Hindu and Muslim communities lost their livelihoods. The musicians decided to appeal to the emperor directly. As he was being taken to the mosque for Friday prayers on a palanquin, the musicians gathered as preplanned and wailed bitterly and carried a bier representing the death of music. Upon inquiry, he was told about the plight of the musicians and how his orders have killed music.

JUDGEMENT: They should pray for the soul of music and see that it is buried well!

REASON: Under Sharia, music is forbidden. Under Aurangzeb, India was an Islamic country with Sharia law.

AFTERMATH: People, both Hindus and Muslims, and even the officials of the government clandestinely took recourse to music.

functioned under the Chief *Qazi;* there were also *Qazis* appointed for the provinces. There was no written law. Sharia was the written law; it is followed by the Muslims for religious edification and for upholding social morality. *Jizyah* was the tax levied on non-Muslims that was abrogated by Akbar—but was again invoked into law by Aurangzeb. However, in the ultimate analysis, it is the king who was the law.

An elaborate revenue system was in place.[6] *Jagir* and *zamindari* were the main forms of endowment of land to military and other officials who would have to contribute revenue both in money and kind for the standing army of the emperor. Severe penalties and punishments were imposed if the tax was evaded.

Persian was the legal language during the Mughal period. However, Urdu was increasingly used as the working language and to this day, our legal jargon includes a sizeable Urdu legal vocabulary. For instance, *kotwali, kotwal, daroga, vakil, vakalatnama, zamindar, zamindari, jagir, chaudhary, lambardar, sardar, malik, diwan,* etc., are some examples of the Urdu words in legal use.

Law in Colonial India

Soon after Vasco da Gama had established the sea route and landed in India in 1498, European traders travelled to India and conducted brisk business. Eventually, trade and commerce resulted in greater political participation. Several European countries such as Portugal, France, and Holland established colonies and commenced governance. The UK, however, overshadowed every other country and from its East India Company, grew an empire that captured and ruled the entire sub-continent. They did it more by the power of law than by the strength of their troops. For, at the height of their power, they merely had 70,000 troops. From Afghanistan to Malaysia, and from Iran to South China Sea, they ruled with the power of law—which helped their business and they enjoyed unparalleled economic bounty at home (Case 1.7).

---

[6]For a short exposition, see http://drgokuleshsharma.com/pdf/mughal%20rule.pdf (6.7.2010)

CASE 1.7

HISTORICAL CASE OF EAST INDIA COMPANY*

FACTS: On 31 December 1600, Queen Elizabeth, by a Royal Charter, created 'The Honorable Company of Merchants of London Trading into the East Indies', subsequently also known as East India Company and British East India Company. The charter granted monopoly of trade to the company for fifteen years, which enjoyed further extensions till 1708 when a rival company challenged the monopoly. The deadlock was resolved when both the companies agreed to merge as United Company of Merchants of England Trading to the East Indies. From trade it developed political and military relationships until several territories were directly controlled by the company. The military and political power was effectively established after the Battle of Plassey in 1757 by Robert Clive. The British Government too cooperated with the company, granting it monopolies, powers of political administration, maintenance and command of standing army, and also judicial powers. However, in 1857, there marked a rebellion that is considered as the decisive war of independence and the end of the Company's rule.

JUDGEMENT: Dissolution of the East India Company. The British Parliament passed Government of India Act, 1858, according to which India came under the direct rule of the British Crown; the Parliament of United Kingdom would legislate and its Government would take over the rule of the Indian Dominions, and effectively dissolve the Company.

REASON: The charters and regulations given to the company failed to stem financial rot and administrative corruption. Although the Company suffered financial loss, the shareholders rolled in the colonial wealth. The opium trade with China, of which the company had monopoly, wrecked havoc on the Chinese population. However, it is the atrocities meted out to the natives that attracted attention and outrage in civilised Britain. Hence, the Parliament—which is the supreme law maker—had to intervene and legislate so that both the executive and judiciary would act responsibly.

AFTERMATH: Firm establishment of the British rule in India with military, political, administrative, and legal system. It paved the way for the rule of law as understood in modern times. When India got independence, it was only logical to follow the established system, for it gave India its national unity and identity.

---

*See for a very useful account: http://www.britannica.com/EBchecked/topic/1 76643/East-India-Company; http:// en.wikipedia.org/wiki/Company_rule_in_India; (26.2.2010) http://www.newworldencyclopedia.org/entry/ British_East_India_Company; http://india_resource.tripod.com/eastindia.html (26.2.2010).

Law in Independent India

India made unique history by winning its political independence from the colonial powers in a bloodless manner in 1947. By 1950, it had given a Constitution to itself and thereby established for itself, a sovereign and democratic republic. It had a legislature, executive, and independent judiciary, all of which constituted from the mother of all Parliaments, the Westminster-British Common Law, Precedent, and the entire Indian legislation since the Privy Council Charter of 1726, the first legislation signed by King George I for the judicial administration of the towns called Calcutta, Bombay, and Madras—lock, stock, and barrel.

Apart from the system, it also included the English language both for writing and usage, the court buildings and furniture, maces, wigs, and all the court paraphernalia. The East India Company Regulating Act of 1773 had brought the Company under government control. The rest is history—a legal history that systematically established the colonial rule.

India obtained independence but the legal tradition continued. The Constitution of India was based on British Common Law. The UK does not have a written Constitution. Since the *Magna Carta*[7] of 1215, when the king's powers were taken away and a charter was formed, the Constitution has grown through parliamentary legislation and judicial precedent, the Case Law. India also adopted the precedents of the US, which too was basically based on the British Common Law.

Unfortunately, what we fail to understand is that the British made laws for India in Britain to further their colonial interests, which purely lay in conducting commerce and protecting their benefits. The natives were not merely subjects of the law, as should be in any law-abiding country, but they were subjected to it as servants or slaves to their master. This subservience still continues. As in many countries, there is no participation of the concerned people of society in the form of jury, which makes justice not just a technical issue but a social responsibility. In India, it is only technicalities; justice remains a distant and unattainable goal.[8]

So, what would managers like you do? In today's India, companies are afraid of litigation. Apart from time-consuming procedures, the costs are prohibitive. Companies cannot afford the costs without passing these on to their customers. This will adversely affect business. Hence, it is the manager's responsibility not to get caught in litigation, settle disputes through arbitration and reconciliation, and out-of-court settlements. But again, in the real world where money matters are of prime importance, disputes are inevitable. The only option that a manager has is to be well informed and fully prepared to face the legal challenges.

1.6 THE NATURE OF THE INDIAN LEGAL SYSTEM

And, for the better management of the said United Company's affairs in India, be it further enacted by the authority aforesaid, that, for the government of the Presidency of Fort William in Bengal, there shall be appointed a Governor-General, and four counsellors; and that the whole civil and military government of the said Presidency, and also the ordering, management, and government of all the territorial acquisitions and revenues in the kingdoms of Bengal, Behar, and Orissa, shall, during such time as the territorial acquisitions and revenues shall remain in the possession of the said United Company, be, and are hereby vested in the said Governor-General and Council of the said Presidency of Fort William in Bengal, in like manner, to all intents and purposes whatsoever, as the same now are, or at any time heretofore might have been exercised by the President and Council, or Select Committee, in the said kingdoms.

– East India Company Act, 1773 (13 Geo. III, c. 63) para VII[9]

MANAGER'S TAKEAWAY

- When in doubt, take recourse to the historical perspective of a legal aspect.
- Take the issues of law seriously and not casually.

---

[7] For a brief understanding see, http://en.wikipedia.org/wiki/Magna_Carta.
[8] For a very good critical account see V.T. Joshi and Anil Chawla, 'Indian Judiciary and Review of the Constitution of India' in http://www.samarthbharat.com/judiciary.htm (24.2.2010)).
[9] For full text document see: http://projectsouthasia.sdstate.edu/Docs/history/primarydocs/Political_History/ABKeithDoc009.htm (24.2.2010).

We have till now discussed the development of law in India. You will notice that the current Indian legal system that we follow has no relationship to its ancient legal heritage. Its origin can be dated to the date of the Charter of East India Company, and all the laws made since concerning Her or His Majesty's subjects. In other words, the Common Law of Great Britain became the basis of our legal system. This tradition, namely, the Common Law continued in independent India.

The nature of the Common Law consists of a body of judicial tradition that has been built and nourished in the society through customs and court decisions. All the English-speaking countries with British legal tradition have adopted this system. India, which came under its influence during its colonial days, has not only continued the common law tradition but also further refined it by borrowing best of the Civil Law from France and the International Law from the United Nations Organisation's principles on human rights, environmental protection, intellectual property rights, and international trade.[10]

Another salient feature of the Indian judicial system is that it is based on the principle of equity. While the law insists purely on strict justice, equity is based on the principle of justice with fairness. For instance, let us state that you mortgaged your land with your neighbour on the condition that if you do not pay your dues on the agreed time you would forfeit your mortgaged property. When the time is up you are not able to redeem yourself. According to Common Law, you would forfeit the property despite the vast disparity between the money that you have to pay to that of the property; but the Equity Court would see that, after evaluating and selling the property and giving the agreed dues to your creditor, you would receive the remainder of the money. Now you as well as your neighbour know that it is a fair justice.

Thus although our judicial system is based on Common Law of the British judicial system in India, India has further improved the system to suit the needs of her citizens. We may analyse our legal system as presented in Table 1.5.

You have seen above some of the salient features of the Indian legal system. There is no jury trial in India as in many other countries. A jury consisting of eminent persons is formed to deliver justice particularly in a criminal case. The judge conducts the proceedings but does not give verdict whether the accused is innocent or guilty; the jury does so. The judge then passes the sentence according to the law. Jury trials were conducted in India from 1860 to 1960. The so-called Nanavati case brought an end to *this* salutary judicial practice (Case 1.8). It can be seen from Case 1.8 how disputes of people when they come before the court of law have been provided defining moments for both application and evolution of the law. Above all, the cases help to test the legal system to its utmost. If the courts then are not able to deal with wishes of the people, then the people use their power to even surpass the law and set up a new benchmark for the. judiciary to follow.

> **MANAGER'S TAKEAWAY**
>
> • Knowledge of the legal system is like a skill to drive; you may not always drive but when you do so, you know not only how to drive but also what rules to follow.
> • One day when you go to create a landmark case, see that you are on the right side.

---

[10]Chief Justice Balakrishna's address at the International Conference of the Presidents of the Supreme Courts of the World,23–24 March 2008: http://www.supremecourtofindia.nic.in/new_links/Abu_Dhabias_delivered.pdf (25.2.2010),

Table 1.5 Indian legal system

Law	Elements
Constitutional and Administrative Law	The Constitution came into force on 26 January 1950. It is both a source of law as well as one that establishes administration and relationship between the federation, its states, and the citizens.
Criminal Law	Criminal justice is administered under Indian Penal Code. Trials are conducted by the court and not the jury. The code has evolved over the years, thanks to some landmark judgements. For instance, homosexuality, was an offence under the old code and yet the courts have been lenient and have taken a kind human view; consequently, it is now amended by the Parliament.
Contract Law	This is in vogue since its inception in 1872 and is the backbone of doing business.
Labour Law	India has an exhaustive volume of labour laws that have been created and evolved in independent India to suit the need of the vast and complex labour force.
Tort Law	Unlike criminal law, its origins lies in the civil law and concerns itself with tortuous liability which is imposed upon the wrong-doer for violating the private rights of another.
Property Law	Ownership, acquisition of ownership, moveable and immovable property, ownership of tangible and intangible property, mortgage and lien, and other ownership-related rights are dealt under property laws.
Trust Law	Holding of a person's property on his behalf by another person; the person upon whom the trust's confidence is placed is the trustee. Trusts are important institutions of business and socially beneficial activity.
Family Law	Hindu, Muslim, Christians, and others do not have one civil code, but it is different for each community.
Nationality Law	Citizenship is well-defined in the Constitution and the Citizenship Act 1955.There is no provision for dual citizenship. Recently, in 2004, Overseas Citizenship of India has been granted to those of Indian origin abroad; but they do not enjoy the political rights or participation in the government.
Law Enforcement	There are several law enforcement agencies functioning under the Ministry of Home Affairs, the basic unit being under the local police station.

CASE 1.8

PETITIONER: K.M. Nanavati vs RESPONDENT: State of Maharashtra

(1962 AIR 605 1962 SCR SUPL. (1) 567)*

FACTS: K.M. Nanavati, a Parsi by birth, was a naval commander and had married English-born Sylvia, and together they had two sons and a daughter. Sylvia, in the long periods of her husband's absence, fell in love with her husband's friend, P.B. Ahuja, belonging to the Sindhi community. Upon his return, Nanavati ascertained the clandestine relationship. He shot Ahuja dead with his service pistol.

JURY: The jury awarded an 8–1 not-guilty verdict.

---

*For full judgement of the Supreme Court see: http://www.indiankanoon.org/doc/1596139/ (27.2.2010). The author recommends the students to study this judgement and note carefully the number of precedents it cites as grounds to dismiss the appellant's appeal.

Contd

Case 1.8 *Contd*

REASON:	The act was a fit of passion and not premeditated.
JUDGE:	The Session's Court judge considered the acquittal unjust and referred the case to the High Court.
JUDGEMENT:	High Court sentenced Nanavati to life imprisonment.
REASON:	Culpable homicide amounting to premeditated murder.
APPEAL:	Nanavati appealed in the Supreme Court.
JUDGEMENT:	The Supreme Court, in its judgement of 4 November 1961, upheld the judgement of High Court and dismissed the appeal.
AFTERMATH:	People and media drummed up support for Nanavati who spent three years in jail until the pressure was so high that the governor had to grant sanction to the petition of pardon presented by a certain Bhai Pratap who belonged to the same community as Ahuja. The sister of the diseased Mamie Ahuja too gave her assent.**
PARDON:	The governor of Maharashtra granted pardon.
UPSHOT:	The practice of trial by jury ended.
EPILOGUE:	Nanavati, along with his wife Sylvia and children, migrated to Canada. He died in 2003.

**For a popular account see: http://en.wikipedia.org/wiki/K._M._Nanavati_vs._State_of_Maharashtra (23.02.2010).

After the Nanavati case, the jury system was abandoned because it can be swayed by public opinion, lack of jurisprudential knowledge, and commitment. However, the higher courts, the High Court and the Supreme Court, have a Bench on which the judges themselves are the members. The number of judges on a Bench is decided by the respective Chief Justices of the High Courts or of the Supreme Court, depending upon the need of the case.

1.7 THE ADMINISTRATIVE STRUCTURE OF THE INDIAN LEGAL SYSTEM

The Supreme Court, in the exercise of its jurisdiction, may pass such decree or make such order as is necessary for doing complete justice in any cause or matter pending before it, and any decree so passed or order so made shall be enforceable throughout the territory of India in such manner as may be prescribed by or under any law made by Parliament and, until provision in that behalf is so made, in such manner as the President may by order prescribe.

– The Constitution of India, Art. 142(1)

The above text from the Constitution of India not only makes its jurisdiction clear over the entire territory of India but also precedes any law to be made by the Parliament in safeguarding the liberty of the citizens. You learnt earlier how the Supreme Court asserted itself after the imposition of the Emergency in 1975. Today, the Supreme Court of India takes active interest in the issues that matter to the citizens concerning their liberty, human rights, privacy, and the chosen way of life in marriage and live-in partnerships.

Delhi is the seat of the Supreme Court. It is also sometimes known as Union Judiciary, to denote its federal character (Figure 1.5). It has a chief justice and 25 justices and they hold office till the age of 65. They are appointed by the President of India.[11]

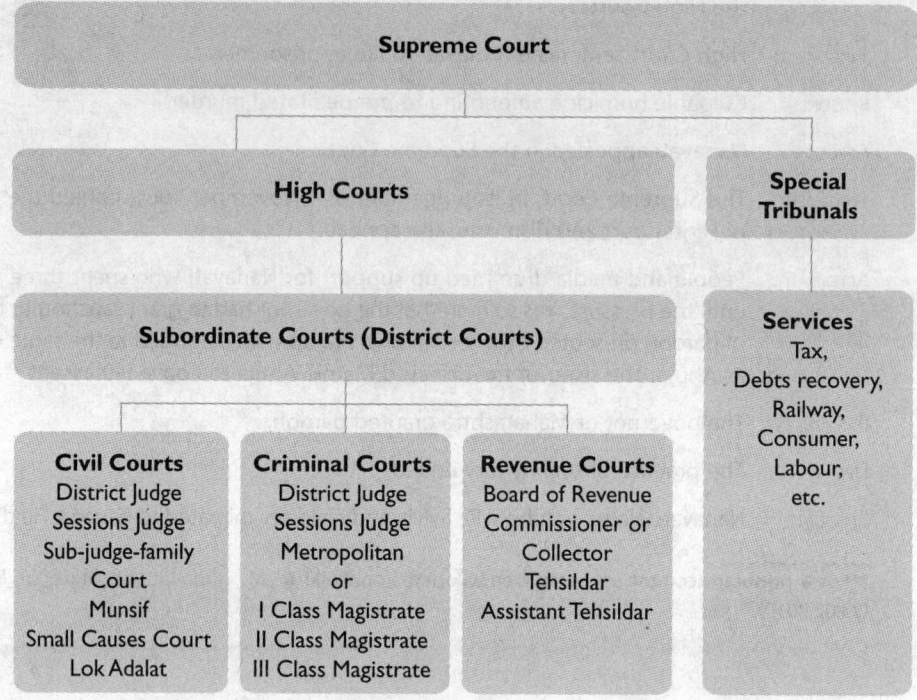

Figure 1.5 Structure of judiciary

Supreme Court

The Constitution of India (Part V, Chapter IV) provides for a court known as the Supreme Court of India. It functions as follows:

(a) the guardian of the Constitution and ultimate interpreter of law of the land;

(b) the federal court—the highest court in the country—having highest jurisdiction in the whole of the country;

(c) the highest appellate court—receives appeals against the judgements of the High Courts of the states and territories of India;

(d) the court that takes writ petitions—orders of the court in the event of serious breach of citizens' rights;

(e) the highest institution of justice endowed with enormous discretionary powers; and

(f) the court of records and supervises every High Court.

High Court

High courts are generally found in state capitals. In the case of smaller states, it is clubbed with a neighbouring one with an additional bench. For example, the High Court for Goa,

---

[11]Articles 124–147 deal with Supreme Court and its powers.

a small neighbouring State of Maharashtra, is a Bench of the Bombay High Court and is situated at Panaji, Goa. The high court is headed by a Chief Justice, who along with his Justice colleagues, is appointed by the President of India.

Lower Courts

Each High Court has its subordinate courts dealing with civil, criminal, and revenue matters at the district level. They also function at metropolitan levels. These lower courts are headed by the respective *munsifs,* magistrates, collectors, *tehsildars,* etc., as the case may be.

What you get to appreciate about the judicial system of India is that it is a singular element of our country that unites it under one system of law. These days, the Supreme Court is highly conscious about the social issues, environmental issues, and international issues. It has remained a watchdog over the legislature and has taken upon itself the active role to defend and protect basic freedoms, life, and property of the people. In this respect, the case presented at the end of this chapter, on Minerva Mills, is an instance of such determination of the Supreme Court. However, here as we shall see in Case 1.9, which too is an equally landmark case, that ensures possession of property as an inalienable right of our Constitution, which cannot be amended even by the Parliament lest its *basic structure should change.*

This case became a landmark in protecting the right to property of the individuals, irrespective of the noble motives of acquisition and redistribution of land to the poor and the needy, Although Mrs Indira Gandhi found it difficult to accept the decision since her party programme had suffered a setback, she acknowledged being bound to socialism and that the party's concept of socialism did not require nationalising

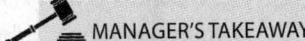

MANAGER'S TAKEAWAY

- You may appreciate the exact and exhaustive administrative structure of the Indian legal system.
- You may truly have faith in our Supreme Court as the defender of our Constitution.

CASE 1.9 PETITIONER: Kesavananda Bharati and Others vs RESPONDENT: The State of Kerala

DATE OF JUDGEMENT: 23 April 1973*

FACTS: The Government of Kerala introduced land reforms, under the 25th Amendment to the Constitution, which included acquisition and redistribution of land to the landless. In several litigations that followed from the owners of the land who lost their property, the courts consistently upheld the rights of the owners. Swami Kesavananda Bharati of Kerala challenged the 25th Constitutional Amendment brought and passed by the Congress Government led by Mrs Indira Gandhi in 1971.

JUDGEMENT: The Parliament cannot make this Amendment.

REASON: Because such an Amendment that restricts the right to property will alter the *Basic Structure of the Constitution.* The Constitution is supreme and changing of its structure is contrary to its very own existence.

*See: http://indiankanoon.org/doc/257876/; http://www.legalserviceindia.com/articles/thyg.htm (27.2.2010).

everything. The Supreme Court of India, time and again, had to deal with such cases and in each, it has never avered in upholding the right to property.

The relevance of this and similar cases to business is of utmost importance. Without the principle right to private property, business will cease to exist.

1.8 RELATIONSHIP BETWEEN BUSINESS AND LAW

Contingent contracts to do or not to do anything if an uncertain future event happens cannot be enforced by law unless and until that event has happened. If the event becomes impossible, such contracts become void.[12]

– The Indian Contract Act, 1872, Chapter 3, para 32

You buy a railway ticket to travel and you are in business contract with the largest public sector railway in the world. The law ensures that you are a *bona fide*, i.e., true and authentic, customer of the Indian Railways. The law will impinge upon the Indian Railways the responsibility of your travel.

Business is an exchange of goods and services that takes place under several conditions. Quite commonly, a business deals with *if-then* formula: If you book and pay immediately for a foreign holiday package tour by Cox & Kings, then you get an 'early bird' discount of 20 per cent and a free gift. A certain condition is to be fulfilled *if and only if an* event occurs. For instance, Amir makes a contract with Bharat to sell the flat, only if Chetan to whom the offer is made first, refuses to buy within an agreed period. In this case, no law can be enforced until the stipulated time has not elapsed.

MANAGER'S TAKEAWAY

- No business is valid without it being, at the same time, legal.
- Legal framework is a manager's boundary.

You see that the law is kept at abeyance only for a while with a given person. However, it is already applicable with whom there is an ongoing agreement. Thus, whether you are concerned immediately or at a future date, the law is always there to legitimise or de-legitimise your deal or contract.

CASE 1.10	PETITIONER: Dabur India Ltd vs RESPONDENT: K.R. Industries

DATE OF JUDGEMENT: 16 May 2008*

FACTS: Dabur, the reputed manufacturer of hygiene products, has a tooth powder product called *Dabur Lal Dant Manjan*. After failing to get relief from the Delhi High Court in a matter concerning copyright violation of its tooth powder carton, it filed an appeal in the Supreme Court of India. It was alleged that K.R. Industries had marketed a similar tooth powder called 'Sujata' whose packing, colour, and blurb imitated that of the Dabur product, thus, causing deception.

*For full case and citations see: http://www.indiankanoon.org/doc/1327080/ (25.2.2010).

Contd

[12] See the Act: http://www.corecentre.co.in/Database/Docs/DocFiles/indian_contract.pdf (25.2.2010).

Case 1.10 *Contd*

JUDGEMENT: Appeal dismissed.

REASON: There was no clear evidence to establish the copyright infringement. After citing several cases, it was found that since the respondent was not selling the product in the jurisdiction of the High Court in Delhi, but was doing so in Andhra Pradesh, the Court did not find merit in the appeal.

The relationship between law and business may be well brought out in Case 1.10 where there is a dispute between two manufacturers. The only authority in the land that can conclusively solve the dispute and impart justice is the law of the land administered by a court of law.

Copyrights are increasingly becoming a thorny issue in the fierce competitive business environment. Every aspect of business from contract to carriage, from company formation to its dissolution, from labour to salaries, from sale and purchase to information technology, from taxation to international trade, and much more, is in the domain of law. In fact, no business can be conducted without law. Every business deal must be unconditionally legal. We shall see in the rest of this book how every chapter will deal with the relationship between law and business.

Case 1.11 discusses the issue of government regulation.

CASE 1.11 | **Government Regulation—Jurisprudence in Action**

REGULATION:
'To regulate' implies 'to control'. The elected government is the manager of the affairs of the people. It puts into practice what the legislature enacts into laws. Judiciary is the adjudicator of the people and judges all matters independent of the government. It also makes sure that the laws enacted by the legislature are according to the will of the people enshrined in the Constitution of the people.

In business and industry, government regulation is the supervision of privately owned businesses or private activities by government or government agencies. The process of regulation is designed to serve public interest. Such agencies control health and safety standards, prices, standards of service, and other aspects of business. The objective of regulations is to control certain outcomes, whether by affecting them or by stopping them, as is necessary. Some examples of regulatory control include market entries, prices, wages, development approvals, pollution control, employment of certain people, reservation of jobs, securities exchange, essential goods, agricultural policies, control of monopoly, information, etc.

Government regulations are a way of implementing the laws. Sometimes these regulations are known as bylaws—both concepts are synonymous. Government appoints agencies for definite activities such as power, banking, securities, investigation, water resources, forests, industry, commerce, etc. All these go to form the organs of the government and they work through committees, commissions, and scores of regulatory authorities as per their purposes.

Contd

Case 1.11 *Contd*

Government regulation may be carried out at all levels: by local (municipal), regional, or central government. Local governments and authorities are given responsibility to regulate some activities by the national governments. For example, local authorities may be responsible for ensuring that buildings meet the required standards of design and safety, for inspecting food shops to check the standards of cleanliness or for visiting farms to make sure the animals are being looked after properly.

Central government has to make sure that regulations are observed, and new ones introduced if necessary by passing new laws. The range of regulations is large in most countries: it may include items such as the time spent by children in school, the school curriculum, the way in which businesses are conducted, or the speed at which motor vehicles may travel on the roads. Relations between workers and management, and conditions of employment are generally the subject of government regulation. Discrimination because of sex, colour, age, or nationality is illegal. Governments often set up special commissions to study the need for new laws, where extra regulation may be required.

The process of regulation does not stop at the national level. International institutions such as United Nations Organisation, the World Trade Organisation, and the World Court of Justice, all give rise to the formation of regulatory authorities.

REFORM

Reform is the need to change. In winter, you wear woollen clothes to save you from cold. In summer, you change to lighter clothes to keep you cool. You change according to need. It is counterproductive to continue with something that is of neither use nor significance. So also is the case with regulations; these change according to the circumstances. The government employs policies and regulations, which work for the people; regulations which do not serve public interest need reform, or change.

DEREGULATION

Deregulation is to free what has been controlled. India followed a controlled system, a licensing system of economic policy that controlled not only industry but also health, education, and several other areas. In early 1900s, the world political and economic situation changed. Correspondingly, India adopted the logic of market economy and deregulated its economic policy.

LIBERALISATION

Liberalisation is to decontrol and allow individual and natural choices. A mere deregulation was not enough. It had to have a complete change of the model of management. This led to total decontrol or liberalisation. Private individuals and firms were free to operate in a competitive and open market. Liberalisation led the market to relate to the forces of demand and supply.

However, liberalised business has its own logic. It also needs certain regulation. Thus, for instance, the Reserve Bank of India comes out with certain statutory regulations to correct a financial course. The finance minister of India introduces several budgetary regulations annually and enacts them in laws. Likewise, all ministries—as per the need of the times—direct various regulatory bodies that they operate to put in new modes of control to meet new challenges.

Regulation is significant if it is useful.

1.9 PRINCIPLE OF COMMERCIAL JURISPRUDENCE

To strive towards excellence in all spheres of individual and collective activity so that the nation constantly rises to higher levels of endeavour and achievement.

– Constitution of India, Article 51, A

Economic well-being of the people is achieved through every form of work and wealth creation. The Constitution of India in Article 51 enumerates the duties of every citizen. This along with Article 21, which lays down the single fundamental principle of the protection of life, liberty, and property of every citizen, epitomises jurisprudence. Business pursuit is part and parcel of it. Anything that vitiates the principles under these articles of our Constitution is contrary to it both in letter and spirit.

The above may be explained through the most fundamental principle in jurisprudence called the Doctrine of the Public Trust. It is based on the principle of stewardship. It consists of the belief that all resources are given by Nature and that the people and, in turn, the State are not its owners but stewards or care takers. No one can claim to be the ultimate owners of air, water, earth, forests, sea, and other natural endowments. It becomes the duty of the governments to allow to use these resources for the benefit of all and not to use for private ownership.

This principle of public trust is present in both the forms of law: Common as well as Civil. In fact, this is the fundamental principle of all time, the very beginning of the rule of law. It is also the fundamental principle of democracy. It mandates affirmative action by the State in the management of the resources and at the same time makes it every citizen's duty to see that the State upholds its duty. In Case 1.12, the principle of public trust is exemplified beyond doubt.

CASE 1.12   PETITIONER: M.I. Builders Pvt. Ltd vs RESPONDENT: Radhey Shyam Sahu and Others

DATE OF JUDGEMENT: 26 July 1999*

FACTS: Lucknow Nagar Mahapalika or the Lucknow City Corporation granted permission to construct an underground commercial complex, and requisite agreements were made with regard to the cost of construction and leasing which gave free hand to the builder. This was challenged on the ground that it is a public park and the planned commercial construction would only further worsen the situation of congestion and will be a public hazard. The High Court of Allahabad set aside and quashed the agreement between the builder and Lucknow Nagar Mahapalika and ordered the latter to restore the park within three months. The builder M.I. Builders Pvt. Ltd, filed a petition in the Supreme Court.

JUDGEMENT: Upheld the judgement of the High Court and declared the agreement between the Mahapalika and the builder as unreasonable, unfair, and atrocious to the public interest.

*For complete judgement and citations see: http://www.indiankanoon.org/doc/1937304/ (27.2.2010).

Contd

Case 1.12 *Contd*

> REASON: Mahapalika is the trustee for the proper management of the parks for the public and that it vitiated the public trust. The agreement between the builder and the Mahapalika disregarded the historical importance and environmental necessity. By allowing the construction of commercial complex, the Mahapalika has deprived people the public good and thus betrayed public trust. It also violated its own constitution and the Municipal Act.

From Case 1.12 it is clear that the philosophy of social and economic justice along with the preservation of natural resources and their judicious use is the principle under which a responsible government and any other agency should function. Entrepreneurs, industrialists, and businesses cannot act against the interest of the people; neither do they have the right to misuse common resources that Nature endows. The rule of law demands that business can function only in the interest of the people and maintain the public trust.

1.10 SOME CONSTITUTIONAL ASPECTS

We, the people of India, having solemnly resolved to constitute India into a [sovereign socialist secular democratic republic] and to secure to all its citizens: justice, social, economic and political; liberty of thought, expression, belief, faith and worship; equality of status and of opportunity; and to promote among them all fraternity assuring the dignity of the individual and the [unity and integrity of the nation]; in our constituent assembly this twenty sixth day of November, 1949, do hereby adopt, enact and give to ourselves this constitution.

– Constitution of India, Preamble

Our Constitution is our first law. All laws derive their legitimacy from it. The text of the preamble of India is our definition of the law from the point of view of its objective. It gives us our identity as Indians. It is considered not only for its length but also for its vision of inclusion of best of jurisprudence. Some of the salient features are presented in Table 1.6.

Perverting the Constitution

MANAGER'S TAKEAWAY

- Public interest above personal interest.
- Business succeeds only with the goodwill of the people, which upholds the public trust.

There are times in the life of a republic when the government tends to take liberty with the people's constitution. There is a provision under Article 123 of the Constitution where the president of the Union or the governor under Article 213 of a State has the right to promulgate a law in the form of an ordinance. This may *only* be done in extreme necessity when the legislature is not in session. But the ordinance may be promulgated only when there is an assured support for it to be replaced by an Act, as soon as the legislature is convened immediately thereafter.

Case 1.13 brings to light how the government of the State of Bihar consistently tried to subvert the Constitution by promulgating ordinances to suit its own ends.

Table 1.6 Salient features of the Indian constitution

Features	Remarks
	Background to the Constitution
Legal history	Laws from the time of colonial rule, particularly after the first war of independence in 1857 when India came directly under British Crown and the British Parliament enacted laws for India.
Act of 1935	The Government of India Act, 1935—by which for the first time in her history—India was conceived as a federal entity. There was a clear separation of powers between the central rule and the provinces. This feature was essentially retained in the new Constitution.
Cabinet mission, 1946	This established the transfer of power. It also formulated the structure of the government.
Indian Independence Act, 1947	A clear demarcation of territory was envisaged for the self-government of the new nation: India.
Drafting of the constitution	A constituent assembly was formed in December 1946.
	The Constitution
Comes into existence	The Parliament adopted the written constitution into law on 26 January 1950.
Structure	Contents: Parts 24, Articles 448, Schedules 15, Appendices 5, and 108 Amendments (the 108th would be the Women's Reservation Bill 2010, which is already passed in the *Rajya Sabha).*
System	Parliamentary Democracy with *Lok Sabha* and *Rajya Sabha,* President as the head of the State of the Union, and the Governors of the States and Union Territories.
System of government	Federal. Clear separation of powers between the Union and the States, and Union Territories. The Central government with prime minister and council of ministers.
Judiciary	Independent. Hierarchical: Supreme Court, High Courts, and lower courts.
Supremacy	Fundamental rights are inalienable and un-amendable.
Unique feature	Directive principles to guide the government in the welfare of the people; guidance to take social and economic measures in the interest of the people.
Citizenship	Recognizes single citizenship
Choice of representatives	Universal franchise
Business	Part XII deals with Finance, Property, Contracts, and Suits; Part XIII deals with Trade and Commerce.

Professor Dr D.C. Wadhwa of Gokhale Institute of Politics and Economics, Pune, tabulated painstakingly, the ordinances promulgated by the government of Bihar, which showed a clear penchant to bypass the houses of State's legislature.

The then Chief Justice, P.N. Bhagwati, one of the most respected luminaries of law, held that: what the constitutional authority cannot do indirectly, it can do directly. It is vigilant

CASE 1.13	Petitioner: D.C. Wadhwa vs Respondent: State of Bihar

(AIR 1987SC 579, 20.12.1986)*

Facts: The Government of Bihar promulgated (a) Bihar Forest Produce (Regulations of Trade) Third Ordinance, 1983; (b) The Bihar Intermediate Education Council Third Ordinance, 1983; (c) The Bihar Bricks Supply (Control) Third Ordinance, 1983; and so on. Dr D.C. Wadhwa in his research included 256 ordinances between 1967 and 1981. He and others petitioned to the Supreme Court pleading that it was a fraud on the Constitution of India.

Judgement: Such promulgation perverts the Constitution.

Reason: Ordinances are essentially a power to meet an extraordinary need. It cannot be used to serve political ends. It is contrary to norms that the Executive should have the power to make a law.

*http://www.manupatrainternational.in/supremecourt/1980–2000/sc1986/s860072.htm.

people like Wadhwa who, through public interest litigation (PIL)[13], ultimately help save our supreme and sacred Constitution that we have given to ourselves. Brick business and forestry are large business ventures in Bihar. There are lobbies of vested-interest business enterprises that pressure governments to take recourse to ordinances. The bureaucrats then find it handed over to them to deal swiftly to entertain the interested parties. The legal course is tedious and exacting. The world has seen horrors by such actions where seemingly the law is followed while it is really perverted. The oft-cited example of the perversion of a Constitution is of the Weimer Republic by Adolf Hitler.

Fundamental Rights and Business Organisations

The knowledge of the fundamental rights of every citizen is an imperative. These rights are also related to the associations and organisations created by the citizens. Business organisations too share in the fundamental rights and it is important for every manager to know about them. (See Table 1.7.)

⚖ MANAGER'S TAKEAWAY

- When in doubt, ask: Is this according to the law of the land? If it is, ask: Is it under an ordinance or an enacted law?
- A manager can also be an exemplary citizen by being vigilant about the affairs of the state.

1.11 MANAGER AND THE LEGAL ENVIRONMENT

TEXT

Subject to the other provisions of this Part, trade, commerce, and intercourse throughout the territory of India shall be free.

– Constitution of India, Part XIII, Article 301[14]

[13]For an excellent article on PIL see: http://www.ngosindia.com/resources/pil_sc.php (11.02.2010)

[14]Constitution of India, Part XIII Trade, Commerce and Intercourse within the Territory of India, Article 301. Also refer to the rest of the provisions.

Table 1.7 Fundamental rights and business organisations

Right	Remark	Business application
Equality	Articles 14 to 18 provide equality before the law without prejudice to caste, creed, sex, birth, etc.	A firm cannot discriminate a person either in employment or payment of wages.
Freedom	Article 19: speech, assembly, association, unions, movement and possession of property, and exercise of profession throughout the Indian territory.	Every employee has these rights.
Protection in respect of conviction	Article 20: No person shall be convicted except for violation of the existing law; no greater penalty to be imposed than the offence; no person shall be prosecuted and punished for the same offence more than once; none can be forced to be witness against himself, i.e., protection against self-incrimination.	A firm cannot take arbitrary action against someone but must always take recourse to law.
Life and liberty	Article 21: None can be deprived of one's life and personal liberty.	No firm can infringe the personal life and liberty of an employee. Thus, forced labour, confinement, confiscation of personal effects of employees is unlawful.
Protection against unlawful detention	Article 22: On arrest, one has the right to be informed of the grounds of detention and must be produced before the magistrate within 24 hours.	The firm and its employees are the subjects of the law.
Protection from exploitation	Articles 23 and 24: Prohibition of traffic in human beings and forced labour.	Firms must respect the human rights.
Freedom of religion	Articles 25 to 28: Profession, practice, and propagation of one's creed is a fundamental inviolable right.	Firms cannot discriminate on religious basis.
Culture and education	Articles 29 and 30: To practice one's culture, develop one's language, and be taught is the basic right.	No cultural or educational discrimination. Only merit matters.
Constitutional remedies	Article 32: Every citizen has the right to move to the court of law to seek legal remedy. The court may use its powers of orders and writs to grant relief to the affected.	Firms too have the fundamental right to seek legal remedy in a court of law whether against its own employees or any others with whom it has a business relation.

You are the manager of a company. Can you confidently say, 'I do not need any law?' Your reasoning is that you are a good person and you do no harm to any one. What about others who do business with you, work for you, provide you with services? Are they all just as law abiding as you? Do you all have the same perspective about law? Do you always hold the same opinion and never have a dispute? At some point there could be some dispute in areas of finance, audit, fulfillment of contracts and agreements, labour problems, personnel problems in workplace, consumer disputes, and so on. These areas form what is known as the legal environment. It is an environment, a surrounding or a context in which business operates according to the law. All parties contracting business have recourse to law as a resort of arbitration and justice when wronged. What a natural environment is for the life and development of living creatures, so is law for the environment where reasonable conduct of business is possible.

Business and Legal Environment

Business is human activity: it creates business relationships—these relationships obtain validity only through the legitimacy of the law. No business can operate without being bound by law. The law ensures one single standard to judge the veracity of all business transactions.

Indian law is a continuance of English law. It is a very well-systematised procedure. As you saw earlier, it is based on constitutional law, which is further supported by the statutory law created by the legislature and further enhanced by the agencies of the government; it is furthered and strengthened by case law and businesses can have full faith in its efficacy. If you possess a degree in law before you join to study business administration, you will not only appreciate how law helps you but you will also gain insight into the functioning of the law, which will help you to take legally right decisions that will be of great benefit for your firm. Knowledge of the legal system makes you comfortable as it is a familiar territory.

Indian judiciary, though ideally one of the best in the world, is often spited for its inordinate delay and haphazardness. Table 1.8 shows some of the conducive and non-conducive factors that, respectively, help or mar the legal environment.

Table 1.8   Factors of the legal environment

Legal environment	
Conducive factors	**Non-conducive factors**
1. System of the rule of law 2. Federal structure that helps uniformity 3. Universal use of english language and translation in local/state languages 4. Based on provable evidence and beyond reasonable doubt 5. High Courts and the Supreme Court have benches instead of jury 6. Lawyers belong to the bar	1. Procedural delays—appeals till they reach the apex court take several years 2. Non-availability of specialised lawyers and legal aid to expedite justice 3. Corruption 4. Costly—in terms of both time and money 5. Problems of legal jargon—only the legal fraternity understand the implications of language in writs, petitions, orders, etc.

Functioning of Court

Try and attend some court proceedings, preferably the cases related to trade and commerce. The entire court atmosphere that you instantly perceive makes you experience the legal environment better than what any book can teach you. The Indian court proceedings are based on arguments presented by the lawyers representing their respective clients. These lawyers are generally members of the bar association. Such a member can practice anywhere in the country. Listening to lawyer-arguments, which are well presented and with definitive logical reasoning, are lessons in themselves. Legal reasoning is precise and logical, or else the arguments will fall on their face and suffer contradictions.

There are single judges or magistrates in the lower courts and tribunals. In the high courts a bench of judges may be appointed for important cases. Indian judges come from a well-systematised cadre of lawyers who are very well versed in law. They are assisted by other court officers who receive the filed cases and fix the dates of hearings. The judge is an impartial referee who gives judgement after weighing the evidences and precedences if any. The judgement is a very well-written document, which evaluates the arguments and applies the constitutional, statutory, and case law as may be the need to cite in corroboration of the conclusion, that is, the judgement. Each judgement is a further step in the furtherance of the case law.

Evidence given by the witnesses normally forms the core of legal procedure. Cross questioning of the witnesses is a practice to ascertain the veracity of facts by the opponents. Thus, the Indian courts give adequate opportunities for the litigants not only to present their case but also to be heard by their opponents.

The interim arrangement of the court has lasted for close to two centuries, and it shall continue in this manner perennially, for the person concerned does not exist to receive justice. However, law has its own logic or wisdom that allows for the things to function as they had been willed by the original owner of the estates, as we will see in the following case of Raja Rajkishore Deb (Case 1.14). Indeed, we may alter the famous saying, 'people may come and people may go but law shall remain'.

CASE 1.14   **The Perennial Case***

HISTORY: Raja Rajkishore Deb was a *zamindar* who lived in late eighteenth century and died early in the following century, in 1825. In 1833, a civil suit was filed over the estate of erstwhile North Kolkata before the Supreme Court; that is, even before Calcutta High Court was formed, which was set up in 1862 and to which the case was transferred. The case is about the will of Raja Rajakishore Deb. He allotted large lands in the city as well as in the rest of the state for maintenance and performance of rituals *(puja)* of the family deities.

One of the relatives challenged the provisions made in the will and filed a case before the then English Supreme Court in Calcutta in 1833. The Supreme Court appointed a receiver to the assets and later when the British established High Courts in Bombay, Madras, and Calcutta, this case was transferred to Calcutta High Court in 1862. After a few decades, it had prepared a scheme for the day-to-day running of the temple and related expenses. There have been generations of receivers to the assets and the scheme continues to this day to the present receiver, a barrister whose name is Gour Roy Chowdhury.

---

*See: http://www.expressindia.com/news/fullstory.php?newsid=65386 (2.3.2010) Posted on April 2, 2006.

Law Is Your Business

As a business manager you have several responsibilities (Table 1.9). However, the legal angle must be your top priority because you do not want, due to your lack of knowledge, to land the firm in a legal tangle. Remember, legal battles cost huge for the firms—which eventually

Table 1.9 Manager's role in different legal matters

Matter	Manager's role
Police complaint	If a complaint has to be lodged (a) Take advice from a senior manager, (b) Appraise the lawyer, and (c) Only then, guided by the above, do the needful.
Police investigation	If the police come to investigate (a) Welcome them and gain time, (b) Consult a senior manager, and (c) Take advice from the lawyer.
Choosing a lawyer	Approach the lawyer appointed by the company in consultation with the senior management (a) Choose the best possible lawyer, (b) Fix the fees, and (c) Make payments as per the hiring contract.
Filing a case	Choose the lawyer as per the above guidelines (a) Check with the lawyer approaching court offices for filling and filing of forms, (b) Pay the court fees, and (c) Attend the hearing of the case, eventhough most of the time, the civil cases do not require the presence of the client, yet attending it will give you a first-hand knowledge of the matter for which you are directly responsible.
Case procedures	Carefully follow the case proceedings from the beginning till the end: (a) Summons: Court summons the disputing parties to place their arguments. If repeatedly one or both the parties are absent, then the court can decree ex parte, that is, without hearing the party, (b) Pleading: The plea of the disputing parties is placed before the court, (c) Proof: Evidence is submitted before the court and arguments are presented in accordance with the law, (d) Judgement: The court, after weighing the arguments and examining the evidence, passes judgement, (e) Execution: The court orders are executed; if appeal to higher court is granted, the case continues; if the orders are not complied, the court may punish for the contempt of the court and may take further action using the administrative machinery of the State. A firm and its managers are liable to be punished for any offence committed.
Employees	As a manager you must realise that your employees are the citizens who enjoy fundamental rights enshrined in the Constitution. Gain legal knowledge in the following subjects: (a) Employee rights (b) Working conditions (c) Social security (d) Job security (e) Wages, allowances, and bonus (f) Trade unions (g) Labour disputes

hike the cost of the products and services you offer and may even cause you to lose the edge over your competitors. There are hundreds of cases of firms whose long and arduous litigation eventually ended in bankruptcy and closure. However, in business, disputes are inevitable and you must be ready to steer your firm quickly and efficiently from becoming a victim of a long litigation.

1.12 PRACTICAL WAYS TO READ AND UNDERSTAND LEGAL LANGUAGE

(4) In case a State Government intends to set up a Special Economic Zone, it may, after identifying the area, forward the proposal directly to the Board for the purpose of setting up the Special Economic Zone: Provided that the Central Government may,

(a) after consulting the State Government concerned;

(b) without referring the proposal for setting up the Special Economic Zone to the Board; and

(c) after identifying the area;

suo moto set up and notify the Special Economic Zone.

– Special Economic Zones Act, 2005[15]

The above text is a simple formation, considering many difficult ones, in the recent Act on Economic Zones, paragraph number 4. The text, however, has all the ingredients which make a perfect legal text and also the flavour that comes through the Latin seasoning—*suo moto* (on its own or without being prompted by someone else). See the sub-clauses that endeavour to exclude nothing in the process of who is actually responsible to take decisions, and also all checks and balances are in place. In one clause, the centre, state, and its authorised board have been designated their bureaucratic function meticulously and without ambiguity. Further, even a business plan is embedded in it: the areas have to be identified, authorisations must be sought, and the actual economic activity has to be set up, even if it means a go-alone strategy by the government. It is a systemic example of simultaneous legal power and bureaucratic set-up.

According to the legal principle, none is excused from the knowledge of law, and yet, legal language is not everyone's cup of tea. Just as other specialised professions and fields have their own technical language, the legal profession is not an exception. In fact, very often it is accused of being most ambiguous and obfuscating. Apart from the ordinary, day-to-day spoken language, we have developed terms and phrases according to the professions. An IT programmer's language is technically different from that of a dentist; a car manufacturer's is different from that of a chemist in a pharmaceutical company; a psychologist's is different from a physicist; a judge's verdict is different than the report of a surgeon, etc. Let us consider some of the salient features of legal-speak.

Historical Development

A thousand years ago, the English and the French came together mostly due to conquests upon each other—the

> **MANAGER'S TAKEAWAY**
> - Do not procrastinate in legal matters.
> - Develop interest in law.

---

[15]See, The *Gazette of India*, Extraordinary Part II — Sec. I, No. 31, Ministry of Law and Justice, New Delhi, June 2005.

so-called Norman conquests. These two countries had the influence of three languages at the highest order of the state and its functioning, namely, English, French, and Latin. While the former two were considered vernacular, the latter was the official language. Since Latin was not understood commonly, it was used only for official records while the courts functioned in English and French. Definitions and principles were retained in Latin even within English and French discourse at the court and it continues to be to this day in both these countries.

The Legal Language of India

As the British colonised around the globe, their legal system was also established in the colonies. India being the first, it got the entire British Common Law system lock, stock, and barrel. The other big colony, the USA, too was established as per common law. America went on to further develop law and the language in its own characteristic way. However, in the subcontinent too there developed a unique form of common law, due to the inclusive nature of the case law, several Indian characteristics got assimilated. Several terms representing Indian realities such as *adalat, raj, zamindar, diwan, tehsil, taluka, munsib, vakil, vakalatnama, rayyot, bandobust, lokayukta,* etc., were incorporated. Jurisprudence in India is inseparably joined with social concerns; it aims at the development and involves actively in advancing a just and fair society. Acts are made, for instance, to safeguard the labour force, children, and women against exploitation. The courts have taken active part in keeping safe of the environment.

Although the national language of India is Hindi and the States have their own official languages, its legal language is English. Legal English applies to the following:

- Contracts and licenses,
- Court pleadings, summonses, briefs, and judgements,
- Acts of the Parliament and subordinate legislation, statutes, and regulations, and
- Legal correspondence.

Salient Features of Legal Language

There is an anecdote about the complication in legal language caused by a simple comma. Czar Alexander III of Russia once signed the death warrant of a criminal: *Pardon impossible, to be sent to Siberia.* However his wife, Czarina Maria Fyodorovna had different designs; she wanted the prisoner to be set free. She merely manipulated text by changing the comma punctuation: *Pardon, impossible to be sent to Siberia.* No one can claim the absolute mastery over legal language; yet it is important to deal with it seriously since life, liberty, and human possessions depend on it; the entire structure of our society and its future depend on it. Some of the salient features of the legal language are as follows:

Terms and phrases   Legal English has its own lexicon. The glossary at the end of this book is a ready help to you to understand what terms and phrases signify. There are a number of free dictionaries available on the Internet. There are specialised terms: action (lawsuit), *party* (principal in a lawsuit), tort, fee simple, novation, consideration, etc. There are also innumerable technical phrases that are not merely in English but very often in Latin and sometimes in French. For instance *certiorari, habeas corpus, prima facie, mensrea, subjudice* are in Latin; The French are: *estoppel, laches, voir dire,* etc. The system also uses quite archaic phrases such as: *herein, hereto, herewith, whereby, whereas, wherefore,* etc. The reason for this is the story that you read earlier about the changing of punctuation. These phrases are handy to avoid punctuation.

Doublets are another way of clear determination of the state of affairs with greatest possible emphasis. Some of the examples are: null and void, fit and proper. There are times even triplets are used: such as dispute, controversy, or claim; perform and discharge; promise, agree, and covenant; etc.

Formal writing　Legal documentation is a serious affair and it adheres to a system of precise expressions, distinctions, and sub-distinctions, clearly identifying persons, positions, circumstances, time elements, and every other aspect as per the matter under consideration.

Legalese　Legal writing takes the shape of a total technical form. It exceeds popular understanding and is uniquely and essentially legal in nature; the terms and expressions are especially carved out to establish clarity and precision of concepts. Its characteristics consist of being strictly formal, having long sentences, having several modifying clauses and phrases, and defining of legal concepts through Latin or French phrases. Some specific terms of legalese are: without bias to, the said, hereafter, forthwith, aforementioned, etc.

Interpretation　A text is as good as it is understood. The lawyers place arguments before the judge based on the legal principles. These principles are the same for all and yet the lawyers putting forward their arguments have their own perspectives in favour of their clients. The judge, who weighs their arguments and the evidences presented too has the very same principles, pronounces judgement which may favour one against the other or neither. Thus, it is not what is written but how it is interpreted—that is the crux of legal text.

The stereotypical language and its legal interpretations are not without purpose; in fact, it does not make the language as clear as possible so that through it the rights of the people are protected without ambiguity. The formal nature of the texts provides certainty to both its writers and users. The lawgiver does not desire to make the law difficult for the people; its purpose is to serve the people. Since it is important for life, we must make some effort to learn the law of the land because, ultimately, it is the law made by the people, for the people, and of the people. We may do well to remember the opening words of our Constitution: We the people of India... do hereby adopt, enact and give to ourselves this constitution.

If you are not a medical student or doctor then you may not understand one of their textbooks or advanced study books, but you certainly understand a medical report that is published in a newspaper. The former is specialised and you are not expected to understand it but the latter is written in a language that can be understood by everybody. So also, highly technical and judicial matters are comprehended by the people professionally concerned with law but everyone understands when a court passes a judgement whose report can be read and understood by a common man.

As a manager, you are not expected to know everything professional that a lawyer knows, but you are definitely expected to read and understand from a newspaper report. Nevertheless, in your area of management, you should know about the law a little better than a layman. You will do well by knowing how the law of the land applies to your area of management. Thus, if you are a plant manager of a manufacturing company, you should know very well the laws concerning not only, for instance, import or export of such machinery but also laws about the safety and security of the people who work on those machines. If you are a personnel manager, you should know the laws concerning employment of the people, their wages, benefits, promotions, provident fund, retirement, trade unions, and labour disputes.

In this book we will be dealing with laws that deal with each and every area of management.

MANAGER'S TAKEAWAY

- Regular reading of legal texts develops legal knowledge.
- Legal knowledge gives you the power to operate proficiently.

SUMMARY

- Legal theory and nature of jurisprudence—law is made out of the necessity to govern everyone under one standard of equality.
- Definition, scope, and classification of law—The concept of the law consists in imparting justice; the object of a court of law is to follow natural justice, i.e., after giving a fair hearing to the disputing parties pronounces a judgement in accordance with the law.
- Theories of law—Laws are based on a certain philosophy of social, cultural, political, and economic aspects of the people; these philosophies may vary, and so does the application of such law.
- Constituents of law—Custom, that is the traditional manner of a set of behaviour approved by the society at large is the basis of law; other aspects such as legislation, constitution, precedents that arise out of cases, statutes, and regulations, etc., go into making of the legal environment.
- Origins of Indian legal system—It has one of the earliest origins in social customs and religious traditions of the world; among the several invasions, rulers, and governing systems, the British colonial system was the last and provided the legal framework for modern legislation.
- The nature of Indian legal system—Indian Law follows the Common Law system. Further, it has

evolved according to the need of the society with various branches of law. The industry, trade, and commerce law are dealt with in this book in a specific way.

- The administrative structure of the Indian legal system—It is federal in nature; the Supreme Court is the apex court; there are high courts in states and district courts in most districts; and other lower courts and tribunals.
- Relationship between business and law—The relationship exists in commercial contract: explicit and implicit, unequivocal and tacit.
- Principles of commercial jurisprudence—The common good entrusted in public trust is the bedrock of business jurisprudence.
- Some constitutional aspects—The Constitution of India is the supreme will of the people of India, and there is no human law above it for her citizens.
- Manager and the legal environment—The law of the land or the rule of the law, by whatever description, the manager has a standard set for him to follow which is equal and impartial to every citizen in the country.
- Practical ways to read and understand legal language—If the law is so important for business, it behooves a manager to study them for his own convenience.

EXERCISES

1. You go to get a no objection certificate (NOC) for your manufacturing plant from the local au-thorities. You give 5 per cent of the value of the land to the authority to expedite procedures and give you the approvals. But you are *caught in the act red handed*. You argue, saying that everybody pays. They say it is bribe. You fight back and say that the businessmen that you know, they give too. They tell you it is against the law. You counter saying that you never realised that it is against the law since everyone was indulging in it. You even try to buy them off by offering the same amount you offered to the authorities. They refuse and arrest you. You protest saying that arresting is against the law while bribing is not. What do you expect your lawyer to tell you? What kind of judgement do you expect from the judge?

2. Two people discuss among themselves about the law and come to the conclusion that there are no grounds to obey the law. (a) They have not made any laws. (b) They will not recognise any law or follow it. How will you convince them?

3. You are the manager of a company that produces shoes. One day you are invited to give a talk to the local business management institute. You tell them that the biggest problem in the company that you face is litigation. How will you convince the students the relationship between Business and Law?

4. You own the company that has built a hotel by the river. You realise that some local people bring their cattle to graze to the river bank. In addition there are others too, who come and utilise the bank or just sit around. You consider this is a nuisance to your esteemed guests. So you barricade the river bank, thus enabling your hotel guests direct and unhindered access to the river. The locals are peeved by this and file a case against the hotel on grounds of deprivation of public good. They threaten to shut it down if the authorities do not take action. What is your position according to the law?

5. You get a notice from the government stating that under the land acquisition act, the land where your manufacturing plant is situated would have to be acquired for public works, in this case, for building a new national highway. This is going to be a fatal blow to your business, which may have to be closed down because the compensation package by the government is meagre. What measures will you undertake to protect your business interests?

DEVELOPMENT OF LEGAL EDGE

- Start a study circle in your college, university, institute, company, or business establishment with some captivating name such as *Legal Cell, Bar at Law, Court Bench, Legal Eagle,* etc.
- In academic institutions, conduct activities with the purpose of learning law in a practical way: attend real court proceedings, conduct discussions, set up a mock court, start a magazine, etc.

- In a company or business organisation: Start a legal cell, both to educate and for real help of the employees. This will help them understand their situation in a knowledgeable way. Legal knowledge creates consciousness about the organisation and its functioning, which both the employer and employee will appreciate and help cut down on litigation. Remember: *Ignorantia legis nonexcusat*

FURTHER READING

Tripathi, Mani, B.N. (1968), *An Introduction to Jurisprudence, Legal Theory* (15th ed. 2004), (Allahabad Law Agency, Allahabad).

CASE STUDY	MINERVA MILLS

No amendment of this Constitution (including the provisions of Part III) made or purporting to have been made under this article [whether before or after the commencement of Sec. 55 of the Constitution (Forty second Amendment) Act, 1976] shall be called in question in any court on any ground.

– Constitution of India, Article 368 (4)

Introduction

The following case, *Minerva Mills Ltd., and Others vs Union of India and Others* dated 9 May 1980, is considered as one of the landmark cases in Indian legal history.[16] The eminent judges of the Supreme Court forming the five-member Bench were Justices Y.V. Chandrachud, A.C. Gupta, N. Untwalia, P.N. Bhagwati, and P.S. Kailasam. The object of the case is to establish the supremacy of the Supreme Court and to oversee that the laws passed by the legislature are in accordance with the Constitution. The case in point was to decide that the 42nd Amendment Act, Secs 4 and 3, 1, are beyond the amending power of the Parliament under Article 368 of the Constitution and, therefore, void, and whether the Directive Principles of State policy contained in Part IV of the Constitution can have primacy over the fundamental rights conferred by Part III of the Constitution of India, Articles 14, 19, 3 1C, 38, and 368. The importance of the case lies in the fact that at the genesis of this landmark judgement was a business establishment called Minerva Mills.

Background Summary

Mrs Indira Gandhi declared national emergency in 1975. The regime introduced the 42nd Amendment through an Act of the Parliament, which made a fundamental change to the entire character of the Constitution. Article 368 empowers the Parliament to introduce amendments through introduction of the concerned bill that has to find favour with a two-third majority and has to be ratified by the States of the Union. The 42nd Amendment restricted anyone from challenging any amendment made by the Parliament in a court of law. This naturally breached the fundamental rights of the citizen enshrined in the Articles. This made the Parliament superior to the Supreme Court. Thanks to Minerva Mills case, the Supreme Court was able to bounce back with a judgement that empowered itself by claiming that the *judicial review* is the basic feature of the Constitution and no amendment can take it away. Thus, it regained its power to examine the constitutionality of any Act that is passed by the Parliament.

Courting controversy

The following is a historical development where the Supreme Court had to fight against the Parliament of India in a bid to assert the inviolability of the Constitution of India. (Also see Table 1.10.) Ever since the first Amendment to the Constitution, which consisted of the abolition of *zamindari* system till 1980 where the Supreme Court finally resolved the issue of private property and established it as an inviolable fundamental right, it was a great tug of war between the legislature and the judiciary.

Thus, despite daunting controversies, the Supreme Court of India has remained the singular institution that guards and protects the rights of the citizens by upholding the integrity of the Constitution of India.

The Minerva Mills dispute

Minerva Mills Ltd, is a limited company dealing in textiles. On 20 August 1970, the Central Government appointed a committee under Section S of the Industries (Development Regulation) Act, 1951, to make a full and complete investigation of the affairs of the Minerva Mills Ltd., as it was of the opinion that there had been or was likely to be substantial fall in the volume of production. The said Committee submitted its report to the Central Government in January 1971, on the basis of which the Central Government passed an order dated 19 October 1971 under Sec. 18A of the 1951 Act, authorising the National Textile Corporation Ltd, to take over the management of the Mills on the ground that its affairs are being managed in a manner highly detrimental to public interest. This undertaking was nationalised and taken over by the Central Government under the provisions of the Sick Textile Undertakings (Nationalisation) Act, 1974.

Minerva Mills Ltd, the petitioners, challenged the constitutional validity of certain provisions of the Sick

---

[16]AIR 1980 SC 1789, (1980) 3 SCC 625, 1981 1 SCR 206

Table 1.10 Historical perspective of the Supreme Court and Parliament tussle to assert inviolability of the Constitution

Year	Parliament	Supreme Court
1951 First 1955 Fourth 1964 Seventeenth Amendment 1967	Amended the Constitution to abolish *zamindari* and redistribute land.	In the case of Golaknath vs State of Punjab, ruled that the Parliament has no power to abrogate fundamental right to private property.
1969, 1970	Passed bank nationalisation bill.	Invalidated the bank nationalisation.
1970	Abolished title, privileges, and privy purses of the former rulers of India.	Declared it as unconstitutional.
1971 Twenty-fourth to twenty-sixth Amendments	Empowered itself to amend any provision of the Constitution including the fundamental rights.	At the instance of Keshavananda Bharati vs State of Kerala case, ruled that although the amendments were constitutional, the Court reserved for itself the power to reject any Amendment that violates the basic structure of the Constitution.
1975–77 Forty-second Amendment	Under emergency declared by Indira Gandhi, the government passed the Amendment preventing the Supreme Court to abrogate or review any amendment. The Amendment established parliamentary sovereignty.	
1977 1980	Janata Party government reversed the forty-second Amendment and the supremacy of the Supreme Court and constitutional democracy were re-established.	In Minerva Mills case, upheld the fundamental right of the individual or the company to private property and reaffirmed its authority to protect the basic structure of the Constitution.

Textile Undertakings (Nationalization) Act, 1974, and of the order dated 19 October 1971, the constitutionality of the Constitution (Thirty Ninth Amendment) Act which inserted the impugned Nationalization Act as Entry 105 in the Ninth Schedule to the Constitution, the validity of Article 3 1 B of the Constitution and, finally, the constitutionality of Secs 4 and 55 of the Constitution (Forty Second Amendment) Act, 1976 on the ratio of the majority judgement in Kesavananda Bharati's case, namely, though by Article 368 of the Constitution, the Parliament is given the power to amend the Constitution, that power cannot be exercised so as to damage the basic features of the Constitution or to destroy its basic structure.

The Concept of Basic Structure of the Constitution

The basic structure of the Constitution implies its essence. As, for instance, in a cooking recipe, it would remain *basically* the same as long as its traditionally accepted ingredients continued to remain the same despite how elegantly or less elegantly it is presented or eaten. The basic ingredients of a legal code have specific provisions; if these provisions are altered, the code ceases to be what it is intended to be. Let us take the example of legal tender such as a one-rupee note or a one-rupee coin. It does not matter to the value of the money whether note is soiled or the coin is worn out; for these do not erode its value. But if you offer someone only 90 paise and argue that it completes a rupee, intrinsically you are mistaken. So too with law, anything that devalues its intrinsic value, erodes its basic structure.

In all the aforementioned controversial cases, the Supreme Court of India has consistently maintained that the Parliament is within its right to make alterations in the Constitution through the Amendments. At the same time, it has also maintained that the amendments must be such that they do not alter the basic structure of the Constitution. In other words, nothing should impinge on the fundamental rights. Likewise, nothing should alter the definition as enshrined in the Preamble of the Constitution.

Figure 1.6 is a structural list summarized from Table 1.9 of landmark judgements about the basic structure of the Constitution.

If you refer back in the chapter, you will see that the law is distinguished as Civil Law and Common Law. Civil Law is a fixed code and hence has little danger to its basic structure; whereas Common Law finds growth in case law and is susceptible to amendments from the Parliament. What happens when a parliamentary amendment breaches the boundary and endangers the basic structure of the Constitution? In India, the Supreme Court assumes that it is its bounden duty to protect the basic structure of the Constitution. In the earlier-cited instances, it has taken up cudgels with the legislature and has tried to repair the damage.

Nani Palkhivala[17]—The defender of the Constitution

Nanabhoy Palkhivala (1920–2002) has been popularly revered as the defender of the Constitution of India and is best known by the short name of Nani. As the defence lawyer for the Minerva Mills case in which he not only won the case against the government but also established the

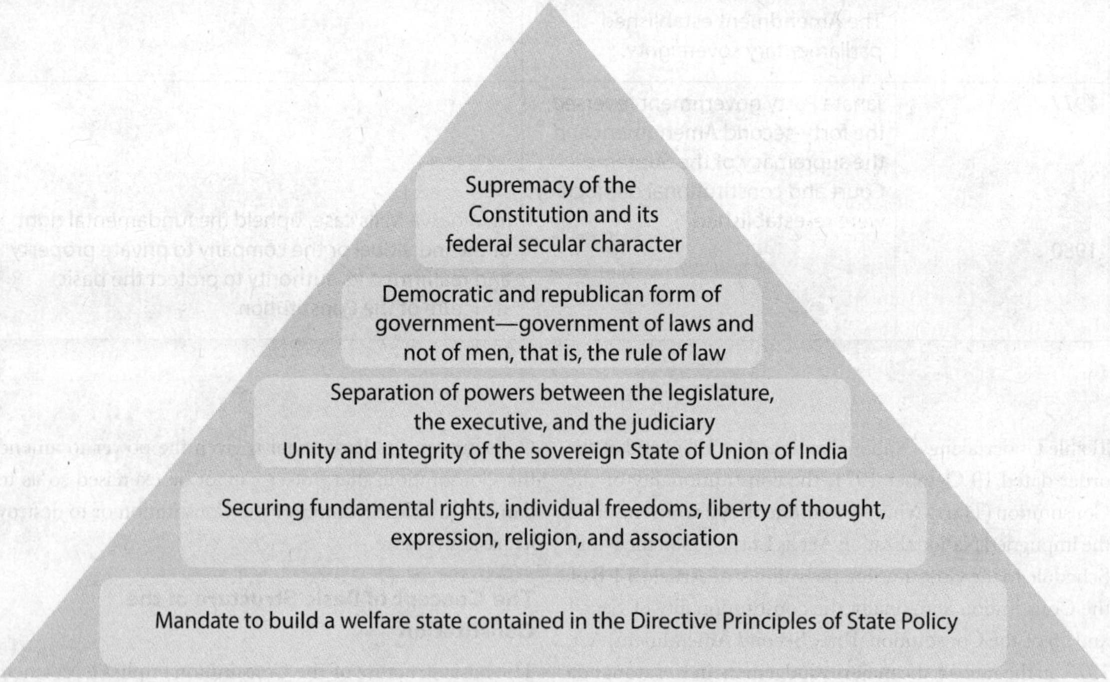

Supremacy of the Constitution and its federal secular character

Democratic and republican form of government—government of laws and not of men, that is, the rule of law

Separation of powers between the legislature, the executive, and the judiciary
Unity and integrity of the sovereign State of Union of India

Securing fundamental rights, individual freedoms, liberty of thought, expression, religion, and association

Mandate to build a welfare state contained in the Directive Principles of State Policy

Figure 1.6   Basic structure of the Constitution

supremacy of the Constitution and restored the judicial review right to the Supreme Court, which, in turn, defended the fundamental rights of the every citizen of India.

Diminutive in stature but holder of a brilliant razor sharp logical mind, one that has attracted people from all walks of life to fill up the court to listen to him, Nani held the Constitution of India as his sacred scripture. 'The Constitution was meant to impart such a momentum to the living spirit of the rule of law that democracy and civil liberty may survive in India beyond our own times and in the days when our place will know us no more.'[18]

Kesavananda vs the State of Kerala was the famous case of protection of the fundamental right to property, which was ably and successfully argued by Palkhivala. He earned international fame for defending a universal right and was highly acclaimed in India for his dedication to the spirit of the Constitution. However, it is the Minerva Mills case that has immortalised him in the annals of Indian jurisprudence. He moved before the bench to declare that Clause (4) of Article 368 of the Constitution, which excludes judicial review of constitutional amendments, was unconstitutional.

Born in a Parsi family in Bombay (now Mumbai), Palkhivala applied for a lecturer's post after his graduation from Bombay University. Since someone was already appointed to the post, he joined the Government Law College of Bombay and later entered the bar and worked with a well-known lawyer, Jamshedji Behramji Kanga. Hardly ten years down the line, he appeared in the Supreme Court to defend the rights of the minority religious communities. He was a multi-faceted person and was a great scholar of Economics and Taxation. On the day India's budget was presented, it was customary that he delivered a lecture which became so famous and drew large crowds that Mumbai's Brabourne cricket stadium had to be hired for the purpose. Several universities, both in India and abroad, conferred honorary degrees on him. The citation of the Princeton University, USA, summed it all up: *Defender of constitutional liberties, champion of human rights.*

Conclusion

The Indian Constitution balances the three wings of the State—Legislature, Executive, and Judiciary—which is held steadfastly with legal reasoning. The logic lying behind our Constitution is that it has been given by the people to themselves and placed on the bedrock of fundamental rights. It obligates the judges to pronounce the validity of the laws. If this right of the court is taken away, then the entire Constitution falls on its face. If the executive is to control the Constitution, then it is as good as the country not having a Constitution at all. The fundamental rights will have no relevance, for one is deprived of their defence in a court of law.

Discussion Questions

1. What was the problem in the Minerva Mills case?
2. What do you understand by a landmark judgement?
3. In what way did the Minerva Mills case bring about such a judgement?
4. How important is any legislation in matters of private property?
5. How are companies and businesses affected by property laws?
6. On what grounds can the government take over a company?
7. Does the government have the right to acquire the property of the people?
8. Does the Supreme Court of India have the powers to overrule the Acts of the Parliament?
9. What kind of bills can the Parliament not enact?
10. What do you understand by the 'basic structure of the Constitution'?

Going Beyond

1. How is private property defined?
2. Does the right to private property come under natural justice?
3. What is the place of private property in capitalism and communism?
4. Can a general referendum make way for overturning our Constitution?

---

[17]Soli J. Sorabjee, 'Palkhivala and The Constitution of India' in http://www.ebc-india.com/lawyer/default.htm (15.7. 2010).
[18]See the quote article in http://en.wikipedia.org/wiki/Nanabhoy_Palkhivala (15.7.2010).

LEGAL LUMINARY

BHIMRAO RAMJI AMBEDKAR—THE ARCHITECT OF THE CONSTITUTION OF INDIA

Soon after the Independence of India, on 15 August 1947, the Constituent Assembly formed a Drafting Committee of the Constitution, consisting of six persons under the chairmanship of B.R. Ambedkar, the most erudite and accomplished scholar of India. He submitted the draft to the Constituent Assembly for discussion on 4 November 1947. The Assembly met to discuss, deliberate, and modify for 166 days; the sessions were spread over a period of 2 years, 11 months, and 18 days. All the sessions were open to the public. The final copies of the Constitution of India, one each in Hindi and English, were handwritten and signed by the 308 members of the Constituent Assembly of India on 24 January 1950, and two days later, on 28 January 1950, it became the supreme law of the people, by the people, and for the people of India. People became their own masters first time ever as the Republic of India. The Constitution of India is the supreme law of the land and nobody, not even the Parliament, has the right to alter its basic structure. It is the longest written constitution of the world which contains 22 parts, 448 articles, 12 schedules and over 100 Amendments.*

It is not just the vast knowledge of jurisprudence that is reflected in the Constitution but also Ambedkar's life experiences that represent the poorest of the poor and the socially, economically, and religiously most discriminated people down the centuries. He was born to *Mahar* caste; they were treated as untouchables. He would never have dreamt of the accomplishments he achieved, had his father not worked in a British military cantonment and sent him to school. Despite myriad humiliations in the class, he studied with the greatest devotion possible. After passing through the famed portals of Elphinstone College, Bombay, in 1908, he went to the United States of America and later joined London School of Economics. He earned doctorates in economics, political science, and law.

His adherence to Buddhism, political engagement, and social movement of leading the *dalits*, the casteless, and untouchables is reflected with great sensitivity and compassion in the Constitution. The clear statements on fundamental rights, human dignity, and care for the children are examples of Ambedkar's vision for India. That our Constitution fully reflects the Human Rights Declaration of the United Nation, speaks of his far-reaching jurisprudence.

---

*See http://indiacode.nic.in (1.5.2010).

PART 2

COMMERCIAL JURISPRUDENCE

2

The Indian Contract Act, 1872

Principle: *Emptor emit quam minimo potest; venditor vendit quam maximo potest.*
The buyer buys as cheaply as he can; the seller sells as costly as he can.

CHAPTER OUTLINE

- Introduction and Interpretation
- Understanding Definitions of Contract Law
- Communication, Acceptance, and Revocation of Proposals
- Agreement
- Offer

- Acceptance
- Rules of Communication of Offer, Acceptance, and Revocation
- Consideration
- *Case Study:* Less for More
- *Legal Luminary:* Rohinton Nariman

2.1 INTRODUCTION AND INTERPRETATION

TEXT

(a) When one person signifies to another his willingness to do or to abstain from doing anything, with a view to obtaining the assent of that other to such act or abstinence, he is said to make a proposal;
(b) When a person to whom the proposal is made, signifies his assent thereto, the proposal is said to be accepted. A proposal, when accepted, becomes a promise.

– Sec. 2a and b, The Indian Contract Act, 1872

It takes two to do business. A business transaction involves at least two parties. It is done through an agreement, which in some cases is very elaborate, and in others it merely signifies the intent of the parties. Though you may hardly realise, when you buy a bus ticket, you have entered into a contract with the transport company–which is similar to buying an apartment with its elaborate documentation on stamp papers. Business is, in short, where a relationship is established between one who promises to deliver a good or service and one who accepts it under agreed terms.

The Indian Contract Act, 1872, is the law upon which the entire business relationship is built. The relationship involves appropriate rights and duties of the contracting parties.

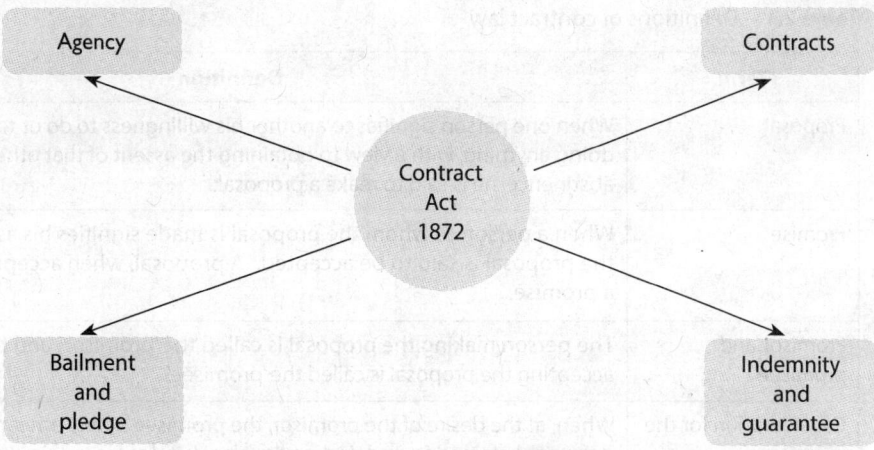

Figure 2.1 Taxonomy of the Contract Act, 1872

The Contract Act deals with the enforcement of such rights and duties. Thus, a contract is an agreement enforceable by law. Despite its length and versatility, the Act may not be completely exhaustive—there are other laws relating to the contract law such as partnership, sale of goods, negotiable instruments, insurance, transport, etc.

The Contract Act, 1872, governs the principles of formation, performance, and enforceability of contracts and the rules relating to contracts and to special types of contracts known as indemnity, guarantee, bailment, pledge, and agency. The Act may be divided into four parts, as depicted in Figure 2.1:

  (i) Contracts
 (ii) Indemnity and guarantee
(iii) Bailment and pledge
(iv) Agency

2.2 UNDERSTANDING DEFINITIONS OF CONTRACT LAW

The Contract Law is the foundation of commercial jurisprudence. The application of the law depends on its interpretation. The tools of the interpretation for the law lie in the definitions of terms defined at the beginning of the Act in Sec. 2, clauses a–j.[1] (See Table 2.1.)

In the tradition of the Common Law of Britain, there is a landmark case (Case 2.1) that is cited as a supreme example of the intention to establish a contract as intact, even though the parties concerned expressly entered into the contractual relationship specifically excluding all the legal aspects. This precedent is cited also in the judgements of the Indian law, which is derived from the British system of law.

Earlier the counsel for Rose & Frank had argued that the companies in question, before the 1913 mutual and legally excluding contract, had conducted business on contracts enforceable by law, and these had never been terminated. However, the judge (House of

[1]The alphabetical order reflects the same as in the Act, Sec. 2.

Table 2.1 Definitions of contract law

Term	Definition
Proposal	When one person signifies to another his willingness to do or to abstain from doing anything, with a view to obtaining the assent of that other to such act or abstinence, he is said to make a proposal.
Promise	When a person to whom the proposal is made signifies his assent thereto, the proposal is said to be accepted. A proposal, when accepted, becomes a promise.
Promisor and promisee	The person making the proposal is called the 'promisor', and the person accepting the proposal is called the 'promisee'.
Consideration for the promise	When, at the desire of the promisor, the promisee or any other person has done or abstained from doing, or does or abstains from doing, or promises to do or to abstain from doing, something, such act or abstinence or promise is called a consideration for the promise.
Agreement	Every promise and every set of promises, forming the consideration for each other, is an agreement.
Reciprocal promises	Promises which form the consideration or part of the consideration for each other are called reciprocal promises.
Void agreement	An agreement not enforceable by law is said to be void.
Contract	An agreement enforceable by law is a contract.
Voidable contract	An agreement which is enforceable by law at the option of one or more of the parties thereto, but not at the option of the other or others, is a voidable contract.
Void contract	A contract which ceases to be enforceable by law becomes void when it ceases to be enforceable.

Lords in this case) did not consider its immediate relevance, but observed the most vivid and implicit action of the parties: the orders given and accepted. Thus, it established beyond any reasonable doubt the bona fide intention between two contracting parties, the existence of a promisor and a promisee, a proposal and an acceptance, and the ensuing consideration between the contracting parties. Case 2.1 fulfilled all the essential aspects of a legal contract enforceable by law.

Salient Features of a Contract

Once you have a grip of the concept of contract law by understanding the meaning of the various terms involved in its definition, the next step is to know its salient features. These are the most outstanding and relevant aspects of a contract. There are ten most important features (Table 2.2) with which you should be familiar as a manager before you enter into a legally binding trade transaction.

CASE 2.1

PETITIONER: Rose & Frank Co. vs RESPONDENT: J.R. Crompton & Bros Ltd

DATE OF JUDGEMENT: (1924) UKHL 2, (1925) AC 445*

FACTS: Rose & Frank Co. was the sole US distributor of carbon paper products of J.R. Crompton. In 1913, both the parties entered into an agreement explicitly writing and signing a document that excluded this business relationship of all legal bindings. It further promised to conduct the business with mutual loyalty and friendly cooperation. But the friendship soured and the relationship broke when J.R. Crompton refused to comply with the supplies. Rose & Frank sued J.R. Crompton and prayed for the enforcement of the agreement.

JUDGEMENT: No legal contract as per the mutual agreement of the parties.

REASON: It is gentleman's agreement, done outside the purview of the law.

APPEAL: Rose & Frank Co. appealed in the higher court for enforcement of agreement.

JUDGEMENT: Upheld the appeal as valid.

REASON: The House of Lords held that the contact of 1913 mutually excluding legal enforcement had no legal force. However, the orders given and accepted constituted enforceable contracts of sale.

*For a brief treatment, see: http://en.wikipedia.org/wiki/Talk:Rose_%26_Frank_Co_v_JR_Crompton_%26_Bros_Ltd; for full text and arguments, see: http://www.bailii.org/uk/cases/UKHL/1924/2.html (08.10.2010).

Table 2.2 Important features that managers must know

Feature	Description
Minimum two parties	Contract implicitly implies a relation between at least two parties: on one side the party that proposes or makes an offer or promises and on the other one that which agrees to the proposal, accepts an offer, or collects what is promised.
Competent parties	It is assumed that the contracting parties must be of legally recognized age, generally 18 years or as per the legal provisions; the validity of the contract belongs to a sound mind; mentally unsound, permanently or temporarily affected with insanity, involuntary, or coerced by force, etc. do not qualify, nor are they competent to contract (Secs 11 and 12 of the Act).
Offer and acceptance	The contracting parties begin their business relationship from an offer made and the same is accepted, thus culminating into a legally binding agreement.
Intention	This is the cornerstone of contract; the intention is present wherever there is an offer and acceptance, irrespective of a written or unwritten statement; even where there is a express contract made to exclude legal enforcement, circumstances must be examined about the intention (see Case 2.1: Rose & Frank Co. vs J.R. Crompton & Bros Ltd)

Contd

Table 2.2 *Contd*

Consideration	It is what one gives and the other gets and has a legal enforceability; it may be in the past, present, or future; it is valid only if it is legal; it must not be illegal, immoral, or opposed to public policy and must not imply injury to the person and property of another.
Free consent	It is the outward expression of inward intention; the invalidating factors are fear, coercion—physical or psychological, fraud, misrepresentation, mistake, etc. (Secs 13 and 14 of the Act).
Lawful object	It is that what it is; it must not be illegal, immoral, or opposed to public policy and must not imply injury to the person and property of another (closely related to no. 5: Sec. 23 of the Act).
Void	A contract ceases to be so, if it has nothing to contract; e.g., as per secs. 24–30 of the Act, agreements in restraint of trade or wagering are not enforceable—such non-enforceable agreements are void.
Certainty and possibility of performance	Contracts are performative acts; if what is contracted is uncertain and the meaning cannot be ascertained, then it is not legally enforceable (Sec. 56 of the Act).
Legal formalities	Normally, if something is legally enforceable, then care is taken to draw some procedure of the contract; however, all business contracts may not need legal documentation or registration with the authorities; even a commuter ticket or a grocery voucher at times serve as legal documents. The advice to the public: demanding bus tickets and vouchers are legal exhortations indicating clear legal formalities.

You as a manager should have them on your fingertips. Apart from this, what must remain imbedded in the mind of a manager are the two inalienable aspects of contract: enforceability by law and intention to be so.

Classification of Contract

Thus far you understood the definition as well as the constituent aspects of a legal contract. However, contract is not just restricted to a single concept. There are different kinds of contracts–which differ according to their validity, formation, and performance (Figure 2.2). It is very important for a manager to discern the kind of contract he might lead the company into signing or agreeing.

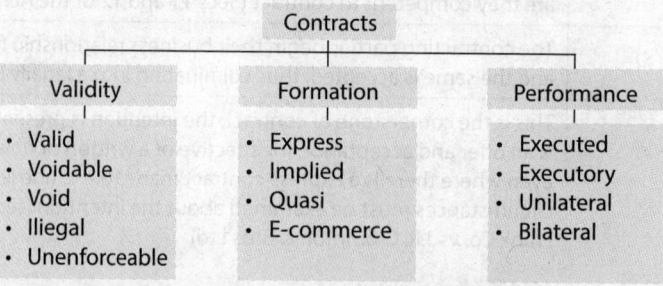

Figure 2.2 Classifications of contracts

Table 2.3 Classification of contracts according to validity

Classification	Description	Example(s)
Valid contract	All those agreements which are enforceable by law; these contain all those salient features which empower them with legal character.	A document deed of acquisition of a company, signed between the concerned parties with all due legal procedure.
Voidable contract	It consists of a missing element in the contract, such as consent. It is thus enforceable by law at the option of one of the parties.	An agreement is made using force by one of the parties. Such contract is valid until the aggrieved party exercises the option to rescind the contract.
Void contract	It is a contract when it ceases to be enforceable by law; there is an apparent contract to begin with, which in reality is non-existent.	A contract entered into without consideration, the give and take of a transaction, is actually not agreement from its inception or *ab initio*.
Illegal contract	It is an agreement that is totally contradictory to what a contract stands for; it is not in accordance with the law. Since it is against the law, it attracts legal action or penalty.	• Any contract forbidden by law; • Involves injury to person or property of another; • Against the legally accepted moral standards or public policies.
Unenforceable contract	These agreements lack certain technical requirements; they are neither void nor voidable but they fail to stand scrutiny of legal procedure.	• Not authorized as per due procedure: unsigned cheque or any negotiable instrument; • Not registered with a competent authority: e.g., the Memorandum of Association as per Companies Act, 1956.

Table 2.3 describes with examples the classification of contracts according to validity.

Validity is that which confers the force of authority. A passport for instance is a valid document of one's identity. The written document of the title of a property deed gives the right of ownership to its possessor if it is registered with the authorities as per procedure. Thus, validity bestows legal character (Sec. 9, The Indian Contract Act).

Going a step further, validity requires the existence of an appearance whereby one can say, 'this is the agreement'. But it may not be practical to have all agreements as written documents. Life would become cumbersome if only written documents are considered valid. Thus, the law recognizes not only written agreements, but also oral, e-mail, and telephonic agreements, and to some extent even certain behaviour through which one can infer of the existence of a contract (Sec. 9, The Indian Contract Act).

A manager is often described as a man of performance. You can learn from Table 2.4 valid contracts and also their formation as occurring in various contexts. To perform is to complete a task. Some of the synonyms used for performance are act, carry out, execute, make, complete, etc.

Table 2.4 Classification of contracts according to formation

Classification	Description	Example(s)
Express contract	An agreement in writing or agreed orally; the offer is made and is accepted.	• A property title deed. • You tell the waiter to serve you a soft drink, and you are served one.
Implied contract	An implied, unlike express, agreement is inferred from the conduct of the parties involved that suggest of an offer and acceptance.	• Take a taxi; just by entering it you enter into an implied agreement. • Parking a car in a paid parking lot.
Quasi contract	The term implies 'as though', in other words, it appears like X but is not X. A contract has intention as its definitional essence. To solve certain practical problems, the law creates an obligation on the principle *a person shall not be allowed to enrich himself unjustly at the expense of another.*	A door-to-door salesman inadvertently leaves behind some of his wares at your house. You use them as your own. Apparently, there is no offer and acceptance either express or implicit, yet the law imposes on you the obligation to pay for the goods that the salesman left behind and you used.
Internet contract	An agreement entered over the Internet.	Today millions of people transact over large commercial networks and sales sites on the Web. Goods and services are bought and sold, money is paid electronically. When disputes arise all the contract laws apply as in the old business models.

From the classification of contracts as in Table 2.5, it is important to understand that legal enforceability is the essential factor—without it contracts are compromised. You as a manager may face enormous legal problems if you are not clear about the nature of the contract. Case 2.2 shows how confusing it can be to determine the nature of a contract and its validity.

Dhurandhar Prasad Singh's case brought thousands of such cases to light and brought hope to so many. Employees often suffer dismissals or termination of service without disputing, and carry on to find another job to earn their livelihoods. However, if set to dispute before a court of law then one sees how the contours of law unfold and exhibit clearly the distinctions and nuances inherent in a contract. As a manager, you will do well to study all the points of an employment contract, the terms and conditions of appointment, before terminating the services of an employee. The consequences of not being attentive in this matter can cost time and money for your company during litigation. It may also tarnish the image of your company and may even have implications for your reputation and assignment.

Table 2.5 Classification of contracts according to performance

Classification	Description	Example
Executed contract	Herein both the parties to a contract have completed their task.	The seller and buyer of an apartment have agreed, produced and registered the documents, and duly transferred the ownership. It is a sale *deed* and is *executed* as per legal norms.
Executory contract	It is an agreement that is not yet carried out into an executed contract; there are still obligations to be met by the parties to complete it. It is a contract that is in the process or stages of completion.	As in the above example of sale of an apartment: when, for instance, in the process of this transaction some things have been done, e.g., payment of caution money has been made, and some things are yet to be done, e.g., signing of the sale deed.
Unilateral contract	At the time of an agreement only one party fulfills the conditions of the contract, and the other is yet to execute.	When you buy a train ticket from Mumbai to Delhi, your part of the contract is complete once you pay for it; the Railways, on the other hand has not yet executed its part of the contract till it transports you to your destination.
Bilateral contract	It is an executory contract where performance by both the contracting parties is called for. There is simultaneity to such a transaction.	The sale and purchase of an apartment involves bilateral performance.

CASE 2.2 APPELLANT: Dhurandhar Prasad Singh VS RESPONDENT: Jai Prakash University and Others

DATE OF JUDGEMENT: 24 July 2001

FACTS: Dhurandhar Singh was appointed by the principal of Ganga Singh College as Routine cum Examination Clerk on 1 August 1977. His services were terminated in the October of the same year as the college got affiliated to the Bihar University. His plea against it was set aside by the High Court, since it saw no contractual validity against the respondent, the Bihar University.

JUDGEMENT: The appellant's case is upheld, against the order of the High Court.

REASON: There is a distinction between void and voidable contract. A void contract is intrinsically a non-contract, a nullity. A voidable contract, of which the above is an example, remains good, until it is set aside.

2.3 COMMUNICATION, ACCEPTANCE, AND REVOCATION OF PROPOSALS

TEXT

The communication of proposals, the acceptance of proposals, and the revocation of proposals and acceptance, respectively, are deemed to be made by any act or omission of the party proposing, accepting or revoking, by which he intends to communicate such proposal, acceptance or revocation, or which has the effect of communicating it.

– Sec. 3, The Indian Contract Act, 1872

In this section, we deal with Sections 3–9 of the Indian Contract Act, 1872.

2.4 AGREEMENT

TEXT

All agreements are contracts if they are made by the free consent of parties competent to contract, for a lawful consideration and with a lawful object, and are not hereby expressly declared to be void. Nothing herein contained shall affect any law in force in India, and not hereby expressly repealed, by which any contract is required to be made in writing or in the presence of witnesses, or any law relating to the registration of documents.

– Sec. 10, The Indian Contract Act, 1872

Communication and acceptance or offer and acceptance are the cornerstones of agreement. Its revocation is an agreement, too; it undoes what is done first and resolves a commercial relation.

By now you have a good idea about the concept of contract. The question that will now cross your mind is: how does a contract come about. For instance, during the festival season in India, television companies advertise attractive offers such as trade-ins, wherein there is a reduction in the price of the new set when an old set is exchanged as part of the deal. You accept the offer. You do the needful by taking your old TV set and depositing with the distributor, and take home a new TV set after making the due payment. However, you may be dissatisfied with the new product for some reason and you may like to cancel the exchange scheme that you had assented to. But the dealer may not agree with your argument and you may drag him to the consumer court. In this manner the story of this product along with the seller and buyer's dispute grows until it is legally resolved.

The aforementioned text and example is a test of the definition of contract that you studied earlier. Actually, how a contract arises and how concerned parties are bound by it is the central issue in this section. You may have seen how a shopkeeper and his customer have a quarrel: they argue and squabble about what one meant but the other misunderstood and vice versa. This shows that there is a difficulty in the agreement of selling and buying. Such situations show to us that a meeting of minds is called for, before goods and services are exchanged. Both the seller and the buyer must mean and understand the same thing in the same sense. Such an understanding of the agreement, the communication between the minds, is known as *consensus ad idem*.

The contract is constituted by a communication of offer, acceptance, and revocation (Figure 2.3). The communication itself may be explicit as through written documents, promissory notes, vouchers, etc., or implicit in the mere exchange of goods and services paid through money.

2.5 OFFER

TEXT

The parties to a contract must either perform, or offer to perform, their respective promises, unless such performance is dispensed with or excused under the provision of this Act, or of any other law. Promises bind the representative of the promisor in case of the death of such Promisors before performance, unless a contrary intention appears from the contract.

– Sec. 37, The Indian Contract Act, 1872

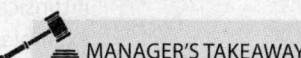

≡ MANAGER'S TAKEAWAY

• To ask oneself the value of a written agreement without the force of law.
• The fact of a trade transaction, with or without a written document, expresses clearly and explicitly of a legally enforceable contract.

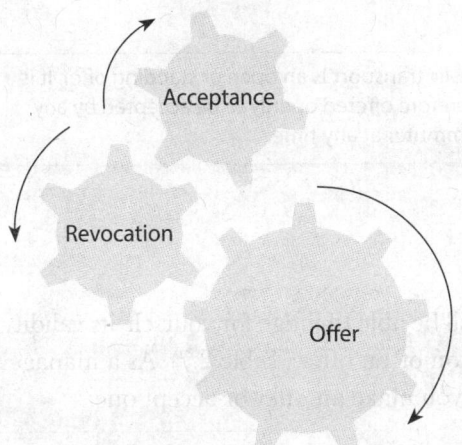

Figure 2.3 Taxonomy of communication of contract—offer, acceptance and revocation

An offer is the starting point of a business transaction. When one tenders, proffers, or proposes to sell or deliver goods or service in exchange for money or an asset, this may be called an offer (Table 2.6). To put it in normal legalese: When one desires to create a legal obligation, communicates to another, his willingness to do or not to do a thing, with a view to obtain the consent of that another person towards such an act or abstinence, the person is said to be making a proposal or offer.

Whereas lawyers study two twin types of offers, namely, act and omission, specific and general. Figure 2.3 will enable you to comprehend better the concept of offer. Next we address the essentials or the salient features of offer.

Table 2.6 Kinds of offer

Category	Sub-category/Explanation	Example(s)
Act	Express: The offerer makes a clear and tangible act of proposal to the offeree.	Orally: Face to face or over telephone; Written: Documents, email, fax, etc.
Act	Implied: Certain type of behaviour or making conventional signs may be sufficient to understand a commercial transaction.	An auto-rickshaw is in queue for passengers near a railway station; the driver does not have to make any extra announcements to let potential passengers know his availability and that the fare would be metered.
Omission	Omission or abstinence: An agreement is made possible by not doing something.	The manager of a bank makes an offer to the client who has borrowed loan from the bank that the latter would not undergo litigation if he pays back the outstanding loan amount as per the newly set regulations.
Specific	Definite offer: An offer made to a particular person or group.	A daily offers its publication to school children for a mere 10% of its actual price.
General	Indefinite offer: An offer made to general public without any specification.	A hotel receives any customer who walks in and asks for hospitality as per tariff.
Cross	When two parties make and exchange identical offers without any prior knowledge, there exists no contract, because it cannot be treated as mutual acceptance. It is a mere accidental occurrence.	You offer to sell your property to X and at the same time you happen to receive from X an offer to buy your property.
Counter	A counter offer is when upon receiving an offer from an offeror, the offeree instead of accepting the offer makes a counter offer. Such an offer nullifies the first offer.	A supplier of automobile spare parts makes an offer to a motor company at a discount of 20% if the products are picked up from its factory. The motor company on the other hand makes a counter offer to buy the factory.

Contd

Table 2.6 *Contd*

Standing, continuing, or open	These offers are general in nature.	Public transport is an open or standing offer. It is therefore offered openly to be accepted by any commuter at any time.

Salient Features of Offer

By knowing the salient features of an offer, you will be able to judge for yourself its validity; and you can also understand the actual constitution of an offer (Table 2.7). As a manager, you must carefully examine these features before you make an offer or accept one.

Table 2.7 Salient features of an offer

Feature	Explanation	Example(s)
Intention to create legal obligation	It is a definite offer where commercial relations are based on legal foundations. It intrinsically presumes legal consequences.	The car dealer has displayed a model of a car in his showroom. It is unambiguously clear it is offered for sale.
Certainty	The offer must entail clarity and transparency of the offer. The terms and conditions must allow definite interpretation, which is understood in the same way by both the seller and the buyer.	One wants to buy the car that he/she has seen and inspected in the showroom and has understood all the terms and conditions of purchase.
(a) To do something (b) To abstain from something	(a) The offerer promises to do something. (b) The offerer abstains from doing something.	(a) The car salesman offers a festival discount if the car is bought within the specified period of the festival season, (b) The car salesman promises not to confiscate the car if the customer promises to repay the outstanding loan before the agreed date.
Communication	An offer must be made known (refer Table 2.6—Kinds of offer) in some form whereby the intention of the offerer to seek an offeree becomes clear.	The car advertisements are direct and clear communication. Its display in a showroom is a further exhibition of intention to sell.
Positive	An offer must have something positive to sell; the communication to sell must be positive.	The new model of the car is now available in seven colours. Negatively: An offeree who has expressed his/her intention to buy car, if he/she fails to confirm within a given period, it would be assumed that it has been accepted. Such a negative condition violates the conditions of a legal offer.

When you study Table 2.7, it becomes analytically clear that if an offer is to have any legal validity it must be clearly communicated, where the minds of the seller and purchaser meet with the same meaning of all the terms and conditions and understood in the same way. There may be short- or long-term negotiations after the offer is made and it is accepted. No contract can be presumed until and unless it is clear to both the parties that a legally enforceable agreement is confirmed. Case 2.3 is a landmark case to understand the operation involved between the offer and its acceptance. There is no contract if one of the above fails. An offer without acceptance is no contract; and acceptance without an offer is a logical impossibility.

The case of Rickmers vs Indian Oil Corporation (Case 2.4) has been cited for making a clear distinction between offer and its acceptance. When the seller has made the offer, the buyer shows intention of entering an agreement. Depending upon the nature of the commercial transaction, long-term negotiations and correspondence may be operated. It may well seem to one of the parties that an agreement has been reached, while the other is very clear that a mutual agreement is still far away. An offer remains a mere offer if it is not taken. It takes two to trade. The legally enforceable contract comes into existence only when both the parties are of one mind to transact business.

CASE 2.3	APPELLANT: M/s Rickmers Verwaltung vs RESPONDENT: The Indian Oil Corporation Ltd*
	DATE OF JUDGEMENT: 19 November 1998

FACTS:	The Indian Oil Corporation (IOC) had an agreement with M/s Tubacero of Mexico. The latter invited offers for shipment. One of the offers it received was from the appellant, M/s Rickmers. To execute the contract, the IOC was supposed to establish a standby letter of credit and Rickmers was supposed to furnish a performance bond. Rickmers did not furnish the bond because IOC did not approve its letter of credit prepared by its bankers and filed a suit for arbitration. The Indian Council of Arbitration directed IOC to deposit monies towards costs of the arbitration. The IOC responded that there existed neither contract nor any binding agreement with Rickmers.
JUDGEMENT:	The Delhi High Court Bench comprising of single judge declared that the petitioner's claim had no merit.
REASON:	The correspondence between the concerned parties clearly showed that they were still negotiating the terms of transaction; there is a clear difference between mutually agreed and signed contract and negotiating a commercial deal.

*M/s Rickmers Verwaltung GmbH vs The Indian Oil Corporation Ltd, on 19 November 1998, http://indiankanoon. org/doc/200909/ (8 November 2010).

Rules of Offer

The aforesaid explanation as well as Case 2.3 illustrate to you a definite need for certain rules to make a valid offer. For instance, if you are a marketing manager, you should not only know what you are selling but how you would sell it. In other words, how do you make an offer to your customers? Following three rules should help you.

CASE 2.4	APPELLANT: Bhagwandas Goverdhandas Kedia vs RESPONDENT: M/s Girdharilal Parshottamdas*

DATE: 1 June 1989

FACTS: The respondents from Ahmedabad entered into a contract with the appellants from Khamgaon through a long-distance telephone call. The appellant disputed that there was a contract.

JUDGEMENT: The appeal is dismissed.

REASON: The contract is complete when the acceptor accepts the proposal of the proposer and conveys back his acceptance, which is duly received by the proposer. Until then the contract is putative or supposed. This was the case between Ahmedabad and Khamgaon. The telephone offer and acceptance is as though the concerned parties are in the presence of each other and there is nothing in the contract law to state otherwise. In this sense, the contract between Ahmedabad and Khamgaon was complete.

*Goverdhandas Kediavs Girdharilal Parshottamdas and Co. see: http://www.indiankanoon.org/doc/1386912/, equivalent citation: 1966 AIR 543, 1966 SCR (1) 656 (9.8.2010).

Rule 1: An invitation to offer is not an offer

You may have read in the papers advertisements from the government or companies under the heading 'Expression of Intention'. The advertisement is put out to invite 'offers', for instance, to supply some specific material. There are terms and conditions set to make the said offer. The fact that your company expresses its intention and complies with all terms and conditions does not imply in any way that the contract is awarded to you. You would have to wait for completion of the due process of awarding such a contract.

For example, public tenders invite offers from interested parties. The applications are furnished, the money deposits are duly made, and on the day of opening the tenders–as per rules and procedures—the contract is granted to a definite party who, according to those who invited the tenders, fulfils their conditions. Now, only if the party that has won the contract formally accepts and fulfils the rest of the conditions, then upon such an agreement does a legally enforceable contract come into existence. Other respondents to the tender are rejected.

Rule 2: Two identical cross offers do not make a contract

The occurrence of cross offers in an increasingly business-oriented society is not an exception. People in similar businesses think alike. However, offering of such proposals does not mean that an agreement has been reached. Only an act of offer and its acceptance confers on it the legal enforceability that is termed as a contract.

Rule 3: Special terms must be notified

You are definitely familiar with the phrase 'fine print'. The labels on products, vouchers, warrantee and guarantee papers, etc. have several terms and conditions in fine print that a customer generally may not read. However, in the event of any dispute, the so-called fine print plays a major role in legal judgements. The importance of the knowledge of the offer is legally imperative both for the offeror and the offeree. The former must specifically notify or communicate the offer and all that it entails; the latter, the offeree, too must inform himself and get familiar with what the acceptance of such an offer involves. The offeree cannot feign ignorance if the legally approved channels of communication of the offer have been made available to the customer.

Invitation to treat Invitation to treat is a peculiar kind of offer that originates from the US where the offeror invites the prospective offerees for a negotiation. It happens while inviting tenders or auctions. Today, invitation to treat is commonplace with companies such as e-Bay, Bazee, etc., inviting customers to bid on the Internet. The most important matter in these cases is that the terms and conditions must be very well communicated to the prospective customers.

Lapse of Offer

The offer becomes invalid and cannot be accepted because the terms and conditions surrounding it are withdrawn or have run out of time. Table 2.8 presents the circumstances under which the offer lapses or slips into invalidity.

In the above manner, the offeror has the freedom to withdraw his offer before anyone accepts it. The provisions of lapse of offer help business people correct their course. However, it may be remembered how Toyota recalled its technically defective cars resulting in the

Table 2.8 Circumstances where the offer lapses or slips into invalidity

Circumstance	Reason	Example
Time	If an offer is conditioned to be accepted within a specified time, it lapses when the time is up.	Festival discounts: These are specified for a time. The offer lapses after the time.
Rejection	The offeree quite simply rejects the offer for his own reasons.	You want to buy a specific house but the price and place do not suit you. So you reject the offer.
Counter offer	In a counter offer, in the first place you reject the offer as made to you, and you make an offer as against the one that you have received.	The offeror has a house for rent which you would like to have, but you go a step further and offer to buy the house instead of renting it.
Death, insanity, etc.	To be alive and to be of sound mind are conditions for a valid offer, failing which the offer lapses.	If the seller of the house dies or loses his mind before the offeree can accept the offer, the same lapses.
Subsequent illegality or destruction of the matter	If what is offered is subsequently declared illegal, it lapses.	You want to book an office in the newly constructed building; but before you accept the offer, it comes to your knowledge that the building has some legal flaws.
Revocation	The offeror withdraws the offer made before anyone accepts it.	A car manufacturer recalls newly launched cars.

customer as well as the company suffering financial losses. If the company had been careful, it would have withdrawn its cars from its showrooms before they were sold.

2.6 ACCEPTANCE

Where a promisor has made an offer of performance to the promisee, and the offer has not been accepted, the promisor is not responsible for non-performance, nor does he thereby lose his rights under the contract.

Every such offer must fulfil the following conditions:

(1) it must be unconditional;

(2) it must be made at a proper time and place, and under such circumstances that the person to whom it is made may have a reasonable opportunity of ascertaining that the person by whom it is been made is able and willing there and then to do the whole of what he is bound by his promise to do;

(3) if the offer is an offer to deliver anything to the promisee, the promisee must have a reasonable opportunity of seeing that the thing offered is the thing which the promisor is bound by his promise to deliver. An offer to one of several joint promisees has the same legal consequences as an offer to all of them.

– Sec. 38, The Indian Contract Act, 1872

You have already come across 'acceptance' when we discussed about the offer—because one cannot be spoken in isolation from the other. Acceptance is the second essential aspect of the completion of contract. Just as the offer is an invitation by the offeror, so also the acceptance is the expression by the offeree of his consent to an agreement (see Figure 2.4).

Figure 2.4 Taxonomy of a contract—Offer and acceptance are communicated unambiguously

In everyday social life, people come across very important contracts—which may not be commercial—that highlight the point that unless a person accepts a proposal, no proposal of the proposer translates into an agreement. For instance, a Muslim marriage is surrounded by great pomp and ceremony, but all of this will turn to naught, if the bride does not express her consent. The moment she accepts bridegroom's proposal, the event turns into marriage. In a similar manner, no matter how sophisticated be the form of offer and the matters concerning negotiation, a legally enforceable contract comes into existence only when the offeror has made his offer and the offeree has accepted the same and communicated his intention to the offeror who in turn gives his assent to the deal. Thus we see that there is to-and-fro communication—it is mutual agreement. There goes a saying among lawyers: acceptance is to an offer what a lighted match is to gun powder.

Salient Features of Valid Acceptance

Just as we studied the salient features of an offer—the first part of the contract—there are corresponding features that show willingness to enter into a commercial relationship which creates a legal environment (Table 2.9).

Table 2.9 Salient features of a valid acceptance

Features	Sub-category/Explanation	Example(s)
Absolute and unqualified	The acceptance of the offer must be in the totality it has been made. The acceptance is a *mirror image* of the offer.	X offers to sell his/her luxury flat for ₹2 crore and Y agrees to buy it. If Y at the instance of paying wants to modify the terms of sale and purchase, then it would be construed as a counter offer.
Acceptance must be communicated to the offeror	(a) Express acceptance: The offeree communicates to the offeror about his acceptance or rejection. (b) Implied acceptance: Generally one cannot imply acceptance, unless a definite tradition has been built by a certain behaviour or form of silence.	(a) The buyer of the flat clearly and *distinctly himself* or as duly authorized by him conveys to the seller that he wants to buy the flat and that the seller receives and assents to the message, b) A dry fruit dealer who has a regular clientele and has established a regular delivery may assume implied acceptance each time he sends the said assortment of dry fruits.
Right acceptor	Only such a person or group can accept an offer to whom it is made.	At a heritage site the entry fee charged is higher for foreigners than for natives. The offer to the native is cheap and to the foreigner is costly. They can respectively accept it or reject it.
Post offer	Acceptance in its logical sense is only possible after an offer has been made. Offer always precedes acceptance.	One cannot write to the owner of a flat and say that you accept to buy the flat when the flat owner has not the slightest intention to sell the flat.
Before lapse	Acceptance is valid only if it is accepted within the specified period.	You cannot demand a discounted festival price from a seller after the festive season is over, saying that he advertised the discount sale during the festival period.
According to the prescribed mode	There are standard and laid-down stipulations of acceptance which may vary from a simple oral deal to a complex documentary deal.	In response to an advertisement for subscription of a magazine, you send in a duly filled coupon as well as the subscription money through money order as stipulated.
Within specified time limit	Generally, acceptance is time bound, unless it is a standing offer. It depends on the offeror's choice, how short or long he may like the offer to run.	Festival discounts are time bound, but public facilities such as commuter transport are standing offers.
In response to an offer	Acceptance is always a response to an offer.	You may apply for the shares of a company only if the issue is offered.
Rejection	The rejected offer by the offeree cannot be accepted again unless the offer is renewed.	

As manager you will face problems similar to those in Case 2.4. It substantiates the relationship between offer, acceptance, and its communication. What can never be adequately underlined is the importance of business communication. Just as communication gaps generate terrible social problems, misunderstandings in business communication can cost your company lucrative deals and loss of enormous amounts of money. You, therefore, need to focus carefully on the rules of communication of offer, acceptance, and revocation.

2.7 RULES OF COMMUNICATION OF OFFER, ACCEPTANCE, AND REVOCATION

Although at this moment you have a fairly good grasp about offer and acceptance and the communication involved, yet it may be tricky to detect *when* exactly during this communication a contract comes into being or lapses and secondly, what means of communication validate a contract (refer Table 2.10).

Table 2.10 Rules of communication of offer, acceptance, and revocation

Offer	Communication	Acceptance
Offer is made when the communication is sent.	Any one of the prescribed forms of communication deemed suitable.	Offer is accepted when the communication is received.
Revocation is made when it is communicated.	Any one of the prescribed forms of communication deemed suitable.	Revocation is complete when the communication is received.
Offer lapses when the prescribed time runs out.	Any one of the prescribed forms of communication deemed suitable.	Acceptance is revoked before it is assented by the offeror and the same is communicated to the offeror.
Offer revoked communicates to the offeree about the revocation.	Any one of the prescribed forms of communication deemed suitable.	Offeree assents to revocation.

Means of Communication

When the law of contract was formulated, apart from face-to-face communication, the only oth ns was of writing letters or sending telegrams through the postal service. Presently, communication has developed and long-distance communication is possible—both aural and visible. These are:

1. Face-to-face in the presence of the concerned parties
2. Exchange of letters and documents
3. Postal services
4. Audio: telephone, mobile, voice over Internet protocol
5. Video: video conferencing, mobile conferencing
6. Internet: instant communication

There is, however, an exception made in communication with the so-called *mail box rule* or *posting rule*. Acceptance takes place when the letter is posted. Case 2.5 happened barely after

CASE 2.5 APPELLANT: **Ramdas Chakrabarti** VS RESPONDENT: **Cotton Ginning Co. Ltd**[*]

DATE OF JUDGEMENT: **1887, Allahabad High Court**

FACTS: Ramdas Chakrabarti denied having received shares he had applied for; but the company claimed to have duly posted the shares.

JUDGEMENT: The contract has come into effect.

REASON: It follows from (Secs. 4 and 5) that a notice of allotment, which is the acceptance of the offer to purchase shares, is communicated to the allottee when it is dispatched, and from that moment there is a complete contract for him. Whether he receives the letter or not is absolutely immaterial.

[*]Ramdas Chakrabarti vs Cotton Ginning Co. Ltd, see: http://www.nls.ac.in/ded/resources/MBL%20I/MBL%20I/ Suggestedanswerforproblembasedquestionincontract%20law.pdf (11.10.2010).

a few years of the Contract Act coming into force, and is an old landmark case from the famed Allahabad Court. It establishes when the communication ends from the offerer and he cannot do anything to revoke it. It is a done deed and the contract takes effect.

The above old case has seen tens of thousands of similar cases ever since. You must take note of the important role communication plays. If you want to promote and safeguard your business, see that the means of communication are working at their best. You will do well to confirm that the communication you have conveyed to your customers has actually reached. Presumption that it will be received and accepted must be avoided.

2.8 CONSIDERATION

Agreement without consideration is void, unless it is in writing and registered or is a promise to compensate for something done or is a promise to pay a debt barred by limitation law…

– Sec. 25, The Indian Contract Act, 1872

So far, you have gone through the technicalities of drawing up a contract. Now you may justifiably ask: What is the real purpose of contract? What is the benefit? It ensures a good deal where you get monetary value in return for goods or services that you offered. It is a quid pro quo, that is, for something that you give, you get something in return. If there is no quid pro quo, nothing in return, then it is called as a *nudumpactum*, a nude contract; it is a bare contract, a void. You may give away something freely as parents give to their children or the philanthropists and social workers and expect no return. However, a business transaction involves a value exchange—which in legal language is termed as *consideration* (see Case 2.6). Every offer comes with a price tag.

The reason stated in the case by Judge Lush—*A valuable consideration, in the sense of the law, may consist either in some right, interest, profit, or benefit accruing to the one party, or some forbearance, detriment, loss, or responsibility, given, suffered, or undertaken by the other*—to this day stands as the definition of consideration.

CASE 2.6

PLAINTIFF: Currie vs RESPONDENT: Misa*

DATE OF JUDGEMENT: 1875

FACTS: Lizardi & Co. sold four bills of exchange to Mr Misa, drawn from a bank. Mr Currie was another of the banking firm and the plaintiff bringing the action. The bills of exchange were sold on 11 February, and by the custom of bill, brokers were to be paid for on the first foreign post-day following the day of the sale. That first day was the 14th February. Lizardi & Co. was much in debt to his banking firm, and, being pressed to reduce his balance, gave to the banker a draft or order on Mr Misa for the amount of the four bills. This draft or order was dated on the 14th, though it was, in fact, written on the 13th, and then delivered to the banker. On the morning of the 14th, the manager of Mr Misa's business gave a cheque for the amount of the order, which was then given up to him. Lizardi failed; on the afternoon of the 14th, the manager, learning that fact, stopped payment of the cheque.

JUDGEMENT: The banker was entitled to recover its amount from Mr Misa.

REASON: A valuable consideration, in the sense of the law, may consist either in some right, interest, profit, or benefit accruing to the one party, or some forbearance, detriment, loss, or responsibility, given, suffered, or undertaken by the other.

*Currie vs Misa, see http://en.wikipedia.org/wiki/Currie_v_Misa#cite_note-0.

A contract is basically a bargain between the contracted parties. The offeror wants to make a living by selling, while the offeree wants to satisfy a desire or need for which he is ready to shell out enough money which he thinks is a good bargain. Then the parties agree on a price and the deal is sealed.

If you are interested in mechanical engineering, you will appreciate well how it functions. Consider a three vee-belt that rotates three wheels; each wheel represents an aspect of the contract, that is, the offeror, offeree, and consideration. Just as the three wheels are brought into motion by the belt, so also the communication brings into motion all the three aspects in a contract. This is the manner in which the commercial machine functions. Just as a machine functions according to the law of mechanics—so also a commercial activity is governed by the enforceable law.

Rules for Consideration

From what has been already brought to your notice, as a student of business management you will appreciate that your sole motivation in your profession is the core matter of a commercial activity. What money you will earn for your company is the motive and purpose of your business management. It is obvious then it must function on some clearly defined rules. Table 2.11 presents the most essential rules of consideration.

If you find Table 2.11a mere enumeration of points regarding payments, it is time that you take a relook at it and reflect seriously. As a manager you will do well to place it somewhere you are sure to see it often. It is recommended you put it up on your company's notice board. For this sums up not only you and your company's charter, but also of all the business and the people in the country and the world. It is the core of economic and legal discourse.

Table 2.11 Essential rules of consideration

Rule	Explanation	Example(s)
At the desire of the offeror	A transaction takes place where something of value is exchanged. The offeror and the offeree agree on a price for the said transaction. Anything other than this, such as a third party or any service rendered voluntarily, is outside the purview of consideration.	Situation A: You see someone stranded on the road with a broken-down car. He offers you ₹500 if you could restart his car. You do the job, and you get the money. Situation B: It is the same case as above, except that you stop out of concern and help the person restart the car. Exchange of money for service is neither offered nor taken.
Move from the offeree or any other person	The consideration must come from the offeree or any authorized person or even a stranger; and if he is someway party to the contract then he has even the right to sue—what matters is that it is paid.	This is a classic example: X by deed of gift transferred property to Y, with the agreement that Y pay Z annuity. However, Y refused to pay Z, pleading that Z had not moved for consideration. The ruling said that the consideration need not necessarily move from the promise.
Must be an act, abstinence, forbearance, or a return promise	This indeed is the definition of consideration; the offeror must get something of value in return for his offer.	X borrows money from Y @ 15%. X fails to pay. Y threatens to sue. X offers to pay a higher rate of interest. Y agrees. This forbearance from Y for a higher rate of interest is the consideration.
May be past, present, or future	Depending on the agreement, the consideration may be honored as one from the past, at present, or to be done in the future.	You may pay your past due electricity bills at present and also pay in advance for the future.
Need not be adequate	The law says that consideration means something in return—whether it is adequate or not. The law is not responsible for bad bargains.	X purchased an antique chair from Y. Later, Y realised that the antique piece was worth several times more. Y sued X. Court rejected the plea on the grounds that it is not for it to fix a price.
Must be real and not illusory	The consideration—may not be adequate—but it must be real. There are four types of unreal considerations:	
	(a) Physical impossibility: One cannot promise what is not within one's powers,	(a) An airlines promises to fly passengers at half the rate but the date of flight is already in the past,
	(b) Legal impossibility: People unrelated to the contract cannot fulfill the obligation.	(b) X owes money to Y. X pays Z, the servant of Y, who discharges him from his obligations,
	(c) Uncertain consideration: The promise is unenforceable if the consideration is uncertain.	(c) X engages B's services and promises to pay a *reasonable* sum.

Contd

Table 2.11 *Contd*

	(d) Illusory consideration: It is a misleading promise that overrides the obligation of the contracting parties.	(d) Two people desert the ship. Captain promises the deserter's salaries will be shared among the rest if they help bring the ship to the port. The promise is unenforceable because the sailors are already under the obligation of their contract to do so.
Must be something which the offeror is not already bound to do.	A promise to do something to which one is already bound by contract adds nothing to it.	A government servant promising to perform public duty.
Must not be illegal, immoral or opposed to public policy	I. The consideration must be lawful else the agreement is void.	
	(a) Forbidden by law: When a certain act is forbidden under statute, rule, or any law and is punishable. A contract contrary to law is void.	(a) X offers Y, a public servant, to grant him a license to manufacture a product that is reserved only for the public sector.
	(b) Defeats the provisions of the law. It may not directly break the law but does not maintain the purpose of the law, hence void.	(b) X and Y agree to take mutual mea- sures which will help them avoid tax.
	(c) Fraudulent: If the purpose of consideration is to defraud third party, then it is a void contract.	(c) When X knowing his property may be attached by Income Tax Department, transfers it to a third party, to be given back to him, when the matter is settled in his favour, e.g., declare him insolvent.
	(d) Injurious to person or property of another. II. Morality is good conduct as practiced in the society of which the law takes cognizance. III. The objective of public policy is the public good. Any consideration against it would result into a void agreement.	(d) X pays Y to get rid of his enemy. A landlord lets his premises to a brothel. Since prostitution is illegal, the rent that he gets is unlawful consideration.
	(a) Trading with an enemy: It will cause harm to people and property of one's own native land.	(a) Countries X and Y are at war. One of the companies conducts arms trade with the enemy country.
	(b) Trafficking in public offices.	(b) X uses his bureaucratic position to grant undue favours and receive consideration for the same.
	(c) Interference with the course of justice: Obstruction of justice is a serious offence and nullifies the contract	(c) X, who was undergoing court proceedings, tried to bribe the opposition's witnesses.

Contd

Table 2.11 *Contd*

	(d) Stifling prosecution: An agreement not to prosecute or coercion to withdraw it, makes such a contract void.	(d) Threat, bribe, influence peddling, coercion, etc. used to obstruct the process of justice.
	(e) Maintenance and champerty: Both considerations of maintenance and champerty are illegal and void.	(e) When a person agrees to give financial or any other assistance to another to enable to bring or defend legal proceedings is called *maintenance*. When a person agrees to assist another in bringing action for the recovery of money or property, it is called *champerty*.
	(f) Marriage brokerage is a void contract. (g) Unfair and unreasonable dealings which are exploitative and are against the public good . (h) Creating interest against public duty.	(f) It is a void contract when it is agreed to procure the marriage of a person for a reward. (g) Company X hires people for short periods and fires them so that it can save on wages and benefits to the workers. (h) X solicits Y, a government bureaucrat, and the former is an effective influence on the latter's decisions which are made in the public interest.

CASE 2.7

PETITIONER: Pankaj Bhargava vs RESPONDENT: Mohinder Nath[*]

DATE OF JUDGEMENT: 2 September 1994

FACTS: Petitioner Pankaj Bhargava complained that the respondents Mohinder Nath and others have violated the undertaking given to the court to vacate the premises rented out to them. The occupants had not paid the rent and rent controller and the tribunal upheld the opinion of the respondents and the court overturned the same holding petitioners' claim that he had rented out the premises for which they failed to pay. The appeal is for remedy and contempt of court.

JUDGEMENT: The respondent is guilty of contempt of court: Imprisonment for two weeks and ₹2,000 fine. If fine is not paid, further imprisonment of another two weeks.

REASON: The appellate authorities, rent controller, and the tribunal failed to appreciate the initial cheque payment made by the respondents as proof of agreed consideration. After examining evidence and proofs, the high court held that the agreement was proper to Delhi Rent Control Act, 1958. The respondents falsely fabricated the case. Further the respondents committed contempt by not complying with the earlier order of this court and continued to remain in possession of the premises of the petitioner.

[*]Pankaj Bhargava vs Mohinder Nath. See link for ful text of the judgement http://www.indiankanoon.org/doc/84188/ (12 November 2010).

Are there instances where consideration is not necessary? Agreement made for the sake of love and affection may be enforceable where the parties have written, signed, and registered the marriage with the authorities, but these may not be any consideration. However, if it is a matter of divorce proceedings and an annuity is decided, then it is a consideration and enforceable by the law. The other instances where consideration is not necessary is payment for voluntary service, promise to pay time-barred debt whose time has elapsed, gifts, and agency. Some of these such as agency will be dealt with later on.

Case 2.7 is instructive for several reasons:

- Firstly, it clearly brings out the principle that the consideration moves from the offeror.
- Secondly, one can traverse with this case from the constitution of the contract to its revocation.
- Thirdly, one can evaluate all the problems that may arise out of not honoring the consideration.
- Fourthly, one can observe how wantonly one can mislead legal procedure; however, the wheels of justice move to deliver justice to the one who relentlessly seeks it.
- Fifthly, disobeying the order of the court leads to its contempt, which is a grave offence for a citizen of a country and a permanent blot on his character.

The lesson for you as a manager from Case 2.7 is that due diligence in all matters of financial obligation is the first duty.

> **MANAGER'S TAKEAWAY**
>
> - Offer, acceptance, communication, and consideration are the 1-2-3-4 timed dancing steps of a manager—if you miss the step, then you are out of sync.
> - Respect the law and the law will protect you in all transactions.

SUMMARY

Introduction and Interpretation

- The Indian Contract Act, 1872 is the law upon which the entire business relationship is built. It governs principles of formation, performance, and enforceability of contracts and rules relating to contracts and to special types of contracts known as indemnity, guarantee, bailment, pledge, and agency.
- All agreements are contracts if they are made by the free consent of the parties.
- Two or more parties are said to consent when they agree upon the same thing in the same sense.
- When consent to an agreement is caused by coercion, fraud, misrepresentation, or undue influence, the agreement is a contract voidable at the option of the party whose consent was so caused.
- Coercion is the committing or the threat to commit any act forbidden by the Indian Penal Code, 1860.
- Undue influence is caused when one of the parties to the contract has a dominant position and draws unfair advantage from it.

Communication, Acceptance, and Revocation of Proposals

- Agreement is the intention to create legal relations—offer, acceptance, consideration, communication, revocation, competency to contract, free consent, lawful object.
- An agreement is made for a lawful consideration and with lawful object.
- Every agreement of which the object or consideration is unlawful is void.
- No action allowed for an illegal agreement: For action arising from a base cause and where there is an equal guilt, the defendant is in a better position.
- An agreement is said to be opposed to public policy when it is injurious to the welfare of the society: e.g., trading with enemy, agreement to commit crime, against public policy, agreements that interfere with the delivery of justice, restraint of trade, etc.

EXERCISES

Communication, acceptance, and revocation of proposals

(i) Examine whether the following offers are valid:

    (a) Amit tells Hari, 'Shama will sell you a camera'. Amit owns several cameras of different ranges of price.

    (b) An auctioneer displays an antique object.

    (c) You enter a bookshop and want to buy on discount the book that is displayed on the shop window.

    Hint: a and b are not offers; find out why c is an offer.

(ii) Amit sent a letter to Bhim offering him to sell the shop. The next day Amit again sent a letter to Bhim revoking the offer. Meanwhile, Bhim accepted the first letter from Amit and confirmed by return post. What is Bhim's remedy as against Amit in the following cases: (a) If Amit's letter of revocation reaches Bhim before latter's letter of acceptance reaches the former; (b) If Bhim's letter is lost in the post; (c) If Bhim's letter of acceptance is posted an hour after the posting of Amit's letter of revocation? Hint: In all cases, there is a concluded contract. See Sec. 4 of the Act and explain.

(iii) Hari applied for the shares of a company. The letter of the allotted shares was sent to him through the agent; but before the letter was handed over to him, he withdrew his offer. Is there a contract between Hari and the company?

Hint: No. See the salient features of offer and acceptance.

(iv) Amit and Bhim divided the family property between them and agreed to contribute ₹10,000 equal shares and invest it in the security of immovable property and pay towards the maintenance of their mother. Can the mother demand that the amount of money invested by her sons be settled in her favour?

Hint: Yes. It was held favorably in the case of Kuer vs Sarla Devi (1947, Bom. L.R. 123) for such settlement.

(v) Comment on the following statements:

    (a) A mere mental acceptance without evidencing through words or conduct does not amount to acceptance in the eyes of the law.

    (b) Performance of the conditions of the proposal is an acceptance of the proposal.

    (c) An agreement may be made in any manner whatsoever, provided the parties are in communication.

(vi) Whereas an offer is not held to be made until it is brought to the knowledge of the offeree, under certain circumstances, acceptance may be so considered.

(vii) Comment on the following:

    (a) No consideration, no contract.

    (b) Insufficiency of consideration is immaterial.

DEVELOPMENT OF LEGAL EDGE

- Conduct a research project of all the important contracts of a company.
- When you conduct a discussion consciously, role-play sometimes as petitioner's counsel and sometimes as the respondent's. Take the role of the difficult position.

FURTHER READING

- The Indian Contract Act, 1872 (easily available in bookshops and law bookshops). This is mandatory while studying the text book.
- Documents and forms: For any document or format of letters of contract; visit http://www.citehr.com.

- Pollock, Fredrick and Dinesh Fardaunji Mulla, 2002, *Indian Contract and Specific Relief Acts.* (12th ed.), Butterworths, New Delhi.

Web resources

- Supreme Court of India: http://supremecourtof india.nic.in/.

- Law Commission of India: http://lawcommissionofi ndia.nic.in/.
- Ministry of Corporate Affairs: http://www.mca. gov.in/.
- All India Reporter: http://airwebworld.com/index. php.

- All acts and documents: http://www.legaldocs.com/.
- Law-related articles and for a: http://www.fi ndlawindia.com/.

CASE STUDY   LESS FOR MORE

Promisee may dispense with or remit performance of promise.[2]

Every promisee may dispense with or remit, wholly or in part, the performance of the promise made to him, or may extend the time for such performance, or may accept instead of it any satisfaction which he thinks fit.

– Sec. 63, The Indian Contract Act, 1872

The Concept of Satisfaction

He *is well paid that is well satisfied*.[3] The question in the following case analysis is how to accept a consideration that falls short of what you have given. In other words, you contract for a certain amount and part with the property, and in the course of time, your client is able to pay less than the contracted amount. Can you be satisfied with the resettlement? Does that not abrogate the previous contract in favour of the new one which would cause you loss? Is it not a self-contradiction to say that you are satisfied with receiving less in lieu of what you have given in excess?

According to the English law if you are *satisfied* with less consideration, it is your business. When you suddenly realise that you have suffered a loss and you regret your action for accepting the lesser deal, then you have an opportunity to bring action against your client.

In India we have generally followed the English case law. Even today citations from English case law are common. Is the concept of satisfaction principle in both the countries also the same? You see at the start of this chapter-end case: Sec. 63 of the Indian Contract Act, 1872, where it is put forward in a few words that you are free to receive your consideration and be satisfied, or you may postpone it if the consideration falls short of your contract, or you may accept less and be satisfied according to your wish. The question is, like English law, does the Indian law allow you to file a suit after you have accepted consideration to your satisfaction, irrespective of its falling short of the contracted amount?

Shylock vs Antonio

The trial of Antonio, the merchant of Venice[4]

William Shakespeare's play *The Merchant of Venice* is a classic example of twists and turns that a contract can generate in a life situation where love and hate relationships dominate and the courtroom drama highlights these with far-reaching consequences.

The play is set in 14th century Venice. Antonio, the protagonist of the play, is a paragon of the quality of loyal friendship. His friend Bassanio needs money to be a suitor to the wealthy heiress called Portia. Antonio, the merchant, who has his ships at sea, has a cash crunch. He approaches Shylock, the cunning Jewish moneylender. Shylock gives him the money he asks for with an explicit written contract that states that if the money is not returned by the specified date, a pound of flesh would be taken off from Antonio's body. Despite protests from Bassanio, Antonio agrees to the contract and gives the money to his friend to go and seek the hand of Portia. Bassanio goes and, in a dramatic fashion, wins the hand of Portia. Time elapses, the ships do not return and Antonio cannot pay back the debt; he becomes insolvent.

Shylock, the creditor, brings action against Antonio. Upon his failure to produce the money, Shylock demands a pound of flesh. Bassanio, who has now returned with a fortune, offers to bail out his friend with the amount doubled. Shylock refuses and sticks to his demand of a pound of flesh. At the right time, there appears a young

---

[2]The title of the Sec. 63 of The Indian Contract Act, 1872.
[3]See next section, Shylock vs Antonio.
[4]For the whole play see, http://shakespeare.mit.edu/merchant/full.html, assessed on 15 October 2010.

lawyer (disguised Portia) to represent Antonio, and produces the famous argument of defence:

Tarry a little; there is something else.
This bond doth give thee here no jot of blood;
The words expressly are 'a pound of flesh:'
Take then thy bond, take thou thy pound of flesh;
But, in the cutting it, if thou dost shed
One drop of Christian blood, thy lands and goods
Are, by the laws of Venice, confiscate
Unto the state of Venice.[5]

The defeated Shylock quickly refers back to the offer made by Bassanio for the defaulted bond. But the young lawyer further buttresses the defence's argument saying that the petitioner has already refused it and cites the Venetian law which states that a person trying to take the life of the citizen of Venice would forfeit half to the government and the other half to the defendant; (in this case Antonio), and leaving his life to the mercy of the Judge, the Duke of Venice.

The operative part of Duke's judgement shows both mercy and justice: Shylock gets life's pardon; Antonio shares the income from the principal till Shylock's death. The rest of the drama ends in a typical Shakespearean romantic comedy: all is well that ends well.

The Case—Twists and Turns of Contract

The Union of India vs Kishorilal Gupta and Brothers[6] is an often-cited case which involves:

- The Arbitration Act, 1940
- The Indian Contract Act, 1872
- Sec. 39 of The Arbitration Act, 1940
- Article 1 36 of The Constitution of India, 1949

The scope of this study is restricted to the Contract Act specifically.

Stage I

Kishorilal & Bros, the respondents, entered into contract with the Union of India, the appellants, with three different contracts for the fabrication and supply of diverse military stores:

> Contract 1: Ladles cook
> Contract 2: Bath ovals
> Contract 3: Kettles Camp

The above contracts contained an arbitration clause. The arbitrators would be nominated from each side.

According to the contracts, the Union of India supplied raw material and the Kishorilal firm supplied the finished goods. But they did not supply all and there arose a dispute. Union of India agreed that in contract 1, there was recovery of raw materials but the other two failed even such recovery of raw material. Union of India rescinded all the three contracts. They accused each other of breach of contract. Finally, they managed to arbitrate and reconcile these disputes.

Stage II

The parties then entered into three fresh contracts on successive dates purporting to settle these disputes on the terms therein contained. By the first two of these settlement contracts, the respondents agreed to pay to the appellant certain moneys in settlement respectively of the disputes relating to the first two original contracts. By the last of these settlement contracts, the respondents agreed to pay to the appellant, in specified installments, certain moneys in settlement of the disputes relating to the third original contract as also the moneys which had then become due on the first two settlement contracts, and had not been paid and further undertook to hypothecate certain properties to secure the due repayment of these moneys. The third settlement contract provided: 'The contracts stand finally concluded in terms of the settlement and no party will have any further or other claim against the other.'

Stage III

The respondents paid some of the installments but failed to pay the rest. They also failed to create the hypothecation. The appellant then referred its claims for breach of the three original contracts to arbitration under the arbitration clauses contained in them. On this reference, an award for a total sum of ₹1,16,446 was made against the respondents in respect of the appellant's claim on the first and the third original contracts, the claim in respect of the second original contract having been abandoned by the appellant, and this award was filed in the High Court at Calcutta. The respondents applied to the High Court for a declaration that the arbitration clauses in the original contracts had ceased to have any effect and the contracts stood finally determined as a result of the settlement contracts and for an order setting aside the award as void and nullity. The High Court held that the first original contract had not been abrogated by the settlement in respect of it, but the third original contract and the arbitration

---

[5]Ibid., lawyer (Portia) retorts the words of the contract for pound of flesh. (14.10.2010).
[6]The Union of India vs Kishorilal Gupta and Bros, 1959 AIR 1362, 1960 SCR (1) 493.

clause contained in it had ceased to exist as a result of the last settlement, and the arbitrator had no jurisdiction to arbitrate under that arbitration clause. As the award was a single and inseverable award, the whole of it was null and void. In this view the High Court set aside the award. The third settlement, properly construed, left no manner of doubt that it was for valid consideration and represented the common intention of the parties to substitute it for the earlier contracts between them. It gave rise to a new cause of action by obliterating the earlier contracts and the parties could look to it alone for the enforcement of their claims. There could, therefore, be no question that the arbitration clause, which whether a substantive or a collateral term, was nevertheless an integral part of the said contracts, must be deemed to exist along with them as a result of the said settlement. It was well settled that the parties to an original contract could by mutual agreement enter into a new contract in substitution of the old one.

The positions in the dispute

Consequently, the Union of India appealed and took the following position:

1. There had been no novation or substitution of the original contract.

2. Even if there had been a novation, the non-performance of the terms of the new contract revived the original contract and hence the arbitration clause exists.

Kishorilal & Bros took the following position:

1. As the appeal had been made to the appellate bench of the HC and in spite of that a special leave had been granted by the SC, it is against the legal procedure and hence the special leave should be revoked.

2. There had been a recession of the old contract and substitution with a new legally enforceable contract.

3. The new contract is legally supported by Sec. 62 and Sec. 63 of the Indian ContractAct, 1872.

4. Non-performance of terms of the new contract did not revive the old contract.

5. Even if the arbitration was alive, the arbitrator was bound to decide the case in terms of the new contract.

The judgement

The bench comprising of three judges—Justices K. Subba Rao, Imam Syed Jaffer, and A.K. Sarkar—delivered a two-to-one judgement in favour of the appellant, the Union of India; Justice Sarkar's being the dissenting judgement (Exhibit A).

Exhibit A   Judgements of Justices Subba Rao and Jaffer and Justice Sarkar

Justices Subba Rao and Jaffer

- The first contention of the respondent is rejected. Reason: The respondent should have raised this issue at the very beginning and not after 5 years, so that the appellant would have had the opportunity to prefer a letters *patent appeal* to the appellate bench of Calcutta HC.
- There was a novation of contract because the receipt given by the appellants and accepted by the respondents and acted on by both proves that they agreed to a settlement of all their existing disputes by the arrangement given in the receipt. It means that by the new settlement, the prior rights of the parties are extinguished. Basically, *consensus ad idem.*
- The second issue is answered, that in case of 'accord and satisfaction by a substituted agreement', prior rights of the parties are extinguished. If a contract is altered,there would be no such clauses in the new

contract enabling you to sue upon that alone, but in case of novation/rescission; you can sue on basis of the new contract alone.

- The logical outcome of discussion of the first issue would be that the arbitration clause perished with the original contract, because it was nonetheless an integral part of the contract and had no existence *de hors* the contract. The new contract stated that the parties gave up the terms of the old contracts, including the arbitration clause. If the dispute is as to whether the contract which contains the clause has ever been entered into at all, that issue cannot go to arbitration. If, however, they entered into a binding contract, such arbitration clause would also confer authority to assess damages. If the contract is superseded by another, the arbitration clause, being a component part of the earlier contract, falls with it.

Contd

- An arbitration clause is a collateral term of a contract. The existence of the contract is a necessary condition for its operation. Also, if the original contract has no legal existence, the arbitration clause will not operate.
- The three contracts were settled and the third settlement substituted all the three contracts which existed previously, extinguishing their arbitration clauses.
- Appeal dismissed with special leave for further appeal.

Justice Sarkar

- The second contract for bath ovals becomes irrelevant for discussion because the appellant withdrew their claim under it from arbitration and no award was made in respect of it.

- The third settlement amounts to a substituted agreement, abrogating the original contract.
- An arbitration clause stands apart from the rest of the contract.
- An accord and satisfaction only releases the parties from the obligations under a contract, but does not affect the arbitration clause in it.
- The third settlement did not alter or rescind the original contract, but only settled the dispute as to its breach and consequences of it.
- The consideration, i.e., the satisfaction, may be executory or executed (promise of performance or actual performance, respectively). Therefore, this was not an accord and satisfaction.
- The appeal is upheld.

The judgement clearly shows the contractual problems. Since the judgement is not unanimous and that the room for further appeal has been granted, there appears no end in sight for the dispute. The appellant, the Union of India, initially had claimed the costs of their raw material. There was no satisfaction given by the respondents. It was disputed. Accord, that is, the agreement or contract and satisfaction, that is, the consideration are dealt deftly in the judgement of Justice Sarkar. The joint judgement of Justices Rao and Jaffer develop the doctrine of contract. To sum, the judgement shows the importance of consideration and satisfaction in a contract. In principle, the consideration may not correspond to the value of the goods, it merely suffices whether the concerned party is satisfied with it. This should raise several questions in your mind.

Satisfaction debate—Complete satisfaction vs less for more

There is certainly confusion in your mind. At the outset of this chapter, you learnt the principle of consideration, wherein, one enters into a contract for a consideration. However, in the above case you get confused whether the appellant is satisfied with the costs of the return of the raw material. As the case progresses, you see the appellant changes his mind and wants full satisfaction. The judgement on the case is also a dissenting one. Hence, what is the ultimate principle of consideration? How a seller is

satisfied by the consideration he receives other than the full satisfaction through full consideration?

Examine the following most celebrated cases in comparison and make up your mind (see Exhibit B).

Conclusion

Apart from the central case, Union of India vs Kishorilal Gupta & Bros you have seen several other cases including a fictional one from Shakespeare. These tell you that a contract is not as simple as it appears. If problems crop up because of it and you fight for the satisfaction of your consideration, litigation may take all your management appetite away. What you have to remember is that the law is there to protect all the parties involved in commerce. As a merchant, you may rightly speculate on anything that is saleable. However, the law is not speculative; it interprets the principles upon which it is based to protect those who live under it.

Discussion Questions

1. What constitutes the dispute in the above cases?
   (a) The Union of India vs Kishorilal
   (b) Pinnel vs Cole
   (c) Punamchand vs Temple
   (d) Shylock vs Antonio

2. What is the importance of consideration to business transactions? Illustrate.

Exhibit B Celebrated Case in Comparison*

British Case Law—Pinnel vs Cole (1602)

The claimant was owed 8 pounds and 10 shillings. The defendant paid 5 pounds, 2 shillings, and 2 pence. The claimant sued for the amount outstanding.

The claimant was entitled to the full amount even if they agreed to accept less. Part payment of a debt is not valid. Consideration for a promise to forebear the balance unless at the promisor's request, part payment is made either:

(a) before the due date, or
(b) with a chattel, or
(c) to a different destination.

Indian Case Law—Hirachand Punamchand vs Lieutenant Temple (1911)

The claimants were money lenders. They lent money to the defendant Lieutenant Temple who was an army officer serving in India. The claimants sought return of the money from the claimant but were unable to get any response; so they contacted his father. Some correspondence happened between the claimant and the father's solicitors. The claimants asked how much the father would be prepared to pay to settle the son's accounts. An amount was agreed upon, which was a substantial amount, although not the full amount due. The claimant promised to send the promissory note relating to the son's debt to the father once they received payment. The father paid, but the claimant retained the promissory note and sued the son to enforce the balance.

The payment made by the father was *sufficient* to discharge the full balance. Where the person making payment in return for discharging the debt owed by another this will amount to good consideration as the existing duty to make payment was not owed by them but a third party.

*For a comparative study, see, http://www.lawjunction.in/resources/projects/contract/Pinnel%20Case.pdf (27 December 2010).

3. Define with examples the concept of satisfaction in the context of the company you are working or want to work for.
4. What are the kinds of situations that make a party accept less than equitable consideration?
5. Why not file a suit for price and recover the consideration rather than take the accord and satisfaction route?
6. Point out the similarities and dissimilarities in the two sets of judgement in Union of India vs Kishorilal case.
7. As a manager, how would you plan to meet the costs of the litigation in the case of Union of India vs Kishorilal?
8. What lessons have you learnt from the above set of cases in your management conditions?

Going Beyond

1. Can you repeatedly and consistently agree and disagree on the same issue?
2. If the law operates on the same principles, how come the judgements differ as in the three-judge bench in the case of Union of India vs Kishorilal.
3. Would it be possible to find a solution to the case of Union of India vs Kishorilal case outside the court. How would you go about it?
4. What insights into contract and satisfaction do you get in Shakespeare's play *Merchant of Venice?*

LEGAL LUMINARY

ROHINTON NARIMAN—SPIRITED CORPORATE LAWYER

His nickname, Company Bahadur, says it all. He is a consummate corporate lawyer and for over two decades, he has been a member of the Bar. Rohinton Nariman was made a senior advocate of the Supreme Court at the young age 36, a singular exception in the history of the Supreme Court. According to a Times of India survey, he stands ninth among the top ten lawyers of India.*

His career took to a flying start as an assistant to the legendary Nani Palkivala in 1980, in the famous Minerva Mills case.** The case was about the basic structure of the Constitution. It gave young Nariman the inner awareness of the Constitution of India and the protection of the fundamental rights.[†]

He has been noted for having a legal library in brain. Sharp intelligence, wit, and dedication mark his this unassuming brilliant counsel of the Supreme Court of India. He is the founder of the Supreme Court Lawyers' Welfare Trust.

The significance of Nariman to you as manager does not lie in his intelligence, success, or pedigree—he is the son of the legendary Padma Vibushan Fali Nariman—but in his attitude to failure. Initially he lost cases. He worked hard. He lost very big cases. He worked harder. He rose to success because he learnt twice from each failure. Moreover, the professional significance for you as manager and a fair warning is that he comes in the rare bracket of those who command a fee starting from ₹2 lakh for mere appearance to ₹25 lakh for a full day's work. If you could avoid paying it, you too would become a 'company bahadur' for your company.

Apart from being the son of his famous father, he is a family man who admits that his greatest joy in life is to gaze at the face of his first born, a baby girl, with wonder and delight. He considers music and books as life and blood.

---

*http://www.legallyindia.com/377-toi-doesnt-like-law-firms-top-10-lawyers-list-09 (2.1.2011).
**See the case in Chapter 1.
[†]For more details see, http://timesofindia.indiatimes.com/india/Indias-top-10-lawyers/articleshow/5426768.cms (2.1.2011).

The Nature of the Indian Contract Act, 1872

Principle: *Contractus legem ex contione accipient.*

Contracts become law from the agreement of their parties.

CHAPTER OUTLINE

- Violable Contracts and Void Agreements
- Void Contracts
- Contingent Contracts
- Performance and Discharge
- Relations Resembling Those Created by Contract or Quasi Contract

- Consequences of Breach of Contract
- *Case Study:* Agreement
- Supervening Beyond Contract
- *Legal Luminary:* The Bhushans

3.1 VIOLABLE CONTRACTS AND VOID AGREEMENTS

All agreements are contracts if they are made by the free consent of parties competent to contract, for a lawful consideration and with a lawful object, and are not hereby expressly declared to be void. Nothing herein contained shall affect any law in force in India, and not hereby expressly repealed, by which any contract is required to be made in writing or in the presence of witnesses, or any law relating to the registration of documents.

– Sec. 10, The Indian Contract Act, 1872

The previous chapter dealt with just one question: Who is capable of making a contract? The entire contract depends on two pillars, namely, *competency* and *consent*. Contracts can be violated, hence they are violable; but they can also be void, that is, upon finding an impediment to a contract, which basically proves that there was no contract at all, that it was void due to a want of an essential condition. What kinds of people are competent to contract. Is a person capable of free consent? You will find the answers to these questions which will help you to determine whether the person or parties you want to sign a contract with is/are competent to do so and that too with free consent.

Capacity to Contract

Every person is competent to contract who is of the age of majority according to the law to which he is subject, and who is of sound mind and is not disqualified from contracting by any law to which he is subject.

– Sec. 11, The Indian Contract Act, 1872

Sections 10 and 11 of the Contract Act have outlined the following essentials as to who can enter a contract, i.e., has the competency to enter a contract:

(a) Attained the age of majority
(b) Sound mind
(c) Not disqualified by law to enter into contract

Minor versus age of majority

One who has not reached the age of majority is called a minor. A minor in India is one who is under the age of 18 years; it is one who has not attained the age of majority or 18 years. When a person is under the wards of court or a guardian appointed under the Guardians and Wards Act, he/she attains the age of majority at 21. The law protects the rights of the minors because they are not able to give a mature consent at such an early age, as they are unaware of the consequences of their actions. Hence, on entering into a contract with a minor, several irregularities may occur. The following is the position of the law vis-à-vis minors:

Void ab initio   If there is a contract with a minor, it is an impediment of law and, hence, any agreement is null and void. The law intends to safeguard the interest of the minor because the minor is not able to make a right choice.

Example   If someone enters into an agreement to grant loan to a minor, such an agreement has no validity from its very inception. The demand for repayment of such a loan will not be considered valid according to the law. Section 65 of the Contract Act asserts that no compensation can be demanded.

No restitution   One cannot demand from a minor to make amends for the benefits obtained under a void agreement because there has been no legal agreement due to the under age of the party.

Example   From the example above, the loan amount cannot be demanded from the minor. However, the Specific Relief Act, 1963[1], provides that such benefit may be returned back to the rightful owner.

Minor's benefit is valid   Although the agreement with the minor may be void *ab initio* yet the benefit accruing to the minor must be upheld.

---

[1]Section 34 of this Act has the provision where, if the minor seeks a cancellation of contract, then she/he may restore all the received benefits.

Example   If by agreement the minor has sold something to another, he has the full right to enforce the promised benefit in his favour. In this manner, the law protects the minor from suffering a loss.

No ratification   A minor makes an agreement. It, however, does not allow him to ratify or endorse it when he comes of age. The reason is clear—because there was no valid agreement in the first place, hence there is nothing to ratify, validate, endorse, or to consent.

Example   The loan granted to a minor cannot be ratified when he attains the age of consent. The reason being not only the contract is void *ab initio*, the consideration given to a minor is also not regarded as consideration in the eyes of the law.

No estoppels   An estoppel is a legal constraint. A minor cannot be constrained or *estopped* from pleading minority.

Example   A minor fraudulently enters a contract impersonating as a major of age. However, the law allows him to reclaim his minority. This absolves the minor of his earlier supposed contract.

Liable for necessaries   A minor is responsible to pay for his *necessaries* supplied to him or to any one who he is legally bound to support. This we will deal under Quasi Contract. However, suffice to say that it is only the property of the minor and not the minor personally that can held liable for such transactions.[2]

Example   The examples of necessaries to a minor are educational and training expenses, medical care, defending a suit against the minor and the like which help her/him to safeguard the interests and future needs.

Specific performance   Only the contract which a lawfully appointed guardian has undergone on behalf of a minor can be considered as a valid contract.

Example   An apprenticeship is signed by the guardian for the minor. It is in the interest of the minor and, hence, binding on him.[3]

Partnership   A minor is not entitled to valid partnership. However, the law allows the minor the benefits and not losses thereof.[4]

Example   If a minor is a *partner* in a company and it is declared bankrupt, the minor partner is not held insolvent.

Torts   Tort is when the contracting party or parties may be held responsible for a transaction.

Example   A minor cannot be sued when a person fails to oblige the surety he has offered on behalf of the minor. One who has offered surety will be responsible.

Shareholder   A minor, since he is not able to contract validly, cannot be issued shares of a company.

---

[2]See Sec. 68 of The Indian Contract Act, 1872.
[3]See Apprentices Act, 1950.
[4]See Chapter 7 covering The Indian Partnership Act, 1932.

Example   A company may refuse to transfer the shares in the name of a minor. A lawful guardian may purchase shares in the name of the minor; but the legal liability lies with the guardian. The company may or may not register shares in the name of the minor, depending on the bylaws of the company.

The case presented below—Case 3.1—contracted by a minor is the benchmark Case for over a century. All the points discussed above have been brought into operation by the courts while deciding the competency of the minors to enter into a contract.

Indian businesses are largely family run. Minors in the family are also made part of the business. The manager, who can again be from the same business family or from outside of it, must know the legal position before enrolling the minors into the family business.

CASE 3.1	Petitioner: Dharmodas Ghose vs Respondent: Mohori Bibi

CASE 3.1

PETITIONER: **Dharmodas Ghose**   VS   RESPONDENT: **Mohori Bibi**

DATE OF JUDGEMENT: 1903 (The Privy Council)*

FACTS: Dharmodas Ghose, a minor entered into a contract for borrowing ₹20,000, of which ₹8,000 was paid to the minor who, in turn, mortgaged the property to the lender. The minor sued the lender to set aside the mortage.

JUDGEMENT: Privy Council declared the contract as void—not just voidable but absolutely void. Further, it held that any money advanced to the minor cannot be recovered.

REASON: Dharmodas Ghose was incompetent to contract due to minority. Such a contract under Secs. 10 and 11 of the Contract Act is void. The minor is also not obliged to repay the sum owned to him.

---

*The case (I. L. R., 30 Cal, 539) has been cited widely for competency to contract for well over a century; one of the innumerable links is: http://www.archive.org/stream/allahabadlawjou00courgoog/allahabadlawjou00courgoog_ djvu.txt where you will find application of this case on several counts. (11 October 2010).

Sound mind

The agreements entered into by persons of unsound mind are void. Section 12 of the Contract Act states that if the person at the time of making a contract is capable of forming a rational judgement as to its effects upon his interests, then it can be construed that it is done with a sound mind. The same section further enumerates that a lunatic, person in a drunken state, or who suffers delirious fevers are of unsound mind. A person who is usually of unsound mind but occasionally of sound mind may make a contract when he is of sound mind. In another instance, a person who is usually of sound mind but occasionally of unsound mind may not make a contract when he is of unsound mind.

For example (a) a lunatic who is of sound mind only at intervals may contract validly at those intervals; (b) a generally sane man at times of acute sickness, like a delirium in high fever, where he is unable to make a reasonable judgement, cannot make a valid contract. Other instances of such temporary inability to make a valid contract are drunkenness, temporary insanity, etc. However, there will be no personal liability of that unsound person.

Insolvent

A person who has been already adjudicated as insolvent is incapable of competent contract. However, contracts entered during the pendency of such adjudication are valid.

Corporations

A corporation legally formed under the law of association is a legal person and enjoys the privileges of a natural person as per the law. A company incorporated under the Companies Act can enter into contract competently. However, the company is constrained by the clauses of the memorandum of association. It is a person in so far as it has identified itself with its objects. Any contracts beyond the purview of its objects are void.[5]

Others

Other persons who are disqualified by law to enter into contract are as below.

Alien enemies   When there is a war between two countries, the citizen of the opposite country becomes an alien enemy.

Foreign sovereigns and ambassadors   These individuals enjoy immunity from law; they cannot be sued in our courts without the permission of the Central government.

Convicts   A person who is found guilty and sentenced to imprisonment is a convict. Such a person is not competent to enter a contract by law during the period of his incarceration.

Consent

Two or more persons are said to consent when they agree upon the same thing in the same sense.

– Sec. 13, The Indian Contract Act, 1872

Consent is to assent or agree to an offer. The above text from the Contract Act is its succinct and apt definition. The essence of the consent is *to agree upon the same thing in the same sense— consensus-ad-idem*. Such consent by people who are not prohibited by law is a free consent. Secs 13 and 14 of the Contract Act deal with free consent.

In the previous section, we detailed who may validly enter into a contract and those who cannot. Those who have been permitted by the established law, bearing capacity to enter into contract are eligible to give consent. Minors, those of unsound mind, aliens of an enemy country, people under the influence of delusion and temporary insanity, etc., cannot give a valid consent and, hence, any act of contract with them is void.

Example for void contract   When a minor enters a contract, it is a mistake because the minor's agreement is considered void in the eyes of the law. In other words, due to the fact that a minor is incapable of a contract, it follows logically there was no contract in the first place.

Example for voidable contract   When a person who can validly contract but is led into it by fraud has two options:

---

[5]We will deal with this theme extensively in Chapter 6 pertaining to The Companies Act, 1956.

(a) If objects to it upon realisation of the fraud then it is voidable contract;

(b) if he continues despite the knowledge of fraud then the contract is valid.

Impediments to free consent

An impediment is a hindrance or an obstacle which prevents something from its proper object. The law clearly defines not merely void and voidable contract that originates from consent but also the obstacles that may arise in giving a free consent.

In common parlance, consent may have numerous synonyms in their usage such as 'agree', 'approve', 'permit', 'sanction', 'authorise', 'bless', etc., but all of them indicate to the decision-making faculty, the fundamental power in humans: to choose. As a manager, you have been taught that the essence of management lies in decision making. You are made responsible for the decisions you take and then implement them. This also shows that before action there is decision; decision is the cause and action is the effect. The decision to do something, the motive, the intention, is the core of law. When two people or more come together with the same intention to decide on something that is in every way similarly understood by both, then they are said to have exchanged their consent and thus a contract comes into existence. Without consent there is no contract. Human as we are, we may make mistakes—one of the parties may misrepresent an object, cause undue influence, or even use force to agree to something. The law protects people from such perils. Beware of the five causes (see Figure 3.1) which make consent invalid.

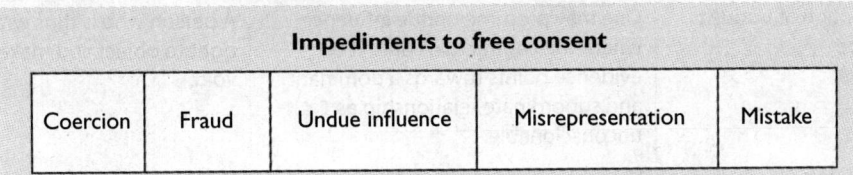

Impediments to free consent				
Coercion	Fraud	Undue influence	Misrepresentation	Mistake

Figure 3.1 Impediments or obstacles which vitiate or invalidate a free consent

Caveat emptor

Table 3.1 is a simplification of the entire gamut of deviation of valid consent. The complexity demonstrates the pitfalls in which a manager may easily fall. It is important that a manager possesses a clear mental model of what is going on when he/she conducts business transactions.

You have seen how the law functions. It does not admit the ignorance of law: *Ignorantia non excusat,* ignorance is not an excuse. In a similar fashion, you cannot give an excuse saying that you consented to buying something without fully knowing what you were buying. The law expects the buyer to be aware of what he buys. *Caveat emptor—buyer be beware—*is an exhortation in this regard.

You can appreciate the wisdom of the judgement: compulsion of law is not coercion (as we see in Case 3.2). This principle, in law, safeguards the sanctity of the law in order to protect the rights of the people. There is no compulsion in so far as one does not break the law. The case also illustrates all the points that you have studied as per Table 3.1 detailing the five impediments to free consent.

Table 3.1 Simplification of the entire gamut of deviation of valid consent

Cause	Explanation	Example/Sub-category
Coercion (Sec. 15)	(a) Committing or threatening to commit an unlawful act. (b) Unlawfully detaining or threatening to detain any property to the prejudice of the party whose consent is being so obtained.	A debtor obtains a letter of confirmation from his creditor at gun point which states that the latter has received his full payment and nothing is due.
Undue influence (Sec. 16)	(a) When one party dominates the will of the other. (b) The dominant party uses its position against the subordinate.	1. Real or apparent authority, e.g., income tax officer as against an assessee. 2. Fiduciary relationship, e.g., a relationship of trust between a creditor and debtor or a solicitor and client or a guardian and ward, etc., the dominant among these can use the confidence bestowed on them to unduly influence those under them. 3. Mental incapacity, e.g., a person with mental balance lost, under delusion, or influence of drugs; undue advantage may be taken of these distressed people to consent to something for which they are not capable.
Presumption of undue influence	One may presume undue influence where the contractual context or evidence points towards a dominant and subordinate relationship as unconscionable.	A person who is thus wronged has the right to object and make the contract void.
Effect of undue influence	Voidable contract	If the discount scheme was not honored by the vendor, the buyer, when he so realises, can cancel his purchase and return the product.
Rescission	A person who undergoes voidable contract can rescind, withdraw, repeal, or cancel the contract. Limitation to the above: (a) If the aggrieved party accepts the contract despite the fraud. (b) The time of rescission is elapsed. (c) A bona fide third party acquires right to the contract.	1. If the buyer accepts the product despite the knowledge of the scheme. 2. The time to claim discount has elapsed. 3. Where a purchaser, after defrauding a vendor, further sells the product to a third party.
Rescission method	When a party decides to rescind a contract: The party must return or restore the benefits obtained under the contract.	1. Give notice to the other party. 2. When the other party cannot be contacted then a public notice, or notice to the concerned authority is issued. 3. Return the received goods.

Contd

Table 3. 1   *Contd*

Fraud (Sec. 17)	It is an intentional misrepresentation of facts.	1. Suggesting something to be a fact, knowing it is false. 2. A person knows it to be false but conceals it. 3. Promise to do without the intention to do so. 4. Fact designed for deception. 5. Something declared by law to be fraudulent.
Silence as fraud	When a person omits to speak when his duty is to do so.	The vendor of FMCGs knows that the price of the television is reduced under a scheme but does not tell his customer, who does not know about the new scheme.
Misrepresentation (Sec. 18)	It is an untrue statement of a material fact which induces the other party into a contract.	1. Unwarranted assertions: When a person asserts a fact which is actually not true because his/her information does not warrant, justify, or merit it, e.g., the sales clerk at a car dealer tells the customer the price of cars will come down in a month, which turns out to be incorrect. The clerk had actually only heard it from his/her friend who had claimed he/she heard it from the top agent. Thus, the clerk's information which does not come from the confirmed source is not warranted. 2. Breach of Duty or Constructive Fraud: Where a person misuses one's position to defraud another who has placed his/her trust in one, e.g., X gives the impression to Y that it is a mere formality of the discussed matter and the former signs the sale deed. However, Y has actually altered the document in his/her own favour. Although one may contend there was no legal or moral obligation on the part of the Y, yet this concealment of information has amounted to a breach of duty. 3. Inducing mistake about the subject matter: When a person

Contd

Table 3.1 *Contd*

		induces another to a contract to mistake as to its subject-matter, e.g., a company makes a bill of exchange with a bank without admitting its liabilities, thus, making it different from what it actually represented. The bank is entitled to recover the amount on the grounds of misrepresentation.
Effect of misrepresentation	When the consent of the party is caused by misrepresentation then it is a voidable contract. (a) Where misrepresentation did not cause consent. (b) Where the misrepresentation caused consent but the party had means to discover it through ordinary diligence.	Three options are possible: 1. Rescind the contract, 2. Deliberately insist on performance to let the person experience his own misrepresentation, or 3. Sue the party for damages.
Mistake (Secs. 14, 20, 21, 22)	It is an erroneous belief.	
	(a) Mistake of Law:	Since ignorance of law is not presumed technically there is no question of such a mistake, except if such a law is not in force in India; in such a case, it would be mistake of fact.
	(b) Mistake of fact: As to identity.	A person who is supposed to be party to a contract but is actually a mistaken identity, resulting in void contract.
	As to subject matter.	• The subject matter ceases to exist before the contract is made. • What the seller purports to sell, he does not have the right to. • Parties to contract do not have the same subject matter in mind. • Parties to the contract are mistaken as to the substance, nature, or quality of the subject matter.
	(c) Mistake about the nature and content of promise.	There is confusion about the character of the deed, e.g., one party may think it is a gift deed while the other thinks it is sale for money. If both the parties are mistaken then it is void; if one defrauds the other then it is void too; if it is due to misrepresentation then it is voidable.

CASE 3.2

PETITIONER: Andhra Sugars Ltd. vs RESPONDENT: State of Andhra Pradesh

DATE OF JUDGEMENT: 29 September 1967*

FACTS: Under the Andhra Pradesh (Regulation of Supply and Purchase) Act, 1961, the proprietor of a sugar factory had to buy sugarcane from cane growers in conformity with the directions of the cane commissioner. Under Sec. 21 of the Act, the state government had the power by notification to tax the purchases of sugarcane for use, consumption, or sale in a sugar factory. The cane growers, of course, were free to sell the sugarcane to anyone they wished, e.g., the sugar factory, the *khandsari,* or make jaggery, which was tax free. However, the law laid down that if the cane farmer made an offer to the factory, the latter will have no choice but to accept it. The petitioners filed writ petitions under Article 32 of the Constitution challenging the validity of Sec. 21 mainly on the ground that as the petitioners or their agents were compelled by law to buy cane from the cane growers, their purchases were not made under agreements and were not taxable.

JUDGEMENT: Petition dismissed with costs.

REASON: Under Act no. 45 of 1961 and the rules framed under it, the cane grower in the factory zone is free to make or not to make an offer of sale of cane to the factory. But if he makes an offer, the factory is bound to accept it. The resulting agreement is recorded in writing and is signed by the parties. The consent of the occupier of the factory to the agreement is not caused by coercion, undue influence, fraud, misrepresentation, or mistake. His consent is free as defined in Sec. 14 of the Indian Contract Act though he is obliged by law to enter into the agreement. The compulsion of law is not coercion as defined in Sec. 15 of the Act. In spite of the compulsion, the agreement is neither void nor voidable.

*Andhra Sugars Ltd vs State of Andhra Pradesh is one of the most cited cases, particularly because the petition claimed that law itself is used in order to elicit or draw consent; the full judgement is available at link: http://www.rishabhdara.com/sc/view.php?case=3407 (29.2010).

3.2 VOID CONTRACTS

All agreements are contracts if they are made by the free consent of parties competent to contract, for a lawful consideration and with a lawful object, and are not hereby expressly declared to be void.

– Sec. 10, The Indian Contract Act, 1872

In legal circles, it is very often spoken about *null and void* agreement, contract, covenant, marriage, treaty, promise, or such terms. Null and void is a double emphasis or a double legal term to emphasise that there was nothing in the said transaction to warrant an agreement. Null implies just nothing and void implies something empty. A null and void contract is just nothing—there was no contract from the beginning because it lacked the essence of a contract; it is also sometimes known as null and void *ab-initio.*

However, in the eyes of the law, a contract may have all the essentials of the contract such as free consent, offer, acceptance, and consideration, and yet there may be those contracts that the law may expressly forbid as void. As per the Contract law, you will see in Table 3.2 those contracts that are void.

Table 3.2 Void contracts

Section	Void agreement	Explanation
11	Incompetent parties	See above: 'capacity to contract' (discussed earlier)
20	Mistake	See above: 'consent' (discussed earlier)
23 24 25	Unlawful object of consideration	See above: 'consideration' (discussed earlier)
26	Restraint of marriage	Legal age of marriage is 21 for boys and 18 for girls; under-age marriages are void; likewise, marriages with conditions such as only for a certain period, etc.
27	Restraint of trade	With enemy country or corporation as per bylaws of the memorandum of association. However, there some exceptions: e.g., sale of goodwill, partnership agreement, service agreements which are mutually agreed upon.
28	Restraint of legal proceedings	Legal redressal is a right and any agreement against it is void. Exceptions are: agreement to refer any dispute to a particular tribunal or arbitration which has already risen.
29	Meaning of contract is uncertain	Ambiguity in meaning of contract renders it void: e.g., say, a car in a showroom carries two price tags—₹2 lakhs and ₹3 lakhs—there is a confusion of consideration.
30	Wager	Wagering agreements are a guess, gamble, or uncertain venture about a future occurrence which if it comes about in one's favour the other would have to part with the money that he/she has put up as his/her stake. Gambling contracts are void as per Indian law.
36 and 56	Contingent on or to do impossible events	Agreement to perform miracles.
57	Agreement to do something illegal	A conspiracy to kill someone—say, contract killing—is not a contract but crime in the eyes of the law.

Restitution

One may enter into a void contract, for instance, as with the minor. A minor may not be legally required to restore, but definitely the duty falls on the guardian to do the needful. One may have benefited from such a contract and has the obligation to restore back: such restoration of benefit is called restitution (refer Case 3.3). The principle on which it is based is that a person who has been unjustly enriched at the expense of another is required to make restitution to that other. It is a principle of natural justice that you cannot unduly enrich yourself at the cost of the other.

Restitution makes justice impartial but fair. The law always upholds that enrichment should not be at the cost of others. Companies have great responsibility towards the people to reimburse if

CASE 3.3

PETITIONER: State of Orissa vs RESPONDENT: Rajballav

DATE OF JUDGEMENT: 6 May 1975*

FACTS: The respondent entered into a contract with the petitioner to construct a godown and received advance payment. He failed to complete the contract and the petitioner cancelled the contract.

JUDGEMENT: Ordered to return the advanced money back to the Government of Orissa.

REASON: Under Sec. 65 of the Contract Act, the government is entitled to recover the amount of money it advanced.

*State of Orissa vs Rajballav, A.I.R. (1976 Ori), 10; also see http://www.indiankanoon.org/doc/699834/ (20 October, 2010)

any undue accruement has taken place. It is fair for a cinema house to reimburse the cine goers if the show is cancelled due to power failure; likewise, for a car company to recall and repair or reimburse any loses suffered by the car owners due to technical faults. A cursory review will prove how our courts and consumer courts are clogged with cases and complaints for restitution.

3.3 CONTINGENT CONTRACTS

A 'contingent contract' is a contract to do or not to do something, if some event, collateral to such contract, does or does not happen.

– Sec. 31, The Indian Contract Act, 1872

Thus far you have studied about contract as a complete and unqualified concept: you did not question expressly whether a contract could depend or rely on some other factors too. Contracts are not absolute; in business these come with conditions. Very often contracts are in the formula of $x \rightarrow y$ *(If x then y)*. For instance, say, X contracts to indemnify Y up to ₹1,00,000 with a premium of ₹10,000 annually if Y's manufacturing unit gets burnt down.

Salient features of contingent contracts are as follows:

Dependence on a future event

The performance of a contingent contract depends on the happening or not happening of a future event.

Example Burning or not burning of a manufacturing unit.

Uncertain event

The event must be uncertain. It may happen or may not happen, as the case may be, for the contract comes into effect.

MANAGER'S TAKEAWAY

- There is no contract without consent.
- The 'fear' (knowledge with awe) of the law is the beginning of wisdom.

Example As in the above example of the manufacturing unit, if it burns down then the insurance for which it has been paying premium comes into operation.

Collateral to the event

A contingent contract necessitates by its very nature of dependency of a condition on a certain surety or a guarantee which is incidental to the contract and not essential.

Example When you take loan from a bank, you keep something of value with the bank as a surety.

Rules for Contingent Contract

From the preceding discussion you may draw certain rules that can assist you when you entering into such a contingent contract.

1. Enforcement of contract on the occurrence of a future uncertain event.
   Example X offers to sell his/her car to Y for a certain price. X also offers to Z to sell the car in the event Y does not buy it. It would then depend upon the refusal of Y for Z to buy the car. Y buys it.
2. Enforcement of contract on non-happening of a future uncertain event.
   Example X offers to pay Y a certain amount of money if the supply fails. The supply fails. Now X will pay Y what he/she has promised.
3. Enforcement of contract contingent upon future conduct of a living person.
   Example X offers pay money to Y if he/she marries Z. But Z marries M, thus making the transaction impossible.
4. Enforcement of contract contingent on a specified event happening within a fixed time. If the specified event does not happen within the specified period, it becomes void.
   Example When the promised supply does not arrive in time, it becomes void.
5. Enforcement of contingent contracts on specified event not happening within a fixed time.
   Example X promises Y to pay if Z does not supply in specified time. Z does not supply.
6. Enforcement of contingent contracts on impossible events—these are void.
   Example See No. 3.

Difference between Contingent Contract and Wager

Many a time, you would have heard that investment speculation in securities, insurance schemes, etc., are nothing better than gambling with an uncertain event of the future. A wager is an agreement between two parties by which one promises to pay upon the happening of some uncertain event in consideration of the other party's promise to pay if the event does not happen. In other words, you bet. You go to the racecourse and lay your bet on a horse to win as per the winning stakes you chose. Your horse wins: you get your reward.

However, in the eyes of the law, there are very clear differences between contingent contract and wagering, as shown in Table 3.3.

Table 3.3 Differences between contingent contract and wagering

Principle of distinction	Contingent contract	Wagering contract
Reciprocal promise	No mutual or reciprocal content	Strictly reciprocal
Condition	Determination of uncertain event—not the sole condition	Determination of uncertain event—the sole condition
Void	Not void	Void
Interest of the parties	Interests of the parties makes the contract	No interests of the parties except a game of chance
Future event	Merely collateral or incidental	Sole determining factor

Case 3.4 clearly exhibits that there is clear distinction in the eyes of the law between a contingent contract and a wager.

CASE 3.4   PETITIONER: The State of Bombay vs RESPONDENT: R.M.D. Chamarbaugwala

DATE OF JUDGEMENT: 9 April 1957*

FACTS: A weekly published from Bangalore, the State of Mysore, had very large circulation in Bombay. There was a prize competition called R.M.D.C. Crosswords and it set up collection centres for forms and fees. According to an amended Act of Bombay legislature, 1952, it was regarded as betting and gambling.

JUDGEMENT: Petition dismissed.

REASON: The prize competitions being of a gambling nature, they cannot be regarded as trade or commerce and as such the petitioners cannot claim any fundamental right under Article 19(1) (g) in respect of such competitions; nor are they entitled to the protection of Article 301.

*The State of Bombay vs R.M.D. Chamarbaugwala, A.I.R. (1957) SC 699, For full judgement see http://www.indiankanoon.org/doc/212098/ (11 January 2010). Note carefully that this is a judgement on an impugned law.

The above judgement set a landmark for the future. Consider how the quiz, game and other such activities have grown from mere hobby pursuits to a multi-crore rupee industry.

3.4 PERFORMANCE AND DISCHARGE

The parties to a contract must either perform, or offer to perform, their respective promises, unless such performance is dispensed with or excused under the provision of this Act, or of any other law.

Promises bind the representative of the promisor in case of the death of such promisors before performance, unless a contrary intention appears from the contract.

– Sec. 37, The Indian Contract Act, 1872

 MANAGER'S TAKEAWAY

- Never forget the contingent factor despite it being incidental.
- Gamble if you want, but never with the law.

This is what the managers do: they perform, and they are held responsible for what they do. In legal field, too, it is performance that matters. Lawyers call it the operative branch. You are free to enter into a contract or not to enter into one; but once you have done so, the responsibility rests on you to *act upon, do, operate, perform, execute, make it happen, carry out, complete,* or *honour* it. The parties to a contract must either perform or offer to perform their respective promises.

Mutual Obligations of the Seller and Buyer

Selling and buying is a mutual commercial relationship. There are rights and duties, and these are not exclusive in their existence but bind both parties mutually. Both parties assume certain duties in anticipation of the performance promised by the other party: the seller sells and receives consideration; the buyer pays and gets goods or services in return.

In international sales transactions, it is often agreed that the seller must ship the goods to the buyer, so that the latter need not pay until he has received the goods and been able to inspect them. Sellers may re-establish the time balance by demanding payment against documents. The buyer receives the documents of title, although the goods themselves may still be with the seller or in transit. The law everywhere protects the time sequence agreed upon by the parties by allowing a party to refuse its own performance as long as the agreed advance performance has not been made by the other party.

The law regarding the performance of contract—Secs 37 to 67—may be classified under three headings (refer Figure 3.2) and these cover:

1. Performance of contract
2. Discharge of contract
3. Remedies for breach of contract

Contract		
Performance	*Discharge*	*Remedies for breach*
Parties to the contract fullfill obligations	The rights and duties created by a contract come to an end	The means given by law for the enforcement of right

Figure 3.2   Classification of contract

Performance of Contract

The parties to a contract must either perform, or offer to perform, their respective promises, unless such performance is dispensed with or excused under the provision of this Act, or of any other law.

Promises bind the representative of the promisor in case of the death of such promisors before performance, unless a contrary intention appears from the contract.

– Sec. 37, The Indian Contract Act

You will see in Table 3.4, a systematic delineation of the performance of a contract.

Table 3.4 Systematic delineation of performance of contract

Salient features	Explanation
Attempted performance or tender	Offer of performance by the promisor in accordance with the terms of contract. If the promisee does not accept, does not perform, then the promisor is neither responsible for non-performance nor does he/she lose his/her rights under the contract. A tender is equal to performance. In order to have this effect, the tender must be an offer in its essential characteristic of unconditional, the whole of what is contracted for, with the proper time, place and manner specified. If unspecified then to have the legal effect, it must be reasonable.
Reciprocal promises and rules	Promises which form the consideration or part of the consideration for each other are called reciprocal promises. It is governed by three rules: (a) To be simultaneously performed—the promisor is not bound to perform unless the promisee is ready and willing to perform, (b) To be performed in the order fixed by the contract, (c) If the order is that one performs first and the other next, the first one cannot claim compensation demanding the second should have performed first.
Who performs contract	(a) Promisor: When a personal consideration is the foundation of the contract, (b) Agent: When personal consideration is not part of the contract, (c) Legal representative: If the promisor dies, (d) Joint promisors: If there are several promisors to the contract.
Who can demand performance	Promisee alone can do it; in the case of his death, his legal representative.
Time of performance	Time is the very essence of contract; it comes about in time just as all the other things in life—nothing can be done outside of it.
Time and place of performance	Parties to the contract, determine the place and time of performance. If time is not determined then it must be done within a reasonable time. If neither place nor time is determined, then the promisor must apply to promisee for one such.
Appropriation of payments	A term in accountancy: Where should the money be entered, e.g., when a debtor owes several debts and pays, not in full, where would the amount be accounted? Rules: (a) It goes where the debtor indicates, (b) If he does not then in account books, the entry on debit side discharged or reduced by the amount included on credit side.
Assignment of contract	Transfer of contractual rights and liabilities to a third party. Rules: 1. Act of the parties: (a) Contracts involving personal skill or other qualifications cannot be assigned, (b) A promisor cannot assign his liabilities and obligations under a contract, (c) Rights and benefits may be assigned if the contractual obligation is not of a personal nature, (d) An actionable claim can always be assigned but always effect in writing. 2. Operation of law: This takes place in the event of death or insolvency.

A business manager will appreciate all the above points well, but above all, he would consider the element of time as the most important feature. However, Case 3.5 shows that time alone and always need not be such indispensable a feature in judging the merit of a complaint.

Although as a manager you may be time-conscious, yet when you make time an essential element of the contract you would have to examine whether you can deliver the promise. Whenever, the time element is the determining factor, there are several issues to the context which need thorough examination. You will appreciate this point when you study the following aspect on discharge of contract.

CASE 3.5

PETITIONER: Hind Construction Contractors   vs   RESPONDENT: The State of Maharashtra

DATE OF JUDGEMENT: 30 January 1979*

FACTS: The appellant entered into a contract with the respondent for the execution of a work—the Alindi aqueduct—the essential term of which being that the contract be completed in 12 months from the commencement of the work. On the ground that the appellant had not completed the work within the stipulated time, the respondent rescinded the contract. The appellant filed suit claiming that rescission was wrongful since the time was not the essential factor and the delay was caused by rains and bad roads. It was upheld by the trial court but declined by the high court. Hence, the appeal filed in the apex court.

JUDGEMENT: Appeal upheld.

REASON: The time element must be read in terms of the entire context of the contract. Such rescission on the part of the respondent-defendant was clearly illegal and wrongful and thereby the respondent-defendant had committed a breach of contract, with the result that there could be no forfeiture of the security deposit. Therefore, the trial court was right in arriving at the conclusion that the appellant-plaintiff was entitled to a refund of their full security deposit.

---

*Hind Construction Contractors vs The State of Maharashtra, A.I.R. (1979) SC 720, was a landmark case in the determination of time as the essential element of contract; for full judgement see link: http://www. courtjudgements. org/hind-construction-contractors-vs-the-state-of-maharashtra/ (2 November 2010).

Discharge of Contract

Where two or more persons have made a joint promise, a release of one of such joint promisors by the promisee does not discharge the other joint promisor, neither does it free the joint promisor so released from responsibility to the other joint promisor or joint promisors.

– Sec. 44, The Indian Contract Act, 1872

Just as the contract is made, so does it come an end. It is logical to assume that a contract is complete when the contracting obligations come to an end, in other words, when it is discharged. However, it is not just fulfilling of the contract that discharges it, there are several other modes by which it gets discharged.

Discharge by performance

This takes place when parties to the contract fulfill their obligation; and as we have seen above such performance may be an actual or attempted one.

Discharge by agreement or consent

This is to say that as you have reciprocally entered into a contract, so can you get out of it with mutual consent. The principle governing this type of discharge of contract is expressed in Latin: *Eodem modo quo quid constituitur, eodem modo destruitur.* A thing may be destroyed in the same manner in which it is constituted.

There are six ways of discharge by agreement or consent:

Novation   When a new contract replaces the old one.

Alteration   When one or more terms of contract are changed.

Rescission   When all or some of the terms of contract are rescinded.

Remission   Acceptance of a lesser fulfillment of promise.

Waiver   One of the parties entitled exercises the right of waiver, i.e., intentionally relinquishes what rightfully belongs to it.

Merger   When an inferior right merges with the superior one.

Discharge by impossibility

You have already learnt that if a contract contains an obligation of something impossible, then it is void. This is based on two legal principles:
Lexicon cogit ad impossibilia—The law does not recognise what is impossible. *Impossibilium nulla obligato est*—What is impossible does not create an obligation.

Impossibility of performance is based on the following aspects:

Initial impossibility   A contract to do impossible thing is void *ab initio*, e.g., where bigamy is forbidden by law, you cannot contract to marry someone who is already married.

Supervening impossibility   It is an impossibility that arises after entering into a contract; hence the characteristic of subsequent or supervening impossibility. There are five such impossibilities to be noted:

Destruction of subject matter of contract   Say, a farmer fails to deliver the promised farm products due to the failure of the crops.

Non-existence or non-occurrence of a particular state of things   For example, people have bought tickets for a cricket match. But the match is cancelled due to rains.

Death or incapability for personal service   For instance, a danseuse who undertook a performance suddenly fell ill.

Change of law or stepping in of a person with statutory authority   A consignment of a particular good was contracted for supply by the importer; however, in the intervening period, the government changed the law and the product was banned from items allowed to be imported.

Outbreak of war   Say, during the war there is no commerce between the parties of the warring countries; the contract is void as long as war lasts and till normal relations come into existence.

Principle: Impossibility of Performance Not an Excuse

Common law upholds the principle that impossibility of performance is not an excuse for non-performance of a contract. The following are some of the excuses which the law does not admit as reason for non-performance of a contract:
(a) Difficulty of performance (impossible task),
(b) Commercial impossibility (unprofitability),
(c) Impossibility due to the failure of a third party (dealer's excuse of non-supply),
(d) Strikes, lockouts, civil disturbance (unless, of course these figured in the contract),
(e) Failure of one of the objects (in case all the objects of the contract not realised), etc.

Doctrine of Frustration

The entire state of affairs of supervening impossibility is although very frustrating, the law in its fundamental reasoning cannot allow these as grounds for non-performance of contracts. Since the above points create quite annoying, trying, exasperating, wearisome, and vexing problems for business, it is famously called *Doctrine of Frustration* in common law.

Discharge by lapse of time   The Limitation Act, 1963, lays down that the contract must be performed within a specified period of time. All transactions are time bound: sale and purchase, insurances, loans, public issues, bonds, debentures, financial instruments, etc. Outside limitation one loses the remedy of law.

Discharge by operation of law   Discharge of contract independent of the wishes of the contracting parties:
(a) Death: Contract terminated on death; liabilities transferred to legal representative.
(b) Merger: Inferior right merges with the superior one.
(c) Insolvency: When the declared insolvent is discharged of contract.
(d) Unauthorised alteration of terms: Material alteration to contract makes the contract void.
(e) Circuity of action: Rights and liabilities, e.g., a bill in the hands of acceptor, the rights and liabilities rest with one and the same person, discharging other parties.

Discharge by breach of contract   Breach of contract consists of breaking or violating the obligations by the contracting parties. (See the section of this chapter covering consequences of breach of contract.)

In the above explanation on the performance of contract—performance, discharge, and remedies—you may have felt rather frustrated with the multitude of minute details. Actually, what you have seen is merely a bird's eye view. These are the sticklers you should be wary of when entering into a contract. It is better to prevent a legal malady rather than seek remedy when both time and money is lost. In the case presented in Case 3.6, you will find a classic illustration of the doctrine of frustrtion. It comes into play because people interact or transact in real time where circumstances keep changing, which naturally affect the contracts. The doctrine of frustration is really an aspect or part of the law of discharge of contract by reason of supervening impossibility or illegality of the act agreed to be done and hence comes within the purview of Sec. 56 of the Indian Contract Act.[6]

The legal experts have very lengthy debates between the principles of the *doctrine of frustration* and the *force-majeure*—a principle that endeavours to support the performance of a contract. It suffices to say that both these are legal instruments where the judges would like to uphold the sanctity of a contract even in extremely difficult conditions.[7]

MANAGER'S TAKEAWAY

- Recognise the sanctity of a contract.
- Keep track of the changing circumstances of a contract.

CASE 3.6 PETITIONER: Satyabrata Ghose VS RESPONDENT: Mugneeram Bangur & Co.

DATE OF JUDGEMENT: 16 November 1953*

FACTS: In 1940, as an integral part of a development scheme of an extensive area of land, started by the defendant company, it entered into a contract with the plaintiff's predecessor for the sale of a plot of land to the latter accepting a small sum of money as earnest. It undertook to construct roads and drains and the conveyance was to be completed soon after the completion of tiled roads on payment of the balance of the price. As a considerable portion of the area comprised in the scheme was requisitioned by the Government for military purposes in 1941, the company wrote to the defendant that the road construction could not be taken up for an indefinite period and required him to treat the agreement as cancelled and receive back his earnest.

JUDGEMENT: The events which have happened here cannot be said to have made the performance of the contract impossible and the contract has not been frustrated at all.

REASON: Having regard to the nature of the contracts the actual existence of war conditions at the time when it was entered into, the extent of the work involved in the scheme fixing no time limit in the agreement for the construction of the roads, etc., and the fact that the order of requisition was in its very nature of a temporary character, the requisition did not affect the fundamental basis of the contract nor did the performance of the contract become illegal by reason of the requisition, and the contract had not, therefore, become impossible within the meaning of Sec. 56 of the Indian Contract Act.

*For full judgement see http://www.indiankanoon.org/doc/1214064/(3 November 2010).

---

[6]Satyabrata Ghose vs Mugneeram & Co. See Head Note of judgement http://www.indiankanoon.org/doc/1214064/ (3 November 2010)

[7]For further enlightenment read article http://www.legalserviceindia.com/article/l289-Doctrine-of-Frustration-&-Force-Majeure-Clause.html which analyses the two principles regarding the performance of a contract or its impossibility. (3 November 2010).

3.5 RELATIONS RESEMBLING THOSE CREATED BY CONTRACT OR QUASI CONTRACT

TEXT

If a person, incapable of entering into a contract, or anyone whom he is legally bound to support, is supplied by another person with necessaries suited to his condition in life, the person who has furnished such supplies is entitled to be reimbursed from the property of such incapable person.

– Sec. 68, The Indian Contract Act, 1872

Quasi Contract

Recall your study about who is competent to enter into a contract. You had learnt that minors, people of unsound mind, etc., were incapable of legally entering into a contract. However, at the same time, the legal system goes out of its way to protect these people on the principle of equity. Although a contract is not possible, yet the law would like to protect these and would not deprive them of the benefits of contract. The law also makes it a point not to burden them with liabilities which, if there are any, are transferred to their legal representatives. The 'contracts' thus entered into only resemble a contracting relationship without actually establishing a contract. Such apparent contracts are termed as quasi contracts. They are also refered to as constructive contracts (see Table 3.5 and Case 3.7). The fundamental guiding principle upon which it operates is: *A person shall not enrich himself unjustly at the expense if another.* Secs. 68–72 of the Indian Contract Act deal specifically with quasi contract.

Table 3.5 Kinds of quasi contracts

Quasi contracts	Explanation	Example
Supply of necessaries (Sec. 68)	If a person is incapable of entering a contract and is supplied by another for his necessaries of life, the latter needs to be reimbursed from the former's property.	Ward or guardian of a minor or a mentally unsound person is to be repaid for his effort from the resources of whom he is taking care. Thus, although there is no legal contract with a minor, the principle of fairness is applied for the service rendered.
Payment by an interested person (Sec. 69)	A person makes a payment which another is bound by law to pay; the former is in his right to be reimbursed.	X holds land on lease granted by Y. However, Y is in land revenue arrears with the government. The government decides to put up the land for auction. If it is sold then X will lose his/her lease, hence he/she pays for it and saves the land from being auctioned. As per the legal maxim, Y is bound to reimburse to X.
Obligation to pay for non-gratuitous acts (Sec. 70)	When a person does or gives anything to the other without the intention of doing it for free or gratuitously, the person who benefits is bound to reimburse.	A salesman inadvertently left behind a vacuum cleaner when he had visited your house as door-to-door sales person. You actually did not buy it, but you used it all the same; you are bound to reimburse the salesman when he returns.

Contd

Table 3.5 *Contd*

Responsibility of finder of goods	When a person finds something valuable belonging to someone who is unknown, it can be retained by him till the rightful owner is found. The principle is: The property will vest in the finder and he can retain the goods as his own against the whole world, except the owner, of course. The finder may sell the goods if: (a) The thing found is in danger of perishing, (b) The owner cannot be found with reasonable diligence. (c) The owner is found but refuses to pay the lawful charges (two-thirds of the value of the thing found).	A jeweller found the diamond ring that he had sold to a customer still on his counter. The customer never returned even after he tried his best and even advertised in the newspaper. There came several claiming to have bought it, but they all failed the test as to how much they paid for it, etc. So, as per the principle, the jeweller may retain the ring.
Mistake or coercion (Sec. 72)	If something is delivered by mistake—under duress, or force—it is to be reimbursed.	A supplier refuses to supply unless a definite excess amount is paid which is illegal. You pay for it because you are in dire need. The supplier is bound to repay you the illegally excessive charges.
Quantum meruit	Principle: One must pay as per quantum merit, i.e., for as much as earned.	You hire someone for a definite work with definite remuneration; but some time before the completion of the work you repudiate the contract. You are bound to pay for the work done.

CASE 3.7

PETITIONER: **Union of India** VS RESPONDENT: **Sitaram Jaiswal**

DATE OF JUDGEMENT: **28 October 1976***

FACTS: In a suit for the recovery of price of Mac Intyre Sleeves, supplied to the appellant, but alleged to have been wrongfully rejected after a considerable time, the respondent/plaintiff sought to make the appellant/defendant liable to compensate by reasons of provisions contained in Sec. 70 of the Indian Contract Act.

JUDGEMENT: Appeal dismissed.

REASON: The three ingredients to support the cause of action under Sec. 70 of the Indian Contract Act are: First, the goods are to be delivered lawfully or anything has to be done for another person lawfully. Second is the thing done or the goods delivered is so, done or delivered not intending to do so gratuitously. Third, the person to whom the goods are delivered enjoys the benefit thereof. Consequently, the respondent in view of the trial court and the division bench of the high court allowing the respondent to go on with the claim under Sec. 70 of the Indian Contract Act became entitled to compensation for the goods accepted.

---

*Union of India vs Sitaram Jaiswal, A.I.R. 1977 SC 329. Also see the link http://indiankanoon.org/doc/1661027/ (3 November 2010).

The debates on quasi contracts are numerous, and the legal community is never sure about how to deal with these precisely. The reason is not because there is any lack of legal application but because a very sensitive understanding of jurisprudence is necessary. It is one of our uncanny characteristics that we take a long time to decide before we accept and when the repudiation comes, all hell seems to break loose. Managers today can ill afford to do it. The cases of non-gratuitous acts are not uncommon at all and managers, just like the courts, have to use their prudence to solve such problems.

3.6 CONSEQUENCES OF BREACH OF CONTRACT

TEXT

When a contract has been broken, the party who suffers by such a breach is entitled to receive, from the party who has broken the contract, compensation for any loss or damage caused to him thereby, which naturally arose in the usual course of things from such breach, or which the parties knew, when they made the contract, to be likely to result from the breach of it. Such compensation is not to be given for any remote and indirect loss of damage sustained by reason of the breach. Compensation for failure to discharge obligation resembling those created by contract takes place when an obligation resembling those created by contract has been incurred and has not been discharged, any person injured by the failure to discharge it is entitled to receive the same compensation from the party in default, as if such person had contracted to discharge it and had broken his contract.

Explanation: In estimating the loss or damage arising from a breach of contract, the means which existed of remedying the inconvenience caused by non-performance of the contract must be taken into account.

– Sec. 73, The Indian Contract Act, 1872

Discharge by Breach of Contract

Breach of contract consists of breaking or violating the obligations by the contracting parties. There are two kinds of such breaches of contract:

Actual breach of contract

(a) At the time when performance is due: X agrees to deliver the consignment on the first day of the new financial year, but he/she refuses or fails to deliver.

(b) During the performance of contract: X has contracted to supply one thousand radial tyres to Y, the retailer. But Y suddenly, when half the stock has already been delivered, refuses to accept the rest.

 MANAGER'S TAKEAWAY

- There is nothing free even when it may seem gratuitous.
- A labourer deserves his quantum meruit.

Anticipatory breach of contract

When a party repudiates its obligation under the contract before its performance, e.g., X contracts to supply electrical appliances to a retailer at the end of the week; but in the middle of the week X informs his client that he would not supply at all.

Remedies for Breach of Contract

In case of breach of contract, the law provides several remedies:

1. Rescission: The injured party may sue to treat the contract as rescinded.
2. Damages: Compensation may be claimed for the loss.
3. *Quantum mruit.* Where there is some breach occurring from both the parties to the contract, a suit may be filed where the quantum merit be judged and remedy granted.
4. Specific performance: The court may direct parties to actually perform the contract.
5. Injunction: It is a restraint order from the court to a party which had breached a negative term, what it promised not to do. The court orders it to restrain from its action.
6. Rectification: When either through fraud or mistake, performance is not possible, either of the parties may file suit for rectification whereby either the contract is corrected or cancelled.

One of the recurring cases is that of rescission. A party to a contract dispenses or cancels the contract. It is annulled; it becomes void. Once the contract is rescinded, it can only be revived or replaced by a new one. It would be a novation, that is, a new one replacing the old one after the rescission of the previous one. Case 3.8 is such a case where it would have to be decided whether there was a novation of a contract in the sense that the new contract replaced or substituted the old one.

A manager faces the cases of rescission both at giving and receiving end on a daily basis. A case of rescission always shows that there lacked good application of mind before the drawing up of the contract. In the case of novations that rescind and replace the old contract, the situation may be different according to the changing circumstances where it would make better business sense to replace the old one with a new one. Rescissions of contract cost both money and time which are in short supply for a manager.

MANAGER'S TAKEAWAY

- Keep in mind the army slogan 'to be always prepared'.

CASE 3.8	PETITIONER: R.N. Kumar vs RESPONDENT: R.K. Soral

DATE OF JUDGEMENT: **13 April 1988***

FACTS: An agreement for distribution of the film *Savere Wali Gadi* was entered into on 19 March 1983 between the petitioner as the distributor and the respondent as the producer. The agreement contained an arbitration clause. A sum of ₹3.40 lakh was paid to the respondent and acknowledged by him earlier to the agreement was deemed to have been adjusted against the first installment. In or about 1984

*R.N.Kumar vs R.K. Soral, 1988 A.I.R. 1205; also see link, http://www.indiankanoon.org/doc/1054312/ (4 November 2010).

Contd

Case 3.8 *Contd*

about ₹3 lakh were further advanced to the respondent. As per the agreement the respondent was to hand over the prints of the film by 10 August 1983, but it was not done. On 11 March 1985, a further agreement was entered into between the parties whereby the respondent agreed to pay a total sum of ₹6.50 lakh to the petitioner for giving up his distribution rights in the first agreement. The first agreement was accordingly irrevocably cancelled and superseded by the subsequent agreement. The respondent took up the matter with Motion Pictures Association to de-register the film in the name of the petitioner. The Motion Picture Association stated that de-registration would be allowed only when the respondent pays ₹6.50 lakh to the petitioner or deposits the amount with the Association. The petitioner's claim before the Association was that the respondent committed breach of the subsequent agreement, and a suit was filed.

JUDGEMENT: Petition was dismissed.

REASON: It is significant to note that the Sec. 10, sub-section (1) gives an option to the parties by the use of expression *may* but the other sub-section if the conditions are fulfilled makes it obligatory for the court to direct filing of an arbitration agreement. Indubitably, in this case there was an arbitration clause in the agreement. The parties have applied for reference. The division bench has reiterated that the original agreement dated 19 March 1983 which ceased to have effect and came to an end by the agreement dated 11 March 1985, stood revived by virtue of the two letters dated 15 July 1985 and 11 September 1995 by the appellant. There was, at all relevant times, a valid and binding contract between the parties. That contract contained an arbitration clause. There was nothing, in view of the reasons indicated above, to disentitle the parties to have their rights adjudicated in terms of an arbitration clause. In the premises the high court was right in the view it took.

SUMMARY

Violable Contracts and Void Agreements

Valid Enforceable by law.

Void Not enforceable by law, due to lack of legal requirements, not covered by law, and other technical reasons.

Voidable Enforceable at the option one party only.

Illegal Contrary to law.

Restitution It is the return of the benefit received from a void contract.

Principle Not to enrich oneself at the cost of another.

Contingent Contracts

Contract on the basis of future event. It is to do or not to do something, if some event, collateral to the contract, does or does not happen. Its performance depends upon happening or not happening of a future event that is uncertain and that it is collateral to the contract.

A wagering contract consists of reciprocal promises whereas a contingent contract may not contain reciprocal promises.

Performance of Contracts

The parties to a contract must either perform or offer to perform their respective promises.

The contract is performed by the promisor; the attempted or tendered performance is also a valid contract.

The promisee or his legal representative can demand performance.

The time and place of contract is important.

The principle of appropriation Where the parties have a current account between them, appropriation impliedly takes place in the order in which the receipts and payments take place and entered in the account.

Relations Resembling Those Created by Contract

Quasi contract An obligation created by law where, in actual fact, the obligation does not come out of a competent agreement.

The basis for quasi-contract is equity.

Principle A person shall not be allowed to enrich himself unjustly at the expense of another.

Kinds of quasi contracts

(a) Claim for necessaries supplied to a person incapable of contract,

(b) Reimbursement of a person paying money due by another in payment of which he/she is interested,

(c) Obligation of a person enjoying benefit of a non-gratuitous act,

(d) Liability of person to whom money is paid or thing delivered by mistake or under coercion.

Consequences of Breach of Contract

A contract gives rise to correlative rights and obligations. A breach of contract consists of infringement or violation of any or all of its terms. It would have no value if there were no remedies to enforce that right in a court of law.

Remedies There are, in all, five remedies:

1. *Rescission* The injured party to contract may sue, rescind, or quash the contract.

2. *Damages* These may arise in the course of rescission:

   (a) *Ordinary damages* Actual damages in the course of rescission.

   (b) *Special damages* These were in the minds of both the parties while contracting as a possible result of breach that may be recovered.

   (c) *Liquidated damages and penalty* Free and fair estimate of the probable loss; a penalty is the estimated damages at the time of the contract; Indian courts allow for only reasonable compensation in such matters.

3. *Quantum meruit* A partly performed contract has become discharged because of the breach by another party. The right is founded on an implied promise by the other party arising from the acceptance of the benefit of that party.

4. *Specific performance* It consists of following court orders in fulfilling the contract.

5. *Injunction* It is a mode of securing specific performance of the negative terms of a contract.

EXERCISES

Violable contracts and void agreements

(i) Amrut is a minor who is supplied for his necessities by a grocer. Amrut makes a promissory note in favour of the grocer. Is the grocer entitled to payment: (a) from the minor personally, (b) against minor's estate?
Hint: (a) No. (b) Yes.

(ii) Aditya sold his iron ore mines in Andhra to Mithun. The latter believed the former's statements about the mines that did not turn out to be true. After several months of work in the mines Mithun realised his mistake of believing Aditya. What remedies does Mithun have?

Hint: Mithun may claim damages. The contract cannot be rescinded. Reason: Parties cannot be restored to their original position.

(iii) Hari & Sons contracted with Mishra Pvt. Ltd., to erect industrial sheds. In calculating the prices of the sheds Hari deducted a particular sum of the shed twice over. Mishra Pvt. Ltd., affixed their seal thus clearly certifying their intention. Is there some remedy for Hari?
Hint: No. The contract is binding.

(iv) Yathish buys a painting from Prakash, an art collector. Both believe the painting in question is genuine; but it actually happens to be fake. What can Yathish do?
Hint: He can do nothing after the event of buying; he should have examined before he bought. Principle: *Caveat emptor*—buyer be beware!

(v) Judge the nature of following agreements:
   (a) A agrees to sell B 100 tonnes of oil.
   (b) A, who is dealer in olive oil only, agrees to sell to B 100 tonnes of oil.
   (c) A agrees to sell to B 100 tonnes of olive oil at a price fixed by C.
   (d) A agrees to sell to B 100 tonnes of oil for ₹5 lakh or ₹10 lakh.
   Hint: (a) Agreement is void due to uncertainty; (b) Agreement is valid; (c) Valid since the price is fixed; (d) Void as there is nothing as the consideration is undetermined.

(vi) Name some persons, other than minors, who are not competent to contract. Illustrate with cases.

(vii) Does a threat to commit suicide amount to coercion?

(viii) What are agreements by way of wagers? What are its legal effects? Is contract of insurance a wager?

Contingent contracts

(i) Amit agrees to pay Bhim a sum of money to marry his daughter Chitra. But she marries Damu. Should Bhim receive money?
Hint: The marriage of Bhim to Chitra becomes impossible as long as she remains married to Damu. Till this contingency lasts he cannot marry her and demand his money.

(ii) Ajit agrees to construct a swimming pool for ₹20 lakh for an upcoming hotel complex. It is agreed that the payment will be done only on the completion of the work. What contingency arises here?
Hint: It is not a contingent contract; see Sec. 31.

(iii) A agrees to pay B a sum of money if a certain ship does not return. The ship does not return. A refuses to pay B.
Hint: See Sec. 33 of the Act.

(iv) Illustrate with case a contingent contract.

(v) Distinguish between wagering and contingent contract discussing the rules regarding enforcement of the same.

Performance of contracts

(i) Yathish, Suresh, and Sandeep promise to pay Damodar ₹3 crore for the supply of building material. Suresh and Sandeep are untraceable. Can Damodar demand his payment from Yathish?
Hint: Yes. Reason: see Sec. 43, (1) of the Act.

(ii) Suresh owes Rahul two separate sums of money:
   (a) ₹10 lakh which is barred by limitation, and
   (b) ₹10.5 lakh which is not barred. Suresh pays Rahul ₹5 lakh on account generally, later Rahul sues for ₹10.5 lakhs. He pleads ₹10 lakh as time-barred and as to ₹10.5 lakh, and ₹50,000 as a part payment. How would you judge Rahul's plea.
   Hint: See Sec. 60 of the Act — both contentions will be wrong. Rahul can appropriate the payment of ₹50,000 towards the first debt and Suresh is bound to pay ₹10.5 lakh that is not barred by limitation.

(iii) A truck dealer promises to deliver the truck to Suman on 1 October. It has been agreed that time is the essence of the contract. The delivery of the truck is delayed by several weeks. What is the position of Suman as against the truck dealer?
Hint: Suman can repudiate the contract, see Sec. 55,(1) of the Act; he can also accept the late delivery and demand some compensation, too, according to Sec. 55,(3); but he would have to notify about this to the dealer.

(iv) Illustrate the provisions of the Indian Contract Act relating the performance of reciprocal promises.

(v) Discuss the law relating to the rights and liabilities of joint promotion in a contract.

Relations resembling those created by contract

(i) Amit and Ashok jointly owe to Chamanlal & Co., ₹25,000. Amit pays all of it without the knowledge of Ashok who, in turn, pays his half of the amount, ₹12,500.

Hint: Chamanlal & Co., is bound to pay the latter amount of ₹12,500 to Ashok; see Sec. 72 of the Act.

(ii) Shashi left his car at his friend's, Sitaram; his landlord seized the car in lieu of his rent. Shashi paid the rent for his friend and got his car delivered. Can Shashi recover the amount from his friend Sitaram?

Hint: Yes. See, Sec. 69 of the Act.

(iii) Consider the following for *quantum meruit:*

(a) Amrit is employed by a publisher to write for a weekly magazine in installments. After a few issues the magazine is closed down.

(b) You have been employed by a company as managing director. After some time it is found out that those who appointed you were not qualified to do so.

Hint: Both you and Amrit can claim money for the work done.

(iv) In quasi contracts, is the promise to pay implied by the law?

(v) Does the law of contract impose any obligation on a person enjoying benefit of a non-gratuitous act of another person done for the former?

Consequences of breach of contract

(i) A supplier from Bombay agrees to supply 100 crates of wine to Brijesh Shah in Gujarat who pays an earnest money of ₹25,000. But there is prohibition of alcohol in Gujarat and hence the supply of liquor is illegal. Can Shah sue the supplier for non-performance as well as get reimbursed?

Hint: The agreement is void *ab initio;* although he may demand reimbursement of his earnest money.

(ii) X agreed to sell Y certain shares to be delivered on 1 March 2010. On that date since the price of the shares had gone down Y refused to accept them. Subsequently, X was able to sell the shares for a higher price than he had agreed to deliver them to Y. Can X sue Y for breach of contract? If so what would be the damages?

Hint: Yes he can sue and get reimbursed equal to the difference between the market price and the contract price on 1 March, 2010; see Sec. 73 of the Act.

(iii) Aditya gives a bond to Arjuna for the repayment of ₹1 lakh at the interest rate of 12 per cent for six months with the stipulation that in the case of default the interest rate will be at the rate of 50 per cent from the date of default. Aditya defaults. Is Arjuna entitled for compensation as per the stipulation?

Hint: No. The stipulation is by way of penalty. The court has the right to fix any compensation. See Sec. 74 of the Act.

(iv) What are the remedies for an aggrieved party of the breach of contract?

(v) When a party to a contract refuses to perform or is disabled from performing his part of it, the other party has the right to rescind it. Discuss this in the light of the Indian Contract Act, 1872.

DEVELOPMENT OF LEGAL EDGE

- Study consumer behaviour from the legal point of view.

- Take interest in consumer issues.

FURTHER READING

- The Indian Contract Act, 1872 (easily available in bookshops and law bookshops). This is mandatory while studying the textbook.

- Shanti Bhushan, 2008, *Courting Destiny,* Penguin Books, Delhi. It helps to deeply understand courts and law from a practicing lawyer's point of view.

Every agreement by which anyone is restrained from exercising a lawful profession, trade or business of any kind, is to that extent void.

Exception 1: Saving of agreement not to carry on business of which goodwill is sold—One who sells the goodwill of a business may agree with the buyer to refrain from carrying on a similar business, within specified local limits, so long as the buyer, or any person deriving title to the goodwill from him, carries on a like business therein, provided that such limits appear to the court reasonable, regard being had to the nature of the business.

– Sec. 27, The Indian Contract Act, 1872

Introduction

'HC Gives Landmark Judgement on Contract Act' was the bold headline in *The Financial Express* of 5 September 2003.[8] The paper reported that the Delhi High Court ruled that a clause in an agreement regulating a mode of trade is enforceable even after expiry of such agreement and would not be affected by Sec. 27 of the Indian Contract Act. The section in question has been quoted above since it is the main issue of this case.

Indian businesses are generally family managed and hence trust runs deep in any agreement or contract. People value mutual trust and goodwill. However, in these days of globalisation the Indian companies in India have to enter into agreements with international companies. Formalisation of contracts takes pre-eminent position before any mutual trust. It is good in the eyes of the law because it is highly significant to safeguard one's interests under the protection of the law.

A contract is essential for any business transaction, ensuring that both parties to the contract abide by the commonly established terms and conditions. Entering an agreement or transaction without a formal contract can be disastrous because it could result in one or both parties escaping their obligations. To protect the interests of both parties, the Indian Contract Act was enacted in 1872. The purpose of Indian contract law is to ensure fair business practices.

The Indian contract law forms the foundation of business law. This is because a bulk of business transactions is based on contracts. The Indian Contract Act has established the general principles for forming, executing,

and enforcing contracts. The case in Exhibit A (between the Knorr-Bremse Group of Germany and Escorts India Ltd of India) will focus the attention on Sec. 27 of the Indian Contract Act, and the judgement of the high court which gives a new direction saying that agreements are enforceable even after they have elapsed. The judgement was passed by Justice R.C. Jain in a case filed by Knorr-Bremse AG of Germany against Escorts Ltd. The court, however, declined to grant interim injunction to the German company against Escorts.

The dispute

According to the technology-sharing agreement between Knorr-Bremse AG and Escorts Ltd, Article I (3) to be precise, Escorts was to take the approval of the Knorr-Bremse before exporting the braking systems to countries where Knorr-Bremse had licensing agreements with other parties or had agents and distributors. Further, there was a caveat in agreement Article 1 (5) which stated that even after the expiry of the agreement period, the clause regulating Escorts' exports of braking systems manufactured with Knorr-Bremse technology would remain enforceable.

Knorr Bremse AG and Escorts Ltd had entered into a license agreement under which the petitioner was given license to manufacture brakes for rail and road vehicles. The license agreement was entered into in 1977, it was amended on 9 January 1987 and with the approval of Government of India vide its letter no., FC II 631 9dated 13 December 1991, the validity of license agreement was extended up to 31 December 1995. No dispute arose between the parties until this date.

---

[8]See link for the five-page report, http://www.financialexpress.com/news/hc-gives-landmark-judgement-on-contract-act/90272/1 (22 November 2010).

Escorts won business deals from Iran as well as Iraq for the supply of braking systems produced with the technological know how of Knorr-Bremse. They did not inform Knorr-Bremse about the business and did not take any cognisance of the trade restricting Artilces 1 (3) and 1 (5). Knorr-Bremse, since they had their own agents in the above-mentioned countries objected to Escorts doing business in those countries. Escorts held that the evocation of trade restrictions was unfair trade practice. The Knorr-Bremse filed suit against the Escorts for violation of trade agreement.

On 28 November 2002, Knorr-Bremse served a legal notice upon the Escorts Ltd, alleging violation of Article 1 (3) of the license agreement. It alleged that Escorts offered to export braking systems manufactured with Knorr-Bremse technology to Iranian railways and Iraq railways through Rites Ltd, without any intimation and consent of Knorr-Bremse. See Exhibit B.

Landmark Judgement by Justice R.C. Jain, Delhi High Court

After hearing the arguments of counsels for both the companies, this Court on a consideration of the above stipulations is prima facie of the view that the restrictions contained in Article 1 (3) do not appear to be in restraint of trade which should attract Sec. 27 of the Contract Act. In so far as the question of survival of the aforesaid stipulations even after the expiry of the agreement is concerned suffice it would be to mention that the respondent (Escorts) having accepted the same with open eyes cannot be allowed to urge that the limitations contained in Article 1 (3) would not survive after the expiry of the license agreement.

In an addendum of sorts to the above judgement the court declined to grant interim relief to Knorr-Bremse AG according to their plea. The judge ruled that even if the negative covenant embodied in the clause of the agreement is valid under German law, it cannot be enforced in India and, therefore, injunction cannot be granted in favour of the plaintiff. The conclusion to the judgement was since Escorts is not debarred from supplying and making their offers for supplying products to other countries, the company should be given a fair chance of competing with them and if they are successful there should be no reason why they should not be allowed to fulfill their commitment for exports.

Aftermath[9]

In 2007, another five years down the line, Escorts and Knorr-Bremse agreed for Arbitration under The Arbitration and

---

Exhibit B   Traders Turned Disputants

Senior counsel C.A. Sundaram for Knorr-Bremse AG, the petitioner	**Senior counsel Shanti Bhushan for Escorts Ltd, the respondent**
So far as exports from India of products manufactured by Escorts with technology of Knorr-Bremse were concerned, Escorts was bound by the conditions of export as laid down in the agreement which survives even after the expiry of the license agreement on the strength of Article 1 (5).	The concerned clauses fall within the purview of Sec. 27 of Indian Contract Act, 1872 and are, therefore, void and illegal as they are contrary to Sec. 27 of the act. The restraint imposed by Article 1 (5) of the agreement between the companies was unreasonable and against the public policy as it imposed absolute restrictions on Escorts to carry out even lawful trade or business. The company is within its rights to freely export the products to other countries, maintained the counsel.

Conciliation Act, 1996, so as to find a settlement. Although the high court judgement proved a landmark judgement, it did not help the disputing companies any better. The tribunal by majority held that it had to confine itself to the authority vested in it by the agreement of the parties as can be culled out from the correspondence exchanged between the parties referred in the order. Since, the arbitral tribunal was constituted to adjudicate the disputes that were the subject matter of proceedings pending before the Delhi High Court, it could not confer upon itself any other jurisdiction and, therefore, could not entertain the counter claim raised by the petitioner.

Recapitulation

The petitioner and respondent had entered into a license agreement under which the petitioner was given license to manufacture brakes for rail and road vehicles. The license agreement was entered into in 1977; it was amended on 9 January 1987 and with the approval of Government of India vide its letter no., FC II 631 (9) dated 13 December 1991, the validity of license agreement was extended up to 31 December 1995. No dispute arose between the parties after expiry of the agreement till the year 2001. On 28 November 2002 the respondent served a legal notice upon the petitioner alleging violation of Article 1 (3) of the license agreement that was followed by the high court judgement.

In the tribunal the petitioner filed the claims and the respondent the counter claims, further stating their original stands. Arbitration is resorted to by the parties to cut the delays and avoid multiplicity of proceedings and litigation between the parties before the courts. If an arbitrator refuses to entertain the counter claim and asks the opposite party to raise a fresh dispute and start procedure *de novo* and to get the dispute referred again to another tribunal, this will only result in multiplicity of proceedings failing the very purpose of the arbitration.

The tribunal set aside the petition and waited for the respondent's response.

Conclusion

Judge R.C. Jain's remark annunciates a fundamental legal principle: Acceptance of contract with *open eyes* and then contesting it does not bespeak of jurisprudence, nay, not even prudence or common sense. Common sense prompts, you get what you see; to turn it around 'to see what you get' may get you into only trouble.

Discussion Questions

1. Identify the legal problems in the above case and apply the appropriate Secs. from the Indian Contract Act, 1872.

2. How would you apply Secs. 3–9 of the Contract Act: communication, acceptance, and revocation of proposals to this case?

3. How would you analyse the arguments put forward by the respective counsels?

---

[9]See, www.http//Escorts Limited vs Knorr Bremse-Ag on 21 November, 2007.htm (4 December 2010).

4. Is there a serious case of breach of contract here? Which Secs. of the Contract Act would apply as a solution?

5. What is the meaning of negative contract? Explain with examples.

6. Do you think that Knorr-Bremse took a principled stand by sticking to articles of their contract?

7. What are the consequences of untenable conditions in trade practices?

8. Do you think restricted trade conditions lead to monopolies? Explain with examples.

9. Why did the petitioner ask for interim injunction?

10. How far do you think arbitration tribunals help in imparting speedy solutions to the disputes?

Going Beyond

1. How do you analyse the judgement of the high court?

2. What kind of international legal implications concerning trade and commerce does this case have?

3. Do you think there is any place for cultural perceptions in international agreements?

4. How would you analyse this case from an ethical perspective?

LEGAL LUMINARY

THE BHUSHANS—FATHER, SON, AND THE JUSTICE OF PEACE

In the basement of the Bhushans' house in Delhi, there have gathered dozens of young college-goers and law students. They discuss animatedly about the burning public issue: political-corporate-judiciary nexus of corruption. The usual politician-criminal nexus is old hat. The axis of corruption is the judiciary.*

There in their midst is Prashant Bhushan, the son of the legal luminary, Shanti Bhushan, to confer and discuss with the group about his initiative called Campaign for Judicial Accountability and Reform (CJAR). He narrates how corruption in judiciary thrives with examples and cases. He is in his early 50s and is already a veteran of Doon Valley Case, Bhopal Gas Tragedy, and the Narmada Agitation Case and has published a book on the Bofors Gun Scam, the worst political-corporate corruption case where business tycoons, international agents, power brokers, business brokers, government and law machineries of India and Sweden were involved.

In the case presented at the end of this chapter senior counsel Shanti Bhushan appeared for the respondent Escorts against the appellants Knorr-Bremse. He represented Raj Narain in an election case against Indira Gandhi, the then prime minister of India. She lost. Consequence: Emergency was declared. Some of his other famous cases were the Mumbai Blast, Parliament Attack, and representing Deve Gowda, the former prime minister. He has also represented the high profile business house case representing Rajendra Singh Lodha regarding the assets of Priyamvadha Birla of Birla Corporation.

In recent years Shanti Bhushan has made his mission to bring accountability in the judiciary. The father-son duo is working indefatigably campaigning for accountability in judiciary. Both the father and son appeared for Transparency International in the provident fund scam of Ghaziabad. For about eight years, a *nazir,* a court official, is alleged to have pilfered money from the provident fund (PF) account for his masters, the judges. The modus operandi was that the *nazir* wrote fake applications and withdrew money from the PF account. A vigilance officer broke the scam. The *nazir* confessed and named many district and high court judges. The name of a sitting Supreme Court judge was also one of them! Apparently, the *nazir* paid sums up to ₹1

---

*http://www.tehelka.com/story_main40.asp?filename=Ne060908thehouseofbhushan.asp (10 December 2010).

Legal Luminary   *Contd*

lakh at a time to the judges. Then he paid for the construction of houses in a few cases, gifted some other judges cell phones and air-conditioners, and even paid for their family shopping. Furniture was shipped to the Kolkata home of the sitting Supreme Court judge's son.

Justice Agrawal, hearing this matter, was not only shell-shocked; Shanti Bhushan further angered him by asking the court to summon the registrar-general as a witness in the case! The judge retorted by saying to him that he was targeting the judiciary and arguing like a street urchin. The junior Bhushan got up at this stage and shot back to the judge that he was twisting his father's argument.**

Shanti Bhushan was born on 11 November 1925. Shanti Bhushan translates to 'jewel of peace'; it could as well mean 'jewel of justice'. He was the law minister in Morarji Desai's Government from 1977–79. His memoirs *Courting Destiny* is considered as a gem for legal eagles.[†]

**http://www.tehelka.com/story_main40.asp? filename=Ne060908thehouseofbhushan.asp (10 December 2010).
[†]Shanti Bhushan, *Courting Destiny*, Penguin Books, Delhi.

Undertaking by the Indian Contract Act, 1872

Principle: *Ex maleficio non oritur contractus.*

No contract arises contrary to law.

CHAPTER OUTLINE

- Indemnity and Guarantee
- Bailment
- Pledge
- Agency, Appointment, and Authority of Agents

- *Case Study*: A Case of Travails of Termination of Agency
- *Legal Luminary:* Fali S. Nariman

4.1 INDEMNITY AND GUARANTEE

A contract by which one party promises to save the other from loss caused to him by the contract of the promisor himself, or by the conduct of any other person, is called a 'contract of indemnity'.

– Sec. 124, The Indian Contract Act, 1872

Understanding Indemnity and Guarantee

Table 4.1 and Cases 4.1 and 4.2 discussed the concepts of indemnity and guarantee.

Kinds of Guarantee

There are three pairs of guarantee[1], as shown in Table 4.2. Some examples of guarantee are promissory note, bank guarantee, letter of credit, etc.

---

[1]Conduct an exercise how these fit into the earlier-referred Case of guarantee (Bank of India vs Stephen).

Table 4.1 Indemnity and guarantee

	Indemnity	**Guarantee**
Definition	It is a contract where a person promises to save the other person from the loss caused by him by the conduct of the promisor himself or by the conduct of any other person. (Sec. 124)	It is an oral or written contract to perform the promise, or discharge the liability, of a third person in case of his default.
Parties involved	It involves two parties: (a) *Indemnifier*: person who gives indemnity (b) *Indemnity holder*: person for whose protection it is given	It involves three parties: (a) *Surety*: person who gives the guarantee (b) *Principal debtor*: person in respect of whose default the guarantee is given (c) *Creditor*: person to whom the guarantee is given
Purpose	Indemnity is for reimbursement.	Guarantee is for the security of the creditor.
Liability	The liability of the indemnifier is primary and arises when the contingent event occurs.	The liability of the surety is secondary and arises when the principal debtor defaults.
Rights against third party	The indemnifier, after performing his part of the promise, has no rights against the third party. He can sue the party only if the assignment is in his favour.	The surety steps into the shoes of the creditor on discharge of his liability, and may sue the principal debtor.

CASE 4.1 PETITIONER: Gajanan Moreshwar Parelkar VS RESPONDENT: Moreshwar Mandan Mantri*

DATE OF JUDGEMENT: 1 April 1942

FACTS: The petitioner got a plot of land from Municipal Corporation of Bombay (1934) on lease. The lease was transferred to the defendant who erected a building on the land. Being in need of money the defendant mortgaged the land to a certain Keshavdas Mohandas. The defendant wanted the transfer of the building from the petitioner and the former agreed to pay off the mortgage. The plaintiff thereafter on several occasions called upon the defendant to procure from Keshavdas Mohandas a release of the plaintiff from his liability under the mortgage and the deed of further charge, but the defendant failed to do so. The plaintiff submits that he executed the mortgage and the deed of further charge at the request of the defendant because the agreement for lease stood in the name of the plaintiff and, therefore, the defendant is liable to indemnify the plaintiff in respect of all liability under the mortgage and the deed of further charge. He, therefore, prays that the defendant be ordered to procure from the mortgagee a release of the plaintiff from all liability under the deed of mortgage and further charge and also that the defendant may be ordered to pay into court the sum required to pay off the whole amount due to the mortgagee under the mortgage and further charge and that the amount so brought into court be utilised for the purpose of paying off the mortgage and further charge.

JUDGEMENT: The defendant is ordered to procure from the mortgagee a release of the plaintiff from all liability under the deed of mortgage and further charge.

*Gajanan Moreshwar Parelkar vs Moreshwar Madan Mantri (AIR 1942, Bom 302); also see the full text of the judgement http://www.indiankanoon.org/doc/1361099/ (3 November 2010).

Contd

Case 4.1 *Contd*

REASON: The liability of an indemnifier arises as soon as the loss or injury to the indemnity holder becomes imminent and is not postponed till the indemnity-holder actually suffers the loss or injury.

REMARK: The judgement in the above case is a watershed in Indian jurisprudence because thus far the Common Law followed the English tradition of the origin of the liability of the indemnifier not until the loss has been suffered. This judgement held that it becomes imminent and is not postponed until actually the loss is suffered.

CASE 4.2   PETITIONER: Union Bank India, Ernakulam   vs   RESPONDENT: T.J. Stephen and Others*

DATE OF JUDGEMENT: 1 February 1989

FACTS: Loan was taken to buy a fishing boat by the defendant with an executed continuing guarantee by three guarantors in 1970. The boat was hypothecated to the bank. The amount was not paid. The bank filed suit for the recovery of debt. The defendants are: (1) Principal debtor and (2) Three guarantors. The court decreed payment declaring the suit against the defendant; this included the guarantors, who contended the order who argued that since the first defendant had acknowledged the debt, there was no obligation on them to pay, because to do so is barred by limitation.

JUDGEMENT: The defendants 2 and 3—guarantors—are also liable for the amounts claimed in the suit by the Bank.

REASON: In a case of continuing guarantee so long as the guarantee has not been withdrawn or so long as the guarantors have refused to perform their obligation under the agreement of guarantee and a suit has been filed within the time prescribed under Article 55 of the Limitation Act, the guarantors are liable for the agreement for the amounts found due to the creditor from the principal-debtor.

REMARK: The above judgement (1990) clearly gave direction in the debt recovery; it seriously stressed on the role of the guarantors. Normally, in India, the guarantor's role is considered a mere formality both by businesses and the public. In the business world, continuous guarantee is a serious issue.

*Union Bank of India, Ernakulam vs T.J. Stephen (AIR 1990, Ker 180), also see the link, http://indiankanoon.org/doc/852865/ (3 November 2010).

Table 4.2   The three pairs of guarantee

1.	*General* Anyone to who it is presented may, on compliance with its terms, hold the guarantor liable.	*Special* Particular person who alone can take advantage of it.
2.	*Absolute* The surety is unconditionally bound to make payment or perform a promise on default by the principal debtor.	*Conditional* It is enforceable on some contingency and the creditor must take necessary steps to fix the liability of the surety.
3.	*Specific* Accountable for one single transaction.	*Continuing* Extends to a series of transactions called 'continuing guarantee'.

Surety's Liability[2]

There are three main liabilities for surety as follows:

Co-extensive   The liability of the surety is co-extensive with that of the principal debtor. For instance, if a person guarantees a loan bond, he is liable not only for the amount of the loan, but also for any interest and charges that may become due.

Conditional   Where there is a condition precedent to the surety's liability, he will not be liable unless that condition is first fullied.

Limitation   A surety has the right to declare his guarantee to be limited to a fixed amount, so that his liability may not extend beyond that specified amount.

Discharge of Surety[3]

Discharge of surety is when the liability comes to an end. Table 4.3 shows the discharge of surety along with the respective sections.

Table 4.3   Discharge of surety

Revocation	Creditor's conduct	Invalidation of contract
Revocation of surety (Sec. 130)	Variance in terms of contract (Sec. 133)	Guarantee obtained by misrepresentation (Sec. 142)
	Release or discharge of principal debtor (Sec. 134)	Guarantee obtained by concealment (Sec. 143)
Death (Sec. 131)	Compounding by creditor with principal debtor (Sec. 135)	
	Creditor's act or omission impairing surety's eventural remedy (Sec. 139)	Failure of a co-surety to join a surety (Sec. 144)
Novation (Sec. 62)	Loss of security (Sec. 141)	Failure of consideration (Sec. 145)

---

[2]Again, conduct a similar exercise to detect the liability in the Case (Bank of India vs Stephen).

[3]The terms in the chart are already familiar and can be understood with further description.

Rights of Surety

A surety has the following rights against the principal debtor.

Right to securities   A surety is entitled to the benefit of every security that the creditor has against the principal debtor at the time when the contract of gurantee is entered into. It is available, irrespective of whether the surety has knowledge of the security or not. If the creditor loses, or without the consent of the surety, parts with any security, the surety is discharged to the extent of the value of that security (Sec. 140).

Right to share dividend   Where a surety had guaranteed a part of the debt that he pays when the principal debtor becomes insolvent, the surety will be entitled to share in the dividends distributed by the official receiver along with the creditor, in proportion with the amount paid by him.

Right to set off   If the creditor sues the surety, the latter shall be entitled to all the rights that the principal debtor has against the creditor.

Conclusion

There is an old and wise saying: Trust, but verify. With necessary change, we may apply the same principle to indemnification and guarantee to business. We may say: Trust, but cover. Business depends on trust. However, when it is the question of protection of capital or assets, then it is prudent to have a cover that guarantees its security. It also helps in enforceability of law.

MANAGER'S TAKEAWAY

- When you take a monetary decision, ask: 'What is the guarantee?'
- The debtor has a very short memory and the creditor a very long one.

4.2   BAILMENT

TEXT

A 'bailment' is the delivery of goods by one person to another for some purpose, upon a contract that they shall, when the purpose is accomplished, be returned or otherwise disposed of according to the direction of the person delivering them. The person delivering the goods is called the 'bailor'. The person to whom they are delivered is called the 'bailee'. Explanation: If a person already in possession of the goods of other contracts holds them as a bailee, he thereby becomes the bailee, and the owner becomes the bailor of such goods, although they may not have been delivered by way of bailment.

– Sec. 148, The Indian Contract Act, 1872

The contracts of bailment and pledge are a special class of contracts. The contract is usually of any economic good. However, the Contract Act alone is inadequate to deal with it; hence, we have other acts such as Carriers Act, 1865, Railways Act, 1989, Carriage of Goods Act, 1925 with which we shall deal later on. Here we are concerned with the fundamental principles of bailment. Bailment, in common parlance, means 'delivery of goods in trust'. The person who delivers such goods is the bailor. The person receiving such goods is the bailee. A bailment of goods as security for the debut incurred is pledge. This is the system of pawning. The classic example from literature is, 'The knight left a jewel as pledge for the borrowed horse'. The bailee will have the custody of goods until the pledge is redeemed.

Salient Features of Bailment

There are four main feature/requisites of bailment:

Contract There is an agreement between the bailor and bailee.

Delivery of possession of goods The delivery of goods by the bailor to bailee for possession. The intention is to control and to exclude others.

Purpose There is a definite purpose why the bailor gives the goods in possession to the bailee. If the goods are delivered by mistake, the bailment does not arise.

Return of specific goods The bailor and the bailee agree that as soon as the purpose is achieved, the goods shall be returned or disposed-off according to the directions of the bailor.

Duties and Rights of Bailor and Bailee

The bailor is bound to disclose to the bailee faults in the goods bailed, of which the bailor is aware, and which materially interfere with the use of them, or expose the bailee to extraordinary risk; and if he does not make such disclosure, he is responsible for damage arising to the bailee directly from such faults.

– Sec.150, The Indian Contract Act, 1872

In all cases of bailment the bailee is bound to take as much care of the goods bailed to him as a man of ordinary prudence would, under similar circumstances, take of his own goods of the same bulk, quantity, and value as the goods bailed.

– Sec. 151, The Indian Contract Act, 1872

Table 4.4(a) & (b) presents the duties and rights of bailor and bailee.

Table 4.3 Duties and rights of bailor and bailee

Bailor	Bailee
(a) Duties	
Disclose known faults of the goods set to bailment. (Sec. 150)	Take reasonable care of the goods bailed. (Sec. 152)
Bear extraordinary expenses of bailment. (Sec. 158)	Not make any unauthorised use of goods. (Sec. 154)
Indemnify bailee for loss in case of premature termination of bailment. (Sec. 159)	Not mix bailor's goods with one's own. (Sec. 155)
Receive back the goods upon the expiry of the bailment. (Sec. 152)	Return the goods upon expiry of the bailment. (Sec. 161)
Indemnify the bailee: when the title of the bailor to the goods is defective and the bailee suffers as a consequence, the bailor is responsible for the bailee. (Sec. 164)	Not set up an adverse title: the bailee must hold goods on behalf of and for the bailor. (Sec. 117)

Contd

Table 4.3 *Contd*

(b) Rights	
Enforcement of rights: the bailor can enforce by suit all the liabilities or duties of the bailee as his rights.	*Delivery of goods to one of several joint bailers of goods*: if several owners of goods bail them, the bailee may deliver them back to or according to the direction of one joint owner without the consent of all, in the absence of the any agreement to the contrary. (Sec. 165).
Avoidance of contract: the bailor may terminate the bailment if the bailee does, with regards to the goods bailed, any act which is inconsistent with the terms of the bailment. (Sec. 153)	*Delivery of goods to the bailor without title*: if a person other than the bailor claims goods bailed, the bailee may apply to the court to stop the delivery of the goods to the bailor to decide the title to the goods. (Sec. 166)
Return of goods lent gratuitously: when the goods are lent gratuitously, the bailor can demand their return whenever he pleases even though he lent them for a specified time or purpose. (Sec. 159)	*Right to apply to court to stop delivery*: if a person, other than their bailor, claims goods bailed the bailee may apply to the court to stop the delivery of the goods to the bailor, and to decide the title to the goods.
Compensation from a wrong-doer: if a third person wrongfully deprives the bailee of the use or possession of the goods bailed or does them any injury, the bailor or the bailee may bring a suit against the third person for such deprivation or injury. (Sec. 180)	*Right of action against trespassers*: if a third person wrongfully deprives the bailee of the use or possession of the goods bailed to him, he has the right to bring an action against that party.
	Bailee's lien: where the lawful charges of the bailee in respect of the goods bailed are not paid, he may retain the goods. This is known as 'particular lien'.

The Law of Lien

Lien implies the right of a person to retain possession of some goods belonging to another until some debt or claim of the person in possession is satisfied. There are two types of lien.

Particular   It is that which is available to the bailee against only those goods in respect of which one has rendered any service involving the exercise of labour or skill.

General   It is the right to retain all the goods or any property of the bailor which is in possession of the bailor until all the claims of the bailee are satisfied.

Termination of Bailment

The termination of bailment takes place in the following conditions:
1. Expiry of the period
2. Achievement of the object—the specific purpose is achieved
3. Right to extraordinary expenses is violated
4. Destruction of the subject matter
5. Gratuitous bailment
6. Death of the bailor or bailee

4.3 PLEDGE

TEXT

The bailment of goods as security for payment of a debt or performance of a promise is called 'pledge'. The bailor is, in this case, called 'pawnor'. The bailee is called 'pawnee'.

– Sec. 172, The Indian Contract Act, 1872

A pledge is a bailment for security. It is a special kind of bailment. The bailment of goods as security for payment of a debt or performance of a promise is called pledge. The bailor is called the pledger or pawnor and the bailee as the pledgee or pawnee (Sec. 172). Although generically same, however, there are the following specific differences between a pledge and a bailment (see Table 4.5).

Table 4.5 Differences between pledge and bailment

Pledge	Bailment
Bailment of goods as security for the payment of specific task	Bailment of goods for general purpose
Pawnee may sell the goods if pawnor does not honour the pledge	Bailee may retain the goods or file suit for his charges
Pawnee has no right to use the goods pawned with him	Bailee may use the goods if the contract so provides

Case 4.3 would never have come to light if the bank manager had applied a wee bit of jurisprudence. It would have saved the bank as well as its customer a litigation that went on almost for a decade. Ten years were lost fighting a case of merely ₹6,500, of which only the interest was in question—that would have been only a few rupees!

CASE 4.3   APPELLANT: Union Bank of India   vs   RESPONDENT: K.V. Venugopalan and Others*

DATE OF JUDGEMENT: 1 November 1990

FACTS: E.V. John had placed money in a fixed deposit on 14 November 1981. On the same day, he had availed of an agricultural loan. On 16 November 1981, the fixed deposit receipt had been produced before the court as security; and accepting the said security, the order attaching the lorry had been vacated. In execution of the decree the court, treating the bank as a garnishee, called upon the bank to deposit the amount and interest thereon, covered by the fixed deposit, in court. In this petition the bank stated that it had the right to retain this money in exercise of its general power of *lien* and appropriate the said money towards amounts due to it under the loan account. The lower court had dismissed the bank's review application.

JUDGEMENT: Bank's review petition dismissed and the ruling of the lower court upheld.

---

*Union Bank of India vs K.V. Venugopalan and others (AIR 1990, Ker. 223), see link, http://indiankanoon.org/doc/1055979/ (11 December 2010).

Contd

Case 4.3 *Contd*

> REASON: When monies are held by the bank in one account and the payer in respect of these monies owes the bank on another account, the banker's lien gives the bank a charge on all the monies of the payer in its hands, so that they may be transferred to whatever account the bank chooses, to set off or liquidate the debt. To put it differently, the banker has the right to set-off one account against the other. The use of the word *lien* in this context is misleading.

4.4   AGENCY, APPOINTMENT, AND AUTHORITY OF AGENTS

An 'agent' is a person employed to do any act for another, or to represent another in dealing with third persons. The person for whom such act is done, or who is so represented, is called the 'principal'.

— Sec. 182, The Indian Contract Act, 1872

Understanding Agency

The best descriptive definition of an agent is a *manager*. He represents his organisation and acts on behalf of his company. The first party is the principal, the chairman, and board of directors of your company. The third party is with whom your company has business and you, between the principal and the third party, are technically an agent. Thus, an agent is a kind of middleman who represents the principal.

> **MANAGER'S TAKEAWAY**
> • Trust is the bedrock of business.
> • There is a proverb that says: Possession is ninetenths of the law.

Today's business is complex. From a simple booking of travel ticket to establishment of large organisations, acquisitions, and their management, agents and agencies play an enormous role. You or your company may not be able to attend to all the transactions or all matters in which it is necessary to be brought into legal relations with other people. You need other persons to legally represent you; these are your agents who mediate on your behalf; they have all the legal power that you have transferred from yourself to them. You have entrusted them with your faith. Your contract with another person to represent you creates a principal–agent relationship.

You may interpret the above textual definition of Sec. 182 in this manner: The essence of a contract of agency is the agent's representative capacity coupled with a power to affect the legal relationship of the principal with the third party. It is this that distinguishes the twin relationship between a principal–agent and an employer–employee one. One is your agent in so far as he creates, modifies, or terminates contractual obligations in your name with the third party. The principle is: *Qui facit, per altum facit per se*, meaning who does an act through another, does it by himself.

Salient Features of Agency/Agent

An agent, having an authority to do an act, has authority to do every lawful thing which is necessary in order to do such act. An agent having an authority to carry on a business, has authority to do every lawful thing necessary for the purpose, or usually done in the course of conducting such business.

— *Sec.* 188, The Indian Contract Act, 1872

Table 4.6 Essential features of agency

Features	Explanation
Agreement between principal and agent	The principal agrees to be represented on his behalf.
Intention of the agent	In his action, the agent has the intention to act on behalf of his principal; this is borne by the fact of his action.
The person of agency	Any person who is legally competent to contract.
Function	The person with the capacity to bind the principal and make him answerable to a third person.
Consideration	Not in the form of salary as to an employee, but as fees, commission, on the basis of work.
Agent is not employee/servant	An employee can work only for his master; an agent works for many principals; for instance, the consultants.

The Contract Act dedicates 56 sections to this subject of contract of agency. The contract of agency is a contract of trust: the principal entrusts his legal obligations to the agent. The day the principal loses his faith, he may withdraw the contract and terminate the agency. In Table 4.6, we present the essential features of agency.

Formation of Agency

An agency may be is formed in the following ways:

Express agreement

Oral agreement   The general everyday transactions, e.g., asking your friend to buy you a cinema ticket.

Written transaction   Where one empowers another to act on his behalf, e.g., power of attorney.

Implied agreement

It arises out of the conduct, situation, or relationship of the parties.

Estoppel   When a person by his statements or conduct willfully leads another person to believe that a certain person is his agent; he is *estopped* from denying subsequently that that person is not his agent.

Holding out   It is an estoppel where the principal is required to confirm the agency subsequently; e.g., your staff buys stationery habitually from one shop; your staff, however, misappropriates the money but you are called on to pay because your prior positive action supports such a transaction.

Necessity   When an agent exceeds his authority in an emergency. For example, you as an agent need to supply perishable goods to a far away place, but due to changed circumstances such as non-availability of transport due to strike or natural calamity, you would have to dispose the goods locally in order to avoid wastage and loss of money

Ratification

When a person acts on behalf of another without the latter's consent; however, later on he agrees or approves or endorses what is done in his name is called ratification. Such a contract may be express or implied and is tantamount to the prior authority. The principal, if he does not ratify it, in other words, rejects it; then the contract is annulled. For instance, X without the authority of Y buys goods for him and further sells them to Z on his own account. Y's conduct here is an implied ratification.

Operation of Law

Through an action of law an agency is set up. For instance, when a company is formed, its promoters become automatically its agents. We shall deal with it in Chapter 5, when we deal with the Indian Partnership Act, 1932.

Authority of Agent

It is very important to understand an agent's authority because he can represent you only as much as you want him to. Would he have your authority in certain actions? Whether the agent is not presumptuous and crosses the limits of his responsibility? He has only what is given to him, but it is merely as described or implied. Due to the problems that may arise, it is important to understand the following concepts.

Agent's authority   Acts of an agent are binding upon the principal and the obligation arising from the contracts entered into are enforceable as though have been entered into by the principal on his own.

Actual authority   Whether implied or expressed, the agent can measure up only to the extent he is asked to do so. He has no authority more than what is granted to him.

Apparent or ostensible authority   It is what a third party perceives. You see a chairman of a company and you assume (because it is apparent to you) that a chairman can decide practically on all matters of business concerning that company.

Agent exceeding his authority   When an agent crosses the limits of his authority, he exceeds it. For instance, you have delegated someone to buy half of the stock from a warehouse; but your agent buys the entire lot, presuming you would like it or perhaps he was induced to do so by the third party. You are within your legal limits for only half of the stock.

Delegation of agent's authority   When a principal authorises someone as his agent, it is delegation; when the agent further authorises the very same task to another then it is called sub-delegation. Although the law does not prohibit sub-delegation, it is very clear on the aspect of responsibility. The sub-agent is responsible to the agent and the agent bears all the responsibility to his principal. In other words, the principal is not liable for the acts of the sub-agent.

Effects of delegation   Regarding delegation to a sub-agent, it primarily depends on how the contract has been entered into. If the principal knows and approves sub-delegation, then the sub-agent's action has the same bearings on the third party as though from the principal. Sub-delegations are not uncommon; it may depend on the nature of business, custom, etc. For example, outsourcing is a business based on agency, the BPO company may further outsource its business.

Substituted agent An agent is given the authority to appoint another person to act for the principal. Such an agent is not a sub-delegated one, but an agent in the full sense of the term for the chosen responsibility. You tell your attorney to appoint an auctioneer to conduct the sale of equipment from your plant. The chosen auctioneer is not sub-agent; he is a substituted one.

Case 4.4 teaches you to be on your guard when you are an agent of business. Today's business complexity demands a chain of agents. To determine a legally enforceable contract, the manager must take care how these contracts are entered into, and how the authority is delegated. This is an essential reason why every manager must know and apply the law.

CASE 4.4

PETITIONER: B. Mahinder Das   vs   RESPONDENT: Mohanlal and Others*

DATE OF JUDGEMENT: 1 June 1938

FACTS: Mohanlal is the owner of the houses on rent. Bhagwan Das & Co, a banking concern, was the appointed agent to lease the said houses. The dispute arose because these agents appointed Mahinder Das as the sub-agent on behalf of Mohanlal the owner, to rent the houses and agreed to pay commission on the rent realized. The rent was paid but not as per agreement. The suit was resisted by the defendants (sub-agents) on the ground that they did not have any contract with the petitioner. The trial court recognised the ownership of the petitioner and decreed in his favour.

JUDGEMENT: The appeal fails and is dismissed.

REASON: The bank was responsible for the loss sustained by the petitioner, because it gave the letter of authority to the sub-agent. The letter of authority was done by the bank and not the petitioner, the owner of the house. The defendant is not responsible to make good the loss of the petitioner.

*B. Mahinder Das vs P. Mohanlal and Others, AIR 1939 All 187 a; also see the link, http://www.indiankanoon.org/doc/1820570/ (15 November 2010).

Having understood both the creation of agency as well as the authority of agent, in other words, what makes an agent and how he can function, you need to understand more about the relationship between the principal and agent which is held by rights and duties.

Rights, Duties, and Liabilities of Principal and Agent

Refer to Table 4.7 to understand better the rights, duties, and liabilities of the principal and agent.

Case 4.5 is an example where the liabilities of the principal take prominence even when the authorised agent has done wrong or overshot his authority. The case was of great interest because of its historical position. It began in early 1940s when India was still under the British rule, and World War II where India to war an ally. Then there came Indian Independence

Table 4.7 Rights, duties, and liabilities of principal and agent

Rights	
Principal	**Agent**
Revoke agency With reasonable notice can cancel or withdraw. *Repudiate* Reject (a) upon concealment of material fact; (b) if the dealings are against the principal's interest. *Secret profits of the agent* The principal has the right over profits undisclosed by the agent.	*Retention* May retain his dues from the monies received. *Remuneration* It is his upon complete discharge of his duties. *Lien* Right to retain property, asset, or documents, etc., against the owner of the property, until what is due to him is paid. *Indemnity* Has right to indemnity by the principal, so as not to cause loss or injury to self. *Compensation* If loss or injury is caused by the principal, the agent has the right to be compensated.
Duties	
Indemnify or compensate agent (a) for a lawful act done by the agent; (b) act done in good faith but caused injury to third person; (c) any injury suffered by the agent caused by the principal.	*Follow instructions or customs* It is obvious from the contract to follow instructions; where there are no express instructions then follow the tradition of the profession.
Compensate for revocation If a lawfully contracted agency is revoked arbitrarily or before time, the agent needs to be compensated.	*Exercise reasonable skill and diligence* A certain standard of professionalism is expected of the agent that he safeguards the interests of his principal: (a) submit correct accounts (b) communicate promptly (c) in emergency, take right action *Avoid conflict of interest* Avoid indulging in the same business as of the principal. *Do not make secret profits* Agent has afiduciary relationship with the principal—hence any profits in excess must be notified and shared as per the contract. *Remit sums* Agent may deduct the amount due to him before remitting entirely what rightfully belongs to the principal. *Do not delegate authority* The agent must not delegate unless it is part and parcel of the contract and done with the consent of the principal.
Liabilities	
Of named principal When the principal is disclosed, then he is directly responsible to the third parts the agent cannot sue or be sued, except when he exceeds his authority.	*Foreign principal* When the agent acts on behalf of a foreign national, he bears full legal responsibility for the contract.

Contd

Table 4.7 *Contd*

Unnamed principal In the event where the existence of a principal is disclosed but remains unnamed, then it is he, and not the agent, who is directly responsible to the third party, unless something is stated specifically in the contract.	*Undisclosed principal* In the case of unnamed principal the agent bears full legal responsibility.
	Agent for minor Agent takes full responsibility even though the principal is disclosed, e.g., a minor, then the legal responsibility lies with the agent.
Undisclosed principal Agent is treated as the principal in so far as the third party is concerned; for some reason, he may disclose himself and take upon himself the liabilities directly; intervention by the principal may cause repudiation by the third party.	*Pretender* An agent who pretends he represents a certain principal is fully responsible contractually to the third party.
	Exceeding authority An agent exceeding his authority is personally liable to the contract in so far as where he has exceeded such authority.
	Specific contract If the contract specifically makes the agent responsible for the contract, then he bears the contractual responsibility before the law.

CASE 4.5

PETITIONER: A. Thangal Kunju Mudaliar vs RESPONDENT: M. Venkitachalam Potti and Others*

DATE OF JUDGEMENT: 20 December 1955

FACTS: The petitioner filed a writ petition in the Travancore High Court against respondent 1 and respondent 2 (Indian Income Tax Investigation Commission) for a writ of prohibition or any other writ prohibiting the respondents from holding an enquiry into the cases registered as evasion cases numbers 1 & 2 of 1126 or from holding an investigation into the income of the petitioner from the year 1940 to the last completed assessment year. The high court held that the respondent had the powers to hold such inquiry.

JUDGEMENT: Appeal dismissed and the judgement of the high court upheld.

REASON: The inquiry was directed only against those persons concerning whom definite information came into the possession of the income tax officer and in consequence of which the income tax officer discovered that the income of those persons had escaped or been under-assessed or assessed at too low a rate or had been the subject of excessive relief. There was definite information leading to discovery within 8 years, or 4 years, as the case may be, of definite item or items of income that had escaped assessment.

---

*A. Thangal Kunju Mudaliar vs M. Venkitachalam Potti, 1956 AIR 246 1955 SCR (2) 1196; it is a five-judge bench judgement and has been cited numerously, see also link, http://indiankanoon.org/doc/407809/ (15 November 2010).

and the new Constitution. The case made transition to new India, where the new states were still in formation until finally the judgement was delivered in 1955. It came under the purview of Constitution of India, Article 14, Travancore Taxation on Income (Investigation Commission) Act, 1124 (Act XIV of 1124), Sec. 5(1)—whether *ultra vires* the Constitution, read along with Sec. 47(1) of Travancore Income Tax Act, 1121 (Act XXIII of 1121); high court jurisdiction—Article 226 of the Constitution—writ petition against authorized official appointed under Sec. 6 of the Travancore Act (XIV of 1124); Investigation Commission—

whether competent under the provisions of the Travancore Act XIV of 1124 to investigate cases not referred to it by the government.

You have witnessed the rights, duties, and liabilities of principal—agent relationship in a contract. Just as you saw the creation of agency, now you are in a position to consider its termination. You have also come across the concept of revocation. Now you are ready to see all the circumstances in which a contract with an agent can be revoked and terminated.

Termination of Agency

It is a deconstruction of agency—the reverse of creation (see Table 4.8).

Table 4.8 Termination of agency

By act of the parties	By operation of law
• Agreement • Revocation by the principal • Revocation by the agent	• Performance of the contract • Expiry of time • Death, or insanity, or insolvency of either party • Destruction of the subject matter • Principal becomes alien enemy • Dissolution of company • Termination of agent's authority

Termination of anency occusion the following circumtances:

Completion of agency business   When the business for which the agency is created is done and over, having completed the business, the agency automatically comes to an end. If the contract of agency is time-bound, at the end of the determined period, the agency ceases to exist. For example, an agency created for the sale of goods within a definite season ends with the end of that season.

Death or insanity   The agency ceases to exist if either the principal or the agent or both are unable to honour the contract due to death or insanity.

Insolvency   If the principal is declared insolvent, the agencies created by him too will lose their validity.

Renunciation   With a reasonable notice, the principal may end an agency. If not, then mere renunciation may compel him to pay compensation to the agent. The principal will also have to compensate for any premature termination.

Revocation   Revocation is the cancellation of authority granted by the principal to the agent. A reasonable notice of revocation and suitable compensation, if the revocation is arbitrary, are the norms of revocation.

At the beginning of this section where we compared your role as manager to an agent, it was to give you the sense of the middleman. Actually, as a manager, you are not an agent of the company—you are an employee. However, as you would have seen, the concept of agent as one who has afiduciary duty towards the principal. Every manager also bears afiduciary duty towards the company. The difference between you as the manager and an agent is that as manager you are in some way the company in and for which you work; whereas an agent is contracted by you to help you in completing a business transaction. The agent will work for you and several others like you; but you will work solely for your company.

Agent, Principal, and the Law

Authority of agent An agent can act on behalf of the principal and can bind the principal.

Agent's duty to principal An agent has the following duties towards the principal to conduct principal's business as per his directions:

- Carry out work with normal skill and diligence
- Render proper accounts—Sec. 213
- Agent's duty to communicate with principal—Sec. 214
- Not to deal on his own account, in business of agency—Sec. 215
- Agent's duty to pay sums received for the principal—Sec. 218
- Agent's duty on termination of agency by the principal's death or insanity—Sec. 209

Remuneration to agent Consideration is not necessary for creation of agency. However, if there is an agreement, an agent is entitled to get remuneration as per contract.

Rights of principal
- Recover damages from the agent if he disregards directions of the principal.
- Obtain accounts from agent.
- Recover moneys collected by the agent on behalf of the principal.
- Obtain details of secret profit made by the agent and recover it from him.
- Forfeit remuneration of the agent if he misconducts the business.

Duties of the principal Pay remuneration to the agent as agreed.
- Indemnify agent for lawful acts done by him as the agent.
- Indemnify agent for all acts done by him in good faith.
- Indemnify agent if he suffers loss due to neglect or lack of skill of the principal.

An agency is terminated:

By the principal Through revoking his authority.

By the agent The agent can terminate the agency under the following circumstances:
- On renouncing the business of the agency.
- Business of the agency being completed.
- Either the principal or agent dying or becoming of unsound mind.
- The principal being adjudicated an insolvent under the provisions of any Act for the time being in force for the relief of insolvent debtors—Sec. 201.

However, an agency cannot be revoked in the following cases:
- Agency coupled with interest—Sec. 202.
- Agent has already exercised his authority—Sec. 203.
- Agent has incurred personal liability.

SUMMARY

Indemnity and Guarantee

Indemnity is a type of contract—if contract is genus then indemnity is its species. It is a contract when a party promises to save the other from loss caused to him by the conduct of the promisor.

Contract of guarantee It is to perform the promise or discharge the liability of a third person in case of his fault.

Surety The person who gives guarantee.

Principal debtor The person in respect of whose default the guarantee is given.

Guarantee is given for the (a) payment of debt, (b) payment of the price of the goods sold on credit; and (c) good conduct or honesty of a person employed in a particular office—called *fidelity guarantee*. *Liability of the surety* is co-extensive with that of the principal debtor, unless it is otherwise provided in the contract.

Rights of surety (a) Against the creditor: before payment of principal debt, surety can file a suit for declaration that the principal debtor shall be the person liable to pay the amount; on payment of the principal debt, the surety steps in the shoes of the creditor; (b) Against the debtor: the surety upon payment or performance of all that he is liable for, is invested with all the rights which the creditor had against the principal debtor; (c) Against the co-sureties who are, in the absence of any agreement to the contrary, liable to contribute equally, that is, as far as their respective obligations.

Discharge of surety It is the freedom from liability by (a) revocation, (b) conduct of creditor: actual release from various terms of liabilities, (c) invalidation: the contract is anomalous due to defects such as misrepresentation and concealment.

Bailment

It is the delivery of goods for some purpose. *Bailor* is the person delivering the goods; *Bailee* is the person to whom the goods are delivered.

Bailments may be for the exclusive benefit of the bailor or exclusive benefit of the bailee or mutual benefit of the bailor and the bailee. Bailments are also classified as gratuitous and non-gratuitous—bailment for reward.

While the bailee has the duty to protect and take care of the goods, the bailor must disclose all the details about the goods.

Lien A right to retain the property of another for a general balance of accounts.

Termination of bailment happens on the expiry of the determined period, on the achievement of the object, or on the inconsistent use of goods bailed.

Pledge is the bailment of goods as security for payment of a debt or performance of a promise. The rule is that it is the owner who can ordinarily create a valid pledge.

Agency, Appointment, and Authority of Agents

The contract that creates the relationship of principal and agent is called an agency. The principal is the one who chooses someone to represent him for a definite business transaction. An agent is the one who is thus chosen to represent the principal. Both the principal as well as the agent must be competent to contract.

Creation of agency Done through express or implied agreement. The implied agency is threefold: estoppel, necessity, and ratification.

Rights, duties, and liabilities of both the principal and agent revolve around the principle of authority that is delegated.

The relation of principal with the third party is primary despite the fact that there is a middleman.

The general rule is that an agent may not sub-delegate; if he does, then the relation between them is that of a principal and agent.

Termination of agency is done by the principal by revoking agent's authority; the agent in turn by renouncing agency; death or becoming unsound in mind of either or both.

EXERCISES

Indemnity and guarantee

(i) A road contractor contracted to buy from Bharat Supplies 100 barrels of bitumen at the rate of ₹5,000 per barrel to be delivered by April 2010. The performance of this contract was guaranteed by CEDA Trading. Soon after, the road contractor contracted to sell back to Bharat Supplies 10 barrels of bitumen at the rate of ₹6,000 per barrel. Is CEDA Trading discharged from its guarantee?

Hint: No, the second agreement is an independent one; his guarantee is good for the first one and he remains the guarantor.

(ii) Arvind & Co. undertakes to build an industrial plant for Bharat Pvt. Ltd, the latter having agreed to supply the materials. The State Bank is the guarantor. Bharat Pvt. Ltd is unable to supply the material and the activity comes to a close. What is the position of the guarantor?

Hint The bank is discharged of the liability; see Sec. 134 of the Act.

(iii) You stand as surety for Raju for his good conduct as he is employed by a bank. But Raju repeatedly misappropriates monies. Are you liable to the bank?

Hint: No; see Sec. 139 of the Act.

(iv) Explain and illustrate with cases, the distinction between contract of indemnity and guarantee.

(v) Comment on the following statements:

(a) A surety is undoubtedly and not unjustly an object of some favour both at law and at equity.

(b) The liability of a surety is co-extensive with that of the principal debtor.

(c) The death of a surety puts an end to the contract of guarantee.

Bailment

(i) A hospital gives its body-scanning machine for repairs to a scientific equipment company for repairs with the stipulation for it to be returned within 48 hours. The company fails even to start the work on the machine. The hospital demands the machine back but the company refuses to part with it unless the charges are paid.

Hint: The Company cannot withhold the machine; the hospital can take back its machine and claim compensation from the company for the breach of contract under Sec. 170 of the Act.

(ii) A young executive is on travel. At the hotel he hands over his belongings and his laptop to the attendant as he checks in. He proceeds to the restaurant for meals. Upon his return to the room he finds that his laptop is missing. Should he be compensated by the hotel?

Hint: The hotel guest can hold the hotel responsible for the loss; see Sec 151 and 152 of the Act.

(iii) A farmer mortgages his land for a loan of ₹1 lakh. Again, at the second instance, he borrows another ₹50,000. The farmer repays the first loan at the stipulated date. He requests for his collateral documents back. The bank refuses on the ground that ₹50,000 is still outstanding. Is the act of the bank justified?

Hint: Yes; see Sec. 174 of the Act.

(iv) When does a bailment come to an end?

(v) When a pledger fails to redeem his pledge, what right does pledgee have in the pledge?

Agency, appointment, and authority of agents

(i) A manager engages an agent to sell old machinery on an agreed commission of ₹1 lakh. The agent tells it for ₹2 lakh and claims 50 per cent of the proceeds as his commission.

Hint: The agent is entitled for the entire commission as promised before.

(ii) Mithra Pvt. Ltd, invited tenders for the supply of cotton. Apollo Traders agreed with the manager of Mithra that they would pay him ₹100 on every bale if the tender was accepted. Accordingly, Apollo quoted ₹100 higher price than they would have quoted. Apollo's tender was accepted. What would happen when Mithra comes to know about it.

Hint: The Company can recover the money as damages.

(iii) X rents out his premises to Y and the contract is terminable at a three-month notice. Z without the knowledge of Y gives the termination notice to X who ratifies the notice and sues Y for ejectment. Is X entitled to get decree?

Hint: No, the notice cannot be ratified on Y; see Sec. 200 of the Act.

(iv) What are the salient features of relationship of agency?

(v) What is the extent of the liability of the principal when his agent exceeds authority? Illustrate with case.

DEVELOPMENT OF LEGAL EDGE

- Provide a case study of a successful commercial agency.

- Drawup a project for your dream agency.

FURTHER READING

- The Indian Contract Act, 1872 (easily available in bookshops and law bookshops)—this is mandatory while studying the text book.
- Documents and forms: For any document or format of letters of contract: http://www.citehr.com.

Web resources

- Supreme Court of India: http://supremecourtofindia.nic.in/.

- Law Commission of India: http://lawcommissionofindia.nic.in/.
- Ministry of Corporate Affairs: http://www.mca.gov.in/.
- All India Reporter: http://airwebworld.com/index.php.
- All acts and documents: http://www.legaldocs.com/.
- Law related articles and for a: http://www.findlawindia.com/.

CASE STUDY   A CASE OF TRAVAILS OF TERMINATION OF AGENCY

Where the agent has himself an interest in the property which forms the subject matter of the agency, the agency cannot, in the absence of an express contract, be terminated to the prejudice of such interest.

– Sec. 202, The Indian Contract Act, 1872

The principal cannot revoke the authority given to his agent after the authority has been partly exercised, so far as regards such acts and obligations as arise from acts already done in the agency.

– Sec. 202, The Indian Contract Act, 1872

When two or more persons have made a joint promise, then, unless a contrary intention appears by the contract, all such persons, during their joint lives, and, after the death of any of them, his representative jointly with the survivor or survivors, and, after the death of the last survivor the representatives of all jointly, must fulfill the promise.

– Sec. 42, The Indian Contract Act, 1872

In the case Tirupati Agencies Pvt. Ltd versus NSK Sales Company Pvt. Ltd, the hearings have been concluded on 9 December 2009.* There are two challenges for you in this case:

1. What would be the judgement by the high court?
2. If the suit moves to the Supreme Court, what would be its judgement?

*See http://www.indiankanoon.org/doc/895861/(5 January 2011)

Table 4.9   In the High Court at Calcutta in the Court of Honorable Justice Sanjib Banarjee

Plaintiff: Tirupati Agencies Pvt. Ltd	Respondent: Nsk Sales Company Pvt. Ltd
Represented by: Anindya Kumar Mitra, senior advocate Abrajit Mitra, advocate Jishnu Chowdhury, advocate	Represented by T. Poornam, advocate A.K. Sil, advocate A.K. Dey, advocate
Claims 1. Introduced NSK's bearings and developed market for their products manufactured in India for thirty years.	Claims 1. Tirupati Agencies was never the sole selling agent in India and what is reflected in the notice of 21 May 2009 is the continuation of a process put into place at lease since 1998. There is no agency of the kind that the plaintiff seeks to set up. The plaintiff's bandying of an unsubstantiated figure of 90 per cent
2. It is not the sole agent for NSK products in India or any of its regions, yet the commercial relationship, borne by their correspondence, was significant.	2. The list appended to the notice to demonstrate that five foremost railway divisions and the Metro Railway in Calcutta were left in the plaintiff's kitty together with the major NTPC units in eastern India and the behemoth of an electricity board, in the largest state in the country.
3. The reason for this suit is NSK's action to prune the number of customers of NSK bearings that it could exclusively deal with.	3. There was no suddenness in termination. The plaintiff should have seen it coming nearly a year before it did. We were under no obligation to continue what is essentially a form of a dealership arrangement. The correspondence between the parties nearly a year back and a communication about 10 days before the notice of 21 May 2009 was issued.
4. It contends that the principle embodied in Sec. 202 of the Contract Act would be applicable to the transaction between the parties hereto is reflected in some of the reliefs claimed in the suit.	4. As indicated, NSK would like to expand distribution channels in India. NSK does not want to terminate or discontinue any relation with TAPL.** However, NSK will not be able to continue to be represented by TAPL in all units of NTPC/SAIL and the different Railway units that TAPL has been doing so far.
5. It seeks an injunction restraining the defendants from supplying bearings to or dealing with the customers referred to in Schedule 'A' to the petition; mandatory injunction commanding the defendants to undertake a host of duties that have been set out; injunction restraining the defendants from interfering with the plaintiff's exclusive agency of NSK bearings in respect of the Schedule 'A' customers till such time that the unexecuted	5. NSK bearings are supplied, by the defendants, directly to automotive original equipment manufacturers and industrial original equipment manufacturers in India.

Contd

**A Japanese agency with which the respondents have started business in India.

Table 4.9 *Contd*

Plaintiff: Tirupati Agencies Pvt. Ltd	Respondent: NSK Sales Company Pvt. Ltd
contracts and the contracts likely to be awarded are fully executed and the existing inventory of bearings at the plaintiff's disposal is exhausted; and, injunction restraining any effect to be given to a notice of 10 June 2009 or any steps being taken by defendants to terminate the exclusive agency in respect of the Schedule 'A' customers.	
6. It has been exclusively entrusted to effect supplies of NSK bearings to the customers listed in Schedule 'A' to the petition. The customers listed in Schedule 'A' include several units of the National Thermal Power Corporation Limited (NTPC), various units of state electricity boards and related entities, divisions and units of the Indian Railways, all plants of the Steel Authority of India Limited and 20 other public and private sector industries.	6. In respect of industrial OEM customers, we directly supply bearings to such parties, but orders may be obtained by the dealers. A dealer may procure an order directly in the name of the defendants from an industrial OEM customer. The supply is thereafter effected by the defendants to the industrial OEM customer directly without the relevant dealer being involved in the delivery or the payment; however, a commission is subsequently paid on such order by *us to the* dealer. We provide after-sales service to large end-users who require constant supply for replacement and the like.
7. There was no 'written agency agreement' and that the terms and conditions of the agency would be borne out and corroborated by the conduct in course of the last decades. In case where the orders are placed by the customers on it directly, the concerned NSK Group company would issue manufacturer's test and warranty certificate for each supply. The concerned respondent also whenever required, would provide an authorization certificate stating that the petitioner is the duly authorized agent for NSK bearings. Copies of a few such authorization letters including that dated 2 July 2008 issued by the respondent no.1 to NTPC are annexed hereto and collectively marked with the letter 'B'.	7. A dealer may obtain an order for replacement from such after-sales service customer, but again the order is directly in the name of us and the supply is made by us to the customer without the dealer coming into the picture. The dealer, however, is paid a commission for having procured the order for us.
8. It required to maintain a stock of reasonable quantity of NSK bearings to meet the urgent needs of customers. This would be evident from letters issued by customers, copies whereof annexed hereto and marked 'D'.	8. There are two other groups of customers '(b)' and '(c)'. Some large end-users like NTPC and the Railways have been clubbed in '(b)' while other smaller end-users and smaller OEM and retail sales customers have been included in '(c)'. These customers obtain NSK bearings from dealers like the plaintiff and the dealers buy the bearings from the company and sell it to such customers at a margin.

Contd

Table 4.9 *Contd*

Plaintiff: Tirupati Agencies Pvt. Ltd	Respondent: NSK Sales Company Pvt. Ltd
9. It would carry out pre-dispatch inspection in India on behalf of the respondents. For this, the respondents have duly authorised the petitioner as would appear from the documents being Annexure 'E' hereto.[†] It has organised itself and its business to deal with the vast majority of NSK customers in India. It submits that there has been no accusation by the defendants as to its performance; on the contrary, it has been recognized and commended by the defendants for its efficiency and impeccable service.	9. It is the sole prerogative of the manufacturers to decide on allocation and dealers can have no say in the matter.

Observations by the Judge

From plaintiff's perspective The plaintiff relies on Secs 202 and 204 of the Contract Act to suggest that as agent it has an interest in the property which forms the subject matter of the agency. The plaintiff urges that in view of its substantial interest, the agency cannot be terminated at the defendant's will or whim or so heavily curtailed that would amount to effective termination. The plaintiff claims that the defendants had given an authority to the plaintiff that it has partly exercised and the authority or agency cannot be revoked. Secs 202 and 204 of the Contract Act provide,

(202) Termination of agency, where agent has an interest in subject-matter. Where the agent has himself an interest in the property which forms the subject-matter of the agency, the agency cannot, in the absence of an express contract, be terminated to the prejudice of such interest.

(204) Revocation where authority has been partly exercised. The principal cannot revoke the authority given to his agent after the authority has been partly exercised, so far as regards such acts and obligations as arise from acts already done in the agency.'

From defendant's perspective The defendants submit that any order that the plaintiff has sought would amount to specific performance that would involve the performance of a continuous duty. The defendants say that compensation would be adequate relief for the plaintiff, particularly since it had valued its alleged loss at paragraph 39 of the plaint. The defendants urge that the arrangement pleaded by the plaintiff would show

that it runs into minute and numerous details and are dependent on the volition of the parties. They say that even if there was an agency that had been granted, it was by its very nature determinable. In short, the defendants invoke every limb of Sec. 14(1) of the Specific Relief Act, 1963. In addition, the defendants say that Sec. 41(e) of the Specific Relief Act would preclude any injunction of the nature sought by the plaintiff being granted.

The Inference by the Judge

About the plaintiff Every dealer of goods is not an agent of the manufacturer. For a dealer or distributor to be regarded as an agent, the relationship needs to be established and will not be presumed for the asking. In order to impress the manufacturer and to further the visibility of its dealership, a dealer may run up an inventory in anticipation of executing future orders. But the fact that a dealer has a huge stock piled up, even of goods that are not easily marketable, will not tell upon the manufacturers' authority to cancel or limit the dealership. As much as a dealer pushing the products that it deals in benefits the manufacturer, it also rakes in profits for the dealer.

Prima facie, the plaintiff is not entitled to any protection of the kind that it seeks by reason of it having amassed a large stock of the defendant's products. The plaintiff is also not entitled to insist that the customers originally on its list cannot be tinkered with by the defendants. The business relating to unexecuted contracts and orders that are likely to be placed on the plaintiff is, however, an entirely different matter.

[†]The list by the plaintiff with the annexure marked is laboriously lengthy.

About the respondent Since the defendants have agreed, to the extent indicated, to allow the unexecuted orders to be worked out, it is the aspect relating to the future orders likely to be placed on the plaintiff following its offers made prior to 21 May 2009, that needs to be protected. It is more than likely that the plaintiff has furnished earnest deposits or made representations to the '(b)' and '(c)' groups of customers that made up its erstwhile list regarding the plaintiffs authority to supply products of the defendant. If such offers are accepted and the plaintiff is prevented from honouring its commitments only by reason of the customers having been taken off the plaintiff's allocated list, unpleasant consequences may visit the plaintiff. The plaintiff would have made the offers or responded to tender enquiries on its reasonable assumption that the plaintiff's bids would ultimately be backed by the defendants if orders were placed pursuant thereto. It is no fault of the plaintiff that some of the customers on the plaintiff s list immediately prior to 21 May 2009 may subsequently have been removed from the new list. The same arrangement as in respect of the unexecuted orders must be made for the orders that the may be placed, in pursuance of offers made prior to 21 May 2009, on the plaintiff by such of the customers that have only gone out of the plaintiff's list following the defendant's decision of 21 May 2009. Sec. 204 of the Contract Act may not strictly apply, but the equitable ethos of the principle embodied therein can be invoked by the plaintiff to seek the defendant's support for executing any of such orders that may be placed on the plaintiff in the reasonable future.

Entitlements Arising through Agency

Entitlement for plaintiff

1. The plaintiff is not entitled to any further order since that would amount to specific performance of a contract, if there is one, that would require constant supervision and that runs into minute details and depends on the volition of the parties.

2. That Sec. 202 of the Contract Act places the kind of agency that it covers on a higher pedestal than the ordinary case of agency does not imply that the interest is created by statute and not by contract. The interest that is referred to in Sec. 202 is an interest created by a contract between the principal and the agent; the statute merely protects such interest.

3. To protection in respect of the unexecuted orders and expected orders as detailed at paragraph 37 of the petition:

(a) To complete the supplies in respect of the unexecuted orders, if subsisting;

(b) To seek further supplies of material from the defendants against prior payment or payment through irrevocable letters of credit, at the defendants' option;

(c) To execute any orders placed on it by customers whose names figured in the plaintiff's allocated list prior to 21 May 2009 and to whom offers have been made by the plaintiff to supply the defendant's products prior to 21 May 2009.

Entitlement for respondent

1. It is also recorded that the defendants have agreed that the plaintiff may exhaust its inventory by effecting supplies therefrom to the customers listed under cover of the defendant's letter of 21 May 2009.

2. The defendants will be obliged to supply the material sought for such purpose and paid for as indicated earlier, subject to availability.

Conclusion

Today, commerce is unthinkable without agencies. An agency is a mediating company. They are actually the link between you and whatever you want to achieve from another person or establishment. They have knowledge of your needs and skills to make you achieve your plans. As a manager, too, you would need hosts of agents and agencies. As mediating entities, agents or agencies work for both you and your client and get consideration from both. A manager's task is to choose a right agent or agency.

Discussion Questions

1. What are the main issues in the case related to the agency and principal?
2. Interpret the three related sections of the contract law with comparative examples.
3. Calculate the business risks an agent takes. Illustrate with examples.
4. Do you think that the suit filed by the plaintiff is justified?
5. What is the legal value of the agency relationship of thirty years between the plaintiff and the respondent?
6. Are implied commercial relationships as good as documented ones?
7. What shortcomings do you find in the respondent's defence?
8. How would you rate the entitlements made by the judge? In what way would you rule differently?

Going Beyond

1. If you were one of the parties to the earlier litigation, how would you propose to recover the costs incurred?

2. Would you propose some amendments to the termination of agency? What would be their nature?

3. Can you suggest an outside-the-court settlement for the earlier case? Give details of negotiation.

LEGAL LUMINARY

FALI S. NARIMAN*— MONUMENTAL AND MEMORABLE

What Sachin Tendulkar is for the sports of cricket, Fali Nariman is for the legal profession. He is the number one and leaves the competition far behind; his fans are innumerable and his worst opponents are his greatest admirers; his honours are numerous and his leadership uncontested. His book, *Memory Fades: An Autobiography*** is education to any ambitious lawyer.

The *Times of India*, that rated him as the number one lawyer in the country, also calls him 'the wise man of the Bar'. No one can be as straightforward as him. The justices on the bench know it that he speaks the truth without ornament. He commands very high fees, at least ₹30 lakh. If someone dare ask him what he does with so much money, he would get a retort: 'That is my business'. Nariman is a quiet philanthropist. He also appears in many cases for the needy for free.

When a person of the brilliance and stature of Nariman appears in the apex court of the country, law is not merely followed but the precedents are created. He appeared first in the Golaknath Case on the basic structure of the Constitution and, like his senior Nani Palkhivala, he created a niche for himself even as his junior. He became the Additional Solicitor General of India in 1971. As the national emergency declared by Indira Gandhi in 1975 suspended the fundamental rights, he resigned immediately in protest; he being the only public official to do so. One of the important cases he argued was to defend the right of press in The Indian Express Case, where the Supreme Court struck down the order of the Delhi government threatening to demolish *The Indian Express* buildings as malafide and violative of the constitutional right of free press. He also appeared in the sensitive case of the conscientious objection to sing the national anthem in the Jehovah Witnesses Case (Bijoe Emanuel Case). He defended the constitutionally guaranteed right of the minority educational institutions in several leading cases culminating in the T.M.A. Pai Case. His greatest contribution lies in protecting the independence of the court and the integrity of the judicial process. He was the lead lawyer in the Second Judges Case where the judiciary took over the right to appoint judges, securing the power of judicial review over legislations specifically exempted from judicial review by Parliament (Ninth Schedule Case), championing the cause of the subordinate judiciary for a better pay and terms of service (All India Judges Association Case).[†]

This brilliant tactician's significance to corporate representation lies in his misjudgement of taking up the defence case of Union Carbide. In an interview with CNN–IBN's Devil's Advocate programme by Karan Thapar[‡] he admits that it was not a case, it was a tragedy. He was relieved when the settlement took place and was free from his brief. Like a professional he took up to defend Union Carbide,

---

*http://timesofindia.indiatimes.com/india/Indias-top-10-lawyers/articleshow/5426768.cms (2 January 2011).

**Fali S. Nariman, Before Memory Fades: An Autobiography, Hay House Publishers.

†http://barandbench.com/brief/1/483/lawyers-who-matter-fali-sam-nariman/(2 January 2011).

Contd

Legal Luminary *Contd*

ambitious to represent a corporation, but rues to this day and considers it a mistake in hindsight. His only consolation is the settlement. If it were not to take place the case would have gone on endlessly, depriving even the currently approved compensation of 470 million dollars. The tragedy today is that more people get qualified for compensation. The more qualified they get the less each party gets entitled. The problem is with the Indian law of torts, in this case, ascertaining the liabilities and fixing the loss to pay interim compensation. Thus Union Carbide is not only a corporate disaster it is also an economic, social, and legal one.

Fali S. Nariman was born on 10 January 1929 in Yangon, Myanmar. He had an impressive academic career studying early in Bishop Cotton School in Shimla and later attended St. Xavier's College, followed by Law College, both in Mumbai. He joined the legal profession under the tutelage of Jamsetjee Kanga who was a mentor par excellence. He prac-

ticed for two decades at Bombay High Court and later joined the Supreme Court as senior counsel.

Nariman held positions and has been honoured both nationally and internationally. He was appointed by the president of India for the *Rajyasabha (1999–2005);* president of Bar Association of India (1991); president of Council for Commercial Arbitration (1994); member of the International Commission of Jurists (1988); member of International Chamber of Commerce (1989); member, London Court of International Arbitration (1988); on the advisory board of United Nations Conference on Trade and Development (1999); chairman of the International Commission of Jurists (1995–1997); etc. He has been awarded the Padmabhusan (1991) and Padmavibhushan (2007), among other honours.[§]

He is the father of Rohinton F. Nariman[||], one of the top ten lawyers of India. Happily married for over half a century, he has a daughter who lives in Mumbai.

[‡]For transcript of the interview see: http://www.thehindu.com/opinion/interview/article488996.ece, you will find the same http:/indialawyers.wordpress.com/category/legal-luminaries/(2 January 2011).

[§]See http:/en.wikipedia.org/wiki/Fali_Sam_Nariman (2 January 2011).

[||]See, Legal Luminary, Chapter 2.

5

The Sale of Goods Act, 1930

Principle: *Tantum bona valent quantum vendi possunt.*
Things are worth what they will sell for.

CHAPTER OUTLINE

- Introduction and Interpretation
- Formation of the Contract
  (Agreement to Sell)
- Goods—The Subject Matter of
  Contract of Sale
- Price
- Conditions and Warranties
- Effects of the Contract

- Performance of the Contract
- Rights of Unpaid Seller Against
  the Goods
- Suits of Breach of the Contract
- Implied Terms, Time, Auction,
  Tax, and Other Matters
- *Case Study:* Less for More
- *Legal Luminary:* Shirish Despande

5.1 INTRODUCTION AND INTERPRETATION

(1) This Act may be called the Sale of Goods Act, 1930.
(2) It extends to the whole of India (except for the state of Jammu and Kashmir).
(3) It shall come into force on the 1st day of July, 1930.

– Sec. 1, (1)–(3), The Sale of Goods Act, 1930

You introduce yourself as a manager and people immediately ask what you sell. The very concept of business will cease if there is no sale. Sales involve commercial relationship. There is exchange of goods and services for money or other assets. Property, ownership, transfer of ownership, rights and duties of buyers and sellers—all of these bind people to a contract. We discussed contract in Chapter 2 in a general way. In this chapter, we shall deal with a particular contract of sale and purchase between the seller and buyer, respectively. You as a manager have no choice but to know this law well, lest you should experience pitfalls.

In 1893, the British Parliament enacted the Sale of Goods Law after repealing part of its Contract Law with the purpose of serving the new business realities. Chapter VII of the Indian Contract Law, Secs 76–123, formed the Sale of Goods Law. To meet the new needs of growing economy, this chapter on sale of goods was repealed to enact a new law on the same lines as the British Law. It does not affect the rights, interests, obligations, and titles acquired or what had already accrued before the enforcement of this Act. Work on the legislation began as early as 1926, carefully examining the case law making new provisions.[1]

When sale of goods is mentioned, remember its classification, as shown in Figure 5.1.

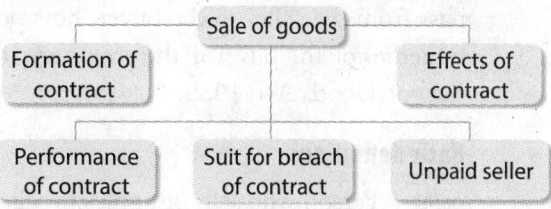

Figure 5.1 Sale of goods classification

Today, objects of virtual world are obviously valuable properties, but in those days people could not comprehend how water, gas, and electricity could be valued. There was doubt whether these objects fell under the definition of goods or property and, hence, saleable and purchasable.

Case 5.1 was a landmark one in the new era under Sale of Goods Act, because until then a lawyer could argue that gas and electricity were not defined as goods. The Law Commission of India recommended for certain amendments so that it is made indubitably clear that electrical energy, water, and gas come under the purview of the definition of goods.[2]

CASE 5.1

PETITIONER: **Rash Behari Singh and Others** vs RESPONDENT: **Emperor***

DATE OF JUDGEMENT: **7 October 1936**

FACTS: The appellants were accused persons who were charged with having been party to a criminal conspiracy to commit theft by dishonest consumption and use of electrical energy belonging to the Calcutta Electric Supply Corporation between the January 1934 and 20 January 1935, and in consequence of such conspiracy, theft was committed at Bharat Laxmi Cinema, Jupiter Cinema, and at other places. It was argued that Sec. 19 (a), Electricity Act, and Rule 31 were necessitated by the fact that there can be no actual property in electrical energy.

JUDGEMENT: The appellants found guilty of conspiracy and theft and sentenced to fine and imprisonment.

REASON: The evidence supplied showed that there was conspiracy to theft and altering of the electricity meter.

*Rash Behari and Others vs Emperor; see http://indiankanoon.org/doc/819989/ (14 December 2010).

---

[1]The Law Commission Report analyses the changes in the new Act and discusses the definition of property in a special way; for more, see http://lawcommissionofindia.nic.in/1–50/Report8.pdf (14 December 2010).
[2]The Commission Report of 1958. See http://lawcommissionofindia.nic.in/1-50/Report8.pdf (14 December 2010).

Agreements for the sale of goods are governed by the general principles of the Contract Law: offer, acceptance, consideration, communication, competence to contract, free consent, and the legality of the object. However, these may not be exhaustive enough to meet some grave challenges in contracts of sale. Hence, the Sale of Goods Act caters to the needs of, for instance, conditions and warranties in a contract; when does the ownership of the goods pass from the seller to the buyer; how does the buyer acquire a good title; fixing of price; remedies of the buyer if the goods are not delivered to him. All of this is the scope of the Sale of Goods Act, 1930.

Basic definitions

Seller   Person who sells or agrees to sell.

Buyer   Person who buys or agrees to buy.

Goods   All kinds of movable property, except actionable claims.

Sale   Where under a contract the property in the goods is transferred from the seller to the buyer, the contract is called a sale.

Agreement to sale   Where the transfer of the property in the goods is to take place at a future time or subject to some condition thereafter to be fulfilled, the contract is called an agreement to sell.

Price   Consideration for the sale of goods in money. (When the consideration is only in goods, then it is 'barter' and not 'sale'.)

Transfer   Transfer of ownership of goods or agreement to that effect.

The Act has found several reviews and amendments to adapt to the new complex course of businesses. In 1993, for instance, the Multimodal Transportation of Goods Act was enacted. As you now study the rest of the chapter, you will be introduced to six different steps to appreciate the practical wisdom enshrined in this Act.

5.2   FORMATION OF THE CONTRACT—AGREEMENT TO SELL

TEXT

A contract of sale of goods is a contract whereby the seller transfers or agrees to transfer the property in goods to the buyer for a price. There may be a contract of sale between one part-owner and another.

– Sec. 4 (1), The Sale of Goods Act, 1930

The seven definitions presented at the end of the preceding section must have given you an orientation about the formation of the agreement to sell. The activity of sale occurs when all those concepts step onto reality. In the Indian Contract Act, 1872 you saw the broad principles of offer, acceptance, consideration, and communication as the essentials of a contract. These and the just visited seven definitions make

 MANAGER'S TAKEAWAY

- Know what you sell.
- Buy what you know.

the sale a reality. In Table 5.1, you will learn all the salient features that go into the formation of contract of sale of goods.

Table 5.1   Salient features of contract of sale

Features	Explanation	Example
Two parties	There must by two parties, buyer and seller, to a contract.	You go to a dealer and buy a computer and pay for it. The dealer is the seller and you are the buyer.
Movable goods	Any goods that are movable and the ownership is transferred. (Immovable property does not come under the Sales of Goods Act.)	When you fly, the airline sells you the service to take you from one place to another; it does not sell you the aircraft. So also when you buy grain, you only buy grain and not the land of the farmer.
Price	Sale is about exchange goods for money. Under Contract Act it is termed as *consideration*, but this consideration must be only in money. Exchange of goods for goods is barter and not sale.	You buy a computer and pay money for it as the price for the value you
Transfer of general property	Property is distinguished as general property and special property. General property consists of as goods owned and special property as goods under possession.	You own a clock. It is general property. You pledge the clock to a pawn shop—the shop owner is in possession of your property which is owned by you; it is a special property for the shop owner.
Valid contract	The principles of valid contract are applicable to sale of contract.	The principles of contract that are enshrined in the Contract Act: offer, acceptance, consideration, communication, and competency to contract.

You may form a mental model of the formation of contract. In other words, you will deal with four main concepts of the formation of a contract (Fig. 5.2).

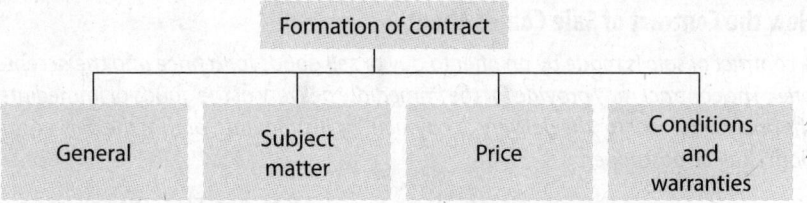

Figure 5.2   The four main concepts of the formation of a contract

Case 5.2 clearly illustrates the transfer of property in goods for a price as the lynchpin of the definition of the contract of sale. The sale comes about only with the transfer of 'ownership': a seller ceases to own and the buyer begins to own.

CASE 5.2	PETITIONER: Union of India vs RESPONDENT: Central India Machinery Manufacturing Co. Ltd*

DATE: 6 April 1977

FACTS: The contract was for the manufacture and supply of wagons. It was provided that the contract would be governed by the standard conditions insofar as they are not inconsistent with the correspondence exchanged between the parties. Under the standard conditions, 90 per cent of the payment had to be made against the company submitting the bill to the purchaser together with the completion certificate and on payment of such 90 per cent price the vehicle in question would become the property of the purchaser. The balance of 10 per cent was to be treated as security for the due fulfillment of the contract. The balance was to be received on the receipt of certificate from the purchaser to the effect that the actual delivery of the vehicle was taken and that the delivery was made in due time. The respondents contended that there was nothing in the special conditions which militated or was inconsistent with the standard condition no. 15. The special conditions, read as a whole, show that the raw materials purchased by the company against 90 per cent of advance payment do not become the property of the railway board or the Union of India because under the express terms of the contract, such advance payment is made towards the contract price of the wagons and not towards price of the materials.

JUDGEMENT: Petition was dismissed.

REASON: Transfer of property in goods for a price is the lynchpin of the definition of 'sale'. The difficulty in distinguishing between the contract of sale and work contract is an age-old one. The test would be whether the thing to be delivered has any individual existence before delivery as the sole property of the party who is to deliver it. If the answer is in the affirmative, it is sale of the thing, otherwise not. Another rule is that if the main object of the contract is the transfer from A to B for a price of the property in a thing in which B had no previous property, then the contract is a contract of sale.

*Union of India vs Central India Machinery (AIR 1977, SC1537). Also see for full text of the judgement, http://www.indiankanoon.org/doc/530386/ (14 December 2010).

How the Contract of Sale Comes About

A contract of sale is made by an offer to buy or sell goods for a price and the acceptance of such offer. The contract may provide for the immediate delivery of the goods or immediate payment of the price or both, or for the delivery or payment by instalments, or that the delivery or payment or both shall be postponed.

– Sec. 5(1), The Sale of Goods Act, 1930

As you have learnt in the Contract Act, no particular form is necessary to constitute a contract of sale. There is offer and acceptance, the communication may be formal, informal, or implied. The sale and transfer may occur immediately before, after, simultaneous, or payment in instalments.

In order to understand exactly how the contract of sale comes about, you must learn some fundamental distinctions. Table 5.2 distinguishes between each of the following:

(a) Sale and agreement to sell
(b) Sale and hire-purchase
(c) Agreement to sell and hire-purchase
(d) Sale and bailment
(e) Sale and contract for work and materials

The table is a logical consequence of the principles of contract that you studied in Chapter 2 which covered the Contract Act, 1872. It goes to prove that both the Contract Act and Sale of Goods Act are complementary and both are based fundamentally on the same principles.

Table 5.2   Fundamental distinctions on how the contract of sale comes about

Distinction between sale and agreement to sell		
Distinction	**Sale**	**Agreement to sell**
Nature of contract	*Executed contract* One of the parties has already performed the contract.	*Executory contract* Both the parties have agreed but are yet to perform the contract.
Creation of right	*Principle* Right on goods against the whole world. Latin: *Jus in rem*—right in possessing the good.	Creates personal right. Latin: *Jus in personam*—against the person in default for fulfilling his part of the contract.
Remedies on breach of contract	The seller has the right to sue for the price of goods, lien, and stoppage.	The seller has the right only to damages to performance of the contract.
Risk of loss	The loss will be borne by the buyer even when the goods are still lying with the seller.	The loss will be borne by the seller since the ownership is not yet transferred to the buyer.
Insolvency of the buyer	Seller is entitled to sue for the price of the goods and can exercise right of lien, stoppage in transit, and resale.	The seller has the right to sue only for damages for non-performance of the contract.
Right of resale	The buyer is the owner. Even if the goods are with the seller, he cannot resell.	The seller may dispose-off the goods as he deems fit; the buyer may sue him only for the breach of contract.
Distinction between sale and hire-purchase		
Distinction	**Sale**	**Hire-purchase**
Nature of contract	Sale and agreement to sell.	Bailment and agreement to sell
Transfer of property in goods	Property in goods is transferred to the buyer immediately at the time of contract.	Property passes to the hirer upon payment of the instalment.

Contd

Table 5.2 *Contd*

Position of the buyer	Owner of the goods.	Bailee till he pays all the instalments.
Power to terminate the contract	Buyer cannot terminate the contract.	May terminate the contract by returning goods to its owner without paying remainder of the instalments.
Risk of loss from insolvency of the buyer	Seller takes the risk.	Owner takes no risk; if the hirer does not pay instalments, the goods are taken back.
Tax payable	Tax is levied at the time of sale and agreement to sell.	Tax is not leviable until it turns into sale.

Agreement to sell and hire-purchase		
Distinction	**Agreement to sell**	**Hire-purchase**
Nature of contract	It is a step towards sale.	Becomes a sale after the completion of the payment.
Transfer of goods	Subsequent to the agreement.	Immediate transfer of goods but the ownership remains with the seller.
Ownership	Buyer can sell or pledge goods.	No ownership rights hence cannot sell or pledge.
Implied conditions and warranties	The buyer can take advantage of conditions and warranties.	Cannot claim beneHts until complete payment is done.
Law	Sale of Goods Act, 1930 is applicable.	Governed by Hire-Purchase Act, 1972.

Distinction between sale and bailment		
Distinction	**Sale**	**Bailment**
Nature of contract	Transfer of ownership from seller to the buyer.	Transfer of possession of goods from bailor to the bailee.
Right	The buyer enjoys all the rights of his property.	Can deal with the goods according to the directions of the bailor.

Sale and contract for work and materials		
Distinction	**Sale**	**Contract for work**
Nature of contract	Delivery of goods.	It is not governed by Sales of Goods Act.*

---

*See Case 5.2 of Union of India vs Central India Machinery, where there was a confusion about sale and manufacturing to deliver.

5.3 GOODS—THE SUBJECT MATTER OF CONTRACT OF SALE

(1) The goods which form the subject of a contract of sale may be either existing goods, owned or possessed by the seller, or future goods.
(2) There may be a contract for the sale of goods the acquisition of which by the seller depends upon a contingency which may or may not happen.
(3) Whereby a contract of sale, the seller purports to effect a present sale of future goods, the contract operates as an agreement to sell the goods.

– Sec. 6, The Sale of Goods Act, 1930

Understanding Goods

It is important to know what the lawgiver has in mind when he refers to 'goods'—what they are and what they are not.

What they are

Every kind of movable property is goods: shares, stocks, crops, trees, goodwill, patents, trade marks, electricity, water, gas, etc.—all that can be exchanged for money.

What they are not

Money and actionable claims are excluded from the claim of goods.

(a) By money, the lawgiver understands that which is a legal tender, the currency. It considers old coins and also foreign currency as goods that can be bought and sold.

(b) Actionable claim implies any debt or beneficial interest in a movable property not in possession, which can be recovered by means of a suit or an action. It is something that is enforceable by the court of law but cannot be sold as goods. It must be noted carefully that although it would logically seem that stocks and shares too are actionable claims, yet the Act specifically considers them as goods.

Classification of Goods

Sec. 6 of the Sale of Goods Act classifies 'goods' under the following categories:

Existing goods   These are the goods that are owned or possessed by the seller at the time of sale.

Specific goods   These are identified and agreed upon at the time of sale.

Ascertained goods   Specific goods that become ascertained subsequent to the contract.

Unascertained or generic goods   These are not identified and agreed upon at the time of sale but defined only by description and may form a part of the lot.

Future goods   These are not possessed by the seller at the time of the contract but will be produced, procured, and supplied by him in the future. It is similar to the goods in an agreement to sell.

Contingent goods   These are of two types as follows.

Contingent goods   The acquisition and supply of these goods depends upon certain conditions, such as arrival of a consignment. The seller is not liable for such goods since it is specifically under conditions.

Contingent and future goods   The procurement of contingent goods depends on a contingency, whereas it is not so in a future contingency. The parties are liable for production or procurement of goods. The promise, for instance, to produce and supply spare parts, must be delivered in the future.

Case 5.3 brings to light the problems one confronts in the subject matter of contract of sale. The problems get compounded in situations where there was no law determining a course of action in a particular commercial activity, and then suddenly a law is made to be implemented.

CASE 5.3	Petitioner: Badri Prasad vs Respondent: State of Madhya Pradesh*

Date: 11 October 1968

Facts: The appellant entered into a contract in respect of certain forests in a *jagir* in Madhya Pradesh. He was entitled to cut teak trees with over 12-inch girth. After the passing of the Abolition of Proprietary Rights (Estates, *Mahals*, Alienated Lands) Act, 1950, a notification was issued vesting the estate in the State. The appellant was prohibited from cutting timber in exercise of his rights under the contract. After some negotiations, a letter was written on 1 February 1955, to the appellant, on behalf of the State, that the appellant's claim to cut trees under the contract would be considered only if he gave up his claim to a sum of ₹17,000 which he had already paid under the contract and was willing to pay a further sum of ₹17,000. The appellant, by his letter dated 5 February 1955 expressed his willingness to pay the additional sum but reserved his right to claim a refund of the first sum. The state government rejected the appellant's right to cut trees. He then filed a suit claiming specific performance of the contract on the grounds: (1) The forest and trees did not vest in the State under the Act; (2) Even if they vested, the standing timber, having been sold to the appellant, did not vest in the State; and (3) In any event a new contract was completed on 5 February 1955, and the appellant was entitled to its specific performance.

Judgement: Appeal fails and dismissed.

Reason: The forest and trees vested in the State under the Act. The plaintiff was entitled to cut teak trees of more than 12-inch girth. It had to be ascertained which trees fell within that description. Till this was ascertained, they were not 'ascertained goods' within Sec. 9 of the Sale of Goods Act. The contract was not to sell the whole of the trees. It is extremely doubtful whether the letter, dated 1 February 1955 is an offer. It seems to be an invitation to the plaintiff to make an offer. Be that as it may, even if it

*Badri Prasad vs State of Madhya Pradesh (AIR 706, 1970); for full text also see http://www.indiankanoon.org/doc/1963535/ (14 December2010).

Contd

Case 5.3 *Contd*

> is treated as an offer there was no unconditional acceptance by the letter dated 5 February 1955. The plaintiff expressly reserved his right to claim a refund of ₹17,000. According to the letter of the Divisional Forest Officer dated 1 February 1955, the plaintiff had to give up his claim to ₹17,000, which he had already paid, and had to pay a further sum of ₹17,000. It is rightly held that the alleged acceptance of the offer made on 1 February 1955 was conditional and qualified.

Before the law about estates came into existence, the entrepreneur in the case had had no problem in his trade. The sudden appearance of the law, which determined and restricted his trade, made matters difficult for him. The lesson that you can learn from the case is that it is difficult to adapt to a new set of laws in a thus-far ongoing trade that functioned without such legislation. In the given case, while the law has solved the problems of proprietary rights and that of trees, it appears the trader got an additional one!

Effects of Destruction of Goods

You know that there are various kinds of goods and equally various ways to deliver them. But goods can age, depreciate, perish, or be damaged. So what is the fate of the contract in such cases? We may consider it in the following two ways.

Goods perishing before the contract

In the case of a contract for the sale of specific goods, that have been damaged or perished without the knowledge of the seller the contract is null and void. The reason for this being *impossibility of performance.* The subject matter of the contract is perished or no more there; the contract cannot be carried out.

Example   A trader in cement sells 100 bags of the product. He is, however, unaware that due to extreme moisture in the warehouse the cement is hardened and is of no use for construction. The merchandise has lost its commercial value. The contract does not stand.

Criteria
(a) Specific or ascertained goods.
(b) Goods must have perished before the contract is made.
(c) The seller has no knowledge of the perished goods at the time of contract.

Goods perishing after the contract but before the sale

In an agreement to sell specific goods, if subsequently the goods perish without the fault of the seller and before the ownership of the goods is transferred, the agreement is void. If the ownership or the title is already passed to the buyer then it becomes his liability.

Example   You go to the dealer to buy a car and make an agreement for sale. You have been notified that your desired car has arrived. In the meantime, someone takes it for a trial drive and crashes it. You know naturally that that particular car is not yours.

Criteria

(a) It must be an agreement to sell and not actual sale.

(b) Goods must be specific.

(c) Goods must have been damaged or perished beyond the recognition of the contract.

(b) The destruction must take place without the fault of either party.

Document of Title to Goods

Thus far you have been told umpteen times about being owner, entitled, holder, proprietor, etc., all of which makes what you have bought or purchased—only yours against the whole world—so to speak. In the ordinary course of business, you may receive a voucher, bill, document, receipt, cash memo, bill of lading, lorry receipt, railway receipt, dock warrant, and several such acknowledgements with which you can prove—and prove so well in a court of law—that you, and you alone, are the owner of such goods. With these you have a title to goods.

Examples with explanation

(a) Bill of lading: Acknowledgement receipt of goods on board of a ship which is signed by the captain of the ship or his authorized representative.

(b) Dock warrant: Document issued by the dock owner.

(c) Warehouse-keeper's or wharfinger's certificate: Document issued by warehouse keeper.

(d) Railway receipt: Document issued by railways acknowledging receipt of goods.

(e) Delivery order: Document of the owner of the goods to the holder of the goods asking the latter to deliver the goods to the person named in the document.

Criteria

(a) Must be used in the ordinary course of business.

(b) The undertaking to deliver the goods to the possessor of the document should be unconditional.

(c) The possessor of document, by virtue of holding such document, must be entitled to receive the goods unconditionally.

5.4 PRICE

(1) The price in a contract of sale may be fixed by the contract or may be left to be fixed in manner thereby agreed or may be determined by the course of dealing between the parties.

(2) Where the price is not determined in accordance with the foregoing provisions, the buyer shall pay the seller a reasonable price. What is a reasonable price is a question of fact dependent on the circumstances of each particular case.

– Sec. 9, The Sale of Goods Act, 1930

Price is what you pay for the value of goods; what you have seen in the Contract Act as *consideration*. It is the consideration for the transfer or agreement to transfer the property in goods from the seller to the buyer. It is not essential that it should be fixed at the time of sale, but you know that it is always payable.

Modes of Fixing the Price

(a) Express statement in the contract.
(b) To be fixed at a later period of time.
(c) Ascertained in the course of dealings. For example, percentage-based commission or discount.
(d) None of the above, but to be fixed reasonably; court may also do such reasonable valuation.
(e) Parties to the contract agree upon a third party—a valuator—to fix the price. Sometimes experts are called upon to assess and fix a 'market price'.

Precaution at Price Fixing

There are often disputes based on price. To avoid these, the following precautions could help:

Price escalation clause
Due to inflation, sellers often demand in their contract for a clause on price escalation. Thus the seller will be able to charge a price not at the time of contract but of the time of delivery of goods. Real estate dealers very often adopt this cause to offset their escalating costs.

Earnest money or security deposit

At times the buyer is asked to pay a part of the payment in advance. This works as a security for the performance of the contract. If the buyer fails to execute the deed, he forfeits his claim on the earnest money; if the seller fails to deliver he would have to return the money. This must be distinguished from money paid in instalments—which is payment in stages and is recoverable in the case of failure by the seller.

Time stipulation

Time of payment is very important; it may be paid before, during, or after a contract; but it is always determined when.

Mode of payment

Any of the negotiable instruments such as cash money, cheque, or draft may be utilized for payments.

5.5 CONDITIONS AND WARRANTIES

A stipulation in a contract of sale with reference to goods which are the subject thereof may be a condition or a warranty.

– Sec. 12, The Sale of Goods Act, 1930

Stipulation is a prerequisite a provision, or qualification that is attached to a contract. Condition in law is very often known by a qualifying clause $p \rightarrow q$. Warranty is an assurance or guarantee in contract to fulfill the obligations of sales of goods; it is a promise of what is claimed to be with guarantee to repair or replace during the stipulated period. (Refer to Figure 5.3 and Table 5.3.)

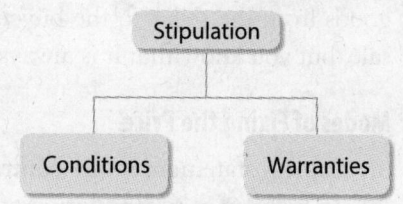

Figure 5.3 Conditions and warranties as stipulation

Table 5.3 Distinction between condition and warranty

Distinction	Condition	Warranty
Stipulation	Essential to the main purpose of the contract, e.g., hotel room will be booked only if payment reaches in advance.	Collateral to the main purpose of contract, e.g., The goods will be replaced only if there is a technical fault within six months.
Breach	Breach gives right to repudiate the contract and also to claim damages, e.g., if the promised goods have not been delivered as per contract, one has the right to rescind the contract and claim loss.	Breach gives right to damages only, e.g., the failure to replace goods results in paying only the damages.
Treatment (Sec. 13)	Breach of condition may be treated as breach of warranty.	Breach of warranty is not breach of condition.
Express (similar in both)	Conditions which have been well-announced, articulated, or written into a contract.	As directly communicated in the contract.
Implied (Secs 14–17)	1. Condition as to title: a) In case of sale: seller has the full right to sell; b) In case of agreement to sell has the right to sell when the property has to be transferred.	1. Quiet possession: a characteristic of title; the buyer has the enjoyment of the goods.
	2. Sale by description: the goods shall correspond with the description, e.g., quality and quantity of goods.	2. Freedom from encumbrances: the buyer has the complete freedom over it and no third party is involved, e.g., when one and the same house is sold to two people, there is an encumbrance.
	3. Condition as quality and fitness: although *caveat emptor* applies, the seller must ensure reasonably good quality.	3. Quality or fitness of usage of trade: the goods bought are of reasonable quality and fit for the purpose for which they have been bought.
	4. Condition as to merchantability: the goods must be free from any latent or hidden defects.	4. Disclose dangerous nature of goods: the seller shall declare if the goods sold by him are capable of causing harm, e.g., when pesticides are sold the buyer must clearly be told of its poisonous nature.
	5. Condition implied by custom: goods have their particular purpose which is implied without expressly saying while buying, e.g., a car is bought for commuting.	

Contd

Table 5.3 *Contd*

	6. Condition implied by sample: there is typical expected nature of product—bulk corresponds to individual specimen, buyer is able to satisfy himself with the specific product, and that it is free from defects. 7. Condition as to wholesomeness: the goods be speak of their integrity as whole and complete and not partial and unfit.	

After going through Case 5.4, you may be able to appreciate the intricacies involved in conditions and warranties after going through Case 5.4 presented next. The judge has to meticulously scrape the differences that lie between these two concepts and the implications of description of goods when the contract was made. Conditions in a contract are very serious since the law demands replacement or goes by the exact description of goods to the contract. Warranties, on the other hand, do not always involve the manufacturer directly, and the dealer is only liable for the damages if they are of technical kind and is not liable for the negligence of the buyer.

Indeed, complying with the description is the safest option for the seller.

CASE 5.4

PETITIONER: Antony Thomas vs RESPONDENT: Ayuppunni Mani*

DATE OF JUDGEMENT: 28 October 1959

FACTS: The respondent had undertaken to deliver to the appellant 125 bundles of cashew nuts and received ₹4,000 in part payment of the price. The suit was for the refund of the said sum with interest at 6 per cent per annum. The appellant rejected the goods on the ground that the bad nuts exceeded the stipulated maximum of twenty per cent. The question for consideration is whether he was entitled to reject the goods as he did.

JUDGEMENT: Appeal is dismissed.

REASON: The answer depends on whether the stipulation regarding the bad nuts was a condition or a warranty. Sec. 12 of the Indian Sale of Goods Act, 1930, deals with conditions and warranties as follows:

1. *A stipulation in a contract of sale with reference to goods which are the subject thereof may be a condition or warranty.*
2. *A condition is a stipulation essential to the main purpose of the contract, the breach of which gives rise to a right to treat the contract as repudiated.*
3. *A warranty is a stipulation collateral to the main purpose of the contract, the breach of which gives rise to a claim for damages but not to a right to reject the goods and treat the contract as repudiated.*

*Antony Thomas vs Ayuppuni Mani (AIR 1960 Ker 176), also for full text see http://www.indiankanoon.org/doc/332073/ (15 December 2010).

Contd

Case 5.4 *Contd*

Whether a stipulation in a contract of sale is a condition of a warranty depends in each case on the construction of the contract. A stipulation may be a condition, though it may be called a warranty in the contract. It is clear that a condition is a more vital undertaking than a warranty, and that the consequences that flow from its breach are different. The *comparative degree of gravity* spells a condition as distinct from one, which amounts only to a warranty. The distinction is of great importance. The breach of a condition entitles the injured party to repudiate the contract, to refuse the goods, and, if he has already paid for them, to recover the price. The only remedy for the breach of a warranty is the recovery of damages. The sale was by description, and there is an implied condition that the goods shall correspond with the description. The section on which he relies is Sec. 15 of the Indian Sale of Goods Act, 1930, which provides that *where there is a contract for the sale of goods by description, there is an implied condition that the goods shall correspond with the description.* The general principle of this implied condition is clear and founded on the consensual basis of the law of contract. The stipulation is definite, and there are no words which indicate any room for elasticity in complying with the stipulation. The sale was, therefore, a sale by description and that there was an implied condition that the goods must comply with the description.

The Principle of Caveat Emptor

Subject to the provisions of this Act and of any other law for the time being in force, there is no implied warranty or condition as to the quality or fitness for any particular purpose of goods supplied under a contract of sale…

– Sec. 16, The Sale of Goods Act, 1930

The object of Case 5.4 was primarily to determine the return of the payment made for goods—which did not bespeak the description of goods, i.e., being defective over a certain limit. The case was judged on the laws governing conditions and warranties. However, if the counsel to the respondent were to direct his arguments and made the judge to consider it from the point of view of the principle *of caveat emptor,* he could have easily succeeded.

Caveat emptor—buyer beware—stands for the practical skill and judgement of the buyer in his choice of goods for purchase. It is the business of the buyer to judge for himself that what he buys has its use and worth for him. No one is forced to buy. He must use his freedom to buy with prudence. Once bought, and if the buy is not up to his expectations, then he alone is to blame and no one else.

The purchase manager of a large company has to take crucial decisions as to the purchases required for the company. For instance, buying a manufacturing plant from a foreign country would involve an agreement to sale for several million dollars. In order to make such a monumental decision, he would have to rely on inputs of data from several agencies and consultancies. Upon analysis of this data, finally, the purchase department has to come to a point where his decision would be awaited. Once such a decision is taken the purchase mechanism sets in. Yet despite all the hard work, the decision to buy such a plant may go awry: it may be found that the plant machinery involves exclusive requirement of personnel from the importing country or that certain technical specifications were not factored in when the purchase decision was made. All of these elements may add up heavily to the costs, which were unforeseen before and therefore lead to litigation. Unfortunately, such litigation, apart from delaying the business, would do nothing else to mitigate the problem because the legal principle is well-annunciated: *buyer beware.*

The earlier-mentioned Sec. 16 of the Act further states five exceptions to the rule or the principle of caveat emptor.

Fitness for buyer's purpose—Sec. 16(1) It happens when the buyer expressly or by implication makes known to the seller the reasons for his purchase and his dependence on the seller's skill and judgement of the goods of their quality and quantity—the description corresponds to the goods. Thus, the seller must supply goods that are fit for the buyer's purpose.

Sale under a trade or patent name—Sec. 16(1) If the goods are of trade or patent mark, there is no implied condition of the reasonableness or fitness of the product; by the very essence of a trademark or patent, the correspondence of description to the goods is taken for granted. The seller is bound to sell goods of merchantable quality.

Merchantable quality—Sec. 16(2) There is a custom or tradition where a seller has been dealing in goods which are according to the accepted description. For instance, a bicycle would be one that is technically made for transport by paddling and that is in condition corresponding to its product description. It is a reasonably good product and the buyer may well assume it to be so.

Usage of trade—Sec. 16(3) An implied warranty or condition as to its quality and fitness for a particular purpose may be annexed by the usage of trade.

Consent by fraud It happens when the seller knowingly conceals the defects which could not be discovered by the buyer with reasonable application of skill and judgement at the time of purchase. The consent is obtained by fraud and, hence, the seller cannot charge the buyer for his negligence to examine.

5.6 EFFECTS OF THE CONTRACT

TEXT

Goods must be ascertained. (1) Where there is a contract for the sale of unascertained goods, no property in the goods is transferred to the buyer unless and until the goods are sanctioned. Property passes when intended to pass. (2) Where there is a contract for the sale of specific or ascertained goods, the property in them is transferred to the buyer at such time as the parties to the contract intend it to be transferred.

– Secs 18 and 19(1), The Sale of Goods Act, 1930

Secs 18–30 of the Sale of Goods Act deal with effects of contract. The essence of the effect of sale of goods contract is 'transfer of property' from the seller to the buyer (Table 5.4).

MANAGER'S TAKEAWAY

- Integrity of goods: quality and quantity.
- Honesty in price: money for value (seller), value for money (customer).

Transfer of Property in Goods

Some basic concepts at the beginning of this new theme are as follows.

Proprietary rights The property rights pass from the seller to the buyer.

Property in goods   The ownership of goods.

Possession of goods   The physical custody or control of goods.

Significance of transfer of property

Table 5.4 presents the significance of transfer of property.

Table 5.4   Significance of transfer of property

Significance	Meaning	Example
Ownership	The ownership passes from the seller to the buyer, with all the rights thereof.	The buyer, now owner, may do with the goods what he likes; if these goods are not supplied or are damaged while not in his possession, he may even sue the seller.
Risk	Once the ownership passes from seller to the buyer, so does the risk. In case of damage or any other limitation, the rightful owner bears the risk.	Unless otherwise mentioned in the contract specifically who would bear the risk of damage or loss, inevitably its on the rightful owner/buyer.
Action against third parties	The third parties involved in the delivery of goods are liable for action from the owner.	If the goods are damaged or destroyed by a third party, the rightful owner may take action against them.
Suit for price	The seller can sue the buyer for price.	The seller can sue only when the buyer has become the owner.
Insolvency	The official receiver or assignee takes over the goods.	It depends who has become insolvent—buyer or seller—and decide accordingly.

Passing of Property

Two things are essential for transfer of property (see Figure 5.4). These are (a) goods must be ascertained, and (b) Intention to pass property in the goods.

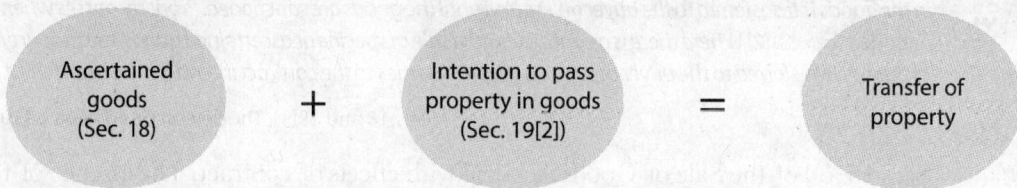

Ascertained goods (Sec. 18)   +   Intention to pass property in goods (Sec. 19[2])   =   Transfer of property

Figure 5.4   Essentials for transfer of property

Salient Features of Transfer of Property

Table 5.5 presents the features of transfer of property.

Case 5.5—goods sent on approval—the problem was how long is long enough to approve or return the goods.

Table 5.5 Features of transfer of property

Features	Explanation	Example
Specific goods Secs 20–22	The goods identified and agreed upon: • There should be an unconditional contract. • Goods should be in deliverable state.	You place an order for 1,000 bags of cement. You agree with the seller/factory and you are promised that the goods will be delivered.
Sale of goods on approval	When the goods are delivered to the buyer on approval basis, from the moment of approval the goods transferred to the ownership of the buyer.	A book seller sends a consignment of books to the library; the librarian approves some and keeps them and sends back the rest.
Sale of unascertained goods (Sec. 23)	The goods are not transferred to the buyer until and unless they are ascertained.	You buy 100 bags of cement and pay for it and take it away; you promise to take another 100, but you have not ascertained unconditionally, that is, you may take them if you need—there is no contract for the next 100 bags.
Appropriation	It is a process of selection of goods which can be done either by the seller or the buyer: • by the seller to sell. • by the buyer to purchase. When they both do it, then the contract comes into being.	The cement dealer selected 100 bags that you approved, paid, and took away. Upon your consent, he sets apart another 100 bags, but you failed to take them away and they got damaged. You are liable for the damage because you had consented to take them although the payment was pending.
Reservation of tight of disposal (Sec. 25)	Whether property in goods is specific or appropriated as long as the seller has certain conditions, the ownership will not be transferred until those conditions are fulfilled.	The seller draws upon the buyer, a bill of exchange for the price and sends him the bill of exchange along with the railway receipt to secure acceptance of the bill; the buyer is required to honour the bill for taking delivery of the goods. The seller reserves the right of disposal till the bill of exchange is accepted by the buyer—only then the property in goods will pass to the buyer.
Transfer of title to goods	Only the owner of the property in goods can transfer the ownership-title to goods. Principle: *Nemo dat quad non habet*—No one can give a better title than he himself has. This ensures ownership; and only an owner can dispose it according to his will to another. Title by estoppel: The buyer may obtain title if the owner has no objection to a third party selling the property in goods. Sale by mercantile agent allows the transfer of title.	You steal a car and sell it to your friend. Your friend has the car but does not have the title to it. By stealing a car you cannot own its title, and what you do not own you cannot transfer. The car belongs neither to you nor your friend who physically has it: it can only belong to its rightful owner who can claim title to it. X sells you a box of dry fruits in the presence of Y who is the real owner who, by an act of omission, leads you to believe X is the owner. You buy goods from mercantile agent who furnishes documents of bona fide sales in the ordinary course of business or with the express consent of the owner.

CASE 5.5

PETITIONER: Hoogly Chinsurah Municipality vs RESPONDENT: Spence Ltd*

DATE OF JUDGEMENT: 18 July 1977

FACTS: Hoogly Chinsurah Municipality contracted with Spence Ltd to buy a tractor on the condition that if the municipality was not satisfied, it would reject the tractor. The municipality took possession of the tractor and after using it for a month and a half it rejected it. The suit was filed upon the unwillingness of the tractor company to accept it.

JUDGEMENT: Appeal dismissed.

REASON: The municipality had not only used the tractor but also a reasonable time had elapsed. Hence, the property in the tractor had already passed to the municipality and, therefore, it could not reject it.

*AIR 1978 Cal. 49; also see http://www.indiankanoon.org/doc/698178/ (15 December 2010).

It pays to use common sense. If you have got goods on approval basis, and you use as though you are going to keep them, then the approval is implied. In the earlier case, had the municipality only test-used the tractor and rejected the offer within a day or two, their claim would have been upheld if they were to prove certain defects in the tractor. It is also beneficial if a definite approval time is fixed in the contract to avoid such problems.

5.7 PERFORMANCE OF THE CONTRACT

TEXT

It is the duty of the seller to deliver the goods and of the buyer to accept and pay for them, in accordance with the terms of the contract of sale.

– Sec. 31, The Sale of Goods Act, 1930

The performance of contract is a simple transaction where the seller delivers the goods and the buyer pays. If there is something more complex, then this is stated in the contract as special terms.

Seller Delivers goods and receives consideration.

Buyer Accepts and pays for the goods.

Terms Contract can have terms of delivery and payment.

Delivery of Goods

Delivery of goods may be defined as voluntary transfer of possession of goods from seller to the buyer. It is distinguished in three ways as presented in Figure 5.5.

MANAGER'S TAKEAWAY

- Be aware of your ever-changing role as buyer and seller.
- Make sure you have the title of the properties in goods, both when you buy and sell.

Actual delivery The goods are handed over by the seller to the buyer or to his authorized agent; it has the effect of putting the goods in the possession of the buyer: Sec. 33.

Symbolic delivery The goods are too bulky and unwieldy such as large machinery, where a symbolic passing of documents or keys and the like demonstrate the transfer of goods.

Constructive or delivery by attornment A third party (bailee) who is in possession of the goods of the seller at the time of sale acknowledges to the buyer that he holds the goods on his behalf: Sec. 36(3).

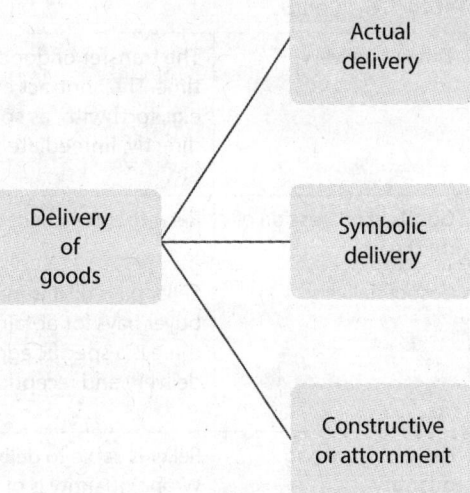

Figure 5.5 Delivery of goods

Delivery of goods and payment of the price are concurrent conditions. But in the world of seller–buyer interaction, it adjusts itself to the prevailing conditions. Rules of delivery, as mentioned in Table 5.6, are in this perspective.

Table 5.6 Rules for delivery of goods

Rule	Definition	Example
Part delivery	Goods being delivered as part of the whole; if the part is severed from the whole then the transfer is not of the whole but only partial.	(a) Whole: You buy 100 bags of cement, and you are at the moment delivered only ten—but you are the owner of the whole. (b) Partial: You want only 100 bags of cement, but you pay only for ten and take ten; rest of the 90 bags are not part of the sale of goods.
Buyer to apply for delivery	Unless the buyer places his demand, there is no sale of goods, unless there is a contract to that effect. It is a logical impossibility to supply you something that you have not asked for.	Suddenly there arrives a truck with 100 bags of cement to your doorstep. You only wonder who placed the order. On the other hand, if you have a contract for regular supply of 100 bags of cement at the beginning of every month then it is a standing order and you will receive it until you expressly cancel it.
Seller's duty to deliver	Seller must make the goods deliverable.	You order cement, it follows that it must be there to be taken by you.

Contd

Table 5.6 *Contd*

Time of delivery	The transfer of goods happens in time. The contract of delivery has terms, e.g., forthwith, as soon as possible, directly, immediately, reasonable time,* etc.	Depending on your order you get the supply of cement, as you have a particular schedule that is agreed upon.
Goods in possession of third party	Refer to attornment above.	
Cost of delivery	Seller pays till it is made deliverable; buyer pays for obtaining delivery, unless there is a specific agreement about delivery and reception.	Your company forwards coal as export with the agreement of Free On Board, that is, you pay until it is put on board; it implies that the buyer will pay for rest of its journey by sea or air as the case may be.
Delivery of wrong quantity	Seller is liable to deliver agreed quantity. Wrong quantity is of three kinds: *Short delivery:* quantity delivered less than what is agreed. *Excess delivery:* the delivered quantity overshoots the order. *Delivery of mixed goods:* apart from the goods of contracted description other types too are included in the delivery.	Short delivery is when you get 50 bags of cement instead of 100. Excess delivery is when you get more than 100 bags of cement while your order is just for 100. Mixed delivery is when along with your order for conventional cement of 100 bags, you get also white cement, water-proofing cement, etc.
Delivery in instalments	Delivery of goods in stages instead of immediate and complete. The rule is for full and immediate delivery; however, a buyer-seller agreement can work out for a delivery in stages. If the seller repudiates contract, the buyer is relieved of his obligation to accept the balance of the goods; if the buyer repudiates the contract then the seller is not liable to deliver the balance instalments.	If your cement supplier, who supplies your total purchase of thousand bags of cement in ten instalments, and then becomes erratic in supply or sends defective goods, does not follow the agreed schedule, etc., which tantamount to repudiation of contract, then you may stop the instalments.
Delivery to carrier or wharfinger	The seller is authorised or obliged as per the contract to deliver goods to the carrier—surface, sea, or air transporter; there may also exist a third person—wharfinger, for the safe custody goods.	Your iron ore is loaded on board of a sea carrier by the seller and is also insured for its safety. If it is lost before its boarding, the seller has the right to sue the insurance company.
Kinds of delivery conditions**	F.A.S.: Free alongside ship. F.A.R.: Free alongside rail.	The seller notifies the buyer that the goods have been delivered by ship. The seller notifies the buyer that the goods have been delivered by rail.

Contd

*A reasonable time to deliver perishable goods will be sooner than the non-perishable ones.

**Although this rule may be separately considered as types of contract in respect to delivery of goods from seller's perspective, it is placed in this column to let the student understand it as the seller's obligation.

Table 5.6 *Contd*

	F.O.B.: Free on board.	The seller notifies the buyer that the goods have been delivered on board.
	F.O.R.: Free on rail.	The seller notifies the buyer that the goods have been delivered by rail.
	C.I.F.: Cost, insurance, and freight.	The seller notifies the buyer that the goods have been delivered and insurance and freight costs have been paid.
	Ex-ship contract	The seller delivers the goods to the buyer's destination.
	Risk of deterioration in transit	Depending on the contract, respectively, seller and buyer are responsible for liability.

Rights and Duties of the Buyer

TEXT

Where goods are delivered to the buyer, which he has not previously examined, he is not deemed to have accepted them unless and until he has a reasonable opportunity of examining them for the purpose of ascertaining whether they are in conformity with the contract.

– Sec. 41, The Sale of Goods Act, 1930

The acceptance or rejection by the buyer creates certain rights and duties. The law protects the buyer in terms of his rights to examine the goods and at the same time obliges him to be a responsible buyer by limiting him to certain liabilities when he rejects the goods (refer Table 5.7).

Case 5.6 covers not only the right to examine goods, but also other aspects of delivery of goods that you would have noticed under the rights and duties of the buyer. You have also seen how often the principle of *caveat emptor* has been referred. There also arise issues of what the seller will do if his goods are not accepted by the buyer. The biggest problem for the seller is what to do with the goods that have been transported to distant places. Exporters very often suffer from these problems. Companies in the developed countries often reject goods from the companies in developing countries. More often than not the reasons are familiar: Sub-standard quality, adulteration, and delayed arrival.

 MANAGER'S TAKEAWAY

- Use all your skills when you buy.
- Use all your knowledge when you sell.

Table 5.7 Rights and duties of the buyer

Rights	Duties
Receive delivery as per contract (Secs 31–32)	Accept the goods (Sec. 31)
Reject goods when not as per contract (Sec. 37)	Apply for delivery (Sec. 35)
Repudiate (Sec. 38[1])	Demand delivery at reasonable time/hour (Sec. 36)
Receive notice of insurance (Sec. 39[3])	Accept instalment delivery (Sec. 38[2])

Contd

Table 5.7 *Contd*

Examine goods before accepting (Sec. 41)	Responsibility of risk in the course of transportation (Sec. 40)
Against the seller for breach of contract to suit for (Sec. 57) (a) Price (b) Specific performance (Sec. 58) (c) Breach of warranty (Sec. 59) (d) Repudiation of contract before date (Sec. 60) (e) Interest (Sec. 61[1])	Intimate the seller on rejection of goods (Sec. 43)
	Take delivery (Sec. 44)
	Pay the price (Sec. 55)
	Damages for non-acceptance (Sec. 56)

CASE 5.6

PETITIONER: Dharampal & Co., Agra VS RESPONDENT: Firm Kila Gatla Ram Chandra Rao & Co., Vizianagaram*

DATE OF JUDGEMENT: 29 January 1980

FACTS: The suit for recovery of ₹1,850 as damages from the respondent firm was decreed by the trial court and future interest at the rate of 4 per cent per annum. A contract was entered into between the parties by means of a telegram for the purchase of 250 bags of peas at the rate of ₹37 per bag, deliverable F.O.R. at Vizianagram. The buyer, namely the respondent, indicated in the telegram that the peas should be friable at 6 1/2.** This agreement was made on 3 February 1962. On the same day, a wagon was indented by the plaintiff for the dispatch of goods. He received the wagon on 14 February 1962 and loaded the peas and dispatched the same day. The wagon reached Vizianagram on 16 February 1962. Meanwhile the plaintiff had also sent a *hundi* to the defendant and dispatched the R.R. (railway receipt) for collection through bank. The defendant did not receive or accept the goods at Vizianagram and he also did not honour the *hundi* or take the R.R. from the bank. The defendant's stand was that the peas sent were not of the contracted quality and therefore, he sought to repudiate the contract. The plaintiff had to send a messenger to Vizianagram who took delivery of the consignment of the goods after paying demurrage to the Railways and sold it to a local dealer at a lower rate with the result that he incurred loss in the price of the goods also. He, therefore, in this suit claimed a sum of ₹833 as demurrage, ₹142 as miscellaneous expenses, and ₹875 as the difference in price, totaling a sum of ₹1,850. The plaintiff's stand was that the defendant could not refuse to take delivery of the goods and was not entitled to repudiate the contract. He was afforded an opportunity of examining the goods but he did not avail of the same. The quality of the goods sent was according to the contract.

---

*Dharampal & Co., Agra vs Firm Kila Gatla Ram Chandra Rao & Co. Vizianagaram, (AIR 1980 All 316); also see http://www.indiankanoon.org/doc/1980471 (22 December 2010).
**Friability technically implies that which is pulverizable, turned into powder.

Contd

Case 5.6 *Contd*

JUDGEMENT: The appeal upheld.

REASON: The Allahabad High Court upheld the verdict of the trial court which held that the time was not the essence of the contract and the quality of the goods supplied was not inferior to the contracted quality, the plaintiff suffered damages as claimed and the court had territorial jurisdiction to try the suit. Lastly, it was held that the plaintiff was entitled to the damages and the suit was accordingly decreed. The lower appellate court formulated two points for consideration. The first point was about the territorial jurisdiction of the court at Agra to try the suit. This was held in the affirmative and in favour of the plaintiff. The second point was whether the contract was in respect of the goods of specific description and the plaintiff failed to satisfy the defendant about the quality of goods, if so, its effect. This was answered by holding that the goods contracted for purchase, were of specific description and the plaintiff failed to satisfy the defendant about the quality of the goods and as such was not entitled to any amount claimed by way of damages.

5.8   RIGHTS OF UNPAID SELLER AGAINST THE GOODS

The seller of goods is deemed to be an 'unpaid seller' within the meaning of this Act—(a) When the whole of the price has not been paid or tendered. (b) When a bill of exchange or other negotiable instrument has been received as conditional payment, and the conditions on which it was received has not been fulfilled by reason of the dishonour of the instrument or otherwise.

– Sec. 45(1), The Sale of Goods Act, 1930

If your responsibilities as manager are that of a salesperson or an agency responsible for billing and receiving payments or a small entrepreneur going for collection of payments for the goods you deal in, then you face a barrage of problems: delays, postponements, bargaining for reduction, complaints about goods and delivery, bouncing of cheques, fraud, plain lies, and myriad excuses to part with money. The property has passed from you to the customer and while he enjoys the benefits, you remain unpaid.

As mentioned earlier and in Sec. 45 of the Sale of Goods Act, these define an unpaid seller: One who is not paid, and even if paid, the payment is conditional. All the negotiable instruments are essentially conditional and until they are honoured, the seller remains bereft of payment. Paragraph 2 of the same section further declares that the term *seller* holds good also for one who is the representative of a seller such as an agent who has the responsibility to sell goods and collect payments.

Rights of an Unpaid Seller

From what has been said in this chapter and from the earlier chapters on Contract Law, you may logically infer the rights of a seller. To give further impetus to your imagination, Figure 5.6 will help imbed a new mental model.

In this way, the seller is protected by the law. The right to lien is very important since it still has the custody of goods in the possession of the seller. He also has the right to stop all transport. Finally, he has the right to resale of goods, depending on the contracted time period

Stage I: Distinction rights of unpaid seller

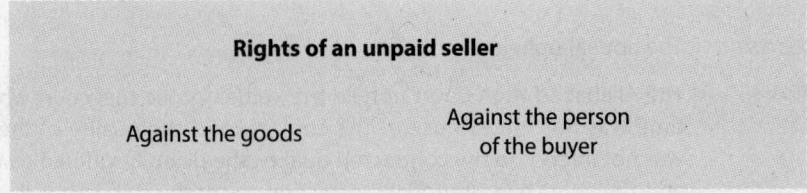

Stage II: Rights of unpaid seller against goods

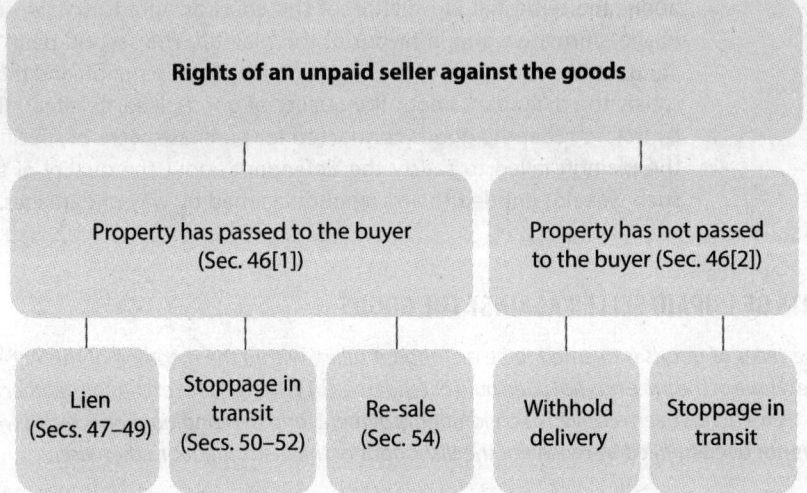

Stage III: Rights of unpaid seller against goods

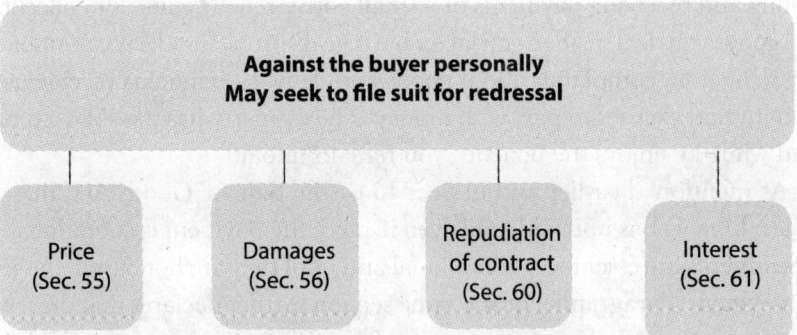

Figure 5.6 Rights of an underpaid seller

and the nature of the goods, such as perishability and in cases of insolvency of the buyer. The second category of rights which is directly against the buyer ensures that the seller can demand redressal through the court of law for price, damages, repudiation of contract, and interest.

Case 5.7 clearly demonstrates that the right of resale can be exercised only when the goods being still unascertained, and no property has passed from the seller to the buyer. In the earlier model of the unpaid seller, each category may be examined to find out the nuances of the sections of the law regarding this important issue.

CASE 5.7

PETITIONER: P.S.N.S. Ambalavana Chettiar & Co.,   vs   RESPONDENT: Express Newspapers Ltd, Bombay*

DATE OF JUDGEMENT: 10 November 1967**

FACTS: Suit under Indian Sale of Goods Act, Secs 18 and 54(2): Sale of unascertained goods: When property passes; repudiation of contract, vendor's right of resale when arises. On 13 November 1951, the respondent agreed to sell to the appellants a stock of 415 tonnes of newsprint in sheets then lying in the respondent's godown. On 26 November, the parties varied the contract by agreeing that the appellants would buy only 300 tons out of the stock of 415 tonnes. After taking delivery of a part of the newsprint, the appellants refused to take delivery of the balance and repudiated the contract on 29 March 1952. On 21 April the respondent, after notice to the appellants, resold the balance at a lesser rate. The suit filed by the respondent claiming from the appellants the deficiency on resale was decreed.

JUDGEMENT: The claim of the respondent unsustainable.

REASON: As the respondent was not a pledger of the newsprint, the respondent had no right to sell the goods under Sec. 176 of the Indian Contract Act. 1872. A seller can claim as damages the difference between the contract price and the amount realized on resale of the goods where he has the right of resale under Sec. 54(2) of the Indian Sale of Goods Act, 1930. But this statutory power of resale arises only if the property in the goods has passed to the buyer subject to the lien of the unpaid seller. Under Sec. 18 of the Sale of Goods Act, it is a condition precedent to the passing of property under a contract of sale that the goods are ascertained. In the present case, when the contract was originally entered into for the sale of 415 tonnes there was an unconditional contract for the sale of specific goods in a deliverable state and the property in those goods then passed to the appellants.

*AIR 1968, SC 741; also see http://www.rishabhdara.com/sc/view.php?case=3439 (22 December 2010).
**Bombay because the Case being in 1968, before it being renamed as Mumbai.

5.9 SUITS OF BREACH OF THE CONTRACT

TEXT

Where there is a breach of warranty by the seller, or where the buyer elects or is compelled, by reason of such breach of warranty, to treat any breach of a condition on the part of the seller as a breach of warranty, the buyer is not only entitled to reject the goods; but also may—(a) Set up against the seller the breach of warranty in diminution or extinction of the price; or (b) Sue the seller for damages for breach of warranty.

– Sec. 59, The Sale of Goods Act, 1930

You are already familiar with breach of contract by the buyer and the unpaid sellers rights from the preceding. You also must have noted how a seller may seek remedy against the goods as well as against the person of the buyer. Just as the seller has the right to sue the buyer, like with the

MANAGER'S TAKEAWAY

• Creditors have good memory.
• Debtors have short memory

law gives opportunity to the buyer wherein the event of any breach of contract from the seller's side warrants a suit against him.

For remedies against the breach of contract by the buyer, see Figure 5.7.

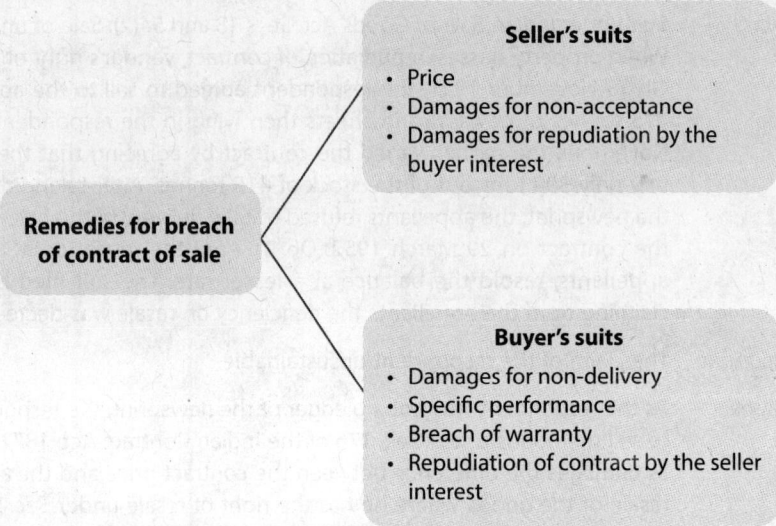

Figure 5.7 Remedies for breach of contract

Table 5.8 clearly shows the remedies or suits available for the buyer against the seller for any breach of contract.

Table 5.8 Remedies against seller for breach of contract

Damages for non-delivery	Seller wrongfully neglects or refuses to deliver. The assessment will be done upon the criteria of availability in the market and the comparative difference in price; if for resale, then the loss differential.
Price	The buyer has paid but the goods are not delivered. Remedy: He can recover the amount paid.
Specific performance	When the goods are ascertained, the buyer may seek the very same goods; just damages would be adequate.
Breach of warranty	The buyer has to accept the goods; but he may institute breach of warranty: (a) in extinction or diminution of the price; (b) sue the seller for breach of warranty.
Repudiation of contract before the due date	When the seller repudiates the contract before the delivery date, the buyer: (a) may sue the seller for rescinding the contract and claim damages for anticipatory breach; (b) may wait till the due date and accordingly take action by demanding damages for the stipulated delivery.

CASE 5.8   PETITIONER: Sitaram Srigopal vs RESPONDENT: Smt. Daulata Devi (Dead) By Heirs*

DATE OF JUDGEMENT: 1 October 1979

FACTS: On 26 August 1950, Tulsiram Shaw sold 1540 'value sluice water flanged and drilled to B.S.T.C.4'. specific goods for a sum of ₹35,200 to the partnership firm of Sitaram Srigopal. The latter paid the entire price in cash to the former. Tulsiram Shaw further promised to hand over the release order of the goods and/or delivery order by 28 August 1950, to enable the firm to take delivery of these goods from Panagarh. Tulsiram neglected or refused to deliver the said release order in spite of demands by Sitaram Srigopal. On the preceding allegations, Sitaram Srigopal instituted a suit in the high court of Calcutta against the original defendant, Tulsiram Shaw, on 15 January 1951, for specific performance by the defendants to deliver the said specific goods on the ground that these goods were not readily available in the market and were of some big value and, therefore, damages would not afford adequate relief for the loss of the goods. In the alternative, the plaintiff claimed refund of the price of ₹35,200 with interest at 6 per cent per annum and a further sum of ₹1,32,559 as damages being the difference between the contract price and the market price of the goods on the date of the breach, namely, the end of August 1950. The suit was resisted by the original defendant, who, in his written statement, pleaded that he was, at all material times, ready and willing to deliver the release order to the plaintiff and had, in fact, offered to do so, but the latter requested the defendant to cancel the contract and refund the amount of ₹35,200 by cheque on 21 September 1950, but the plaintiff declined to accept it. During the pendency of the suit, the original defendant died on 15 November 1959 and his widow, Smt. Daulata Devi and heirs were impleaded as defendants in place of the deceased.

JUDGEMENT: Appeal fails. Dismissed with costs.

REASON: It is clear from the above conspectus that the evidence produced by the plaintiff was not cogent, convincing, and reliable to establish, either that the goods in question comprised were in brand new condition, or the market price of goods of similar specifications in August 1950. In view of the circumstantial evidence on the record, the court below was not wrong in holding that the market price of the goods in question in August 1950 was the same at which they were purchased by the plaintiff from Tulsiram Bhagwandas and, consequently, the plaintiff was not entitled to any damages, apart from the refund of ₹35,200 which was the price paid by him.

*Sitaram Srigopal vs Smt. Daulata Devi (Dead) By Heirs, AIR 1979 SC 1225, (1979) 4 SCC 351; also see http://www.indiankanoon.org/doc/221867 (23 December 2010).

MANAGER'S TAKEAWAY
- Those smart commendations made in the course of the sale do not bind the seller.
- One should not buy something in ignorance.

Case 5.8 that establishes whether the goods are readily available in the market, the measure of damage is, prima facie, the difference between the contract price and the market price at the time when the goods ought to have been delivered, or if no time was fixed at the time of refusal to deliver. In all the cases, the buyer must establish the difference.

From what has been said earlier in this chapter thus far, it has been established that if the seller and buyer are aware of their rights and duties, most of the problems would not arise at all. It is the lack of awareness as well as their practice that puts them to go through disputes and litigation. This hampers smooth business. Look at Figure 5.8. Play with this bilateral relationship between the seller and the buyer, juxtapose the roles; it is a good exercise for the manager whose role frequently changes as seller and buyer.

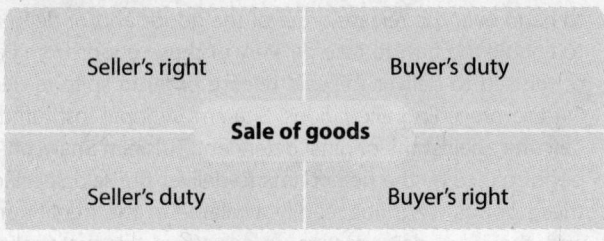

Figure 5.8   Sale of goods

5.10   IMPLIED TERMS, TIME, AUCTION, TAX, AND OTHER MATTERS

TEXT

The sale is complete when the auctioneer announces its completion by the fall of the hammer or in other customary manner, and, until such announcement is made, any bidder may retract his bid.

– Sec. 64(2), The Sale of Goods Act, 1930

Sotheby's in England is the world's most famous auction house where articles of antiquity, celebrity objects, highly rated paintings, and collector's items are auctioned. Closer home, near Fort Mumbai, early hours of the morning are the most exciting as kinds of fresh flowers are auctioned. In the similar way before the sunrise throughout the length and breadth of the country, all the life's essentials such as vegetables, fruits, fish, and scores of other materials are auctioned.

Auction is public sale. When you go to a shop to buy a wrist watch, it is an individual, private sale; it is between you the buyer and the seller. At an auction an article of sale is exhibited publicly. The auctioneer is an agent of the owner of the article who performs the role of a salesman for the former. There are a number of prospective buyers for one and the same article. They announce their bids or their offer, in terms of money. The auctioneer announces the same loudly. The bids are raised one by one until all others give up and finally one is left with the highest bid. The auctioneer ceremoniously announces the last bid thrice adding to good measure the count 1, 2, and 3. Then the last act of the ceremony: A knock, by bringing down the hammer that signals the contract is consummated. The bid can be retracted before the fall of the hammer; once the hammer falls, the bid is sealed and the article is considered sold.

Procedure of an Auction

Figure 5.9 shows the procedure of an auction.

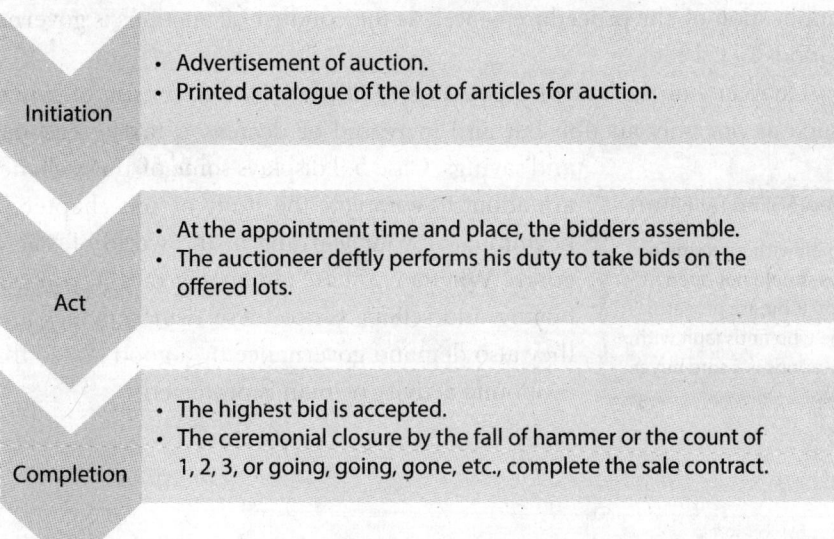

Figure 5.9 Auction

Rules of Auction Sale

Auction calls for certain regulations to make the offer and acceptance, contract of sale of goods, and the passing of those goods to the rightful owner (refer to Table 5.9). Strict

Table 5.9 Rules of auction sale

Rule	Explanation
Sale of goods in lots—Sec. 64(1)	Each lot of sale is prima facie deemed to be the subject of a separate sale.
Completion of sale—Sec. 64(2)	Transfer of goods: Formal conclusion at the fall of hammer or any customary sign of closure. A bidder may revoke his bid prior to such a closure, but will forfeit the security deposit.
Seller's bid—Sec. 64(3) and (4)	Can the seller himself bid? Yes, provided such a right is expressly reserved. The bidding can be done by the seller or his representative. However, a secret agent or representative employed to hike the auction price is fraudulent and against the law.
Reserve price—Sec. 65	Reserve price is the fixed price below which the owner is not willing to sell. If the bids fall short of the reserve price, the auctioneer can withdraw.
Knockout	The bidders form a group to avoid competition with the understanding of disposing the lot among themselves.
Damping	It consists of adversely influencing the bidders from bidding: declaring the goods as defective, obstructing examination of goods, intimidating, etc. These actions are contrary to the law.
Implied warranties	There are some inherent or implied warranties in auction: (a) Authority to sell (b) Without defect and clear title (c) Give goods against the price (d) Guarantees possession by the bidder

application of the procedure as well as the conduct of auctions is governed by the Sale of Goods Act, 1930.

Chapter 7 of the Sale of Goods Act, 1930, Secs 62–66, consists of miscellaneous matters such as not only auction but also increased or decreased taxes, reasonable time, repeal, and savings. Case 5.9 displays some of these elements. Though you are about to complete the study of this chapter, in reality it is the beginning of your learning in the world of sale and purchase of goods. Whether you are a manager or not, you cannot live without buying and selling. Since these twin activities are so close to life, they also demand governance by a good law so that this important economic activity of man is protected.

🔨 MANAGER'S TAKEAWAY

- A man without a smiling face should not open a shop (Chinese proverb).
- One who finds fault with the goods is a sure buyer.

CASE 5.9

PETITIONER: **Consolidated Coffee Ltd** vs RESPONDENT: **Coffee Board, Bangalore***

DATE OF JUDGEMENT: **15 April 1980**

FACTS: The Coffee Board of India is a statutory corporation. Export of coffee outside India is particularly controlled under the Act and the Rules by the Coffee Board. Coffee can be exported either by the Coffee Board directly to parties outside India or the Coffee Board authorizes other exporters to effect such exports. For effecting exports through other exporters, the Coffee Board periodically conducts auctions known as 'export auctions' and it follows a procedure in that behalf. To be able to bid at these auctions, exporters have to get themselves registered with the Board.

The Coffee Board issued a circular dated 7 February 1977 to the registered exporters of coffee, by which it took the view that in order to avail of the benefit of Sec. 5(3) of the Central Sales Tax Act as amended by Amendment Act 103 of 1976, in respect of the coffee sold by it at the export auctions, the registered exporters (bidders) should satisfy three conditions: (a) they must have an export contract (i.e., either agreement or order) from a foreign buyer; (b) they must have it on hand at the time when they participate in the export auction; and (c) they should give proof of the export of the coffee purchased at the auction.

The petitioners, who are registered exporters of coffee, therefore, have filed under Article 32 of the Constitution raising an important question of proper construction of Sec. 5(3), of the Central Sales Tax Act as amended by Amending Act (103 of 1976) and also challenging the constitutional validity of the circular dated 7 February 1977, issued by the Coffee Board, whereby it required the petitioners and other registered exporters of coffee to furnish contingency deposits or bank guarantees equal to the amount of sales tax in respect of the exempted sales under the said Sec. 5(3) of the Central Sales Tax Act and praying for its cancellation or withdrawal and consequential reliefs.

---

*Consolidated Coffee Ltd vs Coffee Board, Bangalore 1980 AIR 1468, 1980 SCR (3) 625; also see http://www. indiankanoon.org/doc/1542029/ (20 December 2010).

Contd

Case 5.9 *Contd*

REASON: Sec. 5(3) of the Central Sales Tax Act as amended by the Amendment Act 103 of 1976 is not ultra vires to Article 286(2) of the Constitution and the said provision neither creates any legal Action nor is it beyond the power or authority conferred on Parliament by Article 286(2) of the Constitution. [645A-D] It is true that the word deemed has been used in Sec. 5(3) but the same word has been used not merely in Sec. 5(1) but also in the other two Sec.s 3 and 4 of Chapter II of the Central Sales Tax Act which has the heading 'Formulations of Principles' for determining when a sale or purchase of goods takes place in the course of inter-state trade or commerce or outside a State or in the course of export or import.

In the penultimate sales (sales of coffee effected to registered exporters at export auctions conducted by the Coffee Board) the property in the coffee sold there passes to the buyer immediately upon payment of full price, weight, and setting apart of coffee for delivery to the buyer under Cls. 19 and 20 of the Auction Conditions and it would be at this stage, i.e., just before this stage is reached that the agreement with or order from a foreign buyer must be available or produced in order to attract Sec. 5 (3) of the Central Sales Tax Act, 1956. [674C-D]

Exporters' assessments or recoveries, if made in conformity with judgement, need not be disturbed. Similarly, contingency deposits or bank guarantees already obtained by the Coffee Board from the registered exporters, if they are contrary to judgement, will be refunded or released forthwith, as the case may be, by the Coffee Board.

SUMMARY

Introduction and Interpretation

The Sale of Goods Act, 1930 was part of the Indian Contract Act, 1872. In their function, both are complementary to each other. The new law was to define the new facets of the business of sale of goods. A contract of sale of goods is a contract whereby the seller transfers or agrees to transfer the property in goods to the buyer for a price.

Formation of the Contract (Agreement to Sell)

Sale   Under a contract the property in goods is passed to the buyer.

Agreement to sell   Transfer of property in goods is to take place sometime in the future fulfilling certain conditions.

A *contract of sale* is made by offer or to buy goods for a price and acceptance of such offer.

Property in goods is the subject matter of sale; goods may be existing, future, or contingent.

Price is the consideration for the goods in property. It is expressed in terms of money. It may be determined mutually at a future date or through an independent source.

Conditions and warranties   A stipulation in a contract of sale with reference to goods. The conditions and warranties may be express or implied.

Caveat emptor   'Let the buyer beware', puts the onus of the sale of goods on the buyer.

Effects of the Contract

Transfer of property in goods is the effect of contract of sale. It involves ownership, risk, action against third party, price, and insolvency.

Primary Rules for Transfer of Property in Goods

Specic goods   Ascertained goods, transfer is immediate—must be in deliverable state.

Unascertained goods Future goods—property passes only when goods, according to the description, are unconditionally appropriated to the contract and the buyer is given a notice.

Goods sent on approval Passed to the buyer on approval or after a reasonable time if approval has not been forthcoming.

Performance of the Contract

It is the duty of the seller to deliver the goods.

It is the duty of the buyer to accept and pay for the goods.

Delivery of goods Transfer of property in goods from seller to the buyer; it may be actual, symbolic, or constructive.

Rules Delivery of goods and payment of the price are concurrent conditions; other circumstances are: part delivery, buyer to apply for delivery, seller's duty to deliver, time of delivery, goods in possession of third party, cost of delivery, delivery of wrong quantity, delivery in instalments, delivery to carrier or wharfinger.

Kinds of delivery F.A.S., F.A.R., F.O.B., F.O.R., C.I.F., Ex-ship contract, risk of deterioration in transit.

Rights of the buyer To receive delivery as per contract, reject goods when not as per contract, repudiate, receive insurance notice, against the seller for breach of contract—price, specific performance, breach of warranty, repudiation before date.

Duties of the buyer To accept the goods, apply for delivery, demand delivery at reasonable time, accept delivery in instalments, responsibility of risk, give notice to seller on rejection, take delivery, pay the price, damages for non-acceptance.

Rights of unpaid seller against goods A seller of goods is deemed to be an unpaid seller:

When the whole price is not paid; and Bills of payment or negotiable instruments received as conditional.

Rights against goods and rights against the person of the buyer. When the property has passed to the buyer then rights of lien, stoppage in transit and resale; and when property has not passed then rights of with-hold delivery and stoppage in transit.

Against the buyer personally Suits for price, damages, repudiation, and interest.

Suits of breach of contract Breach of contract may be committed either by the seller or the buyer.

Seller's remedies Suit against price, damages for non-acceptance, damages repudiation by the buyer, and suit against interest.

Buyer's remedies Damages for non-delivery, specific performance, breach of warranty, repudiation of contract by the seller, and suit against interest.

Implied Terms, Time, Auction, Tax, and Other Matters

Auction Offer of goods to several bidders; the highest bidder getting the goods.

With a customary closure, auction comes to an end and the property in goods is transferred to the bidder.

Procedures of auction At the initiation stage: advertisement and catalogue.

At the action stage: bidders' assembly and the actual auction.

The completion is when the highest bid is accepted and the property in goods passes to its new rightful owner.

EXERCISES

Introduction and interpretation

Make a classification of the Sale of Goods Act, 1930. Formation of the contract (Agreement to sell)

(i) You possess some goods of which you have no immediate knowledge or you have forgotten about it. An acquaintance of yours lays his hands on it and sells it to you. Eventually you know that what you bought was already yours. But your acquaintance argues that the sale has taken place. Do you have a legal remedy?

Hint: It is not only a legal contradiction but also a logical one. You cannot buy your own property. For selling and buying, there should be two distinct parties.

(ii) X sold 1,000 quintals of sugar to Y. The government requisitioned the entire lot in public interest. Y wants to sue X for breach of contract. What legal advice can you give to Y.
Hint: The contract becomes void (Sec. 8 Sale of Goods Act); it also becomes void because of supervening impossibility. (Sec. 56 of the Contract Act)

(iii) X agrees to buy farm produce from Y whose price would be fixed by Z. But Z refuses to oblige and so Y refuses to sell. X wants to sue him and get his goods. Suggest a remedy to X.
Hint: X cannot approach for legal remedy; see Sec. 10.

(iv) How is a contract of sale made? Illustrate with examples and a case.

(v) Distinguish the following:
   (a) Sale and Agreement to sell.
   (b) Sale of good and Hire purchase agreement.
   (c) Sale of goods and Barter.
   (d) Sale of goods and Pledge.

Effects of contract

(i) Examine whether the property in the goods has passed from the seller to the buyer:
   (a) You offer ₹10 lakh to a car dealer for the car chosen by you. You agree that the car will be delivered to you on the 15th of the month and you will make payment on the 30th of the month.
   (b) Your company orders a tanker to be built. The company pays in instalments on account of price as the carrier is being built.
   (c) A wholesaler agrees to sell 10 tonnes of groundnut oil to a dealer. The wholesaler readies the goods and gives notice to the dealer to take the ordered stock.
   Hint: (a) As soon as you get the delivery of the car; (b) No, the property in the tanker will pass when it is ready; (c) Property passes as soon as the wholesaler gives the notice.

(ii) You want to purchase a second-hand machine which is not in a proper condition. You ask the seller to repair and give it to you. The seller says that you take it, repair it, and pay him with the deducted costs. In the process of repairing, the machine is destroyed without any fault of the technician. Now the seller wants the money from you.

Hint: No the seller is not entitled for the money; see Sec. 19 of the Act.

(iii) You ordered for your company some technical equipment on the basis that you will test it before you pass it. No time for its return was fixed. Even after a lapse of two months you did not communicate to the seller whether you approved it or not. Suddenly one day the equipment breaks down and you want to return it. The seller refuses to accept. You refuse to pay. So he files a suit against your company. What chances do you have?
Hint: Your chances are none. The property has already passed to your company because a reasonable time to reject has elapsed. See, Sec. 24.

(iv) What are the provisions of the Sale of Goods Act with regard to passing of property?

(v) Explain the principle of *Nemo dat qui non habet* with examples.

Performance of contract

(i) Your company orders 20,000 tonnes of steel to be delivered in instalments of 2,000 tonnes every month and you paid for each such delivery. After the delivery of 10,000 tonnes, the quality of the steel deteriorated. So you promptly refused any further instalment giving notice to the company that it is not of the contracted quality. The steel maker did not agree with you stating that the contract was done and you would have to accept the delivery and filed a suit. What are your chances?
Hint: You have the right to contracted goods, you have the right to reject if it is not of contracted quality; see Sec. 38 of the Act.

(ii) Pandit Brothers Ltd, sold 100 tonnes of wheat to Charat Ram & Co., by sample. The delivery was through railway. In the meantime, Charat Ram further sold it by the same sample to Shiv Ganga Mills to be delivered by railways. Shiv Ganga refused to accept the delivery on the charges that the sample and the goods supplied varied vastly in quality. Charat Ram, in turn, told his sourcing company, Pandit Brothers that he is rejecting the delivery. Pandit Brothers contested in the court that the goods had been delivered and that the property in goods had passed to Charat Ram & Co.

Hint: Charat Ram & Co., cannot reject the goods; see Secs 17 and 42.

(iii) Sagar & Sons ordered specific items of gems and jewellery from Bharat Javeri, Mumbai, who along with the ordered goods also included other items of gems and jewellery. What should Sagar do?
Hint: Sagar has the choice of accepting or rejecting; he may accept only the ordered specific goods and reject the rest; see Sec. 37(3) of the sales of Goods Act.

(iv) Delivery does not amount to acceptance. Illustrate with examples.

(v) What remedies are open to a buyer for breach of contract by the seller?

Rights of unpaid seller against the goods

(i) Anand Mills sells 15 tonnes of sugar to Sitaram Trading Company on a two-month credit. The sugar is still in Anand warehouse while the buyer is declared insolvent. The official receiver demands delivery of the goods without payment.
Hint: Anand can exercise the right to *lien*; the company is not bound to deliver until the payment has been received; see Sec. 47.

(ii) Shahid & Co., sold leather F.O.B. to a company in Manchester, U.K. The goods were not ascertained at the time of sale. The ship for some reason left the cargo behind and it lay at the docks for two months. Shahid & Co., brought action against the Manchester company.
Hint: The goods have passed F.O.B. and the goods have been delivered and passed to the buyer; see Sec. 55 of the Sale of Goods Act.

(iii) The Railways is in possession of goods as carrier when an unpaid seller gives notice of stoppage in transit. The buyer also owes money to the Railways. Can the Railways hold the goods in *lien* in violation of the right of stoppage in transit of the seller?
Hint: No, the Railways does not have the right to *lien*; see Sec. 52 of the Sale of Goods Act.

(iv) When is a seller of goods deemed to be an unpaid seller?

(v) Explain the nature of the right to *lien* and the right to stoppage in transit of an unpaid seller.

Suits of breach of contract

(i) You buy some goods from your friend. Although you have paid the price, you are yet to make payment of some other charges like for storage and handling. Your friend retains some of the goods as *lien*. Do you think your friend's stand is valid?
Hint: No, he has no right to *lien* since you have already paid the price of the goods.

(ii) The seller had given a notice to the buyer that the goods sold to him were lying in a warehouse which were ready to be delivered against the payment. When the buyer went to examine the goods, he was just shown two boxes that supposedly contained the goods.
Hint: The seller failed to give a reasonable opportunity to the buyer to examine the goods; see Sec. 41 of the Sale of Goods Act.

(iii) The goods were delivered to the buyer on a sale-or-return basis. The buyer did not want to approve, and then he forgot about it; and when he informed the seller, the latter said it was too late and demanded to consider the goods as sold. The buyer disputed and said he wanted to return the goods. The seller brought a suit against the buyer and petitioned for price for the goods sold as well as the accrued interest.
Hint: The seller will win the case on reasonable time for the price, and on interest for the delay; see Secs 43 and 44 of the sale of Goods Act.

(iv) State the rights and duties of the seller.

(v) What do you understand by reasonable time?

Implied terms, time, auction, tax and other matters

(i) At an auction sale, you make a bid for an antique vase and succeed. While the auctioneer lifts the hammer, there is some sort of accident and the vase falls to the ground and breaks into pieces. Who will bear the loss?
Hint: The owner of the vase; see Sec. 64.

(ii) At a sale by auction without reserve, the auctioneer is told not to sell for less than a certain price. The auctioneer accepts the highest bid that happens to be less than the reserve price.
Hint: The sale is valid; the loss must be borne by the auctioneer and who must make good to the principal, the difference of the bid and the reserve price; see Sec. 64 of the Sale of Goods Act.

(iii) State the rules regarding auction.

DEVELOPMENT OF LEGAL EDGE

- Volunteer yourself to work in the sales department or the dispatching unit of a manufacturing company.
- Experience for yourself how orders are received, how billing, lading, dispatching, transporting is performed and how the seller–buyer communication takes place.

- Make a special note of how legal procedures are taken care of.
- Research how the firm has been faring in its legal responsibilities.
- Make recommendations of improvement (if they are welcome from you—a trainee manager!).

FURTHER READING

- Dinesh Fardaunji Mulla, 2001, *Sales of Goods Act*, 6th ed., Butterworths, New Delhi.
- Krishnamachari & Anita B. Gogia, 2007, *A Short Commentary on the Sale of Goods Act, 1930*, 2nd ed. Jain Book Agency, Delhi.

Web resource

- http://www.vakilno1.com/bareacts/saleofgoods/saleofgoods.htm.

CASE STUDY   LESS FOR MORE

> *There is no implied warranty or condition as to the quality or fitness for any particular purpose of goods supplied under a contract of sale.*
>
> – Sec. 16, The Sale of Goods Act, 1930
>
> *The buyer needs a hundred eyes, the seller not one.*
>
> *– George Herbert*[3]

Introduction

The Indian *bazaar* is a battleground where the buyers fight losing battles. The consumers are wounded and most of them succumb to their miseries. There are only a few who keep on fighting with the help of consumer fora and consumer courts. From buying a home appliance to buying an apartment, from buying stationary to buying manufacturing machinery—no buyer is safe from the problems of defects in quality and deficiency in quantity. The image of Indian goods and services is suspect in the international markets. They are often considered substandard, cheap, and produced illegally and unethically.

There is also a very sensitive ethical dimension to buying and selling. The buyers are made conscious about the ethical responsibilities as to buying goods made by child workers and bonded labourers. Indian carpets, fabrics, handicrafts, fireworks, etc., fall in such category.

The laws, too, are very stringent against sweat shops, products from bonded workers, and child workers. There are laws for quality control, e.g., obtaining the ISI mark. There are also laws for pollution control, emission standards, effluents, and toxins. The laws of weights and measures control the quantity.

For a short moment you might feel elated for being a manager and hence on the winning side of the sellers. However, upon reflection you will realise that in the *bazaar*, whatever be your station in life, you have the opportunity both to buy and sell. As a manager you may be responsible for selling your company's goods and services; but as an individual you are just a normal consumer. You do not

---

[3]George Herbert, Jacula Prudentum, 1651.

have to reflect much further—your company too is a buyer most of the time. Imagine your company to be dealing in the manufacture of tractors. The list of vendors from whom you have to buy would almost seem inexhaustible.

The case of M.S. Padmanabha Iyer vs Devadasan Sylus and Others[4] (see Exhibit A) deals with the transfer of property where the judge in his judgement applies the principle of *caveat emptor*. 'Let the buyer beware' has been an age-old principle which has been diligently applied. However, in our contemporary world, this principle has come under the scanner in multiple ways and has demanded that the onus be not only on the buyer but also on the seller or vendor. In the analysis you will be shown this buyer–seller contradiction and the dilemma that each party faces.

Exhibit A   The Case

The Suit before Travancore High Court

Date of judgement   31 October 1969

Matter   Whether the principles laid down in the Transfer of Property Act in respect of the covenants for the sale of property are applicable to the facts of the present case inasmuch as the Transfer of Property Act—*caveat emptor.*

Appellant   Padmanabha Iyer executed a sale deed of the properties in favour of the grandfather of Devadasan in 1949 for ₹2,000. He received ₹2,000 and gave possession of the two items to Devadasan. Suit for recovery of ₹2,318.

The Respondents   Devadasan Sylus and Others, in the meantime lost two suits concerning the same property with a third and a fourth party as follows. Their contention was that the consideration for the sale deed in favour of Devadasan executed by Iyer had completely failed and that he—Iyer—was liable to compensate Devadasan for the failure of consideration and for the loss and damage caused on account of the breach of contract and warranty of title with six per cent interest from 1 June 1960.

Depositions before the High Court

Appellant: The counsel for Iyer, the appellant's lawyer, presented the following argument: There was no representation in respect of the title made by him to Devadasan and that at that time the rule of *caveat emptor* applied. Devadasan, the respondent, was put to proof of the assignment of the others in favour of Jayalakshmi Ammal, to whom the property was gifted. There was no failure of consideration and there was no cause of action against Iyer. There was no breach of contract or warranty of title. He was not a party to the gift deed of 1951. If full evidence had been given in that suit, it would not have been decided against Devadasan, for failure of consideration and for loss and damage caused on account of the breach of contract and warranty of title with six per cent interest from 1 June 1960.

Background   Iyer was an auction-purchaser who in execution of a decree obtained by the defendant against a third party, Subbiah Mooppanar, who claimed title to the two items independently of the judgement. After purchase, a fourth party, Jayalakshmi Ammal, to whom possession was handed over, sued Devadasan alleging that the property was his, and not that of the judgement-debtor and got a decree. The appellant, Iyer, then sued the defendant, Devadasan, to recover the purchase money. The defendant, among other things contended that there was no fraud on his part and that the plaintiff was not entitled to the purchase money as there was no agreement on defendant's part to refund the purchase money if the title failed. The *munsif* gave judgement in favour of the plaintiff, but the *zilla* court, on appeal, reversed the same.

The gift was a sham one and there was no acceptance of the same. It was alienation in fraud of creditors. The rights of the respondent, if any, had been lost by adverse possession even before the delivery of the gift deed. The respondent, being transferee of only one of the items, could not claim the whole amount as damages.

Respondent   The counsel to Devadasan argued that in the absence of positive law, we have to apply the principles of good conscience and equity. (He sidestepped or ignored completely the caveat emptor.)

Contd

---

[4]M.S. Padmanabha Iyer vs Devadasan Sylus and Others, on 31 1969; also see http://www.indiankanoon.org/doc/1590845/ (17 December October 2010).

Exhibit A *Contd*

The sale includes a contract and hence it is to be construed that the agreement for sale is subsisting even after the completion of conveyance. There is a failure of consideration inasmuch as the agreement to sell is still subsisting and there is failure to convey the property. This sale stands on a different footing: it is an assignment of a debt.

Judgement   It is a clear case wherein the principle of *caveat emptor* has to be applied.

In other words, the judgement upheld the arguments by the appellant. Hence, it can be safely held that as far as the present Case is concerned, the principle of *caveat emptor* alone will apply. One is not convinced with the argument of the respondents, to the effect that the sale includes a contract and, hence, it is to be construed that the agreement for sale is subsisting even after the completion of conveyance.

Analysis of caveat emptor in the contemporary Indian legal environment

The earlier case despite being complicated due to the transfer of property three times, upheld the principle of *caveat emptor* to its first principals. Presently, we are a decade ahead in the twenty first century in a free market economy—unthinkable in the days of the earlier judgement. The roles of the sellers and the buyers have undergone a sea change. It is no more the responsibility of buyers alone. There are laws that protect the interests of the consumers; sellers cannot shirk, anymore, their responsibility reciting the old *mantra* of *caveat emptor*.

Housing woes

Vihaan Flat Owners' Association of Chennai in Tamil Nadu, is a registered body that filed a complaint under the Consumer Protection Act, 1986, in the district consumers' forum in 1992 against the builder for deficiency in services. The forum dismissed their complaint saying they did not come under the definition of 'consumers' under the said Act. Likewise, the state forum upheld the verdict. The Association filed its complaint at the national consumer forum which reversed the state and district verdict saying that the Association was indeed a consumer. The time elapsed in the procedure was ten years: 1992–2002.

The district forum heard the complaint and awarded compensation of ₹3 lakh along with costs. The builder appealed to the state commission which replayed the old record that the flat owners are not consumers in contravention to the ruling of the national commission. This process took 8 years.

To go again to the national commission seems a physical impossibility. The representative who used to attend to the matter of the association in Delhi was a member of the association working in Delhi died. The cost of sending a person to Delhi will mount the costs beyond affordability.[5]

By the old principle of *caveat emptor*, the flat owners would have no case at all. It is true the consumer fora did not apply the Act both in letter and in spirit; it did not do its duty for speedy justice. In spite of all these shortcomings, *caveat emptor* would be a far cry insofar as justice is concerned.

Caveat emptor, capitalism, politics, economics, and policy

Gunnar Trumbull is an associate professor at Cornell University who wrote a book titled *Consumer Capitalism: Politics, Product Markets, and Firm Strategy in France and Germany*[6]. He is commissioned to write. His research in France and Germany shows that for the past four decades *caveat emptor* is redundant and almost dead in Europe. Reason: Consumer protection regulations have evolved to such an extent that *caveat* is turned on its head to demand accountability of the vendor. Indeed, consumer attitudes as well as statutory regulations vary from country to country; however, what has happened in Germany and France—for that matter in all the developed countries—is that the consumer is really the king, for he is protected through very

---

[5]S. Saroja, Caveat Emptor: How Long is too Long? http://www.thehindu.com/life-and-style/society/article952163.eceChennai, 14 December 2010. (20 December 2010).

[6]Gunnar Trumbull, 2006,Consumer Capitalism: Politics, Product Markets, and Firm Strategy in France and Germany, Cornell University Press. For more on Trumbull and his writings see http://drfd.hbs.edu/fit/public/facultyInfo.do;jsessionid=KbmTDQP6s0 vfM1ktdbQ3hG6h1Dsnk2WCKc5kSyCGplxzFFGT Rg7Q!528537621!815275569?facInfo=pub&facId=140863 (20 December 2010).

strong legislation. He can blame a fast food company or a tobacco company for the malady he has suffered because of their products and ends up winning so much money as though he has won a lottery.

What kind of agencies work behind the success of the consumer age? In fact, all stakeholders of the market—manufacturers, distributers, media, policy makers, and judiciary—are consumers. One of the scientific fundamentals to which all consumers are sensitive is comparative testing. Consumers show a great deal of interest in it and are aware its findings and reports. Based on these issues, consumers are able to make informed choices. In addition, the regulatory bodies have stepped in to protect consumers to make up for losses suffered by them. Thus, the shopping experience is to customer advantage. Customers will be able to exercise price–quality trade off; it is not a mere low price and free gift but a well-informed decision on quality.

National Consumer Dispute Redressal Commission

The website of the National Consumer Dispute Redressal Commission (NCDRC) opens with the following paragraph:

The Consumer Protection Act, 1986 (in short, 'the Act'), is a benevolent social legislation that lays down the rights of the consumers and provides for the promotion and protection of the rights of the consumers. The first and the only Act of its kind in India, it has enabled ordinary consumers to secure less-expensive and often speedy redressal of their grievances. By spelling out the rights and remedies of the consumers in a market so far dominated by organized manufacturers and traders of goods and providers of various types of services, the Act makes the dictum, caveat emptor ('buyer beware') a thing of the past.[7]

The object of the commission is to provide inexpensive and speedy redressal of consumer disputes. The commission is represented from national, state, and district levels. The consumer protection act covers goods and services. The goods are those that are manufactured or produced and sold to the consumers through wholesalers and retailers. The services are in the nature of transport, telephone, electricity, housing, banking insurance, medical treatment, etc.

The consumer approaches the commission through its lowest body at the district level with complaint and documentary proof such as invoice, etc. District level complaint for a value up to ₹20 lakh; state commission upto ₹1 crore; national commission over ₹1 crore. The consumer protection is in addition to the normal civil suit. The proceedings are summary in nature, that is, unlike a suit in a court, here the depositions are made and quickly the redressal is awarded. There is always room for appeal both for the aggrieved as well as the defendant.

Conclusion

We saw a consumer forum case, a look on modern take on *caveat emptor* and a statutory body formed under the Act of consumer protection which is against the *caveat emptor*. (Table 5.10 explains the various classifications of consumer protection.) Some of the categories are where consumers can hope to get better hearing and justice than in the *caveat emptor* days. You should note that *caveat emptor* has really

Table 5.10   Classification of consumer protection

Category	Protection
Mutual funds investment	Transparency and correct information.
Ethical buying	Knowledge about the background of the product, e.g., whether it is manufactured with child labour.
Retail protection	Clear information about products on its labels, e.g., expiry date.
Organic products	Certification that the products are wholly and truly organic and not just partially so.
Environmental protection	Information on health and other hazards.
Housing	What legal documents one must have for clear title; what is expected from a builder.

Contd

[7] http://ncdrc.nic.in/ (17 December 2010).

Table 5.10 *Contd*

Taxation	To know exactly what the direct tax collection entails, e.g., capital gains tax.
Transport	What transport entails, e.g., insurance.
Services	What kind of services are available; whether schemes are clear and how they are charged, e.g., excess billing.
Medicine	Responsibility of the pharmaceutical industry to fully reveal the side effects of their products.

become a relic in the consumerist society of today. Today it is more appropriate to say *caveat venditor*—let the seller or vendor beware, because the consumer has the upper hand, both economically and legally. You as a manager, although may happen to be a buyer but generally are labelled as a seller. In business today, you cannot blame anyone except yourself.

Discussion Questions

1. Illustrate what is at stake in the principle of *caveat emptor.*
2. Why is the principle of *caveat emptor* applicable in the case of Padmanabha Iyer vs Devadasan?
3. Do you believe that *caveat emptor* has declined? Explain with examples.
4. Do you think flat owners should be considered as consumers?
5. Discuss the nature of mutual funds and illustrate whether caveat *emptor* is applicable.
6. If the courts can solve civil suits regarding consumer problems, what is the need for another agency called NCDRC whose judgement is merely a summary trial?

Going Beyond

1. Can air, water, earth, and fire be considered as 'goods'?
2. How to defend *caveat emptor* as an ethical principle?
3. Army renders defence service. People pay for this service through taxes. Can the people of the country apply the principle of *caveat emptor*? In other words, how do we check the acceptability of the public services?
4. Is India ready for *caveat venditor*?

LEGAL LUMINARY

MUMBAI GRAHAK PANCHAYAT—EMPOWERED CONSUMER ASSOCIATION

This luminary is a consumer activist. Law, unless it is put into action, remains a dead letter. Waging a lone legal battle is least romantic, but a group can make the law to function with clockwork precision. An individual buyer is at the mercy of the seller; but if it is a united front of the buyers, such an association is definitely the king of all the markets that it surveys. *Mumbai Grahak Panchayat* (MGP)* is in the third decade of its foundation and has been considered by the International Consumer Forum as an organization whose paradigm is replicable anywhere in the world. It is highly respected among the public and feared by the traders. Its only weapon is the law of the land.

The 1980s were a period of shortages. One had to book a two-wheeler at least a decade in advance. The Chetak scooter of Bajaj was a status symbol. The rich and the top bureaucrats could bend rules and use influence to lay their hands on it earlier than others. There came to the fore, a two-wheeler manufacturing company called Lohia Machines Limited (LML). It had collaboration with the Italian

---

*See blog, http://mumbaigrahakpanchayat.blogspot.com/ (21 December 2010).

Contd

Legal Luminary

firm Piaggio. The LML scooter was called LML Vespa as in Italy.

In 1983, LML advertised making an offer to put down deposit ₹500 to book the scooter.[†] The deposit would earn a 9 per cent interest and the amount was to be adjusted against the delivery price. Cancellation of booking after 6 months was to be returned with 6 per cent interest within 60 days. The offer was gobbled up by the public. LML's capital was ₹12 crore; the money collected from depositors was a whopping ₹160 crore. With license for only 1 lakh scooters, it would take LML more than two decades to deliver the goods. To make matters worse, LML did not behave responsibly in making refunds.

In 1983, when a bank clerk or a teacher's salary barely touched a thousand rupees, ₹500 was a lot of money. MGP, which was in its initial years only, dealing with complaints of grocery items, took up the cause on 15 March 1990, the World Consumer Rights Day. There came 700 affected LML depositors for the first meeting. MGP filed a class action against LML before the NCDRC. Not only consumer activists but also several noted lawyers and judges joined to support MGP. The complaint demanded redressal for not only those who expressly joined MGP but also all the affected, about four lakh depositors. The Commission demanded the list of the affected. MGP turned the tables on LML to produce the list. The list alone amounted to 23 cartons that had to be transported on a vehicle. LML was made to refund money at the rate of 18 per cent to those who actively complained and at 12.5 per cent to those who were passive depositors.

To crown the good work of the MGP, a precedent was created in case law. For the first time in India, a group or a class of consumers be came eligible for redressal before the consumer courts. Further, even the Parliament made the necessary amendment to the Consumer Protection Act and in June 1993 ratified the amendment to include one or more consumers having the same interest.

Today, during normal daily life, over 20,000 families in and around greater Mumbai receive their household groceries at their doorstep. MGP has been able to deliver not just essentials of life but also costing those that are organically grown, safe, and reasonable to the extent of gaining upto 20 per cent less of what rest of the consumers pay. It keeps a close watch of the market. Wholesalers, distributors, and agents take careful note of the proceedings of the association. It has established *caveat venditor* and at the same time helps the consumers to be informed (*caveat emptor*). MGP has won awards and acclaim and every member is a proud and happy member of the organization.

The MGP has its humble beginnings in the individual experiences of the following proactive citizens; Bindu Madhav Joshi, Madhu Mantri, Lalita Kulkarni, Dr M. Panajkar, and Advocate Shirish Deshpande—all of whom have stories where they took a positive proactive stand against overpricing and hoarding. These were the turbulent 1970s but there was inspiration to be soaked in through the personalities of Jayaprakash Narayan and Justice M.C. Chagla. Today, the MGP is headed by Advocate Shirish Deshpande, who spearheaded the action against LML.

[**]Picture courtesy, http://www.goodnewsindia.com/Pages/content/institutions/mgp.html (21 December 2010).
[†]For more information of this NGO, see http://www.goodnewsindia.com/Pages/content/institutions/mgp.html (21 December 2010).

The Negotiable Instruments Act, 1881

Principle: *Quod ipsis qui contraxerunt obstat estsuccessoribus corum obstabit.*

That which is paid by the order of another is the same as though it were paid to himself.

CHAPTER OUTLINE

- Introduction and Interpretation
- Notes, Bills, and Cheques
- *Hundi*
- Negotiation
- Presentment
- Dishonour of a Negotiable Instrument
- Discharge of a Negotiable Instrument

- Rules of Evidence, Estoppel, and International Law
- Banker and Customer
- *Case Study:* The Indispensable Sec. 138 of the Negotiable Instruments Act, 1881
- *Legal Luminary:* Sarosh Homi Kapadia

6.1 INTRODUCTION AND INTERPRETATION

TEXT

This Act may be called the Negotiable Instruments Act, 1881.

Local extent. Saving of usages relating to hundis, etc. It extends to the whole of India but nothing herein contained affects the 'Indian Paper Currency Act, 1871, (3 of 1871), Sec. 21, or any local usage relating to any instrument in an oriental language: Provided that such usages may be excluded by any words in the body of the instrument which indicate an intention that the legal relations of the parties thereto shall be governed by this Act and it shall come into force on the first day of March, 1882.

– Sec. 1, The Negotiable Instruments Act, 1881

Chapter 5 was an elaboration of the Contract Act, 1872 concerning business transactions between the seller and buyer. Chapters 2 to 5 discussed that the essence of business is 'consideration'—the price that the buyer pays to the seller. In this chapter, you will study about how this consideration actually operates. Goods and services are bought and sold for money. However, as you know from daily experience, *money* is of various kinds such as currency cash, bank cheques, bank drafts, or documents with undertaking to pay, such as promissory notes and bills of exchange. These methods of payment help the large and complex modern commerce of today to function competently and efficiently.

As a manager of a company you hardly see cash transactions; you mostly deal with 'negotiable instruments', i.e., those documents that stand for value of exchange. By *negotiable*, you commonly understand as something talked or discussed about; something you and another have 'agreed' upon or so. Instrument is a tool, something that has a definite 'mechanism', that serves your purpose. In a negotiable instrument, you have a mechanism, that works systematically, concerning the consideration or payments in commerce. In this chapter you will study three such mechanisms: promissory note, bill of exchange, and cheque. Negotiable instruments are a special class of contracts.

Definition and Nature of Negotiable Instruments

From what has been already stated, it may be formally expressed in the following manner. The negotiable instrument is a document that entitles a person to a sum of money and it is transferrable from one person to another through either delivery or indorsement and delivery. The transfer must have the following characteristics:

(a) Bona fide, and
(b) For a value, the holder in due course gets a good title even though the title of the trans-feror may be defective.

One may take a negative test to examine the validity of the negotiable instrument: *Can a good title be acquired by a thief?* If the answer is in the affirmative, then the instrument is negotiable.

Salient Features of Negotiable Instruments

It is a mundane chore for a manager to deal with negotiable instruments. It is assumed that you know the characteristics of these as much as you know the nature of currency cash. Negotiable instruments are characterised by the features listed as follows.

Freely transferable

To the bearer through delivery; or,
Payable to order by indorsement and delivery.[1]

Title of holder free from all defects

A person taking an instrument bona fide and for value, known as 'holder in due course', gets the instrument free from all defects in the title of the transferor. He is not affected by any defect in the title of the transferor or any of the prior party.

---

[1] *Indorse* in Latin, *in dorsa* implies 'on the back of', normally a note made on the back of a document, cheque, or any negotiable instrument; in other words, an accepting or rejecting remark made on an instrument.

Example:

A sells goods to B.

B makes a promissory note for the price to A.

B complains that the goods are not according to order and refuses to make good the promissory note.

If A sues B, B will win.

But

If A negotiates the note to X, B will lose.

Because X is holder in due course, he is not affected by any defect in the title of the transferor.

Recovery

The holder in due course can sue upon a negotiable instrument in his own name for the recovery of the amount. He does not need to give notice of transfer to the party liable on the instrument to pay.

Presumptions

That the negotiable instruments have some implied conditions, known as 'presumptions' in law, unless contrary has been proved.[2] It is presumed. (Refer to Table 6.1.)

Table 6.1   Presumptions in law

Consideration	Every negotiable instrument—made, drawn, accepted, indorsed, negotiated, or transferred—is for 'consideration'. (Holder may get a decree from court for it.)
Date	It is dated.
Time of acceptance	Accepted within a time period and before its maturity.
Time of transfer	Transfer before maturity.
Order of indorsement	The indorsements are in the order they are made.
Stamp	It is stamped.
Holder presumed to be a holder in due course	Every holder is a holder in due course (Sec. 118).
Proof of protest	In a suit for dishonoured instrument, the court, on proof of the protest presumes the fact of dishonour until such fact is disproved (Sec. 119).

The presumptions are rebuttable by evidence. Any challenge to these demands proof. Figure 6.1 shows the classification of negotiable instruments.

---

[2]For the presumptions, see Secs 118 and 119 of the Act.

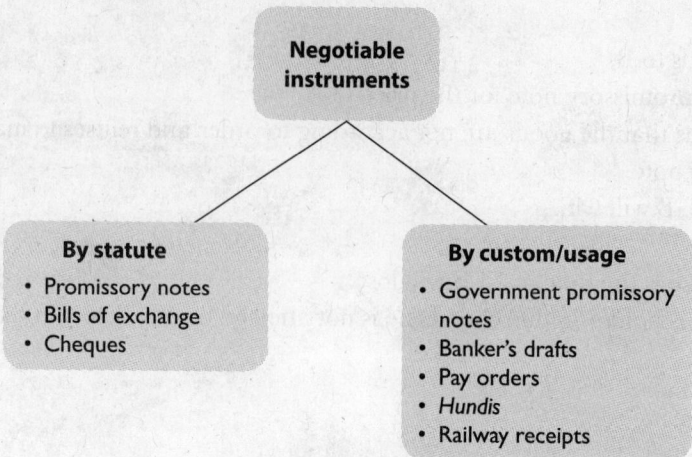

Figure 6.1 Classification of negotiable instruments

Brief History of the Legislation

In 1818, France developed a code of mercantile trading. Several countries adopted this code and in 1882, England enacted the Bills of Exchange Act. A similar process had started in India way back in 1867 under the third Indian Law Commission. The then Law Secretary, Arthur Philips, a member of the Calcutta Bar, redrafted the bill in 1879 and invited objections and suggestions from banks, chambers of commerce, and leading merchants. After several modifications and passing through a select committee, it was eventually enacted into law as the Negotiable Instruments Act, 1881.[3] The following is the time line of the Act.

1881: Enactment of Negotiable Instruments Act.
1882: Came into force in March.
1998: Amendments to Chapters 6(1)–6(10).
2002: The Negotiable Instrument Amendment and Miscellaneous Provisions Act amended the original Act in the following aspects:
   (a) Punishment for dishonouring of cheque: from one year to two years.
   (b) Period for issue of notice by the payee to the drawer increased from 15 days to 30 days.
   (c) Courts granted discretion to waive a month's period for taking cognisance of the case under the Act.
   (d) Accused or witness allowed to be summoned by the court through speed post or courier.
   (e) Provisions for summary trial under the provisions of the Act.
   (f) Offences under the Act compoundable.
   (g) Government-nominated directors exempted from prosecution under Sec. 141 of the Act.

---

[3]See Eleventh Law Commission Report, 1958; http://lawcommissionofindia.nic.in/1-50/Report11.pdf (4 January 2011).

(h) The provisions of the Act subject to Reserve Bank of India Act, 1934, Secs 31 and 32.

Hundis, as indigenous negotiable instruments, too are now acceptable; however, these must confirm to Sec. 1 of the Act, as quoted earlier in the chapter. Regional languages too can be used in all the negotiable instruments; use of Hindi, the national language, is especially encouraged.

Case 6.1 is one of the early ones where a precedent for normal hundi was established. The case goes to show that an instrument for securing payment may become negotiable not only by statute but also by custom or usage. The main advantage of negotiable instrument under the Act is that the property in the instrument and all rights under it pass, by operation of law, to a bona fide transferee for value by mere delivery or by indorsement and delivery without the necessity of the complicated procedure of executing a deed of assignment; further, the rights of the transferee are not in any manner affected by any defect in the title of the transferor.

What becomes clear in Case 6.1 is further establishment of the definition of contract as per the intention of the contract. Any negotiable instrument must essentially express the intention of the delivery mechanism. The regional language does not decide the validity but the usage or custom, which expresses such an intention as to deliver the agreed exchange of value or money. Language should not exclude an instrument if it comes under the Act. Thus, if a hundi, in spite of the name that is given to it in the document by the parties, comes within the definition of the promissory note, bill of exchange, or a cheque, it should be governed by the provisions of the Act alone, not withstanding any usage or custom applicable to it, which may be at variance with such provisions.

MANAGER'S TAKEAWAY

- Promises make debt, and debt makes promises, says a Dutch proverb.
- Good business consists of promises kept.

CASE 6.1

APPELLANT: Jambu Chetty VS RESPONDENT: N.P.L.N. Palaniappa Chettiar*

DATE OF JUDGEMENT: 12 May 1902

FACTS: The appellant brought action against the respondent: the amounts of four hundis drawn by the respondent in favour of the appellant, which were dishonoured by the drawee. The lower court favoured the respondent; hence, the appeal in the Madras High Court. The contention was whether it was a hundi or either a bill or note, thus challenging Sec. 1 of the Negotiable Instruments Act, 1881.

JUDGEMENT: The hundi is governed by the Act.

REASON: The hundi is governed by the Act despite it being at variance with the Act. If a contrary usage were established—an instrument in an oriental language as in Sec. 1—even though it conformed to the requirements of a negotiable instrument as laid down in the Act, would be governed not by the provisions of the Act, but by such usage; but that in the absence of proof of any such usage, such instrument, irrespective of the language, would be governed by the provisions of the Act.

*Jambu Chetty vs N.P.L.N. Palaniappa Chettiar, http://www.indiankanoon.org/doc/795007/ (4 January 2011).

6.2 NOTES, BILLS, AND CHEQUES

Promissory Note

A 'promissory note' is an instrument in writing (not being a bank note or a currency note) containing an unconditional undertaking, signed by the maker, to pay a certain sum of money only to, or to the order of, a certain person, or to the bearer of the instrument.

– Sec. 4, The Negotiable Instruments Act, 1881

Figure 6.2 shows a specimen of promissory note.

₹1,00,000   Date: 11 December 2011

Three months after the date, I promise to pay Mohandas or order the sum of one lakh rupees, for value received.

To Mohandas
1, Birla Mandir Rd,
New Delhi, 110001.   SIGNATURE

Figure 6.2   Specimen of a promissory note

You will be amazed with the number of essential elements this simple-looking promissory note possesses. (See Table 6.2 and also refer to Case 6.2.)

Table 6.2   Essential elements of a promissory note

Essential elements	Explanation	Example
Writing	Exclusively in writing: print or handwritten.	See Figure 6.2
Promise to pay	Express promise to pay.	The term *promise* and no other equivalent such as *debt* or *pro-note*, etc.
Definite and unconditional	The character of the note to pay is absolute.	These are not promissory notes: (a) I promise to pay ₹1,000 when convenient. (b) I promise to pay ₹1,000 in installments. (c) I promise to pay ₹1,000 when goods are delivered. (d) I promise to pay ₹1,000 upon the death of uncle if he has adequately bequeathed...*
Signed by the maker	Maker of the note is one who signs it—which authenticates and gives effect to the contract. Signature implies the will of the person to contract.	Even an agent may sign, if he is authorised to do so, e.g., the power of attorney, the authorised signatory of the contracting person.

Contd

*Since there is no exception to death, it may be seen in a time bracket if the note says '*after* the death of ....'.

Table 6. 2 *Contd*

Certain parties	Two parties must be certain: the payer (maker of the note) and payee, its receiver. A promisor cannot logically pay for himself.	When there is a mistake in the name, it must be ascertained by evidence.
Certain sum of money	The payable sum of money must be certain; not contingent additions or subtractions.	These are not promissory notes: (a) I promise to pay ₹1,000 and all the rest of the sums due to him. (b) I promise to pay ₹1,000 and the fine according to rules. (c) I promise to pay ₹1,000 after deducting any money he owes to me.
Promise to pay money only	Money implies the legal tender; in India, the Indian currency in rupees.	The following are not promissory notes: (a) I promise to pay ₹1,000 and 50 kg of sugar. (b) I promise to pay ₹1,000 and share certificates of TT Company. (c) I promise to pay 20 kg of rice.
Bank note or currency note: not a promissory note	The legal tender as well as the notes by the Reserve Bank of India is currency or money itself.	A promissory note is one that stands for money, it is not money itself like the rupees, dollars, and pounds.
Formalities of number, date, place, consideration, etc.	These aspects formalise and make it into an official document.	There may be a mistake, e.g., concerning the date which may be corrected on evidence; but there is no exception for the fixing of the official stamp as per the Stamp Act, 1899.
Payable on demand or after a definite period of time	'On demand' implies immediately or forthwith.	
It cannot be made payable to bearer on demand	The Reserve Bank of India Act, 1934, prohibits it.	Such a payment is the prerogative of the Reserve Bank of India or the Union government.

CASE 6.2

APPELLANT: Srinivasan vs RESPONDENT: Subbarama Sastrikal*

DATE OF JUDGEMENT: 21 July 1987

FACTS: The problem arose because after execution of the promissory note, on the reverse side of it, on the same day it was recorded under the signatures of both the parties that if the amount is paid within one month the interest need not be paid. It was for this reason alone that the trial court held the promissory note to be one payable otherwise than on demand. The dispute before the Kerala High Court is whether the subject matter of the suit is a promissory note payable on demand or otherwise than on demand. If it is payable on demand, the stamp affixed is sufficient; otherwise it is insufficiently stamped. The subordinate judge found that it is payable otherwise than on demand and, hence, insufficiently stamped and, therefore, inadmissible in evidence. Plaintiff sought to revise that order.

---

*Sreenivasan vs. Subbarama Sastrikal, AIR 1988, Ker 112; See also http://www.indiankanoon.org/doc/507936/ (3 April 2011).

Contd

Case 6.2 *Contd*

JUDGEMENT:	The judgement of the subordinate court set aside.
REASON:	The subordinate judge was clearly in the wrong when he found that the plaintiff was barred from claiming principal and interest for a period of one month and, hence, the note is one payable otherwise than on demand: It is only a promissory note payable on demand and is sufficiently stamped and admissible in evidence.

Bill of Exchange

A 'bill of exchange' is an instrument in writing, containing an unconditional order, signed by the maker, directing a certain person to pay a certain sum of money only to, or to the order of, a certain person or to the bearer of the instrument.

– Sec. 5, The Negotiable Instruments Act, 1881

Mentioned as follows the are the essential characteristics of bill of exchange. (Also see Case 6.3.)

1. It must be in writing.
2. It must contain an order to pay.
3. The order must be unconditional.
4. It requires three persons: drawer, drawee, and payee.
5. The parties must be certain.
6. It must be signed by the drawer.
7. The sum payable must be certain.
8. It must contain order to pay money.
9. The formalities of date, place, and consideration, although not essential, need to be supplied with evidence; the stamp with signature is essential.

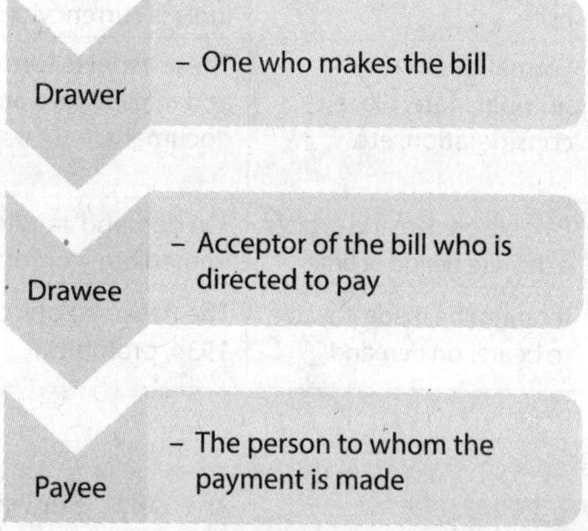

Drawer – One who makes the bill

Drawee – Acceptor of the bill who is directed to pay

Payee – The person to whom the payment is made

Figure 6.3 Parties to a bill of exchange

Figures 6.3 and 6.4 show the parties to a bill of exchange and the specimen of bill of exchange, respectively. Table 6.3 shows the difference between a promissory note and bill of exchange.

CASE 6.3				
APPELLANT:	Alex Mathew	vs	RESPONDENT:	Philip Philip*
DATE OF JUDGEMENT:	20 March 1973			
FACTS:	The trial court found that the Case pleaded by the plaintiff, that there had been borrowings by the first and second defendants, as pleaded in the plaint, for the purpose of the business conducted by the first and second defendants, was not true,			

*Alex Mathew vs Philip Philip, AIR 1973 Ker 210; it is a case that relates to Sec. 118 of the Negotiable Instruments Act, 1881; also see http://www.indiankanoon.org/doc/112603/ (4 March 2011).

Contd

Case 6.3 *Contd*

and that the first defendant had not borrowed any amount as pleaded by the respondent.

JUDGEMENT: Judgement of the trial court upheld.

REASON: Reverting to the plaint, the judge found that the plaintiff himself stated that the sum of ₹5,000 was not paid on 1 August 1942. He also did not bring his Case on the promissory note—Instead he pleaded in his plaint that a sum of ₹4,981 was paid on 16 July 1942. Both the sum and the date are, therefore, contrary to the tenor of the promissory note and the question thus arises whether the plaintiff has not by his own pleading set at naught, the presumption, which would normally have been drawn.

In this connection, the judge could not overlook the fact that the defendant pleaded on the other hand that the promissory note was executed on 27 June 1942. It is obvious that as between the plaintiff and the defendant the issue had to be tried whether the promissory note was executed on 16 July 1942 or on 27 June 1942. Once that issue is tried, it is apparent that if the decision be in favour of the defendant, then the statement of the plaintiff that the sum of ₹5,000 was advanced to the defendant on 16 July 1942 must also fail. The plaintiff, in setting up such a case himself, destroyed the presumption by pleading facts contrary to the plain tenor of the promissory note. The presumption, which could have been drawn, was that the promissory note was executed on 1 August 1942 and that a sum of ₹5,000 was the value for it. Whether or not that sum was paid then or earlier would have, of course, been material if denied by the defendant. The presumption would still have been in favour of the plaintiff. But the plaintiff in the present suit has himself shown that the date which the promissory note bore was not the date on which it was executed and the sum which according to the promissory note was the value, was not the sum which was actually handed over. It is impossible, therefore, to take recourse to the presumption and though the presumption would normally have been drawn, it is the plaintiff who has deprived himself of the presumption by pleading facts contrary to what would be presumed.

Table 6.3 Distinction between promissory note and bill of exchange

Distinction	Promissory note	Bill of exchange
Number of parties	Two parties: maker and payee	Three parties: drawer, drawee, and payee
Difference	Unconditional 'promise' to pay	Unconditional 'order' to pay
Relationship	Maker is 'debtor' and he himself undertakes to pay	Drawee is the creditor who directs the drawee (his debtor) to pay
Acceptance	Not necessary since signed by the maker	Necessity as for validity, signed by the acceptor since he is not the originator of bill
Liability	Primary and absolute	Secondary and conditional

Contd

Table 6.3 *Contd*

Relation	Not immediate—the maker cannot pay himself	Immediate—the drawer and the payee may be the same person
Notice to prior parties	Not required	In case of notification required to do so to holder and all the endorsing parties (in case of dishonouring of bill).
Sets	Sets of copies not required	In duplicates or triplicates or makes multiples (as for foreign bills).
Protest for foreign	No protest required for foreign notes	Foreign bills must be protested as per law from wherever they originate.
Conditional acceptance	No condition can be attached.	Conditional acceptance permitted.
Acceptance for honour	Cannot be paid for honour.	The acceptor can make the payment of a bill.
Payable to the maker	Not possible.	Drawer and payee are one and the same.

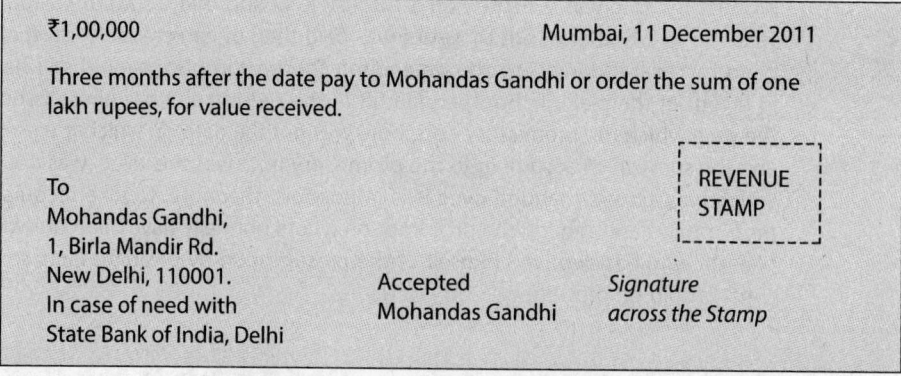

| ₹1,00,000 | Mumbai, 11 December 2011 |

Three months after the date pay to Mohandas Gandhi or order the sum of one lakh rupees, for value received.

To
Mohandas Gandhi,
1, Birla Mandir Rd.
New Delhi, 110001.
In case of need with
State Bank of India, Delhi

Accepted
Mohandas Gandhi

Signature across the Stamp

REVENUE STAMP

Figure 6.4 Specimen of a bill of exchange

A 'cheque' is a bill of exchange drawn on a specified banker and not expressed to be payable otherwise than on demand.

– Sec. 6, The Negotiable Instruments Act, 1881

The cheque is a common form of negotiable instrument both in business and in personal life. (See Figure 6.5 and Case 6.4.) You issue cheques from a savings or current account in a bank. You can issue a cheque in your own name or in favour of others, directing the bank to pay the specified amount to the person named in the cheque. Therefore, a cheque may be regarded as a bill of exchange; the only difference is that the bank is always the drawee in case of a cheque.

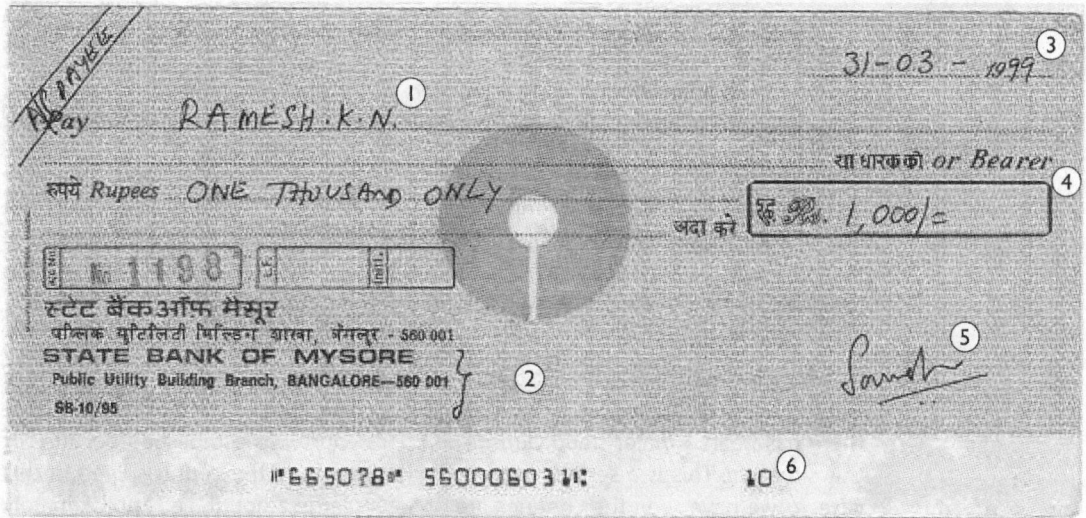

Parts of a cheque:

1. Payee name
2. Drawee, the financial institution where the cheque can be presented for payment
3. Date of issue
4. Amount of currency
5. Signature of drawer
6. Machine readable routing and account information

Figure 6.5 Specimen of a cheque

CASE 6.4

PETITIONER: Bratindranath Banerjee, vs RESPONDENT: Hiten Dalal*
Director, Standard Chartered Bank

DATE OF JUDGEMENT: 28 April 1993

FACTS: The petitioner filed a complaint against the respondent alleging an offence under Sec. 138 of the Negotiable Instruments Act. It is the case of the prosecution that the accused had issued to the said Bank four cheques: (1) cheque no. 985203 dated 24 December 1991 for ₹27 crore (Ex. B); (2) cheque no. 985204 dated 26 December 1991 for ₹14.50 crore (Ex. C); (3) cheque no. 989897 dated 17 February 1992 for ₹17 crore (Ex. D); and (4) cheque no. 023423 dated 27 March 1992 for ₹199,575,000 (Ex. E). It is the case of the prosecution that these cheques were given in discharge of the liability of the accused to the said Bank arising from differences in the contract rates and delivery rates in transactions undertaken at the instance of the accused. It is the case of the prosecution that these cheques, when presented, were dishonoured for reason 'Not Arranged For'. It is the case of the prosecution that in spite of receipt of a notice dated 1 June 1992, the accused has failed to pay the amounts of the said cheques within 15 days thereafter. It is the case of the prosecution that the accused has thus

---

*Bratindranath Banerjee, Director, Standard Chartered Bank vs Hiten P. Dalal, 1994 (4) Bom CR 237; see also http://www.indiankanoon.org/doc/1859635/ (6 March 2011).

Contd

Case 6.5 *Contd*

committed an offence punishable under Sec. 138 of the Negotiable Instruments Act. The accused pleaded not guilty; and among other matters even challenged the court's jurisdiction.

JUDGEMENT: The accused was sentenced to rigorous imprisonment for a term of one year and a fine of a sum of ₹1 lakh, in default to undergo further rigorous imprisonment for a term of 3 months. The sentence of fine is held in abeyance for a period of two months to enable the accused to move an application before this court for permission to pay the same.

REASON: It is beyond reasonable doubt that the accused is guilty under Sec. 138 of the Negotiable Instruments Act. The court has to take judicial note of the fact that there has been a major fraud. *Jurisdiction:* This court was established because of this situation. This is a serious blow to the economy of the country. Even in this case, as we have seen the cheques are of a very large amount, i.e., approximately of ₹78 crore. It is right that there cannot be a better case where a strict sentence must be imposed.

Essential characteristics of a cheque:

1. It must be in writing and duly signed by the drawer. (See the particulars in the above cheque marked 1–6.)
2. It contains an unconditional order.
3. It is issued on a specified banker only.
4. The amount specified is always certain and must be clearly mentioned both in figures and words.
5. The payee is always certain.
6. It is always payable on demand.
7. The cheque must bear a date; otherwise it is invalid and shall not be honoured by the bank.

Table 6.4 presents the differences between a cheque and a bill of exchange.

Table 6.4 Distinction between a cheque and a bill of exchange

Distinction	Cheque	Bill of exchange
Drawee	On specified banker only	Drawn on any—also a banker
Payable	On demand	On demand after expiry date or sight
	On demand to bearer order	Cannot be drawn payable to the bearer on demand
Acceptance	Not necessary	Necessary before payment can be claimed

Contd

Table 6.4 *Contd*

Days of grace	No grace period	Three days for time bills
Presumption	Customer has account with sufficient credit balance	No
Crossing	Crossing—general or specific	No
Stamp	No	It is a must (except demand bills)
Countermand	Possible by the drawer	No
Circulation	Not for circulation; meant for payment	Holders are allowed
Discounting	No	Possible multiple times
Failure to present	Not discharged from liability if not presented (unless he suffers damages by delay in presentment or liquidation of bank)	Drawer and payee are one and the same
Primary liability	Drawer of cheque primarily liable for payment	The drawee or the acceptor is primarily liable
Statutory protection	The banker is protected if he pays a cheque under forged endorsement	No
Noting and protesting	Need not be noted and protested when dishonoured	It is a must
Sets	Not issued in sets	Foreign bills are generally drawn in sets of three or four

Types of cheques

Open cheque   A cheque is called 'open' when it is possible to get cash over the counter at the bank. The holder of an open cheque can do the following:
- Receive its payment over the counter at the bank;
- Deposit the cheque in his own account; or
- Pass it to someone else by signing at the back of a cheque.

Crossed cheque   See top left corner in Figure 6.5. Since an open cheque is subject to risk of theft, it is dangerous to issue such cheques. This risk can be avoided by issuing a type of cheque called 'crossed cheque'. The payment of such cheque is not made over the counter at the bank; it is only credited to the bank account of the payee. A cheque can be crossed by drawing two transverse parallel lines across the cheque, with or without writing 'Account payee' or 'Not negotiable'. Special crossing in the form of writing the bank's name between the crossed lines is a measure for restrictive crossing.

Bearer cheque   A cheque that is payable to any person who presents it for payment at the bank counter is called a 'bearer cheque'. It can be transferred by mere delivery and requires no endorsement.

Order cheque   An order cheque is one which is payable to a particular person. In such a cheque, the word 'bearer' may be cut out or cancelled and the word 'order' may be written.

The payee can transfer an order cheque to someone else by signing his or her name on the back of it.

Also, there are another categorisation of cheques.

Ante-dated cheque A cheque in which the drawer mentions the date earlier to the date of presenting it for payment. For example, a cheque issued on 20 January 2011 may bear a date 1 January 2011.

Stale cheque A cheque which is issued today must be presented before at bank for payment within a stipulated period. After expiry of that period, no payment will be made on it and it is then called a 'stale cheque'.

Mutilated cheque In case a cheque is torn into two or more pieces and presented for payment, such a cheque is called a mutilated cheque. The bank will not make payment against such a cheque without getting confirmation of the drawer. But if a cheque is torn at the corners and no material fact is erased or cancelled, the bank may make payment against such a cheque.

Post-dated cheque A cheque on which drawer mentions a date which is subsequent to the date on which it is presented, it is called a post-dated cheque. For example, if a cheque is presented on 1 January 2011 and bears the date 1 March 2011, it is a post-dated cheque. The bank will make payment only on the date which the cheque bears. Table 6.5 presents the classification of negotiable instruments.

Table 6.5 Classification of negotiable instruments

Type	Explanation
Bearer and order	When it is expressed therein to be so payable—'bearer'. When it is expressed—'order to A'—then to a particular person.
Inland and Foreign	*Inland:* drawn and payable in India. *Foreign:* not originating in India *Usance:* time fixed for the payment for the bills drawn in one country and payable in another.
Payable on demand	*Cheque:* always payable on demand. *Promissory note or bill of exchange:* when it is expressed to be payable 'on demand', 'at sight', or 'at presentment'.
Time	Instruments payable according to a fixed time: 'after sight', 'specified date'.
Accommodation bill	*Trade bill:* when the debtor draws a bill on the creditor who has no immediate money to pay—it accommodates the need of loan to the debtor.
Fictitious bill	When the name of the drawer or the payee or both is fictitious in a bill.
Documentary and clean bill	*Documentary bill:* when the documents of title to the goods and other documents such as invoice, insurance, etc., are annexed to a bill. These are delivered to the buyer only on acceptance or payment of the bill. *Clean bill:* when the documents relating to the title to the goods are not attached.
Escrow	When a negotiable instrument is delivered conditionally, or for a special purpose as a colateral security, or for safe custody only and not for the purpose of transferring absolutely property therein. There is no liability to pay unless conditions are fulfilled.

Contd

Table 6.5 *Contd*

Ambiguous	When one is not sure of the nature of the instrument—whether it is bill of exchange or promissory note—due to faulty drafting. The holder must decide definitely what it is; only then does it become an instrument to be abided by.
Inchoate	An incomplete instrument. A signed instrument with details of amount and date not filled in—helps in business to overcome the prevailing uncertainties: the drawer may put a maximum limit of time and amount; however, if the transferee exceeds the above, then the liability will lie with the drawer of the bill to honour it.*
Undated bills and notes	Although date is most important, yet an instrument that fulfills all the requirements except date is not invalid; it may be filled in with circumstantial evidence—such as date of posting or oral communication; also the holder in due course may insert the date and it would be payable accordingly. Such insertions do not cause material alteration of the instrument.
Bills in sets	According to Secs 132 and 133 of the Act, a bill of exchange may be drawn in parts: two, three, or four. All the parts together make a set and the whole set constitutes only one bill. (See Figure 6.6. Plainly speaking, it is a blank cheque; a manager should desist from such a practice as far as possible.)

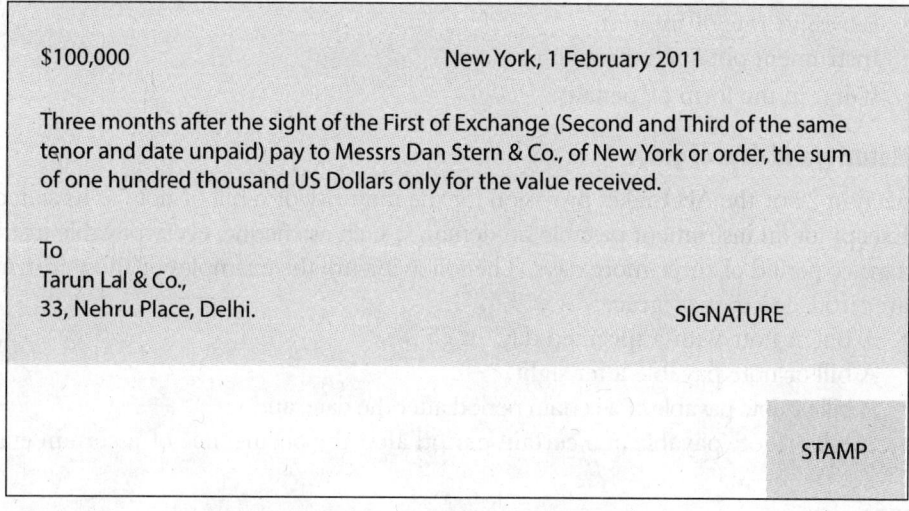

$100,000   New York, 1 February 2011

Three months after the sight of the First of Exchange (Second and Third of the same tenor and date unpaid) pay to Messrs Dan Stern & Co., of New York or order, the sum of one hundred thousand US Dollars only for the value received.

To
Tarun Lal & Co.,
33, Nehru Place, Delhi.   SIGNATURE

STAMP

Figure 6.6   Specimen of bill in sets

All of the above may be good enough, and yet there is a lingering feeling of something amiss: when does the payment actually take place? There is another nagging question: If the payment is not made on time, is there also an interest to be levied on bills and notes? You will find the answers to these questions in the following sections.

Payment in due course

The full form of the above classification should read: payment in due course[4] according to the tenor of the instrument in good faith and without negligence to any person in possession thereof. The term *tenor* is applied to the determined period of time after which the instrument is payable. The five conditions required for the discharge of a negotiable instrument are mentioned below:

1. The payment must be in accordance with the apparent tenor of the instrument.
2. The payment must be made by or on behalf of the drawee or acceptor.
3. The person to whom the payment is made should be in possession of the instrument and should also be entitled to receive payment on it.
4. The payment should be made in good faith without negligence and under bonafide circumstances.
5. There should not be any ground for believing that the possessor is not entitled to receive payment.

Interest on bills and notes

The interest rate will be calculated on the principal money from the date of origin to the date of realisation of the instrument. If the rate of interest is unspecified then, according to Sec. 80 of the Act, it will be fixed at the rate of 18 per cent per annum.

If a party is charged as the endorser of an instrument dishonoured by non-payment, then he is liable to pay interest only from the time that he receives the notice of dishonour. The court will reject the rate of interest in the following cases:

- Excessive rate of interest.
- Instrument obtained through coercion.
- If it is in the form of penalty.

Maturity and days of grace

Section 22 of the Act makes provision for the maturity of a bill or note as its stated due date. Except for an instrument payable on demand, such as cheque, every payable instrument has a grace period of three more days. The following are the examples of those instruments that are entitled to days of grace:

- A bill or note with a specified day,
- A bill or note payable after sight,
- A bill or note payable at a certain period after the date, and
- A bill or note payable at a certain period after the occurrence of a certain event.

6.3 HUNDI

Hundi stems from the Sanskrit root *hund*, that is 'to collect'. In comparison to the modern negotiable instruments, they serve as either promissory notes or bills of exchange. Thus, we may define a hundi as a negotiable instrument that is indigenously developed and is invariably written in any of the Indian vernacular languages (see Table 6.6). There is no explicit mention

---

[4]Sec. 10, The Negotiable Instrument Act.

about the hundi in the Negotiable Instruments Act; however, the case law has always upheld its validity and is treated on par with the instruments in the Act (refer Case 6.5).

Table 6.6   Kinds of hundis

Hundi	Explanation
Shah-jog	Drawn by one merchant on another, asking the latter to pay the amount to a *Shah*. *Shah* is a respectable and responsible person, a man of worth and known in the *bazaar/mandi*. A shah-jog hundi passes from one hand to another till it reaches a *Shah*, who, after reasonable enquiries, presents it to the drawee for acceptance of the payment.
Nam-jog	It is a hundi payable to or to the order of a specified person named in it. It is negotiable like the bill of exchange.
Dharshani	This is a hundi payable at sight. It must be presented for payment within a reasonable time after its receipt by the holder. Thus, it is similar to a demand bill.
Muddati	*Muddati* or *miadi* hundi is payable after a specified period of time; it is similar to a time bill.
Dhani-jog	*Dhani* implies *holder* or *bearer*; it is an instrument payable to the bearer and can be negotiated by mere delivery.
Jawabi	*Jawab* stands for *answer*. It is used to remit money from one place to another. When the payee—the receiver of the money—gets the money, he has to reply to the remitter.
Jokhami	*Jokakam* implies *hurt* or *loss*. It is an instrument which functions as not only payment but also an insurance. It implies a condition that the money shall be payable by the drawee who is the buyer of the goods only in the event of the safe arrival of the goods against which the hundi is drawn.
Firman-jog	*Firman* stands for *order*. It can be negotiated like other instruments payable to order—by endorsement and delivery.

CASE 6.5	APPELLANT: Assistant Commissioner of Income Tax (CIT(A)) vs RESPONDENT: Bissheshwarlal Mannalal & Sons*

DATE OF JUDGEMENT: 16 February 2001

FACTS: Solitary grievance of the Revenue is against CIT(A)'s deleting the addition of ₹45,28,754 made under Sec. 69D on account of borrowings made by the assessees in cash on bundles. The assessee is a Calcutta-based firm and owns a tea garden at Rosekandi in Cachar district of Assam. During the relevant previous year, the assessee had an arrangement with one M/s Batdeodas Satya Narayan, the local moneylender, which had an office at a location near assessee's tea garden, at Janlgang Bazar in Silchar, and under this arrangement, the tea garden office of the firm could borrow money in cash from the local moneylender for meeting local expenses such as labour payments, etc., but immediately upon doing so, the local office would issue internal instructions to the head office to make the payment of the borrowed sum directly to the moneylender. As a matter of fact, the money was given by the moneylender in

*Assistant Commissioner of Income Tax vs Bissheshwarlal Mannalal & Sons, 2002 80 Income Tax Tribunal (ITD) 69 Kol; also see http://www.indiankanoon.org/doc/1891390/ (7 March 2011).

Contd

Case 6.5 *Contd*

exchange of such internal payment instructions issued by the local office to the head office. As a part of this arrangement, head office of the assessee-firm was making instructed payments to the moneylender, by crossed cheques, usually within 2–3 days of such payment instruction being issued by the tea estate office. Thus, effective borrowing period was the time required in implementing the payment instructions issued by the tea estate office to the head office, which worked out to, on an average, less than 3 days. In consideration of these services, the moneylender was charging a flat interest of 75 paise per hundred rupees. On these undisputed facts, the Assessing Officer (AO) was of the opinion that this arrangement by the assessee was in nature of borrowing against hundi and since these borrowings were in cash, Sec. 69D was attracted. Accordingly, the AO made an addition of ₹45,28,754, the total amount of borrowings by the tea estate office during the relevant previous year. In appeal, however, it was held that there were no borrowings by the assessee, as the account credited by the tea garden office was head office remittance and not that of the moneylender. It was further held that even if there was a borrowing, in any case the transaction did not involve any hundi. In coming to this conclusion, the CIT(A) was influenced by the factors that: (i) a hundi is a bill of exchange and therefore, it must have three parties whereas there are only two parties in the present case; (ii) a hundi is generally drawn in vernacular language whereas the payment instructions were issued in English and therefore such a payment construction cannot be construed as hundi; and (iii) even if the payment instruction is treated as hundi, since money is payable on demand, this has to be treated as *darshani* hundi.

JUDGEMENT: The appeal by the Assistant Commissioner of Income Tax is dismissed.

REASON: The entire transaction is fully supported by evidence and confirmation by the moneylender himself, which is placed at page 5 of the paper-book, and PAN number of the moneylender is also placed on record. The repayments are made by the crossed account payee cheques and the identity of the moneylender was not doubted by the Revenue. The Revenue's case hinges on a venial breach of law. CIT(A) action prima facie seems to be unsustainable from this point of view also. However, in the present case, and in view of the findings in the foregoing in the Judgement document, it is not necessary to examine that aspect of the matter.

6.4   NEGOTIATION

When a promissory note, bill of exchange, or cheque is transferred to any person, so as to constitute that person the holder thereof, the instrument is said to be negotiated.

   – Sec. 14, The Negotiable Instruments Act, 1881

Negotiation in colloquial terms implies a communication to settle a certain deal or a problem. In legal terms, negotiation in financial matters involves a give and take or a transfer. Who are the parties to a negotiable instrument what capacity should they possess, and what liabilities do they bear are the issues you will deal with in this section.

MANAGER'S TAKEAWAY

- Be accountable to money's instruments.

Competent Parties

In earlier chapters covering the Indian Contract Act, 1872, you had seen that only those persons who have attained the age of majority, are of sound mind, and are not disqualified by law, have the capacity to enter a contract. Any such person can also become a party to negotiable instrument (refer to Table 6.7).

Table 6.7   Competent parties in negotiation

Person	Particulars
Minor	A minor cannot be an originator of the negotiable instrument. If he does, then it is void. But he can bind all other parties to it so as to draw, indorse, deliver, and negotiate.*
Persons of unsound mind	These are void. Lunatics, idiots, persons suffering from insanity, etc. However, just as in the case of the minors, the others are bound by the liabilities to the instrument.
Corporations	These are artificial legal entities and are liable to the extent those powers are described in the memoranda of rules or the by laws of the association in question.
Agents	A duly authorised agent may make, draw, indorse, accept, negotiate, and deliver a bill, note, or cheque.
Partners	Partners of a trading firm have prima facie authority to bind their co-partners to a negotiable instrument.
Hindu joint family	The *karta* of the family who deals with the outside world has the authority to negotiate on behalf of the family.
Legal representative	Legal representative exercises the powers of negotiable instruments in the event of death of its holder (Sec. 29).

Parties to Negotiable Instruments

Acceptor   One who accepts the bill of exchange.

Acceptor for honour   If a bill is dishonoured by non-acceptance, the holder may allow some other person, the acceptor for honour to accept it for the honour of the drawer or any one of the indorsers.

Drawee   The person on whom the bill of exchange is drawn and who is directed to pay. In case of cheque, the drawee is always a banker.

Drawee in case of need   In a bill of exchange or any indorsement thereon, the name of any person given in addition to the drawee is the drawee in case of need.

Drawer   The person who makes or draws a bill of exchange or cheque.

Holder   Any person entitled in his own name to the possession and to receive or recover the amount due of a promissory note, bill, or cheque.

Indorsee   The person to whom the bill, note, or cheque is indorsed.

---

*Its logic depends on the Law of Contract.

Indorser   The person who indorses the bill, note, or cheque.

Maker   The person who makes a promissory note.

Payee   The person named in the bill, note, or cheque to whom or to whose order, the money has to be paid.

See Table 6.8 for the parties to negotiable instruments.

Table 6.8   Parties to negotiable instruments

Parties to negotiable instruments		
Bill of exchange	**Promissory note**	**Cheque**
Drawer	Maker	Maker
Drawee	Payee	Drawee
Acceptor	Holder	Payee
Payee	Indorser	Holder
Holder	Indorsee	Indorser
Indorser		Indorsee
Indorsee		

Table 6.9 shows the differences between a holder and a holder in due course.

Table 6.9   Differences between *holder* and *holder in due course*

Holder (Sec. 8)	**Holder in due course (Sec. 9)**
Entitled in one's own name:	One is holder in due course if:
(a) to possess thereof	(a) the possessor of the negotiable instrument holds it as payable to bearer or the payee or the indorsee thereof
(b) to receive or recover the amount from the parties thereto	(b) he became the holder before the maturity
	(c) he is its holder in good faith

Caution: However, a holder of a negotiable instrument will not be a holder in due course if:

- the instrument is a gift, unlawful consideration, or illegally obtained.
- obtained after its maturity.
- not obtained bona fide.

Privileges

See Table 6.10, where we show the privileges enjoyed by a holder in due course. (Also see Case 6.6.)

Table 6.10 Privileges enjoyed by a holder in due course

Section of the Act	Privileges
20	Protection against inchoate instrument.
36	Liability of prior parties until the instrument is duly satisfied.
42	Protection against fictitious payee.
43	Protection against the instrument without consideration. In other words, the pleas of absence of consideration cannot be raised against the holder in due course.*
46	The liabilities of the parties that negotiated the instrument to the holder in due course remain undiminished.
53	Any defect in the title of the transferor will not affect the rights of the holder in due course, even if he had the knowledge of the prior defect, provided he himself is not a party to the fraud.
58	Protection against instrument obtained by unlawful means or for the unlawful consideration.
118	Every holder is a holder in due course.
120	Estoppel against denying the original validity of instrument.
121	Estoppel against denying the capacity of payee to indorse.
122	Indorser is not permitted to deny the capacity of prior parties.

CASE 6.6

APPELLANT: U. Ponnappa Moothan Sons, Palghat vs RESPONDENT: Catholic Syrian Bank Ltd, & Others*

DATE OF JUDGEMENT: 18 September 1990

FACTS: Consequent upon the pleading of promissory note and other title deeds relating to her property by defendant no. 5, (mother of defendants 2 to 4) in favour of the respondent bank as security, thereby creating an equitable mortgage, the respondent bank allowed credit facilities like accommodation by way of hundi discount, key loan, and cheque purchases upto a limit of ₹35,00,000 to defendant no. 1, a firm consisting of defendants nos. 2 to 4 as partners. The dispute arose when the first defendant withdrew the amount at various dates. When the respondent bank sent the cheques for collection, the Union Bank of India returned the cheques with the endorsement 'full cover not received'.

www.indiankanoon.org/doc/1077386/ (6 March 2011).

Contd

---

*Sec. 25 of the Indian Contract Act, 1872: 'An agreement made without consideration is void'.

Case 6.6 *Contd*

What is the true meaning and scope of the expression 'holder in due course' as defined in Sec. 9 of the Negotiable Instruments Act, 1881, was the question that arose for consideration in this appeal.

JUDGEMENT: Affirmed the Judgements of the courts below and dismissed the appeal. The respondent bank was a 'holder in due course' and as such entitled to enforce the liability against the appellant-defendant no. 6 and the rest of the defendants.

REASON: The trial court had held that the respondent-bank was a 'holder in due course' and as such entitled to enforce the liability against the appellant-defendant no. 6. In the instant case, there is sufficient evidence establishing the fact that the defendants were allowed credit facilities upto a limit of ₹35,00.000 by the bank and this fact is not in dispute. The pledging of the title deed by the 5th defendant of her properties with the bank with an intention to create an equitable mortgage to secure the repayment of the amounts due from the 1st defendant and the fact that a pro-note for an amount of ₹35,00,000 executed by defendant nos. 2 to 4 in favour of the 5th defendant was endorsed in favour of the plaintiff bank would establish that there was an express contract for providing the credit facilities. It should therefore necessarily be inferred that there is also an implied contract to credit the proceeds of the cheques in favour of defendant no. 1 to his account before actually receiving them. As a question of fact, this aspect is established by the evidence on record. In such a situation the plaintiff need not make enquiries about the transactions of supply of goods etc., that were going on between defendants nos 1 and 6. Even if defendant no. 1 has not supplied the goods in respect of which the cheque in question were issued by defendant no. 6 there was no cause at any rate sufficient cause for the plaintiff to doubt the title of defendant no. 1 nor can it be said that the plaintiff acted negligently disregarding 'red flag' raising suspicion. Viewed from this background, it cannot be said that there was sufficient cause to doubt the title nor there is scope to infer gross negligence on the part of the plaintiff.

There is no material that amounts to rebuttal of the presumption in his favour as provided under Sec. 118(g). On the other hand, the plaintiff has discharged the necessary burden to the extent on him and has proved that he is a holder in due course for valid consideration.

It follows logically to think that if there are privileges then there are duties or liabilities. If the holder in due course has privileges as listed in Table 6.8 then the other parties to the negotiated instrument have liabilities. Refer Table 6.9 for a list of liabilities of the parties to the negotiated instrument.

The above liabilities of the parties may be summed up as the manager's folly. 'Principle of suretyship' (Sec. 38). The holder in due course is also protected from forged indorsement (Sec. 41), and an instrument with a fictitious name (Sec. 42).

MANAGER'S TAKEAWAY

- Signing on a blank cheque is manager's folly.
- All in good faith—but after due verification

Table 6.11 Liabilities of the parties to the negotiated instrument

Parties to the negotiated instrument	Liabilities	Sections of the Act
Drawer	In case of dishonour by the drawee or acceptor, the drawer must compensate the holder*	30
Drawee of cheque	Generally the banker—must honor the cheque by paying it; failure to do so would be further obliged to compensate the drawer.	31
Maker of a note, and acceptor of bill	Liable to pay the amount to the holder on demand; any default in payment results in compensation to the holder.	32
Indorser	Liable to all subsequent holders of an instrument before maturity, in case of dishonour of the instrument.	35
Prior parties to a holder in due course	Every prior party to a negotiable instrument is liable thereon to a holder in due course until the instrument is duly satisfied.	36

6.5 PRESENTMENT

TEXT

In a promissory note or bill of exchange, the expressions "at sight" and "on presentment" mean 'on demand'. The expression "after sight" means, in a promissory note, after presentment for sight, and, in a bill of exchange, after acceptance, or noting for non-acceptance, or protest for non-acceptance.

– Sec. 21, The Negotiable Instruments Act, 1881

The above text may be interpreted as: It is to show the negotiable instrument to the drawee, acceptor, or maker for acceptance, sight, or payment. You will be able to familiarize with the following three kinds of presentment in the next few pages: bills of exchange for acceptance, promissory notes for sight, and negotiable instruments for payments.

Presentment for Acceptance

Table 6.10 discusses the concept of presentment for acceptance. There are two modes of acceptance:

General   When the drawer while accepting the bill does not attach any condition or qualification to it.

Qualified   It qualified when it is subject to some condition or qualification. The holder may refuse such a bill. This will dishonour it. In case he takes it, then it is at his own risk.

---

*Upon the condition that due notice is given.

Table 6.12 Presentment for acceptance

Question	Answer
What is it?	A bill is accepted when the drawee signs it signifying his assent to the order of the drawer and delivered to the holder.
To whom the presentment for acceptance is made?	To the drawee—one or several or: The authorised agent of the drawee; or The legal representative of the drawee, in case the latter has died; or The official receiver or assignee in case the drawee is insolvent.
When is the presentment for acceptance made?	The specified time and before its maturity. In case of acceptance of bill after sight, then within a reasonable period of time.
Where is the presentment for acceptance made?	The specified place; in case no specific place is mentioned, the bill should be presented at the drawee's place of business or residence.
Can the presentment for acceptance be excused?	Yes, if the drawee cannot be found after reasonable search. Yes, if the drawee is dead or insolvent. Yes, if the drawee is fictitious person or not competent of the contract. *Note:* If the presentment for acceptance is excused, the bill is treated as dishonoured.

Presentment for Sight

In the case of a promissory note, the maker himself is the person liable for it. A note payable after certain period after sight must be presented to the maker for sight in order to fix its maturity. In the event of the maker being untraceable, the instrument is dishonoured.

Presentment for Payment

Promissory notes, bills of exchange, and cheques must be presented for payment to the maker, acceptor, or the drawee by or on behalf of the holder. Mentioned below are the rules for presentment for payment:

1. It must be made during the normal hours of business.
2. It must be presented at its maturity.
3. Presentment of promissory note payable by installments must be presented for payment on third day after the due date.
4. The presentment of cheque is at the bank.
5. The delay in presentment is excused if it is beyond the control of the holder.
6. The banker is liable for any negligence in dealing with bill presented for payment.
7. Any person liable to pay and called upon by the holder thereof to pay the amount due on note, bill, or cheque before payment to (a) have it shown, (b) have it delivered up to him, (c) be indemnified against any further claim if lost.[5]

In determining what is a reasonable time for presentment for acceptance or payment for giving notice of dishonour and for noting, one must consider the nature of the instrument

---

[5]See Amendment and Miscellaneous Provisions of the Act, 2002.

and the usual course of dealing with such matters. Reasonable time is usually considered as the business hours of the working days (Case 6.7).

CASE 6.7

APPELLANT: Umiya Pripe Private Limited and Others

VS

RESPONDENT: State of Gujarat*

DATE OF JUDGEMENT: 24 September 2008

FACTS: A criminal suit was filed by respondent against the applicants and others for the offence punishable under Sec. 138 of the Negotiable Instruments Act in the court of learned metropolitan magistrate, Ahmedabad alleging interalia that the cheque for an amount of ₹3 crore was issued by the applicants and when the said cheque was presented, the same came to be dishonoured/returned with an endorsement: insufficient balance. It was the case on behalf of the respondent that thereafter the applicants were served with the legal notice under Sec. 138 of the Negotiable Instruments Act, 1881, and, thereafter, the applicants gave vague reply to the notice but did not make payment, and, therefore, the aforesaid criminal case came to be instituted against the applicants accused for the offence under Sec. 138 of the Negotiable Instruments Act, 1881. The trial court issued summons upon the applicants and others by impugned order dated 09 February 2007 for the offence punishable under Sec. 138 of the Negotiable Instruments Act, 1881. Hence, the applicants have preferred the present criminal miscellaneous application under Sec. 482 of the Code of Criminal Procedure for quashing and setting aside the complaint.

JUDGEMENT: Application succeeds.

REASON: Considering the above case, the impugned complaint filed by the respondent herein against the applicant for the offence under Sec. 138 of the Negotiable Instruments Act is beyond the period of limitation as prescribed under Sec. 142 read with Sec. 138(c) of the Negotiable Instruments Act, 1881 and, therefore, the learned trial court could not have taken cognizance of the said complaint. Under the circumstances, the impugned complaint and the order of the trial court issuing summons in the said complaint deserves to be quashed and set aside.**

---

*Umiya Pipe Private Limited and Others vs State of Gujarat, Gujarat High Court, 24/0902007; see also http://www.indiankanoon.org/doc/102147/ (10 March 2011).

**A relevant and interesting question could be: Which date would be the relevant date for starting the limitation for filing the complaint under Sec. 138 of the Negotiable Instruments Act, 1881?

6.6   DISHONOUR OF A NEGOTIABLE INSTRUMENT

 TEXT

Dishonour by non-acceptance. A bill of exchange is said to be dishonoured by non-acceptance when the drawee, or one of several drawees not being partners, makes default in acceptance upon being duly required to accept the bill, or where presentment is excused and the bill is not accepted. Where the drawee is incompetent to contract, or the acceptance is qualified, the bill may be treated as dishonoured.

– Sec. 91, The Negotiable Instruments Act 1881

 MANAGER'S TAKEAWAY

- The honour of an instrument depends on its backing.
- Time is essential for presentment and acceptance.

Dishonouring a negotiable instrument refers to not accepting a bill of exchange or refusing to payment (see Case 6.8). While the bill of exchange is dishonoured by non-acceptance or non-payment, the promissory note and the cheque are done so by non-payment only. Here you will study three aspects of dishonour: notice of dishonour, noting and protesting, and rules of compensation.

CASE 6.8	

APPELLANT: Indian Overseas Bank vs RESPONDENT: Global Marine Products*

DATE OF JUDGEMENT: 17 September 2002

FACTS: The appellant claimed ₹10,60,277.03 towards packing credit facility due from the first respondent partnership firm from defendants 1 to 8. They also claimed ₹3,40,258.39 being the amount due under foreign demand bills purchased facility, jointly and severally from the defendants 1 to 9. The lower court disallowed the claim made by the appellant against the 9th defendant jointly and severally with the other defendants. The lower court disallowed the amount of ₹1,34,294 and ₹4,50,617 paid by the Export Credit Guarantee Corporation to the appellant after suit on packing credit facility and decree passed for the balance amount against respondents 1 to 8 and charged upon the plaint schedule properties.

The appellant contended that the 9th defendant/9th respondent is liable for the amount due to the appellant under the foreign demand bills purchase facility in this case as per the transaction with the 1st defendant/1st respondent. The 9th respondent is an export house in Delhi having arrangement with the 1st defendant-firm to export the goods of the 1st defendant in their name and it is a private limited company. According to the appellant, an amount ₹3,40,259.39 being the value in Indian rupee of US $12,600 outstanding payment by the foreign buyer of the goods exported by the 1st respondent through the 9th respondent is due. It is the case of the appellant that out of the total amount of US $62,600 due from the foreign buyers M/s Amsea Farms Inc., New York, US $50,000 is paid and the balance amount of US $12,600 remains unpaid.

The plaintiff preferred this appeal challenging the decree and Judgement passed by the lower court disallowing the joint and several decree against the 9th defendant with regard to the claim for foreign demand bills purchase facility and the amount of ₹5,84,913 out of the total claim of ₹9,60,277.03 due as per packing credit facility.

The defendant argued that it is well-settled law that notice of dishonour to the drawer is mandatory and unless and until notice is given, the holder has no cause of action against the drawer of the cheque or bill of exchange under Sec. 30 of the Negotiable Instruments Act unless and until notice to drawer is exempted under Sec. 98 of the Act. Therefore, there is no plea of any notice of dishonour given to them and no exemption is claimed by the appellant in the plaint from giving notice of dishonour, the above claim is not sustainable against them.

*India Overseas Bank vs Global Marine Production, 003 114 CompCas 733 Ker; also see http://www. indiankanoon. org/doc/1524118/ (15 March 2011).

Contd

Case 6.8 *Contd*

JUDGEMENT: Appeal allowed. The decree and Judgement passed by the lower court and decree of the suit for the balance amount of ₹5,84,911 with interest thereon at 16.5 per cent per annum from the date of plaint which is disallowed by the lower court under the packing credit facility account and a joint and several decree is passed against the 9th respondent/9th defendant also for the amount decreed under the count foreign demand bill purchase facility be modified.

REASON: In view of the fact that the 9th respondent was well aware of the dishonour of the bill of exchange and they have acted on the basis of the dishonour of the bill of exchange, the failure to issue the statutory notice as contemplated under Sec. 30 of the Negotiable Instruments Act will not cause any prejudice to the 9th respondent in this case. Therefore, the contention of the 9th respondent that they are not liable for the amount due under the bill of exchange since no notice of dishonour as provided under Sec. 30 of the Negotiable Instruments Act is given to them, is not sustainable and the appellant is entitled to claim exemption of notice to the 9th respondent under clause (c) of Sec. 98 of the Negotiable Instruments Act.

It is clear that the appellant is entitled to a decree against the 9th respondent also for the balance amount of US $12,600 due as per bill of exchange and the lower court was in manifest error in not decreeing the suit jointly against the 9th respondent also in favour of the appellant.

Notice of dishonour   The notice of dishonour is to inform the concerned parties about the accruing liabilities.

- The notice is given by the holder of the instrument or one responsible for it.
- The notice may be written or oral.
- It must be given within a reasonable time.
- The holder has the duty to get it noted and protested by a Notary Public.

Noting and protesting   Noting consists of recording the fact of dishonour by a notary public upon the instrument or a paper attached to it within a reasonable time after the dishonour. When a promissory note or bill of exchange is dishonoured, the holder has the right to sue any or all the parties liable for the instrument.

Noting   The notary notes down the details of dishonour including date, reasons, notary's charges, etc.

Protesting   Having noted the dishonoured instrument, the notary public issues a certificate containing:

- the transcript of the instrument;
- the name of the person against whom the protest is registered;
- the fact and reason for dishonour and its place and time; and
- signature of the notary public.

The noting and protesting helps the holder to possess evidence in the event of a suit.

Rules of compensation   When a negotiable instrument is dishonoured, the party liable to pay becomes bound to pay compensation to the holder or indorsee. The following are the rules for determining compensation (as laid out by Sec. 117):

Compensation to holder   It includes the amount due upon the instrument and expenses incurred in such as presenting, noting, and protesting.

Re-exchange   When the person charged is in a foreign country, the holder is entitled to receive the compensation at the current rate of exchange.

 MANAGER'S TAKEAWAY

- Keep track of the negotiable instruments.
- Keep cheque book stubs to tell you of your financial story.

Compensation to indorser   The indorser is paid with an interest of 18 per cent.[6]

Redraft   A bill is called redraft when the party entitled to compensation may draw a bill upon the party liable to compensate him for the due amount along with all the expenses incurred.

6.7   DISCHARGE OF A NEGOTIABLE INSTRUMENT

Discharge from liability. The maker, acceptor, or indorser, respectively of a negotiable instrument is discharged from liability thereon by:
(a) cancellation: to a holder thereof who cancels such acceptor's or indorser's name with intent to discharge him, and to all parties claiming under such holder;
(b) release: to a holder thereof who otherwise discharges such maker, acceptor, or indorser, and to all parties deriving title under such holder after notice of such discharge;
(c) payment: to all parties thereto, if the instrument is payable to bearer, or has been indorsed in blank, and such maker, acceptor, or indorser makes payment in due course of the amount due thereon.

– Sec. 82, The Negotiable Instruments Act, 1881

Discharge of a negotiable instrument implies a cessation of the liabilities it entails (refer Case 6.9). A negotiable instrument is discharged when all rights of action under it are completely extinguished and it is no more negotiable. This happens when the party ultimately liable on the instrument is discharged from liability. Even a holder in due course does not acquire any rights. There is a real possibility that one or more of the parties involved may be discharged from liability and for the rest who are liable, the instrument is still negotiable. The above text shows that the discharge of a negotiable instrument has two aspect: (a) discharge of the instrument and (b) discharge of a party or parties.

Discharge of an Instrument

There are mainly five modes of discharge as shown in Table 6.11.

Discharge of One or More Parties

Table 6.12 shows the modes of discharge of one or more parties.

[6]Negotiable Instruments Amendment Act, 1998.

CASE 6.9

APPELLANT: Ravi Chandran vs RESPONDENT: Subramanian*

DATE OF JUDGEMENT: 24 June 2005

FACTS: It is the case of appellant that the respondent along with another, had borrowed a sum of ₹90,000 on 4 July 1994, that in order to discharge the said debt, he had issued a cheque dated 19 March 1997 for a sum of ₹1,47,000, which includes interest, that when the cheque was tendered for collection, the same was returned with an endorsement: 'funds insufficient', that even after the issue of mandatory notice, the accused failed to pay the cheque amount and in this view since he had committed the offence under Sec. 138 of the Negotiable Instruments Act, he should be dealt with accordingly. The respondent upon appearance seems to have denied not only the liability but also the issuance of the cheque in favour of the complainant for the alleged discharge of liability.

The trial court, after recording evidence, while scanning the same, came to the conclusion that though the cheque was issued on behalf of Southern Biologicals, the non-inclusion of its owner is not fatal and that the complainant has failed to prove that the cheque was issued by the accused to discharge the liability. Thus concluding, the respondent was acquitted as per the Judgement of 12 November 1998, which is under challenge in this appeal.

JUDGEMENT: The appeal dismissed.

REASON: There is a promissory note, followed by the cheque. It is highly improbable to come to the conclusion that these two documents must have been forged or concocted for the purpose of the case. In this view, the finding of the trial court that the prosecution has failed to prove the issuance of the cheque is not acceptable to me, considering the fact that the cheque belongs to M/s Southern Biologicals, for which the accused was acting as a mandate holder. This finding will not in any way change the result of the case, that is, the acquittal. The case has not been filed against the proper person, in whose account the cheque was drawn. For the foregoing reasons, the appeal deserves dismissal, though not for the reasons recorded by the trial court.

*Ravichandran vs Subramanian, IV (2006) BC 54l; see also http://www.indiankanoon.org/doc/640485/ (20 April 2011).

Table 6.13   Discharge of a negotiable instrument

Mode	Discharge
Payment in due course	It is the normal and most obvious mode: the payment is done and the parties concerned are discharged of their liabilities.
Party primarily liable becomes holder	That he has an absolute title and does not hold conditionally, he as the maker or acceptor becomes its holder in his own right.
Express waiver	The rightful holder renounces in writing or gives up his rights against all the parties to the instrument.
Cancellation	The instrument is cancelled—as willed by the holder or his agent by either expressly cancelling the signature, or destroying the instrument itself.
As in a contract	Discharge through novation, rescission or expiry of its period.

Table 6.14   Modes of discharge of one or more parties

Modes	Discharge
Payment	When the payment is done.
Cancellation	The holder or his authorised agent cancels the name of a party on the instrument.
Release	The holder releases the party in question by any means other than cancellation.
Allowing drawee more than 48 hours	According to Sec. 83 of the Act the holder allows the drawee 48 hours to consider to accept the instrument, all previous parties not consenting to such allowance are discharged.
Non-presentment of cheque	The cheque is not presented by the holder within a reasonable time causing damage to the drawer through delay due to the failure of the bank.
Cheque payable to order	According to Sec. 85 of the Act, a cheque payable to order purports to be indorsed by the payee, the banker is discharged by payment in due course. If it is a bearer's cheque, the drawee is discharged by payment in due course to the bearer.
Draft drawn by one branch on another	The bank is discharged by payment in due course.
Non-consenting parties	According to Sec. 86 of the Act, the holder of a bill of exchange assents in a qualified acceptance, all the previous parties whose consent is not obtained to such consent are discharged from liability.
Operation of law	(a) Court order discharging the insolvent. (b) When a Judgement is obtained against the acceptor, maker, or indorser, the debt under the bill is merged into Judgement debt. (c) Lapse of time.
Material alteration	Renders the instrument void unless parties thereto have consented prior to such alteration.
Payment of altered instrument	The parties to the instrument discharged upon the payment of an apparent tenor of the instrument.

Material Alteration

The material alteration of a negotiable instrument means the changes one does after it has been made.

Essential alterations   These are the ones that change or vitiate the nature of the instrument, i.e., date, sum payable, time of payment, place of payment, and rate.

Non-vitiating alterations   Alterations made prior to the issue of the instrument, correction of an obvious mistake such as 1898 instead of 1998, an alteration of common intention such as 'or order', or a correction with mutual understanding.

Alterations authorised by the Act   Sec. 20—filling blanks of an inchoate instrument; Sec. 49—conversion of a blank indorsement into indorsement in full; Sec. 125—crossing of cheques.

Additionally, Sec. 87 of the Act lays down two clear aspects of material alteration:

(a) No man should be permitted to take the chance of committing a fraud without running any risk of loss by the event when it is detected.

(b) Alteration destroys the identity of the instrument.

Exhibit 6.1 presents the role of presumptions vis-à-vis negotiable instruments.

Exhibit 6.1   It Is Presumed Until the Contrary Is Proved

Presumptions as to negotiable instruments until the contrary is proved, the following presumptions shall be made:

(a) of consideration: that every negotiable instrument was made or drawn for consideration, and that every such instrument, when it has been accepted, indorsed, negotiated, or transferred, was accepted, indorsed, negotiated, or transferred for consideration;

(b) as to date: that every negotiable instrument bearing a date was made or drawn on such date;

(c) as to time of acceptance: that every accepted bill of exchange was accepted within a reasonable time after its date and before its maturity;

(d) as to time of transfer: that every transfer of a negotiable instrument was made before its maturity;

(e) as to order of indorsements: that the indorsements appearing upon a negotiable instrument were made in the order in which they appear thereon;

(f) as to stamp: that a lost promissory note, bill of exchang, or cheque was duly stamped;

(g) that holder is a holder in due course: that the holder of a negotiable instrument is a holder in due course; provided that, where the instrument has been obtained from its lawful owner, or from any person in lawful custody thereof, by means of an SP offence or fraud. or has been obtained from the maker or acceptor thereof by means of an offence or fraud, or for unlawful consideration, the burthen of proving that the holder is a holder in due course lies upon him.

– Sec. 118, The Negotiable Instruments Act, 1881

6.8   RULES OF EVIDENCE—ESTOPPEL AND INTERNATIONAL LAW

Estoppel against denying original validity of instrument: No maker of a promissory note, and no drawer of a bill of exchange or cheque, and no acceptor of a bill of exchange for the honour of the drawer shall, in a suit thereon by a holder in due course, be permitted to deny the validity of the instrument as originally made or drawn.

– Sec. 120, The Negotiable Instruments Act, 1881

You saw in Exhibit 6.1, the text of the law regarding presumptions as to negotiable instruments. Those were the salient features which are essential for a negotiable instrument. Now you will study further conditions to ensure and protect the negotiable instrument. We shall consider these under two headings, namely, estoppel and international law.

MANAGER'S TAKEAWAY

- Manager has the responsibility to protect the identity of the negotiable instrument.
- Shun negligence while issuing an instrument.

Estoppel

It is a legal principle that prevents a person from doing or saying something which would contradict some earlier action or statement that another has relied on and the contradiction of which would hurt that other person. In other words, it is a legal binding that prevents you from changing your mind. The following are the estoppel rules for negotiable instruments:

Estoppel against denying original validity of instrument   According to Sec. 120 of the Act, the maker of a promissory note, the drawer of a bill of exchange or cheque, and the acceptor of a bill for the honour of the drawer are not permitted as against a holder in due course to deny the validity of the instrument as originally made or drawn.

Estoppel against denying capacity of payee to indorse   According to Sec. 121 of the Act, the maker of a promissory note and the acceptor of a bill of exchange payable to order are not permitted as against a holder in due course to say that the payee is incapable of indorsing the instrument.

Indorser not permitted to deny the capacity of prior parties   According to Sec. 122 of the Act, the indorser of a negotiable instrument is not permitted as against a subsequent holder to deny the signature or capacity to contract of any prior party to the instrument.

International Law

The Negotiable Instruments Act, 1881, clearly lays down the rules for foreign negotiable instruments along with illustrations in four sections (Secs 134–137). Table 6.13 presents the rules concerning the foreign negotiable instruments taken verbatim from the Act.

Case 6.10 is worth your attention. Table 6.13 deals with the complex three-fold complaints, which include both criminal and civil liabilities. You will also see how the careful analysis of the sitting judge prevents the wrongdoers from circumventing the law of the land and depriving the innocent of their money. You will see how, in a dramatic fashion, the judge is able to turn around the case and stop the process from miscarriage of justice.

CASE 6.10	APPELLANT: Pale Horse Designs vs RESPONDENT: Natarajan Rathnam*

DATE OF JUDGEMENT: 26 October 2010

FACTS: Criminal Original Petition filed under Sec. 482 Cr.P.C. to call for the records in C.C. nos. 1506, 1507, and 1505 of 2007 on the file of IX Metropolitan Magistrate, Saidapet and quash the criminal proceedings.

The first petitioner M/s Pale Horse Designs is a company registered in the US, of which the second petitioner is the president. Natarajan Rathnam, who figures as the respondent in all the three criminal original petitions, is a non-resident Indian living in the US at No. 3, Parkway Drive, Roselyn Heights, New York.

Natarajan Rathnam, the respondent herein, furnishing a local address in Chennai, namely No. 37, Venkatarathinam Nagar, Adyar, Chennai, as his residential address, has preferred three complaints on the file of the IX Metropolitan Magistrate, Saidapet, Chennai under Sec. 200 Cr.P.C. for alleged offences punishable under Secs 138 and 141

---

*Pale Horse Designs vs Natarajan Rathnam, http://www.indiankanoon.org/doc/1268991/ (25 March 2011)

Contd

Case 6.10 *Contd*

of the Negotiable Instruments Act, 1881, in respect of seven dishonoured cheques drawn on M/s Danvers Savings Bank, One Conant Street, Danvers, MA 01923 in favour of the respondent herein. In respect of two cheques dated 15 June 2006 bearing cheque nos. 002661 and 002663, each for a sum of US $5,000, totaling a sum of US $10,000, the respondent preferred a separate complaint and the same has been taken on file by the above-said IX Metropolitan Magistrate as C.C. no.1506/2007. The said cheques had been presented for collection through the banker of the respondent, namely ICICI Bank Limited, Anna Nagar, Chennai-102, on 9 September 2006 and the same were dishonoured for the reason 'stop payment' instructions issued by the drawer. The said fact of dishonour of the cheques, according to the averments found in the complaint, was intimated to the respondent on 23 August 2006 by memo of the bank dated 21 August 2006 and the original cheques were also returned with a memo dated 25 August 2006. After issuing a legal notice dated 19 September 2006, which was received by the petitioners on 28 September 2006, the respondent preferred the complaint on 31 October 2006 alleging commission of the offences punishable under Secs 138 and 141 of the Negotiable Instruments Act, 1881, since within the time allowed by the said Act after the receipt of the statutory notice, the petitioners/accused did not make payment of the amount covered by the cheques.

With similar averments regarding two more cheques dated 15 February 2006 and 15 April 2006, respectively, bearing cheque nos.002647 and 002649, each one drawn for a sum of US $5,000, which were also presented for collection through ICICI Bank Limited, 3rd Avenue, Anna Nagar, Chennai and returned by the bankers for the reason 'stop payment' instructions been given and contending similar allegations, another complaint was preferred on the very same day, namely 31 October 2006 and the same was taken on file by the IX Metropolitan Magistrate, Saidapet as C.C. no. 1505/2007.

The third complaint was also preferred on the very same day by the respondent herein in respect of three more cheques drawn on 15 March 2006, 15 April 2006, and 15 May 2006 bearing cheque nos. 002658, 002659, and 002660, respectively, each one for a sum of US $5,000, which were also presented for collection through the very same bank and dishonoured for the very same reason. The said complaint was taken as C.C. no. 1507/2007.

In all the three complaints, uniform averments have been made to the effect that the said cheques drawn on Danvers Savings Bank, One Conant Street, Danvers, MA 01923, were issued in favour of the respondent herein/complainant in discharge of a liability in part of the petitioners herein towards the respondent herein/complainant. Since the said complaints were taken on le and registered as calendar cases on the le of the IX Metropolitan Magistrate, Saidapet, Chennai and the said metropolitan magistrate has also ordered issuance of summons to the petitioners/accused, pursuant to which summons were served on them in the USA, they have come forward with all the three criminal original petitions, invoking the inherent powers of the high court under Sec. 482 Cr.P.C, for quashing all the three complaints on the grounds stated in the petitions led by the petitioners.

Contd

Case 6.10 *Contd*

JUDGEMENT:
All the Criminal Original Petitions are allowed and the criminal proceedings in C.C. nos. 1506, 1507, and 1505 of 2007 on the file of the IX Metropolitan Magistrate, Saidapet, are quashed. Consequently, the connected miscellaneous petitions are closed.

REASON:
A combined reading of Secs 1, 11, 12, and 134 to 137 of the Negotiable Instruments Act, 1881, will make it clear that a cheque made/drawn in a foreign country on a drawee bank functioning in the foreign country and made payable therein shall be a foreign instrument and the law of the country wherein the cheque was drawn or made payable shall be the law governing the rights and liabilities of the parties and the dishonour of the cheque. As such the payee cannot select a country and present it through a bank therein for collection to confer jurisdiction on a court functioning therein. If the payee is given such a right to proceed criminally against the drawer by selecting the jurisdiction, the same will encourage forum shopping making the payees to go to a country wherein the dishonour of the cheque is made a criminal offence and wherein the law is more favourable to the payee enabling him to collect the amount covered by the cheque by way of fine or compensation by resorting to criminal prosecution. A person, who is not a citizen of India for an act committed in a foreign country wherein it is not a punishable offence, cannot be prosecuted in India. In this case, none of the petitioners is a citizen of India. The acts constituting the offence, namely, issuance of the cheque, the dishonour of the cheque, and the failure to make payment of the cheque after receipt of the statutory notice, were all committed by them not in India but in USA. Therefore, they cannot be prosecuted in India for the said act as an offence punishable under Sec. 138 of the Negotiable Instruments Act, 1881. The learned IX Metropolitan Magistrate, Saidapet does not have the jurisdiction to entertain the complaint since the offence was not committed within the jurisdiction of the said metropolitan magistrate.

Yet another aspect in this case is worth mentioning. Even the collecting branch which is situated in Anna Nagar, Chennai does not come under the territorial jurisdiction of the IX Metropolitan Magistrate, Saidapet. Only the address of the respondent shown in the complaint and in the statutory notice is in Adyar. The place of issuance of notice shall not be the only criterion conferring jurisdiction on the court. All the transactions were made in USA. The cheques were drawn on a bank in USA. The cheques were payable at the Massachusetts branch, USA. That being so, the respondent, with a view to invoke the provisions of Sec. 138 of the Negotiable Instruments Act, 1881, in order to have a short-cut method of collecting the cheque amount, has chosen to present the cheques in a bank at Anna Nagar, Chennai, Tamil Nadu for collection, issue notice from Adyar, Chennai and prefer the complaint on the file of the IX Metropolitan Magistrate, Saidapet. The said act on the part of the respondent not only amounts to forum shopping but also is an example of abuse of process of the court. Therefore, this court has no hesitation to arrive at the conclusion that in order to avoid miscarriage of justice, to prevent abuse of process of court and to render complete justice, it shall exercise its inherent power under Sec. 482 Cr.P.C, to quash the criminal proceedings in C.C. nos. 1506, 1507, and 1505 of 2007 on the file of the IX Metropolitan Magistrate, Saidapet.

Table 6.15 Rules concerning the foreign negotiable instruments

Rule	Section	Illustration
Law governing liability of maker, acceptor, or indorser of foreign instrument	134: In the absence of a contract to the contrary, the liability of the maker or drawer of a foreign promissory note, bill of exchange, or cheque is regulated in all essential matters by the law of the place where he made the instrument, and the respective liabilities of the acceptor and indorser by the law of the place where the instrument is made payable.	A bill of exchange was drawn by A in California, where the rate of interest is 25 per cent, and accepted by B, payable in Washington, where the rate of interest is 6 per cent. The bill is endorsed in India, and is dishonoured. An action on the bill is brought against B in India. He is liable to pay interest at the rate of 6 per cent only; but if A is charged as drawer, A is liable to pay interest at the rate of 25 per cent.
Law of place of payment governs dishonour	135: Where a promissory note, bill of exchange, or cheque is made payable in a place different from that in which it is made or indorsed, the law of the place where it is made payable determines what constitutes dishonour and what notice of dishonour is sufficient.	A bill of exchange drawn and indorsed in India, but accepted and payable in France, is dishonoured. The indorsee causes it to be protested for such dishonour, and gives notice thereof in accordance with the law of France, though not in accordance with the rules herein contained in respect of bills which are not foreign. The notice is sufficient.
Instrument made, etc., out of India, but in accordance with the law of India	136: If a negotiable instrument is made, drawn, accepted, or indorsed outside India, but in accordance with the law of India, the circumstance that any agreement evidenced by such instrument is invalid according to the law of the country wherein it was entered into does not invalidate any subsequent acceptance or indorsement made thereon within India.	
Presumptions as to foreign law	137: The law of any foreign country regarding promissory notes, bills of exchange, and cheques shall be presumed to be the same as that of India, unless and until the contrary is proved.	

6.9 BANKER AND CUSTOMER

A, the holder of a negotiable instrument payable to bearer, which is in the hands of A's banker, who is at the time the banker of B, directs the banker to transfer the instrument to B's credit in the banker's account with B. The banker does so, and accordingly now possesses the instrument as B's agent. The instrument has been negotiated, and B has become the holder of it.

– Sec. 47(b), The Negotiable Instruments Act, 1881

MANAGER'S TAKEAWAY

- Enjoy the power to sign a cheque as a manager.
- Laxity will land you behind bars.

MANAGER'S TAKEAWAY

- As a manager, put yourself in the shoes of a bank manager.
- Understand the commercial and legal relationship with the customer.

In earlier times, moneylenders extended loans for arbitrary and exorbitant rates of interest. In their place, banks came into existence to provide multifarious financial services under the strict application of the law. Refer to Case 6.11. Banks are essential for commercial needs of both: individuals and firms. They function locally, nationally, regionally, and internationally. Banks are financial agents of the people; people are their customers. Banks manage people's money and through various financial services and financial products, borrow and lend, pay dividends and sureties, and in our times, function with great speed through electronic and Internet banking services. As the transactions between the bank and the customer have become complex, so has relationship between the two. In order to simplify has this relationship to understand banker–customer relationship better, we present it in a question and answer format in Exhibit 6.2.

Exhibit 6.2   Understanding the Banker–Customer Relationship

Q: Who is a banker?

A: A banker is one who acts on behalf of a 'banking company which transacts banking'.* By *banking* it is understood 'accepting for the purpose of lending or investment of deposits of money from the public, payable on demand or otherwise, and withdrawable by cheque, draft, order, or otherwise'.**

Q: Who is a customer?

A: A customer with a bank, in the strict sense, is the one who has an account with the bank that creates banker-customer relation. One may receive services from the bank such as encashing of a cheque issued to him by someone else but it is only holding an account with a bank that creates the said relationship in true sense. Thus, one who has a relationship with a bank due to the maintenance of his account, only that person can be its customer.

Q: What is the nature of banker-customer relationship?

A: The nature of the banker–customer relationship is legal, contractual to be precise. According to financial principle, the banker is the debtor; the customer is the creditor. The relationship is also in reverse if the nature of the transaction is reversed. In other words, when the bank lends, it becomes a creditor to its debtor customer.

Q: What rights and obligations does the banker have in this legal, financial relationship?

A: Briefly, the following are the rights and obligations or liabilities of a banker to its customer:

---

*Sec. 5(b), The Banking Regulation Act, 1949.
**Ibid., Sec. 5(c).

Contd

Exhibit 6.2 *Contd*

Obligation to honour cheques The banker is bound by law to honour the cheque drawn on it by its customer (Sec. 31). The banker is responsible for the wrongful dishonour. The banker would have to compensate the loss appropriately depending on the loss suffered by the customer. The banker is liable to the drawer, who is its lawful customer and not to the payee or the holder because the client relationship exists only with the account holder.

Obligation to maintain records of transactions The banker has the duty to keep exact records by the transactions of the customer. If the banker commits a mistake in entries and the customer contends the same, then the banker is legally estopped from contending that the entries were wrongly made. The banker will not succeed in recovery of the amount in such cases.

Obligation to abide by the instructions given by the customer The instructions, which are within the scope of the banker–customer relationship, given by the customer, must be complied. In the absence of clear instructions by the customer, the banker is bound by the usage and the law (the laws of contract and negotiable instruments) in such instances.

General lien of bankers You have seen while studying the Indian Contract Act, 1872, Sec. 171 stipulates that the banker may, in the absence of a contract to the contrary, retain as a security for a general balance of account, any goods and securities bailed to him by the customer.

Obligation to maintain confidentiality about customer's financial affairs The banker has to preserve and uphold what is entrusted to him by the customer. Failure in this regard will make the bank liable for damages.

Incidental charges and interest The banker has the right to claim incidental charges and interest on money let to the customer as per the rules and regulations contracted and communicated with him when the account was opened.

Right to set-off In the instance of a customer having two accounts with a bank, one showing credit balance and the other debit, the bank can exercise its right to set-off the balance provided the debit and credit balances of two accounts are due by and to the customer in the same right.

Right of appropriation Secs 59–61 of the Indian Contract Act, 1872, direct that if the customer has a current account, appropriation takes place in the order in which the receipts and payments take place and are carried into the account.

Q: **What are the reasons of a banker to dishonour a cheque?**

A: Insufficient funds; cheque: not duly presented, ambiguous, mutilated, materially altered; discrepancy in the signature in comparison with the specimen signature with the bank; cheque having elapsed (overshot the period of six months from the date of issue); banker has a claim for set-off; post-dated cheque which has not achieved maturity.

Q: **When is the banker duty-bound to dishonour a cheque?**

A: A banker must dishonour a cheque by law in case of:
1. Insolvency of the customer in which case the assets of the customer vest in the official receiver.
2. Customer countermands payment.
3. Banker receives the notice of the customer's insanity or death.
4. A legal order has been received by the banker about the customer.

Contd

Exhibit 6.2 *Contd*

5. Customer has given notice of the closure of account.

6. Holder gives notice of the loss of cheque.

Q: **The banker is very much bound by his obligations to the customer. What is the legal protection for the paying banker?**

A: The paying banker is protected under the following circumstances:

Cheques payable to order according to Sec. 85(1), if the cheque payable to order purports to be indorsed by or on behalf of the payee, the drawee the paying banker is discharged by payment in due course. In other words, if the banker pays the amount in accordance with tenor of instrument bona fide and without negligence he has the protection of the law even if the payee may be a forgery or indorsement was without authority.

Cheques payable to bearer According to Sec. 85(2), once a bearer cheque, always a bearer cheque is the rule. A banker is discharged by payment. Any bearer can claim the payment.

Crossed Cheques There are four possibilities follows:

(a) Payment of cheques crossed generally Sec. 126(1): When the payment is done by the drawee bank to another bank; the drawee bank is discharged by the payment.

(b) Payment of cheque crossed specially Sec. 126(1): The drawee banker is discharged by payment in due course of a specially crossed cheque to the banker to whom it is crossed or his agent for collection.

(c) Payment of cheque in due course Sec. 128: If the drawee banker pays a cheque in due course, he is put in the same position as if he had paid to the true owner of the cheque. He may debit his customer despite the amount not reaching the true owner.

(d) Payment of cheque out of due course Sec. 129: When a cheque is crossed generally, and the drawee banker pays otherwise than a banker to whom it is crossed, he is liable to the true owner of the cheque for any loss.

Q: **What is the legal protection for the collecting banker?**

A: The collecting banker is that bank which receives the payment of a crossed cheque on behalf of its customer. There are certain risks involved such as ownership of the customer. The following are the protections of a collecting banker:

(a) Enjoys the privileges of a holder in due course.

(b) Not liable for defective title of the cheque because the banker is only an agent to the customer.

Q: **What liabilities does the customer who is the drawer of a negotiable instrument, from whom all relationships begin bear?**

A: The customer is liable both civilly and criminally. The amended Negotiable Instruments Act of 1998 and 2002, provides for stringent criminal punishment. The offence that a customer can commit is to issue a cheque that lacks sufficient funds. Such cheques bounce; bounced cheques call for criminal liability with provisions for imprisonment upto two years. Section 138 of the Act comes into focus. This question is further answered in the case presented at the end of this chapter.

CASE 6.12

APPELLANT: UCO Bank vs RESPONDENT: Hemchandra Sarkar*

DATE OF JUDGEMENT: 25 April 1990

FACTS: The respondent, who was indenting and lifting goods from textile mills situated in different places. He was maintaining a current account with the appellant bank for this purpose. He filed a suit against the bank for accounts, damages, compensation, and delivery of goods or their equivalent in money, for non-delivery of goods despite receiving payment thereof, contending that there was an oral agreement with the appellant-bank, regarding receipt and payment of bills, etc., and receipt and storage of goods on his behalf, and delivery of goods to him as and when required under the said terms and conditions. The banker constituted himself and acted as an express trustee and/or agent of the respondent in relation to the said goods and documents and thus stood in fiduciary relationship with the respondent. The appellant denying the allegations, contended that it had never acted as an agent, trustee, or depositee of the respondent in respect of the goods and documents and that no fiduciary relationship existed between the parties. The trial court decreed the suit holding that from the evidence and entries in the current account, it could be inferred that there was agreement or arrangement between the parties, and the appellant acted as agent/trustee of the respondent and that there was fiduciary relationship between the parties. The high court, affirming the decree of the trial court held that if the respondent had paid the value of the goods and the appellant bank neither delivered the goods nor rendered accounts, a fiduciary relationship could exist between the respondent and the bank in respect of the goods for which value was paid by the respondent. Hence, this is the appeal by UCO Bank.

JUDGEMENT: The appeal dismissed.

REASON: The courts below were not justified in holding that a fiduciary relationship could exist between the parties in respect of goods for which the suit claim was based. This inference was drawn primarily from the debit entries in the respondent's current account. Collection of bills, remittances to mills, meeting expenses of storing the goods, and debiting the same to the current account even without cheques from the respondent could not lead to an inference that the bank acted as agent of the respondent and that there was fiduciary relationship between parties. There is nothing in this method of operation to take the parties outside the ordinary relationship of banker and customer. This is the normal method of banking operation and the maintenance of the current account in the instant case is not outside this principle.

---

*UCO Bank vs Hemchandra Sarkar, 1990 AIR 1329; also see, http://www.indiankanoon.org/doc/1058782/ (2 April 2010).

SUMMARY

Introduction and Interpretation

A negotiable instrument is one, the property in which is acquired by anyone who takes it bona fide and for value, not withstanding any defect of title in the person from whom he took it.

The property in negotiable instrument passes from one person to another by the process of delivery if payable to bearer and by indorsement and delivery if it is payable to the order.

The holder in due course holds it free from all defects.

There are presumptions in favour of negotiable instruments.

Notes, Bills, and Cheques

Promissory note A negotiable instrument in writing containing unconditional undertaking signed by the maker to pay a certain sum of money only to, or to the order of, a certain person, or to its bearer.

Bill of exchange It is a negotiable instrument in writing containing an unconditional order signed by the maker directing a certain person to pay a certain sum of money only to, or to the order of, a certain person, or to the bearer of the instrument.

Cheque It is a bill of exchange drawn on a 'specified banker' and 'payable on demand'. In case of a crossed cheque, the payment is obtained only through another banker.

Bearer and order instruments A negotiable instrument is payable to the bearer: (a) when it is expressed to be so payable, (b) to a particular person, (c) when it is the only or the last endorsement in blank.

Inland and foreign instruments Any negotiable instrument made and made payable in India is an inland instrument; that which is not is deemed foreign.

Demand and time instruments A negotiable instrument is payable on demand, at sight, or presentment, or as the time is specified on it, a fixed period after date, or after an event.

Maturity and days of grace Maturity is the completion of date or period mentioned in the negotiable instrument; every negotiable instrument, by custom, has three more days after the maturity as grace period.

Payment in due course Payment in accordance with the 'tenor' of the instrument.

Negotiation

The capacity of a person to incur liability as a party to a bill of exchange, a promissory note, or a cheque, is co-extensive with his capacity to contract.

Accordingly, a minor or a person of unsound mind lacks competence to contract. A corporation can exercise only those powers to which it is entitled; an agent too in the similar fashion as the principal allows him and a trading partner equally with his other partner.

The parties involved in negotiable instruments are: maker, payee, holder, indorser, indorsee, drawer, drawee, drawee in case of need, acceptor, acceptor for honour.

A holder in due course is the possessor of a negotiable instrument for consideration. The principle: 'Every holder is a holder in due course' and enjoys privileges to ensure his rights.

Presentation

Presentment is to show a negotiable instrument to the drawee, acceptor, or maker for acceptance, sight, or payment, respectively.

Presentment for acceptance Bills of exchange are presented for acceptance. The acceptance of bill is a sign by the drawee of his assent to the order of the drawer that he will pay the bill at the appointed time.

Presentment for sight A promissory note must be presented for sight before its maturity. The maker's absence on-traceability, or insolvency can dishonour the note.

Presentment of payment Promissory notes, bills of exchange, and cheques must be presented for payment to the maker, acceptor, or drawee, respectively.

Dishonour of a Negotiable Instrument

A bill is dishonoured by non-acceptance or non-payment. A promissory note or a cheque can be dishonoured only by non-payment.

When a negotiable instrument is dishonoured, the holder must give notice of dishonour to all the parties whom he wants to make liable on the instrument.

Contd

Summary *Contd*

If he fails to do so without valid reason then all the concerned parties are discharged of their liabilities.

Discharge of a Negotiable Instrument

A negotiable instrument is said to be discharged when all rights of action under it are extinguished and it ceases to be negotiable or transferrable. It is discharged by payment in due course, by maker or acceptor becoming its holder, by express waiver, and by cancellation.

Liabilities to a negotiable instrument are discharged by cancellation, release, allowing drawee more than 48 hours, delay in presentment of cheque, material alteration, and by the operation of the law.

Rules of Evidence, Estoppel, and International Law

Presumptions The Negotiable Instruments Act, 1881, stipulates definite components for negotiable instruments which are legally termed as 'presumptions' such as consideration, date, and time of acceptance, time of transfer, order indorsements, stamp, holder in due course, and proof of protest.

Estoppel The act lays down rules for various parties of the negotiable instrument that these are prevented from recanting their original statements which have been accepted bona fide.

International law The Act takes cognizance of the liabilities in the event of dishonour of the instruments presuming that the laws regarding the instruments in foreign countries to be the same as in India.

Banker and Customer

Banking is receiving money and lending it to others, or generally consists in managing finances of the clients dealing with commerce. A banker is the 'banking company' or commonly known as just the 'bank'. A customer of the bank is the one who maintains an account with the bank.

The legal relationship between a banker and customer is contractual in nature; it is that of a debtor—the banker or creditor—the customer.

The banker is bound to keep a record of the financial transactions, honour cheques, abide by the instructions of the customer, maintain confidentiality *vis-à-vis* the customer and his interests.

The bank holds the rights of lien, incidental charges, interest on money lent, to set-off, and of appropriation.

Section 85 of the Act lays down rules for protection of the paying banker, and Sec. 131 that of the collecting banker.

EXERCISES

Negotiation

(i) A bill is drawn: *Pay to A or order the sum of ten thousand rupees.* In the margin there is a figure of 1,00,000. Is this a valid bill? If so for what amount? *Hint*: Yes, for ₹10,000 see Sec. 18

(ii) Arun signs as maker, a blank stamped paper and gives it to Bharat, authorizing him to fill it as a promissory note for ₹50,000 to secure an advance which Mohan has to make to Bharat. But he, Bharat, fills up the note for ₹1,00,000 payable to Mohan who has advanced the said amount. Can Mohan recover the money, ₹1,00,000? *Hint*: Yes, see Sec. 20

(iii) A company issued a cheque on its banker with an attached note *provided the receipt form at the bottom is duly signed, dated, and stamped.* Is the cheque valid? *Hint*: No, because a cheque by definition cannot be conditional.

(iv) Draw a promissory note and illustrate its elements.

(v) Describe the concept of 'negotiable instrument'.

Holder in Due Course

(i) Arun sold a mobile to Mithun, who is a minor, and pays for it through cheque. Arun, in turn, indorses the cheque to Vicky, who accepts it in good faith and for value. Upon presentation, it is dishonoured. Who should Vicky sue? *Hint*: Sue Arun; see Sec. 26.

(ii) The director of a company borrowed 15 lakh rupees from a certain businessman and executed a promissory note in his favour. There was no suggestion in the note whether the money borrowed was on behalf of the company for its purposes. In fact, the company used the money. Now on the basis of the promissory not is the company liable for the payment?

Hint: By no means the company is responsible; it is the director. See Sec. 28.

(iii) Bharat obtains Arjun's acceptance to a bill of exchange by fraud. Bharat indorses it to Kumar. Kumar indorses it to Damodar who knows of the fraud. Can Damodar recover the amount from Arjun.

Hint: As far as Damodar is concerned, Kumar is the holder in due course. Damodar may know of the fraud but he is not a party to it. He can recover the money from Arjun in suit. See Sec. 53

(iv) Illustrate the comment: Every holder in due course is a holder, but every holder may not be a holder in due course.

(v) Examine the nature of pleas in the following cases:

  (a) An acceptor of the bill is sued by a holder in due course who pleads that the payee is a minor.

  (b) A maker of promissory note is sued by a holder in due course who pleads saying that the payee could not indorse because he was insolvent.

Presentment

(i) A promissory note is presented for payment ten days after its maturity. Who is held responsible: indorser or the maker?

Hint: The maker; see Sec. 64.

(ii) Amar accepts the bill that is payable only at Bank of Baroda, Parliament Street, Delhi. Is it a valid acceptance? Can the holder treat the bill as dishonoured if he does not agree with this acceptance?

Hint: Both questions answered in the affirmative.

(iii) A indorses a cheque and delivers a cheque to B who keeps it for an unreasonable length of time and then indorses and delivers it to C who presents the cheque for payment within a reasonable time but is dishonoured. Against whom can C enforce payment?

Hint: Against B, see Sec. 73.

(iv) In a bill of exchange if acceptance is refused what steps should the holder take?

(v) Which are the instruments that should be presented for payment; what circumstances make presentment for payment unnecessary?

Dishonour of a Negotiable Instrument

(i) Amar draws on Karan a bill payable three months after sight. It passes several hands till Viraj becomes the holder. When he presents the bill for payment Karan refuses to pay. How can Viraj get his money?

Hint: Viraj can claim money from all the previous holders; Amar and Karan are his principal debtors, the rest of the indorsers are liable as sureties.

(ii) A bill is drawn payable three months after acceptance; it is dated 27 August 2004 and has been accepted for payment on 31 August 2004. When will the bill actually fall due for payment?

Hint: Add three months from day of acceptance for payment +3 days of grace period (Note: November does not have a 31st; hence the last day of the month to be considered), hence on 3 December 2004

(iii) A trading corporation was holding five bills of exchange for five lakhs, all of which were dishonoured. Both the holders and indorses were from the same place. The notice of dishonour was served after three days. What is the fate of this case?

Hint: Delay in notice; see Sec. 106 of the Act.

(iv) Illustrate dishonour, noting, and protesting.

(v) Why is dishonouring of a negotiable instrument a legal offence?

Discharge of a Negotiable Instrument

(i) Arun draws a cheque for ₹50,000 on X Bank which fails before the presentation of the cheque. Can the holder make Arun liable?

Hint: Arun is discharged of his liability; see Sec. 84 of the Act.

(ii) A bill payable with the inscription 'lawful interest' is changed into 20 per cent interest.

Hint: Material alteration causes the bill void; see Sec. 87 of the Act.

(iii) The drawer confirmed that the signature on the cheque was correct, but later denied and insisted that it was forged.
Hint: The banker is discharged of any liability.

(iv) Illustrate the discharge of negotiable instrument.

(v) What alterations to a negotiable instrument do not change their essential characteristics and what changes do?

Rules of Evidence, Estoppel, and International Law

(i) Amar makes a promissory note payable to Sitaram who indorses it to Charan who accepts it in good faith. Having encountered problems Charan sues Amar who proves to him that he made it for an illegal consideration. Can Charan recover the amount?
Hint: Yes; see Secs 58 and 118 of the Act.

(ii) Bharat makes a note payable to bearer. It passes several hands and finally comes to Charan. Upon encountering problems, Charan sues. It was found out that the note was stolen from Bharat. Can Charan enforce payment on the note?
Hint: Yes, for the same reason as the previous.

(iii) What presumptions are made about the negotiable instruments?

(iv) What are the rules of international law concerning negotiable instruments?

Banker and Customer

(i) A cheque is drawn payable to Bharat on order. However, it was stolen and Bharat's signature was forged. The banker, of course, paid the cheque. What is the liability of the banker? What about the forged signature?
Hint: The banker is discharged from liability; see Secs 85(1) of the Act. Forged signature: the banker cannot debit the account of the customer; see Sec. 10 of the Act.

(ii) Who should bear the loss in the case where the bank is presented with a stolen cheque with forged signature?
Hint: The banker; see Sec. 10 of the Act.

(iii) Cheques payable to a company were indorsed by a director to himself in his capacity as director and paid into his personal account with bank for collection. The bank received the money and allowed him to withdraw. Is the bank liable to the company for the conversion of its cheques?
Hint: Yes, the bank is liable because it was negligent.

(iv) If the banker wrongly refuses payment of a cheque, is he liable to the payee in damages?

(v) To what extent is the protection given to a banker who pays a cheque to or collects a cheque on behalf of a person who is not its owner with reference to bearer, order, and crossed cheques?

DEVELOPMENT OF LEGAL EDGE

- Compile all the cases of your firm concerning negotiable instruments. See what patterns develop and suggest solutions to avoid litigation.
- Procure forms for application of dishonour of cheques.

- Periodically have a Q&A session on the Negotiable Instruments Act, 1881, and its amendments.

FURTHER READING

- Krishnamachari Bhashyam, K.Y Adiga, J.C. Verma 2008, *The Negotiable Instruments Act,* 18th ed., Bharat Law House, New Delhi.

Cognizance of offences: Not withstanding anything contained in the Code of Criminal Procedure, 1973 (2 of 1974),

(a) no court shall take cognizance of any offence punishable under Sec. 138 except upon a complaint, in writing, made by the payee or, as the case may be, the holder in due course of the cheque;

(b) such complaint is made within one month of the date on which the cause of action arises under clause (c) of the proviso to Sec. 138;

(c) no court inferior to that of a Metropolitan Magistrate or a Judicial Magistrate of the first class shall try any offence punishable under Sec. 138.

– Sec. 142, The Negotiable Instruments Act

Head note[7a]

The cheque is a negotiable instrument 'par excellence'. You have studied in detail the legal technicalities of this instrument, which undoubtedly is the most indispensable one for business. Likewise explicit, unambiguous, and unequivocal protection is given to the holder, the drawer is held responsible for insufficiency of funds in his account, and the drawee bank's behaviour is closely watched by the law. The key to the legal procedure is payee's complaint. The metropolitan or judicial magistrate, first class and above, exercise the legal jurisdiction. These are the pre-conditions to apply the law of the Negotiable Instruments Act, Sec. 138.

The objective of the Sec. 138 of the Act is to prevent dishonesty on the part of the drawer who may draw a cheque without sufficient funds in his account in his bank and induces the payee or holder in due course to act upon it. The dishonour of cheque is a criminal offence punishable by imprisonment of two years or with fine up to double the amount of dishonored cheque or both.

Scope of Sec. 138

Section 138 of the Negotiable Instruments Act, 1881, creates statutory offence in the matter of dishonour of cheques on the ground of insufficiency of funds in the account maintained by a person with the banker. It falls in the acts that are not criminal in real sense, but are acts that in public interest are prohibited under the penalty, or those where although the proceeding may be in criminal form, they are really only a summary mode of enforcing a civil right. Normally in criminal law, existence of guilty intent—*mensrea*—is an essential ingredient of a crime. However, the legislature can always create an offence of absolute liability or strict liability where *mensrea* is not at all necessary. In a precedent setting case of K.S. Anto vs Union of India, 8 July 1991, it was held: 'Even, though the normal rule is that an act or illegal omission, in order to constitute an offence, must have the requisite mental condition in the form of intention, knowledge, or reasonable belief, that prerequisite could be statutorily dispensed within appropriate cases by creating strict liability offences in the interest of the nation, just like offences under the Prevention of Food Adulteration Act'.[8]

Such is the importance of Sec. 138 of the Act. It is a matter of guarding the monetary interest of all the people. The medium of exchange in world business being primarily based on cheque as the negotiable instrument, whether in regular form or electronic, it is important that the lawgiver makes certain that the bona fide interests of the people are safeguarded and their businesses protected. (See Exhibit 6.3.)

The case relates to the application of the above two Secs: 138 along with 142 which you saw in some detail. While Sec. 138 deals with actual instance of dishonouring the cheque, Sec. 142 deals with the definite procedure so that the legal procedure and jurisdiction is clear. The presentation of a case in the Supreme Court has been reproduced as follows, however, with subheadings so that you appreciate the various aspects of a complete Judgement of the Supreme Court of India in its entirety.

---

[7]The 'Head Note' is the background which the judge narrates in the introduction to a Judgement. Here the same vocabulary is used as an introduction to this Chapter-end case study.
[8]For full Judgement, see http://www.indiankanoon.org/doc/1975822/ (10 April 2011).

Exhibit 6.3 Section 138 of the Negotiable Instruments Act*

Dishonour of cheque for insufficiency, etc., of funds in the account. Where any cheque drawn by a person on an account maintained by him with a banker for payment of any amount of money to another person from out of that account for the discharge, in whole or in part, of any debt or other liability, is returned by the bank unpaid because either the amount of money standing to the credit of that account is insufficient to honour the cheque or it exceeds the amount arranged to be paid from that account by an agreement made with that bank; such person shall be deemed to have committed an offence and shall, without prejudice to any other provision of this Act, be punished with imprisonment for a term which may extend to one year, or with fine which may extend to twice the amount of the cheque, or with both: Provided that nothing contained in this section shall apply unless:

(a) the cheque has been presented to the bank within a period of six months from the date on which it is drawn or within the period of its validity, whichever is earlier;

(b) the payee or the holder in due course of the cheque, as the case may be, makes a demand for the payment of the said amount of money by giving a notice, in writing, to the drawer of the cheque, within fifteen days of the receipt of information by him from the bank regarding the return of the cheque as unpaid; and

(c) the drawer of such cheque fails to make the payment of the said amount of money to the payee or, as the case may be, to the holder in due course of the cheque, within fifteen days of the receipt of the said notice. Explanation for the purposes of this section, 'debt or other liability' means a legally enforceable debt or other liability.

The case in the Supreme Court of India[9]

Bench: Justice Arijit Pasayat
        Justice S.H. Kapadia
Appellent: Prem Chand Vijay Kumar
Respondent: Yashpal Singh and Others
Date of judgement: 2 May 2005
Background: The challenge in this appeal is to the legality of the Judgement rendered by a learned single judge of the Punjab and Haryana High Court holding that the proceedings initiated on the basis of a complaint alleging infraction of Sec. 138 of the Negotiable Instruments Act, 1881, (in short the 'Act') was not maintainable. Therefore, the proceedings were quashed, allowing the petition filed under Sec. 482 of the Code of Criminal Procedure, 1973 (in short 'the Code'). Facts: The following are the facts of the case:

1. The complaint was filed by the appellant alleging that in the year 1995, respondent no.1 had issued a cheque for a sum of ₹5,15,053.72, representing balance amount payable to the appellant for supply of goods to a partnership firm, of which respondents are partners. It was indicated that the total amount payable was ₹49,21,482.72, against which the accused had paid ₹44,06,429/-, leaving balance of ₹5,15,053.72.

2. A cheque drawn on Oriental Bank of Commerce, Ladwa branch (account no. 954) was issued for the same amount on 27 January 1995. The cheque was signed by respondent no. 1, Yashpal Singh, for the firm and respondent no. 2, Nirpal Singh, was a partner in the partnership firm, namely, M/s Sat Guru Rice Traders, New Delhi.

3. The cheque was dishonoured due to inadequacy of funds in the account.

4. Intimation was given on 6 February 1995. Notice was issued by the appellant demanding payment by lawyer's notice dated 17 February 1995. The amount was not paid.

5. The respondents requested the appellant for some time to make the payment. On the request of the respondents, the cheque was again presented on 6 July 1995 and it was again dishonoured due to inadequacy of funds.

6. Intimation in this regard was sent to the appellant on 10 July 1995. Again, lawyer's notice was sent on 24 July 1995. Reply was sent by the respondents on 16 August 1995, refuting the allegations contained in the legal notice. The complaint was lodged on 28 August 1995. Charges were framed.

7. Respondents filed an application for discharge which was dismissed by the trial court by order dated 29 January 2002.

---

[9]This case is reproduced in its entirety; however, it has been divided by sub-headings for the purpose of simplifying the reading of the Judgement. See http://www.indiankanoon.org/doc/1654180/ (4 July 2011).

8. The order was challenged before the high court, which by the impugned Judgement held that the requirements of Sec. 142 of the Act were not met.

Legal Reasoning

Argument by appellant's counsel

In support of the appeal, learned counsel for the appellant submitted that the high court was not right in entertaining the petition under Sec. 482 of the Code. The high court lost sight of the fact that the application was filed by the respondents long after the charges were framed. The high court has erroneously placed reliance on this court's decision in Sadanandan Bhadran vs Madhavan Sunil Kumar (1998 (6) SCC 514)[10]. On the contrary, the decision in Dalmia Cement (Bharat) Ltd vs Galaxy Traders & Agencies Ltd and Ors.(2001 (6) SCC 463)[11] is applicable. The period of limitation has to be reckoned from 10 August 1995, i.e., the date on which the respondents-accused persons replied to the legal notice dated 24 July 1995. As the complaint was filed on 28 August 1995 the same was well within time. It was submitted that the respondent-accused persons categorically stated in their reply dated 10 August 1995 that the first notice had not been served on them.

Argument by respondent's counsel

The learned counsel for the respondent-accused persons on the other hand, submitted that the high court had rightly taken the view that the requirements of Sec. 142 were not met. It was pointed out that the effect of the first notice was lost in view of the fact that the second notice was given. The high court has rightly applied the ratio in Sadanandan Bhadran's case (supra). It is not in dispute that there was issuance and receipt of the lawyer's notices on both the occasions. In fact, the acknowledgement of service of first notice has been filed by the complainant-appellant himself and at all stages the case proceeded on the footing that the first notice had been issued and served. The high court has categorically noted that the first notice had been served on the respondent. With reference to the complaint it was submitted that the appellant himself accepted that the first notice had been served. Therefore, he cannot be permitted to take the different stand that the notice was not served and in any event the second notice did not provide the cause of action.

Judgement by the Two-Judge Bench
Legal reference

For resolution of the controversy, Secs 138 and 142 of the Act are relevant (The judges then quote the above two Sections of the Act verbatim. You may refer to these texts earlier in this Chapter and then follow the Judgement rendered by the bench).

Premises to the judgement

1. In a generic and wide sense (as in Sec. 20 of the Civil Procedure Code, 1908, in short 'CPC') 'cause of action' means every fact which is necessary to establish to support a right or obtain a Judgement. Viewed in that context, the following facts are required to be proved to successfully prosecute the drawer for an offence under Sec. 138 of the Act:

(a) that the cheque was drawn for payment of an amount of money for discharge of a debt/liability and the cheque was dishonoured;

(b) that the cheque was presented within the prescribed period;

(c) that the payee made a demand for payment of the money by giving a notice in writing to the drawer within the stipulated period; and

(d) that the drawer failed to make the payment within 15 days of the receipt of the notice.

Proceeding on the basis of the generic meaning of the term 'cause of action', certainly each of the above facts would constitute a part of the cause of action but clause (b) of Sec. 142 gives it a restrictive meaning, in that, it refers to only one fact which will give rise to the cause of action and that is the failure to make the payment within 15 days from the date of receipt of the notice. A combined reading of Secs 138 and 142 makes it clear that cause of action is to be reckoned accordingly. The combined reading of the above two Sections of the Act leaves no room for doubt that cause of action within the meaning of Sec. 142(c) arises and can arise only once. The period of one month for filing the complaint will be reckoned from the day immediately following the day on which the period of fifteen days from the date of the receipt of the notice by the drawer expires.

---

[10]See Sadanandan Bhadran v. Madhavan Sunil Kumar http://indiankanoon.org/doc/372711/ (4 July 2011).

[11]See Dalmia Cement (Bharat) Ltd, v. Galaxy Traders & Agencies Ltd, and Ors. http://indiankanoon.org/doc/60864/ (4 July 2011).

2. As noted in Sadanandan Bhadran's case (supra), once a notice under clause (b) of Sec. 138 of the Act is 'received' by the drawer of the cheque, the payee or holder of the cheque forfeits his right to again present the cheque as cause of action has accrued when there was failure to pay the amount within the prescribed period and the period of limitation starts to run which cannot be stopped on any account.

3. One of the indispensable factors to form the cause of action envisaged in Sec. 138 of the Act is contained in clause (b) of the proviso to that Section. It involves the making of a demand by giving a notice in writing to the drawer of the cheque 'within fifteen days of the receipt of information by him from the bank regarding the return of the cheque as unpaid'. If no such notice is given within the said period of 15 days, no cause of action could have been created at all.

4. Thus, it is well settled that if dishonour of a cheque has once snowballed into a cause of action, it is not permissible for a payee to create another cause of action with the same cheque.

In Sil Import, USA vs Exim Aides Silk Exporters, Bangalore(1999 (4) SCC 567)[12], it was held that the language used in Sec. 142 admits of no doubt that the magistrate is forbidden from taking cognizance of the offence if the complaint was not filed within one month of the date on which the cause of action arose. Completion of the offence is the immediate forerunner of rising of the cause of action. In other words, cause of action would arise soon after completion of the offence and period of limitation for filing of the application starts simultaneously running.

The Judgement

It is to be noted that though a somewhat confusing statement was made by the respondents regarding the receipt of the first lawyer's notice. Therefore, what was kept alive was a fresh right and not cause of action. Therefore, Sadanandan Bhadran's case (supra) was rightly applied. The impugned Judgement does not suffer from any infirmity to warrant interference.

The appeal is dismissed.

Raison d'être

The conclusion to the above Judgement can be meaningfully performed by stating the rationale behind it, which originated in a landmark Judgement in 2001. The case was ShriIshar Alloy Steels Ltd vs Jayaswals Neco Ltd The three-judge Supreme Court bench consisting of B.N. Agarwal, R.P. Sethi, and K.T. Thomas laid down some of the following principles[13].

The origin   The introduction of negotiable instruments owes its origin to the bartering system prevalent in the primitive society. The negotiable instruments are, in fact, the instruments of credit being convertible on account of the legality of being negotiated and thus easily passable from one hand to another. The source of Indian law relating to such instruments is admittedly the English Common Law. The main object of the Act is to legalize the system by which instruments contemplated by it could pass from hand to hand by negotiation like any other goods. The purpose of the Act was to present an orderly and authoritative statement of the leading rules of law relating to the negotiable instruments.

Preparedness   Before adverting to the various provisions of law as applicable in the case, it has to be kept in mind that the law relating to Negotiable Instruments is the law of the commercial world which was enacted to facilitate the activities in trade and commerce making provision of giving sanctity to the instruments of credit which could be deemed to be convertible into money and easily passable from one person to another. In the absence of such instruments, the trade and commerce activities were likely to be adversely affected as it was not practicable for the trading community to carry on with it the bulk of the currency in force.

Pre-requisite   It has further to be noticed that to make an offence under Sec. 138 of the Act, it is mandatory that the cheque is presented to the 'bank' within the period of six months from the date on which it is drawn, or within the period of its validity, whichever is earlier. It is the cheque drawn which has to be presented to the bank' within the period specified therein.

Post-dated cheque   The post-dated cheque becomes a cheque on the date which is written on the said cheque. The period of six months has to be reckoned from that date. Dishonour of cheque or bouncing of cheque as it is popularly known is untenable for good business. Hence the lawgiver has brought in criminal penal provisions to discourage people from such malpractice. Such strict

---

[12]See In Sil Import, USA v. Exim Aides Silk Exporters, Bangalore, http://indiankanoon.org/doc/781024/ (14 April 2011).

[13]The principles are reproduced from the Judgement; See http://www.rishabhdara.com/sc/view.php?case=17249 (14 April 2011).

provision develops trust in the instrument so that business is conducted unhindered. However, legal pundits have been concerned that despite such stringent provisions, the recovery of the money is not easy; one needs to file civil suit for the same. Litigation takes time; and when business loses time, it loses money.

Discussion Questions

1. Read the two relevant Secs 138 and 142 of the Act and analyse and illustrate in your own words its application to your firm.
2. Elucidate the scope of Sec. 138.
3. What do you understand by 'insufficient funds'?
4. Rephrase the argument and the counter argument of the counsellors of the appellant and the respondent respectively.
5. What are the fundamental principles upon which the judges draw their Judgement?
6. What is the importance of Sec. 138 for business?
7. Why dishonouring of cheques needs not only civil procedure but also a criminal indictment?

Going Beyond

1. What do you understand by legal reasoning? Demonstrate the concept with examples.
2. What assumptions does a judge make before he writes and delivers a Judgement?
3. What are the characteristics of a landmark Judgement?

LEGAL LUMINARY

JUSTICE SAROSH HOMI KAPADIA—LEGAL WIZARD OF FINANCE

On 12 May 2010, the close watchers of the Supreme Court of India suddenly experienced a big difference in the corridors of courts across the country that used to be full of hustle and bustle. They became hushed, somber, and sedate. Reason: Justice Sarosh Homi Kapadia was sworn-in as the 38th chief justice of India by President Mrs Pratibha Patil. The entire establishment seemed to bear out the seriousness and responsibility of the nation's justice system. The new chief justice of India is a finance wizard, logically sound, and legally correct both in its letter and spirit. In the very first address to the legal fraternity, he declared, 'No more frivolous PILs'. His special request to all the judges was to keep abreast with the commercial laws. None can take him lightly and no one will, until he retires on 29 September 2012.*

His career as a lawman runs in clockwork precision: enrolled as an advocate in 1974, practiced in Bombay High Court, both on the original side and appellate side in suits, letters, patent appeals, writs, matters under Negotiable Instruments Act, detention matters, matters under Bombay Rent Act, matters under Bombay Municipal Corporation Act including trials concerning fixation of rateable value, matters under Maharashtra Land Revenue Code including trials concerning valuation of properties for the purposes of fixation of NA assessments, challenge to the validity of notifications fixing standard rent, appeared in AOs, first appeals under the BMC Act, second appeals as also in land acquisition references under the Land Acquisition Act as also in matters under Bombay Land Requisition and Acquisition Act. This is addition to the practice in industrial law and services matters.

He appeared as a counsel for the department in income tax matters, for BMC in matters concerning rateable value and octroi, for Bharat Petroleum Corporation and Hindustan Petroleum Corporation in high court and Supreme Court in connection with service matters including disputes concerning framing of pension rules, for the management and

*See: http://www.lawisgreek.com/tag/justice-sh-kapadia/ (5 April 2010).

Legal Luminary *Contd*

unions in matters under Industrial Disputes Act, 1947, and ULP Act, 1972.

He was appointed as an additional judge of the Bombay High Court (1991), as a permanent judge of the Bombay High Court (1993), as a judge of the special court, Trial of Offences Relating to Transaction in Securities Act, 1992 (1999). During the above period, he decided important matters under PIL pertaining to CRZ, financial matters under RBI and Banking Regulation Act; matters concerning the constitutional validity of the 74th Amendment Act of 1992 dealing with municipalities; matters under the Smugglers and Foreign Exchange Manipulators (Forfeiture of Property) Act, 1976; matters concerning mergers and acquisitions; matters under Payment of Bonus Act; matters under Industrial Disputes Act. In addition to the above, dealt with matters under the Income Tax Act concerning valuation of closing stocks, Accounting treatment to be given to Modvat credit convergence of tax accounting with commercial accounting, etc. As a judge presiding over the special court, he has dealt with civil and criminal matters including matters concerning corroborative value to be given to the report submitted by RBI and JPC vis-à-vis Evidence Act. As a judge of the special court, he has also dealt with accounts and finances of banks and financial institutions, as also accounts of the share and stock brokers as also matters under Contempt of Courts Act where the notified parties had diverted their assets. As a judge of the special court, he has framed investment schemes, schemes dealing with valuation and disposal of shares of notified parties as also distributions of asset of the notified parties under the Act and declaring dividends to the creditors of the notified parties. From chief justice of the Uttaranchal High Court (2003), he was elevated to the bench of the Supreme Court of India in 2003.**

Sarosh Homi was born in Mumbai on 29 September 1947 in a humble family who by the sheer dint of his efforts studied law. In a letter to the highly renowned Justice V.R. Krishna Iyer he wrote, 'I come from a poor family. I started my career as a class *IV* employee and the only asset I possess is integrity'.[†] An enormously hard working judge, he has close to 800 Judgements since he joined as the member of the Supreme Court bench in 2003. He says, 'Even as a judge of the Supreme Court, I have used my knowledge of accounts and economics for the welfare of the downtrodden including tribals and workmen. I hope to fulfill my obligation to the Constitution in the matter of achieving the goal of inclusive growth'.[‡]

It is India's good fortune that she has a chief justice whose qualities of both head and heart are in her highest interest.

** See: http://bombayhighcourt.nic.in/libweb/judges/Kapadia%20S.H..html (5 April2011).
[†] See: http://www.business-standard.com/india/news/newsmaker-s-h-kapadia/394824/(5 April 2011).
[‡] See: http://www.zeenews.com/news626020.html (5 April 2011).

The Indian Partnership Act, 1932

Principle: *Nemo debet in communion invitus teneri.*

No one should be retained in a partnership against his will.

CHAPTER OUTLINE

- Introduction and Interpretation
- The Nature of Partnership
- Relationships of Partners to one Another
- Dissolution of a Firm and Public Notice
- Limited Liability Partnership
- *Case Study:* Taxman's Predicament
- *Legal Luminary:* M.C. Setalvad

7.1 INTRODUCTION AND INTERPRETATION

TEXT

In the Act, unless there is anything repugnant in the subject or context
(a) an 'act of a firm' means any act or omission by all the partners, or by any partner or agent of the firm which gives rise to a right enforceable by or against the firm; '
(b) business' includes every trade, occupation, and profession;
(c) 'prescribed' means prescribed by rules made under this Act; 'Registrar' means the Registrar of Firms appointed under sub-sec. (1) of Sec. 57 and includes the Deputy Registrar of Firms and Assistant Registrar of Firms appointed under sub-sec. (2) of that section;
(d) 'third party' used in relation to a firm or to a partner therein means any person who is not a partner in the firm; and
(e) expressions used but not defined in this Act and defined in the Indian Contract Act 1872, shall have the meanings assigned to them in that Act.

– Sec. 2, The Indian Partnership Act, 1932

We introduce you to this chapter with the definitions of some concepts used in the Act to make you not only realize the importance of these terms but also to impress upon you their full import. Partnership in business is easily understood as two or more people coming together to do business. However, difficulties arise when there are disagreements among them. Although there is no law mandating to register a partnership firm or business—as in the case of company—yet doing so helps in seeking justice in the event of conflict.

You have already studied in previous chapters how the Indian Contract Act, 1872, originally governed all the aspects of commerce and trade. However, as the need rose for more specific governance, the government took steps to legislate further. Chapter XI, Secs 239–266 governed the law relating to partnership. It is based on the English Partnership Act, 1890. All the Common Law countries under the Commonwealth and the USA have adopted the same law. The mind of the lawgiver in this Act is to regulate business as little as possible and grant entrepreneurs the freedom to workout for themselves the various aspects of their business. Hence, the law does not make it compulsory to register partnerships or to make the agreements in writing. The liability is unlimited, and the partners are fully liable for their investments. There is complete freedom to form and administer the partnerships. Partnership is a mere voluntary collective and has no force of law to its constitution. Case 7.1 will demonstrate to you this principle.

CASE 7.1	APPELLANT: Dulichand Lakshminarayan vs RESPONDENT: Income Tax Commissioner, Nagpur*

DATE OF JUDGEMENT: 17 February 1956

FACTS: In connection with the assessment for the assessment year 1949–50 of Dulichand Lakshminarayan, an unregistered firm, an application was made under Sec. 26-A of the Indian Income Tax Act, 1922, before income tax officer, Raigarh, for its registration as a firm constituted under a deed of partnership dated 17 February 1947. In the opening paragraph of the deed, the names and descriptions of the five parties thereto were set out. The signatures of five persons were appended on behalf of five parties, respectively, at the foot of the deed.

It was common ground that out of the five constituent parties, D.L., J.H., and L.C., were separate firms constituted under three separate deeds of partnership. The three different persons who signed the deed on behalf of those three firms, respectively, were partners in their respective firms. The fourth party M.B., was the name of a business carried on by a hindu undivided family of which the person who signed it was the *karta*. The fifth party M.G., was an individual.

The income tax officer rejected the application on the ground that Dulichand Lakshminarayan, constituted under the deed dated 17 February 1947, consisted of three firms, one Hindu undivided family business, and one individual and that a firm or a Hindu undivided family could not as such enter into a partnership with other firms or individual, The assessee's appeal to the appellate assistant commissioner was dismissed but it succeeded before the income tax appellate tribunal who directed registration of the firm.

*Dulichand Lakshminarayan vs Income Tax Commissioner, Nagpur, 1956 AIR 354, 1956 SCR 154; also see http://indiankanoon.org/doc/1718643/ (29 April, 2011).

Contd

Case 7.1 *Contd*

On the application of the commissioner of income tax under Sec. 66(1) of the Income Tax Act, the high court held that on the facts of the case the assessee was not entitled to registration under Sec. 26-A of the Income Tax Act. Hence, the appeal was made in the Supreme Court by the assessee.

JUDGEMENT: The appeal dismissed; the judgement of the high court upheld.

REASON: A perusal of the deed would indicate beyond any doubt that the intention of the parties quite clearly was that each of the three constituent firms, and not the particular member of each of the said three firms who had signed the deed for his respective firm, was to be the partner in the bigger firm constituted under this deed. The contention that only the five individual executants of the deed were the partners of the newly created firm was against the tenor of the deed and was, therefore, without force.

Section 26-A of the Indian Income Tax Act postulates the existence of a firm. The Act, however, does not indicate what a firm signifies or how it is to be constituted. Sec. 26-B of the Act clearly provides, *inter alia*, that 'firm' and 'partnership' have the same meanings, respectively, as they have in the Indian Partnership Act, 1932. Sec. 4 of the Indian Partnership Act (which gives the definitions of 'partnership', 'partner', 'firm' and 'firm name') clearly requires the presence of three elements, namely, (1) that there must be an agreement entered into by two or more persons; (2) that the agreement must be to share the profits of a business; and (3) that the business must be carried on by all or any of those persons acting for all. The general concept of partnership according to both systems of law, English as well as Indian, is that a firm is not an entity or 'person' in law, but is merely an association of individuals and a firm name is only a collective name of those individuals who constitute the firm. In other words, a firm name is merely an expression, only a compendious mode of designating the persons who have agreed to carry on business in partnership. The word 'persons' in Sec. 4 of the Indian Partnership Act, which has replaced Sec. 239 of the Indian Contract Act, contemplates only natural or artificial, i.e., legal persons and, therefore, a firm is not a person, and as such is not entitled to enter into a partnership with another firm, a Hindu undivided family, or an individual and there is no question of registration of a partnership purporting to be one between three firms, a Hindu undivided family business, and an individual as a firm under Sec. 26-A of the Act, as in the present case.

Thus, the concept of partnership is that a firm is not an entity or a person in law but is merely an association of persons and the firm name is only a collective name for individuals who have agreed to carry on business in partnership. (Refer to Table 7.1.) The principle of partnership, in today's common parlance, may be described as 'there is nothing official about it'. The law recognizes its voluntary characteristic and does not want to disturb it by giving it a legal personality. However, recourse to law may be taken by a partnership as would any individual if it is felt that justice has been denied in such a partnership.[1]

> ⚖ MANAGER'S TAKEAWAY
>
> - Understand the term partnership correctly and use it likewise.
> - Partnership is the fundamental principle of the origin of society.

---

[1]See Law Commission of India, 7th Report on Partnership Act, 1932, 1957.

Table 7. 1   Kinds of businesses in India

Type	Liability
Sole proprietorship	Unlimited
Partnership (a) active (b) dormant	Joint and unlimited
Limited liability partnership (Latest development: the Limited Liability Partnership Act, 2008.)	Limited. It is an alternative corporate business vehicle that gives the benefits of limited liability but allows its members the flexibility of organizing their internal structure as a partnership based on an agreement.
Hindu Undivided Family (HUF)	Provision for joint family business
Cooperative	Limited
Family owned business	Unlimited
Private limited company (Pvt. Ltd)	Limited
Limited (Public limited company)	Limited
Public sector unit (PSU) Government owned; founded through legislation and governed through statutes	Limited
Unlimited Company	Liability of the members or shareholders is not limited.
Incorporated Company	Limited

THE NATURE OF PARTNERSHIP

Definition of 'Partnership', 'partner', 'firm', and 'firm name': 'Partnership' is the relation between persons who have agreed to share the profits of a business carried on by all or any of them acting for all. Persons who have entered into partnership with one another are called individually 'partners' and collectively 'a firm', and the name under which their business is carried on is called the 'firm name'.

— Sec. 4, The Indian Partnership Act, 1932

The above text defines essentially what you need to know by 'partnership'. Partnership is defined as the relation between two or more persons who have agreed to share the profits and losses according to their ratio of business run by all or any one of them acting for all. This definition has superseded the previous definition given in Sec. 239 of Indian Contract Act 1872: 'Partnership is the relation which subsists between persons who have agreed to combine their property, labour, skill in some business, and to share the profits thereof between them'. The 1932 definition added the concept of mutual agency. A partnership firm is not a legal entity apart from the partners constituting it. It has limited identity for the purpose of tax law as per Sec. 4 of the Indian Partnership Act of 1932.

In short, there are three aspects to partnership: partners, firm, and firm name.

Partners   Persons entered into partnership are related to each other as partners for conducting business and bound by the law of the land.

Firm   A firm is the collective of those who formed the partnership. It is not a distinctive legal entity apart from the partners like a company.

Firm name   The firm's name is the nomenclature or organization of the partners under one name. The name of the firm should not be such that it exploits government approval or sanction. The intention to name the firm should be clear; it should not cause detriment or imitation of any other similar name to exploit others' goodwill.

Partners

Working partner   One who contributes to the firm through his expertise, knowledge, and manages the affairs of the firm and receives remuneration for the same over and above his partnership share.

Dormant or sleeping partner   Partners who have contributed their share but do not take active part in the running of the firm.

Nominal partner   Nominal partner is a partner only for name sake and he is not the real partner; he has neither claim to any profits nor is he liable to any debts.

Sub-partner   When a partner of a firm shares his partnership with another; it is a private arrangement and he is not deemed to be a partner legally.

Incoming partner   A new partner admitted to the firm with the consent of all the rest of the existing partners (Figure 7.1).

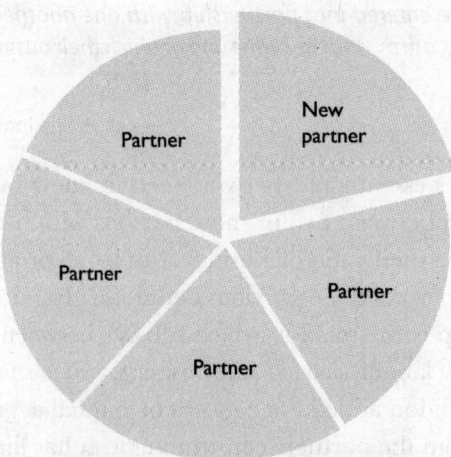

Figure 7.1   Partnership pie-share

Outgoing or retired partner A partner who leaves the firm; the firm carries on with the rest of the existing partners.

Partner by estoppel Partnership shares in the principle of agency; hence, a partner who represents as such is liable whether the person dealing with him knows about it or not.

Partnerships

There are seven criteria to the 'nature of partnership'.

Association of two or more persons At least two and maximum ten (Sec. 11).

Agreement It is a contract (Sec. 5).

Business The purpose of partnership is to conduct business (Sec. 2).

Sharing of profits Shared business calls for shared profits.

Mutual agency A partner is both an agent (binding others by his acts) and a principal (bound by the acts of the partners).

(a) One is an agent of the firm so far as one's external dealings for the purpose of business are concerned: he acts within his responsibility, acts in the name of the firm and for the business of the firm.
(b) One is principal in relation to the other partners among themselves.

Reconstitution Under various circumstances—inclusion of a new one, death of one of the partners, etc—a partnership firm renews itself.

Registration Enlisting with the state authorities. It is voluntary.

It is important for you, as a manager, to know well the succinct definitions of the partnership as listed herein. It contains all essential elements that determine the nature of any partnership.

Kinds of Partnerships

Particular partnership Partnership contracted for the execution of a particular project; it gets dissolved when the purpose for which it was formed is fulfilled.

Partnership-at-will It is a partnership not fixed to a particular period or project, nor is it determined by how it will be dissolved. It may be dissolved whenever notice to that effect is issued expressing the intention of the partners.

Registered partnership It is a partnership registered with a partnership deed, with the registrar of firms.

Illegal partnership A partnership entered into to conduct illegal business or formed illegally, e.g., exceeding the legal number of persons, which is ten.

Distinction of Partnership Firm and Other Associations

Partnership is quite distinct from other human associations. Table 7.2 will help you understand this distinction specifically in the Indian context.

There are other associations with which a partnership firm may be contracted such as co-ownership, clubs, etc., on the basis of the criteria—mode of creation, purpose, nature of interest, shares, etc.—that you have studied above.

Table 7.2 Difference between a partnership firm and other associations

Partnership business	Hindu undivided family business
Arises out of *contract*	Arises out *of status*—born in the family
Registration not compulsory	Must be registered under Company's Act
Membership by consent	Membership by being a family member
No gender discrimination	Female cannot be a business member
A minor is not a full-fledged member	All male members are legitimate
Dissolution upon the death of a member	Unaffected by any death in the family
Partners perform the role of agent to the firm	Only the *karta*—head of the family—is the real agent.
Each members bears unlimited liability	Only the *karta* has unlimited liability; the other members of the family only a liability as per their shares
Partnership business	**Company**
Not a legal person; partners are not distinct from the firm	Legal person and distinct from its shareholders.
Partner as agent	No shareholder acts as an agent
Unlimited liability	Limited liability
Transfer of shares depends upon the decision of all partners	Freedom to transfer shares
Dissolution upon death or incapacity of a partner	Company continues in all eventualities of its members and shareholders
Limited to ten people	Members as many as 50; public company has no limit on shareholders

Formation and Registration of Firm

Formation

Partnership is an agreement, a contract. It may be express—written or oral—or implied which is inferred from the conduct of the parties in business circumstances. Regarding formation of partnership, it should answer the question: 'Who are eligible to form a partnership?'

All All those who are eligible or competent to establish a valid contract can form a business partnership. (Sec. 11, Indian Contract Act, 1872)

Minor   A minor, although not eligible for a valid contract, could become the beneficiary of the partnership with the consent of all the members.

Person of unsound mind   Such a person cannot competently contract; hence he is excluded from forming a valid partnership.

Alien   An alien enemy is deprived legally of such a contract, whereas one who is not the enemy may do so legally.

Corporation   A corporation is a legal entity or a person; it can enter into a partnership as one single person but not as a group.

Registration

You may recall from the preceding paragraphs that a partnership does not have to be registered. But registering with a document deed would put into black and white all the intentions and purposes of the partnership as well as its functioning. You must carefully distinguish the fact that registration only creates an instance or evidence of the existence of partnership, and not a creation of a legal entity. Secs 58 and 59 of the Act lay down following requirements:

(a)   Name of the firm
(b)   Principal place or seat of business of the firm
(c)   Names of other places where business is conducted
(d)   Date on which each partner joined the firm
(e)   Names in full and the permanent addresses of the partners

The information given must be correct under the pain of criminal offence effecting imprisonment. The main effect of the registration of a firm is that it has the advantage to enforce its right through a suit; an unregistered firm lacks such competence.

Case 7.2 amply demonstrates all the aspects you have learnt thus far, and asserts that a firm has no existence without its partners. You will appreciate how the judge carefully studies the legal reasoning of the tribunal as well as the high court and supports the basic principle laid in the concerned Act.

7.3   RELATIONS OF PARTNERS TO ONE ANOTHER

TEXT

Subject to the provisions of this Act, the mutual rights and duties of the partners of a firm may be determined by contract between the partners, and such contract may be express or may be implied by a course of dealing. Such contract may be varied by consent of all the partners, and such consent may be expressed or may be implied by a course of dealing.

— Sec.12(1), The Indian Partnership Act

MANAGER'S TAKEAWAY

The deed of registration drawn and agreed by the partners governs the requisite relationship among the partners. In the event where there is no specific mention of mandatory relationship, Secs 9–17 are applicable. These cover the general duties of the partners, the duty to indemnify for loss caused

- Business partnership is a partnership of economic interest.
- Mutual trust is the foundation of any partnership.

CASE 7.2

APPELLANT: Malabar Fisheries Co., Calcutta vs RESPONDENT: Commissioner of Income Tax*

DATE OF JUDGEMENT: 19 September 1979

FACTS: The appellant, a dissolved firm as originally constituted on 1 April 1959, consisted of four partners and carried on different business in different names and styles. The firm was dissolved on 31 March 1963 and under the deed of dissolution executed by and between the partners, the first business concern was taken over by one of the partners, the remaining concerns by two of the other partners and the fourth partner received, a sum of money in lieu of his respective shares in the assets of all the businesses of the firm. During the four assessment years 1960–61 to 1963–64, the firm had installed various items of machinery in respect of which it received development rebate in its respective tax assessments under Sec. 33 of the Act. On dissolution of the firm on 31 March 1963, the income tax officer took the view that Sec. 34(3)(b) of the Act applied on the ground that there was a sale or transfer of the machinery by the firm within the period mentioned in that Section and, accordingly acting under Sec. 155(5) of the Act he withdrew the development rebate allowed to the firm for the said assessment years, the amending orders being passed against the dissolved firm.

The appeals, preferred by the dissolved firm through one of its erstwhile partners, were dismissed by the appellate assistant commissioner who held that Sec. 155(5) was rightly resorted to since Sec. 34(3)(b) of the Act applied to the case.

The income tax appellate tribunal allowed the appeals by the dissolved firm holding that there was no question of any sale or transfer within the meaning of Sec. 34(3)(b) in a transaction involving the adjustment of the rights of the partners of a dissolved firm, but at the instance of the Revenue (respondent) referred two questions of law to the high court: (a) whether there was only an adjustment of the mutual rights of the partners and the provisions of Sec. 34(3) were not applicable, and (b) whether there was a transfer of assets with in the meaning of the words 'otherwise transferred' occurring in Sec. 34(3)(b) of the Act.

The high court answered the second question in the affirmative and against the assessee holding that a dissolution of a firm amounted to extinguishment of the rights of the firm in the assets of the partnership and accordingly was a transfer within the meaning of Sec. 2(47) of the Act and that, therefore the provisions of Sec. 34(3)(b) applied to the case.

JUDGEMENT: Sec. 34(3)(b) of the Act was not applicable to the case—the judgement of the tribunal is to be upheld.

REASON:
1. There is no transfer of assets involved even in the sense of any extinguishment of the firms rights in the partnership assets when distribution takes place upon dissolution.
2. Sec. 34(3)(b) of the Act is not applicable to the case and the view of the tribunal is upheld.
3. The firm as such has no separate rights of its own in the partnership assets but it is the partners who own jointly in common the assets of the partnership and,

---

*Malabar Fisheries Co., Calcutta vs Commissioner of Income Tax, 1980 AIR 176; also see http://www.indiankanoon.org/doc/1505286/ (30 May 2011).

Contd

Case 7.2 *Contd*

therefore, the consequence of the distribution, division, or allotment of assets to the partners which flows upon dissolution after discharge of liabilities is nothing but a mutual adjustment of rights between the partners and, there is no question of any extinguishment of the firm's rights in the partnership assets amounting to a transfer of assets within the meaning of Sec. 2(47) of the Act.

4. On a plain reading of Sec. 34(3)(b), it will clearly appear that before that provision can be invoked or applied, three conditions are required to be satisfied: (a) that the ship, machinery, or plant must have been sold or otherwise transferred; (b) that such a sale or transfer must be by the assesse; and (c) that the same must be before they expiry of eight years from the end of the previous year in which it was acquired or installed. It is only when these three conditions are satisfied that any allowance made under Sec. 33 shall be deemed to have been wrongly made and the income tax officer acting under Sec. 155(5) will be entitled to withdraw such allowance.

5. Sec. 2(47) gives an artificial extended meaning to the expression 'transfer' for it does not merely include transactions of 'sale' and 'exchange' which, in ordinary parlance, would mean transfers but also 'relinquishment' or 'extinguishment of rights' which are ordinarily not included in that concept.

by fraud, the conduct of business, mutual rights and liabilities, property of the firm, profits, etc. Table 7.3 shows some of these which constitute the essential relationship between the partners.

Table 7.3   Rights and duties

Rights	Duties
Conduct business (Sec. 12a)	Conduct business to the greatest common advantage of the firm
To be consulted (Sec. 12d)	Maintain positive fiduciary relationship
To access of accounts (Sec. 13b)	To indemnify for fraud (Sec. 10)
To share profits (Sec. 13c)	Take upon responsibility diligently (Sec. 12b)
To interest on capital	Not to claim remuneration (Sec. 13a)
To interest on advances (Sec. 13d)	To share losses (Sec. 13b)
To be indemnified (Sec. 13e)	To indemnify for willful neglect (Sec. 13b)
To the use of partnership property (Sec. 15)	To hold and use the property of the firm exclusively for the firm (Sec. 15)
Agent of the firm (Secs 18–19)	To account for personal profits (Sec. 13)
Withhold consent against new partner (Sec. 31[1])	To account for profits in competing business (Sec. 16[b])
No liability before joining (Sec. 31)	To act within authority (Sec. 19[1])
To retire (Sec. 32)	To be liable jointly and severally (Sec. 25).
Not to be expelled (Sec. 33)	Not to assign his rights (Sec. 29)
Of outgoing partner to share in the profits of the firm (Sec. 37)	

Relations of Partners to Third Parties

There are two sets of relationships. First, the relationships between the partners themselves which are implied relationships due to the rights and duties arising out of contracting partnership (Figure 7.2). Second, relations of partners to third parties consist of the business carried on by one or all members of the firm in the name of the firm. They are responsible as a firm to their customers.

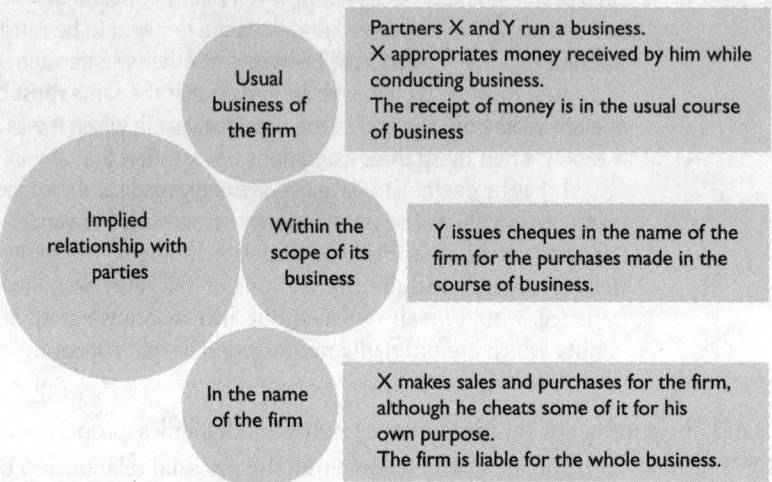

Figure 7.2   Implied relationship between the partners of a firm

Implied relationships

If you read Sec. 19 of the Partnership Act, you will find very clear directions on the relations which are implied and not implied, to make it known to the partners about their powers and their limitations and the third parties to enforce their rights as customers. (Refer Table 7.4.)

Partner's Authority in an Emergency

A partner has authority, in an emergency, to do all such acts for the purpose of protecting the firm from loss as would be done by a person of ordinary prudence, in his own case, acting under similar circumstances, and such acts bind the firm.

— Sec.21, The Indian Partnership Act

Implied authority and third party

Implied authority of the members gives protection of the law to the third parties as mentioned in Table 7.5.

Reconstitution of a Firm

Change is universal and partnership is no exception (Case 7.3). How does the law cope with the change concerning partnership is made amply clear in the following sections of the law. Refer to Table 7.6.

MANAGER'S TAKEAWAY

- Trust the partnership but verify your partner's competence to do business.
- Distrust is a strategy against betrayal.

Table 7.4   Acts within the implied and non-implied authority of a partner

Acts within the implied authority of a partner	Acts within the non-implied authority of a partner
To purchase and sell the goods of the firm.	To submit a dispute for arbitration.
To receive payment and makes receipt for the same.	To open a bank account in one's own name for the firm.
To settle accounts with persons doing business with the firm.	To compromise or relinquish a claim in the name of the firm.
To engage employees.	To withdraw a suit of the firm.
To borrow money on credit in the firm's name.	To admit any liability in a suit of the firm.
To accept, draw, and indorse negotiable instruments for the firm.	To acquire or transfer immovable property in the name of the firm.
To pledge goods to borrow money for the firm.	To enter into a partnership on behalf of the firm.
To employ a lawyer for the firm.	Note: A partner can do the above only with the express consent of all the partners as one single firm with specific authority or as the custom may be.

Table 7.5   Giving protection of the law to the third parties by implied authority of the members

Section	Title	Text
20	Restriction	Any act done by a partner on behalf of the firm that falls within his implied authority, binds the firm.
22	Binding	In order to bind a firm, an act or instrument done or executed by a partner or other person on behalf of the firm shall be done or executed in the firm's name, or in any other manner expressing or implying an intention to bind the firm.
23	Admission	An admission or representation made by a partner concerning the affairs of the firm is evidence against the firm; it is made in the ordinary course of business.
24	Notice	Notice to a partner who habitually acts in the business of the firm of any matter relating to the affairs of the firm operates as notice to the firm, except in the case of a fraud on the firm committed by or with the consent of that partner.
25	Liability	Every partner is liable jointly with all the other partners, and also severally, for all acts of the firm done while he is a partner.
26	Wrongful acts	Where, by the wrongful act or omission of a partner acting in the ordinary course of the business of a firm or with the authority of his partners, loss or injury is caused to any third party, or any penalty is incurred, the firm is liable, therefore to the same extent as the partner.
27	Misapplication	Liability of firm for misapplication by partners: Where—(a) a partner acting within his apparent authority receives money or property from a third party and misapplies it, or (b) a firm in the course of its business receives money or property from a third party, and the money or property is misapplied by any of the partners while it is in the custody of the firm, the firm is liable to make good the loss.

CASE 7.3

APPELLANT: Boda Narayana and Sons vs RESPONDENT: Valluri Venkata Suguana and Others*

DATE OF JUDGEMENT: 21 February 1977

FACTS:
The suit is laid to recover a sum of ₹52,087.47 with interest from the date of suit, on the foot of an equitable mortgage by deposit of title deed made by one late N. V. Narshimham, father of defendants 1 and 2. One of the five purchasers, Venkatakrishna Murthy relinquished his share by mentioning it as 1/8th in favour of the remaining four vendees. Subsequently, some others also became entitled to a share in the property. All of them were made parties to the suit and they are defendants 3 to 8. The defendants maintained that the suit is not maintainable as the plaintiff-partnership firm was not registered and the partner who filed this suit was not authorized to do so.

JUDGEMENT: Petition dismissed.

REASON:
The case law in the instance of Narayanappa vs Bhaskara Krishnappa states** 'The whole concept of partnership is to embark upon a joint venture and for that purpose to bring in as capital money or even property, including immovable property. Once that is done, whatever is brought in would cease to be the exclusive property of the person who brought it in. It would be the trading asset of the partnership in which all the partners would have interest in proportion to their share in the joint venture of the business of partnership. The person who brought it in would, therefore, not be able to claim or exercise any exclusive right over any property which he has brought in, much less over any other partnership property. He would not be able to exercise his right even to the extent of his share in the business of the partnership. His right during the subsistence of the partnership is to get his share of profits from time to time, as may be agreed upon among the partners and after the dissolution of the partnership or with his retirement from partnership or with his retirement from partnership of the value of his share in the net partnership assets as one the date of dissolution or retirement after a deduction of liabilities and prior charges.'

From the treatment given to the property all along, it appears to be clear that the property was always treated as property of the co-owners and not as property of the partnership. Accordingly, the property mortgaged was not the partnership property.

---

*Boda Narayana Murthy and Sons vs Valluri Venkata Suguana and Others; see also http://www.indiankanoon. org/doc/1937918/ (20 May 2011).
**Narayanappa vs Bhaskara Krishnappa, AIR 1304); see also http://indiankanoon.org/doc/1888276/ (20 May 2011). Carefully note the case law quote which places before you the essence of The partnership.

Table 7.6 Law and the change concerning partnership

Section	Title	Text
31(1) 31(2)	Introduction of partner	Subject to contract between the partners and to the provisions of Sec. 30, (minor) no person shall be introduced as a partner into a firm without the consent of all the existing partners. Subject to the provisions of Sec. 80, a person who is introduced as a partner into a firm does not thereby become liable for any act of the firm done before he became a partner.

Contd

Table 7.6   *Contd*

32(1) 32(2) 32(3) 32(4)	Retirement	A partner may retire—(a) with the consent of all the other partners, (b) in accordance with an express agreement by the partners, or (c) where the partnership is at will, by giving notice in writing to all the other partners of his intention to retire. A retiring partner may be discharged from any liability to any third party for acts of the firm done before his retirement by an agreement made by him with such third party and the partners of the reconstituted firm, and such agreement may be implied by a course of dealing between such third party and the reconstituted firm after he had knowledge of the retirement. Notwithstanding the retirement of a partner from a firm, he and the partners continue to be liable as partners to third parties for any act done by any of them which would have been an act of the firm if done before the retirement, until public notice is given of the retirement provided that a retired partner is not liable to any third party who deals with the firm without knowing that he was a party. Notices under Sub-sec. (3) may be given by the retired partner or by any partner of the reconstituted firm.
33(1) 33(2)	Expulsion	A partner may not be expelled from a firm by any majority of the partners, save in the exercise in good faith or powers conferred by contract between the partners. The provisions of Sub-secs. (2), (3), and (4) of Sec. 32 shall apply to an expelled partner as if he were a retired partner.
34(1) 34(2)	Insolvency	Where a partner in a firm is adjudicated an insolvent, he ceases to be a partner on the date on which the order of adjudication is made, whether or not the firm is thereby dissolved. Where under a contract between the partners the firm is not dissolved by the adjudication of a partner as an insolvent, the estate of a partner so adjudicated is not liable for any act of the firm and the firm is not liable for any act of the insolvent, done after the date on which the order of adjudication is made.
35	Death	Where under a contract between the partners the firm is not dissolved by the death of a partner, the estate of a deceased partner is not liable for any act of the firm done after his death.
29(1) 29(2)	Transfer of share	A transfer by a partner of his interest in the firm, either absolute or by mortgage, or, by the creation by him of a charge on such interest, does not entitle the transferee, during the continuance of the firm, to interfere in the conduct of the business or to require accounts or to inspect the books of the firm, but entitles the transferee only to receive the share of profits of the transferring partner, and the transferee shall accept the account of profits agreed to by the partners. If the firm is dissolved or if the transferring partner ceases to be a partner, the transferee is entitled as against the remaining partners, to receive the share of the assets of the firm to which the transferring partner is entitled and, for the purpose of ascertaining that share, to an account as from the date of the dissolution.

7.4   DISSOLUTION OF A FIRM AND PUBLIC NOTICE

The dissolution of a partnership between all the partners of a firm is called the 'dissolution of the firm'.

– Sec.39, The Indian Partnership Act, 1932

Reading the above text you might wonder that it is short and, hence, very simple. However, it implies a very important distinction: 'dissolution of partnership' as distinct from 'dissolution of firm'. Dissolution of partnership implies that due to one or more partners getting out of the firm, the partnership needs to be reconstituted, but the firm does not go out of business.[2] Dissolution of firm implies the closure of the very firm consisting of all the members, resulting in cessation of any further business.

Just as partnerships may be formed with or without legal bindings, so also their dissolution may be effected by the nature of their institution. Consequently, their dissolutions may take place with or without the order of the court. Table 7.7 shows the relevant section texts of the Act.[3]

Table 7.7 Dissolution of a firm with and without the court order

Dissolution without the court order	Dissolution with the court order
A firm may be dissolved with the *consent* of all the partners or in accordance with a contract between the partners. (Sec. 40)	A partner has become of *unsound mind*, in which case the suit may be brought as well by the next friend of the partner who has become of unsound mind as by any other partner. (Sec. 44[a])
A firm is dissolved either (a) by the *adjudication* of all the partners or of all the partners but one as insolvent, or (b) by the happening of any *event which makes it unlawful for the business* of the firm to be carried on or for the partners to carry it on in partnership. Provided that, where more than one separate adventure or undertaking is carried on by the firm, the illegality of one or more shall not of itself cause the dissolution of the firm in respect of its lawful adventures and undertakings. (Sec. 41)	A partner, other than the partner suing, has become in any way permanently *incapable of performing his duties* as partner. (Sec. 44[b])
Contingencies: Subject to contract between the partners a firm is dissolved (a) if constituted for a *fixed term*, by the expiry of that term; (b) if constituted to carry out one or more adventures or *undertakings*, by the completion thereof; (c) by the *death* of a partner; and (d) by the adjudication of a partner as an *insolvent.* (Sec. 42)	A partner, other than the partner suing, is guilty of conduct which is likely to affect prejudicially the carrying on of the business regard being had to the nature of the business. (Sec. 44[c])
Dissolution by notice of partnership at will.(1) Where the partnership is at will, the firm may be dissolved by any partner *giving notice in writing* to all the other partners of his intention to dissolve the firm. (2) The firm is dissolved as from the date mentioned in the notice as the date of dissolution or, if no date is so mentioned, as *from the date of the communication of the notice.* (Sec. 44)	A partner, other than the partner suing, willfully or persistently commits *breach of agreements* relating to the management of the affairs of the firm of the conduct of its business; or otherwise so conducts himself in matters relating to the business that it is not reasonably practicable for the other partners to carry on the business in partnership with him. (Sec. 44[d])

Contd

[2]See preceding on 'reconstitution of a firm' and the relevant portions.

[3]The texts are from the Act; italicized words are the topic of that paragraph.

Table 7.7 *Contd*

	A partner, other than the partner suing, has in any way *transferred the whole of his interest in the firm to a third party*, or has allowed his share to be charged under the provisions of rule 49 of Order XXI of the first schedule to the Code of Civil Procedure, 1908, or has allowed it to be sold in the recovery of arrears of land revenue or of any dues recoverable as arrears of land revenue due by the partner. (Sec. 44[e])
	The business of the firm cannot be carried on save at a *loss*. (Sec. 44[f])
	On any other ground which renders it *just and equitable* that the firm should be dissolved. (Sec. 44[g])

The above texts on the dissolution of partnership or the firm, as the case may be, are quite obvious in their decree. You will do well to read and comprehend the same without further complications. Remember that the law allows partnerships and firms to encourage as much freedom as possible in a business enterprise without needless legal trappings.

Post-dissolution Procedures

When the partnerships are dissolved and the firm is closed, matters do not end there. There are definite rights, liabilities, and obligations towards third parties. Last, but not the least, accounts need to be settled. It will sufffice to know briefly about these important measures (see Table 7.8) about the final matters of your subject under consideration.

Table 7.8 Rights and liabilities of partners on dissolution

Rights of partners on dissolution	Liabilities of partners on dissolution
To wind up business. (Sec. 46)	To give public notice about the closure of the firm. (Sec. 45)
To settle the debts of the firm out of its property. (Sec. 50)	To wind up affairs appropriately and complete incomplete transactions. The following partners do not bear liability: the dead, the insolvent and the dormant. (Sec. 47)
To have personal profits. (Sec. 51)	To settle accounts. (Secs 48, 49, and 55)
To receive return of premium on premature dissolution, if the same was paid at the entry into the firm. (Sec. 51)	To share deficiency at discharge of debts and liabilities at dissolution if assets of the firm are insufficient. (Sec. 48)
To *lien*, to subrogation and to indemnification if partnership contract is rescinded for fraud. (Sec. 52)	
To restrain partners from using firm name. (Sec. 53)	

7.5 LIMITED LIABILITY PARTNERSHIP

TEXT

Sec. 3:
(1) A limited liability partnership is a body corporate formed and incorporated under this Act and is a legal entity separate from that of its partners.
(2) A limited liability partnership shall have perpetual succession.
(3) Any change in the partners of a limited liability partnership shall not affect the existence, rights or liabilities of the limited liability partnership.
Sec. 4:
Save as otherwise provided, the provisions of the Indian Partnership Act, 1932 shall not apply to a limited liability partnership.

– Secs 3 and 4, Limited Liability Act, 2009

Table 7.1, at the beginning of this chapter, discussed the various types of businesses in India. Although the Case Law has been emphatic about unlimited liability as the cornerstone of partnership, certain exigencies and demands have pressed for limited liability partnership. In December 2008, both the houses of Parliament passed the appropriate bill and it was notified in January 2009. It is called the Limited Liability Partnership Act, 2009. It fundamentally changes the nature of partnership from that of a free and voluntary entity to a legal one. However, the lawgiver, in all his wisdom, has not harmed the existing Partnership Act with a new one; it remains as it is, and both are independent of each other.

As a manager in a new economy dominated by information technology and highly competitive professionals, this Act is considered timely and practical. Unlimited liability is highly risky on individual partners but limited liability will only demand it to the extent of their contribution. It will also shield one from the wrongful actions of another. Table 7.9 lists the salient features of the Limited Liability Act, 2009. (Also see Case 7.4.)

Table 7.9 Features of the Limited Liability Act, 2009

Feature	Particulars
Legal entity	It is a corporate body, separate from its partners, who may number two or more to conduct lawful business with the purpose to run a profitable enterprise; it shall be a registered body with perpetual succession.
Rights and duties	These shall be governed by the agreement of the partners; in the absence of any such provision then by the Act itself.
Liability	As agreed to the volume of their contribution, both tangible and intangible.
Third party liability	Unlimited to all partners.
Number of partners	At least two; and two designated partners, of whom one should be Indian.
Audit	It is mandatory to maintain audit of accounts and present the same to the registrar.
Government control	The Central government has the power to investigate the affairs of the company.
Merger	Merger and amalgamation permitted as per the law.
Conversion	A firm, private company, unlisted company is allowed to be converted to limited liability company.
Dissolution	The winding up of the limited liability partnership is either voluntary or by the tribunal is as per the Companies Act, 1956.

CASE 7.4

APPELLANT: Wajid Ali Abid Ali and Others vs RESPONDENT: Commissioner of Income Tax*

DATE OF JUDGEMENT: 10 November 1987

FACTS: The case is about the effect of death of one of the partners of a registered firm during the assessment year on the continued benefit of registration under Sec. 184(7) thereof—Whether a fresh application for registration with partnership deed embodying change in constitution of firm is required.

The assessee was a partnership firm styled as Messrs Wazid Ali Abid Ali, constituted under a deed of partnership, which, *inter alia* provided "that where the deed is silent, it shall be governed by the Indian Partnership Act save and except that on the death or demise of any partner the firm shall not be dissolved but shall be carried on with the remaining partners and that heir and representative of the deceased partner who resides in India on such terms and conditions to which they mutually agree".

An appeal filed by the assessee before the appellate assistant commissioner was dismissed.

The question 'whether, on the facts and in the circumstances of the case, the tribunal was justified in holding that for the period covered by the old constitution the income was assessable in the hands of the assessee as a registered firm?' was referred to the high court, which answered the question in favour of the revenue and in the negative. The assessee appealed to the Supreme Court for relief, as aforementioned.

JUDGEMENT: Appeal fails; petition dismissed.

REASON: On examination of the facts of that case, the high court found that the assessee's contention was right that the firm as found by the tribunal was dissolved and the transactions were carried on with the remaining parties in the course of the winding up and for realization of its dues. The high court accordingly answered rightly in the affirmative and in favour of the assessee. There was, in fact, a dissolution as found by the tribunal and in the facts and circumstances of that case and after the dissolution the firm ceased to exist there should be two separate assessments. The high court was right in answering the question as it did. It appears that the high court was also right in answering the record question in view of the fact that there was a death and as such dissolution of the firm by the manner in which the parties acted, that there is no question of the same firm being continued and the provisions of law could not be said to apply in the light of the facts.

*Wajid Ali Abid Ali vs Commissioner of Income Tax, Supreme Court of India, 1987 AIR 2074; see also http://www.indiankanoon.org/doc/357382/ (25 July, 2011).

Contemporary Significance of Limited Liability Partnership

Normally partnerships happen between individuals. As India surges forward economically, various forms of groups are getting formed in industrial, technological, and service industries. Joint ventures are common. Partnership among companies is becoming common. Therefore, limited liability partnership is significant and a step forward in the Indian economic reforms. The following are some of the points in favour of limited liability partnerships:

Structure It is a 'body corporate' and a 'legal entity' with perpetual succession, operates on the basis of contract has flexibility with regards to detailed legal and procedural requirements, and has the freedom to innovate and experiment with professional and technical expertise.

The limited liability framework is most beneficial in many sectors of new economy including the following:

- Persons and associations providing services of any kind;
- Enterprises in new knowledge- and technology-based fields where the corporate form is not suited;
- For professionals such as chartered accountants, cost and works accountants, company secretaries, and advocates, etc.;
- Venture capital funds where risk capital combines with knowledge and expertise;
- Professionals and enterprises engaged in any scientific, technical, or artistic discipline, for any activity relating to research production, design, and provision of services;
- Small sector enterprises (including micro, small, and medium enterprises); and
- Producer companies in the handloom and handicrafts sector.

Finally, having gone through the essential points of limited liability partnership, you may observe that an amendment regarding liability would have been adequate for the Partnership Act. You must realize that the essence of both the Acts lies in the nature of the liability. The lawgiver intends to grant both total freedom as well as the risk involved in the Partnership Act to the partnership entrepreneurs. The Act of 2009 is essentially different due to the fact of the limited liability, which the partners enjoy as though they are a company. However, procedurally, these enjoy greater freedom than those who come under the Companies Act, 1956, and its amendments. One of the most forward-looking characteristics of limited liability partnership is that it encourages a consultative approach that has been advocated by progressive economists as an ideal model of management.

MANAGER'S TAKEAWAY

- Profits are the secret of sustainability in partnership business.
- If not nourished and nurtured, business relationship sours and hurtles to closure.

SUMMARY

Introduction and Interpretation

Partnership is the relation between two or more persons who have agreed to share the profits of a business carried by any or all of them, acting for all.

The formation of partnership is a contract; it is an extension of the law of agency.

A partnership may be fixed for time, business achievements, or at will.

The Nature of Partnership

Along with its definitional values of being an association of persons to conduct business, it is especially characterized with partners, firm, and the firm's name.

Registration of firm

The firm may or may not be registered. It may be registered with a registrar, after the proper filing of the appropriate form under the Indian Stamp Act. A registration certificate is issued to the firm by the authority. A registered firm has the benefit of the protection of the law.

Relations of Partners to One Another

The relations between the partners are governed by the agreement among themselves; if these are not specifically mentioned, then they are governed under Secs 9–17 of the Act. The partnership is characterized by well spelled out rights and duties.

Relation of partners to third parties

In so far as the relationship of third parties to the partnership firms is concerned, it consists of the partners as the agents of the firm. The third party is not affected by the internal relationship of the partners among themselves.

Kinds of partners

There are many kinds of partners such as actual partner, partner by estoppel, dormant partner, nominal partner, and minor partner.

Reconstitution of a firm

This occurs due to introduction of a new partner, retirement, expulsion, insolvency, or death of a partner.

Dissolution of a Firm

Dissolution may be understood either as disbanding of partnership or as a closure of the firm altogether. Partners may voluntarily dissolve the firm or do so with or without a court order. The dissolution without the order of the court may take place by (a) mutual agreement; (b) compulsory closure due to unlawful business; (c) certain contingencies such as fixed term, adjudication as insolvent, or death, etc.; or by (d) notice of dissolution of partnership at will.

Dissolution by court order may take place due to (a) insanity of a partner; (b) incapacity to conduct business; (c) misconduct; (d) breach of agreement; (e) transfer of interest by a partner; or (f) business loss.

While the partners have rights and duties regarding their share of profits, they also have the responsibility of their liabilities—particularly to the third parties.

Limited Liability Partnership

It is a body corporate formed and incorporated and distinct from its partners. The Limited Liability Partnership Act, 2009 fundamentally changes the nature of partnership from that of a free and voluntary entity to a legal one.

EXERCISES

Introduction and Interpretation

(i) Define partnership and illustrate it by examples.
(ii) Differentiate between partnership and firm.

The Nature of Partnership

(i) Mohammad Ali and Sajjid Ali are two firms who have 15 partners each. They want to merge and amalgamate their firms. Can these conduct legal business?
   Hint: No. See, Sec. 11 of the Companies Act, 1956
(ii) Arun ran a business as a sole proprietor for many years. He found Charan quite agreeable and made him a partner with the conditions: Charan will not invest any capital, not be responsible any loss, may exercise all the powers of a partner, and he would get a monthly remuneration of ₹10,000.

Discuss the legal position of this partnership.
   Hint: Charan is a partner; see Sec. 6 of the Act.
(iii) An unregistered firm sold cement worth ₹50,000 to a certain Biswas who gave a cheque for the amount which bounced. Hira Lal, a partner of the firm, demanded from Biswas to settle money to which the latter responded by paying ₹25,000. In the meantime, the firm was dissolved. It fell to Hira Lal again, who had sued Biswas, to collect the rest of the amount. But Biswas countered it by arguing that since it was an unregistered firm, the suit was barred under Sec. 69 of the Act.
   Hint: No. Interpret Sec. 69 correctly.
(iv) How to establish that partnership exists between two persons?
(v) Explain in detail the registration of a partnership firm.

Relation of Partners to Third Parties

(i) Amit and Subhash are partners. Amit applies for insolvency; however, in the meantime he indorses a bill of the firm. What is the legal position of the indorsee; does he possess a good title to the bill? *Hint:* Yes. Amit is still the lawful partner until his application for insolvency is adjudicated; see Sec. 34 of the Act.

(ii) Anand, Narayan, and Raja are partners. Raja is a dormant partner who retires without giving public notice. Is he liable to the subsequent debts incurred by his two former partners? *Hint:* No. See Sec. 28(1) of the Act.

(iii) Jayanti Lal and Nand Lal are partners of Jayanti Lal Nand Lal & Co. Chaman Lal, the minor son of Nand Lal is admitted as a beneficiary of the firm. Thereafter, Nand Lal meets with an accident and dies, but the firm continues to do business. Jayanti Lal is involved in speculation and loses heavily. The creditors demand their money back both from Jayanti Lal and the minor Cha-man Lal. The lawyers of the deceased Nand Lal informed Chaman Lal, the minor, that his liability will be the capital investment of his father. How to solve this problem and know the legal position of Chaman Lal? *Hint:* The death of a partner dissolves a partnership; any business that is carried thereafter does not involve the minor in anyway.

(iv) Discuss the rights and duties of the partners among themselves. Illustrate with examples.

(v) A partner is the agent of the firm. Discuss with examples.

DEVELOPMENT OF LEGAL EDGE

- Do a business case study of a well-known rm in your locality.
- Investigate whether it has any knowledge about limited liability partnership.
- Do an empirical study about the key ingredients of the success and failure of partnerships in your state.

FURTHER READING

- Jagannatha Sastri & Sankara Sastri (eds.), (1932) *The Indian Partnership Act*, People's Printing and Publishing House, New Delhi.
- The Indian Partnership Act, 1932.
- The Limited Liability Act, 2009: http://www.ebc- (26 July, 2011) india.com/downloads/Limited_ Liability_Partnership_Bill.pdf (26 July, 2011).

CASE STUDY   TAXMAN's PREDICAMENT

After the dissolution of a firm the authority of each partner to bind the firm, and the other mutual rights and obligations of the partners, continue notwithstanding the dissolution, so far as may be necessary to wind up the affairs of the firm and to complete transactions begun but unfinished at the time of the dissolution, but not otherwise; Provided that the firm is in no case bound by the acts of a partner who had been adjudicated insolvent, but this proviso does not affect the liability of any person who has after the adjudication represented himself or knowingly permitted himself to be represented as a partner of the insolvent.

– Sec. 47, The Indian Partnership Act, 1932

Introduction

The case is about a partnership firm that dissolves itself to convert into a registered company and, as a consequence, the members avoid paying tax. The assessing officer charges them that it was done to evade tax and the tribunal awards a judgement in favour of the commissioner of income tax, further strengthening the suspicion about the motives of the entrepreneurs to avoid tax.

In the MBA fraternity of faculty and students there are several witticisms about taxes, one of them being: 'Tax is capital punishment'. It encapsulates the complexity of taxing and being taxed. Corporations do not like taxes because it drains away their liquid asset that is crucial for investment. The taxman, however, collects it telling the taxpayer that it is going to be spent on all the taxpayers for their general benefit. The taxpayer would like to avoid tax and evade it if he can; the tax collector would hound him for doing so. If caught, the tax evader will both lose money as well as freedom.

The assessing officer (AO) of the department of income tax invariably sits on the horns of dilemma. When he assesses, according to his judgement, the income of an individual or of an association such as a partnership firm or a company, particularly if the situation is tricky, he is bound to face problems.

Situation one If he assesses that the assessee must pay tax or more tax than the latter has filed, he is sure that the assessee will file a suit against the commissioner of income tax. The commissioner, in his turn, will pull up the AO for putting the department to litigation and he may receive a negative memo or may be transferred or demoted.

Situation two If he, on the other hand, overlooks the assessee's due diligence failure and his senior officer detects it and complains to the commissioner, who again will pull him up for failing to bring litigation against the assessee to collect the due taxes.

Dilemma He is damned if he causes litigation; damned if he does cause litigation.

Indeed, the subjects of litigation may vary, however, not AO's fate!

In the following case you must make up your mind with whom do your sympathies lie: with the taxman, the business firm, or the court of justice.

Banyan and Berry vs Commissioner of Income Tax

A two-judge bench of the High Court of Gujarat consisting of justices R. Balia and C. Thakkar deliberated the case and delivered the judgement on 21 December 1995.[4]

The Story of Banyan and Berry Partnership/Company

M/s Banyan and Berry was a partnership firm under a deed of partnership executed on 16 November 1982 with sixteen partners. The business of the firm was of contractors, engineers, and builders. A private limited company under the name and style of Banyan and Berry Construction Pvt. Ltd, was incorporated on 16 April 1983. A transfer deed was executed between the firm M/s Banyan and Berry (hereinafter called, 'the firm') and M/s Banyan and Berry Construction Pvt. Ltd, (hereinafter called, 'the company') by virtue of which it was agreed that subject to provisions contained in the agreement, the firm would transfer to the company w.e.f., 1 July 1984, all the assets and liabilities of the firm together with the goodwill thereof with an intention that the firm's business may be taken over as a running concern by the company w.e.f., 1 July 1984. There was specific provision in the agreement to the effect that the benefit of additional claims relating to construction of a dam at Mazam Irrigation Scheme would not stand transferred to the company. The relevant clause of the agreement reads as under:

'The firm was awarded a contract for construction of earthen dam for Mazam Irrigation Scheme in the Sabarkantha district. The said work has been completed and handed over to the state government and the firm has submitted its final bill to the irrigation department, Government of Gujarat. In addition to the final bill so submitted, the firm has also submitted further claims to the Government of Gujarat in connection with the said work notwithstanding anything herein contained benefits of the said claim shall not stand transferred to the company and the vendors shall be entitled to pursue the said claims and retain any amount that may be allowed by the government or otherwise recovered in respect of the said claim or any part thereof and for the purpose of such recovery

---

[4]Banyan and Berry vs Commissioner of Income Tax, 21 December 1995, also 1996 222 ITR 831 Guj; the link http://www .indiankanoon.org/doc/1492714/ supplies the full text of the judgement and is highly recommended for the study (6 October 2011).

Table 7. 10 Questions before the high court

Appellant: Banyan and Berry	Defendant: Commissioner of Income Tax
Whether the tribunal was right in law in holding that the sum of ₹1,48,24,876 became taxable in the hands of the firm which, according to the assessee, stood dissolved through dissolution deed on 16 August 1984?	Whether the tribunal right in law and on facts, in holding that the award amount of ₹14,824,876 is not taxable in the hands of the assessee firm?
Whether, on the facts and in the circumstances of the case, the tribunal was right in law in holding that the case would be governed by the Supreme Court decisions.*	Whether the tribunal is right in law and on facts in holding that the provisions of Secs 28 (iv), 60, and 63 of the Act were not applicable in this case?
Whether the tribunal was right in law in holding that even after the income is taxed protectively or with remarks to that effect in the hands of members of association of persons (AOP), the same income can be validly taxed again in the hands of the firm constituted by same members as partners?	–

the vendors shall be entitled to use the firm name and style and to be in the said name and style.' (Also see Table 7.10 and Figure 7.3)

The conversion of partnership firm into company

* Constitute a firm under the partnership act, 1932
* Dissolve it following procedures of the act

* Apply for conversion
* Acquire directors' identification number (DIN)

* Form members for the company
* Register company under the Companies Act, 1956
* Take incorporation certificate

*The figure is a reminder for what you already studied about the Partnership Act in this chapter and what you will study under Companies Act, 1956 in the following four chapters.

Figure 7.3 Steps for conversion from partnership to company*

Consequences

The aforementioned claims against the State of Gujarat in respect of the contract for construction of an earthen dam for Mazam Irrigation Scheme in Sabarkantha district have on this dissolution of partnership been allotted to and shall be treated as an actionable claim jointly enforceable as tenant in common by the parties hereto and each of the parties hereto shall be entitled to a share in the net amount realized or recovered by any proceedings in respect of the said claims in the same proportion as his share in the profits and losses of the said partnership specified in paragraph 7 of the said deed of partnership of 16 November 1982. For pursuing the said claim under the said dissolution deed, three of the partners were authorized to do all acts, deeds, matters and things about the recovery and relation of the said claims, on behalf of all.

Claims by Banyan and Berry

The facts regarding claim are that the firm was awarded a contract for construction of a dam for Narmada Irrigation Scheme in Sabarkantha district. The work of this contract was completed on 15 May 1984. The firm submitted its final bill to the irrigation department of Government of Gujarat. The firm also submitted a

*McDowell & Co. (1984) 154 ITR 148 (SC) and not by the Supreme Court's decision in CWT vs Arvind Narottam (1988) 173 ITR 479 (SC) and by the Madras High Court's decision in the case of M.V. Valliappan and Anr. vs ITO (1988) 170 ITR 238 (Mad).

further claim in connection with the said work which primarily consisted of price escalation and extra items, as per conditions of the contract. Thereafter, the Government of Gujarat accepted part of the claims and paid two sums, respectively, on 29 June 1984 and 23 November 1984 totalling ₹2,48,944 on 31 May 1985. Since the firm was dissolved, it was claimed that the amounts belong to the partners of the firm in their individual capacity in proportion to their share in the profit of the firm as per the provisions of the dissolution deed of 16 August 1984, and the said amount was assessed in the hands of the partners in the assessment year 1986–87 directly in proportion of their profit ratio. The claims which were not accepted by the government were referred to an arbitrator. The arbitrator made an interim award on 27 August 1986 awarding ₹95,80,700 in favour of the contractors. A final award was made on 27 January 1987 for an additional sum of ₹49,44,570. The two amounts were received on 26 November 1986 and on 5 May 1987, respectively, by the partners of the firm directly. This was in view of the letter of 9 October 1986 written to the officer on special duty, irrigation department, wherein it was requested that in view of the dissolution of the firm, it was necessary to amend the name of the original claimants by including that the claimant firm was dissolved and the names of the 16 partners be added. The Government vide its letter of 26 November 1986 written to the superintending engineer, irrigation department made it clear that there was no objection to the proposal regarding making the payment of interim award to the partners directly in accordance with their share in the partnership deed. Likewise the partners were directly paid the amount of final award as well.

The Taxman's Claims

It may be noticed that construction work at Mazam was completed before transfer of business. The final bill was also submitted and payment thereof was received prior to transfer of business. So also claim for additional sums on account of escalation clause and price of extra claim was lodged with the government prior to said transfer.

The firm did not file any return of income. A notice in respect of the aforesaid sums received by the partners under award under Sec.139(2) by the assessing officer (AO) in response to which the return was filed showing nil income. It was claimed by the assessee that the sum of ₹1,48,24,876 was a capital receipt and not taxable.

The AO brought to tax the above-mentioned sum for the following reasons:

1. The partners received benefit from the business carried on by the partnership firm. The claim arises from the business and there was a direct nexus between the business carried on by the firm and claim which resulted in receiving the sum by the partners. The amount was, therefore, taxable under Sec. 28(iv) of the Act being the value of any benefit or perquisite, whether convertible into any money or not, arising from the business;

2. The amount was taxable under the provisions of Secs 60 and 63 of the IT Act (however, neither the provisions of Secs 60 and 63 were set out in full nor was it explained how these sections can be invoked);

3. The provisions of Sec. 176(3A) provided for taxation of all those receipts which were related to the business activity before its discontinuance.

The award amount received after dissolution of the firm was an integral part of the business receipts of the firm M/s Banyan and Berry. It was, therefore, taxable under Sec. 176(3A).

The assessing authority also held that the claim had arisen from the business and it is a benefit the value of which in terms of money is chargeable as income under Sec. 28(iv) of Act. The AO was also of the view that the provision of Secs 60 and 63 of the Act were also attracted for holding the said sums as taxable. The AO was also of the view that formation of the company, handing over the running business of the firm and dissolution of the firm was made with an ulterior motive to escape the tax liability either in the hands of the firm or in the case of partners under Sec. 176(3A). In these circumstances of the case, the assessee's contention that receipts are not taxable under Sec. 176(3A) was not accepted. Accepting that the assessee has confirmed that the firm is dissolved, it held that it amounted to discontinuance of the business by the firm and attracts the provisions of Sec. 176(3A) of the Act. The receipts were held to be related to business of the firm, receipt of which were deferred due to litigation or dispute. On these proviso it was held that the amount received was income under Sec. 2(24) r/w Sec. 28(iv) and taxable in the hands of assessee under Secs 60, 63, and 176(3A) of the Income Tax Act, 1961, because according to him, Sec. 176(3A) in very unambiguous language provides taxation of receipts which were directly related to business activities before its discontinuance.

Thus, in its ultimate conclusion, the AO accepted dissolution of firm as an existing fact and invoked Sec. 176(3A) to bring the receipts to tax in the hands of the firm.

On appeal, the Commissioner of Income Tax, Ahmedabad found that discontinuation of business under Sec. 176 (3A) should not only be treated from the point of view of continuation or cessation of business but also from the point of view of the person carrying on the business. According to him Sub-sec. (3A) of Sec. 176 is the logical extension of Sec. 189(1) and reading the two provisions together, the firm was liable to be taxed. The CIT (A) did not rest its conclusion on the edifice of treating the dissolution of firm as a device to avoid tax.

Tax Tribunal's take

1. It appears unusual that after the business of the firm was taken over by the company as a going concern on 1 July 1984, except for the outstanding claims which are under consideration, the firm should have been dissolved.
2. The dissolution was not immediate and the firm continued till 16 August 1984, on which date it was dissolved.
3. It has to be remembered that the outstanding claims were not some fringe matters which could be attended to without much effort. We have already noted that the claims were of huge amounts, the amount in the letter of 25 May 1984 from the firm to the executive engineer, irrigation project, alone being ₹1,58,91,625. The follow up of the claim required representation before the arbitrator. Even then it was decided to dissolve the firm, which is far more extreme step than the mere retirement of some partner.
4. Another unusual feature is that even after dissolution, certain important element of the partnership were continued. The claims were treated as an actionable claim, jointly enforceable as tenant in common by the parties thereto.
5. Each of the erstwhile partners was entitled to share in the award in the same proportion as his share in the profits and loss of the firm. Three of the partners were appointed to carry out certain acts on behalf of all the erstwhile partners which included opening of bank accounts.
6. The claim was treated as an outstanding business and we have also come to the same conclusion earlier that the

business of the firm was not discontinued on 1 July 1984.
7. The normal expectation would be that the firm should continue but exactly the opposite took place by its dissolution.

On these precincts, the tribunal concluded that the dissolution of the firm was nothing but a device to avoid tax. The firm was dissolved by a deed but in essence it was a device to avoid tax because there was no purpose in dissolving the firm.

Consequentially, the tribunal held that dissolution of the firm will be ignored for the purpose of assessment of income and it will be treated that the firm continued even after 16 August 1984 and received awards of the arbitrator. In this view of the matter, the sum of ₹1,48,24,876 becomes taxable in the hands of the firm, except to avoid tax.

Having concluded thus, the tribunal found that income should be assessed on the basis of accrual and not on the basis of receipts and as sufficient facts were not available before the tribunal to show when the income accrued, the matter was restored to the file of the CIT (A) for the purpose of ascertaining the year in which the income in question was accrued and restrict assessee only on that part of the income which accrued in the previous year relating to assessment year 1988–89.

Judging by the law

As will be seen presently, the so-called unusual features are the usual state of affairs to come in existence as a result of dissolution. Regarding retaining the claim from the facts, it is obvious that the firm was engaged in construction business as contractor. Construction of the dam at Mazam was a completed work as on the date of transfer of business to the extent of receipt of regular payment of final bill under the contract. Only the claim for escalation and extra claim was pending. No part of business activity relating to the Mazam project was such as could be regarded to be transferred to the company. The claim was disputed. It is also not the case that any other pending claim of any other such completed work was transferred to company and the claim in respect of Mazam dam was treated differently.

In these circumstances, there could not be anything unusual for the partners, who intended to dissolve the firm on transfer of business, not to transfer any pending/disputed claim of a completed work. Likewise, the terms of dissolution were in consonance with Sec. 47 of the Partnership Act.

Even in the absence of said terms the same state would have existed under the said Sec. 47.

The tribunal's approach to treat the dissolution as device to avoid tax because there was no purpose to dissolve is apparently fallacious and is a result of misdirecting oneself in law. The question is whether in the undisputed facts of the case, was it essential to continue with the firm solely for the purpose of realization of a disputed claim when all other business has been transferred to company. No prudent man of common sense would, in fact, in such circumstances, have continued to keep the firm alive, on any commercial principle.

The tribunal has rested its conclusion to hold the dissolution of the firm as a device to avoid tax on the ground of there being no purpose except to avoid the liability of tax which should arise as a result of an award being made in favour of the firm regarding its pending claims about the construction of earthen dam of Mazam Irrigation Scheme which may be received sometime in future, and the terms of dissolution deed which, according to the tribunal, spelt out that certain important elements of the partnership were continued as unusual and those factors were stated to be:

(i)   claims were treated as actionable claim;
(ii) claims were treated as jointly enforceable as tenant in common by the parties;
(iii) partners were entitled to share in the award in the same proportion as each one has share in the profits and loss of the firm; and
(iv) that three of the partners were appointed to do certain acts on behalf of the erstwhile partners which included opening of bank accounts for holding that the said existing partnership after transfer of business to the company still retained the continuing business and the tribunal was also influenced by the magnitude of claim when it repeatedly referred to the fact that the outstanding claims were not some fringe matters which could be attended to without much effort but the claims were of huge amounts, and the follow up of the claim required representation before the arbitrator. The pursuing of the claim was treated by the tribunal as a business of the firm which was to be carried on by it.

The two questions that call for probing at this juncture are whether on the premises aforesaid can reasonably lead to conclusion in law that the dissolution of the firm was not real but was a device to avoid tax and, secondly what is the true scope of applicability of principle.

Principles

The formation and dissolution of partnerships is governed by statutory provisions under the Indian Partnership Act, 1932. The very concept of partnership is founded on agreement between the persons who share the profits of business carried on by all or any of them acting for all. Collectively, persons who have agreed to share the profits of business carried on by them are called a firm. Bringing into existence of a firm depends upon volition of the party. So also its dissolution rests on their volition or on the premise of agreement. The persons cannot be compelled to continue to remain in the same bond of a firm once they decide to dissolve it except as envisaged under the statute. It is not required anywhere under the Act, that a partnership can be dissolved only after the affairs of the firm have been fully wound up and nothing remains to be adjusted between the partners or nothing remains to be discharged as liability by the partners or realization of the outstanding to the firm are adjusted. On the contrary, the scheme of the Partnership Act clearly envisages that in point of time a dissolution of the firm takes place anterior to winding up of affairs of the firm which include finalizing the accounts, discharge of liabilities, outstanding on the date of dissolution of the firm, realization of the outstanding to the firm, and adjustment of accounts of the remainder of the assets of the firm.

Tax planning may be legitimate provided it is within the framework of law. Colourable devices cannot be part of tax planning and it is wrong to encourage or entertain the belief that it is honourable to avoid the payment of tax by resorting to dubious methods. It is the obligation of every citizen to pay the taxes honestly without resorting to subterfuges.[5]

Every man is entitled, if he can, to order his affairs so that the tax attaching under the appropriate Acts is less than it otherwise would be.[6]

Carrying on a trade is the fundamental right guaranteed under Article 19 of the Constitution of India. Right to carry on trade includes not to carry on any trade. How and in what form a business is to be carried is also part of that freedom. Business is carried on individually, collectively, by constituting a partnership firm, forming an AOP, or by company.

---

[5]Mc dowell case: McDowell & Co. Ltd, vs CTO (1984) 154 ITR 148 (SC).
[6]Justice Chinnappa Reddy in his separate opinion examined the ambit and Westminster (1936) AC 1.

Noticing the scheme of provisions of the Partnership Act relating to dissolution makes it apparent that there is nothing abnormal or a contrivance or a thing like device where there is a time lag between the date of dissolution of the firm and winding up of the affairs of the firm as they remain outstanding on the date of dissolution. On the contrary, such a state of affairs is envisaged normally to come into existence as a result of dissolution of firm. It clearly makes out the distinction between dissolution of firm resulting in cessation of its existence and continuing authority of erstwhile partners, not as a firm but as persons in charge to wind up the affairs of firm, to bind each other by their act in the matter of pending actions, realization of assets, etc.

The assessee may stop doing business altogether, and these assets may cease to have the character of business or commercial assets. Then, they take on an entirely different character. They become capital assets, and qua those assets the assessee is not carrying on any business, but qua those assets the assessee may also exploit these assets and receive income. But the income which it receives is no longer business income because no business is being carried on and the assets are not business assets.[7]

Conclusion

The conclusion of the tribunal that the mere realization of an outstanding claim relating to business which was carried on by the firm itself constitutes a business for which the firm ought to have existed until it is realized, is in our opinion, founded on irrelevant consideration and is not supported by any legal principle.

In our opinion, continuation of the authority of the each partner to bind the firm and other mutual rights and obligations of the partners even after dissolution in terms of Sec. 47, does not put the partners (keeping in view that partners and firms are two distinct entities for the purposes of income tax) in more exalted position of a liquidator realizing the assets of the company in liquidation. We have noticed above that even the realization of an asset of a company which took place before actual liquidation but manifesting intention to wind up, was held to be an act of realization of asset and not carrying on business of the company.

Interpretation of Sec. 47

In the case at hand, the firm transferred its business as going concern to the company and it stopped to undertake any further business activity. The settlement of claim of completed work at Mazam with the government remained the only outstanding affair of the firm. The claim was not an accepted claim. The entitlement under the agreement as well as the quantum both were subject matter of determination. It could probably be called only an activity relating to realization of assets of the firm in the course of its winding up but not in any sense be termed as carrying on business. Realization of an asset after dissolution, much less mere persuasion of disputed claim, cannot be termed as 'business' for carrying on which firm ought to continue to exist.

Sec. 47 envisages that after dissolution of the firm, the authority of partners continues. For application of Sec. 47, dissolution of firm is an accepted premise. On the acceptance of that premise, the necessary consequence is that the partners in their capacity as firm when they decided to dissolve the firm stop doing business in the identity of a firm and the assets which belong to the firm on the date of dissolution ceases to have a character of business or commercial assets. They assume the character of capital liable to be applied for payment of debts and distributed amongst the partners in accordance with the terms of agreement to dissolve read with relevant provisions of the Indian Partnership Act. Realization of amount on award having made in favour of the claimant cannot, in the circumstances, be the scope of the oft quoted observation of Lord Tomlin in IRC vs Duke of Co. Ltd (In Liquidation); (1958) 34 ITR 155 (Bom). said to be a realization through carrying on business by the firm. Such realization was by the partners, during winding up of the affairs of the firm.

The tribunal's reasoning that the person must continue to carry on business, not in the ordinary course for earning profit by business activity, but to incur the tax liability, only else it shall be deemed to be a mere device to avoid tax, as if person has no freedom to carry or not to carry on trade. We see no rationale to support this.

As a result of aforesaid discussion, our answer to question nos, 1 and 2 are in negative, that is to say, in favour of the assessee and against the Revenue.

As we have come to the conclusion while dealing with question nos, 1 and 2 referred at the instance of the assessee, the dissolution of the firm cannot be treated as a device to avoid tax and it is in fact come into existence.

---

[7]The general principle laid down by Justice Chagla in: CIT vs National Mills.

Under Sec. 47 of the Partnership Act, also, the authority of partners is only to realize the outstanding of the firm and to bind the firm from their accounts relating to the transaction and the assets once realized, are available for disbursement amongst the partners in their profit sharing ratio. But the firm does not continue to exist.

Operative judgement

Answer to the assessee's questions

Question 1 of the assessee Whether, on the facts and in the circumstances of the case, the tribunal was right in law in holding that the sum of ₹14,824,876 became taxable in the hands of the firm which, according to the assessee, stood dissolved through dissolution deed of 16 August 1984.

Answer is in negative in favour of assessee and against Revenue and we hold that the tribunal was not right in holding that the sum of ₹1,48,24,876 received by partners in pursuance of interim award and final award became taxable in the hands of firm which stood dissolved through dissolution deed of 16 August 1984.

Question 2 of the assessee Whether, on the facts and in the circumstances of the case, the tribunal was right in law in holding that the Case would be governed by the Supreme Court decisions.[8]

We answer the aforesaid question in the negative in favour of assessee and against the Revenue by holding that the tribunal was in error in applying the principle enunciated in McDowell's case.

Question 3 of the assessee Whether, on the facts and in the circumstances of the case, the tribunal was right in law in holding that even after the income is taxed protectively or with remarks to that effect in the hands of members of AOP the same income can be validly taxed again in the hands of the firm constituted by same members as partners?

The question is answered in affirmative in favour of the Revenue and against the assessee.

Answers to the questions referred at the instance of the commissioner of income tax

Question 1 of CIT Whether the tribunal is right in law and on facts, in holding that the award amount of ₹1,48,24,876 is not taxable in the hands of the assessee firm under the provisions of Sec. 176(3A) r/w Sec. 189(1) of the Act?

The answer is in the affirmative that is to say in favour of assessee and against Revenue.

Question 2 of CIT Whether the tribunal is right in law and on facts in holding that the provisions of Secs 28(iv), 60, and 63 of the Act were not applicable in instant case?

The answer is in the in affirmative that is to say in favour of the assessee and against the Revenue.

Final note

You may have appreciated the meticulous legal reasoning rendered by the two-judge bench of the Gujarat High Court. If your company is in trouble with the income tax authorities, you would know now the fundamental principles to be applied. You have been taken through very complex issues from the constitutional right to conduct business to the formation and dissolution of a partnership firm, the establishment of a company, and the tax problems they faced with the income tax authorities. In an increasingly business-dominated world, the knowledge of the principles and procedures of law are an imperative for the manager.

Tax muse

As a muse to this case, an anecdote of Albert Einstein, one of the greatest mathematicians and theoretical physicists, may interest you. He was filing the income tax filing form and found it very tedious. He seemed to have observed that the questions of taxman were very difficult for a mathematician!

Discussion Questions

1. What are the essential facts of the case?
2. What are the main issues to be considered under the law?
3. Elucidate Sec. 47 of the Partnership Act. Discuss instances and cases.
4. Can the commissioner of income tax charge someone with bad intentions of their actions to legitimately save taxes?
5. Do you break laws when you save tax?

---

[8]McDowell & Co., (1984) 154 ITR 148 (SC) and not by the Supreme Court decision in CWT vs Arvind Narottam (1988) 173 ITR 479 (SC), and by the Madras High Court decision in the case of M.V. Valliappan & Anr. vs ITO (1988) 170 ITR 238 (Mad).

6. Enumerate and discuss the principles expounded by the judge.
7. Why are legal principles important?
8. Would you agree with the bench over the judgement? If not, on what grounds would you appeal to the Supreme Court of India?

Going Beyond

1. With which party—the court, the entrepreneurs, commissioner of income tax—do you sympathize?

Sympathy in this instance does not mean the emotional support; your sympathy must be in the way you 'understand' the position of the party you favour.

2. Does the application of legal principle in a court of law change the intention of the lawgiver?
3. What is important in law: motives or actions?
4. Do you see any distinction between avoiding tax and evading tax? Illustrate with examples.

LEGAL LUMINARY

MOTILAL CHIMANLAL SETALVAD—LEGEND OF THE LAW COMMISSION OF INDIA

M.C. Setalvad (1888–1974), as he would normally write his name, was one of the greatest jurists of India who was known for professionalism and for setting impeccable ethical standards in the practice of law. His father, Chimanlal Setalvad, was a renowned advocate in whose path the son trod and distinguished himself at the bar. He had the integrity and courage to address the entire court and admit that his client has no case. Masterly and extremely brief arguments delivered in a stentorian voice mesmerized the court and the peers, and juniors profited enormously from his performance. It showed a great deal of homework, technical preparation, and practice. He stated the facts, presented the evidence, and thus served the law in letter and spirit. He charged very reasonable nominal fees irrespective of the difficulty of the case.*

M.C. Setalvad graduated in law in 1906 and joined his father's law practice and acquired the legal acumen. He became the Advocate General of Bombay in 1937 and continued in this post for full five years. In 1947 he was the member of the most important commission, the Radcliff Commission—for the determination of boundaries between India and Pakistan in the states of Punjab and Bengal. He represented India in the United Nations General Assembly, dealing with the problems of Indians in South Africa, which practised apartheid—discrimination based on one's colour. In 1950, Prime Minister Jawaharlal Nehru appointed him as the Attorney General of India, a position that he held for thirteen years—the longest period for any Attorney General of India.

As far as we are concerned in this book, the importance of Setalvad is due primarily because he was the first chairman of the Law Commission of India, serving from 1955 to 1958. He was responsible for research and reform of the following issues of legislation:

Liability of State in Tort
Sales Tax Limitation Act, 1908
High court benches
British statutes applicable in India
Registration Act, 1908

---

*See: http://bombayhighcourt.nic.in/libweb/references/pdf/M.%20C.%20Setalvad.pdf; also see: http://www.hcmadras. tn.nic.in/jacademy/articles/CANONS%20OF%20JUDICIAL%20ETHICS.pdf.http://www.judgesplot4plot.com/ Plot4Plot/000%20Up%20Dates/06%20CJI.LahotiFirm/CJI.motilal__setalvad.htm (30 June 2011).

Contd

Legal Luminary *Contd*

Indian Partnership Act, 1932
Sales and Goods Act, 1930
Specific Relief Act, 1877
Law of Acquisition and Requisitioning of Land
Negotiable Instruments Act, 1881
Income Tax Act, 1922,
Indian Contract Act, 1872
Judicial reforms

Setalvad wrote a biography published in 1970, titled *My Life—Law and Other Things*. He enunciated in it legal philosophy, and it is relevant for a globalized world.

Motilal Chamanlal Setelvad was born in Ahmedabad in 1884. His dedicated work has well served the judicial system in India. His eldest son Atul Setalvad is a well-known jurist and his grand daughter Teesta Setalvad is a social activist serving the cause of overcoming communal tensions in the country.

The Companies Act— Transition from 1956 to 2013

Principle: *Jus quo Universitates utuntur est idem quod habent privati.*
The law that governs corporations is the same that governs individuals.

CHAPTER OUTLINE

- Introduction and Interpretation
- Objectives and Goals
- Major Thrusts and General Provisions of the Act
- Comparative Analysis of the Provisions of the Companies Act, 2013 with the Companies Act, 1956
- Remarks on the New Act

8.1 INTRODUCTION AND INTERPRETATION

"Company" means a company incorporated under this Act or under any previous company law.

—The Companies Act, 2013, Sec. 2 (20)

Signed into Act

The President of India, Shri Pranab Mukherji, signed the bill passed by the Parliament on 29 August 2013 into *The Companies Act, 2013,* with the subtitle describing its aim: *An Act to consolidate and amend the law relating to companies.* Much of the public missed this historical moment amidst the tumultuous 16th Lok Sabha poll campaign. The law effectively replaces the Companies Act, 1956 along with all its amendments. It has been notified officially in *The Gazette of India* on 30 August 2013. Some of the provisions of the Act have been implemented through notification as of 12 September 2013, some more such notifications are still pending; however, where continuity is in question, the provisions of the Companies Act, 1956 are still in force. Thus the Companies Act, 1956 that you studied in the past remains relevant because the companies have been incorporated and governed by it till now and their continuation and transition to the new act will depend upon it.

Bill's Background

The Companies Bill, 2009 was introduced in the *Lok Sabha* on 3 August 2009 and was subsequently referred to the Department-related Parliamentary Standing Committee on Finance for examination and report. The Committee had submitted its report to the Parliament on 31 August 2010. The report and the recommendations of the aforesaid Standing Committee were examined in the Ministry and a revised draft Companies Bill, 2011 prepared in consultation with the Ministry of Law (Legislative Department) was circulated to the various Ministries and Departments for views and comments. Once the consultations with Ministries and Departments were completed, a *revised Bill as Companies Bill, 2011* was proposed to be introduced in the winter session (2011) of the Parliament after obtaining due approvals. Consequently, upon introduction of the Companies Bill, 2011, the Companies Bill, 2009, pending in the Lok Sabha, was withdrawn.

In 2009, Mr Salman Khurshid, the then minister of Ministry of Corporate Affairs, introduced the Companies Bill in the parliament. It was sent to the Standing Committee for review. On 11 September 2011, Mr Veerappa Moily the minister for Ministry of Corporate Affairs announced that in the coming year a new companies law will be passed to replace the Companies Act, 1956. He said that the ministry has reworked the bill, which was presented in the Parliament in 2009 with more than 300 amendments suggested by the Standing Committee on enactments of law.[1]

Reasons for Review of the Companies Act, 1956

The review of the existing act is required because of the following reasons:

Growth of Companies   After the composition of the Constitution of India, The Companies Act, 1956 was the most important legislation of free India. It replaced the Companies Act of 1913. Fifty years ago India had only about 30,000 companies whose field was generally oriented towards the domestic market; now there is are burgeoning eight lakh companies which are racing towards higher landmarks with global ambitions. Many companies are leaders in the multinational enterprises and own subsidiaries across the globe. Indian multi-nationals acquire and merge dozens of companies from abroad every quarter of the financial year. Several companies even surpass the GDPs of the smaller states and have millions of investors. Hence, the need for a comprehensive and effective company law is of utmost urgency.

Changed Context   In five and a half decades of its existence the Companies Act, 1956 has been amended 24 times indicating quick change of business situations. Major amendments were made in 1993 (twice), 1997, 2000, 2002, 2006, and 2008. Thus the new companies act is overdue at least for the past two decades. The fundamentals of Indian economy started changing from mid 1985 and radically changed in early 1990s. Compared to the business context in 1956 and the first decade of the 21st century it is unthinkable how the laws of over half a century can be meaningfully applied. Indeed, the fundamental principles may be valid, but the case law needs to define its context to be relevant to the globalized trade and commerce.

Globalization: Political, Economic, and Social Change   Internationally there are several political, economic, and social changes which have changed the relationship existing between countries and regions. The political and economic boundaries of Europe have changed

---

[1]http://economictimes.indiatimes.com/topics.cms?query=Companies%20Act (12.092011).

to that of European Union with Euro as its single currency. Eastern Europe has seen political and economic and social upheavals and now they have become robust democracies with promising economic future. The American Continents too have changed and have a leading role in global economic affairs. However, it is the Asian countries which are in a great race towards developed economies. India is in the forefront.

MANAGER'S TAKEAWAY

• There is always a reason to establish the law; circumstances necessitate it.

Apart from the above there are strong international institutions affecting the lives of common man across the globe: United Nations, World Bank, International Monetary Fund, International Court of Justice. International non-governmental agencies, non-profit organizations, etc., have brought the world closer together.

Similarly, technologies, transport, communications, media, and knowledge, etc., have changed the world beyond recognition from that of fifty years ago. Hence the great need to have a relevant law to govern trade and commerce.

8.2 OBJECTIVES AND GOALS

A history of quick amendments to the Companies Act, 1956 clearly showed its shortcomings. There were several approaches which prepared a background for the composition of the new bill.[2] After the amendments there came a slew of committees particularly in the field of corporate governance: Kumar Mangalam Birla Committee, the N.R. Narayana Murthy Committee, and the Naresh Chandra Committee. Commission was also formed under the Chairmanship of J.J. Irani in 2005 which made detailed recommendations as to the formation of a company bill.

Objectives

The Fundamental Objectives are as follows:

• To revise and modify the Companies Act, 1956.
• To make the Companies Act, 1956 compact by deleting provisions that had become redundant over a period of time.

Goals

The proposed company bill has the following ambitious goals[3]

Simplify Corporate Laws   That they are amenable to clear interpretation and provide a framework that would facilitate faster economic growth.

Make the Framework for Regulation   Corporations have to be in tune with the emerging economic scenario; encourage good corporate governance and enable protection of the interests of the investors and other stakeholders.

Grant Greater Autonomy   Allow independent operation and opportunity for self-regulation with optimum compliance costs. There is a need to bring about transparency

---

[2]http://www.mca.gov.in/Ministry/reportonexpertcommitte/chapter1.html (28.07.2011).
[3]Dr J.J. Irani Report on New Company's ACt: http://www.mca.gov.in/report_expert_comt.htm (29.07.2010).

through better disclosures and greater responsibility on the part of corporate owners and managements for improved compliance.

Interests of the Stakeholders   Enable measures to protect the interests of stakeholders and investors, including small investors, through legal basis for sound corporate governance practices.

Self-regulation   Provide a framework for responsible self-regulation through determination of corporate matters through decisions by shareholders, in the background of clear accountability for such decisions, obviating the need for a regime based on Government approvals.

Facilitate Enterprise   Recognize the relevance of a climate that encourages people to set up businesses and make them grow, addresses the practical concerns of small businesses so that people may deal with and invest in companies with confidence, promote international competitiveness of Indian businesses and provide it the flexibility to meet the challenges of the global economy.

Appropriate Legal Framework   Develop different frameworks for corporation on the basis of their size, nature of operations, manner of raising capital, etc. Business entities keep on changing their form and structure from time to time as they grow and also need to adapt to the changing business environment in response to competition, technological change and requirements of operation in the international arena.

Comprehensive Framework   Provide basic principles guiding the operation of corporate entities from registration to winding up or liquidation should be available in a single, comprehensive, centrally administered framework. This is important for the law and practice in corporate law to evolve and to bring about necessary reforms in the application of the framework.

Sectoral Regulation   Give space to sectoral regulators to regulate behaviour of entities in their respective designated domains. It would enable the regulators to concentrate their resources in a more focused manner on the substantive issues affecting their respective sectors.

Smooth Transition   Provide a smooth and seamless transition from one form of business entity to another. Hence a single corporate law framework for application to all companies. The requirements of special companies, e.g., small companies, could be recognized through a scheme of exemptions.

Demarcation of Jurisdiction   Demarcate the respective jurisdictions of Ministry of Company Affairs (MCA) and Securities and Exchange Board of India (SEBI). The Central Government is represented through a Ministry which would be required to exercise the sovereign function and discharge the responsibility of the State in corporate regulation. SEBI, on the other hand, is a capital markets 'regulator having distinct responsibilities in regulation of the conduct of intermediaries' capital market and interaction between entities seeking to raise and invest in capital.

Corporations as Persons Allow corporations to function as economic persons within the Union of India in a manner that contributes to the social and economic well-being of the country as a whole and as such must be subject to the laws pronounced by the Parliament for the welfare of its citizens.

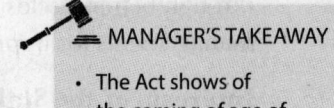

MANAGER'S TAKEAWAY

• The Act shows of the coming of age of corporations in India.

Simplification and transparency are the watchwords. The Companies Act, 1956 served for more than 50 years. Whether the proposed law would have a strong vision for the future is yet to be seen.

8.3.   MAJOR THRUSTS AND GENERAL PROVISIONS OF THE NEW ACT

The Companies Act, 2013 although in volume half of the Companies Act, 1956, it has well focused priorities. These will work as new thrusts for the corporate sector of India:

1. Harmonizes corporate regulation with other sector regulators
2. Ensures of shareholder democracy with due rights to minority
3. Introduces of *e-governance* in all company processes
4. Ensures liability of Board and senior management
5. Brings of new scheme for penalties and punishment for violations
6. Provides specific framework for Merger and Acquisitions of companies
7. Introduces of One Person Company (OPC)
8. Prohibits companies (except NBFC and Banks) from accepting public deposits.
9. Proposes one-third directors to be independent in all listed companies
10. Proposes key managerial personnel (KMP) to include Managing Director (MD), or Executive Officer (CEO), Chief Financial Officer (CFO), and Company Secretary (CS). (Note: No Qualifications have been prescribed for the post of KMP in the case of CS).
11. Makes insider trading a criminal offense
12. Makes consolidation of financial statements of subsidiaries with holding companies mandatory
13. Provides single forum for approval of mergers and acquisitions
14. Provides framework for fair valuation in companies for various purposes
15. Proposes Administration of Investor Education and Protection Fund through a statutory authority
16. Proposes revised framework for regulating insolvency
17. Proposes to establish special courts for offences under the Companies Law
18. Creates National Company Law Tribunal for matters like Merger and Acquisition, amalgamation, reduction of capital, and winding up.

With a very strong emphasis on Corporate Governance and Corporate Social Responsibility it is hoped that the future law would serve the purpose of being timely and visionary.

MANAGER'S TAKEAWAY

• Focus on action achieves the aims.

8.4 COMPARATIVE ANALYSIS OF THE PROVISIONS OF COMPANIES ACT, 2013 WITH THE COMPANIES ACT, 1956

What should a manager know about the Companies Act, 2013? First, a comprehensive idea or a bird's eye view of this complex legislation. As long as the case law continues in its application with those that have suits under the Companies Act, 1956, the importance of the old law is totally relevant. Hence a business manager must know about the essentials of it. It is, of course, obvious why the new law must be studied by a manager because from now on this is the enforceable law. Must a business manager know both the old and the new law? Yes, because of the above stated rationale.

Formation of Company

Minimum/Maximum Members
CA 1956: For private company – 2/50

For public company – 7/

CA 2013: For private company – 2/200

For public company – 7

For one person company (OPC) – 1

Analysis: New: OPC. It is a big motivation for entrepreneurs to move from proprietorships and incorporate their company as OPC

Types of Companies
CA 1956:
1. Public company limited by shares
2. Public company limited by guarantee and having share capital
3. Public company limited by guarantee and having share capital and having no share capital
4. Public unlimited company having share capital
5. Private company limited by shares share capital
6. Public company limited by guarantee and having share capital and having no share capital
7. Public unlimited company having share capital
8. Private company limited by shares
9. Government company
10. Cooperatives

CA 2013: In addition to the above
1. One Person Company (OPC)
2. Nidhi – the Mutual Benefit Company
3. Non-Banking Financial Company (NBFC)
4. Charitable companies – for education, science, promotion of culture, etc.
5. Producer Company

Analysis: The Act 2013 provides for multiple choices that will make Indian companies competitive with the global companies. Science and technological progress in agriculture and food processing industry has been supported by the Act through producer company concept. *Nidhi* and *chit fund* companies which thrived generally in the rural areas now have a corporate avenue.

Memorandum of Association (MOA)

CA 1956: Objects must be stated in MOA; objects incidental to the main objects; and other objects.

CA 2013: Objects of the company to be incorporated; any matter considered relevant to furthering those objects.

Analysis: Objects of the company define the company, hence the MOA for incorporation according to new Act gives focus; easier for ROC to reckon and in matters of dispute serves for clarity.

Name availability

CA 1956: No provision

CA 2013: Section 4 (4) and 4 (5) (i) must file application for the availability of name.

Analysis: For a company its name is brand; there have been innumerable disputes on the issue; the legislation wants to prevent such a predicament.

Articles of Association (AOA)

CA 1956: No provision for entrenchment

CA 2013: Section 5 (3–5) makes such a provision

Analysis: Making a provisions for entrenchment has far-reaching consequences since the company has to abide by its own AOA; these may be amended, of course, with a special resolution in the case of public company; application has to be made to ROC for any changes.

Commencement of Business

CA 1956: A company cannot start business as soon as it is registered unless it complies with the following formalities:

1. **Public Company**
   (a) The company has issue prospectus
   (b) The minimum number of shares which have to be paid for in cash must be allotted
   (c) Every director has paid on his shares an amount equal to what is payable on shares offered to public on application and allotment
   (d) No money is or may become refundable due to failure to apply for or obtain permission for listing from any recognized stock exchange/(s)
   (e) A statutory declaration by the secretary or one of the directors that the above requirements have been complied with is to be filed with ROC.

2. Private Company

(a) The company that has not issued a prospectus

(b) It has filed with ROC a statement in lieu of prospectus at least 3 days before allotment

(c) The above conditions at (c) and (d) in (1) are complied with

CA 2013: Section 11 (1–3) has the provisions that a company having a share capital, public or private, shall not commence any business or exercise any borrowing powers without fulfilling the following conditions:

(a) A declaration is filed by a director with the Registrar that every subscriber to the memorandum has paid the value of the shares agreed to be taken by him and the paid up capital of the company is not less than ₹5,00,000 in case of a public company and not less than ₹1,00,000 in case of a private company on the date of making this declaration

(b) The company has filed with the Registrar a verification of its registered office in such manner as may be prescribed, in accordance with Section 12 (2)

(c) While section 149 of the 1956 Act applied only to public companies having share capital, section 11 of the 2013 Act empowers ROC to initiate action for the removal of the name of the company from the register under Chapter XVIII if the following conditions are satisfied:

   (i) No declaration has been filed with the Registrar as in Point (a) above within 180 days of the date of incorporation of the company and

   (ii) The Registrar has reasonable cause to believe that the company is not carrying on any business or operations.

Analysis: In the new Act the legislator empowers the ROC to monitor both public and private companies the mode of not only incorporating a company but also its operations. The intention is to protect the investors in any form of the company.

Registered Office of the Company

CA 1956: A company must have a registered office:

(a) Either the day on which it begins its operations or 13th day after the date of incorporation.

(b) A notice of change of office must be furnished to the ROC within 30 days of such change.

CA 2013: A company must have its registered office

(a) Either from its day of incorporation or latest by the 15 day from that day.

(b) It must furnish verification of its registered office or in case of change of a due notice to that effect.

(c) Non-compliance concerning registered office or its changed location: The company and every officer who is in default shall be liable to a penalty of

₹1,000 for every day during which the default continues but not exceeding ₹1,00,000

Analysis: Just as an individual's identity is bound to domicile, so also the office of a company, which must be registered with ROC and any further changes in location or name must also be reported.

Bar on Subsidiary Company to Become Member of the Holding Company by Holding Its Shares

CA 1956: Section 42 of the old law barred a subsidiary from being a member of its holding company.

CA 2013: Section 18 (1) states that no company shall, either by itself or through its nominees hold any shares in its holding company

Analysis: It is to check any misuse or obfuscation in monetary transactions and thus maintain both transparency and autonomy in corporate relations of a group.

Service of Documents

CA 1956: All were written documents.
Delivery of documents through post

CA 2013: Any of the existing electronic modes.
Delivery of documents post or courier or electronic

Analysis: Under the old regime of the law service of documents was cumbersome, now the legislator has permitted all kinds of electronic servicing of the documents. The ROC may prescribe a number of options in this regard.

Share Capital

CA 1956: The following are the essential points:

(a) Depository: There was no record of depository

(b) Dividend: Section 87 clarified when the dividend shall be deemed to be due on preference shares in respect to any period.

(c) Variation of shareholders' rights: There was no provision for variation of shareholders' rights where variation by one class of shareholders affects the rights of any other class of shareholders.

(d) Application of premium received on issue of shares: Section 78(2) of the Act permitted all companies to utilize securities premium account *inter alia* for writing off preliminary expenses of or the commission paid or discount allowed on any issue of shares or debentures of the company for providing premium payable on redemption of preference shares or debentures.

(e) Prohibition on issue of shares at discount: Section 29 permitted it.

(f) Filing fees and stamp duty relief for reissue of redeemed preference shares: Section 80 (4) permitted it.

(g) Transfer and transmission of Securities: No such provision but to take recourse to Property Act, 1882 for such transfer.

(h) Applicability of rights issue: Section 81 applied to the public companies only.

(i) Period for which rights fares offer is open: Minimum 15 days maximum 30 days.

(j) Dispatch of notice of rights offer: No provision

(k) Offer of further shares to others: With special resolution; also ordinary resolution and approval from Central Government.

(l) Issue of Bonus Shares:

    (i) A company can issue bonus shares by capitalization of revaluation reserve if the Articles of Association of the company so permits.

    (ii) An unlisted company also could use revaluation reserve for issuing bonus shares.

CA 2013: Corresponding to the above:

(a) Depository: Record of depository; it is an evidence of interest of the owner of shares.

(b) Dividend: Section 43 (b) (ii) (a) speaks of payment of dividends without mention of dividend on preference shares.

(c) Variation of shareholders' rights: Section 48 states that if variation by one class of shareholders affects the rights of any other class of shareholders, the consent of at least 75% of such other class of shareholders shall also be obtained and provisions of this Section shall apply to such variation.

(d) Application of premium received on issue of shares: Section 52(3) eliminates conflict with Accounting Standards by providing that such class of companies whose financial statements comply with Accounting Standards prescribed for such class of companies, cannot utilize securities premium account for writing off preliminary expenses or for writing off the expenses or the commission paid or discount allowed on the issue of preference shares or debentures of the company for providing premium payable on redemption of preference shares or debentures.

(e) Prohibition on issue of shares at discount: Except for sweat shares which may be issued at discount the Act prohibits issue of shares at a discount.

(f) Filing fees and stamp duty relief for reissue of redeemed preference shares: While the old law allowed it, there is no provision in the new law.

(g) Transfer and transmission of Securities: While the old Act did not have a mechanism for this, Section 56 (1) of the new Act provides for transfer by company of such interest by execution of instrument of transfer and delivery of the same to company within 60 days from the date of execution for getting the transfer of interest, registered in transferee's favour.

(h) Applicability of rights issue: While the old Act made provision only for public companies; Section 62 of the new Act applies to all companies public as well as private.

(i) Period for which rights fares offer is open: Minimum 15 days maximum 30 days (Same as the old Act).

(j) Dispatch of notice of rights offer: Section 62 (2) permits through electronic mode; also other modes of dispatch such as post and courier.

(k) Offer of further shares to others: Only through special resolution. No other form such as permission from the Central Government is allowed.

(l) Issue of Bonus Shares: Section 63: No issue of bonus shares by way of issuing by capitalizing reserves created by the reevaluation of the assets.

Analysis: All along the above provisions just one purpose is reflected, that is, customer or investor protection. The legislator realizes that shares make an individual the member of the company, a part owner of the company, and that person must be justly rewarded and he deserves return on his investment.

Registers

Registers are documents concerning the company from inception and incorporation, from MOA and AOA to all the official dealings, accounts, audits, reports, meetings, annual returns and all that concerns the company, up-to-date.

CA 1956: (a) According to Section 138 of the old Act duplicate of the foreign register was to be maintained in India.

(b) Place for registers is the registered office of the company as stated by Section 163.

(c) Inspection of registers: Section 163 states that the company may put up some restriction in this regard, but the documents must be available for inspection for at least two hours a day.

CA 2013: No such provision; it is a logical conclusions since electronic records are maintained with the ROC. However, Section 95 states clearly that the registers are *prima facie evidence* on any matter directed to be filed.

The place for keeping registers and the copies of the annual returns in the new Act are as follows

(a) They may be kept in India, at a place which is not necessarily the registered office.

(b) However, more than 10% of the members must be living in the place; such a matter must be decided by a special resolution; the ROC must have a copy of such a resolution.

(c) No restrictions whatsoever on inspection of documents.

Analysis: The impact of electronic technology has simplified the paper work which is now stored as electronic documents; the signatures are encrypted, the documents are backed up, and all these can be recalled digitally anywhere and at any time. Most of the required information is made available to the investors through the company websites.

Annual Returns

These are documents about the affairs of the company which have to be filed before the ROC on annual basis with definite forms and procedures to be followed.

CA 1956: Section 159 (1) of the Act provided that the five preceding annual returns have given full particulars then in the following years only the changes made need to be filed. The listed companies required to get annual return certified by a *secretary in whole-time practice*. There were no penal provisions for non-compliance for failure to file returns.

CA 2013: Full annual returns to be filed every year by every company. Section 455 (4) of the Act states that if the returns are not filed for two years then the ROC will assign it the status of 'dormant company'. Section 271 (1) (f) states that if returns are not filed for five consecutive years then ROC shall begin proceedings for the winding up of the company. Unlike in the old law only the listed companies needed a certification of a full time company secretary, in the new law even the private companies are covered by the provisions of filing returns. Further, an extract of annual returns in prescribed forms must be attached to the Board's report; this is valid for both public and private companies.

Also, the new provision allows for any correction in returns within 15 days of the filing of the returns. Non-compliance brings the company secretary in question punishable with a fine not less than ₹50,000 and may extend up to ₹5, 00,000.

Analysis: Compliance and disclosure are the two sides of the same coin in corporate control provided by the legislator. While disclosures may be mandatory or non-mandatory as may be provided by the law, compliances are compulsory. As per the form provided by the regulator the annual returns have to be filed, from members, shares, debentures to balance sheet, audited accounts, reports of the annual general meetings, other meetings and their minutes, resolutions, corporate activities such as mergers and acquisitions, subsidiaries—all come under compliances. The effect of compliance ensures a regime of control system.

Annual General Meeting (AGM)

AGM is mandatory for every company irrespective of its type. All associated with the company, the board of directors, the managerial personnel and the shareholders come together to attend to the presentation of the report consisting of all the activities and businesses of the company. Decisions are taken at this meeting through the passage of resolutions such as appointment of board of members, company secretary, auditors, dividends, etc. Resolutions are also passed concerning the future steps to be taken.

CA 1956: (a) Section 162 states that should be conducted during business hours on a working day; it should not be on a public holiday.

(b) Notice of meeting: There is no specific provision. Newspaper ads, post, etc., were used.

(c) Material facts: There was no clarity on the defined matter in the communication for meeting (Section 173)

(d) Quorum: Five members to be present, unless AOA stipulates differently. Meeting will be deemed cancelled if the quorum is not present within half an hour of the scheduled meeting. (Section 174)

(e) Proxy voting: This was allowed without restrictions.

(f) Poll: Members present or by proxy having 10% holding shares in the company may demand a poll on concerned issue of resolution provided on which ₹50,000 or more is paid up share.

CA 2013:

(a) Section 96 (2) reiterates the provision of the old law and further states that the timing of conducting of AGM should be during business hours between 9 am and 6 pm. It should not be on a national holiday.

(b) Notice for meeting: Section 101 permits giving notice through electronic media. A three days' notice is adequate.

(c) Material Fact: According to Section 192 material facts are those by which the members understand the meaning, scope, and implications of the items of business and upon which decisions have to be taken through the passing of appropriate resolutions.

(d) Quorum: Section 102 states, that five members to be personally present in company of less than 1000 members; 15 members in a company that has more than 1000 members but under 5000; 30 members to be personally present for companies with members of more than 5000.

(e) Proxy voting: Section 105 states that a proxy may vote for not more than 50. Further the Central Government may by prescribing rules may restrict certain class of members from certain class of companies from appointing proxies.

(f) Poll: Members present or by proxy having 10% holding shares in the company may demand a poll on concerned issue of resolution provided on which ₹50,00,000 or more is paid up share or even higher as has been prescribed.

Analysis: Under the new Act, AGM has received added importance and that it is not a mere performance of a formality. The interval between two AGMs should cross the limit of 15 months (Section 96). Such an extension should be applied for with the ROC; non-compliance attracts penalty. The AGM is a means to bring public transparency to the company as well as responsibility. The shareholders may use this forum to not only voice their grievances and seek remedy but also give constructive suggestions and changes to be made in the company policy. The notice to AGM has even greater importance since the legislator has made it mandatory that all those business items on agenda for the meeting must be clear to the members. Under Section 102 of the new Act, if any of the officers of the company is responsible for such non-disclosure and profits thereby, then action will be taken against the defaulting officer and compensation made to the company. The new law makes a special provision with regard to move a special resolution by a member. However the member must hold not less than 1% of total voting power on which the aggregate sum not exceeding ₹5,00,000 has been paid up.

Secretarial Standards for Meeting

CA 1956: It did not have any specified secretarial standards prescribed.

CA 2013: The secretarial standards for general as well as board meetings must be followed as specified by the Institute of Company Secretaries and approved in the rules by the Central Government (Section 118)

Analysis: Secretarial standards today are in vogue in international professional practice. It is an effect of formalization. It brings uniformity and conformity to universal practice.

Minutes of the Meeting

Any meeting whether AGM or the board of directors meeting or any of the meetings of the committees of the company is recorded succinctly and yet clearly in the process of the meeting that is taking place. The legislator considers this as the first information and attaches to it complete credibility. There are, of course, secretarial standards and also the trained staff to take such notes that befits its seriousness as the document of decision making.

CA 1956: The old law did not mention it specifically; however in general tradition of conducting corporate business it was taken for granted that minutes were taken and due gravity was granted to that exercise.

CA 2013: Section 118(12) of the 2013 Act provides that if a person is found guilty of tampering with the minutes of the proceedings of meeting he shall be punishable with imprisonment for a term which may extend to two years and with fine which shall not be less than ₹25,000 but which may extend to ₹1,00,000.

Analysis: While in the old days recording the minutes of the proceedings of an official meeting was an art of sorts, these days, one can take recourse to well set templates in the electronic medium. In the next meeting, as the practice is, the minutes of the previous meeting are read by the member secretary and seconded by one of the members. This effectively concludes the last meeting and begins the new one.

Dividend

Dividend consists of the distribution of part of the earning of a company to its shareholders. The board of directors decides the percentage of earnings to be given as dividend and the amount to be re-invested. It is normally calculated as an amount per share on par value of the share; it is also measured as dividend yield, that is, percentage of the share value. Ultimately what it means is that it is what a share holder gets as his returns on investment. The dividend may be paid as interim or final period.

CA 1956: (a) Dividend may be paid, if not out of profits, and then out of reserves, which comes out of accumulated profits from earlier years.

(b) Government can waive off the providing for depreciation.

(c) Payment of dividend through cash or cheque (Section 205 (1)

CA 2013: (a) Same as in the old law; however, the rate of dividend may not exceed the average of the rates at which it was declared in the three years immediately preceding that year.

(b) The law prohibits declaration by a company which has defaulted in payment of deposits (Sections 73 and 74).

(c) The dividend to be paid in cheque or through electronic mode (Section 123 (5))

Analysis: There is always a debate whether dividend has to be paid. There is a double dilemma. From the perspective of the company if dividend is paid then the company has less to invest; if the company does not pay dividend then the investors may not invest. From the perspective of the investor, although the dividend is welcome, since the company would have less to invest the investor is going earn lesser returns on investment. Generally, experts called fund managers putting their financial acumen together are able to calculate a ratio of the profits to be granted as dividend and the rest to be re-invested.

Directors

Director of a company implies a person who holds a responsible position in it. The AOA contains the names of the first directors of a company. There are several directors in a company and this group is called as board of directors; these are collectively responsible for the company. One Man Company, of course, has a single director. One of the directors may be elected as the chairman who is the head of the board of directors. A director who is invested with the executive powers is known as the managing director; at times the chairman and the managing director are one and the same person and goes with the acronym CMD. The Companies Act, 2013 has several innovations with regard to the directorship of a company.

CA 1956: Maximum number of directors in a company was 12. A director may be substituted in the absence of the original one for not less three months. An individual could hold only 15 directorships.

CA 2013: Innovation about directors:

(a) It is mandatory for a listed company to appoint at least one woman director

(b) It is mandatory that every company shall have at least one of the directors who domiciles in India for 182 days or more.

(c) It is mandatory for a listed company to have at least one-third of the total number of directors as independent directors.

(d) The maximum number of directors in a company, whether public or private, is 15; more may be appointed after passing a special resolution.

(e) Limitation of liability of non-executive/independent directors: An independent director or non-executive director, not being promoter or key managerial personnel, shall be held liable only in respect of such acts of omission or commission by a company which had occurred with her/his knowledge, attributable through Board processes, and with her/his consent or connivance or where she/he had not acted diligently.

(f) Declaration by the director: First, the director must furnish a card called Director Identification Number (DIN); secondly, a declaration that he is not disqualified to become a director as per the provisions of the Act.

(g) The board must specify the conditions of the chosen independent director.

(h) The company must determine that not less than two thirds of the directors are liable to retire by rotation; among these the independent directors are not included.

(i) A director may be substituted as an alternate director in the absence of the director for a period not less than three months.

(j) A director shall be disqualified in the event of charged and convicted with an imprisonment of seven years or more. (Section 164)

(k) A director is at default if the company commits specified defaults, such as company failing to file financial statements; further, such a director cannot be reappointed in any company before the elapse of five years.

(l) An individual may hold maximum of 20 directorships; not more than ten those of public companies.

(m) Section 168 deals with the resignation of the director, which should be submitted to the board of directors; upon acceptance of the resignation the board shall inform the ROC, as is prescribed.

(n) Section 169 concerns with the removal of the director which is accomplished through the passing of the resolution and informing the concerned director about it; further the vacancy may be filled through the passing of a resolution by the board of directors.

(o) Section 170 mandates that every register and other documents concerning the directors and the key managerial personnel to be maintained at the registered office of the company.

Analysis: A Company is an artificial person; it cannot function on its own; it needs agents from decision making to its implementation. In other words, a company needs managers, firstly to make decisions collectively through a board of directors and secondly to run operations of the company, the managerial personnel. A director acts on behalf of the company and represents it wherever it should be represented. The decisions and actions do not belong to the director personally, but only institutionally in so far as her/his mandate goes. Thus both the significance and importance of a director of a company is that of responsibility, dependability and accountability. The Companies Act, 2013 also clearly shows the signs of the times: Woman director and independent director. While the former brings vitality and new perspectives the latter brings probity and accountability.

Board Meeting

The meeting of the directors of board of a company is a formal coming together based on an agenda upon which deliberations take place and decisions are taken. One of the meetings that you are now familiar from above is the Annual General Meeting (AGM); but here you are concerned with the decision making body of the company. Unlike AGM, the board meets more frequently. There is a mandatory frequency set for the meetings; apart from that if the board meets more frequently it would be according to the need of the company. There is a prescribed quorum, the mandatory number of directors who must attend the meeting. Among the members there is a presiding member known as chairperson. The deliberations take place and the minutes of the meetings are recorded. The resolutions which are passed are further communicated to the concerned people and organizations. The board functions on the principle of collective responsibility; hence, even a member who may not be present on the particular occasion, yet is bound by the decisions or resolutions of the board.

CA 1956: The board meeting is to be held once in every three calendar months (Section 285) for which a notice must be given. Electronic conferencing such as through video did not exist.

CA 2013: The new Act lays emphasis on board meetings and resolutions to be passed on all issues concerning the company:

(a) First meeting of the company within 30 days of registration.

(b) The meetings can take place and quorum can be attained through video conferencing (Section 174); quorum should consist of 1/3 of the total strength or two directors, whichever is higher.

(c) The notice for the meeting shall be given at least 7 days in advance, and can be done so electronically.

(d) The chairperson and the company secretary have the assigned duties so that the meeting may be conducted in the manner prescribed by the law.

(e) Resolutions must be circulated to all the directors; placing and signing of the registered must be followed.

Analysis: Under the new Law meeting of the board of directors is highly significant. A company is an institution of its members, by the members and for the members; it is a democratic institution. Just as the political representatives of the people meet in the parliament and legislate and execute the laws and policies to govern a country so too the board of directors, who if it is a public company represent the investors, meet to make policies and run the general governance of the company. The processes of the meeting are also democratic: members meet at the appointed time, in a quorum, put to vote the resolutions and thus decide on the principle of majority. A company is a democratic cell and its nucleus consists of the board meetings.

Powers of the Board

CA 1956: The powers of the board in the old law are enumerated in Section 292 of the act; the same powers are continued in the new Act, too.

CA 2013: The new law makes provisions which are similar to the old Act, and also extended further under the rules as follows:

(a) Make calls on shareholders in respect of money unpaid on their shares

(b) Authorize buy-back of securities under Section 68

(c) Issue securities, including debentures, whether in or outside India

(d) Borrow monies

(e) Invest the funds of the company

(f) grant loans or give guarantee or provide security in respect of loans

(g) Approve financial statement and the Board's report

(h) Diversify the business of the company

(i) Approve amalgamation, merger, or reconstruction

(j) Take over a company or acquire a controlling or substantial stake in another company

Further under the Rules:

(k) Make political contributions

(l) Appoint or remove key managerial personnel (KMP)

(m) Take note of appointment(s) or removal(s) of one level below the Key Management Personnel

(n) Appoint Internal auditors and secretarial auditor

(o) Take note of the disclosure of director's interest and shareholding

(p) Buy, sell investments held by the company

(q) Invite or accept or renew public deposits and related matters

(r) Review or change the terms and conditions of public deposit

(s) Approve quarterly, half-yearly and annual financial statements or financial results as the case may be.

Analysis: The quality of governance of a company depends upon the quality of decisions or resolutions that the board approves and implements. The board is responsible for everything what goes on in a company. The danger in modern companies is that the CEOs are very powerful persons as managers in their competencies and hence the board may succumb to their imposing views. Well-known companies such as financial banks and institutions have been the victims of such top-end managers. The result has been a disaster causing financial meltdown, enormous financial scams, and the loss suffered by the investors. A good, competitive, and vigilant board can work wonders for a company. The legislator's insistence on independent directors is a step towards active vigilance and good governance.

Audit

The term with the root *aud* is so familiar, such as *audio, audience, audit* and *auditing* and *auditor* that it needs little explanation except that in the given context it has a common and also a special meaning as may its use suggest. The Latin infinitive *audire* implies *to hear.* A common meaning, for instance, would be to hear music such as at a music concert, and the people gathered in the *auditorium* are denoted as *audience*. *Hearing* also could be a special one. For instance, when a judge summons the parties to a dispute in the court he gives the parties a *fair hearing.* So also a specialist, a professional, whose duty it is to examine his field becomes an auditor and his work is marked as audit or auditing. Every professional field involves audit: management audit, operational audit, technological audit, environmental audit, IT audit, medical audit, etc. It consists of examining of the state of affairs concerning data, statements, records, and their investigation and analysis so that what is examined stands all sorts of scrutiny as may be warranted. The companies, under the Act, 2013 have to undergo financial or accounts audit, both internal as well as external which is independently and impartially conducted and its conclusions should reveal the actual financial state of the health of company. The following key concepts delineate audit in its essence: analysis, assessment, evaluation, check, confirm, inspection, examination, appraisal, inventory, inspection, review, scrutiny, and the like.

CA 1956: The Act assumed that the audit to be external, which is conducted independently of the company management. The company, of course, could maintain an internal audit; however, it was not mandated by the Act.

CA 2013: (a) Section 138 of the Act mandates internal audit. The auditor who could be a chartered accountant or a company secretary must be appointed by the board of directors.

(b) The appointment of auditors is for five years, which is effected through a resolution at the AGM.

(c) Listed companies must follow the principle of rotation of the auditors. If it is an individual he must be rotated after the completion of five year term; if it is an audit firm then after the completion of two five year terms.

(d) Under Section 141 Auditors cannot be appointed who may cause a conflict of interest such as business relationship with the company, a relative is one of the directors, a person convicted for fraud, and if his or his relatives firm is involved as consulting entity.

(e) Duties: It is the duty of the auditor to assess the financial health of the company, to report fraud to the Central Government, must attend general meetings.

(f) Cost Audit: Section 148 empowers the Central Government to cost audit of companies.

Analysis: Good Corporate Governance has been in trend ever since Sarbanes-Oxley Act of 2002.[1] India, too, has introduced reforms and enacted laws to safeguard the interests of the investors. The Ministry for Corporate Affairs with all its statutory bodies is vigilant and enforces rules for disclosures by the companies. The Companies Act 2013, Chapter X, has incorporated mechanisms for accounts and audit. It has increased corporate requirements for performing internal audits.

Corporate Social Responsibility (CSR)

Giving back to the society is a term that describes one's debt to the community from which one is born and brought up and has done well in life and responds by those actions which benefit her/his community. Similarly, a company is not an island for itself; it is a legal person and belongs to the society at large. It uses resources of the earth as well as of the people to make profit. It behoves that such companies do not stop at profits but plough back into the society the fruits of those profits. Just as an individual is expected to be a good citizen so also a company expected to be a good citizen. Corporate responsibility is a dual responsibility: since it utilizes earth's resources it has to make special efforts to be ecologically sustainable in its operations and since it is a part and parcel of the community of people it has the duty respond to the needs of the people. The responsibility towards the people is fulfilled by taking up causes to alleviate poverty, promote healthcare, advance education, and undertake such activities which will benefit the people.

CA 1956: Under the old Act there was no mandate for CSR; it was left to the discretion of the companies to undertake social causes. Many companies used to take to philanthropy, where funds were provided for a certain cause. It was a one-sided activity where aid will be given to passive receivers.

CA 2013: The new Act exhibits the spirit of the times and mandates CSR. It facilitates an interactive undertaking between the company and community. The mandate of the legislator as follows:

Company having:

Minimum net worth of ₹500 crore

Turnover up to ₹1,000 crore

Net profit of at least ₹5 crore

Analysis: It is not that every company is mandated to invest in CSR, although every company may conduct it according to their ability.

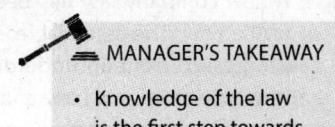

MANAGER'S TAKEAWAY

- Knowledge of the law is the first step towards the wisdom of its application.

8.5 REMARKS ON THE NEW ACT

Jurisprudence has meaning only if it protects liberty, equality, and social harmony. This principle applies to the economic affairs of the people. Creation and sharing of wealth within the boundaries of safeguarding the above three fundamental values is a practical demonstration of jurisprudence. When making laws the legislators must realize that these are made for man and not the other way around.

If the law does not abide by time, justice delays, and that denies justice. The Companies Law is long overdue. For social and economic reasons the bill must be enacted as soon as possible into law.

The objectives and thrusts of the bill are good intentions; whether these will pave a way for the well-being of the companies and make them 'good citizens' for the country and the world is to be seen in the details of the law.

This author would like to propose separate, simple, and concise laws for different companies such as One Person, Small, Partnership, Private, Public, and Listed rather than club them all together under a huge, cumbersome, unwieldy blanket law. One big law discourages smaller enterprises. Further, various regulatory authorities de-motivate them.

The bane of Indian business has been enormous scams and corruption ridden system. The purpose of the law is precisely to see that it does not become cause for it. Ensuring effective administration of the justice is the only way to root out these maladies. Hence, the law must empower the judiciary to serve the cause of clean enterprise.

The legislators got to think beyond the policing strategies to rein in the corporations for fraud through various agencies, audits, and tribunals. There are more intelligent and constructive ways to encourage the enterprise of this country than merely by policing and punishing.

One of the most constructive efforts should be a long term objective to educate and train entrepreneurs, shareholders, managers, and other professionals of business in good corporate citizenship and ethical values. The values of ethics are not only the fabric of a good society but also of good business.

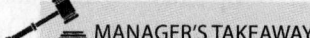

MANAGER'S TAKEAWAY

- Have the enterprise of the country at heart.
- The reputation of a company and the dignity of man go hand-in-hand.

SUMMARY

- A new company law has been the urgent need of the hour. The essential reason being that India progressed from an underdeveloped economy towards a developing one and it has been on a fast take-off stage as the emerging developed economy. Hence, legal instruments were necessary to deal with the contemporary global scenario.
- Guided by clearly set objectives and goals for a globally competitive economy in the context of political, social, and technological world, the new law was enacted to facilitate commerce and trade and make the corporations initiate their own self controls and fix their own responsibilities across the entire cross-section of the stakeholders.
- The major thrusts and general provisions of the Act were to harmonize regulations with

the shareholder democracy. All officers of the company and the key managerial personnel would hold accountability. Make insider trading a criminal offence, encourage transparency in audit, and overall protection of the investors would be supreme.

- The provisions of the Companies Act 2013 are in stark contrast with the old Companies Act 1956.
- Legislation is made after careful consideration of the fundamental values for its basis. It rests on the principles of creation of wealth and its equitable sharing. The Companies Act 2013 may not be the last word in corporate legislation. The statutory bodies have the power to formulate necessary rules to implement the law effectively. Only time will tell the success of this new law.

EXERCISES

(i) A company's paid up capital is ₹40 lakh. Its turnover is ₹20 crore. Will it be defined as a small company?
Hint: See Section 2 (85)

(ii) Read Section 46 with the Companies (Share Capital and Debentures)
Rules, 2014 requires passing of Board Resolution for issuance of share certificates. Under the

Companies Act, 1956 such power could be delegated to Committee of the Board. Companies Act, 2013 is silent on this issue.

Hint: See Section 179 on powers of the Board.

(iii) Investigate whether the following is right or wrong and see if there are some exceptions: As per Rule 3 of the Companies (Management & Administration) Rules, 2014 all the existing companies, registered under the Companies Act, 1956, shall prepare its registers of members as per the provisions of Section 88 of the Companies Act, 2013 within a period of 6 months from the date of commencement of Companies (Management & Administration) Rules, 2014.

Hint: Refer to the above mentioned sections and rules.

(iv) Compare and contrast Section 2 (49) with Section 184 (2). Which definition would you accept? Give reasons; also refer to the website of the Ministry of Corporate Affairs, General Circular to 19/2014 of 12 June 2014.

(v) What are securities? Who can issue them?

DEVELOPMENT OF LEGAL EDGE

- Form an informal group within your class or professional circle.
- Mark the sections of the Act which are relevant to your field of work and conduct a workshop within your group.
- Look out for an opportunity when Chartered Accountants or the Company Secretaries conduct a seminar in your locality and take active participation in it.

FURTHER READING

- Sharay, H.K, *Company Law*, Vth Edition, Universal Law Publishing Co., 2008.
- The Companies Bill, 2011 http://www.mca.gov.in.
- Report, http://www.nfcgindia.org/pdf/21_Report_Companies_Bill, http://220.227.161.86/11489p829-835.pdf.
- MCA's Corporate Governance Voluntary Guidelines, 2009 http://www.nfcgindia.org/pdf/CG_Voluntary_Guidelines_2009_Final.pdf.
- MCA's Corporate Social Responsibility Voluntary Guidelines, 2009 http://www.nfcgindia.org/pdf/CSR_Voluntary_Guidelines_2009.pdf.
- Dr J.J. Irani Report on New Company's ACt, http://www.mca.gov.in/report_expert_comt.htm.

CASE STUDY DLF VS SEBI: A PROBLEM OF CORPORATE DISCLOSURES

The website, www.dlf.in is as sprawling and magnificent as the company's ever expanding mega real estate business. Considered to be one of the largest realty developers in the world, its head Kushal Pal Singh is considered as the richest among his ilk. From apartment townships to five star hotels, from IT parks to golf courses, from malls to corporate offices, from cyber cities to Special Economic Zones, *et al*; think big in real estate and it belongs to the DLF.

The Company

DLF is an acronym that stands for Delhi Land and Finance Housing and Housing and Construction Private Limited. It is familiar with two types of people; first those who love cricket, these are in millions in the country, it is the sponsor of the most successful T-20 version of the game, and those who, particularly in North India, cannot but miss the brand name whether they see apartment blocks, office districts or walk into a mall.

Two people Chaudhary Raghvendra Singh and Makhan Lal Jain Gandharwal of Rohtak in Haryana established the company in 1946 and ventured into realty business by acquiring land first in Delhi and later in their own home state. Their vision as expressed in their website was to build the new India and to be the most valuable real estate company in the world. They professed to abide by the ethical values, and compliance to environmental and legal requirements.

The Money

On Forbes list 2000 (2013), the public company is close to USD two billion whose net income is over USD 220 million and boasts of its chairman as one of the richest business tycoons of India.[4] Trading is done on both the Bombay Stock Exchange as well as on National Stock Exchange. Problems with the market regulator SEBI that banned the company and some of its directors from seeking to raise capital from the public has hit the investors sentiments. Consequently, trading graph has dipped and the stocks have been reduced by 50%. Shareholders, bondholders, and above all the home and office buyers are at the receiving end. Company's appeal to the Securities Appellate Tribunal (SAT) has not brought any relief.[5]

The Case

It began with a complaint to SEBI by one Mr. Kimsuk Sinha on 4 June 2007. He claimed that two Wholly Owned Subsidiaries (WOS) of DLF had defrauded him of ₹34 crores. He prayed for action by the market regulator. DLF had applied for an IPO for raising ₹9,187.5 crores issued the prospectus in May of the same year and filed it with the ROC in June. In the meantime SEBI investigated the matter and passed an order on 10 October 2014 restricting the company and its five directors from accessing the market and prohibited them from dealing with securities for three years. The main reason: Active and deliberate suppression of material information in its prospectus, which was a Red Herring Prospectus (RHP). It misled and defrauded the investors. SEBI's charges against DLF are as follows:

1. Non-disclosure of material information in relation to alleged subsidiaries – the RHP.
2. Non-disclosure of related party transaction.
3. Non-disclosure of outstanding litigation relating to alleged subsidiaries
4. Violation of Disclosure and Investor Protection (DIP) Guidelines
5. Deliberate and active suppression of material information to fraud DLF countered the arguments under the following points:
   (i) SEBI had no jurisdiction beyond attending to the complaint.
   (ii) SEBI denied request to inspect documents which violated the natural justice.
   (iii) The complainant had no legitimate case since he was neither a subscriber of shares in DLF or related to the securities market.
   (iv) The prospectus had adequately disclosed related material to the development of land.
   (v) SEBI took long time to attend to the case and did not allege any motive.
   (vi) DLF acted in good faith.

---

[4]See: http://www.forbes.com/companies/dlf/ (Retrieved 22 December 2014).
[5]See: http://www.livemint.com/Money/trH2jNEFvypHjhsvv11MeK/Should-you-be-worried-about-the-DLF-ban.html?utm_source=cop (Retrieved 22 December 2014).

The Law   Disclosures and Compliances Concerning Raising Money and Lending Loans for the Corporations

1. **Restriction on investment through more than two layers of investment subsidiaries:** The 1956 Act did not impose any restrictions on companies which made investments through multiple layers of investment companies. However, Section 186 (1) of the new Act 2013 restricts a company from making investment through more than two layers of investment companies.

   Reason for the Restriction: The decision to impose a limit on number of investment subsidiaries was taken by the Ministry of Corporate Affairs in the wake of the Purti scam, which exposed the lacunae existing in the Indian corporate regime. Section 186(1) has been introduced with a view to increase transparency in corporate transactions.

2. **Restriction on loans to directors and other persons:** The new Act 2013 has made significant changes to the restrictions relating to provision of loan by a company to its directors. The key changes are as follows:

(a) Under 1956 Act loans made to or security provided or guarantee given in connection with loan given to the director of the lending company and certain specified parties required previous approval of the Central Government. However, section 185 of the new Act 2013 imposes a total prohibition on companies providing loans, guarantee or security to the director or *any other person in whom the director is interested*.

(b) Whilst the restriction contained in the old Act 1956, applied only to public companies, the new Act 2013, has extended this restriction to even private companies.

Reason: The restriction on providing loans to any other person in whom a director is interested is worded broadly and would apply to subsidiaries and other companies within the same group with common directors. Such restriction would create significant difficulties for companies which provide loans, or guarantee or security to their subsidiaries or associate companies for operational purposes. The Ministry for Corporate Affairs addressed this concern by issuing various circulars. Accordingly the companies are now permitted to give loans, guarantee or security with respect to a loan taken by a wholly owned subsidiary, if the loan is utilized by such subsidiary for its principal business activities.

3. **Loans and borrowings of the company**: Section 186 of the 2013 Act restricts a company from providing loans, giving any guarantee or security, or acquiring any securities of a body corporate, exceeding 60% of its paid up share capital, free reserves and securities premium account or 100% of its free reserves and securities premium account, whichever is more. However, a company may overcome such restrictions by passing a *special resolution* at a general meeting. These provisions are substantially the same as contained in Section 372A of the old Act, 1956. However, the following changes have been made:

(a) Section 372A of the 1956 Act was applicable only to public companies. Section 186 of the new 2013 Act additionally applies to private companies.

(b) While old Act restricted a company from giving any loans to other body corporates, the new Act restricts companies from providing loans to any *person or any other body corporate and hence loans to individuals and other non-corporate entities are also covered*.

(c) The new Act requires companies to disclose its loans, investments made, guarantee given or security provided and its purpose, to its members in the financial statement. The Rules however, prescribe that where loan or guarantee is given, or a security has been provided by a company to its *wholly owned subsidiary*, or a *joint venture company*, or an acquisition is made by a holding company, of the securities of its wholly owned subsidiary, the company need not pass a special resolution.

Reason: The restrictions imposed on inter corporate loans are viewed largely as a move to usher in accountability in corporate transactions. The MCA has attempted to bring the Indian corporate legal regime in line with global best practices, by increasing shareholder participation in affairs that directly affect the finances of the company. The 2013 Act also mandates increased disclosure norms to increase transparency in commercial dealings.

4. **Deposits:** Chapter V of the new Act, 2013 lays down provisions relating to deposits which should be read with the Companies **Acceptance of Deposits by Companies** Rules, 2014 Both the new as well as the old Acts provide that a *public company can accept deposits from its members and other persons*, while *private companies can accept deposits only from its members*, it should be noted that old Act permitted a private company to accept deposits from members, directors or their relatives also. The definition of *deposit* as provided under the new Act and the Rules specifically indicate that loans obtained by a company shall also be considered to be a deposit.

Reason: Private companies would be severely restricted in accepting deposits from its members.

5. **Restriction on companies on giving loans for purchase of its shares**: Chapter IV of the new Act deals on this subject.

(a) **The old Law** permitted public companies to provide loans for the purchase of fully paid up shares by trustees for and on behalf of the company's employees. The new Act also permits companies to do so, however subject to a *special resolution*, and certain other requirements, including the requirement that shares have to be valued by a registered valuer.

(b) The new Act does not permit directors holding salaried office or employment to be the beneficiaries of the trust holding the company's shares funded by way of loan from the company.

(c) Voting rights not exercised directly by employees in respect of the employees share scheme is required to be disclosed in the report of the board of directors.

(d) The penalty for non-compliance with these provisions is that an officer in default shall be liable for imprisonment up to three years and shall be subject to a fine ranging between ₹1,00,000 and ₹2,500,000.

Reason: It is to prevent a permanent reduction of liquid assets caused due to payment for shares being made from the accumulated assets of the company itself.

6. **Debentures**: Chapter IV of the new Act 2013 and the Debenture Rules concern this subject. The Act provides:

(a) Secured debentures may only be issued by a company subject to the conditions set out in the Debenture Rules. Some important conditions that a company is required to fulfil include:

• The date of redemption of the secured debentures should not exceed ten years from the date of its issue; however, with respect to infrastructure companies, secured debentures may be issued for a term of up to thirty years

• The charge on the assets or properties should have a value sufficient for repayment of amount of debentures and the interest

• A debenture trustee must be appointed before issue of prospectus or letter of offer for subscription of debentures

• A debenture trust deed must be executed within sixty days of the date of allotment

• The appointment of a debenture trustee mandatory in every public offer regardless of the number of persons to whom the offer was made.

Reason: The Companies Act 2013 has consolidated various provisions of its preceding law. The aim has been singular: to protect the rights of the investors.

Conclusion

The Companies Act, 2013 has brought a change which has moved away from control towards more self-regulation of corporate transactions, disclosures, and compliance. The enhanced standards aim at protecting the rights of the all stakeholders, specifically by facilitating greater shareholder participation when companies obtain or provide loans. The only fear is that excessive regulations and rules may discourage the corporations from conducting the business. Time alone will tell the efficacy of the Companies Act, 2013.

UPDATE

A shareholder has filed a writ petition in the Delhi High Court. It challenges the recent decision by SEBI in May 2013 to allow DLF to raise money through Qualified Institutional Placement (QIP). It raised 1,863 crore which was the largest in the financial year 2014. The Court has given DLF time till 4 February 2015 to reply.[6] How could SEBI allow DLF to raise funds against its own banning the same for fraud while the case is still unresolved?

Discussion Questions

1. State the DLF problem with the market regulator.
2. Give SEBI's reasons to ban company and its directors to seek public funding.

3. What is the special reason to ban the directors from raising debt?
4. What do you understand by disclosures by the company?
5. What is material disclosure?
6. What is related party transaction?
7. What is the jurisdiction of SEBI?

Going Beyond

1. What do you understand by 'doing in good faith'? Illustrate.
2. Should there be a limitation (period of time) on the market regulator? Illustrate with sound reasons.

---

[6]See: http://articles.economictimes.indiatimes.com/2015-01-14/news/58066139_1_dlf-ipo-chairman-kp-singh-capital-market-regulator (Retrieved 16 January 2015).

LEGAL LUMINARY

ARUN JAITLEY, THE VERSATILE LAWYER

Arun Jaitley is a household name in India due to his ubiquitous presence on TV screens. There is no issue that is not familiar to him to comment upon—not just law and politics, policy and strategy but also sports and games, academics, and debates.

He is India's Minister for Finance and also of Ministry for Corporate Affairs. Professionally he is one of the best lawyers of India and as a person in public life one of the most seasoned and astute politicians.

Jaitley would have made an excellent career out of law alone as he was endowed with enormous resources of intellect and willingness to hard work. What made him, an emancipated, enlightened and one inspired by a no less a person than Shri. Jayaprakash Narayan the socialist stalwart, take such a political jump and become a leading light of his party which is considered conservative and fundamentalist? *Perhaps* is a qualification that Jaitley often uses may answer the big question.

What is that *Perhaps*? In 1974 he was elected as the President of the Delhi Students Union called Akhil Bharatiya Vidyarthi Parishad (ABVP). The Union was diametrically opposed to the ruling Congress Party as well as their student union. Getting elected to the Delhi University's union is nothing less than heralding a new political star. Such is the potential of this university student union's president even today. The patron of the union was the erstwhile Jan Sangh, which is presently the Bharatiya Janata Party (BJP). Jaitley's star rose, but at a cost. As emergency was imposed by the government lead by Mrs. Indira Gandhi in 1975, he was incarcerated for his strong views against it. He was lodged in Tihar Jail, Delhi, for 19 months. It is during this period of time which put a stable foundation for the public life. He met here several people who fought against corruption; selfless people who had love for their country more than the pursuit of their own interests.

One's worth is determined by the actions performed; these actions are designated to a position. There are literally scores of positions which Jaitley held and still holds. Some of the following will describe him for what he is worth:

1989–90: Additional Solicitor General, Government of India 13 October

1999–30 September 2000: Minister of State (Independent charge) of the Ministry of Information and Broadcasting

- 10 December 1999–July 2000: Minister of State (Independent Charge) of the Department of Disinvestment (Additional Charge)
- April 2000: Elected to Rajya Sabha
- 23 July 2000–6 November 2000: Minister of State (Independent Charge) of the Ministry of Law, Justice and Company Affairs
- 7 November 2000–1 July 2002: Minister of Law, Justice and Company Affairs
- 20 March 2001–1 September 2001: Minister of Shipping (Additional Charge)
- 29 July 2002–29 January 2003: Member, Court of the University of Delhi
- March 2005–March 2010 1–29 January 2003: Member, Committee on Home Affairs Member, Committee on External Affairs
- 29 January 2003–21 May 2004: Minister of Law and Justice and Minister of Commerce and Industry
- August 2004–May 2009: Member, Committee of Privileges
- August 2004–May 2009: and Member, Committee on Commerce
- August 2009 onwards October 2004–May 2009: Member, Consultative Committee for the Ministry of Home Affairs
- January 2006: onwards Member, Indian Council of World Affairs April 2006 Re-elected to Rajya Sabha

---

[7] See: http://post.jagran.com/search/national-bank-for-agriculture-and-rural-development (24 July 2014).

- August 2006–December 2008: Member, Joint Committee to examine the constitutional and legal position relating to Office of Profit
- August 2006–December 2009: Member, Joint Committee on Offices of Profit
- 3 June 2009: onwards Leader of the Opposition, Rajya Sabha
- July 2009: onwards Member, General Purposes Committee
- August 2009: onwards Member, Joint Parliamentary Committee on Installation of Portraits/Statues of National Leaders and Parliamentarians in Parliament House Complex
- December 2009: onwards Member, Joint Parliamentary Committee on Maintenance of Heritage Character and Development of Parliament House
- August 2012: onwards Member, Railway Convention Committee Member, Joint Parliamentary Committee on Maintenance of Heritage Character and Development of Parliament House Complex[8]

He was an outstanding student throughout his school days in St. Xavier's Delhi; he graduated in Commerce from Sri Ram College of Commerce and his law studies from the Delhi University. He was designated as senior advocate of the Supreme Court in 1989. He addressed the General Assembly of the United Nations in June 1998 on Declaration on Laws relating to Drugs and Money Laundering. He has addressed important and august assemblies and the causes such as on IT Convergence, Broadcasting Laws in India, Disinvestment, and Review of the Functioning of the Indian Constitution. He is a well-travelled and a much desired global personality around the world. Being born and brought up in Delhi, he feels at home in this mega city that is the capital of India.

---

[8]See: http://www.archive.india.gov.in/govt/rajyasabhampbiodata.php?mpcode=27 (Retrieved 20 December 2014).

[i]This Act bearing the names of senators Paul Sarbanes and Michael Oxley of the USA ushered in a new era in corporate governance which called for transparency, accountability, and responsibility in the manner the companies carried out their financial accounts. The purpose of the act was primarily to protect the investors and make corporate disclosures transparent.

The Companies Act, 2013: The Context and Constitution of a Company

Principle: *Nil temere novandum.*

Make no rash innovations.

CHAPTER OUTLINE

- Introduction and Interpretation
  Rationale of the Act
  Aim and Application
  Classification of Companies
- Context of a Company Under the Companies
  Act, 2013
  Special Features of the Act
  Organization of the Companies Act, 2013
  Roles and Responsibilities
  Sections Unchanged from the Companies

- Act, 1956
  Challenges
- Constitution of a Company Under the Companies
  Act, 2013
  Formation
  Incorporation
  Commencement
  Promotion
  One-Person Company
  Nidhi

9.1 INTRODUCTION AND INTERPRETATION

(1) This Act may be called the Companies Act, 2013.

(2) It extends to the whole of India.

(3) This section shall come into force at once, and the remaining provisions of this Act shall come into force on such date as the Central Government may, by notification in the Official Gazette, appoint and different dates may be appointed for different provisions of this Act and any reference in any provision to the commencement of this Act shall be construed as a reference to the coming into force of that provision.

– Sec. 1 (1–3), The Companies Act, 1956

Chapter 8 provided a clear picture of the background of the new Act. We learnt that the new Act aims to consolidate and amend the law relating to companies. Chapters 9, 10, and 11 will discuss this Act in greater depth and detail.

A Brief Remark on the Set-out Principle for this Chapter

Nil temere novandum—Make no rash innovations. When the bill was enacted into law, there were several hasty criticisms in the public domain stating that it is just old wine in a new bottle. But to be fair to the legislators, they have been patient for over six decades and have deliberated and changed as has been necessary by amending the Companies Act, 1956. The serious journey for the new law began in 2008 but with the dissolution of the Lok Sabha in 2009, it relapsed. In 2010, the Standing Committee on Finance re-introduced it; in December 2011, the bill was re-introduced in the Lok Sabha, and another full year elapsed; on 18 December 2012, it was approved with amendments; and on 8 August 2013, it was approved in the Rajya Sabha. It was given the assent by the President of India as has been already stated, on 29 August 2014. This clearly shows that there has been neither haste nor rashness in the legislation of this landmark law. On the contrary, there have also been accolades from the legal and business community that it has been a path-breaking and progressive law that will serve the economic interests of the country in the prevailing global economic environment. The lesson and underlying principle from this approach of slow historical legislation is that we should not let loose on ourselves from laws rashly lest they should become unjust.

Rationale for the New Law

In the course of legislation, which is a response to the behaviour for whom the law is legislated, there are often laws that restrict the companies in their activities. Two such laws are *Monopolistic and Restrictive Trade Practice Act, 1969,* which is generally termed as MRTP Act, and *Competition Act, 2002*. These two acts have their objective to control companies that try to put obstacle in the business of other companies by forming monopolies or dominate market through the formation of cartels; those companies who come together in an unfair collaboration to the detriment of other companies in the similar markets. Again, there are companies that legally come together through the processes of acquisition and amalgamation ostensibly to further the interests of the company, but, in reality, the intention has been to kill competition. For instance, cartelization, a secret agreement between powerful product market leaders to control prices and enjoy a shared monopoly status, is not such a big secret in Indian cement industry. In 2012, the Competition Commission of India slapped a penalty of over ₹ 6,000 crore on the erring companies.[1]

The motivation or the rationale for the new law rose from the fundamental need to meet the new economic challenges of growth, interdependence of the global money markets, trade, and commerce. With over two decades of economic reforms and liberalization, and the acceptance of the policies of free-market economy, India surged forward and has positioned itself as the third largest economy in the world (See Economic Times, 'India displaces Japan to become the third largest world economy in terms of PPP: World Bank'; 30 April 2014; retrieved 25 August 2014).. There has been a dramatic growth of industries where the service sector grew enormously, which made India boast of over a million industries. Growth of companies as

---

[1] See, Prince Mathews Thomas, "CCI, The Cement Cartel of India" [the pun is on CCI which is also the acronym for Competition Commission of India] in Forbes India, 20 July 2002 (http://forbesindia .com/article/briefing/cci-the-cement-cartel-of-india/33354/1 retrieved on 25 August 2014).

well as cooperatives and other free and non-governmental organizations—all contributing to the comprehensive growth of the country required better guidance, governance, and shared responsibility. The Companies Act, 1956, was unable to address these important contemporary issues. The economy as a whole looked for an enabler, a facilitator, a catalyst to usher in a new era of economic growth and prosperity. Normally, laws are enacted to restrict and contain certain states of affairs, but an economic law must motivate entrepreneurs and business establishments in order to further and nurture the enterprise of the nation.

Some salient features of the new law which are quite different from the usual understanding of a law may be enumerated as follows:

1. *Contemporary Needs and Trends*   The Companies Act, 2013, is both written and presented in a contemporary way and addresses all the relevant issues challenging the globalized economic scenario. It puts domestic as well as foreign companies, one-person company (OPC), small company, large company, public company, listed and non-listed companies, all on a level playing field. It also encourages women participation at the highest levels as directors of the board to manage companies. It even envisages a *dormant company* for the benefit of an entrepreneur who registers a company and lets it non-functional until the opportune time when his/her plans and funds are in place. Finally, it recognizes the role of a modern manager.

2. *Governance*   Since a large part of the Act consists of rules and regulations, it helps the officials and managers of the company to understand and follow the law and prevent the companies from several pitfalls and problems. Further, it puts such a system in place that, if followed, one can experience its self-regulatory nature and benefit enormously.

3. *Investor Friendly*   Today, not only financial institutions but also a large section of the public is ardent investors. The Act is particularly protective of the small investors.

4. *Business Friendly*   In short, experts describe the Act as facilitating both large and small businesses. Internationally accepted practices have been incorporated in the Act. It is quite flexible and yet delivers firm and stringent punishments for violations and non-compliance. This approach not only protects the shareholders and other investors but also enables fairness to all the stakeholders in the society, which will promote healthy economic growth of the country.

Aim and Application

The aim of the Companies Act, 2013, is unlike the earlier two Acts, a positive one. It is to facilitate industry, trade, and commerce in the new globalized and commercialized world. It is a scenario where goods and services are produced and supplied across the globe, whether online or offline, whether in real time or virtual time, 24 × 7, 365 days of a year, and the law is a guide for all—producers, service providers, and the consumers.

A law is applicable within its defined jurisdiction, and it is the applicability that makes the law valid. Section 1 (2) of the Act precisely makes it clear: *It extends to the whole of India.* The next clause, Section 1 (3) empowers the Government of India to notify various provisions as and when it deems fit. The legislators in their wisdom to maintain continuity with the Companies Act, 1956, have also applied their minds that the present law is consolidated and eventually amended. Section 1 (4) of the Act specifies the following entities to which the new law is applicable:

TEXT

(a) Companies incorporated under this Act or under any previous company law;

(b) Insurance companies, except in so far as the said provisions are inconsistent with the provisions of the Insurance Act, 1938 or the Insurance Regulatory and Development Authority Act, 1999;

(c) Banking companies, except in so far as the said provisions are inconsistent with the provisions of the Banking Regulation Act, 1949;

(d) Companies engaged in the generation or supply of electricity, except in so far as the said provisions are inconsistent with the provisions of the Electricity Act, 2003;

(e) Any other company governed by any special Act for the time being in force, except in so far as the said provisions are inconsistent with the provisions of such special Act; and

(f) Such body corporate, incorporated by any Act for the time being in force, as the Central Government may, by notification, specify in this behalf, subject to such exceptions, modifications or adaptation, as may be specified in the notification.

– Sec. 1 (4), The Companies Act, 1956

Without application, the law has no reason for its existence. All that you are going to do as a manager is to apply the law, by applying your mind, to its provisions so that the organization that you lead has legal integrity, and protect the interests of the shareholders and the larger circle of stakeholders. Having made these primary remarks, now it is time to move on to examine the new company law in its new context and new components.

MANAGER'S TAKEAWAY

- Be open to the new law, investigate its use, it will succeed only if it delivers what it promises.

9.2 CONTEXT OF A COMPANY UNDER THE COMPANIES ACT, 2013

TEXT

Unless the context otherwise requires, words or expressions contained in these regulations shall bear the same meaning as in the Act or any statutory modification thereof in force at the date at which these regulations become binding on the company.

—Schedule I, Table F—Sec. 1 (2), The Companies Act, 2013

The legislators are conscious that law cannot be applied in vacuum or in a context-free situation. The law is applied given the background of a country with a rule of law and is applied with defined jurisdiction. Those who come under its jurisdiction must comply with its dictates or suffer the consequences. Thus, according to the Companies Act, 2013, all the incorporated companies originate and function as the law prescribes. When a company is incorporated as per law, then there comes into existence a new legal entity with all its rights and duties, and within its parameters, it is perpetual in existence, has a separate existence than from its members, has its own seal, and a citizen of the incorporated world; it is a person, albeit artificial. This is its ambit or domain or context of its origin, existence, and functioning.

Special Elements of The Act

While a lawyer may be interested in the sections and clauses to assist in case law, a business manager would be curious to know the components of the Act, so that she/he is competent to discuss with her/his lawyers the elements of it. The following highlights may stimulate this inquisitiveness.

Composition

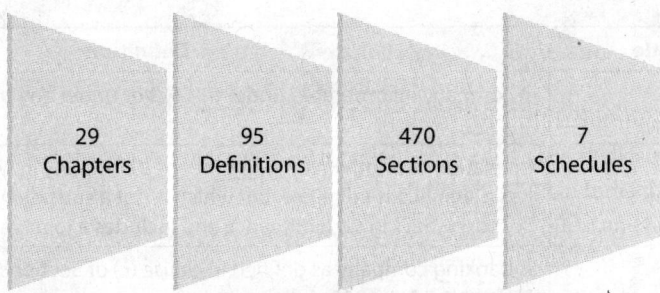

29	95	470	7
Chapters	Definitions	Sections	Schedules

FIGURE 9.1 Composition of the Companies Act, 2013

Status

- President's assent on 29 August 2013
- 98 sections notified on 12 September 2013
- Removal of Difficulties order issued on 20 September 2013 regarding implementation of Sections 24, 58, and 59
- Schedule VII and Section 135 notified on 27 February 2014
- 183 sections notified on 26 March 2014
- Companies first (Removal of Difficulties) Order, 2014 regarding clarification on Section 2(76), the definition of related party
- Companies second (Removal of Difficulties) Order, 2014 regarding clarification on Section 92, the limit on Certification of Annual Return

Organization of the Companies Act, 2013

Building Blocks of the Companies Act, 2013

- Special features
- New law in new context
- New roles and responsibilities
- Stress on self regulation
- Categorization of rules
- Institutions of Governance
- Justice delivery
- Constitution of company to incorporation
- Memorandum and Articles of Association
- Special companies, e.g., charities
- Effects of registration to commencement of business

- Management of the company board and business of the company
- Financial Management
- Shareholder rights
- Internal audit
- Shares
- Share capital
- Debentures
- Powers of nomination
- Acceptance of deposits
- Charges
- Books of accounts Dividend declaration
- Investor education

- Regulatory machinery
- Compliance and penalties
- National Financial Reporting Authority
- Audit
- Investigation of companies
- Protection of employees
- Corporate Social Responsibility
- Tribunals
- Courts and establishments of special courts
- Punishments
- Company Liquidator
- Powers of the Central Government
- Class suits
- Removal of difficulties

Classification of Companies

Section/Title	Definition
2 (20) Company	A company incorporated under this Act or under any previous company law
2 (6) Associate company	In relation to another company, means a company in which that other company has a significant influence, but which is not a subsidiary company of the company having such influence and includes a joint venture company
2 (9) Banking company	A banking company as defined in clause (c) of Section 5 of the Banking Regulation Act, 1949
2 (21) Company limited by guarantee	A company having the liability of its members limited by the memorandum to such amount as the members may respectively undertake to contribute to the assets of the company in the event of its being wound up.
2 (22) Company limited by shares	A company having the liability of its members limited by the memorandum to the amount, if any, unpaid on the shares respectively held by them.
2 (62) One-person company	A company which has only one person as a member.
2 (42) Foreign company	Any company or body corporate incorporated outside India which— (1) has a place of business in India whether by itself or through an agent, physically or through electronic mode; and (2) conducts any business activity in India in any other manner.
2 (45) Government company	Any company in which not less than 51% of the paid-up share capital is held by the Central Government, or by any State Government or Governments, or partly by the Central Government and partly by one or more State Governments, and includes a company which is a subsidiary company of such a Government company.
2 (46) Holding company	In relation to one or more other companies, means a company of which such companies are subsidiary company.
2 (85) Small company	A company, other than a public company,— (a) paid-up share capital of which does not exceed ₹50 lakh or such higher amount as may be prescribed which shall not be more than ₹5 crore; or (b) turnover of which as per its last profit and loss account does not exceed ₹2 crore or such higher amount as may be prescribed which shall not be more than ₹20 crore: (a) Provided that nothing in this clause shall apply to—a holding company or a subsidiary company; (b) a company registered under Section 8; or (c) a company or body corporate governed by any special Act.
8 (1) Charitable company	Where it is proved to the satisfaction of the Central Government that a person or an association of persons proposed to be registered under this Act as a limited company— (a) has in its objects the promotion of commerce, art, science, sports, education, research, social welfare, religion, charity, protection of environment, or any such other object.
455 (1) Dormant company	It is formed and registered under this Act for a future project or to hold an asset or intellectual property and has no significant accounting transaction, such a company or an inactive company may make an application to the Registrar in such manner as may be prescribed for obtaining the status of a dormant company.

141 (3) (*a*) Limited liability partnership	A body corporate other than a limited liability partnership registered under the Limited Liability Partnership Act, 2008. Explanation: The Act gives full force of law to the Limited Liability Partnership Act, 2008. It is an act that speaks both of the trend and need of the times for the small and medium scale enterprises to team up in partnership and benefit the limited liability of a private company and at the same time exercise freedom to agree and contract with the partners flexibly.
406 (1) *Nidhi*	A company which has been incorporated as a Nidhi with the object of cultivating the habit of thrift and savings amongst its members, receiving deposits from, and lending to, its members only, for their mutual benefit, and which complies with such rules as are prescribed by the Central Government for regulation of such class of companies.

Manager's Map

Classification of Companies Under the Act

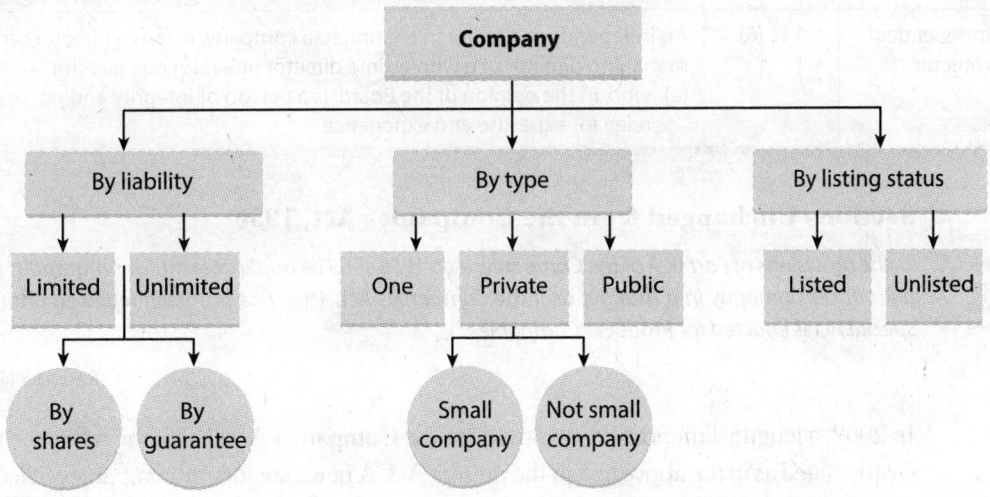

FIGURE 9.2   Organization of the Companies Act, 2013

Roles and Responsibilities

Roles	Reference	Responsibilities
Key Managerial Personnel in Relation to a Company	2 (51)	(i) The Chief Executive Officer or the managing director or the manager; (ii) the company secretary; (iii) the whole-time director; (iv) the Chief Financial Officer; and (v) such other officer as may be prescribed.
Officer	2 (59)	Includes any director, manager or key managerial personnel, or any person in accordance with whose directions or instructions the Board of Directors or any one or more of the directors is or are accustomed to act.

Promoter	2 (69)	(a) who has been named as such in a prospectus or is identified by the company in the annual return referred to in Section 92; or (b) who has control over the affairs of the company, directly or indirectly whether as a shareholder, director, or otherwise; or (c) in accordance with whose advice, directions, or instructions the Board of Directors of the company is accustomed to act: Provided that nothing in sub-clause (c) shall apply to a person who is acting merely in a professional capacity.
Woman Director	149 (1)	Every company shall have a Board of Directors consisting of individuals as directors and shall have— (a) a minimum number of three directors in the case of a public company, two directors in the case of a private company, and one director in the case of a OPC; and (b) a maximum of fifteen directors: Provided that a company may appoint more than fifteen directors after passing a special resolution: Provided further that such class or classes of companies as may be prescribed shall have at least one woman director.
Independent Director	149 (6)	An independent director in relation to a company, means a director other than a managing director or a whole-time director or a nominee director,— (a) who, in the opinion of the Board, is a person of integrity and possesses relevant expertise and experience

Sections Unchanged from the Companies Act, 1956

TEXT

…the provisions of Part IX A of the Companies Act, 1956 shall be applicable mutatis mutandis[2] to a Producer Company in a manner as if the Companies Act, 1956 has not been repealed until a special Act is enacted for Producer Companies

Sec. 465 (1)[2]

In 2002, a lengthy amendment was made to the Companies Act, 1956, the reference to which is clearly stated as in the above text in the present Act. A new category of companies called producer companies was included to the existing ones. So far, there were only three types of companies:

(a) companies limited by shares subdivided into public limited and private limited;

(b) companies limited by guarantees;

(c) unlimited companies.

A producer company is one which deals with primary produce such as agricultural products, animal husbandry, horticulture, handloom, and cottage industry, which generally are carried on by the cooperatives. This legislation would help the association of these producers the benefits of the full-fledged companies.

The said amendment *Part IX A of the Companies Act, 1956* consists of seven chapters, we shall consider this in detail in Chapter 11.

---

[2]Mutatis mutandis stands for the Latin phrase 'with necessary changes when required,' this grants the provision for future amendment as and when it is necessary.

Challenges

You have seen earlier when we considered the rationale of the Companies Act that it is modern, business-oriented, and significant globally. It does not mean, however, that it is absolutely perfect and beyond correction and amendments. The industry and the businesses have found serious problems particularly regarding the rules on compliances, where paucity of time to comply, heavy penalties, and unseen problems have cropped up. While this is from the legally affected side, the problems of implementation both with personnel and infrastructure pose great challenges. The following are some of these challenges:

(a) Out of 470 sections, only about 300 sections have been notified. The seven chapters of *Part IX A of the Companies Act, 1956*, will continue as if nothing has been changed. This will cause confusion in legal as well as commercial community.

(b) The challenges before the auditors are lack of guidance from the regulating authorities. One could say that in the long term, this teething problem may be solved; however, until then if auditors are unable to function or function adequately, the non-compliance will attract very heavy penalty—from ₹ 10 crore for the company to ₹ 3 crore to its officers.

(c) The new Act has the proviso expressly making it illegal for a member of a company to vote for a special resolution if she/he is a related party to the transaction. May be one has to wait for the case law to develop and seek advice of the court of law.

MANAGER'S TAKEAWAY

- The beaten path is a safe path. This concerns the old law. The new law may be described as an area of unchartered waters since one does not know, in spite of its promise, how efficiently it will work. The challenge for a manager is to adapt to the new reality under the new law.

9.3 CONSTITUTION OF A COMPANY UNDER THE COMPANIES ACT, 2013

TEXT

A company may be formed for any lawful purpose by—
(a) seven or more persons, where the company to be formed is to be a public company;
(b) two or more persons, where the company to be formed is to be a private company; or
(c) one person, where the company to be formed is to be One-Person Company that is to say, a private company.

– Sec. 3 (1), The Companies Act, 2013

The above text, Chapter II, Section 3, is precise regarding the three categories of companies: the first two public and private are familiar; the third, OPC, is a new edition in Indian company law. We may divide this section into four stages so that as a manager you would be able to handle this very important and complex legal requirement.

Formation Formation of a company consists of the concerned people coming together to constitute a company with the purpose of establishing a viable business and earn the profits as their reward. The legal process consists of drawing up of Memorandum of Association and the Articles of Association, the documents which are a prerequisite for the formation of a company. *Formation* is the term generally used in the Act for establishing a company, which in this book is further delineated by terms such as *institution* or *constitution* or *establishment* of the company to bring out the import according to the given context.

Incorporation Once the documents of Memorandum of Association and the Articles of Association are complete, they are presented before the Registrar of Companies (ROC) who after examining the documents proceeds to register the new company through which it becomes a legal person and can conduct business in accordance with the law.

Commencement The ROC after due process gives the certificate to the newly established company which permits the promoters of the company to conduct business.

Promotion This consists of putting into practice the business plan which the managers of the company have drawn up.

The above four stages of the process of establishing and advancing the business of the company and strive to achieve its objectives is what you, as a manager, must understand as essence of your organization. You are, of course, assisted by such professionals as company secretary, accountants, auditors for the functioning of the company, and the officers of the government for legal validity of company's actions.

You must realize that throughout the study of the Companies Act, 2013, we would be working still under the shadow, as it were, of the Companies Act, 1956. The defining role of this Act can never go out of vogue, although it is amended and repealed by the lawgiver. As a manager, you would appreciate that the legacy of the old law still remains in the legal expressions and serves as tradition of jurisprudence.

Formation

A company formed under sub-section (1) may be either—
(a) a company limited by shares; or
(b) a company limited by guarantee; or
(c) an unlimited company.

– Sec. 3. (2), The Companies Act, 2013

The above section states the formation of a private company. You have seen different kinds of companies and their classification according to their types in the earlier section, the *Context of a Company in the Companies Act, 2014.* No matter what sort of company, association, or cooperative, if it has to be incorporated, then it must go through the prescribed process with the prescribed documents. The salient features of the formation of such *body corporate* as it is vogue in the legal jargon are as follows:

Mandatory Association In the old dispensation, the Companies Act, 1956, the number of people who could form a partnership company was limited to ten and for banking companies twenty. For the private companies it was fifty. The new Act, 2014, has a latitude of just OPC of one person to 200 associate persons. Further, there could be an association which could be formed for the purpose of without the need for incorporation whose number shall not exceed 100. The Hindu Undivided Family (HUF) establishment is exempted from this. It also applies to the special professions and partnerships, which are governed by the provision of specific laws.

TEXT

Memorandum of Association (MOA) and Articles of Association (AOA) These are the two documents that constitute the charter of a company. In other words, it is a legal deed which gives birth to a new legal entity that receives the seal of approval of the ROC, a body that is created by the Government for the purpose. The MOA has a definite format which the ROC demands. You know most of them from the old Act. Given below are a few with some differences.

Memorandum of Association

The memorandum of a company shall be in respective forms specified in Tables A, B, C, D and E in Schedule I as may be applicable to such company.

– Sec. 4 (6), The Companies Act, 2014

The MOA consists of name of the company, the state in which it is registered and the liabilities of the members as have been usually done under the old law. However, what is new in the current Act is that under Section 4 (1), it does not require the objects clause in the MOA to be classified as

(a) Main objects of the company
(b) The ancillary objects to the main objects
(c) Other objects of the company

The aim was to restrict the company to pursue other objects than in its own main one.

The articles of a company shall contain the regulations for management of the company.

– Sec. 5 (1), The Companies Act, 2014

Articles of Association

An AOA is about the management of internal regulations of the company, relationship to shareholders, and the relationship between the individual shareholders. The Act permits AOA to form retrenchment provisions (5 (3–4)). Generally, companies stick to the format supplied by the Act itself and the forms that the Regulating Authorities provide.

Incorporation

There shall be filed with the Registrar within whose jurisdiction the registered office of a company is proposed to be situated, the following documents and information for registration, namely:—
(a) the memorandum and articles of the company duly signed by all the subscribers to the memorandum in such manner as may be prescribed.

– Sec. 7 (1), The Companies Act, 2014

In addition to the above following conditions, the following clauses *b–g* must be fulfilled:
(b) Declaration by the chartered accountant or company secretary, the professional who has drafted the documents must declare the veracity of the documents.
(c) Affidavit stating all the requisite facts from all the subscribing members.
(d) All the addresses for correspondence.
(e) Personal particulars such as name, surname, nationality, residential addresses, etc.

(f) Similar particulars of the persons in the articles such as Directors, Director Identification Numbers (DIN), proof of identify, etc., as may be prescribed.

(g) Particulars of the persons in the articles as first directors of the company in other firms or corporations, as may be prescribed.

Commencement

The Registrar on the basis of documents and information filed under sub-section (1) shall register all the documents and information referred to in that subsection in the register and issue a certificate of incorporation in the prescribed form to the effect that the proposed company is incorporated under this Act.

– Sec. 7 (2), The Companies Act, 2014

COME LET US FORM

APNA PVT. LTD

I invite you to form a new company called *Apna Pvt. Ltd*. The Hindi term *Apna*, 'our' is quite common. We need to do the following until we set up our company that is private and limited by shares.

1. *Name*: Apna Pvt. Ltd.
2. *Registered Office*: 2121 Mahatma Gandhi Road, Apna Ghar Building, Delhi, 110099.
3. *Shareholders*: 57
4. *Share capital*: A total of ₹100,00,000 of ₹100 each—the initial capital received from the founders of the company (minimum norm is ₹100,000.)
5. *Memorandum of Association*: The document stating all the requisite details such as objects of the company, share holdings, members, etc.
6. *Articles of Association*: It concerns the internal governance of the company with clear rights and duties of the board of directors and other officers of the company
7. *Certificate of Incorporation*: After going through all the formalities before the Registrar of Companies and obtaining the formal certificate
8. *Auditors*: Auditors to be appointed at general meetings and they are supposed to keep check on the financial health of the company.
9. *Accounts*: From cash flow statements to balance sheet and all the aspects of book keeping, readying for the financial year.
10. *Register*: The Company maintains register of members, share ledger, share transfers, charges, debenture holders, etc.
11. *Seal*: An engraved seal which must be impressed on share certificates, all kinds of deeds and financial instruments.
12. *DIN*: Apply and acquire Director Identification Number from the ROC.
13. *DSC*: Apply and acquire Digital Signature Certificate.
14. *e-Filing*: e-Filing with ROC is now in vogue for application and returns.
15. *Duty*: ROC has to be paid fees in stamp duty.
16. *Certification*: ROC sends digitally signed certificates through e-mail to all the directors.

FIGURE 9.3   Requirements for the formation of a private limited company

The certificate of incorporation on prescribed form is granted to the members of the new company after the ROC has scrutinized and validated all the documents with all its prescribed contents.

Under the old Act, a listed company could start business only after the approval by the ROC with regards to the share capital. Now, this has been extended to all the companies. The ROC is empowered to initiate action for removal of the name of the company in case the directors have not filed the declaration related to the payment of the value of shares agreed to be taken by the subscribers to the MOA and that the paid-up capital is not less than the prescribed limits within 180 days of its incorporation.

Promotion

Promoter

'Promoter' means a person—
(a) who has been named as such in a prospectus or is identified by the company in the annual return referred to in section 92; or
(b) who has control over the affairs of the company, directly or indirectly whether as a shareholder, director or otherwise; or
(c) in accordance with whose advice, directions, or instructions the Board of Directors of the company is accustomed to act: Provided that nothing in sub-clause (c) shall apply to a person who is acting merely in a professional capacity.

– Sec. 1 (69), The Companies Act, 2014

The promoter of a company is well defined in the Act by her/his functions:

(a) Appointed by the company and is duly reported in the annual returns to ROC
(b) Is an overseer or controller of the company
(c) Is advisor to the board of directors

The company, from its conception of an idea to its institution or incorporation and to the actual commencing and continuing of the company business, is run by the promoter. The following are some of the salient features of a promoter:

Fiduciary Relationship The promoter is a unique manager with both abilities of ideas and their realization; she/he embodies gifts of entrepreneurship and skills of a manager. Since it is a multifaceted role, the definition of a promoter is difficult. However, there is one element that sets the promoter apart. The essence of the promoter lies in fiduciary relationship. Such a person is one who holds fiduciary relationship to the board of directors as well as to the shareholders. She/he has been legally appointed to hold and manage the assets of the company in trust of others, i.e., all the stakeholders of the company, from members to the last investor. In short, it is not merely a legal relationship but also an ethical one, since the promoter functions not for herself/himself but for others and hence cannot derive private profit.

Disclosure The promoter's prime duty is to disclose; she/he is liable for all contracts made to the third party on behalf of the company; it is both a legal as well as moral obligation.

Remuneration A large portion of the work of the promoter happens to be before the incorporation of the company; since the company does not legally exist, there is no question of any remuneration by the company; again after the commencement of business of the company. A contract with the company may be entered in after the incorporation of the company either with a commission on the services rendered or through the issue of non-issued shares.

CORPORATE LONE RANGER

ONE-PERSON COMPANY

One of the characteristics of the economically emerging India is the highly enthusiastic, knowledgeable, and motivational charged young entrepreneurs. These have set their aspirations to be the recognized business persons of India and of the world. Others, matured through bad experiences of partnerships, want to do something they especially like, work with focus, and be their own boss. OPC is an entrepreneur's dream.

While forming the new company law, the legislators have taken note of the global trend of OPCs and has adopted the same. Further, the legislators have given a huge leeway by exempting several exacting procedures. The advantage is that an OPC is small, quick decisions are possible and easy to manage. On the other hand, as the business grows, there is always a greater opportunity that an OPC can convert to a Private Limited Company. The following are its salient features:

Incorporation: Under 3 (1) (c), anyone, who is a citizen of India and is present in the country for best part of the year, i.e., 182 days, can form an OPC. Rule 1.1 (2) permits registration of five OPCs by a single person.

Memorandum: In the usual format of the memorandum, the name of a nominee, with the latter's consent must be stated, so that in the event of death the nominee will become the owner of the company, which would continue beyond the death of the original creator of the company.

Compliance: Generally, OPC is regarded as a private company as long as the legal obligations are concerned; yet, it has exemptions due to the essential character endowed on it:

(i) No cash flow statement submission (Sec. 2 (40))

(ii) Need not hire a company secretary; annual returns may be filed and signed by the Director himself. (Proviso to Sec. 91 (1)); under same proviso, no annual general meeting, except that the director himself conducts half-yearly meetings and an OPC obviously does not call for a quorum in such meetings (Sections 173, 174, and 175 (5)); further all the provisions of Sections 98, 100–111 concerning the conduct and administration of a private company shall not apply.

(iii) *Conversion:* An OPC, when it is promising and grown, can aspire to be a private or even a public company. Section 18 of the 2013 Act for conversion [Rule 2.4(6)] of the Act makes such provision.

(iv) *Benefits:* Entrepreneur of OPC enjoys the limited liability where the liability is limited to the unpaid subscription money. On the other hand, if he was a sole proprietor, he would stand to lose everything in the event of insolvency.

Small businesses and all the areas of cottage industry could make use of this entrepreneurial opportunity that the law offers. This is one of the ways how the Companies Act, 2013, facilitates and motivates business prowess. The OPCs may also enjoy higher tax benefits than that of private companies and of the sole proprietors. Here seems to be a great opportunity to turn the entire country on an entrepreneurial journey.

NIDHI

INGENEOUS MUTUAL INITIATIVE

Scheme is a term that is familiar even in the remotest and illiteracy ridden villages of India. It is where a group of people come together, pool in their money, and it is lent to member borrowers only. It is used to be an ingenious method to avoid greedy money lenders and difficult banking, where one could save a bit and hope for a small loan to take care of immediate need or emergencies.

The home-grown idea was further innovated by more enterprising people into non-banking and an assured insurance against the requirements of the people. They were named by some local terms which attracted the people to invest in their money. Since these were not under the government control, misuse started and many unscrupulous entrepreneurs decamped with the hard savings by the people.

Nidhi is a vernacular name for treasure or collection of money through savings by individual members. It denotes all those money-saving *schemes* in general. The legislators of the Companies Act have chosen this term to represent such schemes. India is replete with such *schemes*: *Benefit Fund, Mutual Benefit Company, Chit Fund*. The fundamental nature of these organizations is described as *non-banking*. In the interest of customer protection, the successive governments, both State and Central, have legislated laws and have brought these financial establishments under regulation. Following chart shows some of the non-financial banking institutions and their regulators.

Company	Regulator
Chit Funds	Respective State Governments
Insurance Companies	Insurance Regulatory and Development Authority
Housing Financing Companies	National Housing Bank

Venture Capital Fund	Securities and Exchange Board of India
Merchant Banking Companies	SEBI
Stock Broking Companies	SEBI
Nidhi Companies	Ministry of Corporate Affairs

Three main important differences between Non-banking Financial Companies (NBFC) and Banks:
- NBFC cannot accept demand deposits.
- NBFC does not form part of the payment and settlement system and cannot issue cheques drawn on itself.
- Deposit insurance facility of Deposit Insurance and Credit Guarantee Corporation is not available to depositors of NBFC.

Chapter XXVI of the Companies Act, 2013, Section 406, brings the Nidhi Company under the following legislation:

TEXT

In this section, 'Nidhi' means a company which has been incorporated as a Nidhi with the object of cultivating the habit of thrift and savings amongst its members, receiving deposits from, and lending to, its members only, for their mutual benefit, and which complies with such rules as are prescribed by the Central Government for regulation of such class of companies.

– Section 406 (1), The Companies Act, 2013.

Rules:

Some of the draft rules by Ministry of Corporate Affairs[3] are as follows:
- Nidhi shall be incorporated under the Act and shall be a public company which must have a minimum paid-up equity share capital of ₹10 lakh.
- No preference shares shall be issued.

---

[3]See: http://www.mca.gov.in/Ministry/pdf/NCARules_Chapter26.pdf (Retrieved 21 September 2014)

- Every such company will have Nidhi Limited as part of its name.
- Nidhis shall not admit any body corporate or trust as a member.

Forms:

Three kinds of forms are prescribed:
- Return of statutory compliances
- Registration charges
- Half-yearly returns

Requirements

- Not less than 200 members
- Net-Owned Funds (NOF) of ₹10 lakh or more
- Unencumbered term deposits of not less than 10% of the outstanding deposits as specified in rule 14; ratio of NOF to deposits of not more than 1:20.

General restrictions or prohibitions.— No Nidhi shall—

- Carry on the business of chit fund, hire purchase finance, leasing finance, insurance, or acquisition of securities issued by any body corporate
- Issue preference shares, debentures, or any other debt instrument by any name or in any form whatsoever

- Open any current account with its members
- Acquire another company by purchase of securities or control the composition of the Board of Directors of any other company in any manner whatsoever or enter into any arrangement for the change of its management, unless it has passed a special resolution in its general meeting and also obtained the previous approval of the Regional Director having jurisdiction over such *Nidhi.*

Acceptance of deposits by Nidhis

A Nidhi shall not accept deposits exceeding twenty times of its NOF as per its last audited financial statements.

Conclusion

With time, *Nidhis* have grown into large financial institutions and have been brought under the regulator. Experts may conclude that the regulator has effectively terminated a scheme that was of the people, by the people, and for the people. As luck may have it, small-scale *Nidhis* still continue both in rural as well as urban poverty segments. However, the idea of the future would be to resurrect the old idea of small, self-run, flexible, non-profit, savings scheme that is still prevalent in the Indian Villages. *What do you think you can do about it?*

 MANAGER'S TAKEAWAY

- We live in new age, an age of management, it is where the principles of economics are discovered and applied through deft management in the area of production of goods and services, their trade, and commerce. It is wealth creation with the watchwords such as *transparency, accountability, disclosure,* and *social responsibility.*

SUMMARY

The Companies Act, 2013, is an innovation in legislation to advance both business and governance of the corporations. It is also an effort to balance between companies of many members and the individual entrepreneur. India is rapidly progressing and is already the third largest economy in the world. To meet the economic challenges, just one sort of corporation is not the answer. The act classifies several types of companies so that entrepreneurs have a choice to conduct their enterprise.

The Context of a Company under the Companies Act, 2013, comprises the following essential features:

(a) Special Features of the Act
(b) Organization of the Companies Act, 2013
(c) Roles and Responsibilities
(d) Sections Unchanged from the Companies Act, 1956
(e) Challenges

The study of the Act along with rules and regulations by the statutory agencies makes this act as a rule driven rather than control and penalties.

The Constitution of a Company under the Companies Act, 2013, has both classical as well as new elements:

(a) Formation
(b) Incorporation
(c) Commencement
(d) Promotion

The company is an independent legal entity, independent of its members. These originate and function as law prescribes.

EXERCISES

(i) Is a company required to alter its Articles of Association as per the new format under the Companies Act, 2013?
Hint: Section 5 (6 and 9)

(ii) A public company has three directors: (a) one of whom is an Independent Director whose office is not liable to retire by rotation; (b) another is a Managing Director appointed for a fixed term; and (c) third one is the Promoter Director/Director-Appointed Pursuant to share purchase agreement/nominee director, etc., whose office also is not liable to retirement by rotation. How to comply with retirement by rotation?
Hint: Section 152 (6 and 7)

(iii) A public limited company incorporated received certificate of commencement of business (CCOB) in March 2014. As per the provisions of Section 165 of the Companies Act, 1956, every company limited by shares shall, within a period of not less than one month nor more than six months from the date at which the company is entitled to commence business, hold a general meeting of the members of the Company which shall be called the statutory meeting.
Hint: Look at the dates for the application of the Old Act and the New Act; 'e-form' is available on MCA website.

(iv) What is a red herring prospectus? Illustrate with example/case.

(v) What is the impact of the change after Companies Act, 2013 on incorporation?

DEVELOPMENT OF LEGAL EDGE

- Specialize in your area of management.
- Develop a legal attitude to your area of interest.
- Attend a serious course on leadership development.

FURTHER READING

- Devdutt Pattanaik (2013) *Business Sutra: A Very Indian Approach to Management.* Aleph Book Company.
- Peter F. Drucker (1954). *The Practice of Management* (paperback 2006) HarperBusiness; Reissue edition (3 October 2006)

| CASE STUDY | ZOOZOOS CEASE TO SMILE |

When there is an income tax, the just man will pay more and the unjust less on the same amount of income.

— Plato

Introduction

The *Vodafone* ads with ZooZoos characters, whether on billboards, print, or electronic media bring a broad smile to the viewers. The white *dramatis personae* of this ad blitz consist of humanoids in white, ballooned bodies, and eggheads; they play various emotive and zestful situations to promote the product. It is considered as one of the most successful ads created by the Indian subsidiary of *Ogilvy & Mather.*

Objective of the Case

After *Bharti-Airtel, Vodafone* is the largest telecommunications multinational company in India. It is in dispute with the Department of Income Tax for a huge sum of USD 2.5 billion. Although the Supreme Court of India gave its verdict in 2002, still the legal attrition continues. The tax authorities are adamant that the firm owes to it USD 3.3 billion in taxes and fines.

The above saying of Plato that honest people pay more taxes and the dishonest evades them is what still commonly believed is not wholly untrue. In the curious case of *Vodafone*, however, one really does not know who is fair or unfair, whether it is the tax payer firm or the tax-collecting department of the Government of India.

It is a suitable case for *Foreign Company* under the Companies Act, 2013. In the first place, it would make clear the status of *Vodafone* as a foreign company, and this defined identity may help settle its dispute with taxation laws in India. The Supreme Court of India has given its verdict. The objective here is to analyze this case in the light of the Companies Act, 2013.

Background to the Dispute

In 1992, Hutchison Whampoa and the Max Group, both telecommunications multinationals, came together to start a brand named *Max Touch* which later in 2000 became *Orange.* In 2005, Essar joined and started services in various states of India. In 2007, Vodafone bought 67% of the stakes in Hutchinson Essar for USD 11.2 billion. The rest of the 33% was with some Indian companies such as Essar itself

which is the owner, the Hinduja Group, and the Piramal Group. That is, in short, the merger and acquisition story of the major companies involved in the deal.

The deal was accomplished in Cayman Islands, a tax-free haven, and also Mauritius, the recognized investment route to avoid double taxation. Vodafone got a notice for USD 2.5 billion in taxes. The tax authorities argued that in the take-over deal, Vodafone purchased assets of Essar, an Indian company. This transaction attracts tax.

Vodafone contested this argument by saying that the Indian tax authorities do not have jurisdiction over this transaction; even if the tax is to be paid, it is for Hutchison to pay its capital gains tax.

In the Bombay High Court, Vodafone lost the suit which it challenged in Supreme Court of India.

The Verdict of the Supreme Court

Vodafone International Holdings versus *Union of India*, a three-bench Supreme Court of India judgement, 20 January 2012, is seen to be an important verdict.

Reasons:

The Apex Court rejected the conclusions of the Bombay High Court which had stated that the routing of the whole transaction between the parties through their subsidiaries in Mauritius and Cayman Islands was with the intention of evading of tax.

The Court further maintained that acquisition of shares may carry the acquisition of controlling interest which is purely a commercial concept and the tax can be levied only on the transaction and not on its effect.

Vodafone, on purchase of the shares got all those rights, and the price paid by Vodafone is for all those rights, in other words, control premium paid, not over and above the share, but is the integral part of the price of the share. On transfer of share situated in Cayman Islands, the entire rights which accompany stood transferred not in India, but offshore and the facts reveal that the offshore holdings and arrangements made were for sound commercial and legitimate tax planning, not with the motive of evading tax.

Verdict:

The Court below, that is the High Court, had come to a wrong conclusion that it failed to distinguish between transfer of shares and the transfer of capital assets within the meaning of Section 2 (14) of the Indian Income Tax Act and the rights and entitlements flow therefrom.

Consequently, the demand of nearly ₹12,000 crore by way of capital gains tax… would amount to imposing capital punishment for capital investment since it lacks authority of law and, therefore, stands quashed.[4]

The case is not over yet. The tax authorities are still of the view that they have a case to pursue.

---

[4]See: for full text http://indiankanoon.org/doc/115852355/ (Retrieved 2 September 2014).

STATUS OF AN INDIAN COMPANY INCORPORATED ABROAD UNDER THE COMPANIES ACT, 2013

The Companies Act, 1956, provided under part XI that such foreign companies which would have established a place of business in India before or after the commencement of the Act had to comply with some of the provisions of Act which included submitting with the registrar charter documents of the place of business in India, its address, details of directors, etc., for registration, accounts of the Indian entity, details of charges made on property in India, etc.

The new Act, 2013, has increased the compliance requirements. Chapter XXII of the New Act, Section 379, onwards provides for provisions of the Act as applicable to such *foreign companies* in which Indian individuals or corporations jointly/severally hold not less than 50% of the paid-up share capital either in the form of equity or preference and have a place of business in India. Section 379 provides:

'Where not less than fifty per cent of the paid-up share capital, whether equity or preference or partly equity and partly preference, of a "foreign company" is held by one or more citizens of India or by one or more companies or bodies corporate incorporated in India, or by one or more citizens of India and one or more companies or bodies corporate incorporated in India, whether singly or in the aggregate, such company shall comply with the provisions of this Chapter and such other provisions of this Act as may be prescribed with regard to the business carried on by it in India as if it were a company incorporated in India.'

The definition of the foreign company as follows:
Section 2 (42) 'foreign company' means any company or body corporate incorporated outside India which–
(a) has a place of business in India whether by itself **or through an agent, physically or through electronic mode***; and*

(b) **conducts any business activity in India in any other manner.**
Further, under the Companies (Registration of Foreign Companies) Rules, 2014, electronic mode is defined to mean:
For the purposes of clause (42) of section 2 of the Act, 'electronic mode' means carrying out electronically based, whether main server is installed in India or not, including, but not limited to

(i) *business to business and business to consumer transactions, data interchange and other digital supply transactions;*

(ii) *offering to accept deposits or inviting deposits or accepting deposits or subscriptions in securities, in India or from citizens of India;*

(iii) *financial settlements, web based marketing, advisory and transactional services, database services and products, supply chain management;*

(iv) *online services such as telemarketing, telecommuting, telemedicine, education and information research; and*

(v) *all related data communication services, whether conducted by e-mail, mobile devices, social media, cloud computing, document management, voice or data transmission or otherwise;*

With the New Act, the need for physical presence has been done away with, as entities with no physical presence yet having any virtual presence would also now come under the net.

The foreign companies will have to file:

- Statements with regard to related party transactions, repatriation of profits, transfer of funds including dividends from the place of business in India and any other related party of the foreign company outside India.
- Get its accounts audited by a Chartered Accountant in India.

- Penalty for non-compliance: ₹1 lakh to ₹3 lakh; additional fine of ₹50,000 for the continuance of offence every day.
- Every officer of such foreign company who is in default shall be punishable with imprisonment for a term which may extend up to 6 months or fine which may not be less than ₹25,000 but which may extend up to ₹5 lakh or both.

Analysis

Arvind P. Datar, a senior lawyer of Madras High Court, titles his article in the reputed daily *The Hindu* as 'Vodafone is a Misunderstood Case'.[5] He seconds the verdict of the Supreme Court judgement where shares are distinguished from assets of a company. He argues that when you buy shares of a company, you do not buy its assets. Hutchison the vendor and Vodafone the buyer, both as foreign companies brought about the closure of the transaction outside India. The telecom licenses and other assets of the company are retained by Hutchison–Essar, the rightful owner.

Whatsoever may be the arguments that support Vodafone and several other foreign companies that invest in India, there is no doubt at all that it loses hundreds of crores of rupees of revenue in direct taxes due to faulty policies of a treaty with Mauritius, which gives tax exemptions to foreign companies investing in India. The policy was a ploy in the days of command economy in India. Now that India pursues a free-market economy, the old institution of routing investment through a third party is a complete contradiction, an anachronism of the past.

On the other hand, the question for a foreign entrepreneur to ask is: Why should the company invest in India, if there is no motivating benefit in it? The question is not unfair, if one considers that a foreign company, although pays no direct taxes, yet the employment they generate, sales tax, excise duties, customs duties, several cesses, and charges that they pay, bring in multiple revenues.

The Supreme Court's verdict has been hailed as a landmark judgement. The courts do not make laws; They interpret them. The Supreme Court has done exactly that both in letter and spirit of the law.

Conclusion

The case is under consideration. The company is being favoured for an amicable settlement.

Discussion Questions

1. What are the facts of the case that favour the Department of Taxes?
2. What are the facts of the case that favour Vodafone?
3. What is tax evasion by foreign companies?
4. What is the difference between tax evasion and tax avoidance?
5. Do you consider the Vodafone case as a misunderstood case? Give reasons.
6. Should the Government of India give tax holiday or rebate as an incentive to invest in India?

Going Beyond

1. What is the role played by Mauritius in avoidance of double taxation?
2. Is the Vodafone tax case a hindrance for foreign companies to investment in India?

---

[5]See: *The Hindu*, 2 March 2012; http://www.thehindu.com/opinion/op-ed/vodafone-is-a-misunderstood-case/article2951103.ece (Retrieved on 15 September 2014)

LEGAL LUMINARY

DR JAMSHED J. IRANI, ERUDITE SCHOLAR AND MANAGER WITH A HEART

For the people of India, Jamshedpur stands for *Steel City*; but for the people of Jamshedpur, it stands for J.J. Irani, the Managing Director of Tata Steel of the Tata Sons Group; for the officers and the employees of Tata Steel, J.J. Irani is Tata Steel. However, for you, as the student of this book, J.J. Irani stands for the Companies Act, 2013, as he was the Chairman of the Committee on whose recommendations the Act is legislated.

Dr Irani, having a commendable service of 43 years in the Tata Sons conglomerate of which 33 years were spent as the Managing Director of Tata Steel at Jamshedpur, was chosen by the Government of India to head the Expert Committee on Company Law in 2004.[7] The Committee consisted of thirteen members and six expert visitors, all of whom were drawn from multidisciplinary backgrounds.

The revision and replacement of the Company Act, 1956, had become imperative due to the changes in the economic conditions of the country and the global economic change. Countries with Common Law, i.e., those affiliated to the substantive law of the United Kingdom, i.e., the Commonwealth Countries had started the exercise as early as 1980s. India too made 24 amendments and seriously tried to replace the old law. Although the Committee recommendations came in early, yet the legislative bodies of the Parliament passed it towards the end of 2012 and got its assent from the President of India in the beginning of 2013.

Under the Chairmanship of Dr Irani, the committee presented its report on the last day of May 2005. He admitted in his letter presenting the report that the Committee had tried for a comprehensive view in the recommendations keeping in mind the changed contemporary business environment. The objective, therefore, was to present such a legal framework that makes India globally competitive. In order to do that India must have a corporate environment, i.e., at once transparent, simple, and globally acceptable. Attention had to be paid to encourage technology-driven industrial environment, corporate autonomy and opportunity for self-regulation, optimum compliance costs, disclosures, and efficiency in governance. The fruit of this hard work has been paid in the enacting of the new company law, the Companies Act, 2014.

Having specialized in Geology from the University of Nagpur, Dr Irani went on to obtain his doctorate from the University of Sheffield, UK, in 1960. All along his academic stages, he proved to be a golden boy, as it were, as he had a string of gold medals. In 1993, his *Alma Mater* conferred on him Doctor of Metallurgy, in recognition of his work at Tata Steel and the impact it had globally. A *Honoris Causa Doctor of Science* was conferred on him by the prestigious Banaras Hindu University in 2004. He has been the pillar of strength to the Confederation of Indian Industry (CII). He has also been associated with the Xavier Institute of Industrial Relations (XLRI), Jamshedpur, Indian Institute of Metals, All India Management Association, Indian Institute of Management, Lucknow. In 1996, he was elected as a foreign member of the Royal Academy of Engineering; further, in the following year, he was awarded knighthood by the Queen of the United Kingdom recognizing his role in strengthening Indo-British Partnership. There are scores of other awards and honours bestowed upon him, and yet he remains an unassuming gentleman in the global business world.

---

[7]See: http://www.companiesact.in/Companies-Act-2013/Committee-Report-on-New-Act (Retrieved 8 September 2014)

The Companies Act, 2013: The Administration and Management of a Company

Principle: *Aequitas neminem cum injuria alterius.*

Equity does not make a person to harm another.

CHAPTER OUTLINE

- Introduction and Interpretation
- Administration of a Company Under the Companies Act, 2013

  Prospectus

  Securities

  Share Capital and Debentures

- Management of a Company Under the Companies Act, 2013

  Accounts

  Audit and Auditors

  Dividend

10.1 INTRODUCTION AND INTERPRETATION

(i) All sums of money received and expended by a company and matters in relation to which the receipts and expenditure take place;

(ii) All sales and purchases of goods and services by the company;

(iii) The assets and liabilities of the company; and

(iv) The items of cost as may be prescribed under Section 148 in the case of a company which belongs to any class of companies specified under that section;

– Sec. 2 (13), The Companies Act, 2013

Money

The above, which is recorded in the books of account, is *money*, as far as a company is concerned. This chapter explains about establishing a company, raising money to build it up through selling and buying of company securities, and thus creating a new world of wealth. In the corporate context, *equity* is another term that is synonymous with the value of money. It may take the form of ownership of interest or claim of a company. For instance, on a balance sheet of the company, it amounts to funds contributed by the shareholders, their earnings, and the losses.

There is a social meaning to the term 'equity' that is expressed by the leading principle of this chapter: *Equity does not make a person to harm another.* The ultimate aim of the Companies Act, 2013, actually goes far beyond the exchangeable equity; it stands for fairness towards the investors and the protection of their investments.

Raising Money

It goes without saying that the companies need a lot of money for their mission to be achieved in a time-bound manner. There are banks and other financial institutions but they cost more money to obtain and furnish them the guarantee or collateral. There may be strong financial institutions that invest money, and at an opportune time, tank their shares, thus making the capitalization volatile. Finally, there is a mega solution: go public. Making Initial Public Offering (IPO) is a contemporary way to get to a very large source of money, through the public who buy shares in the company from a stock exchange. With the assistance of the law, the Companies Act, 2013, all the agencies such as concerned ministries of the Government and its regulators and statutory authorities, a system is in place to tap the funds from the public.

By going public, the company has a double advantage: (a) it does not have to depend on debt by the banks and other financial institutions; and (b) by selling shares to the public, the company is able to spread its risk with the investors.

All this activity by the corporations creates a capital market that deals with equity, shares, preferential shares, securities, scrip, and other similar money wares. Since money is involved both from the institutions as well as the individuals, the appropriate law is the only means to regulate the capital market and be just and fair to all the participants, who are buyers and sellers of securities.

Manager's Map

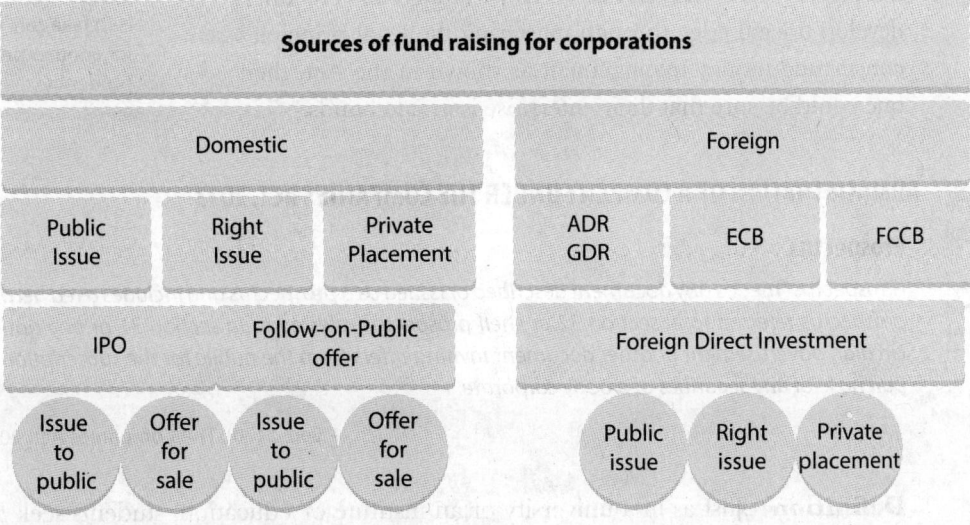

Figure 10.1   Sourcing Funds for the Corporation

Abbreviations

ADR: American Depository Receipt

GDR: Global Depository Receipt

The above are negotiable instruments against the shares of a company.

ECB: External Commercial Borrowings: these are currency borrowings for a short term, usually in foreign currency, and repayable in the same currency.

FCCB: Foreign Currency Convertible Bonds—It is a long-term bond borrowing

Managing Money

Corporate financial management concerns itself with the complex transactions that take place and their efficient supervision to produce optimum results. It functions basically through the application of financial principles to create and maintain value and conduct of proper resource management through good decision-making. Decisions are made on making money, profits, and also on expenditure. Companies exist to make money, maximise its value for themselves, and their shareholders. Money is the scarcest resource and it is the one that can be increased and multiplied if it is put intelligently and smartly to work. Well-known financiers invest their money carefully. One of the first things that a company should be aware and must be wary of is risk. Risk management in the present volatile global financial scenario is imperative. Budgeting of the resources is a wise principle where one tries to spend less and earn more. The saying, companies run on others' money, is commonplace. It is easy to fall into debt trap and end up as insolvent company. Hence, the effort must be to limit debt and create income-producing assets.

> **MANAGER'S TAKEAWAY**
>
> - A manager of finance is bound by fiduciary duty. It consists of a twin relationship of trust, both legal and ethical, between two or more parties. The responsibility is to take care of money for another person, prudently.

The above-mentioned areas concerned with good financial management. The Companies Act, 2013, could be very well illustrated as a charter for such management. If the corporate managers, whom the Act calls as Key Managerial Personnel, develop a legal edge through mastering the legal principles concerning money management as shown in the Act, then one could be sure that their enterprise is in safe hands.

10.2 ADMINISTRATION OF A COMPANY UNDER THE COMPANIES ACT, 2013

Prospectus

TEXT

"Prospectus" means any document described or issued as a prospectus and includes a red herring prospectus referred to in section 32 or shelf prospectus referred to in section 31 or any notice, circular, advertisement or other document inviting offers from the public for the subscription or purchase of any securities of a body corporate.

– Sec. 2 (70), The Companies Act, 2013

Definition Just as in a university or an institute of education, students seek *prospectus*, a booklet that details all about the establishment, the courses it offers, the activities it conducts, the fees structure of the programmes delivered, and so forth. Similarly, a public company may issue a prospectus for the benefit of the investors, whereby they may judge for themselves, the competence of the company to perform and deliver dividends.

At times, the company, for some odd reason, may not be able to supply the complete information, e.g., the quantum or price of the securities, such an incomplete prospectus is considered to be a *red herring* under Section 32 of the Act. The term 'red herring' is a metaphor for something irrelevant that crops up in a considered topic.

Sometimes it may happen that a company issues different types of securities over a certain period of time without the issue of further prospectus; it is as though offered to the investors off the shelf.

Disclosers   Under Section 26 (1), the Regulator has formed rules about the matters to be included or stated clearly in prospectus. These consist of all the particulars of the company, the nature of the shares and their issue, compliance officers, bankers, merchant bankers, stock brokers, credit ratings, dates of opening closing, statement of the board of directors, details of underwriting, consent of all those involved, procedure and time schedule, capital structure—authorised, issued, subscribed, paid up, their description, nominal value, aggregate value, auditor's report, and all the other business activities.

Public Offer   Section 23 of the Act provides how both public and private companies may raise capital:

(i) Public Company through:
- Prospectus
- Private placement
- Rights issue or bonus issue

(ii) Private company through:
- Private placement
- Rights or bonus issue

Change in Contract or Objects   Under Section 27 (1) of the Act, a *special* resolution is required to change the terms of a contract referred to in the prospects or the objects for which the prospectus has been issued. According to the old Act, it would be suffice to take an *ordinary* resolution. Further, Clause 2 of the same section requires the dissenting shareholders to be given an exit offer by the promoters or controlling shareholders.

Sale of Shares by the Members of the Company   Section 28 of the Act directs that the members of a company, after due consultation with the board of directors, may offer a part of their holding of shares to the public. The deed of such an action shall be treated as the prospectus issued by the company. The members shall reimburse the expenses, the incurred expenses to the company.

Global Depository Receipts (GDRs)

"Global Depository Receipt" means any instrument in the form of a depository receipt, by whatever name called, created by a foreign depository outside India and authorised by a company making an issue of such depository receipts.

– Sec. 2 (44), The Companies Act, 2013

*Global Depository Receipt*s are instruments to raise or redeem money abroad through depositories or the related banks. A resolution for the GDRs has to be passed by the board of directors of the company. The company has to take approval of the shareholders prior to such a resolution. These shall be issued by an overseas depository bank appointed by the company and the underlying shares shall be kept in the custody of a domestic custodian bank. The company has to comply with the rules set by the Reserve Bank of India.

In addition to the earlier text of the Section 2 (44), Section 41 of the Act, 2013, asserts that a company may, after passing a special resolution in its general meeting, issue depository receipts in any foreign country in such manner, and subject to such conditions, as may be prescribed. There is a government agency to do this; it is done by the rules laid down by the Securities and Exchange Board of India (SEBI). It drafts rules and regulations for the purpose, thus it deals with foreign convertible bonds and shares. A company is eligible if it complies with the Foreign Exchange Management Rules and Regulations. Even unlisted companies are able to raise capital through GDRs if they comply with the SEBI's specific directives. This is to safeguard any instances of money laundering (Prevention of Money Laundering Act, 2002).

The manner and form of depository receipts are by way of public offering or private placement or any other form prevailing abroad; GDRs may be listed or traded in an overseas listing or trading platform. Shares held by the shareholders of the company may be used for GDRs. A holder of GDRs may become a member of the company with a right to vote.

Private Placement   As we have already seen earlier, it is a method of raising capital by a company that is permitted to both public and private companies. While a listed company offers securities for the public, the private offer of securities or invitation to subscribe shares is done to a selected group of persons. It is done through a private placement offer letter satisfying the conditions laid down by the legislator.

According to Prospectus and Allotment of Securities Rules, 2014, a private placement offer letter shall be accompanied by an application form serially numbered and addressed specifically to the person to whom the offer is made and shall be sent to him, either in writing or in electronic mode within 30 days of recording the names of such persons. Prior to this action, a special resolution by the board of directors that has been previously approved by the shareholders shall be passed. The maximum number of people to whom such offer may be made is 200 during the financial year. Exceptions to this rule are qualified institutional buyers and the employees of the company. The company shall maintain a record of the private placement offers as per Form PAS-5, which must be filed with the ROC. The company offering securities shall not release any advertisements or utilise any media, marketing or distribution channels, or agents to inform the public at large about such an offer.

It is believed that these provisions would bring much desired clarity. However, one cannot but observe the plethora of rules and processes involved, at times, serve as demotivating bureaucratic exercise.

Securities

SECURED WEALTH CREATION

Today, the forces of competition, technology, and globalization have converged to spur innovation and to transform the way business is done in the securities industry.

—Arthur Levitt.

The earlier statement is just a matter of fact; however, if it is made by Arthur Levitt, Chairman of the United States Securities and Exchange Commission, then it has all the importance in the capital market world. He was the longest serving official, from 1993 to 2001, where a quick new world order in geopolitical, economic systems, and cultural sphere swept across the world. The command economy died and the market economy got an unprecedented acceptance. Capital market became the common phenomenon, going far beyond mere banking, creating financial *instruments* that multiplied the securities numerously.

Securities

The economic world is populated with the buyers and sellers of securities that completes the picture of the capital market. They do not buy foods, cars, machinery, houses, or any other goods, in other words, physical assets, but they stand for the *value* of those *assets*. These are the citizens, as it were, of the financial world, so we may generally name them as *financial assets*.

The financial assets, for instance, of a company are sub-divided into *shares*, which are traded on a stock exchange, where both the companies and the interested investors become sellers (*issuers*) and buyers (*investors*), respectively. This is called *primary market*. Further, *secondary market* is where investors are involved and continue the commerce. The purpose of all this buying and selling, which happens globally, round the clock, is, on the one hand, to raise money for companies, and on the other hand, for the investors to earn money. The securities market is also called financial market or capital market. The institutions that deal with such business are called stock exchange. India has stock exchanges in most of its states; however, Bombay Stock Exchange (BSE) and National Stock Exchange of India (NSE) are most prominent; their trading index is known as *Sensex* and *Nifty*, respectively.

Wealth creation through financial securities

A purchase makes many buyers is the principle announced at the beginning of this chapter. It explains the exponential growth in the securities markets around the globe. The wealth created on BSE alone by the major companies is estimated at USD 1.6 trillion.[1]

Debt: A debt security, consisting of any of *debentures, bonds, deposits, notes, commercial paper*, or by any other name, has the characteristic of earning interest upon a contract period of maturity. It is as though one puts some fixed deposit in a bank; however, here a higher rate of interest is awaited. Debt instruments are issued by not only corporations but also governments and their local bodies and international institutions such as World Bank, various Development Banks, and International Monetary Fund.

Equity: Unlike debt securities, which are a loan, equity is a real share or ownership in the company. As an owner, one earns *capital gains* from equity shares. The shares are stocked in a Stock Exchange where daily trading takes place; so, at times, *stocks* is another name for equity shares.

Control of Securities

Securities are serious money. The capital market treats all its customers fairly is most desirable.

---

[1]See: http://timesofindia.indiatimes.com/business/india-business/M-cap-over-1-6tn-markets-at-new-peak/articleshow/42062530.cms (Retrieved, 18 September 2014).

Control and regulation are exercised by the government through legislation and the institution of the statutory bodies, which regularly generate rules and implement regulations and, thus, govern and administer the financial institutions. In India, there are several such control mechanisms: the financial bills passed into acts in the Parliament are supreme; these are further implemented by agencies such as Ministry of Finance, Ministry of Company Affairs, Reserve Bank of India, Securities and Exchange Board of India (SEBI), and Tribunals and Courts set up for the purpose.

Conclusion

Advanced and wealthy nations, such as countries in the Western Europe and North America, are developed on the securities. Japan, one of the most advanced countries, has stakes across the globe with the large footprint of their companies, has one of the most successful and stable securities markets in the world. Japan is the country of the rising sun, that is, a new day in the world begins in Japan and their stock exchange is the first to start a day's business. The Tokyo Stock Exchange is the largest stock exchange in the world.

Share Capital and Debentures

TEXT

The share capital of a company limited by shares shall be of two kinds, namely,
(a) Equity share capital—
(i) With voting rights; or
(ii) With differential rights as to dividend, voting or otherwise in accordance with such rules as may be prescribed; and
(b) Preference share capital:
Provided that nothing contained in this Act shall affect the rights of the preference shareholders who are entitled to participate in the proceeds of winding up before the commencement of this Act.

– Sec. 43, The Companies Act, 2013

"Debenture" includes debenture stock, bonds, or any other instrument of a company evidencing a debt, whether constituting a charge on the assets of the company or not.

– Sec. 2 (30), The Companies Act, 2013

Share capital and debentures

A share is the interest of a member in a company. Section 2 (84) defines share as a share in the share capital of a company. A company limited by shares has share capital that is the amount invested in the company to conduct its business. It may be increased under certain conditions. Shares and debentures (secured debts) are movable property of the company. It is transferrable in any manner according to the provisions of the Articles of Association of the company. It attaches rights and liabilities. Every share has its own distinguishing number (Sec. 46). A certificate is issued under the common seal of the company, specifying the shares held by the person that shall be the *prima facie* evidence of the title of the person to such shares (Sec. 46).

Voting Rights

Every member holding equity shares of the company shall have right to vote on all the resolutions of the company. The preference shareholders shall have voting rights, only applicable to them and in proportion to their shares (Sec. 470).

Application of Premiums

Section (49) stipulates that any calls for further share capital are made on the shares of a class which shall be uniform on all shares falling under that class. If the companies fall short of the accounting standards, then such application is restricted to:

- paying up unissued equity shares of the company as fully paid bonus shares
- writing off the expenses of or the commission paid or discount allowed on any issue of equity shares of the company
- purchase of its own shares or other securities

Prohibition of issue of shares at discount

Section 53 of the Act prohibits expressly the issue of shares by a company at discount. However, Section 54 (a–d) makes an exception to the law with regard to the sweat shares, the shares offered to the employees under some conditions:

- It is to be passed by a special resolution by the company.
- It must specify the number of shares.
- Not less than 1 year has elapsed, since the commencement of the business of the company.
- Listed companies will follow the regulations of SEBI.

Redemption of preference shares

Section 55 of the Act prohibits issue of irredeemable preference shares. If the company is authorised by its articles, it can issue preference shares for not exceeding 20 years. However, the legislator makes an exception regarding infrastructure projects which would be subject to redemption at such percentage as prescribed on an annual basis at the option of such preference shareholders. The so-called infrastructure projects are specified in Schedule VI of the Act.

Transfer and transmission of securities

Section 56 (1) of the Act directs that every company shall, unless prohibited by any provision of the law or the order of the Court, deliver the certificates of all securities allotted, transferred, or transmitted as follows:

- Within a period of 2 months from the date of incorporation
- Within a period of 2 months from the date of allotment
- Within a period of 1 month from the date of receipt by the company of the instrument of transfer
- Within a period of 6 months from the date of allotment in the case of any allotment of debenture

  The company shall intimate the details of the allotment of securities to depository immediately on allotment of such securities.

Impersonation attracts penalty

Section 57 imposes a stiff penalty upon a person who deceitfully personates as the owner of the securities that the person shall be imprisoned for a minimum of 1 year and a maximum of 3 years and shall be liable to fines ranging from ₹1 lakh (as the lowest) and ₹5 lakh (as the highest).

Refusal of registration

According to Section 51 (1), the private and public companies are required to send notice of refusal within 30 days of the receipt of instrument of transfer, and aggrieved party may appeal to the Tribunal against the refusal within the specified number of days. Infringement of this provision attracts a prison term that shall not be less than 1 year and a fine ranging from ₹1 lakh to ₹5 lakh.

The Act also provides for rectification of register of members (Sec. 59 (1)) and publication of authorised, subscribed, and paid-up capital (Sec. 60 (1)).

Provisions incidental to issue of shares

Section 62 deals with the *further issue of capital* where it may want to increase its subscribed capital; Section 63 concerns the bonus shares where a company may issue fully paid bonus shares; Section 64 directs the companies to give notice to Registrar for alternation of share capital.

Power of a company to buy its own shares

Section 68 of the Act permits a company to purchase its own shares or other specified securities out of

- its free reserves
- its securities premium account
- its proceeds of the issue of any shares or other specified securities

The buyback has to be authorised by the articles of the company and a special resolution in this regard has to be passed. The buyback must be completed in one year. Section 70 prohibits buyback in certain circumstances; thus, a company will not buyback through its own subsidiary companies or an investment company.

> **⚖ MANAGER'S TAKEAWAY**
>
> - Companies run on the money invested by the investors. A manager of a company has dual responsibility: *Professional responsibility* has to multiply the value of the shareholders and *Ethical responsibility* ensures that no fraud is played on the shareholders.

10.3 MANAGEMENT OF A COMPANY UNDER THE COMPANIES ACT, 2013

Accounts

"Books of account" includes records maintained in respect of—
(i) All sums of money received and expended by a company and matters in relation to which the receipts and expenditure take place;
(ii) All sales and purchases of goods and services by the company;
(iii) The assets and liabilities of the company; and
(iv) The items of cost as may be prescribed under Section 148 in the case of a company which belongs to any class of companies specified under that section.

– Sec. 2 (13), The Companies Act, 2013

After the definition in Section 2, if you jump to Chapter IX from Section 128 of the Companies Act, 2013, it is all about accounts. In this section, you will briefly study all the important financial matters highlighted. Just as a body does not function without the circulation of healthy blood, so as a company, a body corporate, as the law defines technically, cannot sustain without the money management. The money management of a company is done in two ways:

- *Internally* Book keeping as prescribed by law, internal auditing, maintenance of registers, maintenance of account books in all their categories such as petty cash book, double entry system of accounts keeping, and ledgers.
- *Externally* It consists of external auditors and their reports.

Financial Year

"Financial year," in relation to any company or body corporate, means the period ending on the 31st day of March every year, and where it has been incorporated on or after the 1st day of January of a year, the period ending on the 31st day of March of the following year, in respect whereof financial statement of the company or body corporate is made up

– Sec. 2 (41), The Companies Act, 2013

The above Provision of the Act has made the financial year uniform to all the companies, whether they are Indian or foreign companies with their branches and offices in India. However, the changes are expected to be coming in the form of rules because the foreign companies that follow other patterns of financial year, such as from January to December, would have challenges to meet with the dates.

Maintenance of Account Books

Every company shall prepare and keep at its registered office books of account and other relevant books and papers and financial statement for every financial year which give a true and fair view of the state of the affairs of the company, including that of its branch office or offices, if any, and explain the transactions effected both at the registered office and its branches and such books shall be kept on accrual basis and according to the double entry system of accounting

– Sec. 128 (1), The Companies Act, 2013

The account books reflect the true nature of the company. It is the first information report for both the company management as well as the government regulators. It shows all the money received and spent, sales and purchases, assets and liabilities. Accounts must be kept ready at hand, even at the branches of the companies. The companies may keep books of account electronically. The Act prescribes that the books of account shall be kept up for reckoning for a period of 8 years; if the company is less than 8 years old, then ever since its existence. Vouchers and other related scrips, *challans*, and notes must also be maintained. The books must be available for inspection by the directors during the business hours.

Financial Statements

The financial statements shall give a true and fair view of the state of affairs of the company or companies, comply with the accounting standards notified under section 133 and shall be in the form or forms as may be provided for different class or classes of companies in Schedule III:

– Sec. 129 (1), The Companies Act, 2013

The Act also directs that wherever there are subsidiaries, consolidated accounts shall be prepared; these also include associate and joint venture companies. The regulator provides

Form 9.1 that has to be duly filled and attached to the statement of accounts while filing the returns.

Briefly:

- Prepare its standalone financial statements (Sec. 129 (1))
- Prepare a Consolidated Financial Statements, including all subsidiaries, associates, and joint ventures, whether in India or abroad (Sec. 129 (3))
- Prepare a summary statement for all its subsidiaries, associates, and joint ventures of the salient features of their respective financial statements (Sec. 129 (3))
- Submit the standalone financial statements of subsidiary or these in any number both within and abroad India to the Registrar of Companies (ROC) (Sec. 137 (1)).
- Deliberations on financial report shall consist of extract of annual returns, directors' responsibility statements, declaration by independent directors, explanations on qualifications made, particulars of loans and investments, and the material changes made to the financial statements.
- The board report to be attached will include financial highlights, changes in business, details of directors, key management personnel, new subsidiaries or those defunct, deposit details, orders passed by the regulators or courts or tribunals, and all those matters having an impact on the operations of the company (Sec. 134).
- Financial statements shall be approved by the Board of Directors before they are signed by the directors: Chairperson, two Directors, Chief Finance Officer, Company Secretary, Auditor, and the report of the Board (Sec. 134).

Voluntary Revision of Financial Statements for Board's Report

If it appears to the directors of a company that—
(a) The financial statement of the company; or
(b) The report of the Board, do not comply with the provisions of section 129 or section 134 they may prepare revised financial statement or a revised report in respect of any of the three preceding financial years after obtaining approval of the Tribunal on an application made by the company in such form and manner as may be prescribed and a copy of the order passed by the Tribunal shall be filed with the Registrar.

– Sec. 131 (1), The Companies Act, 2013

If it is concluded that the Financial Statements do not comply with the provisions of Section 129, a revised such document may be drawn up in respect of any of the three preceding financial years after obtaining the approval of the Tribunal on an application made on Form 9.2. The Tribunal, in turn, shall notify the Central Government, Department of Income Tax, or other regulatory bodies and take into consideration their representations. The revision is done only once in a Financial Year. The company board shall record the reasons for the revision of its Financial Statements. The duty of the board shall be to send a copy of the revised Financial Statements and revised auditor's report to the members. In the case of listed company, the same shall be sent to the stock exchanges and regulatory authorities. The revised Financial Statements need to be approved by the members of the company in the general meeting. Section 137 provides that the copies of the Financial Statements shall be filed with the Registrar within 30 days of the general meeting. Additional fees are applicable. OPCs have a time limit of 180 days to do the same.

The challenges of an overload of bureaucratic work seem to be the drawback in the case of book-keeping. In recent times, there has been a public dialogue about these concerns and there are assurances that rules may be reformed to encourage companies to conduct their enterprise.

Audit And Auditors

To audit is to appraise, assess, examine, inspect, review, revise, or conduct an inventory. This may happen in any area of human activity. In financial matters, these are known as financial auditor who re-examine and certify accounting books and financial statements for corporations and other such establishments. This is done not for its own sake but for those who have financial stakes in it. In the case of companies, the stakeholders consist of not only the board of directors, shareholders, and investors but also the society at large in which the business is conducted. The government takes upon itself the responsibility to regulate financial matters by making certain standards of accounting mandatory. The interest of the investors is the supreme goal in the financial controls. An auditor is a professional who does the task of auditing in the sense explained earlier and demonstrates the nature, clarity, and transparency of business transactions. Just as a medical doctor is able to diagnose the health of a person by examining various symptoms, in the same way an auditor is able to verify the financial conduct of a company by the examination of the financial accounts. The Companies Act, 2013, has the following provisions with regard to audit and the auditors.

Appointment of Auditors

TEXT

Every company shall, at the first annual general meeting, appoint an individual or a firm as an auditor who shall hold office from the conclusion of that meeting till the conclusion of its sixth annual general meeting and thereafter till the conclusion of every sixth meeting and the manner and procedure of selection of auditors by the members of the company at such meeting shall be such as may be prescribed.

– Sec. 139 (1), The Companies Act, 2013

The auditor would be appointed with the approval of the members at each annual general meeting for a period of 5 years, which needs to be ratified in the successive annual general meetings. An individual auditor gets only 5 years consecutively, whereas if it is a firm, then not more than two 5-years terms. When these respective terms are complete, they are not eligible for further appointment.

Rotation of Auditors

TEXT

The members of a company may resolve to provide that—
(a) in the audit firm appointed by it, the auditing partner and his team shall be rotated at such intervals as may be resolved by members; or(b) the audit shall be conducted by more than one auditor.

– Sec. 139 (3) (a–b), The Companies Act, 2014

The legislator of the Act has a clear goal, that is, to advance transparency and reduce presumption in profession; to achieve it, the method of mandatory rotation of auditors is provided. The rotation will commence in the case of individuals for every 5 years, and in the case of an audit firm, every 10 years. The auditor or auditor firm cannot be employed in the partner firms of the company. An interval of 5 years is granted as the cooling period after which the re-appointment is possible.

Eligibility, Qualifications, and Disqualifications of the Auditors

A person shall be eligible for appointment as an auditor of a company only if he is a chartered accountant.

— Sec. 141. (1), The Companies Act, 2013

Eligibility In the case of an individual, he/she should be a chartered accountant; in the case of an audit firm, only the partners who are chartered accountants shall be authorised to act and sign on behalf of the firm.

Non-eligibility A company (other than Limited Liability Partnership under 2008); an officer or employee of the company (due to conflict of interest); a partner; a person who has his relative or partner; one who holds security or interest in the company (due to conflict of interest, insider trading); one who is indebted to the company or to its subsidiary; one who has given guarantee or provided security in connection with indebtedness of any third person to the company or its subsidiary; a person or firm that has business relationship with the company or its subsidiary; one whose relative is a director; a person holding full-time auditorship or employment in another company as a director or key managerial personnel; a person who is convicted of fraud and a period of 10 years has not elapsed from the date of conviction; any person whose subsidiary or associate company or any other form engaged in consulting or specialised services.

Powers and Duties of Auditors and Auditing Standards

Every auditor of a company shall have a right of access at all times to the books of account and vouchers of the company, whether kept at the registered office of the company or at any other place and shall be entitled to require from the officers of the company such information and explanation as he may consider necessary for the performance of his duties as auditor and amongst other matters inquire into the following matters

— Sec. 143 (1), The Companies Act, 2013

The duty of the auditor consists of the examination of the following: Loans and advances made to the company; whether the securities are properly secured; whether transactions of the company in the entries of the book prejudicial to the interest of the company and its members; whether personal expenses are charged; nature of the shares allotted.

The auditor shall make a report of all sought and obtained information; whether proper book-keeping has be done; company balance sheet, profit and loss account; compliance of financial statements; comments on financial transactions; comments on qualification of directors, remarks on maintenance of accounts; the financial health of the company, whether it has proper financial control.

The Comptroller of Accounts General of India shall, within 60 days from the date of receipt of audit report, have the right to conduct supplementary audit (Sec. 143 (6)).

Section 144 of the Act prohibits the auditor to render certain services such as accounting and book-keeping services; internal audit; design and implementation of any financial information system; actuarial services; investment advisory services; investment banking services; rendering of outsourced financial services; management services; and any other kind of services as may be prescribed.

Section 145 authorises the auditor to sign audit reports. He has to attend general meetings (Sec. 146); any contravention is punishable by ₹25,000 to ₹5 lakh.

Removal, Resignation of Auditor, and Giving of Special Notice

The auditor appointed under section 139 may be removed from his office before the expiry of his term only by a special resolution of the company, after obtaining the previous approval of the Central Government in that behalf in the prescribed manner: Provided that before taking any action under this sub-section, the auditor concerned shall be given a reasonable opportunity of being heard.

– Sec. 140. (1), The Companies Act, 2013

The company has the power to remove an auditor after going through the procedures in Sec. 140 (1). Natural justice demands, of course, that the auditor is given a fair hearing by the board of directors and that it proceeds in the prescribed manner.

If the auditor resigns, then he shall file within 30 days of his act a statement in the prescribed form with the company and the Registrar of Companies; further he shall file such a statement with the Comptroller and Auditor General (CAG) of India, thereby filing the reasons for his act of resignation. Non-compliance shall attract a penalty of ₹50,000 to ₹5 lakh. A special notice shall be required for a resolution at the annual general meeting for the retiring auditor.

Dividend

DIVIDE AND SHARE

Price is what you pay, value is what you get.

—Warren Buffet

Berkshire Hathaway, the investment company, is known less than its Chairman and the Chief Executive, Warren Buffet. His in-born aptitude to save money has, today, made him, in business, the biggest investor on the stock market and socially one of the biggest philanthropists. Every year at the company's general meeting, over 20,000 shareholders come to listen to his wisdom. A few years ago, he announced to the shareholders that he is not going to pay them dividends but going to buy back those shares for the company. They criticised him for non-payment of dividends. In reply, he reasoned: (a) reinvest in the company for growth; (b) acquire other companies; (c) repurchase shares; (d) pay dividends.[2]

The Companies Act, 2014, is considered to be thus far the most business-friendly, investment-friendly, and investor protection-friendly legislation. Returns on investment are an investor's right just as profit is rightfully deserved by the corporation that runs business.

Chapter VIII, Section 123, of the Act deals with *Declaration and Payment of Dividend*. (a) It shall be paid out of the profits of the company after providing for depreciation in accordance with Schedule II of the Act. The Board of Directors may declare interim dividend during any financial year out of the surplus in the profit and loss account, out of profits of the financial year in which such interim dividend is sought to be declared (Sec. 123 (3)). The dividend has to be deposited in a scheduled bank in a separate account within 5 days of the declaration of such dividend (Sec. 123 (4)). Dividend is paid to the registered shareholder (Sec. 123 (5)). All shares in respect of which unpaid or unclaimed dividend shall be transferred to Investor Education and Protection Fund (Sec. 124). This fund is established by the Central Government (Sec. 125). Right to dividend, rights to shares, and bonus shares to be held in abeyance pending registration of transfer of shares (Sec. 126). The punishment for failure to distribute dividends, which has to be paid within 30 days of declaration of dividends, every director of the company is punishable with imprisonment extending up to 2 years with a fine of ₹1000 every day during which such default continues. However, exception is made for operation of the law; shareholder has given directions to the company regarding payment; there may be a dispute; the sum may be adjusted for some owed dues; any other reason of non-default by the company (Sec. 127).

The Draft Rules for Chapter VIII have the following provisions:

1. The rate of dividend shall not exceed the average of the rates in the three immediately preceding years.
2. Total amount to be drawn from such accumulated profits shall not exceed an amount equal to one-tenth of the sum of its paid-up share capital and free reserves.
3. The amount so drawn shall first be utilised to set off the losses incurred in the financial year.
4. Balance of reserves after such withdrawal shall not fall below 15% of its paid up capital.

Dividends may be in the form of cash and stock, once it is also used to be in property. High-growth companies would prefer to reinvest the dividends into shares. Mutual funds, which have become very popular in India, pay dividend and income received from their portfolio holdings.

There is a simple advice from Warren Buffet, the most successful investor: Rule No. 1: Never lose money. Rule No. 2: Never forget rule No, 1.[3]

[2]See: http://www.businessinsider.in/Warren-Buffett-Does-A-Beautiful-Job-Of-Explaining-Dividends-And-Why-Berkshire-Isnt-Paying-One/articleshow/21299788.cms (Retrieved on 20 September 2014).

[3]See: http://www.businessinsider.in/Warren-Buffett-Does-A-Beautiful-Job-Of-Explaining-Dividends-And-Why-Berkshire-Isnt-Paying-One/articleshow/21299788.cms (Retrieved on 20 September 2014). See for both the quotations from Warren Buffet: http://www.dividend.com/dividend-education/41-inspiring-and-intelligent-investing-quotes/ (Retrieved on 20 September 2014).

MANAGER'S TAKEAWAY

- As a financial manager or fund manager for your company, no wizardry is required; although intelligence and knowledge are most desirable, what is needed is the integrity to manage others' money and pay them dividends

SUMMARY

The old idea that companies work only for money is out; the incorporated companies make money work through its intelligent management. Administration of the corporation and management of money and its various instruments come under the ambit of the Companies Act, 2013. Of particular interest are the following:

- Prospectus

- Securities
- Share Capital and Debentures
- Accounts
- Audit and Auditors
- Dividend

In all these aspects, the company functions according to the law prescribed by the Companies Act, 2013. It deals with raising money from the financial institutions and the general public to the auditing and distribution of dividends to the shareholders.

EXERCISES

i. A company has granted stock options prior to the promulgation of the Companies Act, 2013. Can such stock options be exercisable by the Independent Directors?
   Hint: Section 62 (1) (b); Section 197 (7); Rule 12 (Share Capital and Debentures)

ii. Is there a mandate for Company Secretary to attend the All Board, Committee, and General Meeting?
   Hint: Section 205

iii. Is it mandatory to file the return of appointment of KMPs?
   Hint: Section 203; Rule 3 of the Companies (Appointment and Remuneration of Managerial Personnel) Rules, 2014

iv. The appointment of Cost Auditor shall be for a period of 5/10 years like that of the Statutory Auditor as prescribed under Section 139.
   Hint: Find out the difference between the two auditors? Find out if there are any rules by MCA with regard to the stated periods?

v. Section 124 (6) states that all the shares in respect of which unpaid or unclaimed dividend are transferred to Investor Education and Protection Fund shall also be transferred by the company to Investor Education and Protection Fund. Whether a shareholder can claim back the shares and whether he can attend general meeting and give vote thereat.
   Hint: Find out from the rules.

DEVELOPMENT OF LEGAL EDGE

Collect information from newspapers and magazine clippings in a folder for the following:
- Prospectus
- Securities
- Share Capital and Debentures
- Accounts
- Audit and Auditors
- Dividend

The earlier exercise should be for 30 days after which categorise various trends that develop from the earlier simple research. Pay special attention to securities and dividends.

FURTHER READING

- A.K. Sharma and G.S. Batra (2002) *Indian Stock Market: Regulation, Performance and Policy* (Deep & Deep Publications).
- Concerning Rules and Procedures about disclosures in prospectus and allotment of securities: http://www.icsi.edu/portals/0/PROSPECTUS%20 &%20ALLOTMENT.pdf.
- Share capital and debentures rules: http://perry4law.org/clii/wp-content/uploads/2014/03/Companies-Share-Capital-and-Debentures-Rules-2014.pdf.

CASE STUDY   IN THE NAME OF GODDESS SARADHA BONZI

In the Name of Goddess Saradha

Saradha in the Eastern region of India and Sharadha in the rest of India is one of the names of the most popular goddesses, Goddess Saraswati, who is worshipped mainly for wisdom but also as Durga for courage, which is very significant in Bengal. With 108 different names, which signify people's prayers to be answered by the deity. India is an unfortunate country in so far as its own people exploit each other culturally, politically, and economically with basic, simple, and yet deeply running religious sentiments. From a street hawker to the stock broker, Indians wear their religion on their sleeves. Thus, it is no surprise when Sudipto Sen named his fund-raising venture Saradha, which would immediately evoke in the minds of the customers pious sentiments that would generate unquestionable trust and confidence to invest one's hard-earned money.

Business Operation Model of Saradha

Saradha Group was incorporated in 2006 and got into business with a break-neck speed and went on to establishing a plethora of companies, about 200 of them, with multiple cross-holdings, which completely hoodwinked the regulators beginning from RBI to SEBI, from Ministry of Corporate Affairs to Enforcement Directorate. The business operation model consisted of a forked strategy.

Ponzi Strategy: Money had to be raised. So, it has to be a mass-based scheme. It should be simple to understand and simple to operate. Take money from one and give dividend to another. The method reflects the old saying: *Rob Peter to pay Paul*. Investors are always more than the ones who redeem their investments. So there is no need for creation of wealth through the production of goods and services—just pass on the money. *Saradha* was so widespread both with thousands of collecting agents as well as large sections of the population as investors. It beat the original plan of Charles Ponzi in the depression years in the USA in the 1920s. When Saradha crashed, the locals in Bengal derided with a new name called *Bonzi*, perhaps to categorise its origin from Bengal.

Lull the Law Enforcement:

If low-income group is targeted, it would have a large population under its influence, which will generate political capital and this in turn would keep the law at bay. The net was spread far and wide. From the Ministry of Finance to the State legislatures in the East of the country, from SEBI and RBI to various departments of police in various states, were netted. Celebrities, sports stars, and movie actors, both main stream and vernacular, became the Saradha Group's ambassadors. Companies were formed to run print and visual media enterprises, run hotels, offer tour packages, establish real-estate firms, and even run a huge motor cycle company. All of this great glamour and show further galvanised by the usual Corporate Social Responsibility programmes in health and sports, funding of the popular football sporting clubs made Saradha what people would dream about. The die was completely cast and the powerful Trinamool Congress Party, with its new government, fell prostrate before Saradha. With such political patronage, and the local leaders taking full mileage of the scheme, the simple poor people took one and the other for the same establishment.

Victims of Saradha

The grief has had no bounds. The following two instances multiplied several hundreds of thousands of times may help draw the image of the horrors of the *Saradha* scam.

Victim Number One: Durgavati (name changed), living in a slum of Kolkata, had saved a few thousand rupees from her meagre earnings of sweeping and swabbing in the houses of nearby middle-class apartments. Her husband is a rickshaw puller, but he lived separately. She joined the Saradha scheme and paid 30,000 in instalments. She was proud of herself that she could work and also garner some financial security through the attractive scheme of *Saradha*. As the news of the crash of scheme spread like wildfire, she was the first one to commit suicide, the first victim of *Saradha* scam. It was on 21 April 2013.

Victim Number Two: Five days later, on 28 April 2013, it was reported that a certain Durga Das (name changed) hanged himself. The poor man had invested 60,000 and lost all hope in life as he lost the money.

Multiply the loss, torture, sorrow of the families, all of those millions of people, all from very poor economic background, building a multi-billion rupee empire for the rich, the celebrities, the politicians of all hues and colours, sport stars, and actors. It is a picture of loot and devastation. From the slums of Kolkata to the heights of Assam hills, plains, and rivers, from the backward areas of Bihar to poor but cheerful tribal villages of Odisha and Chhattisgarh, there spread gloom and desperation.

Key People of Saradha

Sudipta Sen:	Sudipto sounds more *Bengali* though Sudipta is used often. Reports say that he was a reformed Naxalite and is the Managing Director of Saradha Group.
Kunal Ghosh:	CEO of Saradha Media Group, Trinamool Congress (TMC) Member of the Parliament, now suspended from the party and is in jail.
Debjani Mukherjee:	One of the Executive Directors of Saradha with powers to sign cheques arrested with Sudipta Sen, lodged in jail.
Srinjoy Bose:	CEO of Bengali daily *Sangbad Protidin*, Rajya Sabha MP of the TMC.
Rajat Majumdara:	Former Director General of Police; TMC Party Leader and its Vice President.
Shankar Barua:	Former Assam Director General of Police, committed suicide after the CBI raid on his premises.
Sadananda Gogoi:	Singer and Film Maker from Assam
Ashok Mohanty:	Former Advocate General of Odisha
Madan Mitra:	Minister for Transport, West Bengal

Patronisers of Saradha

Thus far, to make a very long and sordid story short: It is a unique and ugly scandal entrenched in a political party, the ruling Trinamool Congress of Bengal. The entire media of the country as well as the political opponents of the party are opining that the moral responsibility of this sordid saga lies with party president of TMC, Mamata Banerjee. In early January 2015, the Party announced that it will go to the Supreme Court of India with its grievances against the Government of India and its law-enforcing agencies.

Supreme Court versus Saradha

Acting upon a complaint, the Supreme Court of India slammed the law-enforcing agencies for their complacency.[4] Had they been vigilant, the scam could have been avoided and it would have spared life and life's savings of over 17 lakh people.

---

[4] See: http://timesofindia.indiatimes.com/city/kolkata/SC-slams-Sebi-RBI-for-Saradha-scam/articleshow/33836842.cms (Retrieved 15 September 2014).

SARADHA SCAM IN NEWS HEADLINES

A few random news headlines down below illustrate both the nature as well as the timeline of *Saradha* financial scandal.[5]

23 January 2013:	Anger mounts over Saradha fund crisis as thousands of depositors face ruin (*Daily Mail*)
22 April 2013:	Agents bear brunt of Saradha collapse (*Live Mint*)
22 April 2013:	Promoter at large, no trace of depositors' money on Saradha books (*Live Mint*)
23 April 2013:	*The Telegraph* Company Offices Sealed in Assam
24 April 2013:	Saradha Group Chairman, Sudipta Sen, arrested in Kashmir (*Live Mint*)
24 April 2013:	Business Standard: Mamata sets up fund for duped Saradha investors (Live Mint)
24 April 2013:	Saradha Group Chairman, Sudipto Sen, arrested in Jammu and Kashmir (The Indian Express)
24 April 2013:	Politicos in dock over Saradha scam (Deccan Herald)
25 April 2013:	Corporate Affairs Ministry to probe Saradha Group (The Telegraph)
25 April 2013:	Trinamool cannot wish away its links with Saradha group irrespective of what Mamata says (The Economic Times)
26 April 2013:	Mamata Banerjee vows to repay depositors of Saradha group's Sudipta Sen
26 April 2013:	Saradha chit fund scam: State government failed, but so has centre (The Economic Times)

---

[5] These are random samples from both print and electronic media, at times modified to convey sense of the story. It does not mean other papers did not report; in fact, all the national papers have been covering the story in detail.

30 April 2013:	West Bengal passes new Bill to protect investor interests (Business Line)
18 July 2013:	SC notice to Centre, West Bengal for CBI probe in Saradha scam (Live Mint)
12 August 2013:	SEBI enacts stricter laws on CIS, front-running companies (Business Standard)
21 October 2013:	Sudipta Sen's accounts frozen on laundering charges (Live Mint)
24 November 2013:	TMC MP Kunal Ghosh's bail plea rejected, remanded for 5 days in police custody (Live Mint)
22 February 2014:	Saradha chairman, Sudipta Sen, sentenced to 3 years in jail (Live Mint)
13 January 2014:	Three TV channels owned by Saradha Group to be auctioned (Hindu Businessline)
10 May 2014	SC jolt for Mamata: CBI to probe Saradha scam. The CBI will also probe other Ponzi schemes in West Bengal, Odisha, Tripura, Jharkhand, and Assam (Business Standard)
9 September 2014:	Saradha scam: CBI arrests former West Bengal police Chief Rajat Majumdar (Mint Live)
12 September 2014:	Saradha scam shocker: Mamata Banerjee's aide, TMC MP's link with terror group SIMI, Jamat exposed (One India)
17 September 2014:	Former Assam DGP, under scanner in Saradha scam, commits suicide (Times of India)
21 September 2014:	CBI questions former cabinet minister P. Chidambaram's wife Nalini Chidambaram in Saradha chit fund scam (Times of India)
22 September 2014:	Odisha's former Advocate General, Ashok Mohanty, arrested in chit-fund scam (Times of India)
29 September 2014:	CBI to seek 'clarifications' from Bengal CM's office (Live Mint)

When M.F. Hussein, the most celebrated and the most controversial artist of India painted Saraswati in the nude, it hurt the religious sentiments of both the pious and the radicals of India. He exiled himself and died away from his country. Sudipto Sen designed a logo for his business in the name of the same goddess, an abstract-lined dwelling, coloured in bright gold, and the name of Goddess *Saradha* in bold and large letters, signifying security and promising prosperity.

Questions on the case

1. What are the facts of Saradha chit-fund scheme?
2. Investigate some research figures for savings schemes in India.
3. Note five scams that failed common investors in India.
4. Did political patronage ensure the confidence of the people to invest in Saradha scheme?
5. Can the government legally compensate for the poor who invested in Saradha?
6. What goes wrong in small savings schemes? Can the loopholes be plugged through money management, legal instruments, and government handling?
7. Is there a sure method to make the savings schemes to work successfully for the investors?

Going Beyond

1. Illustrate how spiritual branding works in India.
2. Are political parties a boon or bane in the economic development of the people? Write a letter to the editor of a daily.

LEGAL LUMINARY

RAVI SHANKAR PRASAD: THE GOD'S ADVOCATE

In the tumultuous and unprecedented case of Ayodhya Ram Mandir title suit, Ravi Shankar Prasad represented *Rama Lalla*, the deity to whom the estate belongs. He has argued cases against the high and mighty, the powerful and the corrupt, and has been instrumental in enforcing justice, equally he has defended the famous, espoused the causes of environment and human rights. In the current schedule of the Lok Sabha, first he headed two ministries, namely, Ministry of Law and Justice and Ministry of Communications and Information Technology.

He comes alive on prime time TV across the length and breadth of the country. His mastery over Hindi and English is *par excellence*. As a spokesperson for his Bharatiya Janata Party (BJP), his remarks are factual, his comments are very apt and is a gentleman even when he criticises his bitterest political rivals and their actions.

While he was yet in College, he joined the popular movement led by Jayaprakash Narayan in the early 1970s against the policies of the government led by Indira Gandhi. Later, in the mid-1970s, he, as the student union leader, was jailed during the emergency for being part of the Jayaprakash Narayan's movement. He represented his party in various national and international fora. He was elected as the member of the Parliament in 2000 and was inducted into Ministry of Coal and Mines as a Minister of State in the A.B. Vajpayee Government. Two years later, he became the Minister for State of Law and Justice, and in the following year, he became Minister for Information and Broadcasting. He is known to have introduced far-reaching reforms in each of the earlier areas: modernization in Mines and Coals, fast courts in Law and Justice, and technical advancement in Information and Broadcasting.

On 26 May 2014, he was sworn in as Minister and was given the portfolios for Law and Justice and Communication and Information Technology. He has begun where he has left last. About 287 archaic laws are identified for their eventual repeal.[6] The repealing of the Act too has its own process in the parliament. A bill has to be tabled in the parliament and it has to be passed into law in both the housed of the Parliament. It is an Act to repeal an Act.

To begin with, 72 laws are identified and a bill has been prepared to repeal them. The Minister has asked all the departments across various ministries to send him a list of all those outdated and inapplicable laws. The Law Commission of India will provide a report on this matter.

Born on 30 August 1954, he followed in the footsteps of his illustrious father Thakur Prasad who was a renowned lawyer in Patna. Having completed his degree in law, he began his practice in Patna. His academic qualifications are Bachelor of Art (Honours), Master of Arts in Political Science, and Bachelor of Law. Presently, he is the senior designated lawyer of the Supreme Court of India.

---

[6] See: http://www.thehindu.com/news/national/centre-to-repeal-287-outdated-laws-says-law-minister-ravi-shankar-prasad/article6458352.ece (Retrieved 2 October 2104).

The Companies Act, 2013: The Control and Governance of a Company

Principle: *Nil utile authonestum quod legibus contrartium.*

Nothing is useful nor honourable that is contrary to law.

CHAPTER OUTLINE

- Introduction and Interpretation
- Board of Directors, Directors, and Officers of the Company
    - Control of a Company
    - Board of Directors
    - Key Managerial Personnel (KMP)
    - Independent Director and the Code of Conduct
- Crime and Punishment
- Corporate Social Responsibility
- Control and Governance by Statutory Agencies of the Government
    - National Company Law Tribunal (NCLT)
- National Financial Reporting Authority (NFRA)
    - Serious Fraud Investigation Office (SFIO)

11.1 INTRODUCTION AND INTERPRETATION

Where a Registrar or inspector calls for the books of account and other books and papers under Section 206, it shall be the duty of every director, officer, or other employee of the company to produce all such documents to the Registrar or inspector and furnish him with such statements, information, or explanations in such form as the Registrar or inspector may require and shall render all assistance to the Registrar or inspector in connection with such inspection.

– Sec. 207 (1), The Companies Act, 2013

Inspection and inquiry, as the Act describes, are the means provided by the legislator to administer the regime of good governance to achieve the objectives set by the law. *Trust but verify* is a wise saying. When applied in the context of enforcing the law, it is the most useful principle. The government trusts its citizens because it belongs to its own people. It verifies the activities of the citizens as well as the artificial legal entities that consist of all kinds of human associations recognised by law: establishments, companies, non-profit organizations, and charitable institutions, because it bears the responsibility to do so.

The Companies Act, 2013, empowers the companies to establish self-governance and liberty to act in the interest of all. It allows the companies to draw up their own charter, the Articles of Association, and adhere to it. From the appointment of its directors to the rights of its last employee, all is well-defined and set for fairness and justice.

The Companies Act, 2013, empowers the government to make rules and statutes to enforce the law. Various agencies, from the Registrar of Companies (ROC) to the courts of law and from statutory bodies to control the activities of the companies to imposition of penalties, are established to verify the actions of the company.

Chapter XV of the Act, Section 206–229, is titled as *Inspection, Inquiry, and Investigation*, which delineates the control exercised by the authority of the government. For instance, the ROC after scrutiny of the documents, such as annual returns of the company, upon examination finds discrepancies and inaccuracies or has received reliable information about the company that needs to be checked against facts and comes to the conclusion that an investigation into the matter is indispensable, he may do so as prescribed by the law. The processes commence with a written notice. Then, the investigation may proceed and, if there is any miscarriage of law, it may be investigated, and if not settled as per established law but challenged by the company management, it may be moved to the court of law and justice sought and done.

Thus, the control and governance of the company may be distinguished as internal and external. The internal governance consists of the administration and management of the company by its officers, such as the board of governors, finance and operations officers, executives, and employees. They function in all aspects of running a company and achieving the set objectives. The external control and governance and control are in the domain of the government. The government acts according to the law established by the parliament through various agencies it has established for the purpose. Whether it is the exercise of internal control and governance or the external one, both function systematically under the law.

MANAGER'S TAKEAWAY

- Inspection and inquiry are the means provided by the legislator to administer the regime of good governance to achieve the objectives set by law.

Manager's Map

The Companies Act, 2013		
Company Management	**Companies**	**Government Regulator**
Board of Directors	One Man Company	Ministry of Law
Directors	Limited Company:	and Justice
Independent Directors	Small, Other	Ministry of Corporate
Women Directors	Companies	Affairs
Key Management	Unlimited Company	Ministry of Finance
Personnel	(Public company	Reserve Bank of India
Accountants	Listed company)	Securities and
Auditors	Holding Company	Exchange
Officers	Subsidiary company	Board of India
Employees	Associate company	NEFRA
	Charitable company	Tribunals
	Government Company	Courts
	Producer Company	
	Nidhi Company	
	Dormant company	

Shareholders, Bankers, Underwriters, Merchant Bankers, Bankers, Institutional investors, Brokers and Individual Investors

Figure 11.1 Understanding the Company Act, 2013

11.2 BOARD OF DIRECTORS, DIRECTORS, AND OFFICERS OF THE COMPANY

Control of a Company

TEXT

"Control" shall include the right to appoint majority of the directors or to control the management or policy decisions exercisable by a person or persons acting individually or in concert, directly or indirectly, including by virtue of their shareholding or management rights or shareholders agreements or voting agreements or in any other manner.

– Sec. 2 (27), The Companies Act, 2013

Control, in this context, is to exercise power over an organization. The power is invested in a person or a group of persons known as Board of Directors by virtue of an established law and the/Board, in turn, bears responsibility for the actions before such law. The basis for the exercise of power in a company comes from the contract documents of Memorandum of Articles (MOA) and Articles of Association (AOA) that are endorsed by the legal agency or authority, the ROC, a body corporate established by the Central Government as its statutory body. Empowerment by law is the reason for the exercise of power.

The concept of control is the most important one in the Companies Act, 2013. Chair persons, directors, managers, and other officers of the company should deeply understand the implications of the term. The legislator has empowered the corporations and those who run it with a sense of freedom and responsibility. Self-governance, empowerment, or any other term applicable describes the nature of the new Act.

Control of the company is a democratic exercise in decision-making for the management of the company. A group of individuals is elected by the shareholders of a company to take decisions on their behalf. The head of this group of elected members is given the position of *Chairperson* and the others are known as *Directors*. From their election until their vacation from their positions the group is governed by the rules stated in the Articles of Association, which are in accordance with the stipulations in the company's law. This class of people is known as Board of Directors.

The Board is the head of the company. It decides all the activities of the company and they bear primary responsibility for their actions before the law. As a part of governing the company, they appoint all the officers of the company such as Chief Executive Officer (CEO), Chief Finance Officer (CFO), and Chief Operations Officer (COO) as may be required for the working of the company. These officers are called *Senior Managers* in management jargon. Then, there are other executives of the company who carry on the tasks their seniors may assign them; and, finally, there are employees who actually perform the task. The bigger the company, the longer is the line of command from the board to the last employee. The art of management lies in the effective decision-making of the board and the efficiency of governance.

Today, the control of the companies has evolved and is now commonly referred as *Corporate Governance*. In the past, the experience has not been a good one in controlling the actions of the companies. As a result, there have been economy-crippling financial scams where banks, stock brokers, and other financial institutions caused irreparable damage to the investors. The values of corporate governance consist of ethical action towards all the stakeholders.

It is to understand and balance the interests of all the parties. The stakeholders consist of shareholders, board of directors, management, customers, suppliers, financiers, government, and the whole society. Corporate governance, therefore, is not only a scientific system of control but also a conscientious action that is just and fair to all the stakeholders.

Board of Directors

TEXT

"Board of Directors" or "Board," in relation to a company, means the collective body of the directors of the company.

– Sec. 2(10), The Companies Act, 2013

Every company shall have a Board of Directors consisting of individuals as directors and shall have—
(a) A minimum number of three directors in the case of a public company, two directors in the case of a private company, and one director in the case of a One Person Company; and
(b) A maximum of fifteen directors: Provided that a company may appoint more than fifteen directors after passing a special resolution: Provided further that such class or classes of companies as may be prescribed, shall have at least one woman director.

– Sec. 149, The Companies Act, 2013

Through the realization of the Memorandum of Association and the Articles of Association, a legal entity comes into existence as provided and approved by the law. The members of the Board of Directors are mere agents of this legal (artificial) person who work on the behalf of the company and represent all its members. They may be elected one day and may be dismissed on another day. The new Companies Act, 2013, has a special intention to make the company as democratic as possible so that it exists and functions in the society as a good citizen.

Number of directors:
- Private company: 2
- Public company: 3
- One-Person Company: 1
- Maximum number: 15
- Among them, at least one woman director

Functions:
- Conduct board meetings
- Constitution of committees such as audit, finance, and personnel
- Conduct AGM
- Take decisions in all matters of administration and management of the company

Board Meeting

The Board of Directors has become modern as communication has advanced. The meetings can be conveniently organised through audio-visual means of telecommunications such as video conferencing. The following are the essential features of board meetings:

- First board meeting within 30 days
- Four board meetings every year by each company

- Gap between two meetings—not more 120 days
- Board meeting through video conferencing or audio visual means
- Minimum 7 days' notice
- Quorum—higher of 1/3 or 2

Powers of the Board

Section 149 of the Act empowers the Board of Directors to the following powers:
- All resolutions to be taken at Board Meetings
- Approve Financial Statement and Board Report
- Decision on diversification of Business
- Approving amalgamation, merger, or reconstruction
- Decision on takeover or acquisition in another company
- Issue of securities
- Decision to contribute for political ends
- Fill a casual vacancy in the Board
- Decision to enter into a joint venture or technical or financial collaboration or any collaboration agreement
- Decision to commence a new business
- Decision to shift the location of a plant or factory or the registered office
- Appoint or remove key managerial personnel (KMP) and senior management personnel one level below the KMP
- Appoint internal auditors
- Adoption of common seal
- Take note of the disclosure of director's interest and shareholding

Powers under Section 179:
- To sell investments held by the company (other than trade investments), constituting five percent or more of the paid-up share capital and free reserves of the investee company
- To accept public deposits and related matters
- To approve quarterly, half-yearly, and annual financial statements

Disclosures

(i) *Filing annual returns*: Under Section 92 of the Act, companies are required to prepare an annual return containing the particulars of the entire financial year relating to all the business activities, particulars of holdings, subsidiaries, and associate companies; also, details of promoters, directors, key management personnel, all its committee reports, and details of meetings of board. Attendance details, all legal matters including legal proceedings and penalties.

(ii) *Report to shareholders*: Section 134 (3) mandates in addition to the board reports to be given to shareholders. These consist of an extract of the annual returns [Sec. 92 (3)]; meetings of the board; directors' responsibility statement; declaration of the independent directors; company's policy on appointment of the directors, their remuneration [Sec. (49(6)], including criteria for qualifications, comments, adverse remarks; loans, guarantees, and investments (Sec. 186), related party transactions, state of company affairs; reserves; dividends to be paid, material changes in the financial position; foreign exchange; policy on risk management; corporate social responsibility; formal evaluation on the performance of the board.

Director

"Director" means a director appointed to the Board of a company.

– Sec. 2 (34), The Companies Act, 2013

Appointment:

Where no provision is made in the articles of a company for the appointment of the first director, the subscribers to the memorandum who are individuals shall be deemed to be the first directors of the company until the directors are duly appointed and in case of a One Person Company, an individual being member shall be deemed to be its first director until the director or directors are duly appointed by the member in accordance with the provisions of this section.

– Sec. 152 (1), The Companies Act, 2013

The director is appointed or is an elected member of the board of directors of a company; he is one of the decision-makers for the company. He need not be an employee, such as full-time director of the company or a shareholder. He is, however, duty-bound to be present for the board meetings and vote without proxy. The director is part of the collective decision-making process of the company.

Although the subscribers to MOA and AOA are directors but only until they are ratified in the Annual General Meeting by a special resolution. The director has to be voted individually. For private companies, consent shall be obtained from ROC. Approval of the Central Government is required if it is not according to Schedule V.

One-person Company director will be deemed to be the director from the incorporation of the company itself. The tenure of the full-time director is only for 5 years. Any default in these matters of appointment will attract punishment or imprisonment up to 6 months and fine, ₹500 a day for the period in which the default continues.

Duties of a Director

Subject to the provisions of this Act, a director of a company shall act in accordance with the articles of the company.

– Sec. 166. (1), The Companies Act, 2013

Section 166 (2–7) lays down the duties as follows:
- To act in good faith to promote the objects of the company
- To act diligently and to exercise independent judgement
- Not to involve in any conflict of interest with the company
- Not to gain undue for oneself or for one's relatives or partners or associates
- Not to assign his office
- Any contravention to duty will attract penal procedure and punishable with fine not less than ₹1 lakh extending to ₹5 lakh

Disqualification of the Director

Section 164 (1) lays down the following disqualifications for a director:
- Unsound of mind and stands so declared by court
- Undischarged insolvent; or pending application for insolvency
- Conviction by court for any offence and sentenced to penal punishment until its expiry; serving sentence for more than 7 years disqualifies completely

Illustration

A director is the most important person because he is part of every decision that the company takes and bears legal responsibility for the actions of the company. To understand the role of a director, we may illustrate it as follows:

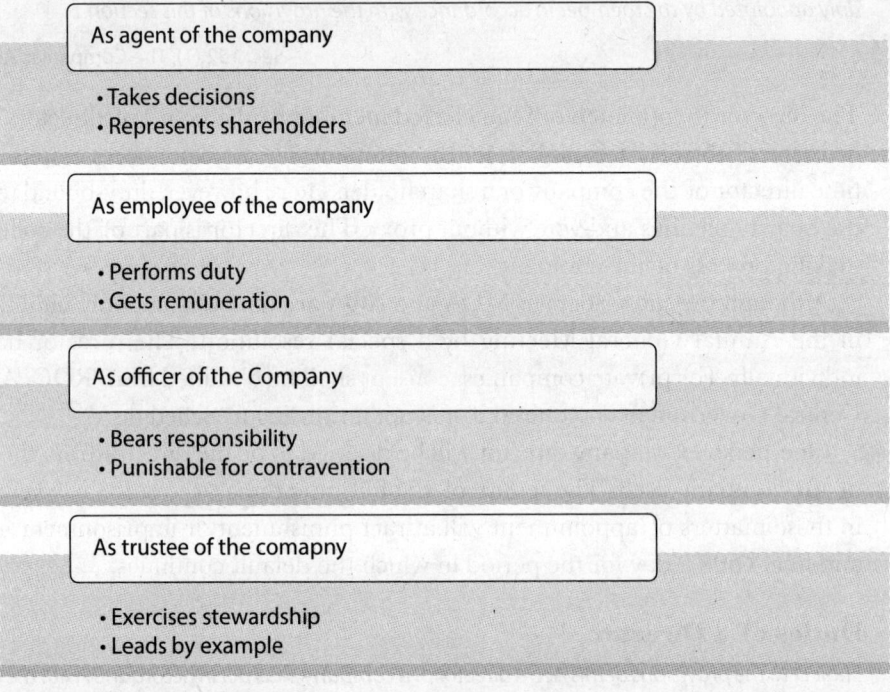

Figure 11.2 Role of a Director

Table 11.1 Kinds of Directors

Designation	Definition	Role
Interested director	Section 2(49): 'Interested director' means a director who is in any way, whether by himself or through any of his relatives or firm, body corporate, or other association of individuals in which he or any of his relatives is a partner, director, or a member, interested in a contract or arrangement, or proposed contract or arrangement, entered into or to be entered into by or on behalf of a company.	Under Section 184 is not supposed to vote or participate in business meeting.

Contd

Designation	Definition	Role
Nominee director	Section149 (6): An independent director in relation to a company, means a director other than a managing director or a full-time director or a nominee director.	He is an independent director who has no interest in the company by way of managing director, any officer of the company, or shares, etc.
Managing director	Section. 2 (54): 'Managing director' means a director who, by virtue of the articles of a company or an agreement with the company or a resolution passed in its general meeting, or by its Board of Directors, is entrusted with substantial powers of management of the affairs of the company and includes a director occupying the position of managing director, by whatever name called.	The AOA endows upon the managing director high powers in the management and administration of the company.
Small shareholder director	Section 151: A listed company may have one director elected by such small shareholders in such a manner and with such terms and conditions as may be prescribed.	*A small shareholder is* one who is holding shares of nominal value of not more than ₹20,000 or such other sum as may be prescribed.
Full-time director	Section 94 includes a director in the full-time employment of the company.	
Officer	Section 2(59): 'Officer' includes any director, manager, or KMP or any person in accordance with whose directions or instructions, the Board of Directors or any one or more of the directors is or are accustomed to act.	It is a general name to any of the directors or managers to signify that they are authorised persons to represent the company.
Resident director	Section 149 (3): Every company shall have at least one director who has stayed in India for a total period of not less than 182 days in the previous calendar year.	Every company would be required to have at least one director who has stayed in India for not less than 182 days in the previous calendar year. This requirement needs to be complied with immediately, i.e., from 1 April 2014.[1]
Director who is officer in default	Section 2(60): 'Officer who is in default', for the purpose of any provision in this Act which enacts that an officer of the company who is in default shall be liable to any penalty or punishment by way of imprisonment, fine, or otherwise, means any of the following officers of a company, namely: (i) full-time director; (ii) KMP; (iii) where there is no KMP, such director or directors as specified by the Board in this behalf and who has or have given his or their consent in writing to the Board to such specification, or all the directors, if no director is so specified; Section 2(60)—'officer who is in default,' (iv) any person who, under the immediate authority of the Board or any KMP, is charged with any responsibility including maintenance, filing, or distribution of	This is a director with liability of penalty or punishment by way of imprisonment or fine. He is not only the usual director or KMP but also one who has been nominated by the BOD. In other words, anyone who exercises authority on behalf of the board. Thus, any decision by such a person in his professional capacity in contravention of the law with his consent or connivance attracts penal proceedings.

[1]See for clarification: http://www.mca.gov.in/Ministry/pdf/General_Circular_25_2014. pdf (Retrieved on 20 September 2014)

Contd

Designation	Definition	Role
	accounts or records, authorizes, actively participates in, knowingly permits, or knowingly fails to take active steps to prevent, any default; (v) any person in accordance with whose advice, directions, or instructions, the Board of Directors is accustomed to act, other than a person who gives advice to the Board in a professional capacity.	
Related party	Section 2(76) is about 'related party', with reference to a company, means— (i) a director or his relative; (ii) a KMP or his relative; (iii) a firm in which a director, manager, or his relative is a partner; (iv) a private company in which a director or manager is a member or director; (v) a public company in which a director or manager is a director or holds along with his relatives, more than 2% of its paid-up share capital; (vi) any body corporate whose Board of Directors, managing director, or manager is accustomed to act in accordance with the advice, directions, or instructions of a director or manager; (vii) any person on whose advice, directions, or instructions a director or manager is accustomed to act: Provided that nothing in sub-clauses (vi) and (vii) shall apply to the advice, directions, or instructions given in a professional capacity; (viii) any company which is: (A) a holding, subsidiary, or an associate company of such company; or (B) a subsidiary of a holding company to which it is also a subsidiary. (ix) such other person as may be prescribed.	
Key managerial personnel	Section 2(51) 'key managerial personnel', in relation to a company, means— (i) the Chief Executive Officer or the managing director, or the manager; (ii) the company secretary; (iii) the full-time director; (iv) the Chief Financial Officer; and (v) such other officer as may be prescribed.	Any officer of the company such as shown in the Act. These are roles assigned as managers of the company given a particular context.
Independent director	Section 149 (6 and 7): An independent director in relation to a company means a director other than a managing director or a full-time director or a nominee director. (7) Every independent director shall, at the first meeting of the Board in which he participates as a director and thereafter at the first meeting	Section 149(4): Every listed public company shall have at least one-third of the total number of directors as independent directors and the Central Government may prescribe the minimum number of independent directors in case of any class or classes of public companies.

Contd

Table 11.1 *Contd*

Designation	Definition	Role
	of the Board in every financial year or whenever there is any change in the circumstances which may affect his status as an independent director, give a declaration that he meets the criteria of independence as provided in sub-section (6).	An independent director and a non-executive director not being a promoter or KMP shall be held liable, only in respect of such acts of omission or commission by a company, which had occurred with his knowledge, attributable through Board processes, and with his consent or connivance or where he had not acted diligently.

Key Managerial Personnel

Definition and Analysis

"Key managerial personnel," in relation to a company, means—

(i) The Chief Executive Officer or the managing director or the manager;

(ii) The company secretary;

(iii) The whole-time director;

(iv) The Chief Financial Officer; and

(v) Such other officer as may be prescribed.

– Sec. 2 (51), The Companies Act, 2013

"Manager" means an individual who, subject to the superintendence, control and direction of the Board of Directors, has the management of the whole, or substantially the whole, of the affairs of a company, and includes a director or any other person occupying the position of a manager, by whatever name called, whether under a contract of service or not.

– Sec. 2 (53), The Companies Act. 2013

The earlier two definitions are technically perfect in the context of the Act, 2013. The legislator has combined the image of *key* and *manager*. *Key* has two functions, to open and to shut. By this term, we also understand something that is main, indispensable, solution, answer, core issue, initiate, and so on. *Manager* is one who handles affairs responsibly; acts to control direct and lead processes; and is the key person. One who has the keys represents power, control, and will to exercise authority and responsibility for taking decisions and implementing the same in action. Further, naming the concept as *key managerial personnel*, the legislator has underscored the essence of management in working in the relationship of a team. Modern enterprise can function well and with success only under coordinated action of a team of well-focused professionals.

There are some more that fit the cap of KMP. The following text with sections mentioned in the brackets define designations of the managerial personnel.

"Chief Executive Officer" means an officer of a company who has been designated as such by it (18).

"Chief Financial Officer" means a person appointed as the Chief Financial Officer of a company (19).

"Company secretary" or "secretary" means a company secretary as defined in clause (c) of sub-section (1) of Section 2 of the Company Secretaries Act, 1980, who is appointed by a company to perform the functions of a company secretary under this Act (24).

"Managing director" means a director who, by virtue of the articles of a company or an agreement with the company or a resolution passed in its general meeting, or by its Board of Directors, is entrusted with substantial powers of management of the affairs of the company and includes a director occupying the position of managing director, by whatever name called (54).

"Whole-time director" includes a director in the whole-time employment of the company (94).

Map of KMP

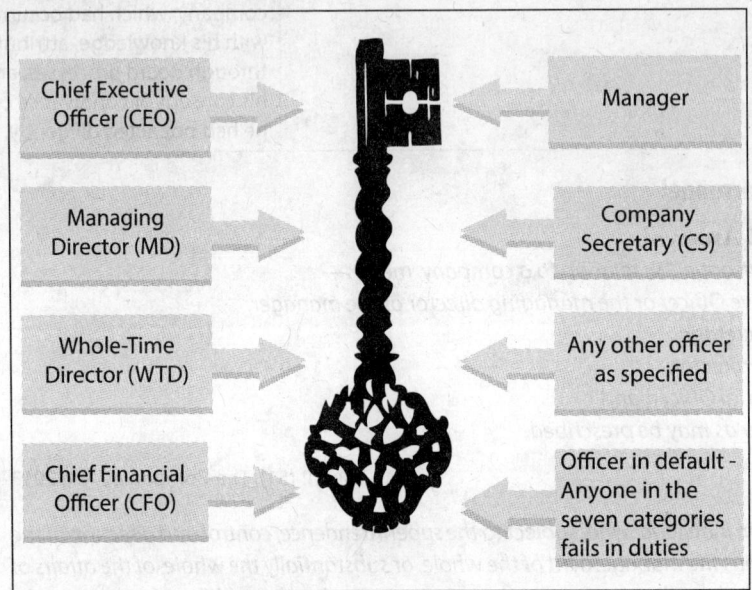

Figure 11.3   Key managerial personnel

Officer in Default: The Negative Category of KMP

"Officer who is in default," for the purpose of any provision in this Act which enacts that an officer of the company who is in default shall be liable to any penalty or punishment by way of imprisonment, fine, or otherwise, means any of the following officers of a company, namely:

(i) whole-time director;

(ii) key managerial personnel;

(iii) where there is no key managerial personnel, such director or directors as specified by the Board in this behalf and who has or have given his or their consent in writing to the Board to such specification, or all the directors, if no director is so specified;

(iv) any person who, under the immediate authority of the Board or any key managerial personnel, is charged with any responsibility including maintenance, filing, or distribution of accounts or records, authorises, actively participates in, knowingly permits, or knowingly fails to take active steps to prevent, any default;

(v) any person in accordance with whose advice, directions, or instructions the Board of Directors of the company is accustomed to act, other than a person who gives advice to the Board in a professional capacity;

(vi) every director, in respect of a contravention of any of the provisions of this Act, who is aware of such contravention by virtue of the receipt by him of any proceedings of the Board or participation in such proceedings without objecting to the same, or where such contravention had taken place with his consent or connivance;

(vii) in respect of the issue or transfer of any shares of a company, the share transfer agents, registrars, and merchant bankers to the issue or transfer.

– Sec. 2 (60), The Companies Act, 2013

The legislator has not only given power to KMP but also makes sure that they act responsibly under the pain of penalty. Every officer of the company who contravenes the law is subject to its rigours. For instance, justice demands that they act fairly without harming the interests of all the concerned stakeholders.

Companies Mandated to Appoint KMP

Section 203 of the Act along with the Companies Rules, 2014, Appointment and Remuneration of Managerial Personnel, mandates:

(a) Every listed company

(b) Public Company having paid-up share capital of ₹10 crore or more

These shall have the following officers:

(i) Managing Director or Chief Executive Officer or Manager or in their absence, a Full-time Director

(ii) Company Secretary

(iii) Chief Financial Officer

Appointment of KMP

Section 203 of the Act concerns itself with the appointment of the KMP. The Board shall appoint the managerial personnel. It shall also impart the terms and conditions of appointment along with terms of remuneration. In the event that a certain KMP falls vacant, the same shall be filled within a period of 6 months from the date of such vacancy.

Limitations

Section 203 (3) bars or limits a full-time KMP from holding office in more than one company. However, with due permission from the Board, one such entity may act as a director of any other company, provided a resolution of the Board is effected and a specific notice has been given to all the directors.

KMP Register

Section 170 (1) mandates every company to maintain a register containing particulars of its directors and KMP. It shall include details of securities held by each of them in the company or its holdings, subsidiaries of company's holding company, or associate companies. Further, the register shall be placed in the registered office of the company. What the register should contain is detailed in Rule 17 of the Companies Rules, Appointment and Qualifications of Directors, 2014.

Filing of Returns with ROC

Rule 18 of the Companies Rules, Appointment and Qualifications of Directors, 2014, Form DIR 12 with the ROC within 30 days from the appointment of any KMP or within the same period if there is any change. This is in accordance with the Section 170 (2) of the Act.

Penalty for Non-compliance

Penalties are imposed both on the company as well as on KMP for any contravention of the law:

(a) The company may be imposed with a penalty of not less than ₹1 lakh which may extend up to ₹5 lakh.

(b) Every officer, director, or KMP of the company will be punishable with a fine of ₹50,000.

(c) With a continuing contravention, the fine may extend up to ₹1,000 every day until the contravention continues.

Conclusion

Experts have given their unstinted support to the concept of KMP. It is going to be prevalent for a long time to come. The positives are seen in the principles of team work and shared responsibility. As modern businesses grow complex and global, such roles of team work and individual as well as collective responsibility are to be admired and encouraged. However, when the wheels of justice move and begin to fix responsibility, it may be naturally anticipated that the buck will not stop anywhere; there will be a dramatic blame game and the buck will only be passed. Time will run out and justice will be delayed. Any denial of justice will prove the rationale of the law as flawed and faulty. Conducting business, making and implementing managerial decisions on ethical principles, which is the real conscience of law, can spell success for KMP.

Independent Director and the Code of Conduct

TEXT

(i) A non-executive director not being promoter or key managerial personnel, shall be held liable, only in respect of such acts of omission or commission by a company which had occurred with his knowledge, attributable through Board processes, and with his consent or connivance or where he had not acted diligently.

– Sec. 149 (12) (ii), The Companies Act, 2013

Independent directors are not a new feature in Indian corporations. However, the Companies Act, 2013, has carved out a special place for an *outside director* in a company. The purpose is to impart impartiality, professional competence, and ethical edification. From stockholders' perspective, such an expert is able to exercise complete neutrality and would help in the administration and management of the company.

Section 149 (8) refers to *Schedule IV* that lays down a clear and simple code of conduct for the professional, the independent director.

The Code is a guide to professional conduct for independent directors. Adherence to these standards by independent directors and fulfilment of their responsibilities in a professional and faithful manner will promote confidence of the investment community, particularly, minority shareholders, regulators, and companies in the institution of independent directors.

Companies to have Independent Directors

- *Every listed public company*
- *Class of companies* Public companies satisfying any one of the following criteria as per the last-audited balance sheet: paid-up share capital of ₹10 crore or more; turnover of ₹100 crore or more; in aggregate outstanding loans, debentures, and deposits, exceeding ₹50 crore
- At least one-third of the total number of directors must be independent directors
- One-year transition period granted to comply with these provisions

Nature

- Disclosure of Independence—First Board Meeting and thereafter at the first meeting of the Board in every financial year or whenever there is any change in the circumstances, which may affect his status as an independent director, give a declaration that he meets the criteria of independence.
- Nominee Director appointed by banks/financial institutions/government/or any other persons shall not be treated as Independent Directors.
- Not entitled to any stock option and may receive remuneration by way of fee provided under sub-section (5) of Section 197.
- Reimbursement of expenses for participation in the Board and other meetings and profit-related commission as may be approved by the members.

Term of Office

- For five consecutive years
- Shall be eligible for reappointment on passing of a special resolution by the company and disclosure of such appointment in the Board's report. *Maximum Tenure:* Two consecutive terms; shall be eligible for appointment after the expiration of 3 years of cessation; shall not during the above-said period of 3 years, be appointed in or be associated with the company in any other capacity, either directly or indirectly; any tenure of an independent director on the date of commencement of this Act shall not be counted as a term

Liability

An independent director is held liable in respect of such acts of omission or commission by a company which had occurred with his knowledge, attributable through Board processes, and with his consent or connivance or where he had not acted diligently.

Data Bank of Available Independent Directors

Independent directors may be selected, after careful study and deliberation as to the requirements of the company from a data bank that is governed by an agency appointed by the government and shall be available on the website for perusal.

Manager's Company Map

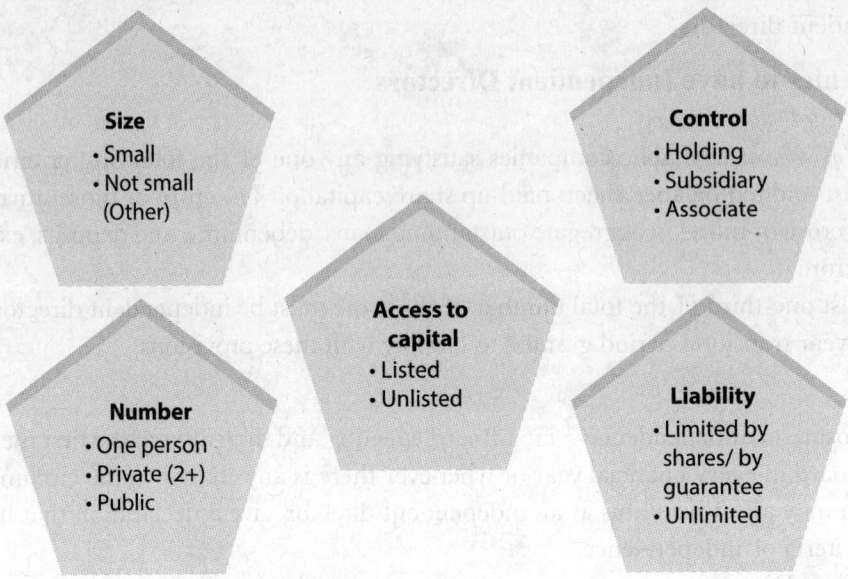

Figure 11.4 Categories of companies

Crime and Punishment

The test of the law lies in its application, in the way it is implemented and above all, wherever necessary, that it is enforced. The reason for enforcement of the law is to protect the rights of others. If a company does not obey the law, it implies it does so at the cost of some customer or investor's right. Law enforcement is the duty of the regulator. The regulator is invested with powers to inspect, investigate, judge, and bring to justice any offender of the law. Above, you have been introduced to three new regulators under the Companies Act, 2013, namely, National Companies Law Tribunal and Appellate Tribunal (NCLT), National Financial Reporting Authority (NFRA), and Serious Fraud Investigation Office (SFIO). Apart from these, there are already existing ones such as Registrar of Companies, Enforcement Directorates of Ministry of Finance, Corporate Affairs and Reserve Bank of India, SEBI, the capital market regulator, and other law enforcement authorities such as Customs and Excise Departments.

The Offender, the Officer who is in default

Under the Companies Act, 2013, the guilty person who is punished is the
The *"officer who is in default,"* for the purpose of any provision in this Act which enacts that an officer of the company who is in default shall be liable to any penalty or punishment by way of imprisonment, fine or otherwise, means any of the following officers of a company.

– Sec. 2(60), The Companies Act, 2013

The Act specifically mentions about imprisonment 76 times and prosecution 25 times. Although, while discussing different roles of the officers of the company, penalties for offences are recorded; the following chart shows some of the offences and punishments which a manager should invariably know.

Section	Offence	Punishment
447	Punishment for fraud	Imprisonment for a term of not less than 6 months but it may extend to 10 years. The liability towards fine is not less than the amount involved in the fraud but it may extend to three times the amount. Where the fraud involves public interest, the imprisonment shall not be less than 3 years. This is without prejudice to the repayment of any debt involved in fraud.
448	Punishment for false statement: Any person making a statement which is false in any material particular knowing it to be false or omission to make material fact knowing it to be material, in relation to any return, report, certificate, financial statement, prospectus statement or other document required by the provisions of this Act or the rules made there under	Imprisonment for a term which shall not be less than 3 years but it may extend to 7 years and with fine which may extend to ₹10 lakh
449	Punishment for false evidence: Any person intentionally gives false evidence upon any examination on oath or solemn affirmation authorised under this Act or in any affidavit, deposition, or solemn affirmation in or about the winding up of any company.	The punishment for the same is as applicable for fraud.
450	Punishment where no specific penalty or punishment is provided: Any company or any officer of the company or any other person contravenes any of the provisions of proposed Act or the rules there under or any condition, limitation, or restriction subject to which any approval is given or granted for which no penalty or punishment is provided elsewhere, then the company and every officer thereof who is in default or such other person.	Such a person is punishable with fine extending it to ₹10,000 and where the contravention is a continuing offence, with a further fine extending it to ₹1000 for every day during which the contravention continues.
451	Punishment in case of repeated default: In the case of repeated default committed for the second or subsequent occasions within a period of 3 years.	The company and every officer thereof who is in default is punishable with twice the amount of fine for such offence, in addition to any imprisonment for the same.

Contd

Section	Offence	Punishment
452	**Punishment for wrongfully withholding of property:** Any officer or employee of a company wrongfully obtains possession of any property including cash or having such property wrongfully withholding it or knowingly applies it for the purpose other than expressed or directed in the articles and authorised by this Act; then he shall on the complaint of the company or any member or creditor or contributory thereof.	Such a person is punishable with fine of not less than ₹1 lakh but it may extend to ₹5 lakh.
453	**Punishment for improper use of the word 'limited' or 'private limited':** Any person carries on trade or business under the name or title of which the word 'limited' or the words 'private limited' or any construction or imitation thereof, unless duly incorporated with limited liability or as a private company with limited liability, as the case may be.	Such a person is punishable with fine of not less than ₹500 but it may extend to ₹2000 for every day during which that name or title has been used.
454	**Adjudication of Penalties:** The Central Government may, by an order published in the Official Gazette, appoint as many officers of the Central Government, not below the rank of Registrar, as Adjudicating Officers for adjudging penalty under this Act in the prescribed manner. The regulations in this behalf are as under: While appointing adjudicating officers, the Central Government shall specify the jurisdiction of each of them. The adjudicating officer may, by an order, impose the penalty on the company and the officers in default stating the non-compliance or default under the relevant provisions of this Act. Before imposing penalty, the adjudicating officer should give a reasonable opportunity of being heard to the company and the officer who is in default. Any person aggrieved by an order made by adjudicating officer may prefer an appeal to the Regional Director having jurisdiction in the matter. Every appeal shall be filed within 60 days from the date of receipt of a copy of the order. The Regional Director after giving the parties to the appeal an opportunity of being heard pass such order as he thinks fit confirming, modifying, or setting aside the order appealed against.	Where the company does not pay the penalty 90 days from the date of receipt of the order, the company is punishable with fine which shall not be less than ₹25,000 but it may extend to ₹5 lakh, where an officer of the company who is in default does not pay the penalty within a period of 90 days from the date of receipt of a copy of the order, such an officer is punishable with imprisonment for 6 months or with a fine of not less than ₹25,000 but it may extend to ₹1 lakh or with both.

Conclusion

The differences between the provisions of the Old and the New Acts are obvious. The adjudication of the penalties by the officers appointed by the Central Government is not just a novelty; it would dispense justice with fairness and equity. At times, the punishments and penalties may seem severe; however, jurisprudence will advocate that firm measures do bring in good results. In all, the punishment serves the public interest.

11.3 CORPORATE SOCIAL RESPONSIBILITY

SHARING IS CARING

Company vs Company

Ram Gopal Verma is a renowned filmmaker from Bollywood whose movies depict violence. In 2002, he produced a gangster movie called *Company*. It typically depicted the notorious Mumbai underworld. One of its characters expresses the principles of this extortion and violence producing *Company* as: *All work for profit. No taxes paid. All money looted. No accounts kept. Anyone can join at any time. No one can leave. One who leaves pays with his life. It is business. It makes profits.* As bizarre as it may sound, it makes a point against business corporations as not being a different from a gangster company. People felt very strongly against companies and still do: *It is just business, they do it only for profit.* This has been the refrain by the common people in the society. In other words, people believe that companies have just one aim, profits at any cost; they have no ethical principles or moral bindings.

The term *company* connotes companionship, friendship, and fellowship. Etymologically, it is a Latin term *com + panis*—to break bread together; in other words to share food, the most basic nourishment, and do it together. In truth, a company consists of ownership of shares. It is also the principle of economic distribution. Sharing expresses the fundamental principle of the existence and sustenance of civilised human society. We may term this phenomenon as the foundation of human society. All the theories of the state are built on this first principle of human existence.

People, Planet, and Profit

Today, companies, having travelled the business road for very long and having to deal primarily with people, have come to realise that they are no different from the people. A man, no matter how poor or how cruel, has some basic goodness. An association of people, such as a company, too, should not be different from that fundamental nature. The company exists because it has the potential for good; the objectives of the company express this truth. Doing this in and for the society is the simple definition of *Corporate Social Responsibility*.

Another truth that the companies have realised, just as the people have, is that they have caused grave damage to the environment. The environmental pollution is mainly blamed on the industries. As a result, the people irrespective of country or region are suffering the consequences. Environmental damage has no limits of boarders.

Thus the objective of a modern company is not merely profits; they have people and the planet Earth as equally the good part of their objectives. Given these new circumstances, starting from the United Nations Organizations to the smallest of nations, prominence has been given to enact laws, advance holistic policies both for the development of the people as well as the protection of environment.

The Law

Every company having net worth of rupees five hundred crore or more, or turnover of rupees one thousand crore or more or a net profit of rupees five crore or more during any financial year shall constitute a Corporate Social Responsibility Committee of the Board consisting of three or more directors, out of which at least one director shall be an independent director.

— Sec. 135(1), The Companies Act, 2013

The Companies Act, 2013, has provided mandatory provisions for the companies in the practice of Corporate Social Responsibility. The above-stated Section 135 and Schedule VII of the Act have the following provisions:

1. The BOD shall appoint Corporate Social Responsibility Committee in which there shall be three or more directors and one among them

shall be an independent director which shall make policy and shall indicate the activities.

2. The Schedule VII specifies these activities as:
   - Eradicating extreme hunger and poverty
   - Promotion of education
   - Promoting gender equality and empowering women
   - Reducing child mortality and improving maternal health
   - Combating human immunodeficiency virus, acquired immune deficiency
   - Syndrome, malaria, and other diseases
   - Ensuring environmental sustainability
   - Employment enhancing vocational skills
   - Social business projects contribution to the Prime Minister's National Relief Fund or any other Fund set up by the Central Government or the State Governments

3. The BOD shall make sure at least 2% of its profits, which are channelized for CSR activities.

4. The draft rules notified by the Ministry of Corporate Affairs lay down that the conducting of the CSR activities shall be through a trust or association or company or a non-profit organization incorporated for the purpose and whose annual returns shall be filed. This has already come into effect since 1 April 2014.

5. The company may also collaborate with other companies in CSR activities.

6. The CSR activities to be conducted only in India.

7. The activities that benefit only the employees of the company are not to be considered as CSR activities.

8. Only those expenditures will be considered as such which are in accordance with the activities listed in Schedule VII of the Act.

9. Board has to state in its reporting the CSR activities and their expenditure.

10. CSR activities must be displayed on the company's website.

Conclusion

Mahatma Gandhi, the Father of the Nation, had the concept of companies to be governed on the principle of trusteeship. Such an ideal would work for the inclusiveness of all in the society, and the companies would be the active part of citizenry. In this regard, the guiding principle has been, *Be the change you want to see in the world*. With insurmountable problems of massive poverty, illiteracy, lack of health care in India, the task of CSR is well cut out for those companies who are willing to see a change for the better.

MANAGER'S TAKEAWAY

The law empowers the organization.

11.4. CONTROL AND GOVERNANCE BY STATUTORY AGENCIES OF THE GOVERNMENT

National Company Law Tribunal (NCLT)

The Central Government shall, by notification, constitute, with effect from such date as may be specified therein, a Tribunal to be known as the National Company Law Tribunal consisting of a President and such number of Judicial and Technical members, as the Central Government may deem necessary, to be appointed by it by notification, to exercise and discharge such powers

and functions as are, or may be, conferred on it by or under this Act or any other law for the time being in force

– Sec. 408, The Companies Act, 2013

Section 407, the one preceding the above text defines the National Company Law Tribunal and Appellate Tribunal, the full form of the name of this quasi-judicial body. The quasi-judicial body, as the term suggests, is one which adjudicates but not to the full extent as would a full-fledged court. Under the Companies Act, 1956, there were two quasi-judicial bodies named Company Law Board (CLB) and Board for Industrial and Financial Reconstruction (BFIR), which are now replaced by one National Company Law Tribunal and Appellate Tribunal. In professional circles, it is known by its acronym NCLT. According to a Supreme Court Judgement in May 2014, the tribunal will have the responsibilities to expedite the merger and acquisition cases in the private sector which is a function of the High Court; it will also deal with the timely unlocking of the distressed corporate assets and take over the process of liquidation of companies which too is a function of the High Court.

Section 407 distinguishes two classes of members to National Company Law Tribunal and Appellate Tribunal: Judicial members and technical members. The tribunal will be headed by a President and the appellate tribunal by a Chairperson.

The objective for the creation of NCLT is to avoid multiplicity of authorities and thus avoid or reduce litigation agencies. There will be adequate number of benches of NCLT across the country so that justice is available to corporations speedily. The technical experts on NCLT are provided for scientific establishment of facts so that right decisions may be taken. It will, for instance, reduce the period of winding up a company from 20 to just 2 years.

While there are, at present, some teething problems about the constitution of the NCLT, there is no doubt about the intention of the legislator to deliver effective, efficient, and speedy justice.

11.5. NATIONAL FINANCIAL REPORTING AUTHORITY (NFRA)

TEXT

The Central Government may, by notification, constitute a National Financial Reporting Authority to provide for matters relating to accounting and auditing standards under this Act.

– Sec. 132 (1), The Companies Act, 2014

Under the stated text, Section 132, the Central Government has set up a new regulatory authority, namely, National Financial Reporting Authority (NFRA). In correspondence to this body, the old Act had National Advisory Committee on Accounting Standards (NACAS) which served as to advise the Central Government on the formulation and to lay down accounting policies and accounting standards for adoption by companies. Unlike NACAS which was merely an advisory body, NFRA is the regulatory authority for auditing and financial reporting.

NFRA is a quasi-judicial body; it has powers to monitor and enforce compliance of auditing and accounting standards. It can investigate the professional and other misconducts which may be committed by the professionals as chartered accountants. Accordingly, its objectives may be summarised as follows:

- Make recommendations on formulation of accounting and auditing policies and standards for adoption by companies and their auditors
- Monitor and enforce the compliance with accounting auditing standards
- Supervise the quality of service of professionals associated with ensuring compliance with such standards and suggest measures required for improvement in quality of service
- Undertake investigation of auditors or audit firms, which conduct audit of 200 companies or more in a year as well as those auditing twenty or more listed companies.
- Impose heavy penalties on those who break the laws and debarment of audit firms for up to ten years.
- May form three committees on Accounting standards, Auditing Standards, and Enforcement; it would have three members and representatives from Corporate Affairs Ministry, Reserve Bank of India (RBI), Securities and Exchange Board of India (SEBI), and central-government-nominated retired Chief Justice of a High Court or a person who has been the Judge of a High Court for at least 5 years.

Central Government shall remain the ultimate authority in all matters concerning the functioning of NFRA.

Serious Fraud Investigation Office (SFIO):

The Central Government shall, by notification, establish an office to be called the Serious Fraud Investigation Office to investigate frauds relating to a company: Provided that until the Serious Fraud Investigation Office is established under subsection(1), the Serious Fraud Investigation Office set-up by the Central Government in terms of the Government of India Resolution No. 45011/16/2003-Adm-I, dated the 2nd July, 2003 shall be deemed to be the Serious Fraud Investigation Office for the purpose of this section.

– Sec. 211(1), The Companies Act, 2013

Serious Fraud Investigation Office (SFIO) is an investigating agency of the Ministry of Corporate Affairs, and thus is directly under the jurisdiction of Government of India. Major and serious fraud probes come under its gambit. Its officers are drawn from multidisciplinary agencies of the government such as IAS, IPS, Income Tax, CBI, CAG, and SEBI. They have thus such experts as from financial sector, capital market, accounts and audit, company law, information technology, forensic audit, customs, and investigation. Initially, the government had decided to form SFIO as early as 2003 as per the recommendations of Naresh Chandra Committee (2002) set up to suggest recommendations on Corporate Governance. The following are a few responsibilities of this quasi-judicial body:

- Detecting and prosecuting or recommending for prosecution white-collar crimes/corporate frauds
- The SFIO will normally take up for investigation only such cases, which are characterised by substantial public interest such as the size of a scam or the number of people affected by the misappropriation or in terms of people affected; further, such investigation should lead to implementation of procedures and reform of system

According to Section 2012 of the Act, the investigation into the fraudulent affairs of a company is ordered by the Central Government if it is convinced of the reports received by it or if it is in the public interest or on request from any Department of the Central Government. It may order to do so under the directorship of the SFIO. The agency upon investigation will submit the report to the Central Government.

From the part of the company that is being investigated, all its officers and employees shall be responsible to provide all information, explanation, documents, and assistance to the officers of SFIO. Any arrests made as a result of the investigation shall be produced before the Metropolitan Magistrate within 24 h (Section 212 (10)). The agency shall provide an interim report of the investigations if the Central Government so demands (Section 212 (11)).

OTHER AREAS OF IMPORTANCE[2]

Insider Trading Section 195 (*1*) states that *no person including any director or key managerial personnel of a company shall enter into insider trading.*

"Insider trading" has been broadly defined to include the acts of subscribing, buying, selling or dealing in securities, or procuring or communicating non-public price sensitive information.

Imprisonment for contravention of the law is up to five years, with or without a fine

Buy-Back of Shares Section 68 (*1*): *Notwithstanding anything contained in this Act, but subject to the provisions of sub-section (2), a company may purchase its own shares or other specified securities.* The law requires a mandatory one-year time period between any type of buy-back, even if the buy-back was achieved through a scheme approved by the tribunal. Buy-back is not possible if the company has made any default in the repayment of deposits or interest, or redemption of debentures, or preference shares, or payment of dividend, or in the repayment of a term loan to a bank or financial institution. However, the buy-back may be possible if the defect is remedied, and a three-year time period has elapsed.

Purchase Minority Shareholding Section 236 (1–7). If an acquisition results in the acquirer holding ninety percent of the issued share capital of the company, it shall be obliged to inform the company

of its desire to purchase the minority shareholding of that company at a price determined according to the provisions of the Act.

Layered Subsidiaries Section 2(*87*) *"subsidiary company" or "subsidiary," in relation to any other company (that is to say the holding company), means a company in which the holding company—*

(i) controls the composition of the Board of Directors; or
(ii) exercises or controls more than one-half of the total share capital either at its own or together with one or more of its subsidiary companies: Provided that such class or classes of holding companies as may be prescribed shall not have layers of subsidiaries beyond such numbers as may be prescribed.

Merger or Amalgamation of Company With Foreign Company Section 234. (*1*) *The provisions of this Chapter unless otherwise provided under any other law for the time being in force, shall apply mutatis mutandis to schemes of mergers and amalgamations between companies registered under this Act and companies incorporated in the jurisdictions of such countries as may be notified from time to time by the Central Government.*

Class Action Suit as Instrument of Investor Protection
Section 125 *(3)(d)*: *reimbursement of legal expenses incurred in pursuing class action suits under sections 37 and*

---

[1]This is not a full treatment of the themes, but here is a mere indicator to the important subjects.

245 by members, debenture-holders or depositors as may be sanctioned by the Tribunal; and (e) any other purpose incidental thereto, in accordance with such rules as may be prescribed:

Enforcement of Shareholder Agreement and Entrenchemnt Section 5 (3). *The articles may contain provisions for entrenchment to the effect that specified provisions of the articles may be altered only if conditions or procedures as that are more restrictive than those applicable in the case of a special resolution, are met or complied with.* Section 5 (4). *The provisions for entrenchment referred to in*

sub-section (3) shall only be made either on formation of a company, or by an amendment in the articles agreed to by all the members of the company in the case of a private company and by a special resolution in the case of a public company. This has now validated the idea of entrenchment and all such contractual agreements by shareholders which bear legal sanction. This provides flexibility for investors to specify that certain provisions of the articles of a company may only be altered if special conditions or procedures are complied with.

 MANAGER'S TAKEAWAY

The legal institutions exist to maintain law and order equally and equitably. Without these, there will be chaos and anarchy.

SUMMARY

- The Companies Act, 2013, is a road map for good governance. There are several types of organizations such as charitable institutions, non-profit organizations, and those which operate for profit, the corporations, with which we are mostly concerned. Here, in these organizations the legislator wants that justice be done to all the stakeholders.
- The company law provides that the corporations be administered and controlled by formalised systems such as Board of Directors, Directors and Officers of the Company, Key Managerial Personnel (KMP), Independent Director, and these will act according

to a Code of Conduct. The contravention of the law attracts penalty and punishment.
- Statutory agencies are established to control and govern. These are:
  - National Company Law Tribunal (NCLT)
  - National Financial Reporting Authority (NFRA)
  - Serious Fraud Investigation Office (SFIO)
- Not all the laws and not all the organs of justice can control everything; but responsible behaviour of the company based on ethical principles can escape all the strictures of the law. Organizations are expected to be socially responsible.

EXERCISES

(i) What is the time limit within which the Board has to appoint an Independent Director and at which meeting whether Board Meeting or General Meeting?
Hint: Section 149(5) and Schedule IV

(ii) The activities of a company, such as Labour Laws and Land Acquisition Act, are required to do as

per statutory obligation under any law, would these be termed as CSR activity?
Hint: Ministry of Corporate Affairs Circular No. 21/2014 dated 18 June 2014.

(iii) What is the relevant financial year, with effect from which such provisions of the new Act relating to maintenance of books of account, preparation, adoption, and filing of financial statements, auditor's report, and Board's report will be applicable?

Hint: MCA Circular No. 08/2014 dated 4 April 2014.

(iv) Are notices of disclosure of interest received from directors in terms of Section 184 of the Companies Act, 2013, required to be filed with the ROC? If yes, in what form?

Hint: Section 117 (3) (g)

(v) Is it mandatory to file the return of appointment of KMPs appointed in terms of Section 203?

Hint: Section 203

DEVELOPMENT OF LEGAL EDGE

- The New Act has served an advantage to women directors. If you are in this category, then develop an interest to educate, train, and be competitive.
- If you are a company, then take the advantage offered by the law to appoint women directors and go a step still further by equally balancing the sex ratio of the employees in your organization.

- If you are not a listed company who does not have the legal obligation for appointment of woman directors, yet having women directors in any company, will reflect the philosophy of our times and the company will be seen in good light.

CASE STUDY · SIXER SAHARA STUMPED BY SEBI

Prologue

Cricket, India's best sports entertainment, is synonymous with its sponsor, the *Sahara* conglomerate under its dashing chief Subrata Roy. Close to 5 years from now, a simple complaint from a small investor woke up the ofted chided as *toothless* regulator, the Securities Exchange Board of India, better known as SEBI, into action that, in cricketing parlance, *stumped* the giant Sahara group with a demand for ₹20,000 crore which had to be distributed to the shareholders of Sahara securities. The firm did not comply. The captain of Sahara Group is cooling his heels in the prison.[3]

The Beginning of the Story

It began with two complaints to SEBI by two small investors: the first was received in the last week of December, 2009, and the second a few days later in the first week of January 2011. The complaints alleged that two companies of the Sahara Group, Sahara India Real Estate Corporation and Sahara Housing Investment Corporation, were raising capital illegally by issuing Optionally Fully Convertible Debentures (OFCD). Upon investigation, SEBI found that these were issued after filing *Red Herring Prospectus* (RHP),

i.e., one that does not fully disclose details which are done in a normal prospectus, with the Registrar of Companies. The securities were issued far above the limit; rules required permission from SEBI for the issuance of securities which has above fifty investors. Investors in Sahara soared over ₹3 crore!

SEBI Demands Refund

After 11 months (November 2010) of the initial complaints, SEBI sends an order asking the twin Sahara companies to refund the money to the investors. SEBI sent the order a second time on June 2011. Sahara challenged it in the Securities Appellate Tribunal. However, the Tribunal upheld SEBI's orders and directed the companies to refund a total amount of ₹25,781 crore to over three crore investors.

Knock on Apex Court's Door

Sahara moved the Supreme Court. The Supreme Court of India passed a landmark order on 31 August 2012. It ordered the two involved companies of Sahara Group to refund the amount and also give all details of the securities and their customers. The only concession that the Apex

---

[3]See some of the links to deal with this story at length: http://www.indiankanoon.org/doc/140793831/; http://www.dnaindia.com/money/report-the-curious-case-of-subrata-roy-highlights-of-the-sahara-sebi-story-1965591; http://www.hindustantimes.com/business-news/sebi-sahara-case-a-saga-of-big-numbers-and-innocuous-names/article1-1189250.aspx.http://www.mondaq.com/india/x/203796/Shareholders/Sahara+vs+SEBIAn+InDepth+Analysis+Of+The+Landmark+Supreme.

court granted was that they may do it in three separate installments with date deadlines.

Sahara complied, but only with the first installment, the other two deadlines elapsed. After the first installment, another ₹24,000 crore was now in default which led SEBI in February 2013 to attach Groups' bank accounts and other properties and also issued summons to the Chairman of the company Subrata Roy and other three directors before it.

More Drama

On 10 April 2013, the chairman and the directors appeared before SEBI. Chairman Roy was dramatic when he came out. He began by chiding SEBI officials before the media for having not even offering him a cup of tea. More was yet to come; the Sahara Group regularly issued full-page advertisements in all the national papers claiming to have cleared the outstanding liabilities, about the phenomenal growth of the company, its vast assets and growing business interests, etc. At the same time, these hit the SEBI the Regulator for making baseless allegations. The drama now was visible full-scale in both print and electronic media. For Sahara sent sixty large truck loads of documents, securities details, etc., to SEBI office in Mumbai that caused a traffic jam and prime-time news slot.

SEBI staidly rejected the public allegations made by Sahara and issued notice in the media cautioning investors and general public against dealing with the Sahara Group. Further, SEBI sent notices to the financial institutions and banks to freeze all accounts. The Regulator also sent notices to district collectors and other authorities for attachment of land, real estate, and other assets. SEBI also brought into action the Department of Taxes, Enforcement Directorate, etc. In May 2013, it initiates the process of refunding the investors as directed by the Supreme Court.

After all the drama, the anti-climax is that SEBI has not been able to disburse money to the investors. Although it is not SEBI's fault, the truth is that the securities and the papers which were dramatically delivered are not in order; false accounts, multiplicity of accounts, and scores of other irregularities have marred and confounded the sordid situation. It is SEBI's turn now to knock on the door of the Apex Court.

The Moment of Truth

The Supreme Court was disappointed, to say the least. In its order, it clearly spells out the reasons as to why it distrusts Sahara Group and directs the company to submit title deeds of its properties worth ₹20,000 crore to be handed over to the securities Regulator, SEBI, within 3 weeks.

On 20 November 2013, SEBI submits before the Supreme Court that Sahara Group had overvalued its assets and has failed to submit original title deals of the properties worth ₹20,000 crore as was ordered by it. The Supreme Court in turn takes umbrage for making a mockery of order and it bars Subrata Roy the Chairman and the three other directors of the Sahara Group from leaving the country and further orders that none of its properties shall be sold. In early January 2014, the Supreme Court contemplates on an investigation by the Central Bureau of Investigation against the Sahara Group to establish the source of ₹22,000 crore it claimed to have refunded the 3.3 crore investors.

Sahara Group frustrated the Supreme Court by its non-cooperative attitude and orders the Chairman of the Group Subrata Roy to appear before it before 26 February 2014. He does not submit himself before the Court. The Court issues a non-bailable warrant for his arrest. The police fail to nab him. On the next day, 27 February 2014, he offers unconditional apology. The very next day, he surrenders to the local police in Lucknow and is promptly sent to jail.

Discussion Questions

1. Lay bear the facts of the Sahara case and shed light on the main three issues.
2. Interpolate the roles played by SEBI the Regulator and the Sahara Group.
3. How would you judge SEBI handling the case?
4. What would you do in the place of the Sahara CEO?
5. Whistle-blowing by an investor. Comment.
6. How would the knowledge of this case help you as manager?
7. Is this case politicised? Comment.

Going Beyond

1. What are the consequences of litigation on:
   - The Company
   - The Employees
   - The Investors
   - Other corporations
   - The economy of the country
2. Give suggestions to make the Market Regulator effective.

FURTHER READING

- Ram Charan (2009). Boards that Deliver: Advancing Corporate Governance from Compliance to Competitive Advantage. Wiley India Ltd. (Paperback)

- Dinesh Kumar Khatri (2010). Security Analysis and Portfolio Management. MacMillan Publishers, India.
- Link: http://www.sebi.gov.in/acts/act122.html

LEGAL LUMINARY

DR NIRMALA SITHARAMAN: RHETORIC AND POLITICS

Rhetoric and Politics have been liberal sciences since the ancient Greek philosophers. Dr Nirmala Sitharaman is a scholar of the highest order, for she holds a doctorate in trade and commerce; she is the well-qualified minister to hold such a portfolio as Ministry of Commerce and Industry—with independent charge—and also Minister of State for Finance and Corporate Affairs; as for rhetoric, she has been the sharpest spokesperson for the Bharatiya Janata Party (BJP) tearing into the arguments of the opposition parties on prime-time television.

She has been an alumnus of Jawaharlal University (JNU), Delhi, and London School of Economics. Her doctoral thesis was focused on Indo-European textile trade within the General Agreement on Tariffs and Trade (GATT) framework. In the United Kingdom (UK), she became a Senior Manager of PricewaterhouseCoopers firm and also had a stint with the British Broadcasting Corporation (BBC).

Dr Nirmala returned to her home state Andhra Pradesh and was placed as Deputy Director of Public Policy Studies in Hyderabad. She fulfilled her interest in education by establishing a school named *Pranav*; she was its Founder Director. Its mission affirms 'quality education for the present and future.' She took active part in women's welfare and empowerment became a member of the National Commission for Women.

Politics was not far away. Her husband, Dr Parakala Prabhakar, was also a scholar from JNU; he came from a highly reputed political family. He was attracted initially to the newly formed Prajarajyam Party in Andhra Pradesh, but soon got disillusioned with it. However, Dr Nirmala Sitharaman felt that the BJP had those economic elements with which she could identify. She joined the Party in 2008 and was immediately elevated to its National Executive which was followed by her appointment as the spokesperson of the Party.

Rhetoric, argumentative, and convincing brought her as the most visible and intellectual face of the BJP. Although a Tamil by birth, she is fluent in Hindi. The Madurai born Dr Sitharaman may well be a loss to the academia but is a big gain to the political economy of the country.[4]

[4]See: http://commerce.nic.in/bio/CIMBiodata.pdf; http://pranavatheschool.org/about/management/; http://articles.timesofindia.indiatimes.com/2010-03-21/india/28136255_1_nirmala-sitharaman-bjp-spokesperson-nitin-gadkari; http://www.bjp.org/organisation/office-bearers; http://www.thehindubusinessline.com/opinion/like-water-on-a-lotus-leaf/article2085256.ece (15 September 2014).

12

The Competition Act, 2002

Principle: Commercium jure gentium commune esse debet et non in monopolium et privatum paucorum quaestum convertuendum.

Commerce, by the law of the nations, ought to be common, and not perverted to monopoly and the private profit of a few.

CHAPTER OUTLINE

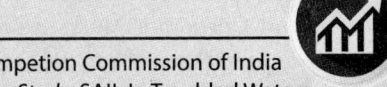

- Introduction and Interpretation
- MRTP versus Competition
- Scope of Competition Act, 2002
- Prohibition of Certain Agreements, Abuse of Dominant Position, and Regulation of Combinations
- Competion Commission of India
- *Case Study:* SAIL In Troubled Waters
- *Legal Luminary:* Arijit Pasayat

12.1 INTRODUCTION AND INTERPRETATION

TEXT

An Act to provide, keeping in view of the economic development of the country, for the establishment of a Commission to prevent practices having adverse effect on competition, to promote and sustain competition in markets, to protect the interests of consumers and to ensure freedom of trade carried on by other participants in markets, in India, and for matters connected therewith or incidental thereto.

– The Competition Act, 2002, Opening paragraph

The Act that is being studied is referred to with its complete title as the Competition Act, 2002 (No. 12 of 2003) as amended by the Competition (Amendment) Act 2007. This Act, when it came into effect, repealed its predecessor, the Monopolies and Restrictive Trade Practices Act, 1969, better known by its acronym MRTP (Fig. 12.1). The four objectives of the Competition Act have been quoted above earlier, but bear repeating. They work on the premise of:

1. Establishment of a commission to prevent adverse effect on competition
2. Promotion and sustenance competition in the market
3. Protection of consumers' interests
4. Freedom of trade

Table 12.1   A comparison between MRTP Act and Competition Act

MRTP Act, 1969	Competition Act, 2002
• Pre-reforms: rigid and reactive	• Post-reforms: simple and transparent
• No administrative and financial autonomy for the commission	• Competition commission is autonomous
• Offences are implicit and undefined	• Offences are well defined
• No power to inquire into foregin cartels	• Regulation is in place

In today's business parlance, the goal of the Act was to create a level-playing field to all the competitors in the market. The Competition Commission of India was established by the Act to promote its objectives.

12.2   MRTP vs COMPETITION

The MRTP Act, 1969 gives a clear idea of how trade and commerce was conducted in the era of command economy, which excelled in putting in place, controls rather than allowing the growth of industry and motivating business. The Act was an instrument that served the objectives of the *license raj*. The government would assess and grant licenses for industry, thus controlling production. Another fallout was that the license holders quickly found out ways to create cartels and monopolies and hence dominated the domestic market.

In 1999, the world economic order had changed and India's own reforms had ushered in free-market reforms which ensured that rolling back to the earlier system was unthinkable. MRTP had to be changed because it did not serve the goals of the new economic order. It was also discovered that our own Constitution in Articles 38 and 39, which come under the Directive Principles, were being read in the new light:

1. That the ownership and control of material resources of the community are so distributed as to best subserve the common good
2. That the operation of the economic system does not result in the concentration of wealth and means of production to the common detriment

A high-level committee under the chairmanship of V.S. Raghavan was set up to examine and give suggestions for a new law. Consequently, the law was enacted in 2002 and was promulgated in January 2003 as the Competition Act, 2002.

12.3   SCOPE OF COMPETITION ACT, 2002

The marketplace is made up of sellers and buyers; each seller competes to win as many buyers as possible over his nearest rival and adopts strategies to outsmart them the rival(s). However, one seller wants to come out on top of everyone else so that he completely dominates the market and wants to achieve the position of a single supplier of goods and services. However, the free-market economy has a fundamental principle of competition: *free and fair*. A market economy based on such a principle stimulates productivity and, innovation, improves the

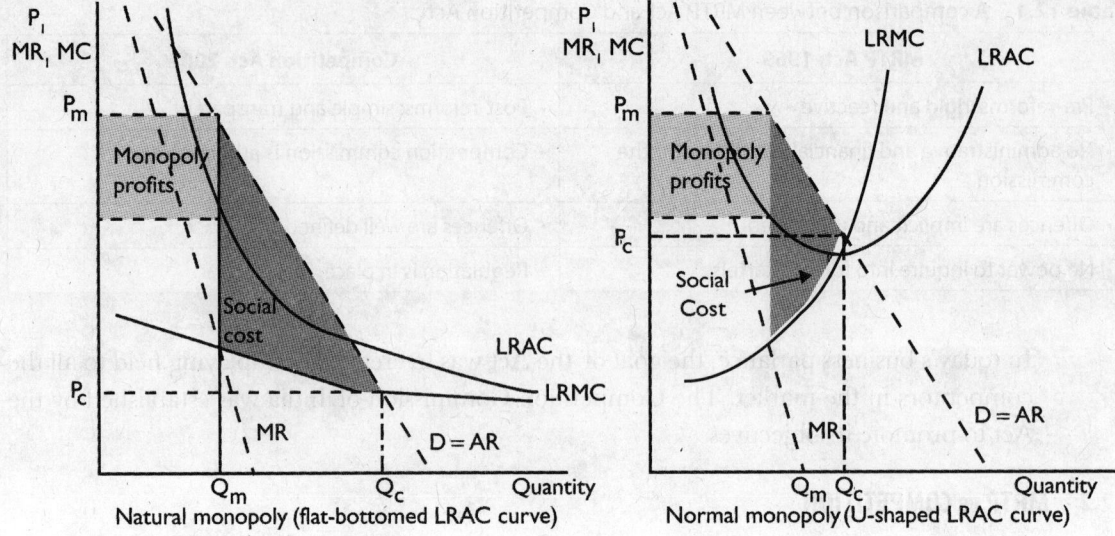

Figure 12.1 Monopoly structure and its social cost

quality, and puts the resources to the best use; it guarantees consumer interests. Thus, it becomes an engine of economic and social development.

In a monopoly, the problem of justice occurs because not only it is unfair to the competitors but also the firm exploits the society as a whole, making it pay a higher price than it would have in a free market environment. (For further explanation, see http://mrski-apecon-2008.wikispaces.com/, 29 August 2011.) Figure 12.2, shows that profit maximizing monopoly will produce at MR = MC, charging a price P_m and producing output Q_m. Under perfect competition, consumers would pay P_c and consume Q_c where P = MC. The welfare loss for society (i.e., social cost) is the area to the left of the social equilibrium point, where marginal social benefit (MSB = D) is equal to marginal social cost (MSC = MC).

The Competition Act, 2002 intends to provide adequate safeguards to all the players in the market. Proper regulation is essential for healthy competition. Hence, the Act provides for a regulatory authority called the Competition Commission of India (CCI).

BOX 12.1   **DEFINITIONS***

ACQUISITION: Directly or indirectly, acquiring or agreeing to acquire
- Shares, voting rights, or assets of any enterprise
- Control over management or the assets of any enterprise

*The definitions are abridged to understand the concepts in this Act. For a full and elaborate description, see the Competition Act, 2002 Sec. 2.

Contd

Box 12.1 *Contd*

AGREEMENT:	Any arrangement, understanding, or action in concert • Whether or not such arrangement, understanding, or action is formal or in writing • Whether or not such arrangement, understanding, or action is intended to be enforceable by legal proceedings
APPELLATE TRIBUNAL:	The Competition Appellate Tribunal established under sub-sec. (1) of Sec. 53A.
CARTEL:	An association of producers, sellers, distributors, traders, or service providers who, by agreement amongst themselves, limit, control, or attempt to control the production, distribution, sale, or price of, or trade in goods or provision of services.
CHAIRPERSON:	The Chairperson of the Commission appointed under sub-sec. (1) of Sec. 8.
COMMISSION:	Competition Commission of India established under sub-sec. (1) of Sec. 7.
CONSUMER:	Any person who • Buys any goods for a consideration which has been paid or promised or partly paid and partly promised, or under any system of deferred payment and includes any user of such goods other than the person who buys such goods for consideration paid or promised or partly paid or partly promised, or under any system of deferred payment when such use is made with the approval of such person, whether such purchase of goods is for resale, for any commercial purpose, or personal use. • Hires or avails of any services for a consideration which has been paid or promised or partly paid and partly promised, or under any system of deferred payment and includes any beneficiary of such services other than the person who hires or avails of the services for consideration paid or promised, or partly paid and partly promised, or under any system of deferred payment, when such services are availed of with the approval of the first-mentioned person, whether such hiring or availing of services is for any commercial purpose or personal use.
DIRECTOR:	The Director General appointed under sub-sec. (1) of Sec. 16 and includes any Additional, Joint, Deputy, or Assistant Directors-General or such officers or other employees in the office of the Director-General.
GENERAL	Deputy or Assistant Directors General appointed under that section.
ENTERPRISE:	A person or a department of the Government, who or which is, or has been, engaged in any activity, relating to the production, storage, supply, distribution, acquisition, or control of articles or goods, or the provision of services, of any kind, or in investment, or in the business of acquiring, holding, underwriting, or dealing with shares, debentures, or other securities of any other body corporate, either directly or through one or more of its units or divisions or subsidiaries, whether such unit, division, or subsidiary is located at the same place where the enterprise is located or at a different place or at different places, but does not include any activity of the Government relatable to the sovereign functions of the Government, including all activities carried on by the departments of the Central Government dealing with atomic energy, currency, defence and space.
EXPLANATION:	For the purposes of this clause: • Activity: Profession or occupation • Article and service: A new article and service: A new service • Unit or division: No relation to an enterprise

Contd

Box 12.1 *Contd*

	1. Plant or factory: Established for the production, storage, supply, distribution, acquisition, or control of any article or goods
	2. Any branch or office established for the provision of any service
GOODS:	Goods as defined in the Sale of Goods Act, 1930 (3 of 1930) and includes:
	1. Products manufactured, processed, or mined
	2. Debentures, stocks, and shares after allotment
	3. In relation to goods supplied, distributed, or controlled in India, goods imported into India
MEMBER:	Member of the Commission appointed under sub-sec. (1) of Sec. 8 and includes the Chairperson
NOTIFICATION:	Notification published in the Official Gazette
PERSON:	• An individual
	• A Hindu undivided family
	• A company
	• A firm
	• An association of persons or a body of individuals, whether incorporated or not, in India or outside India
	• Any corporation established by or under any Central, State, or Provincial Act or a Government company as defined in Sec. 617 of the Companies Act, 1956 (1 of 1956)
	• Any corporate incorporated by or under the laws of a country outside India
	• A cooperative society registered under any law relating to cooperative societies
	• A local authority
	• Every artificial juridical person, not falling within any of the preceding sub-clauses
PRACTICE:	Any practice relating to the carrying on of any trade by a person or an enterprise
PRESCRIBED:	Prescribed by rules made under this Act
PRICE:	In relation to the sale of any goods or to the performance of any services, includes every valuable consideration, whether direct or indirect, or deferred, and includes any consideration which, in effect, relates to the sale of any goods or to the performance of any services, although ostensibly relating to any other matter or thing.
PUBLIC FINANCIAL INSTITUTION:	A public financial institution specified under Sec. 4A of the Companies Act, 1956 (1 of 1956) and includes a State Financial, Industrial or Investment Corporation.
REGULATIONS:	The regulations made by the Commission under Sec. 64.
RELEVANT MARKET:	The market which may be determined by the Commission either with reference to the relevant market, product market, or the relevant geographic market or with reference to both the markets.
RELEVANT GEOGRAPHIC MARKET:	A market comprising the area in which the conditions of competition for supply of goods, provision of services, or demand of goods or services are distinctly homogenous and can be distinguished from the conditions prevailing in the neighbouring areas.

Contd

Box 12.1 *Contd*

RELEVANT PRODUCT MARKET:	A market comprising all those products or services which are regarded as interchangeable or substitutable by the consumer, by reason of characteristics of the products or services, their prices, and intended use.
SERVICE:	Service of any description which is made available to potential users and includes the provision of services in connection with business of any industrial or commercial matters such as banking, communication, education, financing, insurance, chit funds, real estate, transport, storage, material treatment, processing, supply of electrical or other energy, boarding, lodging, entertainment, amusement, construction, repair, conveying of news or information, and advertising.
SHARES:	Shares in the share capital of a company carrying voting rights and includes: • Any security which entitles the holder to receive shares with voting rights • Stock except where a distinction between stock and share is expressed or implied
STATUTORY AUTHORITY:	Any authority, board, corporation, council, institute, university, or any other corporate body, established by or under any Central, State, or Provincial Act for the purposes of regulating production or supply of goods or provision of any services or markets thereof or any matter connected therewith or incidental thereto
TRADE:	Any trade, business, industry, profession, or occupation relating to the production, supply, distribution, storage, or control of goods and includes the provision of any services
TURNOVER:	Includes value of sale of goods or services

Words and expressions used but not defined in this Act and defined in the Companies Act, 1956 (1 of 1956) shall have the same meanings, respectively, assigned to them in that Act.

ANTI-COMPETITION AGREEMENTS*

TIE-IN: ARRANGEMENT	Any agreement requiring a purchaser of goods, as a condition of such purchase, to purchase some other goods.
EXCLUSIVE:	Any agreement, restricting in any manner, the purchaser in the course of his trade from acquiring or otherwise dealing in any goods other than those of the seller or any other person.
EXCLUSIVE: DISTRIBUTION AGREEMENT	Any agreement to limit, restrict, or with hold the output or supply of any goods or allocate any area or market for the disposal or sale of the goods.
REFUSAL TO: DEAL	Any agreement that restricts, or is likely to restrict, by any method, the persons or classes of persons to whom the goods are sold or from whom goods are bought.
RESALE: PRICE MAINTENANCE	Any agreement to sell goods on the condition that the prices to be charged on the resale by the purchaser shall be the prices stipulated by the seller, unless it is clearly stated that prices lower than those prices may be charged.

---

*See Secs 3–6 of the Act.

12.4 PROHIBITION OF CERTAIN AGREEMENTS, ABUSE OF DOMINANT POSITION, AND REGULATION OF COMBINATIONS

TEXT

No enterprise or association of enterprises or person or association of persons shall enter into any agreement in respect of production, supply, distribution, storage, acquisition or control of goods, or provision of services, which causes or is likely to cause an appreciable adverse effect on competition within India.

– The Competition Act, 2002, 3, 1

The earlier text, from Sec. 3(1) of the Act is about prohibition of entering into anti-competition agreements. Sec s 4 and 5 of the Act deal with prohibition of abuse of dominant position and combination of enterprises and person, respectively. They have been explained briefly as follows.

Anti-competition

Anti-competition agreements between companies are also generally known as anti-trust, indicating a breach of trust toward other competitors and all the stakeholders in society. The best of companies, such as Microsoft, Samsung, etc., have been embroiled in anti-trust cases. The anti-trust agreements which companies enter into are of two types: horizontal and vertical (Table 12.2). These agreements are in contravention of the provisions of the Competition Act, 2002.

Table 12.2   Anti-trust agreements

Horizontal	Vertical
Agreements made between two or more competing firms. This is called formation of a cartel which helps in determining the supply as well as the price. Companies dealing with a particular product may come together to form such cartels. Cartels cut competition, raise prices and earn unreasonably high profits leaving customers no option but to buy. Any agreements violating Sec. 3 (1) are void. The reasons (Sec. 3,3) are as follows: (a) directly or indirectly determines the purchase or sale prices (b) limits or controls production, supply, markets, technical development, investment, provision of services (c) shares the market, source of production, provision of services by way of allocation of geographical area of market, type of goods or services, or number of customers in the market, or any other similar way (d) directly or indirectly results in bid rigging or collusive bidding	These are agreements between firms relating to actual or potential relationship of purchasing or selling to each other with a purpose of dominating the market. Since such a relationship does not immediately affect the customers, it is considered as a lesser evil than the horizontal one. Any agreements violating Sec. 3 (1) are void, as are the following: (a) Tie-in arrangement (b) Exclusive supply agreement (c) Exclusive distribution agreement (d) Refusal to deal (e) Resale price maintenance

Prohibition of Abuse of Dominant Position

A dominant position implies that a company, due to its market share and control of infrastructure and technology, is so overriding that the competitors are unable to match its actions or control the prices.

Section 4 of the Competition Act, 2002 prohibits, directly or indirectly, the abuse of dominant position. Examples may be cited of a company that:

(a) directly or indirectly imposes unfair or discriminatory
- (i) conditions in purchase or sale of goods or service
- (ii) price in purchase or sale (including predatory price) of goods or service

(b) limits or restricts
- (i) production of goods, provision of services, or market thereof
- (ii) technical or scientific development relating to goods or services to the prejudice of consumers

(c) indulges in practice or practices resulting in denial of market access in any manner

(d) makes conclusion of contracts subject to acceptance by other parties of supplementary obligations which, by their nature or according to commercial usage, have no connection with the subject of such contracts

(e) uses its dominant position in one relevant market to enter into, or protect, other relevant markets

It must be understood very clearly by you as a manager that the Act is not against companies working hard to become leaders in their field. It is also not against companies becoming dominant in their area and even gaining bigger market share than their competitors. What the Act aims at is that such a dominant position must not be abused, as has been illustrated earlier.

Regulation of Combinations

The acquisition of one or more enterprises by one or more persons or merger or amalgamation of enterprises shall be a combination of such enterprises and persons or enterprises...

– The Competition Act, 2002, Sec. 5

Although the Act is not against any combinations of acquisition, merger, or amalgamations, but if these are strategized to beat competition and establish monopolies thus adversely affecting the competitors, then such activity is illegal. The following are some monetary limits specified for acquisition:

1. The parties jointly have:
   (a) In India, assets of ₹1,000 crore or turnover of ₹4,000 crore
   (b) In India or outside, assets of US $500 million or turnover US $1,500 million
2. The groups jointly have:
   (a) In India, assets ₹4,000 crore or turnover ₹12,000 crore
   (b) In India or outside, assets of US $2 billion or turnover of US $6 billion
3. Direct or indirect contract of acquisition of the acquirer has directly or indirectly control over:
   (a) In India, assets ₹4,000 crore or turnover ₹12,000 crore
   (b) In India or outside, the assets of US $2 billion or turnover of US $6 billion

4. Any enterprise after merger or amalgamation:
  (a) In India, assets ₹1,000 crore or turnover ₹3,000 crore
  (b) In India or outside, the assets are US $500 million or turnover of US $1,500 million

The earlier regulation is to prevent any adverse effect on the other competitors. It must be remembered that it is not mandatory to declare any of these acquisitions, mergers, and amalgamations to the Competition Commission of India. The Act also shows realism vis-à-vis the globalized business scenario by allowing the earlier mentioned activities internationally.

The breach of the Act results in heavy penalty:

If any person, being a party to a combination—
(a) Makes a statement which is false in any material particular, or knowing it to be false; or
(b) Omits to state any material particular knowing it to be material, such person shall be liable to a penalty which shall not be less than rupees fifty lakh and which may extend to rupees one crore, as may be determined by the Commission.

– The Competition Act, 2002, Sec. 44

MANAGER'S TAKEAWAY

- Free market economy is the new world order.
- Transparency is the best policy.

Case 12.1 clearly demonstrates the spirit of the Competition Act, 2002. In the interests of all the competitors in the market, it is watchful but at the same time shows openness to being questioned and challenged. It shows a policy of transparency and dialogue, rather than confrontation and penalization. The petitioners, however, seem to be still in the old frame of mind, where they have to fight by challenging jurisdiction and other strategies.

CASE 12.1 APPELLANT: Aamir Hussain Khan and Others VS RESPONDENT: The Director General Competition Commission of India and Others*

DATE OF JUDGEMENT: 10 August 2010

FACTS: The petitioners challenge the separate show cause notices dated 21 December 2009 issued by the Competition Commission of India, under Sec. 26(8) read with Sec. 3(3) of the Competition Act, 2002.

The commission established under the Competition Act, 2002 (hereinafter referred to as the Act) does not have any jurisdiction to initiate any such proceedings in respect of films for which the provisions of the Copyright Act, 1957 contain exhaustive provisions. The Director General in his response stated in the information that the members of these organizations: 1. United Producers/Distributors Forum (UPDF), 2. Association of Motion Pictures and T.V. Programme Producers (AMPTPP), 3. The Film and Television Producers Guild of India Ltd (FTPGI) are perpetrating cartel-like activity which is violative of provisions of Sec. 3(3) of Competition Act, 2002. It has also been alleged that these Associations/Enterprises, who jointly control approximately 100 per

*Aamir Hussain Khan vs The Director General, UPA 1 wp358-10; also see http://www.indiankanoon.org/doc/1313927/ (29 August 2011).

Contd

Case 12.1 *Contd*

cent of the market share for production and distribution of Hindi Motion Pictures exhibited in Multiplexes, by organizing themselves under the umbrella of UPDF, took a collective decision not to release films to the Multiplexes from 4 April 2009 onwards with the objective to extract a higher revenue sharing ratio from the members of the informant and this cartel-like activity has an appreciable adverse effect on competition in India.

JUDGEMENT: Petition dismissed; appeal allowed.

REASON: Mere issuance of a show cause notice under Sec. 26(8)/Sec. 27, like the issuance of a chargesheet in a departmental inquiry, cannot be treated as pre-judging the issue, merely because the petitioners had raised some of the legal contentions in the replies to the notice issued by the Director General of Investigation and thereafter also the Commission has issued show cause notices. That can never mean that the Competition Commission will not consider the petitioners' objections against maintainability of the proceedings.

The Petitions are dismissed only on the grounds that the petitions challenge show cause notices and that it is open to the petitioners to raise all available contentions, including preliminary objection against legality or otherwise of initiation of the proceedings against the petitioners.

12.5 COMPETITION COMMISSION OF INDIA

(1) With effect from such date as the Central Government may, by notification, appoint, there shall be established, for the purposes of this Act, a Commission to be called the 'Competition Commission of India'.

(2) The Commission shall be a body corporate by the name aforesaid having perpetual succession and a common seal with power, subject to the provisions of this Act, to acquire, hold, and dispose of property, both movable and immovable, and to contract and shall, by the said name, sue or be sued.

The head office of the Commission shall be at such place as the Central Government may decide from time to time.

The Commission may establish offices at other places in India.

– The Competition Act, 2002, Sec. 7, 1–4

Composition of the Commission

The Competition Commission of India (CCI) was established on 14 October 2003. It consists of a chairperson and six members appointed by the central government. These shall be persons of ability and integrity with specialization in subjects such as international trade, economics, business, finance, accountancy, management, and competition matters such as policy and competition. The chairman is chosen by a committee formed by the central government consisting of the Chief Justice of India, the Secretary of Ministry of Corporate Affairs, the Secretary in the Ministry of Law and Justice, and two other experts in the above-mentioned fields. The term of office is for five years. The office is terminated by resignation, insolvency, engagement in other employment, conviction, conflict of interest, abuse of position, inability, and death (Secs 9–11).

Apart from the earlier-mentioned appointed commission, the central government may by notification, appoint a Director General to assist the commission in conducting inquiry into contravention of the any of the provisions of the Act. Further Additional and Joint Deputy or Assistant Director General or such officers may also be appointed (Sec.16). These also will possess similar qualifications and abilities as that of the members of the commission.

Duties and powers of Competition Commission of India

Secs 18–20 deal with a list of duties consisting of inquiry into the practices of the companies, which may contravene the Competition Act. The following is a summary of the duties:

1. Eliminate practices having adverse effects on competition such as the potential level of competition through imports, level of combination in the market, the substitutes available in the market, level of vertical integration, failing businesses, etc.
2. Promote and sustain competition.
3. Protect the interests of the consumers.
4. Ensure freedom of trade carried on by other participants in the market.
5. Conduct inquiry into abuse of dominant position and about combinations.

Procedures

According to Sec. 26 of the Act:

1. On receipt of reference from central government or a state government or any statutory authority, the Director General will commence an investigation of a prima facie case.
2. The Director General will then submit a report to the Competition Commission of India.
3. The Commission then forwards a copy of the report to the concerned parties.
4. If the Director General's office reports that there is no contravention of the Act, the commission shall invite objection or suggestions from the central government, the state government, or the statutory authority, as the case may be.
5. If these agree with the Director General, then the matter is closed. If the said suggestions and objections are made, then the case shall proceed with further inquiry.
6. The time limit for inquiry is one year.

Powers

The Commission has powers to regulate its own procedure (Sec. 36) as follows:

1. It shall be guided by the principles of natural justice and the rules and regulations of the central government.
2. It will exercise same powers as a civil court under the Code of Civil Procedure, 1908:
(a) Summoning and enforcing the attendance of any person and examining him on oath.
(b) Requiring the discovery and production of documents.
(c) Receiving evidence on affidavit.
(d) Issuing commissions for the examination of witnesses or documents.

(e) Requisitioning, subject to the provisions of Secs 123 and 124 of the Indian Evidence Act, 1872 (1 of 1872), any public record or document or copy of such record or document from any office. (Sec. 36, 2)

3. The Commission may call upon the services of the professionals and experts as it deems necessary. (Sec. 36, 3)

4. The Commission may direct any person to produce before the Director General or any other officer authorized by it, such books or documents or related material to be examined. (Sec. 36, 4)

5. The Commission has the powers to rectify its orders, or any mistake apparent from the records. (Sec. 38)

6. Execution of orders: The Commission has the powers to impose monetary penalties. (Sec. 39)

Penalties

Secs 42–48 of the Act deal with penalties, summarized in Table 12.3.

Table 12.3 Offence and penalty

Offence	Penalty
Contravention of the orders of the Commission	Imprisonment up to one year and fine up to ₹1 lakh or both
Failure to comply with the directions of the Commission and the Director General	For every day of default ₹1 lakh
For making false statements or omitting to furnish material information about being party to combination	Above ₹50 lakh to ₹1 crore
Offences relating to furnishing information such as misstatement, omission of material, alteration, etc.	Up to ₹10 lakh

Competition appellate tribunal

The tribunal is established and governed by Sec. 53A–53U. It deals with the complete establishment, composition, and functioning of the civil code procedure as mentioned earlier for the Commission. It consists of a highly reputed legal expert judge who has the ability to be the chairman, in association with two of its members also of the legal fraternity. The term is of five years.

The Appellate Tribunal shall have, for the purposes of discharging its functions under this Act, the same powers as are vested in a civil court under the Code of Civil Procedure, 1908 (5 of 1908) while trying a suit in respect of the following matters, namely:
(a) Summoning and enforcing the attendance of any person and examining him on oath
(b) Requiring the discovery and production of documents

(c) Receiving evidence on affidavit

(d) Subject to the provisions of Secs 123 and 124 of the Indian Evidence

(e) Act, 1872 (1 of 1872), requisitioning any public record or document or copy of such record or document from any office

(f) Issuing commissions for the examination of witnesses or documents

(g) Reviewing its decisions

(h) Dismissing a representation for default or deciding it ex parte

(i) Setting aside any order of dismissal of any representation for default or any order passed by it ex parte

(j) Any other matter which may be prescribed

– The Competition Act, 2002, Sec. 53

Case 12.2 has become a landmark for the protection of customers. The Delhi High Court has dismissed a bunch of writ petitions filed by DLF Ltd and its related entities against the orders of CCI under Secs 26(1) and 33 of the Competition Act. Pursuant to the judgement of Supreme Court in CCI vs SAIL, an order of CCI under Sec. 26(1) directing the Director General to carry out an investigation into a matter that cannot be appealed before the Appellate Tribunal. Therefore, interested parties seek to challenge such order under Sec. 26(1) of the Competition Act before writ courts under Article 226 of the Constitution.

CASE 12.2   APPELLANT: DLF Limited and Others   vs   RESPONDENT: Additional Director General*

DATE OF JUDGEMENT: 4 January 2011

FACTS: The challenge in these writ petitions is to the order dated 20 May 2010 passed by the Competition Commission of India ('CCI') under Sec. 26 (1) of the Competition Act, 2002 ('Act'), an order dated 20 September 2010 passed by the CCI under Sec. 33 of the Act and an order dated 2 December 2010 passed by the CCI directing a further inquiry. The further relief is for quashing of the investigation report dated 13 October 2010 of the Additional Director General ('ADG') of the CCI. An alternative prayer is for a direction to the CCI to decide the jurisdictional issues raised by the Petitioners as a preliminary objection in accordance with the principles of natural justice. A further alternative prayer is for a direction to the CCI not to proceed with the inquiry till all the documents are supplied to the Petitioners.

JUDGEMENT: Petitions disposed with order (below)

REASON: It is directed that upon the documents being provided to the Petitioners on or before 7 January 2011, the Petitioners will be granted two weeks' time thereafter to file their objections to the ADG's Investigation Report. In other words, the objections will be filed on or before 21 January 2011. The CCI WP (Civil) will reschedule the hearing fixed for 6 January 2011 to 14 February 2011 or any other date as soon thereafter as may be convenient to the CCI. In view of the need for the proceedings before

*See http://lobis.nic.in/dhc/SMD/judgement/06-01-2011/SMD04012011CW222011.pdf; also see http://indiankanoon.org/doc/1694565/ (1 September 2011).

Contd

Case 12.2 *Contd*

> the CCI to be concluded expeditiously, as mandated by the SAIL judgement,* it is directed that the said time schedule should be strictly adhered to by the parties.
>
> A distinction was drawn, however, between this and an adjudicatory speaking order which was to be passed by the CCI 'upon due application of mind' by responding to 'all contentions raised before it by the rival party'.
>
> _____
> *See the Chapter End Case where the Court distinguished between the order to be passed by CCI while forming a prima facie opinion under Sec. 26, 1 and other orders.

The customers who had invested with DLF housing were aggrieved. They alleged that DLF was abusing its dominant position by delaying delivery of apartments and changing its plans. For instance, it had increased the number of floors in the project without informing the people who had already bought flats there. They also complained that the agreements that the apartment buyers were made to sign were very one-sided because they were drafted in such a way that consumers could not understand certain terms and DLF had cleverly retained the power to change the terms. Further, DLF had sold the apartments even before getting the appropriate clearances from the authorities.

 MANAGER'S TAKEAWAY

- Competition advocacy is the new mantra.
- Market dominance is an outdated idea.

SUMMARY

Introduction and Interpretation

- Competition Act, 2002 replaced MRTP Act, 1969 with the objective to promote and sustain completion in markets and protect the interests of the consumers.
- A Commission and a Tribunal to enable the objectives were established.

Prohibition of Certain Agreements, Abuse of Dominant Position, and Regulation of Combinations

- The Act wants to safeguard free trade by prohibiting certain strategies by the companies to form cartels or such strategies which are detrimental to competition. Horizontal and vertical agreements are such strategies which restrict trade, hinder fair pricing and also obstruct the natural course of supply, and demand due to controls exercised by the monopolistic behaviour of combined strength of the companies.

- In similar fashion, all kinds of market domination to the detriment of other competitors is prohibited.
- The Act does not discourage market leadership or the growth in market share; what it actively prohibits is the abuse of such leadership or dominance.

Competition Commission of India and the Competition Appellate Tribunal

- The Act is empowered to function through two high-powered institutions:
  - The Competition Commission of India which may act upon the complaints by the aggrieved competitors and consumers or may launch inquiry on its own upon observation that the objects of the Act are endangered.
  - The Competition Appellate Tribunal is created to supply legal remedy to the aggrieved. It is hoped that the Tribunal functions efficiently and promptly.

EXERCISES

Introduction and Interpretation

(i) What do you understand by the concept of competition in terms of market competition? Give reasons for its desirability or undesirability with examples.

(ii) What constitutes competition policy? Site some examples in the competition law which is the result of such policies.

Prohibition of Certain Agreements, Abuse of Dominant Position and Regulation of Combinations

(i) Which of the following agreements are competitive and anti-competitive?
- Agreement to limit production and supply
- Agreement to allocate markets
- Agreement to fix price
- Bid rigging or collusive bidding
- Conditional purchase/sale (tie-in arrangement)
- Exclusive supply/distribution arrangement
- Resale price maintenance
- Refusal to deal

Hint: All are anti-competitive.

(ii) A firm, after conducting the market survey of its product, found that if it acquired its nearest competitor, it would be the market leader in that product. It proceeded to acquire the other company as per all the legal requirements in the Company Law, 1956. It received a notice from the Competition Commission of India. What would be found in the notice?
Hint: See Sec. 6 of the Act.

(iii) The builders in a city tacitly come to an arrangement to manage the prices of real estate; this they do without any formal or written agreement.

After you have bought a piece of real estate to run a franchise business, you learn from your fellow traders about the silent fraud. What remedy does the buyer have?
Hint: There is remedy; see Secs 2 (b) and 3 of the Act.

(iv) What constitutes abuse of dominance?

(v) What do you understand by regulation of combinations?

Competition Commission of India

(i) The Central Government or State Government cannot make a reference to the CCI for inquiry.
Hint: It can; see Sec.19 (1) b of the Act.

(ii) A company complained to the CCI about the unfair means adopted by another company and its subsidiary in winning the contracts and depriving it and others from such a business opportunity. Can the CCI take up the case?
Hint: Yes; see Sec. 29 (1) of the Act.

(iii) The Competition Appellate Tribunal gave an adverse ruling against a respondent company where CCI was the petitioner. The aggrieved party moved the High Court, pleading that the time given by CCI to file the requisite information was inadequate. The CCI countered saying that it had given the stipulated time as per the Competition Act, 2002. What are the chances of the aggrieved company?
Hint: See procedure for investigation 29 (1) of the Act; also see chapter end case in this chapter.

(iv) What are the orders that the Commission can pass in the case of anti-competitive agreements and abuse of dominance?

(v) What are the duties and powers of the CCI

DEVELOPMENT OF LEGAL EDGE

Research Project

Choose a segment of industry or service in your city and:

- Conduct a survey to determine the dominant company.

- Determine the strategies followed by the company against its competitors.

- Determine the different income groups and the manner in which they fare with the said product or service.

- Determine the economic and social costs or gains.

Film for Discussion

Anti TRUST, written by Howard Franklin and directed by Peter Howitt (2001)

It is not difficult to find out the allusions made in the movie to Microsoft and its founder Bill Gates. However, your discussion should focus on the issues not only big companies—Google, Apple, and others—who are facing lawsuits but also about the Indian companies who are now global leaders in their respective businesses.

Manager's Special Interest

To appreciate competition, discover its various meanings for yourself by reading and compiling the history of competition law.

FURTHER READING

1. The Competition Act, 2002: http://www.cci.gov.in/images/media/competition_act/act2002.pdf?
2. CUTS International and National Law University Jodhpur, (2008). 'Study of Cartel Case Laws in Select Jurisdictions, Learnings for the Competition Commission of India', http:// www.cci.gov.in/images/media/completed/cartel_report1_20080812115152. pdf.
3. Vijay Kumar Chaurasia (2011). 'International Cooperation: Application and Enforcement' Issues, http://www.cci.gov.in/images/media/ResearchRe-ports/VijayKrChaurasia.pdf.

CASE STUDY — SAIL IN TROUBLED WATERS

The advantages of perfect competition are three-fold: allocative efficiency, which ensures the effective allocation of resources; productive efficiency, which ensures that costs of production are kept at a minimum; and dynamic efficiency, which promotes innovative practices. These factors by and large have been accepted all over the world as the guiding principles for effective implementation of competition law.[1]

The Law

Section 19(1)	Section 26(1)
The Commission may inquire into any alleged contravention of the provisions contained in sub-Sec. (1) of Sec. 3 or sub-Sec. (1) of Sec. 4, either on its own motion or on: (a) 29[receipt of any information, in such manner and] accompanied by such fee as may be determined by regulations, from any person, consumer, or their association or trade association; or (b) A reference made to it by the Central Government or a State Government or a statutory authority.	On receipt of a reference from the Central Government or a State Government or a statutory authority or on its own knowledge or information received under Sec. 19, if the Commission is of the opinion that there exists a prima facie case, it shall direct the Director General to cause an investigation to be made into the matter: Provided that if the subject matter of information received is, in the opinion of the Commission, substantially the same as or has been covered by any previous information received, then the new information may be clubbed with the previous information.

---

[1]Quote from the judgement: Competition Commission of India vs Steel Authority of India, http://www.indiankanoon.org/doc/864375/ (1 September 2011).

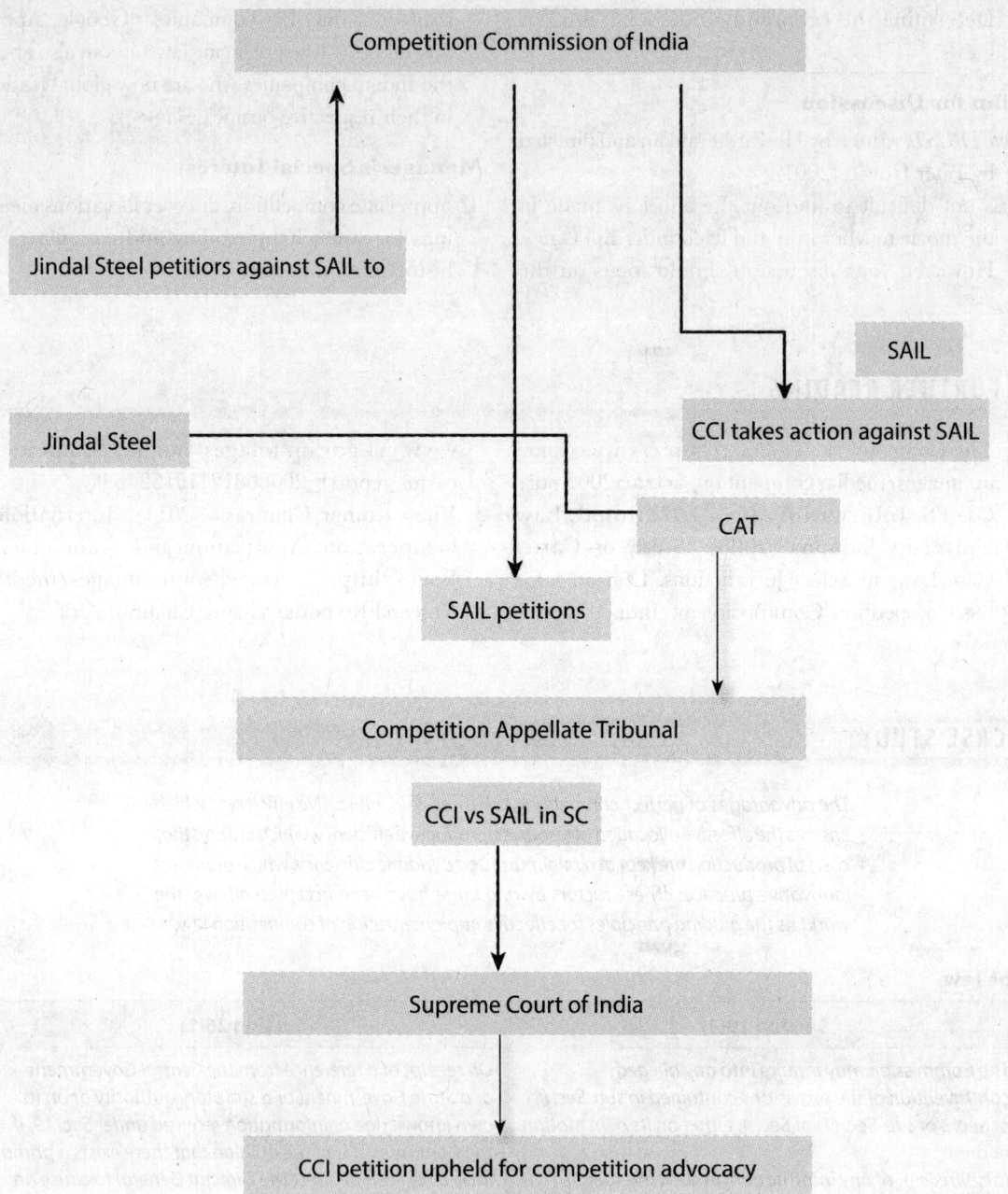

Competition Commission of India

Jindal Steel petitiors against SAIL to

SAIL

Jindal Steel

CCI takes action against SAIL

CAT

SAIL petitions

Competition Appellate Tribunal

CCI vs SAIL in SC

Supreme Court of India

CCI petition upheld for competition advocacy

The Words

Jindal Steel had led a complaint before CCI alleging anti-competitive practices and abusive dominance by SAIL while it entered into an exclusive supply agreement with Indian Railways. Upon receipt of the complaint, CCI issued a notice to SAIL to furnish certain information within two weeks from the date of receipt of such notice. SAIL requested for an extension of six weeks to file the required information. CCI, in its meeting, deliberated on the request and decided not to grant further extension. In the said meeting, CCI also formed a prima facie opinion on the existence of the case and directed the Director General to inquire into the matter pursuant to its powers under Sec. 26(1) of the Competition Act, 2002. SAIL challenged this direction before the Tribunal, claiming that CCI could not have formed a prima facie case without hearing it first. SAIL also contended that CCI has not recorded any reasons while forming the prima facie case and that the time provided by CCI to file information was inadequate. While filing the appeal before Tribunal, SAIL did not plead CCI as a party. CCI, thus, filed an application before Tribunal for as pleading itself as a necessary and proper party and also assailed the very maintainability of appeal.

The Tribunal, in its detailed order, holding that even the direction to inquire was appealable under Sec. 53 A (1) of the Act noted that CCI could not have directed the Director General to inquire into the complaint without having first heard SAIL. It further noted that CCI was neither a necessary nor a proper party in appeals filed by an aggrieved party before the Tribunal. The Tribunal also noted that CCI did not record any reasons while declining to grant extension of time and hence it in violation of principles of natural justice.

The Case

In the Supreme Court of India

Bench: K.S. Radhakrishnan, Swatanter Kumar
Competition Commission of India vs. Steel Authority of India Ltd (SAIL) Date: 9 September 2010

The Questions to be Determined

1. Whether the directions passed by the Commission in exercise of its powers under Sec. 26(1) of the Act forming a prima facie opinion would be appealable in terms of Sec. 53A(1) of the Act?
2. What is the ambit and scope of power vested with the Commission under Sec. 26(1) of the Act and whether the parties, including the informant or the affected party, are entitled to notice or hearing, as a matter of right, at the preliminary stage of formulating an opinion as to the existence of the prima facie case?
3. Whether the Commission would be a necessary, or at least a proper, party in the proceedings before the Tribunal in an appeal preferred by any party?
4. At what stage and in what manner can the Commission exercise powers vested in it under Sec. 33 of the Act to pass temporary restraint orders?

5. Whether it is obligatory for the Commission to record reasons for formation of a prima facie opinion in terms of Sec. 26(1) of the Act?
6. What directions, if any, need to be issued by the Court to ensure proper compliance in regard to procedural requirements while keeping in mind the scheme of the Act and the legislative intent?

The principles

Legislative intent

The provisions of Secs 26 and 53A of the Act clearly depict the legislative intent that the framers never desired that all orders, directions, and decisions should be appealable to the Tribunal. Sec. 53A, against a direction for investigation, as that itself is an appealable right independent of any decision or order which may be made or passed by the Commission.

Clarity of language

The language of Sec. 53A is clear and the statute does not demand that we should substitute 'or' or read this word interchangeably for achieving the object of the Act. On the contrary, the objective of the Act is more than clear that the legislature intended to provide a very limited right to appeal. The orders which can be appealed against have been specifically stipulated by unambiguously excluding the provisions which the legislature did not intend to make appealable under the provisions of the Act.

Natural right vs statutory right

It is well known that right of appeal is not a natural or inherent right. It cannot be assumed to exist unless expressly provided for by statute. Being a creature of statute, remedy of appeal must be legitimately traceable to the statutory provisions. Sec. 13 provides a right of appeal to a party aggrieved by an order under sub-Sec. (2) of Sec. 11 or Sec. 12 and no other. The principle of 'appeal being a statutory right and no party having a right to file appeal except in accordance with the prescribed procedure' is now well-settled.

Expressum facit cessare tacitum

A statute is stated to be the edict of Legislature. It expresses the will of Legislature and the function of the Court is to interpret the document according to the intent of those who made it. It is a settled rule of construction of statute that the provisions should be interpreted by applying the plain rule of construction.

The Courts normally would not imply anything that is inconsistent with the words expressly used by the statute. *Expressum facit cessare tacitum*—'Express mention of one thing implies the exclusion of the other' (Expression precludes implication).

Reason to appeal

One of the parties before the Commission would, in any case, be aggrieved by an order where the Commission grants or declines to grant extension of time. Thus, every such order passed by the Commission would have to be treated as appealable as per the contention raised by the respondent before us as well as the view taken by the Tribunal.

The meaning and language of Sec. 53A of the Act and also on the principle is that they are not orders which determine the rights of the parties. No appeal can lie against such an order. Still the parties are not remediless as, when they prefer an appeal against the final order, they can always take up grounds to challenge the interim orders/directions passed by the Commission in the memorandum of appeal. Such an approach would be in consonance with the procedural law prescribed in Order XLIII Rule 1A and even other provisions of Code of Civil Procedure.

Litigant has a right to know

A litigant who approaches the Court with any grievance in accordance with law is entitled to know the reasons for grant or rejection of his prayer. Reasons are the soul of orders. A judgement without reasons causes prejudice to the person against whom it is pronounced, as that litigant is unable to know the ground which weighed with the Court in rejecting his claim and also causes impediments in his taking adequate and appropriate grounds before the higher court in the event of challenge to that judgement.

The Legal Reasoning

The above principles that are consistent with the settled canons of law would be adopted in this case. Against the backdrop of these determinants, we may refer to the provisions of the Act. Sec. 26, under its different sub-sections, that requires the Commission to issue various directions, take decisions, and pass orders, some of which are even appealable before the Tribunal.

Even if it is a direction under any of the provisions and not a decision, conclusion, or order passed on merits by the Commission, it is expected that the same would be supported by some reasoning. At the stage of forming a prima facie view, as required under Sec. 26(1) of the act, the Commission may not really record detailed reasons, but must express its mind in no uncertain terms that it is of the view that the prima facie case exists, requiring issuance of direction for investigation to the Director General. Such a view should be recorded with reference to the information furnished to the Commission.

The power under Sec. 33 of the Act, to pass a temporary restraint order, can only be exercised by the Commission when it has formed prima facie opinion and directed investigation in terms of Sec. 26(1) of the Act, as is evident from the language of this provision read with Regulation 18(2) of the Regulations.

Having examined various legal issues arising in the present case, we will now revert back to the facts of the case in hand. It is clear that Jindal Steel, the informant, had made a reference to the Commission. The Commission had initiated proceedings and asked for further information from the informant and, thereafter, had even issued notice calling upon SAIL to submit its views and comments.

From the records, it is clear that parties had appeared before the Commission. SAIL had failed to file the reply and prayed for extension of time, which was declined by the Commission in its order dated 8 December 2009. The Director General was asked to conduct the investigation, but liberty was granted to SAIL to file its views and comments during the pendency of the investigation. Since further time was declined, SAIL preferred an appeal before the Tribunal, which resulted in passing of the order impugned in the present appeal.

It must be rejected that the Commission is not a necessary or proper party before the Tribunal. On the contrary, the Regulations and even the interest of justice demands that for complete and effective adjudication, the Commission be added as a necessary and proper party in the proceedings before the Tribunal. The direction issued by the Commission was set aside by the Tribunal and further time was granted to SAIL to file its further reply in addition to what has been filed on 15 December 2009, and the Tribunal then directed the Commission to consider all such material and record a fresh decision.

There is no statutory obligation on the Commission to issue notice for grant of hearing to the parties at the stage of forming an opinion under Sec. 26(1) of the Act unless, upon due application of mind, it finds it necessary to invite parties or experts to render assistance to and produce documents before the Commission at that stage. One cannot agree with the view expressed by the Tribunal that the inquiry commences as soon as the aspects highlighted in sub-Sec. (1) to Sec. 19 are fulfilled and brought to the notice of the Commission.

It is obvious that Regulation 18(2) was not brought to the notice of the Tribunal which resulted in error of law, particularly, when examined in the light of other provisions and scheme of the Act as well. The Commission, vide its order dated 8 December 2009, had, for reasons stated therein, declined the extension of time to SAIL. This order of the Commission cannot be stated to be without jurisdiction or suffering from any apparent error of law.

However, the Tribunal, in exercise of its judicial discretion, had interfered with the said order and granted further time to SAIL unconditionally. SAIL should pay a sum of ₹25,000 to the informant for seeking extension of time. The cost shall be conditional, where, after the additional reply filed by SAIL is taken on record, the Commission shall apply its mind to form a prima facie view in terms of Sec. 26(1) of the Act, if the report of the Director General has not been received as yet. In the event that the report prepared by the Director General during the period 8 December 2009 to 11 January, 2010 has been received, the Commission shall proceed in accordance with the provisions of the Act and the principles of law enunciated in this judgement giving proper notice to the informant as well as to SAIL and pass appropriate orders.

The Directions

The Court Order was as follows:

A. Regulation 16 prescribes limitation of 15 days for the Commission to hold its first ordinary meeting to consider whether prima facie case exists or not and in cases of alleged anti-competitive agreements and/or abuse of dominant position, the opinion on existence of prima facie case has to be formed within 60 days. Though the time period for such acts of the Commission has been specified, still it is expected of the Commission to hold its meetings and record its opinion about the existence or otherwise of a prima facie case within a period much shorter than the stated period.

B. All proceedings, including investigation and inquiry, should be completed by the Commission/Director General most expeditiously and while ensuring that the time taken in completion of such proceedings does not adversely affect any of the parties as well as the open market in purposeful implementation of the provisions of the Act.

C. Wherever during the course of inquiry the Commission exercises its jurisdiction to pass interim orders, it should pass a final order in that behalf as expeditiously as possible and, in any case, not later than 60 days.

D. The Director General in terms of Regulation 20 is expected to submit his report within a reasonable time. No inquiry by the Commission can proceed any further in the absence of the report by the Director General in terms of Sec. 26(2) of the Act. The reports by the Director General should be submitted within the time as directed by the Commission but in all cases not later than 45 days from the date of passing of directions in terms of Sec. 26(1) of the Act.

E. The Commission as well as the Director General shall maintain complete 'confidentiality' as envisaged under Sec. 57 of the Act and Regulation 35 of the Regulations. Wherever the person's confidentiality is breached, the aggrieved party certainly has the right to approach the Commission for issuance of appropriate directions in terms of the provisions of the Act and the Regulations in force.

The Judgement

- The scheme and essence of the Act and the Regulations are clearly suggestive of speedy and expeditious disposal of the matter.
- The Competent Authority shall frame Regulations providing a definite, time frame for completion of investigation, inquiry, and final disposal of the matters pending before the Commission. Till such Regulations are framed, the period specified of 60 days (see Directives C) shall remain in force and we expect all the concerned authorities to adhere to the period specified.
- This appeal is partially allowed. The order dated 15 February 2010 passed by the Tribunal is modified to the above extent. The Commission shall proceed with the case in accordance with law and the principles enunciated (in the directives).

The Final Word

Competition Act, 2002 is fairly a new legislation until it matures with case law. In the above case, the Court clearly wanted to set a precedent. Initially, it remarked on the new order of the globalized and competitive economy. It dwelt on the merits of competition with its social and economic consequences.

The court expounded various legal principles upon which it would base its judgement. It clearly defined the scope and powers of the CCI and the Tribunal and their statutory nature where appeals are not a natural right. However, not giving an opportunity to explain to the litigant without adequate time cannot serve the purpose of the existence of these agencies.

The Court passed its judgement not only basing itself upon the principles it annunciated but also giving clear directives how the respective parties must conduct themselves.

Discussion Questions

1. Enumerate the number of parties in this case and explain their relationship to each other.

2. What are the main issues dealt in this case?

3. Examine each principle and its applicability to the case.

4. Are you sure that natural justice is not legal justice?

5. What would you do differently if you were the manager of SAIL or Jindal Steel?

6. Are the directives of the Court realistic? How would you think of them from a manager's perspective?

7. Would you make any amendments to the Court's judgement? Explain with reasons and precedents from other cases.

Going Beyond

1. Can you detect a new attitude that the Supreme Court adopted in this case? Analyse your answer if 'Yes' or give reasons if your answer is 'No'.

2. Why is the concept of natural justice important?

3. How would you debate the proposition: Monopoly is good for the stability of the economy?

LEGAL LUMINARY

JUSTICE ARIJIT PASAYAT—CHAIRPERSON, COMPETITION APPELLATE TRIBUNAL

A highly learned man, a scholar and an indefatigable worker, Justice Pasayat came into the limelight during the controversial Special Investigation Probe of the Gujarat riots of 2002. Normally, in the ordinary course of his profession, he had dealt with taxation, corporate affairs and, Constitutional matters. However, it has been an extraordinary run to have delivered over 2500 judgements as a judge of the Supreme Court. It has been considered a world record.

The Competition Act, 2002 lists a wide range of qualifications for the chairperson and members of the Appellate Tribunal such as:

(1) The Chairperson of the Appellate Tribunal shall be a person, who is, or has been a Judge of the Supreme Court or the Chief Justice of a High Court.

(2) A member of the Appellate Tribunal shall be a person of ability, integrity, and standing having special knowledge of, and professional experience of not less than twenty five years in, competition matters including competition law and policy, international trade, economics, business, commerce, law, *finance, accountancy, management, industry, public affairs, administration or in any other matter which in the opinion of the Central Government, may be useful to the Appellate Tribunal.*

– The Competition Act, 2002, 53 D, (1&2)

Justice Pasayat's curriculum vitae has it all.

Educational

- Graduation with Honours in English
- First rank in LLB from M.S. College, Cuttack
- Degree in B.Com.
- Excelled in Charted Accountancy (CA)

Professional

- Practised law since 1968 especially in the field of taxation and Constitutional Law
- Appointed Additional Judge of the Orissa High Court in 1989
- Permanent Judge of the same court in 1990
- Acting Chief Justice of Orissa in 1999 for Legal Education
- Chief Justice of Kerala High Court in 1999
- Chief Justice of Delhi High Court in 2000

Legal Luminary *Contd*

- Judge of the Supreme Court in 2001 till his retirement in 2009
- Presently, the Chairperson of the Competition Appellate Tribunal

Arijit Pasayat was born in 1944 in Orissa. He is the son Biswanath Pasayat, an eminent jurist from Orissa and a well-known leader of the freedom movement of India. The State of Orissa has honoured its son of the soil with a Doctorate in Law from Utkal University, Bhubaneshwar, and LLD from Fakir Mohan University, Balasore.

The Sick Industrial Companies Repeal Act, 2003 and Guidelines on Insolvency

Principle: *Id solum nostrum quod debitisdeductis nostrum est.*

That only is ours which remains to us after deduction of debts.

CHAPTER OUTLINE

- Introduction and Interpretation
- The Sick Industrial Companies Act,
- 1985 and 2003 within the Context of The Companies Act, 1956
- Agencies to Deal with Sick Companies and Dispute Resolution

- Guidelines on Insolvency
- *Case Study:* Second Thouhgts on Industrial Sickness
- *Legal Luminary:* Vettath Balakrishna Eradi

13.1 INTRODUCTION AND INTERPRETATION

This Act may be called the Sick Industrial Companies (Special Provisions) Act, 1985.

– Sec. 1 of the Act

This Act may be called the Sick Industrial Companies (Special Provisions) Repeal Act, 2003.

– Sec. 1 of the Act

To begin with, the Act of 1985 and its Repeal Act in 2003 would initially seem confusing. Therefore, to avoid confusion and clarify doubts, a brief overview of these two short Acts is provided in the following paragraph.

A committee of experts was formed in 1981 under the chairmanship of Shri T. Tiwari to make recommendations to the government regarding the alarming growth rate of sick industrial units in both the government and private sectors. Based on the recommendations, a law was enacted titled Sick Industrial Companies (Special Provisions) Act, 1985. It came to be popularly known by its acronym SICA. In 1987, the Board of Industrial and Financial Reconstruction (BIFR) and the Appellate Authority for Industrial and Financial Reconstruction (AAIFR) were established. Furthermore, in 1991 and 1993 more amendments were introduced to determine the industrial problems or *sickness*.

The SICA seemed to have problems as increasingly companies took this route to exit. This Act not only saved them from difficult legal procedures but also allowed them to obtain financial relief which, in turn, burdened the banks. Another factor that forced reform was the piling up of the non-performing assets (NPAs). Hence, in 2003, the Sick Industrial Companies (Special Provisions) Repeal Act was enacted. This replaced the institutions created by the SICA, and the National Company Law Tribunal (NCLT) was responsible for their revival and rehabilitation. Furthermore, any appeal against the order of this agency would be expedited by the National Company Law Appellate Tribunal (NCLAT). You are quite familiar with the NCLT from Chapters 8–10 that deal with the Companies Act, 1956.

Consequently, now you should clearly realize how several laws are inter-related. The Companies Act, 1956, is the core of corporatization in India. To augment it as per requirement, it has been amended several times and in the near future is scheduled to be replaced by a new Act. However, there have been several other Acts to support this Act. The Sick Industrial Companies (Special Provisions) Act, 1985, and its Repeal Act in 2003 are mere phases of its evolution. Therefore, in this chapter both these Acts will be considered in tandem to understand the complete import of the legislative intent.

Objectives of SICA

1. To evaluate the economic viability of sick industrial companies with a view either to rehabilitate them, if the public interest so demanded and if their rehabilitation was possible, or to close them down, if continuing them would be impossible
2. To stop the continued drain of public and private resources for the overall economy of the country
3. To protect employment as far as possible

Industrial Sickness

'Sick industrial company' means an industrial company (being a company registered for not less than five years) which has, at the end of any financial year, accumulated losses equal to or exceeding its entire net worth.

[Explanation—To clear doubts, it is hereby declared that an industrial company existing immediately before the commencement of the Sick Industrial Companies (Special Provision) Amendment Act, 1993 (12 of 1994), registered for not less than five years and having at the end of any financial year accumulated losses equal to or exceeding its entire net worth, shall be deemed to be a sick industrial company.]

– SICA, Sec. 3, 1(0)

Sec. 23 of SICA clarifies the meaning of industrial sickness. It is the accumulated losses of an industrial company that, at the end of any financial year, have resulted in a depletion of 50 per cent or more of peak net worth of the immediately preceding four financial years. A company in such a financial position is considered to be a potentially sick industrial company. The following factors categorize a company as sick:

(a) A company should be engaged in any scheduled industry, any industry specified in First Schedule to the Industries (Development and Regulation) Act, 1951.

(b) Scheduled industries include metallurgical industries, telecommunication, transportation, chemicals, textiles but not financial services and software technology.

(c) To avail the criteria of 'sickness', such a company should have, at the end of any financial year, accumulated losses equal to or exceeding its entire net worth.

Causes of Sickness

According to the Tiwari Report, the causes of industrial sickness are distinguished and classified as enumerated in Table 13.1.

Table 13.1   Internal and external causes of industrial sickness

Internal	External
Planning Inadequate technical know-how, location disadvantage, outdated production process	*Infrastructural bottlenecks* Non-availability/ irregular supply of critical raw materials or other inputs, chronic power shortage, transport problems
Economic viability High cost of inputs, uneconomic size of project, under-estimation of financial requirements, undue large investment in faxed assets, overestimation of demand	*Finance constraints* Owing to credit restrains policy, delay in disbursement of loan by the government, unfavourable investments, fear of nationalization
Implementation Cost overruns resulting from delays in obtaining licenses/sanctions, etc., inadequate mobilization of finance.	*Government control, policies, etc.* Price controls, fiscal duties, abrupt changes in government policies, procedural delays on the part of the financial/ licensing/other controlling or regulating authorities (banks, RBI, financial institutions, government departments, licensing authorities, Competition Commission, etc.).
Production management Inappropriate product mix, poor quality control, high costs, lack of adequate and timely modernization, high wastage, and poor capacity utilization	*Marketing constraints* Liberal licensing policies, restrain of purchase by bulk purchasers, changes in global marketing scenario, excessive tax, and market recession
Labour management Excessive high wage structure, inefficient handling of labour problems, excessive manpower, lack of component personnel	*Extraneous factors* Natural calamities, political situations such as war, strikes, multiplicity of labour unions
Marketing management Dependence on limited number of customers, poor sales realization, defective pricing policy, weak market organization, lack of market feedback and market research, lack of knowledge of marketing techniques	
Financial management Poor resource management and financial planning, liberal dividend policy, application of funds for unauthorized purposes, deficiency of funds, overtrading, inadequate working capital, lack of effective collection machinery	
Management Over-centralization, lack of professionalism, lack of management information system, lack of adequate controls, lack of timely diversification, excessive expenditure on R&D, incompetent and dishonest management	

Case 13.1 is an example of how some companies took the fraudulent route to take undue advantage of SICA. Once the claim gets admitted under SICA, the company may claim relief from all legal procedures against it enforced by its opponent.

13.2 THE SICK INDUSTRIAL COMPANIES ACT AND THE REPEAL ACT

The previous section discussed how the best intentions of the legislator in the provisions of the Act were misused and abused. Next, SICA and its Repeal Act within the context of the Companies Act, 1956 will be considered comparatively to understand how the loopholes in the original Act are plugged by the Repeal Act. It will provide deeper knowledge into this law and on how to use its provisions as per the legislative intent **a**nd not misuse it.

MANAGER'S TAKEAWAY

- A manager nurtures the company as a mother would nurture her child.
- A mother does not abandon her sick child.

The above development as described in Table 13.2 proves the importance of ongoing reforms in company law. The failure of SICA was not due to the good intent of the legislator but due to the outdated nature of the proposals. A holistic view of the Indian industry and markets is necessary before taking steps to legal provisions. The motivation emanating from laws should help the industry to succeed and should not attempt to take recourse to insolvency and closure.

CASE 13.1

PETITIONER: **Saketh India Ltd** vs RESPONDENT: **W. Diamond India Ltd***

DATE OF JUDGEMENT: **30 April 2010**

FACTS: Appellant sought the rejection of the plaint under Order VII Rule 11(d) of the CPC on the ground that it had been declared a sick industrial unit in terms of Sec. 3(1)(o) of the Sick Industrial Companies (special Provisions) Act, 1985 (SICA).

JUDGEMENT: Appeal dismissed

REASON: We must immediately take note of the fact that SICA has been repealed by the Sick Industrial Companies (Special Provisions) Repeal Act, 2003. Although it is yet to be notified, it is significant that provisions akin to Sec. 22 are conspicuous by their absence in the new scheme of revival of sick companies inserted in form of Part VIA, namely, 'Revival and Rehabilitation of Sick Industrial Companies.'

A holistic reading of Sec. 22(1) of SICA makes it manifestly clear that the Parliament's intention was to insulate sick companies only against proceedings for winding up or for execution, or distress or the like or for enforcement of any security or guarantee. In the case in hand, despite several opportunities granted to the appellant, it has miserably and perhaps deliberately failed to substantiate that the claim mentioned in the suit has been reflected in the scheme placed before the Board for Industrial and Financial Reconstruction (BIFR) but even more poignantly, that a scheme was, in fact, pending before BIFR. If an appeal is pending, the question is has BIFR failed to grant or has withdrawn registration under SICA. The conduct of the appellant is nothing more than an abuse of SICA.

---

*Saketh India Ltd vs W. Diamond India Ltd; see http://www.indiankanoon.org/doc/428003/ (30 August 2011).

Table 13.2 Ongoing reforms in company law

SICA, 1985	Companies Act, 1956	Repeal Act, 2003
Vitiation of objective Determination of and providing remedy to sick units misused as official exit route, resulting in loss to creditors.	Many provisions of SICA incorporated in Chapter VI A, Secs 424A–424L to function under NCLT and for further remedy to NCLAT	Objective has been to plug the loopholes of SICA and provide speedy remedy to sick companies
Sec. 3, 1(o) Sick industrial company An industrial company (being registered for not less than 5 years) that has, at the end of any financial year, accumulated losses equal to or exceeding its entire net worth.	*Sick industrial company* An industrial company that has at the end of any financial year 2(46AA) accumulated losses exceeding 50 per cent of the average net worth during 4 years; or has failed to repay debts to its creditor(s) in three consecutive quarters on demand made in writing for such repayment.	*No-moratorium period* The holiday period of 5 years has been deleted. Accumulated losses should exceed 50 per cent of the average net worth during the last four years. Inability to repay its creditors for three consecutive quarters on demand made by them in writing indicates weak liquidity status of the company, hence potentially sick. Any one of the two conditions is sufficient to make the company sick.
Sec. 4 to 14 Constitution and procedures of the BIFR and Appellate Authority	Omitted	BIFR and Appellate authority replaced by NCLT and NCLAT, respectively
Sec. 15 Reference to the Board	Sec. 424A is parallel to Sec. 15 of SICA. Now the company is required to submit a scheme of *revival and rehabilitation* at the time of making reference to the NCLT. Such a reference has to be made within 180 days after the Board of Directors coming to know about 60 days of the final adoption of accounts. Furnish a certificate from auditor on the panel approved by NCLT giving reasons for such reference. Sec. 424A (5) provides that NCLT has to examine, as a preliminary issue, whether the company is a sick industrial company under Sec. 2(46AA) even before considering the viability of the scheme of revival and rehabilitation.	*Reference* has to be made even when banks and financial institutions take over the assets under the Securitization and Reconstruction of Financial Assets, Enforcement and Security Act, 2002. Auditor's certificate adds to the authenticity of such a reference.
Sec. 19 Rehabilitation by providing financial assistance	Similar provisions incorporated in Sec. 424E	No change

Contd

Table 13.2 *Contd*

Sec. 20 Board was required to *record and forward* its opinion for winding up of the sick industrial company to the High Court.	The Tribunal can itself order the winding up of the company, if it is of the opinion that the sick company is not likely to revive, the Tribunal can appoint any officer of the operating agency to act as the liquidator. Moreover, the Tribunal can also sell off assets of the sick company and distribute the proceeds in accordance with Sec. 529A	Sec. 20(2) of SICA becomes redundant as the Tribunal can itself order the winding up instead of merely forwarding its opinion to the High Court. This power was earlier vested with the High Court
Sec. 22 *Suspensions of legal proceedings, contracts*, etc., thus providing complete immunity from legal suits, recovery proceedings, and winding up petitions made during the inquiry and implementation of the scheme	*Recovery proceedings* and suits against the sick industrial company can continue even if inquiry is pending with NCLT or revival and rehabilitation scheme is pending for preparation or implementation	*No protection to sick industrial company against suits or legal proceedings* for recovery of money or execution against property. However, winding up proceedings may be retained as these are with the same Tribunal.
Sec. 33 *Penalty* for certain offences	*Penalty* of imprisonment up to 3 years and fine up to ₹10 lakh for violation of orders of the tribunal, making false statements or giving false evidence, or attempt to tamper with the records of reference or appeal.	Following changes incorporated: Limit of fine fixed up to ₹10 lakh. Tampering with the records of reference or appeal recognized as a *punishable offence.*

The issues that you have appraised yourself in a comparative study of the Acts and in Case 13.2 systematically prove the difficulties faced in SICA and the attitude of the companies to circumvent the intention of the legislator. You may also appreciate how the judge meticulously sieves through the evidence before him. In the full length of the judgement, he examines similar cases of various high courts in the country and, in this manner, further strengthens the case law.

MANAGER'S TAKEAWAY

- As a manager, be sincere in presenting the case through your counsel.
- A strategy to puzzle the judge will fail almost all the time.

13.3 AGENCIES TO DEAL WITH SICK COMPANIES AND DISPUTE RESOLUTION

Company Law Board[1]

Under the Companies Act, 1956, Sec. 10(E) constituted an independent body called Company Law Board (CLB). The notification was issued as No. 364 dated 31 May 1991. The CLB is

---

[1]http://www.clb.nic.in/ (1 September 2011).

CASE 13.2

APPELLANT: Paschim Petrocham Ltd   vs   RESPONDENT: Authorized Officer, Kotak Mahindra Bank Ltd*

DATE OF JUDGEMENT: 11 January 2010

FACTS: In the year 2001, the petitioner filed a reference before the BIFR under Sec. 15(1) of SICA, 1985, which was registered as No. 291 of 2001 and ICICI Bank being a secured creditor and party to the said reference. Meanwhile, by way of deed of assignment in the month of May 2005, the creditor Bank ICICI assigned their secured rights and debts to Kotak Mahindra Bank Ltd (KMBL) and the BIFR issued certain directions by declaring the company as sick and appointed the Industrial Development Bank of India as the operating agency under Sec. 17(3) of the Act to prepare a rehabilitation scheme as per the guidelines.

The respondent had published the said notice of possession in two leading newspapers on 1 July 2009, and accordingly on 17 July 2009, an authorized officer of KMBL informed the Chairman, BIFR, New Delhi, that in view of third provison to Sub-sec. (1) of Sec.15 of the Sick Industrial Companies (Special Provisions) Act, 1985 (SICA, 1985), reference pending before the Honorable Bench stood abated.

According to the petitioner, the above decision of BIFR declaring the petitioner as sick industry entails all assessment of the sick company to be under the complete control, command, and custody of the BIFR; therefore, the respondent bank is a party to the above adjudication and such a decision is binding to them and they cannot act contrary to BIFR and without the consent of BIFR no proceedings can be taken under the Securitization and Reconstruction of Financial Assets (SARFAESI) and Enforcement of Security Interest Act, 2002.

JUDGEMENT: Petition dismissed.

REASON: Sec. 35 of SARFAESI, 2002, a later enactment, categorically lays down that the provisions of the Act shall have effect notwithstanding anything inconsistent therewith contained in any other law for the time being in force or any instrument having effect by virtue of that law and thus the provision overrides Sec. 22 of SICA, a previous enactment having come into being in 1985 and, therefore, notwithstanding the abatement provided by the third proviso to Sec. 15 (1) of SICA, introduced by virtue of Sec. 41 read with the schedule to the SARFAESI Act, the effect of Sec. 22 of SICA no more survives Sec. 35 of the SARFAESI Act.

Reference as found in Sec. 15 under Chapter III of SICA, 1985, exists beyond Sec. 15 and continues at various stages of Secs 16–19 and ultimately its life comes to an end in Sec. 20, in case if the scheme prepared as provided under Sec. 18 for revival of the sick industrial unit fails.

It is to be noted that the Repeal Act, 2003, namely the SICK Industrial Companies (Special Provisions) Repeal Act, 2003, was enacted by the Parliament to repeal the SICK Industrial Companies (Special Provisions) Act, 1985, but as provided in Sec. 1(2) of the Repeal Act, still no date is notified by the central government by notification in the official gazette bringing the enactment into force.

In view of the above, it is held that the impugned notice dated 23 June 2009 issued by the respondent is not bad or illegal.

---

*Paschim Petrocham Ltd vs Authorized Officer Kotak Mahindra Bank Ltd, SCA/8015/2009 48/49; also see http:// www. indiankanoon.org/doc/1834544/ (3 September 2011).

a quasi-judicial body, exercising equitable jurisdiction, which was earlier being exercised by the high court or the central government.

CLB has the power to regulate its own procedures. Accordingly, it has framed Company Law Board Regulations, 1991, prescribing the procedure for filing the applications/petitions before it. The central government has also prescribed the fees for making applications or petitions before CLB, under the Company Law Board (Fees on Applications and Petitions) Rules 1991. The Board has its principal bench at New Delhi and four regional benches located at New Delhi, Mumbai, Kolkata, and Chennai.

Since 1 April 2008, matters falling under Secs 247, 250, 269, and 388B of the Companies Act, 1956, are being dealt with by the principal bench and the rest by the regional benches.

In terms of Sec. 10(F) of the Companies Act, any person aggrieved by any decision or order of CLB may file an appeal to the high court within 60 days from the date of communication of the decision or order of CLB to him on any question of law arising out of such order.

Board for Industrial and Financial Reconstruction

The Sick Industrial Companies (Special Provisions) Act, 1985, was enacted with a view to securing the timely detection of sick and potential sick companies owning industrial undertakings; the speedy determination by a body of experts of the preventive, ameliorative, remedial, and other measures that need to be taken with respect to such companies; and the expeditious enforcement of the measures thus determined and for matters connected therewith or incidental thereto.

The board of experts named the Board for Industrial and Financial Reconstruction[2] (BIFR) was set up in January 1987 and became functional with effect from 15 May 1987.

AAIRFR

It was constituted in April 1987. Government companies were brought under the purview of the SICA in 1991 when extensive changes were made in the Act including, *inter alia*, changes in the criteria for determining industrial sickness.

NCLT and NCLAT[3]

Before the Companies (Second Amendment) Act, 2002, corporations were required to apply to high courts for proceedings such as merger and amalgamation, reduction of capital, and winding up of companies. But since the high courts are over-burdened, delays were inevitable. Even the winding-up petitions before the various high courts had been pending for a very long time. Similarly, various matters before the CLB, the BIFR, and the AAIFR had been pending for a very long period.

The Companies (Amendment) Act, 2002, consistent with the underlying objectives, and in the backdrop of the experience of administration of the SICA and the winding-up process,

---

[2]http://bifr.nic.in/; http://business.gov.in/closing_business/bifr.php (1 September 2011).

MANAGER'S TAKEAWAY

- When in doubt ask, even if it be the highest court in the land.
- The law is made to serve society equally and justly.

the Companies (Second Amendment) Act, 2002, provided for setting up of the NCLT, whereby all matters relating to companies that were earlier, managed by various high courts, the CLB, the BIFR, and the AAIFR were managed by the NCLT. Pending matters with the high courts and the CLB were transferred to the NCLT.

However, this did not solve the problem of backlog of cases. Furthermore, the appeals clogged the high courts. Hence, an appellate court was required, which was established as NCALT, 3 under the Companies Act, 1956 (Case 13.3).

CASE 13.3

APPELLANT: Union of India vs RESPONDENT: R. Gandhi*

DATE OF JUDGEMENT: 1 May 2010

FACTS: The respondent, a member of Madras Bar Association, challenged the constitutional validity of the Companies (Second Amendment) Act, 2002, and especially the power to constitutive the NCLT and National Company Appellate Tribunal. Parliament does not have the legislative competence to vest intrinsic judicial functions that have been traditionally performed by the high courts for nearly a century in any tribunal outside the judiciary.

The Union of India submitted that it had constituted a high-level committee on law relating to Insolvency of Companies under the chairmanship of Justice V. Balakrishna Eradi, a retired judge of this court, with other experts to examine the existing laws relating to the winding up proceedings of the company to remodel it in line with the latest developments and innovations in corporate laws and governance and to suggest reforms to the procedures at various stages followed in insolvency proceedings of the company to avoid unnecessary delay, in tune with international practices in the field. The Madras High Court, by its order dated 30 March 2004, held that the establishment of NCLT and NCLAT and vesting in them the powers hitherto exercised by the high courts and CLB were not unconstitutional. Nevertheless, the Madras High Court concluded that various provisions of Parts 1B and 1C suffered from constitutional infirmities, which had to be sufficiently amended to establish NCLT and NCLAT.

The Union of India moved the Supreme Court.

JUDGEMENT: Order in favour of the petitioner.

REASON: Upheld the judgement of Madras High Court and cleared the doubts by asserting that the constitutional power of the Parliament to constitute tribunals for adjudication of disputes. The legislative competence of the Parliament to provide for creation of courts and tribunals can be traced to Articles 245, 246, and 247 of the Constitution, read with various entries in the Union List (List I of Seventh Schedule) and the Concurrent List (List III of Seventh Schedule), which is in no way affected or controlled by Article 323A or 323B of the Constitution.

* http://www.indiankanoon.org/doc/748977/ (20 September 2011).

3http://www.lawadmissions.info/index.php?option = com_content & view = article & id = 302: national-company -law-tribunal--appellate-tribunal & catid = 61:courts-and-tribunals & Itemid = 37 (1 September 2011).

13.4 GUIDELINES ON INSOLVENCY

The District Courts shall be the Courts having jurisdiction under this Act: Provided that the State Government may, by notification in the Official Gazette, invest any Court subordinate to a District Court with jurisdiction in any class of cases, and any Court so invested shall within the local limits of its jurisdiction have concurrent jurisdiction with the District Court under this Act.

– The Provincial Insolvency Act, 1920, Sec. 3(1)

Introduction

The legal meaning of the terms 'bankruptcy', 'insolvency', 'liquidation', and 'dissolution' can leave an individual confused despite a history of nearly three centuries of legislation. In common law parlance, bankruptcy is not synonymous with insolvency.

(a) Insolvency refers to a person who is unable to pay his debts when called upon to do so.
(b) Bankruptcy is the legal process that an insolvent has to undergo.
(c) Liquidation refers to the situation when after the payment of its debts and liabilities, a company's net assets are divided among its shareholders. The division is made according to the terms on which the company was established. Generally, preferred shareholders are paid out at face value, or par, before the balance is shared between ordinary shareholders.
(d) Dissolution is the reverse of formation of a company, and this legal process is known as winding-up.

Winding-up of companies is in the jurisdiction of the courts, which can sometimes take as long as twenty-five years, even after the company has actually been declared insolvent. On the other hand, supervisory restructuring at the behest of the BIFR is generally undertaken using receivership by a public finance institution (Case 13.4).

Laws Governing Insolvency

The laws relating to insolvency provide a collection of legal and administrative instruments and institutional structures followed by rehabilitative, distributive, and penal objectives. The earliest Act governing insolvency and bankruptcy was the Government of India Acts of 1759 and 1800; their regular amendments continued till 1848. The insolvency laws are distinguished as *personal insolvency* and *corporate insolvency*. Personal insolvency deals with individuals and partnership firms regulated by the Provisional Insolvency Act, 1920, and the Presidency Towns Insolvency Act, 1908. In addition, corporate insolvency is governed under the following:

(a) Secs 391–394, 433–483; 528–545 of the Companies Act, 1956 Dispute redressal under CLB, NCLT, and NCLAT.
(b) Sick Industrial Companies (Special Provisions) Act, 1985 Dispute redressal under BIFR.
(c) Asset Reconstruction under Securitization and Reconstruction of Financial Assets and Enforcement of Security Interest Act, 2002 (SARFASEI).

(d) Sick Industrial Companies (Special Provisions) Repeal Act, 2003
   Dispute redressal under tribunal.

(e) Recovery of debts due to Banks and Financial Institutions Act, 1993
   Dispute redressal under tribunal.

CASE 13.4

APPELLANT: **Dunlop Factory Employees Union** vs
RESPONDENT: **Dunlop India Ltd and Others***

DATE OF JUDGEMENT: 21 December 2004

FACTS: Petitioner filed a Writ Petition under Article 226 of the Constitution of India for issuance of a Writ of Declaration, thereby declaring the sale of Dunlop land at Ambattur on 17 June 2004 by the first respondent in favour of the sixth respondent—VN Devadoss—as null and void.

Dunlop India Ltd, the first respondent was faced with financial issues; therefore, a reference was made to BIFR for framing a scheme. Originally, Industrial Development Bank of India was appointed as the operating agency and thereafter it was replaced by State Bank of India. During the course of the proceedings, the petitioners also took part. It was decided that it was necessary to sell some of the immovable properties belonging to the first respondent in order to facilitate rehabilitation.

JUDGEMENT: Petition dismissed.

REASON: The petitioners have not pointed out any infirmity in the sale. The petitioners are also not able to show how they are aggrieved by the sale, especially when the extract from the documents filed shows that the sale itself was made only to enable the restart of the company, which will be to the advantage of the workers. It is also stated that the first respondent has paid some amount to the workers from out of the proceeds obtained from the sale. The petitioners have not mentioned the pendency of the suit when they filed the writ petition. They had all along been party to the entire rehabilitation proceedings, which culminated in the decision to sell the surplus property, which included the property at Ambattur. If the petitioners were aggrieved, they ought to have challenged the Scheme in the year 2002. Even if the sale deed is vitiated by some procedural irregularity or illegality, the suffering party would be the purchaser and not the workers.

---

*Dunlop Factory Employees Union vs Dunlop India Ltd, see http://www.indiankanoon.org/doc/720047/(3 September 2011).

Jurisdiction

The Presidency Insolvency Act, 1920, is applicable to Kolkata, Mumbai, and Chennai, and the Provisional Towns Insolvency Act, 1908, is applicable to the rest of the country. In law, insolvency is a proceeding in pursuance of which the court takes possession of the property of a debtor who is unable to pay his debts or discharge his liabilities and distributes it equally among his creditors. The official assignee appointed by the government under the Presidency Insolvency Act takes charge of the property of the debtor, realizes it, and distributes it equally amongst the creditors. The proceeding for insolvency may be initiated by any of the creditors or the debtor himself.

Objectives of Insolvency Legislation

1. To restore the debtor company to profitable trading where this is practicable; to maximize the return to creditors as a whole.
2. To bring to book those guilty of mismanagement, and where appropriate, deprive them of the right to be involved in the management of other companies.
3. To provide a battery of legal and administrative instruments and institutional structures:
   (a) Rehabilitative
   (b) Distributive
   (c) Penal

Procedures

1. File petition under the given or chosen Act.
2. All the company documents and audits are attached to the petition.
3. The dispute redressal agency, such as a board or tribunal, will examine debts for which it will appoint a receiver.
4. The board or tribunal will hear all the concerned, particularly the creditors.
5. Upon adjudication of all facts and examination of evidence, the board or tribunal may pass the order of insolvency.
6. The board or tribunal, after making an assessment, may make arrangement so that as many creditors are paid from the resources of the company; a time limit may also be fixed for such an arrangement.

Effects

1. Insolvency of a company suspends the rights of the directors or the company in dealing with its assets other than with the regulation of the court. Fraudulent preferences or transfers made during the insolvency or transfer of shares are avoided.
2. Only the official liquidator can enter into fresh legal contracts on behalf of the company who records each legal proceeding pending with leave of the court.
3. The decree will have to be passed against the official liquidator and, in the event of an unsecured claim, only proofs in insolvency are the appropriate remedy as unsecured creditors shall have to participate in insolvency.
4. Only secured creditors can prove against the official liquidator outside of the procedure of the insolvency law in normal civil proceedings.
5. Remedies of persons in contractual relationships are also only available with leave of the court as no execution distress or warrant can be issued or executed against the company without the leave of the court.
6. When more than one insolvency actions are initiated, all liquidation matters are determined by proofs of insolvency before the official liquidator regulated by the company court. Multiple insolvency matters are effectively consolidated in a single winding-up action or procedure.

MANAGER'S TAKEAWAY

- An athlete never competes to lose; hence, do business to succeed.
- There is no greater motivation than success.

Compromises and Arrangements

The procedures of winding-up are lengthy and time-consuming. The companies have the choice for alternative solutions. They may make an *arrangement*. The board of directors, along with the shareholders and creditors, may find a solution to amicably settle the issues concerning winding-up. However, if applied for relief under any of the dispute redressal agencies, it must be allowed. Withdrawal from such a process is not possible.

SUMMARY

Introduction and Interpretation

- The Companies Act, 1956, required an augmentation due to the increasing problems in the industry, especially the ones making loss, and hurtling towards bankruptcy and insolvency. A package for revival and rehabilitation of sick industry was required. It came in the form of the Sick Industrial Companies (Special Provisions) Act, 1985, and its Repeal Act in 2003. The objectives were to evaluate the economic viability of the companies, stop the drainage of resources and NPAs, and protect employee interest. BIFR was instituted to adjudicate sick industrial matters.

The Sick Industrial Companies Act of 1985 and 2003 within the Context of the Companies Act, 1956

- Companies detected the weaknesses of SICA, abused it as an easy route to exit, benefited from all legal procedures, and gained financially by the grants from the government. The NPAs resulted in overburdening of the nationalized banks, which

needed to finance the sick industries. The Repeal Act of SICA, 2003, and the amended Companies Act, 1956, instituted agencies such as NCLT and NCLAT for dispute resolution.

Agencies to Deal with Sick Companies and Dispute Resolution

- Starting from CLB under the Companies Act, 1956, BIFR of SICA was found inadequate because companies had to seek appeal in the high court. This was resolved by the formation of NCLT and NCLAT. However, the problems of clogged courts and surfeit of cases continue to persist.

Guidelines on Insolvency

- It is a step-by-step manual to be followed in case of insolvency. It differentiates the various concepts connected with insolvency such as bankruptcy, dissolution, and liquidation. Furthermore, it deals with corporate insolvency and various agencies such as BIFR, NCLT, NCLAT, etc., which render dispute redressal mechanism. The procedures for the purpose are also laid out in the manual.

EXERCISES

Introduction and Interpretation

(i) Problem: TIM, a limited company, has been operating for three years. Having lost the market for its products and having become heavily dependent on creditors, the members decided to approach BIFR. Would the company get relief?
Hint: No, see Sec. 3 (o) of SICA, 1985.

(ii) Problem: As per the audited report of a company, it has accumulated losses of more than 60 per cent of its net worth during the immediate earlier two financial years. The board of directors passes a resolution for the company to be declared as sick and seek rehabilitation. What is your advice?
Hint: No, it cannot be declared sick; see Sec 23 of SICA.

(iii) Question: Explain the mandate of BIFR under SICA.

(iv) Question: Comment on the shortcomings of SICA.

The Sick Industrial Companies Act of 1985 and 2003 within the context of the Companies Act, 1956

(i) Problem: SRNT Ltd made reference to NCLT by furnishing a certificate from the auditor giving reasons for such reference. What is involved here?
Hint: Revival and Rehabilitation: Sec. 424 A of the Companies Act, 1956; also see Sec. 15 of the SICA.

(ii) Problem: Who can order winding up?
Hint: See Sec. 20(2) of the SICA.

(iii) Problem: Sridhar Ltd applied for sick industrial company with prima facie documents. The company was operating for the last seven years. Will it be declared sick?
Hint: Yes; see section 3, 1(0) of SICA.

(iv) Question: How was SICA misused?

Agencies to deal with sick companies and dispute resolution

(i) Problem: TISR Ltd received a notice from its creditor bank, a scheduled bank, that it has evidence as to the bad health of the company and advises its Board to determine the measures to declare itself sick and apply for revival and rehabilitation. As a company secretary what would be your legal advice to a company whose status has been declared as sick?
Hint: Reference may be made by Central and State Governments, statutory bodies and scheduled banks; see Sec. 15, 2 of the SICA.
Hint: Rehabilitation by giving financial assistance: see Sec. 19 of the SICA.

(ii) Problem: Under pendency of inquiry into the sick company, the income tax commissioner filed a suit against a company for non-payment of tax when the company was functioning normally. Sec. 22 of SICA provides relief by suspending legal proceedings.
Hint: If there is a prima facie case it will be allowed suspension of legal proceedings; however, see Chapter End Case where the court holds to the contrary.

(iii) Question: What is the role of BIFR with regard to a sick company?

(iv) Question: Can the high court replace the National Companies Appellate Tribunal?

DEVELOPMENT OF LEGAL EDGE

Project
Objectives:
- To know clearly the industrial problems in the state.
- To help entrepreneurs in their strategies.
- Divide your team or class *state-wise*.
- Identify sick companies in their various states of winding up.

- Make a concerted effort to obtain the data on the experience loss or gain of shareholders and creditors.
- Make a special list of the institutional or bank creditors and their activities *vis-à-vis* the winding up or insolvent companies.
- Have the data published on the web or a local newspaper or magazine.

FURTHER READING

Book
- Avtar Singh, *Law of Insolvency*, 4th edn, Eastern Book Co. India, 2004.

Acts
- Sick Industrial Companies (Special Previsions) Act, 1985.

- Sick Industrial Companies (Special Previsions) Repeal Act, 2003.
- Industries (Development and Regulation) Act, 1951 (IDR Act).

Web resources
http://business.gov.in.

| CASE STUDY | SECOND THOUGHTS ON INDUSTRIAL SICKNESS |

When an industrial company has become a sick industrial company, the Board of Directors of the company shall, within sixty days from the date of finalization of the duly audited accounts of the company for the financial year as at the end of which the company has become a sick industrial company, make a reference to the Board for determination of the measures which shall be adopted with respect to the company:

Provided that if the Board of Directors had sufficient reasons even before such nalization to form the opinion that the company had become a sick industrial company, the Board of Directors shall, within sixty days after it has formed such opinion, make a reference to the Board for the determination of the measures which shall be adopted with respect to the company.

– Sick Industrial Companies (Special Provisions) Act, Sec. 15, 1

Second Thoughts

When you are sick, you go to the doctor. However, the doctor's remedy is a long way off in coming. You try to look for an alternative. Upon second thoughts you hit upon an idea and you want to pursue it. But you cannot go ahead because some of the important things are with your first doctor and unless he releases these you have little hope about realizing your alternative.

A similar situation is experienced in this present case. A sick company duly goes to seek help from the remedial institution called BIFR with which you got acquainted in this chapter earlier on. In the meantime the members of the company think there is a way out of trouble with some agreements with the creditors. A new *arrangement* may be made. However, they would have to first seek permission from BIFR to release them from their obligations towards it. BIFR replies in the negative, so they need to go to the high court.

The Case

Ashok Organic Industries Ltd vs Asset Reconstruction, in the Bombay High Court, the Bench consisting of Justice F Rebello and Justice S Vazifdar, on 25 January 2008.[4]

Background

The Company, Ashok Organic Industries Ltd, made a reference to the BIFR under the provisions of the Sick Industrial Companies (Special Provision) Act, 1985, herein after referred to as SICA. They were informed by a letter dated 15 May 2002.

During the pendency of these proceedings before BIFR, the company resolved on 9 December 2005 that the subject to the sanction of the appropriate court as may be required under law and subject to such permission of such authority as may be necessary, a scheme of arrangement between Ashok Organic Industries Ltd and its shareholders and creditors and Mr Pankaj Kadakia, Ashok Kadakia, and Anil Kadakia in their dual capacity as promoters and guarantors be made on a broad basis as referred to in the scheme of arrangement. A petition under Secs 391 and 394 of the Companies Act, 1956 was filed praying that the arrangement embodied in the Scheme be sanctioned with or without modification and to declare the same as binding on the petitioner and its secured and unsecured creditors. The petition was presented on 9 January 2006. On 20 October 2005 in the company application, directions were issued to convene a meeting of the equity shareholders, and secured and unsecured creditors of the petitioner company for the purpose of considering the scheme. Pursuant to the meeting held on 12 December 2005, the chairman of the committee submitted a report, which indicated that the scheme was approved by the requisite majority in numbers of equity shareholders of the petitioner company representing more than three-fourth in value of equity shareholders present at the said meeting and voting. Similarly, in so far as the secured creditors were concerned, 80.05 per cent of the total secured debtors voted in favour of the scheme of arrangement and one secured creditor voted against the scheme, who represented 19.95 per cent of the secured debtors. The scheme, therefore, was approved by the

---

[4]Ashok Organic Industries vs Asset Reconstruction Company, 2008 (3) BomCR 78, 2008 (110) Bom L R 531; also see http//:www.indiankanoon.org/ doc/405057/ (1 September 2011).

requisite majority because the number of secured creditors of the petitioner company had more than three-fourth of value of the secured debtors. Similarly, in so far as unsecured creditors were concerned, 99.91 per cent of the unsecured creditors voted in favour of the scheme of arrangement. The Regional Director filed an affidavit setting out that the scheme is not prejudicial to the interest of the shareholders and unsecured/secured creditors.

The Prayer

Whether an industrial company that has made a reference under Sec.15 of SICA can, during the pendency of such reference, apply to this court for sanctioning a scheme of arrangement or compromise with its creditors and shareholders and whether this court can take cognizance of such an application during the pendency of the reference and pass necessary orders thereon as are permissible in law?

Reasoning

It is difficult to accept the submission of the learned counsel appearing on behalf of the respondents that both the company court and BIFR exercise concurrent jurisdiction. If such a construction is upheld, there shall be chaos and confusion. A company declared to be sick in terms of the provisions of SICA continues to be sick unless it is directed to be wound up. Till the company remains a sick company with regard to the provisions of Sub-sec. (4) of Sec. 20, BIFR alone shall have the jurisdiction as regards the sale of its assets till an order of winding up is passed by a company court.

It is, therefore, not permissible to have recourse to any provisions other than SICA, 1985, to supply any mechanism for sanctioning a scheme impermissible under SICA, 1985 (or indeed even to facilitate a scheme under SICA, 1985) for this would defeat the Parliament's intention that SICA alone would completely and exhaustively cover all aspects relating to sick industrial companies, including schemes in respect thereof.

It must be remembered that revival or rehabilitation is not the only purpose of SICA, 1985. The recovery or realization of the dues of banks and financial institutions is also an important object. The Supreme Court has held that once a reference under Sec.15 of SICA, 1985, is registered, it is mandatory for BIFR to conduct an inquiry under Sec. 16.

Thus, until the mandatory and complete process under SICA, 1985 is exhausted, no other authority or court would have the jurisdiction to pass any order with respect to the sick industrial company, particularly such orders as to provide for its financial restructuring or for a compromise or arrangement with its members and creditors something expressly covered by Sec. 18(1) and (2) of SICA, 1985. This is not a matter of choice for the sick industrial company; once the provisions of Sec.15 of SICA, 1985, are attracted, reference to BIFR is mandatory and cannot be avoided. Once that reference is made, the entire process up to Sec. 20 must necessarily follow.

Answer to the Prayer—Petition Dismissed

Considering the above discussion, it has to be held that once an industrial company makes a reference under Sec.15 of SICA, the company court would have no jurisdiction to sanction the scheme of arrangement of compromise with its creditors and shareholders and it will also not have jurisdiction to take cognisance of such an application during the pendency of the reference.

Discussion Questions

1. What are the problems faced by the petitioner?
2. What is the role of the respondent in this case?
3. What are the issues the High Court Bench must deal with?
4. What would you do if you were a member of the affected company?
5. If you were the CEO of Ashok Organic Industries Ltd, what would be your suggestion to the board of directors?
6. As a manager how would you prepare yourself to refer the sick unit case to SICA and the related adjudication agencies?

Going Beyond

1. Does the High Court judgement solve any problems? Illustrate your comments.
2. What would be the scenario without SICA for the sick industries?
3. How would you implement the above judgement?

LEGAL LUMINARY

JUSTICE VETTATH BALAKRISHNA ERADI—A MAN OF MANY PARTS

In December 2010, when Justice Eradi passed away at the age of 88, the loss was felt not only in the legal fraternity but also in the social, cultural, and spiritual organizations where he held responsible posts. He was the recipient of a host of awards: the National Press of India Golden Jubilee Award (1992), the Rajiv Gandhi Excellence Award (1992), the Shiromani Award (1993), and the National Citizenship Award (1995).*

Justice Eradi (1922–2010) was the Chairman of the Core Group constituted by the Department of Company Affairs, which resulted in the formation of the NCLT and the NCLAT.

As he graduated with distinction from the Madras Christian College, in 1941, Justice Eradi showed his cultural inclination by bagging the first rank in Sanskrit. After his law degree from the Madras Law College, he practised law and later became a judge in the Kerala High Court in 1967. In 1981, he was elevated to the Bench of the Supreme Court of India where he served till his retirement in 1987. He headed numerous commissions and chaired committees, and it is impossible to produce the entire list here due to space constraints. However, he was best known as the Chairman of the Ravi and Beas Waters Tribunal for the adjudication of the dispute regarding sharing of the Punjab River waters between Punjab, Haryana, and Rajasthan. He was the first President of the National Consumer Disputes Commission (NCDRC), 1999.**

*http://supremecourtofindia.nic.in/judges/bio/51_vberadi.htm (2 September 2011).
**http://supremecourtcaselaw.com/jus_vberadi.htm (2 September 2011).

Law of Carriage of Goods

Principle: *Qui cedit a etretinetnihilagit.*

One who transfers, and yet retains, the transfer is not effective.

CHAPTER OUTLINE

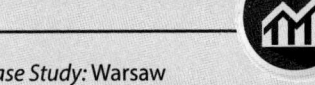

- Introduction and Interpretation
- Definitions
- Carriage of Goods by Land, Sea, and Air

- *Case Study:* Warsaw Convention in Action
- *Legal Luminary:* Mamata Banerjee

14.1 INTRODUCTION AND INTERPRETATION

TEXT

Whereas it is expedient not only to enable common carriers to limit their liability for loss of or damage to property delivered to them to be carried but also to declare their liability for loss of or damage to such property occasioned by the negligence or criminal acts of themselves, their servants, or agents..,

– The Carriers Act, 1895, Preamble

Carriers are pivotal elements in trade and commerce. The sheer number of ministries for transports such as surface transport, shipping, railways, and aviation demonstrates high engagement by the government. The mega infrastructure of transport around the globe is a proof for the same. Carriers are the transporters of goods. Life would be impossible without them, as we depend on them for simple things such as the morning newspaper, household groceries, and stationery.

In law, carriage of goods implies the transportation of goods by land, sea, or air. The scope of study, in this chapter, consists of the relevant laws governing the rights, responsibilities, liabilities, and immunities of the carriers and of the companies—agencies or persons—employing these services from the carriers. The contract law imposes, on the carriers, the obligation not only to carry goods but also to carry them safely and to deliver them in good condition to the owner or the agent. The carrier is always liable for the loss of goods and for any damage to the goods, unless proved that the loss or damage had resulted from a cause that formed an exception to the rule. According to the law of bailment, the carrier is considered to be the bailee who is liable to the bailor on failing to deliver the goods intact.

The rights and liabilities of transporters, by carriers through land, sea, and air, and consignees, are based on express or implicit contract. In the ordinary course of business, acceptance of goods for carriage and delivery implies the making of a contract of carriage. The right to claim freight depends on this contract and obliges the carrier to carry the goods safely to their destination. At the same time the law of bailment is also relevant: owners of the goods can enforce the law by suing the carrier for loss or damage to their goods.

Laws Governing the Carriage of Goods

By land

(a) the Carriers Act, 1865
(b) the Railways Act, 1989
(c) the Carriage by Road, 2007

By sea

(a) the Indian Bills of Lading Act, 1856
(b) the Carriage of Goods by Sea Act, 1925
(c) the Merchant Shipping Act, 1958
(d) the Marine Insurance Act, 1963

By air

the Carriage by Air Act, 1972

As per Case 14.1, the carriers cannot put untenable conditions that are in contravention with the law. Catalogues, warrantees, guarantees, and vouchers very often consist of what is known as *fine print*. These are terms and conditions that the customers receive and also agree without understanding their legal import. However, in the following case, beginning from trial court through to the Supreme Court, judgement has always been consistent on the basis that such a condition is in contravention with the law.

CASE 14.1	APPELLANT: M.G. Brothers Lorry Service vs RESPONDENT: Prasad Textiles*

DATE OF JUDGEMENT: 20 April 1993

FACTS: The respondent entrusted a consignment of goods for being transported from Guntur to Vijayawada to the appellant on 1 May 1969 under a Way Bill. As the appellant failed to deliver the goods at Vijayawada, the respondent gave a notice of claim on 20 June 1969 and thereafter instituted suits for recovery of damages from the appellant.

*M.G. Brothers Lorry Service vs Prasad Textiles, 1984 AIR 15, 1983 SCR (2)1027; also see: http://www. indiankanoon.org/doc/1980603/ (2 September 2011).

Contd

Case 14.1 *Contd*

Upon appeal, the trial court and the high court dismissed the appeals. Hence, petition was filed in the Supreme Court. It examined the legitimacy of Condition 15 of the Way Bill, which read 'No suit shall lie against the firm in respect of any consignment without a claim made in writing in that behalf and preferred within thirty days from the date of booking or from the date of arrival at the destination by the party concerned.'

JUDGEMENT: Appeal dismissed

REASON: Sec. 10 of the Carriers Act, 1865, provides as follows: *No suit shall be instituted against a common carrier for the loss of, or injury to, goods entrusted to him for carriage, unless notice in writing of the loss or injury has been given to him before the institution of the suit and within six months of the time when the loss or injury first came to the knowledge of the plaintiff.* The Carriers Act, 1865, as the Preamble states, was enacted because it was thought as an expedient not only to enable common carriers to limit their liability for loss of or damage to property delivered to them to be carried but also to declare their liability for loss of or damage to such property occasioned by the negligence or criminal acts of themselves, their servants, or their agents. Therefore, it is important to know that the Act was passed to serve both the purposes, that is, to limit the liability as well as to declare the liability of the carriers.

In relation to this, it appears that the construction of Condition 15 of the Way Bill had no limitation of liability expressed or intended but what was provided was that no suit shall lie against the firm unless a particular claim was made in a particular manner within a particular time.

Thus, Condition 15 must be held to be void in view of Sec. 23 of the Indian Contract Act because its object was to defeat the provisions of Sec. 10 of the Carriers Act. This conclusion, in our opinion, follows from the construction of Section and Condition 15 of the Way Bill.

14.2 DEFINITIONS

The following are textual definitions with citations from the Acts of their origin. These clearly define the concepts that would be helpful in not only in understanding their meaning but also in their reference to other concepts and in their relationship, classification, and context.

 MANAGER'S TAKEAWAY

- To ask oneself the value of a written agreement without the force of law.
- No matter how clever the fine print is, the law is always wiser.

Bland Carriage by Road Act 2007, (Sec. 2 a–k)

COMMON CARRIER: Person engaged in the business of collecting, storing, forwarding, or distributing goods to be carried by goods carriages under a goods receipt; or in transporting goods upon hire from place to place by motorized transport on road, for all persons indiscriminatingly; or by including a goods booking company, contractor, agent, broker, and courier agency engaged in the door-to-door transportation of documents, goods, or articles using the services of a person, either directly or indirectly; or to carry or accompany such documents, goods, or articles without including the government.

CONSIGNOR:	Person named as consignee in the goods forwarding note.
CONSIGNEE:	Documents, goods, or articles entrusted by the consignor to the common carrier for carriage, the description or details of which are given in the goods forwarding note.
CONSIGNMENT:	Person, named as consignor in the goods forwarding note, by whom or on whose behalf the documents, goods, or articles covered by such forwarding note are entrusted to the common carrier for carriage thereof.
GOODS:	(i) Containers, pallets, or similar articles of transport used to consolidate goods (ii) Animals or livestock.
GOODS FORWARDING NOTE:	Document executed under Sec. 8.
GOODS RECEIPT:	Receipt issued under Sec. 9.
PERSON:	Any association or body of persons, whether incorporated or not, a road transport booking company, a contractor, and an agent or a broker carrying on the business of a common carrier.
PRESCRIBED:	Prescribed by rules made under the Carriage by Road Act, 2007.
REGISTERING AUTHORITY:	State Transport Authority or a Regional Transport Authority constituted under Sec. 68 of the Motor Vehicles Act, 1988.
REGISTRATION:	Registration granted or renewed under Sub-sec. (5) of Sec. 4.

Carriers Act, 1865

PRIVATE CARRIER:	One who carries his own goods; in case he carries others' goods, he is governed by bailment.
GRATUITOUS CARRIER:	One who carries goods without charges.
SCHEDULED GOODS:	Those enumerated in the schedule of the Act.
DANGEROUS GOODS:	Incumbent on the consignor to declare dangerous goods—explosives, acids, poisons, etc.

Railways Act, 1989 (Sec. 61–102)

RATE BOOKS:	Every railway station and places concerned for receiving goods for carriage must maintain a rate book and must be available to people who want to refer to it.
FORWARDING NOTE:	Every person entrusting goods to railways shall execute a forwarding note as is prescribed by the central government.
RAILWAY RECEIPT:	Every dispatch and reception of goods by railways will be done through the issue of a receipt with prima facie evidence of the weight and number of packages stated therein.
DELAY OR DETENTION IN TRANSIT:	Railways do not bear responsibility for reasons beyond its control. If proved, the plaintiff can claim only the value of the goods lost and not its profit value.
OWNERS RISK RATE:	If the owner bears the risk of damage, the freight rates will be lower.
RAILWAY RISK RATE:	If the railways have to bear the liability for goods carried, the freight rates will be higher.
CARRIAGE OF ANIMALS:	Railways bear no responsibility for loss, damage, and death of any animals. (Railways are exempt from several liabilities that the normal common carriers bear, e.g., not well packed, badly loaded, delay due to accidents, riots, etc.)
DEFINITIONS:	Indian Bills of Lading Act, 1856
AFFREIGHTMENT:	A contract of carriage of goods by sea.
SEAWORTHINESS:	Ship is reasonably fit to encounter the perils of the seas; the undertaking is absolute.
COMMENCEMENT OF VOYAGE:	Loading of cargo, proceed and complete the voyage with reasonable dispatch.

NON-DEVIATION OF VOYAGE:	Ship's voyage in the usual and the customary manner without deviating from the prescribed route; upon default, may suffer rescinding of contract.
CHARTER PARTY:	Contract for hiring the whole ship.
BILL OF LADING:	Document issued when goods are delivered for carriage to a general ship that offers to carry goods of all such merchants who desire to use it for the carriage of goods; the position of the owner of a general ship is that of a common carrier. (a) Dirty bill: With conditions. (b) Through bill: In case where goods are to be carried partly by sea and partly by land. (c) Received bill: Receipt of goods by the ship owner. (d) On-board bill: Goods have been already loaded on board.
MATE'S RECEIPT:	After the exchange of bill of Lading, the master of the ship hands over a receipt to the consignor to acknowledge that the goods have been received on the ship.

Carriage by Air Act, 1972

CONVENTION:	Warsaw convention (1929) for the unification of rules relating to international carriage by air.
AMENDED CONVENTION:	Convention amended at The Hague (1955).
HIGH CONTRACTING PARTY:	All the parties' signatories to the convention and the subsequent adherents.
INTERNATIONAL CARRIAGE:	Carriage in which the place of departure and the place of destination are situated within territories of the high contracting parties.
AIRWAY BILL:	It is a consignment note made by the consignor to the carrier.

14.3   CARRIAGE BY LAND, SEA, AND AIR

On land, the most common modes of carriage are road and rail. These are governed by their respective Acts as mentioned above. The duties, rights, and liabilities of these are similar to those of sea and air in so far as they come under the category of common carriers and are governed by their own respective Acts (see Case 14.2 and also Table 14.1).

 MANAGER'S TAKEAWAY

- Carriers involve a multiplicity of relations, thereby complicating legal issues.
- Meticulous planning, from package to insurance, is required before the agreement to carriage is signed.

CASE 14.2   APPELLANT: General Traders Ltd and Others   VS   RESPONDENT: Pierce Leslie (India) Ltd and Others*

DATE OF JUDGEMENT: 20 April 1993

FACTS: *S.S. Lucky Three* of Panama Flag is a vessel owned by the first defendant's company, which carries on business at Hong Kong besides other regions. The said vessel was chartered by M/s General Traders Limited (second defendant), a West Indies-based concern, under Charter Party dated 8 January 1972. M/s Cashew Corporation of India Ltd,

---

*General Traders Ltd vs Pierce Leslie (India) Ltd; AIR 1987 Ker 62; see also: http://www.indiankanoon.org/doc/1161210/ (8 September 2011).

Contd

Case 14.2 *Contd*

a Government of India undertaking (CCI for short), engaged defendant No. 2 to transship 15,000 bags of raw cashew nuts of Kenyan origin from Mombasa to Calicut. On receiving the consignment, the Master of the ship drew three bills of lading, Exts. B2, B3, and B4. The vessel arrived at the port of Calicut at 9.40 a.m. (IST) on 23 February 1972. Calicut is not a roadstead port; there is some distance between the piers and the place nearest from there where the ship can reach. Hence, barges were used to transport goods from the ship to the piers. M/s Malabar Steamship Company, Bombay (the third defendant), with the branch office at Calicut, carried out lightering work as local agents of defendant No. 2 company. However, in the course of the lightering process, a number of bags of cashew nuts were jettisoned from the barges and a few other bags fell into the sea during unloading of the goods on the piers. Thus, there was a shortage of 1,350 bags of cashew nuts upon delivery, besides the shortage of 4,369 kilos of raw cashew nuts as 284 bags were delivered in a torn and slack condition. The total loss was estimated to be ₹1,99,537.90. The suit is for recovery of the said amount with interest.

The loss and/or damage caused to the consignment, according to the plaintiff, was entirely due to the negligence on the part of defendant No. 2 as well as their agent, defendant No. 3, in discharging the cargo from the steamer to the lighters when the weather was not conducive enough for transshipment, and that the lighters or barges used by defendant No. 3 were unfit and unseaworthy, or at any rate, unsuitable to protect the cargo in rough weather. According to the plaintiffs, the haste in discharging the cargo into the lighters despite the bad weather was only on account of the imprudent anxiety of defendant No. 2 to somehow empty the steamer of its cargo and leave the port at the earliest. By reason of the said act or omission, misfeasance, malfeasance, and non-feasance, the defendants are jointly and severally liable to make good the loss, contended the plaintiffs. The further contention is that plaintiff 2 were the insurers of the said consignment and they paid the amount of loss to plaintiff 1 and thereby were subrogated to the rights and remedies of the insurer, and hence, plaintiff 1 had no objection in granting a decree in favour of plaintiff 2.

Will the liability of a carrier of goods by sea cease on discharge of the cargo from the tackles of the vessel? Can the owner of a ship escape liability, if the ship is chartered by another under a Charter Party? Are the defendants entitled to the defence of 'act of God' in this particular case?

JUDGEMENT: Petition dismissed

REASON: The non-production of the *log-book* of the ship has been very scathingly commented against by the lower court, and an adverse inference was drawn against the defendants for not producing the ship's log book and for keeping the log books in the lighters as well. Therefore, there is no evidence about the 'act of God'.

Discharge from the vessel is intended to deliver the goods to the consignee and until the consignee is in a position to take delivery of the goods, the discharge from the vessel is not incomplete.

It is not open to the defendants to question the correctness of the terms of the assignment or subrogation as between plaintiffs 1 and 2 in this case.

Therefore, there is no substance or merit in the aforesaid point raised on behalf of the appellant.

Table 14.1 Rights, duties, and liabilities of a common carrier

Duties	Rights	Liabilities
Receive and carry goods from all and sundry	Agreed remuneration	*Strict liability* Insurer of goods: warrants to take the goods safely Exceptions: (a) Damage or loss caused by acts of God, such as natural calamities (b) Damage or loss caused by enemies of state (c) Deterioration and loss due to natural inherent causes of goods such as perishable articles (d) Damage and loss due to consignor's defective packing, etc.
Carry goods safely	*Lien* Enforce law both on consignor and on consignee	
Carry goods through customary route without deviation	Recover damage for which he is not liable	
Obey the instructions of the consignor	Limit liability when making the contract	
Deliver goods within the agreed-upon time and the designated place	Recover losses if the consignee does not accept goods	
	Refuse goods if: (a) Carrier is already full or if there is insufficient place (b) Consignor is unwilling to agree to freight charges (c) Not the carrier's usual goods (some are specialized in only some type) (d) Not the regular route (e) Dangerous goods (f) Goods are not properly packed (g) Consignor refuses to disclose the contents of parcels	

SUMMARY

Introduction and Interpretation

In law, carriage of goods implies the transportation of goods by land, sea, or air. The carrier is always liable for the loss of goods and also for any damage to the goods, unless it can be proved that the loss or damage had resulted from a cause that formed an exception to the rule. The rights and liabilities of transporters—land, sea, and air carriers, and consignees—are based on express or implicit contract.

Definitions

The definitions in Sec. 2 of this chapter are to clarify the legal concepts in carriage of goods as intended by the legislator.

Carriages by Land, Sea, and Air

Carriages by land, sea, and air are governed by their respective laws, although a common thread of duties, rights, and liabilities runs through them. The fundamental law underlying the respective laws is the law of contract.

EXERCISES

Introduction and interpretation

(i) What are the laws that govern carriages by land, sea, and air? Comment briefly.

(ii) Why do land, sea, and air have different laws of carriage?

Definitions

(i) What is Airway Bill?

(ii) What is Bill of Lading?

(iii) Define what is meant by common carrier.

(iv) Define what is meant by charter party.

Carriages by land, sea and air

1. Which of the following come under the category of 'Act of God' that damage goods transported by a carrier:

   (a) Landslide due to excessive rainfall

   (b) Curfew in the city

   (c) Air crash

   (d) Ship lost in the storm at sea.

   Hint: 'a' and 'd'.

2. A merchant booked merchandise at the risk of the railways. Due to negligence of the staff, the goods were loaded improperly and got damaged. Does the merchant have a remedy?

   Hint: Yes; see Sec. 74 of the Railways Act, 1989.

3. M.V. Princess, a carrier, issued a bill of lading acknowledging the receipt of a container. The agent noted details such as weight, value, and contents of the container on the bill of lading. The bill of lading was negotiated to the bona fide purchaser. Upon delivery it was found that it was a wrong container. The purchaser took an action. Will he succeed?

   Hint: Yes; he may, but the carrier in the meantime should find the right container! (It shows that even a straight forward case such as these can turn complicated.)

4. To what extent is an air carrier liable for the damage and loss of goods and for causing death?

5. Does the negligence of the pilot make the carrier responsible for the damage and loss of property and life?

DEVELOPMENT OF LEGAL EDGE

Export–Import Project:
Objective: To draw a brief manual on export and import–carriage and carriers.

• Form a group of not more than 4 people.

• The manual should not exceed 20 pages.

• The manual may be printed and distributed in your city for people in the export–import business.

FURTHER READING

• The Carriers Act, 1865.
• The Railways Act, 1989.

• The Carriage by Road, 2007r.
• The Indian Bills of Lading Act, 1856.

- The Carriage of Goods by Sea Act, 1925.
- The Merchant Shipping Act, 1958.
- The Marine Insurance Act, 1963.

- The Carriage by Air Act, 1972.

Web resources

http://indiacode.nic.in/.

CASE STUDY　　　WARSAW CONVENTION IN ACTION

An Act to give effect to the Convention for the unification of certain rules relating to international carriage by air signed at Warsaw on the 12th day of October, 1929 and to the said Convention as amended by the Hague Protocol on the 28th day of September, 1955 and to make provision for applying the rules contained in the said Convention in its original form and in the amended form (subject to exceptions, adaptations and modifications) to non-international carriage by air and for matters connected therewith

– The Carriage by Air Act, 1972, Preamble

In the supreme court of India

Bench: Justice G.S. Singhvi and Justice H.L. Dattu
Trans Mediterranean Airways vs M/s Universal Exports and Others
Date: 15 September 2011[1]

Introduction

The appellant is an international cargo carrier, with its principal place of business at Beirut, Lebanon.

Respondent No.1 is a garment exporter and respondent No.2 is an accredited International Air Transport Association agent.

This appeal is filed under Sec. 23 of the Consumer Protection Act, 1986 (CP), against the order of the National Consumer Disputes Redressal Commission, New Delhi (National Commission), dated 15 January 2004, whereby the National Commission has directed the appellant to pay a sum equivalent to US $71,615.75 with 5 per cent interest from the date of the complaint, till its realization, and imposed costs of ₹1 lakh for deficiency of service.

Task of the Court

1. By this appeal, we are called upon to examine and reconcile the area of operation of the CP Act on the one hand, and the Carriage by Air Act, 1972 (CA Act) along with the Warsaw Convention of 1929 (Warsaw Convention) on the other hand. The appellant and the respondents–respondent No. 1, and respondent No. 2– hereinafter, for the sake of brevity, are referred to as 'appellant carrier', and 'consignor', respectively.

2. Whether the National Commission under the CP Act has the jurisdiction to entertain and decide on a complaint filed by the consignor claiming compensation for deficiency of service by the carrier, in view of the provisions of the CA Act and the Warsaw Convention, or whether domestic laws can be added to or substituted for the provisions of the conventions.

3. Whether the appellant can be directed to compensate the consignor for deficiency of service given the facts and circumstances of the case.

Background of the Case

The agent made out three airway bills for shipping of garments to Spain on behalf of the consignor through the appellant-carrier. In the consignee column the airway bills from Bombay to Amsterdam were dated 25 August 1992 and the consignment through the appellant-carrier reached Amsterdam on 30 August 1992. From Amsterdam, the consignments were sent to Madrid by road on the following day, and they reached Madrid on 03 September 1992 and were cleared by the Customs Authorities. The appellant-carrier delivered the consignment to M/s Liwe Espanola, as according to them, that was the only recognizable address available from the documents furnished by the consignor.

---

[1]Trans Mediterranean Airways vs M/s Universal Exports and Others (Civil Appeal No 1909, 2004; judgement: 15 September 2011) see also: http://www.indiankanoon.org/doc/791637/ (3 September 2011).

After 9 months from the date of shipment, the agent made inquiry regarding two of the three airway bills. As there was no response, the agent made further inquiry again after four months. In response to the query, the appellant-carrier informed the Consignor that on finding the full name and complete postal address of the consignee as M/s Liwe Espanola, the appellant-carrier has delivered the goods to the same. It was at this stage that the consignor claimed that the consignee of the said consignment was Barclays Bank, Madrid, which had only one branch in Madrid. As the appellant-carrier had wrongly delivered the consignment to the address mentioned in the Block column instead of routing it through Barclays Bank, it can be considered as deficiency of service. Accordingly, the consignor instituted a complaint under Sec. 12 of the CP Act before the National Commission inter alia, claiming compensation for the alleged deficiency of service by the appellant-carrier and the agent for not delivering the said consignment to the consignee.

The National Commission, after considering the entire evidence on record, has come to the conclusion that the services rendered by the appellant-carrier was deficient and thereby it was liable to pay compensation equivalent to US $71,615.75 with 5 per cent interest from the date of the complaint till its realization, and imposed costs of ₹1 lakh. It is the correctness or otherwise of this order, which is called in question in this appeal.

The Case before the Supreme Court

On merits, it was the case of the consignor before the National Commission that the services offered by the appellant-carrier and the agent were deficient and that the consignment meant for the consignee was not delivered to the notified person. It was also the case of the consignor that in view of the conditions of contract on the reverse of the airway bill, it was required for the appellant-carrier to have delivered the consignment to the consignee only, and in case of any doubt regarding the address of delivery, the appellant-carrier was required to enquire with the consignor and not deliver the consignment to any other person other than the notified party. Therefore, it was contended that there is a deficiency of service by the appellant-carrier.

The National Commission, in the impugned order, has concluded that the agent was not only the agent of the consignor but also of the appellant-carrier; hence, any mistake committed by the agent would make the principal (appellant-carrier) liable for such damages. Furthermore, it is

held by the National Commission that the appellant-carrier was duty bound to have contacted the consignor in case it was not able to locate the address of the consignee or in the event, the consignee refused to accept the consignment. It is held that it is not open to the appellant-carrier to have delivered the consignment to the notified party without informing the consignor.

Analysis of Convention

India is a signatory to the Warsaw Convention of 1929, which is an International Agreement governing the liability of the air carrier with respect to international carriage of passengers, baggage, and cargo by air. (See Exhibit A.) Under that convention 'international carriage' means any carriage in which, according to the contract made by the parties, the place of departure and the place of destination, whether or not there should be a break in the carriage or trans-shipment, are situated either within the territories of two High Contracting Parties or within the territory of a single High Contracting Party, if there is an agreed-upon stopping place within a territory subject to the sovereignty, suzerainty, mandate, or authority of another power, even though that power is not a party to the Convention. The Convention states that when an accident occurring during international carriage by air causes damage to a passenger, or a shipper, or a cargo, there is a presumption of liability of the carrier.

The carrier, however, is not liable if it proves that it or its agent had taken all necessary measures to avoid the damage or that it was impossible for him or them to take such measures. The Convention balances the imposition of a presumption of liability on the carrier by limiting his liability for each passenger to 1,25,000 gold francs. There is no limitation of liability if the damage is caused by the wilful misconduct of the carrier, or by such default, on his part as, in accordance with the law of the court ceased of the case, is equivalent to wilful misconduct.

The Convention also contains detailed provisions regarding documents of carriage. A diplomatic conference that adopted a protocol to amend the provisions of the Warsaw Convention was held at Hague in September 1955, under the auspices of International Civil Aviation Organization. The Hague Protocol was opened for signature on 28 September 1955 and more than the required number of states have ratified the protocol, which came into force between the ratifying states on 1 August 1963.

Exhibit A   Indian Carriage Act, 1972, Sec. 3

Application of convention to India

1. The rules contained in the First Schedule, being the provisions of the Convention relating to the rights and liabilities of carriers, passengers, consignors, consignees, and other persons, shall, subject to the provisions of this Act, have the law enforced in India in relation to any carriage by air to which those rules apply, irrespective of the nationality of the aircraft performing the carriage.

2. The Central Government may, by notification in the official gazette, certify who are the high contracting parties to the Convention, in respect of what territories they are parties and to what extent they have availed themselves of the provisions of Rule 36 in the First Schedule; and any such notification shall be conclusive evidence of the matters certified therein.

3. Any reference in the First Schedule to the territory of any high contracting party to the Convention shall be construed as a reference to all the territories in which he is a party.

4. Any reference in the First Schedule to agents of the carrier shall be construed as including a reference to servants of the carrier.

5. Every notification issued under Sub-section (2) of Sec. 2 of the Indian Carriage by Air Act, 1934 (20 of 1934), and in force immediately before the commencement of this Act shall be deemed to have been issued under Sub-sec. (2) of this section and shall continue to be in force until such notification is superseded.

Some of the amendments affected by the Hague Protocol to the Warsaw Convention are as follows:

(a) Simplification of documents of carriage.

(b) An increase in the amount specified as the maximum sum for which the carrier may be liable to a passenger, that is to say, the limits of the liability of the carrier with respect to a passenger has been doubled, and unless a higher figure is agreed to by a special contract, the liability is raised from 1,25,000 gold francs per passenger to 2,50,000 gold francs.

(c) Making the carrier liable when the damage was caused by an error in piloting or in the handling of the aircraft or during navigation.

Acceptance of the Hague Protocol would put our national carrier on the same path as that of its other international competitors, as the passengers will be able to avail the limit of liability guaranteed by the Hague Protocol; the limit being double than that stipulated under the Warsaw Convention.

The Bill seeks to give effect to the above objectives. The preamble to the CA Act, 1972 reads as follows: *An Act to give effect to the Convention for the unification of certain rules of international carriage by air signed at Warsaw on the 12th day of October 1929 and to the said Convention as amended by the Hague Protocol on the 28th day of September 1955 and to make provision for applying the rules contained in the said Convention in its original form and in the amended form (subject to the exceptions, adaptations and modifications) to non-international carriage by air and for matters connected therewith.*

The CA Act was enacted to give effect to the convention for unification of rules relating to international carriage by air signed at Warsaw as amended at Hague in 1995 and by the Montreal Convention of 1999.

Judgement

The protection provided under the CP Act to consumers is in addition to the remedies available under any other statute. It does not disconsider the remedies under another statute but provides an additional or alternative remedy. In the case in point, at the relevant point of time, the value of the subject matter was more than ₹20 lakh, by which the National Commission is conferred jurisdiction for any cause of action that arises under the Act.

It may be pertinent to mention that the Parliament has recognized this fact while passing the Consumer Protection Act, 1986, and the Carriage by Air Act, 1972. Sec. 86 was itself a modification and restriction of the principle of foreign sovereign immunity and thus, by limiting the applicability of Sec. 86s, the Parliament, through these incorrect acts, further narrowed a party's ability to successfully plead foreign sovereign immunity. In the modern era, where there is a close interconnection among different countries as far as trade, commerce, and business are concerned, the principle of sovereign immunity can no longer be absolute in the way that it was earlier. Countries that participated in trade, commerce, and business with different countries ought to be subjected to normal rules of the market. State-owned entities would be able to operate with impunity, the rule of law would be degraded and international trade, commerce, and business will come to a grinding halt. Therefore, we do not hesitate in concluding that the appellant cannot claim sovereign immunity.

The CP Act gives the District Forums, State Forums, and National Commission the power to decide on the disputes of consumers. The jurisdiction, the power, and the procedure of these forums are all clearly enumerated by the CP Act. Although these Forums decide matters after following a summary procedure, their main function is still to decide disputes, which is the main function and purpose of a court. We are of the view that for the purpose of the CA Act and the Warsaw Convention, the consumer forums can fall within the meaning of the expression.

The appellant is an airline carrier of high repute and they effect transportation of goods to various parts of the world including Spain and, therefore, it can safely be presumed that the carriers were fully aware of the consignee's name, which was indicated in the consignee's box and they should have notified the party immediately after the arrival of the consignment. As that has not been done, the National Commission was justified in holding that there is deficiency of service on the part of the carrier in not effecting the delivery of goods to the consignee.

We conclude that the National Commission has jurisdiction to decide the dispute between the parties and it is a Court and that there was deficiency in service by the appellant-carrier. In view of the above discussion, we do not see any merit in this appeal. Accordingly, it is dismissed.

Conclusion

The Bench of the Supreme Court has painstakingly studied the case and has applied the law as precisely and as judiciously as possible. The case should give you the meticulous workings of a legal mind. The case is as new as September 2011; however, it is going to set a benchmark for international trade. If you are a manager involved in carriage protocol and international case then there is no better manual to follow than this case. Study the various nuances of the case by answering the following questions in the spirit that the Bench of the Supreme Court has shown above.

Discussion Questions

1 Delineate the preamble of the Indian Carriage Act, 1972.
2 Spell out in your own words the provisions of Sec. 3 of the CA Act.
3 Enumerate the parties to the case and their relationship.
4 Discuss the issues involved in the case.
5 Elucidate the main points of Warsaw Convention and its relevance to Indian Law.
6 How does the reasoning of the Court evolve into a judgement?
7 Does the above case have any resemblance to the case you know? How would you like to apply the judgement of this case as a precedent?
8 What lessons do you learn from the above case? Make a presentation to the board of directors of your company intimating them about the implications of the case.

Going Beyond

1 What is the importance of international convention about carriage?
2 The above case should be settled in a consumer court. Comment.
3 How does the carriage litigation affect international trade? Illustrate with a case.

LEGAL LUMINARY

MAMATA BANERJEE—MINISTER WITH A CAUSE

Ms Banerjee's entry on this page is based on two counts: her two-term tenure as Minister for Railways and her education—B.Ed, M.A. L.L.B., Ph.D. From her student days to date, she has remained an icon for youth. She is a six-time Member of the Parliament, founder of a political party, and presently the chief minister of West Bengal. Her cause: political and economic empowerment of the people of West Bengal.*

Managers are always advised to have clear objectives and focus on what they do. She has developed her vision from her young days as an activist and then as a youth leader. 'Be proactive, take initiative,' and the like are the oft-touted mantras of success for managers. Ms Banerjee could give a lesson or two about these even to the most celebrated managers.

The lessons she would give may not be to the liking of managers. She spearheaded a movement against the acquisition of 10,000 acres of land in Nandigram, which the government demarcated for Special Economic Zone (SEZ). On March 2007, it resulted in a violent confrontation with the state police, which resulted in the deaths and loss of properties of many people. The planned chemical hub thus had to be shelved. Likewise, in Singur she fought against the Nano Car Project of the Tatas and forced the company to return the acquired land back to the farmers. In 2011, when she became the chief minister, she had a law passed in support of the cause.

However, there are also some lessons that a manager may like. For instance, as soon as she became the chief minister, she immediately started dialogues with the Gorkhaland activists who wanted to carve out a separate hill state from West Bengal. A good start has been made by establishing a Gorkhaland Autonomous Council—the festering and confrontationist campaigns have subsided, resulting in bringing peace to the people of the region. Other reforms in the field of education, pensions, and employee relations are on the anvil.

The British Broadcasting Corporation (BBC) brought out an exclusive programme on Ms Banerjee, which vividly showed how a simple woman single-handedly and against all odds fought against a powerful political colossus such as the Communist government of West Bengal, which had a strong ideology, a dominant trade union might, and an almost unchallenged election strategy.**

Born in a simple family, she has maintained the same lifestyle, identifying herself with the poor, by living in a small single-room house with other members of her family, eating simple food, and dressing in plain cotton saris. People fondly call her *didi* (elder sister). She has written several books. Her hobbies are painting and Ravindra Sangeet, the musical tradition established by Rabindranath Tagore. She is presently the CM of West Bengal.

---

*See the case in Chapter 1.

**See http://www.bbc.co.uk/news/world-south-asia-13374646 (7 September 2011).

15

Consumer-related Laws

Principle: *Quorum ususconsistit in abusu.*

The use of a thing consists in consuming it.

CHAPTER OUTLINE

- Introduction and Interpretation
- Consumer Protection Act, 1986
- Definitions
- Consumer Disputes Redressal Agencies
- Consumer Redressal System
- Allied Consumer Laws
- The Agricultural Produce (Grading and Marking) Act, 1937
- Prevention of Food Adulteration Act, 1954

- Essential Commodities Act, 1955
- Prevention of Black Marketing and Maintenance of Supplies of Essential Commodities Act, 1980
- Standards of Weights and Measures Act, 1976 and Enforcement Act, 1985
- Conclusion
- Hire–purchase Act, 1972
- *Case Study:* All the World's a Stage— A Play in Three Acts
- *Legal Luminary:* Ashok Bhan

15.1 INTRODUCTION AND INTERPRETATION

Consumer dispute means a dispute where the person against whom a complaint has been made, denies or disputes the allegations contained in the complaint.

– Sec. 2 B vi(e), The Consumer Protection Act, 1986,

Consumer Protection Act, 1986, Sec. 2 B vi(e)

You have, thus far, seen how the mercantile law functions as a legal system. This chapter is introduced as the social factor of economic laws so that you may never lose sight of the purpose of such a compendium of laws. The old saying is apt here: the law is made for man and not man for the law. All businesses serve humans and their associations; the mercantile law is made to safeguard the economic interests of the people—consumers—in short, protection of the consumer. An umbrella of laws, as seen in the chapter overview, is your *leit motiv* in this chapter.

The scope of this chapter is the various allied laws concerning the consumer. As a manager, your perspective in this chapter of a consumer is not the conventional individual consumer or a group of consumers, but a company. Every company is also a consumer of goods and services, hires and purchases. The transactions of goods and services are set to definite standards of weights and measures, as the case may be. Whether one is an individual or association or a company, the legislator intends to provide protection against fraud.

15.2 CONSUMER PROTECTION ACT, 1986

This Act shall apply to all goods and services.

– The Consumer Protection Act, 1986, Sec. 1(4)

The General Assembly of the United Nations on 19 April 1985 adopted a set of guidelines for the protection of consumers and authorized the Secretary General to persuade member countries to make policies and enact laws accordingly. The guidelines were as follows:
1. Physical safety
2. Protection and promotion of consumer economic interests
3. Standards for safety and quality of consumer goods and services
4. Measures enabling consumers to obtain redressal
5. Measures relating to specific areas (food, water, and pharmaceuticals)
6. Consumer education and information programme

India promptly enacted the law which expressed the spirit of Articles 14–19 of the Constitution of India. The Act provides for effective safeguards to consumers against various types of exploitations and unfair dealings, relying mainly on compensatory rather than punitive or preventive approach. It applies to all goods and services unless specifically exempted and covers the private, public, and cooperative sectors and provides for speedy and inexpensive adjudication.

The Act is based on the following principles, which express the rights of the consumers:
1. Right to safety—Those that are not hazardous to life and property.
2. Right to be informed—To make an informed choice, one needs to know the quantity, quality, potency, purity, standard, and price of goods or services.
3. Right to choose—The right against restrictive trade practices and encourages the spirit of competition so that the consumer has a true choice.
4. Right to be heard—To uphold the interests of the consumers, the consumer welfare fora are essential. These are non-political, non-commercial, and are free of litigation.
5. Right to redressal—Consumer grievances must be heard and must be compensated. For an individual, the grievance may be relatively small; but when considered across society, its impact may be significant.
6. Right to education—Consumer awareness is the most important aspect in making the law work for the consumer. Ignorance is the cause of exploitation.

15.3 DEFINITIONS

The following definitions have two purposes. They clarify the concepts to create a clear understanding of the issues in the Act and at the same time comprehend the rationale of the Act. The definitions are abridged from the Act, Sec. 2, clause 1 and the bracketed letters are the particular sub-clause reference.

Consumer Any person who:

(i) Buys any goods for a consideration which has been paid or promised or partly paid and partly promised, or under any system of deferred payment, and includes any user of such goods other than the person who buys such goods for consideration paid or promised or partly paid or partly promised, or under any system of deferred payment when such use is made with the approval of such person, but does not include a person who obtains such goods for resale or for any commercial purpose.

(ii) Hires or avails of any services for a consideration which has been paid or promised or partly paid and partly promised, or under any system of deferred payment and includes any beneficiary of such services other than the person who hires or avails of the services for consideration paid or promised, or partly paid and partly promised, or under any system of deferred payment, when such services are availed of with the approval of the first mentioned person *but does not include a person who avails of such services for any commercial purposes* (d).

Goods Every kind of moveable property other than actionable claims and money; it includes stocks and shares, growing crops, grass, and things attached to or forming part of land which are agreed to be severed before sale or under the contract of sale (Sec. 2, 7 Sale of Goods Act, 1930) (i).

Spurious goods and services Such goods and services are claimed to be genuine but are actually not so (oo).

Services Any description that is made available to potential users and includes, but not limited to, the provision of facilities in connection with banking, financing insurance, transport, processing, supply of electrical or other energy, board or lodging or both, housing construction, entertainment, amusement or the purveying of news or other information, but does not include the rendering of any service free of charge or under a contract of personal service (o).

Complaint Any allegation in writing made by a complainant (c).

Complainant (i) A consumer or (ii) any voluntary consumer association registered under the Companies Act, 1956 (1 of 1956) or under any other law for the time being in force; or (iii) the central government or any state government, (iv) one or more consumers, where there are numerous consumers having the same interest; (v) in case of death of a consumer, his legal heir or representative, who or which makes a complaint (b).

Restrictive trade practice A trade practice that tends to bring about manipulation of price or conditions of delivery or affect the flow of supplies in the market relating to goods or services in such a manner as to impose on the consumers unjustified costs or restrictions and shall include:

(a) Delay beyond the period agreed to by a trader in supply of such goods or in providing the services which has led or is likely to lead to rise in the price.

(b) Any trade practice that requires a consumer to buy, hire, or avail of any goods or, as the case may be, services as condition precedent to buying, hiring, or availing of other goods or services (nnn).

Unfair trade practice   A trade practice that, for the purpose of promoting the sale, use or supply of any goods or for the provision of any service, adopts any unfair method or unfair or deceptive practice including any of the following practices (r). Examples: Misleading statements, advertisements written or oral, false representation of services, misleading standards of quantity and quality, old goods as new, false characteristics of goods, exaggeration of uses of goods, warranties which do not exist, price misrepresentation, disparaging other goods and services, announcement of schemes and gifts which are unintended, etc.

Defect   Any fault, imperfection, or shortcoming in the quality, quantity, potency, purity, or standard, which is required to be maintained by or under any law for the time being in force under any contract, express, or implied or as is claimed by the trader in any manner whatsoever in relation to any goods (f).

Deficiency   Any fault, imperfection, shortcoming, or inadequacy in the quality, nature, and manner of performance which is required to be maintained by or under any law for the time being in force or has been undertaken to be performed by a person in pursuance of a contract or otherwise in relation to any service (g).

Person   Person includes an individual or any of the following:

(i) A firm, whether registered or not
(ii) A Hindu undivided family
(iii) A co-operative society
(iv) Every other association of persons, whether registered under the Societies Registration Act, 1860 (21 of 1860) or not (m)

Dispute   A dispute where the person against whom a complaint has been made denies or disputes the allegations contained in the complaint (e).

Legal Framework

You will deal with two aspects under the legal framework: first, the agencies involved in consumer grievance redressal; and second, the procedures developed to approach these agencies.

15.4   CONSUMER DISPUTES REDRESSAL AGENCIES

Under Sec. 4 of the Act, the central government establishes the Central Consumer Protection Council and the states likewise form a council at the state level and also at the district level of the states. The aim of the councils is to achieve the objectives of the Act by ensuring the customers their rights.

Sections 9–28 of the Consumer Protection Act deal with the establishment, jurisdiction, and functioning of the District Forum, State Commission, and the National Commission—the agencies to deal with consumer redressal (Figure 15.1 and Case 15.1).

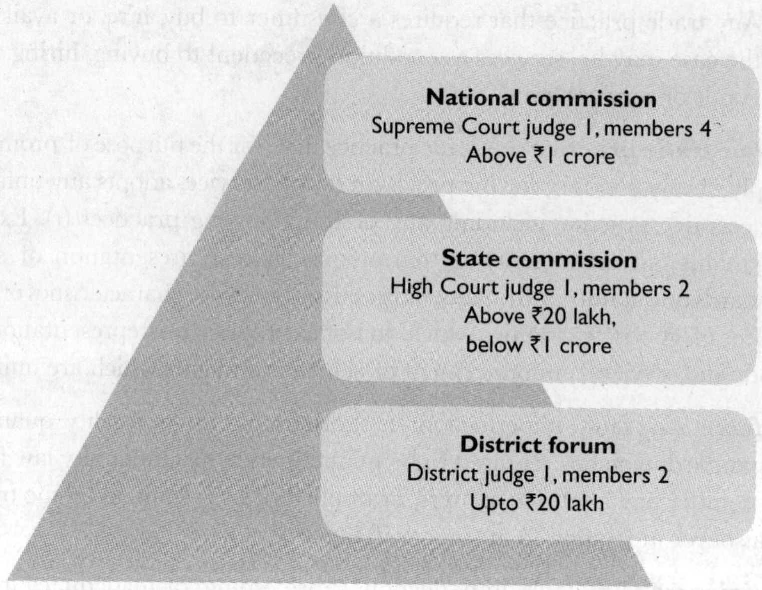

National commission
Supreme Court judge 1, members 4
Above ₹1 crore

State commission
High Court judge 1, members 2
Above ₹20 lakh,
below ₹1 crore

District forum
District judge 1, members 2
Upto ₹20 lakh

Figure 15.1 Consumer protection hierarchy

CASE 15.1 APPELLANT: Birla Technologies Ltd vs RESPONDENT: Neutral Glass and Allied Industries

DATE OF JUDGEMENT: 15 December 2010*

FACTS: This appeal is filed against the judgement passed by National Consumer Disputes Redressal Commission on the deficiency in service, under Sec. 2(1)(d)(ii) of The Consumer Protection Act, 1986.

The appellant had sent a detailed proposal for the purpose of developing certain computer software for the respondent at a cost of ₹36 lakh on 11 February 1998. The problem arose as more time was needed to develop the modules and thus escalate the price. The respondent complained increasingly about the defective modules. A complaint against the appellant came to be filed on 26 June 2003 before the State Consumer Disputes Redressal Commission. The case went through State commission and through to National commission.

The Commission held that the 'goods' purchased by the respondent from the appellant were being used by the respondent for a commercial purpose and, therefore, the respondent was not a 'consumer' within the meaning of Sec. 2(1)(d)(i) of the Act. However, the National Commission further held that notwithstanding such findings, the respondent was entitled to maintain a complaint under the Act with respect to the deficiency in service during the one year warranty period with respect to the said goods relying on Sec. 2(1)(d)(ii) of the Act.

JUDGEMENT: The appeal is allowed. Complaint dismissed with costs assessed at ₹50,000.

REASON: The parties may avail the legal remedies available to them.

---

*Birla Technologies Ltd vs Neutral Glass and Allied Industries; see also: http://www.indiankanoon.org/doc/1679311/ (20 September 2011).

District forum   Each district of a state has a consumer forum which is headed by a person qualified to be a district judge with two more members, of which one shall be a woman.

The jurisdiction of the district forum is restricted to the value of goods or services and the compensation claimed is not more than ₹20 lakh.

State commission   It is set up by the state under a sitting or a retired judge of the high court with two more members to assist him, one of whom shall be a woman.

The jurisdiction in terms of value of goods and services and compensation, if any, shall exceed ₹20 lakh and shall be less than a crore.

Appeal   It will hear appeals against the orders of the district fora.

National commission   It is set up by the central government. It is headed by a sitting or a retired judge of the Supreme Court of India and consists of four more members, one of who shall be a woman.

The jurisdiction in terms of the value of goods and services or compensation will be over ₹1 crore.

Appeal   It will hear appeals against the orders of the state commission.

15.5 CONSUMER REDRESSAL SYSTEM

Filing a complaint   Under Sec. 9A of the Act a complaint may be filed on a complaint form or even on a simple paper, which must have the following important details:
(a) The name and address of the complainant and the opposite party
(b) Facts of the case
(c) Documents in support of the allegations
(d) The relief which the complainant is seeking
(e) It must be signed by the complainant or his authorized agent
(f) Please note: no lawyer is required

Limitation period   Under Sec. 24A of the Act, the grievance must be filed with any of the redressal *fora* within the 2 years from the date on which the cause of action has arisen.

Procedure on admission of complaint   Under the Consumer Protection Amendment Act, 2002, Secs 13, 18, and 22, upon admission of the complaint, the appropriate authority shall refer a copy of the same to the opposite party, directing him to present his version within 30 days, which may be extended by another 15 days. In the event the opposite party denies and fails to do anything about it, the authority shall conduct necessary investigation within 45 days and then issue an appropriate order.

Final orders   Under Sec. 24 of the Act, the orders of the agencies will be final if no appeal has been preferred against such orders.

Appeals   Under Sec. 15 of the Act, appeals against the district forum will be made to the state commission.

Under Sec. 19 of the Act, the state commission appeals will be made to the central commission.

Enforcement of orders   Under Sec. 25 of the Act, the authority may take such action as attachment of the property not complying with the orders, and will appropriately execute the order in favour of the aggrieved.

Penalties   Under Sec. 27A, the penalties for not complying with an order may be not less than ₹2000 and not above ₹10,000, and imprisonment ranging from a month extended to three years; both fines as well as imprisonments may be imposed.

Dismissal of frivolous or vexatious complaints   Under Sec. 26 of the Act, the authorities have the power to dismiss as well as to penalize frivolous or vexatious complaints and to impose fine not exceeding ₹10,000.

15.6   ALLIED CONSUMER LAWS

Food is the first basic need of man. Hence, it is no surprise if the legislator gives it the utmost priority both in our Constitution as well as the laws enacted thereafter.

These laws, orders, and rules aim at the protection of the consumers' interests with special reference to food. Some of these enactments are the Agricultural Produce (Grading and Marking) Act, 1937; the Prevention of Food Adulteration Act, 1954; the Monopolies and Restrictive Trade Practices Act, 1969; the Standard of Weights and Measures Act, 1976; Bureau of India Standards Act, 1986; the Prevention of Food Adulteration Act, 1954; the Fruit Products Order, 1955; the Meat Food Products Order, 1973 ; the Vegetable Oil Products (Control) Order, 1947; the Edible Oils Packaging (Regulation) Order, 1998; the Solvent Extracted Oil, De-oiled Meal, and Edible Flour (Control) Order, 1967; and the Milk and Milk Products Order, 1992. The Constitution of India contains a number of provisions that go a long way in protecting the rights of the consumers. These provisions include Article 21 which deals with the right to life and personal liberty; Article 47 guarantees the right to health, and Article 48-A aims at a pollution-free environment for all citizens. The Supreme Court has held that the right to life under Article 21 includes the right to a healthy and safe environment. Several Acts and Orders have prevailed in India to safeguard food safety and the health of the consumer.

You are expected to study these laws in two ways:

Business discipline   As a business management student you are expected to study these laws along with other aspects of business in the courses of customer relations, sales and marketing, pricing, advertising, ethics, and across several other disciplines wherever consumer is the target.

On-the-job   You are expected to apply very carefully all the legal aspects concerning consumers from manufacturing of goods until they are bought by the customer and beyond. Similarly, as a service provider, your application of the law goes beyond merely rendering the services; you are expected to check the quality of the services that you offer.

MANAGER'S TAKEAWAY

- For a manager Customer is the definition of a consumer.
- As a manager always remember that the customer is king.

From all the laws mentioned in the interest of the consumer, you will consider the highlights of the most important ones as given below. These are merely the highlights.

15.7 THE AGRICULTURAL PRODUCE (GRADING AND MARKING) ACT, 1937

Agricultural Produce (Grading and Marking) Act, 1937, was enacted to achieve the following objectives:

(a) Grading and standardization of agricultural commodities
(b) Regulation of marks and marking practices
(c) Market research and surveys
(d) Training of personnel in agricultural marking

The Act provides for the establishment of a Directorate of Marking and Inspection to look into the above objectives.

The main commodities graded are vegetable oil, ghee, butter, eggs, wheat flour, rice, cotton, potatoes, *gur*, maize, honey, and ground spices. Laboratory facilities for fixing grade standards for the new products and for the existing grade standards, when necessary, are provided by the Central Agmark Laboratory at Nagpur and by sixteen regional Agmark Laboratories in Kolkata, Mumbai, Chennai, Kanpur, Kochi, Bengaluru, Patna, Rajkot, Guntur, and other centres. Grading of agricultural produce at the farmer's level and that of *kapas*—cotton—at the producer's level are undertaken by different grading units and centres in different states. Compulsory grading is done before export in the case of thirty-four commodities. The graded goods are stamped with the seal of the Agricultural Marking Department (AGMARK).

15.8 PREVENTION OF FOOD ADULTERATION ACT, 1954

This law was enacted to eradicate the anti-social evil of food adulteration and to ensure purity in the articles of food. It provides for constitution of a Central Committee for Food Standards to advise the central and state governments on matters arising out of the administration of the Act and to carry out other functions assigned to it.

The Act has some general provisions as regards food and incorporates certain provisions as regards methods of analysis of food. For this purpose, the office of a public analyst has been created. The duty of the public analyst is to analyze the sample of food sent to him. Moreover, the Act provides that a purchaser of any article of food, or a recognized consumer association (whether the purchaser is a member of that association or not), can get such article analyzed by the public analyst. The public analyst shall send the report of the result of analysis of any article of food to the local (health) authority. If the food article as per report is found to be adulterated, prosecution proceedings against the person from whom the sample was taken shall be instituted.

Food Any article used as food or drink for human consumption other than drugs and water and includes:

(a) Any article which ordinarily enters into or is used in the composition or preparation of human food

(b) Any flavouring matter or condiments

(c) Any other article which the central government may, having regard to its use, nature, substance, or quality, declare, by notification in the official gazette as food for the purpose of this Act

Central committee for food standards   There is provision for a Central Committee for Food Standards; it consists of five representatives nominated by the central government to represent the consumers' interests, one of whom shall be from the hotel industry.

Remedy   The purchaser or the consumer, or any recognized consumer association can send any article of food to the public analyst for an analysis report after informing the vendor at the time of purchase his or its intention to have such article so analyzed (Sec. 7). The public analyst shall deliver a report to the local health authority of the result of the analysis of any article of food submitted to him for analysis (8). On receipt of the report of the analysis to the effect that the article of food is adulterated, the local health authority shall initiate measures of prosecution against the persons from whom the sample of the article of food was taken. The person or persons who sent for analysis or the public analyst, either or both of them, may make an application to the court within a period of ten days from the date of receipt of the copy of the report to get the sample of the article of food kept by the local health authority analyzed by the Central Food Laboratory (9).

Penalties under Sec. 16   Sec. 16 of the Act provides that subject to the provisions of sub-Sec. (1-A), if any person, whether by himself or by another person on his behalf, imports into India or manufactures for sales, or stores or distributes any article of food which is adulterated or misbranded or the sale of which is prohibited under any provision of this Act or any rule made there under or by an order of the Food Health Authority and whether by himself or by any other person on his behalf, imports into India or manufactures for sales, or stores, or sells or distributes any adulterant which is not injurious to health be punishable with imprisonment for a term which shall not be less than six months but which may extend to three years, and with fine which shall not be less than ₹1000.

Penalty under Sec. 16 (1-A)   This measure provides that if any person, whether by himself or by any other person on his behalf, imports into India or manufactures for sale, or stores, sells, or distributes any article of food which is adulterated within the meaning of any of the sub-clauses (e) to (l) (both inclusive) of clause (i-a) of Sec. 2 or any adulterant which is injurious to health shall, in addition to the penalty to which he may be liable under the provisions of Sec. 6, be punishable with imprisonment for a term which shall not be less than one year but which many extend to six years and with fine which shall not be less than ₹2000.

Criminal liability   If such article of food or adulterant, when consumed by any person, is likely to cause his death or is likely to cause such harm on his body as would amount to grievous hurt within the meaning of Sec. 320 of the Indian Penal Code shall be punishable with imprisonment for a term which shall not be less than three years but which may extend to term of life and with fine which shall not be less than ₹5000.

15.9 ESSENTIAL COMMODITIES ACT, 1955

This Act empowers the central government in the public interest to achieve the following objectives:
(a) Regulate production, supply, distribution, storage, transport, etc
(b) Control price of commodities that have been declared under the Act, as essential;
(c) Ensure compliance of the provisions of the Act and the orders passed
(d) Award penalties for those who commit offences under the Act
(e) The Act was amended in 1986

Implementation   The Essential Commodities Act is being implemented by the state governments/UT administrations by availing of the delegated powers under the Act. The state governments/UT administrations have issued various Control Orders to regulate various aspects of trading in essential commodities such as food grains, edible oils, pulses kerosene, sugar, etc. The central government regularly monitors the action taken by the state governments/UT administrations to implement the provisions of the Essential Commodities Act, 1955.

Powers to control production, supply, distribution, etc. of essential commodities (Sec. 11)   If the central government is of the opinion that it is necessary or expedient so to do for maintaining or increasing supplies of any essential commodity or for securing their equitable distribution and availability at fair prices, or for securing any essential commodity for the defence of India or the efficient conduct of military operations, it may, by order, provide for regulating or prohibiting the production supply and distribution thereof and trade and commerce therein (1).

Penalties Sec. 12 (1)   If any person contravenes any order made under section (a) he shall be punishable, (i) in the case of an order made with reference to clause (h) or clause (i) of sub-Sec. (2) of that section, with imprisonment for a term which may extend to one year and shall also be liable to a fine, and (ii) in the case of any other order, with imprisonment for a term which shall not be less than three months but which may extend to seven years and shall also be liable to a fine, provided that the court may, for any adequate and special reasons to be mentioned in the judgement, impose a sentence of imprisonment for a term of less than three months; (b) any property in respect of which the order has been contravened shall be forfeited to the government; (c) any package, covering, or receptacle in which the property is found and any animal, vehicle, vessel, or other conveyance used in carrying the commodity shall, if the court so orders, be forfeited to the government.

A number of quality control orders have been issued under the Essential Commodities Act, 1955 such as the Fruit Products Order, 1955; the Solvent Extracted Oil, De-oiled Meal and Edible Flour (Control) Order, 1967; Milk and Milk Products Order, 1992; Meat Food Products Order, 1973; the Vegetable Oils Control (Regulation) Order, 1998; and the Edible Oils Packaging (Regulation) Order, 1998.

15.10 PREVENTION OF BLACK MARKETING AND MAINTENANCE OF SUPPLIES OF ESSENTIAL COMMODITIES ACT, 1980

This Act is a supplement to the Essential Commodities Act, 1955. It deals with certain malpractices indulged in by unscrupulous elements like black-marketeers, hoarders, and profiteers with stringent penal provisions.

Under this Act, the central government, state government, and specified officials of the government have been empowered to order detention of a person who is found to be acting in any manner prejudicial to the maintenance of supplies of commodities essential to the community.

The maximum period for which any person may be detained in pursuance of any detention order cannot exceed 6 months from the date of detention. However, the person detained has a right to know the grounds of his detention, unless disclosure of the grounds is considered against the public interest in general.

Furthermore, the law grants protection to the authorities for having taken action in good faith. It provides that no suit or other legal proceeding shall lie against the central government or a state government, and no suit, prosecution or other legal proceeding shall lie against any person for anything in good faith done or intended to be done in pursuance of this Act.

15.11 STANDARDS OF WEIGHTS AND MEASURES ACT, 1976 AND ENFORCEMENT ACT, 1985

As the title of the Act suggests, it aims at introducing standards in relation to weights and measures used in trade and commerce. The ultimate objective is to serve the interests of the consumers. The Act, therefore, is essentially a consumer protection measure as every article of manufacture, subject to the standards of weights and measures under the Act, ultimately finds its application or use by or for the benefit of the consumer.

The amendment of the Act in 1986 has empowered the consumer associations to make a complaint under the Act.

The Act makes special provisions as regards packaged commodities. Besides, the Standards of Weights and Measures (Packaged Commodities) Rules, 1977 have been framed. Nowadays, commodities, including foodstuffs, are being made available in a ready-to-use condition, off the shelf, in packages. This trend of making a large number of items available in a pre-packed condition is picking up very fast. Here comes the question of protecting the interests of consumers. As the commodity is pre-packed, a consumer does not know at the time of purchase about the quantity, quality, type, number, and size of the contents (Table 15.1).

Table 15.1   Standards of weights and measures

Mass	Kilogram (kg), gram (g), milligram (mg)
Length	Metre (m), centimetre (cm), millimetre (mm)
Area	Square metre (m^2)
Capacity	Kilolitre (kl), litre (l or L), millilitre (ml)
Temperature	Degree Celsius (°C) or Degree Kelvin (°K)
Volume	Cubic metre (m^3), cubic centimetre (cm^3), cubic millimetre (mm^3)

Provisions

1. Provides to prescribe specification of measuring instruments used in commercial transaction, industrial production and measurement involved in public health and human safety. The specifications are given in the Standard of Weights and Measures (General) Rules, 1987

2. Regulation of inter-state trade and commerce in weights and measures and commodities sold, distributed, or supplied by weights or measures

3. Regulation of pre-packed commodities sold or intended to be sold in the course of inter-state and commerce

4. Approval (before manufacture) of models of weights and measuring instrument intended to be manufactured after the commencement of the proposed legislation

5. Control and regulation of export and import of weights and measures and commodities in packaged form

6. Establishment of an Indian Institute of Legal Metrology to provide training in legal metrology to inspectors and others

7. Surveys and collection of statistics for facilitating planning and enforcement of the proposed legislation

8. Inspection of weighing and measuring instruments during their use to prevent fraudulent practices

9. Powers of inspectors to search, seize, and forfeiture of non-standard weight or measure

10. Power to file case in the court for prosecution

11. Power to compound certain cases before or after the institution of the prosecution cases

12. Appeal provisions

13. Prescribe fee for various services rendered

14. Power to make rules for implementing the provisions of the Act

15.12 CONCLUSION

The above provisions have been merely a glimpse into the mind of the legislator about the priority for human life and its protection. It is the human face of the law. All goods and services are oriented towards fulfilling the needs of man.

Human desires and needs form the foundation of man's economic pursuit, to satisfy one's wants, and to live a life worthy of human dignity.

15.13 HIRE–PURCHASE ACT, 1972

Important Note

This Act was intended to come into force on 1 June 1973. The notification was rescinded and was supposed to come into force on 1 September 1973, but even this was rescinded. Since the notification of the Act is still pending, the cases are

MANAGER'S TAKEAWAY

- A nation's character is known by the way it treats its citizens under the rule of law.
- A manager's character is known by the concern he has for the people in the goods and services he is responsible to provide for them in accordance with the law.

dealt as before in reference to the Indian Contract Act, 1872 with which you are familiar. However, the knowledge of the yet to be operational law, apart from its academic interest, should never be underestimated since its spirit is still functional through the law of contract.

TEXT

'Hire purchase agreement' means an agreement under which goods are let on hire and under which the hirer has an option to purchase them in accordance with the terms of the agreement and includes an agreement under which
(i) possession of goods is delivered by the owner thereof to a person on condition that such persons pay the agreed amount in periodical installments,
(ii) the property in the goods is to pass to such person on the payment of the last of such installments, and
(iii) such person has a right to terminate the agreement at any time before the property so passes

– Hire–Purchase Act, 1972, Sec. 2 (c)

Modern business involves ubiquitous schemes of hire-purchase from fast moving consumer goods to real estate, from personal and commercial vehicles to industrial plants and infrastructure. Hire-purchase has a twofold activity: sale of goods and financing the price of the goods. The method consists of a gradual payment for the goods purchased; until every installment is paid the status of the purchased goods is on hire. Upon completion of the payments, the goods are transferred to the buyer as his property. In the language of the Indian Contract Act, 1872, which was further bifurcated by the Sale of Goods Act, 1930, the two aspects of the hire-purchase are bailment and sale of goods.

Rights and Duties of the Hirer

Hirer, the one who hires, is the person who has obtained or is to obtain possession of the goods from the owner under a hire-purchase agreement. When one hires something, he agrees to pay a percentage of the total price periodically. Purchase price is the sum total of all the money that the hirer pays to the owner. The rights and duties of the hirer are as shown in Table 15.2.

Rights and Duties of the Owner

According to Sec. 2 (f) the owner is the one who lets or delivers possession of goods to a hirer under a hire-purchase agreement. Owner's rights and duties are as shown in Table 15.3. According to Sec. 25, if the hirer goes insolvent, the owner may bring a suit against him and the court may appoint a receiver or liquidator who would have same rights as the hirer in respect of the goods.

As has been observed earlier on, Case 15.2 clearly brings out the obvious relation between the hirer and the owner. The essence of the hire-purchase agreement is that the property in the goods does not pass at the time of the agreement but remains with the intending seller. It passes later when the intending buyer pays the entire amount of the price; until then the seller is the true owner bearing full responsibility before the law.

 **MANAGER'S TAKEAWAY**

- Rereading a hire–purchase agreement is the first step towards attending a consumer grievance.
- The right question to ask is: What is the essence of contract?

Table 15.2   Rights and duties of the hirer

Rights	Duties
Purchase with rebate Sec. 9 provides for rebate. The rebate shall be equal to two-thirds of an amount which bears to the hire-purchase charges the same proportion as the balance of the hire-purchase price not yet due bears to the hire-purchase price.	Comply with agreement: Sec. 13 obligates the hirer to honour the agreement and pay the installments on time.
Terminate agreement Sec. 10 provides that the hirer at any time during the hiring has period the right to terminate the agreement by returning the goods and the due installments.	Care of goods: Sec. 14 makes the hirer responsible to take care of the goods with prudence.
Appropriate payments Sec. 11 provides wherever there are more than one hire-purchase agreements with the same owner, the hirer may appropriate the amounts to such agreements as he likes.	Unauthorized use forbidden: Sec. 15 forbids unauthorized use than stated in the agreement; in case of loss, it must be borne by the hirer.
Assign and transmit Sec. 12 permits the hirer to assign and transmit his title with the consent of the owner whose duty is to consent; failure to do so empowers the hirer to go ahead without the owner's consent. The owner has no right to ask for any consideration in lieu of his consent.	Provide information: Sec. 16 makes the hirer responsible to provide any information about the goods to be made available within 14 days of receiving a request from the owner.
Refund on seizure of goods Sec. 17 provides refund on seizure of goods in case the goods are seized by the owner according to Sec. 19. The hirer is liable to get interest in the event the owner fails to pay within 30 days.	

Table 15.3   Rights and duties of the owner

Rights	Duties
Terminate agreement on payment default According to Sec. 18 (1) where the hirer defaults on payment more than once may, upon notice of a week, terminate the agreement. However, if the hirer is ready to settle the payment with interest, he may retain the goods.	Supply a true copy of the agreement, signed by him immediately after the execution of the agreement.
Terminate agreement on unauthorized use Sec. 22 provides for termination of agreement for breach of use.	A copy of agreement to the surety.
Rights on termination Sec. 17 allows retaining the hirer if the latter has paid his dues and claims the goods.	Give the hirer information: the amount paid by or on behalf of the hirer; the amount due and unpaid with dates; the amount which to become payable with dates.
Seizure of goods Sec. 19 permits the owner to seize goods upon default in payment by the hirer.	The hirer must do the agreement in writing.

CASE 15.2

APPELLANT: K.L. Johar and Company   VS   RESPONDENT: Deputy Commercial Tax Officer

DATE OF JUDGEMENT: 11 October 1964*

FACTS: The appellant carried on hire–purchase business in Motor vehicles. The course of business was that the price of the vehicle would be paid by the appellant to the motor dealer and the vehicle would be hired out to the intending purchaser. The latter had to pay the hire money in installments and when all the installments according to the agreement had been paid, he would exercise the option of purchasing the vehicle by a final payment of ₹1. It was clearly laid down in the hire–purchase agreement that for the duration of the hire the vehicle would remain under the ownership of the appellant. The sales tax authorities in Madras imposed sales tax on the appellant for the assessment year 1955–56 and 1956–57. The hire–purchase transactions were treated as sale transactions under Explanation 1 to Sec. 2(h) of the Madras General Sales Tax Act, 1939. The appellant's writ petition before the Madras High Court challenging the said assessment failed, but a certificate of fitness to appeal to the Supreme Court was granted.

JUDGEMENT: Uphold the appeal in so far as that the sales tax authorities will determine the price in accordance with what we have said above and thereafter proceed to levy sales tax according to law.

REASON: So far as the dealer is concerned, the whole price is paid by the appellant. The agreement also shows that the appellant is the owner of the vehicle and the intending purchaser is merely a hirer. The vehicle has to be registered in the name of the appellant, though the fact of registration by itself in one name or another may not be determinative of the ownership of the vehicle. The agreement clearly shows that there was no sale by the dealer to the intending purchaser of the vehicle at the time of the hire–purchase agreement. This gives power to the appellant to retake possession of the vehicle and determine the agreement. Now if the property in the vehicle had passed to the intending purchaser at the time of the hire–purchase agreement, it would not have been open to the appellant to take possession of the vehicle or to insist on payment of arrears or to become entitled to everything that had been paid up to that day. Under the law all that the appellant would have been entitled to was to realize the loan he had given by filing a suit and then attaching and selling the vehicle. These two clauses are, therefore, clear indication of the fact that there was no sale by the dealer to the person who wanted to purchase the vehicle at the time of the hire–purchase agreement, and that at that time the sale was by the dealer to the appellant.

This case brings out the true nature of the payment made as hire in hire-purchase agreement. Part of the amount is towards the hire and part towards the payment of price, and it would be for the sales tax authorities to determine in an appropriate way the price of the vehicle on the date the hirer exercises his option and becomes the owner of the vehicle after fulfilling the terms of the agreement.

It is, therefore, for the sales tax authorities to find out the price of the vehicle on which tax has to be paid in either of the ways indicated by us above or such other way as may be just and reasonable.

---

*K.L. Johar & Co. vs Deputy Commercial Tax Officer, 1965 AIR 1082, 1965 SCR (1) 112; also see: http://www.indiankanoon.org/doc/1367601/ (20 September 2011).

SUMMARY

- All goods and services are produced for the consumers. The law sets safeguards against physical safety, standards of goods and services, qualitative and quantitative measures, and safety in specific areas such as food and medicine. The law also promotes consumer awareness, information, and education.
- It is the intention of the legislator to make consumer law applicable as simply and effectively as possible. To avoid delay and promote quick redress District Consumer Fora, State Commission, and National Consumer Redressal Commission have been formed and empowered to deal with the disputes. The hierarchical legal framework is meant to work efficiently to provide justice to the satisfaction of the consumers.
- There are several consumer-allied laws, which ensure that the determined areas of consumers are served. Thus, for instance, there are separate laws for agricultural grading, essential commodities, action against black marketers, maintenance of supply of essential commodities, the standards of weights and measures, etc.
- Although the Hire–Purchase Act's notification is under pendency, the need and urgency of the law cannot be undermined. Millions of transactions take place every day, as if under this law, on the principle of bailment.

EXERCISES

(i) Kirit is an MBA student in a reputed management institute. He found that several of the faculty members were not good at teaching. He felt that he is a clear loser for he has paid quite a high fee. He wants to file a complaint in the consumer forum. What is your advice?

Hint: Education does not come under the Act; this was held in a case N Taneja vs Calcutta District Forum; see AIR 1992, Cal. 95.

(ii) Savita is a clerk in the Government Electricity Department who got herself treated at an ESI hospital. She felt that the doctor who treated her was negligent. Can she find redress?

Hint: Probably not; although the service falls under the ambit of the Act the allegation of negligence need to be proved with accordance with a responsible body of medical persons.

(iii) Mittal invested in shares and deposited in a participant bank of depository for Demat; however, the bank delayed endlessly to demat the shares. Can Mittal claim consumer protection?

Hint: Yes. In Indusind Bank Ltd vs Vimal Mittal it was held that he was a consumer; see II 2007, CPJ 161 (NC).

(iv) What is the legal framework of Consumer Protection Law?

(v) In the light of Sale of Goods Act and the principle of bailment, is the Hire and Purchase Act superfluous? Discuss.

DEVELOPMENT OF LEGAL EDGE

Project—Consumer Protection

Objective Voluntary service to gain experience in consumer matters

- The District Consumer Fora as well the State Consumer Redressal Commissions lack resources personnel, that there is no adequate staff, which delays dispute redressal.
- Volunteering yourself to aid the Forum Officer or the State Commissioner would give you admirable experience in consumer-related problems.
- This experience will help you to prevent most of the mistakes that managers commit and the consumers pay for them.
- A well-documented report on your work will be a most valuable research report which will not only help lawmakers, but also business people and citizens who are consumers.

FURTHER READING

Books

- VK Agarwal, *Consumer Protection Law and Practice*, 6th edn, Bharat Law House Pvt. Ltd, 2009.
- SS Singh and Sapna Gandhi, *Consumer Protection in India: Some Reflections*, IIPA, New Delhi, 2005.

Web resources

The link for the following laws:

- http://www.indiacode.nic.in.
- http://www.legaldocs.com.

- Consumer Protection Act, 1986.
- Essential Commodities Act, 1955.
- Prevention of Black Marketing and Maintenance of Supplies of Essential Commodities Act, 1980.
- Standards of Weights and Measures Act, 1976.
- Standards of Weights and Measures Enforcement Act, 1985.
- Hire–Purchase Act, 1972.

CASE STUDY ALL THE WORLD'S A STAGE—A PLAY IN THREE ACTS

> *All the world's a stage,*
> *And all the men and women merely players;*
> *They have their exits and their entrances...*[1]

Legal Basis of the Case

Consumer Protection Act, 1986, Sec. 27 *Where a trader or a person against whom a complaint is made or the complainant fails or omits to comply with any order made by the District Forum, the State Commission, or the National Commission, as the case may be, such trader or person, or complainant shall be punishable with imprisonment for a term which shall not be less than one month but which may extend to three years, or with fine which shall not be less than two thousands rupees but which may extend to ten thousand rupees, or with both.*

Consumer Protection Act, 1986 (Sec. 17b*) Notwithstanding anything contained in the Code of Criminal Procedure, 1973 (2 of 1974), an appeal under Sec. 27, both on facts and on law, shall lie from (a) the order made by the District Forum to the State Commission; (b) the order made by the State Commission to the National Commission...*

The constitution of India article 226 *...every High Court shall have power, throughout the territories in relation to which it exercises jurisdiction, to issue to any person or authority, including in appropriate cases, any Government, within those territories directions, orders or writs, including 1 [writs in the nature of habeascorpus, mandamus, prohibition, quo warranto and certiorari, or any of them, for the enforcement of any of the rights...]*

Act I

The prayer The petitioner invokes the extraordinary jurisdiction of this Court under Article 226 of the Constitution of India and accordingly prays for issuance of a writ of certiorari calling for the records relating to the order dated 11 December 2002 in R.P. No. 188 of 2002 on the file of the A.P. State Consumer Disputes Redressal Commission, Hyderabad and quash the same.

The Plot The writ petitioner is a builder who undertook to develop and construct residential flats in the premises bearing Municipal Door No. 1-2-412/5, Valmeeki Nagar, Domalguda, Hyderabad. The second respondent/ complainant was a tenant in the said building. That as per the agreement dated 21 August 1996 executed between the writ petitioner and the second respondent, the second respondent has agreed to vacate the premises and deliver possession of the building subject to the condition that the builder provides a three bedroom flat on the southeast corner of the first floor of the proposed building along with car parking facility at a concessional rate of ₹2,00,000. Admittedly, the writ petitioner herein did not deliver the southeast corner flat after completing the construction of the flats. It was alleged by the second respondent that the writ

---

[1] William Shakespeare, *As You Like It*, Act II, Scene vii; retrieved from: http://www.poemhunter.com/poem/all-the-world-s-a-stage/ (07 September 2011).

petitioner herein was trying to negotiate with third parties to sell the said southeast corner flat and in those circumstances, he filed the complaint before the District Forum as against the petitioner to complete the construction work and deliver possession of the southeast corner flat to him and also for grant of injunction and for a compensation of ₹100,000.

The writ petitioner herein opposed the complaint on various grounds. The case set up by the writ petitioner was that pursuant to the Development Agreement dated 2 September 1996 between the owner of the site and the builder, certain flats including the southeast corner flat went to the share of the owner and hence the agreement between the writ petitioner and the second respondent's contract was deemed impossible to perform and hence the complaint petition should be dismissed.

That after due enquiry, the District Forum disposed of the complainant by order dated 17 August 2000 directing the builder to (a) execute and register conveyance deed and deliver possession of southeast corner flat of the first floor of the building within three months of payment/deposit of ₹2,00,000 and other expenses by the complainant; (b) to pay compensation at the rate of ₹5,500/- per month from 5 May 1999 towards rent till the date of delivery of the possession of the flat to the complainant; and (c) to pay costs of ₹1000. The appeal preferred by the writ petitioner before the A.P. State Consumer Redressal Commission, Hyderabad was dismissed on 21 March 2001 confirming the order of the District Forum. The revision petition was also dismissed by the National Consumer Dispute Redressal Commission, New Delhi. S.L.P preferred by the writ petitioner was also dismissed by the Hon'ble Supreme Court. In the result the order passed by the District Forum attained finality.

Act II

Thereafter, the second respondent herein filed complaint purporting it to be under Sec. 27 of the Consumer Protection Act, 1986 (Act 68 of 1986) (for short 'the Act') against the writ petitioner for punishing him for his failure to comply with the order passed by the District Forum and to execute and enforce the order dated 17 August 2000 passed by the District Forum. The writ petitioner opposed the said petition inter alia contending that the owner of the building filed Civil Suit O.S. No. 783 of 2001 on the file of the first Senior Civil Judge, City Civil Court, Hyderabad against the petitioner for perpetual injunction, and in I.A. No. 532 of 2001 the Court granted temporary injunction

restraining the builder from transferring or alienating flats allotted to her share and it is under those circumstances, the writ petitioner was not in a position to comply with the order passed against the builder.

The District Forum having taken the relevant facts into consideration passed order dated 7 December 2001 which reads as follows:

'The District Forum in an enquiry under Sec. 27 cannot finalize a draft of sale deed. We have to split this part which can be taken up in a Civil process under Sec. 25 of the C.P. Act.'

Under the facts and circumstances discussed above, the ends of justice in this case will be served by sentencing the respondent/opposite party to pay a fine of ₹5,000 (Rupees five thousand only) within one month from the date of receipt of this order. The penalty petition filed by the petitioner/complainant is accordingly disposed of. Regarding compensation and costs awarded by this Forum in the main C.D. shall also be paid within one month from the date of this order by the respondent.

That aggrieved by the said order passed by the District Forum, the second respondent herein invoked the jurisdiction of the State Commission under Sec. 17(b) of the Act with a prayer to set aside the order passed by the District Forum and punish the petitioner and send the records to the civil Court directly for execution of the sale deed and delivering possession of the flat.

The State Commission upon hearing the parties disposed of the revision petition by an order dated 11 December 2002 and the operative portion of the order reads as follows:

'Accordingly we set aside the order of the District Forum and convict the respondent and sentence him to suffer imprisonment for a period of two years. This punishment will be imposed on Mr. Mallikarjuna Reddy, Managing Director of Megacity Builders, Gaganmahal, Hyderabad. However, as a measure of indulgence we are inclined to grant him a month's time from today to comply with the order of the District Forum. In default alone this order will be given effect to and in case the order of the District Forum dated 17 August 2000 is complied in all respects within the said period the conviction and sentence imposed on the respondent shall not be given effect to.'

This writ petition by the petitioner herein is directed against the said order. The impugned order is challenged on various grounds.

Act III

In the first place, it is well settled that where proceedings are taken before a Tribunal under a provision of law, which is ultra vices, it is open to a party aggrieved thereby to move the High Court under Article 226 for issuing appropriate writs. In the second place, the doctrine has no application in a case where the impugned order has been made in violation of the principles of natural justice.

It says that subject to the other provisions of the Act, the State Commission shall have jurisdiction to entertain complaints where the value of the goods or services and compensation, if any, claimed exceeds ₹20 lakh but does not exceed ₹1 crore; and appeals against the order of any District Forum within the State; and to call for the records and pass appropriate orders in any 'consumer dispute' which is pending before or has been decided by any District Forum within the State. Even that power of the State Commission is restrictive and may be exercised only in case where the District Forum has exercised the jurisdiction not vested in it by law, or has failed to exercise a jurisdiction so vested or acted in exercise of its jurisdiction illegally or with material irregularity.

In our considered opinion, the order passed by the District Forum under Sec. 27 of the Act punishing a trader or a person against whom a complaint is made or the complainant as the case may be on the ground of failure to comply with any order made by the District Forum is final and no remedy under the Act is available as against the said order. Therefore, the revision filed under Sec. 17(b) of the Act challenging the legality and correctness of the order passed by the District Forum under Sec. 27 of the Act is not maintainable.

Climax

The petitioner voluntarily expressed the willingness to pay the said amount to the second respondent herein. We consider that interests of justice would be met by directing the writ petitioner to deposit the said amount of ₹13,00,000 in full and final settlement of all the claims and demands of the second respondent within a period of two months from today in the District Forum, which amount shall be permitted to be withdrawn by the second respondent. We are conscious of the fact that, strictly speaking, it was not necessary for this Court to pass any such order directing the writ petitioner to deposit the amounts particularly having set aside the impugned order passed by the State commission on various grounds. However, this Court is not only a Court of law but also a Court of equity and by invoking the equitable jurisdiction under Article 226 of the Constitution of India we direct the writ petitioner to deposit the said amount of ₹13,00,000 in the District Forum, which would subserve the interest of justice.

The Message

Court is not only a court of law but also a court of equity.

Discussion Questions

1. Outline the major issues in this case.
2. Describe the dramatic turn of events in the case.
3. Express your legal opinion on the orders of the District Forum and the State Commission, respectively.
4. In what way did the builder make an assessment of himself throughout the three stages?
5. Explain in your own words the three points of legislation on which this case is based.
6. Explain clearly on what principles does the judge base his legal reasoning.
7. Discuss your opinion about the judgement.

Going Beyond

1. What is the use of any outcome from this case?
2. If you were the builder in this case, how would you proceed to solve your problem?
3. If you are one of the managers of this real estate company, what would be your advice to the CEO?

LEGAL LUMINARY

JUSTICE ASHOK BHAN—CHAIRMAN, NATIONAL CONSUMER DISPUTES REDRESSAL COMMISSION

Justice Ashok Bhan is the Chairman of the National Consumer Disputes Redressal Commission. The greatest problem in the Commission, he admits, is the huge pendency of cases.* He expressed his concern over the inadequacy of the infrastructure—offices, libraries, transport—inadequate staff, and inadequate funds to meet the needs of the litigants. The most neglected are the district forums. Another problem is that the cases drag on for years, which completely defeats the purpose of speedy justice to the consumers. If matters are directly taken at the industrial level, then problems of quality and quantity may be radically solved. Generally, the consumers are not sufficiently aware of their rights. Too much of small print and disclaimers are a hazard to which the consumers pay very little attention. Even the lawyers aiding the consumers are not sure about the consumer protection law. The law schools would have to make a concerted effort in education about the laws related to the consumers.

Justice Bhan is a former Judge of the Supreme Court of India, and former Chairman of the National Legal Services Authority. He has also formerly been the Chief justice of the Karnataka High Court, and Judge in the Punjab and Haryana High Court, prior to which he was the Senior Counsel for the Department of Income Tax, Government of India for 27 years, and Senior Standing Counsel for the Chandigarh Administration for seven years. He was appointed as the Additional Advocate General of Punjab in 1979. Justice Bhan is an advocate of the Lok Adalat method of Alternate Dispute Resolution, for speedy redressal of disputes.

Ashok Bhan was born in 1943. He studied law and was a lecturer in the faculty of law at Punjab University from 1969 to 1979. Thereafter, he became the Additional Advocate General of Punjab. He retired as a judge of the Supreme Court in 2001.

---

*Justice Bhan in a interview with *Halsbury's Law Monthly* http://www.halsburys.in/where-we-are-lagging-is-enforcement.html (20 September 2011).

Economic Laws of Land and Property

Principle: *Dominium non potestesse in pedenti.*
A right to property cannot be in suspension.

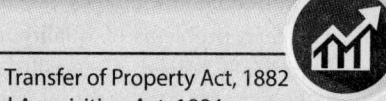

CHAPTER OUTLINE

- Introduction and Interpretation
- Special Economic Zones Act, 2005
- Establishment of Special Economic Zone
- Authorities and Officials
- Facilities and Incentives
- Property Laws

- The Transfer of Property Act, 1882
- Land Acquisition Act, 1894
- Stamp Act, 1899
- Registration Act, 1908
- *Case Study:* Public Cause vs Public Good
- *Legal Luminary:* Anand Sharma

16.1 INTRODUCTION AND INTERPRETATION

No person shall be deprived of his property save by authority of law.

– Article 300A, Constitution of India

The scope of this chapter includes special economic laws. Among these, the Special Economic Zones Act, 2005, also called the SEZ Act 2005, is specifically discussed because of its relevance to you as a manager. You are led through the allied laws of property and entitlement. Ever since her independence, India has grown economically and is considered to be one of the leading emerging economies of the world. Economic development depends on industrial growth. Faster industrial development demands not only large resources of land, but also less bureaucracy and less legal requirements, which help in unhindered and rapid industrialization.

The very title of the Act, the SEZ Act 2005, denotes areas or zones of land set aside for the special purpose of economic activity. The need of emerging economies such as Brazil, Russia, India, China, and South Africa is to set aside adequate space to speed up economic progress through production, trade, and commerce fairly unhindered. To achieve this purpose, government policies of these countries want to assist by removing most of the laws relating to excise and customs tax and render them free to operate in an area set aside for the purpose. India drafted its Special Economic Zone (SEZ) Policy in 2000 with the main objective of providing an internationally competitive environment for exports. The law was enacted in 2005 because mere government policy without the backing of a law might not provide enough confidence to investors. A legal framework always ensures stability, continuity, and purpose.

Although industrial development is in the interest of public good, vast problems have cropped up in the acquisition of land for such development. In a highly populous country like India, land is a relatively scarce resource, which is more often than not owned by poor farmers. Land being their only resource of sustenance, acquiring land for industries has usually met with stiff resistance from them.

The Urban Land Ceiling and Regulation Act, 1976 was enacted for the purpose of overcoming the scarcity of land in the urban areas, for better planning, and for discouraging undue speculation. Large expanses of land in the cities used to be in the hands of a few. Through this law, the government sought to acquire land in the interest of the public good. However, the Urban Land Ceiling and Regulation Act could not be put into practice by the states because of the extreme dissatisfaction of the land owners and the lack of urban planning by the government, thereby indicating the difficulty of land acquisition.

Title of the property, whether land or any other such as stocks and shares, needs legal certification. This is achieved through registration. The process of registration is finalized by paying money to the registry and it is identified by government revenue stamps. The value of the stamp depends on the value of the property.

For you as a manager, this chapter highlights the fact that land resource management must be considered with several allied laws in the context of all the laws of business. There is no resource, property, or ownership upon the Earth as best as the land.

16.2   SPECIAL ECONOMIC ZONES ACT, 2005

(1) A SEZ shall, on and from the appointed day, be deemed to be a territory outside the customs territory of India for the purposes of undertaking the authorized operations.
(2) A SEZ shall, with effect from such date as the central government may notify, be deemed to be a port, inland container depot, land station, and land customs stations, as the case may be, under Sec. 7 of the Customs Act, 1962.

– The SEZ Act, 2005, 53, 1 and 2

Salient Features

A SEZ may be established under this Act, either jointly or severally by the central government, state government, or any person for manufacture of goods or rendering services or for both or as a free trade and warehousing zone [Sec. 3 (1)].

16.3   ESTABLISHMENT OF SPECIAL ECONOMIC ZONE

Who can set up SEZ?   A SEZ may be established under this Act, either jointly or severally by the central government, state government, or any person for manufacture of goods or rendering services or for both or as a free trade and warehousing zone (Sec. 3, 1) (Case 16.1). In case a state government intends to set up a SEZ, after identifying the area, it may forward the proposal directly to the board for the purpose of setting up the SEZ (Sec. 3, 4).

Identification of area   Any person who intends to set up a SEZ may, after identifying the area, make a proposal to the state government concerned for the purpose of setting up the SEZ (Sec. 3, 2).

Developing procedure   The state government may forward, on receipt of the proposal from a developer, together with its recommendations to the board within the prescribed period. The board will further communicate its decision about approval/modifications/rejection to the central government. The central government shall grant a letter of approval if the proposal is approved. The central government may approve more than one developer

CASE 16.1	
	PETITIONER: Oswal VS RESPONDENT: Union of India*
	DATE OF JUDGEMENT: 10 January 2011

FACTS: The petitioners are private limited companies engaged in the business of recycling of plastic scrap into plastic granules and agglomerates and agro products at their units in the Kandla SEZ. The claim that they are governed by the provisions of the SEZ Act, 2005, and the same read with SEZ Rules, 2006. Respondent number 3 is the administrative head of the SEZ and respondent number 4 is the office of the custom based at Kandla SEZ, which is under the control of respondent number 1.

In contrast, the respondents have filed sworn affidavits from laboratories that nullify the certificates given by the petitioners and Deputy Commissioner of Customs. Respondent number 2 herein says that the report of sample of plastic scrap/waste in CAPET Ahmedabad is doubtful and the report of the Kandla Customs Laboratory is contradictory.

JUDGEMENT: Interim relief granted to the petitioner.

REASON: The submission is *prima facie,* found to be not acceptable for the simple reason that it came into force after the SEZ Act, 2005, wherein specific authorities are provided. The Customs Authorities seem to have been rendered *functus officio* so far as the matter pertaining to the conduct of a unit situated in SEZ is concerned.

Show Cause Notice can satisfy the court about its *locus standi* and its jurisdiction; the Authority cannot be allowed to usurp the power to issue Show Cause Notice. Otherwise, the entire object and purpose of the establishment of SEZ will stand frustrated.

Hence ad-interim relief is granted in terms of paragraph 9(HH) subject to the compliance of all the provisions and subject to further orders by this court in respect of any duty or tax payable by the petitioners in case the petitions fail.

*Oswal vs Union of India; see http://www. Indiankanoon.org/doc/869920/ (5 October 2011).

in a SEZ in cases where one developer does not have in his possession the minimum area of contiguous land as may be prescribed for setting up a SEZ. In such cases, each developer shall be considered as a developer in respect of the land in his possession.

Provision of infrastructure   Any person who, or a state government that, intends to provide any infrastructure facilities in the identified area or intends to undertake any authorized operation may, after entering into an agreement with the developer, make a proposal for the same to the board for its approval. Such person or the state government, who has been granted the letter of approval, shall be considered as a co-developer of the SEZ. The developer shall then submit the exact particulars of the identified area to the central government and there upon that government after satisfying that the requirements are fulfilled, shall notify the specifically identified area in the state as SEZ. The developer shall, after the grant of the letter of approval under of Sec. 3 (10) submit the exact particulars of the identified area referred to in sub-Secs (2–4) of that Section, to the central government and there upon that government may, after satisfying that the requirements under Sec. 3 (8) and other requirements as may be prescribed, are fulfilled, notify the specifically identified area in the state as SEZ. This is provided that an existing SEZ shall be deemed to have been notified and established in accordance with the provisions of this Act and the provisions of this Act shall, as far as may be, apply to such a zone accordingly.

Documents

(a) Location of the proposed zone with details of existing infrastructure and that proposed to be established
(b) Area of the proposed SEZ and its distance from the nearest sea port/airport/rail/road head, and so on
(c) Financial details and mode of financing the project and viability of the project
(d) Details of foreign equity, if any
(e) Whether the zone will allow only certain specific industries or will be a multiproduct zone

State government   The following will be provided by the state government:
(a) The area proposed under SEZ shall be free from any environmental restrictions.
(b) Water, electricity, and other services would be provided as required.
(c) Full exemption shall be given in electricity duty and tax on sale of electricity for self-generated and purchased power.
(d) Exemption from state sales tax, octroi, mandi tax, turnover tax and taxes, duty, cess, and levies on supply of goods from Domestic Tariff Area to SEZ units.
(e) Single-point clearances system and minimum inspections requirement under state laws/rules would be provided.
(f) Generation, transmission, and distribution of power shall be allowed within the SEZ.
(g) The zone will be declared as a Public Utility Service under the Industrial Disputes Act, 1947.
(h) All powers under the Industrial Dispute Act, 1947, shall be delegated to the Development Commissioner. Sec. 11(1) of the SEZ Act, 2005, provides that 'the Central Government may appoint any of its officers not below the rank of Deputy Secretary to the Government of India as the Development Commissioner of one.'

Approval by the central government   The Government of India, after considering the above proposals, may grant in-principle approval for the setting up of SEZs. The in-principle approval shall be valid for a period of one year. However, this validity period may be extended by the Department of Commerce as and when necessary. According to Sec. 3(7) of the SEZ Act, 2005, the board of approval may accept, modify, or reject the proposal depending on various circumstances. In case of acceptance, approval is valid for a period of three years within which time effective steps shall be taken by the developer to implement the project. However, this time period can be extended by the Department of Commerce depending on various circumstances.

16.4   AUTHORITIES AND OFFICIALS

Board of approvals   The board of approval is established by the central government (Sec. 8, 1). It will consist of one officer not below the rank of additional secretary from the Ministry or Department of Commerce and two officers not below the rank of a joint secretary to the Government of India; one officer not below the rank of joint secretary to the Government of India with financial services; such officers not exceeding ten nominees of the state government—Sec. 8, 1 (a–d).

Members   State nominee; director general of Foreign Trade; Development Commissioner; and a professor of an Indian Institute of Management.

Development commissioner   He is the overall in-charge of the SEZ and authorized to:
(a) Take all steps to discharge his functions under this Act to ensure speedy development of the SEZ and to promote export
(b) Guide the entrepreneurs in setting up of units in SEZ
(c) Ensure and take suitable steps for the effective promotion of exports from SEZ
(d) Ensure proper coordination with the central government or state government departments concerned or agencies
(e) Monitor the performance of the developer and the units in SEZ
(f) Discharge such other functions as may be assigned to him by the central government under this Act or any other law for the time being in force
(g) Discharge such other functions as may be delegated to him by the Board

Unit approval committee   All the requests for setting up of units in the SEZ are approved at the zone level by the Approval Committee consisting of the Development Commissioner after a discussion with the customs authorities and representatives of the state government. All post-approval clearances in matters related to importer–exporter code number, change in the name of the company or implementing agency, broad-banding diversification, and so on are provided at the zonal level by the Development Commissioner. There is a separate unit to monitor the performance of the SEZ units periodically and it is governed by the Approval Committee. SEZ units are liable for penal action under the provision of the Foreign Trade (Development and Regulation) Act, in case of any violation in the rules formulated by the Approval Committee (Secs 13 and 14).

16.5 FACILITIES AND INCENTIVES

Single-window clearance   Chapter V deals with single-window clearance that deals with the constitution of the approval committee, powers and functions of the approval committee, setting up of unit, cancellation of letter of approval to entrepreneur, setting up and operation of and offshore banking unit, setting up of an international financial services centre, single application form return, agency to inspect, single enforcement officer or agency for notified offences, investigation inspection search or seizure, designated courts to try suits and notified offences, appeal to high court, and offences by companies.

Setting up and operation of offshore banking unit   An application for setting up and operating an offshore banking unit (branch of a bank) in a SEZ may be made to the Reserve Bank. The Reserve Bank shall, if satisfied that the applicant fulfils all the conditions specified, grant permission to such an applicant for setting up and operating an offshore banking unit.

Setting up of international financial services centre   The central government shall approve only one international financial services centre in a SEZ.

Special fiscal provisions for SEZs   Chapter VI deals with special fiscal provisions for SEZ such as exemptions, drawbacks, and concessions to every developer and entrepreneur. Provisions of the Income Tax Act, 1961, can be applied with certain modifications in relation to developers and entrepreneurs, duration of goods or services in SEZs, transfer of ownership and removal of goods, and domestic clearances by units.

SEZ authority   Chapter VII deals with the constitution of SEZ authority, officers of the authority and other staff, special provision for transfer of officers or other employees to the authority and the functions of the authority, grants and loans by the central government, constitution of fund and its application, accounts and audit, directions by the central government, returns and reports, power to supersede authority, members, officers, and other employees of the authority.

It should be noted that the concept of SEZ has been met with significant criticism and opposition in the entire country, especially by

(a) Those who lost their lands through the application of the Land Acquisition Act, 1894
(b) Those who advocate for environmental protection
(c) Other industries that do not have the same infra-structural facilities, fiscal concessions, and customs exemptions
(d) SEZ policy opponents for creating tax haven enclaves and loss of revenue to the country

Social economists suggest an all-inclusive and holistic industrial development.

MANAGER'S TAKEAWAY

- Think critically about the benefits and losses before adopting a legal provision or a policy stipulation.
- When something special is offered, consider its period of validity.

16.6   PROPERTY LAWS

TEXT *'Transfer of property' means an act by which a living person conveys property, in present or in future, to one or more other living persons, or to himself, and one or more other living persons, and 'to transfer property' is to perform such an act.*

– The Transfer of Property, Sec. 5

In the forty-fourth Amendment to the Constitution of India, property was detached from the fundamental rights. Apart from Article 300A, which expressly states that none can deprive another of his properties, the spirit of the entire Constitution of India is based on the protection of dignity of life and the inalienability of one's property. The Transfer of Property Act, 1882, is an allied Act of the Contract Act, 1872, and the Sale of Goods Act, 1930. Similarly, there are other Acts such as the Land Acquisition Act, 1894; the Registration Act, 1908; Easements Act, 1882; the Urban Land Ceiling and Regulation Act, 1976 (which is recommended for repeal due to its non-performance); the Benami Transactions Prohibition Act, 1988; and the state-wise rent Acts. For you at this stage, it is sufficient to know that all these Acts are important because whenever a law is enforced, its interlinking relationship is logical.

16.7   THE TRANSFER OF PROPERTY ACT, 1882

Living person   The transfer of property is between living persons. Living person can be a company, an association, or a body of individuals, whether incorporated or not, but nothing herein contained shall affect any law for the time being in force relating to the transfer of property to or by companies, associations, or bodies of individuals. Living person is a wider term than natural human beings. It includes juristic persons such as companies and others such as associations or body of individuals irrespective of whether registered or not.

Transfer   A process or an act by which something is made over to another. It does not, however, mean that the making over of the thing should always be absolute. I may transfer my book to you for a day. I may also transfer it to you absolutely either by sale, gift, or in exchange of your book. In either case, what is primarily essential is that I have to hand over the book to you. This act of handing over the book to you is the transfer of the book.

Conveyance of property   Transfer of property has special technical meaning in the Transfer of Property Act. Only five conveyances are considered transfer of property for the Act. Three modes convey absolute title, for example, sale, gift, and exchange. Two convey limited interest, for example, mortgage and lease. Transfer can be in the present or future, but the transferor and the transferee must be a living person. The only exception is Sec. 13 of the Transfer of Property Act.

Exception to transfer of property according to Sec. 13—Transfer for benefit of unborn person   Where, on a transfer of property, an interest therein is created for the benefit of a person not in existence at the date of the transfer, subject to a prior interest created by the same transfer, the interest created for the benefit of such a person shall not take effect, unless it extends to the whole of the remaining interest of the transferor in the property.

Illustration   A transfers property of which he is the owner to B in trust for A and his intended wife successively for their lives, and, after the death of the survivor, for the eldest son of the intended marriage for life, and after his death for A's second son. The interest so created for the benefit of the eldest does not take effect, because it does not extend to the whole of A's remaining interest in the property.

Sale of immovable property—Sec. 54   Sale is a transfer of ownership in exchange for a price paid or promised or part-paid and part-promised. Such transfer, in the case of tangible immovable property, can be made only by a registered instrument. It takes place when the seller places the buyer or such a person as he directs, in possession of the property. A contract for the sale of immovable property is a contract that a sale of such property shall take place on terms settled between the parties. It does not, of itself, create any interest in, or charge on, such property.

Mortgage—Sec. 58   A mortgage is the transfer of an interest in a specific immovable property for the purpose of securing the payment of money advanced or to be advanced by means of loan, an existing or future debt, or the performance of an engagement that may give rise to a pecuniary liability. The transferor is called a mortgagor, the transferee a mortgagee, the principal money and interest of which payment is secured for the time being are called the mortgage money, and the instrument (if any) by which the transfer is effected is called a mortgage deed.

Charges—Sec. 100   Where immovable property of one person is by act of parties or operation of law made security for the payment of money to another and the transaction does not amount to a mortgage, the latter person is said to have a charge on the property; all the provisions herein before contained that apply to a simple mortgage shall, so far as may be, apply to such charge.

Leases of immovable property—Sec. 105   A lease of immovable property is a transfer of a right to enjoy property, made for a certain time, express or implied; or in perpetuity, in consideration of a price paid or promised; or of money, a share of crops, service, or any other thing of value, to be rendered periodically or on specified occasions to the transferor by the transferee, who accepts the transfer on such terms.

Exchanges—Sec. 118   When two persons mutually transfer the ownership of one thing for the ownership of another—neither thing nor both things being money only—the transaction is called an exchange. A transfer of property in completion of an exchange can be made only in a manner provided for the transfer of such a property by sale.

Gifts—Sec. 122   Gift is the transfer of certain existing movable or immovable property made voluntarily and without consideration, by one person, called the donor, to another, called the donee, and accepted by or on behalf of the donee. Acceptance must be made during the lifetime of the donor and while he is still capable of giving. If the donee dies before acceptance, the gift is void.

16.8 LAND ACQUISITION ACT, 1894

Declaration of intended acquisition   Declaration that land is required for a public purpose—(i) Subject to the provisions of Part VII of this Act, 4 [when the 6 (appropriate government)] is satisfied, after considering the report, if any, made under Sec. 5-A, sub-sec. (2),] that any particular land is needed for a public purpose, or for a company, a declaration shall be made to that effect under the signature of a secretary, to such government or of some officer duly authorized to certify its order 5 and different declarations may be made from time to time in respect of different parcels of any land covered by the same notification—The Land Acquisition Act, 1894, Sec. 6.

This Act has been highly contentious and has become very controversial as the central and state governments and their agencies apply increasingly for more land from the most unwilling owners such as farmers and householders. In 1894 when the legislation for acquisition of land was enacted, the population was less and the land resources were very high. The acquisition of land by the government did not affect the common people. In an industrially fast-developing country such as India, the situation is reversed. It is hoped that this law will be changed in the nearest future possible to avoid attrition, disputes, agitations, and bloodshed. A new bill as an amendment for the Acquisition of Land Act was introduced in 2007 in the Lok Sabha; however, it has not yet been passed. The important salient features of the procedures involved are described in the following sections.

Notification—Sec. 4(1)   The process of acquisition begins with the issuance of preliminary notification. The notification published in the official gazette and in two daily newspapers circulating in that locality of which at least one shall be in the regional language. Furthermore, it is also necessary that the notification has to be affixed in conspicuous places of that locality.

Filing of objections   The main objective of issuing preliminary notification is to call for objections, if any, against such acquisitions from the owners or others who have certain interest in the property, thereby providing them with an opportunity to raise their claims against the move of the government for acquiring their lands. The persons aggrieved by such notification shall file their objections within thirty days from the date of preliminary notification.

Final declaration—Sec. 4(1)   After receipt of objections, the concerned authority shall consider those objections, and if found unsatisfactory, a final declaration rejecting the claims will be issued. According to Sec. 6 of the amended Act, the final declaration shall be issued by the authority within a period of one year from the date of issuance of preliminary notification. According to Sec. 6(2) of the Act before the amendment, the time stipulated under the Act for final declaration was three years from the date of publication of the preliminary notification. The final declaration has to be published as required.

Award—Sec. 11   It states that after receiving the objections, the authority will have to hold an inquiry. Under Secs 8 and 9, it is necessary that the actual extent of land proposed to be acquired and the value of the land have to be assessed before starting the inquiry. On completion of the inquiry, an award will be passed to that effect and published by the competent authority. After passing the award, the collector or the deputy commissioner shall send notice to the owners or their representatives who were not present personally at the time of passing of the award.

Time limit   Once the inquiry is concluded, it is the duty of the competent authority to pass the award within two years from the date of publication of the declaration under Sec. 6, as envisaged under Sec. 11A of the Act. If the authority fails to adhere to the time schedule prescribed under the Act, the entire proceedings initiated for land acquisition will lapse. After passing of the award, the deputy commissioner or any other competent authority may take possession of the land immediately, which shall there upon vest absolutely with the government, free from all claims, whatsoever.

Special powers—Sec. 17   This confers special powers on the concerned authority wherein passing of award may be dispensed with and yet permits to take possession of the land notified for acquisition. Further holding of inquiry can also be waived, as envisaged under Sec. 5A of the Act. However, such powers can be exercised only in case of urgency. After passing of the award, the person whose land has been proposed to be acquired can give his consent for such acquisition and agree to receive the compensation.

Compensation—Sec. 30   It provides for settlement of dispute pertaining to apportionment of the compensation amount is available. In such a situation, the deputy commissioner should refer the matter to the court. The claimant will be entitled to the compensation, which is determined based on the market value of the land determined as on the date of preliminary notification. According to Sec. 34, if there is delay in payment of compensation beyond one year from the date on which possession is taken, interest at the rate of 15 per cent per annum shall be payable from the date of expiry of the said period of one year on the outstanding amount of compensation till the date of payment.

Possession of the land as final   The government, under Sec. 16 of the Act, is at liberty to withdraw from acquisition of land except in cases provided under Sec. 36. However, if the land has already been possessed, then the government will have no authority to withdraw from such acquisition.

16.9   STAMP ACT, 1899

Objective   The government wants to charge for its various services, starting from postal delivery to transfer of property. Citizens too have come to accept something stamped or sealed as trustworthy. People trust documents on stamp paper similar to how they have confidence in currency coins and bills or notes. There are various stamps for various services, such as share brokers, property deals, and revenue-related deals. All these are instruments of revenue collection to the government.

Basis for the law   The Constitution of India has provided provisions for levying taxes. Tax is levied in the form of stamps on instruments recording the transactions. This form of taxation has been found to be convenient for collection and supervision. The Stamp Act is a fiscal statue dealing with tax on transactions. Article 246 and the seventh schedule are relevant with regard to the legislative power to levy stamp duties. Articles 265, 268, and 269(e) are relevant mainly regarding the distribution of revenue. The proceeds of stamp duty leviable in any financial year shall be assigned to the state. Under Article 246, such stamp duties as are mentioned in a list are levied by the union, but under Article 268, the state in which they are levied collects and retains the proceeds. As the revenue from stamp duty is assigned to the state in which they are collected, each state government has prescribed by rule that stamps purchased in the state alone should be used for instruments executed in it.

Stamp duty on negotiable instruments   Tax is levied in the form of stamp in respect of transactions in instruments such as bill of exchange, letter of credit, debenture, policy of insurance, agreement or memorandum of agreement, lease cum sale, sale of property, deposit of deeds, conveyance, and so on as defined in Schedule 2 of the Stamp Act. As provided in the Stamp Act, all duties with which any instruments are chargeable shall be paid and such payment shall be indicated on such instrument by means of impressed stamps or stamps issued by the government. An instrument to be duly stamped should be stamped with a stamp not only of the amount required by the law but also in the manner prescribed by the law.

Paying for stamps   Stamps have various uses (Table 16.1). The stamp duty payable on an instrument may also be paid in cash by challan in a banking treasury or a treasury counter signed by an officer empowered by state government or by a demand draft or by pay order drawn on a branch of any scheduled bank. Instruments may be stamped with an adhesive stamp.

Table 16. 1   Types of stamps and their use*

Stamp	Use
Revenue	
Court fee	
Judicial stamp	Used for transaction with the judiciary
Non-judicial stamps	Used since 1928. Used for contracts, agreement sales, deed, wills, lease, rent, and so on
Fiscal (adhesive)	Used in non-judicial documents for financial transactions

Contd

---

*The use of stamps is ubiquitous; if you get confused about its use, the images will clear your doubts. See http://www.ksphc.org/stampit/info (3 October 2011).

Table 16.1 *Contd*

Insurance	Used in insurance departments to authenticate policies
Foreign bill	Stamp duty in respect of import paid to India
Share transfer	Used in transaction of shares by financial institutions
'Broker's stamp	Used in respect of transaction through brokers
Notary	Used at notarization of documents

Note: Apart from the above mentioned stamps used in the government departments, embossing and franking of these stamps are also in vogue. It is both efficient and convenient rather than having documents pasted and stamped with seals separately.

All stamps are available in suitable and varied denominations. Each state of India has regulations regarding stamp duty. The states also have the power to increase or decrease the stamp duty.

16.10 REGISTRATION ACT, 1908

Inspector of Registration—(1) The State Government shall appoint an officer to be the Inspector General of Registration for the territories subject to such Government. Provided that the State Government may, instead of making such appointment, direct that all or any of the powers and duties hereinafter conferred and imposed upon the Inspector General shall be exercised and performed by such officer or officers, and within such local limits, as the State Government appoints in this behalf.

– The Registration Act, 1908, Sec. 3

Any document requiring legitimacy in matters of property, sale, brokering, and the like needs to be registered with the central or state governments. There are various authorities who perform this task, such as the registrar or sub-registrar or anyone authorized officially (Case 16.2).

Compulsory registration of documents—Sec. 17 Under this section, there are a number of documents or instruments enumerated that are required to be compulsorily registered:

(a) Instruments by which an immovable property is gifted.

(b) Instruments that create, declare, assign limit, or extinguish any right, title, or interest—vested or contingent—in any immovable property, exceeding ₹100 in value. However, if these are testamentary instruments, for example, wills and codicils, then these are not covered.

(c) Instruments that acknowledge receipt/payment of any consideration on account of any creation, declaration, assignment, limitation, or extinction of any right, title, or interest are covered. The testamentary instruments are not covered.

(d) Leases of immovable properties that are made annually exceeding a term of one year or reserving a yearly rent.

(e) Instruments transferring or assigning any decree or order of a court or any award if it creates, declares, assigns, limits, or extinguishes any right, title, or interest—vested or

CASE 16.2

PETITIONER: Thiruvengada Pillai vs RESPONDENT: Navaneethammal and others*

DATE OF JUDGEMENT: 19 February 2008

FACTS: Specific performance: validity of stamp paper, opinion of experts Sec. 54 of the Indian Stamp Act, 1899; the Indian Stamp Rules, 1925; Sec. 45 of the Indian Evidence Act, 1872.

Plaintiff-Appellant alleged that the first defendant agreed to sell suit property by an agreement and received some amount as advance. Plaintiff issued a notice to execute the sale deed and receive the balance amount. Defendant denied the agreement and executed the sale deed in favour of a second defendant. Plaintiff filed a suit for specific performance. Defendant contended that the sale agreement put forth by the plaintiff was forged and concocted. Trial court dismissed the suit on the ground that the sale put forth by plaintiff was false. High court allowed the second appeal filed by the second defendant restoring the decision of the trial court. Hence, the present appeal.

Is the agreement of sale executed on two stamp papers purchased on different dates and more than six months before the date of execution not valid? Was the first appellate court justified in comparing the disputed thumb impression with the admitted thumb impression and recording a finding about the authenticity of the thumb impression, without the benefit of any opinion of an expert? Did the high court err in reversing the judgement of the first appellate court in the second appeal? Held, the Indian Stamp Act, 1899, nowhere prescribes any expiry date for use of a stamp paper. No impediment for a stamp paper purchased more than six months before the proposed date of execution being used for the document.

JUDGEMENT: Appeal dismissed

REASON: The trial court had analyzed the evidence properly and had dismissed the suit by giving cogent reasons. The first appellate court reversed it by wrongly placing onus on the defendants. Its observation that when the execution of an unregistered document put forth by the plaintiff was denied by the defendants, it was for the defendants to establish that the document was forged or concocted, is not sound proposition. The first appellate court proceeded on the basis that it is for the party who asserts something to prove that thing; and as the defendants alleged that the agreement was forged, it was for them to prove it. But the first appellate court lost sight of the fact that the party who propounds the document will have to prove it. In this case, plaintiffs came to court alleging that the first defendant had executed a Page 0954 agreement of sale in favour. The first defendant having denied it, the burden was on the plaintiff to prove that the first defendant had executed the agreement and not on the first defendant to disprove it. The issues also placed the burden on the plaintiff to prove the document to be true. No doubt, the plaintiff attempted to discharge his burden by examining himself as also the scribe and one of the attesting witnesses. However, the various circumstances enumerated by the trial court and high court referred to earlier, when taken together, rightly create a doubt about the authenticity of the agreement and dislodge the effect of the evidence. The decision of the high court, reversing the decision of the first appellate court, does not call for interference. There is no merit in this appeal and the same is accordingly dismissed.

*Thiruvengada Pillai vs Navaneeethammal and others, in the Supreme Court of India; see also http://www. lawinhk.com/ (3 October 2010).

contingent—in any immovable property, exceeding ₹100 in value, for example, court orders dealing with mergers, demergers, arrangements, and so on (Secs 391–394 of the Companies Act, 1956); again testamentary instruments are exempted.

(f) Documents containing contracts to transfer for consideration of any immovable property in part performance of a contract (Sec. 53A of the Transfer of Property Act, 1882), which have been executed on or after 24 September 2001, must be registered. It has been further provided that if such documents are not registered, then they shall not have any effect for the purposes of Sec. 53A of the Transfer of Property Act, 1882.

Non-compulsory registration of documents The following need not be compulsorily registered:

(a) Instruments relating to shares in a company where all the shares of the company consist of immovable property

(b) Some court decrees

(c) Any endorsement on a mortgage deed acknowledging the payment of the whole or part of the mortgage money and any other receipt for the payment of the money due under a mortgage when the receipt does not extinguish mortgage

Penalties Chapter XIV discusses the penalties for incorrectly endorsing, copying, translating, or registering documents, false statements, delivering false copies of documents, false impersonation, and abetment. The registering officer may conduct under the Indian Penal Code, 1860.

The above issue is merely a pointer. You are recommended to read this Act carefully because all your activities concerning various instruments of contract, sale, brokering, and so on will have a day-to-day occupation with registration processes of one kind or the other. You are further advised to read and understand the Indian Easements Act, 1882, which concerns itself with leave and licenses, an indispensable activity of the company management. The Rent Act, which is specific to each state, is another important law you should know for the benefit of your company.

MANAGER'S TAKEAWAY

- A document is a legal instrument that a manager should assiduously guard.
- Only a signed, sealed, and stamped document is a legal instrument.

SUMMARY

- There are several laws of property and land. The SEZ Act, 2005 suddenly seemed to have increased the public consciousness dramatically against acquisition of large sizes of lands for quick industrialization.
- In the context of SEZ, the following allied laws ensure justice and safeguard the rights of citizens, associations, and the corporations:

SEZ Act, 2005
Transfer of Property Act, 1882
Land Acquisition Act, 1894
Stamp Act, 1899
Registration Act, 1908

- Land acquisition is a difficult issue as it is tied with people's emotions and livelihoods such as those of farmers. The transfer of property ensures the correct manner of conveyance of rights and entitlements thereof. Registration of property ensures legal title. This title is endorsed through documents that are stamped, sealed, and signed. Stamp duty is a means for the government to levy tax for the services it renders.

EXERCISES

(i) Sitaram got a notice from the government saying that land under a certain survey number that happens to be his would be acquired for the highway project. He filed a suit claiming that he has no knowledge of any public notification. He contended that if there were such a notification, he would have filed objections under Sec. 5A of the Act. The government contended that it has the right to dispense with Sec. 5A as per Sec. 17 (4).

Hint: Yes, under the said section the government cannot dispense the right of the people for objections.

(ii) A company acquired land in SEZ as per the law. However, after some time they pressurized the adjutant owners to sell their properties to the company.

Hint: The land acquisition must be carried out as per the law of SEZ by making proposal to the state government or to the Board of Approval.

(iii) Mohan went to the sub-registrar and signed for his brother in a sale deed without having any prior power of attorney. In fact, he acted as if he was his brother.

Hint: Impersonation is a criminal offence; he will be penalized under Sec. 62 of the Stamp Act, 1908.

(iv) Is SEZ a short-term law? It does not have the same place among laws of property as that of Acquisition of Property and Transfer of Property.

(v) Narrate the various uses and instances of the Stamp Duty Act for a private limited company.

DEVELOPMENT OF LEGAL EDGE

- Take up a summer internship at a SEZ of your interest
- Encourage others to do the same.
- At the end of the internship collate your reports.

- When back in your training institutes, make presentations focusing on the legal problems confronted at the zone.

FURTHER READING

Web resources

- Special Economic Zones Act, 2005.
- Transfer of Property Act, 1882.
- Land Acquisition Act, 1894.
- Stamp Act, 1899.

- Registration Act, 1908 http://www.indiacode.co.in.
- Latest Case Law on Land Acquisition Act, 1894 http://revenueharyana.gov.in/html/acts_rules/land%20acquesition%201894.pdf.
- SEZ http://www.sezindia.nic.in.

CASE STUDY   PUBLIC CAUSE VS PUBLIC GOOD

Nothing is good for everyone, but only relatively to some people.[1]

THE SEZ ACT, 2005 States

3. (1) A SEZ may be established under this Act, either jointly or severally by the central government, state government, or any person for manufacture of goods or rendering services

or for both or as a Free Trade and Warehousing Zone. 4. (*1*) The developer shall, after the grant of letter of approval. 6. The areas falling within the SEZ may be demarcated by the Central Government or any authority specified by it as:

---

[1]Andrei Cide, The Counterfeiters, (2.4) (1925), transl. Dorothy Bussy.

The processing area for setting up Units for activities, being the manufacture of goods, or rendering services,

The area exclusively for trading or warehousing purposes, or The non-processing areas for activities other than those specified under clause (*a*) or clause (*b*).

51. (1) The provisions of this Act shall have effect notwithstanding anything inconsistent therewith contained in any other law for the time being in force or in any instrument having effect by virtue of any law other than this Act.

Petitioner and His Cause

Mohan Lal Sharma was a municipal employee. After his retirement, he dedicated himself to public cause: fighting against land grab. He raised the issue through a Public Interest Litigation against the land allotted to developers through the SEZ Act, 2003, in the State of Rajasthan. The land was not only sold cheap, but was also sold to people with interests, which did not speak of any public good as per the stated objective of the SEZ.

Under Sec. 6 (1) of the State Act of 2003, the State of Rajasthan has to identify and notify the area to be developed as a special economic zone whereas under Sec. 6 of the said Act, the state government has been entrusted with the duty to select a developer for the purpose of development of the zone, and under Sec. 6 (3) of the said Act, the state government is required to prescribe the procedure to select the developer.

The land involved was a whopping 13,000 bighas for projects such as IT City, Bio Tech City, and Knowledge City. A Memorandum of Understanding (MoU) was signed between the government and the developer Mahindra and Mahindra, the renowned industrial group. The charge of the Public Interest Litigation petitioner is that the land, which is commercially highly valuable, was transferred to the developer for free. He pleaded with the High Court of Rajasthan to set aside the MoU. The petitioner's commercial estimate of the land was Rupees one crore per bigha. He pleaded stating that this is a land grab in the garb of SEZ, depriving the state of its legitimate revenue.

The State and the Public Good

The counsel for Mahindra and Mahindra countered the claims of the petitioner in the following manner:

The Central Act of 2005 is a parliamentary legislation covering the field of SEZ, which is subsequent to the State Act of 2003 and, therefore, by virtue of the doctrine of parliamentary supremacy, the plea raised by the learned counsel for the petitioner that execution of MoU, and so on is in contravention of the provisions of Sec. 6 of the State Act of 2003 should not be accepted by the court. After pointing out to the court that the substratum of the writ petition is the alleged violation of the State Act of 2003, it was argued that there are no factual averments or grounds relating to violation of the Central Act of 2005, and as the challenge to the allotment of land to respondent number 5 proceeds on a fundamental legal misconception, the petition should be dismissed.

Adjudicator of Cause and the Good

Chief Justice JM Panchal and Justice M Rafiq of the High Court of Rajasthan heard the arguments of the counsels from either side, elaborating their respective positions. They came to the following conclusion:

The record thus does not indicate that the land was allotted in a surreptitious or clandestine manner. Nor does the record show that there is any scam as is sought to be made out by the petitioner. It would not be out of place to state that the so-called scam is a figment of the imagination of the petitioner, which has no factual basis at all. As noticed earlier, several decisions taken under the Central Act of 2005 are not challenged by the petitioner at all. Therefore, the court will have to proceed on the footing that those decisions are valid. Once the decisions taken under the Central Act of 2005 are treated to be valid, this court finds that nothing remains to be done in the instant public litigation. The petition will have to be carried to its logical conclusion by dismissing the same.

The Moral of the Case

Although prudence may convince the fairness of a cause, justice demands fidelity to the application of the law.

Discussion Questions

1. What are main issues in this case?
2. What is the relationship of the disputing parties?
3. How do you evaluate a land resource?
4. What do you understand by the term land use?
5. How would you evaluate the judgement of the Rajasthan High Court?
6. Are you aware of any anti-SEZ movements? Is this judgement relevant to them?

Going Beyond

1. Analyze the SEZ development in India and assess their far-reaching consequences.
2. What are the criteria to judge public good in the Indian socio-economic context?

LEGAL LUMINARY

ANAND SHARMA—LAW TEACHER WHO BECAME CABINET MINISTER

Born and brought up in Shimla, Anand Sharma was one of the youngest MPs to be elected at the age of mere 31 years and part of the pot boiler of Indian politics in the seething heat of New Delhi.

In May 2009, he took the responsibility of the Ministry of Commerce and Industry. Under this ministry, the first thing that he initiated was the opening up of the thus-far-stalled Doha Round talks regarding trade and commerce.

As the minister for commerce and industry, the SEZs come under Sharma's direct responsibility. He has been reported saying: 'about 100 million young people will enter the job market and emphasis on manufacturing is the critical part of creating employment for them.' This provides a glimpse into the priority he has set for his ministry.

The India–ASEAN agreement, India–Korea CECA, India–Malaysia CECA, and India–Japan CEPA were also signed during Sharma's tenure. As a measure of simplifying the foreign investment policy regime, he released a consolidated Foreign Direct Investment Policy document. Anand Sharma brings to his ministerial assignment a vast reservoir of knowledge in international affairs. He has considerable experience in representing his party and India at diplomatic interactions at all levels and has either led or been a member of delegations to over 90 countries. He has been a key organizer of several major international conferences, including the First Non-Aligned Youth Conference in 1985 in New Delhi, which was attended by delegates from 82 countries, and has been sent by the Prime Minster of India as special envoy for various sensitive assignments.

Anand Sharma has studied law and was a law faculty at the University of Shimla. His education stood him in good stead and now he is conversant with parliamentary and legislative procedures. As a member of the panel of chairpersons for the Rajya Sabha, he has presided over sittings of the House. Sharma was born in Shimla in 1953 and became a very active political activist in the Congress party. To commemorate 125 years of the foundation of the Congress party, he wrote the book *Journey of a Nation: Indian National Congress*. He takes keen interest in work relating to autism and disabilities. He is interested in sports and games and loves both Indian and Western classical music. He was elected to the Rajya Sabha on 24 April 1984.

PART 3

FINANCIAL JURISPRUDENCE

Laws of Securities Contract Regulation

Principle: *Nummus est mensura rerum communtandarum.*
Money is the measure of things that are exchanged.

CHAPTER OUTLINE

- Introduction and Interpretation
- The Securities Contracts Regulation Act, 1956
- Other Important Sections
- The Securities and Exchange Board of India, 1992
- Insider Trading
- *Case Study*: Insider Trading
- *Legal Luminary*: Gangumolu Venkata Ramakrishna

17.1 INTRODUCTION AND INTERPRETATION

TEXT

An act to prevent undesirable transactions in securities by regulating the business of dealing, therein, by providing certain other matters connected therewith.

– The Securities Contracts (Regulation) Act, 1956, sub-heading to the title of the Act

Objective

The objective of this chapter is singularly focused on the prevention of undesirable and fraudulent transactions taking place in the capital market. The Securities Contracts Regulation Act, 1956, and the Securities and Exchange Board of India (SEBI) Act, 1992, are the main pillars of the edifice of securities transactions business in India. There are other allied Acts supportive of these two important Acts. Some are already covered in previous chapters and the others will occur in subsequent chapters. These as follows:

(a) Depositories Act, 1996
(b) Foreign Exchange Regulations Act, 1973
(c) Arbitration and Conciliation Act, 1996
(d) Companies Act, 1956

(e) Debt Recovery Act (Bank and Financial Institutions Recovery of Dues Act, 1993)
(f) Banking Regulation Act
(g) Benami Prohibition Act
(h) Indian Penal Code
(i) Indian Evidence Act, 1872
(j) Indian Telegraph Act, 1885

However, in this chapter, the scope is limited to highlight two important Acts that govern the securities contract.

Scope

The scope of this chapter is the Acts governing the capital market of India: the Securities Contracts Regulation Act, 1956, and the SEBI Act, 1992. Despite several drawbacks, mainly due to financial scams, and much less due to the global financial meltdown, the capital market has been doing remarkably well. The primary markets have expanded greatly and the secondary markets are virtually teeming with investors. A plethora of business news channels, in English as well as in the state languages, are an indicator that the ever-growing middle class of India is turning capital market savvy. In such a scenario, the managers of the large and small corporations, commercial establishments, trading institutions, bankers, financial institutions, etc., have their attention fixed on the indexes of the stock exchanges, particularly that of the Bombay Stock Exchange (BSE), which has become the monetary indicator of the health of the nation's economy.

Understanding Capital Market and Securitization

Capital market As already seen while dealing with the Companies Act, 1956, the capital market is a market for sale and purchase of securities. It consists of exchange, both in primary and secondary share or stock markets (see figures 17.1 and 17.2).

Securities Securities are financial instruments. These instruments consist of the following:
(a) Debt: banknotes, bonds, and debentures
(b) Equity: common stocks
(c) Derivatives: contracts such as forwards, futures, options, and swaps
Securities are *fungible* in character. Fungibility is the property of a good whose individual units are capable of mutual substitution without value variance. For instance, you need a change of ₹100 and you are given ten notes of ₹10. Stocks are infinitely divisible and they can be exchanged for value.

Stock exchange The agency of capital market where buyers and sellers in securities do business, through physically present brokers, through telephone, or electronically over the Internet. The term 'share bazaar' is used in common parlance for trading in capital market. There are stock exchanges in all the major cities of India. The BSE and National Stock Exchange (NSE) are the most common ones.

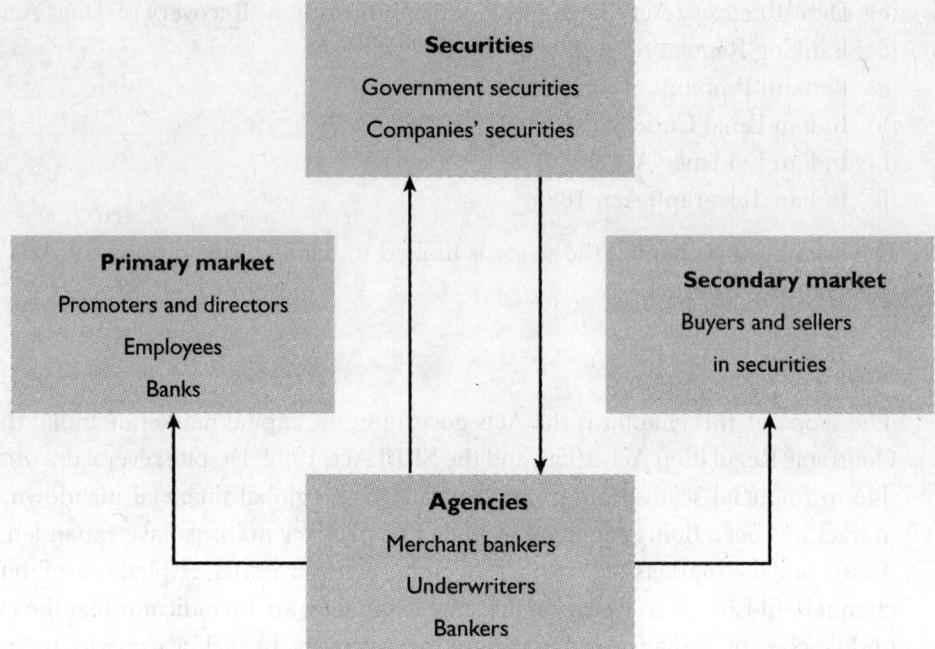

Figure 17.1   Capital market structure

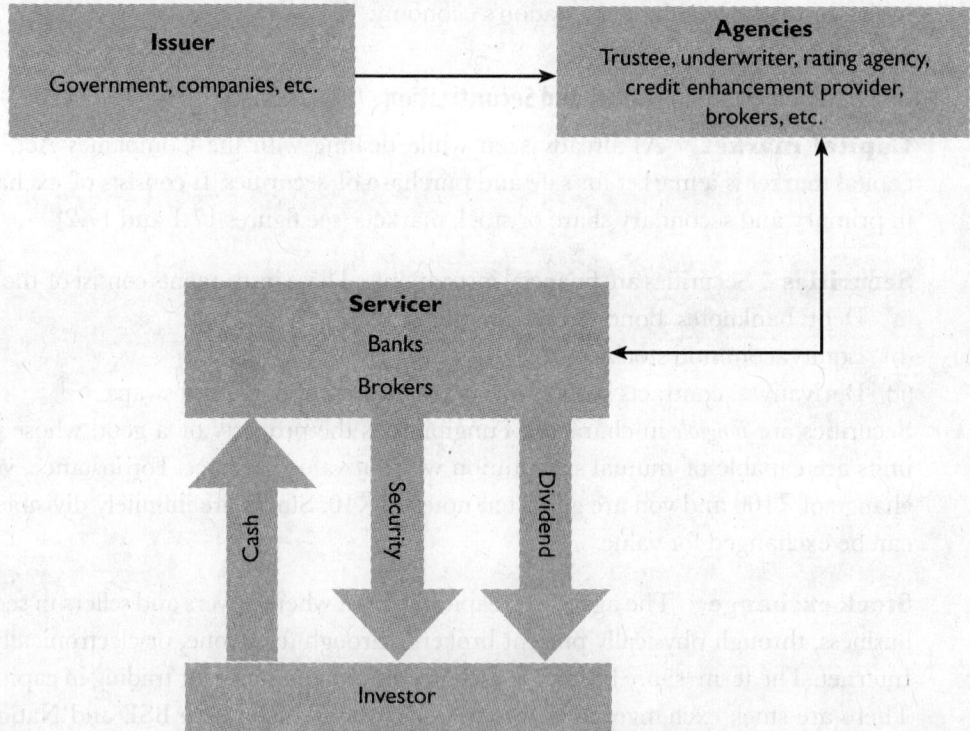

Figure 17.2   Trading relationship in the capital market

Issuer   For instance, a company registers itself through listing and sells securities. The issuers may be domestic or foreign governments, corporations, investment trusts, etc. These are legal entities and are bound by the securities exchange regulator.

Initial public offerings   A private company goes public by listing itself on the stock exchange to raise funds from the public. Generally companies take assistance from agencies such as investment banking firms and underwriters.

Listing   A company registers itself on a stock exchange to trade its stock.

Securitization   It is a process of making securities available to the capital market. An issuer creates financial instruments or securities. For instance, an issuer of mortgage-backed securities can combine mortgages into a large pool and then divide them into small units based on the inherent risks of default and make them available to investors. This process creates liquidity by enabling smaller investors to purchase shares in a larger asset pool. Thus, securitization is the rationale or the fundamental logic of the capital market.

Primary market   It is the market when the issues or shares are sold for the first time. The members of the company and those related to them get the first opportunity to buy the primary shares and preference shares. Furthermore, if the company issues to the public—initial public offering (IPO)—where new shares or stocks are sold directly to the public for the first time.

Secondary market   This market deals with the existing securities that are bought and sold perpetually.

Raising funds   Raising funds is the objective of the government or corporations for their projects. This is done either from investors or from creditors. Figure 17.2 shows the relationship between borrowers and investors.

Aim of Regulation

As you saw above, there are two main Acts—the Securities Contracts Regulation Act, 1956 and the SEBI Act, 1992—to govern the activities of the capital market. The SEBI is the regulator who implements the laws from the said Acts by creating rules and regulations in the trading of securities. The chapter-end case study lists the top ten financial scams of India, which have happened despite the laws and regulations. It has mainly happened for the following reasons:

(a) Lack of diversity in financial instruments
(b) Lack of control over the fair disclosure of financial information
(c) Rampant insider trading
(d) Manipulation of security prices
(e) Inadequacy in the exercise of statutory powers of SEBI (very few convictions)
(f) Unwieldy brokers and sub-brokers
(g) Indifferent institutional investors
(h) High cost of transactions
(i) Informal trading in the primary market before the issue comes in the market

You will see how SEBI, the capital market regulator, tries to control this capital giant despite several problems as cited earlier that are, in fact, not due to the regulatory authority or its will but due to the lack of financial ethics of the traders. Of interest, here, is the application of the law and not the behaviour of the traders.

17.2 THE SECURITIES CONTRACTS REGULATION ACT, 1956

TEXT

…(a) 'Contract' means a contract for or relating to the purchase or sale of securities; [(aa) 'corporatization' means the succession of a recognized stock exchange, being a body of individuals or a society registered under the Societies Registration Act, 1860 (21 of 1860), by another stock exchange, being a company incorporated for the purpose of assisting, regulating, or controlling the business of buying, selling, or dealing in securities carried on by such individuals or society; (ab) 'demutualization' means the segregation of ownership and management from the trading rights of the members of a recognized stock exchange in accordance with a scheme approved by SEBI].

– The Securities Contracts Regulation Act, 1956, Sec. 2, (a) and (aa)[1]

Corporatization and Demutualization (Sec. 2)

This is essentially about the organization of stock exchanges. You notice that this Act is legislated in the same year as that of the Companies Act, 1956. You have also dealt with several principal points when you studied about the company, its formation and management. The principles of a body corporate apply to stock exchanges, too. This Act wants to corporatize and demutualize the stock exchanges. Under *corporatization*, the Act intends to convert a stock exchange into a corporate entity limited by shares and under *demutualization*, which is a process of separating ownership, trading, and management in a stock exchange.

The Act was amended through the promulgation of an amendment called Securities Laws (Amendment) Act, 2005. The purpose of this Amendment was to corporatize and demutualize all recognized stock exchanges, delisting of securities, appeals against orders of the Securities Appellate Tribunal (SAT), penalties to furnish information, return, and other allied matters.

Under Sec. 4A, all stock exchanges must submit a scheme of corporatization and demutualization to the securities regulator SEBI, which may, after judging it on merits, approve the same or reject by passing an order. The main points to be approved or restricted for the stock exchange are as follows:
(a) Voting rights of the shareholders who are also stock brokers
(c) The right of shareholders or stock broker to appoint representatives on the governing board
(b) The number of representatives on the board

The regulator after inquiry has the powers to withdraw the recognition.

---

[1] The italics as well as the square brackets are as in the Act.

Powers of the SEBI to Call for Information (Sec. 6)

Under Sec. 6 of the Act, SEBI may call for information from the stock exchanges:

(a) Returns are filed with SEBI by every stock exchange on a prescribed form giving information on current affairs including volume and value of transactions, short deliveries, and decisions taken by the board.

(b) Maintenance of books of accounts, which SEBI is free to inspect.

(c) The SEBI may call for explanation relating to affairs of an exchange from any of its members; it may also set up an inquiry whenever necessary.

(d) The SEBI may call for information from any officer of the stock exchange.

(e) File annual report to SEBI.

SEBI also undertakes regular inspection of all exchanges and special investigation whenever market conditions warrant.

Power of Stock Exchange to Make By-laws (Sec. 9)

Just as companies have the right to draw the articles of association, which enable them to formulate their own rules and regulations for effective functioning and management, the Act gives powers to stock exchanges to make by-laws for the regulation and control of contracts. All of these must have approval of the SEBI. The by-laws may concern the following:

(a) The opening and closing of markets and the regulation of the hours of trade

(b) Clearing the house of periodical settlement of contracts and differences thereunder; the delivery and payment of securities, the passing on of delivery orders, and the regulation and maintenance of such clearing house

(c) Publication by the clearing house of all the particulars submitted to SEBI

(d) Regulation and prohibition of blank transfers

(e) The number and classes of contracts in respect of which settlements shall be made or differences paid through the clearing house

(f) The regulation or prohibition of *budla* transactions or carryover facilities

(g) The fixing, altering, and postponing of days of settlement

(h) Determination and declaration of market rates, including opening and closing highest and lowest rates for securities, and

(i) The levy of fees, penalties fines, etc.

These and several others concern the securities contracts and their proper conduct of business and settlements, and the stock exchanges may draw detailed by-laws that will be examined and approved by the SEBI (Case 17.1).

Listing of Securities (Sec. 21) and Rule 19 (1)

Section 21 of the Act states that where the company has applied for listing of securities with recognized stock exchange, it must comply with the listing agreement. The Securities Contracts (Regulation) Rules, 1957, Rule No. 19 (1) states the following requirements:

(a) Memorandum and articles of association and, in the case of a debenture issue

(b) Copy of the trust deed

| CASE 17.1 | APPELLANT: A. Vaidyanathan vs RESPONDENT: Union of India and Others |

DATE OF JUDGEMENT: 6 August 1998*

FACTS: The prayer in the writ petition (Madras High Court) is to issue a writ of declaration declaring Rule 8(2) of the Securities Contracts (Regulation) Rules, 1957, as unconstitutional and directing the second respondent to grant membership to the petitioner without imposing any unreasonable and arbitrary terms.

The Securities Contract (Regulation) Act, 1957 Rules: Rule 8(2): No person eligible for admission as a member under Sub-rule (1) shall be admitted as a member unless: (a) he has worked for not less than two years as a partner with, or as an authorized assistant or authorized clerk or remisier or apprentice to, a member, or (b) he agrees to work for a minimum period of two years as a partner or representative member with another member and to enter into bargains on the floor of the stock exchange and not in his own name but in the name of such other member; or (c) he succeeds to the established business of a deceased or retiring member who is his father, uncle, brother, or any other person who is, in the opinion of the governing body, a close relative, provided that the rules of the stock exchange may authorize the governing body to waive compliance with any of the foregoing conditions if the person seeking admission is, in respect of means, position, integrity, knowledge, and experience of business in securities, considered by the governing body to be otherwise qualified for membership.

The petitioner claimed that he is well qualified with a B's degree in Engineering and Master's Diploma in Business Management. He is fully qualified to take up a career in the business of dealing in securities. However, by virtue of certain provisions of the Securities Contracts (Regulation) Act, 1956 and the Rules made thereunder and by virtue of the by-laws/Articles of Association of the Stock Exchanges, the entry of proficient men into this field of business—as broker—was effectively being prevented by vested interests.

JUDGEMENT: Petition dismissed.

REASON: The Act provides for regulatory measures, such as recognition, withdrawal of recognition, direction to make rules, power to suspend business, and power to supersede the governing body. As it could be seen in the preamble to the Act, the Securities Contracts (Regulation) Act is an Act to prevent undesirable transactions in securities by regulating the business of dealing therein, by prohibiting options and by providing for certain other matters connected therewith. Thus, the said Act is purely regulatory in character.

Applying the tests laid down by the series of Supreme Court decisions, these regulatory measures by itself are sufficient in the absence of any other factor, such as financial assistance, control of management, and policies. State protected monopoly status and public functions, so as to come to the conclusion that the first respondent company is an authority amenable to writ jurisdiction under Article 226 of the Constitution.

We hold that Rule 8(2) of the Securities Contracts (Regulation) Rules, 1957 is constitutionally valid and I accordingly dismiss the writ petition as devoid of any merit

---

*A. Vaidyanathan vs Union of India and Others; see http://www.indiankanoon.org/doc/435548 (2 October 11).

(c) Copies of all prospectuses or statements in lieu of prospectuses issued by the company at any time

(d) Copies of offers for sale and circulars or advertisements offering any securities for subscription or sale during the last five years

(e) Copies of balance sheets and audited accounts for the last five years, or in the case of new companies, for such short period for which accounts have been made up with all the testimonials from dividends, vendors, promoters, underwriters, brokers, agents, secretaries, treasurers, directors, general managers, contracts, agreements, collaborations, and all other particulars that the company deals with

(f) In addition, a brief history of the company since its incorporation giving details of accounts that have been made about including reorganization, reconstruction, amalgamation, and letters of consent of the Controller of the Capital Issues

The said list is very long to be reproduced here. It suffices for you as a manager to know that listing on stock exchange includes every document and information that you have till the filing of the application.

Revised Clause 49 of the Listing Agreement

The 1990s saw a revolution in corporate governance. There was a great impact on the management of companies by Cadbury Report on Corporate Governance in the UK and Sarbanes–Oxley Act in the USA. In 2002, the SEBI felt the need to reform. It appointed a committee under the aegis of N.R. Narayana Murthy, the Chairman of Infosys. The origin of the revision of Clause 49 is the report of this committee. This clause in the listing agreement of the listed companies is the bedrock of corporate governance. In a special circular,[2] SEBI replaced the existing clause of 2000 with a new one in 2004. It will be discussed in detail within corporate governance as a separate discipline. Herein, you will be acquainted with its legal implications only.

Objective

The objective of the elaborate Clause 49 of the listing agreement was to introduce some basic corporate governance practices in Indian companies. It specified the minimum number of independent directors required on the board of a company. The setting up of an audit committee, and a shareholders' grievance committee, among others, were made mandatory as were the Management's Discussion and Analysis section and the Report on Corporate Governance in the Annual Report, and disclosures of fees paid to non-executive directors. A limit was placed on the number of committees that a director could serve on.

Compliance Report

The practical application of the Clause 49 of the listing companies is the nature of the compliance report. Table 17.1 reveals what is expected of a listed company and how it must show due diligence by filing a systematic report. The headings of the compliance report are the legal provisions of reforms introduced by SEBI.

---

[2]SEBI/CFD/DIL/CG/1/2004/12/10.

Table 17.1 Application of Clause 49

Clause 49	Provisions	Remarks
I	*Composition of Board of Directors* Powers to lay down code of conduct to all board members, management personnel	Optimum combination of executive and non-executive or independent is • Half in case there is executive chairman • One-third in case there is non-executive chairman *Independent director* is: • Non-executive • Receive remuneration • No other material or pecuniary benefit from the group and its subsidiaries or associates • Not related to directors, promoters one level below board • Not partner or executive of audit firm, internal audit, or legal firm • Not supplier, service provider • *Company secretary* Prepare and finalize code for board and management personnel and get their approval
II	*Audit committee* • To review financial statements • To review directors' responsibility statement • To review whistleblower mechanism • To review internal management performance of statutory and Internal auditors adequacy of internal control	• Minimum three members; two-third shall be independent directors • Auditors must be financially literate having accounting-related financial management expertise • Meetings: quarterly *Obligations* • Discussion and analysis of financial conditions and operational results • Significant related party transactions • Review of internal control and weaknesses issued by auditors • Review of terms of remuneration
III	Subsidiary companies	• At least one independent director on the Board of Directors of the holding company shall be a Director on the board of material non-listed Indian subsidiary company • Audit committee of the holding company to review financial statements • Minutes of the subsidiaries to be tabled at the holding company meetings
IV	Disclosures	*Related to party transactions to be placed before the audit committee:* • A summary statement of all transactions in the normal course of business • Details of material individual transactions not in the normal course of business • Details of material individual transactions together with the managements, justifications *Accounting treatment* Prescribed accounting standard is to be followed *Risk management* Lay down company procedures and their reviews

Contd

Table 17. 1 *Contd*

		Proceeds from public issues, rights issues, preferential issues All disclosures of raising of money *Remuneration of directors* • All pecuniary relationships and transactions • All elements of remuneration packages to individuals, salaries, benefits, etc. • Incentives linked to performance criteria • Service contracts, notice periods, severance fees, etc. • Stock option details *Management* Directors' report: • Industrial structure and development • Opportunities and threats, risks, and concerns-outlook • Internal controls • Financial performance • Human resource development *Shareholders* Shareholders must be provided with information: • Resume of the new director • Quarterly results and other details on company website • Redressal of the shareholders • Expediting share transfers
V	CEO/CFO certification	Managers to be appointed under Companies Act, 1956 *Obligations of CEO/CFO* • Review of financial statements and the cash flow statement • Accept responsibility for establishing and maintaining internal controls for financial reporting and effectiveness, disclosure to audit committee, proposed measures for rectification
VI	Report on corporate governance	Separate section in the annual report on corporate governance: Detailed compliance report Mandatory and non-mandatory compliance reports
VII	Compliance (under Sec. 642 (1), Companies Act, 1956)	File the compliance report on prescribed Annexure:
	Annexure IA	Information to be placed before the board of directors
	Annexure IB	Quarterly compliance report on corporate governance
	Annexure IC	List of items to be included in the Report on Corporate Governance in the Annual Report of Companies
	Annexure ID	Non-mandatory requirements
	Compliance certificate	Obtain Companies Compliance Certificate under its Rules 2001 On prescribed Form, Rule 3

Appellate Tribunal (Sec. 22a)

When a stock exchange refuses listing or is unable to grant listing within the stipulated time, the company may approach the SAT. The Tribunal has the following powers:

(a) Summoning and enforcing attendance of any person and examining him on oath
(b) Requiring discovery and product of documents
(c) Receiving evidence on affidavits
(d) Issuing commissions for the examination of witnesses or documents
(e) Reviewing orders
(f) Dismissing an application for default or deciding ex parte
(g) Setting aside any order of dismissal of any application for default or any order passed by it ex parte

17.3 OTHER IMPORTANT SECTIONS

Sec. 22 C   This allows either the appellant or any person authorized by him, such as a company secretary or a legal practitioner, to appear in person. Furthermore, if the appellant is not satisfied with the Tribunal, he may appeal in the high court.

Sec. 23   It deals elaborately on penalties, such as trading outside the stock exchange, failure to file returns, failure to redress investor grievances, failure to segregate securities or monies of clients, failure to comply with the listing conditions, and for excess dematerialization of unlisted securities.

Sec. 27 A   It deals with the right to receive income from collective investment schemes such as mutual funds (27B).

Concluding sections   The Act concludes (Sec. 28) by announcing the exceptions to who it does not apply to, such as the Reserve Bank of India. Section. 31 states the power of SEBI to make regulations.

17.4 THE SECURITIES AND EXCHANGE BOARD OF INDIA, 1992

TEXT

An Act to provide for the establishment of a Board to protect the interests of investors in securities and to promote the development of, and to regulate, the securities market and for matters connected therewith or incidental thereto

– The SEBI Act, 1992, Preamble

Prior to this Act, the Central Government administered the regulations of the Securities Contract (Regulation) Act, 1956. With enactment of the SEBI Act, 1992, the complete authority to regulate and administer the Securities Contract is given to the board established according this Act. The Act has been amended in 1995, 1999, and 2002 for the sake of investor protection. Furthermore, an Ordinance called

MANAGER'S TAKEAWAY

- Understanding of securities is to understand property in depth.
- Raising capital through securities contract is the cornerstone of modern business.

Subscriber Education and Protection Fund, 2004, was proclaimed to be administered under SEBI. The acronym SEBI for the Securities and Exchange Board of India has become popular; it is also known as the Market Regulator.

SEBI has its headquarters in Mumbai, the Bandra-Kurla Complex, with a very impressive building, SEBI Bhavan; with regional offices at Delhi, Kolkata, Chennai, and Ahmedabad. SEBI consists of one chairman and five members, one each from the Departments of Finance and Law of the Central Government, one from the Reserve Bank of India, and two other persons. Its regional offices in Delhi, Kolkata, and Chennai have been constituted under the SEBI Act to administer its provisions. The Central Government has the right to terminate the services of the Chairman or any member of the Board. The Board decides all questions in its meeting by majority vote, with the Chairman having a second or casting vote.

Section 11 of the Act lays down the duty of the Board to protect the interest of investors in securities and to promote the development of and to regulate the securities market by such measures. It empowers the Board to regulate the business in stock exchanges to register and regulate the working of stock brokers, sub-brokers, share transfer agents, bankers to an issue, trustees of trust deeds, registrars to an issue, merchant bankers, underwriters, portfolio managers, investment advisers, etc.

It also empowers SEBI to register and regulate the working of collective investment schemes including mutual funds, to prohibit fraudulent and unfair trade practices and insider trading, to regulate takeovers, to conduct enquiries and audits of the stock exchanges, etc.

All stock exchanges are required to be registered with SEBI under the provisions of the Act. Under Sec. 12 of the Act, all the stock brokers, sub-brokers, share transfer agents, bankers to an issue, trustees of trust deed, registrars to an issue, merchant bankers, underwriters, portfolio managers, investment advisers, and other such intermediaries who may be associated with the securities markets are obliged to register with the Board, and the Board has the power to suspend or cancel such registration.

The Board is bound by the directions given by the Central Government from time to time on questions of policy and the Central Government has the right to supersede the Board. The Board is also obliged to submit a report to the Central Government every year, giving true and full account of its activities, policies, and programmes. Anyone aggrieved by the Board's decision is entitled to appeal to the Central Government.

You will study in detail the provisions of the Act while studying Securities, Portfolio Management, Capital Market, Derivatives, Corporate Governance, etc.

17.5 INSIDER TRADING

According to Sec. 12A, no person shall directly or indirectly:

(a) use or employ, in connection with the issue, purchase, or sale of any securities listed or proposed to be listed on a recognized stock exchange, any manipulative or deceptive device or contrivance in contravention of the provisions of this Act or the rules or the regulations made thereunder.

(b) employ any device, scheme, or artifice to defraud in connection with issue or dealing in securities that are listed or proposed to be listed on a recognized stock exchange.

(c) engage in any act, practice, or course of business, which operates or would operate as fraud or deceit upon any person, in connection with the issue, dealing in securities which are listed or proposed to be listed on a recognized stock exchange, in contravention of the provisions of this Act or the rules or the regulations made thereunder.

(d) engage in insider trading.

(e) deal in securities while in possession of material or non-public information or communicate such material or non-public information to any other person, in a manner that is in contravention of the provisions of this Act or the rules or the regulations made thereunder.

(f) acquire control of any company or securities more than the percentage of equity share capital of a company whose securities are listed or proposed to be listed on a recognized stock exchange in contravention of the regulations made under this Act—the Securities Exchange Board of India, 1992, Sec. 12 A.

The above text, comprising a full-fledged Chapter VA inserted by the SEBI (Amendment) Act, 2002, Sec. 7 (w.e.f. 29 October 2002), is about prohibition of manipulative and deceptive devices, insider trading, and substantial acquisition of securities or control.

Understanding Insider Trading

The term 'insider' as a general term is not difficult to understand. It stands for someone who has privileged information that the rest of the public does not have. Within a company or within a stock exchange, there are several people who, because of their position and nature of work, have such information on stocks that, if used, can profit to the disadvantage of the public investors. Such misappropriation of information on securities is a breach of the fiduciary relationship of trust and confidence.

Legal Insider Trading vs Illegal Insider Trading

Legal insider trading occurs when corporate insiders, such as officers, directors, or employees, buy or sell stocks within the confines of company policy stated in the memorandum of articles concerning trading in shares.

Illegal insider trading concerns the buying and selling in securities of a listed company. The officers, directors, members of management, employees, auditor, advisor, consultant, analysts, etc., stand in fiduciary duty to the investors from the public. The insiders, due to their position, have such information that the public investor does not have. If an insider then uses this information to his own personal profit to the detriment of a common investor, a breach of fiduciary trust is committed. It is unjust and against the established law, the SEBI Act.

SEBI Regulation against Insider Trading

Regulation 3 of the SEBI Act, 2002 prohibits dealing, communication, and counselling on matters relating to insider trading, as follows:
(a) Unpublished price-sensitive information
(b) Dealing in the securities of another company or an associate of that other company while in possession of any unpublished price-sensitive information

Insiders   Directors and substantial shareholders have to disclose their holding to the company periodically:
(a) Temporary insiders such as lawyers, accountants, investment bankers
(b) Relatives (parents, siblings, spouses, grandchildren) of connected persons, as well as the companies, firms, and trust
(c) Persons deemed to be connected to persons holding more than 10 per cent

The problem of privileged information is difficult to control. Price-sensitive information is communicated and spread out through very loosely connected and informal networks of brokers, clients, and even friends, and through electronic networks. Furthermore, a complex and subtle nexus of company officials, brokers, traders are difficult to regulate. These individuals are very often privy to strategic policy decisions or developments that may influence the valuation of a company's scrip on the bourses.

Duties of a Listed Company

Under SEBI's prohibition of insider trading, the following are the duties of every listed company:
(a) Appoint a senior-level employee, generally the company secretary, as the compliance officers
(b) Set up an appropriate mechanism to frame and enforce a code of conduct for internal procedures
(c) Abide by the Code of Corporate Disclosure practices as specified in Schedule (ii) to the SEBI (Prohibition of Insider Trading) Regulations
(d) Initiate the information received under the initial and continual disclosures to the stock exchange within 5 days of their receipts
(e) Specify the close period
(f) Identify price-sensitive information
(g) Ensure adequate data security of confidential information stored on the computer
(h) Prescribe the procedure for the pre-clearance of trade and entrus the compliance officers with the responsibility of strict adherence of the same

Penalties for Offences of the SEBI Act and Insider Trading

Chapter VI A Sec. 15A, whose provisions have been inserted in the amended Act in 1995, have elaborate penalties and have been imposed (Table 17.2).

Table 17.2 Penalties for offences of SEBI Act and insider trading

Offence	Penalty
Sec. 15A Failure to furnish information, returns, etc.	₹1 lakh for each day during which such failure continues or 1 crore, whichever is less
Sec. 15B Failure by any person to enter into agreement with clients	₹1 lakh for each day during which such failure continues or 1 crore, whichever is less
Sec. 15C Failure to redress investors' grievances	₹1 lakh for each day during which such failure continues or 1 crore, whichever is less
Sec. 15D For certain defaults in case of mutual funds	₹1 lakh for each day during which such failure continues or 1 crore, whichever is less
Sec. 15E Failure to observe rules and regulations by an asset management company	₹1 lakh for each day during which such failure continues or 1 crore, whichever is less
Sec. 15F Failure in case of stock brokers registered under the Act	Five times the amount of brokerage charged in excess of the specified brokerage, whichever is higher
Sec. 15G Penalty for insider trading	₹25 crore or three times the amount of profits made out of insider trading, whichever is higher
Sec. 15H Failure to disclose acquisition of shares and takeovers	₹25 crore or three times the amount of profits made out of insider trading, whichever is higher
Sec. 15HA Fraudulent and unfair trade practices	₹25 crore or three times the amount of profits made out of insider trading, whichever is higher
Sec. 15HB Contravention where no separate penalty has been provided	Up to ₹1 crore

There was a paradigm shift in securities contract as the global economy became favourable to market economy. India saw sweeping changes and reforms in the capital market especially after the enactment of the SEBI Act, 1992 and its subsequent amendments. New benchmarks were introduced under the influence of policy changes suggested by the International Monetary Fund and the World Bank. This was coupled with a few capital market scams that shook the confidence of an economy on its reform course. SEBI, therefore, had all the intention to ensure that Indian stock market was one of the best in the world.

Brokers from all the stock exchanges of India agitated against the regulation brought out by SEBI to impose levy on the basis of different trade levels (Case 17.2). They challenged the regulation and appealed in the Supreme Court.

MANAGER'S TAKEAWAY

- A regulatory agency does not legislate; it implements what is legislated to control an activity.
- It is a salutary practice to challenge the validity of a regulation if its benefit goes only to the investor.

CASE 17.2

APPELLANT: BSE Brokers Forum and others vs RESPONDENT: Securities and Exchange Board of India

DATE OF JUDGEMENT: 2 January 2001*

FACTS: Writ petitions questioning the validity of Regulation 10 of the Securities and Exchange Board of India (Stock Brokers and Sub-brokers) Regulations, 1992 read with Schedule III thereof as also letters dated 7 November 1992 and 7 January 1993 issued by the SEBI were filed in various High Courts in the country.

The controversy in this petition emerges from Regulation 10 read with Schedule III of the said Regulations which reads thus: 10 (1) Every applicant eligible for grant of a certificate shall pay such fees and in such manner as specified in Schedule III:

Provided that the Board may, on sufficient cause being shown, permit the stock broker to pay such fees at any time before the expiry of six months from the date on which such fees become due.

(2) Where a stock broker fails to pay the fees as provided in Regulation 10, the Board may suspend the registration certificate, whereupon the stock broker shall cease to buy, sell, or deal in securities as a stock broker.

SEBI denied that Regulation 10 of Schedule III to the Regulations is either ultra vires of the Act or unconstitutional. Justifying the fee levied by them, the Board contended that it had to render multifaceted and multitude of services contemplated under Sec. 11(2) of the Act.

JUDGEMENT: Petition dismissed.

REASON: The facts involved are matters pertaining to the securities market with its own intricacies. The question involved mainly pertains to the legislative competence, nature, and reasonableness of the levy. We are not called upon to decide or to recommend as to what is the best way to levy the impugned fee. So long as the Legislature has the legislative competence to levy and the Board has not exceeded its statutory authority in imposing the levy, we need not go into other niceties of the levy which are not in the realm of our jurisdiction. We have examined the reasonableness of the levy qua the statutory power of the Board and its quantum with reference to the need of the Board and not with reference to whether it is the best available method of levy.

*BSE Brokers and others vs Securities and Exchange Board of India: see http://www. indiankanoon.org/doc/749233/ (3 October 2011).

SUMMARY

- The objective of securities contract regulations is to prevent undesirable and fraudulent transactions in the stock exchanges. The Securities Contracts Regulation Act, 1956, and the SEBI Act, 1992, are the main pillars of the edifice of securities transactions business in India. The SEBI is the regulator who implements the laws from the said Acts by creating rules and regulations in the trading of securities.

- The principles of a body corporate apply to stock exchanges too. Under *Corporatization*, the Act intends to make a stock exchange as a corporate entity limited by shares and under *Demutualization*, to have a process of separating ownership, trading, and management in a stock exchange.
- Sec. 21 of the Act provides that where company has applied for listing of securities with recognized stock exchange, it must comply with the listing agreement.
- The Clause 49 of the revised SEBI Regulation concerning listing agreement is the foundation for corporate governance. The essence of corporate governance is compliance to the Regulations of SEBI. Regulation 3 of the SEBI, 2002 prohibits dealing, communication, and counseling on matters relating to insider trading:
- Unpublished price-sensitive information
- Dealing in the securities of another company or associate of that other company while in possession of any unpublished price-sensitive information.
- There are heavy penalties for insider trading and other offences of non-compliance.

EXERCISES

(i) A listed company allotted shares. SEBI ruled against it and directed the company to refund the money to the investors.
Hint: The allotment of shares will become void if permission is not granted by SEBI.

(ii) SEBI detected price manipulation in shares of a company and promptly charged the company under Secs 3 and 4 of the Act for fraudulent and unfair practices and directed the company not to raise money from the public. The company contended that the charges were false as the company does not control the movement in shares. The company is a manufacturer of consumable goods. The price movement of shares was merely due to the volatility in the market. How would you judge?
Hint: Set aside SEBI order not to raise funds. See: Videocon International Ltd vs SEBI (Securities Appellate Tribunal); see also: indiankanoon.org/doc/1034691/.

(iii) Naresh, the CFO of a listed company, passes on share price information decided in the board meeting to his wife. Accordingly, she buys the said shares and optimally disposes them off for very high profit. Upon being charged of insider trading, the CFO contends that the information was already out before the trading started, hence there is no question of depriving the public of necessary information. How would you judge?
Hint: Guilty; see Rajiv B. Gandhi, Sandhya R. Gandhi vs SEBI, 2008 84 SCL 192 SAT; see also: http://indiankanoon. org/doc/1281030/.

(iv) What powers does the Securities Exchange Market Regulator exercise? Explain with examples.

(v) In the context of a listed company, explain Clause 49 of the listing agreement of the SEBI Regulation of Securities Contract.

DEVELOPMENT OF LEGAL EDGE

- Do a project research on SEBI website: http://www.sebi.gov.in. Condense the Act, rules, regulations, and circulars as per the need for your company,
- Based on the earlier prepare portfolio management

- Make a model Corporate Governance Compliance Report.
- Feel free to do all the three together in brief or treat each one as an independent project.

FURTHER READING

Book

G.V. Ramakrishnan, *Two Score and Ten, My Experiences in Government*, Academic Foundation.

Legal Texts

* The Securities Contract Act, 1956.
* The Securities and Exchange Board of India Act, 1992.

* Rules
* Regulations
* Prohibition of Insider Trading, 1992.
* Revised Clause 49 of SEBI Regulation.
* Circulars

Web resources

http://www.sebi.gov.in/sebiweb/.

CASE STUDY

The Worst Kept Secret

An 'Insider' means any person who is or was connected with the company or is deemed to have been connected with the company, and who is reasonably expected to have access, by virtue of such connection, to unpublished price-sensitive information in respect of securities of the company or who has received or has had access to such unpublished price-sensitive information.

– SEBI Regulation, 1992, 2(e)

'Connected person' means any person who:
(i) is a director, as defined in Clause 13 of Sec. 2 of the Companies Act, 1956 (1 of 1956) of a company, or is deemed to be director of that company by virtue of sub-clause (10) of Sec. 307 of that Act, or
(ii) occupies the position as an officer or an employee of the company or holds a position involving a professional or business relationship between himself and the company and who may reasonably be expected to have an access to unpublished price-sensitive information in relation to that company

– SEBI Regulation, 1992, 2(c)

The Inside Plot

The story takes place in the context of a company takeover. Bayer AG, the well-known German company, wanted to take over ABS Industries Ltd. Rakesh Agarwal was the managing director of ABS. He conducted high-level negotiations with the buyer company Bayer. Naturally, he was privy to all information; importantly, the price-sensitive information, which, if used as privileged information, without its public knowledge, could alter the course of trading.

Agarwal understood the importance of what he knows. He knew that SEBI is highly vigilant when takeover negotiations, amalgamations, or rearrangements are going on. To escape the vigilant market regulator, Agarwal conceived and executed a smart plot.

First, he took his brother-in-law into confidence. The announcement that ABS would be sold was not yet made. He made I.P. Kedia, his brother-in-law, to buy all the ABS shares from the stock market only to be sold through the open offer making enormous profit. The negotiations were over and ABS was taken over by Bayer.

SEBI outsmarted the duo and surreptitiously followed the trial and trends in trading. SEBI charged Rakesh Agarwal and his brother-in-law for violating under Secs 3 and 4 of the SEBI Prohibition of Insider Trading Regulations, 1992.

Rakesh Agarwal rebutted the charges saying that what he did was in the interest of the company and has not personally gained anything. His plan was to acquire 51 per cent of the ABS through Bayer and execute it accurately.

SEBI would have nothing of it. It directed Rakesh Agarwal to deposit ₹34 lakh with Investor Education and Protection Funds of Stock Exchange, Mumbai and NSE in equal proportion of ₹17 lakh each. The purpose of this deposit was to compensate if any investor made a claim.

The Appeal

Rakesh Agarwal filed an appeal in the SAT, Mumbai. He asserted that his action must be seen as one done in the interest of the company.

The Judgement[3]

The charge against the appellant is that of violating the SEBI regulations on insider trading. Though much has been said in the order about the acquisition of shares by Mr Kedia on behalf of the appellant, ultimately it has boiled down to the purchase of only 1,82,500 shares by Mr Kedia during the period 9 September 1996 to 1 October 1996.

The SEBI regulations on insider trading seek to prohibit persons who, by virtue of their connection with a company, received unpublished, sensitive information from using such information/dealing in the securities of the company based on such information to make secret profits/personal.

Appellant denied he had breached Regulation 3 and rendered himself liable for penalty. In this regard, the Appellant submitted that:

(a) There is no allegation or averment that the appellant made profit, direct or indirect, as a result of the impugned share transaction.

(b) There is no allegation or averment that the appellant undertook the impugned share transaction for the purpose of making any profit.

(c) There is no allegation or averment that the appellant has acted in a manner disadvantageous to the shareholders.

(d) There is no allegation or averment that, in all, the actions of the appellant have caused detriment to the shareholders of the company.

(e) The averment in the findings of investigation relied upon in the Show Cause Notice, issued by the Adjudicating Officer, on the basis of directions issued by the Chairman dated 21 June 2000 (the 'Show Cause Notice') indicates that even according to the department, the acquisition of the impugned shares was undertaken with a view to enable Bayer in reaching its 51 per cent target.

Insider trading takes place when insiders or other persons who, by virtue of their position in office or otherwise, have access to unpublished price-sensitive information relating to the affairs of a company, and deal in securities of such company or cause the trading of securities while in possession of such information or communicate such information to others who use it in connection with the purchase or sale of securities. Thus, insider trading prejudices the smooth functioning of the securities market and undermines investors' confidence.

SEBI had submitted that from a bare reading of Regulation 3, it is clear that prohibition of insider trading by an insider is an absolute offence and that benefit or gain is not an ingredient of the offence. It is difficult to accept the version of SEBI. Once SEBI's view is accepted, the very purpose of imposing prohibition on insider dealing in the securities on the basis of the unpublished price-sensitive information would become meaningless. If an insider, based on the unpublished price-sensitive information, deals in securities for no advantage to him over others, how can it be said to be against the interest of investors. In my view, taking into consideration the very objective of the SEBI regulations prohibiting the insider trading, the intention/motive of the insider has to be taken cognizance of.

It is established that the person who had indulged in insider trading had no intention of gaining any unfair advantage; the charge of insider trading warranting penalty cannot be sustained against him.

The appellant was frantically trying to get a joint venture partner to strengthen the company, when the particular industry was facing problems. The partner was Bayer. It put stiff condition of holding 51 per cent capital in the company. The appellant's intention in acquiring the share was to facilitate the entry of Bayer for the betterment of the company and its other shareholders, employees, etc. The object was not to gain unfair personal gain. It is true that in the process the shares, which he purchased at a lower price, fetched a higher price when offered in the public offer. But this gain was only incidental, and certainly not by cheating others. If the appellant's intention was to make money in the process, he could have cornered much more shares and profited considerably. His bona fide is evident from the fact that he had instructed Mr Kedia to buy even 1,20,000 shares at ₹80 when the public offer response was not that warm, so as to meet the deficiency, if any, in obtaining 20 per cent shares by Bayer in the public offer.

[3]Rakesh Agarwal vs Securities and Exchange Board of India, (2004) 1 CompLJ 193 SAT, 2004 49 SCL 351 SAT; see also: http://www.indiankanoon.org/ doc/863433/ (3 October 2011). The judgement text is abridged.

In any case, as stated in this order since the SEBI has not made out a case to hold the appellant guilty of indulging in insider trading, no action is called for under Sec. 11, 11B of the Act read with Regulation 11 of the SEBI regulations on insider trading. Therefore, that part of the order directing 'Rakesh Agrwal to deposit a sum of ₹34,00,000 with Investor Protection fund of BSE and NSE to compensate the investors who may come forward at a later period of time seeking compensation for the loss incurred by them in selling at a price higher than the offer price' cannot be sustained.

Final judgement   The said part of the order is set aside.

SEBI has the power to order adjudication under Sec. 15G and launch prosecution under Sec. 24. In case the appellant is aggrieved by the order of the adjudicating officer or the decision of the competent court in the criminal complaint, the appellant is not short of appellate remedies.

Conclusion

Of course, it is for you to judge the merits and demerits of this case. The Market Regulator SEBI found no sympathy in the media. The media voiced the footlessness of the regulator. SEBI has drawn flak for several cases. One such case of Hindustan Lever Ltd (HLL) for purchasing eight lakh shares of Brooke Bond Lipton India Ltd from the Unit Trust of India just a month before the merger of the two companies was announced. SEBI charged HLL of insider trading. In the Appellate Authority of the Finance Ministry, HLL contended that the company cannot be an insider trader to itself; the purpose of buying the shares was solely to preserve the parent company, that is, maintain 51 per cent stake. As per the merger, there was no secret about it as it was already published by various entities. Thus, very often the fate of the market regulator has been discomforting.

The Ten Worst Financial Scams of India

Insurance scam, 1947   Immediately after winning independence, despite great patriotism and idealism of a new nation, India's financial health suffered a great blow, which would have lasting and debilitating consequences for its economy in general and financial policies, in particular. India had continued the British legacy of free-market economy and the insurance sector was no different. There were a handful insurance companies who played fiddle to the most favoured companies and ignored the common citizens. To safeguard the public interest the government nationalized the insurance sector by founding Life Insurance Corporation of India by passing an Act in the parliament.[4] The nationalization spree continued till the economic reforms of 1991.

Securities scam, 1991   Harshad Metha, known as Big Bull securities broker for making the capital market most bullish in its history, cleverly manipulated the loopholes in banking system. He used the Ready Forward scheme of the banks to procure large amounts of money to buy shares at highly inflated prices. The markets soared, the banks smelt the rat. But it was too late. The money was gone, so did Mehta who went to prison eventually. But he made a comeback in 1998 with a Website offering trading tips. Result: another stock exchange collapse. He died later.

Companies scam, 1992   C.R. Bhansali was an imaginative man who floated over 100 companies that attracted large sums of money from the public. More money came in as Bhansali offered ever-increasing rates of interest from the very same receipts. To his bad luck and to those who lent money to him, the stock market collapsed. He went to prison for three months, only to escape and never to be found again.

Unit Trust of India, 1998   This Government of India undertaking had a flagship scheme called US-64 with an investor base of 20 million. The chairman and other officials acted in a selective way, which helped some favoured people to amass money. The sheer size of the common people who invested the money in the scheme forced the government to bail out with a phenomenal of ₹4,000 crore.

Home Trade, 2000   The brand Home Trade was an overnight wonder finance portal, which was most visible anywhere in the country with eye-catching ads with endorsements from sports and film stars. The brainchild of a certain Sanjay Agarwal, Home Trade was created to deal in gilts. Apart from the usual story of brokers and bankers duping the innocent investors, it also involved Provident Funds of Seamen. The scam amount was put to be ₹3,000 crore.

Ketan Parekh   He was a qualified chartered accountant turned stock broker, who identified high-end stocks and traded on small stock exchanges—Kolkata, Ahmedabad, etc.—with numerous *benami* accounts. By the time he was found out and a few banks went bankrupt, he had laid waste over ₹1,500 crore.

Telgi stamp paper scam The sheer numbers of this scam are mindboggling: 14 states, 125 banks, 1000 employees, and money ₹30,000 crore. Reserve Bank of India later put the figure to ₹200 crore which no one believed. Abdul Karim Telgi simply bribed the security press in Nasik, got the stamp paper printed, and sold it.

Dinesh Dalmia, 2001 He was the MD of DSQ Software Ltd. The company issued 13 lakh shares, which were allotted to four companies on preferential basis. A stock depository dematerialized and helped in delivery of the shares. This is picture perfect—except that shares were not listed on any stock exchange. Incredulously simple!

IPO, 2004 Initial Public Offerings oversubscribed over 40 times! The operators opened *benami* accounts in thousands to purchase IPOs. Then sit pretty for a while and hope to sell and make huge profits.

Satyam, 2009 Satyam was a formidable Forbes 500 company, second only to Infosys. Ramalinga Raju, its chairman, surprised the world by saying that he has been cooking accounts for several years and that the balloon had swelled to ₹12,000 crore. In his own words, it is a tiger which he cannot dismount. He is lodged in jail. The company after a skilful handling by the government has gone to the business house of Mahindras.

Discussion Questions

1. Define insider trading as relevant to this case.
2. How was insider trading determined in the above case?
3. What relationship is involved among the main characters in the case?
4. Do you think giving price-sensitive information with the intention to benefit your company is not insider trading?
5. Do you think that the appellant has presented a foolproof argument?
6. What is SEBI's contention in framing the charges against the appellant?
7. Upon which principle does the judge base his legal reasoning?
8. QWhat are the main points the judge notes to his conclusion?

Going Beyond

1. As a CEO of your company, in your social conversation, what can be construed as price-sensitive information? Give examples.
2. If a managing director gives price-sensitive information to his colleagues in the company, can it treated as leading to insider trading?

LEGAL LUMINARY

GANGUMOLU VENKATA RAMAKRISHNA—FIRST CHAIRMAN OF THE SEBI

Member of the Planning Commission, Chairman of SEBI), Chairman of the Disinvestment Commission, Chief Secretary of Andhra Pradesh, Diplomatic Mission on Economic Affairs at Indian Embassy in Washington, USA, India's Ambassador to European Union, Padma Shri Gangamolu Venkata Ramakrishna has been an indomitable and exceptional bureaucrat of India. His book, *Two Score and Ten, My Experiences in Government*,* is a powerful case study for every Indian Administrative Service officer of his 50 years of public service; it is also an example for every manager to emulate.

G.V. Ramakrishna, as he is generally known, or in closer circles just GVR, has been a forthright and clear thinker. He has expressed himself in the above-mentioned book, articles, and several interviews. As the reforms in Indian Economy began, a new ministry was formed for disinvestment. He was its chairman; the media called him the strongman. He announced that disinvestment or privatization of public sector should be done prudently. He insisted that a cure must be found for sick units.** Privatization means selling the majority shareholding of the Government companies and giving management control to private companies. However, he held that disinvestment should consist of selling some minority shares without transferring the management control. Furthermore, if the government shareholding is below 51 per cent then the company is not a public sector company. There is no accountability, checks, and balances. The problem becomes acute because in such a scenario the minister will be using his rights as the largest single shareholder; thus turning the public sector into a private *zamindari*. Such has been the strength of mind of this public administrator.

SEBI was established in 1988 by the Government of India through an executive resolution, and was subsequently upgraded as a fully autonomous, statutory body, in the year 1992 with the passing of the SEBI Act on 30 January 1992. The obvious objectives were to protect the interests of the investors in securities and develop the securities market. In those early days, SEBI had meagre powers to deal with the problems. As scam after scam hit the financial market, stringent and comprehensive regulations were brought in, prescribed registration norms, the eligibility criteria, the code of obligations, and code of conduct for different intermediaries, such as bankers, brokers, sub-brokers, registrars, portfolio managers, credit rating agencies, underwriters, etc., were developed. As the time passed and the Chairmen came and went, several commissions such as Kumara Managalam Birla and N.R. Narayana Murthy were appointed and their recommendations were accepted to form a very good code of corporate governance. SEBI, presently, after two decades is considered as one of the exceptional market regulators in the world. G.V. Ramakrishna has every right to be proud of his prodigious institution.

G.V. Ramakrishna was born in 1930. He studied to be a biochemist and worked in a Bangalore hospital doing research in hematology. He went to Harvard and obtained Master's in Public Administration. He joined the Indian Administrative Service in 1952. Ever since, he has been in public service to the extent that he has served four prime ministers after his retirement.

---

*GV Ramakrishna, *Two Score and Ten: My Experiences in Government*, Academic Foundation.
**See the interview in http://www.rediff.com/money/2004/jun/09inter.htm (4 October 2011).

Banking Laws

Principle: *Quicquid solvitur, solvitur secundum modum solventis.*

Money paid is to be applied according to the intention of the party paying it.

CHAPTER OUTLINE

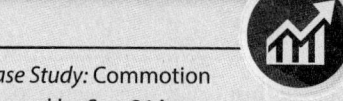

- Introduction and Interpretation
- Banking Regulation Act, 1949
- Reserve Bank of India Act, 1934
- Conclusion

- *Case Study:* Commotion Caused by Sec. 21A
- *Legal Luminary:* Dr Manmohan Singh

18.1 INTRODUCTION AND INTERPRETATION

TEXT

'Banking' means the accepting, for the purpose of lending or investment, of deposits of money from the public, repayable on demand or otherwise, and withdrawable by cheque, draft, order or otherwise.

– Banking Regulation Act, 1949, Sec. 5(b)

For a manager, a bank stands for wealth management. In the post-economic reform era in India, private banks have grown and have become a key factor in industrial development. Banking itself is a leading industry and financial managers are highly valued. Corporations and banks work hand in hand to create wealth. Banks supply capital to entrepreneurs. The following are some of the services offered by banks:

(a) Brokerage

(b) Core banking: current accounts, time deposits, liquidity management

(c) Lending products: margin lending, credit cards, mortgages, financing projects

(d) Asset management: financial and non-financial (real estate, commodities, art, etc.), structured and alternative investments

(e) Consulting: wealth structuring, tax and trusts, etc.

Modern India has a varied and diversified pattern of banking system. The nation's central bank is the Reserve Bank of India (RBI), which is the supreme monetary authority. The entire banking system is unified, regulated, and structured to function under RBI. There are several banks such as nationalized banks, private banks, commercial banks, and cooperatives. Banks have permeated the life of the nation whether urbanor rural, industrial or agricultural. With the high prevalence of technology, electronic banking has become a way of life for ordinary Indians, rich or poor.

The importance of banking, apart from the above general usage for business and industry, is an inevitable and inseparable parameter in wealth creation. For this purpose, banking is not only carried out at the national level but also increasingly at the international level. Major foreign banks are a common sight along with the Indian banks.

The entire banking activity takes place within a definite legal framework, which has been developed through the banking laws since 1872. Box 18.1 provides a chronological account of all the banking-related Acts. This demonstrates that banking is a highly regulated activity, and whether national or international, all banks have to function under the law and submit themselves to the authority of RBI.

BOX 18.1   CHRONOLOGICAL LIST OF BANK ACT

The Acts, from 1872 to 1949, are the foundation laws of banking. The laws enacted later are a development upon these laws to serve the contemporary interests and the evolution of the banking laws.*

1872	Indian Contracts Act
1881	Negotiable Instruments Act
1882	Powers-of-Attorney Act
1891	Bankers' Books Evidence Act
1923	Official Secrets Act
1934	Reserve Bank of India Act
1939	Commercial Documents Evidence Act
1944	Public Debt Act
1949	Banking Regulation Act
1951	State Financial Corporations Act
1955	State Bank of India Act
1959	State Bank of India (Subsidiary Banks) Act
1964	Industrial Development Bank of India Act
1970	Banking Companies (Acquisition and Transfer of Undertakings) Act

---

*Several more laws need to be enacted, particularly in the field of electronic banking, Internet banking, bank data security, corporate banking, stock trading, etc., which are at present managed through statutory rules, regulations, and circulars mainly by RBI and other statutory bodies

Contd

Box 18.1 *Contd*

1972	Hire–Purchase Act
1976	Regional Rural Banks Act
1978	High Denomination Bank Notes (Demonetization) Act
1980	Banking Companies (Acquisition and Transfer of Undertakings) Act
1981	Export–Import Bank of India Act
1981	National Bank for Agriculture and Rural Development Act
1982	Chit Funds Act
1983	Public Financial Institutions (Obligation as to Fidelity and Secrecy) Act
1984	Banking Service Commission Act
1987	National Housing Bank Act
1989	Small Industries Development Bank of India Act
1993	Industrial Finance Corporation (Transfer of Undertaking and Repeal) Act
1997	Industrial Reconstruction Bank (Transfer of Undertakings and Repeal) Act
2003	Industrial Development Bank (Transfer of Undertaking and Repeal) Act

The Scope

The scope of this chapter is very limited. It will offer an overview of two basic laws: Banking Regulation Act, 1949, and the Reserve Bank of India Act, 1934. All the allied laws mentioned in Box 18.1 have their own significance. However, our understanding of them would be limited if we do not first comprehend the two basic laws that would be treated here.

18.2 BANKING REGULATION ACT, 1949

In addition to the business of banking, a banking company may engage in any one or more of the following forms of business, namely, (a) the borrowing, raising, or taking up of money; the lending or advancing of money either upon or without security; and drawing, making accepting, discounting, buying selling, collecting and dealing in bills of exchange, hundies, promissory notes, coupons, drafts, bill of lading, railway receipts, warrants, debentures, certificates, scripts and other instruments, and securities whether transferable or negotiable or not; the granting and issuing of letters of credit, travellers' cheques and circular notes; the buying, selling and dealing in bullion and specie; the buying and selling of foreign exchange including foreign bank notes; the acquiring, holding, issuing on commission, underwriting and dealing in stock funds, shares, debentures, debenture stock bonds, obligations, securities and investments of all kinds; the purchasing and selling of bonds, scripts or other forms of securities on behalf of constituents or others; the negotiating of loan and advances; the receiving of all kinds of bonds, scripts or valuables on deposit or for safe custody or otherwise; the providing of safe deposit vaults; the collecting and transmitting of money and securities.

– Banking Regulation Act, 1949, Sec. 6(1)(a)

We may sometimes wonder whether the Contract Act and the Negotiable Instrument Act are not adequate to deal with banking. Indeed, they had been until 1949 when the banking law was promulgated, and they continue to do so. The need, however, was for regulation. The main objectives of the Act are to safeguard the interest of the depositors, control the abuse of power by the banks, and advance the interest of the Indian economy. The Act does not replace the two fundamental laws of contract and negotiable instruments. This Act regulates banks; it does not purport to codify another law on banking.

Provisions of Banking Regulation Act

In the above text of Sec. 6 (1)(a), we read the essential function for which the basic concept of banking stand. However, there are several other businesses for which banking stands. A bank is a company and is organized as such; it is different from other businesses in so far as the products are financial. It stands as a conduit between other companies and their business. The following provisions of the Act will clearly express the legislative point of view.

Business of Banking Companies (Sec. 6)

(a) Act as agents as for any government or local authority or any other person or persons; the carrying on of agency business of any description, including the clearing and forwarding of goods, giving of receipts and discharges, and otherwise acting as an attorney on behalf of customers. The exception is that the bank cannot be a managing agent, a secretary, or treasurer of a company.

(b) The bank also deals with contracting for public and private loans and for negotiating and issuing the same.

(c) It effects insuring, guaranteeing, underwriting, participating in managing, and carrying out of any issue, public or private, of the state, municipal or other loans or of shares, stock, debentures or debenture stock of any company, corporation or association, and the lending of money for the purpose of any such issue.

(d) It carries on transacting every kind of guarantee and indemnity business.

(e) It manages the selling and realizing of any property that may come into the possession of the company in satisfaction or part satisfaction of any of its claims.

(f) It acquires by holding and generally dealing with any property or any right, title, or interest in any such property that may form the security or part of the security for any loans or advances or that may be connected with any such security.

(g) It undertakes and executes trusts; undertakes the administration of estates as executor, trustee, or otherwise.

(h) It establishes and supports aids in the establishment and support of associations, institutions, funds, trusts, and conveniences calculated to benefit employees or ex-employees of the company or the dependants or connections of such persons.

(i) It grants pension and allowances and makes payments towards insurance; subscribing to or guaranteeing moneys for charitable or benevolent object, for any exhibition, or for any public, general, or useful object.

(j) It acquires, constructs, maintains, and alters any building or works that are necessary or convenient for the purpose of the company.

(k) It sells, improves, manages, develops, exchanges, leases, mortgages, disposes, or turns into account or otherwise deals with all or any part of the property and rights of the company.

(l) It does all such other things as are incidental or conducive to the promotion or advancement of the business of the company or any other form of business which the central government may, by notification in the official gazette, specify as a form of business in which it is lawful for a banking company to engage.

Apart from this, specific agency services such as collection of securities, issuing of letters of credit or guarantee, portfolio management, merchant banking, money exchange, collection of dues, cesses, telephone bills, municipal taxes, safe custody for valuables, and several other general utility services are also taken care of.

Reserve fund (Sec. 17)

Every banking company incorporated in India shall create a reserve fund and out of the balance of profit each year, as prepared under Sec. 29 of the Act and before the declaration of any dividend, transfer to the reserve fund a sum equivalent to not less than 20 per cent of such profit. The Central Government may relax this law upon the recommendation of RBI.

RBI's power to control loans and advances (Sec. 20.5)

RBI is empowered to issue directives to banking companies to determine the policy in relation to loans and advances.

Accounts and balance sheet and audit (Secs 29, 32, 35)

Every banking company incorporated in India, with respect to all transactions by it and through its branches in India, shall prepare a balance sheet and a profit and loss account as on the last working day of the accounting year as given in Forms A and B in the Third Schedule of the Act.

The balance sheet and the profit and loss account as prepared in terms of Sec. 29 of the Act are subject to audit. These auditors are statutory auditors, whose appointment or removal is subject to the approval of RBI.

RBI to undertake inspection (Sec. 35 and variables)

The RBI may conduct inspection in the following matters:

(a) Requirement as to maintaining paid-up capital and reserve (Sec. 11)

(b) Licensing of banks (Sec. 22)

(c) Restriction on opening new and transfer of existing places of business (Sec. 23)

(d) Suspension of business (Sec. 37)

(e) Winding up by high court (Sec. 38)

(f) Power of high court in voluntary winding up (Sec. 44)

(g) Procedure for amalgamation of banking companies (Sec. 44A)

(h) Power of RBI to apply to the central government for suspension of business by a bank and prepare a scheme for reconstitution or amalgamation (Sec. 45)

Power of the Central Government (Sec. 36AB)

The Central Government has the power to acquire the banking company in certain cases, which are as follows:

(a) Failure of the bank to comply with the direction given to it by RBI relating to policy matters under Secs 21 and 35A of the Act; the bank being managed in a manner that is detrimental to the interest of the depositors, etc.

(b) The Central Bank has the power to make schemes in consultation with RBI in such matters as transfer of assets and liabilities of the acquired bank, board management matters, service condition of the employees, compensation payable to the shareholders, etc.

Tribunal (Sec. 36H)

The tribunal shall consist of a chairman who has been a judge of high court and two other members, one of who has commercial banking experience and the other who is a chartered accountant. The tribunal shall have the powers of the civil court (36A1).

It must be kept in mind that banking has a long history and culture of its own in India. It is natural that everything cannot be comprehensively legislated. *Hundies* and other practices have a deeper foundation in the ancient system of Indian banking and tradition than in modern legislation. With the financial reforms of the 1990s, the Indian banking culture has made adjustments and, wherever necessary, has adopted a total paradigm shift, for instance, in internal banking, foreign exchange, institutional investments in securities, etc. International banking practices, such as those concluded in Basel I and Basel II Accords, dilution of the government stake in banks, increase in innovative perpetual debt, etc., are integrated into the banking system.

Goods and passenger transporter vehicles form a very large chunk of the Indian economy (Case 18.1). Bank hypothecation for loans to finance motor vehicles is common.

The courts strictly adhere to the principles laid down mainly in the Bank Regulation Act, 1949. Prior to this Act, the courts depended on the Usurious Loans Act, 1918. It is commonplace even today that the courts refer to this Act in their judgements.

CASE 18.1	APPELLANT: Punjab National Bank vs RESPONDENT: Kishanlal Soni
	JUDGEMENT DATE: 08 November 1995*
FACTS:	The appellant claimed that it was entitled to recover the loan taken on 11 January 1973 by respondent No. 1 amounting to ₹33,600 for purchasing a Matador mini-bus. The rate of agreed interest was alleged to be at the rate of 5 per cent above the rate fixed by RBI or a minimum of 11 per cent per annum. Accordingly, respondent No. 1 executed a promote. Respondent No. 1 was required to repay the loan in 48 monthly instalments at

*Punjab National Bank vs Kishanlal Soni and Others, AIR 1997 MP 27; see also: http://www.indiankanoon.org/doc/539604/ (14 October 2011).

Contd

Case 18.1 *Contd*

the rate of ₹800 per month. Respondent No. 2 was made the guarantor of the repayment of loan by executing a deed of guarantee. The mini-bus was hypothecated with the bank. The appellant further alleged that respondent No. 1 did not pay the loan as stipulated and was a defaulter. The rate of interest declared by RBI was 7 per cent up to 23 July 1974 and it was increased to 9 per cent from that date. It was also claimed that the amount may be paid to the appellant after auctioning the hypothecated vehicle. There was further prayer for a grant of interest at the rate of 14 per cent per annum pendentelite and by way of future interest from the date of decree.

Respondent No. 1 filed his written statement. He admitted to having taken the loan but denied that the rate of interest was the same as alleged by the appellant. He denied that he was liable to pay compound interest. He pleaded the suit was barred by the time and the rate of interest wastoo high. Respondent No. 2 denied his liability to pay on the ground that he was the guarantor.

JUDGEMENT: The appeal was upheld.

REASON: The pleadings of the appellant indicate that the principal amount claimed by it was ?33,600. It claimed interest on it as per the contractual rate, that is, 5 per cent more than the rate fixed by RBI from time to time. The appellant was entitled to 5 per cent plus 7 per cent, that is, 12 per cent up to 23 July 1974 and 9 per cent plus 5 per cent, that is, 14 per cent from 23 July 1974 by way of interest. Similarly, it pleaded that the appellant was entitled to a refund of the amount deposited by it by way of insurance on various dates.

Obviously, the appellant shall be entitled to interest on these amounts from the date they have been paid. Since we have held that Sec. 21A of the Banking Regulation Act, 1949, applied at the time of passing decree appeal the court cannot apply 'the act' for any purpose. In view of the above conclusion, the appellant was entitled to charge the agreed rate of interest on the principal amount advanced. It was also entitled to recover the premium charges it was required to deposit with interest at the agreed rate from the date of deposit. The agreement dated 11 January 1973 is in the form of promissory note. It clearly provides for quarterly rates. The letter of hypothecation also shows that agreement was for quarterly rests. In view of such a situation, the appellant was clearly entitled to charge on the principal sum interest at contractual rate with quarterly rests.

A decree for recovery of ₹53,063.47 shall follow; however, so far as interest pendente lite and future interest are concerned, it will be recovered on ₹36,527.75 at 5 per cent more than RBI from time to time subject to a minimum of 11 per cent, subject to further condition that the appellant shall produce the relevant notification at the time of execution if it claims more than 11 per cent on this amount during the pendency of the suit and thereafter till realization.

18.3 RESERVE BANK OF INDIA ACT, 1934

Establishment and Incorporation of Reserve Bank

TEXT

A bank to be called the Reserve Bank of India shall be constituted for the purposes of taking over the management of the currency from the (central government) and of carrying on the business of banking in accordance with the provisions of this act.

The bank shall be a body corporate by the name of the Reserve Bank of India, having perpetual succession and a common seal, and shall by the said name sue and be sued.

– Reserve Bank of India Act, 1934[1]

RBI was nationalized in 1949. The organization of the bank is entrusted to a Central Board of Directors consisting of 20 members: the governor and four deputy governors, one government official from the Ministry of Finance, ten nominated directors by the government to give representation to important elements in the economic life of the country, and four nominated directors by the central government to represent the four local boards with headquarters at Mumbai, Kolkata, Chennai, and New Delhi. Local boards consist of five members each appointed by the central government for a term of four years to represent territorial and economic interests and the interests of cooperative and indigenous banks.

After World War I, and later, the depression year, British India suffered acute economic and financial problems. The following are the some basic provisions of RBI, which is the monetary authority (Figure 18.1 and Case 18.2).

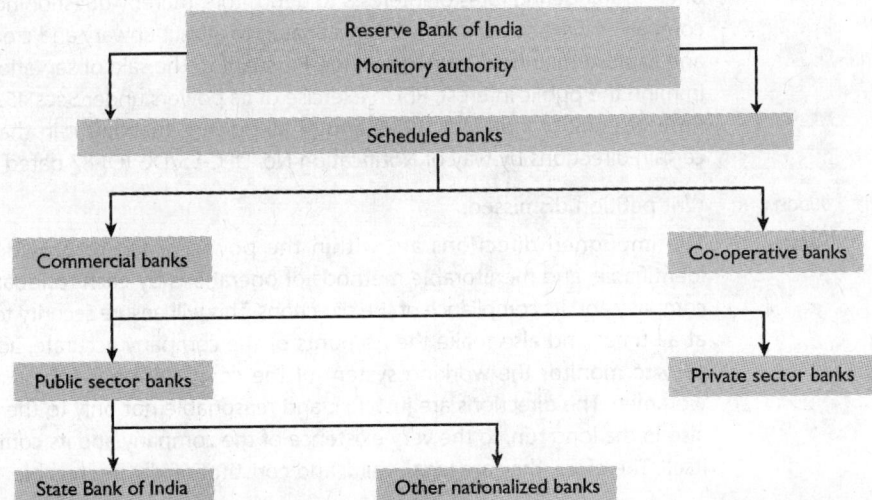

Figure 18.1   The seal of the Reserve Bank and its structure as the monetary authority in India

Body corporate (Secs 3–19)

The body corporate was established in April 1935 with a share capital of ₹5 crore. The share capital was divided into shares of ₹100 each fully paid, which was entirely owned by private shareholders in the beginning. The government held shares of a nominal value of ₹2,20,000. The Reserve Bank of India Act, 1934, was commenced on 1 April 1935. The Act of 1934 (II of 1934) provides the statutory basis for the functioning of the bank.

---

[1]The original section heading and numbers have been retained unchanged as part of the text to preserve the full import of the establishment of the Reserve Bank of India.

CASE 18.2   PETITIONER: Peerless General Finance and Investment Co. Ltd   VS   RESPONDENT: RBI

JUDGEMENT DATE: **30 January 1992***

FACTS: Prayer by the petitioner: whether the Reserve Bank of India Act, 1934: Secs 45K (3), 45J, 45I and 45L:

- Residuary non-banking companies, receiving deposits under the saving schemes.
- Directions issued by the Reserve Bank: such companies to deposit with public sector banks or invest in unencumbered securities the aggregate amounts of liabilities to depositors.
- To disclose the same as liabilities to secure return of the money to depositors.
- Such directions whether statutory in nature—whether ultra vires of Sec. 45K (3)—Whether violative of Articles 14 and 19(1)(g) of the Constitution of India.

Respondent's position: The savings schemes are run by residuary non-banking companies to prevent the exploitation of ignorant investors while simultaneously taking care to protect the thousands of employees working in such companies. There is grave concern at the mushroom growth of the financial investment companies offering staggering rates of interests to depositors, thereby questioning whether these companies were speculative ventures floated to attract unwary and credulous investors and capture their hard-earned savings. Pursuant to the said observations and keeping in mind the public interest, RBI in exercise of its powers under Secs 45J and 45K of the Reserve Bank of India Act, 1934, and of all powers enabling it in that behalf, issued certain directions by way of Notification No. DFC-55/DG (O)-87 dated 15 May 1987.

JUDGEMENT: Writ petition dismissed.

REASON: The impugned directions are within the power of RBI to provide tardy, stable, identifiable, and monitorable methods of operations by each residuary non-banking company and its compliance of the directions. This will ensure security to the depositors at all times and also make the accounts of the company accurate, accountable, and easy to monitor the working system of the company itself and continuance of its workmen. The directions are just, fair, and reasonable not only to the depositors, but also in the long run, to the very existence of the company and its continued business itself. Therefore, they are legal, valid, and constitutionally permissible.

*Peerless General Finance vs Reserve Bank of India; 1992 AIR 1033, 1992 SCR (1) 406; see also: htt://www. indiankanoon.org/doc/1316639/ (12 October 2011).

MANAGER'S TAKEAWAY

- In layman's terms, bankruptcy of a bank is a self-contradiction.
- The dilemma of a bank manager is that if he takes risk-giving loan, he may cause loss to the bank; if he does not take risk-giving loans, his bank has no business.

The bank was constituted with the following objectives:
(a) To regulate the issue of bank notes
(b) To maintain reserves with a view to securing monetary stability
(c) To operate the credit and currency system of the country to its advantage

Furthermore, Chapter II, Secs 3–19, deals extensively with organization and management: qualification and appointment of directors, composition of central and local boards, their constitution and functions, disqualifications and vacation of office, meetings, and business that the bank may transact and may not transact.

Bank of issue (Sec. 21)

Among all the functions of the RBI as the monetary authority of India, the very first function is that it is the bank of issue. It has the sole right to issue bank notes of all denominations. The distribution of ₹1 notes and coins and small coins all over the country is undertaken by the Reserve Bank as the agent of the Government. It has a separate Issue Department, which is entrusted with the issue of currency notes. The assets and liabilities of the Issue Department are kept separate from those of the Banking Department. Originally, the assets of the Issue Department were to consist of not less than two-fifths of gold coin, gold bullion or sterling securities, provided the amount of gold was not less than ₹40 crore in value. The remaining three-fifths of the assets might be held in rupee coins, Government of India rupee securities, eligible bills of exchange, and promissory notes payable in India. Since 1957, RBI is required to maintain gold and foreign exchange reserves of ₹200 crore, of which at least ₹115 crore should be in gold. The system as it exists today is known as the minimum reserve system.

Banker to the government (Secs 20–45)

Chapter III of the Act consists of the central banking functions. Accordingly, the essential function of RBI is to act as the government banker, agent, and adviser. The Reserve Bank is the agent of the Central Government and of all state governments in India (except that of Jammu and Kashmir). The Reserve Bank has the obligation to transact government business: to keep the cash balances as deposits free of interest, to receive and to make payments on behalf of the government, and to carry out exchange remittances and other banking operations. RBI helps both the union and the state governments float new loans and manage public debt. The bank makes loans and advances to the governments for 90 days, makes loans and advances to the state and local authorities, and acts as the advisor to the government on all monetary and banking matters.

Bankers' bank and lender of the last resort

According to the provisions of the Banking Companies Act of 1949, every scheduled bank is required to maintain with the Reserve Bank a cash balance equivalent to 5 per cent of its demand liabilities and 2 per cent of its time liabilities in India. By an amendment of 1962, the distinction between demand and time liabilities was abolished and banks have been asked to retain cash reserves equal to 3 per cent of their aggregate deposit liabilities. The minimum cash requirements can be changed by RBI. The scheduled banks can borrow from RBI based on eligible securities or obtain financial accommodation in times of need or stringency by rediscounting bills of exchange. Since commercial banks can always expect RBI to come to their aid in times of banking crisis, the Reserve Bank becomes not only the banker's bank but also the lender of the last resort.

Controller of credit

According to the Banking Regulation Act of 1949, RBI can ask any particular bank or the entire banking system not to lend to particular groups or persons based on certain types of securities. Since 1956, selective controls of credit are increasingly being used by the Reserve Bank.

(a) Every bank has to obtain a licence from the RBI to do banking business within India. The licence can be cancelled by the Reserve Bank if certain stipulated conditions are not fulfilled.

(b) Every bank will have to obtain the permission of the Reserve Bank before it can open a new branch.

(c) Each scheduled bank must send a weekly return to the Reserve Bank showing, in detail, its assets and liabilities. This power of the bank to call for information is also intended to give it effective control of the credit system.

Custodian of foreign reserves

According to the Reserve Bank of India Act of 1934, RBI was required to buy and sell at fixed rates any amount of sterling in lots of not less than ₹10,000. After India became a member of the International Monetary Fund in 1946, the Reserve Bank has had the responsibility of maintaining fixed exchange rates with all other member countries of the International Monetary Fund. Besides maintaining the rate of exchange of the rupee, RBI has to act as the custodian of India's reserve of international currencies. The vast sterling balances were acquired and managed by the bank. It has the responsibility of administering the exchange controls of the country.

Other functions

The Reserve Bank of India Act, 1934, deals with various other vast and comprehensive functions:

(a) Collection and furnishing credit information (Secs 45A–45G)

(b) Provisions relating to non-banking institutions receiving deposits and financial institutions (Secs 45H–45QB)

(c) Prohibition of acceptance of deposits by un-incorporated bodies (Sec. 45R–45T)

(d) Regulation of transactions in derivates, money market instruments, securities, etc. (Sec. 45U–45X)

(e) General provisions (Sec. 46–58A), such as contribution by the Central Government to the Reserve Bank Fund, national industrial credit, housing credit, certain exemptions from taxes, rural credit, liquidation of banks, power of the board to make regulations, etc.

Penalties (Secs 58B–58G)

The Act deals in detail with a comprehensive set of penalties from offences by companies. It lays down powers of RBI to impose fines. Thus, for instance, according to Sec. 58B (1):

Whoever in any application, declaration, return, statement, information or particulars made, required or furnished by or under or for the purposes of any provisions of this Act, or any order, regulation or direction made or given thereunder or in any prospectus or advertisement issued for or in connection with the invitation by any person, of deposits of money from the public willfully makes a statement which is false in any material particular knowing it to be false or willfully omits to make a material statement shall be punishable with imprisonment for a term which may extend to three years and shall also be liable to fine.

18.4 CONCLUSION

In an economically emerging India, RBI performs various developmental and promotional functions, which at one time were regarded as outside the normal scope of central banking. Accordingly, the RBI has helped in the setting up of the the Industrial Finance Corporation of India and the State Financial Corporation of India; it set up the Deposit Insurance Corporation in 1962, the Unit Trust of India in 1964, the Industrial Development Bank of India in 1964, the Agricultural Refinance Corporation of India in 1963, and the Industrial Reconstruction Corporation of India in 1972. It has developed the cooperative credit movement to encourage savings, to eliminate moneylenders from villages, and to route its short-term credit to agriculture. RBI has set up the Agricultural Refinance and Development Corporation to provide long-term finance to farmers.

MANAGER'S TAKEAWAY

- People trust in RBI.
- A manager is a custodian of the interests of the people.

SUMMARY

- Banking is essentially the business of accepting, for the purpose of lending or investment, of deposits of money from the public, repayable on demand or otherwise. The public would be able to withdraw by means of cheque or similar instrument.
- RBI is the supreme monetary authority under whose regulation all banking and non-banking financial institutions function. It is the bank of issue through which all forms of money are issued and regulated according to the policies set by the Central Government. Hence, RBI is known as not only the nation's banker but also the bankers' banker.

EXERCISES

(i) A farmer took a loan from the bank, which he could not repay due to the losses he suffered and thus even defaulted on interest. The bank sued the farmer. The farmer said that since he suffered loss, no liability can be applied to him. What remedy does the lending bank has?
Hint: In Indian Bank vs Balasubramania 1984 56 Comp Cas 41 Mad, it was held that the bank is justified in enforcing the law for the recovery of the loan.

(ii) According to a bank circular, the bank's staff was divided into several categories based on seniority scheme. The staff contended saying that the bank does not have such powers. What do you think?

Hint: See, Sec. 58, the Reserve Bank of India Act, 1934 gives the RBI and through it to other banks under it to do so.

(iii) Is a licence required for a co-operative bank or a primary credit society for transacting banking business?
Hint: See Sec. 22 (1) (b) of the Banking Regulation Act, 1949

(iv) What are the salient features of the Banking Regulation Act, 1949? Discuss with a case.

(v) How does RBI affect you if you are a mutual funds manager?

DEVELOPMENT OF LEGAL EDGE

Conduct a research project on credit cards to measure the legal and economic consequences both on the banks and agencies who issue credit cards and on the consumers. Some parameters for the survey:
- Determination of area or city
- Categorization of credit card drawing limits

- Categories of consumers
- Consumer behaviour traits
- Volume of complaints in consumer fora
- Findings.

FURTHER READING

- Banking Regulation Act, 1949.
- Reserve Bank of India Act, 1934.

Web resource
- http://rbi.org.in.

CASE STUDY — COMMOTION CAUSED BY SEC. 21A

[21A. Rate of interest charged by banking companies not to be subject to scrutiny by courts. Notwithstanding anything contained in the Usurious Loans Act, 1918 (10 of 1918), or any other law relating to indebtedness in force in any state, a transaction between a banking company and its debtor shall not be reopened by any court on the ground that the rate of interest charged by the banking company in respect of such transaction is excessive.]

– Banking Regulation Act, 1949—Amendment inserted by

Act No. 1 of 1984, w.e.f. 15 February 1984

The above text was a later insertion through an amendment to Banking Regulation Act, 1949, a mere square bracket addition, stating that irrespective of what may have contained about xing an interest rate in the earlier act called Usurious Loans Act, 1918—usury implies charging of interest—has caused emotional and financial distress to the debtors since they are prevented from asking the court to redress their grievance concerning the rate of interest for the loans that they have borrowed.

Usury Laws

Usury is the practice of charging exorbitant, excessive, and illegal rates of interest. The moneylenders of India have been the most notorious since through usury on defaulting

they could grab the land of farmers and make them bonded labourers for generations ahead. In Germany, one of the heinous charges levelled against the Jews by the Nazis was usury, which led to the holocaust, the genocide of six million Jews.

Being *usurious* is the practice of usury, an act of charging illegal interest. Laws have been created to prohibit excessive interests on loans and to limit the maximum rate of interest. In India the Usurious Loans Act, 1918, was enacted with the objective to safeguard the debtors. The act also wanted to prevent the civil courts from being used for the purpose of enforcing harsh and unconscionable loans with interest at usurious rates. RBI has periodically reviewed this issue.[2] The Banking Regulation Act, 1949, further strengthened it with an additional insertion, that

---

[2]See report of the Technical Group set up to review legislations on Money Lending Acknowledgement, http://rbi.org.in/scripts/PublicationReportDetails. aspx?UrlPage=&ID=513 (8 October 2011).

is Sec. 21A, where it is again stressed that courts should not be used to settle usury matters.

Today, one of the easiest loan instruments is the credit card. Even a cursory knowledge from the daily newspapers and television news channels will show excessive fees charged by credit cards. Consumer protection fora across the globe deal with millions of complaints against credit cards. No wonder then credit cards are also termed as *extortion cards*.

Usury is condemned in all religions as a social sin and spiritual decadence; in social and business environment it is castigated as a serious ethical flaw. Even in the literature such as *The Divine Comedy* by Alighieri Dante and *The Merchant of Venice* by William Shakespeare, it is portrayed as evil personified.

In the Andhra High Court

State Bank of Hyderabad and Others vs Advath Sakru and Others[3]
Bench: Justice L Rao, Justice P Sharma and Justice P V Reddi
Date: 26 March 1994

Note

There are several petitions involved in this case. Our concern is not how each petition fared but to study the legal principles enunciated by the high court. The lower court, having received the petitions, recommended the case to the high court to establish legal validity and its application. Numerous cases were filed. If the case law could establish with rigorous interpretation of the Sec. 21A of the Banking Regulation Act, 1949, it would serve the public interest. The clear annunciation would help people not to get into unnecessary litigation.

The judgement of the Andhra High Court is abridged for the purpose with the sources cited already in the footnote.

The Question before the Court

The main point that was debated before the Division Bench was regarding applicability of Sec. 21A of the Banking Regulation Act, 1949, to the transactions entered into between a banking company and its debtors (see Table 18.1).

Table 18.1   Debate of applicability of Sec. 21A of Bending Regulation Act

Banking company's contention	Debtors' contention
After coming into force of Sec. 21A of the Banking Regulation Act, 1949, courts are prohibited/debarred from reopening the transactions entered into between the banking company and its debtor invoking the provisions of Usurious Loans Act, 1918, irrespective of the fact whether the transaction was entered into prior to Sec. 21A of the Act coming into force.	Sec. 21A is only prospective and not retrospective in the sense that it will not be applicable to the transactions entered into prior to the coming into force of the Act, irrespective of the fact whether the suit was filed prior to or after coming into force of Sec. 21A of the Act.
It is also contended that Sec. 21A will be applicable to a suit filed prior to the coming into force of the said provision and pending on the said date, as well as to a suit filed subsequent to the coming into force of Sec. 21A of the Act. In other words, it was contended that irrespective of the fact that the transaction took place earlier to the coming into force of Sec. 21A of the Act and whether the suit in respect of the said transaction is filed prior to the said date or not, the said provision will debar or prohibit the court from reopening the transaction and scaling down the interest by applying the provisions of Act 10 of 1918.	In any event, it is contended that Sec. 21A has no application to the suits filed prior to the coming into force of the said provision irrespective of the fact that the suits are pending on that day. It is also contended that the moment the suit is filed, the right to have the transactions reopened under the provisions of Act 10 of 1918 accrued or acquired by the debtors and the said right is a vested right and the same cannot be defeated by Sec. 21A of the Act.

---

[3]State Bank of Hyderabad and Others vs Advath Sakru and Others, AIR 1994 AP 170, 1993 (1) ALT 608; also see http://www.indiankanoon.org/doc/1142004/ (8 October 2011).

Issues before the High Court

As the issue is important to public interest the Division Bench held that it should be decided by the high court. The following questions were put before the above-mentioned Andhra High Court, with the bench comprising three judges:

1. Whether Sec. 21A of the Banking Regulation Act, 1949, applies to transactions that were entered into prior to its commencement, even though suits were instituted subsequent thereto?
2. Whether it applies only to transactions entered into after the commencement of Central Act 1 of 1984?
3. Whether it applies only to suits that were pending on the date of commencement of Central Act 1 of 1984?
4. Whether it applies to suits instituted and in which decrees were passed before the commencement of the Act?
5. Whether it applies only to suits instituted after the commencement of the Act irrespective of the date of the transaction?
6. Whether it makes any difference if the loan was an agricultural and not a commercial loan?

Guiding Principle

Constitutional validity of Sec. 21A is, therefore, not an issue. Indeed, in our opinion, the competency of the Parliament to enact the said provision could never have been doubted.

Legal Reasoning

With regard to the views expressed by different high courts and also in view of the fact that the banking companies are bound by the directions issued by RBI in respect of charging interest, violation of which will entail penal consequences, the Parliament stepped in to set at rest the controversy and enacted Sec. 21A to enable the banking companies to charge interest as per the directions issued under the provisions of the Regulation Act, 1949. Therefore, the intention of the Parliament is clear that the laws relating to indebtedness prevailing in the respective states and the provisions of the Usurious Loans Act, 1918, should not be made applicable to the banking companies, which are bound to charge the rates of interest as directed by RBI under the provisions of the Banking Regulation Act, 1949. If this is to be construed otherwise, there will be conflict with reference to the actions taken pursuant to the respective laws themselves. If the banking companies are bound to charge the interest as per the directions of RBI under the provisions of the Regulation Act, 1949, it cannot be said at the same time that the transactions can be reopened by the courts and the rates of interest are scaled down as per the different laws relating to indebtedness of the respective states and the Usurious Loans Act on the ground that the rate of interest charged is impermissible. Parliament wanted to rectify this issue and, therefore, according to the learned counsel for the banks, the intention of enacting Sec. 21A is made clear by necessary implication that the Parliament wanted to divest the court of the power to give relief under the respective debt laws of the states as well as under the provisions of the Usurious Loans Act, 1918.

Therefore, it follows that in the case of a banking company, *a fortiori*, its claim to interest at the agreed rate for the period prior to the suit cannot be ignored and the court is bound to grant interest at that rate. The court has no discretion in the matter.

Conclusion

1. Sec. 21A of the Banking Regulation Act, 1949, applies to all transactions entered into between the banking company and its debtor, irrespective of whether the transaction was entered into prior to its commencement or after.
2. Sec. 21A of the Banking Regulation Act, 1949, applies to suits pending on the date of coming into force of the said section.
3. Sec. 21A applies to pending appeals, irrespective of the fact whether a decree was passed giving relief to the debtor or not.
4. Sec. 21A makes no distinction between an advance made for agricultural purpose or for commercial purpose and it equally applies to both.

Epilogue

The epilogue to the case consists of the disposal of various petitions led before the court to which it gave its orders based on the merit of each case. The importance of this case lies in the fact that the High Court Bench handed down a very clear and unambiguous interpretation of Sec. 21A of the Banking Regulation Act, 1949. Henceforth, every case of usurious loans and matters related to their interest can be decided referring to this judgement. This judgement may be considered as a fine work in case law of India.

Discussion Questions

1. What is the basic question posed to the court?
2. Why in your opinion did the particular section of the Act need interpretation?
3. What is the legal basis for the section in question?
4. What problems does the banking company face while lending?

5. What problems do debtors face when banks change rules half-way?
6. How serious do you think is the problem about interest rates in the country?
7. How can RBI regulate and thus prevent litigation for the bank customers?

Going Beyond

1. Elucidate the modes of modern-day usury.
2. Write an essay on *Loan Sharks* from a legal perspective.
3. From the management point of view, is Sec. 21A practical? Illustrate with current examples.

LEGAL LUMINARY

DR MANMOHAN SINGH—THE REFORMIST RESERVE BANK GOVERNOR

'My top most priority is to deal with India's massive social and economic problems, so that chronic poverty, ignorance and disease can be conquered in a reasonably short period of time.'*

This quote by Dr Manmohan Singh describes both the vision and the task of his public life. In the early 1970, he was a lecturer at Delhi University and also worked for United Nations Conference on Foreign Trade and Development (UNCTAD). It so 'happened' that Lalit Narayan Mishra was the then Minister for Trade who 'happened' to travel to Chile for a UNCTAD meeting, where a young Professor Manmohan Singh, too, 'happened' to represent UNCTAD as the economist from India. The minister discovered Manmohan—the rest is history.

Lalit Narayan Mishra, upon his return from the Chile UNCTAD meeting, appointed Dr Singh as the Advisor of Ministry of Foreign Trade (1971–1972). That was followed by a similar post of Advisor of Ministry of Finance (1972–1976). In 1976, he was made the Honorary Professor of Jawaharlal Nehru University, New Delhi. From 1976 to 1980, he was posted to RBI as one of the directors where he served as the Director for Industrial Development Bank of India. From 1977 to 1980, he was Secretary, Ministry of Finance (Department of Economic Affairs, Government of India). In 1982, he was appointed as the Governor of RBI, a post he held till 1985.

It was followed by Deputy Chairman, Planning Commission of India, for the next two years, followed by a unique placement called Secretary General, South Commission, Geneva, from 1987 to 1990. In the following year, he was appointed as the Advisor to Prime Minister of India on Economic Affairs; that again was followed by a short stint as the Chairman of the University Grants Commission. History was made again when Prime Minister Narasihma Rao rediscovered the impeccable and indefatigable bureaucrat and appointed him as the Finance Minister of India from June 1991 to May 1996. In the Thirteenth Lok Sabha he was the Leader of the Opposition in the Rajya Sabha (1998–2004). History was made a third time when Mrs Sonia Gandhi, the President of the Congress party, proposed his name for prime ministership, which was seconded and endorsed by the entire party. He was the Prime Minister of India from 2004 till 2014.

For a manager or for an aspiring manager, there is no other stellar role model than Dr Manmohan Singh. It must be the most unique and mystifying experience to have one's signature on a currency note. The governors of the Reserve Bank are in themselves unique personalities. It is the pinnacle of the best of carriers in the world—to be the custodian of the wealth of a nation. Managers with sterling qualities and unique abilities of both body and mind happen to accomplish it.

---

*See http://en.wikipedia.org/w/index.php?title=Manmohan_Singh&action=edit (12 October 2011).

Contd

Legal Luminary *Contd*

During his tenure as the Governor of the Reserve Bank, Dr Singh introduced comprehensive legal reforms in the banking sector. A new chapter was also introduced in the Reserve Bank of India Act, 1934, through which the Urban Banks Department was set up.* This was merely the beginning. When he became the Finance Minister, he unleashed such monumental reforms that it may well be called the Economic Liberation of India. After her political liberation, India vacillated on her economic ideology; she faltered and floundered. In a highly changing world, Dr Singh adopted a course of reform and liberalization of the economy and changed the very basis of economics of the country. In a short time, India's economic rise was only rivalled by that of China. Dr Manmohan Singh was rightly honoured as the architect of the new economy.

In 1947, upon at the Partition of India, Dr Singh's family migrated from Pakistan to Amritsar in Punjab and young Manmohan made it to school by the sheer dint of his will to succeed in a poor, cruel world full of adversity. Despite the setback of losing his mother early in life, he always excelled in his studies and obtained his Master's degree in Economics from Punjab University in Chandigarh. He earned a scholarship from Cambridge and completed his doctorate in Economics at St John's. Presently, there is a scholarship established at St John's in his name. The laurels and honours both in academic and in public life are far too numerous to list here. He has an academically distinguished wife, Mrs Gursharan Kaur. They have three daughters, who have won equal academic distinctions in their own right.[†]

Manmohan Singh has been recognized by the world leaders as a 'Man of Wisdom' and a person of impeccable personal honesty and integrity.

---

*See http://www.rbi.org.in/scripts/history.aspx (12 October 2011).
[†]See http://www.knowledgebase-script.com/demo/index.php (12 October 2011).

Laws of Insurance

Principle: *Ejus est periculem cujus est dominium aut commodum.*

Risk is with whom the property belongs, or who reaps the advantage.

CHAPTER OUTLINE

- Introduction and Interpretation
- Insurance Act, 1938: As Amended by Insurance (Amendment) Act, 2002
- Conclusion
- Insurance Regulatory and Development Authority Act, 1999
- Actuaries Act, 2006
- Actuary
- Institute of Actuaries in India
- Actuary Mandated By IRDA
- *Case Study:* Mediclaim—A Case of Common Claim
- *Legal Luminary:* Renu Sud Karnad

19.1 INTRODUCTION AND INTERPRETATION

'Indian insurance company' means any insurer being a company:

that is formed and registered under the Companies Act, 1956 (1 of 1956);

in which the aggregate holdings of equity shares by a foreign company, either by itself or through its subsidiary companies or its nominees, do not exceed twenty-six perc ent paid up equity capital of such Indian insurance company; and

whose sole purpose is to carry on life insurance business or general insurance business or re-insurance business

– Insurance Act 1938, Amendment Act Sec. 7A, (a,b,c)

Insurance-related Acts

In this chapter, your attention will be drawn to the laws of insurance. The first Act legislated for insurance in India was the Provident Insurance Societies Act, 1912 related to life insurance business, and later in 1928 the same law was extended to cover rest of the insurance businesses. More was expected of the law to be delivered as the insurance business increased appreciably. The process of introducing a new bill started in 1935; as a result, a comprehensive law was enacted called the Insurance Act, 1938. Immediately after the independence of India the Employees State Insurance Act, 1948 came into effect, which was amended as the Employees State Insurance Amendment Act, 1989, about 245 foreign insurers and provident societies were nationalized by the Life Insurance Act, 1956 and thus the Life Insurance Corporation (LIC) was instituted. The General Insurance Business Nationalization Act, 1972 came into effect; with that the General Insurance Corporation (GIC) was established. The Nationalization Act was amended as the General Insurance Business Nationalization (Amendment) Act, 1985. The economic reforms and market liberalization of the early 1990s made it necessary for the government to do the same to the insurance businesses. Thus, the Insurance Act, 1938, as amended by the Insurance (Amendment) Act, 2002, ushered in not only private businesses to take part but also enabled cooperative societies to do so. In the meantime, as the economic reforms progressed it became necessary for the government to appoint a statutory regulatory body, just as it did for the capital market by creating Securities and Exchange Board of India. The Insurance Regulatory and Development Authority Act, 1999 came into existence with the focused objectives to regulate and develop the insurance businesses in an economically forward surging India. The Insurance Regulatory and Development Authority is well known in the country through its acronym IRDA.

Insurance business began in India with the establishment of a company called Oriental Life Insurance Company in Calcutta in 1818. The company failed in 1834. In 1829, a company called Madras Equitable started operating in the British Madras Presidency. Three companies, Bombay Mutual (1871), Oriental (1874), and Empire India (1897) started their operations in Bombay Presidency. The other companies were Albert Life Assurance, Royal Insurance, Liverpool, and London Globe Insurance.[1]

Scope

The scope of this chapter is limited to only two Acts: the Insurance Act, 1938 [as amended by the Insurance (Amendment) Act, 2002] and the Insurance Regulatory and Development Authority Act, 1999. With the help of these two laws, the insurance businesses of India have become greatly improved. The individual insurance products, such as life insurance, property and vehicle insurance, health insurance, marine insurance, etc., would be a logical conclusion whatever provisions the IRDA provides through rules, regulations, and circulars.

Understanding Insurance

The term 'assurance' was originally used to imply protection against financial loss. People run the risk of untimely death, adverse health conditions, damage or loss of property due to fire and other unforeseen causes, professionals such as performing artists or sports persons of injury, harm to businesses, and similar other situations where one seeks a cover for the losses suffered. A scheme to cover beforehand such financial losses assures people against their fears and when misfortune befalls, and their losses would be made good to the extent they had planned and paid for. At a later stage, the term 'insurance' came into vogue in

---

[1]For more details see http://www.irda.gov.in/ADMINCMS/cms/NormalData_Layout. aspx?page=PageNo4&mid=2 (14 October 2011).

the place of assurance. In their connotation, these terms are synonymous and may be used interchangeably. The term 'insurance', however, immediately and directly refers to the underlying principle of indemnity, a guarantee or cover of compensation for the loss suffered (Figure 19.1).

The following are the salient features of insurance that include definition, constituents, and basic principles.

Insurance contract   Insurance is constituted through a contract between two parties, one of which undertakes to make good a loss of the other, in consideration of a sum of money, upon the occurrence of the specified event, such as fire, burglary, sickness, death, etc.

Insurer and insured   These are the parties of the insurance contract.

Policy Policy is document as evidence to the contract of insurance. Insurance was known as annuity due to the practice of annual renewal.

Risk   It is the danger, peril, jeopardy, or loss from which the insured wants to be indemnified for his interests.

Premium   The consideration for which the insurer undertakes to indemnify the insured against the risk.

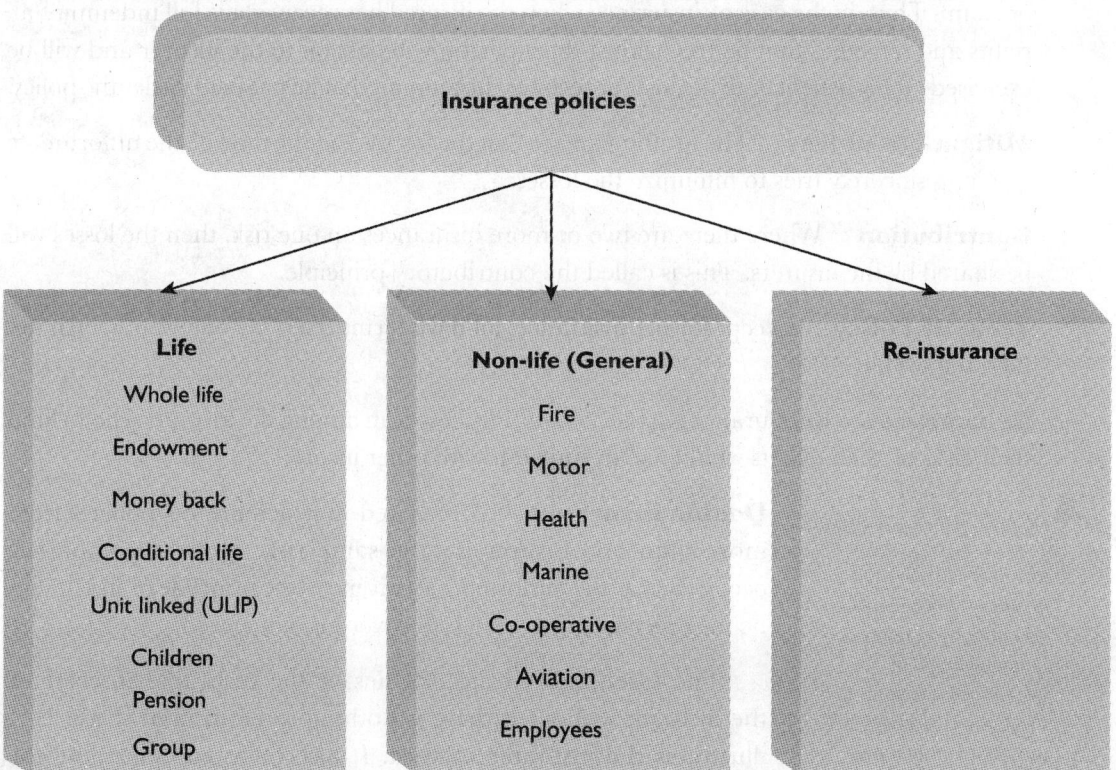

Figure 19.1   Classification of insurance policies

Good faith   This is the basic principle of insurance. The insured must disclose to the insurer all the material truthfully, so that the risk may be calculated and the right premium can be fixed.

Insurable interest   Anything that is insured is the subject matter of insurance; the interest of the insured in the subject matter is the insurable interest. A contract of insurance, therefore, without insurable interest is void. The insurer always has something at stake. The truck owner insures his vehicle and the hirer of the truck insures his goods, as a truck owner would worry about the safety of his truck and the hirer of the truck would worry about the safety of his goods loaded on to it. Thus, different people have different insurable interests.

Causa proxima   It implies the nearest cause of an occurrence. When the damage to the interests of the insured is assessed by an actuary, it will be performed on the principle of the proximate cause, the nearest cause that brought about the misfortune. For instance, a building is gutted in fire and it gets worse due to gushing winds, etc. Fire is the primary cause and the gushing wind is the secondary cause that aggravated it.

Indemnity   The insurance contract consists of a policy, which will make good a loss suffered by the insured, exactly to the amount made in the policy. It is against the law to make profit out of a loss-making incident. This is the nature of insurance frauds.

Subrogation   It implies to put oneself into the place of another in respect to a legal right or claim. Thus, in the case of insurance when the insured has received his full indemnity, all rights and remedies that he has against third person will pass on to the insurer and will be exercised for his benefit until the insurer recoups the amount that he has paid under the policy.

Mitigations of loss   The insurer expects that the insured, at the time of the unfortunate incident, sincerely tries to minimize the losses.

Contribution   Where there are two or more insurances on one risk, then the losses will be shared by the insurers. This is called the contributory principle.

Term of policy   Except for life insurance, all have terms fixed for one year, which are then renewable.

Reinsurance   Reinsurance is a business-to-business plan among the insurers who to limit their risks of their clients would like to spread it with other insurers.

MANAGER'S TAKEAWAY

- Insuring risk is a good business idea because it is limited by indemnity.
- Innovativeness in insurance business is to make the customers feel protected at their own future misfortunes.

Double insurance   An insured may acquire his policies from more than one insurer for the same risk. However, upon the occurrence of the misfortune, according to the principle of indemnity, he may receive only enough to cover his damages.

The essence of insurance lies in the insurable interest of the insured; without it there is nothing to be insured. Case 19.1 illustrates the insurable interest. It also helps to determine the insurable interest.

CASE 19.1   APPELLANT: S. Mehtab Singh, S. Jot Singh and others   vs   RESPONDENT: National Fire and General Insurance

DATE OF JUDGEMENT: 2 April 1962*

FACTS: Mehtab Singh owned a motor vehicle that was registered to carry goods. This vehicle was sold by Mehtab Singh to Puran Singh. But curiously enough, the insurance policy was taken for this vehicle on 28 February 1959 by Mehtab Singh for the period from 16 February 1959 to 15 February 1960. This vehicle met with an accident on 21 June 1959 and on 12 December 1959, the present petition was fied by Mehtab Singh and Puran Singh, among other things, claiming an insurable interest.

The defence set up by the insurance company was that Mehtab Singh had no insurable interest as he had sold out the truck before the policy was taken.

JUDGEMENT: Petition fails: case was dismissed.

REASON: The contention that the petition of Mehtab Singh should have been allowed because he bad an insurable interest in the vehicle fails because the moment the vehicle was transferred by Mehtab Singh to Puran Singh, no interest whatever was left in Mehtab Singh *vis-a-vis* the vehicle.

*S. Mehtab Singh S. Jot Singh and Others vs National Fire and General Insurance; AIR 1963 P H 103, 1963 33 CompCas 830 P H; see also: http://indiankanoon.org/doc/188958 (14 October 2011).

19.2   INSURANCE ACT, 1938—AS AMENDED BY INSURANCE (AMENDMENT) ACT, 2002

TEXT

Same as hereinafter provided, no person shall, after the commencement of the Insurance (Amendment) Act, 1950 (47 of 1950), begin to carry on any class of insurance business in India and no insurer carrying on any class of insurance business in India shall, after the expiry of one year from such commencement, continue to carry on any such business unless he is:
(a) A public company;
(b) A society registered under the Co-operative Societies Act, 1912 or under any other law for the time being in force in any state relating to co-operative societies; or
(c) A body corporate incorporated under the law of any country outside India not being of the nature of a private company.

– The Insurance Act, 138 Amendment, 1999, 2C (1)

The Insurers

As a manager of an insurance concern, you are an insurer. With the Amendment Act,1999, the monopoly of the nationalized insurers, LIC and GIC, came to an end. The insurance sector was open for business to public companies as well as to registered co-operative societies under the Co-operative Societies Act, 1912 and corporations incorporated outside India. Today, these corporations have tie-ups with the indigenous companies to run very successful businesses. Any Indian company can conduct business in special economic zone (Special Economic Zone Act, 2005) area. (Figure 19.2 shows the taxonomy of the Insurance Act, 1938.)

Under provisions of the IRDA Act, 1999, the insurers should get their registration renewed annually before 31 March; the application for the same must reach the authority before

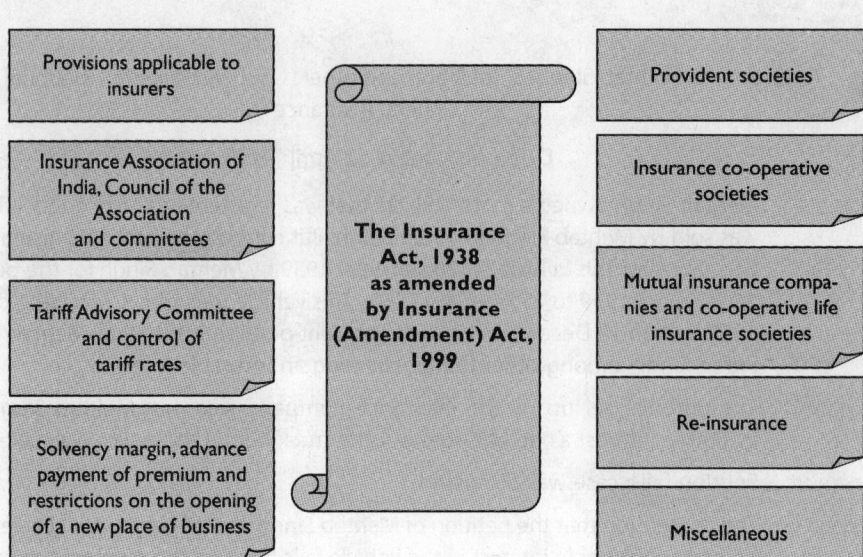

Figure 19.2 Taxonomy of Insurance Act, 1938 as amended by the Insurance (Amendment) Act, 1999

31 December of the proceeding year accompanied by prescribed fee of ₹50,000. The authority shall examine the health of the insurance company. The insurer shall not use the existing name. A capital base of minimum ₹100 crores for life and general insurance and ₹200 crore for reinsurance business is prescribed.

A public company may start an insurance company with the approval of the central government. The accounts of each class of insurance are to be maintained as per prescribed rules, authenticated, audited, actuaries to be entered, and returns filed with all necessary documents and abstracts.

According to Secs 27–28 B and 31, the assets of the insurer must be kept with the Reserve Bank of India or with specified authorities. The authority maintains vigilance on appointment of managers, agents, and the remuneration paid to every person. The authority can order investigation, appoint staff for the purpose, and give directions to the insurer such as dismissing managerial personnel if they are acting against the interests of the policyholders. It may also order closure of foreign insurers for unfair trading and harming the public interest. It has the right to search and seize any documents, books, vouchers, and reports to help investigation. In the public interest, the authority has the right to prepare schemes for amalgamation or transfer of business.

The Central Government has the powers to appoint an administrator and a tribunal. The provisions of Sec. 52H–J gives the powers of a civil court to the tribunal. The tribunal may order the winding up of the companies as per the Companies Act, 1956. The Central Government may impose counter measures against any foreign insurer if its native country imposes similar sanctions against Indian companies.

The Act also makes other provisions with regard to the Insurance Association of India, council of the association and committees, tariff advisory and control of rates, solvency margin and advance payment of premium, provident societies, insurance operative societies, mutual insurance companies, etc. (Case 19.2).

CASE 19.2   APPELLANT: Nipha Exports (P) Ltd   vs   RESPONDENT: Employees' State Insurance

DATE OF JUDGEMENT: 31 March 2003*

FACTS: The petitioner is engaged in the manufacturing of machinery, it is covered under the provisions of the act. Vide notice dated 4 September 2002 (Annexure P-I), the Regional Director of the Corporation called upon it to show cause against the proposed levy of damages on account of its failure to pay contribution on due dates. He directed the petitioner to appear on 8 October 2002. A statement showing delay in the payment of contribution amount and proposed damages was annexed with the show cause notice. The petitioner's prayer was to quash the order dated 18 December 2002 passed by the Regional Director of the Employees' State Insurance Corporation for levy of damages under Sec. 85-B of the Employees' State Insurance Act, 1948.

JUDGEMENT: Petition dismissed.

REASON: In exercise of the power vested in it under Sec. 97, the corporation framed the regulations. Regulation 31 of the regulations specifies the time for payment of the contributions. Regulation 31-A provides for levy of interest. Regulation 31-B provides the mode of recovery. Regulation 31-C prescribes the rate of damages on contributions or any other amount due, but not paid in time. Sec. 85-B of the Act and Secs 31, 31-A, 31-B, and 31-C of the Regulations, which have bearing on the petitioner's prayer for quashing the impugned order, are reproduced below:

> 85-B: Power to recover damages: When an employer fails to pay the due amount in respect of any contribution or any other amount payable under this act, the corporation may recover from the employer by way of penalty such damages not exceeding the amount of arrears, as may be specified in the regulations.
>
> We are further of the view that the quantum of damages (5–25 per cent for different defaults) imposed by the regional director is not unreasonable or excessive warranting interference by this court. A look at the statement sent by the regional director along with notice Annexure P-1 shows that the petitioner had delayed the payment of contributions, etc., on forty two different occasions between April 2000 and March 2002. On most of the occasions, the delay was for more than two months. Therefore, the regional director was justified in imposing damages at the rates specified in Sec. 31-C of the Regulations.

---

*Nipha Exports (P) Ltd vs Employees State Insurance, (2003) IIILLJ 789 P H; see also, indiankanoon.org/doc/716978/ (12 October 2011).

19.3 CONCLUSION

Thus, the Insurance Act, 1938 (Amendment, 2002) is a comprehensive Act and incorporates all the aspects of globalized insurance businesses. However, the increased business and the growth in insurance companies created a need for a regulator. In the following section, you will be acquainted with a similar regulator as you did when you studied Securities and

Exchange Board of India. The Act is called the Insurance Regulatory and Development Authority Act, 1999.

19.4 INSURANCE REGULATORY AND DEVELOPMENT AUTHORITY ACT, 1999

TEXT

3. (1)…Authority to be called 'the Insurance Regulatory and Development Authority'. (2) The authority shall be a body corporate by the name aforesaid having perpetual succession and a common seal with power, subject to the provisions of this act, to acquire, hold, and dispose of property, both movable and immovable, and to contract and shall, by the said name, sue or be sued

Insurance Regulatory and Development Authority Act, 1999, Sec. 3 (1, 2)

Establishment and Incorporation of Authority

The above text establishes IRDA in law (Secs 3–12). The authority comprises of a chairman, five whole-time members, and four part-time members.

IRDA has its headquarters in Hyderabad, Andhra Pradesh. The core functions of IRDA are:
(a) Licensing of insurers and insurance intermediaries
(b) Financial and regulatory supervision
(c) Control and regulation of premium rates
(d) Protection of the interests of the policyholders

Apart from IRDA, there are three more regulators:
(a) Tariff Advisory Committee: It regulates and controls the rates, benefits terms, and conditions offered by the insurance companies functioning in India.
(b) Ombudsman: The arbiter for the smooth functioning of the insurance companies. Their function is to address and redress all complaints relating to settlements of claims. Any policyholder having grievance against any insurance company may approach the Ombudsman.
(c) Insurance association of India: All the insurance companies operating in India are its members. It has two councils: Life Insurance Council and General Insurance Council.

Duties, Powers, and Functions of IRDA (Sec. 14)

In keeping with its objectives, IRDA has the duty to regulate, control, promote, and ensure healthy development of insurance and re-insurance business (Case 19.3). The main functions of IRDA are:

MANAGER'S TAKEAWAY

- In insurance matters, first impressions are lasting impressions.
- Always look for clear reasons why a judge of the higher court should overturn the judgement of the lower court.

(a) To issue, modify, and cancel the registration certificate of the insurer and the applicant
(b) To safeguard the interests of the policyholders, such as insurable interests, settlement of claims, surrender value of the policy, etc.
(c) To specify the code of conduct for the surveyors
(d) To determine the qualifications and training of agents and intermediaries
(e) To levy fees and charges for the work

CASE19.3   APPELLANT: Akshit Kapoor   vs   RESPONDENT: Union of India and Others

DATE OF JUDGEMENT: 12 December 2003[*]

FACTS: The issue involved is with regard to the categorization of insurance surveyors and loss assessors and particularly those with regard to motor insurance claims.

The circular dated IRDA/SLA/1/2001 dated 11 September 2001 was issued by the chairman of the IRDA. This circular is impugned in the present writ petitions along with the subsequent circular of 24 May 2003, whereby the limits prescribed for the categories has been enhanced. The circular dated 11 September 2001 prescribed the financial limits of categories of surveyors and loss assessors for various departments of the insurance companies including motor (public and private).

We are only concerned with the surveyors and loss assessors in respect of motor (public and private). The limits for the variation categories that have been prescribed for this department are as under:

Category 'A'   above ₹1.5 lakh

Category 'B'   up to ₹1.5 lakh

Category 'C'   up to ₹75,000

The same circular dated 11 September 2001 carries three 'notes' that read as under:

1. Category A surveyor will be eligible for jobs falling under the financial limits of Category B. Similarly, category B surveyor will be eligible for jobs falling under the financial limits or category C.

2. Category C surveyor shall not be eligible for the limits of categories B. Category B surveyor shall not be eligible for the limits of category A surveyors.

3. Financial limits are based on the estimated value of the loss in the opinion of the insurer.

Subsequently, in 2003, by the circular dated 24 May 2003, these limits were with regard to Motor Insurance Claims, the following revision was made: 'Motor'

• Category 'C', the existing limit of ₹75,000 would be enhanced to ₹1 lakh.

• Category 'B', the existing limit of ₹1.5 lakhs would be enhanced to ₹2 lakhs.

• Category 'A', surveyors would be permitted to undertake survey in respect of claim of over ₹1 lakh.

The petitioners in each of the writ petitions fall within the category are that they are not being permitted to act as surveyors/loss assessors in limits falling under category 'B'. As such, they are challenging the categorization of surveyors/loss assessors made by the said circular dated 11 September 2001 and the subsequent revision of 24 May 2003 as being contrary to the regulations and the said statutory provisions as well as the terms of the individual licenses. their grievance is that category 'A' surveyors/ loss assessors are being prevented from operating in the area in which category 'B' surveyors operate.

JUDGEMENT: Petition disposed off in favour of the appellants.

---

*Akshit Kapoor vs Union of India and Others; AIR 2004 Delhi 203, 109 (2004) DLT 224, 2004 (72) DRJ 652: also see http://www.indiankanoon.org/doc/1906055/ (12 October 2011).

Contd

Case 19.3 *Contd*

> Reason: It is apparent that the circular itself permits category 'A' surveyors/loss assessors to be eligible for jobs falling within the financial limits of category 'B' (excluding the area of operation of category 'C' surveyors). This fact is further strengthened by the revised circular of 25 April 2003, which clearly stipulates that category 'C' surveyors are to operate up to a limit of ₹1 lakh. The upper limit of category 'B' is ₹2 lakh, whereas in category 'A', surveyors would be permitted to undertake surveyors in respect of any claim over ₹1 lakh. This means that apart from category 'C', category 'A' surveyors would be able to operate in the areas in which category 'B' surveyors are permitted to operate. However, beyond ₹2 lakh, it is only category 'A' surveyors who shall operate exclusively.
>
> In this view of the matter, the position is crystal clear and as category 'A' surveyors survives. The respondent insurance companies shall permit the petitioners to carry on their work as surveyors within the financial limits of category 'A' and also category 'B' but, only over and above the limit of category 'C' surveyors in terms of the circulars.

(f) To conduct investigations and enquiries relating to the issues concerning insurance business

(g) To regulate and control business not controlled by Tariff Advisory Committee (Sec. 64, Insurance Act, 1938)

(h) To regulate investment funds by the insurance companies

(i) To regulate maintenance of margin of solvency

(j) To adjudicate and settle disputes between intermediaries and insurers

(k) To supervise the functioning of Tariff Advisory Committee

The Ombudsman

The office of the ombudsman[2] was created in 1998 by a Government of India notification. The objective was to address and redress the grievances of the policyholders. The appointment of the ombudsman is organized by the governing body of the Insurance Council, comprising the chairpersons of IRDA, LIC, GIC, and representatives of the central government. An ombudsman is chosen from judicial services, insurance industry, or civil services. The term of office is for three years or until the age of 60 years, whichever is earlier; no reappointment is allowed. Ombudsman's territorial jurisdictions are divided into 12 geographical areas of the country and are situated them in main cities.

Functions of ombudsman   The ombudsman has two-fold functions: conciliation and award-making.

Conciliation

(a) Partial or total repudiation of claims by the insurance companies

(b) Dispute with regard to premium

---

[2]See http://www.irda.gov.in (14 October 2011).

(c) Dispute on the legal language of the policy regarding claims

(d) Delay in settlement of claims

(e) Non-issuance of any insurance document to the policyholder after the receipt of premium

Award-making Award-making is to pass an award within a period of three months from the receipt of the complaint. If the policyholder is not satisfied with the award, he may seek redressal in Consumer Forum or Court.

19.5 ACTUARIES ACT, 2006

The objects of the Institute shall be

to promote, uphold, and develop the standards of professional education, training, knowledge, practice, and conduct amongst actuaries;

to promote the status of the actuarial profession;

to regulate the practice by the members of the profession of actuary;

to promote, in the public interest, knowledge and research in all matters relevant to actuarial science and its application; and

to do all such other things as may be incidental or conducive to the above objects or any of them.

Actuaries Act, 2006, Sec. 5

Just as a chartered accountant is a professional in taxation, or a company secretary in company law, or an auditor in financial accounting, so also an actuary is a professional in insurance who assesses the financial risks and uncertainties. Thus, he is an important element in the business of insurance. His expertise is to mathematically and statistically calculate, evaluate, and assess the likelihoods of adverse events and to quantify probabilities of risk with a purpose of minimizing losses. The insurance business in India grew exponentially with the availability of loans for real estate, housing, motor vehicles, industrial establishments, and businesses. Thus, the need was felt for highly qualified experts to develop professional standards and application of actuarial science.

19.6 INSTITUTE OF ACTUARIES IN INDIA

Through an Act of the parliament, the Actuaries Act, 2006, Institute of Actuaries of India was established to achieve the objectives it set forth as has been shown in the above text, Sec. 5 of the Act. Thus far, the Actuarial Society of India formed in 1944 had conducted actuary. With this Act, it was effectively dissolved and all its assets and liabilities were transferred to the Institute of Actuaries of India.

19.7 ACTUARY MANDATED BY IRDA

Every insurer shall furnish to the authority with his returns under Sec. 15 or Sec. 16, as the case may be, a statement certified by an auditor approved by the authority with respect to general insurance business, or an actuary approved by the authority with respect to life insurance business, as the case may be, of his assets and liabilities assessed in the manner required by this section as on 31 March of the preceding year.

Insurance Regulatory and Development Authority Act, 1999, Sec. 36(2)

Actuary is mandated by IRDA through the following regulations:

(a) IRDA (Appointed Actuary) Regulations, 2000: This regulation clearly mentions the power that the appointed actuary will enjoy. It also mentions the duties and obligations of the appointed actuary.

(b) IRDA (asset, liabilities, and solvency margins of insurer) Regulations, 2000: The actuary shall have access to all information or documents in possession of the insurer. He also has the right to attend the meetings of the management including board meetings and can speak on and discuss matters concerning solvency, actuarial advice.

Acturial Duties

(a) To render actuarial advice to the management of the insurer, in particular in the areas of product design and pricing, insurance contract wording, investments, and reinsurance

(b) To ensure the solvency of the insurer at all times

(c) To use actuarial techniques to manage and regulate the affairs of a general insurance company

(d) To review and frame reinsurance arrangements

(e) To analyze the effects of policies

The Institute of Actuaries India and several other universities and institutions offer courses for professionally trained actuaries. The demand is very high and India falls short in supply of actuaries by about 25 per cent.[3]

> **MANAGER'S TAKEAWAY**
> - In a financial transaction self-regulation is a myth.
> - Finding loopholes in a regulation can lead to profit or litigation.

SUMMARY

- Insurance is a financial instrument against the risk of any financial loss. People insure life, property, and anything that is valuable and that cannot be risked for loss. The acts governing insurance in India are as follows:
  - Provident Insurance Societies Act, 1912
  - Insurance Act, 1938
  - India Employees State Insurance Act, 1948
  - Life Insurance Act, 1956
  - Employees State Insurance Amendment Act, 1989
  - General Insurance Business Nationalization Act, 1972.

- Insurance Act, 1938, as amended by the Insurance (Amendment) Act, 2002, which undid the nationalization of insurers and established the IRDA that presently acts as the statutory body to govern and rule the insurance sector.

- Among other principles, the pivotal principle that works for insurance is that of indemnity. In simple terms, it implies to make good the loss.

- The IRDA, the insurance regulator, has powers to form rules, regulations, and send circulars concerning provisions available to the insurers. It may take help from such institutionalized professionals as ombudsman and actuaries.

---

[3]See http://www.rediff.com/money/2007/mar/21spec.htm; for institutes see http://dget.nic.in/cirtes/csc/courses/Actuary%20as%20a%20career.pdf (11 October 2011).

EXERCISES

(i) A part of the house is gutted by fire. It was insured for ₹50,000. The estimated loss by the insurance firm is ₹40,000. How much will the insured get?

Hint: The estimated amount by the insurer. Principle: indemnity.

(ii) Karan took a life insurance on himself. The insurance agent questioned whether he suffered from any mental illness to which he answered in the negative. It happened that after a couple of years Karan was indeed admitted to a psychiatric institute for mental illness. Would he get his medical bills paid by the insurer?

Hint: First ascertain whether the concealment was intentional. If proved the concealment was intentional then the contract is void *ab initio*.

(iii) Grains exported by a company were insured against the perils of the sea such as drowning due to storms or destruction by fire. However, the grains rotted due to the closure of containers. Can the insurance be affected?

Hint: Apply the principle of *Causa Proxima*.

(iv) Enumerate the basic principles of insurance with examples.

(v) Explain insurable interest and illustrate it with a case.

DEVELOPMENT OF LEGAL EDGE

Project—Unit Linked Insurance Products

• The opening up of the insurance sector competition by private companies in Unit Linked Insurance Products has been very popular.

Objective To develop a legally sound management programme

• IRDA has issued guidelines w.e.f. June 2006. Refer IRDA Website: http://www.irda.in

Training

• Do a full course at Institute of Insurance: refer http://www.insuranceinstituteofindia.com or a short one in actuaries: refer http://www.actuariesindia.org/.

FURTHER READING

Acts

• Insurance Act, 1938.
• Insurance Act, 1938: as amended by the Insurance (Amendment) Act, 2002.

Web resources

• http://www.irda.gov.in IRDA Website has everything concerning insurance and its regulation; however, it is advisable to subscribe IRDA journal and supplements to the journal for up to date information.
• Actuary: http://dget.nic.in/cirtes/csc/courses/Actuary%20as%20a%20career.pdf.

CASE STUDY   MEDICLAIM—A CASE OF COMMON CLAIM[+]

Hypogamglobulinemias

A general insurance policy shall clearly state provision for cancellation of the policy on grounds of misrepresentation, fraud, non-disclosure of material facts or non-cooperation of the insured.

Any breaches of the obligations cast on an insurer or insurance agent or insurance intermediary in terms of these regulations may enable the authority to initiate action against each or all of them, jointly or severally, under the act and/or the insurance Regulatory and Development Authority Act, 1999.

— IRDA Regulation, 2002, 7(1) and 11(4)

Objective

As the title claims, it is a common case of medical claim. However, the impact of the judgement in this case is applicable to millions of people who have medical insurance policies whether as private individuals, as earning individuals, or as groups of people such as labourers, industrial workers, etc. The case is important for you as a manager, whether you are a manager of a business establishment or of an insurance company.

At Stake

The case is about the decision whether renewal of a Mediclaim policy on payment of the amount of premium would be automatic.

Legal Background

The parliament enacted the General Insurance Business (Nationalization) Act, 1972 (for short, the 1972 Act) to provide for the acquisition and transfer of shares of insurance companies and undertakings of other insurers to serve better the need of the economy by securing the development of general insurance business in the best interest of the community and to ensure that the operation of the economic system does not result in the concentration of wealth to the common detriment, for the regulation and control of such business and for other matters connected therewith or incidental thereto.

Appellants are the two subsidiary insurance companies of GIC of India, carrying on the insurance business in terms of the 1972 Act. The general insurance companies had a monopoly over the business of general insurance, whereas LIC of India, constituted under the LIC Act, 1956 enjoyed the monopoly in respect of the business of life insurance.

The business activities of the insurance companies are governed by the Insurance Act, 1938 (for short, the 1938 Act). In terms of the provisions of the said Act, an authority known as Insurance Regulatory and Development Authority (the Authority) was constituted by the Central Government in exercise of its power conferred upon it by clause 2(c) of Sec. 114 of the 1938 Act.

The parliament also enacted the Insurance Regulatory and Development Authority Act, 1999. By the 1999 Act, the parliament inserted Sec. 24A in the 1972 Act directing cessation of the exclusive privilege of the corporation and the acquiring companies in relation thereto. In exercise of the powers conferred by clause 2(c) of sub-sec. (2) of Sec. 114A of the 1938 Act read with Secs 14 and 26 of the 1999 Act, the authority made regulations known as Insurance Regulatory and Development Authority (Protection of Policyholders' Interest) Regulations, 2002.

Matter before the Court

Respondent 1 obtained the Mediclaim policy from the appellant in April 1995 and renewed annually upon payment of the requisite amount of premium. After over three years, namely, in July 1998, he suffered a coronary disease and was admitted in the Escorts Heart Institute and Research Centre where he underwent 'angioplasty'. A claim made by him was paid by the appellant. In January 2001, he was once again admitted to the Escorts Heart Institute and Research Centre and once again underwent 'angioplasty'. The amount claimed was duly reimbursed by the appellant to the respondent. In May 2002, he was hospitalized in Holy Family Hospital for a minor operation and the medical expenses claimed to that effect were reimbursed by the appellant. In April

---

[+]This case is an abridged Supreme Court case: United India Insurance Company and Others vs Manubhai Dharmasinhbhai Gajera, (16 May 2008); see also: indiankanoon.org/doc/1894467/ (12 October 2011). The case brings out all the legal principles from the Acts, the regulations of IRDA to make it a model judgement for claims on the insurers.

2002, he underwent a by-pass surgery; he submitted his claim that, however, was not paid.

On 3 April 2003, the respondent approached the appellant for renewal of the policy and issued a cheque toward payment of the premium for the purpose of renewal of the policy w.e.f. 6 April 2003, which was refused on the purported ground of 'high claim ratio'. After serving notice, the said respondents filed a writ petition that was allowed by the learned Single Judge of the Delhi High Court by his order dated 7 January 2005 directing the appellant to renew his Mediclaim insurance policy.

Agreement in Policy

The insured has an option under the existing Mediclaim insurance policy to continue the cover by payment of renewal premium in time in respect of the sum insured.

In case of renewal without break in the period, the Mediclaim insurance policy will be renewed without excluding any disease already covered under the existing policy, which may have been contracted during the period of the expiring policy. Renewal of Mediclaim insurance policy cannot be refused on the ground that the insured had contracted disease during the period of the expiring policy, so far as the basic sum insured under the existing policy is concerned.

In cases where the insured seeks an enhancement of the amount of sum insured at the time of renewal, the option to renew will not extend to the amount of such enhancement and renewal in respect thereof will depend upon the mutual consent of the contracting parties.

Renewal of a medical claim insurance policy cannot be refused, despite timely payment of the renewal premium, on the ground that continuance of the cover would become more onerous or burdensome for the insurer due to the insured contracting a covered disease during the period of the existing policy.

The insurer may refuse renewal, even in cases where the insured has an option to renew the policy on payment of the renewal premium in time, on the grounds such as misrepresentation, fraud, or nondisclosure of material facts that existed at the inception of the contract and would have vitiated the insurance of the cover at its inception or non-fulfillment of obligations on the part of the insured or any other ground on which the performance of the promise under the contract is dispensed with or excused under the provisions of the Indian Contract Act or any other law or when the insurer has stopped doing business.

Lower Court's Ruling

The insurance companies will renew their respective policies from the date on which they expired, on payment of the renewal premium payable by them under the scheme, without excluding the diseases that may have been contracted by them during the period of their existing policies for the concerned year. The rule is made absolute accordingly with costs.

In the Supreme Court

For the appellants Appellants made their submission through the Solicitor General of India:

1. The high court committed a serious error in holding that the contract of insurance is no longer in the realm of contract;
2. The insurance companies must function having regard to 'commercial expedience' consideration in view of Sec. 24A of the Act; and
3. Assuming that the appellant is a 'State' within the meaning of Article 12 of the Constitution of India, the same by itself would not mean that it cannot enter into a contract with the policy holder on its own terms, particularly when such terms have been approved by the authority.

For the respondents Two learned counsels made submissions for the respondents:

The insurance companies having regard to their obligations not only in terms of the constitutional provisions, but also the provisions of the 1938, 1972, and 1999 Acts; the regulations framed there under and the guidelines issued, are bound to renew their Mediclaim policies from time to time on the same terms and conditions.

IRDA Guidelines

The requirements specified by the authority are:-

1. Design and rating of products must always be on sound and prudent underwriting basis. The contingencies insured under the product should be clear and provide transparent cover, which is of value to the insured.
2. All literature relating to the product should be in simple language and easily understandable to the public at large. As far as possible, a similar sequence of presentation may be followed. All technical terms should be clarified in simple language for the benefit of the insured.

3. The product should be a genuine insurance product of an insurable risk with a real risk transfer. 'Alternate risk transfer' or 'financial guarantee' business in any form will not be accepted.

4. The insurance product should comply with all the requirements of the Protection of Policyholders' Interests Regulations, 2002.

5. Insurers should use as far as possible, similar wordings for describing the same cover or the same requirement across all their products. For example, clauses on renewal of insurance, basis of insurance, due diligence, cancellation, arbitration, etc., should have similar wordings across all products.

6. The pricing of products should be based on appropriate data and with technical justification.

7. The terms and conditions of cover shall be fair between the insurer and the insured.

8. Margins built into rates shall be consistent with the experience of the insurer in respect of commission, management expenses, contingencies, and profit.

9. Insurer should take necessary steps in ensuring that competition will not lead to unprincipled rate cutting and other improper underwriting practices.

Guidelines 7 and 25 of the Guidelines issued by the IRDA on 'File and Use': requirements for general insurance products read as under guidelines 7:

Till the tariffs are in force, it will not be necessary for any insurer to file information on any product that complies with tariff rates, terms, and conditions. With respect to products that package insurance covers that are governed by tariffs, with those that are not, the insurer should file such products and confirm that the section governed by tariffs complies with tariff rates, terms, and conditions for the portion that is governed by tariffs, as long as tariffs remain in force.

Policy Cover

The policy covers reimbursement of:

Hospitalization/ domiciliary hospitalization expenses for illness/diseases or injury sustained. In the event of any claim becoming admissible under this scheme, the company/ TPA will pay to the hospital/nursing home or the insured person the amount of such expenses as would fall under different heads mentioned below, and as are reasonable and necessarily incurred thereof by or on behalf of such insured person, but not exceeding the sum insured aggregate in the schedule hereto:

(i) Room, boarding expenses as provided by the hospital/nursing home;

(ii) Nursing expenses

(iii) Surgeon, anaesthetist, medical practitioner, consultants, specialists fees

(iv) Anaesthesia, blood, oxygen, operation theatre charges, surgical appliances, medicines and drugs diagnostic materials and X-ray, dialysis, chemotherapy, radiotherapy, cost of pacemaker, artificial limbs and cost of organs, and similar expenses.

(N.B.1. Company's liability in respect of all claims admitted during the period of insurance shall not exceed the sum insured per person mentioned in the schedule.)

What would be covered under the policy and what would not are matters governed by the Acts, regulations, and guidelines. The limited liability of the insurance provides for a third-party administrator, who is engaged for the purpose of health services and may not only oversee the claim, but may also disburse it.

Application of Law

Keeping in view the aforementioned legal principles, we may notice the fact of each case.

The insurer in SLP (c) No.9877entered into a contract of Mediclaim insurance in 1990 for a sum of ₹90,000 from 1992 to 2002. He had been making payments of the premiums regularly. His policy had been renewed every year. It was also renewed for the period 4 October 2001 to 3 October 2002. The insured's wife, son, and daughter-in-law have also entered into such policies since 1992. Their policies had also been renewed from time to time without any change in terms.

On or about 9 September 2002, respondent 1 handed over a cheque for a sum of ₹6,377 by way of renewal of insurance policy. As no action thereon was taken, a reminder was sent. A legal notice was also issued. The legal notice was refused to be accepted by the divisional manager. In response thereto, only on 30 September 2002, the appellant stated that the policy would be renewed by loading of 300 per cent premium. A sum of ₹18,982 was deposited. A receipt acknowledging the sum of ₹6,377 was also issued. Despite issuance of the said sum, the policy was not renewed. Strangely enough, only on 3 October 2002, the appellant stated that the said policy could be renewed subject to exclusion of the diseases specified therein. It was in the aforementioned situation that the writ petition was filed.

In SLP (c) No.10205 of 2004, the second respondent, who is a practicing consultant neurologist and physician since 1961, had taken Mediclaim insurance for himself his wife and his family members since 1992–1993. He was diagnosed with hypogamglobulinaemias in August-September 1999. Despite the same, the policy was renewed. By a letter dated 26 July 2002, appellant informed him that his Mediclaim policy, which was to expire on 13 August 2002 would be renewed subject to the exclusion of the disease septicaemia with hypogamglobulinaemias and was advised that the next premium will be accepted after loading of 100 per cent with 5 per cent excess for each and every claim. It is at that juncture, the writ petition was filed.

Respondent 3 in SLP (c) No. 10205 of 2004 had taken a Mediclaim policy and accident insurance policy in 1988. By a letter dated 15 January 2002, the Mediclaim policy for the year 2002–2003 was refused to be renewed and he was asked to renew his policy in another company. The policy was cancelled.

The Judgement

Each of the aforementioned cases clearly shows that the action on the part of the authorities of the appellant was highly arbitrary. Respondents though were not entitled to automatic renewal, but indisputably, they were entitled to be treated fairly. We have noticed hereinbefore some of the clauses contained in the prospectus as also the insurance policy. When a policy is cancelled, the conditions precedents therefore must be fulfilled. Some reasons therefore must be assigned. When an exclusion clause is resorted to, the terms thereof must be given effect to. What was necessary is a pre-existing disease when the cover was inspected for the first time. Only because the insured had started suffering from a disease, the same would not mean that the said disease shall be excluded. If the insured had made some claim in each year, the insurance company should not refuse to renew insurance policies only for that reason. The words 'incepts for the first time' as contained in clause 4.1 as also the words 'continuous and without break' if the renewal premium is paid in time, must be kept in mind as also the reasons for cancellation as contained in clause 7 (1)(n) thereof.

Renewal of a Mediclaim policy subject to just exceptions should ordinarily be made, but the same does not mean that the renewal is automatic. Keeping in view the terms and conditions of the prospectus and the insurance policy, the parties are not required to go into all the formalities. The very fact that the policy contemplates terms for renewal, subject of course to payment of requisite premium, the same cannot be placed at par with a case of first contract.

We would like to observe that keeping in view the role played by the insurance companies, it is essential that the regulatory authority must lay down clear guidelines by way of regulations or otherwise. No doubt, the regulations would be applicable to all the players in the field. The duties and functions of the Regulatory Authority, however, are to see that the service provider must render their services keeping in view the nature thereof. It will be appropriate if the Central Government or the general insurance companies also issue requisite circulars.

Appellants before us, being subsidiaries to the GIC, cannot ignore the statutory provisions. They are bound by the directions issued by the Central Government.

We would request the IRDA to consider the matter in depth and undertake a scrutiny of such claims so that in the event it is found that the insurance companies are taking recourse to arbitrary methodologies in the matter of entering into contracts of insurance or renewal thereof, appropriate steps in that behalf may be taken.

Conclusion[5]

The above case illustrates the plight of the common people. In fact, the insurance scenario has changed completely with the private companies now enjoying a bigger market share than the nationalized companies. In this environment with numerable players in the market the role of IRDA, the insurance regulator becomes very important. Its mission statement is to protect the interests of the policyholders and to regulate, promote, and ensure orderly growth of the insurance industry and for matters connected therewith or incidental thereto.[6] The lawgiver would be satisfied if this mission is accomplished.

Discussion Questions

1. State the main issue of the case and its multiplication in each instance.
2. Discuss the status of the insurers as nationalized firms and their objectives.

---

[5]Conclusion is by the author.
[6]See: http://www.irda.gov.in.

3. What is the perspective of the judge of these nationalized insurance companies?
4. Do you think periodic free health checkups for the Mediclaim policyholders could impact the claims?
5. How the services of an actuary would serve this case?
6. What is your business plan for a company from the policyholders' point of view?
7. What is your business plan as a manager of an insurance company?

Going Beyond

1. Enlighten the relationship that should exist between the insurer and the insured.
2. As a manager of a public insurance company how would you prioritize the business to deliver profits to your company without litigations of claims?
3. How would you as a senior manager examine a case for claims, which may be termed as high claim ratio?

LEGAL LUMINARY

RENU SUD KARNAD—MD, HDFC

Renu Sud Karnad is among the most powerful business women in India. Some examples to support the proposition:*

- Managing director: Housing Development Finance Corp. Ltd since 1 January 2010
- Chairperson: Sparsh BPO Services Ltd
- Executive director: Home Loan Services India
- Non-executive director: Indraprastha Medical Corp. Ltd
- Independent director: Bosch Ltd
- Independent director: ONGC Corp. Ltd
- Director: Akzo Nobel India Ltd
- Director: Gruh Finance Ltd
- Director: HDFC Asset Management Company Ltd
- Director: Credit Information Bureau of India
- Director: HDFC General Insurance Co. Ltd
- Director: Mother Dairy Fruits and Vegetables Ltd
- Director: Torrent Pharmaceuticals Ltd
- Advisor: Swiss Technology Venture Capital

Mrs Karnad joined HDFC in 1978. Twenty years later, she was appointed on its board of directors. She has been through all the ranks and departments of the company. She is the brand custodian of this powerful institution and has been able to set up and systematize organization's communication strategy and nurturing of public image. The most successful sector of HDFC, the mortgage sector has been her brainchild.

Mrs Karnad has earned numerous awards. In all the rankings by different organizations, she has been considered as one of the powerful women in business management. Business and economy magazine has conferred on her the most influential women in Indian business. The *Wall Street Journal Asia* honoured her as among the Top Ten Powerful Women to Watch Out For in Asia.

People in the know feel that her success lies not only on her keen and analytical intellect but also on her humane approach and the most infectious smile in the finance industry that exudes personal confidence and professional excellence.

Mrs Karnad is Parvin Fellow of Woodrow Wilson School of International Affairs, Princeton, New Jersey, USA; law graduate from the University of Bombay and post-graduate in economics from Delhi University. She enjoys her home and kitchen, and loves music.

She is a perfect role model for every aspiring Indian manager.

*See: http://www.hdfc.com/pdf/renu_sud_karnad.pdf (14 October 2011).
**Photo courtesy: http://businesstoday.intoday.in/story/most-powerful-women-in-indian-business/17/3105.html (14 October 2011).

Laws of Taxation

Principle: *De jure decimerum, originem ducens de jure patronaturs, eune cognition spectat ad legem cilem,*
i.e., communem.

With regard to the right of taxes, deducing its origin from the right of the patron, then
the cognizance of them belongs to the civil law; that is, the common law.

CHAPTER OUTLINE

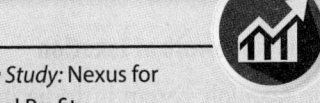

- Introduction and Interpretation
- Central Board of Revenue Act, 1963
- Income Tax Act, 1961
- Other Major Laws of Taxation

- *Case Study:* Nexus for Global Profit
- *Legal Luminary:* Pranab Mukherjee

20.1 INTRODUCTION AND INTERPRETATION

TEXT

No tax shall be levied or collected except by authority of law.

– The Constitution of India, A. 265

Context of Taxation

Wherever there is an organization taking care of common interests of its members, certain contribution is demanded by the former from the latter towards meeting the expenses of those interests. Tax to the government is one such contribution. Only the duly instituted government according to the constitution has the right to impose or levy taxes. If any other agency, other than the one approved by such constitutional authority, collects, taxes, the act amounts to extortion and is unjust and illegal. The law shall be enforced against such action.

The levying of taxes is done according to a well-conceived system called taxation. Laws of taxation govern the system of taxation whose objective is to collect revenues to pay for the costs of running a government for rendering services such as the national defence force, education, health, national infrastructure, industry, commerce, welfare, pensions, and numerous other services.

The government develops ways and means to raise revenues. Revenue collection is mainly carried out through direct taxes and indirect taxes. One of the simplest ways to understand the complex system of taxation is to understand whether a particular tax is direct or indirect. Taxation is direct when a certain determined percentage of your income or wealth has to be paid to the revenue department of the government. Taxation is indirect when you spend your money on goods and services and a certain determined percentage from there is accounted to the revenue department of the government. In short, the tax on your income or wealth is direct tax; the tax on your expenditure is indirect tax.

To maintain equity between the rich and the poor the government levies tax only above a certain determined income; it is done progressively in higher slabs and proportionate percentages. In India the entire agricultural sector, religious societies, non-profitable organizations, etc., are exempt from direct taxes. Indirect taxes, on the other hand, are paid by all who purchase goods and services.

Just as individual citizens do, incorporated companies too pay direct taxes, known as corporate tax, and indirect taxes. You as a manager need to know the basic system of taxation. The rates and items of taxation change annually with the budgetary proposals, which are moved to become law. The important aspect of taxation that must be known is the system of application of law.

Legal Framework of Taxation

The taxation system in India has a federal structure. The Central Government, through the Ministry of Finance and the statutory agencies operating under it, levies wealth tax and tax on personal and corporate income. These are direct taxes. The indirect taxes are through custom duties, excise duties, and central sales tax (Figure 20.1). The states impose state sales tax, stamp duty, and other state-level taxes. Local bodies such as corporations, municipalities, and *panchayats* too have a system of collecting dues for various services rendered by these local bodies. Nothing

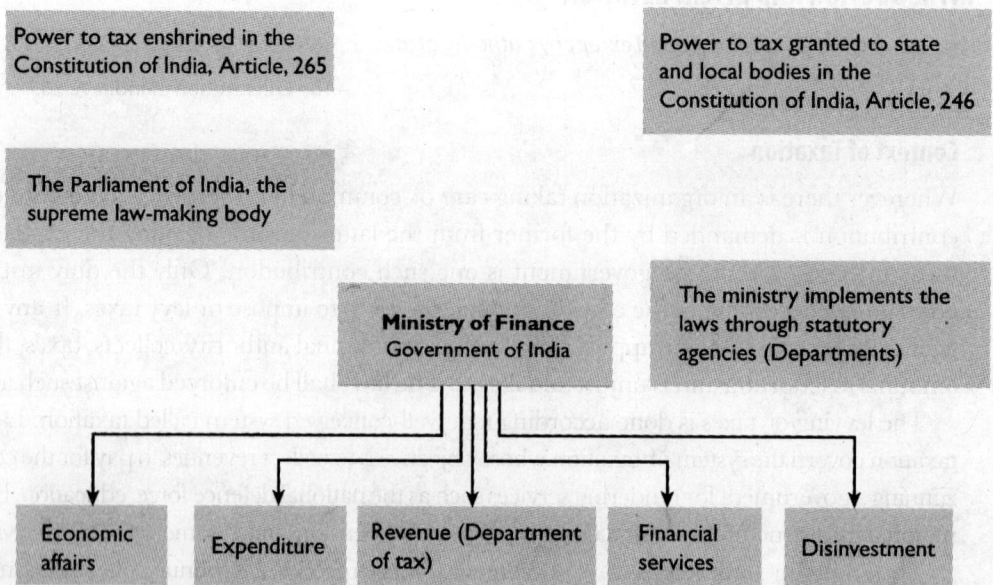

Figure 20.1 Legal framework of taxation under the constitution and the organs of the government

of the above is arbitrary; every levy, duty, excise, customs, toll, and tariff is governed by a definite law. Table 20.1 exhibits the governing laws and their respective implementing authorities.

Table 20.1 The governing laws and the respective implementing authorities

Act	Authority
Direct taxes	
Income Tax Act, 1961	Central Board of Direct Taxes (CBDT) (Central Government)
Wealth Tax Act, 1957	CBDT (Central Government)
Gift Tax Act, 1958	CBDT (Central Government)
Indirect taxes	
Central Excise and Salt Act, 1944	Central Board of Excise and Customs (CBEC) (Central Government)
Customs Act, 1944	CBEC (Central Government)
Central Sales Tax Act, 1956	Central Government
Respective States Sales Tax Acts	Respective state governments

Reforms in Taxation

Economic reforms began in the late 1980s and reached their peak in the 1990s. Taxation lies at the core of government policies because all policies for economic development are also a means for greater government revenues. Tax reforms, therefore, go hand in hand with the economic policies. In 1991, the government appointed a committee known as the Raja Chelliah Committee on Tax Reforms. The Committee, under the chairmanship of Raja Chelliah, submitted important recommendations for tax reform. The objective of the Committee was to rationalize and simplify the system of taxation. The following are some of the reforms implemented by the government, most of which affect Indian companies:

(a) Drastically reducing customs and excise duties
(b) Lowering of corporate tax rates
(c) Removing distinction between widely held and closely held companies
(e) Extending Modified Value Added Tax (MODVAT) to more industries
(e) Simplifying income tax return filing procedures
(f) Levying taxes on services such as insurance, stock brokering, and telephones
(g) Introducing of value added tax (VAT)

Scope

The scope of this chapter is limited to only the context of the system of legislation in India. Only two Acts, the Central Board of Revenue Act, 1963, and the Income Tax Act, 1961, will be highlighted to illustrate the earlier-mentioned context. Taxation is an ongoing process. The particulars of levies, customs, duties, excise, etc., change in the financial statement of the Minister of Finance at annual budgetary exercise in the parliament. Traditionally, the budget is presented in the parliament on the last working day of the month of February. The financial year for taxation spans from 1 April to 31 March.

In the larger perspective, you will appreciate that knowing the taxation system and the authority behind it will give you the right direction as a manager to take the right decisions for your company. Good managerial decisions will have a threefold effect:

- Save money through saving tax
- Save the company from tax litigation
- Make the company strong for successful business

For other details on taxation, there are other professionals—company secretary, chartered accountant, internal auditor—who help citizens work in a lawful and responsible manner.

Taxation is nothing new to India. It has been prevalent since the ancient times. Chanakya, the iconic economist of India, in his work *Arthashastra* laid down a practical principle for the success of tax regime. The recently issued commemorative coin of 150 years of modern taxation in India has the embossed image of Chanakya on the reverse and before him a lotus with a bee, expressing the principle of taxation. Chanakya held that tax should be collected from the public in the same way as the bee collectes nectar from flowers—they take away only a bit of it and also help to pollinate flowers and fruits. However, down through the ages, under various rulers and regimes, taxation has not been like a bee on a lotus flower. India's freedom struggle got into its final and powerful phase when Mahatma Gandhi marched to Dandi (1930) in protest against the salt tax. The Chanakya principle helps build a country; colonial taxation exploits a country.

Case 20.1 is considered very important as it is also applicable in several other Acts such as: the Salt Cess Act, 1953, the Customs Act, 1962, the Central Excise Tariff Act, 1955, the Finance Act, 1996, and several others. Further understanding can be gained by referring to some of these Acts. For a manager dealing with the issues cited in the case above, particularly that of debonding, this insight would be very helpful.

CASE 20.1	APPELLANT: **Commissioner of Central Excise** vs RESPONDENT: **Siv Industries Ltd**

DATE OF JUDGEMENT: 11 December 1997*

FACTS: The issue in the appeal relates to the levy of duty on the finished goods that were earlier manufactured in the 100 per cent Export Oriented Unit (EOU) of the respondents and that were cleared for domestic tariff area (DTA) on debonding of the unit.

Respondents Plea: Incurred heavy losses exceeding ₹805 lakh (therefore) to consider waiver of all/any penalties.

Petitioner's Contention: (1) The undertaking shall pay all customs and excise duties on the imported and indigenous capital goods, raw materials, components, consumables, and spares in stock as well as on the finished goods in stock, together

*Commissioner of Central Excise vs Siv Industries Ltd (in Customs Excise and Gold Tribunal, Tamil Nadu); 1999 (112) ELT 251 Tri Chennai; also see http://www.indiankanoon.org/doc/610076/ (15 October 2011).

Contd

Case 20.1 *Contd*

with all penalties and other charges as per the Customs Act and Rules, before the issue of the final debonding letter.

(2) The undertaking shall also deposit a penalty of 10 per cent of the c.i.f. value of imported capital goods, towards non-fulfillment of export obligation, with the import licensing authority with whom it had executed a local undertaking in respect of the 100 per cent EOU. This penalty shall be paid before the issue of the final debonding letter.

Subject to the approval of BOA, EOU/EPZ units may be debonded on their inability to achieve export obligation value addition or other requirements. Such debonding shall be subject to such penalty as may be imposed and payment of duties of customs and excise are applicable at the time of debonding.

JUDGEMENT: The appeal was upheld.

REASON: The permission to clear the goods to the DTA is provided for in the scheme itself and the question of the Development Commissioner allowing the goods to be cleared does not protect him with any power other than that of verification for compliance with the requirement of the scheme. He performs the functions like those performed by the appraiser or the AC of the Customs where the goods are allowed to be cleared after verifying that the requirements of law have been complied with. The goods cleared to the DTA did not acquire a different hue for reason of the same having been allowed to be taken out of the EOU, after verification regarding fulfilment of the requirements of the scheme. The power to permit clearance of the goods is with the Ministry of Commerce, Government of India, who fixes the percentage and which percentage can be varied by them. In the view of the above matter, we hold that the case law cited by the respondents is distinguishable and plea of the respondents that duty should be paid under the provision to Sec. 3 of the Central Excise Act, 1944, is not sustainable. We, therefore, allow the plea of the department for levy of duty in terms of the proviso to Sec. 3 of the Central Excise Act, 1944.

20.2 CENTRAL BOARD OF REVENUE ACT, 1963

An Act to provided for the constitution of separate Boards of Revenue for Direct Taxes and for Excise and Customs and to amend certain enactments for the purpose of conferring powers and imposing duties on the said Boards.

– Preamble, Central Board of Revenue Act, 1963

Department of Revenue[1]

You have already seen in the previous section that the Ministry of Finance functions under the Central Government, which derives its powers from the Constitution of India and from the

MANAGER'S TAKEAWAY

- A wise manager complies with all the laws and regulations of trade and commerce.
- Doing legal homework and seeking prior advice may save money and trouble for your company.

---

[1]See for details http://incometaxindia.gov.in; http://www.cbec.gov.in; both these websites are a comprehensive and sure and ready guide.

Parliament, the law-making body. Of the five departments under this ministry, the Department of Revenue deals with taxation. The department is headed by the Secretary of Revenue and exercises control over both direct and indirect taxes and their respective agencies: CBDT and CBEC. Each of these boards is headed by their respective chairpersons; these are the ex-officio Special Secretaries to the Government of India (Figure 20.2 and Case 20.2).

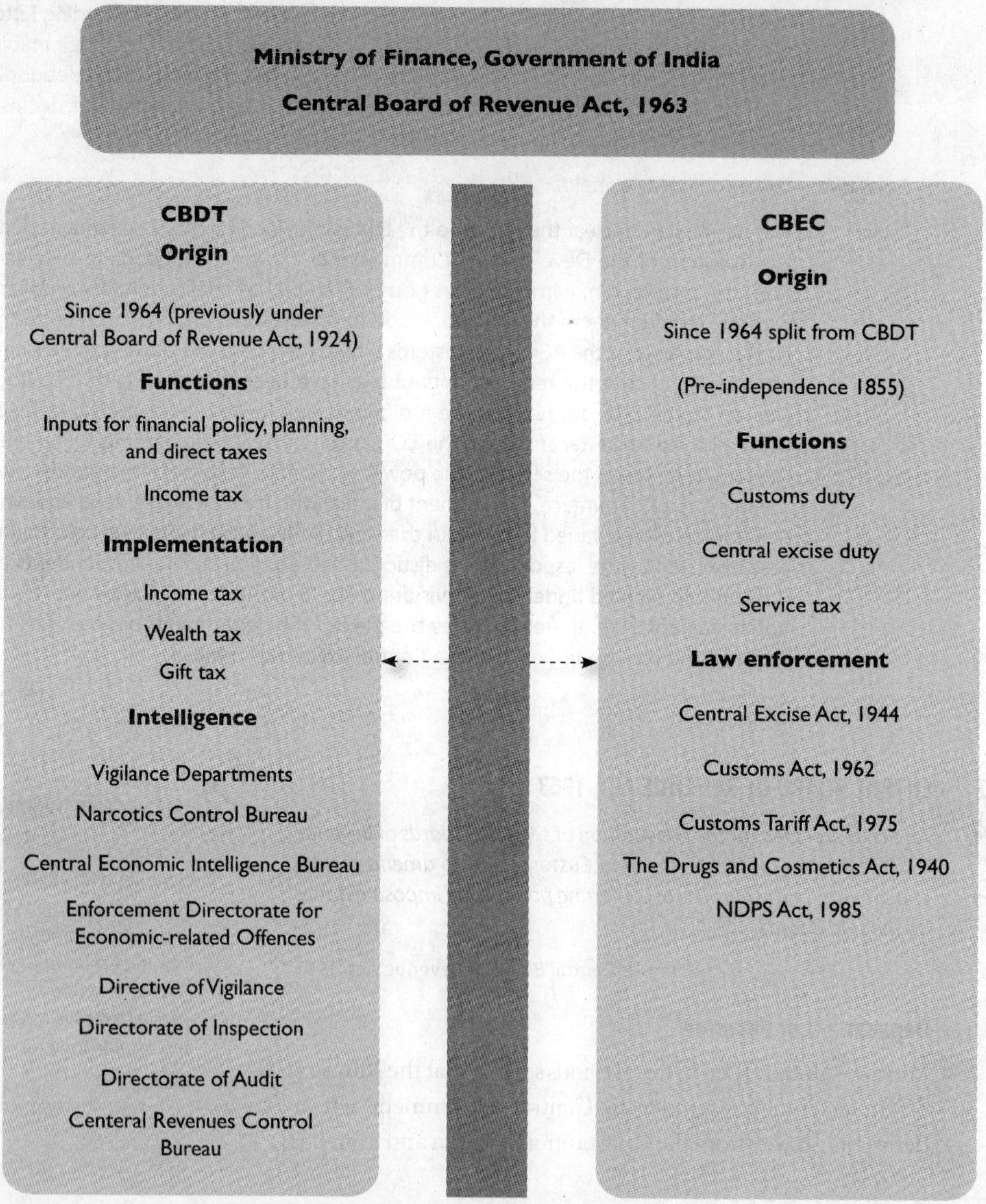

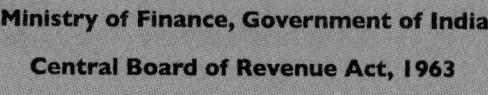

Ministry of Finance, Government of India

Central Board of Revenue Act, 1963

CBDT	CBEC
Origin	**Origin**
Since 1964 (previously under Central Board of Revenue Act, 1924)	Since 1964 split from CBDT
	(Pre-independence 1855)
Functions	**Functions**
Inputs for financial policy, planning, and direct taxes	Customs duty
Income tax	Central excise duty
Implementation	Service tax
Income tax	**Law enforcement**
Wealth tax	
Gift tax	Central Excise Act, 1944
Intelligence	Customs Act, 1962
Vigilance Departments	Customs Tariff Act, 1975
Narcotics Control Bureau	The Drugs and Cosmetics Act, 1940
Central Economic Intelligence Bureau	NDPS Act, 1985
Enforcement Directorate for Economic-related Offences	
Directive of Vigilance	
Directorate of Inspection	
Directorate of Audit	
Centeral Revenues Control Bureau	

Figure 20.2 The Central Board of Direct Taxes and the Central Board of Excise and Customs are the two departments of the Revenue Board of the Ministry of Finance under the Central Board of Revenue Act, 1963

CASE 20.2

APPELLANT: Union of India and others   vs   RESPONDENT: Seth R. Dalmia

DATE OF JUDGEMENT: 27 February 1973*

FACTS: CBDT (regulation of transaction of business) Rules 1964—Rule 4—Whether approval, by the Central Government of distribution of the business of board by chairman must be expressed in the shape of an order.

PETITIONER: Six notices were issued to the respondent under Sec. 148 of the Income Tax Act for reopening the assessments for 3 assessment years. The notices recited that they were issued after obtaining the necessary satisfaction of the CBDT.

Respondent: The respondent filed a writ petition in the High Court challenging the said notices inter alia on the ground that sanction of the CBDT was not taken before the notices were issued as required by Sec. 151 of the Act.

The High Court accepted the said contention and did not decide the other grounds raised in the petition. The High Court also held that as no formal order was passed changing the allocation with the previous approval of the Central Government, the sanction issued by CBDT was without jurisdiction and authority.

Hence, the appeal.

JUDGEMENT: Appeal was upheld.

REASON: The impugned notices were issued in due compliance with the requirements of Rule 4 of CBDT (regulation of transaction of business) Rules, 1964; we do not find it necessary to consider the provisions of this Act for the purpose of these appeals.

The appeals are accordingly allowed and the judgement and orders appealed from are set aside. The High Court will now proceed to dispose of the writ petitions in accordance with law on the other grounds raised therein.

*Union of India and Others vs Seth R. Dalmia; 1975 AIR 1017, 1975 SCR (3) 735; also see http://www.indiankanoon.org/doc/782147/ (16 October 2011).

Constitutional Validity

Article 246 of the Constitution of India allocates powers of taxation between the federal parliament and the state legislatures. The same is further illustrated with clear enumeration in Schedule VII of the Constitution of India with three different lists. While List I enumerates 13 heads for the Parliament and List II enumerates 19 heads for the states, List III, where both the Parliament and the state legislatures can make tax laws concurrently, is thus far without any enumerated heads. Table 20.2 provides Lists I and II.

Taxation, Tax Problems, and Solutions

It is clear that the subject on taxation laws, their application, the problems of taxation, and their solution are impossible to be delineated in this chapter comprehensively. However, the following factors are very important for you to know:

Table 20. 2   Constitutional validity to enact laws of taxation

List I Competency of the Parliament	List II Competency of the State legislature
Income	Land revenue, maintenance of land records, survey for revenue purposes, records of rights, and alienation of revenues
Custom duties—export	Agricultural income
Excise—liquor, drugs, opium	Succession to agricultural income
Corporation	Agricultural Estate duty
Capital value assets	Taxes on land and buildings
Estate duty—other than agricultural land	Taxes on mineral rights
Succession of property	Excise for goods manufactured within the state—alcohol, hemp, etc.
Freight by land, sea, air	Taxes on entry of goods
Stamp duties, stock exchange transactions, futures trading	Taxes on electricity
Sale purchase of newspapers, advertisements	Taxes on advertisements other than on newspapers, radio, and television
Sale/purchase of goods other than newspapers	Taxes on goods by road and inland waterways
Consignment of goods in interstate trade or commerce	Taxes on goods and passengers carried by roads and inland waterways
Residuary taxes not listed in other lists	Motor vehicle taxes
	Taxes on animals and boats
	Toll tax
	Professional tax, trade, callings, and employments
	Capitation taxes
	Taxes on luxuries, entertainment, betting, and gambling
	State stamp duty

Direct taxes—CBDT

Various intelligence agencies
Indian Revenue Service
Directorate of Income Tax (DIT)

Indirect taxes—CBEC

Central excise
Customs, tariffs
Narcotics

For further information on taxation, both direct and indirect, the following two websites provide the immediate sources of information and also of solutions:

- http://incometaxindia.gov.in.
- http://www.cbec.gov.in.

These websites may be used as a ready guide for all the queries on taxation. The main reason why you should refer to these websites is that not only do the financial laws change every year, but also that all the departments of the Central Board of Revenue make renewed rules, regulations, and release circulars.

20.3   INCOME TAX ACT, 1961

Every persons, if his total income or the total income of any other person in respect of which he is assessable under this Act during the previous year exceeded the maximum amount which is not chargeable to income-tax, shall, on or before the due date, furnish a return of his income or the income of such other person during the previous year, in the prescribed form and verified in the prescribed manner and setting forth such other particulars as may be prescribed. Explanation: In this sub-Sec.,'due date' means: (a) where the assessee is a company, the 4 [30th day of November] of the assessment year; (b)where the assessee is a person, other than a company

– The Income Tax Act, 1961 (1995), Sec. 139 (1) (a)(b)

Background of Indian Income Tax

As has been already explained above, the history of Indian taxation dates back to the ancient times. The Chanakya principle of taxation has also been explained. Taxes, particularly highly unjust and burdensome, have caused people's anger against the rulers and have brought down kingdoms and empires irrespective of their power and might. The Mughal Empire expanded and prospered as long as its rulers ruled well and followed the Chanakya principle. *Aurangzeb's jeziah,* the religious tax on non-Muslims, was one of the main causes of the eventual collapse of the kingdom. It seemed that the British rule in India would never end until the salt tax was imposed, against which Mahatma Gandhi led a march from Sabarmati to Dandi in protest and laid the foundation for Purna Swaraj, the total independence of India. The sun set on the British Empire, much against the prophecy of Prime Minister Winston Churchill.

 MANAGER'S TAKEAWAY

- When confronted with a legal problem, first study the legal context: the governing Act and authority.
- On receiving a notice/show cause notice from Income Tax Authorities, first study the matter in consultation with your counsel.

To understand the present taxation regime in independent India, it may help to follow a timeline, which is explained as follows:[2]

1860   After the Sepoy Mutiny in 1852, the British Crown abolished the East India Company administration and imposed direct rule; the laws for India were made at Westminster, the Parliament of Great Britain. Tax was mainly to defray the losses of the mutiny and was implemented only for five years.

---

[2]See http://finance.indiamart.com/taxation/.

1877 Taxation was revived to finance the losses of the famine of the previous year.

1886 The Act was an improvement of the Act of 1860. It defined the agricultural income and exempted it from assessment for income tax. It continues to be so to this day.

1918 This Act began a new model of taxation. The special feature of this Act was the aggregation of income from various sources. It classified the sources of income under six heads. This was the determining factor of the income tax rate. The Act sought to remove disparities in taxation. It also introduced the concept of *accruing* or *arising* income received in British India.

1922 First the All India Income Tax Committee was formed, which made necessary recommendation. In this manner, the practice of committee formation began in India. The concept of direct taxes was first formed in this committee. Thus far, the provincial govern-ments collected the revenues. This Act, for the first time, introduced the concept of federal or Central Government tax. Another important change was with regard to the year of assessment. It established the charge in the year of assessment on the income of the previous year.

1961 The Act of 1922 continued in India for almost one-and-a-half decades after independence. The government wanted a comprehensive Income Tax law and the Law Commission of India made its recommendations accordingly. As a result the Income Tax Act, 1961, which is presently in force, was ushered in.

With the economic reforms and liberalization policies of the 1990s, reforms to the taxation laws were necessary. In 1997, a tax reform committee was formed under the chairmanship of Raja J. Chelliah. The committee's recommendations on restructuring, lowering slabs of taxation, and rationalization have been implemented in the successive financial statements of the finance ministry in the budgetary provisions of the Parliament. In 2003, a task force under Kelekar was formed. The result was the introduction of PAN and TAN cards; exemption of dividend income was implemented.

Income Tax

As is already known, income tax is of two kinds: personal income tax and corporate income tax (Figure 20.3).

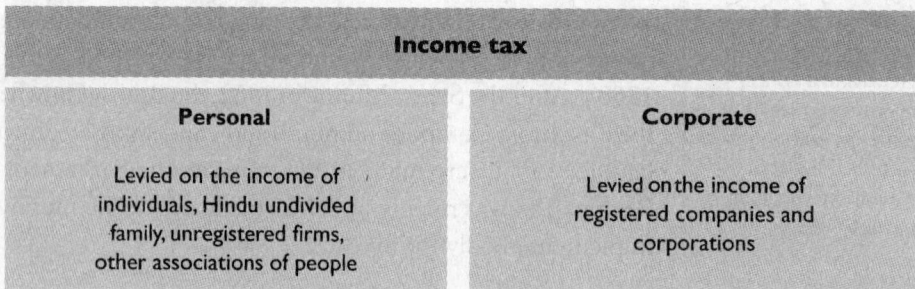

Figure 20.3 Income tax as personal and corporate tax

Income Tax Rate

The income tax rate[3] is the percentage of tax to be paid of the assessed annual income. It applies both to individual persons and to corporate bodies.

Personal income rate   Earnings above ₹2,00,000 is taxable. The slab of taxation is as follows:
From the taxable income upto ₹5,00,000 @ 10%
From ₹5,00,000 upto ₹10,00,000 @ 20%
Above ₹10,00,000 @ 30%

For senior citizens of the age sixty years or more but less than eighty years:
Earnings above ₹2,50,000 is taxable. The slab of taxation is as follows:
From the taxable income upto ₹5,00,000 @ 10%
From ₹5,00,000 upto ₹10,00,000 @ 20%
Above ₹10,00,000 @ 30%

For senior citizens of the age eighty years or more:
Earnings above ₹5,00,000 is taxable. The slab of taxation is as follows:
From ₹5,00,000 upto ₹10,00,000 @ 20%
Above ₹10,00,000 @ 30%

Personal income rebate   The law, however, is considerate and provides rebates on the tax to be paid. The following are some examples:

(a) From FY 2010–11 the IT form has been made simpler and will consist of only 2 pages for individuals.

(b) Tax exemption of ₹20,000 on investment in tax saving infrastructure bonds. Exemption of up to ₹1,00,000 is already allowed under specific savings instruments.

(c) Introduction of a new section in e-TDS/TCS form, namely: PAO/DDO code; state name; ministry name; name of the utility (for return purpose), and PAO/DDO registration no. 3 per cent education cess valid on income tax, including 10 per cent surcharge if applicable. Tax exclusion will be specified for donations to the Central Government Health Scheme.

(d) Subsidiary tax relief offered to guarantee that the supplementary IT to be paid, inclusive of additional charge on surfeit earnings of over ₹10,00,000, is restricted to a sum by which the earnings is above this mentioned sum.

(e) Income tax exemption on agricultural income, associated persons, and body of individuals.

Capital gains tax   Gains arising on the transfer of capital assets are subject to tax as capital gains. Capital assets include property of any kind, but exclude personal effects other than jewellery, inventories held for the purpose of business, and agricultural land situated more than 8 km from a town with a population of 10,000 or more. Capital gains arising from the transfer of depreciable assets that form part of a block of assets are treated as short-term capital gains and computed by deducting from the sale price the following amounts.

---

[3]The rates are as per 2012–2013 budgetary provisions: see http://law.incometaxindia.gov.in.

Corporate Taxation

Basis   The income of the companies is taxed on the basis that companies are legal persons. A company means an Indian company or a body corporate incorporated by or under the laws of a foreign country. A company is treated as resident if it is an Indian company or if during the years the control and management of its affairs are situated wholly in India.

Companies are taxed at flat rates and dividends distributed are included in the taxable income of shareholders. However, a domestic company receiving dividends from another domestic company is entitled to deduct the amount of dividends received to the extent of the dividends it distributes to its own shareholders before the due date for filing the return (Case 20.3).

Individual shareholders   Individual shareholders are permitted to deduct dividends received from Indian companies to a specified extent. Tax is withheld from the dividends distributed, and shareholders get full credit for that amount against their tax liability, but they do not get credit for the underlying corporate tax paid by the company. Residents receiving dividends from foreign companies get credit for foreign tax paid to the extent of the Indian tax on the doubly taxed income, either unilaterally or under treaty.

Territoriality   A resident company is taxed on its worldwide income. A non-resident company is taxed only on income that is received in India, arises in India, or is deemed to arise in India, subject to treaty provisions.

System   The following are the guidelines the Department of Income Tax follows for corporations:

(a) Domestic companies are permitted to deduct dividends received from other domestic companies in certain cases.
(b) Inter-company transactions are honoured if negotiated at arm's length.
(c) Special provisions apply to venture funds and venture capital companies.
(d) Long-term capital gains have lower tax incidence.
(e) Liberal deductions are allowed for exports and for the setting up of new industrial undertakings under certain circumstances.

CASE 20.3   APPELLANT: Commissioner of Income Tax   VS   RESPONDENT: Bokaro Steel Ltd

DATE OF JUDGEMENT: 18 December 1998*

FACTS: The appellant appealed against the Tribunal's justification in five instances of respondent's where money received as not income to be assessed.

JUDGEMENT: Appeals dismissed

REASON: We have to consider whether the amounts received by the assessee under these five heads can be treated as income of the assessee for the relevant assessment years. The Tribunal has held that all these amounts received by the assessee have gone to reduce the cost of construction. These are in the nature of capital receipts that can be set off against the capital expenditure incurred by the assessee during the

*Commissioner of Income Tax vs Bokaro Steel Ltd (Supreme Court 2544–45 of 1988, etc.); also see http://www.indiankanoon.org/doc/222318/ (20 October 2010).

Contd

Case 20.3 *Contd*

relevant assessment years. This view has been upheld by the High Court and hence the department has come by way of the present appeals. During these assessment years, the respondent assessee had invested the amounts borrowed by it for the construction work, which were not immediately required, in short-term deposits and earned interest. It has been held in these proceedings that the receipt of interest amounts to income of the assessee from other sources.

Unless there is real income, there cannot be any income tax. The entry that was initially made as interest was reversed the next year because, in fact, the nature of the transaction was changed and the assessee did not receive any real income.

(f) There are liberal deductions for setting up enterprises engaged in developing, maintaining, and operating new infrastructure facilities and power-generating units.

(g) Business losses can be carried forward for 8 years, and unabsorbed depreciation can be carried indefinitely—no carry-back is allowed.

(h) Speculative tax provisions apply to activities carried on by non-residents.

(i) A minimum alternative tax on corporations has been proposed by the Finance Bill, 1996.

(j) Dividends, interest, and long-term capital gain income earned by an infrastructure fund or company from investments in shares or long-term finance in enterprises carrying on the business of developing, monitoring, and operating specified infrastructure facilities or in units of mutual funds involved with the infrastructure of power sector is proposed to be exempted from tax.

Accounting   According to the Companies Act, 1956, accounting must be on an accrual basis. This is also adopted for tax purposes. Dividends are taxed in the year in which they are declared, and capital gains are taxed in the year in which the capital asset is transferred. However, certain deductions, such as statutory dues, bonuses, or commissions to employees, as well as interest on borrowings from public financial institutions, are permitted only on a cash basis. These are allowed if paid within the due date for filing returns. The deductions for contributions to approved retirements funds are permitted only on a cash basis and if they are paid within the specified due dates applicable to the funds.

Inter-company transactions   The inter-company transactions are accorded the same tax treatment as transactions with unrelated parties. However, there are measures to be taken on the following:

(a) In cases of payments to specified related parties, the assessing officer is empowered to disallow as much thereof as is considered excessive or unreasonable with respect to the fair market value, legitimate business needs, and benefits derived.

(b) Where, due to close connection with non-resident, the transaction produces less than ordinary profits to the resident, the assessing officer can substitute reasonable profits for the profits shown.

(c) Where, by design, an income-producing asset is transferred to a non-resident while the resident continues to have power to enjoy the income or obtains the income in the guise of a loan or repayment of a loan, the income may be taxed in the hands of the transferor.

(d) No capital gain or loss is recognized on transfer of capital assets between a company and its 100 per cent subsidiary if the transferee is an Indian company, provided the relationship continues for at least 8 years.

(e) The base for calculating depreciation remains unchanged in the case of transfer of depreciable assets between a company and its 100 per cent subsidiary if the transferee is an Indian company, irrespective of the actual transfer price.

(f) Advances or loans given by a closely held company to its shareholders are treated as dividends. A closely held company is a private company, a company whose shares are not listed on any stock exchange in India or a company with more than 50 per cent, and 60 per cent in the case of manufacturing companies, of whose shares are beneficially held throughout the year by other closely held companies.

Inventory evaluation   All methods of inventory with sound commercial accounting principles are allowed for tax purposes, provided these are adopted consistently at the beginning and end of the accounting periods over the years. In practice, inventory is usually valued at cost or market value, whichever is lower. Reserves for obsolescence cannot be deducted. Obsolete items are usually reflected by lower year-end values where the valuation is lower than the cost and market value.

Capital gains   Short-term capital gains are taxed at the same rate as other income. Long-term gains are taxed at 30 per cent for domestic companies and at 20 per cent for foreign companies. Long-term capital gains income of venture capital funds or venture capital companies from the transfer of equity shares of venture capital undertaking is wholly exempt from taxation. No capital gains tax is assessed on the transfer of assets between a parent company and its wholly owned subsidiary, provided this relationship continues for at least 8 years from the date of transfer and the capital asset is not converted by the transferee company as its stock-in-trade inventory at the time of transfer. In addition, there is no capital gains tax on transfers in cases of specified amalgamations or when buildings, land, and plant and machinery are sold upon the relocation of an industrial undertaking from an urban to a non-urban area if the sale proceeds are reinvested in similar assets in the new area within a specified period. Furthermore, no capital gains tax is imposed on transfers abroad by one non-resident to another of shares or bonds issued abroad by Indian companies under specified schemes or on transfers of shares in Indian companies by one foreign company to another in an amalgamation if at least 25 per cent of the shareholders of the amalgamating company become shareholders of the amalgamated company and the transfer is exempt from capital gains tax in treatment of losses arising on transfer of capital assets.

Interest   Interest is taxable on accrual basis on the following:

(a) By industrial undertakings in India on borrowings from approved foreign financial institutions.

(b) At approved rates on debts incurred in a foreign country for purchase outside India of raw materials or machinery and equipment.

(c) On approved foreign currency loans from sources outside India.

(d) Payable by Indian financial institutions or banks at approved rates on borrowing from foreign sources.

(e) Any other interest from foreign borrowings where the funds are utilized in a business in India is subject to tax. A lower tax rate of 10 per cent applies to interest on bonds issued abroad by Indian companies under approved schemes.

Inter-company dividends   A domestic company receiving dividends from another domestic company is entitled to deduct them when computing its taxable income, to the extent covered by the dividends it distributes to its own shareholders before the due date for filing its returns. Dividends received by foreign companies from Indian companies are taxed at 20 per cent or a lower treaty rate. A lower tax rate of 10 per cent applies to dividends in certain cases. Dividends received by a venture capital funds or company from venture capital undertakings are wholly exempt from taxation.

Royalties and service fees   Royalties and fees for technical services received by Indian companies from Indian concerns are taxable in full. However, 50 per cent of royalties and fees for technical services received by Indian companies and other residents in convertible foreign exchange from foreign governments or foreign concerns are exempt from tax.

Non-taxable incomes of companies   Some of the incomes of companies that are not taxed are as follows:
(a) Interest on tax-free bonds
(b) Agricultural income, other than that taxed by the states
(c) Payments made by Indian companies engaged in the business of operation of aircraft to a foreign enterprise, provided the agreement is approved by the Central Government
(d) Subsidies received by tea, rubber, coffee, and cardamom companies from their boards for re-plantation, replacement, rejuvenation, or consolidation
(e) Income of non-resident companies, non-resident news agencies shooting cinematographic films in India and not having an Indian shareholder
(f) Profits from a new industrial undertaking setup in SEZ, IT parks, and 100 per cent export-oriented companies for five consecutive years

Business expenses   All business expenses are deductible if they are laid out or expended wholly and exclusively for the purpose of the business, provided they are not of capital nature or that they are not personal expenses.

Conclusion

One of the main characteristics of the Indian taxation system is that it has covered all the bases of indirect tax comprehensively, resulting in very high taxes. Corporations have to disburse large amounts of money to the CBEC. In the beginning, before the Income Tax Act, 1961, a company was required to pay income tax on behalf of the shareholders on dividends paid to them, and each shareholder got a credit to this effect. Since 1961, companies have been treated as independent entities and shareholders are not given any credit. There was a steady development in the method of corporate taxation. This will be considered in the next section 'Other Major Laws of Taxation'.

20.4   OTHER MAJOR LAWS OF TAXATION

MANAGER'S TAKEAWAY

- Unless there is real income, there cannot be any income tax.
- Lower taxes cause less corruption; higher taxes cause revolution.

1944	Central Excise Act
1947	Business Profits Tax Act
1948	Capital Gains Act
1949	Professions Limitation Act
1953	Estate Duty Act
1956	Central Sales Act
1956	Central Sales Tax Act
1956	Sales Tax Laws Validation Act
1957	Wealth Tax Act, which has a regular history of being passed and repealed
1958	Gift Tax (provisions have ceased since 1 October 1998)
1961	Voluntary Surrender of Salaries (exemption from taxation) Act
1962	Customs Act
1964	Companies (profits) Surtax Act
1964	Taxation Laws (Continuation and Validation of Recovery Proceedings Act)
1969	Central Sales Tax (amendment)
1974	Interest Tax Act
1980	Hotel Receipts Tax Act
1986	Taxation Laws (amendment and miscellaneous provisions) Act
1987	Expenditure Act
1987	Expenditure Tax Act
1989	Direct Tax Laws (amendment) Act
1992	Cess and Other Taxes on Minerals (validation) Act
1992	Cess and Other Taxes on Minerals (validation) Act
1994	Service Tax, imposed under Finance Act,
2000	Direct Tax Laws (Miscellaneous) Repeal Act
2002	Foreign Aircraft (exemption from taxes and duties on fuel and lubricants) Act
2005	National Tax Tribunal Act
1995	Transaction Tax Act (in the Income Tax Act)
2005	Central Value Added Tax Act

Objective

The objective of listing all these Acts is to impress upon you the length and breadth, the complexity and difficulty of dealing with the laws of indirect taxation. Furthermore, there are statutory authorities behind each of these Acts to implement them, who further issue rules, regulations, and circulars. There is an almost equal amount of state legislation, which brings forth the problems managers have to face in the area of excise, customs, sales tax, VAT, etc. To illustrate the complexity of the tax problem, here is a short note on VAT, which is implemented both at the central level—Central Value Added Tax (CENVAT) and Modified Value Added Tax (MODVAT)—and at the state level—every state of India has introduced it.

Value Added Tax

Value added tax (VAT) was introduced in 1999; it came into effect on 1 April 2005. It was supposed to have been implemented at least a decade before to adjust to the logistics of economic reforms and market liberalization. Road blocks, mostly of political nature, were insurmountable. Now despite VAT being there for more than half a decade, problems even now remain insurmountable.

Concept Value added tax is a rationalized taxation system. It is a multi-point sales tax with credit or set-off for tax paid on purchases. It is basically a tax on the value addition on the product. The burden of tax is ultimately born by the consumer of goods. In many aspects, it is equivalent to the last point on sales tax. It can also be called a multi-point sales tax levied as a proportion of valued added.

The advantage of this form of taxation is that a set-off is given for input tax as well as for tax paid on previous purchases. Other taxes such as turnover tax and surcharge tax are eliminated.

Central Sales Tax Act, 1956 Rationalization would imply a logical end to the Central Sales Tax, but it is not so. So would it cause double taxation? The answer is in the affirmative. In other words the central sales tax paid by a businessman will not be allowed to be set off against the local output tax payable. The problem with the central sales tax system is that it is highly complex with multiplicity of rates and too many details to be absorbed. It is hoped that gradually it will be repealed and states would be paid compensation for their losses.

State value added tax All the states have drafted their own separate VAT Act and as per the current situation, every state has a separate VAT Act with different provisions not corresponding with each other.

Manufacturer The manufacturer purchases raw material after paying full tax on the rate applicable on such material. The input tax suffered by him would be adjusted or set off from the sale of the finished product. The tax adjustment of input credit of the goods purchased within the state would be available on the sales made within the state and also on the inter-state sales subject to the tax payable.

Trader The trader is required to collect tax on the sales made by him and the tax liability would be set off or adjusted from the purchase or input tax credit of the goods locally purchased in that state.

Issue of invoice The issue of invoice is mandatory. No set-off or input credit would be allowed unless the original tax invoice is produced, wherein tax is clearly charged separately in the invoice.

Accounting The basic account books required for the purpose of the VAT Act are Purchase and Sale Register, which form the basis for the calculation of tax payment. The assessee would be required to enter the value of goods in the goods account and the amount of tax in the tax account separately.

Capital goods   Set-off is available on the tax-paid goods at the time of purchase of capital goods under the VAT Act.

Export   Export would be zero rated. Tax paid on raw material used in the manufacture of goods for export is to be refunded by the state government.

Registration   All importers, manufacturers, exporters, and dealers are required to seek mandatory registration under the new VAT Act.

Audit of account   Every dealer having a turnover of over ₹40 lakh is required to get the account audited by a chartered accountant and submit the audit report within the stipulated time. Failure to do so would attract penalty proceedings.

Penalties   Penalties for failure to register, file return, pay tax when due, failure to maintain records, for making misstatements, etc., attract a fixed sum of money (as the case may be in each state) and a certain percentage per annum as may be specified by the government.

Conclusion

VAT must be understood as tax payable on the amount of value added to goods purchased or service rendered or manufactured for sale. It is calculated after deducting the amount of tax paid on purchases admissible for input tax credit from the tax levied on sale price. To claim input tax credit purchases must be supported by tax invoice, where the tax element must be shown separately.

The Central Sales Tax Act, 1956, was operated under multiplicity of rates. The entire system was cumbersome—from assessments to verifications—which paved opportunities for corruption. VAT is supposed to overcome these problems. Credit or set-off is given for tax paid on eligible purchases. The system is oriented to be transparent, accountable, and efficient. It is dealer friendly only if the dealer assesses himself honestly and maintains correct records. The onus of tax administration is on the government, who can use computer technology to cross-check and balance fraud, such as bogus invoices.

MANAGER'S TAKEAWAY

Generally the government accepts one's declaration on taxable income.
• Maintenance of records of business transactions is the major step to prevent taxation problems.

Service Tax

Case 20.4 discusses service tax, which also comes under VAT.

CASE 20.4   Appellant: Coca Cola and others   vs   Respondent: The Commissioner of Central Excise

Date of Judgement: 26 August 2009*

Facts: The appeal was admitted on the following questions:

(a) Whether services of advertising and marketing procured by the appellants in respect of advertisements for aerated waters are covered by the definition of the

*Coca cola vs Central Commissioner of Excise; see http://www.indiankanoon.org/doc/1796997/.

Contd

Case 20.4 *Contd*

words 'input services' as defined in Rule 2(1) of the CENVAT Credit Rules, 2004, when admittedly the appellants manufacture concentrates exclusively used for the manufacture of the respective aerated waters advertised by the appellants?

(b) Whether the advertisement or sales promotion of aerated waters undertaken by the manufacturer of concentrate is covered by the inclusive part of the definition of 'input service' contained in Rule 2(1) of the CENVAT Credit Rules, 2004? What has to be established in the present appeal is whether the appellants, who are manufacturers of non-alcoholic beverage bases (concentrates), are eligible to avail credit of the service-tax paid on advertising services, sales promotion, market research, and the like availed by them and utilize such credit towards payment of excise duty on the concentrate. As of now judicially recognized, service tax is VAT which, in turn, is destination-based consumption tax in a sense that it is on commercial activities and is not a charge on the business but on the consumer. Just as excise duty is a tax on value addition on goods, service tax is on the value addition by rendition of service.

JUDGEMENT: The Orders of the Excise Commissioner and Tribunal set aside.

REASON: The credit is availed on the tax paid on the input service, which is advertisement and not on the contents of the advertisement. Thus, it is not necessary that the contents of the advertisement must be that of the final product manufactured by the person advertising, as long as the manufacturer can show that the advertisement services availed have an effect of or impact on the manufacture of the final product and establish the relationship between the input service and the manufacture of the final product. The manufacturer thereby can avail the credit of the service tax paid by him. Once the cost incurred by the service has to be added to the cost, and is so assessed, it is recognition by revenue of the advertisement services having a connection with the manufacture of the final product. This test will also apply in the case of sales promotion.

Having thus arrived at the conclusion on the meaning of the expression of input services and that a manufacturer can avail of the credit of the service tax paid by him for payment of CENVAT duty, the question referred for our consideration will have to be answered as follows:

(a) The question is answered in the affirmative in favour of the assessee and against revenue and question.

(b) The question again answered in the affirmative in favour of the assessee and against revenue.

In the light of the above, the impugned order of the Commissioner, Central Excise, Bombay III dated 31 July 2006 and the order of the tribunal dated 16 April 2007 are set aside, the matter is restored to the file of the Commissioner, Central Excise to pass appropriate order in the light of what was set out in the judgement.

SUMMARY

- No tax shall be levied or collected except by authority of law. The Indian Constitution has a well-developed system of taxation for the central, state, and local authorities to execute. The Central Board of Revenue Act, 1963, established the taxation authority, which is executed by the departments of the Ministry of Finance. The department is headed by the Secretary of Revenue, which exercises control over both direct and indirect taxes and their respective agencies, i.e., CBDT and CBEC, respectively. Each of these boards is headed by its respective chairpersons; these are the ex-officio Special Secretaries to the Government of India.

- Income Tax Act, 1961, is the governing act for taxation in India. It is augmented annually by the Finance Act passed through the introduction of the budgetary bill. The tax is direct and indirect, which is charged to persons and corporations. Income tax rates vary, depending on proposals in the financial statement or budget, which when passed becomes law. Corporate taxation concerns companies.

EXERCISES

(i) You have received x sum of money as dividend on equity fund. Do you have to pay tax on it?
Hint: Yes, @ 5 per cent for funds bought after 2012.

(ii) You have taken housing loan and the house is still being built and you are paying your EMIs amounting to ₹1.5 lakh. Do you get emption from tax?
Hint: No. The exemption comes into play only when the construction is paid for.

(iii) Suresh is a trader who was shocked to receive a notice from the Income Tax Office to pay 'professional tax'.
Hint: The professional tax is a State matter and it has slabs as per earnings per month and the tax is charged as per month as may be fixed by the State.

(iv) Illustrate with examples the system of taxation.

(v) Discuss the various aspects of corporate taxation.

DEVELOPMENT OF LEGAL EDGE

Project—State VAT

Objective   To understand the VAT system and its implementation in your state.

Usefulness   It will be useful to both traders and manufacturers in your state.

Nature of work   Produce a 30–50 page VAT manual

Training   Organize in your town or city a VAT training day for traders.

(It is a good business proposition to print the manual and sell it in your state.)

FURTHER READING

Book
- Girish Ahuja and Ravi Gupta, *Concise Commentary on Income Tax, 12th edn*, Bharat Law House Pvt. Ltd, 2011.

Acts
- Central Board of Revenue Act, 1963.
- Income Tax Act, 1961.
- Any of the relevant laws on taxation.

Web resources
- http://incometaxindia.gov.in.
- http://www.cbec.gov.in.
- http://finmin.nic.in/.

For commentary and further information
- http://www.nishithdesai.com/Research-Papers.
- http://law.incometaxindia.gov.in/DIT/.

CASE STUDY NEXUS FOR GLOBAL PROFIT

Economic nexus is an important aspect of the principle of Attribution of Profits.[4]

Introduction

This case, Director of Income Tax (international taxation) Mumbai vs Morgan Stanley and Co, has been considered as a landmark judgement because it clarified pestering issues in the new economy such as: the status of Permanent Establishment (PE) concerning non-resident overseas companies, Transfer Pricing, Attribution of Profits, and Double Taxation.

By clearly identifying a distinction between *stewardship* and *deputation,* it laid to rest the uncertainty that the mere existence of a fixed place of business is not enough to prove the PE of a non-resident company from overseas. Once such a status is decided, issues regarding transfer pricing, attribution of profits, and taxation are resolved by the applicable laws.

Terms to Understand the Case

Arm's length transaction It is a transaction in which the buyers and sellers of a product act independently and have no relationship to each other. It ensures that both parties in the deal act in their own self-interest and are not subject to any pressure or duress from the other party. It is quite illustrative in the real estate market. When determining the fair market value of a piece of property, the price for the property must be obtained through a potential buyer and seller operating through an arm's length transaction; otherwise, the agreed-upon price will likely differ from the actual fair market value of the property This contrasts with a situation in which the two parties are not strangers. For example, it is unlikely that the same transaction involving a father and his son would yield the same result, because the father may choose to give his son a discount. In short, arm's length implies neutrality and impartiality in a transaction.

Attribution of profits The taxation of intra-company dealings.

Permanent establishment (PE) It is a fixed place of business that generally gives rise to income or VAT liability in a particular jurisdiction. The terms of reference are mentioned in income tax treaties between countries. PE is characterized by a fixed place of business with a fixed geographic point and all the normal facilities of a normal enterprise. The essential characteristic of PE is that it gives rise to payment of income tax—anything else is unrelated to the concept of PE.

Tax treaty It is a bilateral agreement between two countries to resolve issues involving double taxation of active or passive income. The rate of tax is fixed as per the terms of reference in the treaty. Normally it is done on the basis of policy on withholding taxes. Example: Two countries may agree to a withholding tax on dividends of 10 per cent, each one of them reciprocating it by the agreed percentage.

Double taxation It is a taxation principle referring to income taxes that are paid twice on the same source of earned income. It occurs because corporations are considered separate legal entities from their shareholders. As such, corporations pay taxes on their annual earnings, just as individuals do. When corporations pay out dividends to shareholders, those dividend payments incur incometax liabilities for the shareholders who receive them, even though the earnings that provided the cash to pay the dividends were already taxed at the corporate level. Tax treaties avoid double taxation—Double Tax Avoidance Agreement (DTAA).

Transfer price It takes place when divisions of a company transact with each other. Transactions may be trade or services of labour between different departments. Transfer of prices is used when individual entities of larger multi-entity firms are treated and measured as separately run entities. In managerial accounting, when different divisions of a multi-entity company are in charge

---

[4]Principle upon which the Supreme Court judgement of Director of Income Tax (International) Mumbai vs Morgan Stanley & Co is based by Justices A. Pasayat and S. Kapadia (9 July 2007).

of their own profits, they are also responsible for their own *Return on Invested Capital*. Hence, when divisions are required to transact with each other, a transfer price is used to determine costs. Transfer prices tend not to differ much from the price in the market because one of the entities in such a transaction will lose out. They will either be buying for more than the prevailing market price or selling below the market price, thereby affecting their performance.

Before the Supreme Court of India

Bench: Justice Arijit Pasayat and Justice S. Kapadia
Petitioner: Director of Income Tax (International Taxation), Mumbai
vs
Respondent: Morgan Stanley & Co. Inc.[5]
Date: 9 July 2007

The Issue

We are concerned with the articles in DTAA between India and the United States, which have implication on transfer pricing legislation. The said treaty either advocates application of arm's length principle or provides a mechanism for avoiding double taxation on income.

Morgan Stanley Group, the Petitioner

Morgan Stanley Group (MS Group) is one of the world's largest diversifying financial services companies. It is a world-wide leader in investment banking and it is ranked amongst the top institutions in merger and acquisitions, underwriting of equity and related transactions. It has a major presence in major securities market, with traders in numerous countries around the world offering a unique distribution of products. It has three main lines of business, namely securities investment management, investment banking, and credit services. Morgan Stanley and Company (MSCo) is an investment bank engaged in the business of providing financial advisory services, corporate lending, and securities underwriting. One of the group companies of Morgan Stanley, Morgan Stanley Advantages Services Pvt. Ltd (MSAS), entered into an agreement for providing certain support services to MSCo. Morgan Stanley and Company outsourced

some of its activities to MSAS. The said MSAS was set up to support the main office functions in equity and fixed income research, account reconciliation, and providing IT-enabled services such as back office operation, data processing, and support centre to MSCo.

On 19 May 2005, MSCo (applicant) filed its advance ruling application in Form 34-C inviting its advance ruling. The basic question relating to the transaction between the applicant and MSAS on which advance ruling was sought was two-fold, namely whether the applicant had a PE in India under Article 5(1) of DTAA on account of the services rendered by MSAS under the Services Agreement dated 14 April 2005 entered into by MSAS with the applicant and, if so, the amount of income attributable to such PE.

Department of Income Tax

According to the Department, the applicant should be regarded as having a fixed place in India under Article 5(1) as the applicant proposes to carry on its business through MSAS in India. According to the Department, MSAS was the PE of MSCo in India. They had a fixed place of business in Mumbai. According to the Department, the nature of the activities proposed to be performed by MSAS in Mumbai indicated that the said company represented the business presence of MSCo in India. The Department also submitted that MSAS legally and financially dependedon the applicant and consequently MSAS constituted an agency PE of the applicant under Article 5(4) of DTAA.

Authority's Ruling Challenged

By the impugned ruling delivered on 13 February 2006 by the Authority for Advance Ruling (AAR) it was held, *inter alia*, that the applicant cannot be regarded as having a fixed place of business PE under Article 5(1) of DTAA; that MSAS cannot be regarded as an agency PE under Article 5(4) of DTAA; and that the applicant would be regarded as having a PE in India under Article 5(2)(l) if it were to send some of its employees to India as stewards or as deputationists in the employment of MSAS. It is against this ruling of the AAR that the applicant and the department came to this court in appeal by way of special leave petition.

---

[5]The case is an abridgment of the full judgement see link: indiankanoon.org/doc/584977/ (22 October 2011); for a short and good commentary see http://www.nishithdesai.com/Research-Papers/WTDBAJT.pdf.

Legal Basis—Articles 5 and 7 of DTAA[6]

Article 5—*Permanent establishment (PE)*

It is a fixed place of business through which the business of an enterprise, wholly or partly, is carried out. It includes physical place, building, factory, office management, and all those things, people, operations, and services that an enterprise in the normal course of business possesses.

The fact that a company that is a resident of a contracting state controls or is controlled by a company that is a resident of the other contracting state, or that carries on business in that other state (whether through a PE or otherwise), shall not of itself constitute either company a PE of the other.

Article 7—**Business profits**

The profits of an enterprise of a contracting state shall be taxable only in that state unless the enterprise carries on business in the other contracting state through a PE situated therein. If the enterprise carries on business as aforesaid, the profits of the enterprise may be taxed in the other state but only so much of them as is attributable to:

(a) that PE;

(b) sales in the other state of goods or merchandise of the same or similar kind as those sold through that PE; or

(c) other business activities carried on in the other state of the same or similar kind as those effected through that PE.

When determining the profits of a PE, expenses that are incurred for the purposes of the business of the PE shall be allowed as deductions, including a reasonable allocation of executive and general administrative expenses, research and development expenses, interest and other expenses, incurred for the purposes of the enterprise as a whole (or the part thereof, which includes the PE), whether incurred in the state in which the PE is situated or elsewhere, in accordance with the provisions of and subject to the limitations of the taxation laws of that state. However, no such deduction shall be allowed in respect of amounts, if any, paid (otherwise than towards reimbursement of actual expenses) by the PE to the head office of the enterprise or any of its other offices, by way of royalties, fees, or other similar payments in return for the use of patents, know-how, or other rights, or by way of commission or other charges for specific services performed or for management, or except in the case of banking enterprise, by way of interest on money lent to the PE.

Analysis

The concept of PE was introduced in the 1961 Act as part of the statutory provisions of transfer pricing by the Finance Act of 2001. In Sec. 92-F (iii) the word 'enterprise' is defined to mean 'a person including a PE of such person who is proposed to be engaged in any activity relating to the production.' Under the CBDT circular No.14 of 2001 it has been clarified that the term PE has not been defined in the Act but its meaning may be understood with reference to the DTAA entered into by India. Thus, the intention was to rely on the concept and definition of PE in the DTAA. However, vide Finance Act, 2002, the definition of PE was included in the Income Tax Act, 1961 (IT. Act) vide Sec. 92-F (iiia), which states that the PE shall include a fixed place of business through which the business of the MNE is wholly or partly carried on. This is where the difference lies between the definition of the word PE in the inclusive sense under the IT Act as against the definition of the word PE in the exhaustive sense under DTAA. This analysis is important because it indicates the intention of the Parliament in adopting an inclusive definition of PE so as to cover service PE, agency PE, software PE, Construction PE, etc.

Stewardship activity

However, the question that arises for determination in the present case is the nature of activities performed by stewards and deputationists deployed by MSCo to work in India as employees of MSAS. Under Article 5(2)(l), furnishing of services through a fixed place in India can constitute a PE. The AAR in the impugned ruling has held that the stewards and deputationists are proposed to be sent by the MSCo from the USA. According to the AAR there is a flow of service from MSCo to MSAS when the former deputes its own employees to work in India in MSAS. Therefore, according to the AAR the service agreement between MSCo and MSAS dated 14 April 2005 would fall under Article 5(2)(l) and consequently the transfer pricing regulation would apply for evaluating the charges payable by MSCo

---

[6]The case is an abridgment of the full judgement see link: indiankanoon.org/doc/584977/ (22 October 2011); for a short and good commentary see http:// www.nishithdesai.com/Research-Papers/WTDBAJT.pdf.

to MSAS in India for such service contract. This ruling has been challenged by the applicant.

Article 5(2)(l) of DTAA applies in cases where MNE furnishes services within India and those services are furnished through its employees. In the present case we are concerned with two activities, namely stewardship activities and the work to be performed by deputationists in India as employees of MSAS. A customer like MSCo who has world-wide operations is entitled to insist on quality control and confidentiality from the service provider. For example in the case of software PE a server stores the data that may require confidentiality. A service provider may also be required to act according to the quality-control specifications imposed by its customer. It may be required to maintain confidentiality. Stewardship activities involve briefing of the MSAS staff to ensure that the output meets the requirements of MSCo. These activities include monitoring of the outsourcing operations at MSAS. The objective is to protect the interest of MSCo. These stewards are not involved in day-to-day management or in any specific services to be undertaken by MSAS. The stewardship activity basically protects the interest of the customer. In the present case as held hereinabove, MSAS is a service PE. It is in a sense a service provider. A customer is entitled to protect its interest in terms of both confidentiality and quality control. In such a case it cannot be said that MSCo has been rendering the services to MSAS. In our view MSCo is merely protecting its own interests in the competitive world by ensuring the quality and confidentiality of MSAS services. We do not agree with the ruling of the AAR that the stewardship activity would fall under Article 5(2)(l). To this extent we find merit in the civil appeal filed by the appellant (MSCo) and accordingly its appeal to that extent stands partly allowed.

Deputation activity

As regards the question of deputation, we are of the view that an employee of MSCo when deputed to MSAS does not become an employee of MSAS. A deputationist has a lien on his employment with MSCo. As long as the lien remains with MSCo, the said company retains control over the deputationist's terms and employment. The concept of a service PE finds place in the U.N. Convention. It is constituted if the multinational enterprise renders services through its employees in India provided the services are rendered for a specified period. In this case, it extends to

2 years on the request of MSAS. It is important to note that where the activities of the multinational enterprise entails it being responsible for the work of deputationists and the employees continue to be on the payroll of the multinational enterprise or they continue to have their lien on their jobs with the multinational enterprise, a service PE can emerge. Applying the above tests to the facts of this case shows that on request/requisition from MSAS the applicant deputes its staff. The request comes from MSAS depending upon its requirement. Generally, occasions do arise when MSAS needs the expertise of the staff of MSCo. In such circumstances, generally, MSAS makes a request to MSCo. A deputationist under such circumstances is expected to be experienced in banking and finance. On completion of his tenure he is repatriated to his parent job. He retains his lien when he comes to India. He lends his experience to MSAS in India as an employee of MSCo as he retains his lien and in that sense there is a service PE (MSAS) under Article 5(2)(l). We find no infirmity in the ruling of ARR on this aspect. In the above situation, MSCo is rendering services through its employees to MSAS. Therefore, the department is right in its contention that under the above situation there exists a Service PE in India (MSAS). Accordingly, the civil appeal filed by the department stands partly allowed.

Profit attribution

An important question that arises for determination is whether AAR is right in its ruling when it says that once the transfer pricing analysis is undertaken there is no further need to attribute profits to a PE. Computation of income arising from international transactions has to be done keeping in mind the principle of arm's length price. Charges paid or payable by MSCo to MSAS under the service contract have to be accounted as income at arm's length price. There are different methods for determining appropriate transfer pricing. Under Sec. 92C(1) of the IT Act, arm's length price in relation to international transaction has to be determined by any of the following methods:

(a) Comparable Uncontrolled Price Method;
(b) Resale Price Method;
(c) Cost Plus Method;
(d) Profit Split Method;
(e) Transactional Net Margin Method; and
(f) Such other method as may be prescribed by CBDT.

Conclusions from the Analysis

Under the impugned ruling delivered by AAR, remuneration to MSAS was justified by a transfer pricing analysis and, therefore, no further income could be attributed to the PE(MSAS). In other words, the said ruling equates an arm's length analysis with attribution of profits. It holds that once a transfer pricing analysis is undertaken; there is no further need to attribute profits to a PE. The impugned ruling is correct in principle insofar as an associated enterprise, which also constitutes a PE, has been remunerated on an arm's length basis taking into account all the risk-taking functions of the enterprise. In such cases nothing further would be left to be attributed to the PE. The situation would be different if transfer pricing analysis does not adequately reflect the functions performed and the risks assumed by the enterprise. In such a situation, there would be a need to attribute profits to the PE for those functions/risks that have not been considered. Therefore, in each case the data placed by the taxpayer has to be examined as to whether the transfer pricing analysis placed by the taxpayer is exhaustive of attribution of profits and that would depend on the functional and factual analyses to be undertaken in each case. Lastly, it may be added that taxing corporates on the basis of the concept of Economic Nexus is an important feature of Attributable Profits (profits attributable to the PE).

Judgement

To conclude, we hold that the AAR was right in ruling that MSAS would be a Service PE in India under Article 5(2)(l), though only on account of the services to be performed by the deputationists deployed by MSCo and not on account of stewardship activities.

As regards income attributable to the PE (MSAS) we hold that the Transactional Net Margin Method was the appropriate method for determination of the arm's length price in respect of transaction between MSCo and MSAS. We accept as correct the computation of the remuneration based on cost plus mark-up worked out at 29 per cent on the operating costs of MSAS. This position is also accepted by the Assessing Officer in his order dated 29 December 2006 (after the impugned ruling) and also by the transfer pricing officer vide order dated 22 September 2006.

As regards attribution of further profits to the PE of MSCo where the transaction between the two are held to be at arm's length, we hold that the ruling is correct in principle provided that an associated enterprise (that also constitutes a PE) is remunerated on arm's length basis taking into account all the risk-taking functions of the multinational enterprise. In such a case nothing further would be left to attribute to the PE. The situation would be different if the transfer pricing analysis does not adequately reflect the functions performed and the risks assumed by the enterprise. In such a case, there would be need to attribute profits to the PE for those functions/risks that have not been considered.

The entire exercise ultimately is to ascertain whether the service charges payable or paid to the service provider (MSAS in this case) completely represents the value of the profit attributable to his service. In this connection, the department has also to examine whether the PE has obtained services from the multinational enterprise at lower than the arm's length cost. Therefore, the department has to determine income, expense, or cost allocations with regard to arm's length prices to decide the applicability of the transfer pricing regulations.

Economic nexus is an important aspect of the principle of attribution of profits[7]

In the light of the above discussion, the impugned ruling by AAR stands modified to the extent indicated hereinabove. Accordingly, both the civil appeals filed by the applicant (MSCo) and by the department are partly allowed.

Landmark in Case Law

The judgement by the two renowned justices of the Supreme Court has been acclaimed as the landmark judgement in the complex taxation world. The distinction made between stewardship and deputation (see Figure 20.4) will go a long way to clear hundreds of cases that have great international bearing due to the tax treaties involved. Furthermore, it is a positive step in integrating the global business.

Before the Supreme Court's decision in the Morgan Stanley case, despite the fact that transactions were concluded on an arm's length basis, the income attributable to the Indian PE was still uncertain since the tax authorities

---

[7]Author's emphasis.

could go beyond the arm's length consideration attributable to an Indian PE. The Supreme Court has put this to rest.

Discussion Questions

1. Point out very clearly the facts of the case and illuminate the main issues.
2. Upon what grounds did the Supreme Court of India view the issues?
3. Discuss PE within the legal framework of DTAA.
4. Explain Transfer Pricing as affecting this case.
5. How did the Supreme Court consider the Attribution of Profits?
6. Analyse the distinction made by the Supreme Court between stewardship and deputation.
7. What benefits did parties to the case acquire after the judgement?

Going Beyond

1. Delineate the legal reasoning of the Supreme Court of India in the above case.
2. How can the distinction Stewardship and Deputation solve the problems of Attribution of Profit and avoid Double Taxation?
3. How can BPOs benefit from the above judgement?

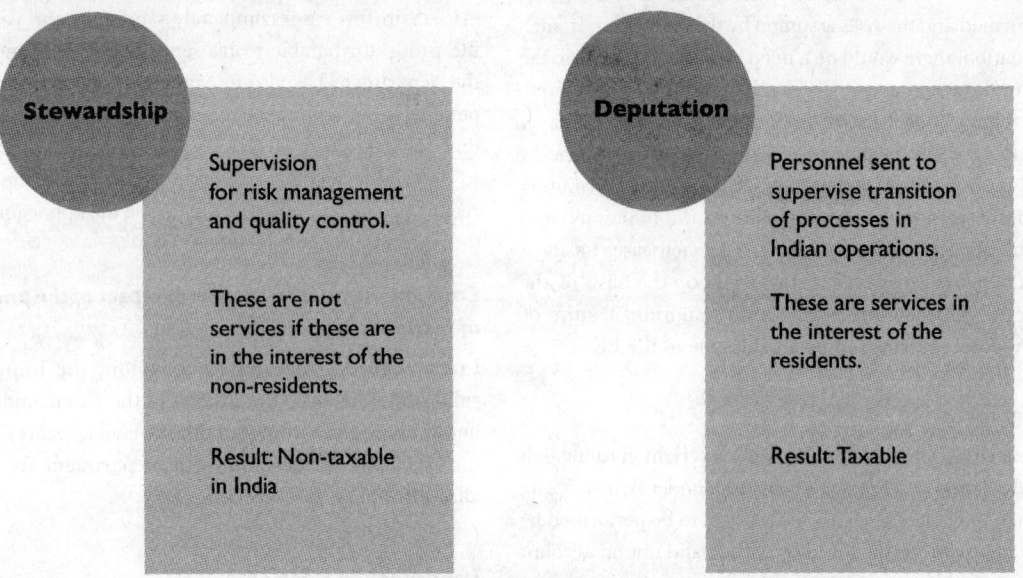

Figure 20.4   Status of the PE in India

LEGAL LUMINARY

PRANAB MUKHERJEE—MONEY MATTERS MOST

If one were to seek all the knowledge, skills, and experience of a manager in one person, it would be Pranab Mukherjee, the President of India. His forte: decision-making. His ability: negotiation. His USP: reach across political and ideological boundaries.

Pranab Mukherjee is an alumnus of Calcutta University, where he obtained master's degrees in history and political science and also earned his LLB. He joined a college in Birbhum district as a lecturer. For a short while, he entered journalism and worked for *Desher Dak*, a well-known Bengali publication. From being a social worker and a journalist, he was nominated to the Rajya Sabha by the Congress Party in 1969. In 1973, he became Minister of State for Industrial Development. Ever since, he has been a regular member of the Congress Party government.*

He was just 47 years when he was made the Minister for Finance in 1982 in Mrs Indira Gandhi's cabinet. The magazine *Euromoney* rated him as the best Finance Minister. Narasimha Rao, the economic reformer prime minister, appointed him as the Vice Chairman of the Planning Commission and later as Minister for External Affairs. In 2004 he became the leader of the House in Lok Sabha, in 2006 the Minister for External Affairs, and in 2009 again the Minister of Finance, Government of India.**

India's Civil Nuclear Agreement with the USA has been attributed to his negotiating skills. Only the signatories to Nuclear Non-Proliferation Treaty could have such an agreement. India is not a signatory to this organization. He exercised his considerable abilities in the formation of the Intellectual Property Rights Act as well as the National Rural Employment Guarantee Act.

Pronob Kumar Mukho padhyaya—his name in Bengali—was born in 1935. His father, Kamda Kinkar Mukherjee, was on the highest decision-making body, the All India Congress Committee (AICC); he was a member of the Legislative Council and President of District Birbhum in West Bengal. His mother's name was Rajlakshmi Mukherjee. Pranab Da, as he is popularly known in Bengal, is married to Suvra Mukherjee. They have three children. He loves Rabindra Sangeet and, for a man who has very little time to spare, gardening is his hobby.

---

*See http://www.pranabmukherjee.in/ (22 October 2011).

**For all the details of positions he held, see http://india.gov.in/govt/loksabhampbiodata.php?mpcode=4195 (22 October 2011).

The Laws of Foreign Exchange and Prevention of Money Laundering

Principle: *Usus est dominium fiduciarium.*
Use is a fiduciary domain.

CHAPTER OUTLINE

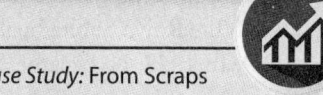

- Introduction and Interpretation
- Foreign Exchange Management Act, 1999
- Prevention of Money Laundering Act, 2002
- *Case Study:* From Scraps to Swiss Banks
- *Legal Luminary:* Savak Sohrab Tarapore

21.1 INTRODUCTION AND INTERPRETATION

An Act to consolidate and amend the law relating to foreign exchange with the objective of facilitating external trade and payments and for promoting orderly development and maintenance of foreign exchange market in India

– Foreign Exchange Management Act, 1999 Preamble

It shall also apply to all branches, offices and agencies outside India owned or controlled by a person resident in India and also to any contravention there under committed outside India by any person to whom this Act applies

– Foreign Exchange Management Act, 1999, Sec. 1(3)

Scope

The scope of this chapter is to acquaint you with two Acts: Foreign Exchange Management Act, 1999 and Prevention of Money Laundering Act, 2002 (PMLA). Both these Acts come under the Directorate of Enforcement under the Ministry of Finance, Department of Revenue. The foreign exchange market is a global monetary market, volatile in character. So it demonstrates a very high risk factor. Another essential feature is that foreign exchange involves currencies, debts, loans, and other financial instruments beyond the borders of a country. Therefore, the issue is concerned with sovereign rights of the nations and their rights over their currencies.

In 1989, a group of countries formed an inter-governmental organization that eventually came to be known as the Financial Action Task Force (FATF) with its headquarters in Paris, France. The membership of this group has steadily increased with over forty countries being signatories. Today, India is one of them. The purpose of FATF is three-fold:

(a) Strengthen the international banking system
(b) Combat money laundering
(c) Put an end to terrorist financing

Further, the United Nations in its General Assembly in 1998 urged its member states to legislate laws against money laundering. With this background, India too brought in legislation for the prevention of money laundering in 2002.

Foreign Exchange Act, 1999

Foreign Exchange Act, 1999 (FEMA) has replaced the Foreign Exchange Regulation Act, 1974 (FERA). FERA was a preventive Act and hence carried criminal liabilities. It succeeded in merely listing offences and criminal liabilities. Due to its negative perspective, it was considered draconian. With the economic liberalization of India, such exigency of criminal liability became redundant; therefore, a new law was needed to manage foreign exchange and fix liability for civil offences. The preamble of the Act amply demonstrates that intent when it states its objective as to facilitate trade, manage payments, and promote development of foreign exchange market in India.

FEMA has a positive perspective and seeks to make foreign trade transactions easier. The language of the Act itself changed from *regulation* to *manage*. The business of foreign exchange involves buying and selling of currencies and debt instruments by individuals, businesses, and governments. It is the world's largest *liquid* market. The global market situations are extremely volatile and the fluctuations in rates of exchange are in a constant flux. In other words, the market risk is the highest in the global money market. The need for a very high quality of management is an absolute imperative. The central bank of each country is endowed with the management responsibility. In India, the Reserve Bank of India (RBI) develops mechanisms for managing foreign exchange. One of the most important mechanisms is the convertibility of the Indian rupee on current account and capital account.

Main Feature—Mechanism for Convertibility of the Indian Rupee

All the exchange transactions depend on one single feature of the Act: the convertibility of the Indian rupee, which is distinguished as convertibility on current account and convertibility on capital account. The Reserve Bank of India manages all the mechanisms of foreign exchange. (Table 21.1).

India has full convertibility of the Indian rupee on current account, whereas only partial convertibility on capital account. The RBI set a committee under the former RBI Governor S.S. Tarapore to review the aspect of capital account convertibility. This was mainly to cater to the need of foreign investment. It addressed the comprehensive tasks as follows:

Table 21.1 Mechanisms of foreign exchange

Current account	Capital account
Allows free inflow and outflow of currency for following purposes: • Buy and sell currency • Pay and receive payment for import and export of goods and services • Utilize exchange for travel, studies, health treatments, gifts, etc.	It allows converting local financial assets into foreign financial assets and vice versa at the market-determined rates of exchange. All the developed countries have it as it is desirable for a globalized free trade. The RBI has certain restrictions in place to safeguard the country's economic interests to avoid disadvantages that could occur due to a free-flow system. The restrictions of convertibility on capital account are reviewed regularly as follows: • Remittances from NRIs • Foreign investments, etc. The incoming money is allowed. The following are the restrictions on outflow of money: • Foreign establishments wanting to repatriate funds • Individuals and companies taking funding abroad above a certain limit

1. To review the extant regulations that straddle current and capital accounts, especially when items in one account have implication for the other account and to iron out the inconsistencies in such regulations
2. To examine existing repatriation/surrender requirements in the context of current account convertibility and management of capital account
3. To identify areas where streamlining and simplification of procedure are possible and to remove the operational impediments, especially in respect of the ease with which transactions at the level of authorized entities are conducted, so as to make liberalization more meaningful
4. To ensure that guidelines and regulations are consistent with regulatory intent

With these and other tasks, it is hoped that the full convertibility of the Indian currency will be achieved in the interest of the national enterprise at the global level. Such a situation will also envisage the necessity of having such a law called Foreign Exchange Management Act (Case 21.1).

CASE 21.1

APPELLANT: Vijay Kumar Mallik vs RESPONDENT: Union of India

JUDGEMENT DATE: 18 December 2002[*]

FACTS: This application has been filed for quashing the entire criminal prosecution initiated as against the petitioner including the order dated 31 May 2002, whereby the learned Special Judge took cognizance for the offences under Sec. 56 of the Foreign Exchange Regulation Act, 1973 r/w Secs 49(3) and (4) of the Foreign Exchange Management Act, 1999.

---

[*]Vijay Kumar Mallik vs Union of India, 2003 (2) JCR 362 Jhr; also refer: http://www.ndiankanoon.org/doc/1296591/ (22 October 2011).

Contd

Case 21.1 *Contd*

> A case has been filed against the accused persons, including the petitioner, for defrauding a huge amount of Government money of upto ₹7,09,92,000 during the period 1980–90 on the basis of fake allotment letters; the petitioner took an active part in getting money by way of certain foreign exchange remittance in total of US $3,15,000 and £1000.
>
> The Petitioner contended that it was a gift in the names of five children and that the bank accounts were opened on their names.
>
> Respondent contended that it was not actually a genuine gift but was suspected to be involved in violations of the provisions of Foreign Exchange Regulation Act.

JUDGEMENT: Petition dismissed.

REASON: There cannot be any bar for a criminal trial even if no opinion has been formed in the adjudication proceeding, and also for the same the entire criminal proceeding cannot be thrown away when there is no denial about the allegation made in the complaint. Where a Court has jurisdiction to try, it is immaterial whether it has taken cognizance of the offence without even being empowered to do so.

21.2 FOREIGN EXCHANGE MANAGEMENT ACT, 1999

TEXT

Save as otherwise provided in this Act, rules or regulations made there under, or with the general or special permission of the Reserve Bank, no person shall:
(a) deal in or transfer any foreign exchange or foreign security to any person not being an authorized person;
(b) make any payment to or for the credit of any person resident outside India in any manner;
(c) receive otherwise through an authorized person, any payment by order or on behalf of any person residing outside India in any manner.
Explanation: For the purpose of this clause, "financial transaction" means making any payment to, or for the credit of any person, or receiving any payment for, by order or on behalf of any person, or drawing, issuing or negotiating any bill of exchange or promissory note, or transferring any security or acknowledging any debt

– Foreign Exchange Management Act, 1999, Sec. 3 (a-d)

The Salient Features

The following are the salient features of FEMA.

Regulation and management of foreign exchange (Secs 3–9) It concerns mainly of holding foreign exchange in any liquid or asset form outside India other than as provided in the Act. Further, it deals with current account and capital account transactions.

MANAGER'S TAKEAWAY

- The existence of a law expresses a current need.
- Better enterprise and better trade will have lesser regulations.

Authorized person (Secs 10–12) Upon application, the RBI may authorize anyone as a dealer and dealing in foreign transactions. It has the power to revoke the application if the due compliance fails. The RBI has the power to issue directions and conduct inspection of the authorized persons.

Contraventions and penalties (Secs 13–15)   The RBI, through its adjudication authority, may impose a penalty of ₹2 lakh, which may extend to up to ₹5,000 for each day after the first day during which the contravention continues. Failure of payment will attract civil imprisonment. A warrant for arrest of the defaulter may also be issued.

Adjudication and appeal (Secs 16–35)   For the purpose of adjudication, the Central Government is authorized to appoint officers of such authority, which is published in the Official Gazette with specified jurisdiction. The Adjudicating Officers are from the Enforcement Directorate of the Ministry of Finance. Anyone aggrieved by the order of the Adjudicating Authority may appeal to a special Director of Enforcement. The Authority has the power of a civil court, which are conferred on the Appellate Tribunal.

Directorate of Enforcement (Secs 36–38)   The Central Government will establish the Directorate of Enforcement (See Case 21.2). It will have the power of search and seize. The officers will not be below the rank of assistant director. The Directorate of Enforcement[1] has its headquarters in Delhi. There are two special directors, one additional director, and two deputy directors at the head office. There is also a legal wing at the headquarters. In India, there are ten zonal offices in the major cities and eleven sub-zonal offices in the secondary cities.

CASE 21.2   APPELLANT: Dr S. Ramakrishna   vs   RESPONDENT: Enforcement Directorate*

DATE OF JUDGEMENT: 21 April 2012

FACTS: The challenge in this petition is to an order dated 22 August 2002, passed by the Special Director, Enforcement Directorate (ED) informing the Petitioner that the adjudication proceedings in respect of the Memo. No. T– 4/2-BAN/2000 (SCN I & II) of 28 February 2000 and 27 March 2001 would be held in accordance with the procedure laid down in the Rules of the Adjudication Proceedings and Appeal Rules, 1974 and accordingly fix the case for personal hearing before him on 12 September 2002. Also challenged are all the consequential proceedings upon passing of the aforementioned order, including the adjudication order dated 17 February 2005 passed by the Special Director finding the Petitioner guilty and levying a penalty of ₹10 lakh for contravention of W.P.(C) 4311/2007 page 1 of 20 Secs 18(2) and 18(3) of the Foreign Exchange Regulation Act, 1973 (FERA) and the orders dated 7 February 2006 and 19 January 2007 passed by the Appellate Tribunal of Foreign Exchange (Appellate Tribunal).

The adjudication order was passed on 17 February 2005, levying a penalty of ₹50 lakh on the Petitioner. The appeal filed by the Petitioner before the Appellate Tribunal came up for hearing on 2 January 2006 when the question of predeposit of the penalty amount was considered. By the impugned order dated 7 February 2006, the Appellate Tribunal required the Petitioner to furnish an unconditional bank guarantee

---

*Dr S Ramakrishna vs Enforcement Directorate,W.P.(C) 4311/2007; also visit: http://www.indiankanoon.org/doc/1024789/.

Contd

---

[1]For provisions and functions of the directoraterefer: http://www.directorateofenforcement.gov.in.

Case 21.2 *Contd*

of ₹25 lakh in favour of the Special Director, ED, within 45 days as a condition to the appeal being taken up for hearing. The Petitioner's application for the modification of the above order was dismissed and the appeal itself was dismissed by the Appellate Tribunal on 19 January 2007. According to the Petitioner this was done despite his demonstrating lack of financial capacity to comply with the order dated 7 February 2006 passed by the Appellate Tribunal.

Meanwhile, the Foreign Exchange Management Act, 1999 (FEMA) was enacted. Under Sec. 49(3) of FEMA, no court could take cognizance of an offence under FERA and no Adjudicating Officer could take notice of any contravention under Sec. 15 of FERA 'after expiry of the period of W.P.(C) 4311/2007 page 2 of 20, two years from the date of the enactment' of the FEMA. In other words, after 31 May 2002 the Adjudicating Officer could not take notice of any contravention under Sec. 51 of FERA.

JUDGEMENT: Direction to place the petition before the Appellate Tribunal and to dismiss the petition upon proof of money deposited is provided.

REASON: Above observations are based on surmises and conjectures and are not borne out by the records of the case. A decision directing the furnishing of a bank guarantee of ₹25 lakh cannot possibly be based on such surmises and conjectures. The Appellate Tribunal erred in approaching the matter casually without adverting to the specific pleadings. Consequently, this Court holds that the Petitioner has been able to demonstrate lack of financial capacity to furnish bank guarantee to the tune of ₹25 lakh as a precondition to his appeal being entertained.

Considering the facts and circumstances, therefore, both the orders dated 17 February 2006 and 19 January 2007, passed by the Appellate Tribunal W.P.(C) 4311/2007 page 19 of 20, are hereby set aside.

As the appeal has been dismissed only on the ground of failure to comply with the order dated 7 February 2006 and as it does not involve any substantial question of law for which a statutory appeal may be filed, this Court directs that subject to the Petitioner depositing, within a period of four weeks from today, a sum of ₹1 lakh, the petitioner's appeal will be heard by the Appellate Tribunal. The said appeal will now be placed for hearing before the Appellate Tribunal on 1 June 2010 or any day thereafter when the Appellate Tribunal sits. On that date, if the Petitioner is not able to produce proof of having deposited a sum of ₹1 lakh, within a period of four weeks from today, his appeal before the Appellate Tribunal will automatically stand dismissed.

21.3 PREVENTION OF MONEY LAUNDERING ACT, 2002

TEXT

Whosoever directly or indirectly attempts to indulge or knowingly assists or knowingly is a party or is actually involved in any process or activity connected with the proceeds of crime and projecting it as untainted property shall be guilty of offence of money laundering

– Prevention of Money Laundering Act, 2002, Sec. 3

MANAGER'S TAKEAWAY

- Foreign exchange business is fraught with legal problems.
- The adjudication process is tedious and expensive.

The Preamble of the Act clearly announces the context of this legislation. The United Nations Organization (UNO) made a declaration adopting the resolution S-17/2, Political Declaration, and Global Programme of Action. A special session of the General Assembly of UNO was held from 8–10 June 1998 where it called upon the member states to legislate anti-money laundering law. In India, the Prevention of Money Laundering Act (PMLA) 2002 came into effect, belatedly, in 2005.

Money laundering occurs mainly in the following three ways:

Phase I   Initially, the money enters from some unaccounted and illegal source.

Phase II   It moves through a complex network of day-to-day transactions, camouflaged as though its source is untainted to the extent that it is undetectable and becomes *clean*. For instance, this money is used in *benami* transactions, put in trusts, issued against invoices, run through banks where criminals have a stake in the banking company, etc. Through these public institutions the money is *laundered*, made clean.

Phase III   The third phase is the logical follow-up of the above; it returns to the legitimate economic field.

Salient Features of the Act

Money laundering is an offence that threatens the financial system and undermines the integrity and sovereignty of a country. The PMLA has effect, notwithstanding anything contained in any other law.

Proceeds of crime [Sec. 2. (1)]   Any property derived or obtained, directly or indirectly, by any person as a result of a criminal activity relating to a scheduled offence or the value of any such property. By property it is meant any property or assets of every description whether corporal or incorporeal, tangible or intangible, deeds, instruments evidencing title to or interest in, such property and assets, wherever located. The schedule to the Act lays down some of these crimes: drug trafficking, murder, homicide, extortion, robbery, forgery of a valuable security, counterfeiting of currency, arms and ammunition trafficking, etc.

Attachment of property   If the appointed Authority has a reason to believe that any person is in possession of any proceeds of crime, then the order for provisional attachment of such property for a maximum period of 90 days may be in effect as per the second schedule of the Income Tax Act, 1961.

Survey If the Authority has the reason to believe that an offence under Sec. 3 is committed, it may inspect related records, check and verify proceeds, and demand for any further information that may be required, such as place marks of identification, inventory of property, and record and statement of any person.

Search and seizure   When the Authority has a reason to believe that a person committing offences constituting money laundering, it can exercise the power of search and seizure of buildings, places, vessels, vehicles, aircraft, break open locks, seize records, property, extract copies, etc. The Authority must file application for requesting of retention within 30 days before the adjudicating authority. Similarly, the search of the persons in the presence of two witnesses is also allowed.

Adjudication (Secs 5, 17, and 18) Upon the reception of the application, the adjudicating authority must within 30 days serve a notice on the person asking him to declare his sources of income and to show the cause as to why the properties should not be declared as involved in money laundering and confiscated.

Vesting of property (Sec. 8) Once the property is confiscated, the rights and title in such confiscated property shall vest absolutely on the Central Government, free from all encumbrances. The government may appoint an administrator to manage the said properties.

Records Banks, financial institutions, and other intermediaries must maintain records of all transactions that are integrally connected to each other. The institutions follow the following norms:

(a) Identification of customer according to Know Your Customer (KYC) norms
(b) Recognizing, handling, and disclosing suspicious transactions
(c) Appointment of Money Laundering Reporting Officer (MLRO)
(d) Staff training
(e) Maintenance of records
(f) Audit of transactions

The contravention of these provisions attracts a fine of ₹10,000 to ₹1 lakh (see Case 21.3).

Authorities The government has the power to appoint adjudication authorities and appellate tribunal, and also transfer to a special sessions court to try money laundering offences (see Case 21.3).

Auditor The auditor has the duty to enlighten his clients about the possible transactions under the Act.

MANAGER'S TAKEAWAY

- Business in foreign exchange involves both civil and criminal liabilities.
- Clearing the basic problems with the adjudicating authority is a valuable solution to business ills.

CASE 21.3

APPELLANT: Pareena Swarup VS RESPONDENT: Union of India

DATE OF JUDGEMENT: 30 September 2008[*]

FACTS: Ms Pareena Swarup, member of the Bar, has filed this writ petition under Article 32 of the Constitution of India by way of Public Interest Litigation seeking to declare various sections of the Prevention of Money Laundering Act, 2002 such as Sec. 6 that deals with adjudicating authorities, composition, powers, etc., Sec. 25 that deals with the establishment of Appellate Tribunal, and Sec. 27 that deals with composition, etc.

According to the Petitioner, the statutory provisions of the Act and the Rules, more particularly, relating to the constitution of Adjudicating Authority and Appellate

*Pareena Swarup vs Union of India (Supreme Court, Writ Petition 634/2007); refer also: http://www.indiankanoon. org/doc/132042/ (1 November 2011).

Contd

Case 21.3 *Contd*

Tribunal are violative of basic constitutional guarantee of a free and independent judiciary; therefore, it is beyond the legislative competence of the Parliament. The freedom from control and potential domination of the executive are the necessary preconditions for independence. With these and various other grounds, the Petitioner has filed this public interest litigation seeking to issue a writ of certiorari for quashing the above said provisions that are inconsistent with the separation of power and interfere with the judicial functioning of the Tribunal as ultra vires of the Constitution of India.

JUDGEMENT: Petition disposed off, with orders to Union of India to implement.

REASON: Rule 3(3) of Adjudicating Action Adjudicating Authority Rules, 2007 has been completed. Rules, 2007 does not amend to specify the 'academic Amended explicitly specify the qualification' for the Member Rule as per qualifications of from the field of finance and annexure A member from the field accounting by inserting a sub– of finance or clause direct the respondent-Union of India to implement the above provisions, if not so far amended as suggested, as expeditiously as possible but not later than six months from the date of receipt of a copy of this Judgement. The writ petition is disposed of accordingly.

SUMMARY

- Foreign Exchange Management Act, 1999 was enacted to facilitate external trade and payments by promoting orderly development and maintenance of foreign exchange market in India. Economic reforms have made it possible to make the Indian rupee to be fully convertible on current account. However, certain economic conditions prevailing in the country do not still allow the full convertibility on the capital account. Several restrictions in this regard are spelled in FEMA, 1999. To implement the provisions, the Enforcement Directorate is made responsible while there is another adjudication authority to settle disputes and grievances.
- Prevention of Money Laundering Act, 2002 was introduced due to the recommendations by the UNO. India is also a signatory to Financial Action Task Force (FTAF), which further accentuates its international obligation to prevent money laundering so that the money is not channelized for terrorist activities. Thus, when the Enforcement Directorate has enough reason to believe that there exists a prima fasciae case of money laundering, it initiates action. One of the actions is to nail the proceeds of crime and confiscate the property involved. The Authority has well-defined power to survey, inspect, search and seize property, and file case for adjudication.
- Thus, FEMA 1999 and PMLA 2002 are often in correlation mainly due to the foreign transitions.

EXERCISES

(i) You are an NRI who had eventually acquired citizenship of your host country, the USA. Now you want to return to India and set up a branch of your company in India.

Hint: Approval by RBI; approach Foreign Investment Promotion Board (FIPB).

(ii) You were fined an exorbitant sum by the Enforcement Directorate after a prima fascie case against you. You defaulted on the imposed fine saying that you do not have so much money to furnish. What is your legal remedy?

Hint: First consider the powers of the Authority under Sec. 13 (2) under the Act; next, you may file your grievance before the Tribunal.

(iii) A customer of your bank has opened several accounts and has been depositing money in them regularly. You suspect the money is coming from tainted sources. What would you do?

Hint: Maintain records and their interconnectedness

(iv) Illustrate with examples the convertibility of the Indian Rupee and its legal implications.

(v) What do you understand by Adjudication Authority? Illustrate with a case.

DEVELOPMENT OF LEGAL EDGE

Project—Newspaper Clipping

Objective   To develop a pattern of legal environment concerning foreign exchange and money laundering.

Purpose   To orient managerial decisions legally.

Method   Newspaper clippings of a theme are a classical method to deliver an emerging image on the subject. As the image emerges, you will be able to map and direct your activities.

Guide   Investigate and analyse.

FURTHER READING

Book
- Ashok Saxena, *Foreign Exchange Management Manual*, 10th edn (in three volumes), Bharat House Pvt. Ltd, 2011.

Web resources
- For Acts, Rules, Regulations, Circulars refer the Website: http://www.directorateofenforcement.gov.in.

CASE STUDY   FROM SCRAPS TO SWISS BANKS

Whosoever directly or indirectly attempts to indulge or knowingly assists or knowingly is a party or is actually involved in any process or activity connected with the proceeds of crime and projecting it as untainted property shall be guilty of the offence of money laundering.

– Prevention of Money Laundering Act, 2002, Sec. 3

From Rise to Fall[2]—Hassan Ali Khan Saga

Hassan Ali Khan has been quite a common name in India until the spotlight fell upon *this* Hassan Ali Khan, the son of Ghousudin Ali Khan of Hyderabad, an excise officer. Hassan may well have been a bureaucrat's son, but he began his career as a scrap dealer. However, this scrap dealer was quite an enterprising one who earned an annual income of ₹30 lakh. That is not impossible, of course, for the hardworking entrepreneurs if the scraps amount to thousands of tonnes of stuff. What is almost impossible to believe is that such an entrepreneur would have US $8 billion staked away in UBS Zurich, Switzerland. On its own, such money deposited in the bank whether national or foreign should not be an issue, irrespective of the

---

[2]The story of Hasan Ali Khan is followed by both print and electronic media. This is merely a summary output of this case in context. Some of the links are: http://taxguru.in/general-info/hassan-ali-khan-indias-largest-tax-defaulter-les.html; http://in.news.yahoo.com/hassan-ali-khan; http://groups.goodle.com/ group/alt/politics/thread/360ceea6f2a6f-; http://www.asianage.com/business (this has the best assembled chronological news).

staggering amount. However, what was most staggering was the ₹50,000 crore that the Enforcement Directorate of the Revenue Department, Ministry of Finance imposed on him as tax.

In the meantime, what Hassan Ali Khan was doing was quite spectacular. He was racing horses. He was breeding horses in his stud farm in Pune. He had a passion for costly cars. He threw large and lavish parties; industrialists and politicians of the highest class were entertained by him. When he told everyone that he was a descendant of the royal family of Nizam of Hyderabad, the world renowned rich and royal family, none doubted it. One of the reasons for his wealth he attributed to have come from the Nizam's Jewellery, and he claimed so even in the court through his counsel.

Hassan was not a mean businessman. He loved his business just as he loved his high octane lifestyle. From metal trading to car rentals, he dealt in antiques and even exported rice and onions to the Middle East. Since early 1990s, people knew that he was doing business in foreign exchange. Perhaps, his fall started when the State Bank of Hyderabad complained that he had duped the bank, and he was arrested. There were also other individual cases against him. However, from all of these case in the end he walked out free, as no one testified against him.

Then people started to speak about his dealings in weapons and his name was linked to the world's biggest arms dealer Adnan Khashoggi. It went even further when people suggested his ultimate selling point has been to be a conduit between the foreign banks and the Indian politicians and industrialists. In a letter rogatory in 2007, the Enforcement Directorate sought some information and documents from the Swiss bank, which was promptly refused by the bank, observing that not paying taxes in India is not relevant to Swiss laws. The authorities pursued him in 2007 and he deposed before them. In the following year in December, the Income Tax department sent him a notice for defaulting ₹50,000 crore. That is when the media picked up and painted him as the *Billion Dollar Bandit*.

In March 2011, Hassan Ali was arrested and put on trial. The Mumbai Sessions Court observed that the Enforcement Directorate had failed to present any material evidence for the charges levelled against Hassan Ali regarding the stashed away wealth in Swiss Bank. The judge granted bail to the accused on a surety of ₹75,000 and the Enforcement Department received a reprimand for not doing its homework well.[3]

Chastised by the verdict, the Enforcement Department appealed in the Bombay High Court, which was again the repeat of the Sessions Court. In the meantime, someone had filed a Public Interest Litigation (PIL) in the Supreme Court highlighting the enormous loss to the public exchequer. In law, therefore, the Enforcement Department was compelled to produce the status report of their investigation. It did so by filing the appeal petition before the Supreme Court, which is the subject matter of consideration in this Chapter.

From High Court to Supreme Court

Disputants: Union of India vs Hassan Ali Khan[4]
Court: The Supreme Court of India
Bench: Justice Altamas Kabir and Justice Surinder Singh Nijjar
Date: 30 September 2011

The Special Leave Petition out of which this appeal arises has been filed against the judgement and final order dated 12 August 2011, passed by the Bombay High Court in Criminal Bail Application whereby the High Court granted bail to the Respondent Hassan Ali Khan.

The allegation against the Respondent (and the other accused) is that they have committed an offence punishable under Sec. 4 of the Prevention of Money Laundering Act, 2002 (PMLA). The said case has been registered on the basis of a complaint filed by the Deputy Director, Directorate of Enforcement, Ministry of Finance, Department of Revenue, Government of India, on 8 January 2007, on the basis of Enforcement Case Information Report based on certain information and documents received from the Income Tax Department.

On the said date, the Income Tax Department carried out a search in the premises owned and/or possessed by the Respondent and a sum of ₹88,05,000, in cash was found in his residence at Peddar Road, Mumbai, which was seized. A number of imported watches and some jewellery were also found and seized during the search.

The search also revealed that the Respondent had purchased an expensive car, worth about ₹60 lakh. It also appears that the documents that were recovered by

---

[3]The High Court Case: Hassan Ali Khan vs Union of India; refer to the link: http://www.indiankanoon.org/doc/744839/ (30 October 2011).
[4]For the full text of the case refer to the link: http://www.indiankanoon.org/doc/3764/ (30 October 2011) Note: this case has been abridged with minor insertions such as short forms, etc.

the Income Tax Department contained several transfer instructions said to have been issued by the Respondent for transfer of various amounts to different persons from the bank accounts held by him outside India.

The said amounts forming the subject matter of the instructions issued by the Respondent ran into billions of dollars. The Income Tax Department assessed the total income of the Respondent for the assessment years 2001–2002, 2006–2007, and 2007–2008 as ₹11,04,12,68,85,303. Furthermore, during the investigation, the Directorate of Enforcement also obtained a document said to have been signed by the Respondent on 29 June 2003, which was notarized by one Mr Nicolas Ronald Rathbone Smith, Notary Public of London, on 30 June 2003.

Further, an investigation was conducted under the Foreign Exchange Management Act, 1999, hereafter referred to as 'FEMA'. Show-cause notices were issued to Respondent No.1 for alleged violation of Secs 3A and 4 of FEMA for dealing in and acquiring and holding foreign exchange to the extent of US $80,004,53,000, equivalent to ₹36,000 crore approximately in Indian currency, in his account with the Union Bank of Switzerland AG, Zurich, Switzerland.

Inquiries also revealed that Hassan Ali Khan had obtained at least three passports in his name by submitting false documents, making false statements, and by suppressing the fact that he already had a passport. In addition to the above, it was also indicated that investigations had revealed that he had sold a diamond from the collection of the Nizam of Hyderabad and had routed the sale proceeds through his account in Sarasin Bank in Basel, Switzerland, to the Barclays Bank in the United Kingdom.

Based on the aforesaid material, the Directorate of Enforcement, Mumbai Zonal Office, arrested the Respondent on 7 March 2011, and, thereafter, he was produced before the Special Judge, PMLA, Mumbai, on 8 March 2011, and was remanded in custody.

Subsequently, by an order dated 11 March 2011, the Special Judge, PMLA, rejected the prayer made on behalf of the Directorate of Enforcement for remand of the Respondent to its custody and released him on bail.

However, as a public interest litigation was pending in this Court in which the Directorate of Enforcement was required to file a status report in respect of the investigations carried out in connection with the case; the fact that the Respondent had been released on bail was brought to the notice of this Court and this Court stayed the operation of the bail order and authorized the detention of the Respondent in custody, initially for a period of four days.

The Union of India thereupon filed a Special Leave Petition and upon observing that the material made available on record prima facie discloses the commission of an offence by the Respondent punishable under the provisions of the PMLA, this Court vide order dated 29 March 2011, disposed of the appeal as well as the Special Leave Petition and set aside the order dated 11 March 2011, of the Special Judge, PMLA, Mumbai, and directed that the Respondent be taken into custody.

Thereafter, the Respondent was remanded into custody from time to time and the complaint came to be filed on 11 May 2011. A further prayer for bail was thereafter made on behalf of the Respondent on 1 July 2011, but the same was dismissed by the Special Judge, PMLA, Mumbai, on the same day.

The said order of the Special Judge, PMLA, Mumbai, rejecting the Respondent prayer for bail was challenged before the Bombay High Court in Bail Application on 2 July 2011. After a contested hearing, the Bombay High Court, by its order dated 12 August 2011, granted bail to the Respondent; and the said order is the subject matter of the present proceedings before this Court.

Exhibit A presents from Counsel-to-petitioner and Counsel-to-Respondent orders.

Exhibit A Counsel-to-Petitioner and Counsel-to-Respondent Orders

Counsel to Petitioner

- The high court failed to appreciate the astronomical amounts of foreign exchange dealt with by the Respondent for which there was no accounting and in respect whereof the Income Tax Department had for the Assessment years 2001–2002 to 2007–2008 assessed the total income as ₹11,04,12,68,85,303.

- The transfer of the huge sums from one bank to another was one of the methods adopted by persons involved in money laundering to cover the trail of the monies, which were the proceeds of crime.
- The large sums of unaccounted money, with which the Respondent had been dealing, attracted the attention of the Revenue Department and on investigation

Contd

Exhibit A *Contd*

conducted under the Foreign Exchange Management Act, 1959, (FEMA), showed that cause notices were issued to the Respondent for alleged violation of Secs 3A and 4 thereof for acquiring and holding foreign exchange and dealing with the same to the extent of US $80,004,53,000, equivalent to ₹36,000 crore, approximately, in Indian currency, in his account with the Union Bank of Switzerland, AG, Zurich, Switzerland.

- The enormous sums of money held by the Respondent in foreign accounts in Switzerland, United Kingdom, and Indonesia and the transactions in respect thereof prima facie indicated the involvement of the Respondent in dealing with proceeds of crime and projecting the same as untainted property, which was sufficient to attract the provisions of Sec. 3 of the PMLA, 2002.
- Under Sec. 24 of the aforesaid Act, when a person is accused of having committed an offence under Sec. 3, the burden of proving that the monies involved were neither proceeds of crime nor untainted property, is on the accused.
- As the money acquired by the Respondent besides being the proceeds of crime, is also connected with transactions involving the international arms dealer, Adnan Khashoggi. The learned ASG submitted that the same became evident from the notarized document that had been obtained by the Directorate of Enforcement during the course of investigation, which had been signed by the Respondent on 29 June 2003, at London and notarized by Mr Nicolas Ronald Rathbone Smith, Notary Public of London, England, on 30 June 2003.
- Respondent used different passports that he had acquired by submitting false documents to open bank accounts in foreign countries and to engage in the laundering of tainted money that brought such transactions squarely within the scope and ambit of Sec. 3 of the PMLA, 2002. Sec. 3 of the Act by itself was an offence as it provides that any person directly or indirectly attempting to indulge in or knowingly assisting or knowingly being a party or actually involved in any process or activity connected with the proceeds of crime and projecting it as untainted property, would be guilty of the offence of money-laundering.

- The provisions of Sec. 45 of the aforesaid Act make offences under the said Act cognizable and nonbailable.

Counsel to Respondent

- Firstly, an offence that did not form part of the scheduled offences referred to in Sec. 45 of the PMLA would not attract the provisions of Sec. 3 of the said Act.
- Whatever be the amounts involved and if the same had been unlawfully procured, it might attract the provisions of the Income Tax Act or FEMA, but that would not satisfy the two ingredients of Sec. 3, which entails that not only should the money in question be the proceeds of crime, but the same had also to be projected as untainted property.
- All that has been disclosed against the Respondent is that he dealt with large sums of money, even in foreign exchange and operated bank accounts from different countries, which in itself would not indicate that the monies in question were the proceeds of crime.
- At no stage has it been shown that the said amounts lying in the accounts of the Respondent in Switzerland, United Kingdom, and Indonesia have been projected as untainted money.
- Once bail had been granted, even if the special leave petition is maintainable, the power to cancel grant of such bail lies with the High Court or the Court of Sessions under Sec. 439(2) Cr.P.C. and, consequently, all the principles laid down by this Court relating to cancellation of bail, would have to be considered before the order granting bail could be cancelled.
- Even though the offences were alleged to have been committed by the Respondent as far back as in 2007, till he was arrested on 7 May 2011, there had been no allegation that he had in any manner interfered with the investigation or tampered with any of the witnesses.
- The apprehension expressed on behalf of the appellant that there was a possibility of the Respondent absconding to a foreign country on being released on bail, was without any basis, since such attempts, if at all made, could be secured by taking recourse to various measures.
- In the absence of any provisions in the PMLA that

Contd

Exhibit A *Contd*

the provision thereof would have retrospective effect, the provisions of the PMLA could not also be made applicable to the Respondent.

- Once it is accepted that the PMLA, 2002 would not apply to the Respondent the provisions of Sec. 45 thereof would also not apply to the Respondent's

case and his further detention would be unlawful.

- The PMLA had been introduced in the Lok Sabha on 4 August 1998, and all the offences alleged to have been committed by the Respondent were long prior to the said date.

From High Court Ruling to Supreme Court Ruling

Case needs different handling

Having carefully considered the submissions made on behalf of the respective parties and the enormous amounts of money that the Respondent had been handling through his various bank accounts and the contents of the note signed by the Respondent and notarized in London, this case has to be treated a little differently from other cases of similar nature.

Projecting the money to be untainted

It is true that at present there is only a nebulous link between the huge sums of money handled by the Respondent and any arms deal or intended arms deals, there is no attempt on the part of the Respondent to disclose the source of the large sums of money handled by him. There is no denying the fact that allegations have been made that the said monies were the proceeds of crime and by depositing the same in his bank accounts, the Respondent had attempted to project the same as untainted money.

Burden of proof on the respondent

The said allegations may not ultimately be established, but having been made, the burden of proof that the said monies were not the proceeds of crime and were not, therefore, tainted shifted to the Respondent under Sec. 24 of the PMLA, 2002: 'When a person is accused of having committed the offence under Sec. 3, the burden of proving that proceeds of crime are in tainted property shall be on the accused.'

High court's failure

The high court failed to focus on other parts of the prosecution case. It is true that having a foreign bank account and also having sizeable amounts of money deposited therein does not ipso facto indicate the commission of an

offence under the PMLA, 2002. However, when there are other surrounding circumstances that reveal that there were doubts about the origin of the accounts and the monies deposited therein, the same principles would not apply. The deposit of US $700,000 in the Barclays Bank account of the Respondent has not been denied.

Massive income

In addition, we cannot ignore the fact that the total income of the Respondent for the assessment years 2001–2002 to 2007–2008 has been assessed at ₹11,04,12,68,85,303 by the Income Tax Department and in terms of Sec. 24 of the PMLA, the Respondent had not been able to establish that the same were neither the proceeds of crime nor untainted property. In addition to the above is the other factor involving the notarized document in which the name of Adnan Khashoggi figures.

Respondent's behaviour does not favour bail

Lastly, the manner in which the Respondent had procured three different passports in his name, after his original passport was directed to be deposited, lends support to the apprehension that, if released on bail, the Respondent may abscond.

Pronouncement of judgement

Taking a different view of the circumstances that are peculiar to this case and in the light of what has been indicated herein above, we are of the view that the order of the high court needs to be interfered with. We, accordingly, allow the appeal and set aside the judgement and order of the high court impugned in this appeal and cancel the bail granted to the Respondent.

Conclusion

Searching questions need to be answered in India about the financial accountability. Equally, all the organs of the Government such as the Ministry of Finance and all its departments bear a special duty towards making such accountability transparent and just. The enormous proportion of this case in mere terms of money itself is mind boggling. The common man of India could do well without the fairy tales of the ilk of Hassan Ali Khan.

Discussion Questions

1. What conclusions do you draw from the facts of the case?
2. What are the legal issues involved? Prioritize them and explain according to their seriousness.
3. Cogently restate the arguments by the Union of India (Enforcement Directorate).
4. Cogently restate the arguments by the Respondent's counsel.
5. Why did the Sessions Court and the High Court grant bail to Hassan Ali?
6. Why did the Supreme Court deal with the case differently?
7. What lesson do you draw for yourself as a manager from the case by clearly illustrating the principles involved?

Going Beyond

1. How would you see this case in the perspective of the following persons?
   (a) Small entrepreneur
   (b) Manager of an import–export company
   (c) Senior manager of an Indian multinational company
   (d) Amateur lawyer
   (e) Politician
   (f) Salaried person with ₹6 lakh per annum income.
2. What lessons do you learn from the case as a citizen of India?

LEGAL LUMINARY

SAVAK SOHRAB TARAPORE—AN ECONOMIST WITH AN EYE FOR DETAILS

True to character, Savak Sohrab Tarapore, a monetary economist dedicated himself completely to the Reserve Bank of India. He joined the RBI in 1961 as a Research Officer and retired in 1996 as a Deputy Governor. As a workhorse of the RBI, he has been ubiquitous in all the important committees even after retirement:

   1997   Capital Account Convertibility
   1998   Committee on Banking Sector Reforms
   2000   Advisory Group on Transparency of Monetary Policy
   2001   Unit Trust of India Inquiry
   2004–05   Committee on Procedures and Performance Audit of Public Services
   2006   Committee on Fuller Capital Account Convertibility

In each of the committee reports, he used to pour his heart and mind. Even on weekends, he would go through every detail of the report several times. Thus, there stuck to him the phrase 'stickler for details'. All of these amounting to an impeccable record in the service of the nation.

As a columnist and a noted speaker, Tarapore's views are keenly observed. His speeches have been published in the book form entitled, India's Monetary Policy in the Crucible of Reform,* which proficiently deals with themes such as debts, public finance, foreign exchange, and monetary policy.

This legal luminary views that the pace of implementation of the recommendations on capital account convertibility should be determined by the

*S S Tarapore and Gangadhar Darbha, India's Monetary Policy in the Crucible of Reform, Vision Books, 2000.

Contd

Legal Luminary *Contd*

prevailing circumstances. He feels that although compliance has been achieved, more is desirable. Considering the volatility in the currency market the same is expected of the rupee also. Rising of the short-term interest rate is a good measure. India cannot suddenly expose itself completely on convertibility unless it feels its monetary foundations are very strong. The macro economics of the country must be strong, in which case the currency can be fully convertible on capital account also. One of the most insistent signals for the strong foundation is to see fiscal discipline by way of reducing and maintaining least fiscal deficit. Fiscal profligacy and unbridled inflation are not the paths to progress. Capital account convertibility must be seen as a system of keeping the macro economics sound.[†]

Savak Sohrab Tarapore was awarded the Doctor of Law (honoriscausa) by the Sheffield University in 1996. He wanted to become a professional musician but a chance meeting with a Reserve Bank official made him commit to this unique and most important monetary institution of India.[‡]

---

[*]S.S. Tarapore photo courtesy: http://www.inclusion.in/index.php?option=com_content&view=article&id=656&Itemid=72.
[†]See his interview in http://www.rediff.com/money/dec/19cac.htm (22 October 2011).
[‡]Refer http://www.business-standard.com/india/news/newsmaker-ss-tarapore/253360/(22 October 2011).

PART

4

LABOUR AND INDUSTRIAL JURISPRUDENCE

The Laws of Wages

Principle: *Omnium contribution sarciatur quod pro omnibus datum est.*
That which is given for all shall be compensated for by the contribution of all.

CHAPTER OUTLINE

- Introduction and Interpretation
- The Payment of Wages Act, 1936 and the (Amendment) Act, 2005
- Wage-related Acts

- *Case Study:* Standardization Award
- *Legal Luminary:* International Labour Organization

22.1 INTRODUCTION AND INTERPRETATION

The industrial revolution that started in Great Britain came to India through colonial channels. Along with it came into existence the labour legislation whose objectives where in the interest of British employers. Labour was cheap in India. Therefore, the Indian textiles were priced lower and posed a threat to the indigenous textile centres at Manchester and Lancashire. As a protectionist measure, the Factories Act, 1883 was introduced under the pressure of the British textile lobby. It made labour costlier and thus raised the prices of Indian textiles. The intention of the legislation was to be a protectionist; however, its salutary effect was welfare-oriented. For the first time in India, the workday was regulated as eight hours, child labour was abolished, and night employment of women was restricted. After Independence, India became one of the founding members of the International Labour Organization (ILO) of the UNO, supporting the policies it has legislated: Abolition of Forced Labour Act, 1930 and 1957, Equal Remuneration Act, 1951, and Against Discrimination (Employment and Occupation) Act, 1958.

Scope

The scope of dealing with wage laws in this chapter may be small due to the large number of Acts and the related and allied laws. Yet, a discussion on a few essential Acts and their quintessential features will justify the importance of these laws. The principle every labourer deserves his wages will become clear as we realize the importance of labour to the economy. In the present-day industrial world, the issue of labour and wages is very complex as the consciousness of the workers has taken a central role in the world economy. The terms 'human resource', 'human capital', 'hard skills', and 'soft skills' show enormous development in the use and understanding of human competencies. Competency, another commonly used term of our times, is one of the main factors that determine wages.

In this sense, it would be out of place to suggest that a manager is so called because of his competency or expertise to organize all the factors of production in such a way that they result in maximum benefit not only to the shareholders but also to the workers. A manager is a worker in the modern sense of a developed competency. Thus, when you see yourself as a worker you will be able to appreciate what is delineated in this chapter and it will go a long way in your work of decision-making and implementation.

22.2   THE PAYMENT OF WAGES ACT, 1936 AND THE (AMENDMENT) ACT, 2005

TEXT

'Wages' means all remuneration (whether by way of salary, allowances or otherwise) expressed in terms of money or capable of being so expressed which would, if the terms of employment, express or implied, were fulfilled, be payable to a person employed in respect of his employment or of work done in such employment...

– The Payment of Wages Act, 1936, Sec. 2(vi)

The definition further expands its scope by including anything that could be considered as wages in return for the service or work rendered. It repeats at every instance of the term, 'Any', thereby emphasizing the wages or remuneration in any form:

(a) Any remuneration payable under any award or settlement between the parties or order of a court

(b) Any remuneration to which the person employed is entitled in respect of overtime work or holidays or any leave period

(c) Any additional remuneration payable under the terms of employment (whether called a bonus or by any other name)

(d) Any sum which by reason of the termination of employment of the person employed is payable under any law, contract, or instrument that provides for the payment of such sum, whether with or without deductions, but does not provide for the time within which the payment is to be made

(e) Any sum to which the person employed is entitled under any scheme framed under any law for the time being in force, but does not include the following:

   (i) Any bonus (whether under a scheme of profit-sharing or otherwise) that does not form part of the remuneration payable under the terms of employment or that is not payable under any award or settlement between the parties or order of a court

   (ii) The value of any house—accommodation or of the supply of light, water, medical attendance, or other amenity, or of any service excluded from the computation of wages by a general or special order of the state government

   (iii) Any contribution paid by the employer to any pension or provident fund, and the interest that may have accrued thereon

(iv) Any travelling allowance or the value of any travelling concession

(v) Any sum paid to the employed person to defray special expenses entailed on him by the nature of his employment

(vi) Any gratuity payable on the termination of employment in cases other than those specified in sub-clause (d)

The above may be classified under the following three classic headings:

- Wages as remuneration for the work and services rendered
- Bonus, the additional benefit—pension, provident fund—given to the workers
- Gratuity—the benefits and payments made when the service period is over or at the termination of employment

From the above, it is understood that the legislator's intent is to safeguard the interest of the worker by making provisions for wages and benefits and thus provide economic security. Refer to Figure 22.1 that shows what these Acts deal with and to Box 22.1 for a classificating of these Acts.

Some Salient Features of the Act

The Act clearly lays down the essential elements in the payment, its mode, and its enforcement. Some of the salient features are as follows.

Responsibility for payment of wages (Secs 3–6)   All wages required to be paid under the law must be disbursed to the workers. The responsible people for such payment are: the

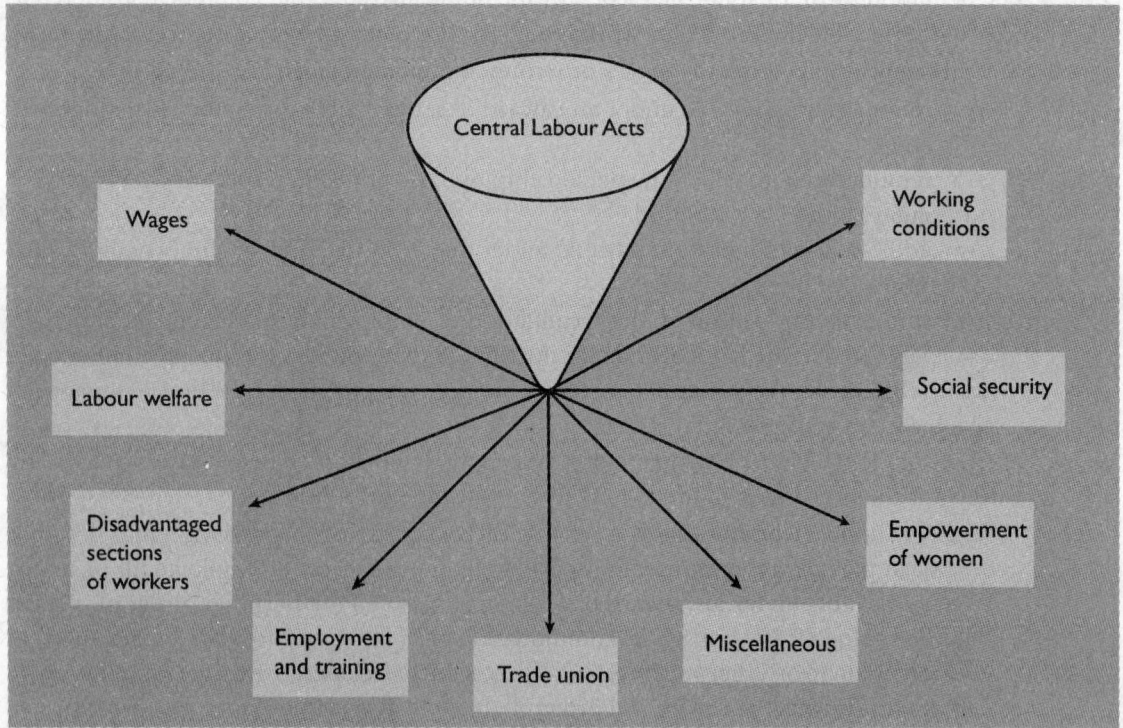

Figure 22.1   Central Labour Acts

BOX 22.1

CLASSIFICATION OF LABOUR ACTS

Trade Unions

1926   The Trade Unions Act

1946   The Industrial Employment (Standing Orders) Act

1947   The Industrial Disputes Act

2001   The Trade Unions (Amendments) Act

Wages

1936   The Payment of Wages Act

1948   The Minimum Wages Act

1958   The Working Journalist (Fixation of Rates of Wages) Act

1965   The Payment of Bonus Act

2005   The Payment of Wages (Amendment) Act

Working Conditions

1948   The Dock Workers (Regulation of Employment) Act

1948   The Factories Act

1951   The Plantation Labour Act

1952   The Mines Act

1955   The Working Journalists and Other Newspaper Employees' (Conditions of Service and Miscellaneous Provisions) Act

1958   The Merchant Shipping Act

1961   The Motor Transport Workers Act

1966   The Beedi and Cigar Workers (Conditions of Employment) Act

1976   The Sales Promotion Employees (Conditions of Service) Act

1979   The Inter-State Migrant Workmen (Regulation of Employment and Conditions of Service) Act

1981   The Cine Workers' Welfare Fund Act

1981   The Cinema Workers and Cinema Theatre Workers (Regulation of Employment) Act

1986   The Dock Workers (Safety, Health, and Welfare) Act

1996   The Building and Other Construction Workers (Regulation of Employment and Conditions of Service) Act

1997   The Dock Workers (Regulation of Employment) (inapplicability to Major Ports) Act

Contd

Box 22.1 *Contd*

Empowerment of Women

1961   The Maternity Benefit Act

1976   The Equal Remuneration Act

Deprived and Disadvantaged Workers

1933   The Children (Pledging of Labour) Act

1976   The Bonded Labour System (Abolition) Act

1986   The Child Labour (Prohibition and Regulation) Act

Social Security

1923   The Workmen's Compensation Act

2000   The Workmen's Compensation (Amendments) Act

1948   The Employees' State Insurance Act

1952   The Employees' Provident Fund and Miscellaneous Provisions Act

1996   The Employees' Provident Fund and Miscellaneous Provisions (Amendment) Act

1972   The Payment of Gratuity Act

2008   The Unorganized Workers' Social Security Act

Labour Welfare

1946   The Mica Mines Labour Welfare Fund Act

1972   The Limestone and Dolomite Mines Labour Welfare Fund Act

1976   The Beedi Workers' Welfare Fund Act

1976   The Beedi Workers' Welfare Cess Act

1977   The Beedi Workers' Welfare Cess Act Rules

1976   The Iron Ore Mines, Manganese Ore Mines, and Chrome Ore Mines Labour Welfare Fund Act

1976   The Iron Ore Mines, Manganese Ore Mines, and Chrome Ore Mines Labour Welfare Cess Act

1981   The Cine Workers Welfare Fund Act

1981   The Cine Workers Welfare Cess Act

1993   The Employment of Manual Scavengers and Construction of Dry Latrines Prohibition Act

Employment and Training

1959   The Employment Exchanges (Compulsory Notification of Vacancies) Act

1961   The Apprentices Act

Contd

Box 22.1 *Contd*

Miscellaneous

1855   The Fatal Accidents Act

1942   The Weekly Holiday Act

1943   The War Injuries (Compensation Insurance) Act

1943   The War Injuries Ordinance Act

1962   The Personal Injuries (Emergency) Provisions Act

1963   The Personal Injuries (Compensation Insurance) Act

1974   The Coal Mines (Conservation and Development) Act

1988   The Labour Laws (Exemption From Furnishing Returns and Maintaining Register by Certain Establishments) Act

1991   The Public Liability Insurance Act

The above acts and a few more central laws, in addition to their amendments and rules, further the state labour laws, and the machinery of its implementation suggests the enormity of the task. This demonstrates to you that dealing with your employees calls for the order of the law at every turn. Ignoring or ignorance about the labour laws will be the greatest undoing of any manager.

employer, the manager, the contractor, or any person designated with such responsibility as in establishments.

Wage period (Secs 4 and 5)   The wage period shall not exceed one month. The payment must be done before the 7th or 10th day of the month.

Medium of payment (Amendment Sec. 6)   The payment may be done in currency, using cheques, or by crediting the bank account. Wages in kind is not allowed.

Deduction from wages (Secs 7 and 8)   Only the deductions authorized by law can be made from the wages of workers. No fine may be levied unless it is done through previous approval by the government, in which case notices must be given with specifications of fines. A show cause notice to the effect is mandatory. The fine shall not exceed 3 per cent of the total wages of the worker. All fines must be recorded in the employer's register. Other deductions are: absence of duty, damage or loss caused; there are deductions for services such as house rent, deductions of recovery of advances, deductions for recovery of loans, and deductions for insurance schemes. Further deductions are for payable income tax, deductions set by court orders, insurance premiums, and any deduction permitted by the worker in writing. The limit of aggregate deductions should not exceed 75 per cent of the wages and those of the cooperatives not more than 50 per cent.

Maintenance of registers and records (Sec. 13–A)   According to the amendment to the Act, an employer shall maintain particulars of the employees in a prescribed register book, which must be retained for three years after the last entry is made. It should contain the following details:

(a) Work details
(b) Wages paid
(c) Deductions from wages
(d) Any receipts given by the workers

Enforcement of the Act (Sec. 14) Inspectors are appointed by the government by notification in the official gazette for the purpose of payment of wages in respect of all factories within assigned local limits. The inspector has the following functions:

(a) Ascertain provisions of the law are followed
(b) Inspect work establishments
(c) Supervise wage payment
(d) Examine any record or register; seize copies and documents if needed
(e) Do not compel anyone for any incriminating information

MANAGER'S TAKEAWAY

- A labourer deserves his wages.
- A manager in conspiracy with a labour inspector can cause havoc to the employees.

Penalties (Sec. 20) The following are the penalties as per the Amendment of 2005 (also see Case 22.1). The fine in Indian rupees is as follows:

(a) Delaying payment of wages: ₹1,500 to ₹7,500
(b) Not complying to form of payment: ₹3,750 for each offence
(c) Obstructing inspector from performance of duty: ₹1,500 to ₹7,500
(d) Additional fine for not paying on fixed date: ₹750 per day
(e) Subsequent offence: 1 to 6 months imprisonment—₹3,750 to ₹22,500

CASE 22.1

APPELLANT: Modi Industries Ltd   vs   RESPONDENT: Additional Labour Commissioner

DATE OF JUDGEMENT: **12 April 2011***

FACTS: Petitioner failed to pay the wages of the workers for the month of December 1992, which ought to have been paid to them by the 10th of the following month. The workers approached respondent No. 1, the Additional Labour Commissioner, for securing payment of their wages. Respondent No. 1 acting under Sec. 3 of the Uttar Pradesh Industrial Peace (Timely Payment of Wages) Act, 1978, gave a notice requiring the Petitioner to give information in Form 3 prescribed under Rule 4 (1) of the Rules framed under the Uttar Pradesh Act of 1978.

The Petitioner put in appearance and filed a reply raising various pleas justifying non-payment of the wages within time. Respondent No. 1, however, disagreed with the contentions raised by the Petitioner and issued a certificate on 10 February 1993 for recovery of ₹13 lakh as arrears of land revenue in respect of wages for the month of December 1992, which is a subject matter of challenge in the Writ Petition. Another

*Modi Industries Ltd vs Additional Labour Commissioner; (1994) ILLJ 482 All; see also: http://www.indiankanoon.org/doc/275531/ (29 October 2011).

Contd

Case 22.1 *Contd*

certificate was issued on 23 February 1993 for ₹20 lakh in respect of wages of the employees for the month of January 1992, which has been challenged in the Writ Petition of 1993.

JUDGEMENT: Heard learned counsel for parties. Judgement reserved.

REASON: In the meantime, the property of the petitioner shall not be auctioned for a period of two weeks provided salary of workers for the month of December 1992 is paid within the aforesaid period. The attachment of the property, however, shall continue except for the bank account and the finished goods. The entire amount in the bank account of the petitioner shall be placed in the hands of the Additional Labour Commissioner, Ghaziabad. As far as the finished goods are concerned, the petitioner may be permitted to sell the same under supervision and the amount so received from the sale of finished goods, along with the amount in bank, shall be first utilized for the payment of wages of the workers under the supervision of the above officer. Respondent Nos. 4 to 7 and their members shall permit the officers of the petitioner to enter inside the premises of the factory and to facilitate the payment of wages in dispute as directed by this order. I do not find any justification for non-payment of wages. However, considering the facts and circumstances and in the interest of both the parties, the period for making payment of the whole amount covered by both the Writ Petitions, i.e., ₹13 lakh plus ₹20 lakh, totalling to ₹33 lakh, was extended upto 30 April 1993.

Both the Writ Petitions have no merits and subject to the aforesaid observation/directions are dismissed.

22.3   WAGE-RELATED ACTS

The Minimum Wages Act, 1948

TEXT

Minimum rate of wages:

(1) Any minimum rate of wages fixed or revised by the appropriate Government in respect of scheduled employments under Sec. 3 may consist of:

(i) a basic rate of wages and a special allowance at a rate to be adjusted, at such intervals and in such manner as the appropriate Government may direct, to accord as nearly as practicable with the variation in the cost of living index number applicable to such workers (hereinafter referred to as the 'cost of living allowance') or

(ii) a basic rate of wages with or without the cost of living allowance, and the cash value of the concessions in respect of supplies of essential commodities at concession rates, where so authorized or

(iii) an all-inclusive rate allowing for the basic rate, the cost of living allowance, and the cash value of the concessions, if any.

(2) The cost of living allowance and the cash value of the concessions in respect of supplies of essential commodities at concession rates shall be computed by the competent authority at such intervals and in accordance with such directions as may be specified or given by the appropriate Government.

– The Minimum Wages Act, 1948, Sec. 4

The Minimum Wages Act prescribes minimum wages for all employees in all establishments or for those working at home in certain employments specified in the schedule of the

Act. Central and state governments revise minimum wages specified in the schedule. The Minimum Wages Act, 1948, has classified workers as unskilled, semi-skilled, skilled, and highly skilled.

For the purposes of coordinating work between committees and sub-committees, boards have been set up at the central and state levels, who advise the government in the matter of fixing and revising minimum wages. Law is enforced through an inspector appointed through a notification in the official gazette. Inspection and awarding penalties in case of infringements of the provisions of the law are powers granted to the inspecting officer. The government has the power to make appropriate rules.

Payment of Bonus Act, 1965

Eligibility for bonus: Every employee shall be entitled to be paid by his employer in an accounting year, bonus, in accordance with the provisions of this Act, provided he has worked in the establishment for not less than thirty working days in that year.

Disqualification for bonus—Notwithstanding anything contained in this Act, an employee shall be disqualified from receiving bonus under this Act, if he is dismissed from service for:

(a) fraud;

(b) riotous or violent behaviour while on the premises of the establishment; or

(c) theft, misappropriation, or sabotage of any property of the establishment.

— The Payment of Bonus Act, 1965, Secs 8 and 9

The Payment of Bonus Act provides for the payment of bonus to persons employed in certain establishments on the basis of profits or on the basis of production or productivity. The Act is applicable to establishments employing 20 or more persons. The minimum bonus that an employer is required to pay even if he suffers losses during the accounting year is 8.33 per cent of the salary.

According to the law, bonus is not a right but an obligation of an establishment to allow them to share in the good that they have created. It literally implies something that is added to the good, which is profit or surplus. The law lays down clear provisions for the computation of bonus through the amendments carried out in 1985. The schedules of the Act have details for the determination of bonus based on such computation.

Sec. 29 deals with the offences against the Act and Sec. 30 deals with the cognizance of such offences. The labour inspectors and commissioners enforce the law and award penalties as prescribed in the Act. The penalty involves both imprisonment upto six months and a fine of up to ₹1000.

Payment of Gratuity Act, 1972

Payment of gratuity:

(1) Gratuity shall be payable to an employee on the termination of his employment after he has rendered continuous service for not less than five years:

(a) upon his superannuation or

(b) upon his retirement or resignation or

(c) upon his death or disablement due to accident or disease: Provided that the completion of continuous service of five years shall not be necessary where the termination of the employment of any employee is due to death or disablement:

[Provided further that in the case of death of the employee, gratuity payable to him shall be paid to his nominee or, if no nomination has been made, to his heirs, and where any such nominees or heirs is a minor, the share of such minor, shall be deposited with the controlling authority who shall invest the same for the benefit of such minor in such bank or other financial institution, as may be prescribed, until such minor attains majority.] Explanation: For the purpose of this section, disablement means such disablement as incapacitates an employee for the work that he was capable of performing before the accident or disease resulting in such disablement.

—Payment of Gratuity Act, Sec. 4

Gratuity, such as provident fund or pension, is a social benefit. However, it finds its place here because it is achieved as a consequence of the wage earner. The Payment of Gratuity Act provides a scheme for the payment of gratuity to all employees in all establishments employing ten or more employees to all types of workers. Gratuity is payable to an employee on his retirement or resignation at the rate of 15 days salary of the employee for each completed year of service subject to a maximum of ₹10,00,000.[1] Gratuity is based on the principle that the employee has contributed to the establishment through his service and he should get benefit of it at the end of his serving period.

The 1987 Amended Sec. 4 makes provision for compulsory insurance of employer's liability to pay gratuity. The companies enrolling the services of 500 employees have to set up a gratuity fund. Each employee who has completed one year of service is required to make a nomination. The nomination may be in favour of the family members; it may be modified after giving the employer a due written notice. Sec. 9 imposes penalties for non-payment of gratuity upto six months of imprisonment and a fine of upto ₹10,000. (See Case 22.2).

MANAGER'S TAKEAWAY

- Manager who decides to give minimum wages must be prepared to receive minimum work.
- Benefits given to workers over and above the wages may not be the right of an employee, yet it is an implicit and inherent liability of the employer in view of the principle of wages.

CASE 22.2

APPELLANT: Mangalore Ganesh Beedi Workers' Association vs RESPONDENT: State of Karnataka and Others

DATE OF JUDGEMENT: 3 June 2003*

FACTS: The Government of Karnataka issued a draft notification and invited suggestions/objections from the affected/likely to be affected persons to the revision of minimum rates of wages in respect of workers employed at the Beedi industry in the State of Karnataka. The Karnataka Beedi Industries' Association (Regd.) submitted its suggestions/objections. The Government of Karnataka, after receipt of objections and suggestions, sought the opinion/comments of the Labour Department and sectored its opinion. The opinion of the Labour Department as well as ejections/

*Mangalore Ganesh Beedi Workers' vs State of Karnataka and Others; 2003 (5) KarLJ 26, (2003) IIILLJ 861 Kant; see also: http://www.indiankanoon.org/doc/1971257/ (29 October 2011).

Contd

[1] The limit laid down under section 4(3) of the Payment of Gratuity Act, 1972 [as amended by the payment of Gratuity (Amendment) Act, 2010, with effect from 24 May 2010] is ₹10,00,000.

Case 22.2 *Contd*

suggestions received from the Karnataka Beedi Industries Association (Regd.) and others were placed before the Karnataka State Minimum Wages Advisory Board by the government for its consideration. The Advisory Board, after considering the suggestions and objections received and the opinion of the Labour Department, recommended revision at the rate of 3 paise per point for every increase of the Consumer Price Index over and above 1,513 points for the purpose of payments of Variable Dearness Allowance (VDA). The state government, after considering the recommendation of the Advisory Board, revised the minimum rates of wages to come into effect from 1 November 1996 for workers employed in any employment at the Beedi Manufacturing Industries in exercise of power conferred on them under subsec. (1)(b) of Sec. 3 read with Subsec. (2) of Sec. 5 of the Act and the same was published in the Karnataka Gazette, Notification No. LD 2'49 LMW 93, Bangalore, dated 24 October 1996 fixing revision at the rate of 3 paise per point for every increase of the Consumer Price Index.

The managements of the Beedi Manufacturing Industries, being aggrieved by the above revision of minimum wage effected by the Government of Karnataka, preferred a Writ Petition assailing the validity of the notification.

Opposing the Writ Petitions, the trade unions representing the workmen of the Beedi Manufacturing Industries filed their statements of objection contesting the correctness of the contentions of the petitioners' and supporting the impugned notification and the revision of the minimum wages.

A Single Judge of this court by a common order impugned in these Writ appeals allowed the Writ Petitions filed by the management of Beedi Manufacturing Industries and quashed the notification issued by the Government of Karnataka under Secs 3 and 5 of the Minimum Wages Act, 1948, revising the rates of minimum wage in the Beedi Manufacturing Industries. Being aggrieved by the said judgement of the learned Single Judge, the State of Karnataka and the concerned trade unions representing the workforce at the Beedi Manufacturing Industries filed these Writ appeals.

JUDGEMENT: Allow Writs Petitions of the Beedi Workers' Association, set aside the judgement of the Single Judge, dismiss the Writ Petitions of the Management of Beedi Industries.

REASON: Since the directive as contemplated under Article 43 of the Constitution enjoins upon the state to implement its obligation by effective legislation or economic organization or in other way, to secure to all workers, a living wage condition of work ensuring a decent standard of life and full enjoyment of leisure, social, and cultural opportunities, interpretation to be placed by the court should also be persuasive. Statute is not to be understood and interpreted merely from the lexicographic angle. The court must not forget, while reviewing the minimum wage notification, the will and in-built policy of the law-maker as discernible from the object and the scheme of the enactment.

One more factor that weighs with us not to interfere with the fixation of minimum wages is that the Act is a beneficial piece of social legislation, which protects the day-today living conditions of the workers employed at the lowest level of wages in sweated labour. It is trite, though the minimum wages are fixed statutorily, it does not measure up either to the fair wage or to the living wage, particularly due to the high rate of increase in the Consumer Price Index.

Contd

Case 22.2 *Contd*

The management of Beedi Manufacturing Industries have utterly failed to produce any permissible ground to quash the impugned minimum wage notification.

We cannot sustain the judgement of the learned Single Judge impugned in these Writ appeals. In the result, we allow the Writ Appeal of the Beedi Workers' Association and set aside the order of the learned Single Judge and dismiss the Writ filed by the management of the Beedi Manufacturing Industries.

SUMMARY

- The problem of the payment of wages is to be seen through the main anchoring law: the Payment of Wages Act, 1936. The Minimum Wages Act, 1948, is equally important. Other closely related laws for anything to be paid in the form of benefits in addition to the salary are the Payment of Bonus Act, 1965, and the Payment of Gratuity, 1972. Labour laws are implemented through the officially appointed authority such as the Labour Inspector and the Labour Commissioner. A slew of central laws along with the state laws as well the related rules and regulations help enforce the law of full and fair wages.
- The onus of payment of wages is on the employer, and hence misrepresentation, misstatement, or anything depriving of the wages to the employees is punishable with resulting penalties of imprisonment and fine.

EXERCISES

(i) An employer slaps a fine on his employee on the first of the month and he wants to deduct it on the first pay day, the seventh of the month.

Hint: The employer is forbidden to do so; see: Sec. 8 (6) of the Act.

(ii) An employer reviewed the wage structure of his employees due to which certain allowances were cancelled. However, the difference compared to the previous wage structure was not very different. What legal remedies are available to the employees to protect themselves from such revisions which in the long run may result in the deduction of their wages?

Hint: See the provision under Sec.15 of the payment of Wages Act, 1936

(iii) An employer got a show cause notice from the Collector for paying less gratuity than his due, specifying the due amount compounded with interest thereof. What should the employer do?

Hint: Pay. See Sec. 8, especially provision 1 of the Payment of Gratuity Act, 1972, Amendment 1987.

(iv) Define wages under the Payment of Wages Act, 1936, and illustrate it with a case.

(v) What constitutes the minimum rate of wages under the Minimum Wage Act, 1948?

DEVELOPMENT OF LEGAL EDGE

Project—Campaign against Bonded Labour

Objective   To assist NGOs related to the eradication of bonded labour in India.

Method   Volunteer yourself with an NGO engaged in the work of eradication of bonded labour.

Report   Make a project report and publish it in the local newspaper.

FURTHER READING

The following are some comprehensive guides:
- Universal's Legal Manual, Labour & Industrial Law Manual, Universal Law Publishing Co., 2011.
- H.L. Kumar, *Employer's Rights Under Labour Laws*, 4th edn), Universal Law Publishing Co., 2011.

CASE STUDY   STANDARDIZATION AWARD

The State Government may, by notification in the Official Gazette, appoint... any Commissioner for Workmen's Compensation or other officer with experience as a Judge of a Civil Court or as a stipendiary Magistrate to be the authority to hear and decide for any specified area all claims arising out of deductions from the wages, or delay in payment of the wages...

– The Payment of Wages Act, 1936, Sec. 15

Supreme Court of India

Bench: Justice P.B. Gajendra Gadkar
          Justice K.N. Wanchoo
          Justice K.C. Das Gupta
Petitioner: Shri Ambica Mills Co. Ltd
Respondent: Shri S.B. Bhatt and Others
Date: 12 December 1960[2]

The Agenda

Under Sec. 15 of the Payment of Wages Act, 1936, the Authority in exercising its jurisdiction, made exclusive by Sec. 22 of the Act, has necessarily to consider various questions incidental to the claims falling thereunder and, although it would be inexpedient to lay down any hard and fast rule for determining the scope of such questions, care should be taken not to unduly extend or curtail its jurisdiction. Whether a particular employee was an operative or one above the rank of an operative and below that of clerk and, therefore within Clause 5 of the agreement, was a question intimately and integrally connected with wages as defined by the Act and as such fell within the jurisdiction of the Authority under Sec. 15 of the Act.

The Background

The appellant, Shri Ambica Mills Co. Ltd, is a textile mill at Ahmedabad. Three of its employees named Punamchand, Shamaldas, and Vishnuprasad made an application to the Authority under Sec. 16 of the Act and prayed for an order against the appellant to pay them their delayed wages.

It appears that an award called the Standardization Award that covered the mill industry in Ahmedabad was pronounced by the Industrial Tribunal on 21 April 1948, in Industrial Reference No. 18 of 1947. This award fixed the wages for different categories of workers working in the textile mills at Ahmedabad, but left over the question of clerks for future decision.

Among the operatives whose wages were determined by the award, the case of hand-folders was specifically argued before the Industrial Tribunal. The Labour Association urged that the rate of ₹36–9–0 awarded to them was too low and it was pointed out on their behalf that they did the same work as cut-lookers did in Bombay where a head cut-looker was given ₹52 and a cut-looker ₹42–4–0.

On the other hand, the mill owners contended that the rate should have been fixed at ₹34–2–0 instead of ₹36–9–0.

The Tribunal found it difficult to decide the point because enough evidence had not been produced before it to show the kind of work that hand-folders were doing at Ahmedabad; that is why the Tribunal was unable to raise the wage of hand-folders to that of cut-lookers in Bombay. However, it made a significant direction on that behalf in these words: 'At the same time', it was observed, 'we desire to make it clear that if there are persons who are doing cut-looking as well as folding, they should be paid the rate earned by the cut-lookers in Bombay.'

On 11 July 1955, the present respondents moved the Authority under Sec. 16 of the Act. They urged that

---

[2]Shri Ambica Mills Co. Ltd vs Shri S.B. Bhatt and Others; 1961 AIR 970, 1961 SCR (3) 220; see also: http://www.indiankanoon.org/doc/1734620/ (29 October 2011). The case is abridged with added subheadings for better comprehension.

they were semi-clerks and occupied a position lower than that of a full-fledged clerk and higher than that of an operative, and as such they were governed by Clause 5 of the Agreement and were entitled to increment provided by the said clause.

This claim was resisted by the appellant on several grounds. It was urged that the present applications were barred by *res judicata*, that the Authority had no jurisdiction to entertain the applications, and that on the merits the respondents were not semi-clerks as contemplated by Clause 5 of the Agreement.

On these contentions, the Authority raised four issues. It held against the respondents and in favour of the appellant on issues 1 and 2, which related to the plea of *res judicata* and the status of the respondents. In view of the said fidings, the Authority thought it unnecessary to decide on the two remaining issues that dealt with the quantum of amount claimed by the respondents.

The finding of *res judicata* was recorded against Punamchand and Vishnuprasad. Shamaldas had not made any previous application and so no question of *res judicata* arose against his application. His application was dismissed only on the ground that he could not claim the status of a semi-clerk. The same finding was recorded against the two other respondents. It appears that at the trial before the Authority the parties filed a joint Pursis that enumerated the duties performed by the respondents in paragraphs.

The Authority took the view that 'the duties performed by them cannot be said to be the duties of persons doing the routine work of writing, copying and making calculations.' In the result, it was held that the respondents were governed by the Standardization Award and did not fall under the subsequent agreement.

Argument Against

The applications made by the respondents' Union on behalf of the three employees were incompetent under Sec. 15 of the Act and the Authority exceeded its jurisdiction in entertaining them. It is true that this point was not specifically urged before the Authority, but it appears to have been argued before the appellate Authority and the High Court, and it is this contention that raises the problem of construing Sec. 15 of the Act. The case for the appellant is that the jurisdiction conferred on the Authority under Sec. 15 is a limited jurisdiction, and it would be unreasonable to extend it on any inferential ground or by implication. The scheme of the Act is clear. The Act was intended to regulate the

payment of wages to certain classes of persons employed in industry, and its object is to provide for a speedy and effective remedy to the employees in respect of their claims arising out of illegal deductions or unjustified delay made in paying wages to them. With that object, Sec. 2(vi) of the Act has defined wages. Sec. 4 fixes the wage period. Sec. 5 prescribes the time of payment of wages. Sec. 7 allows certain specified deductions to be made. Sec. 15 confers jurisdiction on the Authority appointed under the said section to hear and decide for any specified area claims arising out of deductions from wages, or delay in payment of wages, of persons employed or paid in that area. It is thus clear that the only claims that can be entertained by the Authority are claims arising out of deductions or delay made in payment of wages. The jurisdiction thus conferred on the Authority to deal with these two categories of claims is exclusive; Sec. 22 of the Act provides that matters that lie within the jurisdiction of the Authority are excluded from the jurisdiction of ordinary civil courts. Thus, in one sense the jurisdiction conferred on the Authority is limited by Sec. 15, and in another sense it is exclusive as prescribed by Sec. 22.

Counter Argument

The respondent Union contends that they are governed by Clause 5 of the subsequent agreement. It is common ground that both the award and the agreement are in operation in respect of the persons governed, respectively, by them, so that it is not disputed by the appellant that the persons who are specified by their designation under Clause 5 would be entitled to the benefit of the said clause and would not be governed by the award.

If an employee is called a cut-looker by any mill he would naturally fall under Clause 5; in other words, all the specified categories of employees named by designation in that clause would not be governed by the Award though at one stage they were treated as operatives, but they would be governed by Clause 5 of the agreement; if a person bearing that designation applies under Sec. 15 of the Act, his application would be competent.

Analysis

The appellant's argument, however, is that when the last part of Clause 5 refers to other employees 'who have not been included above but who can properly fall under the above category' no designation is attached to that class, and in such a case it would be necessary to enquire whether a particular employee can properly fall under the said category, and that, it is urged, means that such an employee cannot apply under Sec. 15 but must go to the industrial court under the ordinary industrial law.

Thus, the controversy between the parties lies within a very narrow compass. An employee designated as a cut-looker can apply under Sec. 15 and obtain relief from the Authority; an employee not so designated but falling under the said category by virtue of the work assigned to him, it is said, cannot apply under Sec. 15 because the Authority cannot deal with the question as to whether the said employee properly falls under the said category or not. In our opinion, on these facts, the question as to whether a particular employee is an operative falling under the Award or one who is above an operative and below the clerk falling under Clause 5 is a question that is so intimately and integrally connected with the problem of wages as defined under Sec. 2(vi) that it would be unreasonable to exclude the decision of such a question from the jurisdiction of the Authority under Sec. 15.

If a contract of employment is admitted and there is a dispute about the construction of its terms that obviously falls within Sec. 15 of the Act, what is the difference in principle where a contract is admitted, its terms are not in dispute, and the only point in dispute is which of the two subsisting contracts applies to the particular employee in question. If the appellant's argument were to prevail, it would lead to this anomalous position that if a general contract of employment provides for payment of wages to different categories of employees and describes the said categories by reference to the duties discharged by them, none of the employees can ever avail himself of the speedy remedy provided by Sec. 15 of the Act. In such a case, every time a dispute may arise about the duties assigned to a particular employee before his wages are determined. In our opinion, to place such an artificial limitation on the limits of the jurisdiction conferred on the Authority by Sec. 15 is wholly unreasonable. That is the view taken by the High Court in the present case and we see no reason to differ from it.

Judgement

The petitioner has strenuously contended that it is unfair to give the same pay to the three workmen who are doing the work of cut-lookers only for a part of the time and were substantially doing the work of bleach-folders; that, however, has no relevance in determining the present dispute. The only point that calls for decision is whether or not the work done by the three respondents takes them within the category of cut-lookers specified under Clause 5, and as we have already pointed out, on

an earlier occasion the Authority has found in favour of two of the three respondents when it held that they were folders doing cut-looking. If the said finding amounts to *res judicata* it is in favour of the two respondents and not in favour of the appellant; that is why the learned petitioner's counsel did not seriously dispute the correctness of the decision of the High Court on the question of *res judicata*. In the result, the appeal fails and is dismissed with costs. Appeal dismissed.

Conclusion

One thing that clearly stands out is the narrow compass of this case stated by the Supreme Court Bench. It needs to be appreciated that the Bench made a concerted effort to work within this narrow compass focusing *res judicata* in favour of the respondents. *Res judicata* is a very useful legal principle. It literally stands for matter that is already judged. The case or suit is already judged; hence, it becomes redundant to proceed on similar lines and deliver the same judgement. In other words, when both or either of the parties approach the same court for the adjudication of the same matter or issue, the court will say *res judicata*, and strike down the case. However, the principle is not as simple as it sounds thus far. It must fulfil some conditions, for instance: same suit, same cause of the suit, same parties, and that the parties had been given full and fair hearing. The principle serves undue multiplication of litigation.

The above case is a landmark case where the Supreme Court, the highest appellate court, took up the matter because the *res judicata* as far as the same judgement was concerned was at lower courts. The Court may also have come to the conclusion that a full and fair hearing was required. Finally, the Court also wanted to demonstrate that not only justice has to be done, but also it must be **seen** that it is done with the finality of the highest appellate court.

Discussion Questions

1. Delineate Sec. 15 of the Act.
2. Relate other sections mentioned in the case to Sec. 15.
3. Analyze the two main issues in this case on the basis of the related sections.
4. Explain in your own words the legal reasoning on behalf of the petitioner and respondents.
5. Analyze the judgement delivered by the Bench of the Supreme Court.
6. What is the importance of this case for workers in India?
7. What lessons do you learn as a manager dealing with a similar case?
8. Write a short note on *res judicata*.

Going Beyond

1. What do you understand by the following terms: wage, subsistence wage minimum wage, just wage and family wage?

2. On Labour Day, deliver a speech at a public meeting

of workers, which includes the following proposition: Wages for labour must be such that one may provide for himself the means to develop worthily his own material, social, cultural, and spiritual life and that of his dependants.

LEGAL LUMINARY

INTERNATIONAL LABOUR ORGANIZATION

According to Juan Somavia, ILO Director-General,[*] 'the primary goal of the ILO today is to promote opportunities for women and men to obtain decent and productive work, in conditions of freedom, equity, security and human dignity.'

At the very outset, you may rightly query, 'how can an organization be a legal luminary?' A brief reflection may tell you that it is a legal entity, a person in its own right since 1919. Furthermore, it was awarded the Nobel Peace Prize in 1969, the year it celebrated its 50 years of yeoman service to the workers of the world. The organization has the following four objectives:

(a) To promote and realize standards and fundamental principles and rights at work

(b) To create greater opportunities for women and men for decent employment and income

(c) To enhance the coverage and effectiveness of social protection for all

(d) To strengthen tripartism—government, worker, employer—and social dialogue.

It has worked for over 90 years by promoting decent work, livelihoods, and dignity. It has been able to shape the labour policies internationally based on its objectives.

It functions extensively in achieving the following goals:

1. Formulation of international policies and programmes to promote basic human rights, improve working and living conditions, and enhance employment opportunities

2. Creation of international labour standards

backed by a unique system to supervise their application

3. An extensive programme of international technical cooperation formulated and implemented in active partnership with constituents, to help countries put these policies into practice in an effective manner

4. Training, education, and research activities to help advance all of these efforts

The origin of ILO lies as an agency of the League of Nations, which came into existence at the end of World War I in Versailles, France. It became a part of the UN, which was formed after World War II. Presently, it functions in all the countries of the world and provides extensive data on labour statistics, which help governments and regional organizations in the formulations of the policies and enactment of laws. With 183 member countries and the workforce in them, it is an organization of enormous proportions.

India has a very close relationship with ILO. All our enactments of law have a stamp of ILO and it has been able to produce exemplary legislation. India faces one of the highest and the most acute labour problems in the world: child labour, bonded labour, human trafficking, and other problems related to decent human work, adequate pay, and dignity of the human being.

ILO, headquartered in Geneva, has worldwide centres of learning and training. The present thrust of the organization is towards making decent work a strategic international goal and to promote fair globalization.[†]

---

[*]The quote is taken from: http://www.ilo.org/global/about-the-ilo/mission-and-objectives/lang--en/index.htm (2 November 2011).

[†]For all the information on ILO refer to http://www.ilo.org.

23

The Laws of Workers' Social Security

Principle: *Spondet peritiam artis, et imperitia culpae enumerator.*

Everyone is responsible for skill in his profession, for want of such skill is regarded as a fault.

CHAPTER OUTLINE

- Introduction and Interpretation
- The Workmen's Compensation Act, 1923 and Amendments Act, 2000

- Related Social Security Acts
- *Case Study:* Contracting
- *Legal Luminary:* Babu Jagjivan Ram

23.1 INTRODUCTION AND INTERPRETATION

(1) The Central Government shall formulate and notify, from time to time, suitable welfare schemes for unorganized workers on matters relating to:

(a) life and disability cover;

(b) health and maternity benefits;

(c) old age protection; and

(d) any other benefit as may be determined by the Central Government.

– The Unorganized Workers' Social Security Act, 2008, Sec. 3

Scope

The scope of this chapter is welfare of the workers. Although it is beyond the capacity of this chapter to handle even the essential aspects, it is hoped that you will have a clear concept about the legal aspects of the fundamental laws of workers' social sphere, from earning their minimum livelihoods and caring for their sickness to their needs of housing and cultural aspirations. As a manager performing the duties of an employer, knowledge about the Workmens' Compensation Act, 1923 is essential. Being conscious of the seriousness of this Act will make you knowledgeable in the enforcement of the other related Acts.

Workers' Social Security—A Constitutional Obligation

Under the influence of the International Labour Organization, with which you acquainted yourself in the last chapter, India has steadily moved to enact laws of utmost importance to the workers in India. The Constitution of the India in Articles 41, 42, and 43 places responsibilities on the states of the union to provide security and insurance to the employed, and benefits to the unemployed. It lays emphasis on the conditions of labour, provision of provident fund, employers' liability of compensation to workers, and old age and maternity benefits.

In recent years, extensive legislation has been passed both at the centre as well as in the states. Some of the central Acts are as follows:

Workmen's Compensation Act, 1923
Workmen's Compensation (Amendments) Act, 2000
Employees' State Insurance (ESI) Act, 1948
Employees' Provident Fund and Miscellaneous Provisions Act, 1952
Employees' Provident Fund and Miscellaneous Provisions (Amendment) Act, 1996
Payment of Gratuity Act, 1972
Unorganized Workers' Social Security Act, 2008

Organized and Unorganized Workers

The biggest problem in India is that the organized labour force comprises only about 10 per cent and 90 per cent falls into the category of unorganized labour. One of the reasons for this is that the vast masses of labour are engaged in agriculture. Even in urban areas, the existence of unorganized labour is astronomical. These are mainly involved in infrastructure projects and are employed as semi-skilled and unskilled labourers. A large percentage of child labour is engaged both in rural and urban areas. The enormity of the problem has paralyzed all the schemes introduced by the government.

One of the major legislation to stem the tide of unorganized labour has been the introduction of the National Rural Employment Guarantee Act, 2005. The law is a guarantee of employment of 100 days a year for the rural people, who are idle in the non-agricultural season. The Central Government has introduced National Rural Employment Guarantee Act schemes with the help of the state governments who disburse ₹100 per day as minimum wages.

The Unorganized Workers' Social Security Act, 2008 is further strengthened by the Domestic Workers Act, 2008, thus bringing domestic workers under welfare security to make them eligible for bonus, pension, and maternity benefits.

23.2 THE WORKMEN'S COMPENSATION ACT, 1923 AND AMENDMENTS ACT, 2000

TEXT

Employer's liability for compensation:
(1) If personal injury is caused to a workman by accident arising out of and in the course of his employment, his employer shall be liable to pay compensation in accordance with the provisions of this Chapter, provided that the employer shall not be so liable:
(a) in respect of any injury that does not result in the total or partial disablement of the workman for a period exceeding three days; and

(b) *in respect of any injury, not resulting in death, caused by an accident, which is directly attributable to*

   (i) *the workman having been at the time thereof under the influence of drink or drugs,*

   (ii) *the willful disobedience of the workman to an order expressly given or to a rule expressly framed for the purpose of securing the safety of workmen, or*

   (iii) *the willful removal or disregard by the workman of any safety guard or other device that he knew to have been provided for the purpose of securing the safety of workmen.*

– The Workmen's Compensation Act, 1923

The Workmen's Compensation Act, 1923 was the first Act that thought about the welfare of workers by making provision for the liability of the employer, however, with caveats to safeguard the interest of the latter, too. Before this law, the only law that existed was the Fatal Accidents Act, 1855, which allowed the employer several defences against the death of a worker, such as assumed risk of employment and personal action. This left the defendants of the worker without support. The following are some of the salient features of the Act.

Schedules

In the Workmen's Compensation Act, there are two Schedules, I and II, which comprise an exhaustive list of injuries and hazards suffered by the worker for which the employer is liable (Secs 2 and 4). Schedule III (Sec. 3) makes a list of the occupational diseases and the amount of compensation. Schedule IV lists the factors for lump sum compensation, for instance, in the event of the disablement or death of the worker.[1]

Rules of compensation (Sec. 4)

This section deals with the compensation to be paid when due and penalty in the event it is not complied, which amounts to, with interest, 6 per cent per annum. If the salary payment is delayed due to neglect by the employer, then 50 per cent of the amount due shall be recovered.

Computation of wages (Sec. 5)

(a) If the worker is in continuous employment of not less than 12 months preceding accident, he comes in the category of compensation that shall be 1/12th of the total wages that are due.

(b) If the service is less than one month, then the compensation shall be the average monthly amount.

(c) In other cases, the compensation shall be thirty times the total wages earned in respect of the last continuous period of service immediately preceding the accident from the employer who is liable to pay compensation.

Distribution of compensation (Sec. 8)

(a) Payment of compensation for injury or death must be deposited with the commissioner for compensation; any disbursement done directly shall not be deemed as payment of compensation.

---

[1]You are strongly recommended to study these lists in the schedules; in addition you need to carefully study the Employer's Liability Act, 1938.

(b) The employer may make advances on account of payment of an equal amount of three months of wages.

(c) In the event of disablement caused by injury, the compensation is to be deposited with the commissioner who will pay it to the workman.

(d) The commissioner may use his discretion in cases where children are neglected or, due to variance in circumstances of any dependant or any other sufficient cause, vary his earlier orders with regard to distribution or investment of compensation.

Notice and claim (Sec. 10)

(a) No claim for compensation shall be entertained by the commissioner unless the notice of accident has been given in writing by the workman; the notice shall also be served on the employer.

(b) Claim for compensation shall be preferred to the commissioner within two years of the occurrence of accident or in case of death within two years of the occurrence of death. In certain cases, the commissioner has the power to use his discretion even when notice is not given due to sufficient cause.

Enforcement of the Act (Secs 19–30)

The state government by notification in the official gazette appoints the commissioner. One has the right to appeal in the high court against the orders that the commissioner has given. The government has the powers to make rules to enforce the law (Secs 32, 34).

23.3 RELATED SOCIAL SECURITY ACTS

Employees' State Insurance Act, 1948

TEXT

Establishment of ESI Corporation:

(1) With effect from such date as the Central Government may, by notification in the official gazette, appoint in this behalf, there shall be established for the administration of the scheme of ESI in accordance with the provisions of this Act, a Corporation to be known as the ESI Corporation.

(2) The corporation shall be a body corporate by the name of ESI Corporation having perpetual succession and a common seal and shall by the said name sue and be sued.

– The Employees' State Insurance Act, 1948, Sec. 3

MANAGER'S TAKEAWAY

- Manager's dilemma: Whether to support the worker or the employer?
- If companies allow, workers' participation in management problems can be solved without resorting to litigation.

If Workmen's Compensation Act was the first step toward the welfare of the workers, this Act about their insurance was a big step toward ensuring greater safety from disease and want. It provides benefits in sickness, maternity benefits, and other similar cases. Its funding is done both through the financial contributions by the employees as well as the employers. (See Case 23.1.) However, the best thing that happened as a result of this legislation was the establishment of the Employees' State Insurance Corporation, which is today most recognizable through its acronym ESI.

The constitution of ESI corporation The institution of the statutory body called the ESI Corporation is established under

CASE 23.1 Petitioner: R. Gopala Krishnan vs Respondent: The Manager, Karaska Roadways*

Date of Judgement: 3 September 2007

Facts: The appellant/workman was under employment of the respondent on 30 April 1989 as a driver of vehicle No. T.A.I. 2368, which met with an accident, due to which, lower two-third of the left hand, i.e., from slightly above the elbow of the appellant had to be amputated. On the date of accident, the risk of the workman was covered under a policy of insurance by the respondent. The appellant/workman was earning a salary of ₹2200 per month and was aged 45 years on the date of accident.

The lower court held that due to amputation of the lower two-thirds of the left hand of the appellant/workman, he suffered 80 per cent loss of earning capacity and assessed compensation under Sec. 4 (1)(c) of the Act on the ground that the amputation below the shoulder fell within the category enumerated under part II of Schedule I of the Act.

Being aggrieved by the order dated 12 July 1995 passed by the commissioner for Workmen's Compensation, Jagdalpur awarding compensation of ₹67,776 to the appellant/workman against the respondents, i.e., the employer and the insurance company, appellant/workman has filed this appeal under Sec. 30 of the Workmen's Compensation Act, 1923 (henceforth 'the Act').

Judgement: Appeal succeeds.

Reason: The employer was in default in paying the compensation due under the Act within one month from the date it fell due, therefore, the Lower Court ought to have awarded simple interest at the rate of 12 per cent per annum. In the present case, it is not disputed that under the policy of insurance the risk of the workman under the Act was covered.

Although the insurance company has deposited a sum of ₹67,640 on 31 January 1996 yet in view of the default made by the employer the insurer is liable to pay interest at the entire amount awarded. Deducting the above amount from ₹84,720, the remaining amount of ₹17,080 shall be paid by the respondent 2, i.e., the insurance company within a period of one month from today. The insurance company shall also be liable to pay simple interest at the rate of 12 per cent per annum from 12 July 1995, the date of impugned order till realization on the entire sum of ₹84,720.

---

*R. Gopalakrishna vs The Manager, Karaska Roadways; 2008 (1) MPHT 103; see http://www.indiankanoon.org/doc/1999599/ (2 November 2011).

Sec. 3 of the Act as is shown in the aforementioned text. Section 4 deals with the constitution of the ESI Corporation consisting of the following:

(a) A chairman, a vice chairman, and not more than five members appointed by the Central Government

(b) One person each representing each of the states in which the Act is in force to be appointed by the concerned state government

(c) One person appointed by the Central Government as its representative

(d) Ten persons representing employees

(e) Ten persons representing employers

(f) Two persons representing the medical profession

(g) Three members of the parliament of whom two shall be members of the Lok Sabha and one of the Rajya Sabha

(h) Ex-officio member: director of the ESI Corporation

Contributions to ESI   Secs 38–45B deal with all the employees in factories and establishments to whom the Act applies and those who contribute to the ESI Corporation. It is done both by the employees and their employers. The rates of contributions are predetermined according to the rules of the Act, i.e., rule 51. The corporation is responsible for the management of the insurance.

Benefits   Secs 46–73 of Chapter V of the Act lay down in detail the benefits under six heads of classification: sickness, maternity, disablement, dependant's benefit, medical benefit, and funeral expenses.

Adjudication of disputes and claims   Secs 74–83 make provision for the establishment of Employees' Insurance Court. It lists all the matters with regard to disputes and claims to be decided by the court. (See Case 23.2.) The Employees' Insurance Court has the following powers:

(a) To summon and enforce the attendance of the witnesses

(b) To compel, discover, and produce documents and material objects

(c) To administer oath and record evidence

BOX 23.1

GAP IN WORKER WELFARE

The heartrending picture of the boy, Dinabandhu, exhibiting the election photo ID card of his father, Surendra Sethi who died in Alang, the ship breaking yard on Gujarat coast, which is considered one of the most hazardous workplaces in India. There is big gap between the law and the welfare of the workers.

Courtesy: Frontline, Vol. 24, Issue 22, 3 November 2007: http://hindu.com/fiine/fl2422/stories/20071116505108300.htm. For better understanding of workers' problems and environmental hazards, see the above as well as the website http://www.indiatogether.org/2004/sep/ddz-alang.htm (1 November 2011).

Employees' Provident Funds and Miscellaneous Provisions Act, 1952 and (Amendment) Provisions Act, 1996

Employees' Provident Fund Schemes:

(1) The Central Government may, by notification in the official gazette, frame a scheme to be called the Employees' Provident Fund Scheme for the establishment of provident funds under this act for employees or for any class of employees and specify the establishments or class of establishments to which the said scheme shall apply and there shall be established, as soon as may be after the framing of the scheme, a fund in accordance with the provisions of this act and the scheme.

(1A) The fund shall vest in, and be administered by, the central board constituted under Sec. 5A.

(1B) Subject to the provisions of this act, a scheme framed under subsec. (1) may provide for all or any of the matters specified in schedule II.

(2) A scheme framed under subsec. (1) may provide that any of its provisions shall take effect either prospectively or retrospectively on such date as may be specified in this behalf in the scheme.

– The Employees' Provident Funds and Miscellaneous Provisions Act, 1952[2]

CASE 23.2

APPELLANT: Regional Director ESI   vs   RESPONDENT: L. Ranga Rao and others*

DATE OF JUDGEMENT: 24 June 1981

FACTS: The respondent before us were applicants before the Employees Insurance Court. Their son Sudhindra Kumar was an employee of M/s Mysore Breweries Ltd, Yeshanthpur, Bangalore. He was working as a refrigerator operator in the said factory. On 10 August 1978 when he was on his way to the factory to join duty in the third shift, which was to commence at 10.00 p.m., he was run over by an unidentified motor vehicle causing his death at the spot. Unfortunately, the vehicle could not be traced and, therefore, the respondents could not approach the claims tribunal constituted under the Motor Vehicle Act.

They moved the Employees Insurance Court under Sec. 75 of the Act claiming the benefits payable under the Act on the ground that their son died as a result of an employment injury.

The Regional Director of the ESI Corporation contested the application contending inter alia that the employee was killed in a road accident while walking on a public road and not travelling in a vehicle provided by the employer and, therefore, his death was not out of and in the course of his employment.

But the Insurance Court did not accept the contention of the Regional Director. It held that the death was in the course of the employment and the dependents are entitled to the benefits payable under the Act.

The ESI Corporation has preferred this appeal challenging the order of the Insurance Court.

JUDGEMENT: Lower Court verdict upheld; petition dismissed.

REASON: With regard to the facts and circumstances of the case, we are of the view that the order of the Insurance Court is perfectly justified and does not call for interference.

Before parting with the case, we think it is right to observe that the corporation should not be a litigant in each and every case. The Act is designed to confer benefits on the disabled employees and their dependents in distress. The machinery for implementing the scheme of state insurance is provided in the shape of the corporation and subsidiary agencies. The benefits due to the employees and their dependents have to be promptly worked out and delivered to them and it should be the primary concern of the corporation.

---

*Regional Director ESI vs L. Ranga Rao and others; ILR 1981 KAR 1255, 1981 (2) KarLJ 197, (1982) ILLJ 29 Kant; also see http://www.indiankanoon.org/doc/320209/.

---

[2]Several of the square brackets and number qualifications are removed for flow of the text for the sake of better comprehension.

The provident fund legislation was yet another step in the direction of social security, whereby employees would be encouraged to save for the sake of the family. These were deposit-linked schemes for the employees. This Act was originally intended only for factory and establishment workers but now has been amended to include a larger class and number of employees.

Under Sec. 6 of the Act, the principal duty is laid upon the employer to put the Employees' Provident Fund and Family Pension Schemes into operation and to make contributions of both the employer and the employees' share to the fund, and deduct from the wages of the employees their share. (See Case 23.3.)

The administration of the scheme is provided in Sec. 5A to be under Central Board. Sec. 7 deals with the determination of funds due from employers and their recovery and employees' provident fund. The Board appoints inspectors for the purpose of administration. The Central Government has powers to adjudicate on various statutory issues of doubt or difficulty.

⚖ MANAGER'S TAKEAWAY

- A worker's wages are not just the salary but also the instruments that secure his welfare.
- Before going to the court against an employee, the employer must do a serious analysis of both the settlement of the workers' dues and the costs of litigation and its long-term consequences.

CASE 23.3

APPELLANT: Ajanta Offset and Packaging Ltd vs RESPONDENT: The Regional Director of Provident Fund[*]

DATE OF JUDGEMENT: 25 March 2004

FACTS:

The petitioner is aggrieved by an order dated 27 May 1974 communicating coverage of the petitioner under the provisions of the Employees' Provident Funds and Family Pension Funds Act, 1952, now known as the Employees' Provident Fund and Miscellaneous Provisions Act, 1952. The petitioner is also aggrieved by a memorandum dated 24 November 1976 sent by the Regional Provident Fund Commissioner demanding a sum of ₹42,562.40 plus ₹989.25 on account of damages for delayed remittances of provident fund dues from April 1974 to February 1976.

In their counter affidavit, the respondents have denied the averments made by the petitioner. The most important fact that has been brought out by the respondents in their counter affidavit is that a date of hearing was given to the petitioner pursuant to the show cause notice on more than one occasion. Finally, on 2 November 1976, the petitioner was heard when its representative discussed the case and thereafter requested for an adjournment. The adjournment was declined because the petitioner had asked for adjournments on three previous occasions. On the basis of the material available on record, the Regional Provident Fund Commissioner passed an order on the same date, i.e., 2 November 1976 confirming the damages levied against the petitioner. Pursuant to the order dated 2 November 1976, the impugned demand 24 November 1976 was raised. This led to the filing of the present writ petition.

---

[*]Ajanta Offset and Packaging Ltd vs The Regional Director of Provident Fund; 110 (2004) DLT 757, 2004 (74) DRJ 293; http://www.indiankanoon.org/doc/1971828/ (3 November 2010).

Contd

Case 23.3 *Contd*

JUDGEMENT: Petition dismissed and passed order accordingly

REASON: We are of the view that framing of the table of damages by the government is a salutary measure for the guidance of the officers of the government who act under Sec. 14-B. Under the table, the amount of damages is related to the delay in payment of the contributions. This method of determining damages is entirely reasonable and it shows that no officer acting under Sec. 14-B can act arbitrarily, but must follow this reasonable guideline made by the government. The quantum of damages was, therefore, reduced to 50 per cent of the demand made at the time of the show cause notice. Reasons have been given why the contentions made by employer could not be accepted in full and why a partial relief for those reasons should be given namely by reducing the damages by 50 per cent.

The writ petition requires dismissal and it is ordered accordingly. The bank guarantee furnished by the petitioner for the amount in dispute should be encashed forthwith. The petitioner will be liable to pay and the respondent is entitled to recover the disputed amount with interest at the rate of 9 per cent per annum from 22 February 1977, the date on which an interim order was made in favor of the petitioner, till its recovery. The respondent will be entitled to costs of ₹5000.

SUMMARY

- Social welfare of the workers is the constitutional duty of the government, particularly, the states (A 41, 42, and 43). Laws with regard to compensation, insurance, and provident fund are central to the social welfare of the workers. The aim of such legislations is the protection of the workers and their dependents.
- The Workmen's Compensation Act, 1923 makes the employer liable for the welfare of the employees.

Clear provisions have been made through the detailed schedules for the items that need to be compensated. Similarly, insurance and provident fund that are financed by the contributions of both the employees and employer are to be managed according to the respective acts.

EXERCISES

(i) Ramesh is a worker in a foundry. He worked for a half a day and then got ill and eventually died of heart attack after a couple of days. Is he eligible for compensation?

Hint: Yes; see Schedule II of the Workmen's Compensation Act, 1923.

(ii) A person died while working on an electricity pole. The work was submitted by the Electricity Department to a contractor. Who should pay the compensation to the dependents of the dead?

Hint: See Sec. 12 of the Workmen's Compensation Act, 1923.

(iii) You are managing a very small enterprise; although you have over twenty persons working for you and you are supposed to pay for the provident fund of your employees, the financial situation does not allow you to do so. What is your way out?

Hint: Certain establishments are exempt from the Act; see Sec. 16 Amendment Act, 1988.

(iv) State the salient features of the Workmen's Compensation Act, 1923 and explain the role of the employer.

(v) How does the ESI Act, 1948 provide the adjudication of disputes and claims?

DEVELOPMENT OF LEGAL EDGE

Project—Compensation Guide

Objective Ready Human Resource Reference

Method Make a systematic list of the four schedules of the Workmen's Compensation Act, 1923

Benefit Circulate to establishments employing more than twenty persons.

FURTHER READING

Book

• *Compliances Under Labour Laws, A User's Guide to Adhere with the Provisions Under Various Employment Related Acts*, Universal Publications (2011).

Acts

• http://labour.nic.in.

CASE STUDY   CONTRACTING

Contracting

(1) *Where any person (hereinafter in this section referred to as the principal) in the course of or for the purposes of his trade or business contracts with any other person (hereinafter in this section referred to as the contractor) for the execution by or under the contractor of the whole or any part of any work, which is ordinarily part of the trade or business of the principal. The principal shall be liable to pay to any workman employed in the execution of the work any compensation, which he would have been liable to pay if that workman had been immediately employed by him; and where compensation is claimed from the principal, this act shall apply as if references to the principal were substituted for references to the employer except that the amount of compensation shall be calculated with reference to the wages of the workman under the employer by whom he is immediately employed.*

(2) *Where the principal is liable to pay compensation under this section, he shall be entitled to be indemnified by the contractor, 2[or any other person from whom the workman could have recovered compensation and where a contractor who is himself a principal is liable to pay compensation or to indemnify a principal under this section he shall be entitled to be indemnified by any person standing to him in the relation of a contractor from whom the workman could have recovered compensation,] and all questions as to the right to and the amount of any such indemnity shall, in default of agreement, be settled by the commissioner.*

(3) *Nothing in this section shall be construed as preventing a workman from recovering compensation from the contractor instead of the principal.*

(4) *This section shall not apply in any case where the accident occurred elsewhere than on, in or about the premises on which the principal has undertaken or usually undertakes, as the case may be, to execute the work or which are otherwise under his control or management.*

– Workmen's Compensation Act, 1923, Sec. 12

The Way It Happened

The facts of the case are that one Ram Chander was working along with other workmen with the Appellant Corporation and respondent contractor on work for extraction of geltus and carrying them by rope way. The agreement was entered into between the Appellant Corporation and respondent contractor on 2 December 1985 to execute the contract. When Ram Chander was working on the span, he fell down on a stone on 15 June 1989 at about 12.45 p.m. and thereafter he was taken to Rampur Hospital where he died at 3 p.m. due to the injuries suffered by him in the mishap. A report of the accident was lodged by Shyam Chand, brother of the deceased, in Nitmand police station. The claimants who were the first party before the commissioner below are the parents of the deceased and filed claim application under Secs 4 and 4-A of the Workmen's Compensation Act.

Submission by HP Forest Corporation

In its written statement, the Appellant Corporation, second party, stated that the deceased was not their employee and there existed no relationship of employee and employer between them. It was stated that the relationship of the claimants with the deceased was not within the knowledge of the Appellant Corporation and that the deceased may be under the employment of respondent contractor, and if he had died while working with him, it was his obligation and duty to lodge the report with the police and to pay compensation to the dependants of the deceased. The respondent contractor had not informed the Appellant Corporation with regard to the employment of Ram Chander on his work. It was further stated that it was the duty of the respondent contractor to supply the names and particulars of the workmen who were engaged in the work by him as per the terms of the agreement executed by him with the Appellant Corporation. The Appellant Corporation denied the liability to pay the compensation to the claimants.

Submission by the Contractor

The respondent contractor in his written statement also denied the employment of Ram Chander by him on his work and contended that he was merely the labour supply mate of the Appellant Corporation on commission basis and it was the Appellant Corporation alone who was the employer of the labour. He also stated that the work was executed by him on behalf of the Appellant Corporation who was the main employer of the labour and, therefore, he also denied the liability to pay the compensation to the claimants.

Questions

1. Was the deceased Ram Chander an employee of the second party?
2. Did the accident occur when the deceased was in the employment?
3. If issue Nos. 1 and 2 are proved in favour of the first and second party of the first party, then how much compensation is to be given to them?
4. If issue No. 3 is in favour of the applicant then who out of the second party is liable to pay the amount of compensation?

Verdict of the Lower Court

The parties went to trial. The commissioner, on appreciation of the evidence, came to the conclusion that the deceased Ram Chander, while setting the span in order, fell down and died and at the relevant time he was performing the work of the Appellant Corporation, which the respondent contractor was carrying on its behalf. Consequently, compensation under Sec. 4 of the act was determined to the tune of ₹1,35,828 and was ordered to be paid to the mother of the deceased and not to the father for the reason that under the Hindu Succession Act, 1956, the father would not get the share of the deceased who was unmarried at the time of the death. The commissioner below also held that if the amount of compensation determined in his order was not deposited after one month of the announcement of the order then the Appellant Corporation would be liable for 50 per cent penalty and interest at the rate of 6 per cent per annum on the said amount of compensation.

The Appeal

The above appeal by the H.P. State Forest Corporation (Appellant Corporation) under Sec. 30 of the Workmen's Compensation Act, 1923 is directed against the order dated 18 November 1992 of commissioner under the Workmen's Compensation Act, 1923, Sub Division Ani, whereby claim of ₹1,35,828 filed by the claimants was allowed for the death of their son Ram Chander who died while in the employment of the Appellant Corporation and respondent contractor. The prayer was for award of interest and penalty provided under the provisions of the act which, according to them, was not awarded by the commissioner accordingly.

The Judge's Judgement

We have perused the provisions of Sec. 12 of the Act and interpreting the provisions thereof, four essential conditions have to be satisfied before Sec. 12 can be applied. The four conditions are thus:

(i) That the person (called the principal) is carrying on a trade or business and, in the course of or for the purpose of that trade or business, engages a contractor to execute the work.

(ii) That work is ordinarily a part of the trade or business of the principal.

(iii) The accident that gives rise to the liability for compensation must have occurred on, in or about the premises on which the principal has undertaken, or usually undertakes, to execute the work or which is in his control or management.

(iv) The accident must have occurred while the workman was in the course of his employment in executing the work.

The finding recorded by the commissioner would show that the above conditions are satisfied in this case. The employee Ram Chander was doing the work of repairing the span, which was established for carrying the geltus and the said work was assigned to the respondent contractor by Appellant Corporation and, therefore, the Appellant Corporation was the principal employer of the deceased.

In the circumstances, Sec. 12 of the Act is applicable to the facts of the case and there cannot be any doubt about the legal position that the opposite party No. 1, i.e., the Appellant Corporation is also responsible to pay compensation payable under the Act to the workman even if the workman was engaged actually by the second party, i.e., the respondent contractor.

The commissioner committed a serious error of law in awarding the interest and penalty if the award amount of compensation was not deposited before him within one month of the order. To this extent, the finding of the commissioner is wholly unjust and untenable. Compensation becomes payable on the date of the accident and not on the date of determination of the amount thereof.

We hold that the claimants are entitled to the amount of compensation of ₹1,35,828 awarded by the commissioner along with 50 per cent penalty and interest at the rate of 6 per cent from the date of the accident of Ram Chander who admittedly died on 15 June 1989. The entire amount together with interest and penalty shall be deposited with the registry office by the Appellant Corporation within three months from this date and the Appellant Corporation shall be at liberty to get the indemnification of the amount from the respondent contractor under Sec. 12(2) of the Act.

The finding of the commissioner below that under the Hindu Succession Act, 1956 claimant Sheesh Ram, father of the deceased will not be entitled to get the share of the compensation is not found to be legal and valid. It appears that the commissioner below has not cared to read the definition of dependant under Sec. 2(1)(d) of the Act where under a parent is entitled for compensation being dependant of the deceased workman. In the present case, the deceased was unmarried at the time of his death. Both the claimants are, therefore, held entitled to share the entire amount of compensation together with interest and penalty in equal shares. No other submissions have been made by the learned counsel on either side.

For the aforesaid reasons and observations, the appeal is allowed in part and the order of the commissioner below shall stand modified to the extent indicated above.

Conclusion

In the above case, you see very clearly the role of the employer, the outsourced service, and the worker. Matters become painful when the worker is dead and the dependants have to make the rightful claim. A pertinent question is to ask is that if you were the Director of the H.P. Forest Department what things would you do differently than the person in the above case did. Would you not be in a dilemma that your reporting Authority may disapprove it? Thus, as a consequence, if you allow it you will be questioned, if you do not you will be questioned.

Discussion Questions

4. Tell the story in the case according to facts.
5. How many parties are involved in the above case? Highlight their relationship.
6. Summarize in your own words Sec. 12 of the Workmen's Compensation Act, 1923.
7. Discuss in detail the role of the principal and the contractor.
8. How would you apply Sec. 12 of the Act to this case?

9. Explain the stand taken by the lower court.

10. Analyze the legal reasoning of the judge.

11. As a manager, what legal lessons do you learn from the case?

Going Beyond

1. How do you ethically justify the disowning of a worker by an employer, so that one does not have to part with the legal compensation?

2. Discuss contract as an agreement of employment and the issues governing it.

LEGAL LUMINARY

BABU JAGJIVAN RAM—INDEPENDENT INDIA'S FIRST MINISTER FOR LABOUR

Jagjivan Ram, born in 1908, is as much a part of India's history as Baba Saheb Ambedkar. Both came from the underprivileged classes of the Indian society, both were erudite and dedicated themselves to the cause of the depressed classes. Ambedkar's fame lies in the fact that he was the father of the Constitution of India. Jagjivan Ram's fame lies in the fact that under his ministership, most important labour laws were enacted:

The Minimum Wages Act, 1946 The Industrial Disputes Act, 1947 The ESI Act, 1948 The Provident Fund and Miscellaneous Act, 1952

Babu Jagjivan Ram's father was from Bihar, and worked for the British Army. His mother was his mentor and despite several difficulties in his school, she encouraged him to study. For lower caste children, the pitcher for drinking water was separate from the others. Jagjivan broke the pitcher of the lower caste again and again until finally the school gave in and all the children could drink from the same pitcher. Later on, when he joined Benaras Hindu University, he faced similar discrimination and his counter action stopped it once and for all. He graduated in Science from the University of Calcutta and wanted to be a scientist. However, the social problems were so pressing, particularly those of the workers, that he built a workers' organization. This brought him to close to the great heroes of freedom movement, especially Subhash Chandra Bose and Chandrashekar Azad. In 1934, there was an earthquake in Bihar. Jagjivan Ram rushed to his home state and organized relief work. Herein he met Mahatma Gandhi for the first time and his life changed completely, as history bears witness. He was one of the leaders of the Quit India Movement started by the Mahatma and was incarcerated in the jail for it by the British Government. In Independent India, despite his young age, Jagjivan shouldered important ministries in the government.

1946–1952	Union Minister of Labour
1952–1956	Union Minister for Communications
1956–1962	Union Minister for Transport and Railways
1962–1963	Union Minister for Transport and Communications
1966–1967	Union Minister for Labour, Employment and Rehabilitation
1967–1970	Union Minister for Food and Agriculture
1970–1974 & 1977–1979	Union Minister of Defence
1974–1977	Union Minister for Agriculture and Irrigation
1977	Founding Member Congress for Democracy party, aligned with Janata Party Deputy Prime Minister of India.

Amidst his busy schedule, he served as President of the Bharat Scouts and Guides from September 1976 to April 1983.

Contd

Legal Luminary *Contd*

Along with Shachi Rani Gurtu, he wrote the book *Jagjivan Ram on Labour Problems* (1951) and he wrote another book called *Caste Challenge in India* (1980). He died in 1986. His memorial is known as Samata Sthal or Equality Place, a term that summarizes the life and struggles of Jagjivan Ram. A postal stamp was released in his honour in 1991. His daughter Meira Kumar was the Speaker of the Lok Sabha from 2009 to 2014.

The Laws of Industrial Relations

Principle: *Qui in suo utitur, nemini facit injuriam.*

He who uses his legal rights harms no one.

CHAPTER OUTLINE

- Introduction and Interpretation
- The Trade Unions Act, 1926, and Amendments Act, 2001
- The Industrial Disputes Act, 1947

- *Case Study:* Dispute over Conciliation and Settlement
- *Legal Luminary:* George Fernandes

24.1 INTRODUCTION AND INTERPRETATION

The Taj Mahal of Agra is the signature monument of India. As the legend goes, the Taj was built by the best architects, engineers, artisans, and labourers of the time. As beautiful and romantic as its glory and splendour is, equally gory and violent was the fate meted out to all those who built it to disable them from replicating or repeating the feat, thereby making it exclusive and the only one of its kind in the world.

Such a cruel reward for the workers of such a magnificent monument is unthinkable today. Thanks to the admission of workers' rights in the aftermath of the industrial revolution, there are labour laws, labour unions, and laws in place for the employers. The instruments of justice provide not only for wages but also for social securities and they seek the holistic development of the faculties of workers, based on the principles of equality and freedom, without discrimination of gender, race, caste, or creed.

Industrial Relations

In common parlance, industrial relations is understood as the employer-employee relationship through the medium of employees' trade union. Until the economic reforms of the 1990s, during the entire twentieth century, India was mired in industrial action commonly known as strikes. Strikes are refusal to work and have been usually resorted to pressurize the management. However, with industrial growth and free market economic policies, industrial disputes have found negotiated settlements. For the redressal of grievances, labour courts and Labour Lok Adalat or Labour Ombudsman have been established. (Table 24.1 shows the various parties to industrial relations.)

From the management point of view, industrial relation concerns human resource management. Management science has made it possible to develop harmonious labour relationships, formulate goal-based teams, establish strategies through employer–employee cooperation, establish a common mission, and develop related skills. Good human resources management not only stops employees from resorting to industrial action but also makes the enterprise understand and appreciate the true value and worth of human capital. This treatment of employees as capital allows the employer to realize it is an invaluable resource, which must be protected and promoted to result in a win–win situation for the industry.

From the legal point of view, two more factors come into play: the government and the trade unions. In case of a dispute between the employees and the employer, the law is the arbiter, authority, or the umpire. The government enforces the law and the trade unions plead on behalf of the employees. The tribunals, the appellate tribunals, and the courts of the land dispense justice and award relief or punishment as appropriate.

The importance of good industrial relations can never be adequately over-emphasized. Good relations will result in uninterrupted production, which renders continuous employment, in turn, resulting in reward for workers and profits for the enterprise. Excessive and continuous adverse industrial action has eventually led to factories being closed down, resulting in the loss of livelihoods of the workers.

Scope

The scope of this chapter is limited to two Acts: The Trade Union Act, 1926, and the Industrial Disputes Act, 1947. It discusses the essential elements of its implementation,

Table 24.1 Parties to industrial relations[*]

Government	Employer	Workman	Trade union
In relation to any industrial dispute concerning any industry carried on by or under the authority of the Central Government	In relation to an industry carried on by or under the authority of any department of the Central Government or a State Government, the authority prescribed in this behalf, or where no authority is prescribed, the head of the department; in relation to an industry carried on by or on behalf of a local authority, the chief executive officer of that authority	Any person (including an apprentice) employed in any industry to carry out any manual, unskilled, skilled, technical, operational, clerical, or supervisory work for hire or reward, whether the terms of employment be express or implied, and for the purposes of any proceeding under this Act in relation to an industrial dispute, includes any such person who has been dismissed, discharged, or retrenched in connection with, or as a consequence of, that dispute, or whose dismissal, discharge, or retrenchment has led to that dispute, but does not include any such person	A trade union registered under the Trade Unions Act, 1926

[*]The Industrial Disputes Act, 1947, Sec. 2 (a i), (g i,ii), (rr iv, s), (q).

which will help in knowing in advance that any decision taken in relation to the employees will have serious legal consequences. One will be unable to report to one's authorities about the existing problems in a company if one cannot articulate the same legally.

24.2 THE TRADE UNIONS ACT, 1926, AND AMENDMENTS ACT, 2001

'Trade Union' means any combination, whether temporary or permanent, formed primarily for the purpose of regulating the relations between workmen and employers or between workmen and workmen, or between employers and employers, or for imposing restrictive conditions on the conduct of any trade or business, and includes any federation of two or more Trade Unions: Provided that this Act shall not affect:

(i) *any agreement between partners as to their own business;*

(ii) *any agreement between an employer and those employed by him as to such employment; or*

(iii) *any agreement in consideration of the sale of the goodwill of a business or of instruction in any profession, trade, or handicraft.*

– The Trade Unions Act, 1926, Sec. 2 (h)

The development of organization of the employee association has become familiarized since the founding of the International Labour Union in 1919. The philosophy of such an organization of workers has come to be known as trade unionism. It consists of the fundamental assumption that workers have a just right to their performance in an enterprise. Individually, workers might find themselves helpless in fighting for their rights; however, if united, they can stand against the employers' unjust practices. Thus, it is a collective bargain against the management of an enterprise or a company that runs such an enterprise for the wages and welfare benefits of the members of the trade union.

With the above-mentioned law in place in 1926, the Indian Trade Unions have grown and multiplied and have had enduring effects on the Indian industries. Most of the trade unions have affiliations with the major political parties in India, thus providing them with a greater say in the shaping up of the industrial and labour policies and legislation.

The law of trade union comes under the general category of the right of human association enshrined in the constitution. The other types of associations, other than trade unions, which are appropriately placed within the ambit of the law are:

- The Societies Registration Act, 1860
- The Cooperative Societies Act, 1912
- The Companies Act, 1956

The above-mentioned Acts have their own objectives and are different from the Trade Union Act. Hence, trade unions are legal only if they are formed under the Trade Union Act, 1926. The following are the essential characteristics of this Act.

Registration of a trade union

Under Sec. 4, at least seven members or more may apply for registration of a trade union by subscribing their names to the rules of the trade union and comply with the Act with respect to registration. Under Sec. 5, those desirous of the application must submit the details regarding their names, occupations, and addresses. Under Sec. 6 of the Act, registration is possible only if the executive is constituted and the requisite rules are formed (see Case 24.1). Under Sec. 8, the Registrar has the power to call for further particulars. The Registrar, upon being satisfied, may register the trade union (Sec. 8) and issue a certificate of registration on the prescribed form (Sec. 9). The characteristics of the registered trade union are (Sec. 13) as follows:

CASE 24.1

APPELLANT: The Registrar of Trade Unions   VS   RESPONDENT: The Government Press Employees' Union

DATE OF JUDGEMENT: 29 January 1975[*]

FACTS: The employees of the Pondicherry Government Press constituted themselves into the Government Press Employees' Union and, under Sec. 5 of the Trade Unions Act, applied to the Registrar of Trade Unions, Pondicherry, for registration of the trade union.

The Commissioner of Labour, Pondicherry, sent a communication to the Secretary of the Government Press Employees' Union regretting his inability to register the trade union under the Trade Unions Act, 1962. The ground given by the Registrar for refusing to register the application was, 'the present functions of the Government Press, Pondicherry, do not come within the meaning of trade or business.'

Aggrieved by this order, the Secretary of the Government Press Employees' Trade Union filed an appeal with the District Judge, Pondicherry, impugning the order of the Registrar.

Consequently, the learned District Judge set aside the order of the Registrar of Trade Unions and allowed the appeal with costs.

It is against this judgement that the Registrar of Trade Unions, Pondicherry, has preferred this petition.

JUDGEMENT: Petition dismissed.

REASON: The Division Bench deliberately refused to decide whether the workmen in an industry conducted by the government would be governed by the Trade Unions Act, 1926: If workmen in a government undertaking such as the Government Press of Pondicherry had exclusively and without joining hands with the civil service exercising sovereign and regal functions formed an association, the Division Bench would have regarded them as 'workmen' within the meaning of the Trade Unions Act entitled to have their Trade Union registered under Sec. 6 of the Act.

I have little hesitation in holding that the respondent (Government Press, Employees' Union) is an association of workmen employed in an 'industry', irrespective of whether it is an industry conducted by the government or the private sector and is, therefore, entitled to registration under Sec. 6 of the Act.

I am clear, in my mind, that the workmen employed in an industrial undertaking, such as the Government Press, Pondicherry, are 'workmen' entitled to the benefits of the Trade Act of 1926. Consequently, the Unions Act confirmed the judgement of the court below and dismissed this petition with costs.

---

[*]The Registrar of Trade Unions vs The Government Press Employees' Union; (1975) 2 MLJ 347; see also: http://www.indiankanoon.org/doc/1486162/ (29 October 2011).

(a) It becomes a body corporate by the name under which it is registered and becomes a distinct body separate from the members.

(b) It has perpetual succession and common seal.

(c) It has the power to acquire movable and immovable properties.

(d) It has the power to contract.

(e) It can sue or be sued.

Cancellation of registration of a trade union

Section 10 empowers the Registrar to cancel registration if the registration is obtained by fraud, has ceased to exist, or contravened or rescinded some rule. In such an event if the trade union feels aggrieved, it can appeal in the court, where the proceedings must begin within 60 days of the appeal.

Rights and privileges of a registered trade union

The following are the rights and privileges of a registered trade union:

(a) Every registered trade union has all the above-mentioned characteristics of a body corporate (Sec. 13).

(b) A trade union may form a separate fund for the civic and political interest of its members (Sec. 16).

(c) An office bearer of the trade union is granted immunity in civil suits in respect of the funds spent on the objects of the trade union (Secs 17 and 18).

(d) An agreement between the members of the registered trade union shall not be void or voidable merely by reason of the fact that any of the objects of the agreement is in restraint of trade (Sec. 19).

(e) An office bearer of the trade union has the right to inspect its books (Sec. 20).

(f) Minors, who have completed the age of 15 years, are eligible to be members of a trade union (Sec. 21).

Duties of a registered trade union

(a) If there is any change in the address of the head office, it must be notified to the Registrar of the trade unions in writing (Sec. 12).

(b) The funds of the trade union may be spent only on its objects stated and approved in the application of its registration (Sec. 15).

(c) A separate fund may be formed for the purposes of civic and political interests (Sec. 16).

(d) Not less than one half of the total number of office bearers shall be persons actually engaged or employed in an industry with which the trade union is connected. The other half of the office bearers may be social or political workers (Sec. 22).

(e) Every trade union must file returns on the prescribed form (Sec. 28).

Amalgamation of trade unions

Any two or more registered trade unions may become amalgamated together as one trade union with or without the dissolution or division of the funds of such trade unions (Sec. 24–26).

Dissolution of a trade union

A trade union stands dissolved when signed by seven of its members and by its Secretary and sent to the Registrar within 14 days after the resolution of dissolution is passed (Sec. 27).

Penalties

Small fines ranging from ₹5 to ₹500 are levied if (Sec. 31)
(a) Annual returns are not filed
(b) Notice of change of address is not furnished
(c) Notice of change of name or amalgamation is not forwarded to the Registrar

24.3 THE INDUSTRIAL DISPUTES ACT, 1947

TEXT

'Industrial dispute' means any dispute or difference between employers and employers or between employers and workmen, or between workmen and workmen, which is connected with the employment or non-employment or the terms of employment or with the conditions of labour, of any person.

The Industrial Disputes Act, 1947, Sec. 2(k)

> **MANAGER'S TAKEAWAY**
> - In union there is strength.
> - Lingering question in the mind of the manager: How to deal with a trade union?

Meaning and Objectives of the Act

The Industrial Disputes Act, 1947, provides for setting up of labour courts, industrial tribunals, and national tribunals. These are set up by the central and state governments or by the administrations of union territories for dealing with matters that cover the central and the state domains, respectively. It, however, depends on the central government to refer a matter for which it is the appropriate government to a labour court or an industrial tribunal constituted by the state government.

Labour courts deal with matters pertaining to the discharge and dismissal of workmen, application and interpretation of standing orders, propriety of orders passed under standing orders, legality of strikes of lock-outs, etc. Industrial tribunals deal with collective disputes such as wages, hours of work, leave, retrenchment, and closure as well as all matters falling under the jurisdiction of labour courts.

The central government may set up a national tribunal for adjudication of industrial disputes, which, in its opinion, involve questions of national importance or are of such nature that industrial establishments in more than one state are likely to be interested in such disputes.

The Main Objectives

The main objectives of the Act are obvious from the previous section relating to the settlement of industrial disputes and thus administer justice are as follows:
(a) Secure industrial peace through the administration of justice

(b) Endeavour to re-establish employee–employer relationship

(c) Ameliorate the employees' condition

Important Issues of Dispute

Prohibition of strikes and lock-outs (Secs 22–23)

(a) No person working in public utility will go on strike without giving the employer a notice of 6 weeks in advance.

(b) No employer carrying on any public utility service shall lock-out without giving a notice of 6 weeks in advance.

(c) A strike is illegal if it is in contravention to Secs 22 and 23 of the Act. Section 25 expressly prohibits any person from knowingly expending money in direct furtherance of the strike or lock-out.

(d) Section 24 deals with the penalties ranging from ₹50 to ₹1000 and imprisonment of upto 6 months.

Lay-off and retrenchment (Sec. 25)

(a) Lay-off means no employment is provided for person who is legally employed. Laying-off may be with an agreement, with full wages, or may be due to absence due to temporary disablement, being on maternity leave, etc.

(b) Retrenchment is the termination of service. The worker may be given a month's notice in writing. It must indicate the reason, the worker must be paid, and notice must also be given to the appropriate government authority. The principle followed in retrenchment is: last come, first go.

Adjudication Machinery

Conciliation officers

These officers fall under Sec. 4 and are entrusted with the duty of mediating in and promoting the settlement of industrial disputes. They may be appointed for a specified area, or for specified industries in a specified area, or for one or more specified industries, either permanently or for a limited period. It is the duty of these officers to bring both the employees and employers together and help them resolve their differences. If the dispute is settled, they shall send a report, to that effect, to the appropriate government.

Board of conciliation

According to Sec. 5, the Board of Conciliation consists of a chairman and two or four other members. Where a dispute has been referred to the board, it shall, without delay, investigate the dispute and perform all such things as it thinks fit for the purpose of inducing the parties to come to a fair and amicable settlement of the dispute.

Court of inquiry

Under Sec. 6, it is to inquire into any matter appearing to be connected with or relevant to an industrial dispute. It shall, thereafter, report about it to the government usually within a period of 6 months from the commencement of its inquiry. Such a court may consist of one independent member or of such a number of independent members as the appropriate government may deem fit; where it consists of two or more members, one of them shall be appointed as the chairman.

Table 24.2 discusses the different types of courts.

Table 24.2 Types of courts

(Sec. 7) Labour court	(Sec. 7A) Industrial tribunal	(Sec. 7B) National tribunal
Established by the government through notification in the official gazette. Schedule II deals in detail with matters of the court.	Established by the government through notification in the official gazette. Schedule III deals in detail with matters of the court.	Established by the government through notification in the official gazette.

Award

An award implies any interim or final determination or settlement (Sec. 10) by the labour court or industrial tribunal or the national tribunal. It shall be published in the official gazette (Sec. 17), noting both the award and minutes of any dissent.

The Act also makes it obligatory for an employer to set up a grievance settlement authority in an industrial establishment in which fifty or more workers have been employed in the preceding 12 months. This authority shall have the responsibility to settle industrial disputes concerning an individual worker employed in that establishment.

Under the Industrial Disputes Act, 1947, the central government is the appropriate government for the investigation and settlement of industrial disputes with regard to the departmental undertakings of the central government, major ports, mines, oil fields, cantonment boards, banking and insurance companies, the Life Insurance Corporation of India, the Industrial Finance Corporation of India Limited, the Oil and Natural Gas Corporation Limited, the Indian Airlines, Air India, the Airport Authority of India, and all air transport services. However, in relation to other industrial establishments, the state government is the appropriate government. (See Case 24.2.)

MANAGER'S TAKEAWAY

- Disputes are nipped in the bud to ensure the company's health.
- Careless interpretation of legal language is the surest way to lose a case.

Central Government Industrial Tribunals (CGITs) have been set up in different parts of the country. Currently, there are 17 CGITs to whom industrial disputes could be referred to for adjudication. These CGITs-cum-labour courts are located at New Delhi, Mumbai (2 CGITs), Bengaluru, Kolkata, Asansol, Dhanbad (2 CGITs), Jabalpur, Chandigarh, Kanpur, Jaipur, Lucknow, Nagpur, Hyderabad, Chennai, and Bhubaneshwar. Out of these 17 CGITs, the CGITs in Mumbai-I and Kolkata have been declared as National Industrial Tribunals.

The Organization of the Chief Labour Commissioner (Central) acts as the primary conciliatory agency in the Central Government for industrial disputes. The Regional

Labour Commissioners (Central) and Assistant Labour Commissioners (Central), on behalf of the Chief Labour Commissioner (Central), act as Conciliatory Officers in different parts of the country.[1]

CASE 24.2

APPELLANT: M/s Msco Pvt Ltd   VS   RESPONDENT: Union of India and Others

DATE OF JUDGEMENT: 31 October 1984[*]

FACTS: The appellant imported some stainless steel plates at a concessional rate of import duty under a notification that provided: (i) that the importer should import the goods for the manufacture of all or any of the articles specified in that notification; (ii) that the articles so manufactured had to be sold to industrial units for their use; (iii) that in case of violation of any one of the conditions mentioned above, the importer was liable to pay, in respect of such quantity of goods as is not proved to have been utilized as per the notification, an amount equal to the difference between the duty leviable on such quantity but for the exemption contained in the notification and that already paid at the time of importation. The appellant submitted a certificate that the goods imported by him under the notification had been consumed and/or utilized as per the notification. Although However, the Assistant Collector of Customs rejected the said certificate and held that the appellant was liable to pay the deficient duty in respect of the goods that had been sold to hospitals/nursing homes since they were not 'industrial units' within the meaning of the Customs Act, 1962. The Collector of Customs (Appeals) confirmed the order in appeal. The revision petition of the appellant before the Customs, Excise, and Gold (Control) Tribunal also failed.

The appellant contended before court that the word 'industrial units' contained in the notification should be given the same meaning as is assigned to the word 'industry' in the Industrial Dispute Act, 1947.

JUDGEMENT: The appeal is dismissed.

REASON: The appellant relies upon the meaning assigned to the word 'industry' in the Industrial Disputes Act, 1947, in support of its case. The expression 'industry' is no doubt given a very wide definition in Sec. 2 (j) of the Industrial Disputes Act, 1947. It reads thus: '2 (j) "industry" means any business, trade, undertaking, manufacture, or calling of employers and includes any calling, service, employment, handicraft, or industrial occupation or avocation of workmen'. The above definition is given in the context of the subject matter with which the Industrial Disputes Act, 1947,

---

[*]M/s Msco Pvt Ltd vs Union of India and Others; 1985 AIR 76, 1985 SCR (1)1146; see also: http://www.indiankanoon.org/doc/1893181/ (29 October 2011).

Contd

---

[1]See links: http://labour.nic.in/cgit/; http://labour.nic.in/cgit/annexureA.htm.

Case 24.2 *Contd*

is concerned. The pith and substance of this act is to provide for the settlement of disputes between employers and employees in institutions, establishments, industrial, or business houses or factories of various kinds.

It indicates that the meaning given to the expression 'industry' in the Industrial Disputes Act, 1947, cannot be relied upon while construing other statutes or statutory instruments and it should be confined to the Industrial Disputes Act, 1947. In our view, in the notification under which the exemption is claimed by the petitioner, the word 'industry' refers to the place where the process of manufacture or production of goods is carried on and it cannot in any event include 'hospitals, dispensaries, or nursing homes'.

The decision of the Tribunal does not call for any interference. The appeal was, therefore, rejected.

SUMMARY

- Management of industrial relations is the most important element in the contemporary local and global industry. The trade unions, associations of the workers formed for demanding higher wages, and benefits are part of the integral industrial culture. The trade union movement in India has evolved from mere protests associations to well-programmed organizations with two-fold objectives: promotion of workers' interests and promotion of workers' development programmes as stakeholders in society.

- The Trade Unions Act, 1926, and the Industrial Disputes Act, 1947, complement each other in their objectives to eliminate unrest in the industry and promote beneficial relationship between employees and employers. Both have well-defined adjudication mechanisms and the central government is responsible for making any rules and regulations. The hierarchy of labour-oriented courts are set up to dispense justice.

EXERCISES

(i) The employees of a company producing essential goods went on a strike without notice. The strike went on for several weeks. An NGO started helping the striking workers by providing money and provisions. Do you think the NGO performed a legal service?
Hint: No, because furtherance or support to an illegal strike is unlawful.

(ii) During the pendency of the proceedings of the Court of Enquiry, the employer proceeded with lock-out. The trade union filed a case challenging the employer's action. Will the trade union succeed?
Hint: No, pendency in proceedings does not take away employer's right to lock-out.

(iii) An Industrial Tribunal failed to serve proper notices to the parties while making an award. Is the award binding?
Hint: No awarding is binding without proper notices to the parties.

(iv) What are the privileges, rights, and duties of a trade union?

(v) Describe the adjudication machinery.

DEVELOPMENT OF LEGAL EDGE

Project—Labour Court and Labour Lok Adalat Texts and Cases

Objective To update the liaison officers and HR managers

Method Small and handy manual to be a ready reference

Benefit HR Managers, Liaison Officers, Public Relations Officers in the industrial and public sectors

FURTHER READING

Acts
• http://labour.nic.in.

Labour Court
• http://labourandemployment.gov.in/ilc_a/lokadalat.htm.
• http://labour.nic.in/cgit/.
• http://labour.nic.in/cgit/annexureA.htm.

Book
• P.L. Rao and P.R.K. Raju, *Industrial Relations in India*, Excel Books, 2010.

Web resources
• S.R. de Silva, Elements of a Sound Industrial Relations System, ILO Bangkok, see http://www.ilo.org/public/english/dialogue/actemp/downloads/publications/srseleme.pdf.

CASE STUDY DISPUTE OVER CONCILIATION AND SETTLEMENT

(k) 'Industrial dispute' means any dispute or difference between employers and employers or between employers and workmen, or between workmen and workmen, which is connected with the employment or non-employment or the terms of employment or with the conditions of labour, of any person.

(e) 'Conciliation proceeding' means any proceeding held by a conciliation officer or Board under this Act.

(p) 'Settlement' means a settlement arrived at in the course of conciliation proceeding and includes a written agreement between the employer and workmen arrived at otherwise than in the course of conciliation proceeding where such agreement has been signed by the parties thereto in such a manner as may be prescribed and a copy.

– The Industrial Disputes Act, 1947, Sec. 2, (k), (e) (p)

Introduction

This case of General Manager, Security Paper Mills vs R.S. Sharma and Others (the Union Members) adjudicated by Single Bench Judge Justice E.S. Venkataramiah, is an oft-cited case for the Industrial Disputes Act, 1947.[2] The objective of the case here is to highlight, albeit negatively, the manager's role in industrial relations.

The Dispute

In the course of conciliation proceedings under the provisions of the Industrial Disputes Act, 1947, a settlement was arrived at on 29 June 1973 between the management of the Security Paper Mill, Hoshangabad, the appellant, and the SPM Employees Union, Hoshangabad. One of the terms of the settlement related to the incentive benefit entered into on behalf of the workmen and other non-operative officers and staff of the Security Paper Mill at Hoshangabad.

When the above settlement was in force, the Government of India, by its letter dated 29 December 1975, reduced the rate of group incentive benefit payable by restricting the entitlements of the non-operative officers and staff with effect from 1 January 1976 to 25 per cent of the rate applicable to industrial workmen for gazetted officers and to 50 per cent for non-gazetted industrial staff.

When the said order was challenged, the CGIT-cum-labour court held that the modification of the incentive benefit made by the Government of India was illegal.

After that the management entered into an agreement with one of the trade unions named SPM Employees Union on 11 April 1979, reducing the rate of incentive benefit to 50 per cent to the non-operative employees, i.e., administrative staff and accounts staff, and paid the benefit accordingly. The said agreement was not entered into during the course of any conciliation proceedings and, in fact, there were no conciliation proceedings pending at the time when the agreement was entered into.

The respondents, who belonged to the non-operative staff and who were not the members of the Union and parties to the agreement, challenged the validity of the agreement before the Authority under the Payment of Wages Act on the basis of the settlement of the year 1973. Although allowing the claim for ₹1,93,357.85 and cost at the rate of ₹10 per worker, it did not, however, allow any compensation.

In appeal, the Industrial Court affirmed the decision of the authority under the Payment of Wages Act but disallowed the costs at the rate of ₹10 per worker. Hence, the appeal is by special leave by the management alone, i.e., Security Paper Mills, Hoshangabad.

Verdict of the Industrial Court

A distinction is made in the Industrial Disputes Act, 1947, between a settlement arrived at in the course of conciliation proceeding and a settlement arrived at by agreement between the employer and workman otherwise than in conciliation proceeding both with regard to the procedure to be followed in the cases and with regard to the persons on whom they are binding. If a settlement of the dispute or of any of the matters in dispute is arrived at in the course of the conciliation proceeding, the Conciliation Officer shall send a report thereof to the appropriate government or an officer authorized in that behalf by the appropriate government together with a Memorandum of Settlement signed by the parties. Even though a Conciliation Officer is not competent to adjudicate upon the disputes between the management and its workmen, he is expected to assist them to arrive at a fair and just settlement. He has to play the role of an advisor and friend of both the parties and should ensure that neither party takes undue advantage of the situation. Any settlement arrived at should be a just and fair one.

In the case just discussed, the agreement entered into on 11 April 1979 between the Management and SPM Employees Union is not binding on the respondents and, therefore, cannot have the effect of depriving them of their right under the settlement dated 29 June 1983 as long as it is in operation because: (a) it is not indicated that the SPM Employees Union, which had entered into an agreement, could represent the respondents and that the respondents were parties to it; (b) no plea of termination or bringing to an end in some manner known to the law of the earlier agreement under Sec. 19(2) was taken by the management; and (c) apart from the bare assertion that the agreement dated 11 April 1979 reducing the incentive benefit was fair and just and, therefore, it should not be interfered with, no material was placed by the management before the Authority under the Payment of Wages Act or the Industrial Court to indicate that the said agreement was fair and just.

Judgement by the Supreme Court of India

There was no evidence to indicate that the respondents were the members of the SPM Employees Union, which had entered into the agreement dated 11 April 1979. Since it is not shown that SPM Employees Union, which had entered into the agreement, could represent the respondents herein and that the respondents were parties to it, the agreement was not binding on them.

The settlement arrived at in the course of conciliation proceeding on 29 June 1973, which was binding on the appellant and the respondents herein, would remain in operation until it is terminated or brought to an end in some manner known to law. Sec. 19(2) of the Industrial Disputes Act, 1947, provides that a settlement shall be binding on the persons on whom it is binding for such a period as is agreed upon by the parties and if no such period is agreed upon for a period of 6 months from the date on which the memorandum of settlement is signed by the parties to the dispute and shall continue to be binding on the parties after the expiry of the period aforesaid until the expiry of two months from the date on which a notice in writing of an intention to terminate the settlement is given by one of the parties to the other party or parties to the settlement. No notice given under Sec. 19(2) shall have effect unless it is given by a

---

[2]General Manager, Security Paper Mills, Hoshangabad vs R S Sharma and Others; 1986 AIR 954, 1986 SCR (1) 281; also see http://www.indiankanoon. org/doc/1394570/.

party representing the majority of papers bound by the settlement in view of the provisions contained in Sub-Sec. (7) of Sec. 19 of the Industrial Disputes Act, 1947. No such plea of termination under Sec. 19(2) is considered in this case by the management. The agreement was entered into on 11 April 1979 between the management and SPM.

The Employees Union, which is not binding on the respondents, cannot have the effect of depriving them of their right under the settlement dated 29 June 1973, as long as it is in operation.

The contention, therefore, fails.

The Authority under the Payment of Wages Act and the Industrial Court were, therefore, right in rejecting the defence of the management. The appeal, therefore, fails and it is dismissed with costs.

Conclusion

The fundamental objective of the Industrial Dispute Act, 1947, is to promote positive justice. In other words, the law provides an instrument to settle matters of dispute through conciliation rather than confrontation in a court of law. Flooding the courts with cases under this law defeats its benevolent purpose. The legislator's intention is that employees and their trade unions would amicably negotiate with the employers for a fair and just settlement. A manager would do well to read, study, understand, and reflect Sec. 2 of the Act where a new language is introduced to solve disputes in an innovative way, through discussion, negotiation, and dialogue that advances the employee–employer relationship. The legislator would like to place the confidence in the abilities of the employees and employers to sort out and settle their differences and build and advance their mutual cooperation. Dragging themselves to the court would revert them back to the old ways of understanding justice that is imposed by the Authority.

Discussion Questions

1. Enumerate the facts of the case and relation of the involved.
2. Why do you think conciliation and settlement failed?
3. Analyze the legal reasoning of the Industrial Court.
4. How will you fit in it the principles of settlement?
5. How does conciliation work?
6. How would you analyze the judgement of the Supreme Court?
7. What lessons as a manager do you learn from this case?

Going Beyond

1. Would you follow the same course of legal action as the manager of the Security Paper Mills chose? Give reasons in both cases if you would follow or would not.
2. Discuss the fundamental principles of dispute settlement.
3. Analyze the intention of the legislator in the Industrial Dispute Act, 1947.

LEGAL LUMINARY

GEORGE FERNANDES—THE FIERY PETREL OF TRADE UNIONISM

Anti-establishment. Single-minded. Fearless. These three characteristics marked this trade union leader turned politician turned minister in the Union Government of India. He was a self-made young man in the rough and tumble of Bombay (now Mumbai) who lived a tough life. He joined the socialist trade union movement and steeped himself in its philosophy so intensely that there emerged a man with strong socialist ideals and a powerful and emotive sense of the social injustice meted out to the workers. The workers of India struggled for everything in life, from birth to death, from making a livelihood to obtaining a modicum of food, shelter, and safety. Fernandes felt that the workers were in need of social liberation. With this ideal, for two decades, in the 1950s and the 1960s, George Fernandes became a household name as he organized strikes and bandhs, bringing governments and companies to their knees to accede to the demand of the workers. In 1974, riding at the pinnacle of his power as union leader, as President of the All India Railwaymen's Federation, he led the Railway Strike that stunned the country for the sheer ferocity of the power of his union under his leadership. He was the most strident leader who directly challenged Mrs Indira Gandhi, the then Prime Minister, who was at the height of her power. She declared National Emergency in mid-1975 and put all the opposition leaders behind bars. Fernandes went underground, but was eventually arrested and put on one of the most infamous trials in the country called the Baroda Dynamite Case.

Soon after the Emergency was lifted, Fernandes joined the electoral politics, making Muzaffarpur, Bihar, as his constituency from where he won in succession from 1977 to 2009 until old age and ill health did not permit him any further, although he was made a Rajya Sabha Member from Bihar in 2009 only to retire in 2010 due to acute illness. He held some very important ministries: Minister for Industries (1977), where he ordered IBM and Coca-Cola out of the country for investment irregularities; Minister for Railways (1989), where he introduced the most challenging rail track, now called Konkan Railway; Minister for Defence (1998), where India conducted nuclear tests at Pokhran and fought a war against Pakistan known as the Kargil War.

George, born in an upper middle-class family in Mangalore, Karnataka, in 1930, developed a keen interest in writing from an early age. In Bombay, he went in search of a job as a journalist and found one as a proofreader. The influence of Dr Ram Manohar Lohia, one of the greatest socialist leaders of India, changed his life permanently and he became involved in the trade unionist movement. However, he never gave up his first love: writing. He has been the editor of vernacular publications such as in Kannada and Konkani and also in Hindi and English. His books are: *What Ails the Socialists* (1972), *The Kashmir Problem*, *Railway Strike* (1974), *Dignity for All: Essays in Socialism and Democracy* (1991), and *George Fernandes Speaks* (1991), an autobiographical account. All his life, he has been surrounded by controversies, insurmountable problems, and is now fighting a grave illness. He is perhaps the only politician who rejected personal security. He has always lived life on his own terms.[*]

---

[*]With inputs from: http://www.daijiworld.com/chan/achievers_view.asp?a_id=24; http://en.wikipedia.org/wiki/George_Fernandes; http://www.mapsofindia.com/mangalore/people-culture-festivals/george-fernandes.html (29 November 2011).

PART

5

ASPECTS OF NEW ECONOMY AND JURISPRUDENCE

Laws Related to Information and Communication

Principle: *Omnia libere et legaliter facienda.*

All things are to be done freely and legally.

CHAPTER OUTLINE

- Introduction and Interpretation
- Information Technology Act, 2000
- Telecom Regulatiory Authority of India Act, 1997

- *Case Study:* An Incredible Tale of the 2G Spectrum Scandal
- *Legal Luminary:* Kapil Sibal

25.1 INTRODUCTION AND INTERPRETATION

TEXT

An Act to provide legal recognition for transactions carried out by means of electronic data interchange and other means of electronic communication, commonly referred to as 'electronic commerce', which involves the use of alternatives to paper-based methods of communication and storage of information, to facilitate electronic filing of documents with the Government agencies and further to amend the Indian Penal Code, the Indian Evidence Act, 1872, the Bankers' Books Evidence Act, 1891, and the Reserve Bank of India Act, 1934, and for matters connected therewith or incidental thereto.

Whereas the General Assembly of the United Nations by resolution A RES 51 162, dated 30 January 1997 has adopted the Model Law on Electronic Commerce adopted by the United Nations Commission on International Trade Law;

And whereas the said resolution recommends inter alia that all states give favourable consideration to the said Model Law when they enact or revise their laws, in view of the need for uniformity of the law applicable to alternatives to paper-based method of communication and storage of information;

And whereas it is considered necessary to give effect to the said resolution and to promote efficient delivery of Government services by means of reliable electronic records.

– Information Technology Act, 2000, Preamble

The above text unambiguously lists the objectives, uses, and the need for regulation for all the transactions carried on by the new information technologies. The law is modeled on the

United Nations Commission on International Trade Law, 1996 (UNCITRAL). It makes provisions for the legal treatment of the users of electronic communication and paper-based communication. The World Trade Organization also has geared itself up to handle its work in this area. Truly, the enactment of laws concerning information technology and communication by the member countries of the United Nation Organization has heralded the establishment of a new legal order of global trade and commerce through the use of the new technologies.

The laws related to information technology (IT) and communication are three dimensional so far as they include three elements: technology, law, and human beings. For a business manager, it is a waltz between business, law, and technology. With the development of these twin technologies of information and communication, the world has gone ahead of its own industrial revolution and has created what is known as digital revolution. Our contemporary age is commonly called Cyber Age, where all the tools that humans use have connectivity to some satellites in space. Even common people use cyber technology for their work and leisure. Television, computer, cellular phone, ATM, Internet, tablet, and all the technological gadgets that mark our age are the tools of creation and transfer of data, data management, communication systems without which normal life would be impossible. With an announcement saying 'Systems are down', everything from airports to banking, from commercial bookings to paying your bill at the grocer's come to a standstill. With so much at stake and so many possibilities of disputes, conflicts, and crime, the enacting of the law to regulate technology-related behaviour becomes an imperative.

Scope

The scope of this chapter is limited to the core understanding of two main laws: IT Act, 2000 and the Telecom Regulatory Authority of India Act, 1997 (TRAI Act, 1997). These two Acts and their enforcing authorities complement each other as the transactions performed through the said technologies come under their compass of functioning. Your focus will be directed on two aspects: legal elements and legal authorities of enforcement.

25.2 INFORMATION TECHNOLOGY ACT, 2000

Legal recognition of electronic records:
Where any law provides that information or any other matter shall be in writing or in the typewritten or printed form, then, notwithstanding anything contained in such law, such requirement shall be deemed to have been satisfied if such information or matter is:
(a) Rendered or made available in an electronic form; and
(b) Accessible so as to be usable for a subsequent reference.

– IT Act, 2000, Sec. 4 (a)(b)

Legal Elements

Authentication of electronic records (Sec. 3) It is a process to confirm the identity of the person to prove the integrity of information. The technique involved consists of

(a) Asymmetric crypto system, a private key for creating digital signature
(b) Electronic record to authentication by any subscriber

(c) Digital signature, typical data received or sent in electronic form

(d) Hash function, an algorithm to map or translate one set of bits into another

(e) Electronic signature consists of authentication by the subscriber of an electronic record by using one of the techniques of signature creation

E-Governance (Secs 4–10)   The following are the elements that formulate the functions of E-Governance:

(a) Legal recognition of electronic records

(b) Legal recognition of electronic signatures

(c) Use of electronic records and signatures in Government and its agencies

(d) Delivery of services by service provider

(e) Retention of electronic records

(f) Audit of documents in electronic form

(g) Publication of rules, regulations in the Electronic Gazette, the Official Gazette of the Government

Sections 6–8 do not confer the right on individuals or agencies to insist upon electronic data for any transaction. Section 10 empowers the government to make necessary rules. The section further states that in a contract formation, the communication proposals, their acceptance, their revocation, or acceptances as the case may be are expressed in electronic form or by means of an electronic record; such contracts shall not be deemed to be unenforceable solely on the ground that such electronic form or means was used for that purpose.

Attribution of electronic records (Secs 11–13)   An electronic record shall be attributed to the originator if sent by:

(a) The originator himself

(b) The person who is authorized by the originator

(c) The information through an automatic system organized and authorized by the originator

Secure records and electronic signatures (Secs 14–16)   An electronic signature or record is secured if:

(a) The signature creation data, at the time of affixing signature, were under the exclusive control of signatory and no other person.

(b) The signature creation data were stored and affixed in such exclusive manner as may be prescribed.

Regulation of certifying authorities (Secs 17–39)   The Central Government may, by notification in the Official Gazette, appoint the controller of certifying authorities and also deputies, assistants, and other officers according to the provisions of the Act. They will have powers to:

(a) Recognize foreign certifying authorities

(b) Issue license for electronic signature certificates

(c) Grant, reject, or suspend licenses

(d) Delegate powers of the controller

Duties of subscribers (Secs 40–42)   When the Digital Signature Certificate has been accepted by a subscriber, which is to be listed in the Digital Signature Certificate, he shall generate the key pair by applying the security procedure. The subscriber shall be deemed to have accepted a Digital Signature Certificate if he publishes or authorizes the publication of a Digital Signature Certificate, then he is obliged to hold the private key corresponding to public key that all information in the key is true.

Penalties, compensation, and adjudication (Secs 43–47)   In this respect, the provisions of the Act are as follows (also see Table 25.1):

(a) Penalties for damage of computer systems: ₹1 crore
(b) Failure to furnish information, return, etc.: ₹1.5 lakh
(c) The adjudication is administered by the duly appointed officers by the Central Government

Cyber Appellate Tribunal

Establishment of the cyber appellate tribunal (Secs 48–64)   The Act empowers the Central Government to establish by official notification in the Official Gazette, the formation of one or more as the need demands to appoint Appellate Tribunals. The Act provides the formation and functioning of these tribunals. The appeals from the Appellate Tribunal shall be filed in the High Court within 60 days from the date of communication of order or decision by the Cyber Appellate Tribunal.

Table 25.1   Offences for adjudication before the tribunal (Secs 65–78)

Offences	Punishment
Tampering with computer source documents (Sec. 65)	Imprisonment: up to 3 years Fine: ₹2 lakh or both
Computer-related dishonesty, fraud, etc. (Secs 66, 43)	Dishonesty: Sec. 24 of Penal Code of 1860 Fraud: same as above
Sending offensive messages through communication services (Sec. 66A)	Imprisonment up to 3 years with fine
Receiving stolen computer resource or communication (Sec. 66 B)	Imprisonment up to 3 years with fine of ₹1 lakh
Identity theft (Sec. 66 C)	Imprisonment up to 3 years with fine of ₹1 lakh
Cheating by personating by suing computer resource (Sec. 66D)	Imprisonment up to 3 years with fine of ₹1 lakh
Violation of privacy (Sec. 66E)	Imprisonment up to 3 years with fine of ₹2 lakh or both
Promotion of terrorism (Sec. 66F)	Imprisonment for life
Publishing transmitting obscene material (Sec. 67)	Imprisonment for 5 years and fine up to ₹10 lakh
Publishing transmitting sexually explicit material	Imprisonment up to 7 years and fine of ₹10 lakhs

Contd

Table 25.1 *Contd*

Publishing or transmitting of sexually explicit material depicting children (Sec. 67B)	First conviction: imprisonment up to 5 years and fine of ₹10 lakh Subsequent conviction: imprisonment up to 7 years and fine up to ₹10 lakhs
Prevention and retention of information by intermediaries (Sec. 67 C)	Imprisonment up to 3 years and fine
Failure of comply any regulation (Sec. 68)	Imprisonment up to 3 years and fine of ₹one lakh or both
Hacking into critical information infrastructure, the Government declared protected data (Sec. 70)	Imprisonment up to 10 years and fine
Misrepresentation	Imprisonment up to 2 years and fine of ₹1 lakh
Breach of confidentiality and privacy (Sec. 72)	Imprisonment up to 2 years and fine of ₹1 lakh
Disclosure of information in breach of lawful contract (Sec. 72A)	Imprisonment up to 3 years and fine of ₹5 lakh or both
Publishing electronic signature	Imprisonment up to 2 years and fine of ₹1 lakh
Publication for fraudulent purpose (Sec. 74)	Imprisonment up to 2 years and fine of ₹1 lakh

Section 76 empowers the officers to confiscate all the electronic equipment of the offenders. Section 77A empowers the Court to compound offences and may be punished under the Criminal Law Procedure, 1973. Offences up to 3 years imprisonment are bailable. (Refer Case 25.1)

CASE 25.1   PETITIONER: Hindustan Unilever Employees   VS   RESPONDENT: The Inspector of Factories

DATE OF JUDGEMENT: 8 June 2011 *

FACTS: The petitioner union has come forward to file the present writ petition seeking for a direction to the first respondent Inspector of Factories to consider the complaint, dated 20 February 2009 sent by the union and to take action against the second respondent for removing 'Optional Lock System' in the computerized attendance system maintained in the second respondent factory and for a consequential direction to the second respondent to keep all statutory records and registers prescribed under the provisions of the Factories Act, 1948 and Rules made there under.

It was stated that for computerizing the Time Attendance System (TAS), permission will have to be required from the Inspector of Factories and pursuant to the said the computerized system was introduced during 2003–2004. In the software utilized 97–102 by the second respondent, whenever the workmen registered their names,

*Hindustan Unilever Employees vs Inspector of Factories; see also: indiankanoon.org/doc/1993343/ (28 October 2011).

Case 25.1 *Contd*

it was programmed in such a way that registration will be directly rejected. Utilizing the said programme and with a view to victimize the workers, the registration was locked. Therefore, the petitioner union stated that such procedure was illegal and they should discontinue the TAS computerized system and that the original card system should be introduced.

In respect to these allegations, the first respondent had stated that in terms of Sec. 4 of IT Act, 2000, the Chief Inspector of Factories and Boilers, Puducherry had given permission to the second respondent to maintain the following registers in a soft copy by letter dated 23 September 2000.

(i) Muster Roll Form No. 23

(ii) Over Time Register Form No. 10

(iii) Register of national and festival holidays Form No. 6

(iv) Register of compensatory holidays Form No. 9

(v) Register of adult workers Form No. 12

(vi) Register of leave with wages Form No. 15

As there is provision under IT Act, 2000 to maintain records in electronic format, such permission was granted with a direction that they should take print out of all soft copies and should be preserved as required under the Puducherry Factories Rules, 1964 and must be presented to the first respondent during their inspection. It was also stated that other disputes between the petitioner and the second respondent are covered by the Industrial Disputes Act, 1947 and that the petitioner union must seek remedy under the said Act.

JUDGEMENT: Petition dismissed.

REASON: As contended by the respondents, the union has agreed for the introduction of TAS system of attendance by a settlement. Therefore, it is too late for the petitioner to question the same. Even otherwise, under Rule 104, the Chief Inspector of Factories can grant exemption with respect to any of the provisions contained under Rules 97–102 with respect to any factories subject to such conditions. These rules relate to the right of workman to have leave with wages. Apart from this, Sec. 4 of IT Act, 2000 grants legal recognition of electronic records. Sec. 4 reads as follows: 'Legal recognition of electronic records: where any law provides that information or any other matter shall be in writing or in the typewritten or printed form, then, notwithstanding anything contained in such law, such requirement shall be deemed to have been satisfied if such information or matter is:

(a) Rendered or made available in an electronic form; and

(b) Accessible so as to be usable for a subsequent reference.'

In case of violation of any of the provisions of the Factories Act or Rules made thereunder, it was always open to the workmen or through their representative to complain to the appropriate authority and seek redressal.

In the light of the stand taken by the respondents, it is unnecessary to entertain the writ petition. Hence, the writ petition will stand dismissed.

25.3 TELECOM REGULATORY AUTHORITY OF INDIA ACT, 1997

TEXT

Establishment and incorporation of Authority:
(1) With effect from such date as the Central Government may, by notification appoint, there shall be established, for the purposes of this Act, an Authority to be called TRAI.
(2) The Authority shall be a body corporate by the name aforesaid, having perpetual succession and a common seal, with power, subject to the provisions of this Act, to acquire, hold and dispose of property, both movable and immovable, and to contract, and shall, by the said name, sue or be sued.
(3) The Authority shall consist of a Chairperson, and not less than two, but not exceeding six members, to be appointed by the Central Government.
(4) The head office of the Authority shall be at New Delhi.

– TRAI Act, 1997, Sec. 3

The Department of Telecommunications (DOT) under the Ministry of Communications and IT is the concerned authority for all matters relating to telecom. It is responsible for formulating the developmental policies; granting licenses for various telecom services; promoting standardization, research, and development, as well as private investment in the sector.

The main aim of the regulator is to facilitate quick growth of the telecom sector. Hence, its strategy is to provide for a transparent policy environment. The regulator is responsible for tariff, interconnections, direct-to-home services, mobile number portability, etc.

Salient Features of TRAI Act, 1997

An independent regulatory body called as TRAI was established in 1997, under TRAI Act, 1997. TRAI Act, 1997 was amended by TRAI (Amendment) Act, 2000. By the Amendment Act, an Appellate Tribunal known as the Telecom Disputes Settlement and Appellate Tribunal has been set up to protect the interests of service providers and consumers of the telecom sector. The following are some of the essential elements of the Act:

TRAI establishment and incorporation (Secs 3–10)   As in the above text, it is clear that TRAI is established as per the Act.

(a) It is a body corporate with all its characteristics of perpetual succession, common seal with powers to hold and dispose of property, both moveable and immoveable, and to sue and be sued.

(b) It consists of a chairperson with well-defined powers and being assisted by other officers.

Functions of TRAI (Sec. 11)   The section enumerates the functions of TRAI as to

(a) Recommend the need and timing for introduction of new service provider

(b) To recommend the terms and conditions of licence to a service provider

(c) Ensure technical compatibility and effective interconnection between different service providers

(d) Regulate arrangement among service providers of sharing their revenue derived from providing telecommunication services

(e) Ensure compliance of terms and conditions of licence

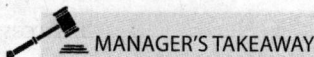 **MANAGER'S TAKEAWAY**

- IT is manager's challenge and India's pride.
- IT permeates every walk of life; law is no exception.

(f) Recommend revocation of licence for noncompliance of terms and conditions of licence

(g) Lay down and ensure the time period for providing local and long distance circuits for telecommunication between different service providers

(h) Facilitate competition and promote efficiency in the operation of telecommunication services so as to facilitate growth in such services

(i) Protect the interest of the consumers of telecommunication service

(j) Monitor the quality of service and conduct the periodical survey of such provided by the service providers

(k) Inspect the equipment used in the network and recommend the type of equipment to be used by the service providers

(l) Maintain register of interconnect agreements and of all such other matters as may be provided in the regulations

(m) Keep register maintained under Clause (l) open for inspection to any member of public on payment of such fee and compliance of such other requirements as may be provided in the regulations

(n) Settle disputes between service providers

(o) Render advice to the Central Government in the matters relating to the development of telecommunication technology and any other matter reliable to telecommunication industry in general

(p) Levy fees and other charges at such rates and in respect of such services as may be determined by regulations

(q) Ensure effective compliance of universal service obligations

(r) Perform such other functions including such administrative and financial functions as may be entrusted to it by the Central Government or as may be necessary to carry out the provisions of this Act

While discharging the functions, the Regulator shall not act against the interest of the sovereignty and integrity of the country, friendly relations with foreign states, public order, decency, and morality. It shall ensure transparency at all levels.

Powers of TRAI (Secs 12, 13) The Regulator can exercise the following powers to:

(a) Call upon any service provider at any time to furnish in writing such information or explanation relating to its affairs as the Authority may require

(b) Appoint one or more persons to make an inquiry in relation to the affairs of any service provider

(c) Direct any of its officers or employees to inspect the books of account or other documents of any service provider

The Regulator has the power to issue directions to the service providers as is necessary.

Settlement of disputes (Secs 14–19) The Regulator shall be directed by the principles of natural justice. It may involve the following:

(a) Summoning and enforcing the attendance of any person and examining him on oath

(b) Requiring the discovery and production of documents

(c) Receiving evidence on affidavits

(d) Issuing commissions for the examination of witnesses or documents;

(e) Reviewing its decisions

(f) Dismissing an application for default or deciding it ex parte

(g) Setting aside any order of dismissal of any application for default or any order passed by it ex parte

(h) Any other matter which may be prescribed

The applicant has the right to legal representation and if aggrieved by the decision may appeal to the High Court. The orders passed by the Regulator or High Court are to be executable as a decree.

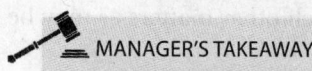

MANAGER'S TAKEAWAY

- Transparency is the basis of regulation.
- One who knowingly accepts the benefits of a contract or conveyance is estopped to deny the validity or binding effect on him of such contract or conveyance.

Penalty (Sec. 20)   The penalty for willful failure to comply with the orders of the Regulating Authority or the High Court shall be punishable with fine extending to ₹1 lakh; a subsequent conviction shall bear the penalty of ₹2 lakh and continued contravention will attract a fine of additional ₹2 lakh for every day during which the default continues.

Powers of the Central Government (Sec. 25)   The Central Government may issue the Regulating Authority such directions as it may think necessary in the interest of the country, its foreign relations and its people (refer Case 25.2).

CASE 25.2		
Petitioner: Shyam Telelink Ltd vs **Respondent:** Union of India		

Date of Judgement: 5 October 2010*

Facts: This appeal under Sec. 18 (1) of TRAI Act, 1997 is directed against an order dated 9 April 2003 passed by the Telecom Dispute Settlement and Appellate Tribunal whereby, Petition No. 24/2001 filed under Sec. 14 (a) (i) read with Sec. 14 A (1) of TRAI Act, 1997.

The appellant's case before the Tribunal and also before us (Supreme Court of India) is that, it was ready to commence commercial operations in the last week of February 1999 and had sought permission of the respondents to do so. Permission was, however, denied on the ground that certain technical deficiencies remained to be removed and certain conditions for the grant of permission remained to be fulfilled.

In the meantime, the Union of India appears to have offered a Migration Package to all the Telecom Operators in July 1999. Under this package, which was offered to the appellant, Shyam Telelink Ltd on 22 July 1999, the fixed licence fee was to stand replaced by a revenue-sharing arrangement w.e.f. 1 August 1999 subject to the stipulation that at least 35 per cent of all outstanding dues including interest payable as on 31 July 1999 and liquidated damages in full is paid by the appellant on or before 15 August 1999. Migration Package further provided that the company shall have to accept all the conditions stipulated in the package and that all proceedings instituted by the licensee or their associations against the Union of India shall have to be withdrawn.

*Shyam Telelink Ltd vs Union of India; see also: indiankanoon.org/doc/805666/ (23 October 2011).

Contd

Case 25.2 *Contd*

The prayer was upon consideration turned down with the result that the appellant paid 35 per cent of the outstanding licence fee and interest amounting to ₹2.36 crore on 16 August 1999. It also paid the full amount of ₹7.30 crore toward liquidated damages as demanded by the Government.

Commercial operations in Rajasthan were finally started by the appellant company on 5 June 2000. In March 2001, a demand was raised by the respondent for payment of a further amount of ₹70 lakh as liquidated damages for the delay in the commissioning of the service. Aggrieved by the demand of ₹8 crore toward liquidated damages out of which the appellant had already paid ₹7.30 crore on 16 August 1999, the appellant approached the Tribunal for redress.

The respondent contested the petition before the Tribunal, inter alia, on the ground that the petitioner appellant was not entitled to question any demand arising out of the agreement executed between the parties after it had unconditionally accepted the Migration Package, under which it agreed to deposit without demur the outstanding licence fee as also the liquidated damages payable under the licence agreement.

It was further pointed out by the respondent that the computation of actual liquidated damages could be undertaken only after the appellant had commenced commercial operations. The actual charges after such computation were according to the respondent determined at ₹29.86 crore, but the demand was restricted to ₹8 crore in terms of the explicit limitation prescribed under the licence. An amount of ₹7.3 crore having already been paid under the Migration Package, a demand for payment of ₹70 lakh only was raised by the respondent.

The Migration Package that contained a specific stipulation that the acceptance of the package will be deemed as a full and final settlement of all existing disputes whatsoever irrespective of whether they are related to the present package or not could not be questioned by the petitioner appellant.

JUDGEMENT: The petition dismissed.

REASON: The Tribunal was, therefore, perfectly justified in holding that the commercial operations were started only on 5 June 2000, and that for the intervening period, such operations could not be commenced on account of deficiencies that were attributed entirely to the defects in the system that the appellant had installed.

The Tribunal was also justified in our opinion in holding that the denial of permission to the appellant was neither arbitrary nor malafide especially when the conditions in the licence agreement requiring the appellant to arrange and install suitable equipment to meet the prevailing technical specifications by Telecommunication Engineering Centre were not complied with nor were all performance tests required for successful commissioning of the services carried out by the licensor before the services are commissioned for public use.

As a general principle, one who knowingly accepts the benefits of a contract or conveyance is estopped to deny the validity or binding effect on him of such contract or conveyance. This rule has to be applied to do equity and must not be applied in such a manner as to violate the principles of right and good conscience.

For the reasons set out by us hereinabove, we have no hesitation in holding that the appellant was not entitled to question the terms of the Migration Package after unconditionally accepting and acting upon the same. In the result, this appeal fails and is hereby dismissed.

- IT Act, 2000 is modeled on the United Nations Commission on the International Trade Law, 1996. It makes provisions for legal treatment of the users of electronic communication and paper-based communication. The objectives are to support e-commerce and e-governance. Authentications by digital signature, the private key, and the public key are the newly introduced technical innovations. Legal recognition is granted to electronic records. A certifying Authority is appointed by the Central Government. Adjudication and penalties too are part of the law enforcing machinery.
- The TRAI Act, 1997 is a progressive legislation to promote and standardize research and development in communications technology. The Authority is a body corporate with all the essential characteristics that belong to it. It has wide ranging powers in its sphere to introduce, regulate, price, and manage all activities proper to its functioning. Transparency and fairness are its goals. It has the responsibility to maintain national harmony and integrity, as well as the friendly relations with all the countries of the world. It has to be also responsible guardian of public decency in all communication technology and of moral embodiment. The TRAI has wide ranging powers of inspection, summons, and examination of concerned persons under oath. Failure to comply with the orders of the Authority is dealt appropriate penalties.

EXERCISES

(i) An employee was found manipulating the computer system that caused high loss to a national company. Under what law would he be booked?

Hint: Secs 406, 420, and 468 IPC, and 43(g) of the Information Technology Act, 2000.

(ii) A cable operator failed to pay back the loans. The creditor enforced the law pleading for re-payment. The debtor argued saying that his loans are covered by surety. What is your opinion about it?

Hint: The court found no substance in the argument of the debtor and ordered to repay (Sicom Ltd vs Harjinder Singh, AIR 2004 Bom 337, IV (2004) BC 350, 2004 (5) BomCR 304.

(iii) An association of small hotel owners complained to the Authority that they are unable to bear the extra charges levied against them along with the establishments of the big hotel owners who serve their guests with the television networks. While the small hoteliers employ cable service, the big hoteliers have direct contract with the broadcasters; hence the TRAI levies must be for the big hoteliers.

Hint: It is for the Authority to fix charges, see Sec. 11 of the Act.

(iv) State the salient features of the IT Act, 2000.

(v) What are the functions of TRAI? Illustrate with a case.

DEVELOPMENT OF LEGAL EDGE

Project—New definitions

Objective To learn new legal vocabulary and definitions from the new Acts.

Method Select and list all the definitions from Sec. 2 of both IT Act, 2000 and TRAI Act, 1997.

The resulting booklet should be small, easy to handle which will be useful to anyone in IT and Tele-communication businesses.

FURTHER READING

Acts, Policies Regulatory Authority, Rules, and Regulations

• http://www.trai.gov.in/trai_act.asp.

Books

• Vakul Sharma, *IT Law and Practice and Emerging Technology Cyber Law and E-Commerce*, Universal Publications, 2011.

Web Resources

• http://www.topnews.in/companies/trai.

CASE STUDY   AN INCREDIBLE TALE OF THE 2G SPECTRUM SCANDAL

Notwithstanding anything contained in the Indian Telegraph Act, 1885, the Authority may, from time to time, by order, notify in the Official Gazette the rates at which the telecommunication services within India and outside India shall be provided under this Act including the rates at which messages shall be transmitted to any country outside India: provided that the Authority may notify different rates for different persons or class of persons for similar telecommunication services and where different rates are fixed as aforesaid the Authority shall record the reasons there for.

While discharging its functions under Subsec. (1), the Authority shall not act against the interest of the sovereignty and integrity of India, the security of the state, friendly relations with foreign states, public order, decency, or morality.

The Authority shall ensure transparency while exercising its powers and discharging its functions.

– The TRAI Act, 1997, Sec. 11 (2)(3)(4)

Introduction

Financial scams are a regular feature in India. However, there has never been a bigger, sinister, and brazen one than the 2G Spectrum Scandal. Unlike other scams, it is a straightforward and simple scam. The Minister of Telecommunication decides, against the advice of the Ministry of Finance and even the Prime Minister, to undercharge mobile telephony by allocating licences on an old price rate. Furthermore, he throws all sane principles of justice, first come first served, and arbitrarily allocates. This results in a shortfall of a staggering ₹1.76 lakh crore. The scam cropped up in an uncanny investigation of a lobbyist by the Department of Income Tax. However, it is due to the very high public interest-oriented Dr Subramanian Swamy who is credited to have brought before Court of Law and Advocate Shanti Bhushan, a former Minister for Law, who has convincingly and with great perseverance has been able to make the Supreme Court monitor the case. The case is presented below in an abridged version

from the judgement of the apex court. Exhibit A on the Minister of Telecommunication sets up the background for the case.

In the Supreme Court of India

The Bench   Justices G.S. Singhvi and Justice Kumar Ganguly

Appellant   Centre for PIL and others

Respondent   Union of India and others

Date   16 December 2010

Initiation

On 4 May 2009, appellant submitted detailed representation to the Chief Vigilance Commissioner (CVC) pointing out irregularities committed in the grant of UASL (Basic Cellular). After 5 days, one Shri A K Agarwal made a complaint to the CVC to highlight how manipulations were made by some of the applicants for getting the licences and how the exercise undertaken by the DOT for grant of

Exhibit A   When People's Manager Loses Sight of the Law

On 17 November 2010, the *Times of India* ran a story in its front page titled: '2G scam: How A Raja robbed the nation'.* The report by the Comptroller Auditor General (CAG) was tabled in the Parliament. Its conclusions stunned the entire country. The Minister for Telecommunications Mr A Raja along with a host of telecommunication companies, lobbyists and top bureaucrats had spun a saga of incredible proportions in terms of not only the sheer amount of money but also the exposure of administrative rot and corporate corruption.

A short passage from the report was reproduced in the above-mentioned daily: 'The entire process of allocation of Unified Access Service licences (UASLs) lacked transparency and was undertaken in an arbitrary, unfair and inequitable manner. The Honorable Prime Minister had stressed on the need for a fair and transparent allocation of spectrum, and the ministry of finance had sought for the decision regarding spectrum pricing to be considered by an empowered group of ministers**. Brushing aside their concerns and advices, DOT, in 2008, proceeded to issue 122 new licences for 2G spectrum at 2001 prices, by flouting every canon of financial propriety, rules, and procedures' Result: the estimated loss of ₹1.76 lakh crore.

As soon as A Raja became the Minister for Telecommunication in 2007 fresh applications, in addition to the old ones, were invited for the grant of spectrum (frequency bandwidth for telecommunication) allocation. The Prime Minister through a letter advised the Minister to follow a policy of auctioneering rather than arbitrary allocation. The Minister replied saying that auctioning will discriminatorily reduce the playing field for the new entrants.

Furthermore, the Ministry of Finance warned the Minister that fixing the price for allocation of licences on the 2001 price base without indexation or current evaluation would question the very sanctity of continuing with the old price. The Minister had an answer to this also. He replied saying that these kinds of observations merely confuse the issue and obfuscate legitimacy and integrity.

The Minister, A Raja, who is charge sheeted by the Central Bureau of Investigation (CBI) as the mastermind of undervaluing the spectrum, favoured companies who were largely ineligible for licences to run mainly mobile networks. Even before mid-November 2010, the media was agog with corruption stories related to 2G frequency to telecom operators it is the tabling of the CAG report. With the mounting pressure that resulted in the loss of face for the Government in general and disgrace for the minister, he resigned. In early February 2011, he was arrested and sent into custody charged with criminal conspiracy, cheating and forgery under the Indian Penal Code and abuse of official position and corruption under the Prevention of Corruption Act.

A short list of the high-profile people involved the case are

1. Kanimozhi Karunanidhi, the daughter of former Chief Minister of Tamil Nadu Mr M Karunanidhi, and leader of the DMK party, which is the Government's coalition partner
2. Siddharth Behura, the Telecom Secretary
3. R.K. Chandolia, A Raja's Personal Secretary
4. Sanjay Chandra, MD of Unitech Wireless
5. Shahid Balwa, Promoter, DB Realty and Swan Telecom
6. Vinod Goenka, Promoter and MD DB Realty and Swan Telecom
7. Gautam Doshi, Group MD, Anil Dhirubhai Ambani Group
8. Hari Nair and Surendra Pipara, Senior Vice Presidents, Anil Dhirubhai Ambani Group[†]

There are several more from the areas of cinema, journalism, etc.

The investigations have shown that the bribe paid for undervaluing run into hundreds of crores of rupees by each company. However, in the court, the various agencies such as Central Board of Direct Taxes, CBI, and TRAI are presenting different figures. Furthermore, the current Minister for Telecommunications has denied of any loss to the exchequer.[‡]

---

*See also: http://articles.timesofindia.indiatimes.com/2010-11-17/india/28257643_1_spectrum-pricing-2g-transparent-allocation.

**Normally, a committee formed by a group of ministers to deliberate an issue; in this case the electronic for telecommunication technology.

[†]Until November 2011, although some of these are out on bail, the minister himself was not released.

[‡]See http://www.ndtiv.com/article/india/2g-spectrum-scam.

Contd

Exhibit A *Contd*

A Raja, the disgraced Minister of Telecommunications, is a politician belonging to the DMK party of Tamil Nadu, which is a partner in the coalition Government of United Progressive Alliance at the Centre. The 2G scam attributed to the former minister is considered as one of the worst in the world for the abuse of power in the public office. There has never been such a great failure of management in all its aspects in the history of Independent India.

UASL has resulted in serious financial loss to the public exchequer.

The CVC got conducted an inquiry under Sec. 8 (d) of the Central Vigilance Commission Act, 2003 and noticed some grave irregularities in the grant of licences. On 12 October 2009, a copy of the report prepared on the basis of the said inquiry was forwarded by the CVC to the Director, CBI to investigate into the matter to establish the criminal conspiracy in the allocation of 2G Spectrum under UASL policy of DOT and to bring to book all wrong doers. On receipt of the aforesaid communication from the CVC, CBI registered FIR No. RC-DAI-2009-A-0045 dated 21 October 2009 against unknown officials of DOT and unknown private persons/companies and others for offence under Sec. 120 B IPC read with Secs 13 (2) and 13 (1) (d) of the Prevention of Corruption Act, 1988.

Prayer by Appellant

Feeling aggrieved by refusal of the Division Bench of the Delhi High Court to entertain, the writ petition filed by them for a court monitored investigation by the CBI or a Special Investigating Team into what has been termed as '2G Spectrum Scam' for unearthing the role of respondent No. 5, Shri A Raja, then Union Minister of the DOT, senior officers of that department, middlemen, businessmen, and others, the appellants have invoked the jurisdiction of this Court under Article 136 of the Constitution.

Submission by Appellant's Counsel

Shri Prashant Bhushan, learned counsel for the appellants argued that the allocation of spectrum on 10 January 2008 has resulted in huge loss to the public exchequer and, therefore, a thorough probe is necessary by an independent agency so that all the persons who may be found guilty are brought before law and punished.

Bhushan extensively referred to the documents produced by the parties before the High Court and this Court including the letter dated 20 November 2009 of the Joint Secretary of Income Tax and the report of the CAG and argued that the Court should direct the CBI to conduct investigation on various issues including the grant of permission for use of dual/alternate technology to three operators a day before the policy decision was announced to the public by means of the press release dated 19 October 2007, the change of cutoff date from 25 September 2007 to 1 October 2007, issue of letter of intents by DOT on 10 January 2008, gross violation of the policy of first come first served, non-compliance of the rollout and other obligations by the licensees, failure of the TRAI and DOT to ensure that the licensee complied with the conditions on which they were permitted to use the spectrum and huge loss caused to the public exchequer by manipulative mechanism as also sale of equities by different licensees to foreign companies.

Bhushan referred to Paragraph 6.3 1, (iv) of TRAI recommendation to show that no proposal for permission for merger and acquisition could be entertained till the fulfillment of rollout obligations, but DOT acted in contrast with TRAI recommendation without complying with fifth proviso to Sec. 11 of the Act and as a result of that the licensees violated the conditions of licence with impunity. Shri Bhushan submitted that the grant of licences on the basis of 2001 price in the garb of implementing the recommendations made by TRAI has resulted in loss to the public exchequer to the tune of more than ₹1.76 lakh crore.

Submission by Respondent's Counsel

(K K Venugopal for CBI, Gopal Subramanian the Solicitor General for TRAI, Harin P. Raval for Central Board of Direct Taxes.)

The Court should not make any order which may cast any reflection on the ability of the CBI to conduct the investigation into a case in which allegations of corruption have been leveled against various functionaries of the Government. The CBI has always conducted investigations objectively and, therefore, there is no reason to think that the investigation in the present case will not be fair and impartial or that any attempt will be made to shield any one.

The UASL were granted in 2008 on the price fixed in 2001 because the TRAI had recommended that the new entrant should not be subjected to discriminatory treatment and there should be level playing field for all the applicants.

The recommendations made by the TRAI were approved by the Government and as such the same cannot be termed as illegal or arbitrary. The TRAI is an expert body established for rapid growth of telecommunication services and there is no reason to doubt the credibility of the recommendations made by it on 28 August 2007 for grant of licences on the principle of first come first served basis by treating the 2001 price as the bench mark.

The loss indicated in the report of CAG is based on assumptions and at this stage the Court may not make the said recommendations as the basis for recording a finding whether any loss has been caused to the public exchequer and/or magnitude of the loss.

The Central Government has, after considering the recommendation made by the TRAI, already initiated action for cancellation of the licences of the ineligible applicants and also those who failed to comply with the conditions of licence including rollout obligation.

The counsel referred to the provisions of the Prevention of Money-Laundering Act, 2002 and the Foreign Exchange Management Act, 1999 and argued that soon after receiving complaint, which was forwarded by the Ministry of Finance, the Director General Income Tax (Investigation) sought permission from the Union Home Secretary for putting on surveillance the telephone lines of Ms Niira Radia and her associates and on the basis of the approval granted by the latter, telephone lines of Ms Niira Radia and her associates were put under surveillance.

After completion of the recording, a detailed investigation is being conducted under the supervision of the Director General Income Tax (Investigation). He invited the Court's attention to the report, which was produced in a sealed envelope to show that serious efforts are being made by the Department to find out whether there has been violation of the provisions contained in the two Acts and loss has been caused to the public exchequer. The counsel assured that the Department will produce report on the basis of further investigation conducted by it.

The Government of India and the CBI would have no objection to a Court monitored investigation by the CBI, but submitted that there is no reason for appointment of a Special Investigation Team.

Judgement

In our opinion, the Division Bench of the High Court committed a serious error by dismissing the writ petition at the threshold ignoring that the issues raised by the appellants, whose bonafides have not been doubted, are of great public importance.

We are, prima facie, satisfied that the allegations contained in the writ petition and the affidavits filed before this Court, which are supported not only by the documents produced by them, but also the report of the Central Vigilance Commission, which was forwarded to the Director, CBI on 12 October 2009 and the findings recorded by the CAG in the Performance Audit Report, need a thorough and impartial investigation.

The CBI should probe how licences were granted to large number of ineligible applicants and who was responsible for the same and why the TRAI and the DOT did not take action against those licensees who sold their stakes/equities for many thousand crores and also against those who failed to fulfill rollout obligations and comply with other conditions of licence.

The CBI shall conduct the investigation without being influenced by any functionary, agency, or instrumentality of the state and irrespective of the position, rank, or status of the person to be investigated or probed.

The CBI shall, if it has already not registered first information report in the context of the alleged irregularities committed in the grant of licences from 2001 to 2006–2007, now register a case and conduct thorough investigation with particular emphasis on the loss caused to the public exchequer and corresponding gain to the licensees/service providers and also on the issue of allowing use of dual/alternate technology by some service providers even before the decision was made public vide press release dated 19 October 2007.

The CBI shall also make investigation into the allegation of grant of huge loans by the public sector and other banks to some of the companies, which have succeeded in obtaining licences in 2008 and find out whether the officers of the DOT were signatories to the loan agreement executed by the private companies and if so, why and with whose permission they did so.

The Directorate of Enforcement/concerned agencies of the Income Tax Department shall continue their investigation without any hindrance or interference by any one.

Both the agencies, i.e., the CBI and the Directorate of Enforcement shall share information with each other and ensure that the investigation is not hampered in any manner whatsoever.

The Director General, Income Tax (Investigation) shall, after completion of analysis of the transcripts of the recording made pursuant to the approval accorded by the Home Secretary, Government of India, handover the same to CBI to facilitate further investigation into the FIR already registered or which may be registered hereinafter.

The progress reports based on the investigations conducted by the CBI and the Enforcement Directorate shall be produced before the Court in sealed envelopes on 10 February 2011.

The case is to be listed for further consideration on 10 February 2011.

Conclusion

The case is not yet concluded. The Supreme Court of India with this order has practically taken over the case for its systematic process, development, and progress. The order to the agencies is a clear indication that the executive or the Government has failed in its duty to aid the process of justice. It is noteworthy that the Supreme Court took a serious view of the High Court for not allowing the earlier petition concerning 2G scam before it. Although some of the accused are now released on bail, the case will continue because of the directions given by the Supreme Court of India. The saying, no matter howsoever high one may be the law is yet above all. It highlights the rational principle for the functioning of the system of law. For those within its system, although they may be the very lawmakers or the guardians of the law, yet it works for them if their actions are in accordance with it or against them if their actions are in conflict with it, as the case may be.

Discussion Questions

1. How did the 2G scam originate?
2. Who are the main persons and corporations and Government agencies involved in the case and their legal relationship?
3. How is the Telecom Minister responsible under the law? What went wrong with the minister in the current case?
4. What is the importance of this case to the people of India?
5. Analyze the submissions made by the respective counsels in the case.
6. Discuss the directions given by the Supreme Court of India highlighting its aim of probity in public interest.
7. A minister is a manager of the interests of the public, in this case the spectrum for mobile telephony, the spectrum frequency bandwidth which is a rare technological resource. State the failures in the management of this resource by the minister and his team of bureaucrats and make recommendations to the Ministry of Telecommunication, the DOT, and TRAI for successful management.

Going Beyond

1. Do you think the 2G scam a sufficient ground for the Central Government to resign? If yes, why did the legislators not table a motion of noconfidence in the Parliament?
2. What are the economic and legal consequences of this case?
3. Lay down a guide of rules and regulations for a private company for liaison with a ministry of the Government.

LEGAL LUMINARY

KAPIL SIBAL—THE MULTI-TASKING MINISTER

Lightning intelligence, indulgent smile, silver speech. Kapil Sibal, the Senior Lawyer of the Supreme Court of India, the Union Minister with multiple portfolios, from the political constituency of Chandni Chowk and the world famous Red Fort, the historical nerve centre of India's capital. People say, he is a typical Punjabi: open hearted, open minded and liberal, with a great sense of humour. There is hardly a day without Kapil Sibal on TV; hence, he is a household name in the entire country. It is so because of the very important portfolios that he has been managing:

- Minister for Science and Technology, 2004
- Minister for Earth Science, 2004
- Minister of Human Resource Development, 2009
- Minister of Communications and IT, 2010

In addition, Sibal is the spokesperson for his government, sometimes the party; he heads several groups and commissions.

Sibal understands education; he understands technology as a means to that end. When he announced that he has initiated to develop a touch screen tablet with a scheme of public–private partnership, which would cost ₹1,500 only, many expressed doubts that a Nano Car model for IT may not work. It worked. Sakshat, as the tablet is called, is being distributed to schools nationwide. He has strived to raise the general level of education in India by introducing the continuous and comprehensive evaluation system and has encouraged advanced and professional education by establishing new institutes of engineering, management, and technology across the country.

Kapil was born in 1948 to a post-partition refugee family from West Punjab, where his father was a highly respected advocate and a politician. The young Kapil embodied the very same passion from his father for law and public life. He graduated from the prestigious St. Stephen's College and obtained his master's from the Harvard Law School, USA. In 1989, he was appointed as the Additional Solicitor General of India. He has been the President of the Supreme Court Bar Association on three occasions, between 1995 and 2002. Roli Books published his collection of poems titled *I Witness*, in 2008. He has two sons who are also highly qualified lawyers.*

---

*See http://kapilsibalmp.com

Laws Related to Intellectual Property Rights

Principle: *Ubi jus ibi remedium.*

Where there is a right, there is a remedy.

CHAPTER OUTLINE

- Introduction and Interpretation
- The Copyright Act, 1957
- The Patent Act, 1970

- The Trademarks Act, 1999
- *Case Study:* Battle of the Patents
- *Legal Luminary:* Vandana Shiva

26.1   INTRODUCTION AND INTERPRETATION

Members

TEXT

Desiring to reduce distortions and impediments to international trade, and taking into account the need to promote effective and adequate protection of intellectual property rights, and to ensure that measures and procedures to enforce intellectual property rights do not themselves become barriers to legitimate trade;

Recognizing, to this end, the need for new rules and disciplines concerning:

(a) The applicability of the basic principles of GATT 1994 and of relevant international intellectual property agreements or conventions;

(b) The provision of adequate standards and principles concerning the availability, scope and use of trade-related intellectual property rights;

(c) The provision of effective and appropriate means for the enforcement of trade-related intellectual property rights, taking into account differences in national legal systems;

(d) The provision of effective and expeditious procedures for the multilateral prevention and settlement of disputes between governments; and

(e) Transitional arrangements aiming at the fullest participation in the results of the negotiations;

Recognizing the need for a multilateral framework of principles, rules and disciplines dealing with international trade in counterfeit goods;

Recognizing that intellectual property rights are private rights;

Recognizing the underlying public policy objectives of national systems for the protection of intellectual property, including developmental and technological objectives;

Recognizing also the special needs of the least-developed country Members in respect of maximum flexibility in the domestic implementation of laws and regulations in order to enable them to create a sound and viable technological base;

Emphasizing the importance of reducing tensions by reaching strengthened commitments to resolve disputes on trade-related intellectual property issues through multilateral procedures;

Desiring to establish a mutually supportive relationship between the WTO and the World Intellectual

Property Organization (referred to in this Agreement as WIPO) as well as other relevant international organizations…

> – Preamble, Agreement on Trade-related Aspects of Intellectual Property Rights, 1994[1].

TRIPS and India

The above text from the preamble of the Agreement on Trade-related Aspects of Intellectual Property Rights (TRIPS) clearly states the will of the member countries. It is one of the most important agreements in the current global trade and commerce affairs among the member countries of the World Trade Organization (WTO). Under the initiative of the United Nations Organization, the World Intellectual Property Organization was formed consisting of the members of the WTO, with the following two objectives[2]:

(a) To give statutory expression to the moral and economic rights of creators in their creations and the rights of the public in access to those creations.

(b) To promote as act of the government policy, creativity, and the dissemination and application of its result and to encourage fair trading, which would contribute to economic and social development.

India has been a WTO member since 1995 and, as an emerging economic power with the highest and well-educated human resource, it generates a very high volume of creativity, particularly in the field of information technology, media, entertainment, designing, engineering, industrial and agricultural patents, trademark registrations, geographical indications (for products such as *neem, basmati* rice, etc.), integrated circuits layout designs, undisclosed information and trade secrets that have commercial value (confidential data), technology transfer and transition agreements to develop such technology indigenously.

India is also a member of two treaties: the Paris Convention for the Protection of Industrial Property (relating to patents, trademarks, designs, etc.) of 1883 and the Berne Convention for the Protection of Literary and Artistic Works (relating to copyright) of 1886. Apart from these, India is also a member of the Patent Cooperation Treaty, which facilitates the obtaining of patents in several countries by filing a single application.

The Department of Industrial Policy and Promotion[3] is the concerned agency with legislations relating to patents, trademarks, designs, and geographical indications. (Figure 26.1 shows the various marks used to signify the legal ownership of intellectual property rights.) These are administered through the Office of the Controller General of Patents,

---

[1]See http://www.wto.org/english/docs_e/legal_e/27-trips.pdf (p. 320).

[2]See http://www.wipo.int/export/sites/www/about-ip/en/iprm/pdf/ch1.pdf (p. 3.).

[3]http://www.ipindia.nic.in.

Figure 26.1   Commonly used letters of the alphabet found on books, products, and brands

Designs and Trade Marks, subordinate office, with headquarters at Mumbai. The other related Acts and offices are as follows:

(a) The Patents Act, 1970, amended in 1999, 2002, and 2005 through the Patent Offices at Kolkata (HQ), Mumbai, Chennai, and Delhi.

(b) The Designs Act, 2000, through the Patent Offices at Kolkata (HQ), Mumbai, Chennai, and Delhi.

(c) The Trade Marks Act, 1999 through the Trade Marks Registry at Mumbai (HQ) Chennai, Delhi, Kolkata, and Ahmedabad.

(d) The Geographical Indications of Goods (Registration and Protection) Act, 1999, through the Geographical Indications Registry at Chennai.

(e) Copyright is protected through the Copyright Act, 1957, as amended in 1999—administered by the Department of Higher Education.[4]

(f) Layout of transistors and other circuitry elements is protected through the Semi-conductor Integrated Circuits Layout-Design Act, 2000, administered by the Department of Information Technology.[5]

(g) New varieties of plants are protected through the Protection of Plant Varieties and Farmers' Rights Act, 2001, administered by the Department of Agriculture and Cooperation.[6]

The Controller General of Patents, Designs and Trade Marks is also incharge of the Office of the Patent Information System, Nagpur, and the Intellectual Property Training Institute, Nagpur.

An Intellectual Property Appellate Board has been set up at Chennai to hear appeals against the decisions of Registrar of Trademarks, Geographical Indications, and the Controller of Patents.

Article 39 of the TRIPs Agreement mandates protection of test data submitted to regulatory authorities for obtaining marketing approvals against unfair commercial use. A committee under the chairmanship of the Secretary, Department of Chemicals and Petro-chemicals, has examined this issue and submitted its report to the government.

---

[4]http://education.nic.in/CprAct.pdf.

[5]http://www.mit.gov.in/download/siclda.pdf.

[6]http://agricoop.nic.in/PPV&FR%20Act,%202001.pdf.

Knowledge Economy

The emergence of knowledge economy is the basis for intellectual property rights (IPR), which is protected by the law of the land. In the traditional economy, the classical factors—land, labour, capital, and production—along with monetary management, built an economic structure that was modelled as free market and styled as capitalistic. A revolution, akin to the industrial revolution, took place with the emergence of information technology, which functioned on the sole resource of human knowledge and technological prowess. Every byte of information came to be data managed; the solutions were not sought from the planning of classical economy, but through the computations of systems management. The revolution got accentuated with digitalization of the information, which worked with speed, efficiency, and preciseness, hitherto believed to be impossible.

The knowledge-based property multiplied exponentially, along with that so too did the need to protect it from fraudsters, hackers, and cyber thieves. IT enabled the common people to use such a tool wherein replication and distribution of data became the easiest thing to do, thus endangering the creative work of the people, which was want only and freely made available. The very nature of the new technology made this possible globally due to the seamless possible connectivity and communication.

Intellectual Property Identifier

The letter C within a circle or an R, or the two letters TM on any product, writings such as books, or creations such as photographs, paintings, sketches, etc. is akin to the physical boundary walls between neighbours or territorial borders between two states or countries marking ownership and the rights thereof. The ownership of tangible properties such as land, house, vehicles, and other privately or commonly owned properties is physical. However, products of creativity of mind such as books, paintings, new inventions, computer programmes, images, movies, etc. are intangible, their origin lies in the human genius, the ingenious creations, and innovative inventions that equally belong to some owner or the other. These are an intellectual property (IP). Similar to physical properties being protected from being stolen or damaged or in any way misappropriated, IP is also legally protected. Similar to an owner having a right over his tangible property, the owner of IP exercises unique right over the products of his creativity. He has intellectual property rights over it (see Figure 26.2).

Scope

The sheer enormity of the range of IPR makes it difficult to know everything about it. However, you will be able to grasp both the context and methodology involved in the enforcement of law in this special new area. Hence, only three main Acts, which are as follows, will be considered in a digest approach:

(a) The Copyright Act, 1957
(b) The Patents Act, 1970
(c) The Trade Marks Act, 1999

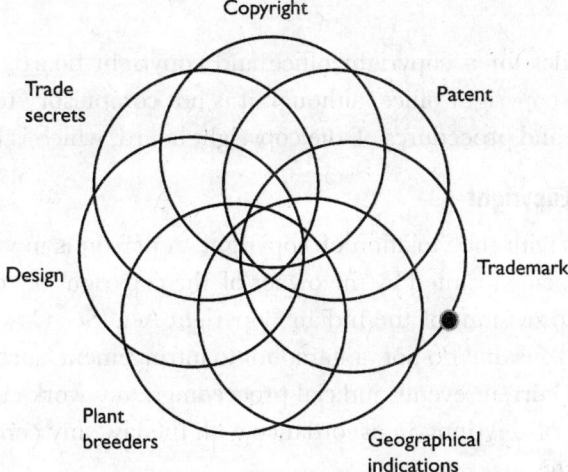

Figure 26.2 Intellectual property

In other words, this chapter will present a short overview of the acts and this will be highlighted with a case each.

26.2 THE COPYRIGHT ACT, 1957

TEXT

No Copyright except as provided in this Act. No person shall be entitled to copyright or any similar right in any work, whether published or unpublished, otherwise than under and in accordance with the provisions of this Act or of any other law for the time being in force but nothing in this section shall be construed as abrogating any right or jurisdiction to restrain a breach of trust or confidence.

– The Copyright Act, 1957, Sec. 16

Copyright issues at times become so highly complicated, because of the complexities involved in ownership and because of the owners' relationship with others, that one can easily lose sight of the meaning of the term.

Meaning of Copyright

Section 14 of the Act annunciates the meaning of copyright as to reproduce the work of any material form [14(1)]. In other words, copyright shorn of all details quite simply means 'the right to copy'. Plagiarism, for instance, is the stealing of IP from its owner. Plagiarism happens commonly when writers, journalists, students, etc. use the method of copy and paste without acknowledging the author from whom such material is sourced. Acknowledgement of sources and documentation thus saves one from such contravention of the law.

Terms of Copyright

Section 2 deals with the concepts of copyright, which can be inferred as ownership terms, and pertains to such as all forms of writing, painting, architecture, images, cinema, and sounds and music. This question will help you determine copyright. Does this—word, deed, or thought—belong to me? If it does not, it never was. If it does, it is yours.

Copyright Office

Section 9 provides for a copyright office and copyright board. One may register one's copyright at the copyright office, although it is not compulsory to do so. Section 12 deals with the powers and procedures of the copyright board, which is headed by a chairman.

Infringement of Copyright

Section 51 deals with the violation of copyright. A person is in violation of the Act when without licence being granted by the owner of the copyright or registrar of copyrights, he infringes on the provisions of the Indian Copyright Act. (See Case 26.1.) However, Sec. 52 deals with those Acts that do not tantamount to infringement, such as private use, research, newspapers and current events, judicial proceedings, any work created by secretariat of a legislature, copy of anything in accordance with the law, any ceremony held by local and state authority, etc.

Civil Remedies for Infringement of Copyright

Section 54 states that the copyright owner may sue in a district court having for jurisdiction and will be entitled to remedy.

Penalty for the Breach of Copyright

According to Sec. 63, the infringement of copyright is punishable with imprisonment for a term not less than six months, that may extend to three years, and with a fine not less than ₹50,000. Infringement of copyright in computer programming, results in imprisonment from 7 days to 3 years and a fine of not less than ₹50,000, which may extend to ₹1,00,000. Now look at the Case 26.1 between Super Cassettes Ltd vs Myspace Inc and Others.

CASE 26.1	APPELLANT: Super Cassettes Industries Ltd vs RESPONDENT: Myspace Inc. and Others
	DATE OF JUDGEMENT: 29 July 2011 *

FACTS: The plaintiff has filed the instant suit for restraining infringement of copyright, damages, etc. The plaintiff claims to be the owner of the copyright in the repertoire of songs, cinematograph films, sound recordings, etc. The plaintiff claims to have over 20,000 Hindi non-film songs and around 50,000 songs in regional languages.

Defendant No. 1 is stated to be a social networking and entertainment Website that offers various entertainment applications including sharing, viewing of music, images, and cinematograph works having its base in the USA. Defendant No. 2 is the owner of defendant No. 1, which is stated to be a division of News Corporation, Fox Interactive media, which offers border-free online network that caters to consumers by giving them platform or tools.

*Super Cassettes Industries Ltd vs Myspace Inc. see http://www.indiankanoon.org/doc/216257/(08 November 2011).

Contd

Case 26.1 *Contd*

> The plaintiff contends that the defendants' basic point of attraction in running this Website is to make available the multimedia content including songs, pictures, and clips, which can be seen and shared by the user over the Internet space. The said website of defendant No. 1 not only includes recently released infringing material but also the material that has not yet been released or is authorized for broadcast through the authorized distribution channels.

> JUDGEMENT: Interim order of restraint.

> REASON: The plaintiff has been able to make out a prima facie case as the plaintiff is the owner of the copyright in the works enumerated in the plaint. The plaintiff has also been able to establish prima facie that the acts of the defendants are infringing in nature as the same are permitting the Web space or a place on Internet for profit. The prima facie case thus is in favour of the plaintiff. The balance of convenience lies in favour of the plaintiff as the defendants would be less inconvenienced if they are directed not to infringe on the plaintiffs works, as it is their own case is that the defendants are doing business from multifarious jobs on the Internet and those works of the plaintiff are not a means of profit.

> Consequently, the present case warrants the grant of interim injunction for the purposes of prevention of infringement of the plaintiffs works. The defendants, their agents, representatives, servants, their officers, or any person on their behalf are restrained from modifying the works (more specifically the works of the plaintiff), permitting the place for profit within the meaning of Sec. 51 (a)(ii) of the Act and resulting in infringement of copyright of the plaintiff.

26.3 THE PATENT ACT, 1970

TEXT

Register of patents and particulars to be entered therein:
(1) There shall be kept at the patent office a register of patents, wherein shall be entered
(a) the names and addresses of grantees of patents;
(b) notifications of assignments and of transmissions of patents of licences under patents, and of amendments, extensions, an revocations of patents; and
particulars of such other matters affecting the validity or proprietorship of patents as may be prescribed.
(2) No notice of any trust, whether express, implied or constructive, shall be entered in the register, and the Controller shall not be affected by any such notice.
(3) Subject to the superintendence and direction of the Central Government, the register shall be kept under the control and management of the Controller.
(4) For the removal of doubts, it is hereby declared that the register of patents existing at the commencement of this Act shall be incorporated in, and form part of, the register under this Act.

– The Patents Act, 1970, Sec. 67

MANAGER'S TAKEAWAY

- In the information age, knowledge is a commodity of monetary value.
- Copyrights, patents, and trademarks bear legal character when officially registered and hence are legally enforceable.

The following is a brief summary of the salient features of the Patent Act, 1970.

Patent [Sec. 2 (m)]

Patent is a certificate of official recognition for an invention. It confers a guarantee and the exclusive right to manufacture and sell such an invention for a period determined by legal process. Not all inventions are patentable (Secs 3 and 4), such as those that are frivolous, and are contrary to public order and morality.

Application for patent (Secs 6–11)

The first and true inventor, individually or jointly, may apply for application; it can be done through any assignee or a legal representative. Secs 25–28 allow for opposition to be granted to patents by sending a notice to the Controller of Patents.

Grant of patent (Secs 43–53)

Having performed the process of examination of the validity of the application and its approval, the Controller of Patents makes an official grant of patent with the mention of the date of grant, the rights of the patentee, and the term of the patent, which is generally for twenty years.

Surrender and revocation of patents (Secs 60–62)

A patentee, by giving notice to the Controller of Patents, may surrender his patent. After the procedure of investigation and publication, the Controller may revoke the patent. The power to revoke is also granted to the Appellate Board upon a petition by any interested person or by the Central Government. The high court may revoke a patent in a suit for infringement of the patent. The Central Government may revoke the patent in public interest.

Register of patents (Secs 67–72)

As seen in the above text, a register is maintained in the patent office with complete particulars of the patents. The register is both in hard and soft copies and is open for the public to examine on payment of the prescribed fee.

Working of patents (Secs 82–94)

The objective of patent grant is to ensure the rights of the inventor and at the same time make available its benefits to the public at a reasonably affordable price.

It is regrettable though that the Indian patent offices take over a decade to complete the process of patenting, which is unfair to the inventor. Fast processing has been recommended as the applications are mounting in the offices of the Controller of Patents. Now look at Case 26.2 between Bayer Corporation and Others vs Union of India and Others.

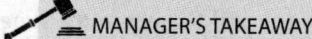

MANAGER'S TAKEAWAY

- Patents remain the most controversial issue in IPR.
- According to the Patent Act, 1970, Sec. 156, a patent shall have, to all intents, the like effect as against government as it has against any person.

CASE 26.2	Appellant: Bayer Corporation and Others	vs	Respondent: Union of India and Others

Date of Judgement: 1 December 2009*

Facts: In the writ petition, the appellants, Bayer Corporation, sought directions inter alia to restrain the Drug Controller General of India (DCGI), respondent No. 2 herein, from granting a drug licence to Cipla Ltd, respondent No. 3 herein (a generic drug manufacturer), to manufacture, sell, and distribute its drug 'sorafenibtosylate', prescribed for the treatment of advanced renal cell carcinoma.

According to Bayer, it learned on July 2008 that Cipla had announced the introduction inter alia of a drug 'Soranib', which was a substitute for Bayers' drug 'sorafenibtosylate'. On 31 July 2008 Bayer wrote to the DCGI inter alia requesting that marketing approval be not granted to Cipla for its drug 'Soranib'. It was pointed out that the proprietary rights to the molecule 'sorafenibtosylate' are vested in Bayer Health Care LLC, a wholly owned subsidiary of appellant No. 1. It alone had the marketing rights to sell the drug in India. Bayer Corporation, along with Bayer HealthCare LLC, asked the DCGI to acknowledge their patent rights and not grant marketing approval to Cipla for launching the generic version of 'sorafenibtosylate'.

Initially an interim ex-parte order was passed by learned Single Judge on 7 November 2008 restraining the DCGI from passing a final order on the application made by Cipla for grant of marketing approval for Soranib. Cipla then applied for vacation of the order. Cipla characterized Bayer's contention that an application for grant of marketing approval under DCA was 'circumscribed by and controlled by a registered Patent' as 'completely untenable' inasmuch the Patents Act and the DCA 'operate in completely different fields and there is no overlap'.

The DCGI in its counter affidavit submitted that the writ petition was 'entirely misconceived'. It was not within the scope of DCA to not grant the said licence on the alleged ground of violation of the provisions of the Patents Act. The DCGI contended that the schemes of the Patents Act and the DCA were completely different and that 'these legislations operate in separate areas and do not overlap with each other'. It was stated by the DCGI that it had asked Cipla to furnish comments on the objections raised by Bayer and that it was yet to receive a reply from Cipla.

The learned Single Judge negated the above contentions of Bayer.

Judgement: Petition dismissed.

Reason: The manufacture or marketing of spurious drugs under the DCA attracts penal consequences whereas the Patents Act itself does not envisage penal consequences in the event of an infringement of a patent. Therefore, by accepting Bayer's contention that every generic drug would be a spurious drug, this court would be subjecting manufacturers of generic versions of patented drugs to prosecution under the DCA although the Patents Act does not provide for such a consequence. This is yet another reason why the attempt at bringing in patent linkage on the basis of the existing provisions of the Patents Act and the DCA cannot be countenanced.

This court does not find any ground having been made out to reverse the well-reasoned judgement of learned Single Judge in which we fully concur. The appeal is accordingly dismissed.

---

*Bayer Corporation and Others vs Union of India and Others; The Patent Act, 1970 Secs 48 and 156; see also http://www.indiankanoon.org/doc/1123372 (15 November 2011).

26.4 THE TRADE MARKS ACT, 1999

TEXT

'Registered trade mark' means a trade mark which is actually on the register and remaining in force.

– The Trade Marks Act, 1999, Sec. 2 (w)

Registered trade mark is exactly what the phrase describes: it is a well-designed word or words or a symbol through which a commercial commodity is marked for distinct identification of the product to distinguish it from similar other products so that the public knows exactly the product they are buying. Registering it gives it official certification. Thus, a trade mark has the following functions:

(a) Identification of the product and its origin

(b) Guarantee of the unchanged product characteristics

(c) Advertising and publicizing of products through the trade mark

(d) Creation of a definite image of the product in the minds of the public

Consider the following essential features of trade mark.

Registration of trade mark (Secs 3–17)

The Central Government appoints the Controller General of Patents, Designs and Trademarks. The register contains all the particulars from application, date, and grant of registration of trademarks or designs. The registration procedure is as per the prescribed standards. Once the application is accepted, it will be publicized for any objections from the public with a notice period of three months. The registered trade mark shall be for a period of ten years upon whose expiry one may apply for renewal with the prescribed fee.

Effects of trade mark registration (Secs 27–36)

The registration of the trade mark is a prima facie evidence of the validity thereof. The proprietor of the registered trade mark shall have the exclusive right to use and obtain relief in respect of infringement of the trade mark.

Appellate board (Secs 46–47)

The Central Government establishes the Appellate Board, to be known as the Intellectual Property Appellate Board. The penalties for offences and procedural details are provided in chapter XII from Secs 100 to 150. Falsification of trade mark or deception is an offence that attracts a penalty of not less than ₹50,000 and may extend to ₹2 lakh or imprisonment up to six months and a fine of ₹50,000.[7] Now look at Case 26.3 between Macleods Pharmaceuticals Ltd vs Tidal Laboratories Pvt Ltd.

> **MANAGER'S TAKEAWAY**
>
> • What's in a name? asked William Shakespeare and suggested that by whatever name a rose be called, it would always smell as sweet. Wrong. Today, even flowers are branded.
> • A manager should be conscious about the identity of his company even when he is not on duty.

---

[7]For managers dealing with trade mark use in brand management, Chapter XII of the Act is very important and must be read and discussed to acquire practical comprehension.

CASE 26.3   APPELLANT: Macleods Pharmaceuticals Ltd   vs   RESPONDENT: Tidal Laboratories Pvt. Ltd

DATE OF JUDGEMENT: 27 October 2005*

FACTS: This is the ad-interim application. The matter has been argued at length by both the learned Counsel and both wanted the matter to be heard at the ad-interim stage and not at the final stage. In that view of the matter, I am required to grant a detailed reasoned order which I accordingly pass herein.

The present application for ad-interim is moved by the plaintiff on cause of action of passing off under the provisions of the Trade and Merchandise Marks Act, 1999. The plaintiffs are seeking an injunction from this court restraining the defendant from in any manner using the impugned trade mark named 'Rabemax' or any other mark deceptively similar to the plaintiffs' trade mark of 'Rabemac' so as to pass off the plaintiffs' product as that of the defendant.

Sometime in or about 21 March 2002 the plaintiffs claimed to have filed an application for registration of the mark 'Rabemac' under Application No. 10899361 under Clause V of the Schedule to the Trade Marks Act. The mark of the plaintiffs has been advertised and application is pending for registration.

The next contention advanced by the learned Counsel for the defendant that the goods that are manufactured by the plaintiff and the defendant use a common molecule 'Rabeprozale sodium'. Thus, the word 'Rabe' is used both by the plaintiff and the defendant to indicate that the goods are manufactured from the said molecule Rabeprozale sodium. 'Rabe' as a prefix is being used by many parties and has nothing special about the same insofar as the plaintiffs are concerned. The plaintiffs appealed to the court with a false case that they have been using the mark since 2001 and/or that the figures shown were the same for the entire period of 2002–2003. Admittedly the licence to manufacture the drug has been received by the plaintiff in September 2002 and thereafter the sales commenced only from October 2002.

JUDGEMENT: Application rejected for the ad-interim relief.

REASON: The plaintiff is also not entitled to ad-interim orders because as far back as on 14 May 2003 the defendant had intimated to the plaintiff that they have filed their application for registration of the mark Rabemax in relation to their goods. The plaintiff did not oppose the application before the Trade Mark Registry and even did not file a suit for passing off for almost two years. The only explanation given in the plaint was that the goods of the plaintiffs were not available in the market from September 2003 till October 2005. The defendants have produced the sales figures of sales during this period, which run to about ₹1,24,93,698. In that view of the matter, it is not possible to accept the contention of the plaintiff that the defendant entered the market only in October 2005. The plaintiff permitted the defendant to use the mark from November 2002 till date and the use of their respective marks by the plaintiff and the defendants has been concurrent since October/November 2002. At this ad-interim stage no case is made out for grant of any ad-interim injunction. Thus, the application was rejected for ad-interim reliefs.

---

*Macleods Pharmaceuticals Ltd vs Tidal Laboratories Pvt Ltd and Others; 2006 (32) PTC 221 Bom; also see http://www.indiankanoon.org/doc/993661/ (25 November 2011).

SUMMARY

- IP is an intangible asset. The rights of its owners are easily contravened due to the technological advantage in the information age. International treaties and laws of the land are geared towards the objective of protecting IPR in the form of copyright, patents, trademarks, designs, geographical indications, agricultural plants, seeds, etc.
- In India, several important legislations have been passed to protect IPR, with the main ones being as follows:

The Copyright Act, 1957: There is a Copyright Board established by the Central Government and under it there is the Registrar of Copyright who controls the copyright office. The infringement of copyrights gives rise to civil remedies such as injunction or damages and also penalties and fines.

The Patents Act, 1970: Patent is granted only for inventions that are new and useful. One applies for patents with all the details and the Patent Office grants the certificate with the particulars of the patent, with a duration of twenty years of exclusive use for the patented object's manufacture and sale.

The Trade Marks Act, 1999: A trade mark is a visual symbol in the form of a word, device, or label. One contravenes the law when a trade mark is imitated deceptively to resemble, generally, a successful similar trade mark. The authority for trademarks is called the Controller General of Patents, Designs and Trade Marks. The office of the authority maintains a register of trademarks. He is the proprietor of the trade mark who has applied and registered it. The effect of trade mark registration allows the proprietor to take proceedings against infringement.

EXERCISES

(i) A plaintiff sued for a permanent injunction and damages claiming that the defendant has infringed copyrights of his film. But the defendant proved that the plaintiff is not the owner of all the copyrights of the film. What remedy will the plaintiff obtain?

Hint: Final relief may not be granted, although an ad-interim one is possible till the Registrar directs suits for proceedings. See: Warner Bros Entertainment vs Santosh V.G. + CS (OS) No.1682/2006.

(ii) Sriman applied for trade mark with a word 'India', which the Registrar refused to accept. Sriman went to the court. What remedy would he receive?

Hint: Court will not entertain the petition as it is for the Registrar to do so. See Sec. 108 of the act.

(iii) What do you understand by Intellectual Property Rights? Shed light upon TRIPS.

(iv) Elucidate the legal perspective on copyright.

(v) Explain the procedure for the grant of patent.

DEVELOPMENT OF LEGAL EDGE

- Rajiv Gandhi School of Intellectual Property Law, IIT Kharagpur.
- Recommended course in IPR.

FURTHER READING

Book

- Tamali Sen Gupta (Roger Blanpain, editor), *Intellectual Property Law in India*, Aspen Publications, 2011.

Agreement on Trade-related Aspects of IPR

- http://www.wto.org/english/docs_e/legal_e/27-trips.pdf.

Other Legal Documents of WTO

*   http://www.wto.org/english/docs_e/legal_e/
    legal_e.htm#TRIPs.

CASE STUDY	BATTLE OF THE PATENTS[8]

Bajaj Auto vs TVS Motor Company Ltd
Rights of patentees:
(1) Subject to the other provisions contained in this act, a patent granted before the commencement of this act, shall confer on the patentee the exclusive right by himself, his agents or licensees to make, use, exercise, sell, or distribute the invention in India.
(2) Subject to the other provisions contained in this act and the conditions specified in Sec. 47, a patent granted after the commencement of this act shall confer upon the patentee
(a) where the patent is for an article or substance, the exclusive right by himself, his agents or licensees to make, use, exercise, sell or distribute such article or substance in India;
(b) where a patent is for a method or process of manufacturing an article or substance, the exclusive right by himself, his agents or licensees to use or exercise the method or process in India.

– The Patents Act, 1970, Sec. 108, Sec. 48

Bajaj Auto Ltd	**TVS Motor Company Ltd**
• Listed company, public limited	• Listed, public limited
• Headquarters: Pune	• Headquarters: Chennai
• Products: two wheelers and three wheelers	• Products: mainly two wheelers
• Revenues of approximately ₹17,000 crore	• Revenue: approximately ₹7,000 crore
• Employees: over 10,000	

Legal Basis of the Suit

Reliefs in suits for infringement: The reliefs which a court may grant in any suit or infringements include an injunction (subject to such terms, if any, as the court thinks fit) and, at the option of the plaintiff, either damages or an account of profits.

– The Patents Act, 1970, Sec. 108

It is a suit filed under Sec. 108 of the Patents Act, 1970, for the relief of permanent injunction in respect of the plaintiffs patent No. 195904 and/or from using the technology/invention described in the said patent and/or manufacturing, marketing, selling, offering for sale, or exporting two or three wheelers, including the proposed

---

[8]Bajaj Auto Ltd vs TVS Motor Company Ltd; (2008) ILLJ 726 Mad, MIPR 2008 (1) 217; also see http://www.indiankanoon.org/doc/1058259 (25 November 2011). The abridgement of this judgement is limited to only Secs 48 and 108 of the Patents Act, 1999.

125-CC FLAME motorcycle containing an internal combustion engine or any internal combustion engine or product that infringes the plaintiffs patent No. 195904, claiming of damages for infringement of patent to the extent of ₹10,50,000.

Pending the said suit, the plaintiff therein, namely Bajaj Auto Limited, has filed a suit praying for an order of temporary injunction restraining the respondent from in any manner infringing the applicant's patent No. 195904 and/or from using the technology/ invention described in the said patent and/or manufacturing, marketing, selling, offering for sale, or exporting two or three wheelers, including the proposed 125 cc FLAME motorcycle containing an internal combustion engine or any internal combustion engine or product that infringes the plaintiffs patent No. 195904.

TVS Motor Company Limited has filed the suit on the basis of a groundless threat of infringement under Sec. 106 of the Patents Act, for declaring that the threats held out by the defendant on 1 and 3 September 2007 that the plaintiff is infringing the defendant's patent No. 195904 and that the defendant is proposing to take infringement action against the plaintiff are unjustified, for declaring that the plaintiffs product TVS Flame, which uses 2 spark plugs with screw-fitted sleeve and 3 valves, does not infringe patent No. 195904 of the defendant, for permanent injunction restraining the defendant from continuing the issuance of threats that the plaintiff is infringing the defendant's patent No. 195904 directly or indirectly in any manner including by way of circulars, advertisements, communications orally or in writing to the plaintiff or any other person, and thereby interfering with the launch and sale of product TVS Flame apart from directing the defendant to compensate the plaintiff with a sum of ₹1 crore or as determined by this Court as damages sustained on account of the unjustified threats made by the plaintiff.

Analysis

It is an admitted fact that the plaintiff has been issued with patent rights for both process and product. The process is for preparation of low-glycaemic sweets for a term of twenty years from 13 February 2003. Similarly, they are also entitled to patent for the product for twenty years from July 2004. Thus, the plaintiff has discharged his initial responsibility by proving that they are protected by the certificate issued by the authorities under the Patents Act, 1970. In other words, the plaintiffs have established a prima facie case on the strength of their two certificates. In such circumstances, Sec. 48 of the Patents Act, 1970,

will hold the field according to which a patent granted under this act shall confer upon the patentee the exclusive right to prevent third parties from the act of making, using, selling, or importing that product in India if the subject matter of the patent is a product. Similarly, if the subject matter of the patent is a process, the patentee has the exclusive right to prevent third parties from the act of using the process for sale, selling for those purpose the product obtained directly by that process in India. Therefore, the plaintiff, having obtained the patent for both the process and product under the Patent Act, 1970, has the statutory right to prevent third parties from infringing those rights.

When third parties infringe the rights granted under the Patent Act, then Sec. 108 of the act will come into operation according to which, in case of infringement, the court may grant the reliefs including injunction and ordering the goods to be seized, forfeited, or destroyed.

In the context of the facts and situation of the present case, I am of the considered view that the contention that triable issues against the patent must be found out by the court before granting an order of injunction is not sustainable, in the light of the amended provision of Sec. 48 of the Patents Act, 1970 (Amended Act 38 of 2002 with effect from 20 May 2003), by which a patentee is given an exclusive right to prevent third parties from using its patent and product.

Keeping in view the Statement of Objects and Reasons stated above and also the salient features of the Bill, Sec. 48, has been amended to give better rights to the patentees and the entire aspect has to be considered in that angle too. Since the purpose is the concept of globalization and for the development of the 'intellectual property system in India' on par with international practice, such rights are given. In contrast, the triable issue against patent sought to be raised on behalf of the respondent is that the specifications in various stages differ and therefore the applicant itself is not aware of its invention, which prima facie I have found as not correct. In such factual situation, the question of raising a triable issue against the patent granted to the applicant at this stage does not arise.

The object of Patent Law is to encourage scientific research, new technology and industrial progress. Grant of exclusive privilege to own, use, or sell the method or the product patented for a limited period stimulates new inventions of commercial utility. The price of the grant of the monopoly is the disclosure of the invention at the Patent Office, which, after the expiry of the fixed period of the monopoly, passes into the public domain.

Principle

The fundamental principle of Patent Law is that a patent is granted only for an invention that is new and useful. That is to say, it must have novelty and utility. It is essential for the validity of a patent that it must be the inventor's own discovery as opposed to mere verification of what was already known before the date of the patent.

Judgement

I have taken into consideration while arriving at such a conclusion the novelty stated to have been achieved by the applicant by way of patent, coupled with its enablement, as proved by putting the product in the market and that has earned usage in a large extent and both novelty and enablement have been established by the applicant for the purpose of granting the order of injunction in favour of the applicant/plaintiff.

Conclusion

Even a cursory case as this case would reveal that patents present the greatest challenge to manufacturers of the highly commercial automotive industry. The importance of this industry also suggests its global problems of IPR of its designs and products. Commercially successful patents immediately attract copycats and unlawful imitators. Today, the global industries in the areas of not only manufacturing but also in fashion, cinematography, software development, art and architecture, etc., find themselves amidst claims of patents. TRIPS is a good beginning in matters of the protection of IPR internationally. However, more work needs to be done through multilateral agreements and common treaties to coordinate the actions in support of IPR uniformly across the globe.

Discussion Questions

1. Delineate the two important Secs 48 and 108 against the issues involved in this case.
2. What is the position taken by each of the contestants in this case?
3. Independently judge the merit of their positions.39
4. Could this case have been avoided? How?
5. Highlight the points of the analysis by the judge?
6. What is the fundamental principle of patents and how is it applied in the case?
7. What lesson do you learn as a manager that may be applicable to a similar case that you know from experience?

Going Beyond

1. What are the problems faced in IPR in the age of Information Technology, especially from the perspective of the Internet?
2. Your son/daughter is a school student. He/she wrote an essay but someone else stole it away and it was published in the school magazine. Create the entire scenario to educate the children, teachers, and parents about IPR.
3. Is your organization or learning institute involved in IPR infringements (unlicensed software, plagiarized papers, cases, etc.). Suggest steps to stop such piracy and contravention of law.

LEGAL LUMINARY

VANDANA SHIVA—EXPOSED VARIABLES

According to Dr Vandana Shiva, 'the primary threat to nature and people today comes from centralizing and monopolizing power and control. Not until diversity is made the logic of production will there be a chance for sustainability, justice and peace. Cultivating and conserving diversity is no luxury in our times: it is a survival imperative.'*

Shiva is an outstanding academician who does not need an introduction in the following areas: academics, environmental problems, business globalization, international economics, ecology, feminism, human development, biodiversity, documentaries, democracy, justice, international policy-making, physics, and the philosophy of science. There is hardly any national or international award that she has been not awarded, except only the Nobel Prize. She is the definition of a prolific writer, with already 20 books and scores of scientific papers in a life that spans six decades. This

*See http://www.rightlivelihood.org/v-shiva.html.

Contd

Legal Luminary *Contd*

indomitable, indefatigable lady with an infectious smile, a true daughter of the Himalayas, hails from Dehradun, Uttarakhand.**

From what has been said above, the reason for Shiva finding this space in the profile of legal luminaries is obvious. She may have well belonged equally worthily in all the areas that have been mentioned above. However, here, for managers she is highly relevant, especially in the field of IPR. Her two works—*Patents, Myths, and Reality;* and *Earth Democracy, Justice, Sustainability, and Peace*—make a framework not only matters concerning IPR, but also for the fundamental moral responsibilities of the people and for justice and peace in an increasingly peace-threatened world. For managers, there are lessons to be drawn as to how to deal with global commerce and at the same time do justice to the acute problems of sustainability, in other words, resource management, food supply, knowledge economy, and all the major problems put in the big picture of the world.

The range of her academic prowess coupled with an active leadership in environmental and feminists issues is a rare combination of a thinker and activist on the world stage. Vandana Shiva graduated in physics and obtained her master's in the philosophy of science; she earned her PhD degree with the dissertation Hidden Variables and Locality in Quantum Theory. The heading of her present profile as Exposed Variables is meant to point to her ability to combine multidisciplines

and the versatility of her engagements on the international level. In Bengaluru, she conducted research in science and technology at the Indian Institute of Science and at the same time rendered her service at the Indian Institute of Management. In Dehradun she founded a Research Foundation in 1982 that characteristically spanned across multiple disciplines: science, technology, and ecology. The foundation's objectives were to work at the grassroots and acquire and apply knowledge on the principles of sustainability. She raised these real local issues of the people to the forum of WTO and put them in the context of TRIPS, as she intensively dealt with IPR issues and made an in-depth impact on biodiversity. Her foundation successfully challenged the bio-piracy of *Neem, Basmati*, and Wheat. Similarly, she has carried out campaigns in the areas of biotechnology and genetic engineering in Africa, Asia, and Latin America, and in Europe. A student of St Mary's School in Nainital and later of Convent of Jesus and Mary, Dehradun, she is now the most sought-after person in the portals of the famous universities of the world. One among them is the Bernheim Chair for the Study of Peace and Citizenship at the Univesitelibre de Bruxelles, Belgium. It is not possible to fit into this tiny profile all the books and literature produced by Shiva, nor is it possible to enumerate all her awards and accolades. The message from this luminary to a manager is to develop a holistic and scientific view of the world.

**See http://cd.planet-diversity.org/fileadmin/files/planet_diversity/Programme/Workshops/Women_for_Biodiversity/Shiva_Vandana.pdf.

Laws Related to Environmental Protection

Principle: *Ad vid majorem vei ad casus fortuitous non tenetur quis, nisi sua cupla intervenerit.*

No one is held to answer for the effects of a superior force or of accidents unless his own fault has contributed to it.

CHAPTER OUTLINE

- Introduction and Interpretation
- The Environment Protecton Act, 1986
- Acts Related to Environmental Protection

- *Case Study*: Taj Mahal—
  The Empress of World Monuments in Peril
- *Legal Luminary:* M.C. Mehta

27.1 INTRODUCTON AND INTERPRETATION

An Act to provide for the protection and improvement of environment and for matters connected there with:

Whereas the decisions were taken at the United Nations Conference on the Human Environment held at Stockholm in June, 1972, in which India participated, to take appropriate steps for the protection and improvement of human environment;

And whereas it is considered necessary further to implement the decisions aforesaid in so far as they relate to the protection and improvement of environment and the prevention of hazards to human beings, other living creatures, plants and property;

Be it enacted by Parliament in the Thirty-seventh Year of the Republic…

— The Environment (Protection) Act, 1986, Preamble

That we live in an endangered world is an understatement. It clearly exhibits the mismanagement and lack of management of Earth's resources: soil, water, air, green cover, rivers, lakes, and oceans. As a result, life on Earth is endangered. Nature has both the means and the time to take care of itself. It is we and all that enables us to live that are directly affected. Our mindless misuse of resources has landed us with few sustainable choices. If these are not made early enough, we will pay the price through nothing less than life itself.

United Nations Environment Programme

In 1972, the United Nations Organization (UNO) held a conference on the human environment, which gave an impetus to all the member countries to provide legislation for the protection of the environment. A direct consequence of this conference was the establishment of the United Nations Environment Programme (UNEP). Under this programme, the UNEP conducts wide-ranging activities, particularly in the developing and underdeveloped countries. Areas such as atmosphere, ecosystems, environmental science, climate change, etc. are researched and the knowledge is disseminated. The UNEP conducts activities such as approaches to climate change, disasters and conflicts, ecosystem management, resource efficiency, etc.

According to the above-mentioned areas and programmes, the UNEP has initiated several treaties and protocols that are binding on the member nations. Some of the well-known international environmental agreements are as follows:

1. Convention for the Conservation of Antarctic Marine Living Resources, Canberra, 1980
2. Basel Convention on the Control of Trans-boundary Movements of Hazardous Wastes and their Disposal, Basel, 1989
3. Convention for the Protection of the Natural Resources and Environment of the South Pacific Region, Nouméa, 1986
4. Convention on Assistance in the Case of a Nuclear Accident or Radiological Emergency (Assistance Convention), Vienna, 1986
5. Convention on Biological Diversity, Nairobi, 1992
6. Convention on the Conservation of Migratory Species of Wild Animals, Bonn, 1979
7. Convention on the Protection and Use of Trans-boundary Watercourses and International Lakes (ECE Water Convention), Helsinki, 1992
8. FAO International Code of Conduct on the Distribution and Use of Pesticides, Rome, 1985
9. International Treaty on Plant Genetic Resources for Food and Agriculture
10. Montreal Protocol on Substances that Deplete the Ozone Layer, Montreal, 1989
11. The Kyoto Protocol is a protocol to the United Nations Framework Convention on Climate Change, 1997, ratified by 191 member countries

Constitutional Mandate

The 42nd Amendment Act to the Constitution of India, 1976, has introduced the principle of environmental protection under:

Article 48A: The state shall endeavour to protect and improve the environment and to safeguard the forests and wildlife of the country.

Article 51A: It shall be the duty of every citizen of India to protect and improve the natural environment, including forests, lakes, rivers, and wild life, and to have compassion for living creatures.

With the constitutional mandate and directives in place, India has proceeded with the statutory framework of Acts, rules, and regulations. It has also established the judicial machinery necessary to adjudicate disputes and to aid redressal. Tribunals and appellate tribunals have been established. The central government has a full-fledged cabinet rank ministry dedicated to the environment, the Ministry of Environment and Forests (MoEF).

Scope

The scope of this chapter is limited to considering some aspects of the Environment Protection Act, 1986. The other related laws, rules, and regulations are listed to provide an understanding of the expanse of the legal provisions and the statutory machinery for the enforcement of the laws of protection of the environment. Although it is not possible to go through all the sections of all the laws, yet a fair idea of not only the enormity of laws but also the seriousness of the issues involved in industry affecting these laws and regulations will be obtained.

27.2   THE ENVIRONMENT PROTECTON ACT, 1986

TEXT

(1) Subject to the provisions of this Act, the Central Government shall have the power to take all such measures as it deems necessary or expedient for the purpose of protecting and improving the quality of the environment and preventing controlling and abating environmental pollution. (3) The Central Government may, if it considers it necessary or expedient so to do for the purpose of this Act, by order, published in the Official Gazette, constitute an authority or authorities by such name or names as may be specified in the order for the purpose of exercising and performing such of the powers and functions (including the power to issue directions under Sec. 5 of the Central Government under this Act and for taking measures with respect to such of the matters referred to in Sub-sec. (2) as may be mentioned in the order and subject to the supervision and control of the Central Government and the provisions of such order, such authority or authorities may exercise and powers or perform the functions or take the measures so mentioned in the order as if such authority or authorities had been empowered by this Act to exercise those powers or perform those functions or take such measures.

– The Environment (Protection) Act, 1986, Sec. 3

The Environment Protection Act, 1986 (EPA), has given the central government extensive powers to formulate rules and regulations and to establish authorities for the sake of supervision and control of all the measures that it decides to take. The EPA has the powers to control and regulate the discharge of pollutants, the handling of hazardous substances, and the response to accidents and disasters, and to punish offenders who endanger the environment and human health.

The environmental protection measures [(Sec. 3(2)]   It provides for the following measures:

1. Coordination of actions by the state governments, officers, and other authorities:
    (a) under this Act, or the rules made there under, or
    (b) under any other law for the time being in force, which is relatable to the objects of this Act
2. Planning and execution of a nation-wide programme for the prevention, control, and abatement of environmental pollution

3. Laying down standards for the quality of environment in its various aspects

4. Laying down standards for emission or discharge of environmental pollutants from various sources whatsoever: provided that different standards for emission or discharge may be laid down under this clause from different sources with regard to the quality or composition of the emission or discharge of environmental pollutants from such sources

5. Restriction of areas in which any industries, operations, or processes, or class of industries, operations, or processes shall be or shall not be carried out subject to certain safeguards

6. Laying down procedures and safeguards for the prevention of accidents that may cause environmental pollution and remedial measures for such accidents

7. Laying down procedures and safeguards for handling of hazardous substances

8. Examination of such manufacturing processes, materials, and substances as are likely to cause environmental pollution

9. Carrying out and sponsoring investigations and research relating to problems of environmental pollution

10. Inspection of any premises, plant, equipment, machinery, manufacturing, or other processes, materials, or substances and giving, by order, of such directions to such authorities, officers, or persons as it may consider necessary to take steps for the prevention, control, and abatement of environmental pollution

11. Establishment or recognition of environmental laboratories and institutes to carry out the functions entrusted to such environmental laboratories and institutes under this Act

12. Collection and dissemination of information with respect to matters relating to environmental pollution

13. Preparation of manuals, codes, or guides relating to the prevention, control, and abatement of environmental pollution

14. Such other matters as the Central Government deems necessary or expedient for the purpose of securing the effective implementation of the provisions of this Act

Prevention, control, and abatement of environmental pollution (Secs 7–13)

These sections deal with both the industry and the government officials:

(a) Persons carrying on industry operation, etc., not to allow emission or discharge of environmental pollutants in excess of the standards (Sec. 7)

(b) Persons handling hazardous substances to comply with procedural safeguards (Sec. 8)

(c) Furnishing of information to authorities and agencies in certain cases (Sec. 9)

(d) Powers of entry and inspection (Sec. 10)

(e) Power to take sample and procedure to be followed in connection therewith (Sec. 11)

(f) Environmental laboratories (Sec. 12)

Furthermore, the government has the right to prepare reports by its analysts. Sec. 15 deals with penalties for contravention of the provisions of the Acts, rules, and directions.

Offences by the companies (Sec. 16)

1. Where any offence under this Act has been committed by a company, every person who, at the time the offence was committed, was directly in charge of, and was responsible to, the company for the conduct of the business of the company, as well as the company, shall be deemed to be guilty of the offence and shall be liable to be proceeded against and punished accordingly: provided that nothing contained in this sub-section shall render any such person liable to any punishment provided in this Act, if he proves that the offence was committed without his knowledge or that he exercised all due diligence to prevent the commission of such offence.

2. Not withstanding anything contained in Sub-sec. (1), where an offence under this Act has been committed by a company and it is proved that the offence has been committed with the consent or connivance of, or is attributable to any neglect on the part of, any director, manager, secretary, or other officer of the company, such as director, manager, secretary, or other officer shall also deemed to be guilty of that offence and shall be liable to be proceeded against and punished accordingly.

Principles of Environment Protection

The following public interest litigation case in the Supreme Court of India advocated by the world-renowned environmental protectionist and human rights activist, M.C. Mehta, brought out a benchmark judgement where the principles of environment protection were delineated and enforced. The twin principles of polluter pays and public good, sometimes expressed as public trust, have been expounded and applied. You would benefit through analysing the rewards of these two principles. As a manager, if the public good or the public trust is kept, it would go a long way in ensuring the social responsibility of a company towards the stakeholders in society. When such a perspective is lost, then disregard for nature sets in and law will be enforced and the civil and criminal liabilities would have to be enforced by the law (Case 27.1).

 MANAGER'S TAKEAWAY

- Polluter pays.
- The public trust or public good is an inviolable natural right.

CASE 27.1

PETITIONER: M.C. Mehta vs RESPONDENT: Kamal Nath and others[*]

DATE OF JUDGEMENT: 13 December 1996

FACTS : Span club was built after encroaching upon 27.12 *bighas* of land, including substantial forest land, in 1990. The land was later regularized and leased out to the company on 11 April 1994. The regularization was carried out when Kamal Nath was the Minister of Environment and Forests.

The swollen river Beas changed its course and engulfed the Span club and the adjoining lawns, washing it away. For almost five months now, the Span Resorts

---

[*]M.C. Mehta vs Kamal Nath and others, (Supreme Court Bench J. Kuldip Singh and J.S. Sagnhnar Ahmad); see also: http://www.indiankanoon.org/doc/1514672/ (23 November 2011).

Contd

Case 27.1 *Contd*

management had been moving bulldozers and earthmovers to turn the course of the Beas for a second time.

Three private companies, one each from Chandigarh, Mandi, and Kullu, moved in one heavy earth mover (hired at the rate of ₹2,000 per hour), four earth movers, four bulldozers (rates varying from ₹650 to ₹850 each per hour), and thirty-five tractor trolleys; a security ring has been thrown all around.

Another worrying thought is that of the river eating into the mountains, leading to landslides, which are an occasional occurrence in this area. Last September, these caused floods in the Beas and property estimated to be worth ₹105 crores was destroyed.

Once they succeed in diverting the river, the Span management plans to go in for landscaping the reclaimed land. However, as of today, they are not so sure. Even they confess the river may just return.

JUDGEMENT: Petition disposed in accordance with the Court Order.

REASON: The Public Trust Doctrine primarily rests on the principle that certain resources such as air, sea, waters, and the forests have such a great importance to the people as a whole that it would be wholly unjustified to make them a subject of private ownership. The said resources being a gift of nature, they should be made freely available to everyone irrespective of the status in life. The doctrine enjoins upon the government to protect the resources for the enjoyment of the general public rather than to permit their use for private ownership or commercial purposes.

Coming to the facts of the present case, a large area of the bank of river Beas, which is part of a protected forest, has been given on a lease purely for commercial purposes to the motels. We have no hesitation in holding that the Himachal Pradesh Government committed patent breach of public trust by leasing the ecologically fragile land to the motel management. Both the lease and transactions are in patent breach of the trust held by the state government. The second lease granted in 1994 was virtually of the land, which is a part of the river bed.

The public trust doctrine, as discussed by us in this judgement, is a part of the law of the land.

The prior approvals granted by the Government of India, Ministry of Environment and Forest, by the letter dated 24 November 1993 and the lease deed dated 11 April 1994 in favour of the motel are quashed. The lease granted to the motel by the said lease deed with respect to 27 *bighas* and 12 *biswas* of area is cancelled and set aside. The Himachal Pradesh Government shall take over the area and restore it to its original natural conditions.

The river bank and the river basin shall be left open for public use.

27.3 ACTS RELATED TO ENVIRONMENTAL PROTECTION
Laws to Save the Environment

The concerns of survival and sustainability were taken up seriously by the community of the world's nations at the United Nations Conference on the Human Environmental problems in 1972 in Stockholm. India, as a member of the UNO, had participated actively and thereafter passed legislation keeping abreast with the world community of nations with appropriate legislation. Table 27.1 gives a list of those legislations. The relevance of all these laws is obvious to a manager as all these laws are primarily applied to industries and their allied fields, because it is the industry that has failed to manage the Earth's resources sustainably.

Table 27.1 Acts related to environment protection

Year	Act	Objectives
General laws of environment		
1986	EPA	To protect and improve environmental quality, control and reduce pollution from all sources, and prohibit or restrict the setting and operation of any industrial facility on environmental grounds To provide public liability insurance to provide immediate relief to affected persons handling hazardous substance
1991	The National Environmental Tribunal Act	To hear appeals about classes of industries and the safeguards to be exercised
1995	The National Environment Appellate Authority Act	To award compensation for damages arising from handling hazardous waste
1997	The National Environment Appellate Authority Act	To hear appeals of classes of industries with respect to restrictions of areas to be carried out under EPA, 1986
2002	The Biological Diversity Act	To provide for the conservation of biological diversity sustainable use of its components and fair and equitable sharing of the benefits arising out of the use of biological resources and knowledge associated with it
Laws of forest and wildlife		
1927/1984	The Indian Forest Act and Amendment	Concerns the forests produce, transit, and the levy on them
1972/1991	The Wildlife Protection Act	To protect birds, animals, and related matters concerning their habitat
Laws of water		
1882	The Easement Act	Concerns the water resources, which are a state property, ownership as attached to land for individuals
1897	The Indian Fisheries Act	To protect the fish stock both in coastal and in inland water bodies; using of explosives or chemicals to harvest fish attracts criminal penalty
1956	The River Boards Act	To establish interstate cooperation along with the Central Government to resolve disputes
1970	The Merchant Shipping Act	To control the waste arising from ships
1974	The Water Prevention and Control Pollution Act	To prevent and abate water pollution; standards for water quality; standards for effluents; constitution of the Central Pollution Control Board (CPCB)

Contd

Table 27.1 *Contd*

1977	The Water Prevention and Control of Pollution Cess Act	To levy cess and collect fees on water-consuming industries and local authorities
Air		
1948/1987	The Factories Act	To regulate work environment of workers and application of hazardous processes
1982	The Atomic Energy Act	To regulate radioactive waste
1988	The Motor Vehicles Act	To manage and dispose hazardous waste

In addition to the above Acts (Table 27.1), the Authority set up under each Act regularly makes rules and regulations. These are notified in the official gazette both as hard copy and soft copy and are available on the Government of India websites. If you as a manager are dealing with one of the industries that come under these laws, you would appreciate not only the Acts but also would update yourself with the rules and regulations, which function as day-to-day and mandatory compliances. You may also gather the requisite information specifically applicable to the industry operating under your watch from the State Pollution Control Board.

SUMMARY

- The problems of environmental pollution and destruction are due to mismanagement or lack of management of the natural resources. Industry is the culprit here. The laws initiated by the UNO and enacted by the member countries despite their best intention have problems of enforcing them. As a result, pollution of air, water, and soil have reached enormous proportions.
- India has enacted several laws to use the natural resources sustainably and for the public good. India's environmental laws are mandated by the Constitution of India itself. The EPA, 1986 is the basis of all the environmental laws. The Ministry of Environment and Forests is responsible for the protection of environment and through its departments and boards controls and enforces the laws. Tribunals and appellate tribunals deal with disputes and redressal. The courts in the country have not only given landmark judgements to protect the environment but also played an active role in monitoring the work of various agencies in the implementation of their orders.
- Public interest litigation by the citizens of the country has gone a long way to bring business establishments and industries under the purview of the law.

EXERCISES

(i) Your company was indicted and fined for causing pollution and was ordered out of the city to be relocated far away from the city. You were also supposed to discard the polluting machinery and install new environmentally friendly technology. The court order further asked the company to reinstate all the employees. You plead praying that all of this is beyond the means of the company.

Hint: Court orders are generally absolute; see the Chapter-end case for further deliberations on the Court Order. Information Technology Act, 2000.

(ii) Your company has been charged by the State Pollution Control Board for letting out untreated effluents in the river. You contest the show cause notice in the National Environment Appellate Authority. What is your legal remedy?

Hint: You will lose the case; see EPA 1986.

(iii) A bakery in the midst of a residential area emitted so much smoke, day and night, that after sometime the neighbours developed respiratory problems. One could not chase away the baker because many did want him to continue. How to deal with this problem?

Hint: The baker must go; see Gobind Singh vs Shanti Swarup; AIR 1979 SC 143.

(iv) Explain the principle of 'public good' through the illustration of a case.

(v) Do you think the principle 'polluter pays' is helpful? Illustrate with examples.

DEVELOPMENT OF LEGAL EDGE

Project I—Collaboration with Pollution Control Board

If yours is an educational or management institute, developing a linkage or collaboration on specific areas with the State Pollution Control Board.

Areas of collaboration

- Research in industrial effluents
- Medical solid waste
- Mining-related pollution
- Urban pollution in construction industry
- Marine hazardous waste
- Ship breaking
- Transport of hazardous material
- Computer hardware-related toxins

Project II

If you are an executive in an industry, write a case study on the environmental status of your company.

Steps to be taken

- Make an application to the appropriate authorities of the company, for example, the Board of Directors, about the case study clearly stating its objectives and method.
- Obtain a written permission to conduct the research and the allotted time limit.
- Upon completion of the case study submit it to the same authorities to whom you applied and from whom you got the permission.
- If you are called upon to help, extend your full cooperation.
- If you are unduly harassed you may after proper legal advice blow the whistle.
- This way you will help the intent of the rule of law in the country to protect environment for the public good.

FURTHER READING

Web resources

- For further information on all the acts, rules, and regulations of all the above stated laws in the section Acts Related to Environmental Protection, refer to the following website: http://moef.nic.in.

Book

- P.B. Sahasranaman, *Handbook of Environmental Law in India*, Oxford University Press (India).

CASE STUDY TAJ MAHAL—THE EMPRESS OF WORLD MONUMENTS IN PERIL

Introduction and Objective

In the Supreme Court of India

Bench: Justice K. Singh and Justice F. Uddin[1]

Petitioner: M.C. Mehta

RESPONDENT: Union of India and others

Date: 30 December 1996

In the annals of environmental case law, this case is the supreme example of probity, concern for environment, and fear about its consequences. As a manager, this case will show you how polluting industries destroy everything in their path: health, life, and all that it holds dear—(dwellings, cities, monuments, soil, water, air, etc). For a manager to lose sight of these serious concerns is to be blind to what is evidently obvious. In contrast, being good to the environment is tantamount to being good to oneself. The lesson of this case: Environmental protection is not only a legal obligation but also the utmost moral duty, the ethical imperative.

What Justice Kuldip Singh Says about Taj Mahal[2]

Taj Mahal, The Taj, is the 'King Emperor' amongst the World—Wonders. The Taj is the final achievement and acme of the Moghul Art. It represents the most refined aesthetic values. It is a fantasy, like grandeur. It is the perfect culmination and artistic interplay of the architects' skill and the jewelers' inspiration. The marble-in-lay walls of The Taj are amongst the most outstanding examples of decorative workmanship. The elegant symmetry of its exterior and the aerial grace of its domes and minarets impress the beholder in a manner never to be forgotten. It stands out as one of the most priceless national monument, of surpassing beauty and worth, a glorious tribute to man's achievement in architecture and engineering.

What Others Say

The Taj is threatened with deterioration and damage not only by the natural causes of decay but also by changing the social and economic conditions that aggravate the situation with even more formidable phenomena of damage or destruction. A private sector preservation organization called the 'World Monuments Fund' (American Express Company) has published a list of 100 most endangered sites (1996) in the world. It has included the Taj in the list by stating: The Taj Mahal (Agra, India), Marble Tomb for Mumtaz Mahal, wife of emperor, Shah Jahan, is considered the epitome of Mughal monumental domed tombs set in a garden. The environment of Agra is today best with problems relating to the inadequacy of its urban infrastructure for transportation, water, and electricity. The dense pollution near the Taj Mahal is caused by residential fuel combustion, diesel trains and buses, and back-up generators. Construction of the proposed Agra Ring Road and Bypass that would divert the estimated daily 6,50,000 tons of trans-India truck traffic awaits financing. Strict controls on industrial pollution established in 1982 are being intensively enforced following a 1993 Supreme Court Order. The Asian Development Bank's proposed $300 million loan to the Indian government to finance infrastructure improvement would provide the opportunity to solve the chronic problems. Agra contains three World Heritage Sites, including the Taj Mahal.

What the Petitioner Says

According to the petitioner, (M.C. Mehta) the foundries, chemical/hazardous industries, and the refinery at Mathura are the major sources of damage to the Taj. The sulphur dioxide emitted by the Mathura Refinery and the industries when combined with oxygen, with the aid of moisture in the atmosphere, forms a sulphuric acid rain called 'Acid rain', which has a corroding effect on the gleaming white marble. Industrial/refinery emissions, brick kilns, vehicular traffic, and generator sets are primarily responsible for polluting the ambient air around the Taj Trapezium (TTZ). The petition states that the white marble has yellowed and blackened in places. It is inside the Taj that the decay is more apparent. Yellow pallor pervades the entire monument. In places, the yellow hue is magnified by ugly brown and black spots. Fungal deterioration is worst in the inner chamber where the original graves of Shah Jahan and Mumtaz Mahal lie. According to the petitioner, the Taj, a monument of international repute, is on its way to degradation due to atmospheric pollution and it is imperative that preventive steps are taken and soon.

---

[1]The case is abridged except for the independent boxed item; the text of the case is widely available on the Internet; for easy access see http://www.indiankanoon.org/doc/1964392/ (22 November 2011).

[2]Ibid; these are the opening words of Justice K Singh; he also quotes other eloquent admirers such as Lord Roberts, another poet, etc.

The petitioner has finally sought appropriate directions to the authorities concerned to take immediate steps to stop air pollution in the TTZ and save the Taj. The Report of the Expert Committee called 'Report on Environmental Impact of Mathura Refinery' (Varadharajan Committee) published by the Government of India in 1978 has been annexed along with the writ petition. Paragraph 4.1 of the conclusions therein is as follows: 'There is substantial level of pollution of sulphur dioxide and particulate matter in the Agra region. The possible sources are all coal users consisting of two power plants, a number of small industries mainly foundries (approximately 250), and a railway shunting yard. As far as suspended particulate matters are concerned, because of the use of coal, contribution will be substantial. Although the total amount of emission of sulphur dioxide from these sources may be small, on account of their proximity to the monuments, their contribution to the air quality of the zone will be considerably high.'

What the Committee Says

The Varadharajan Committee made the following recommendations: steps may be taken to ensure that no new industry including small industries or other units that can cause pollution are located northwest of the Taj Mahal.

Efforts may be made to relocate the existing small industries, particularly the foundries, in an area south east of Agra beyond the Taj Mahal, so that emissions from these industries will not be in the direction of the monuments.

Similar considerations may apply to large industries, such as fertilizer and petrochemicals. Such industries that are likely to cause environmental pollution may not be located in the neighbourhood of the refinery.

No large industry in the Agra region and its neighbourhood are established without conducting appropriate detailed studies to assess the environmental effect of such industries on the monuments. Location should be so chosen as to exclude any increase in environmental pollution in the area.

The Committee wishes to record its deep concern with regard to the existing level of pollution in Agra. An appropriate authority must be created that could monitor emissions by industries as well as the air quality at Agra continually. This authority should be vested with powers to direct industries causing pollution to limit the level of emission and specify such measures as are necessary to reduce the emission, whenever the pollutant level at the monuments exceeds acceptable limits. Recommendations

made in regard to reduction of existing pollution levels at Agra should be converted to a time-bound programme and should be implemented with utmost speed.

Studies should be undertaken by competent agencies to explore the possibility of protecting the monuments by measures, such as provision of a green belt around Agra in the region between Mathura and Agra.

Although assurances have been obtained from India Oil Corporation Ltd that adequate precaution would be taken to contain the pollution on account of using coal in the power plant, the Committee is of the opinion that till such time this problem is studied in depth and suitable technologies have been found to be satisfactorily in use elsewhere, the use of coal in the refinery power plant should be deferred.

What National Environment Engineering Research Institute Says

The National Environment Engineering Research Institute (NEERI) gave an 'Overview report' with regard to the status of air pollution around the Taj in 1990. Relevant part of the report is as follows.

The sources of pollution, including small-scale and medium-scale industrial units, are scattered all around Taj Mahal. High air pollution load is thus pumped into the Taj airshed. Sudden increases in concentration level are often recorded in all directions in both gaseous and particulate pollutants depending on the local microclimatic conditions.

On four occasions during the five-year air quality monitoring, the 4-hourly average values of 802 at Taj Mahal were observed to be higher than 300 |ig/m^3, i.e., ten-folds of the promulgated CPCB standard of 30 |ig/ m^3 for sensitive areas. The values exceeded even the standard of 120 |ig/m^3 set for industrial zones. Statistical analysis of the recorded data indicates that 40 per cent (cumulative percentage level) has crossed the standard set for sensitive receptors/zones.

The suspended particulate matter levels at Taj Mahal were invariably high (more than 200 |ig/m^3) and exceeded the national ambient air quality standard of 100 |ig/m^3 for suspended particulate matter for sensitive locations barring a few days in monsoon months.

Another study during 1985–1987 brought to the fore that the overall status of the ambient air quality within the trapezium has significantly deteriorated over this period.

The impact of the air quality on the Taj has been stated as follows.

The rapid industrial development of Agra and Mathura region has resulted in acidic emissions into the atmosphere at an alarming rate. This causes serious concern on the well being of Taj Mahal.

The gaseous pollutants being acidic in nature, significantly impact both the biotic and the abiotic components of the ecosystem such as plants and building material such as marble and red stone.

What the Order of the Court Says

This Court on 8 January 1993 passed the following order: We have heard Mr M.C. Mehta, the petitioner in person. According to him, the sources of pollution in Agra region as per the report of Central Pollution Control Board are iron foundries, ferro-alloyed industries, rubber processing, lime processing, engineering, chemical industry, brick refractory, and vehicles. He further states that distant sources of pollution are the Mathura Refinery and Ferozabad Glass Industry. It is necessary to have a detailed survey done of the area to find out the actual industries and foundries that are working in the region.

We direct the UP Pollution Control Board to get a survey done of the area and prepare a list of all the industries and foundries that are the sources of pollution in the area. The Pollution Board after having the survey done shall issue notices to all the foundries and industries in that region to satisfy the Board that necessary anti-pollution measures have been undertaken by the said industries/foundries. The Pollution Board after doing this exercise shall submit a report to this Court on or before 5 May 1993.

A copy of this order should be sent to the Chairman and Secretary, UP Pollution Control Board for compliance and report as directed.

What the UP Pollution Control Board Says

The affidavit further states that notices were issued to the aforesaid 511 industries/foundries as directed by this Court.

Although Mathura Refinery is included in the list of 511 industries, we are not dealing with the refinery in this judgement. The Mathura Refinery is being dealt with separately. All the foundries/industries are represented before us through the national chamber of Industries and Commerce, UP, Agra, UP Chamber of Commerce and the Glass Industries Syndicate. Some of the individual industries have also been represented through their learned counsel.

What the Supreme Court Bench Says

The precautionary principle and the polluter pays principle have been accepted as part of the law of the land. Article 21 of the Constitution of India guarantees protection of life and personal liberty. Articles 47, 48 A, and 51A(g) of the Constitution are as follows:

The state shall regard the raising of the level of nutrition and the standard of living of its people and the improvement of public health among its primary duties and in particular, the state shall endeavour to bring about prohibition of the consumption except for medicinal purposes of intoxicating drinks and of drugs that are injurious to health. Article 48A mentions about the 'Protection and improvement of environment and safeguarding of forest and wild life'. The state shall endeavour to protect and improve the environment and to safeguard the forests and wildlife of the country.

Article 51A(g): To protect and improve the natural environment including forests, lakes, rivers and wild life, and to have compassion for living creatures.

Apart from the constitutional mandate to protect and improve the environment, there are numerous post-independence legislations on the subject, but the following are the more relevant enactments for our purpose are: The Water (prevention and Control of pollution) Act, 1974 (also known as the Water Act); the Air (Prevention and Control of Pollution) Act, 1981 (also known as the Air Act); and the Environment Protection Act, 1986 (also known as the Environment Act).

The Water Act provides the constitution of the CPCB by the Central Government and the constitution of the State Pollution Control Board by the Central Government and the constitution of the State Pollution Control Boards by various state governments in the country. The Boards function under the control of the governments concerned. The Water Act prohibits the use of streams and wells for disposal of polluting matters and also provides for restrictions on outlets and discharge of effluents without obtaining consent from the Board. Prosecution and penalties have been provided, which include sentence of imprisonment. The Air Act provides that the CPCB and the State Pollution Control boards constituted under the Water Act shall also perform the powers and functions under the Air Act. The main function of the Boards, under the Air Act, is to improve the quality of the air and to prevent, control, and abate air pollution in the country. We shall deal with the Environment Act in the later part of this judgement.

What the Order of the Supreme Court Bench Says

The Supreme Court provided the following order and direction:

1. The industries (292) shall approach/apply to the Gas Authority of India Ltd (GAIL) before 15 February 1997 for grant of industrial gas connection.

2. The industries that are not in a position to obtain gas connections and also the industries that do not wish to obtain gas connections may approach/apply to the Corporation (UPSIDC)/Government before 28 February 1997 for allotment of alternative plots in the industrial estates outside TTZ.

3. The GAIL shall take the final decision in respect of all the applications for grant of gas connections by 31 March 1997 and communicate the allotment letters to the individual industries.

4. Those industries that applied neither for gas connection nor for alternative industrial plot shall stop functioning with the aid of coke/coal in the TTZ with effect from 30 April 1997. Supply of coke/coal to these industries shall be stopped forthwith. The District Magistrate and the Superintendent of Police shall have this order complied with.

5. The GAIL shall commence supply of gas to the industries by 30 June 1997. As soon as the gas supply to an industry commences, the supply of coke/coal to the said industry shall be stopped with immediate effect.

6. The Corporation/Government shall finally decide and allot alternative plots, before 31 March 1997, to the industries that are seeking relocation.

7. The relocating industries shall set up their respective units in the new industrial estates outside TTZ. The relocating industries shall not function and operate in TTZ beyond 31 December 1997. The closure by 31 December 1997 is unconditional and irrespective of the fact whether the new unit outside TTZ is completely set up or not.

8. The Deputy Commissioner, Agra, and the Superintendent (Police), Agra, shall effect the closure of all the industries on 31 December 1997 that are to be relocated by that date as directed by the court.

9. The UP State Government/Corporation shall render all assistance to the industries in the process of relocation. The allotment of plots, construction of factory buildings, etc. and issuance of any licence/permissions, etc., shall be expedited and granted on priority basis.

10. To facilitate shifting of industries from TTZ, the state government and all other authorities shall set up unified single agency consisting of all the departments concerned to act as a nodal agency to sort out all the problems of such industries. The single-window facility shall be set up by the UP State Government within one month from today. The Registry shall communicate this direction separately to the Chief Secretary, Secretary (Industries), and Chairman/ Managing director, UPSIDC, along with a copy of this judgement. We make it clear that no further time shall be allowed to set up the single-window facility.

11. The state government shall frame a scheme for the use of the land, which would become available on account of shifting/relocation of the industries before 30 June 1997. The state government may seek guidance in this respect from the order of this Court dated 10 May 1996 in I.A. No. 22 in Writ Petition (Civil) No. 4677 of 1985.

12. The shifting industries on the relocation in the new industrial estates shall be given incentives in terms of the provisions of the Agra Master Plan and also the incentives that are normally extended to new industries in new industrial estates.

13. The workmen employed in the above-mentioned 292 industries shall be entitled to the rights and benefits as indicated hereunder:

    (a) The workmen shall have continuity of employment at the new town and place where the industry is shifted. The terms and conditions of their employment shall not be altered to their detriment.

    (b) The period between the closure of the industry in Agra and its restart at the place of relocation shall be treated as active employment and the workmen shall be paid their full wages with continuity of service.

    (c) All those workmen who agree to shift with the industry shall be given one year's wages as 'shifting bonus' to help them settle at the new location. The said bonus shall be paid before 31 January 1998.

    (d) The workmen employed in the industries who do not intend to relocate/obtain natural gas and opt for closure shall be deemed to have been retrenched by 31 May 1997, provided they have been in continuous service (as defined in Sec. 25-B of the Industrial Disputes Act, 1947) for not less than one year in the industries concerned before the said date. They shall be paid compensation in terms of Sec. 25F(b) of the Industrial Disputes Act. These workmen shall also be paid, in addition, six years' wages as additional compensation.

(e) The compensation payable to the workmen in terms of this judgement shall be paid by the management within two months of the retrenchment.

(f) The gratuity amount payable to any workman shall be paid in addition.

Before parting with this judgement, we may indicate that the industries in the TTZ other than 292 industries shall be dealt with separately.

The Court directed the board to issue individual notices and also public notice to the remaining industries in the TTZ to apply for gas connection/relocation within one month of the notice by the Board. The Board shall issue notice within one month from today. The matter to come up for further monitoring in this respect before this Court is on 4 April 1997.

The Court also indicated by order dated 10 May 1996 has stopped the operation of all the brick kilns in the TTZ with effect from 15 August 1996. The court by order dated 4 September 1996 directed that the fly-ash produced in the process of the functioning of thermal plants may be supplied to the brick kilns for the construction of bricks. This would be a useful step to eliminate the pollution caused by flyash.

What the Court Monitoring Says

This Court is separately monitoring the following issues for controlling air pollution in TTZ:

(a) The setting up of hydrocracker unit and various other devices by the Mathura Refinery.

(b) The setting up of fifty-bed hospital and two mobile dispensaries by the Mathura Refinery to provide medical aid to the people living in the surrounding areas (Court order dated 7 August 1996).

(c) Constructions of Agra bypass to divert all the traffic, which passes through the city. Under directions of this Court, 24-km stretch of the bypass shall be completed by the end of December 1996 (Court order dated 10 April 1996).

(d) Additional amount of ₹99.54 crore sanctioned by the Planning Commission to be utilized by the State Government for the construction of electricity supply projects to ensure 100 per cent uninterrupted electricity to the TTZ. This is necessary to stop the operation

of generating sets, which are the major source of air pollution in the TTZ (Court orders dated 10 April 1996, 10 May 1996, 30 August 1996, 4 September 1996, and 10 September 1996).

(e) The construction of Gokul Barrage, water supply work of Gokul Barrage, roads around Gokul Barrage, Agra Barrage and water supply of Agra Barrage, have also been undertaken on a time schedule basis to supply drinking water to the residents of Agra and to bring life into river Yamuna, which is next to the Taj (Court order dated 10 May 1996 and 30 August 1996.).

(f) Green belt as recommended by National Environment Engineering Research Institute has been set up around the Taj. Pursuant to continuous monitoring of this Court, the Green Belt has become a reality.

(g) This Court suggested to the Planning Commission by order dated 4 September 1996 to consider sanctioning separate allocation for the city of Agra and the creation of separate cell under the control of Central Government to safeguard and preserve the Taj, the city of Agra and other national heritage monuments in the TT.

(h) All emporia and shops functioning Within the Taj premises have been directed to be closed.

(i) Directions have been issued to the Government of India to decide the issue, pertaining to declaration of Agra as heritage city within two months. We are mentioning these issues dealt with by this Court because it may be necessary to monitor some of these matters to take them to a logical extent.

This Court may look into these matters on 4 April 1997. The issue relating to 292 industries is thus disposed of.

Conclusion

The significance of this case is enormous to the survival of humanity. Saving a monument or an animal such as tiger or rhino, or a forest or a river is connected directly and immediately with human survival. The rational explanation for the protection and promotion of the environment is always at its best when seen through these living metaphors for survival. The governments of the people and the industries, the manner in which they are acting against nature is most definitely irrational. If the industries behaved conscientiously and ethically and the government policies reflected the interested of the people, then the courts would not have to intervene and even monitor the progress of their directives and orders.

Discussion Questions

1. What are the significant issues placed before the court by M.C. Mehta?
2. Briefly illustrate the findings of the Varadharajan Committee and NEERI, and assess the environmental factors affecting the Taj Mahal.
3. Discuss the Constitutional basis for the premises of the Supreme Court's judgement.
4. Discuss in detail the role of the industries in Agra contributing to the environmental destruction.
5. Can relocation of industries be a permanent solution to environmental destruction?

6. Discuss the court order in relation to its monitoring areas.
7. Critically analyse the implementation and consequences of the court order.

Going Beyond

1. From what perspective would you judge the above case if you were one of the proprietors of the 292 to polluting industrial units?
2. What are the implications when a court says that it is going to monitor the progress of a case and the implementation of its orders?
3. Why is environmentally saving the Taj Mahal important?

LEGAL LUMINARY

M.C. MEHTA—A SYMBOL OF LOVE OF NATURE

M.C. Mehta Environment Foundation,[*] established in 2000, is a non-profit and non-governmental organization, which works for the twin objectives of environmental protection and citizens' rights. It concerns itself mainly on research and training on social and environmental issues. It welcomes especially young lawyers and scientists. Apart from the internationally acknowledged case against the deterioration of the World Wonder Monument, M.C. Mehta is also known for the following landmark cases and their far-reaching consequences:

The River Ganges pollution   This case, which began against two polluting industries, expanded to more than one lakh industries and three hundred towns in eight states of the country. The Supreme Court ordered the closing of industrial plants and the imposition of financial responsibility against the polluters. The Court ordered nearly 250 towns and cities to build sewage treatment plants, and 600 tanneries operating in highly congested residential areas were relocated to a planned leather complex in the State of West Bengal. The case saw a record

number of lawyers, more than 1,200, who appeared against Mr Mehta in the course of the case.

Vehicular air pollution   M.C. Mehta filed a suit to reduce air pollution in Delhi; in 1984, the city was ranked as the fourth most-polluted city in the world. The Supreme Court ordered recommendations for the nationwide control of vehicular pollution. Consequently, lead-free gasoline and compressed natural gas were introduced for the first time in the country.

Relocation of polluting industries in Delhi
Apart from vehicular traffic pollution, another major pollutant was the emissions and effluents from the industries operating in Delhi in violation of the Master Plan and Environmental laws, resulting in severe environmental problems and hazards to the people of Delhi. The Supreme Court ordered the concerned authorities to identify industrial areas in the neighbouring states to which hazardous industries could be relocated. As a consequence of this case, about one lakh polluting industries shifted out of Delhi, allowing the citizens of Delhi to breathe easily.

---

*For details about M.C. Mehta and his foundation, visit mcmef.org/.

Contd

Legal Luminary *Contd*

Environmental awareness and education

M.C. Mehta's work has had amazing outcomes: Environment and its protection studies have become compulsory subjects in schools, colleges, and universities throughout India.

There are scores of achievements by M.C. Mehta and his foundation. Ironically, it demonstrates that the more his achievements, the more are the failures of industries, governments, officials, and managers, but which are ultimately in the good interests of the people.

Mahesh Chander Mehta was born in 1946 in Rajouri, Jammu and Kashmir. His love of nature was evident right from the early years. He walked to school, 15 km a day, crossing a couple of rivers and several hills. He obtained his post-graduation in political science and his law degree from the University of Jammu and Kashmir. He initially practised at the high court of his home state and later in 1983 joined the Supreme Court. He has won innumerable awards nationally and internationally for his contribution towards environmental protection.

PART

6

JUDICIAL AND SOCIAL JURISPRUDENCE

Business and Criminal Liability

Principle: *Crimen omnia ex se nata vitiat.*
A crime vitiates all things proceeding from it.

CHAPTER OUTLINE

- Introduction and Interpretation
- Acts Related to Criminal Liability of Business
- Classification of Evidence

- *Case Study:* Those Who Trust This Court Will Not Have Cause for Despair
- *Legal Luminary:* R.S. Pathak

28.1 INTRODUCTION AND INTERPRETATION

Cheating and dishonestly inducing delivery of property: Whoever cheats and thereby dishonestly induces the person deceived to deliver any property to any person, or to make, alter or destroy the whole or any part of a valuable security, or anything which is signed or sealed, and which is capable of being converted into a valuable security, shall be punished with imprisonment of either description for a term which may extend to seven years, and shall also be liable to fine. Of fraudulent deeds and dispositions of property

– The Indian Penal Code, 1860, Sec. 420

The general criminal law of India is found in the Indian Penal Code (IPC), 1860. Just as it is applicable to natural persons, so also it is appropriate for artificial persons such as companies. As a company itself is imperceptible and operates through its agents, the law vicariously, that is, as it is related by virtue of holding office or employment or any other agency relationship in the company, is appropriated to be applied to those who represent the company and bear legal, whether civil or criminal, liability.

Corporate Criminal Liability

After having gone through the past 27 chapters you may ask the perfect question: The actual *legal party*, that acts, performs acts of commission and omission, is the company; therefore, is it not then in the interest of the natural justice that it is the company that should bear the punishment and not the board of directors or managers? To make it clear: If I kill someone, it is I who will be charged with murder, and I will be punished for it; just because my family members are closely related to me they are not liable for punishment. Therefore, if there is no vicarious principle of justice amidst natural individuals, why should it exist between the company, which is a legal entity, and its agents, board of directors, managers, employees, and other agents related to the company?

The burial of a child victim of the Bhopal Gas Tragedy, 1984. The spine-chilling image depicting the horrors of the tragedy travelled around the world and people reacted with great sorrow at the disaster and anger at the Union Carbide (India), a concern of DOW of the USA.

Understanding Vicarious Liability

The above question of vicarious justice conceals the answer to vicarious liability. The principle may be expressed in common language. A master is (vicariously) liable for the acts of his servant to an outsider, if the outsider suffers any loss. For instance, your driver meets with an accident. You are then directly liable to pay the damages that the vehicle has caused. Thus far, it is a matter of civil law. However, if your driver culpably kills the person in the said accident, the criminal liability will lie with the driver. Thus, to understand vicarious liability one must distinguish between civil liability and criminal liability. While the former is vicariously applicable, the latter is specific to the person who acts criminally.

In the case of corporate criminal liability, the target of the criminal liability is not the company but the agents, who decide and act on behalf of the company, who will be held vicariously liable for the acts of the company. When you studied the Companies Act, 1956, you must have come across this aspect of criminal justice. If it is found that a director or official of a company (Sec. 5) is responsible for acts of connivance or neglect, he shall be deemed guilty and the law will be applied accordingly.

Indian Penal Code and Vicarious Corporate Criminal Liability

You are aware from the study of the Negotiable Instruments Act, 1881, that its Amendment in 1989 brought a sea change in vicarious criminal liability. Sec. 138 deals with cheque bouncing, which was made a criminal offence. This made the cheque to be one of the most acceptable negotiable instruments. Further, Sec. 141 made directors, managers, and other officer's of a company liable if the offence is attributable to any neglect on their part. A relief in the matter of Secs 138 and 141 of the Act is that these offences are bailable. Further, relief from personal appearance has also been granted. Although these measures seem to dampen the criminal liability, the actual application of IPC can be severe.

Sections 406 and 420 of the IPC are presently used quite extensively against the companies where directors find themselves being booked under criminal liability of theft and stealing. The economic offences are widespread as a result not only the directors of the company face severe charges and nonbailable warrants, but also the cabinet rank ministers find themselves behind the bars. The Satyam scam and the 2G scam, and the former corporate crime and the latter ministerial crime, have led the company boss as well as ministers, legislators, heads of state governments to face the harsh realities offered by the Indian Criminal Code.

The debate that only natural persons should be held culpable has been going on for a long time. However, as corporations are taking centre stage in life, and that they are, after all, associations of the people, mere being a corporation should not be a facade for illegal activities. This debate is gaining more ground as corporate crime has grown and has become complex.

Scope

The scope of this chapter is like an indicator needle. It merely points out the principle of the criminal liability of the corporations. However, the chapter-end case about the Bhopal Gas Tragedy of 1984 should be a notorious example of the utter criminality and total disregard for human lives. Corporations cannot afford to dodge the law and criminal behaviour. This case is a blot on the corporate world. Even after more than 25 years, the case is still not settled and the parent company, DOW of the USA is a pariah among the corporations of the world.

28.2 ACTS RELATED TO CRIMINAL LIABILITY OF BUSINESS

The Indian Penal Code, 1860

TEXT

Punishment for criminal breach of trust: Whoever commits criminal breach of trust shall be punished with imprisonment of either description for a term which may extend to three years, or with fine, or with both.

– The Indian Penal Code, 1860, Sec. 406

You will realize that all businesses are based on legal contract, which in turn is based on trust. Any breach of trust attracts not only civil liability but also criminal liability. In Chapter XVII, Secs 378–462, of the Indian Penal Code, 1860, deal with the offences against property, the sole object in business.

Table 28.1 is an indicator of offence where business practice may be involved. Businesses deal with property, whether tangible or intangible, goods or services, intellectual property or physical property. The Criminal Code lays down the general principles and the different individual Acts that you have studied in the past chapters and enforces the law in their given sphere of operation. For instance the Information Technology Act, 2000, that you studied in Chapter 26 has offences and punishments specific to the Act.

Example   The goods that were hypothecated have been misappropriated. This is clearly a breach of trust. What is the criminal liability involved here? Firstly, it is not an actual transfer of property, even though the owner is in possession of it. He is holding the property as a trustee, which is the principle of hypothecation, on behalf of the person from whom the money is taken. The offence of breach of trust of the property in question must belong

Table 28.1 IPC sections and the respective offences

IPC secs	Offences
378–382	Theft
378–389	Extortion
390–402	Robbery and dacoity
403–404	Criminal misappropriation of property
405–409	Criminal breach of trust
410–414	Receiving of stolen property
415–420	Cheating
421–424	Fraudulent deeds and disposition of property
425–440	Mischief
441–462	Criminal trespass

to a person other than the person to whom the property is entrusted. It follows that if the hypothecated property is sold, the liability for criminal breach of trust is evident. However, it depends upon the terms of hypothecation.

Principle The principle of jurisprudence regarding liability depends upon *mensrea*, that is, the guilty mind. In a voluntary, wilful, and deliberate action, it is the intention or the motive of such an action that counts for legal liability. This liability may be distinguished as civil and criminal. While civil liability is against individuals and attracts damages, criminal liability is a crime against society and attracts punishment, imprisonment, and also payment of damages. Procedures for these liabilities are different too. The criminal liabilities follow the Criminal Code and the Criminal Code of Procedure (Cr.PC).

The Indian Evidence Act, 1872

'Evidence' means and includes:
(1) All statements which the Court permits or requires to be made before it by witnesses, in relation to matters of fact under inquiry; such statements are called oral evidence;
(2) All documents produced for the inspection of the Court; such documents are called documentary evidence.
'Proved': A fact is said to be proved when, after considering the matters before it, the Court either believes it to exist, or considers its existence so probable that a prudent man ought, under the circumstances of the particular case, to act upon the supposition that it exists.

– The Evidence Act, 1872 Sec. 3 (1)(2)

This Act was a system changer in the adjudication process in India. It brought about a uniform standard to support a case with evidence. Before the existence of this law, the courts followed different standards in the prosecution depending on the communities, religious background, caste, and social position of the people. This Act instituted a single standard of evidence to be produced in the court, independent of the background of the person to be prosecuted. The introduction of this Act initiated the essence of the system of justice, impartiality. It defined justice as equality for all before the law and none to be above it.

28.3   CLASSIFICATION OF EVIDENCE

Evidence consists of all those facts that verify, substantiate, and support any data, information, and material that indicate, verify, and confirm what is to be proved and established beyond a reasonable doubt. Under the Evidence Act, 1872, Sec. 3 includes all statements that the court permits or requires to be made before it by witnesses in relation to matters of fact under inquiry and all documents produced for the inspection of the court. Table 28.2 is a classification of evidence.

Table 28.2   Classification of evidences

Primary evidence Immediate evidence of the principal fact. For example, eye witness account	**Secondary evidence** It is a substitute to primary evidence; supportive in nature. For example, copies and exhibits, etc.
Real evidence It is addressed directly to the senses of the court. For example, production of murder weapon	**Personal evidence** Testimony of the witnesses
Direct evidence It indicates the precise point of the principal fact. For example, eye witness who encountered crime	**Circumstantial evidence** Series of other facts that indicate to the principal fact; it confirms the context of the principal fact
Judicial evidence Testimony given by witnesses in the court or the documents produced and read by the court	**Extrajudicial evidence** Not directly proved by the court, but which serves as a link between judicial evidence and the fact requiring proof
Original evidence It has its own probative force. For example, eye witness account	**Hearsay evidence** It is not actually perceived by the witness but stated by him as he had heard it through someone else

The judge according to his jurisprudence has the discretion to permit material that he would regard as proper material of admissible evidence and to reject others that may not aid in the adjudication of a case. There are also other processes such as cross-examination of witnesses, verification of documents, sworn affidavits, etc., all amounting towards proving a case beyond reasonable doubt.

The Code of Criminal Procedure, 1973

Procedure on order being made absolute and consequences of disobedience:

(1) When an order has been made absolute under Sec. 136 or Sec. 138, the Magistrate shall give notice of the same to the person against whom the order was made, and shall further require him to perform the act directed by the order within a time to be fixed in the notice, and inform him that, in case of disobedience, he will be liable to the penalty provided by Sec. 188 of the Indian Penal Code (45 of 1860).

(2) If such act is not performed within the time fixed, the Magistrate may cause it to be performed,

and may recover the costs of performing it, either by the sale of any building, goods or other property removed by his order, or by the distress and sale of any other movable property of such person within or without such Magistrate's local jurisdiction and if such other property is without such jurisdiction, the order shall authorise its attachment and sale when endorsed by the Magistrate within whose local jurisdiction the property to be attached is found.

– The Code of Criminal Procedure, Sec. 141 (1)(2)

The above text is given to your perusal with a special and emphatic objective: you shall never disobey an order of the court. As a manager your primary responsibility to your company is to obey court orders. Disobedience has enormous legal and reputational repercussions for your company. Disobeying a court order is a crime called contempt of the court, which is a serious offence with very stiff punishments depending upon the nature of the order.

Judicial procedure   There are essentially five elements of judicial procedure as follows:

Summons   To enable the litigants to present their case before the court with their petitions and claims.

Pleadings   Both the plaintiff and the defendant present their versions of dispute before the court through their counsels.

Proof   Presentation of evidence to draw a conclusion of the case.

Judgement   Drawing of the conclusion by the judge; the decision of the court.

Execution   Enforcement of the decree or the order of the court.

Arrest   In a criminal case situation the first step that the law takes is to stop the criminal from what he is doing. For this purpose, the police will apprehend, detain, and produce him before a magistrate with the complaints against him within 24 hours of his arrest. The further legal procedure as to the crime will proceed under the magistrate's directives. Investigation of the crime will be conducted. The person will be charged and produced before the court for trial. During the trial, evidence will be produced for and against him by the prosecution and defence after examining the evidence; the judge will accordingly convict him or acquit him as the case may be.

Arrest without warrant   Generally, the procedure to arrest a person consists of the police obtaining an order to detain and arrest the person in question from the appropriate magistrate. However, there are certain situations where an immediate arrest, without a warrant, is provided by the Criminal Code. Under Sec. 41, the provision is made for the following situations:

(a) A person who is concerned in any cognizable offence or against whom a reasonable complaint has been made or credible information has been received or reasonable suspicion exists of his having been so concerned

(b) If a person is found in possession of any implement of house braking without lawful excuse

(c) If a person is proclaimed offender

(d) If a person is found in possession of a property suspected to be stolen and there is reasonable suspicion of his committing the offence

(e) If a person obstructs a police officer in execution of his duty or has escaped or attempts to escape from lawful custody

(f) If a person is reasonably suspected of being a deserter from any armed forces of the Union

(g) A person against whom a reasonable complaint has been made or credible information has been received or reasonable suspicion exists of having been concerned in any act committed outside India, which would have been a punishable offence committed in India and for which he is under any law relating to any extradition, or otherwise, liable to be apprehended or detained in custody in India

(h) A person who, being a released convict, commits a breach of any rule made under Sub-sec. (5) of Sec. 365

(i) A person for whose arrest any requisition, whether written or oral, has been received from another police officer, provided that the requisition specifies the person to be arrested and the offence or other cause for which the arrest is to be made and it appears from there that the person might lawfully be arrested without a warrant by the officer who issued the requisition.

All the above situations can arise within a company. Now look at Case 28.1 between Iridium India Telecom Ltd and Motorola Inc. and Others.

MANAGER'S TAKEAWAY

- *Actus non facitreum, nisi mens sit rea.* (The act itself does not constitute guilt unless done with a guilty intent.)
- Procedure is the mode by which a legal right is enforced.

CASE 28.1   PETITIONER: Iridium India Telecom Ltd   VS   RESPONDENT: Motorola Inc. and Others[*]

DATE OF JUDGEMEMNT: 12 December 2003

FACTS: The two motions sought orders in the nature of attachment before judgement and injunction for obtaining security for a decree that might be passed in the appellants pending suit. Among others, the suit claims are (1) US $12,04,90,000 with further interest at the rate of 5 per cent per annum on US $9,03,30,000 and (2) a sum of ₹3,77,21,54,857 with further interest at the rate of 12 per cent per annum on the principal amount of ₹48,11,00,000.

This motion taken out by respondent No. 1 herein seeks through prayer (a) to produce and rely upon the documents listed in the schedule annexed to the motion. Prayer (b) seeks that Ravi Parthasarthy, Managing Director of ILFS, who has verified the plaint and who has filed an affidavit on 4 August 2003, be ordered to attend cross-examination.

The appellants object to both these prayers being granted.

JUDGEMENT: Petition disposed off, according to the Court Order.

REASON: This is a matter where both parties are attributing dishonesty to the other. It is the case of the appellants that they have been cheated and the entire project was a

---

[*]Iridium India Telecom Ltd vs Motorola Inc. and Others; 2004 (1) Bom CR 479; see also: http://indiankanoon.org/doc/456019/ (23 November 2011). Later the case was appealed in the Supreme Court see Iridium India Telecom Ltd vs Motorola Incorporated and Ors (AIR 2011 SC 20, [2010] 160 Comp Case 147), which upheld the judgement of the High Court.

Contd

Case 22.1 *Contd*

fraud. As against that, the respondents contend that there was no fraud and that the appellants had complete knowledge about the scheme. The documents have a bearing on the knowledge of the appellants. It would not be proper that the judgement be pronounced without these documents being considered or else it will leave a lacuna in the evidence on record.

Prayer (a) of Notice of Motion No. 3462 of 2003 is allowed. The respondent No. 1 is permitted to produce these documents in appeal. In view of this order, the appellant will be at liberty to file their response to these documents.

As far as prayer (b) of this motion is concerned, we cannot but note that the motion was decided, as always by the learned Single Judge, only on affidavits and having considered the facts that there is no need for any oral evidence at the motion stage. We are, therefore, not inclining to entertain prayer (b) of the motion.

Respondent No. 1 is to pay the costs of the motion quantified at ₹50,000 to the appellants within 4 weeks from today.

SUMMARY

- Corporations are legal parties that can sue and be sued both with civil and criminal liabilities. The Indian Penal Code, 1860, the Indian Evidence Act, 1872, and the Code of Criminal Procedure collectively provide for criminal justice, whether of the humans or of the legal entities such as human associations and corporations.
- The Penal Code lays down elaborate situations and instances of criminal liabilities. It is found that while a plaintiff files suit also the criminal repercussions are shown by making relevant criminal sections as part of the complaints. However, it is the Evidence Act that lays down clear instructions of procedure from arrest, investigation, pleading, trial, and execution of court orders to the procedures that the police and the official of law should follow.
- The Code of Criminal Procedure further sees that justice may not be miscarried and its applications are quite rigorous.

EXERCISES

(i) Your group of MBA juniors had a physical fight with the MBA seniors. Seniors were careful with their fisticuffs; and none of us could prove before the institute's authorities that they had harmed us. The seniors produced two of their members as severely injured, one with a fractured hand and the other with a stab wound on the shoulder. Legal action is threatened. What is going to happen to you?
Hint: Criminal proceedings under Secs 320 and 325 of the Indian Penal Code.

(ii) You are the manager of a company. Your company is continuously getting inflated telephone bills. May be some employees are misusing the phone or they may be some kind of racket going on which you do not know. What is your legal remedy?
Hint: File a First Information Report (FIR) with the Police under Sec. 379 of the Penal Code.

(iii) A public company carries on business for more than 6 months after the number of its members is reduced below the mandatory seven members. Is the company or its directors legally liable?
Hint: See Sec. 4, 5 of the Companies Act, 1956; the Registrar of companies also can take legal action.

(iv) Under which situations a person may be arrested without warrant?

(v) Analyze legal evidence.

DEVELOPMENT OF LEGAL EDGE

The Bhopal Project

Objective For self-awareness of the Corporate Social Responsibility.

Method Write a critical paper titled Ethical and Legal Perspectives of the Bhopal Tragedy.

Bhopal Gas Tragedy Link

http://legacy.bhopal.net/gda/facts.html/. (There are hundreds of other websites that are easily searchable on the Internet).

FURTHER READING

Acts, Rules, Regulations

• http//:www.mha.nic.in.

Book

• K .C. Khera, 30 Years Digest on Evidence Indian Evidence Act 1872, Jain Book Publication, New Delhi.

CASE STUDY — THOSE WHO TRUST THIS COURT WILL NOT HAVE CAUSE FOR DESPAIR

Like all other human institutions, this court is human and fallible. What appears to the court to be just and reasonable in that particular context and setting need not necessarily appear to others in the same way. Which view is right, in the ultimate analysis, is to be judged by what it does to relieve the undeserved suffering of thousands of innocent citizens of this country[1].

Subject to the provisions of any law made by Parliament or any rules made under article 145, the Supreme Court shall have power to review any judgement pronounced or order made by it.

– The Constitution of India, Act 137

In the Supreme Court of India

Bench: Justice R.S. Pathak, Chief Justice
   Justice E.S. Venkataramaiah
   Justice Ranganath Misra
   Justice M.N. Venkatachalliah
   Justice N.D. Ojha
Petitioner: Union Carbide Corporation
RESPONDENT: Union of India
Date: 4 May 1989

The Main Issue

The Bhopal Gas Leak Disaster (Registration and Processing of claims) Act, 1985: Court giving reasons for the overall settlement order dated 14 February 1989—Compelling duty both judicial and humane to secure immediate relief to the victims.

Facts of the Case

The Bhopal Gas Leak Tragedy that occurred at midnight on 2 December 1984, by the escape of deadly chemical fumes from the appellant's factory, was a great industrial disaster and it took an immediate toll of 2,600 human lives and left tens of thousands of innocent citizens of Bhopal physically affected in various ways. As per the figures furnished by the Union of India in its amended plaint, a total of 2,660 persons suffered agonising and excruciating deaths whereas around 30,000 to 40,000 persons sustained serious injuries as a result of the said disaster.

Legal proceedings for the recovery of compensation for the victims were initiated against the multinational company first in US Courts and later in District Court at Bhopal in Suit No. 113 of 1986. The present appeals concern with the order dated 4 April 1988 passed by the Madhya

---

[1]This text consist of the last few lines of Justice R S Pathak's judgement of this case, Union Carbide vs Union of Indian; 1990 AIR 273, 1989 Sec (2) 540. The heading is the last sentence of this judgement and the following bold italicized lines prior to it. The abridged case brings out one of the best pieces of Indian jurisprudence in the hour of worst human tragedy caused by a careless and callous Corporation, the Union Carbide.

Pradesh High Court whereby it modified the interlocutory order dated 17 December 1987 made by the District Judge and granted interim compensation of ₹250 crore. Both the Union of India and the Union Carbide Corporation have appealed to this Court against that order.

The basic consideration motivating the conclusion of the settlement was the compelling need for urgent relief. Considerations of excellence and niceties of legal principles were greatly over-shadowed by the pressing problems of survival for a large number of victims. The instant case is the one where damages are sought on behalf of the victims of a mass disaster, and having regard to the complexities and the legal question involved, any person with an unbiased vision would not miss the time consuming prospect for the course of the litigation in its sojourn through the various courts, both in India and later in the United States.

This Court considered it as a compelling duty, both judicial and humane, to secure immediate relief to the victims. In doing so, the Court did not enter upon any forbidden ground. What this Court did was in continuation of what had already been initiated. The range of choice for the Court in regard to the figures was, therefore, between the maximum of US $426 million and the minimum of US $500 million.

Having regard to all the circumstances, including the prospect of delays inherent in the judicial process in India and thereafter in the matter of domestication of the decree in the United States for the purpose of execution, the Court directed that US $470 million, which upon immediate payment and with interest over a reasonable period and pending actual distribution among the claimants, would aggregate very nearly to US $500 million or its rupee equivalent of approximately ₹750 crore, which the Attorney General had suggested be made on the basis of the settlement.

The settlement proposals were considered on the premises that the Government had the exclusive statutory authority to represent and act on behalf of the victims and neither counsels had any reservation for this. The order was also made on the premises that the Bhopal Gas Leak Disaster (Registration and Processing of Claims) Act, 1985, was a valid law.

There might be different opinions on the interpretation of laws or on questions of policy or even on what may be considered wise or unwise; but when one speaks of justice and truth, these words mean the same thing to all men whose judgement is uncommitted.

Earlier Settlement

The Bhopal Gas Leak tragedy that occurred at midnight on 2 December 1984, by the escape of deadly chemical fumes from the appellant's pesticide-factory was a horrendous industrial mass disaster, unparalleled in its magnitude and devastation and remains a ghastly monument to the de-humanizing influence of inherently dangerous technologies. The tragedy took an immediate toll of 2,660 innocent human lives and left tens of thousands of innocent citizens of Bhopal physically impaired or affected in various degrees. What added grim poignancy to the tragedy was that the industrial enterprise was using methyl isocyanate, a lethal toxic poison, whose potentiality for destruction of life and biotic-communities was, apparently, matched only by the lack of a pre-package of relief procedures for management of any accident based on adequate scientific knowledge as to the ameliorative medical procedures for immediate neutralization of its effects.

It is unnecessary for the present purpose to refer, in any detail, to the somewhat meandering course of the legal proceedings for the recovery of compensation initiated against the multinational company initially in the Courts of the USA and later in the District Court at Bhopal in Suit No. 113 of 1986. It would suffice to refer to the order dated 4 April 1988, of the High Court of Madhya Pradesh which, in modification of the interlocutory order dated 17 December 1987, made by the learned District Judge, granted an interim compensation of ₹250 crore. Both the Union of India and the Union Carbide Corporation appealed against that order.

This Court by its order dated 14 February 1989, made in those appeals directed that there shall be an overall settlement of the claims in the suit, for US $470 million and termination of all civil and criminal proceedings.

The Review Under Article 137 of the Constitution

It appears to us that the reasons that persuaded this Court to make the order for settlement should be set out, so that those who have sought a review might be able to effectively assist the Court in satisfactorily dealing with the prayer for a review. The statement of the reasons is not made with any sense of finality owing to the infallibility of the decision; but with an open mind to be able to appreciate any tenable and compelling legal or factual infirmities that may be brought out, calling for remedy in Review under Article 137 of the Constitution.

The points on which we propose to set out brief reasons are the following:

(a) How did this Court arrive at the sum of US $470 million for an overall settlement?

(b) Why did the Court consider this sum of US $470 million as 'just, equitable, and reasonable'?

(c) Why did the Court not pronounce on certain important legal questions of far reaching importance said to arise in the appeals owing to the principles of liability of monolithic and economically entrenched multinational companies operating with inherently dangerous technologies in the developing countries of the third world—questions said to be of great contemporary relevance to the democracies of the third world?

The present case is the one where damages are sought on behalf of the victims of a mass disaster and, having regard to the complexities and the legal questions involved, any person with an unbiased vision would not miss the time consuming prospect for the course of the litigation in its sojourn through the various courts, both in India and later in the United States.

Justice: Principle of Hope in Despair

In the present case, the compulsions of the need for immediate relief to tens of thousands of suffering victims could not, in our opinion, wait till these questions, vital though they be, are resolved in the due course of judicial proceedings. The tremendous suffering of thousands of persons compelled us to move into the direction of immediate relief that, we thought, should not be subordinated to the uncertain promises of the law, and when the assessment of fairness of the amount was based on certain factors and assumptions not disputed even by the plaintiff.

A few words in conclusion: A settlement has been recorded upon material and in circumstances that persuaded the Court that it was a just settlement. This is not to say that this Court will shut out any important material and compelling circumstances that might impose the duty on it to exercise the powers of review.

Like all other human institutions, this court is human and fallible. What appears to the court to be just and reasonable in that particular context and setting need not necessarily appear to others in the same way. Which view is right, in the ultimate analysis, is to be judged by what it does to relieve the undeserved suffering of thousands of innocent citizens of this country. As a learned author said:

Wallace Mendelson: Supreme Court Statecraft—The Rule of Law and Men.

If a decision is wrong, the process of correction must be in a manner recognized by law. Here, many persons and social action groups claim to speak for the victims, quite a few in different voices. The factual allegations on which they rest their approach are conflicting in some areas and it becomes difficult to distinguish the truth from false-hood and half-truth, and to distinguish as to who speaks for whom. However, all of those who invoke the corrective-processes in accordance with law shall be heard and the court will do what the law and the course of justice requires. The matter concerns the interests of a large number of victims of a mass disaster.

The Court directed the settlement with the earnest hope that it would do them good and bring them immediate relief; for, tomorrow might be too late for many of them. But the case equally concerns the credibility of, and the public confidence in, the judicial process. If, owing to the pre-settlement procedures being limited to the main contestants in the appeal, the benefit of some contrary or supplemental information or material, having a crucial bearing on the fundamental assumptions basic to the settlement, have been denied to the Court and that, as a result, serious miscarriage of justice, violating the constitutional and legal rights of the persons affected, has been occasioned, it will be the endeavour of this Court to undo any such injustice. But that, we reiterate, must be by procedures recognized by law. Those who trust this Court will not have cause for despair.

Conclusion

The settlement of US $470 million, having been reconfirmed by the apex court, has ended neither the tragedy nor the dispute. The most emotional part of this tragedy is that even after a generation the young mothers, born after the tragedy, produce toxic milk and hence are prevented from breast feeding their children. Social intercourse and marriages are shunned from certain *contaminated* people. Awful deformities and disabilities afflict people. While Union Carbide may have ceased to exist in India, its parent company, DOW, is doing business around the globe. It is, however, not exonerated either by the law or by the people. It has lost its moral reputation and has been called and reviled as the Butcher of Bhopal. Its bid to be the sponsor of the London Olympics 2012, has been condemned by India and it will be forced to exit the same under the threat of the boycott of the Olympics.

Discussion Questions

1. Briefly sketch the Bhopal Gas Tragedy.
2. Discuss the reasons for compensation.
3. On what basis did the High Court make the specific settlement?
4. Do you think the judgement of the Supreme Court was of any help to the suffering?
5. Do you think delay in settlement of compensation has added to the existing suffering?
6. State the management failures of the Union Carbide.
7. Having now gained so much knowledge of an industrial disaster what measures hazardous industries must take to prevent human tragedy on large scale?

Going Beyond

1. Clearly analyze the jurisprudence of this judgement.
2. What is the Ethical or Social Responsibility of a Corporation before and after the disaster it causes?
3. What is the role of corruption in allowing harmful industries?

LEGAL LUMINARY

JUSTICE R.S. PATHAK—MR INTEGRITY

Justice R.S. Pathak (1924–2007) was the judge at the International Court of Justice at Hague. He was the Chief Justice of India from 1986 to 1989. He became the judge of the Supreme Court of India in 1978. He became the judge of the High Court at a very young age (37 years). The area of his work mainly concerned Constitutional Law, Income Tax, Sales Tax, Civil Law, Industrial Disputes Law, etc. His brilliant career as jurist spanned fifty years in which he dedicated his service to the institution of justice that he most loved.

You have already seen the way he presided over the Bench of the Supreme Court in the landmark case of Bhopal Tragedy in the chapter-end case. He was erudite in all his works of judgement. The following are the most avidly read works by him in the legal world:

(a) *International law in transition: essays in memory of Judge Nagendra Singh (Book) 1992 (two editions)*

(b) *The case concerning the military personnel database (Ercola v. Filova), judgement of 30 March 1996 World Championship Jessup Cup Round, 1996*

(c) *Report of the Justice R.S. Pathak Inquiry Authority: in the matter of the independent in quiry committee report on the United Nations oil-for-food programme relating to contract no. M/09/54 and contract no. M/10/57 (Book), 2006.*

Justice Pathak was a man of learning, humility, and a perfect example to follow for the lawmen. As the Chief Justice of India, he travelled to every high court and local bar and bench to hear first-hand the problems facing his fraternity. As a result, he discovered great legal minds in various high courts and selected the best of them to the Supreme Court. His legal views were most respected internationally. Thus, there was no surprise when he was chosen as the judge at the International Court of Justice.

Raghunandan Swarup Pathak was born in 1924 and he completed his early education in St Joseph's High School and Ewing Christian College, both at Allahabad, and law at the University of Allahabad. His father, Gopal Swarup Pathak, was the Vice President of India. Justice Pathak died of a heart attack in 2007.

Alternative Dispute Resolution

Principle: *Deliberandum est diu quod statuendum est semel.*

That which is to be resolved once and for all, that should long be deliberated upon.

29.1 INTRODUCTION AND INTERPRETATION

TEXT

An act to consolidate and amend the law relating to domestic arbitration, international commercial arbitration, and enforcement of foreign arbitral awards, as also to define the law relating to conciliation and for matters connected therewith or incidental thereto.

Preamble:

Whereas the United Nations Commission on International Trade Law (UNCITRAL) has adopted the UNCITRAL Model Law on International Commercial Arbitration in 1985;

And whereas the General Assembly of the United Nations has recommended that all countries give due consideration to the said Model Law, in view of the desirability of uniformity of the law of arbitral procedures and the specific needs of international commercial arbitration practice;

And whereas the UNCITRAL has adopted the UNCITRAL Conciliation Rules in 1980;

And whereas the General Assembly of the United Nations has recommended the use of the said rules in cases where a dispute arises in the context of international commercial relations and the parties seek an amicable settlement of that dispute by recourse to conciliation;

And whereas the said model law and rules make significant contribution to the establishment of a unified legal framework for the fair and efficient settlement of disputes arising in international commercial relations;

And whereas it is expedient to make law respecting arbitration and conciliation, taking into account the aforesaid model law and rules.

– The Arbitration and Conciliation Act, 1996, Introduction along with Preamble

Historical Background

At the very outset, it must be made clear that the ancient system of arbitration and conciliation, implying mediation and reconciliation of disputes without the dispute redressal of a court litigation system, still exists in India. The panchayat, literally the five elders of a tribe or a village, hears publicly the grievances of the people and solves their problems through mutual negotiation and resolution of disputes. This system still works, albeit with the difficulties of procedural authority and abiding solutions. However, in recent years, there have been encouraging developments in the dispute redressal system with the convergence of the traditional indigenous redressal systems, which has been modernized through the establishment of the Lok Adalat, the people's court, and Lokayukta, the people's ombudsman. The system will be complete from the grassroots of panchayats to the state levels of Lokayukta to the federal Lokpal at the centre when such a bill would be enacted into law.

One of the earliest Acts in modern India introduced by the British was known as the Bengal Regulation Act, 1772. The court could provide reference for arbitration with the consent of the parties for all trade-related matters, such as accounts, partnership deeds, breach of contract, etc. With the coming of the Arbitration and Conciliation Act, 1996, some of the existing laws had to be streamlined to accommodate the new provisions. Accordingly, the Code of Civil Procedure of 1908 has been amended by the introduction of the Sec. 89(1) making provision to settle disputes outside the court. The Act gives it an international character under the mandate of UNCITRAL. However, the old and new systems are complementary and this shows the unique Indian approach to adjudication. In fact, the Lok Adalat system was already accepted in the mainstream justice system under the National Legal Service Authority Act, 1987.

Alternative Dispute Redressal

There was a system of arbitration well in place even before the Arbitration and Conciliation Act, 1996, which is demonstrated by the repeal of three laws at its enactment. They are:

(a) The Arbitration Act, 1940
(b) The Arbitration (Protocol and Convention) Act, 1937
(c) The Foreign Awards Recognition and Enforcement Act, 1961

Domestic arbitration is defined as an alternative dispute resolution mechanism in which the parties settle the disputes through the intervention of a third party and without having recourse to the court of law. It is a mode in which the dispute is referred to a nominated person who decides the issue in a quasijudicial manner after hearing both sides. Generally, the disputing parties refer their case to an arbitral tribunal and the decision arrived at by the tribunal is known as an award.

International commercial arbitration implies an arbitration relating to disputes arising out of legal relationships, whether contractual or not, considered as commercial under the law in India and where at least one of the parties is

(a) An individual who is a national of, or habitually resident in, any country other than India
(b) A body corporate that is incorporated in any country other than India

(c) A company, an association, or a body of individuals whose central management and control is exercised in any country other than India

(d) The government of a foreign country

Arbitration is still a developing mechanism in India. Large and small corporations have not yet realized the potential of settling disputes through arbitration and conciliation, which has escalated costs and prolonged the time of grievances and redressal.

29.2 ARBITRATION AND CONCILIATION ACT, 1996

TEXT

Arbitration agreement:

(1) In this part, 'arbitration agreement' means an agreement by the parties to submit to arbitration all or certain disputes, which have arisen or which may arise between them in respect of a defined legal relationship, whether contractual or not.

(2) An arbitration agreement may be in the form of an arbitration clause in a contract or in the form of a separate agreement.

(3) An arbitration agreement shall be in writing.

(4) An arbitration agreement is in writing if it is contained in:

(a) a document signed by the parties;

(b) an exchange of letters, telex, telegrams, or other means of telecommunication that provide a record of the agreement; or

(c) an exchange of statements of claim and defence in which the existence of the agreement is alleged by one party and not denied by the other.

(5) The reference in a contract to a document containing an arbitration clause constitutes an arbitration agreement if the contract is in writing and the reference is such as to make that arbitration clause part of the contract.

– Arbitration Act, 1996, Sec. 7

The above text of the Act, Sec. 7, clearly states the essence of arbitration arising out of a contract. Fundamental to arbitration, even before it takes place, is an agreement to undergo arbitration. It is an agreement that is in writing, signed by both the parties, about a contract, which both agree now to approach through a compromise formula. The salient features of the Act are as follows:

Non-interference by judicial authority (Sec. 5)   This section states that no judicial authority shall intervene except where so provided by law in the Act.

Administrative assistance (Sec. 6)   To facilitate the conduct of arbitral proceedings, the parties or the arbitral tribunal with the consent of the parties, may arrange for administrative assistance by a suitable institution or person.

Interim measures (Sec. 9)   The court may set some interim measures, such as appointment of a guardian for a minor or for a person of unsound mind; preservation or sale of goods, which are the subject matter of arbitration; securing the amount in dispute in arbitration; and interim injunction or the appointment of a receiver.

Appointment of arbitrators (Secs 11 and 12)   The procedure for appointment of arbitrators can be set out by the parties in their agreement. However, his position may be challenged in the circumstances where justifiable doubts are expressed about his independence and impartiality or lack of qualifications agreed by the parties.

Settlement (Sec. 30)   It is not incompatible with an arbitration agreement for an arbitral tribunal to encourage settlement of the dispute and, with the agreement of the parties; the arbitral tribunal may use mediation, conciliation, or other procedures at any time during the arbitral proceedings to encourage settlement (1). If, during arbitral proceedings, the parties settle the dispute, the arbitral tribunal shall terminate the proceedings and, if requested by the parties and not objected to by the arbitral tribunal, record die settlement in the form of an arbitral award on agreed terms (2).

Arbitral award (Sec. 31)   The award must be in writing and shall be signed by the members of the arbitral tribunal. It must state the reasons thereof. Unless otherwise agreed by the parties, where and in so far as an arbitral award is for the payment of money, the arbitral tribunal may include in the sum for which the award is made interest, at such rate as it deems reasonable, on the whole or any part of the money, for the whole or any part of the period between the date on which the cause of action arose and the date on which the award is made (7a).

Setting aside an award (Sec. 34)   An arbitral award may be set aside because of the following reasons:

(a) Incapacity of the party
(b) Invalidity of agreement
(c) Want of proper notice
(d) Award deals with dispute not referred to arbitration
(e) Defective composition of the arbitral tribunal
(f) The dispute incapable of settlement by arbitration under the law
(g) Arbitral award in conflict with public policy

Enforcement of award (Sec. 36)   An award is enforceable in the same way as a decree or order of the court.

Foreign award (Part II)   The enforcement of foreign award is under the Geneva Convention, 1937 and New York Convention, 1958, which have the same provisions. The interested person at the time of application must file the award and the agreement on which it is based and evidence that the award is a foreign award.

🔨 MANAGER'S TAKEAWAY

- Arbitration is the opportunity to choose your judge.
- For corporations, arbitration is both equity and corporate social responsibility. Its benefits are long-term bonus.

There is no doubt that the Arbitration and Conciliation Act has been a landmark legislation, which serves both internal and external dispute resolutions. Today, more and more people, organizations, and nations realize the benefits of arbitration in their relationship. It is a more versatile tool for serving justice than the courts of litigation, which cost money and endless disputes.

    Now look at Case 29.1 between Bhagwandas Auto Finance Ltd and others and HDFC Bank Ltd.

CASE 29.1 APPELLANT: Bhagwandas Auto Finance Ltd and others vs RESPONDENT: HDFC Bank Ltd

DATE OF JUDGEMENT: 21 January 2011 *

FACTS: This appeal is directed against an order dated 17 December 2009; disposing of these three applications filed before the Honorable First Court under Sec. 9 of the Arbitration and Conciliation Act, 1996. The said applications were filed by the respondent HDFC bank.

The given three agreements contain arbitration Clause 30, which is set out here under: all disputes, differences, and/or claim arising out of or touching upon this agreement whether during its subsistence or thereafter shall be settled by arbitration in accordance with the provisions of the Arbitration and Conciliation Act, 1996 or any statutory amendments thereof and shall be referred to the sole arbitrator of an arbitrator nominated by the bank. The award given by such an arbitrator shall be final and binding on the borrower and guarantor to this agreement.

The disputes and differences having been arisen in respect of the subject matter of the three agreements, the petitioner has invoked the arbitration agreement in each case and has brought the present proceedings under Sec. 9 of the said Act.

The three petitions were filed by the HDFC Bank under Sec. 9 of the Arbitration and Conciliation Act, 1996 inter alia on an allegation that the agreement for loan cum hypothecation agreement was entered into between the Bank and the appellant herein in terms of the said agreement. In terms of the said agreement, the bank sanctioned and disbursed the loan with respect to three agreements that was required to be paid by the respondent along with interest. The loan amount was utilized by the appellant/respondent and, subsequently, it appears that the appellant deliberately failed and neglected to pay the outstanding dues or any part thereof. Hence, the Bank pleaded that they have suffered substantial loss and in these circumstances, the applications filed under Sec. 9 inter alia for appointment of receiver, injunction, and other ancillary reliefs. The court held as follows:

There will be an order directing the receiver appointed by the order dated 18 February 2009, to take possession of the vehicles being the subject matter of the agreements covered by the three petitions. Till such time that the receiver takes possession of the vehicles, the respondents will remain restrained from dealing with, disposing of, alienating, encumbering, or parting with possession of any of the vehicles or parts thereof in favour of any other person. The receiver will be paid a remuneration of 300 GM in each petition by the petitioner, subject to the petitioner being entitled to claim such amount in the relevant reference. The receiver will keep the vehicles at a place to be provided by the petitioner, but the petitioner will not be entitled to use the vehicles without the previous leave of the arbitral tribunal. The petitioner may apply before the arbitral tribunal for sale of the vehicles, if necessary.'

Being aggrieved, this appeal has been filed.

JUDGEMENT: Petition dismissed.

REASON: It appears that the Honorable First Court correctly came to the conclusion that a court under Sec. 9 of the 1996 Act would not be exercising its jurisdiction as a court within the meaning of the expression 'No court or other authority', but it would derive its power from the Arbitration Agreement that appears to fall outside the scope of the bar under Sec. 18 of the said Act.

Contd

Case 29.1 *Contd*

Accordingly, we affirm the order on such point that the Court does not finally adjudicate upon any matter under Sec. 9 of the 1996 Act. Such arrangement has been made at any interim measure, the other question which has been urged before us with regard to the forum selection clause. We also find that in this case, the said forum selection clause is clear and unambiguous. It further appears that the lending bank is situated at Kolkata. The forum selection clause also made it clear that any competent court in Kolkata would have the jurisdiction to adjudicate the disputes.

We find that no ground has been made out by the appellant to interfere with the order passed by the Honorable First Court and in our considered opinion the said order does not suffer from any illegality or irregularity. For the discussions and reasons stated by us, we affirm the said judgement and/or order of the learned trial court and we find that there has been no grounds has made out by the appellant to interfere with the order passed by the honorable first court and in our considered opinion, the said order does not suffer from any illegality or irregularity.

For the reasons stated here in above, the appeal is dismissed.

SUMMARY

- Arbitration and conciliation were the system of justice before the introduction of the Common Law in India under the British Government. Presently, there is an increasing effort to assimilate the traditional system with the scientific or systematic approach of the common law and the case law. Panchayat, Lok Adalat under Lokayukta, and Lokpal are going to *Indianize* the adjudication system in India. It is an evolving process.

- The Arbitration and Conciliation Act, 1996, is a part of both indigenous as well one that is initiated by the UNCITRAL, 1985. The objective of the Act is to administer speedy, satisfying, and expensive system of grievance redressal.

EXERCISES

(i) Your Company's arbitration has become so complicated that it appears to you that regular court procedure would be simpler and surer. How will you solve your dilemma?

Hint: For unforeseeable complexity see: Guru Nanak Foundation vs M/s Rattan Singh and Sons; AIR 1981 SC 2075, 2076.

(ii) You and your respondents agreed for arbitration of the business problem. However, in the middle of the arbitration, you realized that you do not see any hope for settlement. What is your next step?

Hint: Apart from abandoning the arbitration, Sec. 9 offers interim measures from the court.

(iii) Two litigants are involved in a banned narcotics dispute. Can it be solved by arbitration?
Hint: The Act allows only those that are permitted under it for arbitration; narcotics disputes are of criminal liability and come under the penal code

(iv) Compare and contrast court litigation and arbitration. Give reasons why Alternative Dispute Redressal is a better alternative.

(v) What are the salient features of the Arbitration Act, 1996? Illustrate it in the context of Indian arbitration history.

DEVELOPMENT OF LEGAL EDGE

Project Study course in arbitration and conciliation. **Objective** Dispute handling for the managers.

Method Attend a course at the Indian Institute of Arbitration and Mediation.

FURTHER READING

Acts, Rules, and Regulations
• http://business.gov.in/legal_aspects/arbitration_conciliation.php.

Book
• O.P. Malhotra and Indu Malhotra, *The Law and Practice of Arbitration and Conciliation*, Lexis, Nexis Butterworths Wadhwa, Nagpur, 2006.

Law Commission of India
• Law Commission of India, 176th report on the Arbitration and Conciliation (Amendment) Bill, 2001.
• http://lawcommissionofindia.nic.in/arb.pdf.

Ministry of Law and Justice
• http://lawmin.nic.in/.

CASE STUDY   THE ARBITRAL AWARD

(3) An arbitral award on agreed terms shall be made in accordance with Sec. 31 and shall state that it is an arbitral award.

(4) An arbitral award on agreed terms shall have the same status and effect as any other arbitral award on the substance of the dispute.

– The Arbitration and Conciliation Act, 1996, Sec. 30 (3)(4)

The Suit[1]

Court: Allahabad High Court
Judge: Justice A. Jog
Petitioner: Indian Institute of Technology
RESPONDENT: Anushree Constructors and others
Date: 11 September 1999

The Indian Institute of Technology, Kalyanpur, Kanpur, a body corporate was established by and under the Institutes of Technology Act, 1961, to provide education and research in various branches of engineering.

The working department of the Institute floated tenders on 8 October 1987 for eight different works. Tenders of M/s Anushree Contractors and Consultant Associate Private Ltd,

New Delhi, called the contractors (respondent), were accepted and works were awarded as per details given. For each contract, articles of agreements were executed by the institute and the contractor. Details of articles of agreements, except Clause 55, are not necessary for the purpose of the present petition, which was provided for arbitration, in case of dispute and/or difference arising between the parties. Clause 55 as quoted in paragraph 14 of the writ petition reads as:

'(a) All disputes and differences arising between the parties to this agreement in the matter of meaning and interpretation of these articles of agreements and conditions, whether giving rise to any claim settlement concerning the works, during or after the construction of building, shall be referred to a sole arbitrator by mutual

---

[1]Indian Institute of Technology vs Anushree Constructors and others; (27 November 2011). 1999 (4) AWC 3493; also see http://www.indiankanoon.org/doc/1943820

agreement of parties to this contract, falling which the President, for the time being, of the Indian Institute of Engineers may be appointed as a sole arbitrator, and the award of such arbitration shall be final and conclusive and binding on the parties hereto. The submission shall be deemed to be submission to arbitration under the meaning of the Arbitration Act, 1940 or any statutory modification re-enactment thereof for the time being in force.'

The agreement containing aforequoted arbitration clause is admitted to the parties.

The Dispute

It is alleged, on behalf of the institute that inordinate delay was committed by the contractor in executing works and the works were completed after various extensions of times. It is also alleged that there were several defects in the constructions and consequently last payment was withheld. The contractor had written various letters to the institute with regard to non-payment of contract money under several heads. The validity and justification of the stand taken by the either party is not subject matter of the writ petition and hence details are not required to be mentioned to appreciate the controversy and the issue arising in the present case.

Contractor filed claim before the Arbitrator Institute, filed objections/ counter claim.

Award was given by the sole arbitrator. Awarded Institute has to pay ₹35,70,455, inclusive of past interest re-reference charges, pendents lite, and future interest at the rate of 18 per cent from the date of the award counter claim of the Institute, and was not considered by the arbitrator on the ground that it was not referred to him by the director of the institute vide letter dated 25 January 1996.

Application (4/Ga) filed by the Institute to set aside award filed in court (case 12/70 of 1997; photostat copy duly attested by counsel for 'contractor' and not disputed by institute as record of this writ petition).

Title of the said application reads as

'Application for setting aside the arbitral award under Sec. 34 of the Arbitration and Conciliation Act, 1996'..

The contractor filed objections against the said application (4/Ga).

District Court

The court finds that:

(i) The subject-matter of the dispute is not capable of settlement by arbitration under the law for the time being in force, or

(ii) The arbitral award is in conflict with the public policy of India.

Explanation   Without prejudice to the generality of sub-clause (ii) of clause (b), it is hereby declared, for the avoidance of any doubt that an award is in conflict with the public policy of India if the making of the award was induced or affected by fraud or corruption or was ink violation of Sec. 75 or Sec. 81.

High Court

Clause 3.04 of the award clearly mentioned that when fact of commencement of the New Act was brought on record, institute raised no objection to the applicability of the provisions of the New Act.

Institute allowed the arbitrator to proceed on the basis that it had no objection to the applicability of the New Act. By not raising objection to the applicability of the New Act before the arbitrator, institute explicitly agreed for proceedings to be carried in accordance with the provisions of the New Act.

Perusal of objection of the petitioner under Sec. 34, the New Act (paper 4Ga) shows that petition is filed in under Sec. 34 of the New Act.

At this belated stage (i.e., in writ proceedings) objection on this ground, after award is rendered, is not permissible. Petitioner is estopped from raising the said objection now. It will give institute leverage to abuse 'process of law'. Institute is to gain at the cost of the contractor by a delay. This court cannot permit itself to be used as a tool for exploiting a party.

Petitioner is now estopped under the law from raising this issue.

The institute has not come forward to make offer to deposit 'arbitral amount' with this court or district judge to prove it's bonafide. Unfortunately, bonafide of the Institute are lacking.

The petitioner institute having agreed by not raising objection and there being 'agreement to the contrary' as contemplated under Sec. 85 (2)(a) of the New Act, the petitioner can have no valid grievance when award is delivered on the basis of its own representation. Arbitrator committed no wrong by proceeding on the basis that the New Act is applicable to the case between the parties.

The parties agreed to have the matter adjudicated by the arbitrator as per provisions of the New Act as permitted under Sec. 85 (2)(a) New Act. Petitioner's grievance cannot be entertained after the 'award' is given. It will cause enormous inconvenience and injury to the other side, and on this ground, this court can refuse to entertain the writ petition under Article 226 of Constitution of India, which is a discretionary jurisdiction and not as of course.

Pronouncement

The writ petition is devoid of merits and deserves to be dismissed.

Conclusion

It may shock you that a prestigious and world renowned IIT, Kanpur, admirably chose arbitration, but failed at conciliation and went into regular litigation only to be rapped for its intransigence. Today, reputed institutes of management plan to setup arbitration, mediation, and conciliation cells as legal aid to corporations.

The corporations would like to repose faith in the educational institutions as just and good arbitrators.

Even managers can see their primary roles as arbitrators. Motivation and persuasion at workplaces do wonders to cut down employer–employee disputes. Actions taken initially will nip large and harmful industrial disputes in the bud. A manager can exercise the same skills of an arbitrator as one appointed by the court.

Discussion Questions

1. State clearly the issues involved in the case.
2. What is the status of the institute as a body corporate?
3. Why did the parties agree for arbitration?
4. What sections in the Arbitration and Conciliation Act, 1996 apply to this case?
5. What do you understand by award and how it is applied in this case?
6. Analyse the legal reasoning by the Allahabad High Court.
7. What lessons do you learn from this case and would you like to apply to the similar situations you face?

Going Beyond

1. What compels the parties in arbitration to abandon the process?
2. Critically analyse whether arbitration is just another way of prolonging cases.
3. Examine whether arbitration and conciliation is a viable approach to seek justice in India.

LEGAL LUMINARY

MOHANDAS KARAMCHAND GANDHI—ARBITRATOR PAR EXCELLENCE

M.K. Gandhi (1869–1948), the simple attorney who became the Father of the Nation, is the world's most inspirational leader and social and political philosopher. The singular secret of his success is described in his own words in his autobiography *My Experiments with Truth*, in Chapter 14, 'Preparation for the Case', pp. 84–85.*

The year's stay in Pretoria was a most valuable experience in my life. Herein it was that I had opportunities of learning public work and acquired some measure of my capacity for it. Here, it was that the religious spirit within me became a living force and I too acquired a true knowledge of legal practice. Here, I learnt the things that a junior barrister learns in a senior barrister's chamber, and I also gained confidence that I should not after all fail as a lawyer.

It was likewise here that I learnt the secret of success as a lawyer. Dada Abdulla's was no small case. The suit was for £40,000. Arising out of business transactions, it was full of intricacies of accounts. Part of the claim was based on promissory notes, and part on the specific performance of promise to deliver promissory notes. The defence was that the promissory notes were fraudulently taken and lacked sufficient consideration. There were numerous points of fact and law in this intricate case.

Both parties had engaged the best attorneys and counsel. I, thus, had a fine opportunity of studying their work. The preparation of the plaintiff's case for the attorney, and the sorting of facts in support of his case, had been entrusted to me. It was an education to see how much the attorney accepted, and how much he rejected from my preparation, as also to see

---

*The autobiography of Mahatma Gandhi is available in very inexpensive editions, and freely circulated on hundreds of websites; the highly recommended website is: http://www.mkgandhi-sarvodaya.org; for full text of the biography as well as images you may see, for example: http://d3vilsheaven.com/wp-content/uploads/2011/05/My-experiments-with-truth.pdf.

Contd

Legal Luminary   *Contd*

how much use the counsel made of the brief prepared by the attorney. I saw that this preparation for the case would give me a fair measure of my powers of comprehension and my capacity for marshalling evidence.

I took the keenest interest in the case. Indeed, I threw myself into it. I read all the papers pertaining to the transactions. My client was a man of great ability and reposed absolute confidence in me and this rendered my work easy. I made a fair study of book keeping. My capacity for translation was improved by having to translate the correspondence, which was for the most part in Gujarati.

As I have said before, although I took a keen interest in religious communion and in public work and always gave some of my time to them, they were not then my primary interest. The preparation of the case was my primary interest. Reading of law and looking up law cases, when necessary, had always a prior claim on my time. As a result, I acquired such a grasp of the facts of the case as perhaps was not possessed even by the parties themselves, in as much as I had with me the papers of both the parties.

I recalled the late Mr Pincutt's advice: 'facts are three-fourths of the law'. At a later date, it was amply borne out by that famous barrister of South Africa, the late Mr Leonard. In a certain case in my charge, I saw that though justice was on the side of my client, the law seemed to be against him. In despair, I approached Mr Leonard for help. He also felt that the facts of the case were very strong. He exclaimed, 'Gandhi, I have learnt one thing, and it is this that if we take care of the facts of a case, the law will take care of itself. Let us dive deeper into the facts of this case.' With these words, he asked me to study the case further and then see him again. On a re-examination of the facts, I saw them in an entirely new light, and I also hit upon an old South-African case bearing on the point. I was delighted and went to Mr Leonard and told him everything, 'Right,' he said, 'we shall win the case. Only we must bear in mind which of the judges takes it.'

When I was making preparation for Dada Abdulla's case, I had not fully realized this paramount importance of facts. Facts mean truth, and once we adhere to truth, the law comes

to our aid naturally. I saw that the facts of Dada Abdulla's case made it very strong indeed, and that the law was bound to be on his side. But I also saw that the litigation, if it were persisted in, would ruin the [page 85] plaintiff and the defendant, who were relatives and both belonged to the same city. No one knew how long the case might go on. Should it be allowed to continue to be fought out in court, it might go on indefinitely, and to no advantage of either party. Both, therefore, desired an immediate termination of the case, if possible.

I approached Tyeb Sheth and requested and advised him to go to arbitration. I recommended him to see his counsel. I suggested him that if an arbitrator commanding the confidence of both parties could be appointed, the case would be quickly finished. The lawyers' fees were so rapidly mounting up that they were enough to devour all the resources of the clients, big merchants as they were. The case occupied so much of their attention that they had no time left for any other work. In the meantime, mutual ill-will was steadily increasing. I became disgusted with the profession. As lawyers, the counsels on both sides were bound to rake up points of law in support of their own clients. I also saw for the first time that the winning party never recovers all the costs incurred. Under the Court Fees Regulation, there was a fixed scale of costs to be allowed as between the parties, the actual costs as between attorney and client being very much higher. This was more than I could bear. I felt that my duty was to befriend both parties and bring them together. I strained every nerve to bring about a compromise. At last, Tyeb Sheth agreed. An arbitrator was appointed, the case was argued before him, and Dada Abdulla won.

But that did not satisfy me. If my client were to seek immediate execution of the award, it would be impossible for Tyeb Sheth to meet the whole of the awarded amount, and there was an unwritten law among the Porbandar Memans living in South Africa that death should be preferred to bankruptcy. It was impossible for Tyeb Sheth to pay down the whole sum of about £37,000 and costs. He meant to pay not a pie less than the amount, and he did not want to be declared bankrupt. There was only one way. Dada Abdulla should allow him to pay in moderate installments. He was equal to the occasion

---

**Young lawyer, Mahatma Gandhi in South Africa.

Contd

Legal Luminary *Contd*

and granted Tyeb Sheth installments spread over a very long period. It was more difficult for me to secure this concession of payment by installments than to get the parties to agree to arbitration. But both were happy over the result, and both rose in the public estimation. My joy was boundless. I had learnt the true practice of law. I had learnt to find out the better side of human nature and to enter men's hearts. I realized that the true function of a lawyer was to unite parties driven asunder. The lesson was so indelibly burnt into me that a large part of my time during the twenty years of my practice as a lawyer was occupied in bringing about private compromises of hundreds of cases. I lost nothing thereby, not even money, certainly not my soul.

Basic Rights and Business

Principle: *Homo vocabulum est naturae; persona juris civilis.*
Man is a term of nature, a person of civil law.

CHAPTER OUTLINE

- Introduction and Interpretation
- Basic Rights in Indian Context

- *Case Study:* The Trial of Dr Binayak Sen—From Jail to Bail
- *Legal Luminary:* Dr Binayak Sen

30.1 INTRODUCTION AND INTERPRETATION

(1) All human beings are born free and equal based on dignity and rights. They are endowed with reason and conscience and should act towards one another in a spirit of brotherhood.

(2) Everyone is entitled to all the rights and freedoms set forth in this Declaration, without distinction of any kind, such as race, colour, sex, language, religion, political or other opinion, national or social origin, property, birth, or other status. Furthermore, no distinction shall be made based on the political, jurisdictional, or international status of the country or territory to which a person belongs, whether it is independent, trust, non-self-governing, or under any other limitation of sovereignty.

(3) Everyone has the right to life, liberty, and security of person.

(4) No one shall be held in slavery or servitude; slavery and the slave trade shall be prohibited in all their forms.

(5) No one shall be subjected to torture or to cruel, inhuman or degrading treatment or punishment.

(6) Everyone has the right to recognition everywhere as a person before the law.

(7) All are equal before the law and are entitled without any discrimination to equal protection of the law. All are entitled to equal protection against any discrimination in violation of this Declaration and against any incitement to such discrimination.

(8) Everyone has the right to an effective remedy by the competent national tribunals for acts violating the fundamental rights granted him by the constitution or by law.

(9) No one shall be subjected to arbitrary arrest, detention, or exile.

(10) Everyone are entitled in full equality to a fair and public hearing by an independent and impartial tribunal, in the determination of his rights and obligations and of any criminal charge against him.

(11) (1) Everyone charged with a penal offence has the right to be presumed innocent until proved guilty according to law in a public trial, at which he has had all the guarantees necessary for his defence.

(2) No one shall be held guilty of any penal offence on account of any act or omission that did not constitute a penal offence, under national or international law, at the time when it was committed. Nor shall a heavier penalty be imposed than the one that was applicable at the time the penal offence was committed.

(12) No one shall be subjected to arbitrary interference with his privacy, family, home or correspondence, or to attacks upon his honour and reputation. Everyone has the right to the protection of the law against such interference or attacks.

(13) (1) Everyone has the right to freedom of movement and residence within the borders of each state.

(2) Everyone has the right to leave any country, including his own, and to return to his country.

(14) (1) Everyone has the right to seek and to enjoy in other countries asylum from persecution.

(2) This right may not be invoked in the case of prosecutions genuinely arising from non-political crimes or from acts in contrast with the purposes and principles of the United Nations.

(15) (1) Everyone has the right to a nationality.

(2) No one shall be arbitrarily deprived of his nationality nor denied the right to change his nationality.

(16) (1) Men and women who have attained an age of 18 years majority, without any limitation due to race, nationality, or religion, have the right to marry and to form a family. They are entitled to equal rights as to marriage, during marriage, and at its dissolution.

(2) Marriage shall be entered into only with the free and full consent of the intending spouses.

(3) The family is the natural and fundamental group unit of society and is entitled to protection by society and the state.

(17) (1) Everyone has the right to own property alone as well as in association with others.

(2) No one shall be arbitrarily deprived of his property.

(18) Everyone has the right to freedom of thought, conscience, and religion; this right includes freedom to change his religion or belief, and freedom, either alone or in community with others and in public or private, to manifest his religion or belief in teaching, practice, worship, and observance.

(19) Everyone has the right to freedom of opinion and expression; this right includes freedom to hold opinions without interference and to seek, receive, and impart information and ideas through any media regardless of frontiers.

(20) (1) Everyone has the right to freedom of peaceful assembly and association.

(2) No one may be compelled to belong to an association.

(21) (1) Everyone has the right to take part in the government of his country, directly or through freely chosen representatives.

(2) Everyone has the right of equal access to public service in his country.

(3) The will of the people shall be the basis of the authority of government; this will shall be expressed in periodic and genuine elections, which shall be by universal and equal suffrage and shall be held by secret vote or by equivalent free voting procedures.

(22) Everyone, as a member of society, has the right to social security and is entitled to realization, through national effort and international co-operation and in accordance with the organization and resources of each state, of the economic, social, and cultural rights indispensable for his dignity and the free development of his personality.

(23) (1) Everyone has the right to work, to free choice of employment, to just and favourable conditions of work, and to protection against unemployment.

(2) Everyone, without any discrimination, has the right to equal pay for equal work.

(3) Everyone who works has the right to just and favourable remuneration ensuring for himself and his family an existence worthy of human dignity, and supplemented, if necessary, by other means of social protection.

(4) Everyone has the right to form and to join trade unions for the protection of his interests.

(24) Everyone has the right to rest and leisure, including reasonable limitation of working hours and periodic holidays with pay.

(25) (1) Everyone has the right to a standard of living adequate for the health and well-being of himself and of his family, including food, clothing, housing and medical care, and necessary social services, and the right to security in the event of unemployment, sickness, disability, widowhood, old age, or other lack of livelihood in circumstances beyond his control.

(2) Motherhood and childhood are entitled to special care and assistance. All children, whether born in or out of wedlock shall enjoy the same social protection.

(26) (1) Everyone has the right to education. Education shall be free, at least in the elementary and fundamental stages. Elementary education shall be compulsory. Technical and professional education shall be made generally available, and higher education shall be equally accessible to all based on merit.

(2) Education shall be directed to the full development of the human personality and to the strengthening of respect for human rights and fundamental freedoms. It shall promote understanding, tolerance, and friendship among all nations, racial or religious groups, and shall further the activities of the United Nations for the maintenance of peace.

Parents have a prior right to choose the kind of education that shall be given to their children.

(27) (1) Everyone has the right freely to participate in the cultural life of the community, to enjoy the arts and to share in scientific advancement and its benefits.

(2) Everyone has the right to the protection of the moral and material interests resulting from any scientific, literary, or artistic production of which he is the author.

(28) Everyone is entitled to a social and international order in which the rights and freedoms set forth in this Declaration can be fully realized.

(29) (1) Everyone has duties to the community in which alone the free and full development of his personality is possible.

(2) In the exercise of his rights and freedoms, everyone shall be subject only to such limitations as are determined by law solely for the purpose of securing due recognition and respect for the rights and freedoms of others and of meeting the just requirements of morality, public order, and the general welfare in a democratic society.

(3) These rights and freedoms may in no case be exercised contrary to the purposes and principles of the United Nations.

(30) Nothing in this Declaration may be interpreted as implying for any state, group or person any right to engage in any activity or to perform any act aimed at the destruction of any of the rights and freedoms set forth herein.

– The Universal Declaration of Human Rights, 1948, all the 30 Articles that are adopted
by the United Nations General Assembly[1]

You have been given above the text of the Universal Declaration of Human Rights to read, reflect, and to make it your own as a manager in the global world of commerce and trade. The objective is to instill in you the foundation of the new charter of humanity.

After World War II, humanity looked at itself with a renewed sense of human worth and resolved to invest itself with inalienable human dignity, freedom, and liberty. It established a new world order.[2] As a result, today, sovereign states, despite all their rights of national

---

[1] See http://www.un.org/en/documents/udhr/#atop.

[2] The League of Nations preceded UNO. It was influenced by the Rights of Man and of the Citizen, France, 1788; it had already developed some of the rights in the Universal Declaration of Human Rights.

sovereignty are bound by the international laws and conventions whose foundation is based on this declaration.

Human rights have not yet been established. In contrast, we see them being abused publicly in custodial deaths or brutalities on the streets. Genocides, human trafficking, child slavery, child abuse, child prostitution, gender bias, human organ trafficking, political violence, corruption, and criminalization of politics are rampant.

Corporations have great power, both of wealth and of influencing public policy. Some of the global corporations are wealthier than the smaller nation-states. In fact, these corporations have breached the 50 per cent mark and have already overtaken the nation-states. The member nations of the United Nations are aware of this fact and have come together to form common global policies on social, economic, legal, and political affairs. The United Nations Organization (UNO) initiates models of reform in these fields. You have seen the examples of this in the past few chapters. The UNO conducts programmes in the areas of social, health and educational development, science and technology, trade and commerce (for example, World Trade Organization, World Bank, International Monetary Fund), legal initiatives, World Court, etc. It is evolving itself into a world government.

The corporate sector has a greater role to play in world affairs. It is expected that corporations become the good citizens of the world. Social responsibility is expected from them, as more than half the global population is still very poor. It is expected of corporations that they see these poor people as their valuable customers and innovate their businesses to develop partnership with them and empower them socially and economically. All of this is only possible with the rule of law, equity, and justice. The charter of human rights consists only of thirty short articles; however, their enormity is incalculable and most valuable to humanity.

As man evolves, so does the value system in which he lives. There was a time when slavery was acceptable as a normal social condition in the West. Today, it is condemned as ethically and legally unacceptable. Caste system was also a part of the social, economic, and religious order in India; this too has been hearly purged from our society. Although the evil still exists, its encouragement is clearly abhorred by the law. There were heinous customs of *sati*, untouchability, and gender discrimination that have been brought under the ambit of law. Every year 10 December is observed as the Human Rights Day.

Scope

The scope of this chapter is to reflect the above Universal Declaration of Human Rights in the Indian context. These rights find their expression in the Constitution of India, and the laws related to human rights, right to information, and public interest litigation. The bearing of these laws on businesses is obvious. Corporations as legal entities are bound by these laws. From acquisition of lands for companies, claiming licences for mining and other resources, taking responsibility for environment, employment and payment of employees, labour relations, equal work equal pay, gender equality, business morality or ethics of doing business, and all such related issues are related to the basic rights.

30.2   BASIC RIGHTS IN INDIAN CONTEXT

Constitution of India, 1950

TEXT

The state shall not deny to any person equality before the law or the equal protection of the laws within the territory of India.

— The Constitution of India, Article 14

The Constitution of India enshrines in its preamble the dignity of the individual, which is the basic principle of human rights. Further in Part III, it lays down the fundamental rights that are inalienable from the individual person. There are nine fundamental rights ensuring people's justice, liberty, equality fraternity, and dignity.

Right to equality (Articles 14–18)   These grant equality before the law and non-discrimination based on religion, caste, race, sex, or place of birth. It also provides equality of opportunity in matters of public employment.

Right to freedom (Article 19)   It is one of the most important rights granting freedom: of speech and expression, peaceful assembly, to form associations and unions, to move freely throughout the territory of the country, reside and settle in any part of the country, and practise profession, trade and business.

Protection in respect of conviction or offences (Article 20)   It grants three explicit protections: against ex post facto penal code: double jeopardy and self-incrimination.

Protection life and personal liberty (Article 21)   No person shall be deprived of his personal life and liberty.

Protection against arrest and detention (Article 22)   In the event of an arrest, the person has the right to be informed under which provision of the law he has been arrested or detained and shall be produced before the nearest magistrate within 24 hours of such arrest or detention.

Right against exploitation (Articles 23, 24)   Human traffic, forced labour, and child labour are forbidden.

Right to freedom of religion (Articles 25–28)   These articles grant the right to freedom of conscience, practise, and propagation of religion.

Cultural and educational rights (Articles 29, 30)   Culture and educational freedom, to preserve one's language and the right to establish and administer educational institutions, particularly the minorities.

Right to constitutional remedies (Article 32)   The Constitution makes the Supreme Court of India the protector of fundamental rights. Any aggrieved person may directly move the apex court that can give directions, orders, and writs.

Apart from the fundamental rights, there are also directive principles of state policy in Part IV of the Constitution. The rights here include:

(a) Social security

(b) Right to work

(c) Right to just and favourable work conditions

(d)　Right to equal work equal pay

(e)　Right to existence worthy of human dignity

(f)　Right to rest and leisure

(g)　Right to cultural life of the community

(h)　Right to free and compulsory education

(i)　Right to equal justice and free legal aid

The term 'judicial activism' has been used quite frequently in recent years. It is because the Supreme Court has taken keen interest in its duty to be the protector of the fundamental rights. The apex court has been very vigilant particularly in the protection of the rights of the people arrested or detained and those of women and children. The apex court has shown its extreme concern for people who have no food, succumb to starvation and exposure, or are forced to commit suicide, as in the case of poor farmers who are unable to repay their loans.

Protection of Human Rights Act, 1993

An Act to provide the constitution of a National Human Rights Commission, State Human Rights Commission in States, and Human Rights Courts for better protection of human rights and for matters connected therewith or incidental thereto…

– The Protection of Human Rights Act, 1993, Preamble

The Act sets up three institutions for the protection of human rights:

(a)　National Human Rights Commission (NHRC)

(b)　State Human Rights Commission

(c)　Human Rights Courts

A few headlines from the newspapers may enlighten you about the importance of human rights commissions, both at national as well as state level:

(a)　NHRC issues notices to the Maharashtra, Andhra Pradesh, and Kerala governments on farmers' suicide.

(b)　The NHRC asks Punjab government to pay ₹5 lakhs as monetary relief in a case of death in prison.

(c)　The NHRC asks Bihar government to pay ₹3 lakhs as monetary relief in a case of death of an under-trial prisoner.

(d)　The NHRC asks the Delhi government to submit a report on the quacks operating in the National Capital Region.

(e)　The NHRC releases its report for Second Universal Periodic Review of Human Rights in the country.

(f)　The UP government complies with the NHRC recommendations; pays ₹5 lakhs as compensation and moves against the police officials guilty of beating a boy to death.

(g)　Forty labourers allegedly missing after an accident at a construction site in Damoh district; NHRC asks the MP government to respond.

The above clearly and vividly demonstrates to you the functions and powers of the NHRC.

The NHRC conducts the following programmes under the pursuance of the Supreme Court of India:

(a) Abolition of bonded labour
(b) Functioning of the mental hospitals at Ranchi, Agra, and Gwalior
(c) Functioning of the Government Protective Home (Women), Agra
(d) The right to food

There are hosts of other programmes that the Commission conducts, such as child protection, prevention of human trafficking, sexual violence, and sex tourism, rehabilitation of destitute women, abolition of manual scavenging, rights of the disabled, monitoring relief measures to earthquake victims, and several such to alleviate misery and suffering.

Right to Information, 2005

An Act for setting out the practical regime of right to information for citizens to secure access to information under the control of public authorities, to promote transparency and accountability in the working of every public authority, the constitution of a Central Information Commission and State Information Commissions, and for matters connected therewith or incidental thereto.

Whereas the Constitution of India has established democratic Republic;

And whereas democracy requires an informed citizenry and transparency of information that are vital to its functioning and also to contain corruption and to hold Governments and their instrumentalities accountable to the governed;

And whereas revelation of information in actual practice is likely to conflict with other public interests including efficient operations of the Governments, optimum use of limited fiscal resources and the preservation of confidentiality of sensitive information;

And whereas it is necessary to harmonize these conflicting interests while preserving the paramountcy[3] of the democratic ideal;

Now, therefore, it is expedient to provide for furnishing certain information to citizens who desire to have it.

– The Right to Information Act, 2005, Preamble

It is clear from the outset that the Right to Information Act, known by its acronym RTI, is not exclusive from the Protection of Human Rights Act, but it is complementary to it. As the preamble thoroughly demonstrates that in a democratic republic—where the people are sovereign and secrecy and concealment have no place—transparency and correct information serve to communicate all the aspects of governance of the people. Secrecy, non-disclosure, mystery of the ruler, etc. are anomalous to the principles of democracy and the fundamental rights of the citizens who have given a law to themselves by constituting a Constitution. The nation is of the people; they choose their own government and approve all the institutions of legislation, executive, and the judiciary. The right to information is thus a fundamental right of a citizen.

India, under the British government, had a law entitled the Official Secrets Act, 1923, which served the purposes of colonial rulers. It has taken independent India six decades to enact RTI. The right perspective about right to information is that it is an open and transparent channel of communication between the people and their government. The more accessible a channel, the greater is the interaction between the citizens and the governing machinery, the bureaucracy that works for the people. In the bargain, it makes

---

[3]The author interprets that the legislator's intention may have been to use the term *supremacy* (the existence of the term *paramountcy* is doubtful).

the government and all its organs function responsively and responsibly. Today, the law has been also adopted in most of the states of India, and people have become conscious about the workings of the government. Now the fact that people want several other laws in the social, economic, and political areas goes to show that the democratic participation of the people is growing, which demands better management in governance. Some of the pending laws are Judicial Accountability, Right to Food Act, Right to Employment Act, and Lokpal Act. Some reflections will tell you these are nothing but specification of the fundamental rights enshrined in the Constitution of India.

The Act provides for essentially the following:

Secs 3–11   Right to information and obligations of public authorities. The legal reasoning for compliance to requests of information is that whosoever is paid from the public exchequer is bound to give information to the public. In other words, from the President of India to the very least government functionary, in government-related offices, institutions, associations, corporations, etc.

Secs 12–14   These sections deal with the establishment of the Central Information Commission and its functions, responsibilities, and liabilities. For instance, if the Chief Information Commissioner or a Information Commissioner in any way concerned or interested in any contract or agreement made by or on behalf of the Government of India or participates in any way in the profit thereof or in any benefit or emolument arising there from otherwise than as a member and in common with the other members of an incorporated company, he shall, for the purposes of Sub-sec. (1), be deemed to be guilty of misbehaviour (14) (4).

Secs 15–17   These sections deal with how states of the Union of India establish similar commissions on the model of the centre.

Secs 18–20   These sections deal with the powers and functions of the Information Commissions and also the appeals and penalties. For instance, if the State Chief Information Commissioner or a State Information Commissioner in any way, concerned or interested in any contract or agreement made by or on behalf of the government of the state or participates in any way in the profit thereof or in any benefit or emoluments arising there from otherwise than as a member and in common with the other members of an incorporated company, he shall, for the purposes of Sub-sec. (1), be deemed to be guilty of misbehaviour (17) (4).

The most important thing about RTI for you as a manager is to understand its impact on corporations. If your corporation is public sector unit, and other such corporations then you come directly under the purview of RTI, and it will serve you well to know all procedures about the Act.

There is already a very strong debate going on in the country that the publicly listed companies in which people invest their money must be accountable to the people and the provisions of RTI must also be extended to them. Corporation supply goods and services to the people. People have a contract with the companies in similar fashion as they have a contract with their government. People do have a right to know what they buy or what service they subscribe to. It seems reasonable, therefore, that the RTI provisions must be extended to all companies who sell goods and services. The greater the information and more transparent the communication, better are the chances that the business transactions would be ethical.

Public Interest Litigation, Article 32

The right to move the Supreme Court by appropriate proceedings for the enforcement of the rights conferred by this Part is guaranteed.

– The Constitution of India, Article 31 (1)

Understanding public interest litigation   Public interest litigation, PIL for short, is to be clearly understood by its very terms: it is to file a suit, not as a personal dispute or grievance that needs redressal, but a public grievance that affects many people. Complaints need to be made so that the judiciary takes notice and orders the executive to set matters right. Thus, moving the court and petitioning to redress a grievance would help a great number of people. The term 'litigation' does not mean some long-drawn war of attrition but quite simply a legal action initiated in a court of law for enforcement of public interest. You have also studied, earlier on, the terms such as public good or public trust. Thus, a complaint to the court against the destruction of public property, public buildings, parks, water resources, land (for mines or urbanization), environment, prisoners' rights, children's protection, matters of public decency, unauthorized eviction, implementation of welfare laws, etc. is in the interest of the public at large.

Legal basis for PIL   The above text, Article 32 of the Constitution is based on the fundamental right of every citizen to move to the apex court of the nation. The Directive Principles in Part IV of the Constitution are directly related to the Universal Declaration of Human Rights of the UNO.

Qualifications for filing PIL   Any member of the public, acting in good faith and having sufficient interest in instituting an action for redressal of public wrong or public injury. The action is not to be motivated by any personal gain but only by public good.

Methods of filing PIL   Public interest litigation is as old as the courts of law. However, the concept has been strengthened in our times due to the frequency and the quantum of interest. In the past, people used to write simple, earnest letters of concern to the courts, which after judging the concern expressed would accept it as a petition of public interest. Today, people may file petitions that are well drafted and supported by documents and exhibits to prove the point in question. It may be directly handed over to the free legal committee service of the court or through registered letter. Assistance of lawyers and knowledgeable people may be sought (Box 30.1).

There is a ground well in the interest of public good. Highly professional people today give up the trappings of upper-crust living style and have become conscious of the problems

BOX 30.1 **Landmark Cases of PIL**

1. Anil Yadav and others vs State of Bihar and Bachcho Lal Das, Superintendent, Central Jail, Bhagalpur, Bihar (1982) 2 SCC 195:

PETITION: Blinding of undertrial prisoners at Bhagalpur in the State of Bihar. The eyes were pierced with needles and acid was poured into them.

JUDGEMENT: Passed comprehensive orders to ensure that such barbarous and inhuman acts are not repeated.

2. Munna and others vs State of Uttar Pradesh and others (1982) 1 SCC 545:

PETITION: The juvenile undertrial prisoners were sent in the Kanpur Central Jail instead of Children's Home in Kanpur. The children were sexually exploited by the adult prisoners.

JUDGEMENT: In no case except, can a child be sent to jail. The children below the age of 16 years must be detained only in the Children's Homes or other place of safety. A nation that is not concerned with the welfare of the children cannot look forward to a bright future.

3. Labourers Working on Salal Hydro Project vs State of Jammu Kashmir and others (AIR 1984 SC 177):

PETITION: News item in the *Indian Express* with regard to the condition of the construction workers was converted by the court as PIL.

JUDGEMENT: The construction work is a hazardous employment and no child below the age of 14 years can, therefore, be allowed to be employed in construction work by reason of the prohibition enacted in Article 24 and this constitutional prohibition must be enforced by the Central Government.

4. B.R. Kapoor vs Union of India and others AIR 1990 SC 752:

PETITION: Mismanagement of the hospital for mental diseases located at Shahdara, Delhi.

JUDGEMENT: There are acute problems of availability of water, existing sanitary conditions, food, kitchen, medical and nursing care, ill-treatment of patients, attempts of inmates to commit suicide, death of patients in hospital, availability of doctors and nurses, etc. The Union of India is ordered to take over the hospital and model it on the lines of NIMHANS at Bengaluru.

5. Vishaka and others vs State of Rajasthan and others [1997] 6 SCC 241]:

PETITION: Sexual harassment in workplace.

JUDGEMENT: Court gave directions with regard to enforcement of the fundamental rights of the working women under Articles 14, 19, and 21 of the Constitution. The Court also gave comprehensive guidelines and norms and directed for protection and enforcement of these rights of the women at their workplaces.

Contd

Box 30.1 *Contd*

6. Karnataka Industrial Areas Development Board vs Sri C. Kenchappa and others (AIR 2006 SC 2038):

PETITION: Sustainable development.

JUDGEMENT: There has to be balance between sustainable development and environment. Before acquisition of lands for development, the consequence and adverse impact of development on environment must be properly comprehended and the lands be acquired for development that they do not gravely impair the ecology and environment. State Industrial Areas Development Board shall incorporate the condition of allotment to obtain clearance from the Karnataka State Pollution Control Board before the land is allotted for development. The said directory condition of allotment of lands shall be converted into a mandatory condition for all the projects to be sanctioned in future.

of the masses. They work for accountability from the government and work selflessly for the needy in the country.

The issues of human rights, right to information, and public interest litigation have gone unnoticed by corporations. Very often, the perception given by corporations is that these laws are enacted against them. In contrast, these laws may be positively used by corporations to safeguard the rights of their employees instead of giving it in the hands of the unions. Corporations can use the right to information for advancing their entrepreneurial goals rather than involve in corruption. They can also make it their responsibility to utilize public interest litigation to set right their products and practices. Corporations need to rethink about the laws of the country and accept them and follow them.

MANAGER'S TAKEAWAY

- Public interest is a part of corporate social responsibility.
- Nothing is as precious as the human dignity of an employee.

SUMMARY

- Basic rights are: Protection of Human Rights Act, 1993 Right to Information, 2005
- As we evolve as society, we create new rights and broaden the existing ones. All the mentioned Acts above actually stem from the Constitution of India and the Universal Declaration of Human Rights. India

has experienced insurmountable problems in the areas of human rights. The corporations too have contributed to the woes of these rights by infringing their rights of fair wages, amenities, and health care. The problems of land acquisition, environmental problems, etc., are perpetrated by the corporations. Managers need to wake up their conscience.

EXERCISES

(i) Illustrate fundamental rights in the Constitution of India with suitable cases.

(ii) In what way human rights impact businesses?

(iii) How to eradicate slums from the cities?

(iv) Devise a method to include companies under RTI.

(v) What is the constitutional basis for PIL?

DEVELOPMENT OF LEGAL EDGE

Project—File PIL

Objective   Learn by doing

Method   Form a group of employees or students as the case may be:

- Study your local problems
- Prepare a suitable PIL
- Documentation is essential

- Consult legal opinion
- Get permission from employer or the institute of your study
- File the PIL

Motto   Impact the world around you with the instrument of law.

FURTHER READING

Acts, Rules, and Regulations

- Ministry of Law and Justice. http://lawmin.nic.in.

Book

- D.N. Gupt *Human Rights: Acts, Statutes and Constitutional Provisions* Delhi: Kalpaz Publications, 2009.

Web resources

- Usha Ramanathan, Human Rights in India, A Mapping, http://www.ielrc.org/content/w0103.pdf.
- Karnataka Women's Information and Resource Centre, Human Rights Education for Beginners, http://nhrc.nic.in/publications/hredu.pdf.

CASE STUDY   THE TRIAL OF DR BINAYAK SEN—FROM JAIL TO BAIL

I have never seen such oppression from the state government. This literature, what they call sedition, is available in the market.

– Mr Ram Jethmalani, Counsel to Dr Binayak Sen
in the Supreme Court of India, 15 April 2011[4]

The Headnote

Dr Binayak Sen is a paediatrician. He came to be well known for his selfless service to the poor rural tribal people of Chhattisgarh. Working with them he saw their acute problems as their basic rights were trampled. He, thus, naturally took to serve them as a human right activist. Sen worked with the Government to improve the health programmes. However, he criticized the Government for its poor record on human rights. The Government took umbrage of his stance and accused him of not only being a Naxalite or Maoist sympathizer but conspiring with them, sedition and committing treason.

Sen objected the methods employed by the Government in anti-Maoist operations. Finally, the State Government caught up with him and leveled charges against him. The Sessions Court convicted him of the charges and

---

[4]As reported in the daily newspaper: http://www.thehindu.com/news/national/article1698939.ece?homepage=true.

[5]Dr Binayak Sen vs State of Chhattisgarh (Criminal Appeal No 54 of 2011); also see http://www.indiankanoon.org/doc/94313095/ (07 December 2011).

the Chhattisgarh High Court upheld those charges. The following is the trial at the High Court.

The Trial

Court: Chattisgarh High Court[5]

Bench: Justice T.P. Sharma and Justice R.L. Jhanwar

Petitioner: Dr Binayak Sen

Respondent: State of Chhattisgarh

Date: 10 February 2011

Appellant in Cr.A.No.20/2011, Binayak Sen, has been convicted for commission of the offence of sedition punishable under Sec. 124A of the IPC; Secs 8 (1), 8 (2), 8 (3), and 8 (5) of the Chhattisgarh Vishesh Jan Suraksha Adhiniyam, 2005 (for short: 'the Act, 2005'); and Sec. 39 (2) of the Unlawful Activities (Prevention) Act, 1967 (for short: 'the Act, 1967') and sentenced.

The Charges

Sen was arrested on 14 May 2007 under the provisions of the Chhattisgarh Special Public Security Act, 2005 and the Unlawful Activities (Prevention) Act, 1967. The allegations claimed that he had acted as a courier for a Maoist leader, Narayan Sanyal, lodged in the Raipur Jail and then absconded. The charges against him were as follows:

(a)   Treason

(b)   Criminal conspiracy

(c)   Sedition, anti-national activities, and making war against the nation

(d)   Knowingly using the proceeds of terrorism

(e)   Links with the Maoists

The charges were based on the Maoist literature that was found with Dr Sen.

The Prosecution

Additional public prosecutor appearing on behalf of the state has vehemently opposed the applications and contended that evidence adduced on behalf of the prosecution and admission of accused persons by adducing defence witnesses are sufficient to establish the fact that the appellants have committed aforesaid offence, including the offence of sedition. The appellants have been convicted only on 24 December 2010 and there is no likelihood of delay in hearing the appeals.

The Defense

Even as per the prosecution, police has not recorded any such statement and co-accused Piyush Guha has not made any statement before any person or Magistrate other than the police. In these circumstances, even if these facts are admitted that Piyush Guha has made confessional statement relating to the aforesaid three letters, the same would not be admissible in evidence in terms of Secs 24, 25, and 26 of the Indian Evidence Act, 1872 and it cannot be used against appellant Sen and even against co-accused Piyush Guha. Appellant Sen, in connection with private affairs and affairs relating Peoples' Union for Civil Liberties including health of co-accused Narayan Sanyal, visited jail thirty-two times to meet Narayan Sanyal who was in custody at Bilaspur jail and subsequently at Raipur jail with due permission from the jail authorities. As per evidence, superior authority had directed for strict surveillance upon appellant Sen during his visit to jail and meeting with Narayan Sanyal and, therefore, the jail authority used to arrange meetings in a separate room under strict surveillance and control, and all meetings were held in the presence of jail authorities. Appellant Binayak Sen used to talk in Hindi; he had not talked in English or Bengali. The discussions were normal and not relating to commission of any offence. This evidence is even prima facie not sufficient for casting liability upon Binayak Sen for commission of the offence of sedition and any other offences. Binayak Sen is not member of any banned organization, he has not committed offences punishable under the aforesaid provisions of law, he is the member of Peoples' Union for Civil Liberties, and has dedicated his life to bring awareness amongst illiterate people of remote areas towards the atrocities committed by police and public servants. Conducting awareness meetings for illiterate people residing in remote places especially, in forests against the police atrocities and other civil rights, is not offence. By conducting such meetings, the appellant has not attempted to bring into hatred or contempt, or excite or attempts to excite disaffection including disloyalty and all feelings of enmity towards the Government established by law.

While answering the questions put to him, appellant Binayak Sen gave his defence in writing on 23 October 2010, in which he specifically took defence that he is a doctor, specialized in child heath, having degree of MD (Pediatrics), he had also joined faculty of the Centre for Social Medicine and Community Health at Jawaharlal Nehru University in New Delhi and worked for two years. He had worked intensively in the diagnosis and treatment of Tuberculosis and understood many of the social and economic causes of disease. He was strongly influenced by the work of Marjorie Sykes, the biographer of Mahatma Gandhi, who lived at Rasulia centre. He has also worked with Late Shankar Guha Niyogi and the workers of the Chhattisgarh Mines Shramik Sangh. He helped to establish the Shaheed Hospital. He has worked to develop a health programme among the Adivasi population in and around village Bagurmnala, which today is in Dhamtari District. After formation of the State of Chhattisgarh, he was appointed as member of the advisory group on healthcare sector reforms, and helped to develop the Mitanin programme, which, in turn, became the role model for the ASHA of the National Rural Health Mission. He has also worked on human rights, which has been nationally and internationally recognized.

The Judgement

Documentary and oral evidence adduced on behalf of both the parties, explanation given by appellants Binayak

Sen and Piyush Guha in their examination under Sec. 313 of the Code and written defence submitted by appellant Binayak Sen are sufficient for drawing inference that conviction of the appellants under Secs 124A read with Sec. 120B of the IPC; 8 (1), 8 (2), 8 (3), 8 (5) of the Act, 2005; and 39 (2) of the Act, 1967, are prima facie legally sustainable. Considering the nature and gravity of the offence, especially the offence of sedition, we do not find any ground for suspension of sentences and grant of bail to appellant Binayak Sen in Cr. A., No.20/2011 and appellant Piyush Guha in Cr. A. No. 54/2011, during the pendency of appeals.

The Punishment

Table 30.1 lists out the various charges and punishments.

Table 30.1 The punishment

Charges	Punishment
Secs 120 read with 120 B of Indian Penal Code	Life imprisonment and ₹5000 fine, additional one year for non-payment
Sec. 6(1) Chhattisgarh Special Public Security Act, 2005	Rigorous imprisonment for two years; ₹1000 fine and additional three months for non-payment
Sec. 8 (2) Chhattisgarh Special Public Security Act, 2005	Rigorous imprisonment for one year; ₹1000 fine and additional three months for non-payment
Sec. 8 (3) Chhattisgarh Special Public Security Act, 2005	Rigorous imprisonment for three years; ₹1000 fine and additional three months for non-payment
Sec. 8 (5) Chhattisgarh Special Public Security Act, 2005	Rigorous imprisonment for five years; ₹1000 fine and additional three months for non-payment
Sec. 39 (2) Unlawful Activities (Prevention) Act, 1967	Rigorous imprisonment for five years; ₹1000 fine and additional three months for non-payment
The imprisonment is to be undergone simultaneously	

Bail by the Supreme Court

Binayak Sen moved to the Supreme Court challenging the order of the Chhattisgarh Court. He claimed that the High Court has erred as there was no substantial evidence against him. After examining for two days, the Supreme Court of India ruled that there was no sedition charge. The judge said: 'We are a democratic country. He may be a sympathizer (of Maoists). That does not make him guilty of sedition. No case of sedition

is made out on the basis of materials in possession unless you show that he was actively helping or harboring them… If Mahatma Gandhi's autobiography is found in somebody's place, is he a Gandhian?'[6]

Discussion Questions

1. State the facts of the case without becoming emotionally involved in the saga of Dr Sen.

---

[6]This account is as per newspaper reports: http://www.thehindu.com/news/national/article1698939.ece?homepage=true.

2. Analyze the background leading to the trial.
3. What is the role of the state machinery in the case?
4. Did Sen overdo his role and cause undue suspicion?
5. Could Sen not clarify instead of confronting the police in difficult situations such as brutal killings by the Naxals?
6. Could Sen not sympathize with the police and their families who suffered loss of life and property from the Naxals?
7. Analyze critically the judgement of Chhattisgarh High Court.

Going Beyond

1. Discuss about the prisoner of conscience.
2. Do we need non-government organizations?
3. Human rights and corporations: are these compatible?

LEGAL LUMINARY

BINAYAK SEN—HUMAN RIGHTS ACTIVIST

Dr Binayak Sen originally started working as a paediatrician extending health care to poor people in the rural-tribal areas of Chhattisgarh. While he worked with the state government on health sector reform, he also strongly criticized the government on human rights violations during the anti-Naxalite operations, while advocating non-violent political engagement. He was accused of sedition by the Chhattisgarh government (details of his trial have been given in the above case study).

Dr Sen and his wife Illina Sen played key roles in the foundation of the Chhattisgarh Mukti Morcha's Shaheed Hospital which is owned and operated by a workers' organization and a community-based NGO called Rupantar. He is also an advisor to Jan Swasthya Sahyog, a health care organization. He is also the National Vice-President of the People's Union for Civil Liberties (PUCL) and General Secretary of its Chhattisgarh unit. In this capacity, he helped organize numerous investigations into alleged human rights violations carried out during anti-Naxalite operations.

He has been the recipient of several awards. In 2004, he received the Paul Harrison award for a lifetime of service to the rural poor, from his alma mater the Christian Medical College in Vellore, India. He was awarded the R.R. Keithan Gold Medal by The Indian Academy of Social Sciences on 31 December 2007. They describe him as one of the most eminent scientists of India. Dr Sen was selected for the Jonathan Mann Award for Global Health and Human Rights in 2008. He has also been awarded the Gwangju Prize for Human Rights 2011 in memory of the Gwangju Democratization Movement of South Korea. The award announcement remarks "Dr Sen, as an accomplished medical practitioner has distinguished himself by his devotion to providing health services for the poor and by his strong advocacy against human rights violations and structural violence inflicted on the poor in Chhattisgarh, a state in central India."

Although he was often critical of state policy, and particularly the execution of such policy, his engagement with the government was never abandoned.

Glossary

This glossary serves as an elementary concept guide to facilitate the user of the book for immediate reference. Some abbreviations are used, such as (*Lt*) for Latin and (*Fr*) for French.

A fortiori (*Lt*) With a stronger reason; used in argument to describe a proposition that must be true because it is a subcategory of something that is true

A posse ad esse (*Lt*) From possibility to actuality

A posteriori (*Lt*) From what comes after. Inductive reasoning based on observation, as opposed to deductive, or *a priori*

A priori (*Lt*) Prior to experience; something deduced from a principle

Ab Inio (*Lt*) From the beginning

Abandon (Noun—**abandonment**) To intentionally give up a right or property without any plan of reclaiming it in the future; to desert a spouse or child

Abate (Noun—**abatement**; adjective—**abatable**) To decrease, reduce, or diminish; to end, dismiss, or tempo-rarily suspend a lawsuit

Abdicate (Noun—**abdication**) To renounce a responsibility or position; generally used to describe the act of a sovereign giving up a throne or an official renouncing the privileges and duties of his or her office; also used to describe a government or official failing to fulfill responsibilities or duties

Abet To help or encourage someone else to commit a crime

Abolish (Noun—**abolition**) To end or do away with; generally used to describe formally ending an institution, system, or custom, such as slavery or a tax

Abrogate (Noun—**abrogation**) To repeal, revoke, or end; particularly applies to laws, rights, orders, or formal agreements

Abstain To refrain from doing something, such as voting

Abuse of process Using the courts and legal process for some improper purpose, such as initiating a lawsuit for revenge or intimidation

Abuse To misuse; to wrong or mistreat a person or animal physically, mentally, or sexually, corrupt acts; cruel treatment of another

Accept (Noun—**acceptance**) To receive willingly; to agree voluntarily creating a binding contract; implies the right to refuse

Acceptance, conditional Agreeing to accept an offer if a certain condition is fulfilled

Acceptance, implied An agreement that is implied from a person's words and deeds rather than from explicit acceptance of the offer

Accident A chance occurrence or incident; an unforeseen and unintended event; often used to describe unfortunate occurrences

Accord and satisfaction Ending a dispute by forming an agreement (the accord) that one party will pay the other some consideration (the satisfaction, often less than the amount originally agreed to) and that this will discharge any remaining obligation

Accord To give or grant; to agree; a treaty; an agreement between two parties that settles a dispute and provides satisfaction to the wronged party

Account A description of an event

Accountability Responsibility; the state of being answerable for something

Accredit Recognize officially or authorize; to attribute; to send someone to another place (often internationally) as an official envoy

Accrue (1) Accumulate or increase; to receive at regular intervals; to become due. (2) Come into existence as a cause of action

Accuse (Noun—**accusation**) Charge someone with a crime; to institute legal proceedings against a suspected criminal

Accused Someone charged with a crime

Acknowledge (Noun—**acknowledgement**) Admit or confirm; to accept responsibility

Acquiesce Accept without protest; to give implied consent by silence

Acquire (Noun—**acquisition**) Gain or obtain; to become the owner of something

Acquit (Noun—**acquittal**) Set free or release; to absolve of criminal liability

Act of god Something that happens as a result of natural forces that cannot be controlled by humans, such as storms, earthquakes, or floods

Act (Noun—**action**) To do something, usually voluntarily (1) An action or deed. (2) A law or written ordinance passed by the parliament or legislative body

Action (1) A proceeding or an action; the right to pursue a lawsuit. (2) A court proceeding; a lawsuit; a formal complaint brought by one party to prosecute another or demand rights within a court of law

Action at law An action brought in a court of law

Actionable Forming the legal basis of a cause of action

Activism, judicial The practice of making legal decisions based on beliefs about individual rights and attitudes rather than precedent and statute

Actual value A value awarded in condemnation proceedings based on the price that a property would probably fetch from a willing buyer to a willing seller

Actuary Someone who uses statistics to calculate insurance rates

Actus reus (*Lt*) Wrongful act; as opposed to *mens rea*—the wrongful intention or guilty mind

Ad absurdum (*Lt*) To the point of absurdity

Ad hoc (*Lt*) For a particular purpose; example: *ad hoc* committee

Ad hoc (*Lt*) For this; arranged for one particular purpose; e.g., *ad hoc* committee

Ad hominem (*Lt*) To the person; appealing to the emotions instead of to logic and reason

Ad hominem (*Lt*) In an argument appealing to a person's physical and emotional urges, rather than her or his intellect or logic

Ad honorem (*Lt*) In honour; honour not baring any material advantage

Ad idem (*Lt*) Of the same mind

Ad infinitum (*Lt*) To infinity without end repeatedly; forever

Ad interim For the meantime

Ad libitum (*Lt*) At one's pleasure; acronym: *ad lib*

Ad libitur (*Lt*) As desired

Ad litem (*Lt*) For a lawsuit or action

Ad referendum (*Lt*) Subject to reference

Ad rem (*Lt*) To the point

Ad valorem tax (*Lt*) A tax assessed on the value of property

Ad valorem (*Lt*) According to the value; in proportion to value

Addendum Something that is added on; usually written material added to the end of a document

Adequate remedy at law A remedy that provides complete and appropriate relief

Adjective law Rules of procedure; the rules that administer substantive law

Adjourn Postpone; to suspend; to stop with the intent of resuming later

Adjudge Decide; to pass judgement; to sentence

Adjudicate (Noun—**adjudication**) Judge; to formally issue a final judgement in a court proceeding synonymous with adjudge

Administer (Noun—**administration**) Manage; to run (a business or other operation); to make someone take an oath; to enforce a decree

Administrative agency A governmental organization that implements a particular piece of legislation, such as workers' compensation or tax law

Administrative law The body of laws that governs administrative agencies

Administrator A person appointed by a court to handle the estate of someone who dies intestate, i.e., without a will also known as executor

Admissible evidence Evidence that is proper to admit at trial because it is relevant to the matter at hand

Admit (1) Allow in; to accept as evidence (2) To acknowledge

Adopt (1) Make one's own; to accept; to choose. (2) To create a legal parent-child relationship between people unrelated by blood

Adult A fully grown person; one who has reached the age of maturity

Advocate Someone who defends another; a legal counselor or representative

Affect Have an effect on; to influence; to change

Affidavit (*Lt*) A sworn written statement usable as evidence in court

Affirmative action Deliberate and positive efforts to help victims of discrimination by remedying effects of past discrimination and preventing future discrimination; e.g., in India principle of government job reservation or quota for low castes

Agency (1) A relationship in which one person, the agent, is authorized to act on behalf of the other, the principal. (2) A department or group that performs a specific task for the government. (3) A business that provides a specific service, often arranging transactions between customers

Agenda (*Lt*)   Things to be done; example: agenda of a meeting

Agent   A person authorized to act for another person, the principal, in specific or unlimited ways

Agreement   A mutual understanding between two or more parties; a meeting of minds; t often leads to a contract

Aid and abet   To knowingly help someone commit a crime—*accessory* or *accomplice*

Aka   Abbreviation for **also known as** (aka)—*alias*

Alias (*Lt*)   Otherwise; a fake or alternate identity

Alibi (*Lt*)   A defense in which the defendant claims to have been at another place than the scene of a crime when the crime was committed and produces evidence to prove it; that it was physically impossible for him or her to have committed the crime in question

Alien   A foreigner; someone born in another country who has not become a citizen of his or her country of residence—*resident alien*

Alienate (Noun—**alienation**)   To transfer property from one person to another

Allege (Noun—**allegation**)   To claim; to assert; to state in a pleading what one intends to prove at trial

Allocate (Noun—**allocation**)   To distribute for a particular purpose; to assign; to allot; in taxation

Allow   To permit; to acquiesce; to accept as true

Allowance   The amount that is permitted; sum of money paid to someone regularly

Alma mater (*Lt*)   Nourishing mother; One's old school or university

Alter (Noun—**alteration**)   To change or modify

Alteration, material   A change in the language of a contract that affects the rights defined by the contract

Alumnus (*Lt*)   Nursling; former pupil

Amalgamation   When two or more companies combine into one company, the shareholders in the amalgamating companies becoming substantially the shareholders in the amalgamated company. Amalgamation may take place in two ways: (1) By transferring one or more undertakings to a new company. (2) By the transfer of one or more undertakings to an existing company

Amend (Noun—**amendment**)   To fix; to improve; to modify; to revise a document, Bill, Act, etc.

Amicus curiae (*Lt*)   Friend of the court; someone who is not a party to a lawsuit but who has a strong interest in the subject matter of a case and petitions the court for permission to file a brief providing information on the matter to aid the court in rendering its decision; such a brief is called an amicus curiae brief or amicus brief

Amnesty   An official pardon granted by a government

Amortize (Noun—**amortization**)   To spread out the payment of a debt by periodically paying a portion of interest and capital; to pay off a debt such as a mortgage in installments; to write off the cost of an asset over time; e.g., EMI—Equal Monthly Installment

Ancillary   Supplementary, additional or supporting

Annul   To declare something invalid, to abolish

Antitrust   Intended to prevent monopolies and trusts and to promote competition in business

Appeal   To request a higher court to review a case that has been decided by a lower court

Appear (Noun—**appearance**)   To come into court as a party to a lawsuit and submit to the court's jurisdiction

Appellant   One who files an appeal

Appellate court   A court that reviews decisions made by lower courts or administrative agencies and does not hear new cases

Appellate   Having to do with appeals, e.g., Appellate Court

Apportion (Noun—**apportionment**)   Divide something and assign or allocate portions of it to different parties; to distribute legislative seats among the parties to be represented

Appropriate   Take something as one's own; theft is a misappropriation; when used as noun it implies proper or suitable

Arbiter   A referee; someone appointed by a court to settle a dispute by the rules of law or equity, also called *arbitrator*

Arbitrage   A financial transaction in which securities or goods are simultaneously bought in one market and sold in another; profit is determined by price differences in the different markets

Arbitrary   To act with whim or at random; illogical; capricious

Arbitration clause   A clause in a contract that requires disputes under the contract to be submitted to arbitration; such clauses are designed to avoid the litigation of disputes

Arbitration   A form of dispute resolution in which a neutral third party renders a decision after both parties speak for themselves at a hearing; as in arbitration and conciliation

Arbitrator   A neutral person appointed or chosen to settle a dispute by hearing arguments from both parties and then rendering a decision at one's own discretion

Argument   A set of reasons given in logical order intended to persuade hearers of a particular conclusion, e.g., a lawyer presents his arguments before the a court

Argumentum ad hominem (*Lt*) An argument against the man. Directing an argument against an opponent's character rather than the subject at hand

Argumentum ad ignorantiam (*Lt*) Arguing from ignorance

Arraign (Noun—**arraignment**) To produce a defendant into court, charge him or her with an offense, and allow him or her to plead

Arrangement Reorganization as of the share capital of a company by the consolidation of shares of different classes or by the division of shares into shares of different classes or by these both methods

Arrest Use legal authority to deprive someone of liberty; hold, detain, apprehend

Article A clause or paragraph of a legal document

Articles of incorporation A document that creates a corporation; also known as articles of association

Assent To approve; to ratify; to consent

Assess (Noun—**assessment**) Evaluate; to determine a value or price for something; to set a value on property for tax purposes

Asset, intangible Assets that have no physical presence, e.g., trademark or goodwill

Asset Something of value; real or personal property worth money

Assets, capital All property held by a taxpayer

Assign (1) Transfer legal rights or property to someone else. (2) To select or designate

Assignee A person who receives property from another

Association A group of people joined together for a specific purpose

Assume (Noun—**assumption**) (1) To take on a responsibility or power; to receive. (2) To take on something deceitfully, such as a false name. (3) To suppose something to be the case without any proof

Attach To seize a defendant's property before a judgement has been reached at trial as security for any judgement that the plaintiff might receive

Attest Authentication of a document to be true; to sign a document as a witness

Attorney general One who acts as chief legal adviser to the Government and who represents it in legal matters in the court

Attorney A lawyer; an advocate/agent appointed to act for another person

Auction A public sale of goods or property to the highest bidder

Audit A systematic review or inspection of an organization's or an individual's accounts; an **auditor** conducts it

Authenticate Prove that something is genuine or true; to give something legal authority so as to allow it to be admitted as evidence

Authority Legally appointed to act bearing such powers as proper; rights or powers delegated by one person or body to another

Authorize Approve legally or grant permission

Authorized stock issue The number of shares of stock a corporation is allowed to sell under its articles of association

Award Grant, for instance, compensation; the decision given by an arbiter such as injury or mishap that something is true; to confess to a crime

Bad cheque A cheque written on a closed account or on an account with insufficient funds to pay

Bad debt reserve An account used to estimate debts that ultimately will not be paid and will, thus, eventually be deducted for tax purposes

Bad debt An uncollectible debt; a debt owed by an insolvent debtor

Bad faith Deceit; opposite of *bona fide*: good faith

Bail bond A contract between a prisoner, the state, and a third party known as a bail bondsman, in which the bail bondsman agrees to furnish bail for the prisoner in return for a fee and takes the risk that the prisoner will not return for trial

Bail Money or other security given temporarily to the court to allow a prisoner to be released before trial and to ensure that he or she will return for trial; if the prisoner does not return for trial, he or she forfeits the bail

Bailee A person who holds goods or property for someone else for a specific purpose

Bailiff A court officer who keeps who carries out the orders of the court

Bailment The delivery of goods by one person to another for some purpose according to a contract Sec. 148 of the Indian contract Act, 1872

Bailor One who delivers personal property or goods to a bailee

Bailout Financial assistance to an ailing business to save it from

Bait and switch A kind of deceptive advertising in which a merchant advertises a low-priced product to lure customers and then disparages that product or fails to have it in stock in order to persuade them to buy a more expensive item

Balance sheet A financial statement of assets and liabilities

Balance Compare the difference between debits and credits in an account; to compare the value of one thing with another; to distribute weights or values to create harmony or equality

Ballot   A piece of paper or other object used by a voter to cast a vote in an election

Bank   A financial institution that holds money for customers in bank accounts, invests it to earn interest, lends money at interest, issues promissory notes, handles trusts, deals in negotiable securities, and performs other financial services

Bankruptcy   A process in which a court declares a person or business insolvent and orders the debtor's assets to be sold to pay off creditors, at which point the debtor is discharged from any further obligation and may begin anew

Bar   An association or fraternity of legal professionals at state or national level

Bargain   Negotiate the terms of a transaction or agreement

Barratry   The offense of inciting lawsuits or quarrels

Barrister   The full form is barrister at law; lawyer who represents clients in a court of law

Barter   It is an exchange of goods and services for other goods and services without using money

Bearer   One who possesses a document, instrument, or security

Bench   (1) A court; the seat of a judge. (2) The collective body of judges—the Bar

Beneficiary   Someone who benefits from someone else's act, such as a person for whom property is held in trust, the recipient of the proceeds of an insurance policy, or someone named in a will as a recipient of property

Bequeath   To leave a gift of personal property to someone by a will

Beyond a reasonable doubt   Evidence that demonstrates conviction and moral certainty

Bias   A preconceived opinion or prejudice; a condition that renders someone unable to judge a matter impartially

Bid   An offer to buy or sell goods or services at a stated price, common at auctions

Bill   (1) A statement of goods purchased or services rendered and moneys owed for them. (2) A piece of paper currency, e.g., a dollar bill. (3) A draft of a proposed law introduced into the legislature for debate and voting. (4) A pleading submitted by a plaintiff to an equity court stating grounds for a trial

Bill of lading order   A negotiable bill of lading that can be sold, and that causes title to the goods to vest in its holder, who can collect the goods by presenting the bill of lading to the carrier

Bill of lading   A receipt given by a carrier to someone who entrusts goods to the carrier for shipment, serving as a contract between shipper and carrier and giving its holder title to the goods held by the carrier

Bind   To obligate; to place legal duties upon someone

Board of directors   The governing body of a corporation that is elected by shareholders and that sets company policy and appoints officers

Board   A group of people who manage a business or public office

Bona fide   In good faith; genuine; not intending to deceive

Bond bearer   Negotiable instrument payable to its bearer

Bond issue   Raising funds by offering bonds to investors

Bond, surety   A bond issued by a surety promising to perform an obligation if the person who is supposed to perform it defaults

Bond   Written evidence of a debt issued by a company or government in which the issuing body agrees to pay a fixed rate of interest during the period of the loan and to repay the principal at a specified date, called maturity

Bondsman   Someone who serves as surety for a bond

Bonus stock   Common stock offered as an incentive with the purchase of another kind of securities, such as preferred stock or bonds

Bonus   Added benefit

Book value   An asset's official value; usually cost minus depreciation

Book   (1) A document containing the accounts or records of a business. (2) To perform administrative tasks such as recording the name. (3) To make one responsible for a deed, e.g., police booking someone for an offence

Breach   Generally a breach of contract or trust; to break a promise; to fail to perform a duty or observe an agreement. It may be constructive when the concerned party announces beforehand problems regarding fulfilling a contract. The breach is material when a contract is completely broken; it is partial when some of the duties of the contract fail

Bribe   Illegal inducement

Brief   (1) A written document presented to the court and to the opposing counsel by a lawyer that describes the facts of a case, questions of law, and legal arguments in support of client's position. (2) A summary or abstract of a case

Broker   Also known as middleman; a person who brings parties together to negotiate transactions between them in return for a commission

Business judgement rule A rule that exempts corporate executives when it is made in good faith in the interest of the corporation

Business A commercial activity done to earn money

Bylaws The internal rules and regulations made by a corporation or association

Cadit quaestio (*Lt*) The question drops

Call A demand for payment; callable bond, a bond that may be called for payment before it matures

Canon A rule or standard; a body of rules, particularly for governing the conduct of a kind of professionals

Capacity Legal competence, e.g., to contract

Capital punishment The death penalty

Capital Wealth in the form of money and assets; all the assets owned by a business

Capitalization All stock, bonds, and other securities issued by a corporation

Caption The heading of a legal document such as a brief, motion, or pleading, containing the names of the parties, the court, the action, the docket number, and any other required information

Carte blanche (*Fr*) Complete freedom to act as one chooses; unlimited discretionary power

Cartel A coalition of independent producers, industrial corporations, who band together to set prices and restrict competition—creation of monopoly

Case law In common law and civil law: a body of law derived from examination of previously judged cases, including their treatment of a subject and interpretation of legislation

Case A legal action or lawsuit to be decided in a court of law or equity

Casebook A legal text book with cases and legal opinions

Causa mortis (*Lt*) Death cause

Causa (*Lt*) Cause, reason

Cause To make something happen; legally a cause of action, which may be direct, indirect, intervening, superseding, proximate or remote

Cautionary instruction A judge's instruction to the concerned parties for better court behaviour or procedure

Caveat (*Lt*) Let him/her beware

Caveat emptor (*Lt*) Let the buyer beware; the principle that the buyer is responsible for examining merchandise and judging its quality before buying it

Caveat venditor (*Lt*) Let the seller beware

Cease and desist order An order by a court to the litigants to stop doing a particular activity, usually because the activity in question is illegal

Censor Examine offensive content and prohibit

Censure A formal reprimand or expression of disapproval

Certify Approve; certificate, the document of such an approval, e.g., birth and death, stock, deposit, incorporation, occupancy, check, etc.

Certiorari (*Lt*) A writ issued by an appellate court to a lower court requesting the official record of a decision made by the lower court so that the appellate court can review it for errors

Cestui que (*Fr*) The one who; e.g., trust

Cetera desunt (*Lt*) The rest is missing

Ceteris paribus (*Lt*) All else being equal

Chain of title The history of ownership of a property, listed from the original owner to the present one

Challenge Dispute, objection by a lawyer; peremptory or allowed number of challenges given to a juror

Chambers Private office of a judge

Champerty An illegal agreement between parties to a lawsuit

Change To alter or modify; to substitute one thing for another

Character A person's moral qualities; reputation; legal importance when a witness gives evidence

Charge Accuse someone of an offence

Charitable trust A trust whose property must be used for charitable purposes

Charter A document granted by the state permitting the creation of a corporation, city, or university and defining its rights and privileges

Chattel Possession movable or personal property, as opposed to land or real property; something that can be owned

Check Examine; verify, e.g., a document

Chief justice The judge who presides over a court with more than one judge

Circa (**c**.) (*Lt*) Approximately

Circumstantial evidence Indirect evidence drawn from inference or deduction

Citation A reference in a legal document or argument to a legal authority such as a precedent or statute

Civil action A lawsuit brought by a private citizen to protect a private or civil right or to seek a civil remedy; a non-criminal action

Civil court A court handling civil actions, i.e., non-criminal matters

Civil law Law concerned with citizens and private matters

Civil liberties Personal rights and immunities from government

Civil procedure The laws governing procedure and practice

Civil rights The rights of all citizens to personal liberties, freedom, and equality; rights specifically granted through laws enacted by communities, as opposed to civil liberties, which are rights that the government is not allowed to restrict

Civil service The professional staff and workers of a government

Civil The branch of law that handles private matters as opposed to criminal law

Claim A demand for something that one considers one's own, a cause of action, a right enforceable by the court

Clear title A title free of encumbrances; good title

Client An individual or organization that employs a professional to provide that professional's services; someone who employs a lawyer to represent him or her in court, to draft legal documents, to advise, or to provide other legal services

Conclusive evidence Incontrovertible confirmation of facts establishing proof of a case

Code A systematic collection of laws, regulations, or rules, e.g., civil code

Coerce To force someone to act against his or her wishes, through the use of verbal or physical threats or other forms of compulsion

Cognizance Jurisdiction or judicial notice

Cohate Completed, e.g., *cohate lien,* a lien that has been perfected and can be enforced

Co-heir One of two or more heirs inheriting from the same estate

Collateral estoppel A doctrine holding that a judgement on issues litigated by two parties is binding on them for those issues in all subsequent actions with different causes of action

Collateral Something pledged as security for a loan, to be forfeited if the debt is not paid

Collective bargaining Negotiation and dispute resolution over employment matters between a representative group of employees and the employer, as in labour union

Collude Conspire; to agree secretly to commit some fraudulent act

Colour Appearance as opposed to reality; disguise; hiding facts behind a false legal theory

Commit Bind oneself to someone or something

Commitment (1) The act of committing. (2) An obligation

Common law A system of law based on judicial precedent and custom rather than statute and code; the system of jurisprudence used in England and the Commonwealth countries; India is the largest country in the world practicing this law

Commune bonum (*Lt*) The common good

Communi consilio (*Lt*) By common consent

Company A group or association of people with the purpose of running a business or commercial enterprise; a business

Compensate (1) To give someone money to make up for an injury he or she has suffered. (2) To pay someone for work he or she has performed - compensation

Competency Ability to stand trial or serve as a witness

Competent court A court with proper jurisdiction

Complainant A party who brings a legal complaint against another

Complaint (1) The pleading that begins a civil lawsuit, in which the plaintiff sets forth his or her causes of action and demands relief. (2) In criminal law, a charge made before a magistrate that a particular person has committed an offence, in an effort to begin the process of prosecution

Compliance The practice within a business of ensuring that all personnel are following applicable laws, rules, and regulations

Compos mentis (*Lt*) Of sound mind (and judgement) sane and mentally, competent

Compromise Presupposes an existing dispute in which willingness is shown to for settlement or adjustment of claims through mutual concessions

Concealment Intentional withholding of information

Conclusion of law A court's legal conclusions about a case arrived at through application of law

Condemn Declaring someone guilty of a crime

Condition State of affairs; proviso

Condone Reluctant approval

Confer (*cf.*) (*Lt*) Compare

Confess Admittance of committing an act

Confirmation Formal approval, ratification, endorsement

Confiscate Take someone's private property for public use

Conflict of interest Concerns moral dilemma, when two duties are at odds with one another

Conflict of laws Arises out contradictory laws or of confusion of legal jurisdiction

Conform: Comply with stated rules or standards

Conjecture Tentative conclusion or opinion based on limited Information

Conjunctive denial A single collective denial of several facts stated in a complaint

Conscience Individual moral sense; a personal standard that guides a person's view of what is right and wrong

Consent Expression of one's will; voluntary action; essence of a contract

Consequence The result that naturally follows a cause

Conservator Someone appointed by a court to manage an estate, a business, or the personal affairs of someone unable to manage

Consideration A payment made in agreement to an exchange to seal a contract

Consign Entrust goods to someone else, to deliver goods to the custody of a carrier or agent, usually so that they can be sold

Consignee The recipient of consigned goods; the person named as recipient in a bill of lading

Consignment The act of consigning

Consolidated appeal A single appeal filed by more than one appellant whose interests are similar enough to make their combination feasible

Consolidation of actions Combining several related lawsuits into a single action

Consortium An association of several companies that join together to pursue a common object for a specified period of time, in which the members do not assume liability for one another's actions

Conspiracy Two or more people who join together to plan and commit an unlawful act

Constitution A collection of fundamental principles of law according to which a nation or organization is to be governed

Construct An idea composed of various conceptual elements

Constructive contract A contract not intentionally entered into by the parties, that arises legally to prevent injustice—*quasi contract*

Constructive notice Notice implied by law, usually because it is in a public record

Construe To find the meaning in words or actions

Consultant An expert whose services are for hire

Consumer goods Goods bought for personal use by an individual, household, or family, and not intended for resale

Consumer protection laws Laws regulating sales and credit practices intended to protect consumers

Consumer A person who buys goods and services for one's use

Contempt of court Disregard of court's orders

Contingent Depending on something; occurring if some specified condition occurs; provisional, e.g., contingent beneficiary, contingent interest, contingent liability

Contra (*Lt*) Against

Contraband Illegal goods; goods that are illegal to possess, e.g., narcotics or counterfeit money

Contract An agreement between two or more parties. Kinds of contract: bilateral, oral, unilateral, etc.

Contractor A person who contracts to do work for someone else, on an independent basis, using his or her own materials and methods and not under the control of the customer with regard to the details of how the work is done

Contributory Once the winding-up of a company has been set into process, the persons liable to contribute to the assets of the company—members, fully paid-up shareholders—are called contributories

Controversy A dispute that can be litigated in court; a civil action or lawsuit

Convertible securities Bonds or preferred stock that can be exchanged for common stock or another lesser security, generally within the same company

Convey To transfer property from one person to another

Convict One who has been found by a court to be guilty of a crime

Conviction A legal act of finding someone guilty of a crime at the end of a prosecution, including the judgement or sentence

Cooperative A business owned and run by its members for the purpose of mutual help, in which profits and costs are shared

Copyright The legal right to publish, perform, or display a work of literature, art, music, drama, recording, film, etc

Corporation A legal entity, distinct from its members, with perpetual existence and seal

Corrigenda (*Lt*) A list of things to be corrected

Corroborating evidence Supporting facts that agree with the already presented evidence

Corruption Abuse of an official position for personal gain

Costs The expenses involved in taking a case to trial, sometimes awarded to the victorious party; costs usually do not include lawyer's fees

Counterfeit Fake, forged, copied with the intention of passing off as authentic

Court A court of law

Covenant A contract, formal agreement; often produced in writing and signed by all parties

Credit rating A number calculated by examining a person's assets, liabilities, and financial history that tells a lender how likely that person is to pay back a loan

Creditor A person or business to whom a debt is owed

Crime against humanity An attack on or persecution of a group of people who are part of a widespread practice or governmental policy that results in serious attacks on human dignity or degradation of the victims, including widespread rape, murder, torture, or racial, political, or religious persecution

Crime, white-collar A crime usually done by professionals and businesspeople, such as extortion, computer crime, wire fraud, and government contract fraud—felony, misdemeanour

Crime An act that violates criminal law

Criminal law The branch of law that deals with the prosecution and punishment of criminals

Criminal procedure The body of law that governs actions in criminal courts, including investigation, prosecution, and punishment

Culpa (*Lt*) Fault, blame; culpable: deserving blame; culprit: one who commits crime

Cum With

Curriculum vitae (*Lt*) The course of one's life

Custody (1) Responsibility or guardianship of a person or thing. (2) Arrest followed by confinement

Custom The traditional, ordinary, and accepted way of doing things in a particular community; usage that acquires force of law

Customer Someone who buys goods or services

Customs The government agency that collects tariffs and taxes on imports; also the place at an airport, port, or border crossing where imported goods are inspected

Cyber crime A crime committed using computers, networks, or the Internet

Cyber law The field of law that encompasses issues involving computers, networks, and information technology

Cyber space The non-physical territory occupied by the Internet and computer networks

Cyber squatting Registering a trademarked name as a domain name with the intention of selling it to an individual or company that actually owns the trademarked name enforceable by law

Dacoity (*Hindi*) Gang robbery committed by five or more persons (Sec. 391, the Indian Penal Code, 1860)

Damage Harm or loss

Damages Compensation for loss; known as the doctrine of restitution (Sec. 73, the Indian Contract Act, 1872)

Dangerous instrumentality Something that can endanger people by either careless or improper use

Dealer One who buys something to resell it

De bene esse (*Lt*) Used to describe a legal proceeding that is done provisionally and let stand for the time

being, but that can be challenged in the future; e.g., a witness cannot appear to testify

Debenture An unsecured loan instrument issued by a company with good credit ratings and backed by a promise to pay; the holders of debentures are creditors of a corporation and if the corporation dissolves, they receive payment before stockholders

Debtor (1) A person who owes a debt to someone else; see (2) A person subject to bankruptcy proceedings

Decide Come to a conclusion or resolution after deliberation and consideration; to determine something

Decision Conclusion reached after considering facts and applicable law if necessary—a judicial determination or judgement

Declaration (1) A formal announcement or statement. (2) According to common law, the first pleading presented to the court by a plaintiff, similar to a complaint in structure and purpose. (3) As evidence, an unsworn statement made by a witness, a party to a lawsuit, or a person who subsequently died. (4) When entering a country, a statement of goods brought into the country by the person entering

Declaration, dying Last statement before an unforeseen, untimely death which in law has the force of evidence

Declaration against interest An out of court which is so disadvantageous to the person making it that it is presumed to be true

Decree Judgement; judicial decision of a court in equity made after hearing testimony and determining the rights of the parties

Decree nisi A conditional judgement that will be made permanent unless a party can show the cause as to why it should not be

Deduction, standard A standard amount that a taxpayer may deduct from gross income instead of itemizing individual expenses

Deed A written instrument, signed and delivered, by which one person conveys land or property to another

Deed of trust A deed that transfers the title of property to a trustee as a security

De facto In fact, in reality; used to describe a situation that is for all practical purposes the case, though it might not be legal or official—*de jure*

Defalcate Embezzle funds; fail to pay over trust funds or other money held in a fiduciary capacity at the proper time

Defamation Slander, libel; intentional publication or public statement of false information that damages someone's reputation. (Secs 499–502, the Indian Penal Code, 1860)

Default Failure to perform a legal duty or meet an obligation

Default judgement Judgement entered against a defendant who fails to defend himself or herself by responding to the plaintiff's complaint or appearing in court

Defeasance Rendering something null and void, e.g., a deed or a will

Defective pleading Insufficient or inaccurate pleading in substance or form

Defective title Unmarketable title; a title obtained by fraud or not, in fact, entirely owned by the purported owner

Defendant The party against whom a lawsuit is brought; in civil cases, the party who responds to the complaint; in criminal cases, the person against whom charges are brought

Defense A response, reason, or allegation offered by a defendant to a lawsuit as to why the plaintiff has not established a claim and should not receive relief; a denial of the plaintiff's claims or an attack on the validity of the plaintiff's causes of action

Defer Postpone; put off or rearrange at a later date, e.g., deferred compensation, payments

Deficiency Lacking in something

Deficiency judgement A judgement issued against someone who holds a mortgage, imposing personal liability on him or her if a foreclosure sale does not yield enough money to cover the mortgage debt

Deficit Shortfall; a condition brought about by spending more money than is earned; in accounting, the opposite of surplus

Defraud Cheat someone; misrepresent a fact intending for someone to rely on it and thereby harm him or her

Degree (1) The amount, level, or extent of something. (2) A certificate awarded to those who finish a course of study at a university or college

Degree of proof Level of proof needed to convince a court to render a verdict for a particular case; evidence that is beyond reasonable doubt

De jure (*Lt*) By law, by right; the condition of being in compliance with all applicable laws; legitimate and lawful. Cf. *de facto*

Delegate Entrust someone with a task or responsibility; to transfer one's authority to another person. A person appointed to represent someone else

Deliberation Careful consideration of a matter, weighing all arguments and evidence

Delict Violation of the law; a tort, injury, or crime; *Ex delictio*—arising out of a tort

Delinquent Person, neglecting one's duty; failing to pay a debt; guilty of a crime or failure of duty

Delinquent child Juvenile delinquent; a minor below a specified age who tends to commit crimes or otherwise engages in immoral or disobedient behaviour and therefore needs treatment or supervision

Delist (Noun—**delisting**) Delete something from a list; usually refers to removing a security from an exchange for failing to meet the minimum requirements for listing

Deliver Hand over to something to someone else; to voluntarily transfer title or possession of something to someone else's possession or control

Delude Deceive someone or persuade him or her to believe something that is false

Delusion Erroneous belief that is contrary to fact

Demand Claim by right

De minimis (*Lt*) Insignificant or unimportant; not of a level to interest the law

De minimis non curat lex (*Lt*) The law does not care about insignificant matters

Demise Death of a person; conveyance of a property at transfer or at bequeathing

Demit Resign from an office

Demonstrate Prove the truth of something by using evidence and arguing logically

Demur Object to a point of law or fact alleged by the opposing party on the grounds that it does not advance the interests of the party making the statement

Denial Refutation of all allegations as entirely false

Denounce Publicly declaration of someone or something to be morally wrong or evil; to inform against someone, usually in order to allow the authorities to arrest that person

De non apparentibus et non existentibus eadem est ratio (*Lt*) That which does not appear will be presumed to exist

Dependent: Sustained by outside support

Dependent coverage Insurance protection for dependents of the insured

Dependent promise A promise in which the promisor does not have to perform until the other party has done some agreed-upon duty first

Deponent A witness who testifies in the court under oath

Depose Questioning of a witness at a deposition

Depredation Large-scale plunder; pillage

Deputy Someone empowered by a superior to exercise the functions of the superior's office and to act on the superior's behalf

Derelict Neglected; abandoned; homeless person or abandoned property

Derivative action   A lawsuit brought on behalf of a corporation by a shareholder

Derivative mortgage   Sub-mortgage

Derivative tort   (1) A civil action in tort based on an injury caused by criminal conduct by the defendant, where the plaintiff seeks compensation for the injury, independent of a criminal action brought for the same offence. (2) Tort liability imposed on a principal for a wrong done by one's agent

Derogation   Partial repeal or relaxation of a law

Descent   One's family origin; heredity; the transmission of property and goods by inheritance

Detain   Taking into custody; to arrest

Devise   Concerning bequeathing of a property made in a will

Devolve   Transfer from one person to another as a result of the operation of law and without any intentional act by either party; e.g., inheritance

Dictum   Statement or observation made by a judge about a case; it is not the judgement

Direct evidence   Evidence that proves a fact directly, without inference or presumption

Disability   Lack of legal capacity, caused by a condition such as infancy or insanity

Disbar   Expulsion of a lawyer from the bar cancelling to licence to practice law

Discharge   (1) Performance of one's duty. (2) Satisfy a debt; (3) Dismiss or release someone

Disclaimer   Denial of something, usually one's own responsibility; a denial of someone else's claim

Disclose   Release of information by the parties to a case or in taxation matters

Discretion   (1) Freedom and authority to decide how to act; the power given to public. (2) The ability to recognize the difference between right and wrong. (3) A judge's freedom to make decisions one sees fit, bound by the principles of law

Discrimination   Unequal or unfair treatment of people based on gender, race, region, religion, etc.

Dishonour   (1) Disgrace. (2) Refusal to accept a negotiable instrument such as a promissory note or cheque, etc.

Dismiss   (1) Permit to leave. (2) Termination of employment. (3) For a judge to refuse to consider a lawsuit further, thereby ending it before a trial is completed

Dismissal with prejudice   A dismissal that prevents the plaintiff from ever suing on that cause of action again, considered a judgement of the case on its merits and thus *res judicata*

Disqualify   Pronouncing a person ineligible to perform a particular task, usually due to some offence or failure to observe applicable rules

Dissent   Disagreement or contrary opinion used by one or more judges presiding on the same bench

Dissolution   The act of terminating something, such as a business, partnership, or contract; the termination of a corporation's legal existence, etc.

Dissolve   Closure or annulment; ending the legal existence of a corporation

Distribution, corporate   A corporation's paying out money to shareholders, such as accumulated earnings in the form of dividends

Distributive share   A share that an heir receives from an intestate estate or that a partner receives from a dissolved partnership

Disturb   Interfere with peaceful, normal conditions; to throw into disorder; to intrude or interrupt

Dividend   Corporate profits and earnings distributed to shareholders in proportion to the number of shares they own. It may be cumulative, preferred or stock

Divorce   The legal dissolution of a marriage

Document of title   A written document that supplies proof that a person is entitled to receive and hold particular goods

Domain   (1) Total ownership of land. (2) The property owned by a nation or state

Domain name system   The system used to identify information on the Internet by linking domain names with computer-readable addresses

Domicile   (1) Refers to one's legal home; the country or state that a person considers his or her permanent residence, even one is living elsewhere. (2) The place where a corporation conducts its affairs

Double jeopardy   A second prosecution for an offence after the defendant has already been tried for it and acquitted

Dower   In common law, a widow's right to a life estate in her dead husband's property; no longer exists in most states

Due care   The legal duty a person owes to others in order not to be negligent; care that is sufficient and proper for the circumstances

Due process   The guarantee of a fair civil procedure that follows the rules, including the right to be notified about a complaint or charge and the right to be heard in court

Due process of law   Fair judicial treatment guaranteed to every citizen

Dummy corporation   A corporation with no legitimate business purpose

Dump   Sale of goods in quantity at a price far below market value, often in a foreign market

Duplicity Double-dealing; in common law, the error of combining two separate causes of action in one count of a pleading

Earmark A symbol of identification

Earnest Something that one person gives another to mark a promise or bind a contract, such as a token, pledge, or partial payment; e.g., earnest money

Easement A right to use someone else's property for a specific purpose; e.g., easement access: the right to enter another's property. (Sec. 4, the Indian Easement Act, 1882)

Eavesdrop Secretly and unlawfully listening in an to a conversation directly or through the installation of a listening or recording device outside a private place, or intercepting communications over telephones or other devices

Ecclesiastical law Church law

Egalitarian Supporting equality and fair treatment for all people

Ei incumbit prabatio qui dicit, non qui negat (*Lt*) The burden of proof lies on him who alleges, and not on him who denies

Ejectment A common law action brought by a property owner to eject a tenant who has refused to leave at the appointed time or someone claiming the land by adverse possession

Ejusdem generis (*Lt*) Of the same kind; a rule of interpreting statutes holding that if a statute lists a few examples of something, then it will be assumed that it only includes things similar to the examples; e.g., articles that a class of weapons would contain

Element A component of some abstract concept; e.g., equity being an element of law

Embezzle Misappropriate money or funds entrusted to one's care.

Encroach Gradual intrusion into someone else's property or territory.

Encryption Conversion information into code that can only be deciphered with a key

Encumbrance A mortgage, debt, or other burden on a piece of property

Endorse Signing on the back of a cheque or other negotiable instrument to make it payable to someone else; also technically written as indorse. (Sec. 15, the Negotiable Instruments Act, 1881)

Endow Donate; to provide financial support by granting property or an income—an endowment granted for a purpose

End user license agreement A contract presented by a software producer to the product's end user, i.e., the person who has acquired the software in order to use it, stating the terms and conditions associated with using the software—browse wrap agreement, click-wrap agreement, shrink-wrap agreement

Enforce Take action to ensure that a law is upheld

Enfranchise Granting of the right to vote; require someone to do something

Entail (1) Effecting of certain inevitable consequences. (2) Settlement of the inheritance of a property within a specific family line over generations, limiting it to particular descendants—entailment

Entitlement Claim, a right granted; a benefit or right guaranteed by law

Enumerated powers Powers expressly granted by the Constitution to a branch of government

Ee pluribus unum (*Lt*) One out of many

Equality Basic right under the law, the condition of having the same opportunities, rights, privileges, and duties; e.g., equal opportunity of treating employees equally without any discrimination; equal protection to all citizens without discrimination

Equitable (1) Fair, impartial, just. (2) Arising in equity instead of law; e.g., equitable distribution where wealth is distributed fairly

Equity Fairness, justice, impartiality in matters of law

Equity, court of A court that hears cases and makes judgements according to the principles of fairness rather than strict letter of the law

Erroneous judgement A judgement rendered using a mistaken application of the law; also known as error of law

Escape clause A clause in a contract that allows the parties to it to break the contract without penalty if a specified event happens or under specified circumstances

Escheat Taking over of forfeited property

Eschew Avoid

Escrow A conditional deal in the hands of a third party; e.g., escrow account in a bank (the third party) holds the money until the contract is fulfilled where by the seller get the money and the buyer his property

Estate An interest in or ownership of land, all the money, property, and goods that one person owns

Estoppel A restraint or bar; a doctrine that prevents a person from doing or saying something that would contradict some earlier action or statement that another has relied on and the contradiction of which would hurt that other person. (Sec. 116, the Indian Evidence Act, 1872)

Euthanasia Mercy killing, e.g., painlessly killing someone who is suffering from a painful incurable disease or who is in a coma and has no hope of ever waking up

Eviction (1) Actual—Physically expelling the tenant from the property. (2) Retaliatory: Expelling the tenant from the property in retaliation for the tenant's valid complaints about the landlord

Evidence All that is used to prove the truth of an issue in court such as testimony, documents, objects, and anything else that could persuade the judge

Examination Formal testing according to regulations

Exceptio probat regulam do rebus non exceptis An exception proves the rule concerning things not excepted

Exception (1) An objection to a court's ruling or an error. (2) In insurance, a risk that is excluded from a policy. (3) Concerning property, a piece of land that is not included in a transfer of an estate or interest

Exchange (1) The act of giving one thing and receiving something else in return. (2) An institution that facilitates; e.g., bills of exchange, stock exchange, etc. (Sec. 138, the Indian Evidence Act, 1872)

Exchequer The national treasury

Excise A tax on certain actions or occupations, the manufacture and sale of particular items, or the transfer of property; also called excise duty

Exclusionary rule A rule stating that evidence found during illegal or unwarranted searches and seizures cannot be used at trial

Exclusive contract A contract in which a person promises to buy or sell from one source only

Exclusive control Control over something exercised by only one person or agency

Exclusive jurisdiction Power over a kind of lawsuit or person that is held by only one court or tribunal, requiring that all actions of that sort be heard there

Exclusive license A right granted by the owner of a patent to one person or agency to use, make, and sell the patented item

Exclusive use In trademark law, the exclusive right to use a specific mark and other marks

Excommunicate The act of expelling a person from a community

Exculpatory evidence Evidence that clears a defendant of the charge

Ex curia Out of court

Excursus A supplementary agreement or treaty

Excuse To forgive; to release from responsibility

Ex dolo malo non oritur action (*Lt*) A right of action cannot arise out of fraud

Execute (1) Carry out or perform. (2) Sign a legal document and perform any other tasks needed to make it legally binding. (3) Carry out death sentence.

Executive powers The power to enforce and carry out laws granted by the constitution to the executive branch or government

Executor A person chosen by a testator to carry out the will

Exemplar Evidence other than testimony taken from a defendant and used to identify him or her, including fingerprints, voiceprints, blood samples, handwriting samples, etc

Exemplary damages Damages awarded on top of actual damages if the wrong done to the plaintiff by the defendant was aggravated in some way

Exempt Free from obligation or liability; e.g., Tax exemption

Ex gratia Purely as a favour

Exhaustion of remedies Where every possible means to find a solution has failed before bringing the lawsuit or appealing to a higher court.

Exhibit A piece of physical evidence

Exigency Urgent need or emergency

Exile Banishment from a country

Exit Way out

Ex nudo pacto non oritor actio (*Lt*) No cause of action arises from a bare promise

Ex officio By virtue of one's office; implied powers of an office, although they may not be expressly stated; e.g., the chairman of a company is ex-officio chairman of the executive committee

Exonerate Absolve someone from a certain obligation; acquit; release someone from blame

Ex parte On behalf of one party to a case; e.g., a judicial hearing held for the benefit of one party only, without notice to or attendance by an adverse party

Ex parte injunction An injunction issued by a court after hearing only the party requesting it

Expert testimony Opinions sought from an expert to help judge with specialized evidence

Ex post facto (*Lt*) From the point of view of subsequent events; after the fact; retroactive; retroactive laws are against the legal principles

Expressio unius est exclusio alterius (*Lt*) That which is expressed is included and that which is not is excluded

Expropriation The act of dispossessing

Ex proprio motu Voluntarily

Expulsion The act of ejection out of a group or community, dismissal of membership, etc.

Expunge Erasing of objectionable documents, information, remarks, etc. A judge may order for certain reasons to destroy some records

Ex rights Without rights; the condition of a stock sold without rights to purchase more stock from the issuing corporation

Extenuation Mitigation of an act such as to make a crime appear less serious and make the one who committed it appear less blameworthy than would actually be the case

Extinguish Termination of a right or contract by agreement between the parties or by operation of law

Extortion The act of obtaining something out of duress, threat or fear. (Sec. 383, the Indian Penal Code, 1860)

Extradition The act of surrendering the custody of a person to another state where the alleged crime may have taken place

Extrajudicial An event that is not authorized and is outside the court; e.g., extrajudicial confession allegedly made under duress during police interrogation

Ex turpi contractu non oritur action No action arises on an immoral act

Eyewitness One who testifies to what he has actually seen

Fabricated evidence Fictitious evidence created to disguise the truth—a lie. (Sec. 192, the Indian Penal Code, 1860)

Facsimile An exact copy of something, usually a document

Fact (1) Anything, state of things, or relation of things, capable of being perceived by the senses. (2) Conscious mental condition. (Sec. 3, the Indian Evidence Act, 1872)

Factum negantis nulla probation No proof is incumbent on him who denies a fact

Failure of consideration A condition that occurs when a contract's consideration becomes worthless or no longer exists

Failure of justice Miscarriage of justice; a loss of rights or lack of reparation due to the absence of an adequate legal remedy

Failure of proof Inability to prove a side of a case

Failure to state a claim Lack of prayer by the plaintiff, a failure to define and support a cause of action sufficient to support a case in court, resulting in dismissal of the case

Fait (*Fr*) A short order or warrant by a judge to allow a process

Fait accompli Something done and cannot be undone

Fait jus, ruat justicia (*Lt*) Let the law prevail, though the justice fails

Fair Impartial and just; according to stated rules and standards

Fair hearing An administrative hearing authorized in a case where a normal judicial proceeding would not satisfy the requirements of due process, such as a case in which no judicial remedy is available or in which the plaintiff would have to suffer much more harm to be eligible for one

Fair use The legal use of copyrighted materials without the owner's consent or payment of royalties; whether a use is a fair use or an infringement of copyright depends on factors such as who is using the material, the amount used, and whether or not the user acknowledges the copyright

False pretences Intentionally using fraud or misrepresentation to obtain property or money

False representation Intentionally misleading someone either by lying or by failing to disclose a fact when the fact should have been disclosed

False statement A statement made by someone who knows it is false or who makes it recklessly without honestly believing it to be true, intending it to deceive

Fatal error An error at trial that hurts one party's case so badly as to be grounds for a new trial

Federation A union of states that share a central government but also govern themselves independently—the Indian federation consisting of Union and States

Felony A serious crime

Feudalism A social, economic, and governmental system common in medieval India where powerful kings ruled over the vassals who, in turn, ruled over zamindars; using them for military and tax collection purposes

Fiat An arbitrary and authoritative command; a decree

Fiat justicia (*Lt*) Let justice be done

Fiduciary A relationship of trust, particularly in financial matters; someone

Filibuster Excessively long speech used as a delaying tactic in a debate

Financial statement A report of the financial condition of a person or institution, including a balance sheet, an income statement, and charges

Finding of fact After due examination of facts, the court's way of determining a case

Fine Money that a person must pay as a penalty for a crime or wrongful act

Finis finem litibus imponit A fine puts an end to litigation

Firm offer An offer by a merchant to buy or sell goods made in writing and signed, assuring the other party that the offer will be held open for a specified period of time

Fixed assets The property that a business uses in its daily operations and will not convert into cash, such as premises, machinery, etc.

Fixed capital Money permanently invested in a company

Fixed income Regular income that does not fluctuate over a period of time

Fixture Object that is permanently attached to a building or property and is thus regarded as part of the property

Flim-flam Confidential fraud perpetrated with an aim get rich aim

Float The interval between when a cheque is deposited and when the money it represents is deducted from the writer's account

Floating capital Capital kept to meet current expenses, often kept in the form of current assets

Floating debt Short-term debt held by a business or government

Floating interest rate A variable interest rate that changes based on the money market

Forced sale A sale made by order of the court to enforce a judgement against the property owner

Foreclose End someone's right to a property; to take possession of mortgaged property as a result of the property owner's failure to make payments

Forensic medicine A branch of medicine that applies medical principles to the investigation of legal matters, especially the investigation of crimes that result in death

Forensics The application of scientific tests and techniques to the investigation of crimes

Forfeit Lose the right to something as a punishment; a right or thing lost as a penalty

Forfeiture The taking of property without compensation, usually as a punishment for breaking the law

Forgery Counterfeit; copying of a document, signature, work of art, or bank note with the intention of deceiving someone into thinking it is genuine

Forms of action The categories of legal actions available under common law

Forthwith Right away; immediately; at the first opportunity

Fortuitous Happening by chance rather than design

Four corners rule A rule requiring that the meaning of a document and the intention of its creator be determined by considering it as a whole and not in isolated parts

Fraud Intentional misrepresentation of the truth done to deceive or injure; mislead into surrendering a legal right or otherwise being injured. (Sec. 17, the Indian Contract Act, 1872)

Fraus omnia vitiate (*Lt*) Fraud vitiates everything

Free consent Willingly, without force or fear, voluntary—it forms the essence of an agreement, contract or covenant. (Sec. 14, the Indian Contract Act, 1872)

Freehold Property that the owner

Free on board A contractual agreement by a seller to deliver goods to a specified place without expense to the buyer

Freight (1) Goods transported by a carrier such as a truck, train, aircraft, or ship. (2) The cost of transporting goods by a carrier

Frivolous appeal An appeal that has no importance

Frustration Impossibility of performance of a contract, rendering it void. (Sec. 56, the Indian Contract Act, 1872)

Fugitive Someone who absconds or hides in an attempt to evade capture

Fungible Interchangeable; describes goods that are essentially identical to one another and that can replace one another, e.g., oil, grain, or money

Future interest An interest in real or personal property that will begin at some specified time in the future

Futures contract An agreement to buy shares of a commodity at a fixed price but with delivery and payment occurring at an agreed-upon date in the future; if the price of the commodity rises during that period, the seller pays the buyer the difference between the agreed price and the current price, and if the price of the commodity drops, the buyer pays the seller the difference

Gaining wrongfully/losing wrongfully When someone obtains and retains wrongfully/someone is deprived wrongfully (Sec. 23, the Penal Code, 1860)

Gag order An order issued by a judge prohibiting participants in a lawsuit from discussing the case publicly in order to protect the litigants' right to an impartial trial

Garnish Seizure of a person's property or salary to settle debt or claim

Garnishee Third party who is ordered by the court to surrender money or property owed to a debtor so that it can be used to pay the debtor's debt

Geneva Conventions Four treaties created in Geneva, Switzerland, between 1863 and 1949 that set standards for how member nations should treat prisoners of war and civilians during wartime

General power of attorney Legal authorization to represent a person on all general matters, as against particular ones

Gift Anything given freely and willingly; gift deed (Sec.s 122-129, the Transfer of Property Act, 1882)

Good faith Sincere intention to act as promised (Sec. 52, the Indian Penal Code, 1860)

Goods Every kind of movable property (Sec. 27, the Sale of Goods Act, 1930)

Good title A clear title to property that is valid and can be sold without encumbrance

Goodwill An intangible business asset composed of a good reputation with customers, suppliers, and the community at large, good employee morale, the ability to attract customers and clients, good management, and other positive aspects that are difficult to value monetarily but that contribute to the success of a business

Governance The act of control and regulation of the affairs of an organization, institution, nation, state, or group of people

Governing body A group or entity that controls the actions and policies of an institution, nation, state, group, or organization

Government The body that controls, influences, and regulates the affairs of a nation, state

Government company Where the paid up share capital by the government is not less than 5 per cent. (Sec. 617, the Companies Act, 1956

Government servant One employed by the authority of the government. (Sec. 14, the Indian Penal Code, 1860)

Grace period A period between an official due date and the time when an actual penalty will be imposed for failure to pay or perform; in insurance, the time between the due date of a premium and the time when insurance will actually be cut off if payment is not made

Gratis (*Lt*) Free; without charge

Gratuitous (1) Done for free; given without expectation of payment. (2) Unjustified; done without good reason

Gratuity Money or other property given freely, usually in return for some service or favour

Gray market Unofficial trade in something, especially of unissued shares of stock, controlled or scarce goods

Grievance A complaint; an allegation that someone has committed some injury or injustice that deserves recompense

Gross Income or profit, total, before deductions

Guarantee A promise or formal statement that specific conditions are the case or will be met

Guardian A person who looks after the legal and financial affairs or takes care of someone who is unable to look after his or her own because of age or disability

Guilt Culpability—the condition of having committed a crime or wrongful act; the fixing of responsibility for such an act

Habeas corpus (*Lt*) Literally—you must have the body. It is a writ that institutes a court proceeding to determine whether a criminal defendant has been lawfully imprisoned, or to test the constitutionality of a conviction; Only the High Courts and the Supreme Court of India have such powers to issue the writ. (Articles 226 and 32, respectively, the Constitution of India)

Habendum (*Lt*) Conveyance clause defining what estate or interest is granted by it

Habit Fixed course of conduct

Habitual offender A person who regularly commits crimes

Hack Break into a closed computer network by using software or clever programming

Harass (1) To pressure, intimidate, or attack repeatedly; to annoy; to insult or abuse verbally. (2) To bring a criminal prosecution against someone without a reasonable expectation of conviction

Harassment, quid pro quo Concerns sexual harassment in which a superior demands sexual favours from an employee as a condition of his or her continued employment, threatening to fire the employee if the demands are not met

Harassment, sexual Employment discrimination that involves sexual demands and acts, which can involve perpetrators and victims of either sex

Harmless error An error made by an appellate court during a trial that is usually trivial or academic, does not prejudice the rights of the party affected by it, and does not necessitate the reversal of thetjudgement

Hearing A legal proceeding, usually less formal than a trial, in which the parties to a case are given an opportunity to present evidence and testimony to a judge or other official who determines the facts and makes a decision based on the evidence presented

Hearing de novo A fresh hearing, as though the previous one did not exist

Hedge fund A mutual fund or partnership of investors that uses hedging techniques such as arbitrage, futures contracts, and selling short in an attempt to maximize profits

Heir A person legally entitled to inherit an estate if its owner dies without a will

Heretofore Before the present time

Hereunder Within or further on in the document

Holder A person with legal possession of a document of title, promissory note, check, or other instrument, and who is entitled to receive payment on it

Holder in due course A bona fide purchaser who acquires an instrument in good faith, for value, and without notice of any claim against the instrument

Hold harmless Indemnification—assumption of the liability for a situation, thereby absolving another party of any responsibility for it

Holding A court's ruling on an issue presented at trial; a legal principle produced by a court in deciding a case, e.g., 'the court held that…'

Holding company A company that exists solely to own the stock of or manage the affairs of another company

Honour (1) Acceptance of a cheque, credit card, or other form of payment. (2) A title of courtesy given to a judge, as in the phrase 'Your Honour'

Honourable discharge A declaration by the government or employers that the employee is leaving the service with good conduct

Honoris causa (*Lt*) As a mark of respect

Hostile witness A witness who expresses a bias adverse to the party examining him

Human rights The basic rights to which all humans are generally considered to be entitled, which can include life, liberty, freedom of speech, freedom of religion, due process, equal rights, and dignity. (Human Rights Act, 1993)

Hypothecate Pledging of money or property for a particular purpose, often as security for a debt

Ibidem (*Lt*) Often used as abbreviation in footnotes as already cited previous source in *ibid*, the same place

Idem (*Lt*) The same; used when citing a text that is part of the source that has just been cited in the immediately preceding reference

Illegal Forbidden by law

Ignorantia facti excusat (*Lt*) Ignorance of fact is excusable

Ignorantia legis neminem non excusat (*Lt*) Ignorance of law excuses nobody

Illicit Illegal; against rules or custom

Immaterial Irrelevant, not essential

Immaterial evidence Irrelevant evidence, no relation to what is under examination

Immoral Against accepted moral standards

Immunity Exemption or protection from something such as prosecution, duty, or penalty

Impeachment A criminal procedure in which a public official is charged with misconduct

Impediment A condition that prevents one from any valid action

Imperfect title Incomplete title

Impinge The act of intrusion, imposition or invade

Implicate Involving someone in an action which may not be true—incriminate

Implied condition Condition that is not express but follows as logical circumstance, e.g., where there is no express warranty. (Sec. 14, the Sale of Goods Act, 1930)

Impossibility, legal A condition arising when a law makes it impossible for a person to do a particular act; e.g., a minor cannot make a valid will

Impossibilium nulla obligato est (*Lt*) Impossibility is an excuse for the non-performance of an obligation. See **Frustration**

Impostor Someone presents himself as someone else with the intention of deceiving others to gain some benefit

Impound Seize and take legal custody of something, such as a vehicle

Impunity Freedom from punishment

Impute Attribution of charge

Impugn Challenge; dispute atjudgement and appeal in a higher court

In absentia (*Lt*) In absence; not physically present at an event

Inadmissible Not able to be admitted under the rules of evidence

Inalienable Not able to be taken away or given up without consent of the possessor

Inalienable rights Rights such as human rights cannot be taken away from or given up by anyone without his or her consent

In camera (*Lt*) In chambers; done in a judge's private chambers

Incapacity Inability to do or understand something; lack of physical, mental, or legal ability to do a particular task

Incarcerate Imprison

Incendiary Inflammable—more at provocative speech

Inchoate Not yet fully developed; incomplete

Incondite Badly composed document

Incontrovertible Irrefutable, indisputable, or unassailable

Incriminate Implication of a person into a crime

Incriminating evidence Evidence that helps establish the guilt of an accused person

Inculpate Accuse; blame

Incumbent A person who currently holds a particular office. Necessary; required as part of duty or responsibility

Indefeasible Not able to be defeated, annulled, or revoked

Indemnify Pay or reimburse someone for a loss or injury; to take on legal responsibility for someone else's actions; to insure

Indemnity Money given as compensation or reimbursement for a loss or injury; security against legal responsibility for one's own actions; the benefit provided by an insurance policy

Indemnity against liability A promise to take on another person's liability or compensate him or her if and when that liability arises

Indemnity against loss Compensation given to a person when he or she suffers a particular loss—*insure, subrogation*

Indenture Originated in British colonies as an agreement for labour, generally known as indentured servant. (1) A formal agreement conveying real estate from one party to another and binding both parties with obligations. (2) An agreement issuing corporate bonds and debentures, often between a corporation and an indenture trustee, who holds title to the trust property and carries out the terms of the agreement

Independent contractor A person who does a job for another person independently, using his or her own methods and is not under the control of the employer in regard to how the work is accomplished

Independent counsel A person or group of people appointed to investigate accusations of criminal conduct by a high-level public official

Index fund A mutual fund that chooses its stocks according to a stock market index number

Indict Charging a person formally with a crime—indictment

Indictable offence A crime that can be prosecuted by indictment, usually a serious crime

Indigenous Native to a place; an ethnic group that was present in a nation before the current population was created

Indigent Poor; poverty-stricken; destitute

Indigent defendant A criminal defendant who lacks the financial resources to pay for a lawyer to defend him- or herself

Indispensable evidence Evidence that is absolutely necessary to prove a particular fact

Indorse To endorse; to sign a cheque or negotiable instrument in order to transfer its payment to someone else—*indorsement*. (Sec. 16, the Negotiable Instruments Act, 1881)

Industrial dispute Disagreement between employer-employee relationships regarding, wages, working conditions and other terms and conditions. (Sec. 2, the Industrial Disputes Act, 1947)

In extremis (*Lt*) At the outermost limits, e.g., at the point of death; in extreme difficulty

Infer Conclusion through logical reasoning—inference

Inferior court A court whose decisions are subject to review by an appellate cour ; e.g., decisions of a trial court or tribunal may be reviewed by the High Court

Informal contract A contract that is valid without being executed formall; e.g., oral contract

Informed consent Consent given after learning and understanding all the relevant facts needed to make an intelligent decision, required in situations where someone is giving up rights, as when being arrested, or in potentially risky situations, such as surgery

Informer A person who confidentially gives information about a crime to the police

Infra (*Lt*) Below; as in a judgement where the judge refers to some information that is to be found further down in the document; opposite of *supra*: above

Infraction Violation of a law, agreement, or duty

Infringe Encroach or trespass on something; to violate the terms of a contract, right, or law; to violate a copyright, patent, or trademark by using it without permission or payment to the owner—*infringement*

Ingress Entrance; the act of entering or the right of entrance; opposite of egress

Inherent defect A defect built into an object that exists regardless of how it is used

Inherent powers Authority that is an intrinsic part of an office or position and that exists without being expressly granted

Inherent right A right that a person has simply by virtue of being a person and that is not granted from some outside source; e.g., being a member of an association gives a person certain automatic rights

Inherit Receive property or money as an heir after the owner's death; technically refers to receiving property by the rules of

Initial public offering Generally known through its abbreviation IPO. The first set of shares a new company sells on a public stock exchange, usually in an effort to raise money from investors in order to enlarge the company

Injunction A court order prohibiting someone from doing a specified act in order to prevent future injury; it may be mandatory or permanent or temporary. (Sec. 36, the Specific Relief Act)

Injure Harm or damage to a person or property

Injuria non excusat injuriam One wrong does not justify another

Injustice Violation of a right

In loco parentis (*Lt*) In the place of a parent; describes a situation in which someone (e.g., a teacher or counsellor) supervising a minor temporarily assumes the legal obligations normally held by a parent or guardian

Innocent Not guilty

Innuendo Suggestive remark, insinuation or hint; in a libel action, the part of the pleading in which the plaintiff explains the meaning of the allegedly libellous words

In perpetuity Forever; perpetual

In person Describes a situation in which a person actually attends a trial, hearing, or other event, and speaks for himself or herself, instead of allowing an attorney or other representative to appear and speak for him or her

Inquest A judicial investigation into the facts surrounding a death, conducted by a coroner or medical examiner; a court's inquiry into the facts surrounding an incident often made by a jury; sometimes called an inquisition

In re (*Lt*) In the matter of; concerning; in regard to; used to entitle judicial proceedings that do not involve adversaries but instead concern themselves with disposing of some situation, such as the settling of an estate

In rem (*Lt*) Against a thing; describes actions or proceedings concerning property rather than people, used in cases to determine title to or interests in property within the court's territorial jurisdiction and that are brought against the property itself, not against the people who own it

In rem, quasi Describes proceedings brought against a defendant personally but that which concern property, usually claims for money damages such as foreclosures or attachments

Insanity Madness or mental illness; the condition of being mentally ill to the point that one's perceptions and behaviour are seriously impaired and one is not responsible for one's actions

Insider In securities and corporations, someone who has access to information about a business that is not available to the general public, such as corporate directors, officers, and major stockholders; insiders are not allowed to buy and sell stocks in such a way as to take advantage of their privileged position and use it for personal gain

Insider information Information about a corporation that is available only to insiders and not revealed to the general public

Insider trading The illegal buying and selling of stock based on information available only to insiders

Insolvent Financially unable to pay debts—insolvency. (Insolvency Act, 1872)

Insufficient evidence The condition of not having enough evidence to support a claim at trial, determined by the court and resulting in a directed verdict for the defendant

Instrument, financial (1) Any contract that gives rise to a financial asset of one entity and a financial liability or equity instrument of another entity. (2) A tradable asset of any kind, either cash; evidence of an ownership interest in an entity; or a contractual right to receive, or deliver, cash or another financial instrument

Instrument, cash It is a financial instrument whose value is determined directly by markets. It can be divided into securities, which are readily transferable, and other cash instruments such as loans and deposits, where both borrower and lender have to agree on a transfer

Instrument, derivative It is a financial instrument which derives its value from the value and characteristics of one or more underlying entities such as an Asset an Index or an Interest Rate. It can be divided into exchange-traded derivatives and over-the-counter (OTC) derivatives

Insure Agreement to compensate someone for the loss of or damage to someone or something in exchange for payments of money; to assume the risk of loss or damage; to underwrite—*indemnify*

Intangible asset Property that has no physical substance but that nevertheless exists as a right, such as a patent, copyright, or goodwill; also called intangibles

Intention Purpose in one's mind, desire, willed action, voluntary, deliberated action—*intentional*

Intentional tort A tort committed deliberately with an express desire to harm

Inter alia (*Lt*) Among other things; used to avoid listing all the details of a statute or other document while noting that they exist

Interest (1) A right, claim, or title to something. (2) A share or stake in some undertaking; a personal stake in a matter. (3) Money paid at a specified rate on a regular basis for the use of a loan or to delay the date of repayment of a loan

Interest, vested A present interest in property that the owner is allowed to transfer in the present but might not be allowed to actually possess or enjoy until sometime in the future

Interim In the meantime; during intervening time; temporary

Interim order A temporary order issued to handle a matter until a specified event happens or until a final order is issued

Interlocking directors People who serve on the boards of directors of two or more corporations simultaneously, resulting in a situation called an interlocking directorate, which can be used to restrict competition and is often illegal under antitrust law

Interlocutory Temporary; provisional; issued as a temporary stopgap measure while a lawsuit proceeds

International Court of Justice The United Nations' Court seated at The Hague, Netherlands, that provides advice on questions of law and the writing of treaties and settles legal disputes between nations; its decisions are enforceable by the U.N. Security Council

International law The body of law that governs relations between different countries; composed of custom and practice, rules and statutes, international treaties, and other sources

Interpolate Insert words into a document, thereby changing its meaning

Interpret Explain the meaning of something, such as a statute, contract, or other document; to explain the meaning of the language of a law or other legal document without venturing into legal intentions and consequences—*construe, construction*

Interrogate Conduct questioning; to ask questions of someone such as a suspected criminal, often in a close or formal way—*interrogation*

Intervention A procedure in which someone who is not originally a party to a lawsuit enters it to defend his or her own interest in the matter

Intestate Without a valid will at the time of death

Intrinsic evidence Evidence produced by questioning a witness at trial

Intrinsic fraud Fraud that occurs during trial through perjury, forged documents, or hiding or misrepresenting evidence, which affects the outcome of the trial

Intrinsic value The inherent value of a thing, which remains constant regardless of place, time, or special features that affect its market value

Instrument A document by which a right or liability is created. (Sec. 2, the Indian Stamp Act)

Inure (1) To take effect; to benefit someone; to vest. (2) To accustom someone to something

Inventory A detailed list of property, such as goods in stock or the complete contents of an estate

Involuntary Done unwillingly, without choice

Ipso facto (*Lt*) By the very fact itself

Ipso jure (*Lt*) By the very law itself

Isonomy Equality of civil rights

J Abbreviation used for a judge or justice; JJ is used for judges or justices

Jeopardy Risk or danger; the danger of being convicted that is a natural accompaniment to being a defendant in a criminal trial. See also **Double jeopardy**

Joinder The act of uniting parties or causes of action to a lawsuit

Joint and several liability Liability for an enterprise shared by two or more people that can be applied to the group as a whole or to individuals, so that each is individually responsible for performing the entire obligation and each can be sued independently for failure to fulfil it, while at the same time the group is also responsible for the obligation and can be sued as a whole

Judex aequitatem simper spectare debet (*Lt*) A judge ought to always regard equity.

Judex est lex loquens (*Lt*) The is the speaking law

Judge An officer who presides over and decides cases in a court

Judgement The court's final decision in a trial

Judicature The extent of the powers of the court. (Judicature Act, 1873)

Judicial Related to the office of judge, judgements, the administration of justice, or courts; related to the interpretation and application of laws

Judicial activism A form of legal action in which a judge writes opinions and renders decisions based on progressive ideas of social justice instead of basing his or her decisions strictly on judicial precedent and a restrained interpretation of legislation

Judicial authority The power that comes as part of the office of judge; the power to hear cases and render decisions

Judicial immunity A judge's immunity from civil liability for anything done in his or her official capacity

Judicial notice A practice in which the court will recognize certain facts without requiring one of the parties to produce evidence proving them, usually in the case of facts that are universally acknowledged to be true or facts that the judge or jury already know

Judicial review The power of the courts to review the acts of other branches of the government, usually in order to determine that the law is properly applied to a matter, especially in constitutional matters; review by the Supreme Court of acts by the legislature

Judiciary The whole mechanism of the system of justice administration

Jump bail For a criminal defendant to leave the jurisdiction or fail to appear at trial after bail has been posted for him or her, causing whoever posted bail to forfeit it

Juridical Related to legal proceedings, judges, or the administration of justice

Juris (*Lt*) Of law

Jurisdiction (1) The authority or power to make judicial decisions; a court's or judge's power to investigate the facts of a matter, apply law to them, and declare a judgement (2) The territory in which a particular court can exercise its authority; the system of courts within a particular area

Jurisprudence (1) The philosophy or science of law. (2) The body of law formed by cases and interpretations of them

Jurist A scholar of the law; a lawyer or judge

Jury A group of people selected and sworn to hear the evidence in a case and decide what the true facts are; usually composed of a cross Sec. of the community. India has abolished the jury system and replaced by the Bench comprising of one or several judges

Jus cogens (*Lt*) Compelling law; a peremptory norm; in international law, a principle that is widely accepted to be true by a large number of states and individuals; e.g., it is commonly held that genocide, human trafficking, slavery, etc., are wrong

Just Fair; lawful; morally right

Just cause A legitimate or fair reason for doing something

Just compensation Compensation given to an owner whose property is taken through eminent domain that is fair both to the owner, who is losing property, and to the public, who is paying for it

Justiciable Able to be tried in court; presenting real interests instead of merely hypothetical or abstract ones

Justifiable Defensible; able to be proven to be reasonable or correct

Juvenile A child; a person below the age of legal majority

Juvenile court A court that hears cases involving children and teenagers, particularly over juvenile delinquents and neglected children

Juvenile delinquent A minor who commits a crime or engages in regular criminal activity

Kangaroo court A sham court; a court without legal authority that punishes unfairly and without due judicial process

Kickback A payment made by a seller to a buyer or agent in order to persuade him or her to enter into the transaction

Kidnap Unlawfully and forcibly take and carry away a person

Kingpin The key person in an act

Kleptomania A psychological disorder that compels one to steal

Knock down Tapping the article for auction with the auctioneer's hammer

Knockout auction An auction in which the bidders league together to keep the bidding low

Labour dispute A disagreement between employees and their employer about the terms and conditions of employment

Labour relations The relationship between employers and employees, usually as personified by management and employees

Labour union An organization of workers in a particular field that exists to handle disputes between the workers and their employers, working under the assumption that the workers have more power when they join forces and negotiate as a unit

Laches Culpable negligence in asserting or enforcing a claim

Laches, estoppels by Principle prevents a person from suing for a grievance that happened a long time ago

Landmark decision A decision or judgement of the court that changes the established law in an area

Lapse The expiration of a right or privilege due to failure to exercise it or otherwise maintain it

Lata culpa dolo aequiparatur Gross negligence is equivalent to fraud

Latent ambiguity Language that appears to be clear and understandable but that in fact presents ambiguities or confusion when someone tries to apply it

Latent defect A defect in an object that is not apparent on reasonable inspection or through the use of ordinary care

Launder To move money through different businesses, accounts, and banks in order to conceal its origins; obscuring the source of money obtained through illegal means such as drug dealing, racketeering, and other crimes—*money laundering*

Law (1) A system of rules created by a society to regulate behaviour and punish crimes. (2) A statute. (3) The professional field concerned with the rules that regulate society

Law, at Pertaining to law; related to the law or the legal profession

Law enforcement Seeing that people follow laws and catching and punishing lawbreakers; the police enforces the law

Law of the land The established law of a society, especially the principles of due process and other

Law of the sea United Nations Convention on the Law of the Sea; an international agreement that sets rules for the use of the world's oceans, establishing territorial boundaries and governing the management of marine resources

Lawsuit An action at law or equity; a dispute brought before a court for determination

Lease A contract in which the owner of a piece of property allows someone else to possess it exclusively for a specified period of time in return for payment. (Sec. 105, The Transfer of Property Act, 1882)

Leasehold An estate in real property held by lease, usually of a fixed duration

Leave Permission granted by the judge

Legacy A bequest; money or property left to someone by a will

Legal capacity to sue The right to bring a lawsuit; the condition of being of sound mind, being of legal age, and suffering from no legal rest raints or other impediments to bringing a lawsuit

Legal cause The conduct or event that directly causes an injury

Legal detriment Injury or disadvantage caused to someone who acted in such a way as to change his or her legal position or assume a liability or duty based on a promise that another person made but did not keep

Legal duty An obligation required by law

Legalese The formal language used in legal documents

Legal fiction An assumption that certain facts are true that is made by the court in order to render a legal decision without delay

Legal name A person's or association or corporations official name registered with the government

Legal tender Monetary currency such as notes, coins

Legislate Passing of law; legislation, the act of making laws

Lend Let out something temporarily, on the understanding that it will be returned; provide someone with money to be returned eventually with interest

Lender A person or organization that lends something or money

Lessee A person who holds property through a lease; a person who rents property; a tenant

Leaser A person who rents or leases property to someone else

Letter of intent A document that records the intention of the parties to it to enter into a contract or take some other action but that is not itself a formal contract

Letter of the law A strict, literal, word-for-word interpretation of laws and statutes as opposed to the *spirit of the law*

Levy Tax, fee, or fine on someone

Lex (*Lt*) Law

Lex loci (*Lt*) The law of the place

Lex non cogit ad impossibilia (*Lt*) The law does not compel that which is impossible

Lex posterior derogat priori (*Lt*) A later act overrules an earlier act

Liability Legal obligation or duty; an obligation or duty to do something or pay a sum of money; a possible claim against a person or business

Libel A written, printed, or published false and malicious statement that injures someone's reputation; the written form of defamation

Liberty Freedom—fundamental right

License (1) A permit that allows someone to do some act; permission to do something that would be illegal without that permission. (2) Permission to use property owned by someone else, which does not give the licensee an exclusive right of possession

Lien A claim placed on property to act as security for a debt owed by the owner, held until the owner pays the debt and kept if the owner never pays

Limitation A restriction; a restriction of the time in which a lawsuit can be filed; a restriction of who can receive an estate in property or the uses to which an estate may be restricted

Limited Restricted in size, time, or extent

Limited jurisdiction Jurisdiction over only specific kinds of cases or otherwise restricted by statute

Limited liability Liability for corporate losses that is restricted in some way, usually to the amount that an investor or shareholder has placed in the corporation and not reaching personal assets

Limited liability company A business organization, often managed by its members, with limited liability and limited ability to transfer ownership

Limited partnership A form of partnership in which one or more general partners manage the business and are personally responsible for its debts, and one or more limited partners contribute money and earn profits but do not run the business and are not liable for its debts

Line of credit An amount of credit available for a specified time to a consumer that the consumer may access as he or she chooses; a standing loan available for a preset time period

Liquidate (1) Convert assets into cash; to sell assets. (2) To settle; to pay debts; to settle the affairs of a business by determining debts and apportioning assets

Liquidity The amount of cash available to a person or business; the ease with which a person or business can obtain cash

Listed stock Stock in a company that meets the Securities and Exchange Commission's requirements and is traded on an organized stock exchange; also called a listed security

Listing Entering into a contract to place a company's stock on a stock exchange

List price The publicly advertised price of an item

Litigation A lawsuit or legal action; the act of bringing or defending a lawsuit

Living wage A wage sufficient to meet ordinary living expenses—*minimum wage*

Loan shark A person who lends money at extortionate interest rates, usually illegally

Lobby Attempt to influence a politician on a particular issue

Lockout An employer's refusal to allow employees to work during periods of negotiation; the employer's version of a strike

Locus contractus (*Lt*) The place where a contract was made

Long-term capital gain or loss A gain or loss that occurs from the sale of capital assets that have been held for the required length of time, usually at least one year

Loophole An ambiguity in a law; an inadequacy in a law that allows a person to legally avoid complying with it, especially in tax laws

Liquidation A term similarly used as winding-up to mean a process through which the life of the company is ended and assets administered amongst its creditors and members

Liquidator It is a person who appointed by the legal authority to oversee the process of winding up or liquidation of a company

Magistrate A public official with judicial, executive, or legislative power granted by the government, often functioning as a judge over minor matters or a justice of the peace

Magna Carta (*Lt*) Great Charter; an agreement signed by King John in England in 1215, guaranteeing political rights and liberty to his nobles and forming the foundation of English rights and privileges

Mailbox rule A doctrine in contract law stating that an offer is accepted at the time a written acceptance is deposited in the mail

Maintenance (1) The upkeep of property. (2) Providing financial support for another person

Malfeasance Bad conduct; wrongdoing; a wrongful or unlawful act, particularly by a public official

Malicious Intending to do harm; done out of ill will and without justification

Malicious abuse of legal process Intentionally using the legal process for an improper purpose

Malicious arrest Arresting on criminal charges a person who is known not to have committed a crime or arresting a person without probable cause

Malicious prosecution Criminal or civil litigation brought without probable cause and out of malice; if the defendant prevails in such a case, he or she may bring an action for the tort of malicious prosecution

Malpractice Incompetence or improper conduct by professional performing professional duties

Malpractice, legal Failure by an attorney to use the degree of skill or care that should ordinarily be exercised in a situation

Mandamus (*Lt*) A writ issued by a superior court to a lower court, corporation, or officer, ordering it to do some act that is a duty required of it by law

Mandate (1) A judicial order or command directing that some action be taken, especially from a higher court to a lower one. (2) Authority granted to a person to do some act, usually granted to an elected official by the electorate

Mandatory Required; compulsory

Manifesto A public declaration of political principles issued by a sovereign or politician; a formal document issued by an executive officer of a state declaring its reasons for taking some international action

Manifesta probatione non indigent (*Lt*) Manifest things require no proof

Manipulate To influence someone unfairly; to control someone's actions; to buy or sell a security in order to give a false impression about its value and thus influence the purchasing or selling decisions of others

Maritime law The body of laws governing travel and commerce on navigable waters

Marketable title Title to property that is free from encumbrances such that a reasonable person would accept it and that can be sold or transferred without impediment

Material Essential; important; relevant to establishing a cause of action or arriving at a judgement

Material alteration A change to a document that alters its original meaning or its legal effect. (Secs 87–89, the Negotiable Instruments Act, 1881)

Material evidence Evidence with a real bearing on the issues

Material fact A fact that is relevant and important to the matter at hand and that would influence the actions of other parties if made known to them

Material witness A witness who is the only person, or one of very few people, who can testify about a particular fact

Matter of law A question of the proper law to apply to the facts of a case, to be determined by the judge; also called a question of law

Matter of record An issue that can be proven by the official record on which it has been entered

May presume '… the court may presume a fact, it may regard such fact as proved, until and unless it is disproved, or may call for a proof for it.' (Sec. 4, the Indian Evidence Act, 1872)

Mediation A form of alternate dispute resolution in which a neutral third party, the mediator, hears the testimony of both parties to a dispute and tries to help them agree on a solution, but cannot impose a decision on them

Meeting of minds The state of agreement about the terms and conditions of a contract that the parties to it must reach for it to be validly created

Member firm A securities brokerage firm that belongs to a particular stock exchange

Memorandum (1) An informal document that records the details of a transaction, event, or agreement, or discusses some matter. (2) A document that examines the facts of a case and applies the law to it to see whether it has merit or not

Memorandum of understanding A legal document that expresses an agreement between two parties but that is not as formal or binding as a contract

Mens rea (*Lt*) The mental state that occurs when committing a crime, i.e., guilt, criminal intent, or knowledge that a crime is being committed; one of the four mental states in which a crime may be committed, i.e., intentionally, knowingly, recklessly, or negligently

Mental anguish Extreme distress, anxiety, and any other mental pain that is extreme enough to merit damages for the victim

Mental capacity A person's ability to understand what he or she is doing or the effects that other people's actions will have on him or her

Mental cruelty Behaviour by that endangers the mental health

Mercantile law Commercial law; the law that governs merchants, trade, and commerce

Mercy killing Euthanasia; killing a person or animal because continued life would be intolerable due to a painful, incurable illness or severe injury

Merits The legal substance of a claim or defence

Mineral rights The right to take minerals out of a particular piece of land

Minimum wage Minimum Wages Act, 1948

Minor A person below the age of majority

Minutes A transcript of a meeting or event; a record of court proceedings

Misappropriate Dishonestly take something that belongs to someone else and use it for oneself

Miscarriage An unsuccessful outcome, especially due to mismanagement

Miscarriage of justice Errors made by a court that damage the rights of a party sufficiently to warrant reversal of the decision

Mischief Harm; trouble; the act of damaging property or injuring a person intentionally or recklessly

Misconduct Improper behaviour; neglect of duties; mismanagement

Misconduct in office Unlawful or corrupt behaviour by a public official in the conduct of official duties

Miscreant A person who breaks a law or a rule; a person who behaves badly

Misdemeanour A minor crime

Misfeasance Doing a legally required duty in the wrong way

Misrepresent To make a false or inaccurate statement; to give the impression by words or behaviour that a situation is different from what is in fact the case

Mistake An incorrect or wrong action or belief; an act or omission caused by ignorance or misconception about the true situation

Mistake of law An error occurring when a party understands the facts but is ignorant or confused as to how the law applies to them

Mistrial An invalid trial

Misuse To use something in an improper or incorrect way; to use a product in a way not intended or reasonably foreseen by its manufacturer

Mitigate Make punishment less severe

Mitigating circumstances Circumstances that make a crime or offence less serious

Modo et forma (*Lt*) The manner and form

Modus operandi (*Lt*) A way of operating; a way of doing things; especially used to refer to a criminal's habitual methods

Modus vivendi (*Lt*) Way of living

Monopoly Exclusive possession or control of a supply of some commodity or an industry by one or a few people or businesses; a market condition in which a single person or company controls the entire trade in something

Moot To raise an issue for debate; to discuss

Moot case A case that seeks a decision on some issue that has no actual controversy or no practical application because the issue has already been resolved

Moral turpitude Depravity, dishonesty, or vileness; conduct that grossly violates acceptable standards of morality and behaviour

Moratorium A temporary stop to or prohibition of a particular activity; a temporary period in which debtors may postpone payment of debts

Mortality tables Actuarial tables that insurance companies use to determine how long a person is likely to live

Mortgage An interest in real property held by a creditor who lends money to a debtor to purchase the property and takes title to or a lien on the property as security for the loan

Motion A formal application to the court asking for a rule or order in favour of the applicant, such as a grant of summary judgement, of judgement

Motion to suppress In a criminal case, a request to exclude evidence that has been obtained illegally

Motive The reason for doing some act; the idea or circumstances that cause someone to do something

Move To make a motion

Multiplicity of actions Several lawsuits on the same matter brought by different plaintiffs against the same defendant—multiplicity of suits

Mutatis mutandis (*Lt*) The necessary changes having been made

Mutual fund A fund run by an investment company that pools the contributions of various investors who purchase shares in the fund, and invests them in a selection of publicly traded securities

Mutuality of obligation The principle that both parties to a contract are either bound to it or not, but one party cannot be bound if the other is not

Mutuality of remedy The principle that one party cannot receive an equitable remedy that the other party could not also receive

n/a Abbreviation (1) Not available; not applicable. (2) (*Lt*) *Non allocator*; not allowed

Quotation A computerized information system used in trading securities

Native A person who was born in a particular place

Naturalization The process of becoming a citizen of a country if one was not born there

Natural justice Those fundamental principles such as justice to be administered without bias, fair hearing to all the parties concerned and where reasons are provided; it is also known as substantial justice or ethical justice or fundamental justice

Natural law Moral rules and principles believed to govern human behaviour naturally, as an inherent part of human nature, regardless of laws enacted by people

Natural person A human being; an actual person instead of an artificial entity such as a corporation

Natural right Those incidents and advantages as provided by nature, e.g., use and enjoyment of property

Necessary Something indispensable, e.g., conservation of life

Negligence Failure to take due care

Negligence, criminal Negligence that can constitute a crime; such carelessness or disregard for the safety of others that it makes the actor criminally liable

Negligence, gross Failure to use even the slightest care

Negligence, wilful, wanton, or reckless Negligence done with complete disregard to the risks and with conscious indifference to the consequences

Negotiable instrument A legal document signed by its maker that promises unconditionally to pay a specified sum at a specified time to the person who presents it or to order, i.e., 'pay to the order of Mr X'; a check, money order, draft, note, certificate of deposit, or other similar document, as long as it can be transferred to another person

Negotiate Discuss a matter in an effort to reach agreement

Nemo dat quod non habet (*Lt*) No one gives what he does not have. It is one of the principles of the law of contract

Nepotism The practice by a public official or other person with power and influence of giving choice jobs to close relatives; preferential hiring of relatives

New matter In pleading, a new issue with new facts that has not been already alleged by a party and added by an amended or supplemental pleading

Next of kin The living person or people most closely related by blood to someone; the person or people who will take a decedent's estate under the rule of descent and distribution

Nihil ad rem (*Lt*) Nothing to do with the point. It is irrelevant to the case

Nihil obstat (*Lt*) Nothing stands in the way. There is no objection

Nisi (*Lt*) Unless; used to describe an order, judgement, etc., that will take effect unless some specific thing happens

No fault Used to describe a situation in which the fault of the parties is irrelevant to the outcome, such as an insurance policy in which the insurer will pay for damage regardless of whether the insured was at fault in causing it

Nominee A person who has been nominated for a position

Non compos mentis (*Lt*) Not of sound mind; insane

Nota bene (*nb.*) (*Lt*) Note well. Observe carefully

Non bis in idem (*Lt*) Not twice for the same thing. One of the principles where one cannot be punished twice for the same crime

Nonconformity An aspect of some object that does not conform to the prevailing standard for objects of that kind

Nondisclosure Failure to disclose information or reveal facts

Nonfeasance Failure to perform a duty

Non licet (*Lt*) It is not allowed. For instance the judge disallows a faulty argument or irrelevant evidence, etc.

Non liquet (*Lt*) It is not clear

Non sequitur (*Lt*) It does not follow. For instance in a faulty argument the conclusion is in variance with the premises or principle

Notary, public A person with the authority to perform a limited range of legal functions such as administering oaths, witnessing signatures, drawing up contracts or deeds, taking depositions, etc.

Notice Notification; warning or knowledge that a fact exists or that something will occur

Notice, legal Notice that the law requires to be given, such as by advertising in a newspaper; also, notice implied by law such as actual notice or constructive notice

Notice of dishonour Notice that a check or other negotiable instrument has been dishonoured

Null Invalid; void; with no legal force; also called null and void

Numerus clauses (*Lt*) A restricted number

Nudum pactum (*Lt*) A nude pact; an invalid agreement; a contract with illusory benefits or without consideration, hence, unenforceable

Oath The act of swearing that something is true; a promise to tell the truth in court or perform some act, often sworn before a witness or invoking a supreme power

Oath of office An oath sworn upon taking some office, promising to perform the duties of the office properly

Obiter dictum (*Lt*) Something said in passing; incidental remarks or opinions made by a judge that are not essential to judgement in a case

Objection The act of protesting an action or statement of the opposing party in order to draw the court's attention to illegality and impropriety and to preserve the issue for appeal

Obligation A duty; something that a person is required to do; a binding agreement that requires a person to do something

Offence An illegal act; an act that violates criminal laws

Offer To present something to someone to be accepted or rejected; an expression of willingness to do something or pay a sum of money; a promise to enter into an agreement if the promise is accepted

Offer and acceptance The two necessary components of a contract; a proposal by one party that is accepted by the other

Office, public An official governmental position that gives a person holding it some degree of governmental powers to be used to benefit the public

Officer A person who holds an office

Ombudsman An official in a government or company whose job is to hear, investigate, and remedy complaints

Omission The failure to do some duty or required action; the exclusion or leaving out of something or someone; overlooking something or someone. Vomit—to exclude

Onus (*Lt*) Burden; a duty or responsibility

Open court A court open to the public, to which anyone conducting themselves properly may be admitted

Operation of law The automatic effects of law; used in situations when the rights or liabilities of parties are determined by application of law, and not through their own private agreements

Operative Most relevant, meaningful, or significant; describes the word or words that carry the most important meaning in a sentence, or that cause a contract or document to take effect

Opinion, concurring An opinion written by a judge who is part of a bench of judges, agreeing with the conclusion of the majority opinion but not necessarily with the reasoning

Opinion, dissenting An opinion written by one of a bench of judges disagreeing with the majority opinion

Oral Verbal; stated in speech, not in writing

Order A command or direction; a direction issued by a court to direct an action or determine a point of law

Ordinance A law, statute, or rule, usually proclaimed by the President of India when the Parliament is not in session

Original document rule A rule that a party must produce the original of a document offered as evidence unless it is not available

Original jurisdiction Jurisdiction to try and judge a case at its beginning

Out-of-court settlement An agreement reached privately by the parties to a lawsuit, settling their grievances and ending the lawsuit without intervention by the court

Overbroad Used to describe a statute that covers too many situations, i.e., that, while legitimately forbidding certain conduct, inadvertently also prohibits constitutionally protected activities

Overdraft The condition of drawing more money out of an account than it has in it, such as by writing a check for too great an amount

Overhead Operating expenses

Overreaching Using fraud or a superior bargaining position to take advantage of someone else in a commercial transaction

Overrule Reverse or annul; to overturn or void the decision of another court

Overt act In criminal law, an open act done as part of a crime

Over-the-counter market A securities market of dealers who buy and sell securities that are not listed in a securities exchange, done primarily over the telephone or online

p.a. Abbreviation for *per annum*, yearly, annually

Pact An agreement between two or more parties

Par A standard or norm used as a benchmark for comparison; e.g., the face value of a stock, bond, or negotiable instrument, as opposed to market value; also called par value; par above or below as the case may be

Pardon Release a convicted criminal from liability for his or her crime; to absolve

Parity (1) Equality, particularly of pay or status; equivalence of goods. (2) A method of regulating prices for farm goods by making them equivalent to prices set on a particular date. (3) One country's value in terms of another's at a particular rate of exchange

Parliamentary law Rules governing procedure in a legislature; also called parliamentary procedure

Partner A person who shares the profits and risks of some business or other enterprise with one or several other people

Partner, limited A partner whose liability for partnership debts is limited to his or her share of contributed capital, and who has only a limited share of profits or losses

Partner, silent A partner who shares profits and losses but does not participate in the management of the enterprise; also called a dormant partner

Partnership An association between two or more people who call themselves partners and share the profits and risks of a business or some other undertaking

Partnership, limited A partnership with at least one general partner and at least one limited partner

Party A person or entity involved in some transaction or matter; a person or entity on one side of a lawsuit or other dispute

Patent An exclusive right granted by the government to manufacture and sell an invention for a specified period of time.

Patrimony Property inherited from one's father; property inherited from either parent or other ancestors

Pawn To give an object of personal property to another person, called a pawnbroker, as security for a loan

Payment in due course Payment to the holder of a negotiable instrument on or after its maturity date in good faith and with no known defects in title

Payroll A list of all the employees in a company and the amounts they are paid; the total amount a company pays its employees

Pecuniary Related to money

Penal code The codification of criminal law; criminal statutes

Penalty A punishment

Penalty clause A clause in a contract or agreement that describes a penalty for a breach, default, or other infraction, usually not enforceable by a court

Pendente lite (*Lt*) Pending the lawsuit; describes matters that must be put on hold to await the outcome of a lawsuit that will determine how they are settled

Per capita (*Lt*) By heads; according to the number of people; counting individuals and dividing something among them equally

Per curiam (*Lt*) By the court; by a judge's decision

Per diem (*Lt*) By the day; daily allowance of money

Peremptory Absolute; final; indisputable

Peremptory norm A principle of international law that is so important and so widely accepted that no state is permitted to deviate from it, such as the prohibitions on genocide, slavery, or piracy

Perfidy Treachery

Perform To do some act in fulfilment of a promise; to take the required steps to meet an obligation; to accomplish something

Perjury The crime of intentionally lying under oath during a judicial proceeding

Perpetrate To commit a crime or other wrongful act

Per se (*Lt*) In itself; intrinsically; by its very nature

Person A human being; an individual, corporation, partnership, trustee, labour organization, government, or other entity with defined legal responsibilities and rights

Personal liability Liability for a matter extending to an individual's personal funds and property

Persona non grata (*Lt*) Unacceptable person; one who is declared as without status

Per stirpes (*Lt*) By roots or by shoots, by the right of representation, i.e., according to one's lineage or stock

Petition A formal written request to a court asking it to take some judicial action

Place of business A place—domicile—where a business is run

Plagiarize To copy someone else's words or ideas and pass them off as one's own

Plain meaning An interpretation of a statute arrived at by reading its words and interpreting them according to their general, common meaning, usually without considering legislative history or other evidence to determine the intent of the people who drafted it

Plain view Those things that can be immediately seen without special effort because they are sitting out in the open and are unconcealed; incriminating evidence in plain view can be taken by police without a search warrant

Plaintiff A person who files a complaint to start a lawsuit

Plea In criminal law, a defendant's response to the charges brought against him or her

Plead To file a pleading in response to a plaintiff's complaint

Pledge (1) A promise. (2) An object given as security for a promise, contract, debt, or other obligation

Point An argument; a distinct proposition or issue of law; the relevance or reason of some argument

Point reserved A difficult legal issue set aside at trial for later consideration so that the court can proceed with other issues

Policy The principles that guide the actions of a government, business, or other entity or individual

Policyholder A person who owns an insurance policy

Polygraph A lie detector; a device that monitors heart rate, breathing, and other physical aspects of a person being questioned to predict the likelihood that he or she is telling the truth, but with debatable reliability

Ponzi scheme A kind of pyramid scheme in which a perpetrator promises high returns on an investment and uses money submitted by later investors to pay off earlier investors, but eventually runs out of money or disappears and the scheme collapses

Positive law Law created by a government and human institution to run society. See also **Natural law**

Post-date To enter a date on an instrument that is later than the date on which it is written

Post hoc ergo propter hoc (*Lt*) After this, therefore, because of this; the mistaken reasoning that if something happens after an event, it was necessarily caused by that event

Posthumous (*Lt*) After death

Practice Customary action or procedure; the established procedures of law and court proceedings

Prayer It is formal request in a complaint or petition in equity asking for relief for the plaintiff's grievance; also called a prayer for relief or demand for relief

Precedent A previously decided case that serves as a guide for deciding subsequent cases that have similar facts or legal questions

Pre-empt Acting before someone else; forestalling

Preferential Favouring one person or group over another

Preferred stock Stock that received dividends or distributions ahead of common stock

Prejudice Bias; prejudgement not based on actual experience or evidence; injury to a party that results from preconceived notions about the facts

Preliminary hearing An initial hearing on a criminal charge to give the judge a chance to determine whether the prosecution has enough evidence to bring the charge to trial

Premeditate Consider an act before doing it; to think out and plan a crime before committing it

Premium (1) A reward given for services rendered; a bonus; a sum added to wages or interest. (2) The fee paid for an insurance policy

Prerogative A right or privilege that is exclusive to a person, office, or class

Presentment (1) A written accusation of a crime created and signed and presented to the court. (2) The act of presenting a negotiable instrument to the person responsible for paying it in order to receive payment

Presumption An assumption that must be made by a court if certain facts are shown and that will stand until other facts are presented to rebut it

Presumption of innocence The assumption that a person is innocent until proven guilty

Presumptive evidence Evidence that is accepted as true until rebutted by contradictory evidence

Prevaricate Speak evasively; to act in a deceitful manner

Preventive detention Confinement of a criminal defendant before trial without the option of bail in cases where the defendant would pose an immediate risk to the public if released pending trial

Prima facie (*Lt*) First face; at first sight; based on first impressions; the initial view of something, accepted as true until disproved

Prima facie evidence Evidence sufficient to establish a claim or defence until rebutted by contrary evidence

Primary evidence The best and most important evidence in a case

Primary jurisdiction The principle that where an administrative agency has jurisdiction over a dispute, the courts will not hear the case until the agency has heard it first

Principle A fundamental truth, especially a moral truth that serves as a basis for action; a rule of action or procedure

Privilege (1) A right, immunity, or advantage held by only one or a few people, or only by a particular group or class. (2) An exemption from duties or requirements imposed on most people

Privity A relationship between parties that occurs when they share an interest in or right

Privy A person who shares privity with another

Privy council It was the Supreme Appellate Authority for India till October, 1949. It served also other British colonies around the world

Probation A sentencing procedure in which, instead of imprisoning a person convicted of a crime, the court releases him or her to the supervision of a probation officer, with the understanding that a violation of the terms of probation will result in a prison sentence

Pro bono (*Lt*) For the sake of good; describes work done without compensation, for the public good

Procedure The formal steps and methods used in conducting a lawsuit; there are civil and criminal procedures

Proclamation Official or public announcement, especially of some governmental action or policy

Proctor An agent or proxy; a person who manages another person's affairs

Proffer To offer; to offer or hold out something as proof or evidence

Pro forma (*Lt*) For the sake of form; as a matter of form, rather than based on facts

Prohibit To prevent; to forbid by law or rule

Promise A binding declaration that a person will do a certain act, which gives the person receiving the promise the right to expect performance

Promisee A person who receives a promise

Promisor A person who promises something

Promissory Implying or containing a promise

Promissory note A document in which the maker promises to pay a certain sum of money on a specified date

Promote To form a corporation and raise capital for it

Promulgate Announce a statute or rule officially

Proof The use of evidence or argument to establish a fact

Property That which is or can be owned, possessed, used, and disposed of; those things owned by someone. It may be common, intangible, movable, personal public or private

Proprietary Related to ownership

Pro rata (*Lt*) According to the rate; proportional or proportionately

Prosecute Start legal proceedings

Prospective law A law scheduled to be enacted at some future date and that will apply only to cases arising after it is enacted

Prospectus A document issued by a corporation disclosing its financial information to current and prospective investors

Protectionism The policy of limiting trade with foreign nations in an attempt to protect domestic producers

Protective custody The confinement of a person to protect him or her from harm, either self-inflicted or inflicted by others

Protective tariff A duty on imported goods intended to discourage imports and protect domestically manufactured goods

Pro tempore (*Lt*) Abbreviated as *pro tem*, for the time being; temporary or provisional used to describe someone holding an office temporarily

Protocol Proper procedure, behaviour, and etiquette at a diplomatic occasion or government function; the procedural rules for an organization, government, or situation

Provisional remedy A temporary remedy given to a plaintiff to meet a present need while a lawsuit is in progress

Proviso A condition or stipulation added to an agreement or contract

Provoke Cause someone to act, usually by deliberately annoying or irritating

Proxy Substitute, deputy, or agent; a person authorized to act on behalf of someone else, especially someone allowed to vote for stockholders in a corporate election

Public good The well being of the entire community

Public interest An interest or concern important to an entire community or all of society; public interest litigation—a lawsuit in the interest of public good

Purview Within the scope of something, such as a statute

Putative Reputed; generally assumed to be; supposed, e.g., putative spouse

Qualification (1) Eligibility something by meeting a required condition. (2) Restrict the meaning of something; to add reservations to a statement

Quantum meruit (*Lt*) As much as one deserves; used to describe a reasonable sum to pay to a person for some service if the price is not specified in a contract;

used to prevent the unjust enrichment of someone who has received services under circumstances that should have notified him or her that the plaintiff providing the service expected to be paid

Quarantine A period of time, condition, or place of isolation for someone who has been exposed to an infectious disease, intended to prevent the disease from spreading into the community

Quash Reject, suppress, or end; to make something legally invalid

Quasi (*Lt*) Almost, as if; apparently but not actually; seemingly

Quasi contract An obligation similar to a contract imposed by the law when two parties have made no promises to one another but when one party has benefited from services provided by another in such a way that the benefited party would be unjustly enriched if the court did not find the existence of an obligation—implied contract, constructive contract. (Secs 68–72, the Indian Contract Act, 1872)

Quasi easement An implied obligation concerning easement or transfer of property. (Sec. 13, the Indian Easement Act, 1882)

Quasi in rem jurisdiction Jurisdiction based on a defendant's interest in property within the court's jurisdiction, even when the defendant does not actually live there

Quasi judicial Describes the actions and powers of administrative officers and agencies that can perform some judicial tasks, although they are not in fact judges or courts

Quid pro quo (*Lt*) Something for something; giving one valuable thing in exchange for something else

Quorum The minimum number of members or delegates that must be present at a meeting of a body to validate any decisions made or business transacted at that meeting

Quota A fixed number of objects or people that are allowed or desired someplace; a proportional share of something

Quote (1) To copy or read words verbatim from a source, such as a statute or document. (2) To state a price for something or the cost of doing a job; to state an official price for the sale of securities

Quotient Proportion, measure

Quo warranto (*Lt*) A prerogative writ that can be granted by the Supreme Court and High Courts in India to inquire from the other party by what authority he claimed the office, franchise or liberty in order to determine the right. (Articles 32 and 226, the Constitution of India, 1950)

Racketeering Engaging in a conspiracy to commit business fraud, extortion, or coercion

Rate (1) A measure or value relative to some other measure or value; a proportion. (2) A price; a fee; a charge per unit of service or goods; e.g., rate of—exchange, interest, tax, etc.

Ratify Approve, affirm, or confirm something, such as a law or contract; to make something valid

Ratio est legis anima (*Lt*) Reason is the soul of law

Rationale A statement based on principles

Real evidence Evidence consisting of actual things that can be seen and inspected by the jury at trial

Reason (1) A cause, motive, or explanation for something. (2) Common sense; mental ability to think, distinguish between right and wrong, and to discern and interpret facts.

Reasonable belief A belief based on facts, circumstances, and information trustworthy enough to make a person of ordinary intelligence and caution believe something is the case, commonly used when deciding to arrest someone or conduct a search and seizure without a warrant

Reasonable care The care that a person of ordinary prudence and competence would use in a similar situation.

Reasonable doubt Enough uncertainty that a person has committed a crime, based on evidence or lack thereof

Rebut Respond to an argument or claim with contrary arguments and evidence; to refute

Receiver A person appointed by a court to manage property owned by an insolvent person that is the subject of a lawsuit, to hold the property and preserve it for the benefit of those who will ultimately receive it

Receiver pendente lite A person appointed by the court while the case is pending

Receiving stolen property The crime of receiving and accepting property or goods known to be stolen. (Sec. 441 the Indian Penal code, 1860)

Recess A break in a court or legislative session in which official proceedings are adjourned for a definite time

Recidivist A repeat offender; a person who habitually and regularly commits crimes

Reciprocal contract A bilateral contract; a contract in which each party does something for the other

Reciprocal law A law that extends rights and privileges to citizens of another state in exchange for the other state extending its rights and privileges to the first state

Recognizance A promise or obligation to do an act required by law, such as to appear in court on a particular date to answer criminal charges

Recrimination An accusation made by an accused person against his or her accuser, especially in a divorce case

Rectify Set right that had gone wrong

Recuse For a judge to withdraw from hearing a lawsuit because of self-interest, bias, or other inability to render a fair and impartial decision

Redendo singular singulis (*Lt*) Giving each to each; giving one's due

Redeem Buy something back; exchange a negotiable instrument for money; to clear a debt, such as a mortgage; for a corporation to buy back its own stock. Redemption, the act of redeeming

Red herring (1) A misleading clue; a point in a case that might seem important but that is in fact irrelevant to the main issue. (2) In securities, a preliminary prospectus about a future stock issue not yet approved by the Securities and Exchange Board, so-called because usually it is bordered in red to alert investors that it is not yet approved

Reductio ad absurdum (*Lt*) Reduction to the point of absurdity; a method of arguing against a proposition by showing that its ultimate conclusion is absurd

Redundant Unnecessary; superfluous

Reference (1) A citation; a mention of the source of information; a book or other document used as a source of information. (2) A person who provides information about another person, usually to a prospective employer; a letter from a person providing information about another person. (3) The act of referring a matter to another body

Refund A return of money paid to some person or institution, such as to a dissatisfied customer or to a taxpayer who has paid too much in taxes

Register Enter something in an official list or record. Registration—the act of registering in an official record

Registrar The registering officer

Registration of property Official transfer of property according to the Indian Stamp Paper Act, 1899 and the Indian Registration Act, 1908

Registry A book or record in which information is recorded

Regulation A rule created and enforced by an authority; a rule created by a government agency to carry out the requirements of a law; the act of regulating

Rehabilitate Restore a person or business to a normal level of health, freedom, reputation, dignity, finances, or other capacity; to help a criminal improve his or her situation so as to abandon crime in the future

Rehearing A second hearing of a matter that the court has already considered; a retrial or reconsideration by the court in which a matter was originally heard

Reinstate Restore to former status or position

Rejoinder A reply or response; an answer made by a defendant to a plaintiff's rebuttal

Release (1) Set free; to remove restrictions from someone or something. (2) Giving up a claim, right, debt, or interest; a document that gives up a claim, right, debt, or interest

Relief Help, solution, release, resolution, etc., provided by the court's decision or order

Remand To place someone in custody, such as a defendant, while a trial is adjourned

Remedy Court's of compensating someone for an injury or enforcing a right

Remit (1) Referring of a matter to some authority for decision; to send a case back to a lower court. (2) Cancel a debt; to refrain from punishing someone for a misdeed; to forgive. Remission—act of remitting

Renounce Formally abandon a claim or right

Repeal Revoke or annul a law

Replevin An action for the wrongfully seized goods

Replication A plaintiff's reply to a defendant's answer

Represent Act or speak on someone's behalf; make a statement that allows the listener to form a judgement

Reprieve A temporary relief given by a court's decision; order to suspend punishment

Reprimand An official rebuke; formal censure of a person administered by his or her superior or by an organization

Reprisal Retaliation; an act done out of spite or to retaliate for some real or imagined wrong

Repudiate Deny an obligation or refuse to perform a duty, such as that required by a contract; to deny that something is valid; to refuse to accept something

Repugnant Disgusting, revolting

Reputation The opinion about a person held by other people or by the community in general

Res (*Lt*) Thing; a thing or object; the subject matter of a lawsuit

Rescind Revoke or cancel a contract or agreement

Rescission The revocation or cancellation of a contract or agreement; a cancellation of a contract that returns the parties to their condition before they entered into it—to *rescind*

Rescript A written court order providing directions on how to dispose of a case; a short judicial opinion by an appellate court providing reasons for its decision to be sent to the trial court that originally heard the case in question

Reserve Hold back or delay judgement on a matter

Res gestae (*Lt*) Things done; a spontaneous remark or declaration made by a person just after an event but before he or she has had a chance to manufacture a falsehood, which is held to be inherently reliable

Residue The items and money that remain in estate after all testamentary bequests have been made and all debts, taxes, and other costs have been paid; also called a residuary estate

Res ipsa loquitur (*Lt*) The thing speaks for itself

Resist arrest Physical defiance to avoid being arrested by a police officer

Res judicata (*Lt*) An adjudicated matter; a rule that a court's final judgement conclusively settles the rights of all parties involved

Resolution A formal expression of the opinion or intended course of action of a legislative body or other group arrived at through a vote

Respondent (1) The party against whom an appeal is brought—*appellant*. (2) The party against whom an equitable proceeding is brought

Restitution (1) A remedy in which a victim is restored to his or her original state or condition prior to the injury; the act of making good for some wrong; restoration of the status quo. (2) Restoration of stolen property to its owner

Restraining order An order issued with an application for an injunction preventing the defendant from doing a particular act until the court decides whether to issue the injunction

Restrict Limit, confine, or control; to limit freedom of motion or action

Restricted securities Securities acquired from the issuer in a transaction not open to the public and not available to the general public to purchase

Retainer A fee paid to someone, such as an attorney, to secure his or her services for a particular matter or period of time

Retract Withdraw a statement, offer, or promise

Retrial A subsequent trial of the same matter

Retribution (1) Appropriate and just punishment for a crime or misdeed. (2) Recompense; money or another consideration paid as restitution for wrongdoing

Retroactive Made effective as of a date in the past

Retroactive law A law that applies to events that happened before it was passed. See **Ex post facto**

Revert Return to an earlier state; for a property to return to its former owner or his or her heirs

Rider Condition, proviso, qualification

Right of first refusal Entitlement to the first opportunity to do something before the opportunity is offered to others

Right of way (1) The right of a person travelling on a road, in the air, or on a body of water to proceed

ahead of others. (2) An easement that allows a person to pass through someone else's property, usually in order to reach his or her own property; a piece of land that is subject to a right of way

Rogatory letter A letter sent from a judge to another judge in another state or country, asking that he or she question a witness who lives there

Roman law A body of law derived from ancient Rome, foundation of civil law

Royalty A percentage of the proceeds from the sale of a literary work, recording, or other intellectual property that is paid to the author, creator, or owner of the work by the person or company that is selling it

Rule A law, principle, regulation, or standard that prescribes suitable conduct in a given situation; a court order requiring someone to do something—to control; to exercise power over someone or something, to make a judgement in a lawsuit; to make an authoritative statement about the law—ruling

Rule nisi An ex parte order that will become final unless the affected party can show a reason why it should not

Rule of law The belief that a court should make decisions by applying laws or legal and equitable principles to a matter without using discretion in their interpretation and application—supremacy of law

Sale or exchange Phrase used in tax to describe a sale or transfer of property that yields a taxable gain or loss

Sales tax A tax paid on purchased goods, usually a percentage of the cost of an item, collected by the seller on behalf of the government

Salvage The goods retrieved after the destruction or damage of a building or other property, or the value of those goods; the cargo retrieved from a wrecked ship or other vessel

Sanction (1) Official approval of some action. (2) A penalty or threatened penalty for disobeying a law or rule; penalties taken by one nation against another, such as trade restrictions, intended to force it to comply with some standard

Sane Sound mind; in possession of one's mental faculties

Sans frais (*Lt*) Without expense

Scandal An event that is considered morally wrong and causes public outrage

Scope of authority Authority that has been delegated to an agent to allow him or her to carry out the assigned task, including both powers actually authorized by the principal and those that are implied in the task

Schedule A document containing inventory

Scrutiny Close observation; critical and thorough examination

Seal An impression or another substance, or an impression on document, placed on a document to verify that it has been legally executed

Sealed bid A bid for a job submitted by a contractor in a sealed envelope; all sealed bids are opened at the same time and the job is awarded to the lowest bidder

Sealed instrument An instrument signed and sealed by its maker

Search and seizure A search in which the officers conducting the search take evidence of a crime if they find it

Search warrant A written order issued by a judge or judicial official in the state's name, authorizing police to search a particular place for evidence of a crime and seize it if found

Secede Formal withdrawal from a union, an alliance, or a political or religious group

Scrip (1) A written document that acknowledges a debt. (2) Historically, companies short of cash have paid scrip dividends instead of cash dividends. (3) Other examples would be frequent flier miles, vouchers, hampers, etc.

Secured debt A debt that is guaranteed by certain items that the creditor may take if the debtor fails to pay back the loan

Secured transaction A transaction secured with collateral that can be taken by the creditor if the debtor defaults

Self-defence The act of defending oneself against threatened injury

Self-incrimination The act of testifying against oneself or implicating oneself in a crime

Sentence The punishment given by the court to a criminal defendant who has been found guilty of a crime

Sentence, suspended A sentence that is not imposed on the defendant on the condition that he or she does not violate terms specified at sentencing

Sequester (1) Separate or segregate; to hide away; to isolate a jury during a trial. (2) Seize property pending the outcome of litigation or to hold until a debt is paid; to impose spending restrictions on a government; to declare someone bankrupt

Settle (Noun—**settlement**) (1) Resolve a matter; to conclude an estate; to finalize accounts; for the parties to a lawsuit to resolve their dispute on their own before a court reaches a final judgement on the matter after trial, thereby allowing the trial to be cancelled and the lawsuit terminated. (2) To dispose of finally, such as after death; to give property to someone

Shall A modal verb used to create a future tense; as used in statutes and legal documents; generally has an imperative sense, meaning 'must,' though it can also be used in a permissive sense, meaning 'may'

Sharia Islamic law, based on interpretation of the Quran and other sources of Islamic doctrine and tradition

Show cause notice An order by the court made upon the motion of one party requiring the opposing party to appear before it and explain why the court should not take a particular action

Simulated fact An invented fact; a lie

Simulated judgement A judgement on a case of bad debt that appears valid but actually is meant to give unfair advantage to one of the parties or to perpetrate a fraud on third parties

Sine qua non (*Lt*) Without which not; something without which something else cannot happen; a requirement or necessity

Sit Hold a session of a court, a legislature, or other body

Situs (*Lt*) Site, position; the location of a thing; the location of property for tax purposes; the place where a crime or other action takes place

Sole proprietor A person who owns a business alone, without co-owners or partners

Solicit Try to get something from someone; seek favour

Solicitor The head legal officer of government

Solicitor general The attorney who ranks just below the attorney general

Solvent Able to pay debts; having enough money to cover one's expenses—solvency

Sound mind Sane and mentally capable, with unimpaired faculties

Specific performance An equitable remedy in a case of breach of contract, in which the breaching party is required to perform the obligation under the contract

Spirit of the law The actual intention of a law; the meaning it is meant to convey, arrived at through interpretation and possibly consideration of the intentions of those who wrote it, as opposed to the letter of the law

Spoliation Destruction or modification of a document or instrument

Stake An interest, such as in a business. (2) A wager

Stakeholder (1) A person with an interest in a business or transaction. (2) A third party who holds property or money that is the subject of a contest between two other people, such as a lawsuit or a wager

State of mind The mental condition at the time that some event occurs; a person's reasons for acting in a particular way

Status quo (*Lt*)   The usual state of things at a particular time

Status quo ante (*Lt*)   The normal state of things before a particular event occurred

Statute   A formal written law passed by a legislature

Stay   A judicial order that puts some action on hold temporarily

Stay of execution   A judicial order that prevents a judgement from being executed for a period of time

Stipulate   Require or demand something as part of an agreement

Stock   The capital of a business raised by selling shares in the business to people inside or outside the company; an ownership interest in a company or business—*security*

Stockbroker   A person employed by a customer to buy and sell securities on the customer's behalf

Stock certificate   A document that indicates that its holder has an ownership interest in a corporation

Stock market   A stock exchange; the entire marketplace of securities trading facilities; the economic concept of securities trading

Stock option   The right to buy stock at a predetermined price, usually better than market price, during a specified period, offered as incentive or compensation to employees and managers of a company

Stock split   The splitting of single shares into two or more shares apiece, resulting in an increased total number of shares and in the shares held by individual shareholders.

Strike   A refusal to work by a group of employees

Sua sponte   (*Lt*) Of one's own volition; voluntarily

Sub judice (*Lt*)   Under a judge; under consideration by a court

Submit   Present a proposal to the court for approval

Subpoena   An official court document ordering a person to appear in court or at a judicial proceeding at a specified time

Subrogation   The substitution of one person for another with respect to an obligation, legal claim, or debt, with the substituted person assuming all duties of payment or performance and all rights that accompany the claim

Substantiate   Provide evidence to support a contention or prove a fact; to verify; to back up a story

Substantive   Related to actual rights or duties rather than rules or procedures

Substantive evidence   Evidence offered to prove a fact at issue in a trial, as opposed to character evidence about a witness

Substantive law   The part of law that defines rights and duties rather than procedural methods of enforcing

those rights, i.e., the law of contract, tort, property, trusts and estates, etc., as opposed to civil procedure

Subterfuge   A ploy to escape, evade, or conceal something; a deceitful means of accomplishing some goal

Subvert   Work to undermine established authority or overthrow the government

Succession   (1) Several people or things of the same type following one after the other. (2) Inheriting a title or right to property through a will. (3) Following someone in a position, office, or other situation

Sue   Initiate and carry out legal proceedings against someone; to bring a lawsuit against someone

Sufferance   Tolerance; consent to some action implied by failing to object rather than explicitly approving

Suffrage   The right to vote in a public election

Sui generis (*Lt*)   Of its own kind; unique; the only example of its type

Sui juris (*Lt*)   Of one's own right; emancipated; of legal age; having the right to handle one's own affairs and not under the legal control of anyone else

Sub lite (*Lt*)   In dispute

Suit   (1) A lawsuit; a legal action in which a plaintiff appeals to a court to grant him or her a remedy for some injury. (2) An entreaty or appeal to an authority to grant some request

Summary judgement   A judgement that ends a lawsuit without trial in a case where a judge finds that there is no genuine issue of material fact and thus no need to send the matter to a jury

Summon   Notify a defendant that he or she has been sued and must appear in court on a particular day

Summons   An order issued by a court informing a defendant that a lawsuit has been brought against him or her and summoning him or her to appear in court on a particular day to answer the complaint

Suppression of evidence   (1) A court's refusal to admit evidence acquired by unlawful means. (2) A party's refusal or failure to furnish opposing counsel with evidence that might prove unfavourable

Supra (*Lt*)   Above; used in a document to refer to something mentioned earlier in the document. See also **Infra**

Surety   A person who takes responsibility for someone else's debt, agreeing to pay it if the debtor fails to do so

Survivor   A person who remains alive after the death a relative or event

Suspended sentence   A sentence for a criminal offence that is postponed indefinitely unless the convicted person commits another crime within a specified period

Swear   Bind oneself or someone else with an oath

Syndicate A group of people or companies that form an alliance, permanent or temporary, to conduct some business or activity together

Table Expose for public scrutiny; e.g., tabling a report in the parliament

Tacit Implied but not openly expressed

Take over Acquire control over or management of a company

Tamper Interfere with something so as to change it

Tangible evidence Evidence that can be seen or touched, as opposed to testimony

Tangible property Physical things, such as land, buildings, and objects that can be possessed

Tariff A tax or duty imposed on imports and exports

Tax A charge imposed by the government on people and businesses on various activities and possessions, such as income, property, purchased goods, or inheritances, used by the government to fund itself and its programs

Taxable income The amount of income subject to taxes, i.e., gross income minus credits and deductions

Tenancy The condition of being a tenant; an interest in land held by a tenant

Tender Offer or present something to someone; to present someone with money as payment; to offer to perform some service for a price

Tender, legal Valid money

Tenure (1) A right to hold property; the condition of holding property. (2) The time that a person spends in a position or (3) A state of guaranteed permanent employment awarded to professors, teachers, and a few other employees who have worked for an institution a specified period of time

Term (1) A word or expression for something. (2) The duration of something; a fixed period of time; a period of time in which a court is in session

Terminable Able to be terminated

Terrorism The use of violence to achieve political ends in order to intimidate citizens and governments into acquiescing to the demands of the terrorists

Testament A will; the part of a last will and testament that disposes of someone's personal property

Testator A person who writes and executes a will; a deceased person whose property is disposed of according to the terms of his or her will

Test case A lawsuit that serves as a test of the validity of a law, principle, or cause of action

Testify Speak under oath; to give evidence as a witness in a deposition or lawsuit; to serve as proof of something

Testimony The spoken evidence given by a witness under oath in court or at a deposition, or written evidence provided by a witness under oath through an affidavit

Third party A person who is not directly involved in a transaction; someone who is not a party to an agreement

Third party complaint A complaint filed by a defendant in an existing lawsuit against someone who is alleged by the defendant to be liable for damages to the plaintiff

Title A right or claim of ownership of property

Tonnage Capacity of a ship; the amount of cargo a ship can carry

Tort A private injury or wrong; a violation of a socially recognized duty owed to a plaintiff that results in injury to the plaintiff

Trademark A name, word, symbol, or device used by the manufacturer of a product to identify that product and distinguish it from other similar ones produced by competitors- copyright, *patent*, *trade name*

Transaction One instance of conducting business, such as buying or selling an item; an agreement or act involving at least two people that alters their legal rights in relation to one another

Transcript An official, certified, written record of a trial or other proceeding prepared by a court reporter

Trial A formal judicial proceeding in which a judge hears the evidence in a case and decides the rights of the parties in a civil case or the guilt or innocence of the defendant in a criminal case

Trial court The court in which a case is first presented, as opposed to an appellate court

Tribunal A judicial court; a judge's seat or bench; a judge or group of judges with jurisdiction in an area

True copy A copy of a document that is not necessarily an exact duplicate of the original but is close enough to be clearly understood and recognized

Trust, charitable A trust created to benefit a class or the public for educational, charitable, scientific, or religious purposes

Trustee The person who holds the property of a trust and administers it in a fiduciary capacity for the benefit of the beneficiaries

Trust indenture A document containing the terms and conditions governing a trust

Ubi jus ibi idem remedium (*Lt*) Where there is a right there is a remedy

Ultra vires (*Lt*) Beyond the powers; outside one's official authority; used especially to describe actions by a corporation that exceed the powers granted to it by its charter or by state law

Unconscionable Unreasonably detrimental; grossly one-sided; so unfair or oppressive to the interests of a party to a contract as to render the contract unenforceable

Unconstitutional Conflicting with the Constitution of India

Underwrite (1) To insure; to accept the liability for something. (2) To agree to buy all unsold shares from an issue of stocks or bonds. (3) To provide financial support for some enterprise

Undue Improper; unwarranted; exceeding what is necessary

Unethical Not ethical; not according to morals or the ethical standards of a profession

Unfair competition The tort of fraudulently trying to pass off one's goods as those of another company, or to use the reputation of another company to sell one's own product, as through misleading advertising or packaging

Unilateral One-sided; performed by one party in a situation without the participation or agreement of other parties; affecting only one party or group in a particular situation

Union A labour organization that exists to negotiate with employers on behalf of workers in matters such as wages, hours, and workplace safety

United Nations An international organization founded in 1945 to help nations cooperate in matters of human rights, economics, security, and international law

Unlawful entry Entering property without the owner's consent through the use of force or fraud

Unreasonable Arbitrary; excessive; unfair; irrational

Usage A practice that is usual within a particular business

Usufruct The civil law right to use property that belongs to someone else

Usurer A person who lends money at unreasonably high interest

Usurp Take over; to supplant; to take over a position of power by force

Usury Lending money at excessively high interest rates

Vacate (1) To leave; to make empty. (2) To make void; to annul

Valid Properly executed and legally binding; legitimate; acceptable

Valid contact Legally enforceable contract

Valuable consideration Something of value given in exchange for a performance or a promise, which entitles the recipient of the promise to enforce a claim against a promisor who fails to perform

Value (1) Worth; cost or price in money; the price a seller would give a buyer in a bona fide transaction in an open market. (2) A moral principle

Valuation The act of appraising, estimating

Value Variance A discrepancy

VAT Value added tax

Vend Sell

Vendee Buyer

Vendor Seller

Venture capital Funding for a new business that involves risk but has potential for great profits

Veracity Truthfulness

Verba sunt indices animi (*Lt*) Words are indications of the intention

Verdict Judgement by the judge

Verify Confirm the truth, accuracy, or authenticity of something; to attest to the truth of something in an affidavit or other sworn statement

Versus (*Lt*) Against; used in the title of a lawsuit to indicate which party is against which

Vest Accrue; to take effect; to bestow on someone; to give someone authority, power, or a right; to gain a legal right to something; to come into possession of something

Vested interest An interest that is recognized as belonging to someone who has the right to give it away; a personal stake in some matter. (Sec. 19, the Transfer of Property Act, 1882)

Vested right In constitutional law, a right that is so firmly attached to a person that it cannot be taken away by someone else

Veto The act of rejection of an agreement

Vexatious litigation A lawsuit brought without probable cause, out of malice toward the opposing party

Vicarious: Experienced or done through another person

Vicarious liability Liability imposed on one person for the actions of another based on a relationship between them, such as when the corporation is at fault, the responsible members would be made liable for legal action

Vienna Convention on the Law of Treaties An international treaty effective in 1980 that codified and clarified accepted international law on the creation of treaties

Void Invalid; not legally binding; ineffective; empty

Void ab initio Never having had legal validity; void from the beginning

Voidable Able to be annulled or voided due to some irregularity or problem, but valid until that happens

Voidable contract A contract that may be legally voided by one or both parties, but that is valid until voided

Voluntary Done willingly, without the influence of or pressure from someone else, deliberate; of one's own will

Vote An indication of a choice for candidates in an election; an individual ballot or other means of indicating such choice submitted by a voter; the right to vote

Vouch Verify; to confirm that a person is of good character or qualified for a position; to assert that something is true, based on personal experience

Voucher A small printed document that entitles its holder to some good or service; a receipt; a document that authorizes the payment of cash

Wages Compensation for work performed—salary

Wage, living Compensation sufficient to support a family above poverty conditions

Wager A bet; an agreement made by two parties that one of them will pay the other a specific sum if a certain condition occurs

Waive Voluntarily give up a legal right or claim

Wanton Reckless; malicious; deliberate, unprovoked, and in disregard of the safety of others

Warehouse receipt A document issued by a person who runs a warehouse, indicating that the goods have been deposited into his or her care, which serves as a document of title for its holder

Warrant A written order issued by some authority directing someone to do a certain act, particularly an order issued by the state directing a law enforcement officer to arrest someone

Warranty A promise or assurance that something is true, of a certain quality, or useful for a particular purpose; an assurance by one party to a contract that a certain fact is true, given to save the other party the trouble of confirming it, which is in effect a promise to cover any losses suffered by the other party if the fact turns out not to be true

Warsaw convention An international convention that regulates international air transport of people and goods

Watermark (1) A transparent mark on a piece of paper that can be seen when the paper is held to a light, used as a sign of genuineness. (2) A mark on the bank of a body of water that indicates the highest or lowest point to which the water has risen or dropped

Whereas (1) Considering that something is the case; used in legal documents to begin an introductory statement. (2) In comparison to; in contrast with

Whistleblower An employee who reports wrongdoing by his or her employer or co-workers

Will (1) Desire; intention; choice. (2) A document in which a person describes how to distribute his or her property after death

Winding up Concluding the affairs of a corporation or partnership that is being liquidated, including paying off debts and distributing the remaining assets

Withdraw Retreat; to remove or take away; to take money out of an account

Withhold Hold something back; to keep something that is desired by someone else; to deduct income tax from an employee's pay

With prejudice Describes a claim or action that has been dismissed and that may not be brought again as a new action

Without prejudice With no legal rights affected; describes a claim or action that may be brought as a new action after dismissal

Without recourse Having no further rights or possible remedies

Witness A person who has seen or experienced some event; a person who testifies under oath about seeing or experiencing some event, or about the character of someone involved in a lawsuit

World Intellectual Property Organization An agency of the United Nations that promotes creative activity and the protection of intellectual property—WIPO

World Trade Organization (WTO) An international organization that regulates trade among nations

Writ A written command issued by a court or other authority ordering someone to do a particular act

Writ of assistance An equitable remedy that transfers title to property that has been determined by the court to belong to the recipient

Writ of attachment A court order to seize a debtor's property

Writ of certiorari An order of a superior court calling up record of a proceeding in an inferior court for review

Writ of habeas corpus An order issued by a court requiring an imprisoned person to be brought to a stated place at a stated time to examine the legality of his imprisonment

Writ of Mandamus A command used by a higher court to a lower court

Writ of Prohibition A higher court prohibiting the lower court not to accede its jurisdiction

Writ of quo warranto An order issued by as court to show by what warrant he holds an office

Writ of execution A court ordering a law enforcement officer to enforce a judgement by the court

Wrongful act An act that infringes on someone's rights and injures him or her

X The graphic representation of the letter x to mark something; as an indicator; e.g., for signing; a member of the class of x, y, z; usually to indicate a negative sign as opposed to a positive sign

Xenophile One attracted to all that is foreign

Year, month '...it is to be understood that the year or the month is to be reckoned according to the British calendar...' (Sec. 49, the Indian Penal Code, 1860)

Yield Something produced; to give up, surrender

Zenith Highest point

Zone Marked or defined area

Index

About the Author

Daniel Albuquerque, PhD, is the Director of Alternative tech Foundation (AtF) of Biodiversity Conservation India Ltd (BCIL), Bengaluru. Dr Albuquerque, a student of economics and literature, obtained his doctorate from the Julius Maximilian University of Würzburg, Germany. He is currently a visiting professor at various management institutes in India and abroad, such as Banasthali University, Rajasthan, and the Friedrich Schiller University, Jena, Germany.

Dr Albuquerque's work experience spans across academic, corporate, political, and cultural fields, both in India and abroad. He is associated with several business schools in India as part of academic council and other institution-building concerns.

The author has been a member of Franz Brentano Forschung (Research) of Julius Maximilian University of Würzburg, and a member of the United Nations Global Compact for corporate governance based in Villach, Austria. He is the founder of the Seat of Wisdom Educational Society, Goa.

Professor Albuquerque is a prolific writer, with more than ten books and scores of scientific papers to his credit. He has also authored *Business Ethics: Principles and Practices* (OUP).

Related Titles

Corporate Governance | 9780198062233

T.N. Satheesh Kumar Independent Consultant and Trainer

Corporate Governance is a comprehensive textbook that provides an in-depth analysis of the core concepts of the subject and supplements them with relevant examples, exhibits, and case studies.

Key Features
- Expounds on issues and challenges faced by corporates in applications of governance in India as well as abroad
- Contains extensive discussion on the European Union approach to corporate governance
- Provides numerous real-world cases

9780198069836 | **Corporate Social Responsibility**

Madhumita Chatterji Professor, IFIM Business School, Bengaluru

Corporate Social Responsibility explores the core concepts of corporate social responsibility (CSR) and explains them through numerous examples, mini cases, exhibits, and case studies.

Key Features
- Provides a unique comparative study of CSR in four different countries (US, UK, New Zealand, and Indonesia) with real data
- Discusses CSR practices of Indian and global companies such as HUL, ITC, Philips, Satyam, Tata Group, etc.

Business Ethics: Principles and Practices | 9780195699647

Daniel Albuquerque Formerly Professor, Goa Institute of Management, Goa

Business Ethics: Principles and Practices provides a deep insight into the crucial role played by ethics in managerial decision making and the impact of such decisions on the world at large.

Key Features
- Provides exhaustive coverage of various facets of ethics in the business arena
- Follows a highly detailed pedagogy with several pertinent diagrams, mini cases, case studies with questions, and end-chapter review questions
- Offers coverage of technological issues such as cyber ethics and sensitive issues such as gender ethics, human rights, etc.

Other Related Titles

9780195694451 Anil Bhat & Arya Kumar *Management: Principles Processes and Practices*

9780198070733 Udai Pareek & Sushama Khanna *Udai Pareek's Understanding Organizational Behaviour, 3/e*

9780198077053 Meenakshi Raman & Prakash Singh *Business Communication, 2/e*

9780198077039 Paresh Shah *Financial Accounting for Management, 2/e*

9780198075349 Dominick Salvatore & Ravikesh Srivastava *Managerial Economics, 7/e*

9780198064145 B. Muthukumaran *Information Technology for Management*